Guide to U.S. HMOs & PPOs

2023
Thirty-fifth Edition

Guide to U.S. HMOs & PPOs

Detailed Profiles of U.S. Managed Healthcare Organizations & Key Decision Makers

Grey House Publishing

PUBLISHER: Leslie Mackenzie
EDITORIAL DIRECTOR: Stuart Paterson
EDITORIAL ASSISTANT: Margarita Vachenkova
COMPOSITION: David Garoogian
MARKETING DIRECTOR: Jessica Moody

Grey House Publishing, Inc.
4919 Route 22
Amenia, NY 12501
518.789.8700 FAX 845.373.6390
www.greyhouse.com
e-mail: books@greyhouse.com

While every effort has been made to ensure the reliability of the information presented in this publication, Grey House Publishing neither guarantees the accuracy of the data contained herein nor assumes any responsibility for errors, omissions or discrepancies. Grey House accepts no payment for listing; inclusion in the publication of any organization, agency, institution, publication, service or individual does not imply endorsement of the editors or publisher.

Errors brought to the attention of the publisher and verified to the satisfaction of the publisher will be corrected in future editions.

Except by express prior written permission of the Copyright Proprietor no part of this work may be copied by any means of publication or communication now known or developed hereafter including, but not limited to, use in any directory or compilation or other print publication, in any information storage and retrieval system, in any other electronic device, or in any visual or audio-visual device or product.

This publication is an original and creative work, copyrighted by Grey House Publishing, Inc. and is fully protected by all applicable copyright laws, as well as by laws covering misappropriation, trade secrets and unfair competition.

Grey House has added value to the underlying factual material through one or more of the following efforts: unique and original selection; expression; arrangement; coordination; and classification.

Grey House Publishing, Inc. will defend its rights in this publication.

Copyright © 2023 Grey House Publishing, Inc.
All rights reserved

First edition published 1987
Thirty-fifth edition published 2023
Printed in Canada

Publisher's Cataloging-In-Publication Data
(Prepared by The Donohue Group, Inc.)

Names: Grey House Publishing, Inc., publisher.
Title: Guide to U.S. HMOs & PPOs.
Other Titles: HMOs & PPOs | Guide to U.S. HMOs and PPOs | Guide to United States health maintenance organizations & preferred provider organizations
Description: Amenia, NY : Grey House Publishing, 2023- | "Detailed profiles of U.S. managed healthcare organizations & key decision makers." | Includes bibliographical references and indexes.
Subjects: LCSH: Health maintenance organizations—United States—Directories. | Preferred provider organizations (Medical care)—United States—Directories. | LCGFT: Directories.
Classification: LCC RA413.5.U5 H586 | DDC 362.1042580973—dc23

ISBN: 978-1-63700-157-8 Softcover

Table of Contents

Introduction vii
User Guide... ix
User Key xi
Health Insurance Coverage in the United States: 2020..................... xiii
Small Area Health Insurance Estimates: 2019 xlv
Health Insurance Coverage: Early Release of Estimates from the
    National Health Interview Survey, 2021 lix
Demographic Variation in Health Insurance Coverage: United States, 2020 ... lxxxiii
National Uninsured Rate Reaches All-Time Low in Early 2022................ xci
Environmental Scan on Consolidation Trends and Impacts in Health
    Care Markets ci

State Statistics & Rankings
    Health Insurance Coverage.. 3
    Managed Care Organizations Ranked by Total Enrollment................. 13
    Managed Care Organizations Ranked by State Enrollment 21

HMO/PPO Profiles
    State Profiles and Listings by State 27

Appendices
    Appendix A: Glossary of Terms.. 387
    Appendix B: Industry Websites 395

Indexes
    Plan Index 399
    Personnel Index 409
    Membership Enrollment Index.. 429
    Primary Care Physician Index 433
    Referral/Specialty Physician Index 437

Introduction

This 35th edition of *Guide to U.S. HMOs & PPOs* profiles 900 managed care organizations in the United States. It lists current, comprehensive information for HMO, PPO, POS, and Vision & Dental Plans. Comprehensive coverage—from state listings to consolidations in the health insurance industry—is the cornerstone of this new edition.

In addition to detailed profiles of managed healthcare organizations, this edition includes the following important health insurance information:

- Health Insurance Coverage in the United States: 2020—a 31-page report based on data from the Current Population Survey Annual Social and Economic Supplement (CPS ASEC) and the American Community Survey (ACS), with maps, charts, tables, including insurance trends and state comparisons;
- Small Area Health Insurance Estimates: 2019—13 pages of maps, charts and statistics covering states and counties based on the U.S. Census Bureau's Small Area Health Insurance Estimates (SAHIE);
- National Health Interview Survey, 2021—a 22-page report presenting full-year estimates of health insurance coverage for the civilian noninstitutionalized U.S. population based on data from the January–December 2020 National Health Interview Survey (NHIS);
- Demographic Variation in Health Insurance Coverage: United States, 2020—an 8-page report from the Centers for Disease Control and Prevention (CDC) presenting national estimates of different types of health insurance coverage and lack of coverage (uninsured), by selected sociodemographic characteristics, including age, sex, race and Hispanic origin, family income, education level, employment status, and marital status;
- National Uninsured Rate Reaches All-Time Low in Early 2022—a 9-page report from the Office of the Assistant Secretary for Planning and Evaluation (ASPE) examining how the uninsured rate in early 2022 reached an all-time low of 8.0%, indicating that 5.2 million people have gained health insurance coverage since 2020;
- Environmental Scan on Consolidation Trends and Impacts in Health Care Markets—a 10-page report prepared by RAND Health Care discussing trends and impacts of consolidation in health care after the implementation of the No Surprises Act (NSA) of the 2021 Consolidated Appropriations Act, which created protections for those with private health insurance against surprise medical bills;
- State Statistics and Rankings section with state-by-state numbers of individuals covered by type of health plans, and state ranking by number of individuals enrolled in health plans.

Praise for previous editions of *Guide to U.S. HMOs & PPOs*:

> "...of a topic that has grown exponentially more complex each year, this well-organized resource tries its best to keep it simple.... The detailed user guide and five indexes enhance navigation.... Written for both the consumer and the researcher, this work is a vital resource for public, academic and medical libraries."
>
> "...Information is clear, consistently presented, and easily located, making the guide extremely user friendly.... A practical addition to public and medical library collections."
>
> —*Library Journal*

Arrangement

Plan profiles are arranged alphabetically by state. The first page of each state chapter is a State Summary chart of Health Insurance Coverage Status and Type of Coverage by Age. This chart includes a number of categories, from "Covered by some type of health insurance" to "Not covered at any time during the year."

Directly following the State Summary, plan listings provide crucial contact information, including key executives, often with direct phones and e-mails where available, fax numbers, web sites and hundreds of e-mail addresses. Each profile provides a detailed summary of the plan, including the following:
- Type of Plan, including Specialty and Benefits
- Type of Coverage
- Type of Payment Plan
- Subscriber Information
- Financial History
- Average Compensation Information
- Employer References
- Current Member Enrollment
- Hospital Affiliations
- Number of Primary Care and Specialty Physicians
- Federal Qualification Status
- For Profit Status
- Specialty Managed Care Partners
- Regional Business Coalitions
- Employer References
- Peer Review Information
- Accreditation Information

Additional Features

In addition to the detailed front matter, state statistics, and comprehensive plan profiles, *Guide to U.S. HMOs & PPOs* includes two Appendices and five Indexes.
- Appendix A: Glossary of Health Insurance Terms—Includes more than 150 terms such as Aggregate Indemnity, Diagnostic Related Groups, Non-participating Provider, and Waiting Period.
- Appendix B: Industry Web Sites—Contains dozens of the most valuable health care web sites and a detailed description, from Alliance of Community Health Plans to National Society of Certified Healthcare Business Consultants.
- Plan Index: Alphabetical list of insurance plans by seven plan types: HMO; PPO; HMO/PPO; Dental; Vision; Medicare; and Multiple.
- Personnel Index: Alphabetical list of all executives listed, with their affiliated organization.
- Membership Enrollment Index: List of organizations by member enrollment.
- Primary Care Physician Index: List of organizations by their number of primary care physicians.
- Referral/Specialty Care Physician Index: List of organizations by their number of referral and specialty care physicians.

To broaden its availability, the *Guide to U.S. HMOs & PPOs* is also available for subscription online at http://gold.greyhouse.com. Subscribers can search by plan details, geographic area, number of members, personnel name, title and much more. Users can print out prospect sheets or download data into their own spreadsheet or database. This database is a must for anyone in need of immediate access to contacts in the US managed care marketplace. Plus, buyers of the print directory get a free 30-day trial of the online database. Call (800) 562-2139 x118 for more information.

User Guide

Descriptive listings in the *Guide to U.S. HMOs & PPOs* are organized by state, then alphabetically by health plan. Each numbered item is described in the User Key on the following pages. Terms are defined in the Glossary.

1. **U Healthcare**
2. **3000 Riverside Road**
   Sharon, CT 06069
3. **Toll Free: 060-364-0000**
4. **Phone: 060-364-0001**
5. **Fax: 060-364-0002**
6. Info@uhealth.com
7. www.uhealth.com
8. Mailing Address: PO Box 729 Sharon, CT 06069-0729
9. Subsidiary of: USA Healthcare
10. For Profit: Yes
11. Year Founded: 1992
12. Physician Owned: No
13. Owned by an IDN: No
14. Federally Qualified: Yes 08/01/82
15. Number of Affiliated Hospitals: 2,649
16. Number of Primary Physicians: 4,892
17. Number of Referral/Specialty Physicians: 6,246
18. Current Member Enrollment: 204,000 (as of 7/1/01)
19. State Member Enrollment: 29,000

    Healthplan and Services Defined
20. Plan Type: HMO
21. Model Type: Staff, IPA, Group, Network
22. Plan Specialty: ASO, Chiropractic, Dental, Disease Management, Lab, Vision, Radiology
23. Benefits Offered: Chiropractic, Dental, Disease Management, Vision, Wellness
24. Offers a Demand Management Patient Information Service: Yes
    DMPI Services Offered: Vision Works, Medical Imaging Institute

25. **Type of Coverage**
    Commercial, Medicare, Supplemental Medicare, Medicaid
    Catastrophic Illness Benefit: Varies by case

26. **Type of Payment Plans Offered**
    POS, Capitated, FFS, Combination FFS & DFFS

27. **Geographic Areas Served**
    Connecticut, Maryland, New Jersey, Vermont, New York

    Subscriber Information
28. Average Monthly Fee Per Subscriber (Employee & Employer Contribution):
    Employee Only (Self): $8.00
    Employee & 1 Family Member: $10.00
    Employee & 2 Family Members: $15.00
    Medicare: $ 10.00
29. Average Annual Deductible Per Subscriber:
    Employee Only (Self): $200.00

Employee & 1 Family Member: $250.00
Employee & 2 Family Members: $500.00
Medicare: $200.00

30.▶ Average Subscriber Co-Payment:
Primary Care Physician: $8.00
Non-Network Physician: $10.00
Prescription Drugs: $5.00
Hospital ER: $50.00
Home Health Care: $25.00
Home Health Care Max Days Covered/Visits: 30 days
Nursing Home: $5.00
Nursing Home Max Days/Visits Covered: 365 days

31.▶ **Network Qualifications**
Minimum Years of Practice: 10
Pre-Admission Certification: Yes

32.▶ **Peer Review Type**
Utilization Review: Yes
Second Surgical Opinion: No
Case Management: Yes

33.▶ **Accreditation Certification**
JCAHO, AAHC (formerly URAC), NCQA
Publishes and Distributes a Report Card: Yes

34.▶ **Key Personnel**
CFO..............................David Williams
Marketing......................Clarence J. Fist
Medical Affairs...............Samantha Johnson, MD
Provider Services.............Laura Falk

Average Claim Compensation
35.▶ Physician's Fee's Charged: 22%
36.▶ Hospital's Fee Charged: 34%

37.▶ **Specialty Managed Care Partners**
AMBI, Pharmaceutical Treatment, OxiTherapy

38.▶ **Enters into Contracts with Regional Business Coalitions: Yes**
New York Healthcare

39.▶ **Employer References**
Life Science Corporation

User Key

1. **Health Plan:** Formal name of health plan
2. **Address:** Physical location
3. **Toll Free:** Toll free number
4. **Phone:** Main number of organization
5. **Fax:** Fax number
6. **E-mail:** Main e-mail address of health plan, if provided
7. **Website:** Main website address of health plan, if provided
8. **Mailing Address:** If different from physical address, above.
9. **Subsidiary of:** Corporation the health plan is legally affiliated with
10. **For Profit:** Indicates if the organization was formed to make a financial profit. Non-profit organizations can make a profit, but the profits must be used to benefit the organization or purpose the corporation was created to help
11. **Year Founded:** The year the organization was recognized as a legal entity
12. **Physician Owned:** Notes if the organization is owned by a group of physicians who are recognized as a legal entity
13. **Owned by an IDN:** Notes if the organization is owned by an Integrated Delivery Network
14. **Federally Qualified:** Shows if and when the plan received federally qualified status
15. **Number of Affiliated Hospitals:** In-network hospitals contracted with the health plans
16. **Number of Primary Physicians:** In-network primary physicians contracted with the health plan
17. **Number of Referral/Specialty Physicians:** In-network referral/specialty physicians contracted with the health plan
18. **Current Member Enrollment:** The number of health plan members or subscribers using health plan benefits, and date of last enrollment count
19. **State Member Enrollment:** The number of health plan members or subscribers using health plan benefits in that state, and date of last enrollment count
20. **Plan Type:** Identifies the health plan as an HMO, PPO, Other (neither an HMO or PPO) or Multiple (both an HMO and PPO, or an HMO and TPA or POS; see Glossary for definitions of terms). Note: If a plan is both an HMO and PPO with different product information, i.e. number of hospitals or physicians, the plan is listed as two separate entries
21. **Model Type:** Describes the relationship between the health plan and its physicians
22. **Plan Specialty:** Indicates specialized services provided by the plan
23. **Benefits Offered:** Indicates specialized benefits offered in addition to standard coverage for physician services, hospitalization, diagnostic testing, and prescription drugs
24. **Offers Demand Management Patient Information Services:** Notes if Triage and other services are offered to help plan members find the most appropriate type and level of care, and what those services are
25. **Type of Coverage:** Lines of business offered
26. **Type of Payment Plans Offered:** How the insuror pays its contracted providers
27. **Geographical Areas Served:** Geographical areas the health plan services
28. **Average Monthly Fee Per Subscriber:** Monthly premium due to the carrier for each member
29. **Annual Average Deductible Per Subscriber:** The deductible each member must meet before expenses can be reimbursed
30. **Average Subscriber Co-Payment:** The co-payment each member must pay at the time services are rendered
31. **Network Qualifications:** Qualifications a physician must meet to contract with the plan
32. **Peer Review Type:** The type of on-going peer review process used by the health plan

33. ➔**Accreditation Certification:** Specific certifications the health plan achieved after rigorous review of its policies, procedures, and clinical outcomes
34. ➔**Key Personnel:** Key Executives in the most frequently contacted departments within the plans, with phone and e-mails when provided
35. ➔**Physician's Fees Charged:** The percentage of physicians' billed charges that is actually paid out by the plan
36. ➔**Hospital's Fees Charged:** The percentage of hospitals' billed charges that is actually paid out by the plan
37. ➔**Specialty Managed Care Partners:** Specialty carve-out companies that are contracted with the health plan to offer a broader array of health services to members
38. ➔**Regional Business Coalitions:** Notes if physician or business entities have formed for the sole purpose of achieving economies of scale when purchasing supplies and services, and the names of those businesses
39. ➔**Employer References:** Large employers that have contracted with the health plan and are willing to serve as references for the health plan

Health Insurance Coverage in the United States: 2020

Current Population Reports

By Katherine Keisler-Starkey and Lisa N. Bunch
Issued September 2021
P60-274

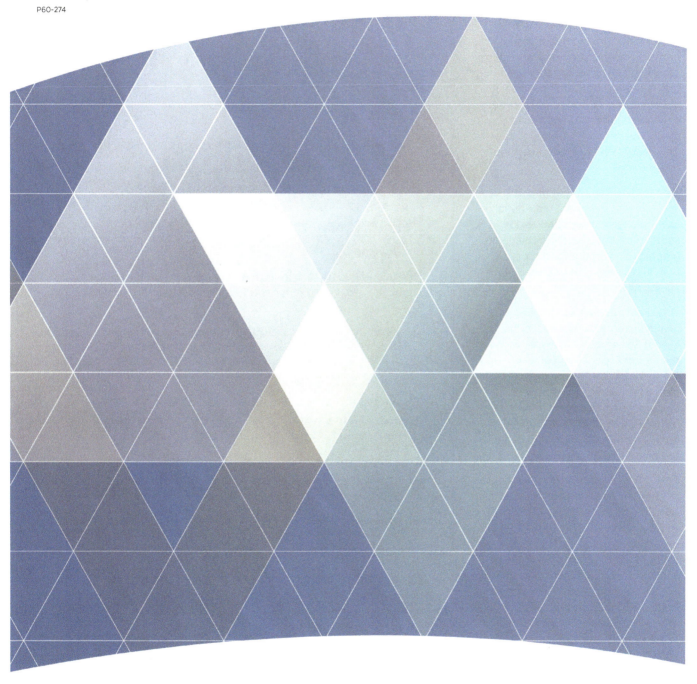

U.S. Department of Commerce
U.S. CENSUS BUREAU
census.gov

Health Insurance Coverage in the United States: 2020

INTRODUCTION

Health insurance is a means for financing a person's health care expenses. While the majority of people have private health insurance, primarily through an employer, many others obtain coverage through programs offered by state and federal governments. Other individuals do not have health insurance coverage at all (The "What Is Health Insurance Coverage?" text box contains more information).

Year to year, the rate of health insurance coverage and the distribution of coverage types may change due to economic trends, shifts in the demographic composition of the population, and policy changes that affect access to care.

This report presents estimates of health insurance coverage in the United States in 2020, a year in which the nation experienced an economic recession related to the COVID-19 global pandemic. The statistics in this report are based on information collected in the Current Population Survey Annual Social and Economic Supplement (CPS ASEC).[1]

The CPS is the longest-running household survey conducted by the Census Bureau. The key purpose of the CPS ASEC is to provide timely and detailed estimates of economic well-being, of which health insurance coverage is an important component. The Census Bureau has integrated improvements to the CPS ASEC as the needs of data users and the health insurance environment have changed.

What Is Health Insurance Coverage?

Health insurance coverage in the Current Population Survey Annual Social and Economic Supplement (CPS ASEC) refers to comprehensive coverage at any time during the calendar year for the civilian, noninstitutionalized population of the United States.* For reporting purposes, the U.S. Census Bureau broadly classifies health insurance coverage as private insurance or public insurance.

Private Coverage

- *Employment-based*: Plan provided through an employer or union.
- *Direct-purchase*: Coverage purchased directly from an insurance company, or through a federal or state Marketplace (e.g., healthcare.gov).
- *TRICARE*: Coverage through TRICARE, formerly known as Civilian Health and Medical Program of the Uniformed Services.

Public Coverage

- *Medicare*: Federal program that helps to pay health care costs for people aged 65 and older and for certain people under age 65 with long-term disabilities.
- *Medicaid*: This report uses the term Medicaid to include the specific Medicaid government program and other programs for low-income individuals administered by the states such as Children's Health Insurance Program (CHIP) and Basic Health Programs.
- *CHAMPVA or VA*: Civilian Health and Medical Program of the Department of Veterans Affairs, as well as care provided by the Department of Veterans Affairs and the military.

Additionally, people are considered uninsured if they only had coverage through the Indian Health Service (IHS), as IHS coverage is not considered comprehensive.

* Comprehensive health insurance covers basic health care needs. This definition excludes single service plans such as accident, disability, dental, vision, or prescription medicine plans.

The 2020 estimates highlighted in this report were collected from February 2021 to April 2021. Respondents were asked to report any health insurance coverage they had during the previous calendar year (2020). People are only considered uninsured if they had no coverage at any time during the year. As a result, people who lost coverage during 2020 are not included in the uninsured rate.[2]

---

[1] The U.S. Census Bureau reviewed this data product for unauthorized disclosure of confidential information and approved the disclosure avoidance practices applied to this release: CBDRB-FY21-POP001-0193.

[2] The CPS ASEC also includes a measure of health insurance coverage held at the time of the interview. Although this measure of coverage cannot predict coverage in a given calendar year, it offers a snapshot of health insurance coverage early in the year when CPS ASEC data are collected. More information is available in Appendix B: Estimates of Health Insurance Coverage 2013–2020, Figure B-5.

> **The Impact of the Coronavirus (COVID-19) Pandemic on the Current Population Survey Annual Social and Economic Supplement (CPS ASEC)**
>
> The U.S. Census Bureau administers the CPS ASEC each year between February and April by telephone and in-person interviews, with the majority of data collected in March. In 2020, data collection faced extraordinary circumstances due to the onset of the COVID-19 pandemic as the Census Bureau suspended in-person interviews and closed both telephone contact centers. The response rate for the CPS basic household survey was 73 percent in March 2020, about 10 percentage points lower than preceding months and the same period in 2019, which were regularly above 80 percent.
>
> During collection of the 2021 CPS ASEC, for the safety of both interviewers and respondents, in-person interviews were only conducted when telephone interviews could not be done. In March 2021, the response rate for the CPS basic household survey improved to about 76 percent, though not quite returning to the prepandemic trend. While the response rate improved, it is important to examine how respondents differ from nonrespondents, as this difference could affect income and poverty estimates. Using administrative data, Census Bureau researchers have documented that the nonrespondents in both 2020 and 2021 are less similar to respondents than in earlier years. Of particular interest, for the estimates in this report, are the differences in median income and educational attainment, indicating that respondents in 2020 and 2021 had relatively higher incomes and were more educated than nonrespondents. For more details on how these sample differences and the associated nonresponse bias impact income and official poverty estimates, refer to <www.census.gov/newsroom/blogs/research-matters/2021/09/pandemic-affect-survey-response.html>.

Estimates of health insurance coverage for 2019 were collected between February and April of 2020, during the first months of the COVID-19 pandemic. In the middle of the collection period, the Census Bureau suspended in-person interviews and closed telephone contact centers to protect the health and safety of staff and respondents. Last year's report included an explanation of the impact of the coronavirus pandemic on the CPS ASEC.[3] In addition, the Census Bureau produced several working papers exploring how changes in CPS ASEC data collection in 2020 may have affected 2019 estimates.[4] "The Impact of the Coronavirus (COVID-19) Pandemic on the Current Population Survey Annual Social and Economic Supplement (CPS ASEC)" text box provides more information. The Census Bureau recommends that users consider the effect of the pandemic on CPS ASEC data collection in interpreting changes in health insurance coverage between 2019 and other years using the CPS ASEC.

Estimates for 2018 were collected in 2019, prior to the pandemic. In order to make the most consistent comparisons, the majority of the estimates in this report focus on changes in health insurance coverage between 2018, prior to the pandemic, and 2020. More information presenting the 2020 coverage estimates in the context of a longer time frame is available in Appendix B: Estimates of Health Insurance Coverage 2013–2020.

HEALTH INSURANCE COVERAGE BY TYPE AND SELECTED CHARACTERISTICS

Highlights

- In 2020, 8.6 percent of people, or 28.0 million, did not have health insurance at any point during the year (Table 1 and Figure 1).

---

[3] More information is available in the "The Impact of the Coronavirus (COVID-19) Pandemic on the CPS ASEC" text box in the report "Health Insurance Coverage in the United States: 2019," <www.census.gov/content/dam/Census/library/publications/2020/demo/p60-271.pdf>.

[4] For additional information related to the impact of COVID-19 on the 2020 CPS ASEC, refer to Edward R. Berchick, Laryssa Mykyta, and Sharon M. Stern, "The Influence of COVID-19-Related Data Collection Changes on Measuring Health Insurance Coverage in the 2020 CPS ASEC," <www.census.gov/library/working-papers/2020/demo/SEHSD-WP2020-13.html>, and Jonathan Rothbaum and C. Adam Bee, "Coronavirus Infects Surveys, Too: Nonresponse Bias During the Pandemic in the CPS ASEC," <www.census.gov/library/working-papers/2020/demo/SEHSD-WP2020-10.html>.

- The percentage of people with health insurance coverage for all or part of 2020 was 91.4 (Table 1).

- In 2020, private health insurance coverage continued to be more prevalent than public coverage at 66.5 percent and 34.8 percent, respectively.[5] Of the subtypes of health insurance coverage, employment-based insurance was the most common, covering 54.4 percent of the population for some or all of the calendar year, followed by Medicare (18.4 percent), Medicaid (17.8 percent), direct-purchase coverage (10.5 percent), TRICARE (2.8 percent), and Department of Veterans Affairs (VA) or Civilian Health and Medical Program of the Department of Veterans Affairs (CHAMPVA) coverage (0.9 percent) (Table 1 and Figure 1).[6]

- Between 2018 and 2020, the rate of private health insurance coverage decreased by 0.8 percentage points to 66.5 percent, driven by a 0.7 percentage-point decline in employment-based coverage to 54.4 percent (Table 1 and Figure 1).[7]

- Between 2018 and 2020, the rate of public health insurance coverage increased by 0.4 percentage points to 34.8 percent (Table 1 and Figure 1).[8, 9]

- In 2020, 87.0 percent of full-time, year-round workers had private insurance coverage, up from 85.1 percent in 2018. In contrast, those who worked less than full-time, year-round were less likely to be covered by private insurance in 2020 than in 2018 (68.5 percent in 2018 and 66.7 percent in 2020) (Figure 3).[10]

- More children under the age of 19 in poverty were uninsured in 2020 than in 2018. Uninsured rates for children under the age of 19 in poverty rose 1.6 percentage points to 9.3 percent (Figure 6).

This report classifies health insurance coverage into three different groups: overall coverage, private coverage, and public coverage (The "What Is Health Insurance?" text box contains more information). In the CPS ASEC, people are considered to be insured if they were covered by any type of health insurance for part or all of the previous calendar year. People are considered uninsured if, for the entire year, they were not covered by any type of insurance.[11]

---
[5] Some people may have more than one coverage type during the calendar year.
[6] The final category includes CHAMPVA coverage and care provided by the VA and the military.
[7] All comparative statements in this report have undergone statistical testing, and unless otherwise noted, all comparisons are statistically significant at the 90 percent confidence level. Standard errors used in statistical testing and margins of errors presented in tables reflect the use of replicate weights to account for the complex sampling design of the CPS ASEC.
[8] This increase was due to growth in the number of people aged 65 and older. The proportion of the population 65 years and older with Medicare coverage decreased between 2018 and 2020, from 93.9 percent to 93.5 percent. However, the percentage of the U.S. population 65 years and older increased between 2018 and 2020.
[9] Throughout this report, details may not sum to totals because of rounding.
[10] In this report, a full-time, year-round worker is a person who worked 35 or more hours per week (full-time) and 50 or more weeks during the previous calendar year (year-round). For school personnel, summer vacation is counted as weeks worked if they are scheduled to return to their job in the fall.
[11] Infants born after the calendar-year reference period are excluded from estimates in this report, with the exception of estimates of coverage at the time of interview (Appendix B, Figure B-5).

In 2020, most people (91.4 percent) had health insurance coverage at some point during the calendar year (Table 1 and Figure 1). More people had private health insurance (66.5 percent) than public coverage (34.8 percent).

Employment-based insurance was the most common subtype of health insurance (54.4 percent), followed by Medicare (18.4 percent), Medicaid (17.8 percent), direct-purchase insurance (10.5 percent), TRICARE (2.8 percent), and VA/CHAMPVA health care (0.9 percent) (Table 1 and Figure 1).

The percentage of people covered by any type of health insurance in 2020 was not significantly different than the percentage in 2018. Although this result seems counter to reports of coverage loss during the COVID-19 pandemic, the CPS ASEC measures coverage in calendar year 2020 based on whether an individual had coverage for all or part of the year during 2020. For example, a person who held coverage in January 2020, but became uninsured later in the year during the COVID-19 pandemic, would still be considered insured in 2020 using the CPS ASEC. Further, individuals losing one type of coverage may also purchase or be eligible for another type of health coverage. People who lose employment-based coverage through job loss might access coverage through the Marketplace, purchase it directly, or they may be eligible for medical assistance through federal and state programs such as Medicaid.

Table 1.
Number and Percentage of People by Health Insurance Coverage Status and Type: 2018 to 2020

(Numbers in thousands. Margins of error in thousands or percentage points as appropriate. Population as of March of the following year. Information on confidentiality protection, sampling error, nonsampling error, and definitions is available at <https://www2.census.gov/programs-surveys/cps/techdocs/cpsmar21.pdf>)

Coverage type	2018 Number	2018 Margin of error[1] (±)	2018 Percent	2018 Margin of error[1] (±)	2019 Number	2019 Margin of error[1] (±)	2019 Percent	2019 Margin of error[1] (±)	2020 Number	2020 Margin of error[1] (±)	2020 Percent	2020 Margin of error[1] (±)	Change (2020 less 2019)	Change (2020 less 2018)
Total	323,668	133	X	X	324,550	132	X	X	325,638	153	X	X	X	X
Any health plan	296,206	641	91.5	0.2	298,438	688	92.0	0.2	297,680	638	91.4	0.2	*-0.5	-0.1
Any private plan[2,3]	217,780	1,222	67.3	0.4	220,848	1,121	68.0	0.3	216,532	1,166	66.5	0.4	*-1.6	*-0.8
Employment-based[2]	178,350	1,283	55.1	0.4	183,005	1,142	56.4	0.4	177,175	1,070	54.4	0.3	*-2.0	*-0.7
Direct-purchase[2]	34,846	647	10.8	0.2	33,170	776	10.2	0.2	34,041	653	10.5	0.2	0.2	*-0.3
Marketplace coverage[2]	10,743	428	3.3	0.1	9,716	417	3.0	0.1	10,804	439	3.3	0.1	*0.3	Z
TRICARE[2]	8,537	508	2.6	0.2	8,534	522	2.6	0.2	9,183	579	2.8	0.2	*0.2	*0.2
Any public plan[2,4]	111,330	962	34.4	0.3	110,687	967	34.1	0.3	113,337	923	34.8	0.3	*0.7	*0.4
Medicare[2]	57,720	401	17.8	0.1	58,779	409	18.1	0.1	59,844	393	18.4	0.1	*0.3	*0.5
Medicaid[2]	57,819	891	17.9	0.3	55,851	927	17.2	0.3	57,921	893	17.8	0.3	*0.6	-0.1
VA or CHAMPVA[2,5]	3,217	182	1.0	0.1	3,221	188	1.0	0.1	2,979	175	0.9	0.1	*-0.1	-0.1
Uninsured[6]	27,462	630	8.5	0.2	26,111	657	8.0	0.2	27,957	612	8.6	0.2	*0.5	0.1

* Changes between the estimates are statistically different from zero at the 90 percent confidence level.
X Not applicable.
Z Rounds to zero.
[1] A margin of error (MOE) is a measure of an estimate's variability. The larger the MOE in relation to the size of the estimate, the less reliable the estimate. This number, when added to and subtracted from the estimate, forms the 90 percent confidence interval. MOEs shown in this table are based on standard errors calculated using replicate weights.
[2] The estimates by type of coverage are not mutually exclusive; people can be covered by more than one type of health insurance during the year.
[3] Private health insurance includes coverage provided through an employer or union, coverage purchased directly, or TRICARE.
[4] Public health insurance coverage includes Medicaid, Medicare, CHAMPVA (Civilian Health and Medical Program of the Department of Veterans Affairs), and care provided by the Department of Veterans Affairs and the military.
[5] Includes CHAMPVA, as well as care provided by the Department of Veterans Affairs and the military.
[6] In the CPS ASEC, individuals are considered to be uninsured if they do not have health insurance coverage for the entire calendar year.
Source: U.S. Census Bureau, Current Population Survey, 2019 to 2021 Annual Social and Economic Supplement (CPS ASEC).

Figure 1.
Percentage of People by Type of Health Insurance Coverage and Change From 2018 to 2020
(Population as of March of the following year)

○ No statistical change between years

Type of Coverage in 2020

Uninsured	8.6
With health insurance	91.4
Any Private Plan	66.5
Employment-based	54.4
Direct-purchase	10.5
Marketplace	3.3
TRICARE	2.8
Any Public Plan	34.8
Medicare	18.4
Medicaid	17.8
VA and CHAMPVA[1]	0.9

Change: 2018 to 2020

Uninsured	+0.1
With health insurance	-0.1
Any Private Plan	*-0.8
Employment-based	*-0.7
Direct-purchase	*-0.3
Marketplace	Z
TRICARE	*+0.2
Any Public Plan	*+0.4
Medicare	*+0.5
Medicaid	-0.1
VA and CHAMPVA	*-0.1

* Denotes a statistically signficant change between 2018 and 2020 at the 90 percent confidence level.
Z Rounds to zero.
[1] Includes CHAMPVA (Civilian Health Medical Program of the Department of Veterans Affairs), as well as care provided by the Department of Veterans Affairs (VA) and the military.
Note: The estimates by type of coverage are not mutually exclusive: people can be covered by more than one type of health insurance during the year. Information on confidentiality protection, sampling error, nonsampling error, and definitions in the Current Population Survey is available at <https://www2.census.gov/programs-surveys/cps/techdocs/cpsmar21.pdf>.
Source: U.S. Census Bureau, Current Population Survey, 2019 and 2021 Annual Social and Economic Supplement (CPS ASEC).

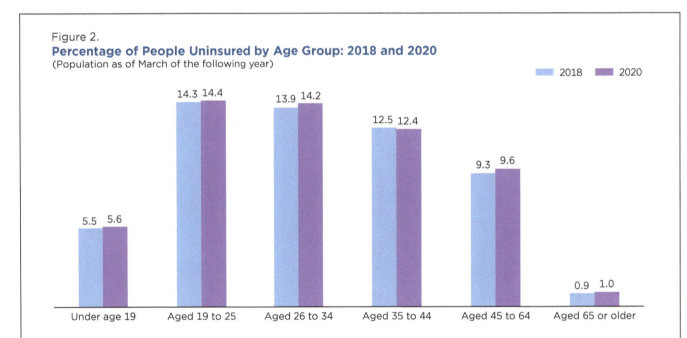

Figure 2.
Percentage of People Uninsured by Age Group: 2018 and 2020
(Population as of March of the following year)

2018 ■ 2020 ■

Age Group	2018	2020
Under age 19	5.5	5.6
Aged 19 to 25	14.3	14.4
Aged 26 to 34	13.9	14.2
Aged 35 to 44	12.5	12.4
Aged 45 to 64	9.3	9.6
Aged 65 or older	0.9	1.0

Note: There were no significant changes between 2018 and 2020 at the 90 percent confidence level. Information on confidentiality protection, sampling error, nonsampling error, and definitions in the Current Population Survey is available at <https://www2.census.gov/programs-surveys/cps/techdocs/cpsmar21.pdf>.
Source: U.S. Census Bureau, Current Population Survey, 2019 and 2021 Annual Social and Economic Supplement (CPS ASEC).

Between 2018 and 2020, of the subtypes of private health insurance, employment-based coverage and direct-purchase insurance decreased, while TRICARE increased. The percentage of people covered by employment-based insurance and direct-purchase insurance decreased by 0.7 percentage points to 54.4 percent and by 0.3 percentage points to 10.5 percent, respectively, in 2020. TRICARE coverage increased by 0.2 percentage points to 2.8 percent in 2020 (Table 1 and Figure 1).

Additionally, the percentage of people covered by a public health insurance plan increased between 2018 and 2020 to 34.8 percent (Table 1 and Figure 1). Of the three subtypes of public health insurance, only the Medicare rate increased between 2018 and 2020. The percentage of people covered by Medicare increased by 0.5 percentage points to 18.4 percent in 2020. This increase in coverage was partly due to growth in the number of people aged 65 and older. The Medicaid rate in 2020 was 17.8 percent, which was not statistically different from 2018.

Age is associated with the likelihood that a person has health insurance coverage. Older adults (those over the age of 65) and children (those under the age of 19) are more likely to have health insurance coverage than those aged 19 to 64, in part because their age makes them eligible for certain public health insurance programs. Medicare provides health coverage benefits for most adults aged 65 and older. Children under the age of 19 may qualify for coverage through Medicaid or the Children's Health Insurance Program (CHIP), and young adults may receive coverage through a parent or guardian's plan until the age of 26.[12]

In 2020, 1.0 percent of adults aged 65 and older were uninsured for the entire calendar year, while 5.6 percent of children under the age of 19 were uninsured in the same period. Among working-age adults, the age group with the largest percentage uninsured for the entirety of calendar year 2020 was those aged 19 to 25 (14.4 percent), followed by those aged 26 to 34 (14.2 percent), adults aged 35 to 44 (12.4 percent), and those aged 45 to 64 (9.6 percent) (Figure 2).[13] Between 2018 and 2020, there were no significant changes in the uninsured rate by age groups.

Selected Social Characteristics

The CPS ASEC can also be used to look at the prevalence and type of health insurance coverage across certain social and economic characteristics, as well as changes in coverage across race and Hispanic origin groups.

Overall, Hispanics had the highest uninsured rate (18.3 percent) in 2020, followed by Blacks (10.4 percent), Asians (5.9 percent), and non-Hispanic Whites (5.4 percent) (Table A-1).[14,15,16]

In 2020, Blacks had the highest rate of public coverage (41.4 percent) followed by Hispanics (35.9 percent), non-Hispanic Whites (33.8 percent), and Asians (27.0 percent). In the same year, non-Hispanic Whites had the highest rate of private coverage (73.9 percent), followed by Asians (72.4 percent), Blacks (54.6 percent), and Hispanics (49.9 percent) (Figure 3).

---

[12] CHIP is a public program that provides health insurance to children in families with income too high to qualify for Medicaid, but who are likely unable to afford private health insurance.

[13] In 2020, the uninsured rate of individuals aged 19 to 25 was not statistically different from the uninsured rate of individuals aged 26 to 34.

[14] Federal surveys give respondents the option of reporting more than one race. Therefore, two basic ways of defining a race group are possible. A group, such as Asian, may be defined as those who reported Asian and no other race (the race-alone or single-race concept) or as those who reported Asian, regardless of whether they also reported another race (the race-alone-or-in-combination concept). The body of this report (text, figures, and tables) shows data using the first approach (race alone). Use of the single-race population does not imply that it is the preferred method of presenting or analyzing data. The Census Bureau uses a variety of approaches. Data for American Indians and Alaska Natives, Native Hawaiians and Other Pacific Islanders, and those reporting two or more races are not shown separately.

In this report, the term "non-Hispanic White" refers to people who are not Hispanic and who reported White and no other race. The Census Bureau uses non-Hispanic Whites as the comparison group for other race groups and Hispanics.

Because Hispanic people may be any race, data in this report for Hispanic people overlap with data for racial groups. Of those who reported only one race, 16.0 percent of White householders, 5.3 percent of Black householders, and 2.7 percent of Asian householders also reported being Hispanic.

Data users should exercise caution when interpreting aggregate results for the Hispanic population and for race groups because these populations consist of many distinct groups that differ in socioeconomic characteristics, culture, and recency of immigration. Data were first collected for Hispanic people in 1972.

[15] The small sample size of the Asian population and the fact that the CPS ASEC does not use separate population controls for weighting the Asian sample to national totals contributes to the large variances surrounding estimates for this group. As a result, the CPS ASEC may be unable to detect statistically significant differences between some estimates for the Asian population.

[16] In 2020, the uninsured rate of non-Hispanic Whites was not statistically different from the uninsured rate of Asians.

Health Insurance Coverage in the United States: 2020

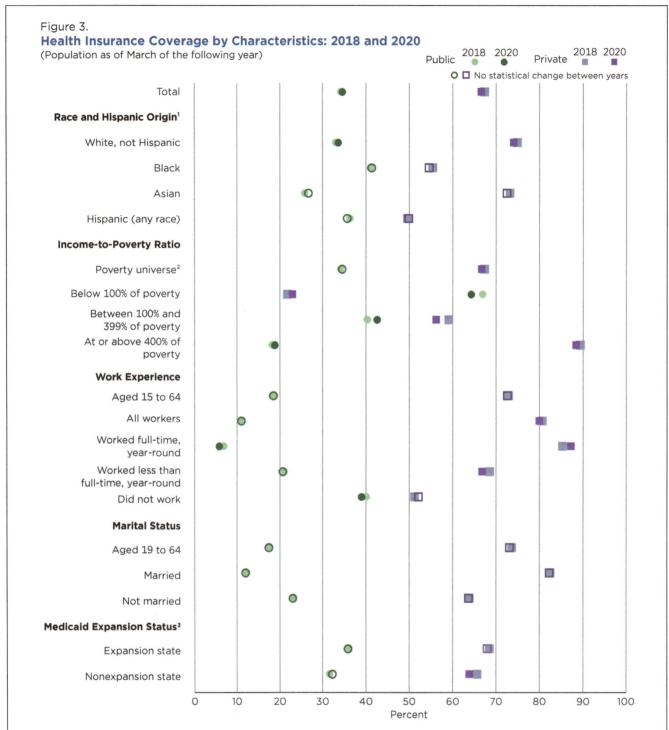

Non-Hispanic Whites experienced changes in health insurance status between 2018 and 2020. Specifically, private coverage decreased by 0.9 percentage points to 73.9 percent, and public coverage increased by 0.6 percentage points to 33.8 percent in 2020. In contrast, there was no significant change in either private or public coverage between 2018 and 2020 for Hispanics of any race, Blacks, or Asians.

Selected Economic Characteristics

For many adults aged 15 to 64, health insurance coverage is related to work status such as working full-time, year-round, working less than full-time, year-round, or not working at all during the calendar year. Workers were more likely than nonworkers to be covered by private health insurance. In 2020, 87.0 percent of full-time, year-round workers were covered through a private insurance plan, compared with 66.7 percent of those working less than full-time, year-round. Those who did not work were the least likely to have private health insurance coverage, at 52.2 percent (Figure 3 and Table A-2).

Overall, between 2018 and 2020, workers' private coverage declined by approximately 0.7 percentage points. However, this decrease was not equal across all types of workers. For example, the percentage of full-time, year-round workers with private coverage increased by 1.9 percentage points, while private insurance coverage rates for those who worked less than full-time, year-round decreased by 1.9 percentage points. There was no statistical change in private coverage for nonworkers between 2018 and 2020.

Rates of public coverage followed a different pattern. Nonworkers were more likely than those working less than full-time, year-round to have public coverage (39.1 percent of nonworkers versus 20.9 percent of less than full-time, year-round workers). Full-time, year-round workers were the least likely to have public coverage, at 6.1 percent. In 2020, public insurance coverage rates decreased by 1.0 percentage point for full-time, year-round workers and 1.0 percentage point for nonworkers compared to 2018.

Many adults obtain health insurance coverage through their spouses, and, therefore, health insurance coverage is related to marital status. Adults aged 19 to 64 who were not married were less likely to have private health insurance than married adults (63.6 percent and 82.1 percent, respectively). There were no changes in private or public health insurance rates between 2018 and 2020 for either married or unmarried people (Figure 3 and Table A-2).[17]

Health insurance coverage and type is also associated with family income-to-poverty ratio, which provides a measure of a family's economic resources.[18] Family resources may determine the ability to afford private health insurance, and families below certain income-to-poverty thresholds may qualify for public health insurance options. Figure 4 shows the public coverage rate, private coverage rate, and uninsured rate for individuals based on their family's income-to-poverty ratio in 2020.

---

[17] Unmarried people include those who were never married, as well as those who are widowed, divorced, or separated. For estimates of health coverage for each of these groups, refer to Appendix Table A-2.

[18] The Office of Management and Budget (OMB) determined the official definition of poverty in Statistical Policy Directive 14. Appendix B of the report, "Income and Poverty in the United States: 2020," provides a more detailed description of how the Census Bureau calculates poverty. More information is available at <www.census.gov/content/dam/Census/library/publications/2021/demo/p60-273.pdf>.

For private insurance, those living in poverty are the least likely to have private insurance (23.2 percent), and each group with a higher income-to-poverty ratio has a higher rate of private insurance. Those living at or above 400 percent of the poverty line are the most likely to have private health insurance (88.2 percent) (Figure 4).

In contrast, those living in poverty are the most likely to have public insurance (64.3 percent), while those living at or above 400 percent of the poverty line are the least likely to have public health insurance (19.1 percent). The percentage of people with public insurance decreases as the income-to-poverty ratio increases.

As the income-to-poverty ratio increases, the percentage of uninsured declines. Those in poverty have the highest rate of people uninsured for the full calendar year (17.2 percent), while those living at or above 400 percent of the poverty line have the lowest rate of people uninsured for all of 2020 (3.4 percent). Other income-to-poverty groups fall between these rates, and those with higher income-to-poverty ratios are less likely to be uninsured.

Changes in health insurance coverage by type were not distributed equally across income-to-poverty ratio groups. For example, people with an income-to-poverty ratio between 100 and 399 percent and those at or above 400 percent of poverty increased their rates of public insurance use between 2018 and 2020 (by 2.2 percentage points and 0.6 percentage points, respectively) (Figure 3).

In contrast, between 2018 and 2020, rates of private insurance decreased for people with an income-to-poverty ratio between 100 and 399 percent

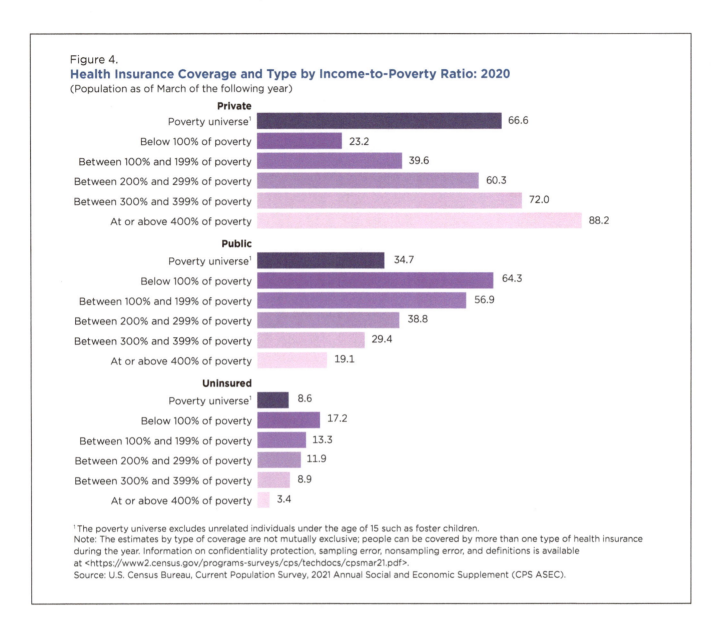

Figure 4.
Health Insurance Coverage and Type by Income-to-Poverty Ratio: 2020
(Population as of March of the following year)

[1] The poverty universe excludes unrelated individuals under the age of 15 such as foster children.
Note: The estimates by type of coverage are not mutually exclusive; people can be covered by more than one type of health insurance during the year. Information on confidentiality protection, sampling error, nonsampling error, and definitions is available at <https://www2.census.gov/programs-surveys/cps/techdocs/cpsmar21.pdf>.
Source: U.S. Census Bureau, Current Population Survey, 2021 Annual Social and Economic Supplement (CPS ASEC).

of poverty and those at or above 400 percent of poverty (by 2.9 percentage points and 1.0 percentage point, respectively). However, those in poverty saw an increase in private health coverage by 1.3 percentage points (Figure 3).

Income-to-Poverty Ratio and Medicaid Expansion Status

The Patient Protection and Affordable Care Act provided the option for states to expand Medicaid eligibility to adults whose income-to-poverty ratio fell under 138 percent of the poverty line.[19] As of January 1, 2020, 35 states and the District of Columbia had expanded Medicaid eligibility ("expansion states"); 15 states had not expanded Medicaid eligibility ("non-expansion states").[20] The uninsured rate in 2020 varied by state Medicaid expansion status. In 2020, among adults aged 19 to 64, those in expansion states had lower

[19] In 2020, the Medicaid income eligibility threshold for adults under the age of 65 in the District of Columbia was 221 percent of the poverty line. More information is available in "Medicaid and CHIP Eligibility, Enrollment, and Cost Sharing Policies as of January 2020: Findings From a 50-state Survey," <https://files.kff.org/attachment/Report-Medicaid-and-CHIP-Eligibility,-Enrollment-and-Cost-Sharing-Policies-as-of-January-2020.pdf>.

[20] The 35 states and the District of Columbia that expanded Medicaid eligibility on or before January 1, 2020, include AK, AR, AZ, CA, CO, CT, DC, DE, HI, IA, ID, IL, IN, KY, LA, MA, MD, ME, MI, MN, MT, ND, NH, NJ, NM, NV, NY, OH, OR, PA, RI, UT, VA, VT, WA, and WV. More information is available at <www.medicaid.gov/state-overviews/index.html>.

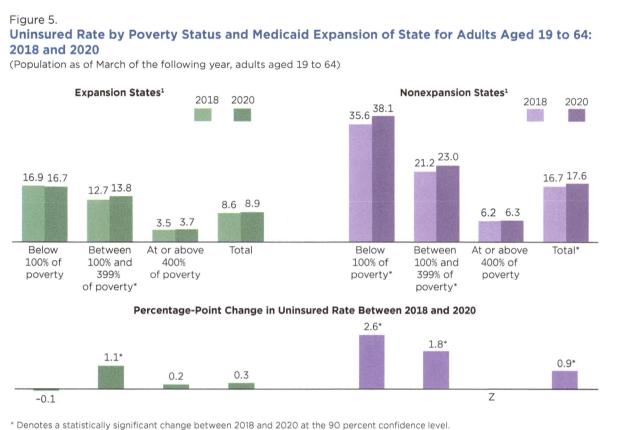

Figure 5.
Uninsured Rate by Poverty Status and Medicaid Expansion of State for Adults Aged 19 to 64: 2018 and 2020
(Population as of March of the following year, adults aged 19 to 64)

* Denotes a statistically significant change between 2018 and 2020 at the 90 percent confidence level.
Z Rounds to zero.
[1] Medicaid expansion status as of January 1, 2020, for 2020 data. Medicaid expansion status as of January 1, 2018, for 2018 data. Expansion states on or before January 1, 2018, include AK, AR, AZ, CA, CO, CT, DC, DE, HI, IA, IL, IN, KY, LA, MA, MD, MI, MN, MT, ND, NH, NJ, NM, NV, NY, OH, OR, PA, RI, VT, WA, and WV. After January 1, 2018, and on or before January 1, 2020, ID, ME, UT, and VA expanded Medicaid. More information is available at <www.medicaid.gov/state-overviews/index.html>.
Note: Information on confidentiality protection, sampling error, nonsampling error, and definitions, is available at <https://www2.census.gov/programs-surveys/cps/techdocs/cpsmar21.pdf>.
Source: U.S. Census Bureau, Current Population Survey, 2019 and 2021 Annual Social and Economic Supplement (CPS ASEC).

uninsured rates (8.9 percent) than those in nonexpansion states (17.6 percent) (Figure 5).

Further, the relationship between poverty status, health insurance coverage in 2020, and the change in coverage between 2018 and 2020 may be related to an individual's state of residence and whether that state expanded Medicaid eligibility (Figure 5).

Uninsured rates were lower for all income-to-poverty groups in expansion states than in nonexpansion states. For people in families living in poverty in nonexpansion states, there was a 2.6 percentage-point increase in the uninsured rate, to 38.1 percent between 2018 and 2020, while there was no statistically significant change in the uninsured rate for those in poverty in expansion states.[21] Among people with family income between 100 and 399 percent of poverty, 23.0 percent of people in nonexpansion states did not have health insurance for the full year, representing a 1.8 percentage-point increase in the percentage of uninsured from 2018. For the same group in expansion states, there was a 1.1 percentage-point increase in the percentage of uninsured to 13.8 percent. For all other income-to-poverty groups, there was no significant change in the uninsured rate between 2018 and 2020.

Health Insurance Coverage by Age and Selected Characteristics

In 2020, 5.6 percent of children under the age of 19 did not have health insurance coverage, which was not statistically different from 2018 (Figure 6). Examining coverage by children's characteristics reveals that changes in health insurance coverage between 2018 and 2020 did not occur equally across groups.

---
[21] Between 2018 and 2020, the change in the uninsured rate of people in poverty living in expansion states was not statistically different from the change in the uninsured rate of people in poverty living in nonexpansion states.

Figure 6.
Percentage of Children Under the Age of 19 Without Health Insurance Coverage by Selected Characteristics: 2018 and 2020

(Population as of March of the following year, children under age 19)

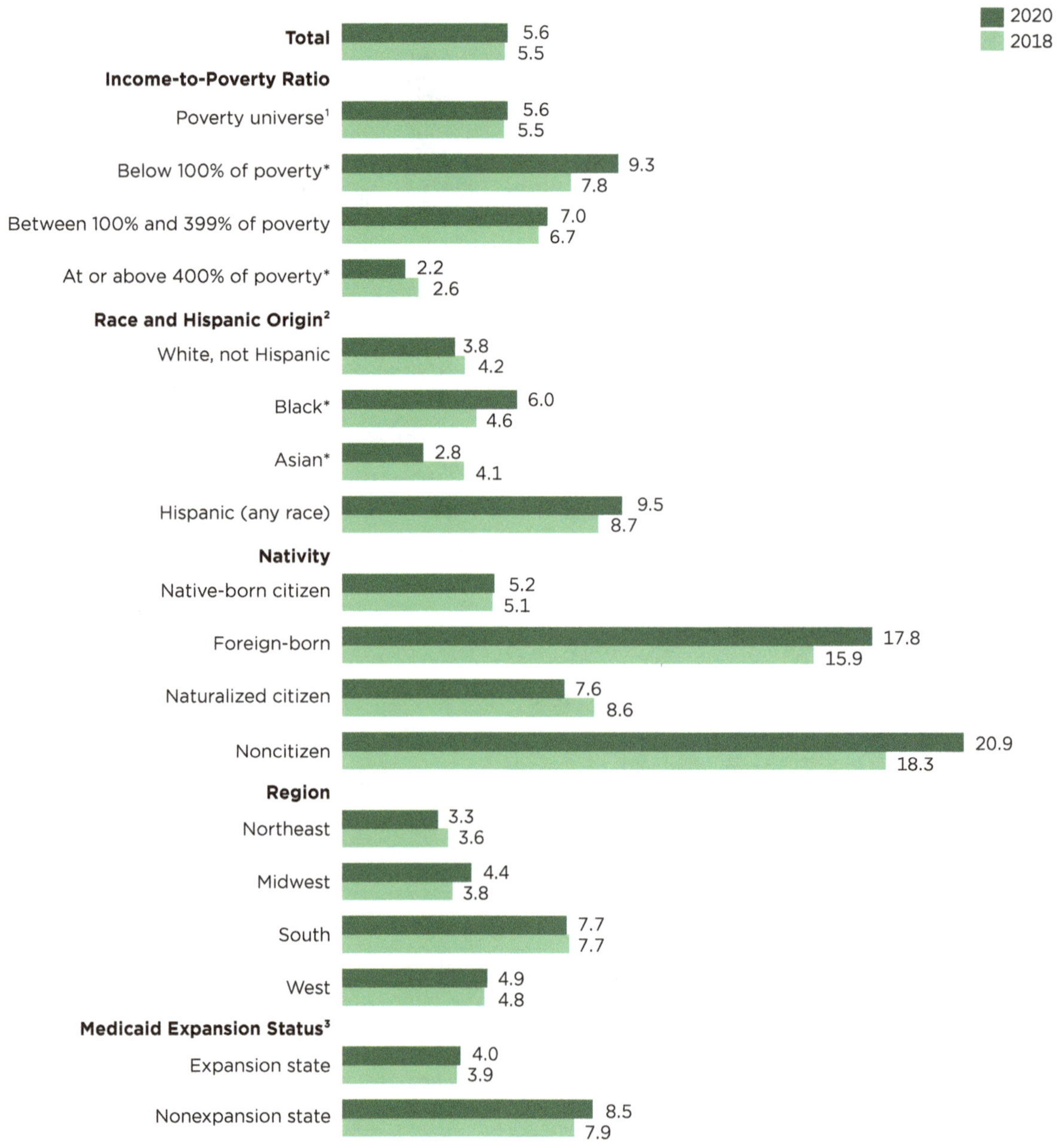

Characteristic	2020	2018
Total	5.6	5.5
Income-to-Poverty Ratio		
Poverty universe[1]	5.6	5.5
Below 100% of poverty*	9.3	7.8
Between 100% and 399% of poverty	7.0	6.7
At or above 400% of poverty*	2.2	2.6
Race and Hispanic Origin[2]		
White, not Hispanic	3.8	4.2
Black*	6.0	4.6
Asian*	2.8	4.1
Hispanic (any race)	9.5	8.7
Nativity		
Native-born citizen	5.2	5.1
Foreign-born	17.8	15.9
Naturalized citizen	7.6	8.6
Noncitizen	20.9	18.3
Region		
Northeast	3.3	3.6
Midwest	4.4	3.8
South	7.7	7.7
West	4.9	4.8
Medicaid Expansion Status[3]		
Expansion state	4.0	3.9
Nonexpansion state	8.5	7.9

* Denotes a statistically significant change between 2018 and 2020 at the 90 percent confidence level.
[1] The poverty universe excludes unrelated individuals under the age of 15 such as foster children.
[2] Federal surveys give respondents the option of reporting more than one race. This figure shows data using the race-alone concept. For example, "Asian" refers to people who reported Asian and no other race.
[3] Medicaid expansion status as of January 1, 2020, for 2020 data. Medicaid expansion status as of January 1, 2018, for 2018 data. Expansion states on or before January 1, 2018, include AK, AR, AZ, CA, CO, CT, DC, DE, HI, IA, IL, IN, KY, LA, MA, MD, MI, MN, MT, ND, NH, NJ, NM, NV, NY, OH, OR, PA, RI, VT, WA, and WV. After January 1, 2018, and on or before January 1, 2020, ID, ME, UT, and VA expanded Medicaid. More information is available at <www.medicaid.gov/state-overviews/index.html>.

Note: Information on confidentiality protection, sampling error, nonsampling error, and definitions is available at <https://www2.census.gov/programs-surveys/cps/techdocs/cpsmar21.pdf>.

Source: U.S. Census Bureau, Current Population Survey, 2019 and 2021 Annual Social and Economic Supplement (CPS ASEC).

Among children living in poverty, 9.3 percent did not have health insurance at any time in 2020, representing an increase of 1.6 percentage points since 2018. For children in families at or above 400 percent of poverty, the uninsured rate decreased by 0.4 percentage points, to 2.2 percent. In 2020, 7.0 percent of children between 100 and 399 percent of poverty did not have health insurance, which is not statistically different from 2018. In both years, the percentage of children without health insurance coverage decreased as the income-to-poverty ratio increased.

The percentage of non-Hispanic White children without health insurance coverage was not statistically different in 2020 compared with 2018. However, the uninsured rate decreased for Asian children (by 1.4 percentage points) and increased for Black children (by 1.4 percentage points), to 2.8 percent and 6.0 percent, respectively. In 2020, 9.5 percent of Hispanic children were uninsured, which is not statistically different from 2018.

In 2020, 5.2 percent of children born in the United States were uninsured. However, among foreign-born children, 17.8 percent were uninsured, including 7.6 percent of children who were naturalized citizens and 20.9 percent of children who were not citizens.[22]

Health insurance rates for children varied by region as well.[23] For example, 7.7 percent of children living in the South were uninsured, while the uninsured rates for children in the Northeast (3.3 percent), Midwest (4.4 percent), and West (4.9 percent) were lower.[24]

Health insurance rates varied for children who lived in expansion states compared to those who lived in nonexpansion states (4.0 percent and 8.5 percent, respectively).

Health insurance outcomes for working-age adults aged 19 to 64 may differ from those in other age groups because they do not qualify for certain programs, such as CHIP, and only qualify for Medicare under limited circumstances. In 2020, 11.9 percent of working-age adults (aged 19 to 64) did not have health insurance coverage, which was not statistically different from 2018 (Figure 7).

The uninsured rate for noncitizen adults aged 19 to 64 increased 2.2 percentage points between 2018 and 2020. In 2020, 33.8 percent of working-age noncitizens did not have health insurance, which is higher than foreign-born adults (22.9 percent), naturalized citizen adults (10.7 percent), and native-born adults (9.6 percent).

The uninsured rate decreased by 1.1 percentage points for working-age adults who worked full-time, year-round, from 9.5 percent in 2018 to 8.4 percent in 2020. However, the uninsured rate increased by 1.8 percentage points for working-age adults who worked less than full-time, year-round to 16.4 percent.

Among working-age adults in 2020, those who were separated (20.2 percent), never married (16.0 percent), divorced (13.2 percent), or widowed (12.1 percent) were more likely to be uninsured than those who were married (8.5 percent).[25]

Health insurance rates for working-age adults also varied by region. For example, 11.3 percent of adults living in the West in 2020 were uninsured, a 0.8 percentage-point increase from 2018. There was no significant change in uninsured rates for working-age adults in other regions.

ADDITIONAL INFORMATION ABOUT HEALTH INSURANCE COVERAGE

State and Local Estimates of Health Insurance Coverage

Since the CPS ASEC produces thorough and timely estimates of income, poverty, and health insurance, the Census Bureau recommends that people use it as the data source for national estimates. However, the Census Bureau also publishes annual estimates of health insurance coverage by state and other smaller geographic units based on data collected in the American Community Survey (ACS). Single-year estimates are available for geographic units with populations of 65,000 or more. Five-year estimates are available for all geographic units, including census tracts and block groups.

Due to the impact of the pandemic on data collection, the standard 1-year estimates from the 2020 ACS will not be released. However, the Census Bureau plans to release experimental estimates developed from the 2020 ACS 1-year data later this year in the form of a limited number of data tables for limited geographies.

---

[22] In 2020, the uninsured rate of native-born children under the age of 19 was not statistically different from the uninsured rate of naturalized citizen children.

[23] For information about how the Census Bureau classifies regions, refer to <https://www2.census.gov/geo/pdfs/maps-data/maps/reference/us_regdiv.pdf>.

[24] In 2020, the uninsured rate of children living in the West was not statistically different from the uninsured rate of children living in the Midwest.

[25] In 2020, the uninsured rate of divorced adults aged 19 to 64 was not statistically different from the uninsured rate of widowed adults aged 19 to 64.

Health Insurance Coverage in the United States: 2020

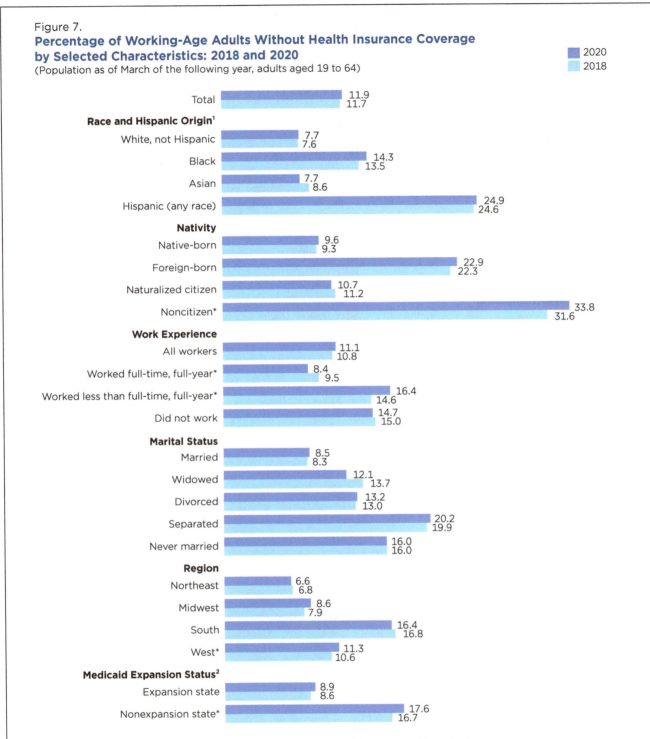

Figure 7.
Percentage of Working-Age Adults Without Health Insurance Coverage by Selected Characteristics: 2018 and 2020
(Population as of March of the following year, adults aged 19 to 64)

* Denotes a statistically significant change between 2018 and 2020 at the 90 percent confidence level.
[1] Federal surveys give respondents the option of reporting more than one race. This figure shows data using the race-alone concept. For example, "Asian" refers to people who reported Asian and no other race.
[2] Medicaid expansion status as of January 1, 2020, for 2020 data. Medicaid expansion status as of January 1, 2018, for 2018 data. Expansion states on or before January 1, 2018, include AK, AR, AZ, CA, CO, CT, DC, DE, HI, IA, IL, IN, KY, LA, MA, MD, MI, MN, MT, ND, NH, NJ, NM, NV, NY, OH, OR, PA, RI, VT, WA, and WV. After January 1, 2018, and on or before January 1, 2020, ID, ME, UT, and VA expanded Medicaid. More information is available at <www.medicaid.gov/state-overviews/index.html>.
Note: Information on confidentiality protection, sampling error, nonsampling error, and definitions is available at <https://www2.census.gov/programs-surveys/cps/techdocs/cpsmar21.pdf>.
Source: U.S. Census Bureau, Current Population Survey, 2019 and 2021 Annual Social and Economic Supplement (CPS ASEC).

The Census Bureau's Small Area Health Insurance Estimates (SAHIE) program also produces single-year estimates of health insurance for all states and all counties. These estimates are based on statistical models using data from a variety of sources, including current surveys, administrative records, and annual population estimates. In general, SAHIE estimates have lower variances than ACS estimates but are released later because they incorporate these additional data into their models.

Small Area Health Insurance Estimates are available at <www.census.gov/programs-surveys/sahie.html>. The most recent estimates are for 2019.

Additional Data

The CPS ASEC is used to produce additional health insurance coverage tables. These tables are available on the Census Bureau's Health Insurance Web site. The Web site may be accessed through the Census Bureau's home page at <www.census.gov> or directly at <www.census.gov/data/tables/2021/demo/health-insurance/p60-274.html>.

For assistance with health insurance data, contact the Census Bureau Customer Services Center at 1-800-923-8282 (toll-free), or search your topic of interest using the Census Bureau's "Question and Answer Center" found at <https://ask.census.gov>.

Data.census.gov

Data.census.gov is the new platform to access data and digital content from the Census Bureau. It is the official source of data for the Census Bureau's most popular surveys and programs such as the ACS, Decennial Census, Economic Census, and more. Through the centralized experience on data.census.gov, data users of all skill levels can search premade tables or create custom statistics from Public Use Microdata files.

The Census Bureau created easy ways to visualize, customize, and download data through a single platform on data.census.gov in response to user feedback. To learn more about data.census.gov, check out the release notes at <https://www2.census.gov/data/api-documentation/data-census-gov-release-notes.pdf>.

In addition to the pretabulated detailed and historical tables available online, data users of all skill levels can create custom statistics from Public Use Microdata files using the Microdata Access Tool (MDAT) available at <https://data.census.gov/mdat>. The MDAT provides data users the ability to create customized tables using public-use data from the CPS ASEC.

Public-Use Microdata

Microdata for the CPS ASEC are available online at <www.census.gov/data/datasets/time-series/demo/cps/cps-asec.html>. Technical methods have been applied to CPS microdata to avoid disclosing the identities of individuals from whom data were collected.

Census Data API

The Census Data Application Programming Interface (API) gives the public access to pretabulated data from various Census Bureau data programs. It is an efficient way to query data directly from Census Bureau servers with many advantages, including the ability to easily download target variables and geographies and immediately access the most current data. Users can find which datasets are currently available via API online at <www.census.gov/data/developers/data-sets.html>.

SOURCE AND ACCURACY OF THE ESTIMATES

The estimates in this report are from the CPS ASEC. The CPS is the longest-running survey conducted by the Census Bureau. The CPS is a household survey primarily used to collect employment data. The sample universe for the basic CPS consists of the resident civilian, noninstitutionalized population of the United States. People in institutions, such as prisons, long-term care hospitals, and nursing homes, are not eligible to be interviewed in the CPS. Students living in dormitories are included in the estimates only if information about them is reported in an interview at their parents' home. Since the CPS is a household survey, people who are homeless and not living in shelters are not included in the sample.

The CPS ASEC collects data in February, March, and April each year, asking detailed questions categorizing income into over 50 sources. The key purpose of the CPS ASEC is to provide timely and comprehensive estimates of income, poverty, and health insurance and to measure change in these national-level estimates. The CPS ASEC is the official source of national poverty estimates calculated in accordance with the Office of Management and Budget's Statistical Policy Directive 14.[26]

The CPS ASEC collects data in the 50 states and the District of Columbia; these data do not represent residents of Puerto Rico or U.S. Island Areas.[27] The 2021 CPS ASEC sample consists of about 90,800 addresses. The CPS ASEC includes military personnel who live in a household with at least one other civilian adult, regardless of whether they live off post or on post. All other armed forces personnel are excluded. The estimates in

---

[26] The OMB determined the official definition of poverty in Statistical Policy Directive 14. Appendix B of the report, "Income and Poverty in the United States: 2020," provides a more detailed description of how the Census Bureau calculates poverty. More information is available at <www.census.gov/content/dam/Census/library/publications/2021/demo/p60-273.pdf>.

[27] U.S. Island Areas include American Samoa, Guam, the Commonwealth of the Northern Mariana Islands, and the Virgin Islands of the United States.

this report are controlled to March 2021 independent national population estimates by age, sex, race, and Hispanic origin. Beginning with 2010, population estimates are based on 2010 Census population counts and are updated annually taking into account births, deaths, emigration, and immigration.

The estimates in this report (which may be shown in text, figures, and tables) are based on responses from a sample of the population and may differ from actual values because of sampling variability or other factors. As a result, apparent differences between the estimates for two or more groups may not be statistically significant. All comparative statements have undergone statistical testing and are statistically significant at the 90 percent confidence level unless otherwise noted. In this report, the variances of estimates were calculated using the Successive Difference Replication (SDR) method.

Beginning with the 2011 CPS ASEC report, the standard errors and confidence intervals displayed in tables were calculated using the SDR method, unless otherwise noted. In previous years, the standard errors of CPS ASEC estimates were calculated using the generalized variance function (GVF) approach. Under this approach, generalized variance parameters were used in formulas provided in the source and accuracy statement to estimate standard errors. Further information on replicate weights, standard errors, income top-coding and data swapping on the public-use file, and changes to the CPS ASEC data file is available at <https://www2.census.gov/programs-surveys/cps/techdocs/cpsmar21.pdf>.

Comments

The Census Bureau welcomes the comments and advice of data and report users. If you have suggestions or comments on the health insurance coverage report, please write to:

Sharon Stern
Assistant Division Chief, Employment Characteristics
Social, Economic, and Housing Statistics Division
U.S. Census Bureau
Washington, DC 20233-8500

or e-mail
<sharon.m.stern@census.gov>.

APPENDIX A.

Table A-1.
Percentage of People by Health Insurance Coverage Status and Type by Selected Characteristics: 2018, 2019, and 2020

(Numbers in thousands. Population as of March of the following year. Information on confidentiality protection, sampling error, nonsampling error, and definitions is available at <https://www2.census.gov/programs-surveys/cps/techdocs/cpsmar21.pdf>)

Characteristic	Total Number	Any health insurance Percent	Margin of error[1] (±)	Private health insurance[2] Percent	Margin of error[1] (±)	Public health insurance[3] Percent	Margin of error[1] (±)	Uninsured[4] Percent	Margin of error[1] (±)
2020 Total	325,638	91.4	0.2	66.5	0.4	34.8	0.3	8.6	0.2
Race[5] and Hispanic Origin									
White	247,763	91.7	0.2	68.6	0.4	34.3	0.3	8.3	0.2
White, not Hispanic	194,230	94.6	0.2	73.9	0.4	33.8	0.4	5.4	0.2
Black	43,427	89.6	0.6	54.6	1.0	41.4	0.8	10.4	0.6
Asian	20,125	94.1	0.6	72.4	1.2	27.0	1.1	5.9	0.6
Hispanic (any race)	61,160	81.7	0.7	49.9	0.9	35.9	0.7	18.3	0.7
Age									
Under age 65	269,802	89.8	0.2	70.0	0.4	22.6	0.3	10.2	0.2
Under age 19[6]	76,156	94.4	0.3	62.2	0.6	35.1	0.6	5.6	0.3
Aged 19 to 64	193,646	88.1	0.3	73.0	0.4	17.7	0.3	11.9	0.3
Aged 19 to 25[7]	29,269	85.6	0.6	69.4	0.9	18.2	0.8	14.4	0.6
Aged 26 to 34	40,916	85.8	0.6	70.4	0.8	18.2	0.6	14.2	0.6
Aged 35 to 44	42,004	87.6	0.5	73.7	0.7	16.3	0.6	12.4	0.5
Aged 45 to 64	81,457	90.4	0.3	75.3	0.5	18.0	0.4	9.6	0.3
Aged 65 and older	55,836	99.0	0.1	49.6	0.8	93.6	0.3	1.0	0.1
Nativity									
Native-born	280,839	93.1	0.2	68.2	0.4	35.4	0.3	6.9	0.2
Foreign-born	44,799	80.7	0.7	55.8	0.9	30.9	0.7	19.3	0.7
Naturalized citizen	22,667	91.7	0.5	63.8	1.0	36.8	0.9	8.3	0.5
Not a citizen	22,132	69.4	1.2	47.5	1.3	24.9	1.0	30.6	1.2
Region									
Northeast	54,771	95.2	0.4	69.1	0.9	37.8	0.9	4.8	0.4
Midwest	67,436	93.8	0.4	71.7	0.8	33.5	0.7	6.2	0.4
South	125,396	88.2	0.4	63.4	0.6	33.6	0.5	11.8	0.4
West	78,035	91.8	0.3	65.0	0.7	35.7	0.6	8.2	0.3
State Medicaid Expansion Status[8]									
Lived in Medicaid expansion state	211,948	93.6	0.2	67.9	0.5	36.1	0.4	6.4	0.2
Did not live in Medicaid expansion state	113,690	87.4	0.4	63.8	0.6	32.5	0.5	12.6	0.4

Footnotes provided at end of table.

Table A-1.
Percentage of People by Health Insurance Coverage Status and Type by Selected Characteristics: 2018, 2019, and 2020—Con.

(Numbers in thousands. Population as of March of the following year. Information on confidentiality protection, sampling error, nonsampling error, and definitions is available at <https://www2.census.gov/programs-surveys/cps/techdocs/cpsmar21.pdf>)

Characteristic	Total							Uninsured[4]	
	Any health insurance								
				Private health insurance[2]		Public health insurance[3]			
	Number	Percent	Margin of error[1] (±)	Percent	Margin of error[1] (±)	Percent	Margin of error[1] (±)	Percent	Margin of error[1] (±)
2019 Total	324,550	92.0	0.2	68.0	0.3	34.1	0.3	8.0	0.2
Race[5] and Hispanic Origin									
White	247,869	92.2	0.2	70.1	0.4	33.5	0.3	7.8	0.2
White, not Hispanic	194,518	94.8	0.2	75.2	0.4	33.0	0.4	5.2	0.2
Black	42,991	90.4	0.5	55.2	0.9	41.8	0.9	9.6	0.5
Asian	19,905	93.8	0.7	74.4	1.1	25.2	0.9	6.2	0.7
Hispanic (any race)	60,517	83.3	0.7	51.6	0.9	35.8	0.8	16.7	0.7
Age									
Under age 65	269,908	90.5	0.2	71.4	0.4	22.0	0.3	9.5	0.2
Under age 19[6]	76,636	94.8	0.3	63.6	0.7	34.3	0.7	5.2	0.3
Aged 19 to 64	193,272	88.9	0.3	74.4	0.4	17.2	0.3	11.1	0.3
Aged 19 to 25[7]	29,605	85.8	0.7	70.8	0.8	17.2	0.7	14.2	0.7
Aged 26 to 34	40,511	86.7	0.5	71.5	0.7	17.8	0.6	13.3	0.5
Aged 35 to 44	41,412	88.6	0.5	75.6	0.7	15.6	0.6	11.4	0.5
Aged 45 to 64	81,744	91.2	0.3	76.7	0.5	17.6	0.5	8.8	0.3
Aged 65 and older	54,642	98.9	0.1	51.6	0.7	93.8	0.3	1.1	0.1
Nativity									
Native-born	279,653	93.5	0.2	69.7	0.4	34.6	0.3	6.5	0.2
Foreign-born	44,897	82.2	0.7	57.7	0.8	30.8	0.7	17.8	0.7
Naturalized citizen	22,750	91.3	0.6	64.0	1.1	36.6	1.0	8.7	0.6
Not a citizen	22,147	72.9	1.1	51.3	1.2	24.9	1.0	27.1	1.1
Region									
Northeast	55,080	95.3	0.4	70.8	0.9	35.9	0.9	4.7	0.4
Midwest	67,486	94.3	0.4	73.2	0.7	33.5	0.8	5.7	0.4
South	124,084	89.0	0.4	65.0	0.6	32.8	0.5	11.0	0.4
West	77,900	92.4	0.4	66.5	0.8	35.4	0.7	7.6	0.4
State Medicaid Expansion Status[8]									
Lived in Medicaid expansion state	205,888	94.0	0.2	69.3	0.4	35.6	0.4	6.0	0.2
Did not live in Medicaid expansion state	118,661	88.4	0.4	65.9	0.6	31.6	0.5	11.6	0.4

Footnotes provided at end of table.

Table A-1.
Percentage of People by Health Insurance Coverage Status and Type by Selected Characteristics: 2018, 2019, and 2020—Con.

(Numbers in thousands. Population as of March of the following year. Information on confidentiality protection, sampling error, nonsampling error, and definitions is available at <https://www2.census.gov/programs-surveys/cps/techdocs/cpsmar21.pdf>)

Characteristic	Total								
	Any health insurance							Uninsured[4]	
				Private health insurance[2]		Public health insurance[3]			
	Number	Percent	Margin of error[1] (±)	Percent	Margin of error[1] (±)	Percent	Margin of error[1] (±)	Percent	Margin of error[1] (±)
2018 Total	323,668	91.5	0.2	67.3	0.4	34.4	0.3	8.5	0.2
Race[5] and Hispanic Origin									
White	247,472	91.8	0.2	69.3	0.4	33.8	0.3	8.2	0.2
White, not Hispanic	194,679	94.6	0.2	74.8	0.4	33.2	0.3	5.4	0.2
Black	42,758	90.3	0.5	55.4	1.1	41.2	0.9	9.7	0.5
Asian	19,770	93.2	0.6	73.1	1.3	26.1	1.1	6.8	0.6
Hispanic (any race)	59,925	82.2	0.6	49.6	1.0	36.5	0.8	17.8	0.6
Age									
Under age 65	270,881	90.0	0.2	70.2	0.4	22.8	0.3	10.0	0.2
Under age 19[6]	77,333	94.5	0.3	61.8	0.7	35.7	0.7	5.5	0.3
Aged 19 to 64	193,548	88.3	0.3	73.5	0.4	17.6	0.3	11.7	0.3
Aged 19 to 25[7]	29,297	85.7	0.6	69.9	0.9	18.3	0.7	14.3	0.6
Aged 26 to 34	40,768	86.1	0.5	71.3	0.8	17.5	0.6	13.9	0.5
Aged 35 to 44	41,027	87.5	0.5	73.7	0.6	16.2	0.5	12.5	0.5
Aged 45 to 64	82,455	90.7	0.3	75.8	0.5	18.1	0.4	9.3	0.3
Aged 65 and older	52,788	99.1	0.1	52.4	0.7	94.1	0.3	0.9	0.1
Nativity									
Native-born	277,848	93.2	0.2	69.1	0.4	34.9	0.3	6.8	0.2
Foreign-born	45,820	81.1	0.6	56.0	0.9	31.2	0.7	18.9	0.6
Naturalized citizen	22,296	91.2	0.6	64.0	1.0	36.4	1.0	8.8	0.6
Not a citizen	23,524	71.4	1.0	48.4	1.1	26.2	1.0	28.6	1.0
Region									
Northeast	55,266	94.9	0.5	69.4	0.9	36.9	0.8	5.1	0.5
Midwest	67,458	94.3	0.4	72.8	0.8	33.3	0.7	5.7	0.4
South	123,391	87.9	0.4	64.2	0.6	33.1	0.4	12.1	0.4
West	77,553	92.3	0.4	65.9	0.8	35.6	0.7	7.7	0.4
State Medicaid Expansion Status[8]									
Lived in Medicaid expansion state	197,396	93.8	0.2	68.4	0.5	36.1	0.4	6.2	0.2
Did not live in Medicaid expansion state	126,273	88.0	0.4	65.6	0.6	31.8	0.4	12.0	0.4

[1] A margin of error (MOE) is a measure of an estimate's variability. The larger the MOE in relation to the size of the estimate, the less reliable the estimate. This number, when added to and subtracted from the estimate, forms the 90 percent confidence interval. MOEs shown in this table are based on standard errors calculated using replicate weights.
[2] Private health insurance includes coverage provided through an employer or union, coverage purchased directly, or TRICARE.
[3] Public health insurance coverage includes Medicaid, Medicare, CHAMPVA (Civilian Health and Medical Program of the Department of Veterans Affairs), and care provided by the Department of Veterans Affairs and the military.
[4] Individuals are considered to be uninsured if they do not have health insurance coverage for the entire calendar year.
[5] Federal surveys give respondents the option of reporting more than one race. Therefore, two basic ways of defining a race group are possible. A group, such as Asian, may be defined as those who reported Asian and no other race (the race-alone or single-race concept) or as those who reported Asian regardless of whether they also reported another race (the race-alone-or-in-combination concept). This table shows data using the first approach (race alone). The use of the single-race population does not imply that it is the preferred method of presenting or analyzing data. The Census Bureau uses a variety of approaches. Data for American Indians and Alaska Natives, Native Hawaiians and Other Pacific Islanders, and those reporting two or more races are not shown separately.
[6] Children under the age of 19 are eligible for Medicaid/CHIP.
[7] This age group is of special interest because of the Affordable Care Act's dependent coverage provision. Individuals aged 19 to 25 may be eligible to be a dependent on a parent's health insurance plan.
[8] Medicaid expansion status as of January 1, 2020, 2019, and 2018, respectively. Expansion states on or before January 1, 2018, include AK, AR, AZ, CA, CO, CT, DC, DE, HI, IA, IL, IN, KY, LA, MA, MD, MI, MN, MT, ND, NH, NJ, NM, NV, NY, OH, OR, PA, RI, VT, WA, and WV. After Jan 1, 2018, and on or before January 1, 2019, VA expanded Medicaid. After January 1, 2019, and on or before January 1, 2020, ID, ME, and UT expanded Medicaid. For more information, refer to <www.medicaid.gov/state-overviews/index.html>.
Note: The estimates by type of coverage are not mutually exclusive; people can be covered by more than one type of health insurance during the year.
Source: U.S. Census Bureau, Current Population Survey, 2019, 2020, and 2021 Annual Social and Economic Supplement (CPS ASEC).

Table A-2.
Health Insurance Coverage Status and Type by Age and Selected Characteristics: 2018, 2019, and 2020

(Numbers in thousands. Population as of March of the following year. Information on confidentiality protection, sampling error, nonsampling error, and definitions is available at <https://www2.census.gov/programs-surveys/cps/techdocs/cpsmar21.pdf>)

Characteristic	Total							Uninsured[4]	
	Any health insurance								
				Private health insurance[2]		Public health insurance[3]			
	Number	Percent	Margin of error[1] (±)	Percent	Margin of error[1] (±)	Percent	Margin of error[1] (±)	Percent	Margin of error[1] (±)
2020									
Total, 15 to 64 years old.............	**210,421**	**88.5**	**0.3**	**72.5**	**0.4**	**18.8**	**0.3**	**11.5**	**0.3**
Disability Status[5]									
With disability.............	15,134	91.0	0.7	45.5	1.2	52.9	1.2	9.0	0.7
With no disability...........	194,199	88.2	0.3	74.4	0.4	16.2	0.3	11.8	0.3
Work Experience									
All workers................	154,502	89.0	0.3	79.8	0.4	11.4	0.3	11.0	0.3
Worked full-time, year-round..............	99,588	91.6	0.3	87.0	0.3	6.1	0.2	8.4	0.3
Worked less than full-time, year-round..............	54,913	84.3	0.5	66.7	0.7	20.9	0.5	15.7	0.5
Did not work at least one week...................	55,920	87.1	0.4	52.2	0.7	39.1	0.7	12.9	0.4
Total, 19 to 64 years old.............	**193,646**	**88.1**	**0.3**	**73.0**	**0.4**	**17.7**	**0.3**	**11.9**	**0.3**
Marital Status									
Married[6]..................	98,821	91.5	0.3	82.1	0.4	12.3	0.4	8.5	0.3
Widowed...................	3,304	87.9	1.5	60.1	2.4	32.6	2.4	12.1	1.5
Divorced...................	18,486	86.8	0.7	65.0	1.0	24.9	0.9	13.2	0.7
Separated..................	3,738	79.8	1.9	53.0	2.3	29.7	2.0	20.2	1.9
Never married..............	69,297	84.0	0.5	63.9	0.6	22.1	0.5	16.0	0.5
Total, 26 to 64 years old.............	**164,377**	**88.5**	**0.3**	**73.7**	**0.4**	**17.6**	**0.3**	**11.5**	**0.3**
Educational Attainment									
No high school diploma......	13,758	68.1	1.4	35.4	1.2	35.4	1.3	31.9	1.4
High school graduate (includes equivalency)......	43,850	83.9	0.6	61.5	0.7	25.8	0.7	16.1	0.6
Some college, no degree.....	23,885	89.3	0.6	72.6	0.8	20.4	0.8	10.7	0.6
Associate degree............	17,799	91.0	0.6	77.7	0.9	16.5	0.8	9.0	0.6
Bachelor's degree...........	41,047	94.1	0.4	87.5	0.5	8.8	0.4	5.9	0.4
Graduate or professional degree....................	24,039	96.5	0.4	92.3	0.5	5.8	0.5	3.5	0.4

Footnotes provided at end of table.

Table A-2.
Health Insurance Coverage Status and Type by Age and Selected Characteristics: 2018, 2019, and 2020—Con.

(Numbers in thousands. Population as of March of the following year. Information on confidentiality protection, sampling error, nonsampling error, and definitions is available at <https://www2.census.gov/programs-surveys/cps/techdocs/cpsmar21.pdf>)

Characteristic	Total								Uninsured[4]	
		Any health insurance								
				Private health insurance[2]		Public health insurance[3]			
	Number	Percent	Margin of error[1] (±)	Percent	Margin of error[1] (±)	Percent	Margin of error[1] (±)	Percent	Margin of error[1] (±)
2019									
Total, 15 to 64 years old	210,228	89.3	0.3	73.9	0.4	18.2	0.3	10.7	0.3
Disability Status[5]									
With disability	15,056	91.6	0.6	47.3	1.3	52.4	1.3	8.4	0.6
With no disability	194,194	89.1	0.3	75.8	0.4	15.6	0.3	10.9	0.3
Work Experience									
All workers	157,181	89.8	0.3	80.8	0.3	11.2	0.3	10.2	0.3
Worked full-time, year-round	112,803	91.1	0.3	85.8	0.3	7.0	0.2	8.9	0.3
Worked less than full-time, year-round	44,379	86.6	0.5	68.2	0.7	21.6	0.6	13.4	0.5
Did not work at least one week	53,047	87.8	0.5	53.2	0.7	39.1	0.7	12.2	0.5
Total, 19 to 64 years old	193,272	88.9	0.3	74.4	0.4	17.2	0.3	11.1	0.3
Marital Status									
Married[6]	100,795	92.4	0.3	83.4	0.4	12.2	0.4	7.6	0.3
Widowed	3,319	86.5	1.7	56.5	2.5	33.5	2.3	13.5	1.7
Divorced	18,290	88.0	0.7	67.4	1.0	23.6	0.9	12.0	0.7
Separated	3,802	81.0	1.8	51.8	2.2	31.4	1.9	19.0	1.8
Never married	67,065	84.3	0.5	65.1	0.6	21.3	0.5	15.7	0.5
Total, 26 to 64 years old	163,666	89.4	0.3	75.1	0.4	17.2	0.3	10.6	0.3
Educational Attainment									
No high school diploma	13,733	71.5	1.3	38.9	1.3	35.9	1.4	28.5	1.3
High school graduate (includes equivalency)	43,630	85.1	0.5	64.2	0.7	24.2	0.7	14.9	0.5
Some college, no degree	24,315	89.8	0.6	73.7	0.8	19.7	0.8	10.2	0.6
Associate degree	17,998	91.6	0.7	79.3	0.9	15.8	0.8	8.4	0.7
Bachelor's degree	40,563	94.7	0.4	87.6	0.6	9.1	0.4	5.3	0.4
Graduate or professional degree	23,428	96.8	0.4	93.2	0.5	5.4	0.4	3.2	0.4

Footnotes provided at end of table.

Table A-2.
Health Insurance Coverage Status and Type by Age and Selected Characteristics: 2018, 2019, and 2020—Con.

(Numbers in thousands. Population as of March of the following year. Information on confidentiality protection, sampling error, nonsampling error, and definitions is available at <https://www2.census.gov/programs-surveys/cps/techdocs/cpsmar21.pdf>)

Characteristic	Total								
		Any health insurance						Uninsured[4]	
				Private health insurance[2]		Public health insurance[3]			
	Number	Percent	Margin of error[1] (±)	Percent	Margin of error[1] (±)	Percent	Margin of error[1] (±)	Percent	Margin of error[1] (±)
2018									
Total, 15 to 64 years old.............	210,794	88.7	0.3	72.8	0.4	18.8	0.3	11.3	0.3
Disability Status[5]									
With disability.............	15,438	90.4	0.7	44.7	1.2	53.9	1.1	9.6	0.7
With no disability..........	194,434	88.5	0.3	74.9	0.4	16.0	0.3	11.5	0.3
Work Experience									
All workers...............	155,221	89.3	0.3	80.5	0.4	11.1	0.2	10.7	0.3
Worked full-time, year-round............	111,950	90.5	0.3	85.1	0.4	7.2	0.2	9.5	0.3
Worked less than full-time, year-round............	43,271	86.2	0.5	68.5	0.7	21.3	0.6	13.8	0.5
Did not work at least one week....................	55,573	86.9	0.4	51.3	0.8	40.2	0.7	13.1	0.4
Total, 19 to 64 years old.............	193,548	88.3	0.3	73.5	0.4	17.6	0.3	11.7	0.3
Marital Status									
Married[6]..................	101,805	91.7	0.3	82.3	0.4	12.6	0.3	8.3	0.3
Widowed...................	3,385	86.3	1.6	55.6	2.2	34.9	2.2	13.7	1.6
Divorced..................	18,683	87.0	0.7	64.7	1.0	25.3	1.0	13.0	0.7
Separated.................	4,200	80.1	2.0	52.4	2.3	29.7	1.8	19.9	2.0
Never married..............	65,475	84.0	0.5	64.7	0.6	21.6	0.5	16.0	0.5
Total, 26 to 64 years old.............	164,250	88.7	0.3	74.2	0.4	17.5	0.3	11.3	0.3
Educational Attainment									
No high school diploma......	15,197	71.0	1.2	37.0	1.2	36.9	1.3	29.0	1.2
High school graduate (includes equivalency)......	44,573	85.1	0.5	64.3	0.7	24.4	0.6	14.9	0.5
Some college, no degree.....	24,977	89.3	0.6	73.8	0.8	19.3	0.7	10.7	0.6
Associate degree............	17,735	91.0	0.6	78.7	0.8	15.8	0.7	9.0	0.6
Bachelor's degree...........	39,255	93.8	0.3	87.2	0.5	8.5	0.4	6.2	0.3
Graduate or professional degree....................	22,514	96.6	0.4	92.9	0.5	5.7	0.4	3.4	0.4

[1] A margin of error (MOE) is a measure of an estimate's variability. The larger the MOE in relation to the size of the estimate, the less reliable the estimate. This number, when added to and subtracted from the estimate, forms the 90 percent confidence interval. MOEs shown in this table are based on standard errors calculated using replicate weights.
[2] Private health insurance includes coverage provided through an employer or union, coverage purchased directly, or TRICARE.
[3] Public health insurance coverage includes Medicaid, Medicare, CHAMPVA (Civilian Health and Medical Program of the Department of Veterans Affairs), and care provided by the Department of Veterans Affairs and the military.
[4] Individuals are considered to be uninsured if they do not have health insurance coverage for the entire calendar year.
[5] The sum of those with and without a disability does not equal the total because disability status is not defined for individuals in the U.S. armed forces.
[6] The combined category "married" includes three individual categories: "married, civilian spouse present," "married, U.S. armed forces spouse present," and "married, spouse absent."
Note: The estimates by type of coverage are *not* mutually exclusive; people can be covered by more than one type of health insurance during the year.
Source: U.S. Census Bureau, Current Population Survey, 2019, 2020, and 2021 Annual Social and Economic Supplement (CPS ASEC).

Table A-3.
Health Insurance Coverage Status and Type by Family Type and Family Income-to-Poverty Ratio: 2018, 2019, and 2020

(Numbers in thousands. Population as of March of the following year. Information on confidentiality protection, sampling error, nonsampling error, and definitions is available at <https://www2.census.gov/programs-surveys/cps/techdocs/cpsmar21.pdf>)

Characteristic	Total								
		Any health insurance						Uninsured[4]	
				Private health insurance[2]		Public health insurance[3]			
	Number	Percent	Margin of error[1] (±)	Percent	Margin of error[1] (±)	Percent	Margin of error[1] (±)	Percent	Margin of error[1] (±)
2020 Total	325,638	91.4	0.2	66.5	0.4	34.8	0.3	8.6	0.2
Household Relationship									
Married couple family	193,596	93.6	0.2	74.8	0.4	29.4	0.4	6.4	0.2
With children under 18 years	106,005	92.6	0.3	75.5	0.6	20.4	0.6	7.4	0.3
Unmarried male reference person	42,018	86.9	0.6	58.9	0.9	36.6	0.8	13.1	0.6
With children under 18 years	10,891	86.2	1.4	54.7	1.9	35.4	1.8	13.8	1.4
Unmarried female reference person	72,338	90.3	0.4	50.2	0.7	50.3	0.6	9.7	0.4
With children under 18 years	31,937	89.3	0.7	41.7	1.1	52.2	1.1	10.7	0.7
Unrelated subfamilies	1,017	86.5	3.8	51.3	6.0	38.3	5.2	13.5	3.8
Secondary individuals	16,670	82.8	0.9	61.3	1.3	25.7	1.0	17.2	0.9
Income-to-Poverty Ratio									
Total, poverty universe	325,156	91.4	0.2	66.6	0.4	34.7	0.3	8.6	0.2
Below 100 percent of poverty	37,156	82.8	0.8	23.2	0.9	64.3	1.0	17.2	0.8
Below 138 percent of poverty	56,337	83.9	0.6	25.3	0.7	64.6	0.8	16.1	0.6
Between 100 and 199 percent of poverty	52,336	86.7	0.6	39.6	0.9	56.9	0.8	13.3	0.6
Between 200 and 299 percent of poverty	50,389	88.1	0.5	60.3	0.9	38.8	0.8	11.9	0.5
Between 300 and 399 percent of poverty	41,655	91.1	0.6	72.0	0.9	29.4	0.8	8.9	0.6
At or above 400 percent of poverty	143,620	96.6	0.2	88.2	0.3	19.1	0.3	3.4	0.2

Footnotes provided at end of table.

Table A-3.
Health Insurance Coverage Status and Type by Family Type and Family Income-to-Poverty Ratio: 2018, 2019, and 2020—Con.

(Numbers in thousands. Population as of March of the following year. Information on confidentiality protection, sampling error, nonsampling error, and definitions is available at <https://www2.census.gov/programs-surveys/cps/techdocs/cpsmar21.pdf>)

Characteristic	Total								
		Any health insurance						Uninsured[4]	
				Private health insurance[2]		Public health insurance[3]			
	Number	Percent	Margin of error[1] (±)	Percent	Margin of error[1] (±)	Percent	Margin of error[1] (±)	Percent	Margin of error[1] (±)
2019 Total	**324,550**	**92.0**	**0.2**	**68.0**	**0.3**	**34.1**	**0.3**	**8.0**	**0.2**
Household Relationship									
Married couple family	197,994	93.9	0.2	75.8	0.4	28.9	0.4	6.1	0.2
With children under 18 years	109,323	93.0	0.4	76.4	0.7	19.7	0.6	7.0	0.4
Unmarried male reference person	40,246	88.0	0.6	61.2	0.8	35.7	0.8	12.0	0.6
With children under 18 years	10,244	86.8	1.3	55.2	1.9	36.0	1.8	13.2	1.3
Unmarried female reference person	69,641	91.1	0.4	51.4	0.7	50.4	0.7	8.9	0.4
With children under 18 years	30,494	91.2	0.7	42.9	1.2	53.2	1.2	8.8	0.7
Unrelated subfamilies	941	90.6	3.6	58.5	6.0	38.2	6.2	9.4	3.6
Secondary individuals	15,728	81.4	1.0	62.1	1.2	23.4	1.1	18.6	1.0
Income-to-Poverty Ratio									
Total, poverty universe	324,048	92.0	0.2	68.1	0.3	34.0	0.3	8.0	0.2
Below 100 percent of poverty	33,879	84.1	0.8	22.9	0.9	66.6	1.0	15.9	0.8
Below 138 percent of poverty	52,816	84.6	0.6	25.2	0.8	65.9	0.8	15.4	0.6
Between 100 and 199 percent of poverty	51,349	85.9	0.6	39.9	1.0	55.5	1.0	14.1	0.6
Between 200 and 299 percent of poverty	48,924	89.0	0.5	63.0	0.9	37.3	0.9	11.0	0.5
Between 300 and 399 percent of poverty	43,078	91.7	0.5	72.6	0.8	29.5	0.8	8.3	0.5
At or above 400 percent of poverty	146,818	97.0	0.2	88.8	0.3	19.2	0.3	3.0	0.2

Footnotes provided at end of table.

Table A-3.
Health Insurance Coverage Status and Type by Family Type and Family Income-to-Poverty Ratio: 2018, 2019, and 2020—Con.

(Numbers in thousands. Population as of March of the following year. Information on confidentiality protection, sampling error, nonsampling error, and definitions is available at <https://www2.census.gov/programs-surveys/cps/techdocs/cpsmar21.pdf>)

Characteristic	Total Number	Any health insurance Percent	Margin of error[1] (±)	Private health insurance[2] Percent	Margin of error[1] (±)	Public health insurance[3] Percent	Margin of error[1] (±)	Uninsured[4] Percent	Margin of error[1] (±)
2018 Total	323,668	91.5	0.2	67.3	0.4	34.4	0.3	8.5	0.2
Household Relationship									
Married couple family	195,914	93.6	0.2	75.3	0.4	29.1	0.4	6.4	0.2
With children under 18 years	109,341	92.6	0.4	75.1	0.7	20.9	0.6	7.4	0.4
Unmarried male reference person	40,495	87.2	0.6	59.0	0.8	36.9	0.7	12.8	0.6
With children under 18 years	10,398	87.2	1.1	53.0	1.8	38.2	1.6	12.8	1.1
Unmarried female reference person	70,093	90.6	0.4	51.3	0.7	50.1	0.7	9.4	0.4
With children under 18 years	31,462	90.2	0.6	43.3	1.1	51.4	1.2	9.8	0.6
Unrelated subfamilies	1,069	86.9	3.4	50.0	5.1	42.4	4.6	13.1	3.4
Secondary individuals	16,097	81.5	1.0	61.6	1.2	23.8	1.0	18.5	1.0
Income-to-Poverty Ratio									
Total, poverty universe	323,172	91.5	0.2	67.3	0.4	34.3	0.3	8.5	0.2
Below 100 percent of poverty	38,056	83.7	0.6	22.0	0.8	66.8	0.9	16.3	0.6
Below 138 percent of poverty	58,204	84.4	0.6	24.7	0.7	65.8	0.7	15.6	0.6
Between 100 and 199 percent of poverty	55,302	86.4	0.6	41.6	0.9	54.4	0.8	13.6	0.6
Between 200 and 299 percent of poverty	50,632	89.2	0.5	64.4	0.8	36.2	0.8	10.8	0.5
Between 300 and 399 percent of poverty	43,624	91.9	0.4	75.1	0.8	27.7	0.7	8.1	0.4
At or above 400 percent of poverty	135,559	96.6	0.2	89.2	0.3	18.5	0.3	3.4	0.2

[1] A margin of error (MOE) is a measure of an estimate's variability. The larger the MOE in relation to the size of the estimate, the less reliable the estimate. This number, when added to and subtracted from the estimate, forms the 90 percent confidence interval. MOEs shown in this table are based on standard errors calculated using replicate weights.
[2] Private health insurance includes coverage provided through an employer or union, coverage purchased directly, or TRICARE.
[3] Public health insurance coverage includes Medicaid, Medicare, CHAMPVA (Civilian Health and Medical Program of the Department of Veterans Affairs), and care provided by the Department of Veterans Affairs and the military.
[4] Individuals are considered to be uninsured if they do not have health insurance coverage for the entire calendar year.
Note: The estimates by type of coverage are not mutually exclusive; people can be covered by more than one type of health insurance during the year.
Source: U.S. Census Bureau, Current Population Survey, 2019, 2020, and 2021 Annual Social and Economic Supplement (CPS ASEC).

APPENDIX B.
ESTIMATES OF HEALTH INSURANCE COVERAGE: 2013 TO 2020

The Current Population Survey Annual Social and Economic Supplement (CPS ASEC) is used to produce official estimates of income and poverty, and it serves as the most widely-cited source of estimates on health insurance coverage and the uninsured.

SURVEY REDESIGN

The Census Bureau has consistently sought to improve measurement of health insurance coverage. The CPS ASEC underwent a two-stage redesign in recent years, including changes to the questionnaire incorporated over the period of 2014 to 2016, followed by changes to post-survey collection processing methods in 2019.[1] Evidence suggests that the redesign effectively addressed known limitations to CPS ASEC health coverage and improved health insurance coverage measurement.[2]

In consideration of these and previous changes in survey design, researchers should use caution when comparing results over time. Due to the differences in measurement, health insurance estimates for calendar year 2013 through 2017 are not directly comparable to previous years. Estimates for calendar years 2018 and beyond may be compared with each other and with 2017 estimates from the 2018 CPS ASEC Bridge File or 2016 estimates from the 2017 CPS ASEC Research File. Although it is not appropriate to directly compare 2018 estimates with earlier years processed with the legacy system, it is helpful to examine the estimates in this report in the context of a longer time period to better understand the changes that occurred in health coverage in 2020.

RECENT CHANGES IN THE HEALTH INSURANCE LANDSCAPE

Changes in health coverage over time reflect economic trends, demographic shifts, and changes in federal and state policy. Several such policy changes are related to the Patient Protection and Affordable Care Act (ACA).

Many of the provisions of the ACA went into effect in 2014, including the establishment of health insurance marketplaces (e.g., healthcare.gov) and the optional expansion of Medicaid eligibility. Over the following years, some states took the opportunity to expand Medicaid eligibility. The first year, 24 states and the District of Columbia expanded eligibility. By 2020, all but 15 states had expanded Medicaid eligibility.

As a result, many people, particularly adults aged 19 to 64, may have become eligible for coverage options under the ACA. Based on family income, some people may have qualified for subsidies or tax credits to help pay for premiums associated with health insurance plans. In addition, people with lower income may have become eligible for Medicaid coverage if they resided in one of the states (or the District of Columbia) that expanded Medicaid eligibility.

Notably, some provisions of the ACA no longer apply. For example, as of 2019 the individual mandate penalty requiring individuals to be covered by health insurance or pay a tax penalty was cancelled at the federal level, although several states and the District of Columbia have state health insurance coverage mandates.

The economic shock related to the COVID-19 global pandemic also may have affected health insurance coverage in the United States in 2020. The Families First Coronavirus Response Act required states, as a condition of receiving increased Medicaid funding, to provide continuous coverage for those enrolled in Medicaid. A recent Centers for Medicare & Medicaid Services report showed that Medicaid enrollment increased dramatically in 2020, after declines in enrollment from 2017 to 2019. Specifically, annual Medicaid enrollment during the period February 2020 through January 2021 increased from 34.0 million to 40.2 million among adults aged 19 and older; Medicaid and the

---

[1] For more information on the survey redesign, refer to Appendix A in Edward R. Berchick, Jessica C. Barnett, and Rachel D. Upton, "Health Insurance Coverage in the United States: 2018," *Current Population Reports*, P60-267, U.S. Census Bureau, Washington, DC, 2019.

[2] Heide Jackson and Edward R. Berchick, "Improvements in Uninsurance Estimates for Fully Imputed Cases in the Current Population Survey Annual Social and Economic Supplement," Inquiry: *The Journal of Health Care Organization, Provision, and Financing*, 2020, and E. R. Berchick and H. M. Jackson, "Health Insurance Coverage in the 2017 CPS ASEC Research File," <www.census.gov/library/working-papers/2019/demo/SEHSD-WP2019-01.html>.

Figure B-1.
Percentage of People Without Health Insurance Coverage: 2013 to 2020
(Numbers in percent. Population as of March of the following year)

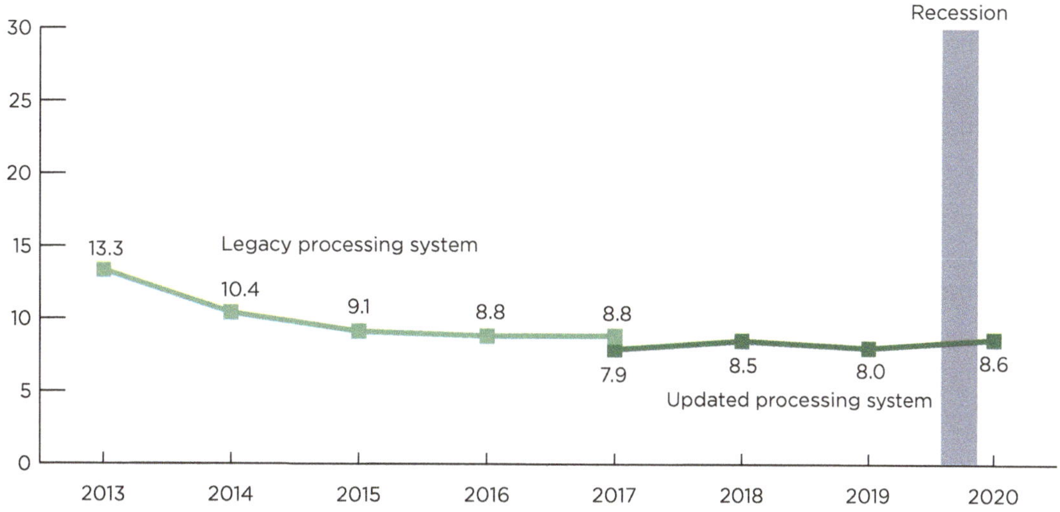

Year	Legacy processing system	Updated processing system
2013	13.3	
2014	10.4	
2015	9.1	
2016	8.8	
2017	8.8	7.9
2018		8.5
2019		8.0
2020 (Recession)		8.6

Note: Information on confidentiality protection, sampling error, nonsampling error, and definitions is available at <https://www2.census.gov/programs-surveys/cps/techdocs/cpsmar21.pdf>.
Source: U.S. Census Bureau, Current Population Survey, 2018 Annual Social and Economic Supplement Bridge File and 2014 to 2021 Annual Social and Economic Supplement (CPS ASEC).

Children's Health Insurance Program enrollment increased from 35.0 million to 38.3 million for children under the age of 19.[3, 4]

The coronavirus pandemic and the related stay-at-home orders during the spring of 2020 also affected how the Census Bureau collected data for the CPS ASEC. The edition of this report released in September 2020 provides an overview of the issues.[5] In addition, the Census Bureau produced several working papers exploring how changes in CPS ASEC data collection in 2020 may have affected 2019 estimates. These analyses revealed that the 2020 CPS ASEC sample differed from the previous year with respect to a number of characteristics that are correlated with health insurance coverage. For example, the 2020 CPS ASEC sample was older, more educated, and more likely to have a disability than the 2019 sample.[6] Researchers should consider the effect of the pandemic on CPS ASEC data collection in interpreting changes in health insurance coverage between 2019 and other years using the CPS ASEC. As a result, no comparisons between calendar year coverage in 2019 (collected in 2020) and other survey years are reported in this Appendix.

Estimates of health insurance coverage: 2013 to 2020

Uninsured Rates

Figure B-1 shows the percentage of people without health insurance coverage from 2013 to 2017, under the legacy processing system, and from 2017 to 2020, using the updated processing system. The uninsured rate declined from 2013 to 2014, when many provisions of the ACA went into effect and continued to decline

---

[3] Appendices A and B of the December 2020 and January 2021 Medicaid and CHIP Enrollment Trends Snapshot are available at <www.medicaid.gov/medicaid/national-medicaid-chip-program-information/downloads/december-2020-january-2021-medicaid-chip-enrollment-trend-snapshot.pdf>.
[4] Throughout this appendix, details may not sum to totals because of rounding.
[5] "The Impact of the Coronavirus (COVID-19) Pandemic on the CPS ASEC" text box in the "Health Insurance Coverage in the United States: 2019," report is available at <www.census.gov/content/dam/Census/library/publications/2020/demo/p60-271.pdf>.

[6] Additional information related to the impact of COVID-19 on the 2020 CPS ASEC is available in Edward R. Berchick, Laryssa Mykyta, and Sharon M. Stern, "The Influence of COVID-19-Related Data Collection Changes on Measuring Health Insurance Coverage in the 2020 CPS ASEC," <www.census.gov/library/working-papers/2020/demo/SEHSD-WP2020-13.html>, and Jonathan Rothbaum and C. Adam Bee, "Coronavirus Infects Surveys, Too: Nonresponse Bias During the Pandemic in the CPS ASEC," <www.census.gov/library/working-papers/2020/demo/SEHSD-WP2020-10.html>.

through 2016.[7] The uninsured rate for 2017 was lower under the updated processing system than under the legacy system. However, the percentage of uninsured increased between 2017 and 2018 by 0.5 percentage points to 8.5 percent.

In 2020, the uninsured rate was 8.6 percent, 0.6 percentage points higher than the uninsured rate in 2017, but not significantly different from the rate in 2018. The CPS ASEC only includes people who had no coverage at all during calendar year 2020 as uninsured. Therefore, people losing health insurance coverage in 2020 are not considered uninsured in 2020.

Private health insurance coverage

The percentage of people with private health insurance coverage from 2013 to 2020 is presented in Figure B-2.[8] As shown, there was an increase in private coverage rates between 2013 and 2015, coincident with the implementation of the ACA, followed by a leveling of private coverage between 2015 and 2017.

Using the updated processing system, there was no statistically significant change in the private coverage rate between 2017 and 2018. However, between 2018 and 2020, the percentage of people with private health insurance coverage at any point during the year declined 0.8 percentage points to 66.5 percent.

Public coverage

Figure B-3 shows the percentage of people with public coverage and Medicaid coverage in the CPS ASEC from 2013 to 2020. Using the legacy

---

[7] There was no significant change in the uninsured rate between 2016 and 2017 using the legacy processing system.

[8] Private coverage includes employer-sponsored insurance, insurance purchased directly by an individual, through a broker or the Marketplace (such as healthcare.gov). The updated processing system further includes TRICARE as private coverage.

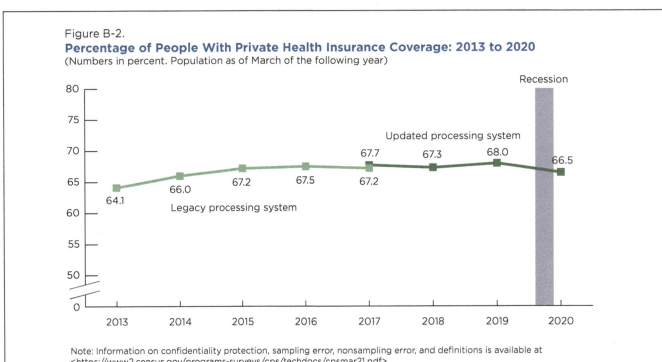

Figure B-2.
Percentage of People With Private Health Insurance Coverage: 2013 to 2020
(Numbers in percent. Population as of March of the following year)

Note: Information on confidentiality protection, sampling error, nonsampling error, and definitions is available at <https://www2.census.gov/programs-surveys/cps/techdocs/cpsmar21.pdf>.
Source: U.S. Census Bureau, Current Population Survey, 2018 Annual Social and Economic Supplement Bridge File and 2014 to 2021 Annual Social and Economic Supplement (CPS ASEC).

Figure B-3.
Percentage of People With Public Coverage and Medicaid Coverage: 2013 to 2020
(Numbers in percent. Population as of March of the following year)

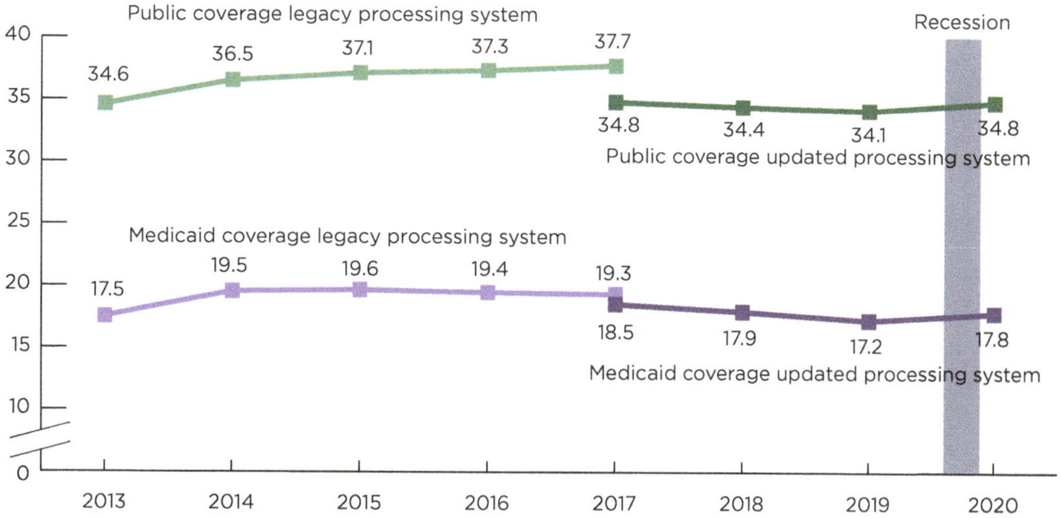

Public coverage legacy processing system: 34.6 (2013), 36.5 (2014), 37.1 (2015), 37.3 (2016), 37.7 (2017)

Public coverage updated processing system: 34.8 (2017), 34.4 (2018), 34.1 (2019), 34.8 (2020)

Medicaid coverage legacy processing system: 17.5 (2013), 19.5 (2014), 19.6 (2015), 19.4 (2016), 19.3 (2017)

Medicaid coverage updated processing system: 18.5 (2017), 17.9 (2018), 17.2 (2019), 17.8 (2020)

Recession shaded in 2020.

Note: Information on confidentiality protection, sampling error, nonsampling error, and definitions is available at <https://www2.census.gov/programs-surveys/cps/techdocs/cpsmar21.pdf>.
Source: U.S. Census Bureau, Current Population Survey, 2018 Annual Social and Economic Supplement Bridge File and 2014 to 2021 Annual Social and Economic Supplement (CPS ASEC).

processing system, public coverage increased from 2013 to 2017.[9] Public coverage rates were lower in 2017 using the updated processing system compared to the legacy processing system. However, TRICARE is defined as private coverage in the updated processing system and not as public coverage as in the legacy system.

Although public coverage rates declined between 2017 to 2018 using the updated processing system, the percentage of people holding public coverage increased by 0.4 percentage points to 34.8 percent between 2018 and 2020.

As with public coverage, the percentage of people with Medicaid coverage declined between 2017 and 2018 by 0.7 percentage points to 17.9 percent under the updated processing system. Although there was no significant difference in Medicaid coverage rates reported in the CPS ASEC between 2018 and 2020, the lack of change masks a 0.4 percentage-point increase in the percentage of working-age adults aged 19 to 64 covered by Medicaid during this same time. Working-age adults may have been more vulnerable to losing coverage during the COVID-19 pandemic than other age groups (Figure B-4).[10]

Current Coverage, or Coverage at Time of the CPS ASEC Interview

The redesigned CPS ASEC also includes a measure of current coverage, health insurance coverage

[9] Under the legacy processing system, public coverage increased annually, except for 2015 to 2016, which was not a significant change.

[10] There was no significant change in the Medicaid coverage rate for children under the age of 19 or for percentage of adults aged 65 and older between 2018 and 2020.

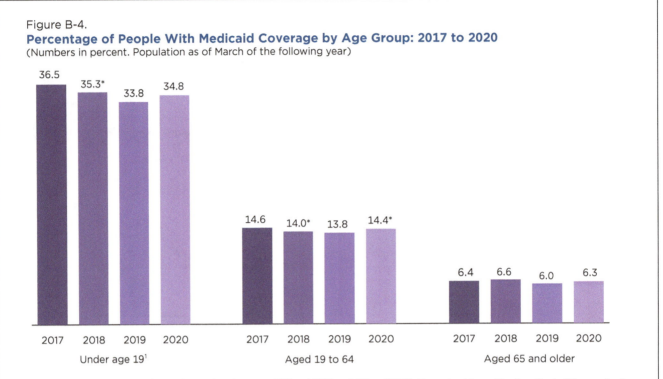

Figure B-4.
Percentage of People With Medicaid Coverage by Age Group: 2017 to 2020
(Numbers in percent. Population as of March of the following year)

* Denotes a statistically significant change from between 2017 and 2018, or 2018 and 2020. Users should consider the effect of the pandemic on 2020 CPS ASEC data collection in interpreting changes in health insurance coverage between 2019 and other years using the CPS ASEC. As a result, no comparisons between calendar year coverage in 2019 (collected in 2020) and other survey years are reported here.
[1] The percentage of children under 19 with Medicaid coverage in 2020 is statistically different from the percentage of children under 19 with Medicaid coverage in 2017.
Note: Information on confidentiality protection, sampling error, nonsampling error, and definitions is available at <https://www2.census.gov/programs-surveys/cps/techdocs/cpsmar21.pdf>.
Source: U.S. Census Bureau, Current Population Survey 2018 Annual Social and Economic Supplement Bridge File and 2019 to 2021 Annual Social and Economic Supplement (CPS ASEC).

held at the time of the CPS ASEC interview. Although this measure of coverage cannot predict coverage in a given calendar year, it offers a snapshot of health insurance coverage early in the year, when CPS ASEC data are collected. A discussion of differences between the primary measure of health insurance coverage (calendar year coverage) and current coverage measured at the time of the interview in the CPS ASEC were discussed in the Research Matters blog, "Current Coverage, Calendar-Year Coverage: Two Measures, Two Concepts," published in 2019.[11]

Figure B-5 illustrates the change in current coverage at the time of the 2019 CPS ASEC interview in early 2019, before the pandemic and pandemic-related changes to data collection, and at the time of the CPS ASEC interview in early 2021.

As shown in Figure B-5, a decline in private coverage over the period was partly offset by an increase in the percentage of people covered by public insurance programs. As a result, the percentage of uninsured in early 2021 (9.1 percent), when the CPS ASEC was collected, was not statistically different from the uninsured rate in early 2019.

---
[11] Sharon Stern, "Current Coverage, Calendar-Year Coverage: Two Measures, Two Concepts," <www.census.gov/newsroom/blogs/research-matters/2019/09/current-coverage.html>.

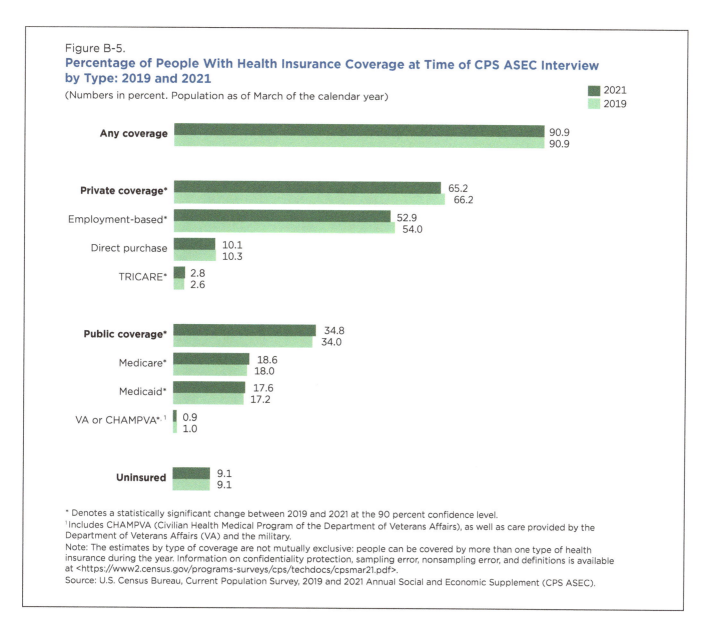

Consistent with calendar year coverage, private coverage in early 2021 declined 1.0 percentage point to 65.2 percent, from early 2019 before the COVID-19 pandemic. This decrease in private coverage was partly driven by a 1.1 percentage-point drop in coverage through employer-sponsored insurance to 52.9 percent, as many individuals may have lost their jobs and their coverage during the pandemic.[12, 13]

In contrast, by early 2021, 34.8 percent of people were covered through public insurance programs, representing an increase of 0.9 percentage points. Between early 2019 and early 2021, Medicaid coverage increased by 0.4 percentage points to 17.6 percent, consistent with reports of increased enrollment. In early 2021, 18.6 percent of people were covered under Medicare, representing an increase of 0.6 percentage points since 2019.[14]

[12] There was no statistical difference between the percent change in private coverage and the percent change in employment-based coverage between early 2019 and early 2021.

[13] For more information regarding job losses during the COVID-19 pandemic, refer to Ryan Ansell and John P. Mullins, "COVID-19 Ends Longest Employment Recovery and Expansion in CES History, Causing Unprecedented Job Losses in 2020," *Monthly Labor Review*, U.S. Bureau of Labor Statistics, June 2021, <https://doi.org/10.21916/mlr.2021.13>.

[14] Between 2019 and 2021, there was no statistical difference between the percent change in public coverage and Medicaid; public coverage and Medicare; or Medicaid and Medicare.

Keiser-Starkey, Katherine and Lisa N. Bunch. "Health Insurance Coverage in the United States: 2020." United States Census Bureau, Current Population Reports, P60-274, U.S. Government Publishing Office, Washington, DC, September 2021.

Small Area Health Insurance Estimates: 2019

Small Area Estimates

Current Population Reports

By Sara Robinson and Katherine Ann Willyard

June 2021

P30-09

INTRODUCTION

This report provides a summary of the 2019 release of the U.S. Census Bureau's Small Area Health Insurance Estimates (SAHIE).[1] SAHIE are the only source of data for single-year estimates of health insurance coverage status for all counties in the United States by selected economic and demographic characteristics (refer to the "Small Area Health Insurance Estimates (SAHIE)" text box).[2]

The 1-year American Community Survey (ACS) provides detailed estimates of health insurance coverage for counties with populations of 65,000 or more.[3] As a data enhancement to the ACS, the SAHIE model-based estimates are a vital source of information for measuring year-to-year change in health insurance coverage at the county level. The data in this report show changes in health insurance coverage between 2018 and 2019, as well as changes in health insurance coverage between 2013 and 2019. In addition, the report provides results on the differences in coverage among selected demographic groups.

---

[1] The Census Bureau's Disclosure Review Board and Disclosure Avoidance officers reviewed this data product for unauthorized disclosure of confidential information and approved the disclosure avoidance practices applied to this release. CBDRB-FY21-077.

[2] There are 3,142 counties in the United States. The SAHIE program does not include Kalawao County, Hawaii, due to insufficient data.

[3] Approximately 73.6 percent, or 2,313 of U.S. counties, do not have detailed 1-year estimates of health insurance coverage. However, the ACS 1-year county-level estimates cover about 85.0 percent of the total U.S. population. The ACS also releases 1-year supplemental tables of health insurance coverage estimates for geographic areas with populations greater than 20,000, but these tables do not provide the same economic and demographic detail as SAHIE.

HIGHLIGHTS

- From 2018 to 2019, for the population under the age of 65, 90.7 percent of (or 2,850) counties did not have a statistically significant change in their uninsured rate. Among counties that experienced changes in their uninsured rates, more saw an increase (237 counties) than a decrease (54 counties).

- Among the population under the age of 65, the estimated county uninsured rate in 2019 ranged from 2.4 percent to 35.8 percent. The median county uninsured rate was 11.0 percent.

- In 2019, 33.6 percent of (or 1,054) counties had an estimated uninsured rate below 10.0 percent for the population under the age of 65.

OVERVIEW OF SAHIE

Each year, the SAHIE program releases timely, reliable estimates of health insurance coverage for the population under the age of 65 by state and county.[4] Federal agencies and programs use SAHIE data to determine eligibility for public health services. The SAHIE program is partially funded by the Centers for Disease Control and Prevention's Division of Cancer Prevention and Control (DCPC). The DCPC's National Breast and Cervical Cancer Early Detection Program and its stakeholders use SAHIE to determine the number of low-income, uninsured women who may be

---

[4] Please refer to the definition of insured at <www.census.gov/programs-surveys/sahie/about/faq.html>.

U.S. Department of Commerce
U.S. CENSUS BUREAU
census.gov

eligible for their program at the state and county levels (refer to the "Why Are Small Area Health Insurance Estimates (SAHIE) Important?" text box).

The SAHIE program produces estimates on health insurance coverage at the state and county levels for the full cross-combination of five income-to-poverty ratio (IPR) categories, all incomes, selected age groups, race/ethnicity (state level only), and sex. These IPR categories are defined as the ratio of family income to the federal poverty threshold (refer to the "How Is Poverty Status Measured?" text box). SAHIE data are used to analyze health insurance status by selected characteristics that reflect the federal poverty thresholds and meet the needs of local, state, and federal assistance programs. For instance, the IPR category 0–138 percent of poverty represents the population that may be eligible for Medicaid coverage if they reside in one of the states that expanded Medicaid eligibility under the Patient Protection and Affordable Care Act (ACA).

County-level SAHIE data also allow data users to take a closer look at the distribution and concentration of the uninsured population within states, regions, and metropolitan areas.[5] Since the SAHIE program produces single-year estimates for all U.S. counties, SAHIE data are used to analyze changes over time in health insurance coverage, as well as geographic variation. The purpose of this report is to highlight several key findings of such analyses.[6]

HEALTH INSURANCE COVERAGE IN U.S. COUNTIES

In 2019, estimated county uninsured rates for the population under the age of 65 ranged from 2.4 percent to 35.8 percent. The median county uninsured rate was 11.0 percent.[7] Figure 1 shows how uninsured rates varied among counties throughout the country. The lightest shade in the map represents counties with the lowest uninsured rates (10.0 percent and below). In 2019, 33.6 percent of (or 1,054) counties had an uninsured rate less than 10.0 percent. The Northeast and Midwest had the highest proportion of counties with low uninsured rates.[8] In 2019, only 18.1 percent of (or 567) counties had uninsured rates greater than 15.0 percent. These counties were primarily located in the South.[9]

---

[5] Reference maps on regions and metropolitan/micropolitan area status are available at <https://www2.census.gov/programs-surveys/sahie/reference-maps/2019/ref1-mp-2019.pdf>.

[6] All data shown are estimates containing uncertainty. Sources of uncertainty include model error, sampling error, and nonsampling error. Unless specifically noted in the text, apparent differences among the estimates may not be statistically significant. All direct comparisons cited in the text have been statistically tested at the 90 percent confidence level. More information is available at <www.census.gov/programs-surveys/sahie/technical-documentation/source-and-accuracy.html>.

[7] The median estimated county uninsured rate differs from the ACS's estimated national uninsured rate, which is 9.2 percent (± 0.1) of the U.S. population under the age of 65 in 2019. The SAHIE program does not produce a national uninsured rate for the United States. SAHIE data are produced using survey estimates from the ACS.

[8] The number of counties with uninsured rates below 10.0 percent by region: Northeast—188 out of 217 counties (86.6 percent); Midwest—554 out of 1,055 counties (52.5 percent); South—213 out of 1,422 counties (15.0 percent); West—99 out of 447 counties (22.2 percent).

[9] Among the 567 counties with uninsured rates above 15.0 percent, 82.5 percent (468 counties) are in the South. The remaining are in the Midwest (57 counties) and West (42 counties). No counties in the Northeast fell into this category.

SMALL AREA HEALTH INSURANCE ESTIMATES (SAHIE)

SAHIE are model-based enhancements of the American Community Survey (ACS) estimates, created by integrating additional information from administrative records, postcensal population estimates, and decennial census data. SAHIE methodology employs statistical modeling techniques to combine this supplemental information with survey data to produce estimates that are more reliable. SAHIE are broadly consistent with the direct ACS survey estimates, but with help from other data sources, SAHIE program estimates are more precise than the ACS 1-year and 5-year survey estimates for most counties. Detailed ACS 1-year estimates are not available for most of these smaller geographic areas. A 2019 ACS map of unpublished counties is available at <https://www2.census.gov/programs-surveys/sahie/reference-maps/2019/ref2-mp-2019.pdf>.

Information on the various input data sources used in producing SAHIE is available at <www.census.gov/programs-surveys/sahie/technical-documentation/model-input-data.html>.

SAHIE are subject to several types of uncertainty. Details on this and the SAHIE methodology are available at <www.census.gov/programs-surveys/sahie/technical-documentation/methodology.html>.

ANNUAL CHANGE IN COUNTY UNINSURED RATES

Between 2018 and 2019, for the population under the age of 65, estimated county uninsured rates significantly decreased in 1.7 percent of (or 54) U.S. counties. More counties experienced a significant increase: 7.6 percent (237 counties). The remaining 2,850 counties did not have a statistically significant change in their uninsured rates.

In 2014, many provisions of the ACA went into effect. From 2013 to 2019, the SAHIE program estimates that 92.7 percent of (or 2,909) counties experienced a significant decrease in their uninsured rates for the population under the age of 65.[10] However, the year-to-year changes in county uninsured rates varied. Figure 2 displays the number of counties where uninsured rates changed from 2013 to 2019. For the periods 2013 to 2014, as well as 2014 to 2015, over 70.0 percent of counties had a significant decrease in their uninsured rates.[11] Between 2015 and 2016, that amount dropped to 20.0 percent of (or 629) counties.

---

[10] When analyzing changes between 2013 and later years, four counties are not included. Bedford County, Virginia, and three counties in Alaska experienced changes in geographic boundaries in 2014. The data for these counties are not comparable to 2013. When analyzing changes between 2017 and later years, three other counties were excluded because of data collection errors in the ACS. For more information, the ACS errata notes are available at <www.census.gov/programs-surveys/acs/technical-documentation/errata.2019.html>.

[11] Between 2013 and 2014, estimated uninsured rates for the population under the age of 65 decreased in 74.1 percent of (or 2,325) counties. Only one county had an increase. From 2014 to 2015, 71.3 percent of (or 2,239) counties experienced a rate decrease. In four counties, the uninsured rate increased. For both periods, the remaining counties had no statistically significant change.

IMPROVEMENTS TO MEDICAID DATA FOR SAHIE

The SAHIE model utilizes Medicaid enrollment data, among other auxiliary data sources. Major policy changes affected Medicaid in 2014 under the Patient Protection and Affordable Care Act (ACA). Such provisions gave states the option to expand their Medicaid eligibility criteria. To capture changes in the Medicaid enrollment data during this period, the SAHIE program incorporates more up-to-date Medicaid data, starting with the updated 2013 release.

In prior data releases, SAHIE used 2-year lagged Medicaid data from the Medicaid Statistical Information System (MSIS) provided by the Centers for Medicare and Medicaid Services (CMS). For example, the 2013 SAHIE model used 2011 Medicaid data. This 2-year lag is reflected in the 2013 SAHIE data, released in March 2015. In prior years, research supported the 2-year lag because Medicaid enrollment was relatively stable. However, with the implementation of the new ACA provisions in 2014, Medicaid enrollment changed substantially across states. As of December 31, 2019, 33 states and the District of Columbia had expanded their Medicaid enrollment criteria.

The current SAHIE process reduces the 2-year lag of the Medicaid data in the SAHIE model by using more timely sources. SAHIE's updated Medicaid data methods combine MSIS data with two additional Medicaid sources: the CMS Performance Indicator Project Medicaid and Children's Health Insurance Program (CHIP) data, and Kaiser Family Foundation's Medicaid and CHIP data. SAHIE's updated data methods also utilize the most recent Internal Revenue Service 1040 tax data and the American Community Survey estimates to approximate the latest county-level and demographic detail within the state-level Medicaid and CHIP totals. More information on recent changes to SAHIE's use of Medicaid data is available at <www.census.gov/programs-surveys/sahie/technical-documentation/model-input-data/medicaid.html>.

UPDATED 2013 SAHIE DATA AVAILABLE FOR COMPARISON

Methodological improvements, which were applied to 2014 SAHIE and subsequent years, were also used to update 2013 SAHIE for comparability purposes. The original 2013 SAHIE data released in March 2015 (as mentioned above), and the updated 2013 SAHIE released in May 2016, are not comparable due to the changes in SAHIE's use of Medicaid data. The updated 2013 SAHIE was released simultaneously with the 2014 SAHIE data in May 2016. Both data sets are available to download from the SAHIE Web site. For more information, refer to the links in the "Why Are Small Area Health Insurance Estimates (SAHIE) Important?" text box.

Figure 1.
Estimated Uninsured Rates for the Population Under the Age of 65: 2019

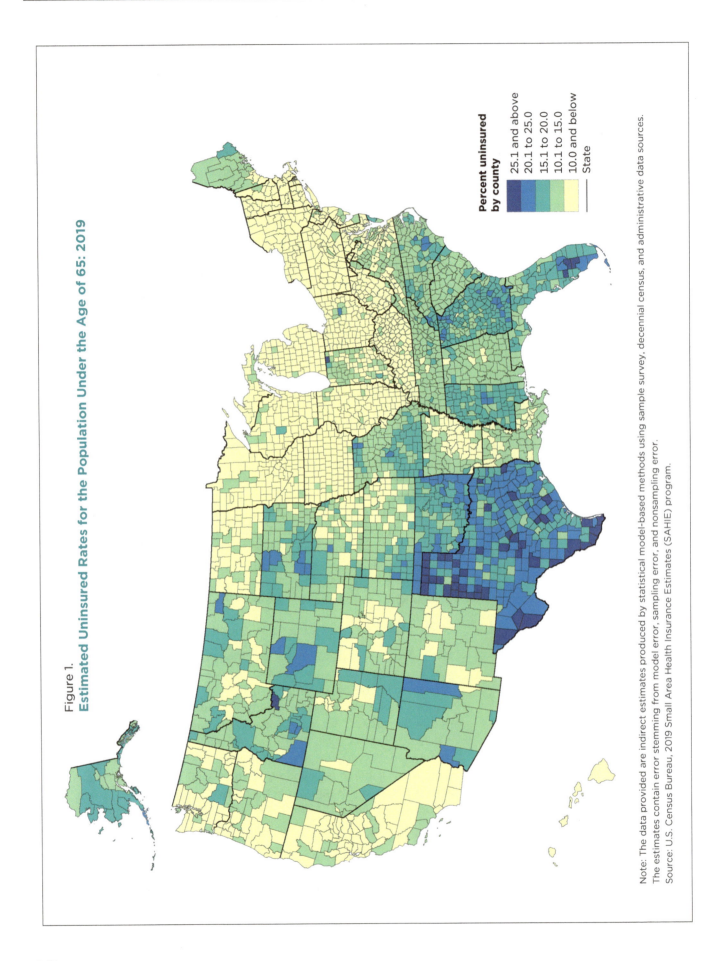

Note: The data provided are indirect estimates produced by statistical model-based methods using sample survey, decennial census, and administrative data sources. The estimates contain error stemming from model error, sampling error, and nonsampling error.
Source: U.S. Census Bureau, 2019 Small Area Health Insurance Estimates (SAHIE) program.

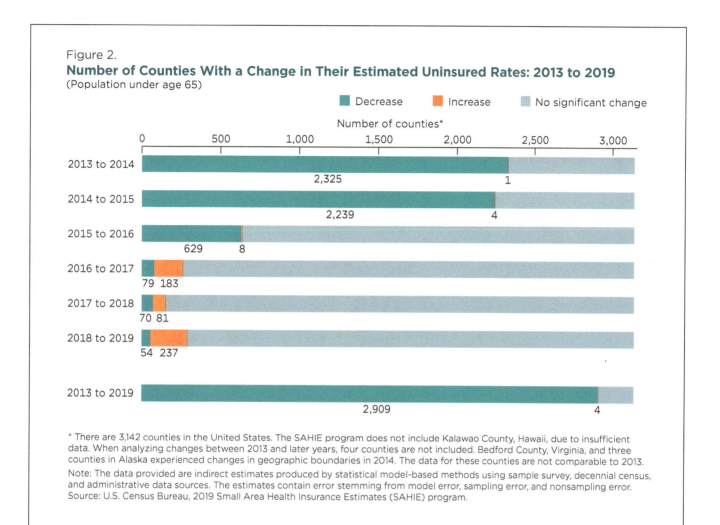

Figure 2.
Number of Counties With a Change in Their Estimated Uninsured Rates: 2013 to 2019
(Population under age 65)

* There are 3,142 counties in the United States. The SAHIE program does not include Kalawao County, Hawaii, due to insufficient data. When analyzing changes between 2013 and later years, four counties are not included. Bedford County, Virginia, and three counties in Alaska experienced changes in geographic boundaries in 2014. The data for these counties are not comparable to 2013.
Note: The data provided are indirect estimates produced by statistical model-based methods using sample survey, decennial census, and administrative data sources. The estimates contain error stemming from model error, sampling error, and nonsampling error.
Source: U.S. Census Bureau, 2019 Small Area Health Insurance Estimates (SAHIE) program.

From 2016 to 2017, over 91.0 percent of (or 2,879) counties did not have a statistically significant change in their uninsured rates; however, unlike during the previous 3 years, more counties (183) saw a significant increase than a decrease (79 counties) in their uninsured rates. Similarly, from 2017 to 2018, more counties (81) saw a significant increase than a decrease (70 counties) in their uninsured rates. This increasing trend continued from 2018 to 2019, as even more counties (237) saw a significant increase than a decrease (54 counties) in their uninsured rates.

Given these trends, estimated uninsured rates have fallen below 10.0 percent in many counties. In 2013, only 130 counties, or 4.1 percent of all counties, had an uninsured rate less than or equal to 10.0 percent. In 2018, the number of counties with uninsured rates less than or equal to 10.0 percent increased to 1,184 counties, or 37.7 percent of all U.S. counties. In 2019, the number of counties with uninsured rates less than or equal to 10.0 percent decreased slightly to 1,054 counties, or 33.6 percent of all U.S. counties.

UNINSURED RATES FOR LOW-INCOME, WORKING-AGE ADULTS

The ACA gave states the option to expand Medicaid eligibility to low-income, working-age adults, aged 18 to 64, living at or below 138.0 percent of poverty. Figure 3 contains two maps. The top map displays state Medicaid expansion status as of December 31, 2019. In 2019, two states expanded Medicaid eligibility—Maine and Virginia—making a total of 33 expansion states and the District of Columbia.[12]

---

[12] Maine expanded their Medicaid program's eligibility on January 10, 2019. Virginia expanded on January 1, 2019.

Small Area Health Insurance Estimates: 2019   Guide to U.S. HMOs & PPOs 2023

Figure 3.
Medicaid Expansion Status by State and Estimated Uninsured Rates for Low-Income, Working Age-Adults by County: 2019

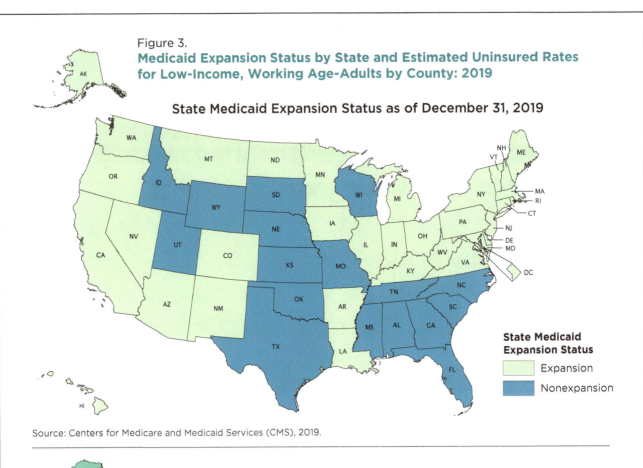

State Medicaid Expansion Status as of December 31, 2019

Source: Centers for Medicare and Medicaid Services (CMS), 2019.

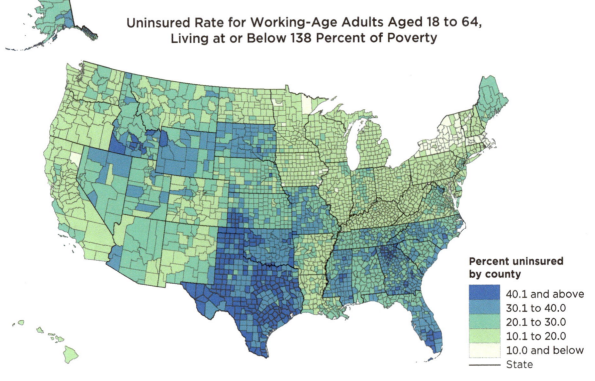

Uninsured Rate for Working-Age Adults Aged 18 to 64, Living at or Below 138 Percent of Poverty

Note: The data provided are indirect estimates produced by statistical model-based methods using sample survey, decennial census, and administrative data sources. The estimates contain error stemming from model error, sampling error, and nonsampling error.
Source: U.S. Census Bureau, 2019 Small Area Health Insurance Estimates (SAHIE) Program.

1

HOW IS POVERTY STATUS MEASURED?

Poverty status is determined by comparing total annual family before-tax income to federal poverty thresholds that vary by family size, number of related children, and age of householder. If a family's income is less than the dollar value of the appropriate threshold, then that family and every individual in it are considered to be in poverty. For people not living in families, poverty status is determined by comparing the individual's total income to their threshold. General information on poverty is available at <www.census.gov/topics/income-poverty/poverty.html>.

The table of federal poverty thresholds is updated annually by the U.S. Census Bureau to allow for changes in the cost of living using the Consumer Price Index (CPI-U). The thresholds do not vary geographically.

SAHIE's primary data input is the estimates of poverty from the American Community Survey (ACS), a continuous survey with people responding throughout the year. Since income is reported for the previous 12 months, the appropriate poverty threshold for each family is determined by multiplying the base-year poverty threshold by the average of the monthly CPI values for the 12 months preceding the survey. More information is available in "How the Census Bureau Measures Poverty" at <www.census.gov/topics/income-poverty/poverty/guidance/poverty-measures.html>.

To determine a family's or an individual's income-to-poverty ratio (IPR), divide a family's or individual's before-tax income by the appropriate federal poverty threshold. Then multiply by 100 to determine how far the family or individual earner is below or above poverty (a family with an IPR of 100 percent is living at the federal poverty threshold).

For example, imagine a family of four, two parents and two children, with a total annual income of $50,000. In 2019, a family of this size had a federal poverty threshold of $25,926. Their income-to-poverty ratio would be:

$$\frac{\text{Total annual income}}{\text{Federal poverty threshold}} = \frac{\$50,000}{\$25,926} = 1.929 = 192.9 \text{ percent of poverty}$$

The family of four is living just below 200 percent of poverty. This means their income is just below twice the determined federal poverty threshold.

SAHIE Income-to-Poverty Ratio Categories: 0-138 percent, 0-200 percent, 0-250 percent, 0-400 percent, 138-400 percent of poverty, and all incomes.

The bottom map displays estimated county uninsured rates for low-income, working-age adults who may be eligible for Medicaid. In 2019, county uninsured rates for this population ranged from 6.1 percent to 61.9 percent. The median county uninsured rate among low-income, working-age adults was 22.1 percent. In states that expanded Medicaid eligibility, 9.2 percent of counties (151 out of 1,647 counties) had an estimated uninsured rate above 20.0 percent, compared to 84.8 percent of counties (1,267 out of 1,494 counties) in states that did not expand it.

CHILDREN HAVE LOWER UNINSURED RATES THAN WORKING-AGE ADULTS

At the state level, SAHIE data show that in 2019, children under the age of 19 had a lower estimated uninsured rate than working-age adults, aged 18 to 64, in all 50 states and the District of Columbia. The difference between the two age groups is even found among U.S. counties, where children had significantly lower uninsured rates than working-age adults in 94.5 percent of all counties (Figure 4). There was only one county where the child population had a significantly higher uninsured rate: Dunn County, North Dakota.

Small Area Health Insurance Estimates: 2019 | Guide to U.S. HMOs & PPOs 2023

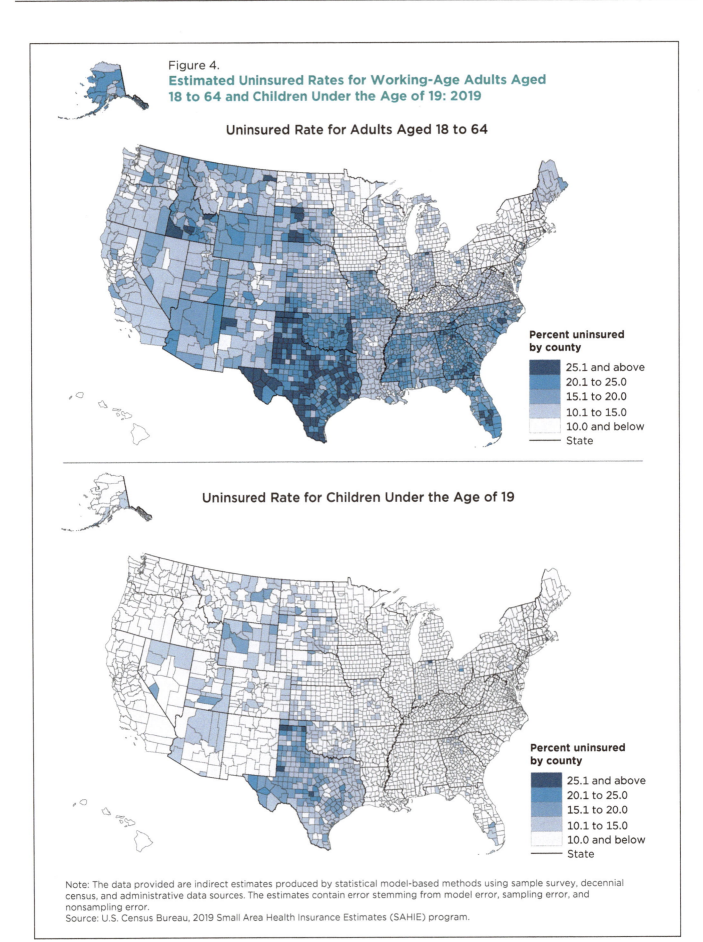

Figure 4.
Estimated Uninsured Rates for Working-Age Adults Aged 18 to 64 and Children Under the Age of 19: 2019

Note: The data provided are indirect estimates produced by statistical model-based methods using sample survey, decennial census, and administrative data sources. The estimates contain error stemming from model error, sampling error, and nonsampling error.
Source: U.S. Census Bureau, 2019 Small Area Health Insurance Estimates (SAHIE) program.

WHY ARE SMALL AREA HEALTH INSURANCE ESTIMATES (SAHIE) IMPORTANT?

The SAHIE program is partially funded by the Centers for Disease Control and Prevention's Division of Cancer Prevention and Control. It has a congressional mandate to provide screening services for breast and cervical cancer to low-income, uninsured, and underserved women through the National Breast and Cervical Cancer Early Detection Program (NBCCEDP). SAHIE data are used as an important consideration when planning and evaluating public policy on health insurance programs, the impact of common illnesses, or serious health conditions for states and the 3,141 counties in the United States. More information about NBCCEDP is available at <www.cdc.gov/cancer/nbccedp/>.

Additional information is available by data release year from 2000 to 2019. For example, you can download annual reports (for 2010–2019 data release years only), data sets, maps, and interactive data tables at <www.census.gov/programs-surveys/sahie.html>.

The online SAHIE Interactive Data Tool provides detailed customized data tables of the insured and uninsured populations by selected year(s) from 2006–2019, geography (state and county), income-to-poverty ratio (IPR) categories, selected age groups (under the age of 65, ages 18–64, ages 21–64, ages 40–64, ages 50–64, and under the age of 19), sex, and race/ethnicity (state level only). These custom tables can be downloaded to a PDF or CSV file. To access the interactive data online, visit <www.census.gov/data/data-tools/sahie-interactive.html>.

Starting in 2008, SAHIE began utilizing the American Community Survey data. For years prior to 2008, the SAHIE program estimates utilized the Annual Social and Economic Supplement to the Current Population Survey. More information is available at <www.census.gov/programs-surveys/sahie/technical-documentation/methodology/methodology-2008-2019.html>.

WORKING-AGE MEN HAVE HIGHER UNINSURED RATES

In every state and the District of Columbia, the 2019 estimated uninsured rate for working-age men, aged 18 to 64, was higher than for working-age women. Working-age men had a significantly higher uninsured rate than women in 1,661 counties (52.9 percent). There were no statistically significant differences in the remaining counties (Figure 5).

STATE UNINSURED RATES VARY BY RACE AND ETHNICITY

The SAHIE program provides health insurance coverage estimates at the state level by race and ethnicity. In 2019, for the population under the age of 65, non-Hispanic Whites had a lower estimated uninsured rate than Hispanics and non-Hispanic Blacks in every state and the District of Columbia. Non-Hispanic Blacks under the age of 65 also had a lower estimated uninsured rate than Hispanics in every state and the District of Columbia (Figure 6 and Appendix Table 1).

Figure 6 also displays how estimated uninsured rates changed from 2018 to 2019 by race and ethnicity across states. Each line represents the magnitude of change for each group. Longer lines indicate a larger change in the uninsured rate. From 2018 to 2019, for the population under the age of 65, uninsured rates for non-Hispanic Blacks saw significant increases in five states and a significant decrease in one state; the remaining states and the District of Columbia did not have a statistically significant change. Uninsured rates for non-Hispanic Whites significantly increased in 20 states and decreased in three states. Twenty-eight states and the District of Columbia did not have a statistically significant change in their uninsured rates. For the Hispanic population, more states had an increase than a decrease in their uninsured rate. One state had a decrease and 12 states had an increase, while the remaining states did not have a statistically different uninsured rate (Appendix Table 1 for statistically significant changes).

Small Area Health Insurance Estimates: 2019

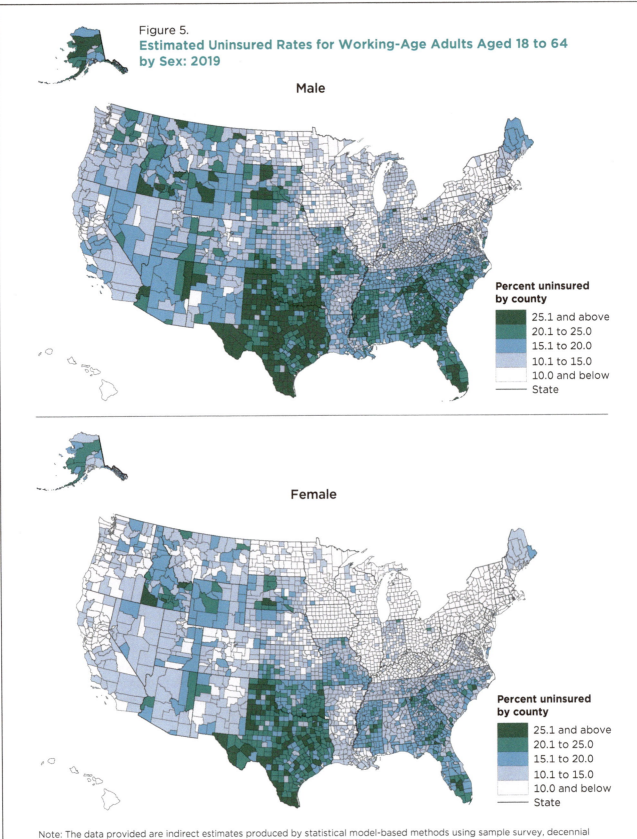

Figure 5.
Estimated Uninsured Rates for Working-Age Adults Aged 18 to 64 by Sex: 2019

Note: The data provided are indirect estimates produced by statistical model-based methods using sample survey, decennial census, and administrative data sources. The estimates contain error stemming from model error, sampling error, and nonsampling error.
Source: U.S. Census Bureau, 2019 Small Area Health Insurance Estimates (SAHIE) program.

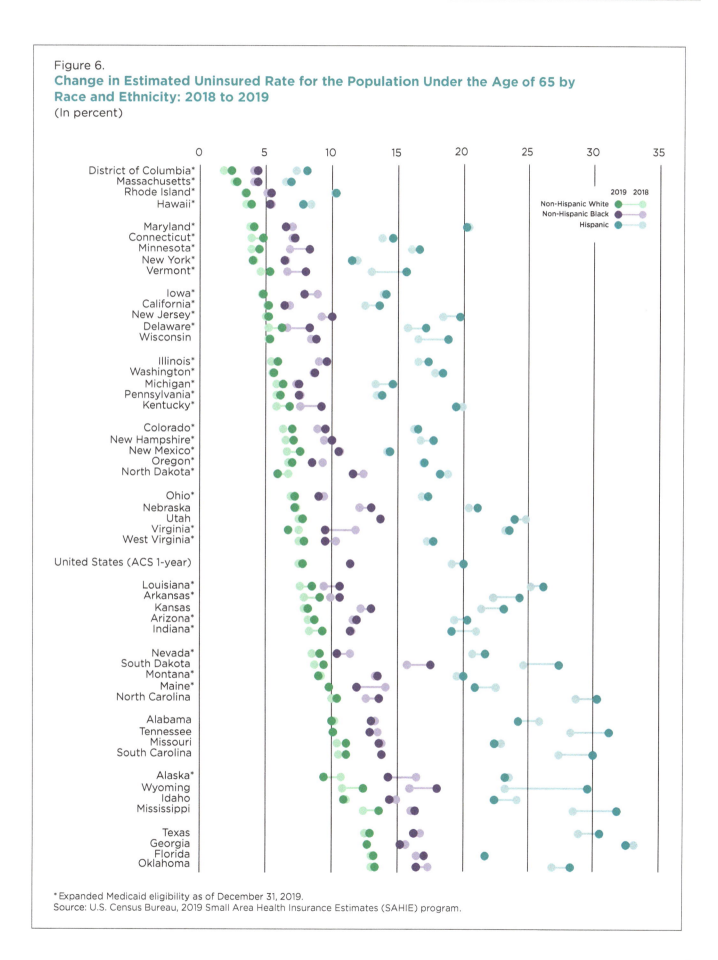

ACKNOWLEDGMENTS

The Small Area Estimates Branch prepared this document with significant contributions from the Small Area Modeling and Development Branch and the Health and Disability Statistics Branch.

CONTACT

For questions related to the contents of this document, including estimates and methodology of the Small Area Health Insurance Estimates (SAHIE) program, contact the Small Area Estimates Branch at (301) 763-3193 or <sehsd.sahie@census.gov>. For questions related to health insurance, income and poverty definitions, the American Community Survey, or other Census Bureau surveys, contact the U.S. Census Bureau Call Center at 1-800-923-8282 (toll free), or visit <https://ask.census.gov>.

SUGGESTED CITATION

Robinson, S. and K. A. Willyard, "Small Area Health Insurance Estimates: 2019," *Current Population Reports*, P30-09, U.S. Census Bureau, Washington, DC, 2021.

Appendix Table 1.
Change in Estimated Uninsured Rate for the Population Under the Age of 65 by Race and Ethnicity: 2018 to 2019

(In percentage points. All data shown are estimates containing uncertainty. Sources of uncertainty include model error, sampling error, and nonsampling error. More information is available at <www.census.gov/programs-surveys/sahie/technical-documentation/source-and-accuracy.html>)

State	Medicaid expansion[1]	Non-Hispanic White 2019	Change	Non-Hispanic Black 2019	Change	Hispanic 2019	Change
Alabama	no	10.0	-0.2	13.0	-0.3	24.2	-1.7
Alaska	yes	9.4	*-1.3	14.3	-2.1	23.2	-0.3
Arizona	yes	8.7	*0.5	11.9	0.3	20.3	*1.0
Arkansas	yes	9.1	*1.2	10.6	0.7	24.3	2.0
California	yes	5.2	0.1	6.4	-0.4	13.6	*1.1
Colorado	yes	7.0	*0.7	9.5	0.6	16.5	0.3
Connecticut	yes	4.8	*0.9	7.2	0.2	14.6	0.8
Delaware	yes	6.2	*1.0	8.3	*1.7	17.1	1.4
District of Columbia	yes	2.4	*0.6	4.4	0.3	8.1	0.8
Florida	no	13.2	0.2	17.0	0.6	21.7	Z
Georgia	no	12.7	Z	15.2	-0.4	32.5	-0.6
Hawaii	yes	3.9	0.4	5.3	-0.1	7.8	-0.6
Idaho	no	10.9	-0.2	14.4	-0.5	22.4	-1.7
Illinois	yes	5.9	*0.5	9.6	0.6	17.3	*0.8
Indiana	yes	9.3	*1.0	11.4	-0.1	19.1	*-1.9
Iowa	yes	4.8	0.1	7.9	-1.0	14.1	0.2
Kansas	no	8.2	0.3	13.0	0.8	23.1	1.7
Kentucky	yes	6.8	*1.0	9.2	*1.6	19.4	-0.5
Louisiana	yes	8.5	*0.9	10.6	*1.2	26.2	1.0
Maine	yes	9.8	Z	11.9	-2.2	20.9	-1.6
Maryland	yes	4.1	0.3	6.5	-0.5	20.2	-0.2
Massachusetts	yes	2.8	*0.2	4.4	0.3	6.9	0.4
Michigan	yes	6.3	*0.5	7.5	0.2	14.6	*1.3
Minnesota	yes	4.5	*0.6	8.3	*1.5	16.6	0.6
Mississippi	no	13.6	*1.2	16.3	0.3	31.8	*3.3
Missouri	no	11.1	*0.7	13.6	-0.2	22.4	-0.5
Montana	yes	9.0	-0.2	13.5	0.2	20.0	0.5
Nebraska	no	7.2	-0.1	13.0	0.9	21.1	0.7
Nevada	yes	9.1	0.6	10.4	-1.0	21.7	1.0
New Hampshire	yes	7.1	0.6	10.0	0.6	17.7	1.0
New Jersey	yes	5.2	0.2	10.0	0.8	19.7	*1.3
New Mexico	yes	7.6	*1.0	10.5	-0.1	14.4	0.2
New York	yes	4.0	-0.1	6.4	-0.1	11.5	-0.4
North Carolina	no	10.4	0.4	13.6	*1.0	30.3	*1.6
North Dakota	yes	5.9	*-0.8	11.6	-0.8	18.2	-0.6
Ohio	yes	7.2	0.3	9.0	-0.4	17.3	0.5
Oklahoma	no	13.3	0.3	16.4	-0.9	28.3	1.4
Oregon	yes	7.0	0.3	8.5	-0.8	17.0	0.1
Pennsylvania	yes	6.1	*0.3	7.5	-0.1	13.8	0.4
Rhode Island	yes	3.5	0.1	5.4	0.3	10.3	0.1
South Carolina	no	11.1	0.6	13.8	Z	30.0	*2.6
South Dakota	no	9.4	0.7	17.5	1.8	27.4	2.8
Tennessee	no	10.1	Z	12.9	-0.6	31.2	*2.9
Texas	no	12.9	*0.4	16.2	-0.5	30.5	*1.6
Utah	no	7.8	0.3	13.7	Z	23.9	-0.9
Vermont	yes	5.3	*0.7	8.0	1.4	15.6	2.6
Virginia	yes	6.7	*-0.8	9.5	*-2.3	23.5	0.3
Washington	yes	5.6	0.1	8.7	0.1	18.4	0.6
West Virginia	yes	7.9	0.4	9.5	-0.8	17.7	0.5
Wisconsin	no	5.3	0.1	8.8	0.4	18.8	*2.3
Wyoming	no	12.4	*1.6	18.0	2.1	29.6	*6.4

* Changes between the estimates are statistically different from zero at the 90 percent confidence level.
Z Represents or rounds to zero.
[1] States that expanded Medicaid eligibility as of December 31, 2019.
Source: U.S. Census Bureau, 2019 Small Area Health Insurance Estimates (SAHIE) program.

Robinson, S. and K. A. Willyard. "Small Area Health Insurance Estimates: 2019." Current Population Reports, P30-09, U. S. Census Bureau, Washington, DC, June 2021.

NATIONAL CENTER FOR HEALTH STATISTICS
National Health Interview Survey Early Release Program

Health Insurance Coverage: Early Release of Estimates From the National Health Interview Survey, 2021

by Robin A. Cohen, Ph.D., Amy E. Cha, Ph.D., M.P.H., Emily P. Terlizzi, M.P.H., and Michael E. Martinez, M.P.H., M.H.S.A.
Division of Health Interview Statistics, National Center for Health Statistics

What's New

- Estimates of health insurance coverage based on data from 2021 are provided, along with selected trends from 2019–2021.

Highlights

- In 2021, 30.0 million people of all ages (9.2%) were uninsured at the time of interview. This was lower than, but not significantly different from 2020, when 31.6 million people of all ages (9.7%) were uninsured.

- In 2021, among adults aged 18–64, 13.5% were uninsured at the time of interview, 21.7% had public coverage, and 66.6% had private health insurance coverage.

- Among children aged 0–17 years, 4.1% were uninsured, 44.3% had public coverage, and 53.8% had private health insurance coverage.

- Among non-Hispanic White adults aged 18–64, the percentage who were uninsured decreased from 10.5% in 2019 to 8.7% in 2021.

- The percentage of people under age 65 with exchange-based coverage increased from 3.7% in 2019 to 4.3% in 2021.

This report presents estimates of health insurance coverage for the civilian noninstitutionalized U.S. population based on data from the 2021 National Health Interview Survey (NHIS). These estimates are being published before final editing and final weighting to provide access to the most recent information from NHIS. Estimates are disaggregated by age group, sex, family income (as a percentage of the federal poverty level [FPL]), race and ethnicity, and state Medicaid expansion status. Detailed appendix tables contain all estimates presented in the figures and additional estimates for selected population characteristics. With 3 years of comparable data available starting with the redesigned NHIS in 2019, this report is now able to provide data on trends, similar to reports using 2018 and earlier data. Quarterly estimates by age group and family income, and more information about NHIS and the Early Release (ER) Program, are available from the NHIS website.

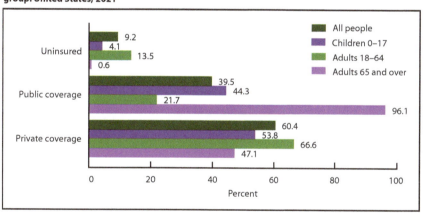

Figure 1. Percentages of people who were uninsured or had public or private coverage, by age group: United States, 2021

NOTES: People were defined as uninsured if they did not have any private health insurance, Medicare, Medicaid, Children's Health Insurance Program (CHIP), state-sponsored or other government plan, or military plan. People also were defined as uninsured if they had only Indian Health Service coverage or had only a private plan that paid for one type of service, such as accidents or dental care. Public coverage includes Medicaid, CHIP, state-sponsored or other government-sponsored health plan, Medicare, and military plans. Private coverage includes any comprehensive private insurance plan (including health maintenance and preferred provider organizations). These plans include those obtained through an employer, purchased directly, purchased through local or community programs, or purchased through the Health Insurance Marketplace or a state-based exchange. Private coverage excludes plans that pay for only one type of service, such as accidents or dental care. A small number of people were covered by both public and private plans and were included in both categories. Data are based on household interviews of a sample of the civilian noninstitutionalized population.
SOURCE: National Center for Health Statistics, National Health Interview Survey, 2021.

- In 2021, among people of all ages, 9.2% were uninsured, 39.5% had public coverage, and 60.4% had private coverage at the time of interview (Figure 1).

- Adults aged 18–64 were the most likely to be uninsured (13.5%), followed by children aged 0–17 years (4.1%) and adults aged 65 and over (0.6%).

- Adults aged 65 and over were the most likely to have public coverage (96.1%), followed by children aged 0–17 years (44.3%) and adults aged 18–64 (21.7%).

- Adults aged 18–64 were the most likely to have private coverage (66.6%), followed by children aged 0–17 years (53.8%) and adults aged 65 and over (47.1%).

Figure 2. Percentages of adults aged 18–64 who were uninsured or had public or private coverage, by year: United States, 2019–2021

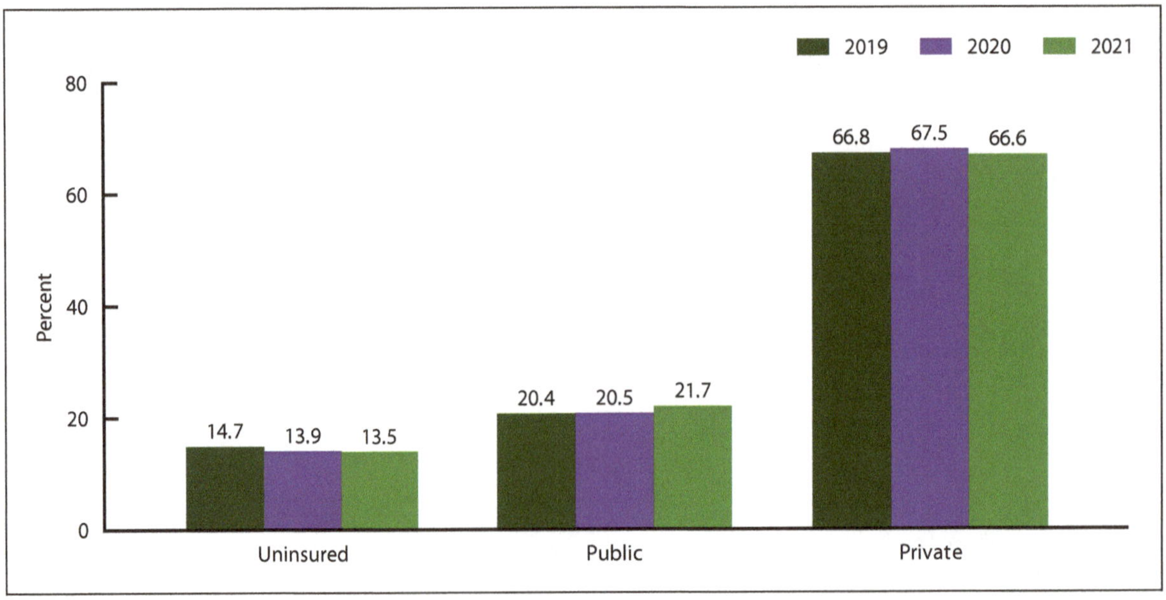

Coverage	2019	2020	2021
Uninsured	14.7	13.9	13.5
Public	20.4	20.5	21.7
Private	66.8	67.5	66.6

NOTES: People were defined as uninsured if they did not have any private health insurance, Medicare, Medicaid, Children's Health Insurance Program (CHIP), state-sponsored or other government plan, or military plan. People also were defined as uninsured if they had only Indian Health Service coverage or had only a private plan that paid for one type of service, such as accidents or dental care. Public coverage includes Medicaid, CHIP, state-sponsored or other government-sponsored health plan, Medicare, and military plans. Private coverage includes any comprehensive private insurance plan (including health maintenance and preferred provider organizations). These plans include those obtained through an employer, purchased directly, purchased through local or community programs, or purchased through the Health Insurance Marketplace or a state-based exchange. Private coverage excludes plans that pay for only one type of service, such as accidents or dental care. A small number of people were covered by both public and private plans and were included in both categories. Due to the COVID-19 pandemic, National Health Interview Survey (NHIS) data collection switched to a telephone-only mode beginning on March 19, 2020. Personal visits (with telephone attempts first) resumed in all areas in September 2020. In addition, from August through December 2020, a subsample of adult respondents who completed NHIS in 2019 were recontacted by telephone and asked to participate again. Response rates were lower and respondent characteristics were different in April–December 2020. Differences observed in estimates between April and December 2020 and other time periods may have been impacted by these differences in respondent characteristics. Data are based on household interviews of a sample of the civilian noninstitutionalized population.
SOURCE: National Center for Health Statistics, National Health Interview Survey, 2019–2021.

- Among adults aged 18–64, the percentage who were uninsured did not change significantly between 2020 (13.9%) and 2021 (13.5%) (Figure 2).
- Among adults aged 18–64, the percentage who had public coverage in 2021 (21.7%) was higher than the percentage who had public coverage in 2020 (20.5%).
- Among adults aged 18–64, the percentage who had private coverage in 2021 (66.6%) was lower than, but not significantly different from, the percentage who had private coverage in 2020 (67.5%).
- Among adults aged 18–64, the percentage who were uninsured decreased from 14.7% in 2019 to 13.5% in 2021. Public coverage increased from 2019 (20.4%) through 2021 (21.7%). No significant trend in private coverage was observed between 2019 and 2021.

Figure 3. Percentages of children aged 0–17 who were uninsured or had public or private coverage, by year: United States, 2019–2021

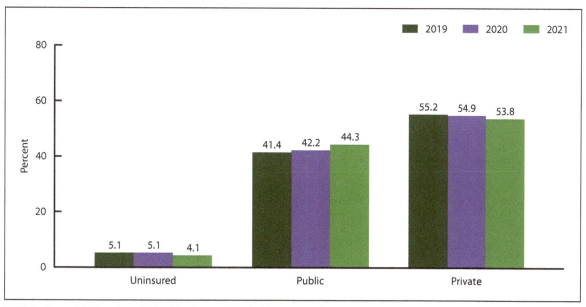

NOTES: People were defined as uninsured if they did not have any private health insurance, Medicare, Medicaid, Children's Health Insurance Program (CHIP), state-sponsored or other government plan, or military plan. People also were defined as uninsured if they had only Indian Health Service coverage or had only a private plan that paid for one type of service, such as accidents or dental care. Public coverage includes Medicaid, CHIP, state-sponsored or other government-sponsored health plan, Medicare, and military plans. Private coverage includes any comprehensive private insurance plan (including health maintenance and preferred provider organizations). These plans include those obtained through an employer, purchased directly, purchased through local or community programs, or purchased through the Health Insurance Marketplace or a state-based exchange. Private coverage excludes plans that pay for only one type of service, such as accidents or dental care. A small number of people were covered by both public and private plans and were included in both categories. Due to the COVID-19 pandemic, National Health Interview Survey (NHIS) data collection switched to a telephone-only mode beginning on March 19, 2020. Personal visits (with telephone attempts first) resumed in all areas in September 2020. In addition, from August through December 2020, a subsample of adult respondents who completed NHIS in 2019 were recontacted by telephone and asked to participate again. Response rates were lower and respondent characteristics were different in April–December 2020. Differences observed in estimates between April and December 2020 and other time periods may have been impacted by these differences in respondent characteristics. Data are based on household interviews of a sample of the civilian noninstitutionalized population.
SOURCE: National Center for Health Statistics, National Health Interview Survey, 2019–2021.

- Among children aged 0–17, the percentage who were uninsured in 2021 (4.1%) was lower than the percentage who were uninsured in 2020 (5.1%) (Figure 3).

- Among children aged 0–17, the percentage who had public coverage in 2021 (44.3%) was higher than, but not significantly different from, the percentage who had public coverage in 2020 (42.2%).

- Among children aged 0–17, the percentage who had private coverage in 2021 (53.8%) was lower than, but not significantly different from, the percentage who had private coverage in 2020 (54.9%).

- Among children aged 0–17, the percentage who were uninsured decreased from 5.1% in 2019 to 4.1% in 2021. Public coverage increased from 2019 (41.4%) through 2021 (44.3%); the observed decrease among children aged 0–17 with private coverage between 2019 and 2021 was not significant.

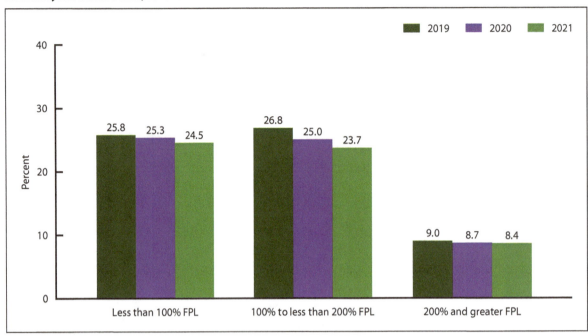

Figure 4. Percentage of adults aged 18–64 who were uninsured, by family income as a percentage of the federal poverty level and year: United States, 2019–2021

NOTES: FPL is federal poverty level. People were defined as uninsured if they did not have any private health insurance, Medicare, Medicaid, Children's Health Insurance Program (CHIP), state-sponsored or other government plan, or military plan. People also were defined as uninsured if they had only Indian Health Service coverage or had only a private plan that paid for one type of service, such as accidents or dental care. Public coverage includes Medicaid, CHIP, state-sponsored or other government-sponsored health plan, Medicare, and military plans. Due to the COVID-19 pandemic, National Health Interview Survey (NHIS) data collection switched to a telephone-only mode beginning on March 19, 2020. Personal visits (with telephone attempts first) resumed in all areas in September 2020. In addition, from August through December 2020, a subsample of adult respondents who completed NHIS in 2019 were recontacted by telephone and asked to participate again. Response rates were lower and respondent characteristics were different in April–December 2020. Differences observed in estimates between April and December 2020 and other time periods may have been impacted by these differences in respondent characteristics. Data are based on household interviews of a sample of the civilian noninstitutionalized population.
SOURCE: National Center for Health Statistics, National Health Interview Survey, 2019–2021.

- In 2021, among adults aged 18–64, the percentage who were uninsured was higher among those with family incomes less than 100% FPL (24.5%) and those with family incomes from 100% to less than 200% FPL (23.7%) compared with those with family incomes at or above 200% FPL (8.4%) (Figure 4).

- No significant differences were observed in the percentage of adults who were uninsured between 2020 and 2021 for any of the family income subgroups shown.

- Among adults aged 18–64 with family incomes from 100% to less than 200% FPL, the percentage who were uninsured decreased from 2019 through 2021; the observed decreases in the percentage of uninsured adults aged 18–64 with family incomes less than 100% FPL or family incomes at or above 200% FPL, between 2019 and 2021 were not significant.

Figure 5. Percentage of children aged 0–17 who were uninsured, by family income as a percentage of the federal poverty level and year: United States, 2019–2021

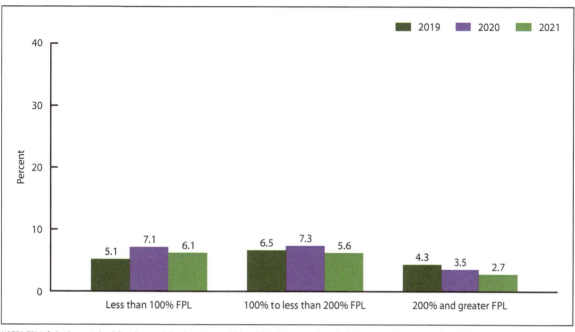

NOTES: FPL is federal poverty level. People were defined as uninsured if they did not have any private health insurance, Medicare, Medicaid, Children's Health Insurance Program (CHIP), state-sponsored or other government plan, or military plan. People also were defined as uninsured if they had only Indian Health Service coverage or had only a private plan that paid for one type of service, such as accidents or dental care. Public coverage includes Medicaid, CHIP, state-sponsored or other government-sponsored health plan, Medicare, and military plans. Due to the COVID-19 pandemic, National Health Interview Survey (NHIS) data collection switched to a telephone-only mode beginning on March 19, 2020. Personal visits (with telephone attempts first) resumed in all areas in September 2020. In addition, from August through December 2020, a subsample of adult respondents who completed NHIS in 2019 were recontacted by telephone and asked to participate again. Response rates were lower and respondent characteristics were different in April–December 2020. Differences observed in estimates between April and December 2020 and other time periods may have been impacted by these differences in respondent characteristics. Data are based on household interviews of a sample of the civilian noninstitutionalized population.
SOURCE: National Center for Health Statistics, National Health Interview Survey, 2019–2021.

- In 2021, among children aged 0–17, the percentage who were uninsured was higher among those with family incomes less than 100% FPL (6.1%) and those with family incomes from 100% to less than 200% FPL (5.6%) compared with those with family incomes at or above 200% FPL (2.7%) (Figure 5).

- No significant differences were observed in the percentage of uninsured children between 2020 and 2021 for any of the family income subgroups shown.

- Among children aged 0–17, the percentage who were uninsured decreased among those with family incomes at or above 200% FPL, from 4.3% in 2019 to 2.7% in 2021; the observed increase in the percentage of uninsured children with family incomes less than 100% FPL —from 5.1% in 2019 to 6.1% in 2021— was not significant. Among children with family incomes from 100% to less than 200% FPL, no trends were observed between 2019 and 2021.

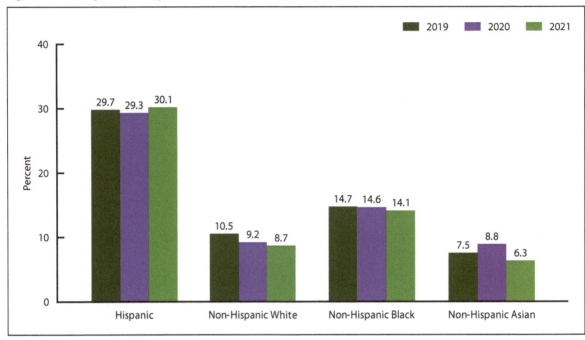

Figure 6. Percentage of adults aged 18–64 who were uninsured, by race and ethnicity and year: United States, 2019–2021

NOTES: People were defined as uninsured if they did not have any private health insurance, Medicare, Medicaid, Children's Health Insurance Program (CHIP), state-sponsored or other government plan, or military plan. People also were defined as uninsured if they had only Indian Health Service coverage or had only a private plan that paid for one type of service, such as accidents or dental care. Public coverage includes Medicaid, CHIP, state-sponsored or other government-sponsored health plan, Medicare, and military plans. Due to the COVID-19 pandemic, National Health Interview Survey (NHIS) data collection switched to a telephone-only mode beginning on March 19, 2020. Personal visits (with telephone attempts first) resumed in all areas in September 2020. In addition, from August through December 2020, a subsample of adult respondents who completed NHIS in 2019 were recontacted by telephone and asked to participate again. Response rates were lower and respondent characteristics were different in April–December 2020. Differences observed in estimates between April and December 2020 and other time periods may have been impacted by these differences in respondent characteristics. Data are based on household interviews of a sample of the civilian noninstitutionalized population.
SOURCE: National Center for Health Statistics, National Health Interview Survey, 2019–2021.

- In 2021, Hispanic adults were the most likely to lack health insurance coverage (30.1%), followed by non-Hispanic Black (14.1%), non-Hispanic White (8.7%), and non-Hispanic Asian (6.3%) adults (Figure 6).
- No significant differences were observed in the percentage of adults aged 18–64 who were uninsured between 2020 and 2021 for any of the race and ethnicity subgroups shown.
- Among non-Hispanic White adults aged 18–64, the percentage who were uninsured decreased from 10.5% in 2019 to 8.7% in 2021; no significant trends were observed for Hispanic, non-Hispanic Black, or non-Hispanic Asian adults aged 18–64.

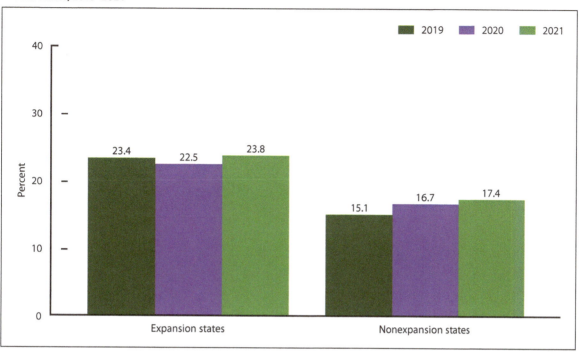

Figure 7. Percentage of adults aged 18–64 who had public coverage, by year and state Medicaid expansion status: United States, 2019–2021

NOTES: Public coverage includes Medicaid, CHIP, state-sponsored or other government-sponsored health plan, Medicare, and military plans. Due to the COVID-19 pandemic, National Health Interview Survey (NHIS) data collection switched to a telephone-only mode beginning on March 19, 2020. Personal visits (with telephone attempts first) resumed in all areas in September 2020. In addition, from August through December 2020, a subsample of adult respondents who completed NHIS in 2019 were recontacted by telephone and asked to participate again. Response rates were lower and respondent characteristics were different in April–December 2020. Differences observed in estimates between April and December 2020 and other time periods may have been impacted by these differences in respondent characteristics. Data are based on household interviews of a sample of the civilian noninstitutionalized population.
SOURCE: National Center for Health Statistics, National Health Interview Survey, 2019–2021.

- In 2021, among adults aged 18–64, those living in Medicaid expansion states (23.8%) were more likely than those living in non-Medicaid expansion states (17.4%) to have public coverage (Figure 7).

- Among adults aged 18–64 living in Medicaid expansion states, no significant difference was observed in the percentage of those with public coverage between 2019 and 2021.

- Among adults aged 18–64 living in non-Medicaid expansion states, the percentage with public coverage increased from 15.1% in 2019 to 17.4% in 2021.

- Among adults aged 18–64 living in non-Medicaid expansion states, no significant difference was observed in the percentage with public coverage between 2020 and 2021.

Figure 8. Percentage of people under age 65 who had exchange-based private health insurance coverage, by selected characteristics: United States, 2021

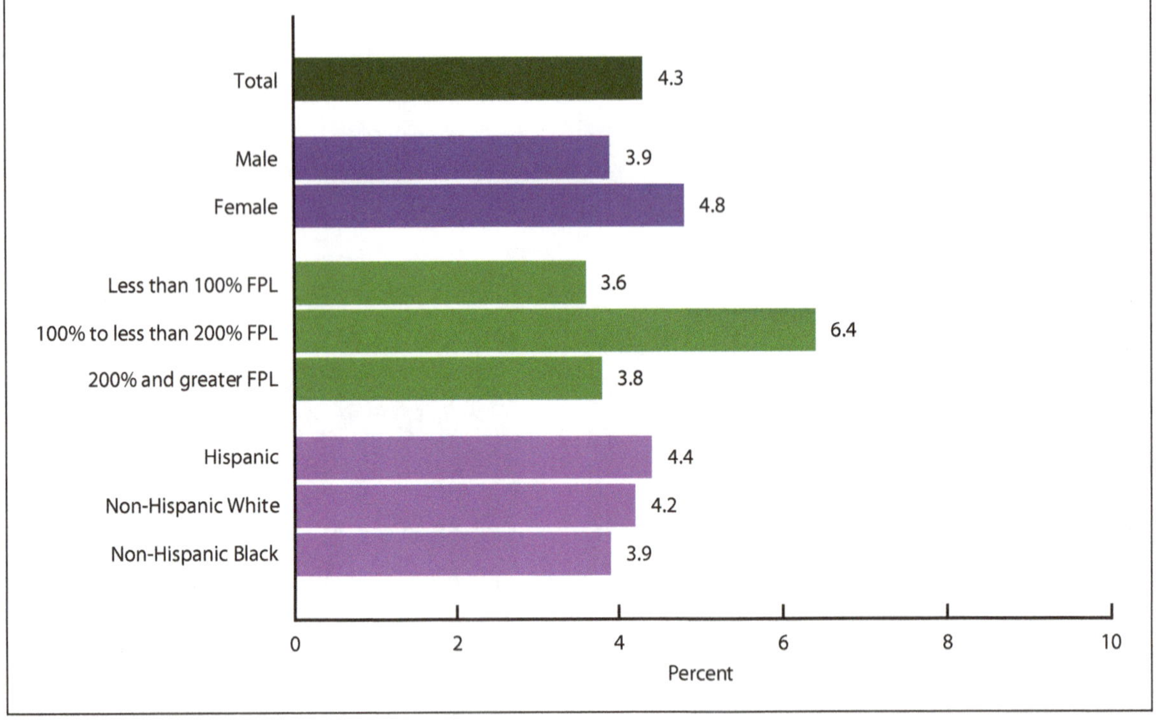

Characteristic	Percent
Total	4.3
Male	3.9
Female	4.8
Less than 100% FPL	3.6
100% to less than 200% FPL	6.4
200% and greater FPL	3.8
Hispanic	4.4
Non-Hispanic White	4.2
Non-Hispanic Black	3.9

NOTES: FPL is federal poverty level. Exchange-based coverage is a private health insurance plan purchased through the Health Insurance Marketplace or state-based exchanges that were established as part of the Affordable Care Act (ACA) of 2010 (P.L. 111–148, P.L. 111–152). Data are based on household interviews of a sample of the civilian noninstitutionalized population.
SOURCE: National Center for Health Statistics, National Health Interview Survey, 2021.

- In 2021, 4.3% of people under age 65 had exchange-based coverage (Figure 8).
- Males (3.9%) were less likely than females (4.8%) to have exchange-based coverage.
- Exchange-based coverage was higher among those with family incomes from 100% to less than 200% FPL (6.4%) compared with those with family incomes less than 100% FPL (3.6%) and family incomes at or above 200% FPL (3.8%).
- The observed differences by race and ethnicity were not significant.

Figure 9. Percentage of people under age 65 who had exchange-based private health insurance coverage, by year: United States, 2019–2021

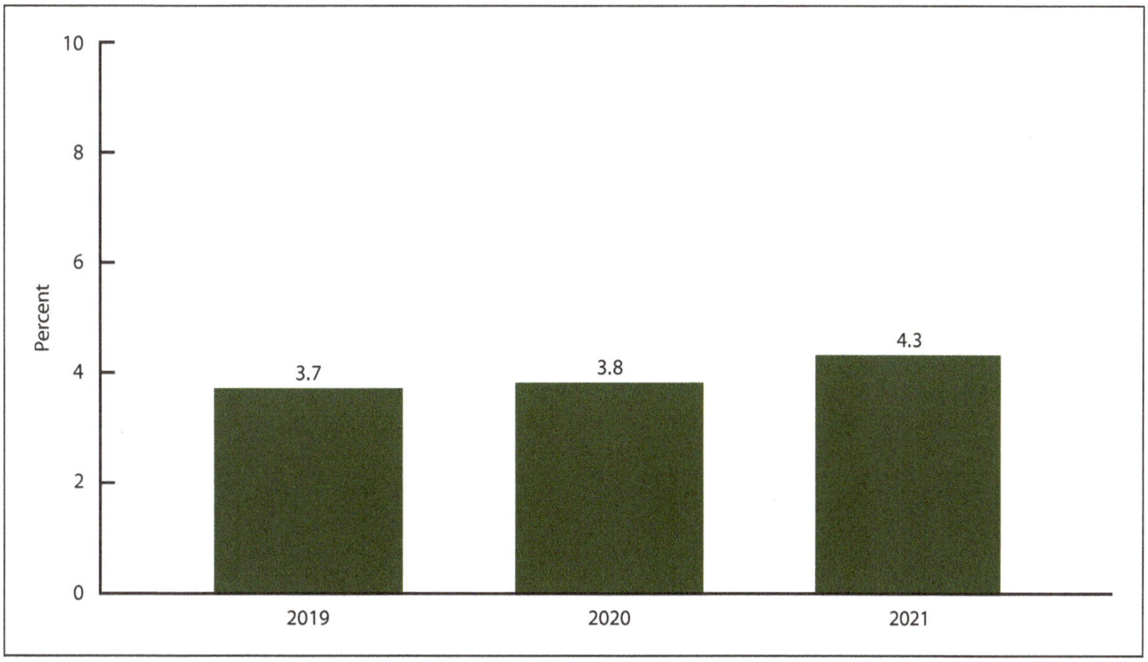

Year	Percent
2019	3.7
2020	3.8
2021	4.3

NOTES: Exchange-based coverage is a private health insurance plan purchased through the Health Insurance Marketplace or state-based exchanges that were established as part of the Affordable Care Act (ACA) of 2010 (P.L. 111-148, P.L. 111-152). Due to the COVID-19 pandemic, National Health Interview Survey (NHIS) data collection switched to a telephone-only mode beginning on March 19, 2020. Personal visits (with telephone attempts first) resumed in all areas in September 2020. In addition, from August through December 2020, a subsample of adult respondents who completed NHIS in 2019 were recontacted by telephone and asked to participate again. Response rates were lower and respondent characteristics were different in April–December 2020. Differences observed in estimates between April and December 2020 and other time periods may have been impacted by these differences in respondent characteristics. Data are based on household interviews of a sample of the civilian noninstitutionalized population.
SOURCE: National Center for Health Statistics, National Health Interview Survey, 2019–2021.

- Overall, the percentage of people under age 65 with exchange-based coverage increased from 3.7% in 2019 to 4.3% in 2021 (Figure 9).

Technical Notes

All estimates in this report are based on preliminary data. The 2021 estimates are being released before final data editing and final weighting to provide access to the most recent information from NHIS. Previously, differences between estimates calculated using preliminary data files and final data files were typically less than 0.1 percentage point.

Data source

Data used to produce this ER report were derived from the Sample Adult and Sample Child components from the 2019–2021 NHIS. NHIS is a nationally representative household survey conducted throughout the year to collect information on health status, health-related behaviors, and health care access and utilization. The NHIS interview begins by identifying everyone who usually lives or stays in the household. Then, one "sample adult" aged 18 and over and one "sample child" aged 17 years and under (if any children live in the household) are randomly selected. Information about the sample adults is collected from the sample adults themselves unless they are physically or mentally unable to report, in which case a knowledgeable proxy can answer for them. Information about the sample child is collected from a parent or adult who is knowledgeable about and responsible for the health care of the sample child. This respondent may or may not also be the sample adult. Data analysis for the 2021 NHIS was based on information collected on 29,696 sample adults and 8,293 sample children. Visit the NHIS website at: https://www.cdc.gov/nchs/nhis.htm for more information about the design, content, and use of NHIS.

Estimation procedures

The National Center for Health Statistics (NCHS) creates survey sampling weights to produce representative national estimates. The base weight is equal to the inverse of the probability of selection of the sample address. These weights are adjusted for household and person-level nonresponse using multilevel models predictive of response propensity. Nonresponse-adjusted weights are further calibrated to U.S. Census Bureau population projections and American Community Survey 1-year estimates for age, sex, race and ethnicity, educational attainment, housing tenure, census division, and metropolitan statistical area status. Point estimates and estimates of their variances were calculated using SUDAAN software (RTI International, Research Triangle Park, N.C.) to account for the complex sample design of NHIS, considering stratum and primary sampling unit identifiers. The Taylor series linearization method was chosen for variance estimation. Trends were evaluated using logistic regression analysis.

Impact of COVID-19 on NHIS sampling and longitudinal follow-up

Due to the COVID-19 pandemic, NHIS data collection switched to a telephone-only mode beginning March 19, 2020. Personal visits (with telephone attempts first) resumed in all areas in September 2020. In addition, from August through December 2020, a subsample of adult respondents who completed NHIS in 2019 were recontacted by telephone and asked to participate again. Response rates were lower and respondent characteristics were different in April through December 2020. Differences observed in estimates between April through December 2020 and other time periods may have been impacted by these differences in respondent characteristics.

All estimates shown meet NCHS standards of reliability as specified in "National Center for Health Statistics data presentation standards for proportions" (1). All differences discussed are statistically significant unless otherwise noted. Differences between percentages were evaluated using two-sided significance tests at the 0.05 level. Lack of comment regarding the difference between any two estimates does not necessarily mean that the difference was tested and found to be not significant. As noted above, the 2020 estimates in this report include approximately 10,000 sample adult respondents who participated in the 2019 NHIS and who also participated in the 2020 NHIS. The tests used to evaluate differences between the 2020 and 2021 estimates are conservative, and do not account for the potential covariance that may be introduced by having a subset of respondents participate in both the 2019 and 2020 NHIS surveys.

2019 questionnaire redesign and comparison of estimates to earlier years

In 2019, the NHIS questionnaire was redesigned to better meet the needs of data users. Due to changes in weighting and design methodology, direct comparisons between estimates for 2019 and earlier years should be made with caution, as the impact of these changes has not been fully evaluated. A working paper entitled, "Preliminary evaluation of the impact of the 2019 National Health Interview Survey questionnaire redesign and weighting adjustments on Early Release Program estimates," available from the Early Release Program homepage, discusses both of these issues in greater detail for three indicators of insurance coverage (lack of health insurance [uninsured], public health plan coverage, and private health insurance coverage). However, the discussion of these health insurance indicators is limited to adults aged 18–64.

Reference

1. Parker JD, Talih M, Malec DJ, Beresovsky V, Carroll M, Gonzalez Jr JF, et al. National Center for Health Statistics data presentation standards for proportions. National Center for Health Statistics. Vital Health Stat 2(175). 2017. Available from: https://www.cdc.gov/nchs/data/series/sr_02/sr02_175.pdf.

Suggested citation

Cohen RA, Cha AE, Terlizzi EP, Martinez ME. Health insurance coverage: Early release of estimates from the National Health Interview Survey, 2021. National Center for Health Statistics. May 2022. DOI: https://dx.doi.org/10.15620/cdc:115983.

Table I. Percentage (and 95% confidence interval) of people who lacked health insurance coverage, had public health plan coverage, and had private health insurance coverage at the time of interview, by age group and year: United States, 2019–2021

Age group (years), year, and 6-month interval	Uninsured[1]	Public health plan coverage[2]	Private health insurance coverage[3]
All ages			
2019	10.3 (9.7–10.8)	37.4 (36.6–38.3)	61.3 (60.2–62.4)
2020	9.7 (9.2–10.3)	38.0 (37.2–38.9)	61.8 (60.8–62.7)
2021 (full year)	9.2 (8.7–9.7)	39.5 (38.8–40.3)	60.4 (59.4–61.3)
2021 (Jan–Jun)	9.6 (8.9–10.3)	39.5 (38.4–40.6)	60.1 (58.9–61.3)
2021 (Jul–Dec)	8.8 (8.3–9.5)	39.6 (38.6–40.6)	60.6 (59.5–61.8)
Under 65			
2019	12.1 (11.4–12.8)	26.0 (25.1–26.9)	63.7 (62.5–64.8)
2020	11.5 (10.9–12.2)	26.4 (25.4–27.3)	64.1 (63.0–65.2)
2021 (full year)	11.0 (10.4–11.6)	27.7 (26.9–28.6)	63.2 (62.1–64.2)
2021 (Jan–Jun)	11.4 (10.6–12.3)	27.8 (26.7–29.0)	62.8 (61.4–64.1)
2021 (Jul–Dec)	10.6 (9.9–11.3)	27.6 (26.6–28.7)	63.5 (62.2–64.8)
0–17			
2019	5.1 (4.5–5.7)	41.4 (39.8–43.0)	55.2 (53.4–57.0)
2020	5.1 (4.3–6.0)	42.2 (40.1–44.3)	54.9 (52.8–57.0)
2021 (full year)	4.1 (3.7–4.6)	44.3 (42.8–45.9)	53.8 (52.1–55.5)
2021 (Jan–Jun)	4.4 (3.7–5.3)	44.7 (42.6–46.8)	53.1 (50.9–55.4)
2021 (Jul–Dec)	3.8 (3.2–4.6)	44.0 (42.3–45.6)	54.4 (52.5–56.4)
18–64			
2019	14.7 (13.9–15.4)	20.4 (19.6–21.2)	66.8 (65.7–67.9)
2020	13.9 (13.2–14.7)	20.5 (19.7–21.4)	67.5 (66.5–68.5)
2021 (full year)	13.5 (12.8–14.3)	21.7 (20.8–22.5)	66.6 (65.6–67.6)
2021 (Jan–Jun)	14.0 (13.0–15.1)	21.6 (20.6–22.7)	66.3 (65.0–67.6)
2021 (Jul–Dec)	13.0 (12.2–13.9)	21.7 (20.6–22.8)	66.9 (65.6–68.2)
65 and over			
2019	0.9 (0.6–1.3)	96.0 (95.5–96.5)	49.1 (47.6–50.7)
2020	0.8 (0.5–1.1)	95.9 (95.3–96.4)	50.2 (48.7–51.7)
2021 (full year)	0.6 (0.4–0.9)	96.1 (95.5–96.5)	47.1 (45.5–48.6)
2021 (Jan–Jun)	0.6 (0.3–1.0)	96.0 (95.1–96.7)	47.4 (45.2–49.7)
2021 (Jul–Dec)	0.6 (0.4–1.0)	96.2 (95.3–96.9)	46.7 (44.9–48.5)

[1]People were defined as uninsured if they did not have any private health insurance, Medicare, Medicaid, Children's Health Insurance Program (CHIP), state-sponsored or other government-sponsored health plan, or military plan. People also were defined as uninsured if they had only Indian Health Service coverage or had only a private plan that paid for one type of service, such as accidents or dental care.

[2]Public health plan coverage includes Medicaid, CHIP, state-sponsored or other government-sponsored health plan, Medicare, and military plans. A small number of people were covered by both public and private plans and were included in both categories.

[3]Private health insurance coverage includes any comprehensive private insurance plan (including health maintenance and preferred provider organizations). These plans include those obtained through an employer, purchased directly, purchased through local or community programs, or purchased through the Health Insurance Marketplace or a state-based exchange. Private coverage excludes plans that pay for only one type of service, such as accidents or dental care. A small number of people were covered by both public and private plans and were included in both categories.

NOTES: Due to the COVID-19 pandemic, data collection switched to a telephone-only mode beginning on March 19, 2020. Personal visits (with telephone attempts first) resumed in all areas in September 2020. In addition, from August–December 2020, a subsample of adult respondents who completed NHIS in 2019 were recontacted by telephone and asked to participate again. Response rates were lower and respondent characteristics were different in April–December 2020. Differences observed in estimates between April–December 2020 and other time periods may have been impacted by these differences in respondent characteristics. Data are based on household interviews of a sample of the civilian noninstitutionalized population.

SOURCE: National Center for Health Statistics, National Health Interview Surveys, 2019–2021.

Table II. Number (millions) of people who lacked health insurance coverage, had public health plan coverage, and had private health insurance coverage at the time of interview, by age group and year: United States, 2019–2021

Age group (years), year, and 6-month interval	Uninsured[1]	Public health plan coverage[2]	Private health insurance coverage[3]
All ages			
2019	33.2	121.4	198.7
2020	31.6	123.5	200.6
2021 (full year)	30.0	128.6	196.5
2021 (Jan–Jun)	31.1	128.4	195.5
2021 (Jul–Dec)	28.8	128.8	197.4
Under 65			
2019	32.8	70.6	172.7
2020	31.2	71.2	173.2
2021 (full year)	29.6	74.7	170.1
2021 (Jan–Jun)	30.8	75.0	169.1
2021 (Jul–Dec)	28.5	74.4	171.0
0–17			
2019	3.7	30.3	40.4
2020	3.7	30.7	39.9
2021 (full year)	3.0	32.0	38.9
2021 (Jan–Jun)	3.2	32.3	38.5
2021 (Jul–Dec)	2.8	31.7	39.3
18–64			
2019	29.0	40.3	132.3
2020	27.5	40.5	133.3
2021 (full year)	26.6	42.7	131.2
2021 (Jan–Jun)	27.6	42.6	130.6
2021 (Jul–Dec)	25.7	42.7	131.7
65 and over			
2019	0.5	50.8	26.0
2020	0.4	52.3	27.4
2021 (full year)	0.4	53.9	26.4
2021 (Jan–Jun)	0.3	53.4	26.4
2021 (Jul–Dec)	0.4	54.4	26.4

[1]People were defined as uninsured if they did not have any private health insurance, Medicare, Medicaid, Children's Health Insurance Program (CHIP), state-sponsored or other government-sponsored health plan, or military plan. People also were defined as uninsured if they had only Indian Health Service coverage or had only a private plan that paid for one type of service, such as accidents or dental care.

[2]Public health plan coverage includes Medicaid, CHIP, state-sponsored or other government-sponsored health plan, Medicare, and military plans. A small number of people were covered by both public and private plans and were included in both categories.

[3]Private health insurance coverage includes any comprehensive private insurance plan (including health maintenance and preferred provider organizations). These plans include those obtained through an employer, purchased directly, purchased through local or community programs, or purchased through the Health Insurance Marketplace or a state-based exchange. Private coverage excludes plans that pay for only one type of service, such as accidents or dental care. A small number of people were covered by both public and private plans and were included in both categories.

NOTES: Due to the COVID-19 pandemic, data collection switched to a telephone-only mode beginning on March 19, 2020. Personal visits (with telephone attempts first) resumed in all areas in September 2020. In addition, from August–December 2020, a subsample of adult respondents who completed NHIS in 2019 were recontacted by telephone and asked to participate again. Response rates were lower and respondent characteristics were different in April–December 2020. Differences observed in estimates between April–December 2020 and other time periods may have been impacted by these differences in respondent characteristics. Data are based on household interviews of a sample of the civilian noninstitutionalized population.

SOURCE: National Center for Health Statistics, National Health Interview Surveys, 2019–2021.

Table III. Percentage (and 95% confidence interval) of people under age 65 who lacked health insurance coverage, had public health plan coverage, and had private health insurance coverage at the time of interview, by sex, age group, and year: United States, 2019–2021

Sex, age group (years), year, and 6-month interval	Uninsured[1]	Public health plan coverage[2]	Private health insurance coverage[3]
Male			
Under 65			
2019	13.2 (12.3–14.1)	24.7 (23.6–25.9)	63.9 (62.4–65.4)
2020	12.3 (11.5–13.2)	25.1 (23.8–26.3)	64.6 (63.2–66.0)
2021 (full year)	12.5 (11.7–13.4)	25.9 (24.9–26.9)	63.5 (62.3–64.7)
2021 (Jan–Jun)	12.7 (11.5–14.0)	26.2 (24.9–27.4)	62.9 (61.4–64.5)
2021 (Jul–Dec)	12.3 (11.3–13.3)	25.6 (24.3–27.0)	64.1 (62.6–65.5)
0–17			
2019	5.1 (4.4–5.8)	42.1 (40.1–44.2)	54.5 (52.2–56.7)
2020	5.8 (4.6–7.3)	42.1 (39.4–44.8)	54.6 (51.8–57.3)
2021 (full year)	3.9 (3.3–4.6)	45.5 (43.5–47.6)	52.9 (50.5–55.2)
2021 (Jan–Jun)	3.8 (2.9–4.9)	45.4 (42.6–48.3)	52.7 (49.8–55.6)
2021 (Jul–Dec)	4.1 (3.1–5.1)	45.6 (43.4–47.8)	53.0 (50.3–55.7)
18–64			
2019	16.3 (15.1–17.4)	18.1 (17.0–19.2)	67.5 (66.1–69.0)
2020	14.8 (13.8–15.9)	18.6 (17.5–19.7)	68.4 (67.1–69.8)
2021 (full year)	15.8 (14.7–16.9)	18.4 (17.5–19.4)	67.5 (66.2–68.8)
2021 (Jan–Jun)	16.1 (14.6–17.8)	18.9 (17.7–20.0)	66.8 (65.1–68.5)
2021 (Jul–Dec)	15.4 (14.1–16.8)	18.0 (16.6–19.5)	68.3 (66.7–69.9)
Female			
Under 65			
2019	11.0 (10.4–11.7)	27.3 (26.2–28.4)	63.4 (62.2–64.7)
2020	10.7 (10.0–11.6)	27.6 (26.4–28.9)	63.6 (62.3–65.0)
2021 (full year)	9.5 (8.9–10.1)	29.6 (28.4–30.8)	62.8 (61.6–64.0)
2021 (Jan–Jun)	10.1 (9.2–11.1)	29.5 (27.9–31.1)	62.6 (60.9–64.3)
2021 (Jul–Dec)	8.9 (8.1–9.8)	29.7 (28.0–31.3)	63.0 (61.4–64.6)
0–17			
2019	5.1 (4.4–6.0)	40.6 (38.5–42.8)	56.0 (53.8–58.2)
2020	4.4 (3.4–5.6)	42.3 (39.5–45.2)	55.2 (52.4–58.0)
2021 (full year)	4.3 (3.7–5.1)	43.1 (40.8–45.4)	54.8 (52.3–57.2)
2021 (Jan–Jun)	5.1 (4.0–6.3)	43.9 (41.0–46.9)	53.5 (50.3–56.8)
2021 (Jul–Dec)	3.6 (2.7–4.7)	42.2 (39.3–45.2)	56.0 (52.8–59.1)
18–64			
2019	13.1 (12.4–13.9)	22.6 (21.6–23.6)	66.1 (64.9–67.3)
2020	13.0 (12.0–14.0)	22.4 (21.3–23.5)	66.6 (65.3–67.9)
2021 (full year)	11.3 (10.6–12.1)	24.8 (23.5–26.1)	65.7 (64.5–66.9)
2021 (Jan–Jun)	11.9 (10.8–13.1)	24.3 (22.7–26.1)	65.8 (64.1–67.5)
2021 (Jul–Dec)	10.8 (9.9–11.7)	25.2 (23.6–26.9)	65.5 (64.0–67.1)

[1]People were defined as uninsured if they did not have any private health insurance, Medicare, Medicaid, Children's Health Insurance Program (CHIP), state-sponsored or other government-sponsored health plan, or military plan. People also were defined as uninsured if they had only Indian Health Service coverage or had only a private plan that paid for one type of service, such as accidents or dental care.

[2]Public health plan coverage includes Medicaid, CHIP, state-sponsored or other government-sponsored health plan, Medicare, and military plans. A small number of people were covered by both public and private plans and were included in both categories.

[3]Private health insurance coverage includes any comprehensive private insurance plan (including health maintenance and preferred provider organizations). These plans include those obtained through an employer, purchased directly, purchased through local or community programs, or purchased through the Health Insurance Marketplace or a state-based exchange. Private coverage excludes plans that pay for only one type of service, such as accidents or dental care. A small number of people were covered by both public and private plans and were included in both categories.

NOTES: Due to the COVID-19 pandemic, data collection switched to a telephone-only mode beginning on March 19, 2020. Personal visits (with telephone attempts first) resumed in all areas in September 2020. In addition, from August–December 2020, a subsample of adult respondents who completed NHIS in 2019 were recontacted by telephone and asked to participate again. Response rates were lower and respondent characteristics were different in April–December 2020. Differences observed in estimates between April–December 2020 and other time periods may have been impacted by these differences in respondent characteristics. Data are based on household interviews of a sample of the civilian noninstitutionalized population.

SOURCE: National Center for Health Statistics, National Health Interview Surveys, 2019–2021.

Table IV. Percentage (and 95% confidence intervals) of people under age 65 who lacked health insurance coverage, had public health plan coverage, and had private health insurance coverage at the time of interview, by family income as a percentage of the federal poverty level, age group, and year: United States, 2019–2021

Family income as a percentage of FPL[1], age group (years), year, and 6-month interval	Uninsured[2]	Public health plan coverage[3]	Private health insurance coverage[4]
Less than 100% FPL[1]			
Under 65			
2019	18.3 (16.2–20.5)	65.3 (63.0–67.5)	18.2 (16.3–20.3)
2020	18.4 (16.0–20.9)	68.3 (65.5–71.1)	15.6 (13.7–17.7)
2021 (full year)	17.8 (15.8–20.0)	66.1 (63.1–69.1)	17.5 (14.9–20.3)
2021 (Jan–Jun)	19.5 (16.5–22.9)	66.0 (62.4–69.4)	16.1 (13.5–18.9)
2021 (Jul–Dec)	16.0 (13.6–18.7)	66.3 (62.1–70.3)	18.9 (15.2–23.1)
0–17			
2019	5.1 (3.8–6.8)	87.8 (85.3–90.1)	8.9 (7.1–11.1)
2020	7.1 (4.2–11.0)	88.0 (84.0–91.4)	7.3 (5.1–10.0)
2021 (full year)	6.1 (4.5–8.0)	87.3 (84.6–89.6)	7.8 (6.1–9.9)
2021 (Jan–Jun)	6.9 (4.5–10.1)	87.3 (83.3–90.6)	7.4 (5.1–10.3)
2021 (Jul–Dec)	5.2 (3.3–7.7)	87.2 (83.9–90.1)	8.3 (5.9–11.3)
18–64			
2019	25.8 (23.0–28.9)	52.3 (49.4–55.1)	23.6 (20.9–26.5)
2020	25.3 (22.3–28.4)	56.3 (52.9–59.7)	20.7 (18.2–23.4)
2021 (full year)	24.5 (21.5–27.6)	54.1 (50.3–57.9)	22.9 (19.3–27.0)
2021 (Jan–Jun)	26.9 (22.7–31.5)	53.4 (48.7–58.1)	21.2 (17.6–25.1)
2021 (Jul–Dec)	22.0 (18.4–25.8)	54.8 (49.9–59.6)	24.8 (19.7–30.4)
100% to less than 200% FPL[1]			
Under 65			
2019	20.1 (18.6–21.6)	47.0 (45.1–48.9)	35.4 (33.6–37.2)
2020	18.9 (17.1–20.9)	50.5 (48.3–52.6)	33.6 (31.6–35.7)
2021 (full year)	17.6 (16.3–19.0)	51.5 (49.6–53.3)	34.1 (32.2–36.0)
2021 (Jan–Jun)	17.8 (15.6–20.1)	52.4 (49.9–54.9)	33.2 (30.5–35.9)
2021 (Jul–Dec)	17.4 (15.5–19.4)	50.5 (48.1–52.9)	35.0 (32.3–37.8)
0–17			
2019	6.5 (5.2–8.0)	70.3 (67.7–72.8)	25.8 (23.1–28.5)
2020	7.3 (5.3–9.8)	72.8 (69.2–76.2)	23.3 (20.2–26.6)
2021 (full year)	5.6 (4.4–7.0)	75.8 (73.3–78.2)	22.3 (20.0–24.8)
2021 (Jan–Jun)	6.2 (4.5–8.4)	77.1 (73.9–80.1)	20.3 (17.3–23.5)
2021 (Jul–Dec)	4.9 (3.3–7.1)	74.4 (70.8–77.8)	24.5 (21.0–28.3)
18–64			
2019	26.8 (24.9–28.8)	35.4 (33.3–37.5)	40.1 (38.3–42.0)
2020	25.0 (22.7–27.4)	38.8 (36.5–41.1)	39.0 (36.7–41.4)
2021 (full year)	23.7 (22.0–25.5)	39.0 (37.1–41.0)	40.1 (38.0–42.2)
2021 (Jan–Jun)	23.8 (21.0–26.6)	39.6 (36.9–42.3)	39.9 (36.8–43.1)
2021 (Jul–Dec)	23.7 (21.2–26.3)	38.4 (35.7–41.3)	40.3 (37.3–43.4)
200% and greater FPL[1]			
Under 65			
2019	7.9 (7.3–8.4)	11.8 (11.2–12.5)	82.0 (81.1–82.8)
2020	7.5 (6.9–8.1)	12.2 (11.5–13.0)	82.0 (81.1–82.9)
2021 (full year)	7.0 (6.6–7.5)	13.0 (12.4–13.7)	81.5 (80.8–82.3)
2021 (Jan–Jun)	7.2 (6.6–7.9)	12.7 (11.8–13.6)	81.8 (80.9–82.7)
2021 (Jul–Dec)	6.8 (6.3–7.5)	13.4 (12.5–14.2)	81.3 (80.2–82.4)
0–17			
2019	4.3 (3.6–5.1)	16.3 (14.9–17.8)	80.7 (79.1–82.2)
2020	3.5 (2.8–4.4)	17.9 (16.2–19.7)	80.2 (78.4–82.0)
2021 (full year)	2.7 (2.3–3.2)	19.0 (17.7–20.4)	80.3 (78.8–81.7)
2021 (Jan–Jun)	2.9 (2.1–3.8)	17.9 (16.2–19.6)	81.2 (79.3–83.0)
2021 (Jul–Dec)	2.6 (2.0–3.4)	20.1 (18.3–22.0)	79.4 (77.3–81.4)

See footnotes at the end of table.

Table IV. Percentage (and 95% confidence intervals) of people under age 65 who lacked health insurance coverage, had public health plan coverage, and had private health insurance coverage at the time of interview, by family income as a percentage of the federal poverty level, age group, and year: United States, 2019–2021—Con.

Family income as a percentage of FPL[1], age group (years), year, and 6-month interval	Uninsured[2]	Public health plan coverage[3]	Private health insurance coverage[4]
200% and greater FPL[1]			
18–64			
2019	9.0 (8.4–9.6)	10.4 (9.8–11.0)	82.4 (81.6–83.2)
2020	8.7 (8.1–9.4)	10.4 (9.7–11.1)	82.5 (81.6–83.4)
2021 (full year)	8.4 (7.9–9.0)	11.1 (10.5–11.8)	82.0 (81.2–82.7)
2021 (Jan–Jun)	8.6 (7.8–9.5)	11.0 (10.1–12.0)	82.0 (81.0–83.0)
2021 (Jul–Dec)	8.2 (7.5–8.9)	11.2 (10.4–12.0)	81.9 (80.8–83.0)

[1] FPL is federal poverty level. Income categories are based on the ratio of the family's income in the previous calendar year to the appropriate poverty threshold (given the family's size and number of children), as defined by the U.S. Census Bureau for that year (Semega JL, Kollar MA, Creamer J, Mohanty A. Income and poverty in the United States: 2018. Current Population Reports, P60–266. 2019 and Semega J, Kollar M, Shrider EA, Creamer J. Income and poverty in the United States: 2019. Current Population Reports, P60–270. 2020). The percentage of respondents under age 65 with unknown poverty status in was 7.6% in 2019, 8.4% in 2020 and 8.7% in 2021. People with unknown poverty status are not shown in this table. Estimates may differ from estimates that are based on both reported and imputed income.

[2] People were defined as uninsured if they did not have any private health insurance, Medicare, Medicaid, Children's Health Insurance Program (CHIP), state-sponsored or other government-sponsored health plan, or military plan. People also were defined as uninsured if they had only Indian Health Service coverage or had only a private plan that paid for one type of service, such as accidents or dental care.

[3] Public health plan coverage includes Medicaid, CHIP, state-sponsored or other government-sponsored health plan, Medicare, and military plans. A small number of people were covered by both public and private plans and were included in both categories.

[4] Private health insurance coverage includes any comprehensive private insurance plan (including health maintenance and preferred provider organizations). These plans include those obtained through an employer, purchased directly, purchased through local or community programs, or purchased through the Health Insurance Marketplace or a state-based exchange. Private coverage excludes plans that pay for only one type of service, such as accidents or dental care. A small number of people were covered by both public and private plans and were included in both categories.

NOTES: Due to the COVID-19 pandemic, data collection switched to a telephone-only mode beginning on March 19, 2020. Personal visits (with telephone attempts first) resumed in all areas in September 2020. In addition, from August–December 2020, a subsample of adult respondents who completed NHIS in 2019 were recontacted by telephone and asked to participate again. Response rates were lower and respondent characteristics were different in April–December 2020. Differences observed in estimates between April–December 2020 and other time periods may have been impacted by these differences in respondent characteristics. Data are based on household interviews of a sample of the civilian noninstitutionalized population.

SOURCE: National Center for Health Statistics, National Health Interview Surveys, 2019–2021.

Table V. Percentage (and 95% confidence intervals) of people under age 65 who lacked health insurance coverage, had public health plan coverage, and had private health insurance coverage at the time of interview, by race and ethnicity, age group, and year: United States, 2019–2021

Race and ethnicity[1], age group (years), year, and 6-month interval	Uninsured[2]	Public health plan coverage[3]	Private health insurance coverage[4]
Hispanic			
Under 65			
2019	22.1 (20.3–23.9)	34.7 (32.7–36.7)	44.3 (42.1–46.4)
2020	22.1 (20.3–24.1)	34.5 (32.4–36.6)	44.7 (42.4–47.0)
2021 (full year)	22.8 (21.0–24.6)	36.1 (34.6–37.5)	42.5 (40.8–44.3)
2021 (Jan–Jun)	23.6 (21.1–26.3)	35.9 (33.8–38.1)	42.0 (39.5–44.6)
2021 (Jul–Dec)	21.9 (19.6–24.5)	36.2 (34.1–38.3)	43.0 (40.6–45.5)
0–17			
2019	7.2 (6.0–8.6)	58.7 (55.9–61.5)	35.4 (32.7–38.1)
2020	7.8 (6.0–10.0)	57.3 (53.7–60.8)	37.0 (33.5–40.7)
2021 (full year)	7.8 (6.6–9.1)	61.2 (59.1–63.3)	32.5 (30.3–34.9)
2021 (Jan–Jun)	7.8 (6.1–9.7)	62.2 (59.1–65.2)	31.6 (28.4–35.0)
2021 (Jul–Dec)	7.8 (6.3–9.6)	60.2 (57.3–63.1)	33.5 (30.1–37.0)
18–64			
2019	29.7 (27.4–32.0)	22.5 (20.4–24.7)	48.8 (46.5–51.1)
2020	29.3 (26.9–31.9)	23.0 (21.0–25.1)	48.6 (46.2–51.0)
2021 (full year)	30.1 (27.9–32.4)	23.7 (22.1–25.4)	47.4 (45.6–49.3)
2021 (Jan–Jun)	31.4 (28.1–34.9)	23.0 (20.3–25.7)	47.2 (44.3–50.1)
2021 (Jul–Dec)	28.8 (25.6–32.2)	24.5 (22.0–27.1)	47.7 (45.0–50.4)
Non-Hispanic White			
Under 65			
2019	9.0 (8.4–9.7)	19.6 (18.7–20.7)	73.3 (72.2–74.3)
2020	7.9 (7.3–8.6)	19.9 (18.9–21.0)	74.3 (73.2–75.5)
2021 (full year)	7.2 (6.7–7.8)	21.6 (20.6–22.6)	73.3 (72.1–74.4)
2021 (Jan–Jun)	7.5 (6.8–8.3)	22.0 (20.6–23.5)	72.7 (71.3–74.1)
2021 (Jul–Dec)	7.0 (6.2–7.8)	21.2 (20.1–22.4)	73.8 (72.3–75.2)
0–17			
2019	4.5 (3.7–5.4)	27.9 (26.1–29.8)	69.3 (67.4–71.1)
2020	3.8 (2.8–5.1)	29.4 (26.9–31.9)	69.1 (66.5–71.6)
2021 (full year)	2.7 (2.1–3.3)	31.5 (29.4–33.7)	68.5 (66.3–70.6)
2021 (Jan–Jun)	2.9 (2.1–4.0)	31.9 (29.1–34.7)	67.9 (65.0–70.7)
2021 (Jul–Dec)	2.4 (1.7–3.4)	31.1 (28.9–33.5)	69.1 (66.8–71.3)
18–64			
2019	10.5 (9.8–11.2)	17.0 (16.1–18.0)	74.5 (73.5–75.5)
2020	9.2 (8.6–10.0)	16.9 (16.0–17.8)	76.0 (75.0–77.1)
2021 (full year)	8.7 (8.0–9.4)	18.5 (17.6–19.4)	74.8 (73.7–75.8)
2021 (Jan–Jun)	9.0 (8.1–9.9)	18.8 (17.5–20.2)	74.3 (72.9–75.6)
2021 (Jul–Dec)	8.4 (7.5–9.4)	18.1 (17.0–19.3)	75.3 (73.8–76.7)
Non-Hispanic Black			
Under 65			
2019	11.6 (10.2–13.0)	42.8 (40.0–45.6)	48.5 (46.0–50.9)
2020	12.0 (10.4–13.8)	42.1 (39.2–45.0)	48.3 (45.3–51.4)
2021 (full year)	11.2 (9.9–12.5)	41.5 (38.7–44.4)	49.4 (46.8–52.0)
2021 (Jan–Jun)	11.8 (9.9–13.8)	40.2 (37.4–43.1)	50.2 (47.2–53.1)
2021 (Jul–Dec)	10.5 (8.7–12.5)	42.8 (39.2–46.5)	48.6 (45.3–51.9)
0–17			
2019	3.5 (2.5–4.9)	64.5 (60.1–68.7)	35.1 (31.1–39.3)
2020	5.1 (2.9–8.1)	65.8 (60.6–70.8)	30.7 (25.9–35.8)
2021 (full year)	3.0 (1.8–4.8)	66.1 (61.4–70.5)	32.6 (28.2–37.4)
2021 (Jan–Jun)	*	66.0 (60.8–70.9)	32.6 (27.4–38.2)
2021 (Jul–Dec)	2.5 (1.2–4.5)	66.3 (60.6–71.6)	32.6 (27.1–38.6)

See footnotes at the end of table.

Table V. Percentage (and 95% confidence intervals) of people under age 65 who lacked health insurance coverage, had public health plan coverage, and had private health insurance coverage at the time of interview, by race and ethnicity, age group, and year: United States, 2019–2021—Con.

Race and ethnicity[1], age group (years), year, and 6-month interval	Uninsured[2]	Public health plan coverage[3]	Private health insurance coverage[4]
Non-Hispanic Black			
18–64			
2019	14.7 (12.9–16.7)	34.3 (31.5–37.1)	53.7 (51.3–56.0)
2020	14.6 (12.7–16.7)	33.1 (30.5–35.9)	54.9 (51.9–57.9)
2021 (full year)	14.1 (12.5–15.7)	32.6 (29.9–35.5)	55.4 (52.8–58.1)
2021 (Jan–Jun)	14.7 (12.5–17.1)	31.0 (28.3–33.9)	56.4 (53.4–59.4)
2021 (Jul–Dec)	13.4 (11.3–15.9)	34.3 (30.7–38.1)	54.4 (51.1–57.8)
Non-Hispanic Asian			
Under 65			
2019	6.6 (5.0–8.7)	17.5 (15.1–20.2)	76.6 (73.5–79.5)
2020	7.7 (5.9–9.9)	19.3 (16.4–22.5)	73.9 (70.5–77.1)
2021 (full year)	5.2 (4.0–6.8)	20.4 (18.1–22.8)	74.9 (72.2–77.4)
2021 (Jan–Jun)	5.1 (3.3–7.4)	21.0 (18.4–23.8)	74.7 (71.2–78.0)
2021 (Jul–Dec)	5.4 (4.0–7.1)	19.8 (16.1–24.0)	75.0 (70.8–78.9)
0–17			
2019	3.2 (1.6–5.7)	24.1 (19.6–29.1)	73.2 (68.2–77.8)
2020	3.4 (1.5–6.3)	29.6 (23.5–36.3)	68.2 (61.5–74.4)
2021 (full year)	1.3 (0.6–2.5)	29.0 (24.0–34.4)	70.9 (65.6–75.7)
2021 (Jan–Jun)	1.3 (0.3–3.5)	30.5 (23.6–38.0)	70.3 (62.9–76.9)
2021 (Jul–Dec)	1.3 (0.4–3.2)	27.6 (21.5–34.4)	71.4 (64.7–77.5)
18–64			
2019	7.5 (5.6–9.9)	15.8 (13.2–18.7)	77.5 (74.2–80.5)
2020	8.8 (6.7–11.4)	16.7 (13.8–20.0)	75.4 (71.8–78.8)
2021 (full year)	6.3 (4.8–8.2)	18.0 (16.0–20.2)	76.0 (73.6–78.2)
2021 (Jan–Jun)	6.1 (3.9–8.9)	18.4 (15.4–21.8)	75.9 (72.1–79.4)
2021 (Jul–Dec)	6.6 (4.8–8.8)	17.6 (14.0–21.7)	76.0 (71.9–79.8)
Non-Hispanic, other races and multiple races			
Under 65			
2019	14.6 (11.4–18.2)	34.5 (28.9–40.3)	52.9 (46.7–59.0)
2020	13.0 (10.1–16.3)	39.2 (34.1–44.6)	51.3 (45.1–57.5)
2021 (full year)	11.0 (8.6–13.8)	40.2 (35.1–45.5)	51.9 (46.3–57.4)
2021 (Jan–Jun)	11.7 (8.1–16.3)	40.1 (34.1–46.3)	50.8 (43.8–57.8)
2021 (Jul–Dec)	10.4 (7.2–14.3)	40.3 (34.0–46.9)	52.9 (46.0–59.8)
0–17			
2019	5.9 (3.5–9.3)	45.3 (38.0–52.8)	50.4 (42.6–58.3)
2020	6.1 (3.0–10.9)	48.5 (41.5–55.6)	49.2 (42.2–56.3)
2021 (full year)	5.0 (2.6–8.6)	49.3 (42.9–55.7)	48.8 (43.8–53.9)
2021 (Jan–Jun)	*	46.3 (39.1–53.6)	48.6 (41.5–55.7)
2021 (Jul–Dec)	*	52.4 (43.3–61.4)	49.1 (41.2–57.0)
18–64			
2019	21.1 (17.0–25.8)	26.2 (20.6–32.5)	54.8 (48.1–61.3)
2020	17.6 (13.7–22.1)	32.9 (25.7–40.9)	52.7 (44.3–61.0)
2021 (full year)	15.5 (12.3–19.3)	33.5 (27.2–40.1)	54.1 (46.1–62.0)
2021 (Jan–Jun)	15.5 (11.1–20.9)	35.4 (27.2–44.3)	52.5 (42.5–62.4)
2021 (Jul–Dec)	15.6 (10.5–21.9)	31.5 (24.5–39.1)	55.8 (46.9–64.4)

*Estimate is not shown, as it does not meet National Center for Health Statistics standards of reliability.

[1]Hispanic origin and race are two separate and distinct categories. People of Hispanic or Latino origin may be of any race or combination of races. Hispanic or Latino origin includes people of Mexican, Puerto Rican, Cuban, Central and South American, or Spanish origin. Race is based on respondents' descriptions of their own racial background. More than one race may be reported. For conciseness, the text, tables, and figures in this report use shorter versions of the 1997 Office of Management and Budget terms for race and Hispanic or Latino origin. For example, the category "not Hispanic, Black or African American, single race" is referred to as "non-Hispanic Black" in the text, tables, and figures. Estimates for non-Hispanic people of races other than White only, Black only, and Asian only, or of multiple races, are combined into the "non-Hispanic, other races and multiple races" category.

[2]People were defined as uninsured if they did not have any private health insurance, Medicare, Medicaid, Children's Health Insurance Program (CHIP), state-sponsored or other government-sponsored health plan, or military plan. People also were defined as uninsured if they had only Indian Health Service coverage or had only a private plan that paid for one type of service, such as accidents or dental care.

[3]Public health plan coverage includes Medicaid, CHIP, state-sponsored or other government-sponsored health plan, Medicare, and military plans. A small number of people were covered by both public and private plans and were included in both categories.

[4]Private health insurance coverage includes any comprehensive private insurance plan (including health maintenance and preferred provider organizations). These plans include those obtained through an employer, purchased directly, purchased through local or community programs, or purchased through the Health Insurance Marketplace or a state-based exchange. Private coverage excludes plans that pay for only one type of service, such as accidents or dental care. A small number of people were covered by both public and private plans and were included in both categories.

NOTES: Due to the COVID-19 pandemic, data collection switched to a telephone-only mode beginning on March 19, 2020. Personal visits (with telephone attempts first) resumed in all areas in September 2020. In addition, from August–December 2020, a subsample of adult respondents who completed NHIS in 2019 were recontacted by telephone and asked to participate again. Response rates were lower and respondent characteristics were different in April–December 2020. Differences observed in estimates between April–December 2020 and other time periods may have been impacted by these differences in respondent characteristics. Data are based on household interviews of a sample of the civilian noninstitutionalized population.

SOURCE: National Center for Health Statistics, National Health Interview Surveys, 2019–2021.

Table VI. Percentage (and 95% confidence intervals) of people under age 65 who lacked health insurance coverage, had public health plan coverage, and had private health insurance coverage at the time of interview, by state Medicaid expansion status, age group, and year: United States, 2019–2021

State Medicaid expansion status[1], age group (years), year, and 6-month interval	Uninsured[2]	Public health plan coverage[3]	Private health insurance coverage[4]
Medicaid expansion states[5]			
Under 65			
2019	9.1 (8.6–9.7)	27.8 (26.7–28.9)	65.0 (63.8–66.2)
2020	8.5 (7.8–9.2)	27.5 (26.3–28.8)	66.0 (64.7–67.4)
2021 (full year)	8.1 (7.5–8.7)	28.9 (27.8–30.0)	65.0 (63.7–66.3)
2021 (Jan–Jun)	8.5 (7.6–9.4)	29.2 (27.8–30.6)	64.4 (62.8–66.0)
2021 (Jul–Dec)	7.7 (7.0–8.5)	28.5 (27.2–29.9)	65.6 (64.1–67.1)
0–17			
2019	3.9 (3.3–4.6)	40.3 (38.3–42.2)	57.6 (55.5–59.7)
2020	3.6 (2.7–4.7)	41.3 (38.9–43.8)	57.3 (54.8–59.8)
2021 (full year)	2.6 (2.1–3.1)	42.7 (40.9–44.6)	57.3 (55.3–59.3)
2021 (Jan–Jun)	2.6 (1.8–3.6)	43.2 (40.7–45.8)	56.7 (54.1–59.4)
2021 (Jul–Dec)	2.5 (1.9–3.3)	42.2 (40.1–44.3)	57.8 (55.5–60.2)
18–64			
2019	11.0 (10.4–11.6)	23.4 (22.3–24.5)	67.6 (66.4–68.8)
2020	10.2 (9.5–11.1)	22.5 (21.5–23.6)	69.2 (68.0–70.4)
2021 (full year)	10.1 (9.3–10.9)	23.8 (22.8–24.9)	67.8 (66.6–69.0)
2021 (Jan–Jun)	10.6 (9.5–11.7)	24.1 (22.7–25.5)	67.2 (65.7–68.7)
2021 (Jul–Dec)	9.6 (8.7–10.6)	23.5 (22.3–24.8)	68.4 (67.0–69.9)
Non-Medicaid expansion states[6]			
Under 65			
2019	17.1 (15.8–18.5)	23.0 (21.5–24.6)	61.4 (59.0–63.8)
2020	17.2 (16.0–18.5)	24.1 (22.5–25.8)	60.5 (58.6–62.4)
2021 (full year)	16.8 (15.6–18.1)	25.5 (24.2–26.8)	59.4 (57.6–61.3)
2021 (Jan–Jun)	17.1 (15.5–18.8)	25.2 (23.7–26.8)	59.6 (57.3–61.9)
2021 (Jul–Dec)	16.5 (15.0–18.0)	25.8 (23.8–27.8)	59.3 (56.5–62.0)
0–17			
2019	7.0 (6.0–8.1)	43.2 (40.1–46.3)	51.5 (47.9–55.0)
2020	7.8 (6.3–9.5)	43.7 (40.0–47.5)	50.5 (46.8–54.3)
2021 (full year)	7.2 (6.1–8.4)	47.5 (44.8–50.2)	46.9 (43.9–49.8)
2021 (Jan–Jun)	7.8 (6.3–9.5)	47.4 (44.0–50.9)	46.4 (42.5–50.3)
2021 (Jul–Dec)	6.5 (5.0–8.4)	47.6 (44.3–50.9)	47.4 (43.6–51.3)
18–64			
2019	21.2 (19.6–22.8)	15.1 (14.0–16.3)	65.3 (63.2–67.3)
2020	20.8 (19.3–22.3)	16.7 (15.3–18.2)	64.3 (62.6–66.0)
2021 (full year)	20.4 (18.9–21.9)	17.4 (16.2–18.5)	64.1 (62.3–65.9)
2021 (Jan–Jun)	20.6 (18.6–22.7)	16.9 (15.7–18.2)	64.5 (62.2–66.8)
2021 (Jul–Dec)	20.1 (18.3–22.0)	17.8 (16.0–19.7)	63.7 (60.9–66.4)

[1]Under provisions of the Affordable Care Act of 2010 (P.L. 111-148, P.L. 111-152), states have the option to expand Medicaid eligibility to cover adults who have incomes up to and including 138% of the federal poverty level. There is no deadline for states to choose to implement the Medicaid expansion, and they may do so at any time. As of January 1, 2019, 33 states and the District of Columbia moved forward with Medicaid expansion.

[2]People were defined as uninsured if they did not have any private health insurance, Medicare, Medicaid, Children's Health Insurance Program (CHIP), state-sponsored or other government-sponsored health plan, or military plan. People also were defined as uninsured if they had only Indian Health Service coverage or had only a private plan that paid for one type of service, such as accidents or dental care.

[3]Public health plan coverage includes Medicaid, CHIP, state-sponsored or other government-sponsored health plan, Medicare, and military plans. A small number of people were covered by both public and private plans and were included in both categories.

[4]Private health insurance coverage includes any comprehensive private insurance plan (including health maintenance and preferred provider organizations). These plans include those obtained through an employer, purchased directly, purchased through local or community programs, or purchased through the Health Insurance Marketplace or a state-based exchange. Private coverage excludes plans that pay for only one type of service, such as accidents or dental care. A small number of people were covered by both public and private plans and were included in both categories.

[5]For 2019, states moving forward with Medicaid expansion included: Alaska, Arizona, Arkansas, California, Colorado, Connecticut, Delaware, Hawaii, Illinois, Indiana, Iowa, Kentucky, Louisiana, Maine, Maryland, Massachusetts, Michigan, Minnesota, Montana, Nevada, New Hampshire, New Jersey, New Mexico, New York, North Dakota, Ohio, Oregon, Pennsylvania, Rhode Island, Vermont, Virginia, Washington, and West Virginia. The District of Columbia also moved forward with Medicaid expansion. Beginning with 2020, two states were added to this grouping: Idaho and Utah. Beginning with 2021, Nebraska was added to this grouping.

[6]For 2019, states not moving forward with Medicaid expansion included: Alabama, Florida, Georgia, Idaho, Kansas, Mississippi, Missouri, Nebraska, North Carolina, Oklahoma, South Carolina, South Dakota, Tennessee, Texas, Utah, Wisconsin, and Wyoming. Beginning with 2020, two states have been removed from this grouping: Idaho and Utah. Beginning with 2021, Nebraska was removed from this grouping.

NOTES: Due to the COVID-19 pandemic, data collection switched to a telephone-only mode beginning on March 19, 2020. Personal visits (with telephone attempts first) resumed in all areas in September 2020. In addition, from August–December 2020, a subsample of adult respondents who completed NHIS in 2019 were recontacted by telephone and asked to participate again. Response rates were lower and respondent characteristics were different in April–December 2020. Differences observed in estimates between April–December 2020 and other time periods may have been impacted by these differences in respondent characteristics. Data are based on household interviews of a sample of the civilian noninstitutionalized population.

SOURCE: National Center for Health Statistics, National Health Interview Surveys, 2019–2021.

Table VII. Percentage and number of people under age 65 who had exchange-based private health insurance coverage at the time of interview, by year and selected characteristics: United States, 2019–2021

Year and selected characteristics	Percent (95% confidence interval)	Number in millions
2019		
Age group (years)		
Under 65	3.7 (3.4–4.0)	10.0
0–17	1.7 (1.4–2.1)	1.3
18–64	4.4 (4.0–4.8)	8.7
Sex		
Male	3.5 (3.1–3.9)	4.7
Female	3.9 (3.5–4.4)	5.3
Family income as a percentage of FPL[1]		
Less than 100% FPL	3.0 (2.2–4.0)	1.1
100% to less than 200% FPL	5.3 (4.6–6.1)	2.8
200% and greater FPL	3.2 (2.9–3.5)	5.8
Race and ethnicity[2]		
Hispanic	3.8 (3.1–4.6)	2.1
Non-Hispanic White	3.6 (3.2–4.0)	5.5
Non-Hispanic Black	2.9 (2.2–3.9)	1.0
Medicaid expansion status[3]		
Medicaid expansion states[4]	3.3 (3.0–3.8)	5.7
Non-Medicaid expansion states[5]	4.3 (3.8–4.9)	4.3
2020		
Age group (years)		
Under 65	3.8 (3.5–4.1)	10.1
0–17	2.1 (1.7–2.5)	1.5
18–64	4.4 (4.0–4.7)	8.6
Sex		
Male	3.1 (2.8–3.5)	4.2
Female	4.4 (4.0–4.8)	5.9
Family income as a percentage of FPL[1]		
Less than 100% FPL	1.9 (1.3–2.6)	0.6
100% to less than 200% FPL	4.8 (4.1–5.7)	2.4
200% and greater FPL	3.7 (3.3–4.1)	6.9
Race and ethnicity[2]		
Hispanic	4.2 (3.5–5.0)	2.4
Non-Hispanic White	3.7 (3.3–4.1)	5.7
Non-Hispanic Black	2.6 (1.9–3.3)	0.9
Medicaid expansion status[3]		
Medicaid expansion states[4]	3.5 (3.2–3.9)	6.2
Non-Medicaid expansion states[5]	4.1 (3.6–4.7)	3.9

See footnotes at the end of table.

Table VII. Percentage and number of people under age 65 who had exchange-based private health insurance coverage at the time of interview, by year and selected characteristics: United States, 2019–2021—Con.

Year and selected characteristics	Percent (95% confidence interval)	Number in millions
2021		
Age group (years)		
Under 65	4.3 (4.0–4.7)	11.6
0–17	2.1 (1.7–2.6)	1.5
18–64	5.1 (4.7–5.5)	10.1
Sex		
Male	3.9 (3.5–4.2)	5.2
Female	4.8 (4.3–5.2)	6.5
Family income as a percentage of FPL[1]		
Less than 100% FPL	3.6 (2.7–4.7)	1.2
100% to less than 200% FPL	6.4 (5.5–7.4)	3.3
200% and greater FPL	3.8 (3.4–4.1)	6.9
Race and ethnicity[2]		
Hispanic	4.4 (3.6–5.3)	2.5
Non-Hispanic White	4.2 (3.8–4.6)	6.4
Non-Hispanic Black	3.9 (3.2–4.8)	1.3
Medicaid expansion status[3]		
Medicaid expansion states[4]	4.0 (3.6–4.5)	7.2
Non-Medicaid expansion states[5]	4.9 (4.4–5.5)	4.4
Jan–Jun 2021		
Age group (years)		
Under 65	4.3 (3.8–4.8)	11.6
0–17	2.1 (1.5–2.9)	1.5
18–64	5.1 (4.6–5.7)	10.0
Sex		
Male	4.0 (3.5–4.5)	5.3
Female	4.6 (4.0–5.3)	6.2
Family income as a percentage of FPL[1]		
Less than 100% FPL	3.6 (2.5–4.9)	1.3
100% to less than 200% FPL	6.0 (4.7–7.5)	3.2
200% and greater FPL	3.8 (3.3–4.5)	7.0
Race and ethnicity[2]		
Hispanic	4.8 (3.8–6.0)	2.7
Non-Hispanic White	4.1 (3.6–4.6)	6.3
Non-Hispanic Black	3.5 (2.5–4.6)	1.2
Medicaid expansion status[3]		
Medicaid expansion states[4]	4.1 (3.5–4.8)	7.3
Non-Medicaid expansion states[5]	4.6 (3.8–5.5)	4.3

See footnotes at the end of table.

Table VII. Percentage and number of people under age 65 who had exchange-based private health insurance coverage at the time of interview, by year and selected characteristics: United States, 2019–2021—Con.

Year and selected characteristics	Percent (95% confidence interval)	Number in millions
Jul–Dec 2021		
Age group (years)		
Under 65	4.4 (3.9–4.8)	11.7
0–17	2.1 (1.6–2.8)	1.5
18–64	5.2 (4.6–5.7)	10.2
Sex		
Male	3.8 (3.3–4.3)	5.0
Female	4.9 (4.3–5.6)	6.7
Family income as a percentage of FPL[1]		
Less than 100% FPL	3.6 (2.4–5.2)	1.2
100% to less than 200% FPL	6.8 (5.6–8.1)	3.4
200% and greater FPL	3.7 (3.2–4.2)	6.8
Race and ethnicity[2]		
Hispanic	4.0 (3.2–5.0)	2.3
Non-Hispanic White	4.3 (3.7–4.9)	6.6
Non-Hispanic Black	4.4 (3.2–6.0)	1.4
Medicaid expansion status[3]		
Medicaid expansion states[4]	3.9 (3.3–4.5)	7.1
Non-Medicaid expansion states[5]	5.3 (4.7–6.0)	4.6

[1]FPL is federal poverty level. Income categories are based on the ratio of the family's income in the previous calendar year to the appropriate poverty threshold (given the family's size and number of children), as defined by the U.S. Census Bureau for that year (Semega JL, Kollar MA, Creamer J, Mohanty A. Income and poverty in the United States: 2018. Current Population Reports, P60–266. 2019 and Semega J, Kollar M, Shrider EA, Creamer J. Income and poverty in the United States: 2019. Current Population Reports, P60–270. 2020). The percentage of respondents under age 65 with unknown poverty status was 7.6% in 2019, 8.4% in 2020, and 8.7% in 2021. People with unknown poverty status are not shown in this table. Estimates may differ from estimates that are based on both reported and imputed income.

[2]Hispanic origin and race are two separate and distinct categories. People of Hispanic origin may be of any race or combination of races. Hispanic origin includes people of Mexican, Puerto Rican, Cuban, Central and South American, or Spanish origin. Race is based on respondents' descriptions of their own racial background. More than one race may be reported. For conciseness, the text, tables, and figures in this report use shorter versions of the 1997 Office of Management and Budget terms for race and Hispanic or Latino origin. For example, the category "not Hispanic, Black or African American, single race" is referred to as "non-Hispanic Black" in the text, tables, and figures.

[3]Under provisions of the Affordable Care Act of 2010 (P.L. 111–148, P.L. 111–152), states have the option to expand Medicaid eligibility to cover adults who have income up to and including 138% of the FPL. There is no deadline for states to choose to implement the Medicaid expansion, and they may do so at any time. As of January 1, 2019, 33 states and the District of Columbia moved forward with Medicaid expansion.

[4]For 2019, states moving forward with Medicaid expansion included: Alaska, Arizona, Arkansas, California, Colorado, Connecticut, Delaware, Hawaii, Illinois, Indiana, Iowa, Kentucky, Louisiana, Maine, Maryland, Massachusetts, Michigan, Minnesota, Montana, Nevada, New Hampshire, New Jersey, New Mexico, New York, North Dakota, Ohio, Oregon, Pennsylvania, Rhode Island, Vermont, Virginia, Washington, and West Virginia. The District of Columbia also moved forward with Medicaid expansion. Beginning with 2020, two states were added to this grouping: Idaho and Utah. Beginning with 2021 Nebraska was added to this grouping.

[5]For 2019, states not moving forward with Medicaid expansion included: Alabama, Florida, Georgia, Idaho, Kansas, Mississippi, Missouri, Nebraska, North Carolina, Oklahoma, South Carolina, South Dakota, Tennessee, Texas, Utah, Wisconsin, and Wyoming. Beginning with 2020, two states have been removed from this grouping: Idaho and Utah. Beginning with 2021, Nebraska was removed from this grouping.

NOTES: Exchange-based coverage is a private health insurance plan purchased through the Health Insurance Marketplace or state-based exchanges that were established as part of the Affordable Care Act of 2010 (P.L. 111–148, P.L. 111–152). Due to the COVID-19 pandemic, data collection switched to a telephone-only mode beginning on March 19, 2020. Personal visits (with telephone attempts first) resumed in all areas in September 2020. In addition, from August–December 2020, a subsample of adult respondents who completed NHIS in 2019 were recontacted by telephone and asked to participate again. Response rates were lower and respondent characteristics were different in April–December 2020. Differences observed in estimates between April–December 2020 and other time periods may have been impacted by these differences in respondent characteristics. Data are based on household interviews of a sample of the civilian noninstitutionalized population.

SOURCE: National Center for Health Statistics, National Health Interview Surveys, 2019–2021.

Cohen, Robin A., Ph.D., Amy E. Cha, Ph.D., M.P.H., Emily P. Terlizzi, M.P.H., and Michael E. Martinez, M.P.H., M.H.S.A. "Health Insurance Coverage: Early Release of Estimates From the National Health Interview Survey, 2021." National Center for Health Statistics, Division of Health Interview Statistics, May 2022.

National Health Statistics Reports

Number 169 ■ February 11, 2022

Demographic Variation in Health Insurance Coverage: United States, 2020

by Amy E. Cha, Ph.D., M.P.H., and Robin A. Cohen, Ph.D.

Objectives—This report presents national estimates of different types of health insurance coverage and lack of coverage (uninsured). Estimates are presented by selected sociodemographic characteristics, including age, sex, race and Hispanic origin, family income, education level, employment status, and marital status.

Methods—Data from the 2020 National Health Interview Survey were used to estimate health insurance coverage. Estimates were categorized by selected sociodemographic characteristics. Additionally, estimates for uninsured people were categorized by length of time since they had coverage, private coverage was further classified by source of plan, and public coverage was categorized by type of public plan.

Results—In 2020, 31.6 million (9.7%) people of all ages were uninsured at the time of the interview. This includes 31.2 million (11.5%) people under age 65. Among children, 3.7 million (5.0%) were uninsured, and among working-age adults (aged 18–64), 27.5 million (13.9%) were uninsured. Among people under age 65, 64.3% were covered by private health insurance, including 56.6% with employment-based coverage and 6.7% with directly purchased coverage. Moreover, 4.0% were covered by exchange-based coverage, a type of directly purchased coverage. Among people under age 65, about two in five children and one in five adults were covered by public health coverage, mainly by Medicaid and the Children's Health Insurance Program (CHIP). Among adults aged 65 and over, the percentage who were covered by private health insurance (with or without Medicare), Medicare Advantage, and traditional Medicare only varied by age, family income level, education level, and race and Hispanic origin.

Keywords: uninsured • private • public • National Health Interview Survey

coverage persist (5,6). Also, previous research has noted differences in health insurance coverage by age, education level, employment status, marital status, and poverty level (7). Population estimates of health insurance coverage are essential to develop and assess federal and state health care coverage programs and policies (8).

This report is updated annually to provide the most current picture of health insurance coverage by demographic characteristics (9). Estimates of the percentage and number of people who were uninsured, had private coverage, and had public coverage at the time of interview are presented. Estimates are also further categorized by duration of being uninsured, source of private coverage, and types of public coverage. For adults aged 65 and over, six mutually exclusive categories of coverage are presented by selected sociodemographic characteristics.

Introduction

Health insurance coverage in the United States is linked to improved health care and health outcomes and is a key measure of health care access (1,2). The passage of the Affordable Care Act (ACA) in 2010 (3) was designed to increase access to health care, improve health, and mitigate health care disparities (4). Although dramatic decreases in the percentage of uninsured people post-ACA occurred, racial and ethnic disparities in health insurance

Methods

Data source

The estimates in this report are based on data from the Sample Adult and Sample Child modules of

U.S. DEPARTMENT OF HEALTH AND HUMAN SERVICES
Centers for Disease Control and Prevention
National Center for Health Statistics

NCHS reports can be downloaded from: https://www.cdc.gov/nchs/products/index.htm.

the 2020 National Health Interview Survey (NHIS). NHIS is a nationally representative household survey of the U.S. civilian noninstitutionalized population. It is conducted continuously throughout the year by the National Center for Health Statistics (NCHS). From each household, one sample adult is randomly selected to answer detailed questions about their health. One sample child, if present, is also randomly selected from each household, and an adult who is knowledgeable and responsible for the child's health answers questions on the child's behalf. Interviews are typically conducted in respondents' homes, but follow-ups to complete interviews may be conducted over the telephone when necessary. However, due to the COVID-19 pandemic, NHIS data collection switched the Sample Adult and Child interviews to a telephone-only mode beginning March 19, 2020 (10). Personal visits to households resumed in selected areas in July 2020 and in all areas of the country in September 2020. However, cases were still attempted by telephone first, and most were completed by telephone.

Additionally, starting in August and continuing through the end of December, a subsample of adult respondents who completed NHIS in 2019 were recontacted by telephone and asked to participate again, completing the 2020 NHIS questionnaire. These reinterviewed participants are included as part of the regular Sample Adult file, and estimates in this report are based on data from both reinterviewed participants and participants sampled only in the 2020 NHIS. The 2020 NHIS Sample Adult (excluding reinterviewed sample adults) and Sample Child response rates were 48.9% and 47.8%, respectively. A nonresponse bias assessment of the 2020 sample detected no biases for estimates of health insurance coverage (11). For more information about the impact of these changes on the 2020 data and general information about NHIS, visit https://www.cdc.gov/nchs/nhis/2020nhis.htm.

Both the Sample Adult and Sample Child modules include a full range of questions addressing health insurance, such as coverage status, sources of coverage, characteristics of coverage, and reasons for no coverage. The sample adult and sample child receive similar sets of health insurance questions, so the Sample Adult and Sample Child files can be combined to create a file that contains people of all ages. Estimates are based on a combined file containing 37,358 people (5,790 sample children and 31,568 sample adults).

In this report, the term "adults" refers to people aged 18 and over, and the term "children" refers to people under age 18 years. The term "working-age adult" refers to people aged 18–64, and the term "older adult" refers to people aged 65 and over.

Insurance coverage

People were considered uninsured if, at the time of the interview, they did not have coverage through private health insurance, Medicare, Medicaid, Children's Health Insurance Program (CHIP), military (TRICARE, Veterans Administration [VA], and CHAMP–VA), other state-sponsored health plans, or other government programs. People were also defined as uninsured if they only had Indian Health Service (IHS) coverage or only had a private plan that paid for one type of service, such as dental, vision, or prescription drugs. Uninsured people were further classified into one of three categories regarding the length of time since they last had coverage (uninsured for less than a year, uninsured for a year or more, and uninsured for unknown duration). Length of time since the person last had coverage was based on the following question: "How long has it been since [you/child's name] last had health care coverage that paid for doctor's visits or hospital stays?"

Private health insurance coverage includes any comprehensive private insurance plan (including health maintenance and preferred provider organizations). These plans include those obtained through an employer, purchased directly, purchased through local or community programs, or purchased through the Health Insurance Marketplace or a state-based exchange. Private coverage excludes plans that pay for only one type of service, such as dental, vision, or prescription drugs. People with private coverage were further classified into three sources of private coverage: employment-based, directly purchased, and other sources. The employment-based category includes plans obtained through an employer, union, or other professional organization. Directly purchased coverage includes exchange-based coverage in addition to plans obtained directly from an insurance company or through a broker. Exchange-based coverage is a private plan purchased through the federal Health Insurance Marketplace or state-based exchanges that were established as part of the ACA (3). The "other sources" category for private health insurance includes plans obtained through a state or local government or community programs, school, parent, other relative, other source not specified, and those who did not respond to the question asking about the source of their private coverage (refused, not ascertained, and don't know).

Public health plan coverage includes Medicaid, CHIP, state-sponsored or other government-sponsored health plans, Medicare, and military plans. For people under age 65, public coverage was categorized into four categories: Medicaid and CHIP, Medicare, other government, and military coverage. The Medicaid and CHIP category also includes those with state-sponsored plans. These categories are not mutually exclusive, and a person may be covered by more than one type of public coverage.

For adults aged 65 and over, a health insurance hierarchy of six mutually exclusive categories was developed. This hierarchy eliminates duplicate responses for both private health insurance and Medicare Advantage, giving preference to the report of Medicare Advantage. Medicare Advantage is another way for people covered by Medicare to get their Medicare Part A and Medicare Part B coverage. Medicare Advantage plans are sometimes called "Part C" and are offered by Medicare-approved companies that must follow rules set by Medicare (12). Older adults with more than one type of health insurance were assigned to the first appropriate category in the following hierarchy:

Private coverage—Includes older adults who have both Medicare and any comprehensive private health insurance plan (including health maintenance organizations, preferred provider organizations, and Medigap plans). This category also includes older adults with private insurance only but excludes those with a Medicare Advantage plan.

Medicare and Medicaid (*dual-eligible*)—Includes older adults who do not have any private coverage but have Medicare and Medicaid or other state-sponsored health plans including CHIP.

Medicare Advantage—Includes older adults who only have Medicare coverage through a Medicare Advantage plan.

Traditional Medicare only (*excluding Medicare Advantage*)—Includes older adults who only have Medicare coverage but do not receive their coverage through a Medicare Advantage plan.

Other coverage—Includes older adults who have not been previously classified as having private, Medicare and Medicaid, Medicare Advantage, or traditional Medicare-only coverage. This category also includes older people who only have Medicaid, other state-sponsored health plans, or CHIP, as well as people who have any type of military coverage without Medicare.

Uninsured—Includes older adults who did not indicate that they are covered at the time of the interview under private health insurance, Medicare, Medicaid, CHIP, a state-sponsored health plan, other government programs, or military coverage. This category also includes older adults who are covered by IHS only or who only have a plan that paid for one type of service, such as dental, vision, or prescription drugs.

Selected sociodemographic characteristics

Sociodemographic characteristics presented in this report include age, sex, race and Hispanic origin, and family income. For adults aged 18–64, estimates are further classified by age and sex because previous studies have found differences in coverage by these demographic subgroups (5,7). Additionally, for adults aged 18 and over, estimates are also presented by marital status and employment status, and for adults aged 25 and over, by education level.

Race and Hispanic origin are shown for five specific groups: Hispanic, non-Hispanic White, non-Hispanic Black, non-Hispanic Asian, and non-Hispanic other and multiple races. People categorized as Hispanic may be any race or combination of races. People categorized as non-Hispanic White, non-Hispanic Black, and non-Hispanic Asian indicated one race only. Non-Hispanic people of multiple or other races (includes those who did not identify as White, Black, Asian, or Hispanic, or who identified as more than one race) are combined into the non-Hispanic other and multiple races category.

Family income as a percentage of the federal poverty level (FPL) was calculated using the U.S. Census Bureau's poverty thresholds for the previous calendar year, which consider family size and age (13). People were classified into five groups based on their family income: less than 100% FPL, 100% to less than 139% FPL, 139% to less than or equal to 250% FPL, greater than 250% to less than or equal to 400% FPL, and greater than 400% FPL. Family income in NHIS was imputed for approximately 23% of people (14).

Categories of education are based on years of school completed or the highest degree obtained for adults aged 25 and over. The high school diploma category includes those who obtained a GED.

Adults aged 18 and over are classified as currently employed if they reported that they either worked or had a job or business at any time during the 1-week period preceding the interview. Adults who are seasonal contract workers or who are working at a job or business, but not for pay, are also considered to be employed. Employment status is categorized as employed, not employed, and not in workforce, with the latter defined as those who are not working and not looking for work. The "not in workforce" category also includes adults who are retired and those who have never worked.

Marital status is based on a series of questions that collect information from sample adults. Sample adults are first asked if they are "now married, living with a partner together as an unmarried couple, or neither." Married sample adults are further asked if their spouse lives in the same residence; if not, they are asked if this is because the sample adult and their spouse are legally separated. Sample adults who are living with an unmarried partner, are neither married nor living with a partner, or don't know or refuse to state their marital status are asked if they have ever been married. Sample adults who are currently living with a partner and have been married are asked their current legal marital status—that is, whether they are currently married, widowed, divorced, or separated. Sample adults who are neither living with a partner nor married but have been married are asked if they are widowed, divorced, or separated. Five mutually exclusive marital status categories were created: married, widowed, divorced or separated, never married, and living with a partner. People may identify themselves as married regardless of the legal status of the marriage or sex of the spouse. People categorized as "never married" includes those who were married and then had that marriage legally annulled. People who are living with a partner (or cohabitating) includes unmarried people regardless of sex who are living together as a couple but do not identify themselves as married. This category may include adults who are currently divorced, widowed, or separated. Adults who are living with a partner are considered to be members of the same family.

Statistical analysis

Percentages and 95% confidence intervals (CI) are presented for prevalence estimates of health insurance coverage based on questions about coverage at the time of the NHIS Sample Adult and Sample Child interviews. The 95% CIs were generated using the Korn–Graubard method for complex surveys (15). Estimates were calculated using the NHIS survey weights and are representative of the U.S. civilian noninstitutionalized population. The weighting adjustment method incorporates robust multilevel models predictive of response propensity. Nonresponse-adjusted weights were further calibrated to U.S. Census Bureau population projections and American Community Survey 1-year estimates for age, sex, race and ethnicity, education level, housing tenure, census division, and metropolitan statistical area status (10). Point estimates and their corresponding variances were calculated using SUDAAN software version 11.0.0, a software package designed to account for the complex sampling design of NHIS.

Respondents with missing data or unknown information were generally excluded from the analysis unless specifically noted. For the types of health insurance coverage shown in this report, the item nonresponse rate was about 0.5%. For items related to details about a type of health insurance coverage, item nonresponse varied. For example, the item nonresponse rate for duration of being currently uninsured and source of private coverage was 10.3% and 2.4%, respectively. Follow-up questions about details of coverage are determined at the time of the interview based on initial survey responses to types of coverage or lack of coverage. So, some respondents may not have received the appropriate follow-up questions for their final insurance coverage classification. For more information on the NHIS health insurance data-editing process after response collection, see the 2020 survey description (10) and the Health Insurance Information webpage (https://www.cdc.gov/nchs/nhis/insurance.htm). All estimates presented in this report met NCHS standards of reliability as specified in "National Center for Health Statistics Data Presentation Standards for Proportions" (16). Otherwise, estimates were not shown if they did not meet NCHS standards of reliability.

Differences in percentages between subgroup characteristics were evaluated using two-sided significance tests at the 0.05 level. Trends by family income (as a percentage of FPL), education level, and age groups for adults aged 18–64 were evaluated using orthogonal polynomials in logistic regression. Terms such as "more likely" and "less likely" indicate a statistically significant difference. Lack of comment regarding the difference between any two estimates does not necessarily mean that the difference was tested and not found to be significant.

This report provides overall and age-specific estimates of the percentages and number of people who were uninsured, had private coverage, and had public coverage at the time of the interview in 2020 in Table 1. The percentage and number of people without insurance are also categorized by duration of being uninsured in this table. In Table 2, for those under age 65, aged 0–17 years, and aged 18–64 years, private coverage is further classified by source, including employment-based, directly purchased, and other and unknown source. Public coverage is also categorized by type, including Medicaid and CHIP, Medicare, other government, and military coverage, by selected sociodemographic characteristics. Additionally, the percentage of people under age 65 with exchange-based coverage, a specific type of directly purchased coverage established under the ACA (3), is presented in Table 3 by selected sociodemographic characteristics. For adults aged 65 and over, six mutually exclusive categories (private, dual-eligible [Medicare and Medicaid], Medicare Advantage, traditional Medicare only, other coverage, and uninsured) are presented by selected sociodemographic characteristics in Table 4. Although the results section focuses primarily on the data shown in the figures, these tables are included for reference at the end of this report.

Results

Uninsured people

In 2020, 31.6 million (9.7%) people of all ages were uninsured at the time of the interview (Table 1). This includes 31.2 million (11.5%) people under age 65. Among children, 3.7 million (5.0%) were uninsured, and among working-age adults, 27.5 million (13.9%) were uninsured (Figure 1). The percentage of working-age adults who were uninsured for a year or more (8.7%) was more than double the percentage who were uninsured for less than a year (4.0%). Among children, the percentage who were uninsured for a year or more (2.3%) was similar to the percentage of those who were uninsured for less than a year (2.0%). Overall and within each duration subgroup, working-age adults were more likely than children to be uninsured.

Private coverage

Among people under age 65, 173.8 million (64.3%) were covered by private health insurance at the time of the interview (Table 1). This includes 56.6% with employment-based coverage, 6.7% with directly purchased coverage, and 1.0% from other sources (Table 2). The percentage of private coverage was highest among non-Hispanic White (74.6%) and non-Hispanic Asian (74.6%) people compared with non-Hispanic people of other and multiple races (51.2%), non-Hispanic Black (48.6%), and Hispanic (44.9%) people (Figure 2). Employment-based coverage was highest among non-Hispanic White people (66.5%), and directly purchased coverage was highest among non-Hispanic Asian people (10.8%).

Exchange-based coverage

Among people under age 65, 10.8 million (4.0%) were covered by exchange-based coverage (Figure 3, Table 3). Females were more likely to have exchange-based coverage (4.6%) than males (3.4%). Exchange-based coverage was highest among non-Hispanic Asian people (7.5%) compared with Hispanic (4.5%), non-Hispanic White (3.8%), and non-Hispanic Black (3.0%) people and non-Hispanic people of other and multiple races (2.5%). Hispanic people were more likely than non-Hispanic Black and non-Hispanic people of other and multiple races to have exchange-based coverage. Exchange-based coverage increased among those with incomes less than 100% FPL (2.3%) through those with incomes 139% to less than or equal to 250% of FPL (6.4%), and then decreased among those with family incomes greater than 400% FPL (2.8%).

Public coverage

Among people under age 65, 71.6 million (26.5%) were covered by public health coverage at the time of the interview (Table 1). This includes 20.7% covered by Medicaid and CHIP, 3.6% by military coverage, and 3.3% by Medicare (Table 2). Public coverage was highest among non-Hispanic Black (42.6%) people compared with

Figure 1. Percentage of people under age 65 who were uninsured at the time of the interview, by duration without coverage and age group: United States, 2020

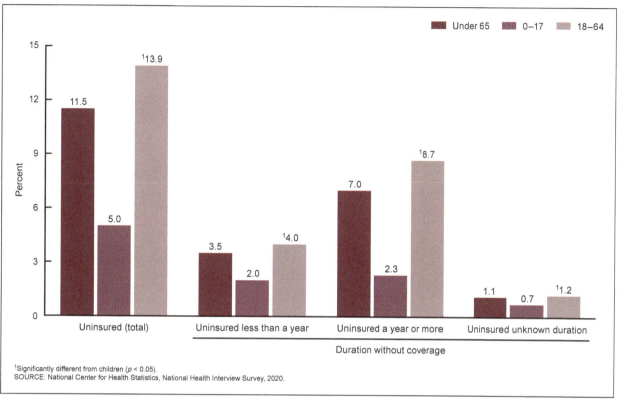

[1]Significantly different from children ($p < 0.05$).
SOURCE: National Center for Health Statistics, National Health Interview Survey, 2020.

Figure 2. Percentage of people under age 65 with private health insurance, by race and Hispanic origin and source: United States, 2020

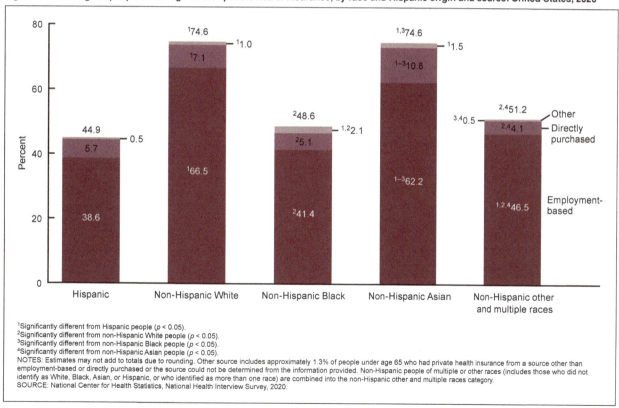

[1]Significantly different from Hispanic people ($p < 0.05$).
[2]Significantly different from non-Hispanic White people ($p < 0.05$).
[3]Significantly different from non-Hispanic Black people ($p < 0.05$).
[4]Significantly different from non-Hispanic Asian people ($p < 0.05$).
NOTES: Estimates may not add to totals due to rounding. Other source includes approximately 1.3% of people under age 65 who had private health insurance from a source other than employment-based or directly purchased or the source could not be determined from the information provided. Non-Hispanic people of multiple or other races (includes those who did not identify as White, Black, Asian, or Hispanic, or who identified as more than one race) are combined into the non-Hispanic other and multiple races category.
SOURCE: National Center for Health Statistics, National Health Interview Survey, 2020.

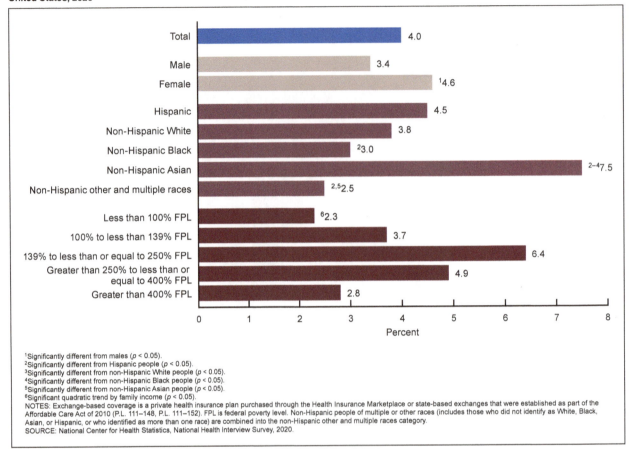

Figure 3. Percentage of people under age 65 with exchange-based coverage at the time of the interview, by selected characteristics: United States, 2020

[1]Significantly different from males ($p < 0.05$).
[2]Significantly different from Hispanic people ($p < 0.05$).
[3]Significantly different from non-Hispanic White people ($p < 0.05$).
[4]Significantly different from non-Hispanic Black people ($p < 0.05$).
[5]Significantly different from non-Hispanic Asian people ($p < 0.05$).
[6]Significant quadratic trend by family income ($p < 0.05$).
NOTES: Exchange-based coverage is a private health insurance plan purchased through the Health Insurance Marketplace or state-based exchanges that were established as part of the Affordable Care Act of 2010 (P.L. 111–148, P.L. 111–152). FPL is federal poverty level. Non-Hispanic people of multiple or other races (includes those who did not identify as White, Black, Asian, or Hispanic, or who identified as more than one race) are combined into the non-Hispanic other and multiple races category.
SOURCE: National Center for Health Statistics, National Health Interview Survey, 2020.

Hispanic (34.3%), non-Hispanic White (20.2%), and non-Hispanic Asian (18.9%) people (Figure 4). Public coverage among non-Hispanic people of other and multiple races (38.6%) was higher than among non-Hispanic White and non-Hispanic Asian people. For Medicaid and CHIP, coverage was highest among non-Hispanic Black (33.9%) and Hispanic (30.4%) people compared with non-Hispanic Asian (15.2%) and non-Hispanic White (14.3%) people. Medicaid and CHIP coverage among non-Hispanic people of other and multiple races (30.7%) was higher than among non-Hispanic White and non-Hispanic Asian people. Similar patterns were observed for Medicare and military coverage. Percentages were higher among non-Hispanic Black people and non-Hispanic people of other and multiple races than other race and Hispanic-origin groups.

Coverage among adults aged 65 and over

Among older adults (aged 65 and over), 39.8% were covered by private insurance (with or without Medicare), 31.8% had Medicare Advantage, 12.1% had traditional Medicare only, 8.7% had some other coverage (including military coverage without Medicare), 6.8% were covered by Medicare and Medicaid (dual-eligible), and 0.7% were uninsured (Table 4, Figure 5).

Summary

This report provides an overall picture of health insurance coverage in the United States by selected demographic characteristics. In 2020, 31.6 million (9.7%) people of all ages were uninsured at the time of the interview. In the United States, very few adults aged 65 and over are without health insurance coverage, because almost all adults in this age group are eligible for health care coverage through the Medicare program (17). Although most people under age 65 had private health insurance either through employment-based coverage or some other source, 11.5% of people under age 65 lacked any type of health insurance at the time of the interview during 2020.

This report provides an annual summary of health insurance estimates categorized by selected sociodemographic measures based on the final NHIS data files. Timely reports and tables on health insurance based on provisional NHIS data are also provided quarterly through the NHIS Early Release Program (https://www.cdc.gov/nchs/nhis/releases.htm).

Note that the information presented in this report is not without some limitations. NHIS responses are self-reported, so may be subject to recall

Figure 4. Percentage of people under age 65 who had public coverage, by type and race and Hispanic origin: United States, 2020

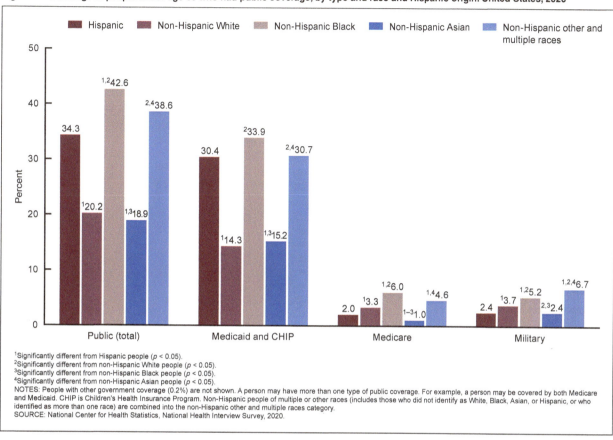

[1]Significantly different from Hispanic people ($p < 0.05$).
[2]Significantly different from non-Hispanic White people ($p < 0.05$).
[3]Significantly different from non-Hispanic Black people ($p < 0.05$).
[4]Significantly different from non-Hispanic Asian people ($p < 0.05$).
NOTES: People with other government coverage (0.2%) are not shown. A person may have more than one type of public coverage. For example, a person may be covered by both Medicare and Medicaid. CHIP is Children's Health Insurance Program. Non-Hispanic people of multiple or other races (includes those who did not identify as White, Black, Asian, or Hispanic, or who identified as more than one race) are combined into the non-Hispanic other and multiple races category.
SOURCE: National Center for Health Statistics, National Health Interview Survey, 2020.

Figure 5. Percent distribution of health insurance coverage among adults aged 65 and over: United States, 2020

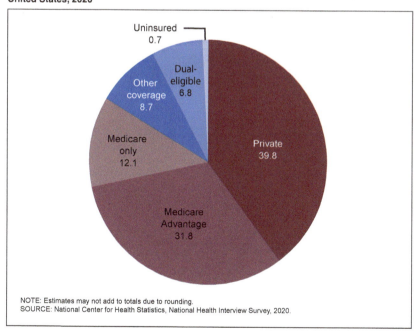

NOTE: Estimates may not add to totals due to rounding.
SOURCE: National Center for Health Statistics, National Health Interview Survey, 2020.

bias. Additionally, item nonresponse for length of time since last had coverage was slightly more than 10%, because 10.3% of those who were uninsured were not eligible to receive the follow-up questions to determine how long they had been uninsured. These respondents were classified as uninsured during the postprocessing editing, or they were only covered by IHS. Lastly, data collection procedures were modified due to the COVID-19 pandemic. Although the 2020 NHIS data file retained some biases after weighting adjustments, notably an underrepresentation of adults living alone and those in the lowest income category, and an overrepresentation of adults living in households with both landline and cell telephones, no biases were detected for estimates of health insurance coverage based on the full sample (11).

One strength of NHIS is that it had a very low nonresponse rate to questions about the type of health insurance coverage (about 0.5%). Additionally, a feature that distinguishes NHIS estimates of health insurance coverage from other survey-based estimates is the use of responses to follow-up questions to evaluate the reliability of the reported health insurance coverage and to resolve conflicting information. Finally, NHIS health insurance coverage information can be analyzed in combination with the other health measures available on NHIS, including health care access and utilization, chronic conditions, and health behaviors.

References

1. Larson K, Cull WL, Racine AD, Olson LM. Trends in access to health care services for US children: 2000–2014. Pediatrics 138(6):1–9. 2016.
2. Institute of Medicine. Coverage matters: Insurance and health care. Washington, DC: The National Academies Press. 2001.
3. Affordable Care Act of 2010. Pub L No 111–148, Pub L No 111–152. 2010.
4. Adepoju OE, Preston MA, Gonzales G. Health care disparities in the post-Affordable Care Act era. Am J Public Health 105 Suppl 5(Suppl 5):S665–7. 2015.
5. Cohen RA, Martinez ME. Health insurance coverage: Early release of estimates from the National Health Interview Survey, 2014. National Center for Health Statistics. June 2015. Available from: https://www.cdc.gov/nchs/data/nhis/earlyrelease/insur201506.pdf.
6. Buchmueller TC, Levison AM, Levy HG, Wolfe BL. Effect of the Affordable Care Act on racial and ethnic disparities in health insurance coverage. Am J Public Health 106(8):1416–21. 2016.
7. Cohen RA, Terlizzi EP, Martinez ME. Health insurance coverage: Early release of estimates from the National Health Interview Survey, 2018. National Center for Health Statistics. May 2019. Available from: https://www.cdc.gov/nchs/data/nhis/earlyrelease/insur201905.pdf.
8. Blewett LA, Davern M. Meeting the need for state-level estimates of health insurance coverage: Use of state and federal survey data. Health Serv Res 41(3 Pt 1):946–75. 2006.
9. Cohen RA, Cha AE, Terlizzi EP, Martinez ME. Demographic variation in health insurance coverage: United States, 2019. National Health Statistics Reports; no 159. Hyattsville, MD: National Center for Health Statistics. 2021. DOI: https://dx.doi.org/10.15620/cdc:106462.
10. National Center for Health Statistics. National Health Interview Survey: 2020 survey description. 2021.
11. Bramlett MD, Dahlhamer JM, Bose J. Weighting procedures and bias assessment for the 2020 National Health Interview Survey. 2021. Available from: https://ftp.cdc.gov/pub/Health_Statistics/NCHS/Dataset_Documentation/NHIS/2020/nonresponse-report-508.pdf.
12. Department of Health and Human Services. Medicare Advantage plans. Available from: https://www.medicare.gov/sign-up-change-plans/types-of-medicare-health-plans/medicare-advantage-plans.
13. U.S. Census Bureau. Poverty thresholds. Available from: https://www.census.gov/data/tables/time-series/demo/income-poverty/historical-poverty-thresholds.html.
14. National Center for Health Statistics. Multiple imputation of family income in 2019 National Health Interview Survey: Methods. 2020.
15. Korn EL, Graubard BI. Confidence intervals for proportions with small expected number of positive counts estimated from survey data. Surv Methodol 24(2):193–201. 1998.
16. Parker JD, Talih M, Malec DJ, Beresovsky V, Carroll M, Gonzalez Jr JF, et al. National Center for Health Statistics data presentation standards for proportions. National Center for Health Statistics. Vital Health Stat 2(175). 2017. Available from: https://www.cdc.gov/nchs/data/series/sr_02/sr02_175.pdf.
17. Social Security Act. Title XVIII: Health insurance for the aged and disabled. 42 USC 1395–1395III. 1965.

Cha, Amy E., Ph.D., M.P.H., and Robin A. Cohen, Ph.D. "Demographic Variation in Health Insurance Coverage: United States, 2020." National Health Statistics Reports, Number 169, February 11, 2022.

HP-2022-23

National Uninsured Rate Reaches All-Time Low in Early 2022

The uninsured rate in early 2022 has reached an all-time low of 8.0% among all U.S. residents, indicating that 5.2 million people have gained health insurance coverage since 2020.

Aiden Lee, Joel Ruhter, Christie Peters, Nancy De Lew, Benjamin D. Sommers

KEY POINTS

- The nation's uninsured rate declined significantly in 2021 and early 2022, reaching an all-time low of 8.0 percent for U.S. residents of all ages in the first quarter (January-March) of 2022, based on new data from the National Health Interview Survey.
- Approximately 5.2 million people – including 4.1 million adults ages 18-64 and 1 million children ages 0-17 – have gained health coverage since 2020. These gains in health insurance coverage are concurrent with the implementation of the American Rescue Plan's enhanced Marketplace subsidies, the continuous enrollment provision in Medicaid, several recent state Medicaid expansions, and substantial enrollment outreach by the Biden-Harris Administration in 2021-2022.
- Uninsured rates among adults ages 18-64 declined from 14.5 percent in late 2020 to 11.8 percent in early 2022. The uninsured rate among children ages 0-17, which had increased during 2019 and 2020, fell from 6.4 percent in late 2020 to 3.7 percent in early 2022.
- Approximately 5.4 percent of adults 18-64 reported having Marketplace coverage in early 2022 compared to 4.4 percent in 2020, reflecting approximately 2 million additional adult Marketplace enrollees – roughly half of the 4 million adults who gained health coverage over this period.
- Changes in uninsured rates from 2020 to 2022 were largest among individuals with incomes below 100% of the Federal Poverty Level (FPL) and incomes between 200% and 400% FPL.
- State-specific analyses using the American Community Survey show that the largest changes in the uninsured rate for low-income adults between 2018-2020 generally occurred in states that recently expanded Medicaid. More recent state estimates beyond 2020 are not yet available.
- Overall, these results highlight the significant gains in health insurance coverage that occurred in 2021 and early 2022 associated with the Biden-Harris Administration's policies to support health insurance expansion. These gains build on the large reductions in the uninsured rate that occurred after the implementation of the Affordable Care Act (ACA) in 2014, which research demonstrates produced improved health outcomes, better access to care, and improved financial security for families.

BACKGROUND

Newly-released federal survey data show the uninsured rate reached an all-time low in early 2022 and suggest that the Biden-Harris Administration's efforts to improve access to affordable health insurance coverage have helped reduce the nation's uninsured rate in 2021 and early 2022.[1] Previous reports indicate that health coverage enrollment related to the Affordable Care Act (ACA) – Marketplace, Medicaid expansion, and the Basic Health Program – reached an all-time high of more than 35 million people in late 2021/early 2022.[2] The 2022 Open Enrollment Period saw an all-time high in Marketplace sign-ups of 14.5 million, following administrative and legislative actions such as an extended 2021 special enrollment period and implementation of expanded Marketplace subsidies under the American Rescue Plan (ARP).[3] In addition, recent adoption of the ACA Medicaid expansion in several states has extended Medicaid coverage to low-income adults up to 138% of the Federal Poverty Level (FPL).

This Data Point examines new National Health Interview Survey (NHIS) data for the first quarter of 2022 to assess changes in health insurance coverage. The report also examines data from the American Community Survey (ACS) to analyze state-level uninsured rates for low-income adults, particularly with respect to states that have expanded Medicaid since 2018.

METHODS

We analyzed newly-released NHIS data from the Centers for Disease Control and Prevention's (CDC).[4] Data are based on household interviews of a sample of the civilian noninstitutionalized population. The NHIS provides a reliable and consistent data source for assessing long-term changes in coverage, as indicated in a 2014 assessment by the White House Council of Economic Advisors.[5] NHIS results in 2020 may not be as reliable for comparisons to survey results before the pandemic, though response rates in 2021 and 2022 have more closely resembled pre-pandemic levels; more details on NHIS data collection can be found in a previous ASPE report.[6] We analyzed changes in coverage over time by age group and income group, as well as source of health insurance coverage.

We also analyzed ACS Public Use Microdata Sample (PUMS) 1-year data to estimate state-level changes in coverage for low-income adults from 2018 to 2020, as the NHIS does not have samples sizes to allow for state estimates for all states.[*] Several states have expanded Medicaid in the past few years, and a comparison of low-income adults' uninsured rates from 2018 to 2020 in these states can provide some indication of expansion effects in these states.

FINDINGS

National Results
Figure 1 shows the national uninsured rates for the U.S. population (all ages) from 2000 through the most recent data. The uninsured rate for Q1 2022 was 8.0 percent, the lowest uninsured rate ever recorded in the NHIS.[7] Prior to 2022, the lowest full-year uninsured estimate in the NHIS was 9.0 percent in 2016, and the lowest quarterly estimate was 8.6 percent in Q1 2016 (note that quarterly estimates are somewhat more

---

[*] We note that the ACS is not as timely as NHIS, and there are survey quality issues in 2020 due to the COVID-19 pandemic. The 2020 ACS 1-year data products do not meet the Census Bureau's statistical data quality standards, and instead the Census Bureau released experimental estimates from the 1-year 2020 ACS data; we use those experimental data products for our analysis in this report.

volatile than full year estimates, given their smaller sample sizes).[8†] The new results correspond to 26.4 million uninsured individuals in Q1 2022, compared to an annual estimate of 31.6 million for 2020, indicating that approximately 5.2 million people gained health care coverage during this time period.[9] This is a conservative estimate of the number of people who gained coverage since 2020, since uninsured rates rose in the second half of 2020; if we compare the Q1 2022 estimate to Q4 2020, the estimated number gaining coverage rises to 7.2 million.

Figure 1 demonstrates that the recent reductions in the uninsured rate built on the large coverage gains that occurred in the first 3 years after implementation of the ACA in 2014 and reversed a temporary increase in the uninsured rate from 2017-2019. Overall, the Q1 2022 uninsured population represents a drop of nearly 22 million from the peak of 48.3 million in 2010.

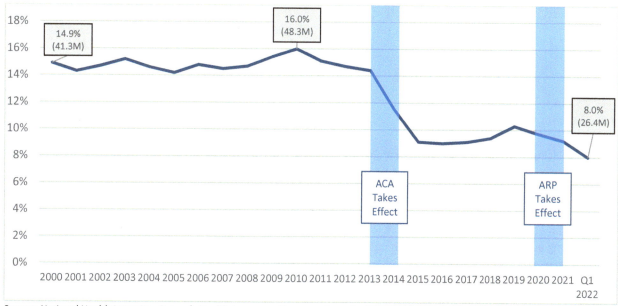

Figure 1. National Uninsured Rate, All Ages (2000 – Q1 2022)

Source: National Health Interview Survey's Health Insurance Coverage Reports, 2000-2021.
https://www.cdc.gov/nchs/nhis/healthinsurancecoverage.htm; Health Insurance Coverage: Early Release of Quarterly Estimates From the National Health Interview Survey, January 2021–March 2022.
https://www.cdc.gov/nchs/data/nhis/earlyrelease/Quarterly_Estimates_2022_Q11.pdf
Note: Beginning in the third quarter of 2004, two additional questions were added to the NHIS insurance section to reduce potential errors in reporting Medicare and Medicaid status, resulting in two methods to estimate uninsurance. Beginning in 2005, all estimates were calculated using Method 2. Please see "Technical Notes" for the Early Release of Health Insurance Estimates Based on Data From the 2010 National Health Interview Survey for more information.

Figure 2 shows quarterly changes in health insurance coverage among adults ages 18-64, for whom the uninsured rate was 11.8 percent in Q1 2022, a 2.7 percentage-point decrease from Q4 2020. Children ages 0 to 17 years also experienced a 2.7 percentage-point decrease in their uninsured rates in the same time frame. If we focus on full-year estimates for 2020 vs. Q1 2022, the change for adults ages 18-64 was 2.1 percentage

---

[†] The NHIS underwent a survey redesign in 2019. While the questions used to assess health insurance coverage did not change, the questionnaire design and sample weighting were revised. A technical paper conducted by the National Center for Health Statistics concluded that the redesign "may have shifted upward by 0.7 percentage points due to the methodological change" the national estimate for the uninsured rate among adults. This upward shift since 2019 means that the Q1 2022 uninsured estimate of 8.0 percent likely represents a record-low by an even larger margin than the 0.6 percentage points compared to Q1 2016 and 1.1 percentage points compared to full-year 2016. See https://www.cdc.gov/nchs/data/nhis/earlyrelease/EReval202009-508.pdf for further details on the NHIS redesign.

points (from 13.9 percent to 11.8 percent) with approximately 4.1 million adults gaining health coverage, and the change for children was 1.4 percentage points (from 5.1 percent to 3.7 percent) with approximately 1 million children gaining health coverage.[10,11]

Figure 2. Uninsured Rate by Quarter, Populations Ages 18-64 and Ages 0-17 (Q4 2020 – Q1 2022)

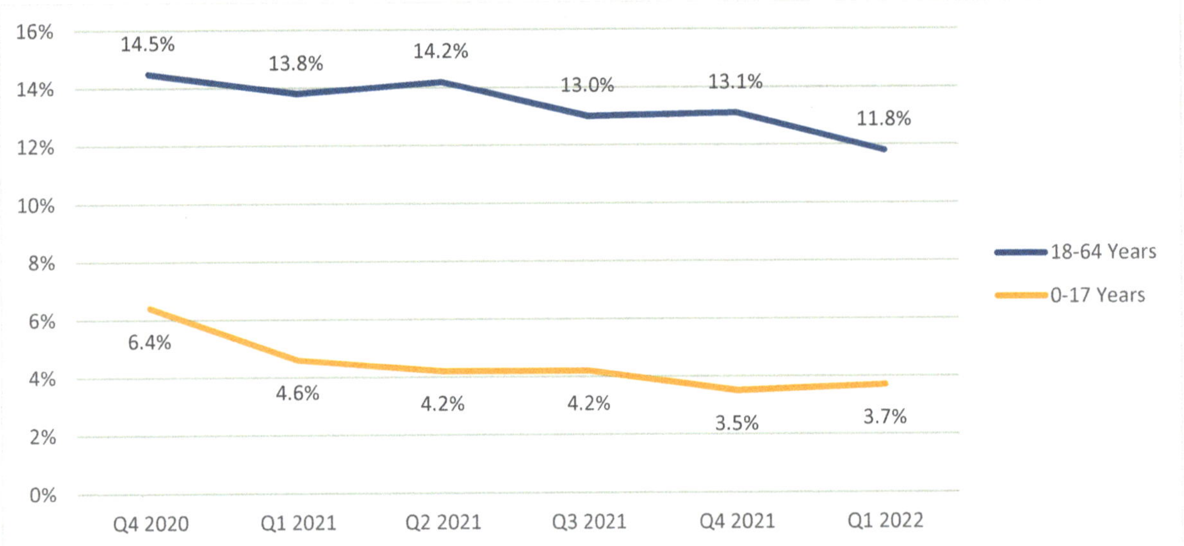

Quarter	18-64 Years	0-17 Years
Q4 2020	14.5%	6.4%
Q1 2021	13.8%	4.6%
Q2 2021	14.2%	4.2%
Q3 2021	13.0%	4.2%
Q4 2021	13.1%	3.5%
Q1 2022	11.8%	3.7%

Source: Health Insurance Coverage: Early Release of Quarterly Estimates From the National Health Interview Survey, October 2020–December 2021. https://www.cdc.gov/nchs/data/nhis/earlyrelease/Quarterly_Estimates_2021_Q14.pdf; Health Insurance Coverage: Early Release of Quarterly Estimates From the National Health Interview Survey, January 2021–March 2022. https://www.cdc.gov/nchs/data/nhis/earlyrelease/Quarterly_Estimates_2022_Q11.pdf

Figure 3 shows the growth in Marketplace coverage (or "Exchange-based private coverage," as the NHIS refers to it) among adults 18-64 since 2019. An estimated 5.4 percent of adults ages 18-64 reported having Marketplace coverage in early 2022, compared to 4.4 percent in 2019. This represents an increase of approximately 2 million adults, or roughly half of the estimated reduction in the adult uninsured population during this period. While survey-based information on Marketplace coverage is not as reliable as official administrative enrollment statistics, this result is consistent with the record-breaking Marketplace Open Enrollment Period for 2022[12] and suggests that Marketplace coverage gains in 2021 and early 2022 were a substantial contributor to the reduction in the uninsured rate.

Figure 3. Percentage of Adults Ages 18-64 with Marketplace Coverage (2019 – Q1 2022)

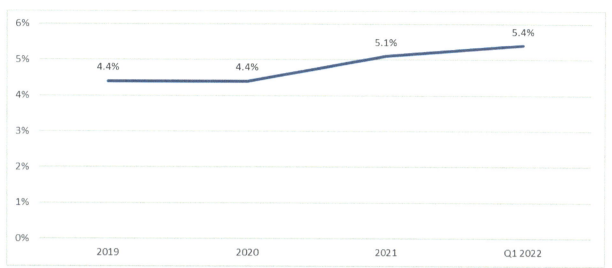

Source: NHIS Interactive Quarterly Early Release Estimates.
https://wwwn.cdc.gov/NHISDataQueryTool/ER_Quarterly/index_quarterly.html

Figure 4 shows that uninsured rates among those under age 65 declined for all income bands since the beginning of 2021. Those with incomes below 100% FPL had the greatest gain in coverage, with uninsured rates decreasing 4.5 percentage points (from 20.0 to 15.5 percent). Uninsured rates for those between 100% and 200% FPL went from 16.6 to 16.0 percent, though when compared to Q2 2021, there was a larger decline from 19.0 to 16.0 percent. Uninsured rates for those with incomes between 200% and 400% FPL decreased 2.0 percentage points (from 11.7 in Q1 2021 to 9.7 percent in Q1 2022). Those with incomes above 400% FPL had the lowest uninsured rate throughout the study period, and it declined modestly from 4.2 to 3.7 percent. In relative terms, these declines represent a 22 percent reduction in the uninsured rate for those below 100% FPL, a 16 percent reduction for those between 100% and 200% FPL (compared to Q2 2021), a 17 percent reduction for those between 200% and 400% FPL, and a 12 percent reduction for those above 400% FPL.

These declines in uninsured rates coincide with the implementation of the ARP subsidies, which were retroactive to January 1, 2021, and boosted the size of premium tax credits for those with incomes between 100% and 400% FPL and extended tax credits to those with incomes above 400% FPL for the first time. Previous ASPE analyses have shown the impacts of the ARP in lowering Marketplace premiums and improving plan affordability through increased access to zero- and low-premium plans on the HealthCare.gov platform.[13,14]

Figure 4. Uninsured Rate Among U.S. Residents Under Age 65, by Income (Q1 2021 – Q1 2022)

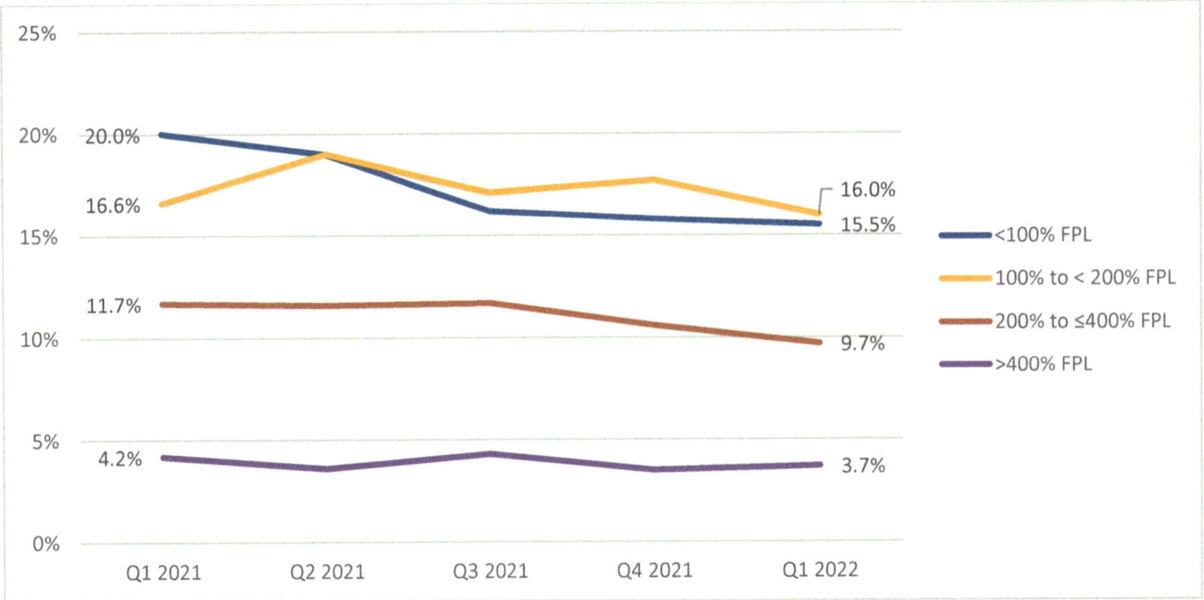

Note: FPL = Federal Poverty Level.
Source: Health Insurance Coverage: Early Release of Quarterly Estimates From the National Health Interview Survey, January 2021–March 2022. https://www.cdc.gov/nchs/data/nhis/earlyrelease/Quarterly_Estimates_2022_Q11.pdf

State Results
Turning to state-specific analyses using the ACS, Table 1 shows state-level changes in uninsured rates for low-income adults ages 18-64 from 2018 to 2020. 18 states saw uninsured rates for this population decrease over this period, with decreases ranging from -0.1 percentage points to -8.4 percentage points. Fifteen of the 18 states experiencing declining uninsured rates have expanded Medicaid. Uninsured rates declined in all 5 states that expanded Medicaid in 2019-2020, with decreases ranging from -1.4 percentage points (Utah) to -8.4 percentage points (Idaho). Future analyses of the 2 states that expanded Medicaid in 2021 (Missouri and Oklahoma) are needed to continue monitoring the coverage impacts of expansion.

Table 1. Uninsured Rates by State Among Adults Ages 19-64, with Incomes Under 138% FPL, 2018 vs. 2020

	Medicaid Expansion Year	Sample Size for 2020	2018	2020*	Percentage Point Change, 2018 vs. 2020
Alabama	n/a	6,734	31.9%	32.2%	0.3%
Alaska	2015	1,078	24.7%	25.2%	0.5%
Arizona	2014	7,844	25.2%	26.5%	1.4%
Arkansas	2014	4,430	22.0%	22.8%	0.9%
California	2014	45,611	17.0%	17.4%	0.4%
Colorado	2014	5,362	18.1%	21.2%	3.1%
Connecticut	2014	3,400	12.7%	11.5%	-1.2%
Delaware	2014	961	11.8%	17.7%	5.9%
District of Columbia	2014	980	8.6%	4.5%	-4.1%
Florida	n/a	19,862	34.1%	34.0%	-0.1%
Georgia	n/a	10,803	37.8%	36.9%	-0.9%
Hawaii	2014	2,108	13.3%	10.3%	-3.0%
Idaho	**2020**	**2,023**	**28.2%**	**19.7%**	**-8.4%**
Illinois	2014	15,190	18.8%	19.2%	0.4%
Indiana	2015	8,207	20.6%	17.3%	-3.3%
Iowa	2014	3,884	13.5%	15.3%	1.7%
Kansas	n/a	3,605	28.2%	29.6%	1.3%
Kentucky	2014	6,387	13.1%	13.1%	0.0%
Louisiana	2016	6,017	19.0%	19.5%	0.5%
Maine	**2019**	**1,610**	**21.3%**	**16.5%**	**-4.9%**
Maryland	2014	5,942	16.7%	15.7%	-1.1%
Massachusetts	2014	7,514	6.7%	7.4%	0.6%
Michigan	2014	13,189	13.9%	14.1%	0.2%
Minnesota	2014	5,051	11.9%	13.6%	1.6%
Mississippi	n/a	4,220	36.4%	32.2%	-4.3%
Missouri	2021	8,164	27.7%	29.4%	1.7%
Montana	2016	1,374	17.1%	16.5%	-0.6%
Nebraska	**2020**	**2,122**	**27.9%**	**25.2%**	**-2.8%**
Nevada	2014	3,321	25.7%	28.5%	2.8%
New Hampshire	2014	1,231	15.9%	15.9%	0.0%
New Jersey	2014	8,156	21.0%	21.1%	0.0%
New Mexico	2014	2,962	19.4%	17.4%	-2.0%
New York	2014	25,769	12.0%	11.9%	-0.2%
North Carolina	n/a	11,696	30.3%	31.2%	0.9%
North Dakota	2014	755	19.8%	20.4%	0.6%
Ohio	2014	14,187	16.2%	15.5%	-0.7%
Oklahoma	2021	6,632	37.5%	40.3%	2.9%
Oregon	2014	4,416	16.8%	16.8%	0.0%
Pennsylvania	2015	16,687	15.2%	15.9%	0.7%
Rhode Island	2014	1,101	8.6%	9.5%	0.9%
South Carolina	n/a	6,161	30.0%	30.0%	0.0%
South Dakota	n/a	1,006	31.3%	35.4%	4.1%
Tennessee	n/a	8,075	29.1%	29.6%	0.5%
Texas	n/a	28,235	44.6%	45.0%	0.4%
Utah	**2020**	**3,484**	**25.0%**	**23.6%**	**-1.4%**
Vermont	2014	808	6.1%	9.0%	2.8%
Virginia	**2019**	**8,626**	**27.4%**	**20.1%**	**-7.2%**
Washington	2014	7,229	16.8%	15.8%	-1.0%
West Virginia	2014	2,508	15.7%	16.8%	1.1%
Wisconsin	n/a	6,373	15.4%	16.7%	1.3%
Wyoming	n/a	569	27.3%	38.4%	11.1%

Notes: States in bold expanded Medicaid between 2018 and 2020.
*The 2020 ACS 1-year data products do not meet the Census Bureau's statistical data quality standards. The Census Bureau released experimental estimates from the 1-year 2020 ACS data, which were used for this analysis; results from the experimental estimates

should be interpreted with caution. For more information, see: https://www.census.gov/newsroom/press-releases/2021/experimental-2020-acs-1-year-data.html
Source: ASPE analysis of 2018 and 2020 American Community Survey (ACS) Public Use Microdata Sample (PUMS) 1-year data.

CONCLUSION

The Biden-Harris Administration took administrative and legislative actions in 2021 that have helped individuals gain and maintain health coverage, including robust outreach efforts and expanded Marketplace subsidies under the ARP. These health coverage gains build on the large reductions in the uninsured rate that occurred after the implementation of the Affordable Care Act (ACA) in 2014. Medicaid enrollment has grown under the continuous enrollment provision passed by Congress as part of the COVID-19 pandemic response, as well as several states' recent Medicaid expansions. With these policies in effect, the U.S. uninsured rate declined throughout 2021 and early 2022, reaching an all-time low of 8.0 percent by the first quarter of 2022. States that expanded Medicaid since 2019 have experienced a decrease in the uninsured rates among low-income adults. Additional information on state-level changes will be available later this year after release of the 2021 ACS.

Research over the past decade demonstrates that the ACA has produced improved health outcomes, better access to care, and improved financial security for families.[15,16,17] Understanding the full nature of these historic gains in health insurance coverage as a result of the ACA and the ARP will be critical to maintaining high health coverage rates, assessing their impact on population health, and building on recent progress to make health insurance affordable and available to all Americans. Future analyses will explore state-level impacts as well as coverage changes by race and ethnicity and other demographic factors.

REFERENCES

[1] Cohen RA, Cha AE. Health Insurance Coverage: Early Release of Quarterly Estimates From the National Health Interview Survey, January 2021–March 2022. Centers for Disease Control and Prevention. National Health Interview Survey. Accessed at: https://www.cdc.gov/nchs/data/nhis/earlyrelease/Quarterly_Estimates_2022_Q11.pdf

[2] Lee A, Chu RC, Peters C, and Sommers BD. Health Coverage Changes Under the Affordable Care Act: End of 2021 Update. (Issue Brief No. HP-2022-17). Office of the Assistant Secretary for Planning and Evaluation, U.S. Department of Health and Human Services. April 2022. Accessed at: https://www.aspe.hhs.gov/reports/health-coverage-changes-2021-update

[3] Lee A, Chu RC, Peters C, and Sommers BD. Health Coverage Changes Under the Affordable Care Act: End of 2021 Update. (Issue Brief No. HP-2022-17). Office of the Assistant Secretary for Planning and Evaluation, U.S. Department of Health and Human Services. April 2022. Accessed at: https://www.aspe.hhs.gov/reports/health-coverage-changes-2021-update

[4] Cohen RA, Cha AE. Health Insurance Coverage: Early Release of Quarterly Estimates From the National Health Interview Survey, January 2021–March 2022. Centers for Disease Control and Prevention. National Health Interview Survey. Accessed at: https://www.cdc.gov/nchs/data/nhis/earlyrelease/Quarterly_Estimates_2022_Q11.pdf

[5] White House Council of Economic Advisors. Methodological Appendix: Methods Used to Construct a Consistent Historical Time Series of Health Insurance Coverage. 2014. https://obamawhitehouse.archives.gov/sites/default/files/docs/longtermhealthinsuranceseriesmethodologyfinal.pdf

[6] Lee A, Chu RC, Peters C, and Sommers BD. Health Coverage Changes Under the Affordable Care Act: End of 2021 Update. (Issue Brief No. HP-2022-17). Office of the Assistant Secretary for Planning and Evaluation, U.S. Department of Health and Human Services. April 2022. Accessed at: https://www.aspe.hhs.gov/reports/health-coverage-changes-2021-update

[7] Executive Office of the President of the United States. 2016. The Economic Record of the Obama Administration: Reforming the Health Care System. https://obamawhitehouse.archives.gov/sites/default/files/page/files/20161213_cea_record_healh_care_reform.pdf

[8] Cohen R, Martinez M, and Zammitti E. Health Insurance Coverage: Early Release of Estimates From the National Health Interview Survey, January-March 2016. Centers for Disease Control and Prevention. National Health Interview Survey. Accessed at: https://www.cdc.gov/nchs/data/nhis/earlyrelease/insur201609.pdf

[9] Cohen RA, Terlizzi EP, Cha AE, Martinez ME. Health Insurance Coverage: Early Release of Estimates From the National Health Interview Survey, 2020. Centers for Disease Control and Prevention. National Health Interview Survey. Accessed at: https://www.cdc.gov/nchs/data/nhis/earlyrelease/insur202108-508.pdf

[10] Cohen RA, Terlizzi EP, Cha AE, Martinez ME. Health Insurance Coverage: Early Release of Estimates From the National Health Interview Survey, 2020. Centers for Disease Control and Prevention. National Health Interview Survey. Accessed at: https://www.cdc.gov/nchs/data/nhis/earlyrelease/insur202108-508.pdf

[11] Cohen RA, Cha AE. Health Insurance Coverage: Early Release of Quarterly Estimates From the National Health Interview Survey, January 2021–March 2022. Centers for Disease Control and Prevention. National Health Interview Survey. Accessed at: https://www.cdc.gov/nchs/data/nhis/earlyrelease/Quarterly_Estimates_2022_Q11.pdf

[12] https://www.cms.gov/newsroom/fact-sheets/marketplace-2022-open-enrollment-period-report-final-national-snapshot

[13] Branham DK, Conmy AB, DeLeire T, Musen J, Xiao X, Chu RC, Peters C, and Sommers BD. Access to Marketplace Plans with Low Premiums on the Federal Platform, Part II: Availability Among Uninsured Non-Elderly Adults Under the American Rescue Plan (Issue Brief No. HP-2021-08). Washington, DC: Office of the Assistant Secretary for Planning and Evaluation, U.S. Department of Health and Human Services. April 1, 2021. Available at: https://aspe.hhs.gov/reports/accessmarketplace-plans-low-premiums-uninsured-american-rescue-plan

[14] Branham DK, Conmy AB, DeLeire T, Musen J, Xiao X, Chu RC, Peters C, and Sommers BD. Access to Marketplace Plans with Low Premiums on the Federal Platform, Part III: Availability Among Current HealthCare.gov Enrollees Under the American Rescue Plan (Issue Brief No. HP-2021-09). Washington, DC: Office of the Assistant Secretary for Planning and Evaluation, U.S. Department of Health and Human Services. April 13, 2021. Available at: https://aspe.hhs.gov/reports/access-marketplace-plans-low-premiums-federal-platform

[15] Gruber J, Sommers BD. The Affordable Care Act's Effects on Patients, Providers, and the Economy: What We Know So Far. Journal of Policy Analysis and Management. 2019; 38(4): 1028-1052.

[16] Mazurenko O, Balio CP, Agarwal R, Carroll AE, Menachemi N. The Effects Of Medicaid Expansion Under The ACA: A Systematic Review. Health Aff (Millwood). 2018 Jun;37(6):944-950. doi: 10.1377/hlthaff.2017.1491. PMID: 29863941.

[17] Creedon TB, Zuvekas SH, Hill SC, Ali MM, McClellan C, Dey JG. Effects of Medicaid expansion on insurance coverage and health services use among adults with disabilities newly eligible for Medicaid. Health Serv Res. 2022 Jul 10. doi: 10.1111/1475-6773.14034. Epub ahead of print. PMID: 35811358.

Lee, Aiden, Joel Ruhter, Christie Peters, Nancy De Lew, Benjamin D. Sommers. "National Uninsured Rate Reaches All-Time Low in Early 2022." Office of the Assistant Secretary for Planning and Evaluation (ASPE), Office of Health Policy, August 2022.

CONTRACTOR PROJECT REPORT
HP-2022-15

Environmental Scan on Consolidation Trends and Impacts in Health Care Markets

HP-2022-15

Prepared for
the Office of the Assistant Secretary for Planning and Evaluation (ASPE)
at the U.S. Department of Health & Human Services

by
RAND Health Care

August 2022

ASPE Executive Summary

The No Surprises Act (NSA) of the 2021 Consolidated Appropriations Act creates protections for those with private health insurance against surprise medical bills. Under Section 109 of the NSA, the Secretary of Health and Human Services must conduct a study by January 1, 2023, and annually thereafter for the following 4 years, on the effects of the Act on any patterns of vertical or horizontal integration of health care facilities, providers, group health plans, or health insurance issuers; overall health care costs; and access to health care.

Responsibility for the Reports to Congress has been delegated to the Office of the Assistant Secretary for Planning and Evaluation (ASPE). We plan two major analytic tasks to set the stage for the reports to the Congress. The first task is to establish a comprehensive baseline report that describes the landscape of market consolidation across the U.S. and analyzes the evidence on the price, cost, and quality effects of consolidation. The attached report from RAND presents the results of these analyses, and the below "Graphics Supplement" provides additional information about the concentration landscape. The second task for the near future will be to develop the analytic models and databases that will allow us to estimate the impact of the NSA provisions on market consolidation, price, quality, and access.

The attached environmental scan discusses trends and impacts of consolidation in health care. Key findings are:

- The literature shows strong evidence that hospital horizontal consolidation increases prices for health care services and increases health care spending.
- While not as thoroughly documented, physician horizontal consolidation has been found to increase prices for health care services.
- Studies also find that insurer horizontal consolidation increases health insurance premiums and increase overall health care spending, with some evidence that it also reduces payment rates to health care providers.
- The literature is less conclusive on questions of how consolidation impacts health care quality and patient access.
- The few existing evaluations on state surprise billing laws do not find direct evidence of those laws on spending, quality, patient access, and consolidation.

Markets for health insurance and health care services are not uniform across the country or over time. The variation in market concentration across geography and over time will influence the local impact of the NSA and will be an important consideration in evaluating the impact of the NSA.

In the attached "Graphics Supplement," we present insurance and hospital market concentration measures across geographic areas and over time, based on ASPE data analyses.

The RAND report is an independent assessment and does not represent the official views of ASPE or HHS.

Graphics Supplement – Health Care Market Concentration Geography

Health insurance, hospital, and physician organization markets have been characterized as highly concentrated for years.[1] This section displays maps of a commonly-used measure of market concentration in the academic literature, the Herfindahl–Hirschman index (HHI),[*] for several health care product markets at several levels of geography.[†] The HHI measures the relative sizes of firms in a market. The measure approaches zero when a market has a large number of firms of equal size (i.e. "perfect competition") and reaches its maximum of 10,000 when the market is a monopoly. The Department of Justice and the Federal Trade commission generally classify markets into three types based on their HHI:

- Unconcentrated Markets: HHI below 1500
- Moderately Concentrated Markets: HHI between 1500 and 2500
- Highly Concentrated Markets: HHI above 2500.[2]

In this supplement, health insurance HHI is calculated using DRG Managed Market Surveyor data and is presented at the county and core-based statistical area (CBSA) level. Adjusted hospital admissions[‡] from American Hospital Association data were calculated at the hospital referral region (HRR) and CBSA level. Hospital referral regions (HRR) are regional health care markets designed by the Dartmouth Atlas Project. HRRs are designed to reflect patterns in inpatient tertiary care referrals, while CBSAs reflect urban commuting patterns. Federal antitrust agencies conduct relevant market analyses on a case-by-case basis, meaning the relevant markets in antitrust enforcement actions may differ from the methodology described here.

Hospital Markets

For at least the past three decades, hospital markets have become increasingly concentrated.[3] Recent increases have occurred across the country. The percentage of hospital referral regions (HRRs) with an HHI <1,500 – meaning unconcentrated – decreased from 23% (71 of 306) in 2008 to 12% (38 of 306) in 2019 (Figure 1).[§] Using another geographic definition for hospital markets, CBSA (or metropolitan area), also shows a decline: 6% (25 of 392) of CBSAs had an HHI < 1,500 in 2008 while in 2019 just 4% (14 of 392) did (Figure 2). The number of CBSAs with HHI < 2,500 declined from 18% (72 of 392) to 13% (50 of 392) over the same period.

---

[*] Herfindahl–Hirschman index (HHI) measures the relative firm size in a market where market share is represented as the sum of squared markets shares in a given market scaled from 0 to 10,000.

[†] Throughout this document market definitions are not necessarily antitrust product markets nor was a full analysis conducted in accordance with the U.S. Department of Justice and Federal Trade Commission Horizontal Merger Guidelines § 5.3 (revised Aug. 19, 2010) that would establish any of these as an antitrust product or geographic market.

There are multiple potential markets for health insurance and health care services. For example, in the context of commercial health insurance, the DOJ has defined markets for individual, small group, large group, and national accounts. With respect to national accounts, it is not necessarily clear that concentration in a single geography is informative of overall competition for a given national account.

[‡] AHA's adjusted admissions measure attempts to capture both inpatient admissions and outpatient volume by scaling based on relative revenue. Adjusted Admissions = Admissions + (Admissions * (Outpatient Revenue/Inpatient Revenue))

[§] The U.S. Department of Justice (DOJ) and FTC merger guidelines classify markets with an HHI below 1,500 as unconcentrated; between 1,500 and 2,500 as moderately concentrated; and over 2,500 as highly concentrated (DOJ and FTC, 2010).

Figure 1. Hospital Referral Region (HRR) Level Herfindahl-Hirschman Index (HHI) For Adjusted Admissions, 2008 and 2019

2008

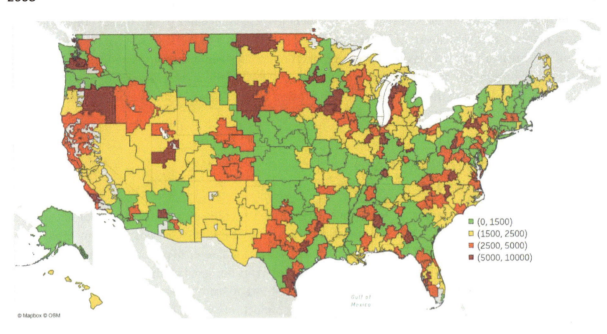

2019

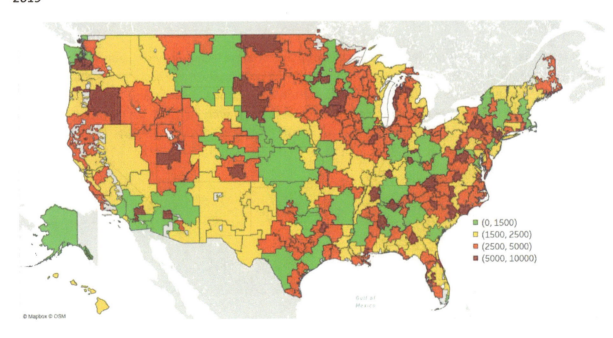

Source: ASPE Anaylsis of AHA Data

Figure 2. Core-based statistical area (CBSA) Level Herfindahl-Hirschman Index (HHI) For Adjusted Admissions, 2008 and 2019

2008

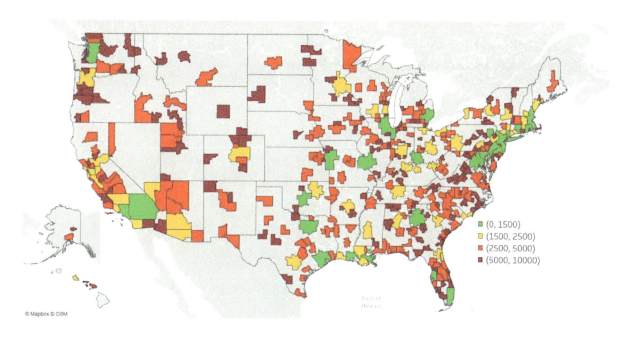

2019

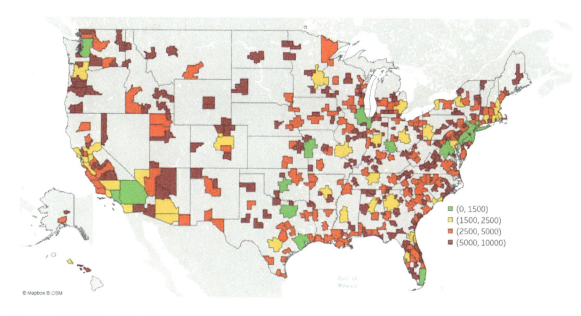

Source: ASPE Anaylsis of AHA Data

Health Insurance Markets

Markets for health insurance are also concentrated. In 2008, 31% of CBSAs had a commercial health insurance HHI below 1,500 (120 of 384) (Figure 3). In 2019, a similar 35% of CBSAs had a commercial health insurance HHI below 1,500 (135 of 384).

In 2008, 27% of CBSAs had a Medicare Advantage enrollment HHI below 1,500 (103 of 384). In 2019, that figure was nearly steady at 26% (100 of 384) (Figure 4).

Figure 3. Core-based statistical area (CBSA) Level Herfindahl-Hirschman Index (HHI) for For Commercial Health Insurance Membership, 2008 and 2019

2008

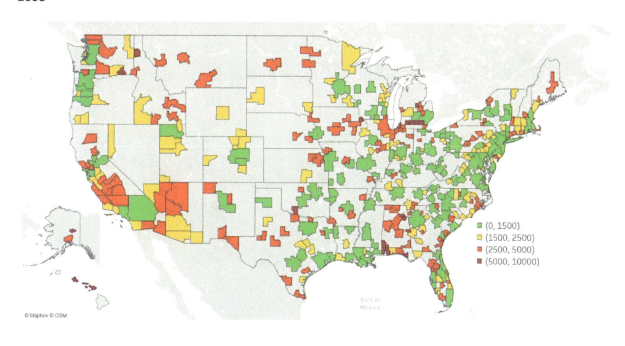

2019

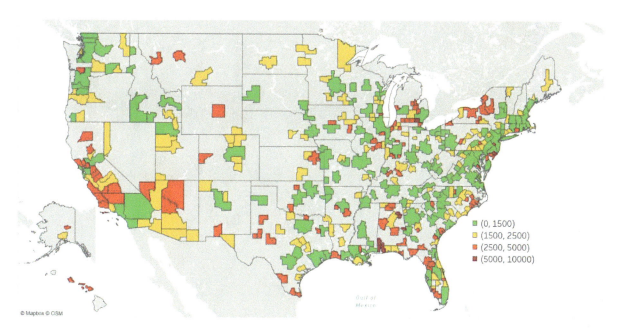

Source: ASPE Anaylsis of Clarivate|DRG Managed Market Surveyor

Figure 4. Core-based statistical area (CBSA) Level Herfindahl-Hirschman Index (HHI) for Medicare Advantage Plan Enrollment, 2008 and 2019

2008

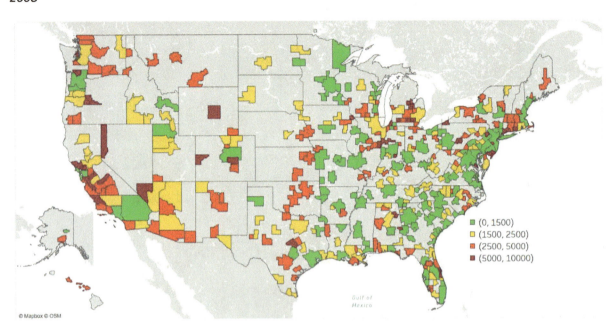

2019

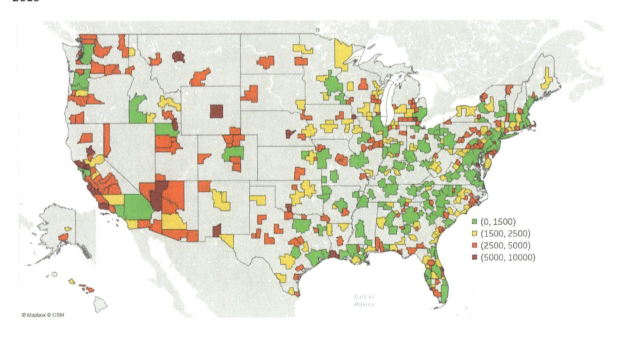

Source: ASPE Anaylsis of Clarivate|DRG Managed Market Surveyor

Combined Commercial Insurance and Hospital Markets

The markets for health insurance and health care services interact. A highly concentrated insurance market gives insurers leverage over providers in negotiating reimbursement rates for providers in their networks. Conversely, providers with high market share can command high prices from insurers. Markets with limited competition for both insurance and providers create the potential for both insurers and providers to raise prices and worsen consumer well-being.

In Figure 5, CBSAs are coded based on the joint HHI measures for commercial insurance and adjusted hospital admissions. The four mutually-exclusive categories are: (1) both commercial health insurance and hospital HHI <1500; (2) at least one of commercial health insurance or hospital HHI >1500; (3) both commercial health insurance and hospital HHI >2500 (but at least one of them ≤5000); and (4) both commercial health insurance and hospital HHI >5000.

In 2019, 28% of CBSAs had both highly concentrated hospital and commercial insurance markets (both commercial health insurance and hospital HHI >5000), down slightly from 32% in 2010.

Insurers with more bargaining power can more effectively negotiate in markets with high levels of hospital concentration than insurers with less bargaining power.[4] However, the evidence is not clear that any benefits of insurer concentration are passed to consumers in the form of lower premiums.[5] How these two highly concentrated markets interact is an important area of research that may require policy attention as both provider and insurance markets grow more concentrated.

Figure 5. Core-Based Statistical Area (CBSA) Level Herfindahl-Hirschman Index (HHI) Levels Of Concentration For Commercial Insurance And Hospital Adjusted Admisisons, 2008 and 2019

2008

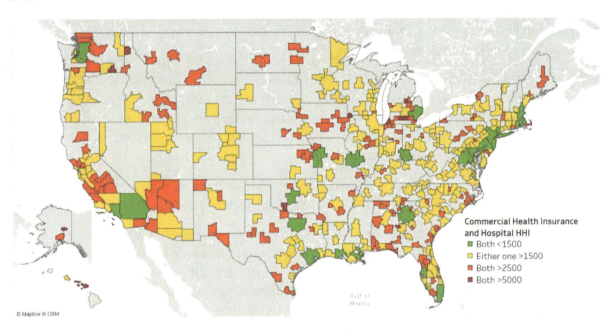

2019

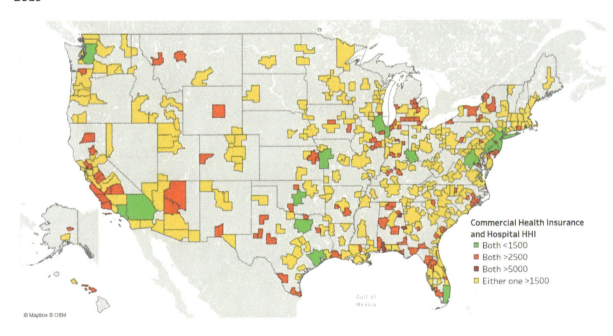

Source: ASPE Anaylsis of Clarivate|DRG Managed Market Surveyor, AHA Data

REFERENCES

[1] Fulton, Brent D. Health Care Market Concentration Trends In The United States: Evidence And Policy Responses. Health Affairs 2017 36:9, 1530-1538

[2] U.S. Department of Justice and Federal Trade Commission, Horizontal Merger Guidelines § 5.3 (2010). https://www.justice.gov/atr/horizontal-merger-guidelines-08192010#5c

[3] Vogt, William B. "Hospital market consolidation: trends and consequences." Expert Voices (2009).
Fulton, Brent D. Health Care Market Concentration Trends In The United States: Evidence And Policy Responses. Health Affairs 2017 36:9, 1530-1538
Gaynor, Martin. "What to do about health-care markets? Policies to make health-care markets work." Brookings Institution (2020). https://www.brookings.edu/wp-content/uploads/2020/03/Gaynor_PP_FINAL.pdf

[4] Barrette, Eric, Gautam Gowrisankaran, and Robert Town. "Countervailing market power and hospital competition." The Review of Economics and Statistics (2021): 1-33.

[5] Scheffler, Richard M., and Daniel R. Arnold. "Insurer market power lowers prices in numerous concentrated provider markets." Health Affairs 36.9 (2017): 1539-1546.

RAND Health Care. "Environmental Scan on Consolidation Trends and Impacts in Health Care Markets." Office of the Assistant Secretary for Planning and Evaluation (ASPE), Office of Health Policy, August 2022.

State Statistics & Rankings

Covered by Some Type of Health Insurance

All Persons		Under 19 Years		Under 65 Years	
State	**Percent**	**State**	**Percent**	**State**	**Percent**
Massachusetts	97.0 *(0.2)*	Massachusetts	98.5 *(0.2)*	Massachusetts	96.5 *(0.2)*
District of Columbia	96.5 *(0.6)*	Rhode Island	98.1 *(0.7)*	District of Columbia	96.1 *(0.7)*
Rhode Island	95.9 *(0.6)*	District of Columbia	98.0 *(0.9)*	Rhode Island	95.2 *(0.7)*
Hawaii	95.8 *(0.4)*	Vermont	97.9 *(0.7)*	Hawaii	95.0 *(0.5)*
Vermont	95.5 *(0.5)*	New York	97.6 *(0.2)*	Vermont	94.4 *(0.6)*
Minnesota	95.1 *(0.2)*	Hawaii	97.2 *(0.7)*	Minnesota	94.2 *(0.3)*
Iowa	95.0 *(0.3)*	Iowa	97.1 *(0.5)*	Iowa	94.0 *(0.4)*
New York	94.8 *(0.1)*	Minnesota	96.9 *(0.4)*	New York	93.9 *(0.1)*
Wisconsin	94.3 *(0.2)*	Washington	96.9 *(0.3)*	Wisconsin	93.2 *(0.3)*
Michigan	94.2 *(0.2)*	Maryland	96.6 *(0.5)*	Maryland	93.1 *(0.3)*
Pennsylvania	94.2 *(0.2)*	Michigan	96.6 *(0.3)*	Michigan	93.1 *(0.2)*
Connecticut	94.1 *(0.3)*	Alabama	96.5 *(0.3)*	Connecticut	93.0 *(0.4)*
Maryland	94.0 *(0.3)*	Connecticut	96.5 *(0.5)*	Pennsylvania	93.0 *(0.2)*
New Hampshire	93.7 *(0.6)*	West Virginia	96.5 *(0.6)*	New Hampshire	92.4 *(0.7)*
Kentucky	93.6 *(0.3)*	California	96.4 *(0.2)*	Kentucky	92.3 *(0.4)*
Delaware	93.4 *(0.6)*	New Hampshire	96.3 *(0.9)*	Washington	92.3 *(0.3)*
Ohio	93.4 *(0.2)*	Wisconsin	96.2 *(0.3)*	Ohio	92.2 *(0.2)*
Washington	93.4 *(0.3)*	Illinois	96.0 *(0.3)*	Delaware	91.9 *(0.8)*
West Virginia	93.3 *(0.4)*	Oregon	95.9 *(0.6)*	North Dakota	91.9 *(0.8)*
North Dakota	93.1 *(0.7)*	Kentucky	95.7 *(0.5)*	West Virginia	91.7 *(0.5)*
Oregon	92.8 *(0.3)*	New Jersey	95.7 *(0.4)*	Illinois	91.4 *(0.2)*
Illinois	92.6 *(0.2)*	Louisiana	95.6 *(0.6)*	Oregon	91.4 *(0.4)*
California	92.3 *(0.1)*	Pennsylvania	95.4 *(0.3)*	California	91.1 *(0.1)*
New Jersey	92.1 *(0.2)*	Delaware	95.2 *(1.4)*	New Jersey	90.8 *(0.3)*
Virginia	92.1 *(0.3)*	Ohio	95.2 *(0.3)*	Colorado	90.7 *(0.3)*
Colorado	92.0 *(0.3)*	Virginia	95.1 *(0.4)*	Virginia	90.7 *(0.3)*
Maine	92.0 *(0.5)*	Idaho	95.0 *(0.8)*	Nebraska	90.2 *(0.5)*
Montana	91.7 *(0.5)*	Tennessee	95.0 *(0.5)*	Maine	89.9 *(0.7)*
Nebraska	91.7 *(0.4)*	Colorado	94.5 *(0.6)*	Montana	89.8 *(0.7)*
Indiana	91.3 *(0.3)*	Maine	94.4 *(1.1)*	Indiana	89.7 *(0.3)*
Louisiana	91.1 *(0.3)*	Nebraska	94.3 *(0.8)*	Louisiana	89.5 *(0.4)*
Arkansas	90.9 *(0.4)*	New Mexico	94.3 *(0.9)*	United States	89.2 *(0.1)*
Kansas	90.8 *(0.4)*	United States	94.3 *(0.1)*	Utah	89.2 *(0.6)*
United States	90.8 *(0.1)*	Kansas	94.2 *(0.7)*	Arkansas	89.1 *(0.5)*
Alabama	90.3 *(0.3)*	North Carolina	94.2 *(0.4)*	Kansas	89.1 *(0.5)*
Utah	90.3 *(0.5)*	South Carolina	94.2 *(0.6)*	Alabama	88.3 *(0.3)*
Missouri	90.0 *(0.3)*	Arkansas	94.1 *(0.7)*	Missouri	88.0 *(0.4)*
New Mexico	90.0 *(0.6)*	Mississippi	93.9 *(0.7)*	New Mexico	88.0 *(0.7)*
Tennessee	89.9 *(0.3)*	Montana	93.8 *(0.9)*	Tennessee	87.9 *(0.4)*
South Dakota	89.8 *(0.7)*	Missouri	93.5 *(0.5)*	South Dakota	87.8 *(0.8)*
Idaho	89.2 *(0.5)*	Indiana	92.9 *(0.6)*	Idaho	87.2 *(0.6)*
South Carolina	89.2 *(0.3)*	Georgia	92.6 *(0.5)*	South Carolina	86.8 *(0.4)*
Arizona	88.7 *(0.3)*	Florida	92.4 *(0.4)*	Nevada	86.6 *(0.6)*
North Carolina	88.7 *(0.3)*	North Dakota	92.2 *(1.5)*	North Carolina	86.6 *(0.3)*
Nevada	88.6 *(0.5)*	South Dakota	92.2 *(1.4)*	Arizona	86.4 *(0.4)*
Alaska	87.8 *(0.8)*	Nevada	92.0 *(0.9)*	Alaska	86.1 *(0.9)*
Wyoming	87.7 *(1.3)*	Utah	91.7 *(0.7)*	Wyoming	85.2 *(1.5)*
Mississippi	87.0 *(0.5)*	Oklahoma	91.4 *(0.6)*	Mississippi	84.6 *(0.6)*
Florida	86.8 *(0.2)*	Arizona	90.8 *(0.6)*	Georgia	84.5 *(0.3)*
Georgia	86.6 *(0.3)*	Alaska	90.6 *(1.3)*	Florida	83.7 *(0.3)*
Oklahoma	85.7 *(0.3)*	Wyoming	89.4 *(1.8)*	Oklahoma	83.2 *(0.4)*
Texas	81.6 *(0.2)*	Texas	87.3 *(0.3)*	Texas	79.2 *(0.3)*

Note: Numbers in thousands; Figures cover civilian noninstitutionalized population in 2019; N/A indicates that data was not available; Z represents or rounds to zero; Margin of error appears in parenthesis and is calculated using replicate weights.
Source: U.S. Census Bureau, American Community Survey, Table HI-05. Health Insurance Coverage Status and Type of Coverage by State and Age for All People: 2019

Covered by Private Health Insurance

All Persons		Under 19 Years		Under 65 Years	
State	Percent	State	Percent	State	Percent
North Dakota	79.1 (1.2)	Utah	78.3 (1.1)	North Dakota	81.1 (1.3)
Utah	78.5 (0.6)	North Dakota	76.2 (2.2)	Utah	80.9 (0.7)
Hawaii	76.1 (0.8)	Rhode Island	73.0 (2.9)	Nebraska	77.9 (0.7)
Minnesota	75.9 (0.4)	New Hampshire	70.9 (2.0)	Hawaii	77.6 (1.0)
New Hampshire	75.6 (1.0)	Minnesota	70.6 (0.9)	New Hampshire	77.6 (1.0)
Nebraska	75.2 (0.7)	Nebraska	69.9 (1.4)	Minnesota	77.1 (0.5)
Virginia	74.6 (0.4)	Wisconsin	69.8 (0.8)	Wisconsin	77.0 (0.5)
Kansas	74.4 (0.6)	Massachusetts	69.7 (1.0)	Rhode Island	76.5 (1.4)
Massachusetts	74.3 (0.4)	Virginia	69.2 (0.9)	Massachusetts	76.3 (0.5)
Wisconsin	74.3 (0.4)	Hawaii	69.1 (1.9)	Kansas	76.2 (0.6)
Maryland	74.0 (0.5)	Kansas	68.7 (1.1)	Virginia	76.1 (0.5)
Rhode Island	73.3 (1.3)	Wyoming	68.1 (3.1)	Iowa	75.0 (0.8)
Iowa	73.2 (0.7)	New Jersey	66.9 (0.7)	Maryland	74.6 (0.6)
District of Columbia	72.6 (1.4)	South Dakota	66.5 (2.0)	South Dakota	74.3 (1.0)
Pennsylvania	71.9 (0.3)	Iowa	66.1 (1.4)	New Jersey	73.9 (0.4)
South Dakota	71.8 (0.9)	Maryland	65.7 (1.1)	District of Columbia	73.8 (1.5)
New Jersey	71.7 (0.4)	Maine	65.6 (2.2)	Colorado	73.5 (0.5)
Wyoming	71.6 (1.6)	Colorado	65.4 (1.0)	Wyoming	73.5 (1.8)
Washington	71.1 (0.5)	Michigan	64.7 (0.7)	Pennsylvania	73.2 (0.3)
Michigan	71.0 (0.4)	Connecticut	64.4 (1.2)	Washington	72.5 (0.5)
Colorado	70.9 (0.5)	Missouri	64.0 (0.9)	Missouri	72.4 (0.5)
Delaware	70.9 (1.4)	Indiana	63.7 (1.0)	Illinois	72.1 (0.4)
Illinois	70.1 (0.4)	Illinois	63.6 (0.7)	Maine	71.9 (0.9)
Idaho	70.0 (0.9)	Ohio	63.5 (0.7)	Connecticut	71.5 (0.7)
Missouri	69.7 (0.5)	Pennsylvania	63.5 (0.7)	Delaware	71.5 (1.6)
Indiana	69.5 (0.5)	Idaho	63.1 (2.0)	Idaho	71.5 (1.1)
Maine	69.5 (0.9)	Oregon	62.8 (1.4)	Indiana	71.4 (0.5)
Connecticut	69.4 (0.6)	Washington	62.5 (1.1)	Michigan	71.2 (0.4)
Ohio	68.9 (0.4)	Nevada	61.8 (1.2)	Ohio	70.8 (0.4)
Vermont	68.8 (1.3)	New York	61.6 (0.6)	Oregon	70.1 (0.7)
Oregon	68.0 (0.6)	Delaware	61.4 (2.8)	Vermont	70.1 (1.5)
New York	67.5 (0.3)	District of Columbia	60.4 (3.6)	New York	69.4 (0.3)
United States	67.4 (0.1)	United States	60.3 (0.2)	United States	69.2 (0.1)
Alabama	66.9 (0.6)	Vermont	60.2 (2.8)	Alabama	68.1 (0.6)
North Carolina	66.6 (0.4)	Tennessee	58.7 (1.1)	Nevada	68.1 (0.7)
Montana	66.3 (0.9)	Alaska	58.2 (2.6)	North Carolina	68.1 (0.4)
South Carolina	66.3 (0.6)	California	57.8 (0.4)	Montana	68.0 (1.1)
Tennessee	66.1 (0.5)	Arizona	57.4 (0.9)	Tennessee	67.9 (0.6)
Georgia	65.8 (0.4)	Montana	57.4 (2.0)	Georgia	67.5 (0.5)
Nevada	65.0 (0.7)	Georgia	57.1 (0.9)	South Carolina	67.4 (0.7)
Alaska	64.8 (1.5)	North Carolina	56.1 (0.8)	California	66.3 (0.3)
California	63.9 (0.2)	South Carolina	56.0 (1.2)	Florida	65.9 (0.4)
Oklahoma	63.9 (0.5)	Alabama	55.5 (1.1)	Alaska	65.2 (1.6)
Kentucky	63.7 (0.6)	Kentucky	55.5 (1.2)	Arizona	64.6 (0.6)
Arizona	62.7 (0.5)	Florida	54.9 (0.7)	Kentucky	64.4 (0.7)
West Virginia	62.6 (1.0)	West Virginia	54.4 (2.1)	Oklahoma	64.3 (0.5)
Florida	62.5 (0.3)	Texas	52.9 (0.5)	Texas	63.3 (0.3)
Texas	61.8 (0.3)	Oklahoma	52.6 (0.9)	West Virginia	62.5 (1.2)
Arkansas	59.3 (0.7)	Louisiana	48.3 (1.2)	Arkansas	60.3 (0.8)
Mississippi	58.7 (0.9)	Arkansas	47.0 (1.5)	Mississippi	59.9 (1.0)
Louisiana	57.8 (0.7)	Mississippi	45.8 (1.6)	Louisiana	58.9 (0.7)
New Mexico	53.7 (0.8)	New Mexico	43.2 (1.6)	New Mexico	53.7 (1.0)

Note: Numbers in thousands; Figures cover civilian noninstitutionalized population in 2019; N/A indicates that data was not available; Z represents or rounds to zero; Margin of error appears in parenthesis and is calculated using replicate weights.
Source: U.S. Census Bureau, American Community Survey, Table HI-05. Health Insurance Coverage Status and Type of Coverage by State and Age for All People: 2019

Covered by Private Health Insurance: Employment-based

All Persons		Under 19 Years		Under 65 Years	
State	Percent	State	Percent	State	Percent
Utah	64.6 (0.7)	North Dakota	66.4 (2.3)	Minnesota	69.8 (0.5)
Hawaii	63.9 (0.9)	Utah	66.2 (1.3)	Wisconsin	69.5 (0.5)
Maryland	63.1 (0.6)	Wisconsin	65.3 (0.8)	New Hampshire	68.8 (1.2)
Massachusetts	63.1 (0.4)	Minnesota	65.2 (0.9)	Utah	68.8 (0.8)
Minnesota	62.6 (0.4)	New Hampshire	64.5 (2.0)	North Dakota	68.3 (1.4)
New Hampshire	62.4 (1.0)	Rhode Island	64.2 (2.9)	Massachusetts	68.1 (0.5)
New Jersey	62.0 (0.4)	Massachusetts	63.8 (0.9)	Iowa	67.6 (0.9)
Wisconsin	61.8 (0.4)	Nebraska	61.3 (1.4)	Nebraska	67.2 (0.8)
North Dakota	61.5 (1.3)	Iowa	60.8 (1.5)	Hawaii	66.9 (1.0)
District of Columbia	61.4 (1.4)	Kansas	60.6 (1.2)	Rhode Island	66.8 (1.6)
Rhode Island	60.7 (1.4)	New Jersey	60.6 (0.7)	Kansas	66.4 (0.7)
Michigan	60.5 (0.3)	Wyoming	59.6 (2.9)	New Jersey	66.4 (0.5)
Iowa	60.1 (0.7)	Michigan	59.4 (0.7)	Maryland	65.6 (0.6)
Nebraska	60.1 (0.7)	Connecticut	59.1 (1.3)	Pennsylvania	65.1 (0.4)
Virginia	60.1 (0.5)	Ohio	58.7 (0.8)	Illinois	64.9 (0.4)
Illinois	59.8 (0.3)	Illinois	58.5 (0.7)	Indiana	64.4 (0.5)
Kansas	59.6 (0.6)	Indiana	58.5 (1.0)	Ohio	64.4 (0.4)
Delaware	59.4 (1.3)	Maine	57.6 (2.2)	Virginia	64.4 (0.5)
Connecticut	59.2 (0.6)	Maryland	57.6 (1.1)	Connecticut	64.2 (0.7)
Ohio	59.1 (0.4)	Pennsylvania	57.6 (0.7)	Michigan	63.7 (0.4)
Pennsylvania	59.1 (0.3)	Virginia	57.5 (0.9)	Washington	63.7 (0.6)
Indiana	58.8 (0.5)	Oregon	56.6 (1.5)	Delaware	63.6 (1.6)
Washington	58.5 (0.5)	Missouri	56.2 (0.9)	Missouri	63.3 (0.6)
Colorado	57.4 (0.5)	Hawaii	56.0 (2.0)	District of Columbia	62.9 (1.5)
Missouri	57.1 (0.5)	Colorado	55.5 (1.1)	Wyoming	62.6 (1.7)
New York	56.9 (0.3)	South Dakota	55.5 (2.3)	Colorado	62.4 (0.6)
Wyoming	55.8 (1.5)	Delaware	54.9 (2.8)	South Dakota	61.8 (1.3)
United States	55.4 (0.1)	Washington	54.9 (1.1)	Maine	61.4 (1.1)
Oregon	55.0 (0.7)	Nevada	53.8 (1.5)	Oregon	61.4 (0.8)
Maine	54.8 (1.0)	Vermont	53.6 (2.7)	Vermont	60.6 (1.5)
Vermont	54.7 (1.2)	Idaho	52.8 (2.0)	New York	60.2 (0.3)
South Dakota	54.4 (1.1)	United States	52.7 (0.2)	United States	60.0 (0.1)
Alaska	54.2 (1.4)	New York	52.3 (0.6)	Nevada	59.4 (0.9)
Georgia	54.2 (0.4)	Tennessee	51.0 (1.1)	Idaho	58.7 (1.2)
Alabama	54.1 (0.6)	West Virginia	50.5 (2.1)	Tennessee	58.4 (0.6)
West Virginia	54.0 (1.0)	Arizona	50.2 (1.0)	Alabama	58.2 (0.7)
Nevada	53.8 (0.8)	California	50.1 (0.5)	Georgia	58.1 (0.5)
Idaho	53.2 (1.0)	Kentucky	49.5 (1.3)	West Virginia	57.4 (1.2)
California	53.0 (0.2)	Georgia	49.0 (0.9)	Kentucky	57.1 (0.7)
Tennessee	53.0 (0.5)	Alabama	48.1 (1.1)	South Carolina	57.0 (0.7)
Kentucky	52.9 (0.6)	South Carolina	47.8 (1.2)	California	56.9 (0.3)
South Carolina	52.5 (0.6)	Montana	47.7 (2.1)	North Carolina	56.7 (0.5)
North Carolina	52.3 (0.4)	North Carolina	46.9 (0.8)	Arizona	56.2 (0.6)
Texas	51.4 (0.3)	District of Columbia	45.9 (3.2)	Alaska	55.0 (1.5)
Oklahoma	50.8 (0.5)	Texas	45.8 (0.5)	Montana	55.0 (1.3)
Arizona	50.6 (0.5)	Alaska	45.7 (2.7)	Oklahoma	54.8 (0.6)
Montana	48.6 (1.1)	Oklahoma	44.7 (0.9)	Texas	54.8 (0.3)
Louisiana	47.6 (0.6)	Florida	43.8 (0.7)	Arkansas	51.4 (0.8)
Arkansas	46.8 (0.7)	Louisiana	42.3 (1.1)	Florida	51.4 (0.4)
Mississippi	46.1 (0.9)	Arkansas	40.2 (1.5)	Louisiana	50.9 (0.7)
Florida	45.8 (0.3)	Mississippi	38.5 (1.7)	Mississippi	50.9 (1.0)
New Mexico	43.7 (0.9)	New Mexico	37.0 (1.7)	New Mexico	46.1 (1.1)

Note: Numbers in thousands; Figures cover civilian noninstitutionalized population in 2019; N/A indicates that data was not available; Z represents or rounds to zero; Margin of error appears in parenthesis and is calculated using replicate weights.
Source: U.S. Census Bureau, American Community Survey, Table HI-05. Health Insurance Coverage Status and Type of Coverage by State and Age for All People: 2019

Covered by Private Health Insurance: Direct Purchase

All Persons			Under 19 Years			Under 65 Years	
State	**Percent**		**State**	**Percent**		**State**	**Percent**
North Dakota	19.0 (1.0)		District of Columbia	13.1 (2.8)		Florida	14.2 (0.3)
Montana	18.5 (0.8)		Utah	11.9 (0.9)		Montana	13.6 (0.8)
South Dakota	17.7 (0.8)		South Dakota	10.5 (1.4)		North Dakota	13.6 (1.0)
Idaho	17.4 (0.7)		New York	10.2 (0.4)		Idaho	12.9 (0.8)
Florida	16.9 (0.2)		Rhode Island	10.0 (1.6)		South Dakota	12.8 (0.9)
Nebraska	16.7 (0.5)		Florida	9.8 (0.4)		Utah	12.5 (0.6)
Wyoming	16.0 (1.2)		Idaho	9.6 (1.2)		Nebraska	12.1 (0.6)
Vermont	15.8 (0.8)		Montana	9.4 (1.3)		District of Columbia	11.7 (1.0)
Kansas	15.6 (0.4)		Nebraska	9.1 (0.9)		Rhode Island	11.7 (0.9)
Rhode Island	15.4 (0.9)		North Dakota	9.1 (1.3)		New York	10.8 (0.2)
Minnesota	15.2 (0.2)		Colorado	7.8 (0.5)		Wyoming	10.8 (1.2)
Maine	15.0 (0.6)		Hawaii	7.8 (1.0)		North Carolina	10.7 (0.3)
Iowa	14.8 (0.3)		California	7.7 (0.2)		Colorado	10.5 (0.3)
Pennsylvania	14.8 (0.2)		Wyoming	7.5 (1.7)		Maine	10.5 (0.7)
Utah	14.8 (0.6)		Missouri	7.3 (0.5)		California	10.4 (0.1)
North Carolina	14.6 (0.3)		Maine	7.2 (1.2)		Vermont	10.3 (0.8)
Wisconsin	14.5 (0.3)		Massachusetts	7.1 (0.5)		Massachusetts	10.2 (0.3)
Oregon	14.3 (0.3)		Nevada	7.0 (0.8)		Kansas	10.1 (0.4)
Massachusetts	14.1 (0.3)		South Carolina	7.0 (0.6)		South Carolina	10.1 (0.4)
New Hampshire	14.1 (0.6)		Kansas	6.9 (0.6)		Hawaii	9.9 (0.7)
South Carolina	14.0 (0.4)		New Jersey	6.9 (0.5)		Alabama	9.7 (0.4)
Delaware	13.6 (0.6)		United States	6.9 (0.1)		United States	9.7 (0.1)
Tennessee	13.5 (0.3)		North Carolina	6.8 (0.4)		Tennessee	9.6 (0.3)
Alabama	13.3 (0.4)		Virginia	6.8 (0.4)		Oregon	9.4 (0.4)
Colorado	13.3 (0.3)		Arizona	6.6 (0.5)		Maryland	9.3 (0.4)
Missouri	13.3 (0.3)		Maryland	6.6 (0.6)		Missouri	9.3 (0.3)
Oklahoma	13.2 (0.3)		Oregon	6.5 (0.6)		Oklahoma	9.3 (0.3)
Virginia	13.2 (0.2)		Tennessee	6.5 (0.5)		Virginia	9.3 (0.3)
Arkansas	13.1 (0.4)		Delaware	6.4 (1.2)		Georgia	9.2 (0.2)
Michigan	13.1 (0.2)		Arkansas	6.2 (0.6)		Pennsylvania	9.2 (0.2)
United States	13.1 (0.1)		Georgia	6.2 (0.4)		Arkansas	9.1 (0.4)
District of Columbia	13.0 (1.0)		Oklahoma	6.2 (0.5)		New Hampshire	9.1 (0.6)
New York	13.0 (0.2)		Pennsylvania	6.1 (0.3)		Michigan	8.9 (0.2)
Hawaii	12.9 (0.7)		Texas	6.1 (0.2)		Wisconsin	8.8 (0.3)
Washington	12.6 (0.2)		Vermont	6.1 (1.1)		Nevada	8.7 (0.4)
Arizona	12.5 (0.3)		Alabama	6.0 (0.6)		New Jersey	8.7 (0.3)
Illinois	12.3 (0.2)		Iowa	5.9 (0.5)		Mississippi	8.6 (0.4)
Maryland	12.3 (0.3)		Michigan	5.9 (0.3)		Texas	8.6 (0.2)
Mississippi	12.3 (0.4)		Washington	5.7 (0.4)		Arizona	8.5 (0.3)
Indiana	12.2 (0.3)		Minnesota	5.6 (0.4)		Connecticut	8.5 (0.3)
California	12.1 (0.1)		Mississippi	5.5 (0.6)		Iowa	8.5 (0.4)
Connecticut	12.0 (0.3)		New Hampshire	5.5 (0.8)		Louisiana	8.4 (0.4)
Georgia	11.8 (0.2)		Connecticut	5.3 (0.4)		Minnesota	8.4 (0.2)
New Jersey	11.8 (0.3)		Illinois	5.3 (0.3)		Delaware	8.3 (0.6)
Kentucky	11.7 (0.3)		Indiana	5.3 (0.4)		Illinois	8.3 (0.2)
Ohio	11.7 (0.2)		Kentucky	5.3 (0.5)		Washington	8.3 (0.3)
Louisiana	11.2 (0.4)		Wisconsin	5.3 (0.3)		Indiana	7.8 (0.3)
Nevada	11.2 (0.4)		Louisiana	5.2 (0.6)		New Mexico	7.6 (0.5)
Texas	10.7 (0.2)		New Mexico	5.2 (0.8)		Kentucky	7.3 (0.3)
New Mexico	10.5 (0.5)		Ohio	5.0 (0.3)		Ohio	7.3 (0.2)
West Virginia	10.2 (0.5)		Alaska	4.7 (1.1)		Alaska	6.4 (0.6)
Alaska	7.4 (0.6)		West Virginia	3.6 (0.7)		West Virginia	5.7 (0.4)

Note: Numbers in thousands; Figures cover civilian noninstitutionalized population in 2019; N/A indicates that data was not available; Z represents or rounds to zero; Margin of error appears in parenthesis and is calculated using replicate weights.
Source: U.S. Census Bureau, American Community Survey, Table HI-05. Health Insurance Coverage Status and Type of Coverage by State and Age for All People: 2019

Covered by Private Health Insurance: TRICARE

All Persons		Under 19 Years		Under 65 Years	
State	Percent	State	Percent	State	Percent
Alaska	9.8 (1.0)	Alaska	13.4 (2.0)	Alaska	9.6 (1.1)
Hawaii	7.8 (0.5)	Hawaii	11.7 (1.2)	Hawaii	7.6 (0.6)
Virginia	7.7 (0.2)	Virginia	8.6 (0.5)	Virginia	6.9 (0.3)
South Carolina	5.0 (0.2)	North Carolina	4.4 (0.3)	South Carolina	3.7 (0.3)
Alabama	4.8 (0.2)	Colorado	4.3 (0.5)	Alabama	3.6 (0.2)
Delaware	4.4 (0.6)	Kansas	4.3 (0.5)	North Carolina	3.6 (0.2)
North Carolina	4.2 (0.2)	Maryland	4.3 (0.4)	North Dakota	3.5 (0.6)
Oklahoma	4.2 (0.2)	Washington	4.3 (0.4)	Colorado	3.4 (0.2)
Washington	4.2 (0.2)	Georgia	4.1 (0.3)	Oklahoma	3.4 (0.3)
Colorado	4.1 (0.2)	Oklahoma	4.1 (0.5)	Washington	3.4 (0.2)
New Mexico	4.1 (0.3)	South Carolina	3.9 (0.4)	Georgia	3.3 (0.2)
Georgia	4.0 (0.2)	North Dakota	3.8 (1.1)	Maryland	3.3 (0.2)
Mississippi	4.0 (0.3)	Montana	3.7 (1.0)	Delaware	3.2 (0.6)
Maryland	3.9 (0.2)	District of Columbia	3.6 (1.6)	Kansas	3.2 (0.3)
North Dakota	3.9 (0.5)	Alabama	3.5 (0.4)	Montana	3.0 (0.5)
Wyoming	3.9 (0.6)	Delaware	3.5 (1.3)	Mississippi	2.9 (0.3)
Kansas	3.8 (0.2)	Mississippi	3.5 (0.6)	New Mexico	2.9 (0.3)
Montana	3.8 (0.4)	Wyoming	3.5 (1.0)	South Dakota	2.9 (0.4)
Tennessee	3.7 (0.2)	Tennessee	3.3 (0.4)	Tennessee	2.9 (0.2)
Florida	3.6 (0.1)	Florida	3.1 (0.3)	Wyoming	2.8 (0.6)
Idaho	3.6 (0.4)	New Mexico	3.1 (0.5)	Florida	2.7 (0.1)
Maine	3.6 (0.4)	Maine	2.9 (0.9)	Nebraska	2.6 (0.3)
Nevada	3.6 (0.3)	South Dakota	2.9 (0.7)	Nevada	2.6 (0.3)
South Dakota	3.6 (0.4)	Nevada	2.7 (0.5)	Idaho	2.5 (0.4)
Arizona	3.4 (0.2)	Nebraska	2.6 (0.4)	Arizona	2.4 (0.2)
Nebraska	3.3 (0.2)	Idaho	2.5 (0.6)	Maine	2.4 (0.4)
Arkansas	3.1 (0.3)	Texas	2.5 (0.2)	Texas	2.3 (0.1)
Texas	2.9 (0.1)	United States	2.5 (Z)	Kentucky	2.2 (0.2)
Kentucky	2.8 (0.2)	Louisiana	2.4 (0.4)	Missouri	2.1 (0.2)
Louisiana	2.7 (0.2)	Arizona	2.3 (0.3)	United States	2.1 (Z)
Missouri	2.7 (0.1)	Arkansas	2.1 (0.4)	Arkansas	2.0 (0.2)
United States	2.7 (Z)	Kentucky	2.1 (0.3)	District of Columbia	2.0 (0.6)
Utah	2.5 (0.2)	Missouri	2.1 (0.3)	Louisiana	2.0 (0.2)
West Virginia	2.5 (0.3)	Vermont	2.1 (0.9)	Utah	1.9 (0.2)
New Hampshire	2.3 (0.3)	West Virginia	2.0 (0.6)	West Virginia	1.8 (0.3)
Vermont	2.3 (0.4)	Utah	1.9 (0.3)	Vermont	1.6 (0.5)
District of Columbia	2.1 (0.5)	California	1.8 (0.1)	New Hampshire	1.5 (0.3)
Oregon	2.1 (0.2)	New Hampshire	1.7 (0.6)	California	1.4 (0.1)
Rhode Island	2.0 (0.3)	Rhode Island	1.7 (0.5)	Oregon	1.4 (0.2)
Iowa	1.8 (0.1)	Indiana	1.5 (0.3)	Indiana	1.3 (0.1)
California	1.7 (Z)	Ohio	1.5 (0.2)	Iowa	1.3 (0.2)
Indiana	1.7 (0.1)	Iowa	1.4 (0.3)	Ohio	1.3 (0.1)
Ohio	1.7 (0.1)	Oregon	1.4 (0.3)	Rhode Island	1.3 (0.3)
Pennsylvania	1.5 (0.1)	Connecticut	1.3 (0.3)	Pennsylvania	1.1 (0.1)
Connecticut	1.4 (0.1)	Minnesota	1.2 (0.2)	Connecticut	1.0 (0.1)
Minnesota	1.4 (0.1)	Pennsylvania	1.2 (0.2)	Illinois	1.0 (0.1)
Wisconsin	1.4 (0.1)	Illinois	1.1 (0.2)	Minnesota	1.0 (0.1)
Michigan	1.3 (0.1)	Michigan	1.0 (0.1)	Wisconsin	1.0 (0.1)
Illinois	1.2 (0.1)	New Jersey	1.0 (0.2)	Michigan	0.9 (0.1)
Massachusetts	1.2 (0.1)	Wisconsin	1.0 (0.1)	Massachusetts	0.8 (0.1)
New Jersey	1.0 (0.1)	Massachusetts	0.9 (0.2)	New Jersey	0.7 (0.1)
New York	0.9 (Z)	New York	0.9 (0.1)	New York	0.7 (Z)

Note: Numbers in thousands; Figures cover civilian noninstitutionalized population in 2019; N/A indicates that data was not available; Z represents or rounds to zero; Margin of error appears in parenthesis and is calculated using replicate weights.

Source: U.S. Census Bureau, American Community Survey, Table HI-05. Health Insurance Coverage Status and Type of Coverage by State and Age for All People: 2019

Covered by Public Health Insurance

All Persons		Under 19 Years		Under 65 Years	
State	**Percent**	**State**	**Percent**	**State**	**Percent**
New Mexico	50.1 (0.8)	New Mexico	57.0 (1.7)	New Mexico	39.8 (1.0)
West Virginia	47.5 (0.8)	Louisiana	51.2 (1.2)	West Virginia	34.6 (1.0)
Louisiana	44.3 (0.5)	Arkansas	51.1 (1.5)	Louisiana	34.5 (0.6)
Arkansas	44.0 (0.6)	Mississippi	51.0 (1.6)	Arkansas	32.9 (0.7)
Kentucky	43.2 (0.5)	West Virginia	47.4 (2.0)	Kentucky	32.2 (0.7)
Vermont	42.0 (1.1)	Alabama	44.7 (1.2)	New York	28.6 (0.3)
Montana	40.6 (0.9)	Kentucky	44.4 (1.2)	Vermont	28.3 (1.4)
New York	39.6 (0.3)	Vermont	43.5 (2.9)	California	28.1 (0.2)
Delaware	39.5 (1.3)	Oklahoma	43.3 (1.0)	Mississippi	28.0 (0.8)
Mississippi	39.4 (0.7)	District of Columbia	42.9 (3.8)	Montana	27.0 (1.1)
Michigan	38.8 (0.3)	California	42.7 (0.4)	Alaska	26.5 (1.5)
Maine	38.6 (0.8)	South Carolina	42.5 (1.2)	District of Columbia	26.3 (1.6)
Oregon	38.5 (0.5)	Montana	42.0 (2.3)	Michigan	26.3 (0.4)
Arizona	38.4 (0.4)	North Carolina	41.4 (0.8)	Oregon	25.6 (0.6)
California	37.8 (0.2)	New York	41.3 (0.7)	Arizona	25.5 (0.5)
Pennsylvania	37.6 (0.2)	Tennessee	40.7 (1.2)	Delaware	25.4 (1.5)
Alabama	37.3 (0.5)	Florida	40.6 (0.7)	Connecticut	25.0 (0.6)
Ohio	37.2 (0.3)	Delaware	39.7 (3.0)	Ohio	24.9 (0.4)
Connecticut	37.1 (0.5)	Georgia	39.2 (0.8)	Alabama	24.7 (0.6)
South Carolina	37.1 (0.4)	Washington	39.0 (1.1)	Massachusetts	24.4 (0.5)
Florida	36.8 (0.2)	Alaska	38.7 (2.7)	Pennsylvania	24.3 (0.3)
Hawaii	36.3 (0.7)	Pennsylvania	38.1 (0.6)	Tennessee	24.1 (0.5)
Rhode Island	36.2 (1.1)	United States	38.1 (0.2)	Washington	23.9 (0.5)
Tennessee	36.2 (0.4)	Oregon	37.6 (1.3)	Rhode Island	23.8 (1.3)
Iowa	36.1 (0.6)	Michigan	37.5 (0.7)	South Carolina	23.8 (0.5)
Massachusetts	36.1 (0.4)	Arizona	37.4 (1.0)	United States	23.6 (0.1)
United States	35.4 (0.1)	Texas	36.9 (0.5)	Iowa	23.4 (0.7)
Alaska	35.2 (1.3)	Connecticut	36.7 (1.3)	Maine	23.3 (1.0)
Washington	35.2 (0.4)	Iowa	36.6 (1.3)	Oklahoma	22.8 (0.4)
North Carolina	34.9 (0.3)	Idaho	36.3 (1.8)	North Carolina	22.5 (0.4)
Oklahoma	34.5 (0.3)	Ohio	36.3 (0.7)	Maryland	22.2 (0.5)
District of Columbia	34.2 (1.4)	Illinois	35.4 (0.7)	Hawaii	21.9 (0.8)
Nevada	33.8 (0.6)	Maine	35.3 (2.1)	Illinois	21.9 (0.3)
Indiana	33.7 (0.3)	Maryland	34.8 (1.0)	Nevada	21.8 (0.7)
Illinois	33.5 (0.3)	Massachusetts	34.6 (1.0)	Indiana	21.7 (0.4)
Maryland	33.5 (0.4)	Hawaii	33.5 (1.7)	Florida	21.1 (0.3)
Wisconsin	33.2 (0.3)	Rhode Island	33.2 (2.5)	Minnesota	20.7 (0.4)
Minnesota	32.9 (0.4)	Indiana	33.1 (0.9)	Georgia	20.6 (0.3)
Idaho	32.5 (0.8)	Nevada	33.0 (1.3)	Colorado	20.5 (0.6)
Missouri	32.2 (0.3)	Missouri	32.7 (1.0)	Idaho	20.0 (0.9)
New Hampshire	32.1 (0.8)	Colorado	32.3 (1.0)	Wisconsin	19.7 (0.4)
New Jersey	31.7 (0.3)	New Jersey	31.5 (0.8)	New Jersey	19.4 (0.4)
Colorado	31.5 (0.5)	Minnesota	31.4 (0.9)	Missouri	18.9 (0.4)
Georgia	31.4 (0.3)	Wisconsin	31.1 (0.8)	Texas	18.6 (0.2)
South Dakota	30.7 (0.9)	Kansas	29.7 (1.1)	Virginia	18.3 (0.4)
Virginia	30.7 (0.3)	South Dakota	29.4 (2.1)	New Hampshire	17.7 (1.0)
Kansas	29.6 (0.4)	Virginia	29.0 (0.9)	South Dakota	17.2 (1.1)
Wyoming	29.2 (0.9)	New Hampshire	28.4 (2.1)	Kansas	16.7 (0.5)
Nebraska	28.3 (0.6)	Nebraska	27.4 (1.5)	Nebraska	15.5 (0.7)
Texas	28.3 (0.2)	Wyoming	24.0 (2.7)	Wyoming	15.1 (1.1)
North Dakota	27.2 (1.0)	North Dakota	20.5 (2.4)	North Dakota	14.6 (1.2)
Utah	20.7 (0.4)	Utah	16.4 (1.0)	Utah	11.1 (0.5)

Note: Numbers in thousands; Figures cover civilian noninstitutionalized population in 2019; N/A indicates that data was not available; Z represents or rounds to zero; Margin of error appears in parenthesis and is calculated using replicate weights.
Source: U.S. Census Bureau, American Community Survey, Table HI-05. Health Insurance Coverage Status and Type of Coverage by State and Age for All People: 2019

Covered by Public Health Insurance: Medicaid

All Persons		Under 19 Years		Under 65 Years	
State	Percent	State	Percent	State	Percent
New Mexico	33.4 (0.8)	New Mexico	56.6 (1.8)	New Mexico	37.0 (0.9)
Louisiana	29.1 (0.5)	Louisiana	50.9 (1.2)	Louisiana	31.6 (0.6)
Arkansas	26.6 (0.6)	Arkansas	50.8 (1.5)	West Virginia	30.0 (1.0)
West Virginia	26.6 (0.8)	Mississippi	50.8 (1.6)	Arkansas	29.1 (0.7)
Kentucky	25.9 (0.6)	West Virginia	46.9 (2.0)	Kentucky	28.3 (0.7)
New York	25.7 (0.3)	Alabama	44.1 (1.2)	New York	26.9 (0.3)
California	25.5 (0.2)	Kentucky	44.0 (1.2)	California	26.4 (0.2)
District of Columbia	24.8 (1.4)	Vermont	43.1 (2.9)	Vermont	25.8 (1.4)
Mississippi	24.0 (0.7)	California	42.2 (0.5)	Mississippi	25.1 (0.8)
Vermont	22.9 (1.1)	South Carolina	42.2 (1.2)	District of Columbia	24.7 (1.6)
Massachusetts	22.0 (0.4)	Montana	41.8 (2.3)	Michigan	23.8 (0.4)
Alaska	21.8 (1.2)	District of Columbia	41.7 (3.8)	Montana	23.6 (1.1)
Connecticut	21.8 (0.6)	Oklahoma	41.6 (1.0)	Connecticut	23.2 (0.6)
Michigan	21.8 (0.3)	New York	41.1 (0.7)	Delaware	23.0 (1.5)
Montana	21.0 (0.9)	North Carolina	41.1 (0.8)	Massachusetts	23.0 (0.5)
Oregon	20.9 (0.5)	Tennessee	40.5 (1.1)	Oregon	23.0 (0.6)
Arizona	20.8 (0.4)	Florida	40.1 (0.7)	Alaska	22.8 (1.4)
Delaware	20.8 (1.1)	Delaware	39.5 (2.9)	Arizona	22.8 (0.5)
Rhode Island	20.4 (1.1)	Washington	38.6 (1.1)	Ohio	22.2 (0.3)
Ohio	20.1 (0.3)	Georgia	38.3 (0.9)	Pennsylvania	22.0 (0.3)
Pennsylvania	20.1 (0.2)	Pennsylvania	37.9 (0.6)	Rhode Island	21.6 (1.2)
United States	19.8 (0.1)	United States	37.6 (0.2)	Washington	21.4 (0.5)
Washington	19.8 (0.4)	Michigan	37.3 (0.7)	Iowa	21.3 (0.7)
Alabama	19.6 (0.5)	Oregon	37.2 (1.3)	Tennessee	21.0 (0.5)
Tennessee	19.6 (0.4)	Alaska	37.1 (2.6)	United States	21.0 (0.1)
Maine	19.5 (0.8)	Arizona	36.5 (1.0)	Alabama	20.7 (0.5)
Iowa	19.4 (0.6)	Connecticut	36.5 (1.4)	Maine	20.2 (0.9)
South Carolina	18.8 (0.4)	Texas	36.4 (0.5)	South Carolina	20.2 (0.5)
Maryland	18.4 (0.4)	Iowa	36.3 (1.3)	Illinois	19.7 (0.3)
Illinois	18.2 (0.3)	Idaho	36.2 (1.8)	Maryland	19.6 (0.5)
Hawaii	18.0 (0.7)	Ohio	36.0 (0.7)	Hawaii	19.5 (0.8)
North Carolina	18.0 (0.3)	Illinois	35.0 (0.7)	North Carolina	19.2 (0.3)
Nevada	17.8 (0.6)	Maine	34.9 (2.1)	Indiana	19.1 (0.4)
Indiana	17.7 (0.4)	Massachusetts	34.4 (1.0)	Minnesota	18.9 (0.4)
Florida	17.3 (0.2)	Maryland	33.9 (1.0)	Nevada	18.9 (0.7)
Minnesota	17.3 (0.4)	Hawaii	33.0 (1.7)	Oklahoma	18.7 (0.4)
Oklahoma	17.3 (0.3)	Nevada	32.8 (1.3)	Colorado	18.1 (0.5)
Georgia	17.2 (0.3)	Rhode Island	32.8 (2.5)	Florida	18.1 (0.3)
Colorado	17.1 (0.5)	Indiana	32.7 (0.9)	Wisconsin	17.6 (0.4)
New Jersey	16.5 (0.3)	Missouri	32.2 (1.0)	Georgia	17.4 (0.3)
Wisconsin	16.5 (0.3)	Colorado	32.0 (1.1)	New Jersey	17.4 (0.4)
Idaho	16.0 (0.7)	Minnesota	31.2 (0.9)	Idaho	17.3 (0.8)
Texas	15.9 (0.2)	New Jersey	31.0 (0.8)	Texas	16.2 (0.2)
Missouri	14.5 (0.3)	Wisconsin	30.7 (0.8)	Missouri	15.6 (0.4)
Virginia	13.6 (0.3)	Kansas	29.4 (1.1)	New Hampshire	14.6 (0.9)
Kansas	13.3 (0.5)	South Dakota	29.0 (2.1)	Virginia	14.5 (0.4)
New Hampshire	13.2 (0.8)	New Hampshire	28.1 (2.1)	Kansas	14.3 (0.5)
South Dakota	13.1 (0.9)	Virginia	27.9 (0.8)	South Dakota	14.2 (1.0)
Nebraska	12.8 (0.6)	Nebraska	27.1 (1.5)	Nebraska	13.4 (0.7)
North Dakota	12.1 (1.0)	Wyoming	23.7 (2.6)	North Dakota	12.4 (1.2)
Wyoming	11.7 (0.9)	North Dakota	20.3 (2.4)	Wyoming	12.3 (1.1)
Utah	9.7 (0.5)	Utah	16.3 (1.0)	Utah	9.8 (0.5)

Note: Numbers in thousands; Figures cover civilian noninstitutionalized population in 2019; N/A indicates that data was not available; Z represents or rounds to zero; Margin of error appears in parenthesis and is calculated using replicate weights.
Source: U.S. Census Bureau, American Community Survey, Table HI-05. Health Insurance Coverage Status and Type of Coverage by State and Age for All People: 2019

Covered by Public Health Insurance: Medicare

All Persons		Under 19 Years		Under 65 Years	
State	Percent	State	Percent	State	Percent
West Virginia	24.3 *(0.3)*	Oklahoma	2.1 *(0.4)*	West Virginia	5.5 *(0.4)*
Maine	23.7 *(0.3)*	Maryland	1.3 *(0.3)*	Kentucky	5.0 *(0.2)*
Florida	22.6 *(0.1)*	Arizona	1.2 *(0.3)*	Arkansas	4.9 *(0.2)*
Vermont	22.5 *(0.4)*	Alaska	1.1 *(0.8)*	Alabama	4.8 *(0.2)*
Delaware	21.6 *(0.3)*	District of Columbia	1.1 *(0.7)*	Mississippi	4.5 *(0.3)*
Montana	21.3 *(0.3)*	Georgia	1.0 *(0.2)*	Maine	4.4 *(0.3)*
Alabama	20.8 *(0.2)*	Rhode Island	0.9 *(0.5)*	Vermont	4.1 *(0.4)*
Arkansas	20.7 *(0.2)*	Virginia	0.9 *(0.2)*	Louisiana	4.0 *(0.2)*
South Carolina	20.7 *(0.2)*	Alabama	0.8 *(0.2)*	Oklahoma	4.0 *(0.2)*
Kentucky	20.5 *(0.2)*	New Jersey	0.8 *(0.1)*	Rhode Island	3.9 *(0.5)*
New Mexico	20.5 *(0.3)*	West Virginia	0.8 *(0.4)*	Michigan	3.7 *(0.1)*
Pennsylvania	20.4 *(0.1)*	California	0.7 *(0.1)*	New Mexico	3.7 *(0.3)*
Hawaii	20.2 *(0.2)*	Florida	0.7 *(0.1)*	South Carolina	3.7 *(0.2)*
New Hampshire	20.2 *(0.3)*	Kentucky	0.7 *(0.2)*	Missouri	3.6 *(0.2)*
Michigan	20.1 *(0.1)*	New Mexico	0.7 *(0.3)*	Tennessee	3.4 *(0.2)*
Arizona	19.7 *(0.2)*	Vermont	0.7 *(0.5)*	Delaware	3.3 *(0.3)*
Mississippi	19.7 *(0.3)*	Indiana	0.6 *(0.1)*	North Carolina	3.3 *(0.1)*
Oregon	19.7 *(0.2)*	Mississippi	0.6 *(0.2)*	Pennsylvania	3.3 *(0.1)*
Rhode Island	19.7 *(0.4)*	Missouri	0.6 *(0.2)*	Florida	3.2 *(0.1)*
Missouri	19.5 *(0.1)*	Texas	0.6 *(0.1)*	Indiana	3.2 *(0.1)*
Ohio	19.1 *(0.1)*	United States	0.6 *(Z)*	New Hampshire	3.2 *(0.3)*
Wisconsin	19.0 *(0.1)*	Wisconsin	0.6 *(0.1)*	Georgia	3.1 *(0.1)*
Iowa	18.9 *(0.2)*	Arkansas	0.5 *(0.2)*	Ohio	3.1 *(0.1)*
North Carolina	18.9 *(0.1)*	Illinois	0.5 *(0.1)*	Montana	3.0 *(0.3)*
Tennessee	18.9 *(0.2)*	Michigan	0.5 *(0.1)*	South Dakota	2.9 *(0.4)*
South Dakota	18.8 *(0.4)*	New York	0.5 *(0.1)*	United States	2.9 *(Z)*
Louisiana	18.7 *(0.2)*	Oregon	0.5 *(0.1)*	Arizona	2.8 *(0.2)*
Oklahoma	18.7 *(0.2)*	Pennsylvania	0.5 *(0.1)*	Maryland	2.8 *(0.2)*
Wyoming	18.6 *(0.4)*	South Carolina	0.5 *(0.1)*	Virginia	2.8 *(0.1)*
Connecticut	18.4 *(0.2)*	Colorado	0.4 *(0.1)*	Idaho	2.7 *(0.3)*
New York	18.1 *(0.1)*	Delaware	0.4 *(0.3)*	Iowa	2.7 *(0.2)*
United States	18.1 *(Z)*	Hawaii	0.4 *(0.2)*	Kansas	2.7 *(0.2)*
Idaho	18.0 *(0.3)*	Iowa	0.4 *(0.2)*	New York	2.7 *(0.1)*
Indiana	18.0 *(0.1)*	Kansas	0.4 *(0.1)*	Oregon	2.7 *(0.2)*
Massachusetts	17.9 *(0.1)*	Louisiana	0.4 *(0.1)*	Wisconsin	2.7 *(0.1)*
Kansas	17.8 *(0.2)*	Maine	0.4 *(0.2)*	Massachusetts	2.6 *(0.1)*
Virginia	17.7 *(0.1)*	Massachusetts	0.4 *(0.1)*	Connecticut	2.5 *(0.2)*
New Jersey	17.6 *(0.1)*	Nebraska	0.4 *(0.2)*	District of Columbia	2.5 *(0.4)*
Nevada	17.5 *(0.2)*	New Hampshire	0.4 *(0.2)*	Illinois	2.5 *(0.1)*
Illinois	17.2 *(0.1)*	North Carolina	0.4 *(0.1)*	New Jersey	2.5 *(0.1)*
Maryland	17.1 *(0.2)*	Ohio	0.4 *(0.1)*	Nevada	2.4 *(0.2)*
Minnesota	17.1 *(0.1)*	South Dakota	0.4 *(0.2)*	Washington	2.4 *(0.1)*
Nebraska	17.1 *(0.2)*	Tennessee	0.4 *(0.1)*	Wyoming	2.4 *(0.4)*
Washington	17.1 *(0.1)*	Washington	0.4 *(0.1)*	Alaska	2.3 *(0.4)*
Georgia	16.4 *(0.1)*	Wyoming	0.4 *(0.2)*	Texas	2.3 *(0.1)*
North Dakota	16.4 *(0.3)*	Idaho	0.3 *(0.2)*	Nebraska	2.2 *(0.2)*
California	15.6 *(0.1)*	Montana	0.3 *(0.2)*	California	2.1 *(0.1)*
Colorado	15.6 *(0.1)*	Nevada	0.3 *(0.1)*	Hawaii	2.0 *(0.2)*
Alaska	14.0 *(0.5)*	Connecticut	0.2 *(0.1)*	Minnesota	2.0 *(0.1)*
Texas	14.0 *(0.1)*	Minnesota	0.2 *(0.1)*	North Dakota	2.0 *(0.3)*
District of Columbia	13.2 *(0.4)*	North Dakota	0.2 *(0.1)*	Colorado	1.9 *(0.1)*
Utah	12.1 *(0.2)*	Utah	0.2 *(0.1)*	Utah	1.4 *(0.1)*

Note: Numbers in thousands; Figures cover civilian noninstitutionalized population in 2019; N/A indicates that data was not available; Z represents or rounds to zero; Margin of error appears in parenthesis and is calculated using replicate weights.
Source: U.S. Census Bureau, American Community Survey, Table HI-05. Health Insurance Coverage Status and Type of Coverage by State and Age for All People: 2019

Covered by Public Health Insurance: VA Care

All Persons		Under 19 Years		Under 65 Years	
State	**Percent**	**State**	**Percent**	**State**	**Percent**
Alaska	4.2 *(0.4)*	Alaska	0.9 *(0.5)*	Alaska	3.1 *(0.4)*
Montana	4.2 *(0.4)*	District of Columbia	0.7 *(1.0)*	Virginia	2.3 *(0.1)*
West Virginia	3.8 *(0.3)*	Virginia	0.7 *(0.1)*	Montana	2.2 *(0.3)*
South Dakota	3.7 *(0.3)*	Iowa	0.3 *(0.2)*	West Virginia	2.2 *(0.3)*
Oklahoma	3.4 *(0.1)*	Kansas	0.3 *(0.2)*	Oklahoma	1.9 *(0.1)*
Wyoming	3.4 *(0.5)*	Maine	0.3 *(0.2)*	Nevada	1.8 *(0.2)*
Maine	3.3 *(0.2)*	West Virginia	0.3 *(0.2)*	South Carolina	1.8 *(0.1)*
North Dakota	3.3 *(0.3)*	Wyoming	0.3 *(0.2)*	South Dakota	1.8 *(0.3)*
South Carolina	3.3 *(0.1)*	Alabama	0.2 *(0.1)*	Arkansas	1.7 *(0.2)*
Arkansas	3.2 *(0.1)*	Arkansas	0.2 *(0.1)*	Colorado	1.7 *(0.1)*
Idaho	3.2 *(0.2)*	Florida	0.2 *(0.1)*	Georgia	1.7 *(0.1)*
New Mexico	3.2 *(0.2)*	Georgia	0.2 *(0.1)*	Maine	1.7 *(0.2)*
Nevada	3.1 *(0.2)*	Hawaii	0.2 *(0.2)*	New Mexico	1.7 *(0.2)*
Arizona	3.0 *(0.1)*	Kentucky	0.2 *(0.1)*	North Carolina	1.7 *(0.1)*
Virginia	3.0 *(0.1)*	Louisiana	0.2 *(0.1)*	Wyoming	1.7 *(0.4)*
Florida	2.9 *(0.1)*	Maryland	0.2 *(0.1)*	Alabama	1.6 *(0.1)*
Oregon	2.9 *(0.1)*	New Mexico	0.2 *(0.2)*	Arizona	1.6 *(0.1)*
North Carolina	2.8 *(0.1)*	North Carolina	0.2 *(0.1)*	Florida	1.6 *(0.1)*
Tennessee	2.8 *(0.1)*	Oklahoma	0.2 *(0.1)*	Idaho	1.6 *(0.2)*
Alabama	2.7 *(0.1)*	Oregon	0.2 *(0.1)*	North Dakota	1.6 *(0.3)*
Kentucky	2.7 *(0.1)*	Rhode Island	0.2 *(0.3)*	Tennessee	1.6 *(0.1)*
Missouri	2.7 *(0.1)*	South Carolina	0.2 *(0.1)*	Hawaii	1.5 *(0.2)*
Nebraska	2.7 *(0.2)*	Texas	0.2 *(Z)*	Oregon	1.5 *(0.1)*
Iowa	2.6 *(0.1)*	United States	0.2 *(Z)*	Washington	1.5 *(0.1)*
New Hampshire	2.6 *(0.2)*	Washington	0.2 *(0.1)*	Kentucky	1.4 *(0.1)*
Colorado	2.5 *(0.1)*	Arizona	0.1 *(0.1)*	Missouri	1.4 *(0.1)*
Delaware	2.5 *(0.2)*	California	0.1 *(Z)*	Texas	1.4 *(0.1)*
Georgia	2.5 *(0.1)*	Colorado	0.1 *(0.1)*	Iowa	1.3 *(0.1)*
Hawaii	2.5 *(0.2)*	Connecticut	0.1 *(0.1)*	Kansas	1.3 *(0.1)*
Vermont	2.5 *(0.2)*	Idaho	0.1 *(0.1)*	Delaware	1.2 *(0.2)*
Washington	2.5 *(0.1)*	Illinois	0.1 *(0.1)*	Louisiana	1.2 *(0.1)*
Kansas	2.4 *(0.1)*	Indiana	0.1 *(0.1)*	Maryland	1.2 *(0.1)*
Mississippi	2.4 *(0.2)*	Massachusetts	0.1 *(0.1)*	Mississippi	1.2 *(0.1)*
Wisconsin	2.4 *(0.1)*	Michigan	0.1 *(0.1)*	Nebraska	1.2 *(0.1)*
Minnesota	2.3 *(0.1)*	Minnesota	0.1 *(Z)*	New Hampshire	1.2 *(0.2)*
Indiana	2.2 *(0.1)*	Mississippi	0.1 *(0.1)*	Ohio	1.2 *(0.1)*
Louisiana	2.2 *(0.1)*	Missouri	0.1 *(0.1)*	United States	1.2 *(Z)*
Ohio	2.2 *(0.1)*	Montana	0.1 *(0.1)*	Indiana	1.1 *(0.1)*
Texas	2.2 *(0.1)*	Nebraska	0.1 *(0.1)*	Vermont	1.1 *(0.2)*
United States	2.2 *(Z)*	Nevada	0.1 *(0.1)*	Wisconsin	1.1 *(0.1)*
Rhode Island	2.1 *(0.2)*	New Jersey	0.1 *(0.1)*	District of Columbia	1.0 *(0.4)*
Michigan	2.0 *(0.1)*	New York	0.1 *(Z)*	Michigan	1.0 *(0.1)*
Pennsylvania	2.0 *(0.1)*	Ohio	0.1 *(0.1)*	Pennsylvania	1.0 *(0.1)*
Maryland	1.9 *(0.1)*	Pennsylvania	0.1 *(Z)*	California	0.9 *(Z)*
Illinois	1.7 *(0.1)*	Tennessee	0.1 *(0.1)*	Minnesota	0.9 *(0.1)*
Connecticut	1.6 *(0.1)*	Utah	0.1 *(0.1)*	Connecticut	0.8 *(0.1)*
California	1.5 *(Z)*	Vermont	0.1 *(0.1)*	Illinois	0.8 *(0.1)*
Utah	1.5 *(0.1)*	Wisconsin	0.1 *(Z)*	Utah	0.8 *(0.1)*
District of Columbia	1.4 *(0.4)*	Delaware	0.0 *(0.0)*	Rhode Island	0.7 *(0.2)*
Massachusetts	1.4 *(0.1)*	New Hampshire	Z *(Z)*	Massachusetts	0.6 *(0.1)*
New York	1.3 *(Z)*	North Dakota	Z *(Z)*	New York	0.6 *(Z)*
New Jersey	1.1 *(0.1)*	South Dakota	Z *(Z)*	New Jersey	0.5 *(Z)*

Note: Numbers in thousands; Figures cover civilian noninstitutionalized population in 2019; N/A indicates that data was not available; Z represents or rounds to zero; Margin of error appears in parenthesis and is calculated using replicate weights.
Source: U.S. Census Bureau, American Community Survey, Table HI-05. Health Insurance Coverage Status and Type of Coverage by State and Age for All People: 2019

Not Covered by Health Insurance at any Time During the Year

All Persons		Under 19 Years		Under 65 Years	
State	Percent	State	Percent	State	Percent
Texas	18.4 (0.2)	Texas	12.7 (0.3)	Texas	20.8 (0.3)
Oklahoma	14.3 (0.3)	Wyoming	10.6 (1.8)	Oklahoma	16.8 (0.4)
Georgia	13.4 (0.3)	Alaska	9.4 (1.3)	Florida	16.3 (0.3)
Florida	13.2 (0.2)	Arizona	9.2 (0.6)	Georgia	15.5 (0.3)
Mississippi	13.0 (0.5)	Oklahoma	8.6 (0.6)	Mississippi	15.4 (0.6)
Wyoming	12.3 (1.3)	Utah	8.3 (0.7)	Wyoming	14.8 (1.5)
Alaska	12.2 (0.8)	Nevada	8.0 (0.9)	Alaska	13.9 (0.9)
Nevada	11.4 (0.5)	North Dakota	7.8 (1.5)	Arizona	13.6 (0.4)
Arizona	11.3 (0.3)	South Dakota	7.8 (1.4)	Nevada	13.4 (0.6)
North Carolina	11.3 (0.3)	Florida	7.6 (0.4)	North Carolina	13.4 (0.3)
Idaho	10.8 (0.5)	Georgia	7.4 (0.5)	South Carolina	13.2 (0.4)
South Carolina	10.8 (0.3)	Indiana	7.1 (0.6)	Idaho	12.8 (0.6)
South Dakota	10.2 (0.7)	Missouri	6.5 (0.5)	South Dakota	12.2 (0.8)
Tennessee	10.1 (0.3)	Montana	6.2 (0.9)	Tennessee	12.1 (0.4)
Missouri	10.0 (0.3)	Mississippi	6.1 (0.7)	Missouri	12.0 (0.4)
New Mexico	10.0 (0.6)	Arkansas	5.9 (0.7)	New Mexico	12.0 (0.7)
Alabama	9.7 (0.3)	Kansas	5.8 (0.7)	Alabama	11.7 (0.3)
Utah	9.7 (0.5)	North Carolina	5.8 (0.4)	Arkansas	10.9 (0.5)
Kansas	9.2 (0.4)	South Carolina	5.8 (0.6)	Kansas	10.9 (0.5)
United States	9.2 (0.1)	Nebraska	5.7 (0.8)	United States	10.8 (0.1)
Arkansas	9.1 (0.4)	New Mexico	5.7 (0.9)	Utah	10.8 (0.6)
Louisiana	8.9 (0.3)	United States	5.7 (0.1)	Louisiana	10.5 (0.4)
Indiana	8.7 (0.3)	Maine	5.6 (1.1)	Indiana	10.3 (0.3)
Montana	8.3 (0.5)	Colorado	5.5 (0.6)	Montana	10.2 (0.7)
Nebraska	8.3 (0.4)	Idaho	5.0 (0.8)	Maine	10.1 (0.7)
Colorado	8.0 (0.3)	Tennessee	5.0 (0.5)	Nebraska	9.8 (0.5)
Maine	8.0 (0.5)	Virginia	4.9 (0.4)	Colorado	9.3 (0.3)
New Jersey	7.9 (0.2)	Delaware	4.8 (1.4)	Virginia	9.3 (0.3)
Virginia	7.9 (0.3)	Ohio	4.8 (0.3)	New Jersey	9.2 (0.3)
California	7.7 (0.1)	Pennsylvania	4.6 (0.3)	California	8.9 (0.1)
Illinois	7.4 (0.2)	Louisiana	4.4 (0.6)	Illinois	8.6 (0.2)
Oregon	7.2 (0.3)	Kentucky	4.3 (0.5)	Oregon	8.6 (0.4)
North Dakota	6.9 (0.7)	New Jersey	4.3 (0.4)	West Virginia	8.3 (0.5)
West Virginia	6.7 (0.4)	Oregon	4.1 (0.6)	Delaware	8.1 (0.8)
Delaware	6.6 (0.6)	Illinois	4.0 (0.3)	North Dakota	8.1 (0.8)
Ohio	6.6 (0.2)	Wisconsin	3.8 (0.3)	Ohio	7.8 (0.2)
Washington	6.6 (0.3)	New Hampshire	3.7 (0.9)	Kentucky	7.7 (0.4)
Kentucky	6.4 (0.3)	California	3.6 (0.2)	Washington	7.7 (0.3)
New Hampshire	6.3 (0.6)	Alabama	3.5 (0.3)	New Hampshire	7.6 (0.7)
Maryland	6.0 (0.3)	Connecticut	3.5 (0.5)	Connecticut	7.0 (0.4)
Connecticut	5.9 (0.3)	West Virginia	3.5 (0.6)	Pennsylvania	7.0 (0.2)
Michigan	5.8 (0.2)	Maryland	3.4 (0.5)	Maryland	6.9 (0.3)
Pennsylvania	5.8 (0.2)	Michigan	3.4 (0.3)	Michigan	6.9 (0.2)
Wisconsin	5.7 (0.2)	Minnesota	3.1 (0.4)	Wisconsin	6.8 (0.3)
New York	5.2 (0.1)	Washington	3.1 (0.3)	New York	6.1 (0.1)
Iowa	5.0 (0.3)	Iowa	2.9 (0.5)	Iowa	6.0 (0.4)
Minnesota	4.9 (0.2)	Hawaii	2.8 (0.7)	Minnesota	5.8 (0.3)
Vermont	4.5 (0.5)	New York	2.4 (0.2)	Vermont	5.6 (0.6)
Hawaii	4.2 (0.4)	Vermont	2.1 (0.7)	Hawaii	5.0 (0.5)
Rhode Island	4.1 (0.6)	District of Columbia	2.0 (0.9)	Rhode Island	4.8 (0.7)
District of Columbia	3.5 (0.6)	Rhode Island	1.9 (0.7)	District of Columbia	3.9 (0.7)
Massachusetts	3.0 (0.2)	Massachusetts	1.5 (0.2)	Massachusetts	3.5 (0.2)

Note: Numbers in thousands; Figures cover civilian noninstitutionalized population in 2019; N/A indicates that data was not available; Z represents or rounds to zero; Margin of error appears in parenthesis and is calculated using replicate weights.
Source: U.S. Census Bureau, American Community Survey, Table HI-05. Health Insurance Coverage Status and Type of Coverage by State and Age for All People: 2019

Managed Care Organizations Ranked by Total Enrollment

State	Total Enrollment	Organization	Plan Type
Alabama	30,000,000	Trinity Health of Alabama	Other
Alabama	502,000	Behavioral Health Systems	PPO
Alabama	90,000	VIVA Health	HMO
Alabama	66,000	North Alabama Managed Care Inc	PPO
Alabama	45,000	Health Choice of Alabama	PPO
Alaska	800,000	Moda Health Alaska	Multiple
Arizona	8,800,000	United Concordia of Arizona	Dental
Arizona	3,500,000	Avesis: Arizona	Multiple
Arizona	1,500,000	Blue Cross & Blue Shield of Arizona	HMO/PPO
Arizona	325,000	Mercy Care Plan/Mercy Care Advantage	Multiple
Arizona	175,000	Arizona Foundation for Medical Care	Multiple
Arizona	130,000	Employers Dental Services	Dental
Arizona	115,000	Health Choice Arizona	HMO
Arizona	50,000	Care1st Health Plan Arizona	HMO
Arkansas	2,000,000	Delta Dental of Arkansas	Dental
Arkansas	650,000	HealthSCOPE Benefits	Other
California	88,000,000	VSP Vision Care	Vision
California	30,000,000	Trinity Health of California	Other
California	12,400,000	Kaiser Permanente	HMO/PPO
California	8,800,000	United Concordia of California	Dental
California	8,500,000	Health Net Federal Services (HNFS)	Multiple
California	7,300,000	Managed Health Network, Inc.	Other
California	6,600,000	Dental Benefit Providers: California	Dental
California	6,100,000	Health Net, Inc.	Multiple
California	5,000,000	eHealthInsurance Services, Inc.	Multiple
California	4,608,507	Kaiser Permanente Southern California	Multiple
California	4,383,328	Kaiser Permanente Northern California	HMO/PPO
California	4,380,000	Blue Shield of California	HMO/PPO
California	3,400,000	Molina Healthcare	Medicare
California	3,000,000	Liberty Dental Plan of California	Dental
California	2,000,000	First Health	PPO
California	2,000,000	L.A. Care Health Plan	HMO
California	758,970	CalOptima	HMO
California	600,000	Health Services Los Angeles County	Other
California	560,000	Partnership HealthPlan of California	Other
California	390,000	Dental Alternatives Insurance Services	Dental
California	346,000	Central California Alliance for Health	HMO
California	338,000	Pacific Health Alliance	PPO
California	335,000	Health Plan of San Joaquin	HMO
California	320,000	Blue Shield of California Promise Health Plan	HMO
California	250,000	Lakeside Community Healthcare Network	HMO
California	245,000	Santa Clara Family Health Foundations Inc	HMO
California	175,000	CenCal Health	HMO
California	150,000	Landmark Healthplan of California	HMO/PPO
California	146,000	Community Health Group	HMO
California	145,000	San Francisco Health Plan	HMO
California	140,000	Alameda Alliance for Health	HMO
California	140,000	Contra Costa Health Services	HMO
California	130,000	Health Plan of San Mateo	HMO
California	128,272	SCAN Health Plan	HMO

State	Total Enrollment	Organization	Plan Type
California	125,000	Premier Access Insurance/Access Dental	PPO
California	123,880	Western Dental & Orthodontics	Dental
California	120,000	Sant, Community Physicians	HMO/PPO
California	97,000	Kern Family Health Care	HMO
California	92,000	Western Health Advantage	HMO
California	90,000	BEST Life and Health Insurance Co.	PPO
California	90,000	Dental Health Services of California	Dental
California	85,000	California Dental Network	Dental
California	49,000	Sharp Health Plan	HMO
California	23,000	Chinese Community Health Plan	HMO
California	18,900	Inter Valley Health Plan	Medicare
California	17,000	Primecare Dental Plan	Dental
California	12,000	Medica HealthCare Plans, Inc	Medicare
California	1,000	On Lok Lifeways	HMO
Colorado	8,800,000	United Concordia of Colorado	Dental
Colorado	636,904	Kaiser Permanente Northern Colorado	HMO
Colorado	636,904	Kaiser Permanente Southern Colorado	HMO/PPO
Colorado	300,000	Boulder Valley Individual Practice Association	PPO
Colorado	236,962	Rocky Mountain Health Plans	HMO/PPO
Colorado	100,000	Denver Health Medical Plan	HMO
Colorado	5,000	Friday Health Plans	HMO
Connecticut	46,500,000	Aetna Inc.	Multiple
Connecticut	30,000,000	Trinity Health of New England	Other
Connecticut	19,000,000	Cigna Corporation	Multiple
Delaware	30,000,000	Trinity Health of Delaware	Other
District of Columbia	100,000	AmeriHealth Caritas District of Columbia	Other
District of Columbia	90,000	Quality Plan Administrators	HMO/PPO
Florida	30,000,000	Trinity Health of Florida	Other
Florida	8,800,000	United Concordia of Florida	Dental
Florida	6,300,000	WellCare Health Plans, Inc.	Medicare
Florida	2,000,000	Liberty Dental Plan of Florida	Dental
Florida	560,000	Simply Healthcare Plans, Inc.	Medicare
Florida	230,000	AvMed	Medicare
Florida	230,000	AvMed Ft. Lauderdale	Medicare
Florida	230,000	AvMed Gainesville	HMO
Florida	135,000	Capital Health Plan	HMO
Florida	111,000	CarePlus Health Plans	Medicare
Florida	108,000	Neighborhood Health Partnership	HMO
Florida	45,000	Preferred Care Partners	Multiple
Florida	42,000	Leon Medical Centers Health Plan	HMO
Georgia	30,000,000	Trinity Health of Georgia	Other
Georgia	8,800,000	United Concordia of Georgia	Dental
Georgia	312,899	Kaiser Permanente Georgia	HMO
Georgia	300,000	Amerigroup Georgia	Medicare
Georgia	68,000	Secure Health PPO Newtork	PPO
Georgia	15,000	Alliant Health Plans	HMO/PPO
Hawaii	252,840	Kaiser Permanente Hawaii	HMO
Hawaii	70,000	AlohaCare	HMO
Idaho	75,000,000	Delta Dental of Idaho	Dental

State	Total Enrollment	Organization	Plan Type
Idaho	30,000,000	Trinity Health of Idaho	Other
Idaho	2,400,000	Regence BlueShield of Idaho	Multiple
Idaho	563,000	Blue Cross of Idaho Health Service, Inc.	HMO/PPO
Illinois	107,000,000	BlueCross BlueShield Association	Medicare
Illinois	30,000,000	Trinity Health of Illinois	Other
Illinois	16,000,000	Health Care Service Corporation (HCSC)	HMO/PPO
Illinois	8,000,000	Blue Cross & Blue Shield of Illinois	HMO/PPO
Illinois	6,200,000	Dental Network of America	Dental
Illinois	3,000,000	Dearborn National	Other
Illinois	2,000,000	Delta Dental of Illinois	Dental
Illinois	2,000,000	Liberty Dental Plan of Illinois	Dental
Illinois	1,500,000	OSF Healthcare	HMO
Illinois	1,100,000	Trustmark	PPO
Illinois	750,000	Meridian Health Plan of Illinois	Medicare
Illinois	475,000	Trustmark Companies	PPO
Illinois	316,000	Preferred Network Access	PPO
Illinois	255,494	Health Alliance Medicare	Medicare
Indiana	79,000,000	Anthem, Inc.	HMO/PPO
Indiana	30,000,000	Trinity Health of Indiana	Other
Indiana	25,900,000	American Specialty Health	HMO
Indiana	13,100,000	Renaissance Dental	Dental
Indiana	1,000,000	CareSource Indiana	Medicare
Indiana	900,000	Anthem Blue Cross & Blue Shield of Indiana	HMO/PPO
Iowa	50,000	Sanford Health Plan	HMO
Iowa	45,000	Medical Associates	HMO
Kansas	26,000,000	CareCentrix: Kansas	HMO
Kansas	5,000,000	PCC Preferred Chiropractic Care	PPO
Kansas	916,695	Blue Cross and Blue Shield of Kansas	HMO
Kansas	400,000	Preferred Mental Health Management	Multiple
Kansas	152,000	ProviDRs Care Network	PPO
Kansas	121,000	Advance Insurance Company of Kansas	Multiple
Kansas	95,000	Health Partners of Kansas	PPO
Kentucky	10,000,000	Humana Inc.	Multiple
Kentucky	1,900,000	CareSource Kentucky	Medicare
Kentucky	1,900,000	CareSource West Virginia	Medicare
Kentucky	300,000	Passport Health Plan	HMO
Louisiana	1,800,000	Blue Cross and Blue Shield of Louisiana	HMO/PPO
Louisiana	80,000	Peoples Health	Medicare
Louisiana	55,000	Vantage Health Plan	HMO
Louisiana	14,000	Vantage Medicare Advantage	Medicare
Maine	3,000,000	Harvard Pilgrim Health Care Maine	Multiple
Maine	936,000	Northeast Delta Dental Maine	Dental
Maine	70,000	Martin's Point HealthCare	Multiple
Maryland	30,000,000	Trinity Health of Maryland	Other
Maryland	12,500,000	Spectera Eyecare Networks	Multiple
Maryland	8,800,000	United Concordia of Maryland	Dental
Maryland	3,500,000	Avesis: Maryland	PPO
Maryland	3,300,000	CareFirst BlueCross BlueShield	HMO/PPO
Maryland	750,552	Kaiser Permanente Mid-Atlantic	Multiple

State	Total Enrollment	Organization	Plan Type
Maryland	250,000	Priority Partners Health Plans	HMO
Maryland	205,000	American Postal Workers Union (APWU) Health Plan	PPO
Maryland	10,000	Denta-Chek of Maryland	Dental
Massachusetts	27,000,000	DentaQuest	Dental
Massachusetts	3,500,000	Avesis: Massachusetts	PPO
Massachusetts	3,000,000	Harvard Pilgrim Health Care Massachusetts	Multiple
Massachusetts	2,900,000	Blue Cross & Blue Shield of Massachusetts	HMO
Massachusetts	1,170,000	Tufts Health Plan	Multiple
Massachusetts	430,000	Allways Health Partners	HMO
Massachusetts	300,000	Medical Center Healthnet Plan	HMO
Massachusetts	250,000	Araz Group	PPO
Massachusetts	200,000	Health New England	HMO/PPO
Michigan	30,000,000	Trinity Health	Other
Michigan	30,000,000	Trinity Health of Michigan	Other
Michigan	14,200,000	Delta Dental of Michigan	Dental
Michigan	8,800,000	United Concordia of Michigan	Dental
Michigan	6,100,000	Blue Cross Blue Shield of Michigan	Multiple
Michigan	4,500,000	DenteMax	Dental
Michigan	900,000	Blue Care Network of Michigan	HMO
Michigan	750,000	Meridian Health Plan	HMO
Michigan	650,000	HAP-Health Alliance Plan: Flint	HMO/PPO
Michigan	650,000	Health Alliance Plan	HMO/PPO
Michigan	596,220	Priority Health	Multiple
Michigan	390,000	SVS Vision	Vision
Michigan	383,000	Health Alliance Medicare	Medicare
Michigan	187,000	Paramount Care of Michigan	HMO/PPO
Michigan	130,000	Golden Dental Plans	Dental
Michigan	90,000	Total Health Care	HMO
Michigan	68,942	Physicians Health Plan of Mid-Michigan	HMO/PPO
Michigan	47,000	Upper Peninsula Health Plan	HMO
Michigan	17,000	ConnectCare	PPO
Michigan	14,000	HAP-Health Alliance Plan: Senior Medicare Plan	Medicare
Minnesota	70,000,000	UnitedHealth Group	Multiple
Minnesota	3,500,000	Avesis: Minnesota	PPO
Minnesota	3,500,000	Healthplex	Dental
Minnesota	2,700,000	Blue Cross & Blue Shield of Minnesota	HMO
Minnesota	150,000	Medica	HMO
Minnesota	147,000	UCare	Multiple
Minnesota	24,176	Hennepin Health	HMO
Mississippi	155,070	Health Link PPO	PPO
Missouri	15,000,000	Centene Corporation	HMO/PPO
Missouri	3,000,000	Liberty Dental Plan of Missouri	Dental
Missouri	1,700,000	Dental Health Alliance	Dental
Missouri	942,000	American Health Care Alliance	PPO
Missouri	60,000	Essence Healthcare	Medicare
Missouri	49,976	Children's Mercy Pediatric Care Network	HMO
Missouri	5,000	Cox Healthplans	HMO/PPO
Montana	300,000	Blue Cross & Blue Shield of Montana	HMO
Nebraska	717,000	Blue Cross & Blue Shield of Nebraska	PPO
Nebraska	615,000	Midlands Choice	PPO

State	Total Enrollment	Organization	Plan Type
Nebraska	150,000	Medica: Nebraska	HMO
Nebraska	54,418	Mutual of Omaha	HMO/PPO
Nevada	2,000,000	Liberty Dental Plan of Nevada	Dental
Nevada	418,000	Health Plan of Nevada	HMO
Nevada	150,000	Nevada Preferred Healthcare Providers	PPO
Nevada	32,000	Hometown Health Plan	Multiple
New Hampshire	3,000,000	Harvard Pilgrim Health Care New Hampshire	HMO/PPO
New Hampshire	936,000	Northeast Delta Dental	Dental
New Jersey	30,000,000	Trinity Health of New Jersey	Other
New Jersey	3,500,000	Horizon Blue Cross Blue Shield of New Jersey	HMO/PPO
New Jersey	3,000,000	Liberty Dental Plan of New Jersey	Dental
New Jersey	1,700,000	Delta Dental of New Jersey	Dental
New Jersey	975,000	CHN PPO	PPO
New Jersey	900,000	QualCare	Multiple
New Jersey	854,000	Horizon NJ Health	PPO
New Jersey	265,000	AmeriHealth New Jersey	HMO/PPO
New Jersey	150,000	Atlanticare Health Plans	HMO/PPO
New Mexico	8,800,000	United Concordia of New Mexico	Dental
New Mexico	550,000	Blue Cross & Blue Shield of New Mexico	HMO/PPO
New Mexico	400,000	Presbyterian Health Plan	HMO
New York	55,000,000	Davis Vision	Vision
New York	30,000,000	Trinity Health of New York	Other
New York	8,800,000	United Concordia of New York	Dental
New York	1,500,000	Excellus BlueCross BlueShield	HMO
New York	1,500,000	Univera Healthcare	HMO
New York	1,326,000	MagnaCare	PPO
New York	700,000	MVP Health Care	Multiple
New York	625,000	Fidelis Care	Multiple
New York	555,405	BlueCross BlueShield of Western New York	HMO/PPO
New York	540,000	Liberty Dental Plan of New York	Dental
New York	500,000	MetroPlus Health Plan	Medicare
New York	400,000	CDPHP Medicare Plan	Medicare
New York	365,000	Independent Health	HMO/PPO
New York	350,000	CDPHP: Capital District Physicians' Health Plan	HMO/PPO
New York	265,000	Affinity Health Plan	HMO
New York	210,000	Nova Healthcare Administrators	Multiple
New York	205,677	Guardian Life Insurance Company of America	HMO/PPO
New York	193,498	BlueShield of Northeastern New York	HMO/PPO
New York	154,162	Aetna Health of New York	HMO/PPO
New York	53,000	GHI Medicare Plan	Medicare
New York	16,000	Elderplan	Medicare
North Carolina	8,800,000	United Concordia of North Carolina	Dental
North Carolina	3,810,000	Blue Cross Blue Shield of North Carolina	HMO/PPO
North Carolina	670,000	MedCost	PPO
North Carolina	40,000	Crescent Health Solutions	PPO
North Carolina	13,000	FirstCarolinaCare	HMO
North Dakota	150,000	Medica: North Dakota	HMO
Ohio	43,000,000	EyeMed Vision Care	Vision
Ohio	30,000,000	Trinity Health of Ohio	Other

17

State	Total Enrollment	Organization	Plan Type
Ohio	1,900,000	CareSource Ohio	Medicare
Ohio	500,000	Aultcare Corporation	HMO/PPO
Ohio	370,000	Ohio Health Choice	PPO
Ohio	300,000	The Dental Care Plus Group	Multiple
Ohio	187,000	Paramount Elite Medicare Plan	Medicare
Ohio	187,000	Paramount Health Care	HMO/PPO
Ohio	144,000	Medical Mutual Services	PPO
Ohio	55,000	MediGold	Medicare
Ohio	52,000	Ohio State University Health Plan Inc.	Multiple
Ohio	26,000	SummaCare Medicare Advantage Plan	Medicare
Ohio	20,000	Prime Time Health Medicare Plan	Medicare
Oklahoma	1,000,000	Delta Dental of Oklahoma	Dental
Oklahoma	830,000	HCSC Insurance Services Company Oklahoma	HMO
Oklahoma	700,000	Blue Cross & Blue Shield of Oklahoma	HMO/PPO
Oklahoma	500,000	CommunityCare	Multiple
Oregon	8,800,000	United Concordia of Oregon	Dental
Oregon	2,400,000	Regence BlueCross BlueShield of Oregon	Multiple
Oregon	2,400,000	Regence BlueCross BlueShield of Utah	Multiple
Oregon	620,848	Kaiser Permanente Northwest	HMO
Oregon	275,000	PacificSource Health Plans	HMO/PPO
Oregon	275,000	PacificSource Health Plans	Multiple
Oregon	250,000	CareOregon Health Plan	Medicare
Oregon	125,000	Managed HealthCare Northwest	PPO
Oregon	54,000	AllCare Health	Medicare
Pennsylvania	30,000,000	Trinity Health of Pennsylvania	Other
Pennsylvania	22,000,000	Value Behavioral Health of Pennsylvania	PPO
Pennsylvania	8,800,000	United Concordia Dental	Dental
Pennsylvania	8,800,000	United Concordia of Pennsylvania	Dental
Pennsylvania	8,000,000	Independence Blue Cross	HMO/PPO
Pennsylvania	5,300,000	Highmark Blue Shield	PPO
Pennsylvania	540,000	Geisinger Health Plan	HMO/PPO
Pennsylvania	265,000	AmeriHealth Pennsylvania	HMO/PPO
Pennsylvania	263,200	Health Partners Plans	Medicare
Pennsylvania	174,309	Valley Preferred	Multiple
Pennsylvania	150,000	UPMC Health Plan	Multiple
Pennsylvania	33,000	South Central Preferred Health Network	PPO
Pennsylvania	2,375	Vale-U-Health	PPO
Puerto Rico	300,000	Medical Card System (MCS)	Multiple
Puerto Rico	180,000	First Medical Health Plan	Multiple
Puerto Rico	126,000	MMM Holdings	Multiple
Rhode Island	70,000,000	CVS Caremark	Other
Rhode Island	1,018,589	Tufts Health Plan: Rhode Island	Multiple
Rhode Island	600,000	Blue Cross & Blue Shield of Rhode Island	HMO
Rhode Island	190,000	Neighborhood Health Plan of Rhode Island	HMO
South Carolina	1,900,000	Delta Dental of South Carolina	Dental
South Carolina	950,000	Blue Cross & Blue Shield of South Carolina	HMO/PPO
South Carolina	330,000	Select Health of South Carolina	HMO
South Carolina	205,000	BlueChoice Health Plan of South Carolina	Multiple
South Carolina	30,000	InStil Health	Medicare
South Dakota	60,000,000	Delta Dental of South Dakota	Dental

State	Total Enrollment	Organization	Plan Type
South Dakota	1,800,000	Wellmark Blue Cross & Blue Shield of South Dakota	Multiple
South Dakota	118,600	DakotaCare	HMO
South Dakota	87,000	First Choice of the Midwest	PPO
South Dakota	63,000	Avera Health Plans	HMO
Tennessee	3,500,000	Blue Cross & Blue Shield of Tennessee	Multiple
Tennessee	518,000	Health Choice LLC	PPO
Tennessee	423,244	Baptist Health Services Group	Other
Texas	8,800,000	United Concordia of Texas	Dental
Texas	6,000,000	Blue Cross & Blue Shield of Texas	HMO/PPO
Texas	5,700,000	HCSC Insurance Services Company Texas	HMO
Texas	5,427,579	USA Managed Care Organization	PPO
Texas	5,000,000	American National Insurance Company	PPO
Texas	3,500,000	Avesis: Texas	PPO
Texas	3,500,000	Galaxy Health Network	PPO
Texas	2,000,000	MHNet Behavioral Health	Multiple
Texas	1,000,000	HealthSmart	PPO
Texas	200,000	Liberty Dental Plan of Texas	Dental
Texas	200,000	Scott & White Health Plan	Multiple
Texas	120,000	Horizon Health Corporation	PPO
Texas	110,000	Community First Health Plans	HMO/PPO
Texas	80,000	Alliance Regional Health Network	PPO
Texas	44,000	Sterling Insurance	Medicare
Texas	42,000	WellCare TexanPlus	Multiple
Texas	22,000	Valley Baptist Health Plan	HMO
Texas	15,000	Seton Healthcare Family	HMO
Texas	1,000	UTMB HealthCare Systems	HMO
Utah	750,000	Intermountain Healthcare	HMO
Utah	177,854	Public Employees Health Program	PPO
Utah	150,000	Opticare of Utah	Vision
Utah	148,000	Altius Health Plans	Multiple
Utah	86,000	University Health Plans	HMO/PPO
Utah	6,000	Emi Health	HMO/PPO
Vermont	930,000	Northeast Delta Dental Vermont	Dental
Vermont	180,000	Blue Cross & Blue Shield of Vermont	PPO
Virginia	68,000,000	Delta Dental of Virginia	Dental
Virginia	24,000,000	Dominion Dental Services	Dental
Virginia	8,800,000	United Concordia of Virginia	Dental
Virginia	7,900,000	Amerigroup	Medicare
Virginia	3,300,000	CareFirst Blue Cross & Blue Shield of Virginia	HMO/PPO
Virginia	2,800,000	Anthem Blue Cross & Blue Shield of Virginia	HMO/PPO
Virginia	551,000	Optima Health Plan	HMO/PPO
Virginia	88,366	MedCost Virginia	PPO
Virginia	30,000	Piedmont Community Health Plan	Multiple
Washington	8,800,000	United Concordia of Washington	Dental
Washington	2,200,000	LifeWise	PPO
Washington	300,000	Community Health Plan of Washington	Multiple
Washington	90,000	Dental Health Services of Washington	Dental
Washington	71,000	Asuris Northwest Health	Multiple
West Virginia	5,300,000	Highmark BCBS West Virginia	PPO
West Virginia	380,000	The Health Plan	HMO/PPO

State	Total Enrollment	Organization	Plan Type
West Virginia	80,000	UniCare West Virginia	HMO/PPO
Wisconsin	1,500,000	EyeQuest	Vision
Wisconsin	340,000	Quartz Health Plan	Multiple
Wisconsin	247,881	Dean Health Plan	Multiple
Wisconsin	205,000	Security Health Plan of Wisconsin	Multiple
Wisconsin	200,000	Care Plus Dental Plans	Dental
Wisconsin	200,000	Wisconsin Physician's Service	Multiple
Wisconsin	150,000	ChiroCare of Wisconsin	PPO
Wisconsin	130,000	Managed Health Services Wisconsin	Other
Wisconsin	119,712	Prevea Health Network	PPO
Wisconsin	118,000	Network Health Plan of Wisconsin	HMO
Wisconsin	80,000	Group Health Cooperative of South Central Wisconsin	HMO
Wisconsin	70,000	Group Health Cooperative of Eau Claire	HMO
Wisconsin	40,000	Health Tradition	HMO
Wisconsin	5,000	Trilogy Health Insurance	PPO
Wyoming	100,000	Blue Cross & Blue Shield of Wyoming	HMO

Managed Care Organizations Ranked by State Enrollment

State	State Enrollment	Organization	Plan Type
Alabama	2,900,000	Blue Cross and Blue Shield of Alabama	HMO/PPO
Alabama	90,000	VIVA Health	HMO
Alabama	45,000	Health Choice of Alabama	PPO
Arizona	1,500,000	Blue Cross & Blue Shield of Arizona	HMO/PPO
Arizona	892,000	Delta Dental of Arizona	Dental
Arizona	325,000	Mercy Care Plan/Mercy Care Advantage	Multiple
Arizona	130,000	Employers Dental Services	Dental
California	4,608,507	Kaiser Permanente Southern California	Multiple
California	4,383,328	Kaiser Permanente Northern California	HMO/PPO
California	4,380,000	Blue Shield of California	HMO/PPO
California	758,970	CalOptima	HMO
California	585,000	First Health	PPO
California	346,000	Central California Alliance for Health	HMO
California	335,000	Health Plan of San Joaquin	HMO
California	250,000	Lakeside Community Healthcare Network	HMO
California	245,000	Santa Clara Family Health Foundations Inc	HMO
California	197,000	Pacific Health Alliance	PPO
California	146,000	Community Health Group	HMO
California	145,000	San Francisco Health Plan	HMO
California	130,000	Health Plan of San Mateo	HMO
California	110,000	Alameda Alliance for Health	HMO
California	92,000	Western Health Advantage	HMO
California	90,074	Kern Family Health Care	HMO
California	49,000	Sharp Health Plan	HMO
California	23,000	Chinese Community Health Plan	HMO
California	12,283	SCAN Health Plan	HMO
California	942	On Lok Lifeways	HMO
Colorado	1,000,000	Delta Dental of Colorado	Dental
Colorado	636,904	Kaiser Permanente Northern Colorado	HMO
Colorado	636,904	Kaiser Permanente Southern Colorado	HMO/PPO
Colorado	236,962	Rocky Mountain Health Plans	HMO/PPO
Connecticut	3,000,000	Trinity Health of New England	Other
District of Columbia	100,000	AmeriHealth Caritas District of Columbia	Other
Florida	230,000	AvMed	Medicare
Florida	230,000	AvMed Ft. Lauderdale	Medicare
Florida	230,000	AvMed Gainesville	HMO
Florida	141,178	Neighborhood Health Partnership	HMO
Florida	135,000	Capital Health Plan	HMO
Florida	111,000	CarePlus Health Plans	Medicare
Florida	42,000	Leon Medical Centers Health Plan	HMO
Georgia	312,899	Kaiser Permanente Georgia	HMO
Georgia	68,000	Secure Health PPO Newtork	PPO
Georgia	15,000	Alliant Health Plans	HMO/PPO
Hawaii	700,000	Hawaii Medical Service Association	HMO/PPO
Hawaii	252,840	Kaiser Permanente Hawaii	HMO

State	State Enrollment	Organization	Plan Type
Idaho	700,000	Trinity Health of Idaho	Other
Idaho	563,000	Blue Cross of Idaho Health Service, Inc.	HMO/PPO
Idaho	151,299	Regence BlueShield of Idaho	Multiple
Illinois	16,000,000	Health Care Service Corporation (HCSC)	HMO/PPO
Illinois	8,000,000	Blue Cross & Blue Shield of Illinois	HMO/PPO
Illinois	3,000,000	Dearborn National	Other
Illinois	1,000,000	Delta Dental of Illinois	Dental
Illinois	316,000	Preferred Network Access	PPO
Illinois	240,000	Meridian Health Plan of Illinois	Medicare
Illinois	220,000	HCSC Insurance Services Company	HMO
Kansas	916,695	Blue Cross and Blue Shield of Kansas	HMO
Kansas	95,000	Health Partners of Kansas	PPO
Kentucky	300,000	Passport Health Plan	HMO
Louisiana	1,800,000	Blue Cross and Blue Shield of Louisiana	HMO/PPO
Louisiana	80,000	Peoples Health	Medicare
Louisiana	55,000	Vantage Health Plan	HMO
Maryland	750,552	Kaiser Permanente Mid-Atlantic	Multiple
Maryland	250,000	Priority Partners Health Plans	HMO
Maryland	205,000	American Postal Workers Union (APWU) Health Plan	PPO
Massachusetts	2,900,000	Blue Cross & Blue Shield of Massachusetts	HMO
Massachusetts	430,000	Allways Health Partners	HMO
Massachusetts	300,000	Medical Center Healthnet Plan	HMO
Massachusetts	200,000	Health New England	HMO/PPO
Massachusetts	160,000	Araz Group	PPO
Michigan	4,500,000	Blue Cross Blue Shield of Michigan	Multiple
Michigan	650,000	HAP-Health Alliance Plan: Flint	HMO/PPO
Michigan	650,000	Health Alliance Plan	HMO/PPO
Michigan	90,000	Total Health Care	HMO
Michigan	68,942	Physicians Health Plan of Mid-Michigan	HMO/PPO
Michigan	47,000	Upper Peninsula Health Plan	HMO
Michigan	36,000	ConnectCare	PPO
Michigan	20,000	Dencap Dental Plans	Dental
Michigan	14,000	HAP-Health Alliance Plan: Senior Medicare Plan	Medicare
Minnesota	2,700,000	Blue Cross & Blue Shield of Minnesota	HMO
Minnesota	245,000	Americas PPO	PPO
Missouri	1,900,000	Delta Dental of Missouri	Dental
Missouri	860,000	American Health Care Alliance	PPO
Missouri	49,976	Children's Mercy Pediatric Care Network	HMO
Missouri	26,000	Med-Pay	Other
Missouri	1,964	Cox Healthplans	HMO/PPO
Missouri	1,500	Dental Source: Dental Health Care Plans	Dental
Montana	300,000	Blue Cross & Blue Shield of Montana	HMO
Nebraska	717,000	Blue Cross & Blue Shield of Nebraska	PPO
Nebraska	28,978	Mutual of Omaha	HMO/PPO
Nevada	150,000	Nevada Preferred Healthcare Providers	PPO

State	State Enrollment	Organization	Plan Type
Nevada	25,576	Health Plan of Nevada	HMO
Nevada	10,000	Hometown Health Plan	Multiple
New Jersey	3,500,000	Horizon Blue Cross Blue Shield of New Jersey	HMO/PPO
New Jersey	900,000	QualCare	Multiple
New Jersey	854,000	Horizon NJ Health	PPO
New Jersey	150,000	Atlanticare Health Plans	HMO/PPO
New Mexico	550,000	Blue Cross & Blue Shield of New Mexico	HMO/PPO
New Mexico	550,000	HCSC Insurance Services Company New Mexico	HMO
New Mexico	468,219	Delta Dental of New Mexico	Dental
New Mexico	400,000	Presbyterian Health Plan	HMO
New York	1,500,000	Univera Healthcare	HMO
New York	928,200	MagnaCare	PPO
New York	625,000	Fidelis Care	Multiple
New York	540,000	Liberty Dental Plan of New York	Dental
New York	500,000	MetroPlus Health Plan	Medicare
New York	365,000	Independent Health	HMO/PPO
New York	350,000	CDPHP: Capital District Physicians' Health Plan	HMO/PPO
New York	265,000	Affinity Health Plan	HMO
New York	197,194	BlueCross BlueShield of Western New York	HMO/PPO
New York	154,162	Aetna Health of New York	HMO/PPO
New York	72,563	BlueShield of Northeastern New York	HMO/PPO
New York	15,000	Elderplan	Medicare
North Carolina	670,000	MedCost	PPO
North Carolina	40,000	Crescent Health Solutions	PPO
North Carolina	13,000	FirstCarolinaCare	HMO
Ohio	370,000	Ohio Health Choice	PPO
Ohio	73,724	SummaCare Medicare Advantage Plan	Medicare
Ohio	55,000	MediGold	Medicare
Ohio	52,000	Ohio State University Health Plan Inc.	Multiple
Ohio	20,000	Prime Time Health Medicare Plan	Medicare
Ohio	5,151	Aultcare Corporation	HMO/PPO
Oklahoma	830,000	HCSC Insurance Services Company Oklahoma	HMO
Oklahoma	700,000	Blue Cross & Blue Shield of Oklahoma	HMO/PPO
Oregon	730,000	Regence BlueCross BlueShield of Oregon	Multiple
Oregon	620,848	Kaiser Permanente Northwest	HMO
Oregon	330,000	Regence BlueCross BlueShield of Utah	Multiple
Oregon	250,000	CareOregon Health Plan	Medicare
Oregon	54,000	AllCare Health	Medicare
Pennsylvania	3,000,000	Independence Blue Cross	HMO/PPO
Pennsylvania	320,000	Gateway Health	HMO
Pennsylvania	174,309	Valley Preferred	Multiple
Pennsylvania	150,000	UPMC Health Plan	Multiple
Pennsylvania	33,000	South Central Preferred Health Network	PPO
Puerto Rico	180,000	First Medical Health Plan	Multiple
Rhode Island	190,000	Neighborhood Health Plan of Rhode Island	HMO
South Carolina	950,000	Blue Cross & Blue Shield of South Carolina	HMO/PPO

State	State Enrollment	Organization	Plan Type
South Carolina	330,000	Select Health of South Carolina	HMO
South Carolina	205,000	BlueChoice Health Plan of South Carolina	Multiple
South Dakota	340,000	Delta Dental of South Dakota	Dental
South Dakota	300,000	Wellmark Blue Cross & Blue Shield of South Dakota	Multiple
South Dakota	63,000	Avera Health Plans	HMO
South Dakota	25,000	First Choice of the Midwest	PPO
South Dakota	24,310	DakotaCare	HMO
Tennessee	3,500,000	Blue Cross & Blue Shield of Tennessee	Multiple
Tennessee	1,400,000	Delta Dental of Tennessee	Dental
Tennessee	518,000	Health Choice LLC	PPO
Texas	6,000,000	Blue Cross & Blue Shield of Texas	HMO/PPO
Texas	5,700,000	HCSC Insurance Services Company Texas	HMO
Texas	3,200,000	Galaxy Health Network	PPO
Texas	1,118,582	USA Managed Care Organization	PPO
Texas	200,000	Liberty Dental Plan of Texas	Dental
Texas	200,000	Scott & White Health Plan	Multiple
Texas	110,000	Community First Health Plans	HMO/PPO
Texas	80,000	Alliance Regional Health Network	PPO
Texas	44,000	Sterling Insurance	Medicare
Texas	12,004	Valley Baptist Health Plan	HMO
Utah	177,854	Public Employees Health Program	PPO
Utah	150,000	Opticare of Utah	Vision
Utah	84,000	Altius Health Plans	Multiple
Utah	65,000	Emi Health	HMO/PPO
Utah	50,000	University Health Plans	HMO/PPO
Vermont	54,023	Blue Cross & Blue Shield of Vermont	PPO
Virginia	2,800,000	Anthem Blue Cross & Blue Shield of Virginia	HMO/PPO
Virginia	2,000,000	Delta Dental of Virginia	Dental
Virginia	551,000	Optima Health Plan	HMO/PPO
Virginia	490,000	Dominion Dental Services	Dental
Virginia	88,366	MedCost Virginia	PPO
Virginia	30,000	Piedmont Community Health Plan	Multiple
Washington	300,000	Community Health Plan of Washington	Multiple
West Virginia	500,000	Highmark BCBS West Virginia	PPO
West Virginia	380,000	The Health Plan	HMO/PPO
Wisconsin	205,000	Security Health Plan of Wisconsin	Multiple
Wisconsin	200,000	Wisconsin Physician's Service	Multiple
Wisconsin	164,700	Managed Health Services Wisconsin	Other
Wisconsin	67,812	Network Health Plan of Wisconsin	HMO
Wisconsin	40,000	Health Tradition	HMO
Wisconsin	15,706	Prevea Health Network	PPO
Wyoming	100,000	Blue Cross & Blue Shield of Wyoming	HMO

HMO/PPO Profiles

ALABAMA

Health Insurance Coverage Status and Type of Coverage by Age

Category	All Persons Number	All Persons %	Under 19 years Number	Under 19 years %	Under 65 years Number	Under 65 years %
Total population	4,823 (2)	100.0 (0.0)	1,154 (5)	100.0 (0.0)	3,988 (5)	100.0 (0.0)
Covered by some type of health insurance	4,354 (13)	90.3 (0.3)	1,114 (7)	96.5 (0.3)	3,523 (14)	88.3 (0.3)
Covered by private health insurance	3,228 (27)	66.9 (0.6)	641 (13)	55.5 (1.1)	2,716 (26)	68.1 (0.6)
Employer-based	2,607 (30)	54.1 (0.6)	556 (13)	48.1 (1.1)	2,322 (29)	58.2 (0.7)
Direct purchase	640 (19)	13.3 (0.4)	69 (7)	6.0 (0.6)	386 (18)	9.7 (0.4)
TRICARE	231 (11)	4.8 (0.2)	40 (4)	3.5 (0.4)	142 (10)	3.6 (0.2)
Covered by public health insurance	1,797 (24)	37.3 (0.5)	516 (14)	44.7 (1.2)	985 (23)	24.7 (0.6)
Medicaid	947 (22)	19.6 (0.5)	509 (14)	44.1 (1.2)	827 (20)	20.7 (0.5)
Medicare	1,003 (10)	20.8 (0.2)	9 (2)	0.8 (0.2)	192 (9)	4.8 (0.2)
VA Care	132 (6)	2.7 (0.1)	2 (1)	0.2 (0.1)	62 (5)	1.6 (0.1)
Not covered at any time during the year	469 (13)	9.7 (0.3)	40 (4)	3.5 (0.3)	465 (13)	11.7 (0.3)

Note: Numbers in thousands; Figures cover civilian noninstitutionalized population in 2019; N/A indicates that data was not available; Z represents or rounds to zero; Margin of error appears in parenthesis and is calculated using replicate weights.
Source: U.S. Census Bureau, American Community Survey, Table HI-05. Health Insurance Coverage Status and Type of Coverage by State and Age for All People: 2019

Alabama

1 Aetna Health of Alabama
151 Farmington Avenue
Hartford, CT 06156
Toll-Free: 800-872-3862
www.aetna.com
Subsidiary of: CVS Health / Aetna Inc.
For Profit Organization: Yes

Healthplan and Services Defined
PLAN TYPE: PPO
Model Type: Network
Plan Specialty: Behavioral Health, Lab, PBM, Radiology
Benefits Offered: Behavioral Health, Dental, Disease Management, Long-Term Care, Physical Therapy, Podiatry, Prescription, Psychiatric, Vision, Wellness, Life, LTD, STD

Type of Coverage
Commercial, Supplemental Medicare, Student health

Type of Payment Plans Offered
POS, FFS

Geographic Areas Served
Statewide

Key Personnel
Market Pres., GA & Gulf . . . . Cynthia Follmer

2 Ascension At Home
St Vincent's Home Health & Hospice
1400 Urban Center Drive, Suite 240
Birmingham, AL 35242
Phone: 205-313-2800
ascensionathome.com
Subsidiary of: Ascension
Non-Profit Organization: Yes

Healthplan and Services Defined
PLAN TYPE: Other
Plan Specialty: Disease Management
Benefits Offered: Dental, Disease Management, Home Care, Wellness, Ambulance & Transportation; Nursing Service; Short-and-long-term care management planning; Hospice

Geographic Areas Served
Texas, Alabama, Indiana, Kansas, Michigan, Mississippi, Oklahoma, Wisconsin

Key Personnel
President. . . . . David Grams
Chair/CEO . . . . James A. Deal

3 Behavioral Health Systems
2 Metroplex Drive
Suite 500
Birmingham, AL 35209
Toll-Free: 800-245-1150
www.behavioralhealthsystems.com
For Profit Organization: Yes
Year Founded: 1989
Total Enrollment: 502,000

Healthplan and Services Defined
PLAN TYPE: PPO
Plan Specialty: Behavioral Health
Benefits Offered: Behavioral Health, Prescription, Psychiatric, Wellness, Worker's Compensation, EAP, Drug Testing

Geographic Areas Served
Nationwide

Network Qualifications
Minimum Years of Practice: 5
Pre-Admission Certification: Yes

Peer Review Type
Utilization Review: Yes
Case Management: Yes

Publishes and Distributes Report Card: Yes

Accreditation Certification
AAAHC, TJC, URAC, CARF
Utilization Review, Pre-Admission Certification, Quality Assurance Program

Key Personnel
Founder/Chairman/CEO. . . . . Deborah L. Stephens
President, Safety First . . . . Danny Cooner
EVP/Chief Clinical Off. . . . . Kyle Strange
SVP/Chief Finanial Off. . . . . Tina Cannon
Medical Director. . . . . William Patterson, MD
EVP/Chief Marketing Off. . . . . Shannon Flanagan
Corp. VP, Business Dev. . . . . Jeff Hill
Public & Corp. Relations . . . . Shannon Flanagan
205-443-5483

Specialty Managed Care Partners
State of Alabama, Drummond Co, MTD Products
Enters into Contracts with Regional Business Coalitions: Yes
Employers Coalition on Healthcare Options (ECHO), Louisiana Business Group on Health (LBGH), Louisiana Health Care Alliance (LHCA)

4 Blue Cross and Blue Shield of Alabama
450 Riverchase Parkway East
Birmingham, AL 35244
Toll-Free: 888-267-2955
www.bcbsal.org
Year Founded: 1936
State Enrollment: 2,900,000

Healthplan and Services Defined
PLAN TYPE: HMO/PPO
Model Type: IPA
Plan Specialty: Behavioral Health, Dental, Lab
Benefits Offered: Behavioral Health, Dental, Physical Therapy, Prescription, Wellness

Type of Coverage
Commercial, Individual, Medicare, Supplemental Medicare

Geographic Areas Served
Statewide

Accreditation Certification
URAC

Key Personnel
President/CEO . . . . Tim Vines

5 Bright Health Alabama
219 N 2nd Street
Suite 401
Minneapolis, MN 55401
Toll-Free: 844-667-5502
Phone: 833-356-1182
brighthealthplan.com
Year Founded: 2016
Number of Primary Care Physicians: 1,500

Healthplan and Services Defined
PLAN TYPE: HMO
Benefits Offered: Wellness

Geographic Areas Served
Statewide

Key Personnel
President/CEO . . . . G. Mike Mikan
Chief Financial Officer . . . . Cathy Smith

6 Health Choice of Alabama
P.O. Box: 382408
Birmingham, AL 35238
Phone: 205-939-7714
Fax: 205-730-2863
info@healthchoiceppo.com
www.healthchoiceofalabama.com
Subsidiary of: St. Vincent's Hospital
Non-Profit Organization: Yes
Year Founded: 1984
Number of Affiliated Hospitals: 90
Number of Primary Care Physicians: 6,200
Total Enrollment: 45,000
State Enrollment: 45,000

Healthplan and Services Defined
PLAN TYPE: PPO
Model Type: Group, Network
Plan Specialty: Chiropractic
Benefits Offered: Chiropractic

Type of Coverage
Commercial

Type of Payment Plans Offered
POS, DFFS, FFS

Geographic Areas Served
Statewide

Specialty Managed Care Partners
Aetna, Superien, MNHO

7 Humana Health Insurance of Alabama
8213 Highway 72 West
Suite C
Madison, AL 35758
Toll-Free: 800-942-0605
Phone: 256-755-3282
Fax: 256-430-3468
www.humana.com
Secondary Address: 2204 Lakeshore Drive, Suite 100, Birmingham, AL 35209, 205-879-7374
Subsidiary of: Humana Inc.
For Profit Organization: Yes

Healthplan and Services Defined
PLAN TYPE: HMO/PPO
Model Type: Network
Plan Specialty: Dental, Vision
Benefits Offered: Dental, Vision, Life, LTD, STD

Type of Coverage
Commercial, Medicare, Medicaid

Geographic Areas Served
Statewide

Accreditation Certification
URAC, NCQA, CORE

Key Personnel
Market VP, GA/AL . . . . John Dammann

8 North Alabama Managed Care Inc
290 Cochran Road SW
Building 700
Huntsville, AL 35824
Toll-Free: 800-636-2624
Phone: 256-532-2755
Fax: 256-532-2756
alabamappo@namci.com
www.namci.com
Mailing Address: P.O. Box: 18788, Hunstville, AL 35804
Non-Profit Organization: Yes
Year Founded: 1991
Number of Affiliated Hospitals: 100
Number of Primary Care Physicians: 13,000
Total Enrollment: 66,000

Healthplan and Services Defined
PLAN TYPE: PPO
Model Type: Network
Plan Specialty: Group Health
Benefits Offered: Behavioral Health, Chiropractic, Physical Therapy, Podiatry, Psychiatric, Vision, PPO Network; Radiology; Durable Medical Equipment; Chemical Dependency Recovery Facilities; Kidney Dialysis Centers

Type of Coverage
Commercial, Individual

Type of Payment Plans Offered
Combination FFS & DFFS

Geographic Areas Served
North Alabama: Colbert, Cullman, Franklin, Jackson, Lauderdale, Lawrence, Limestone, Madison, Marshall, Morgan and Winston

Subscriber Information
Average Subscriber Co-Payment:
  Primary Care Physician: Varies by plan
  Nursing Home: Varies

Network Qualifications
Pre-Admission Certification: Yes

Key Personnel
Executive Director . . . . Sherree Clark
  256-532-2765
  sherree.clark@namci.com
Operations Manager . . . . Debbie Brumbeloe
  256-532-2754
  debbie.brumbeloe@namci.com

Specialty Managed Care Partners
Enters into Contracts with Regional Business Coalitions: Yes
ECHO

Employer References
Huntsville HospitalSunshine Homes

9 Trinity Health of Alabama
Mercy LIFE
2900 Springhill Avenue
Mobile, AL 36607
Toll-Free: 855-367-6562
Phone: 251-287-8427
www.trinity-health.org
Secondary Address: 20555 Victor Parkway, Livonia, MI 48152-7018, 734-343-1000
Subsidiary of: Trinity Health
Non-Profit Organization: Yes
Year Founded: 2013
Number of Affiliated Hospitals: 92
Number of Primary Care Physicians: 7,500
Total Enrollment: 30,000,000

Healthplan and Services Defined
  PLAN TYPE: Other
  Benefits Offered: Disease Management, Home Care, Long-Term Care, Physical Therapy, Psychiatric, Hospice programs, PACE (Program of All Inclusive Care for the Elderly), occupational therapy

Geographic Areas Served
Gulf Coast region

Key Personnel
Executive Director . . . . Michael A. Slubowski
Chief Operating Officer . . . . Benjamin R. Carter

10 UnitedHealthcare of Alabama
33 Inverness Center Parkway
Suite 350
Birmingham, AL 35242
Toll-Free: 888-545-5205
Phone: 205-437-8500
www.uhc.com
Subsidiary of: UnitedHealth Group
For Profit Organization: Yes
Year Founded: 1991

Healthplan and Services Defined
  PLAN TYPE: HMO/PPO
  Model Type: Network
  Plan Specialty: Behavioral Health, Dental, Disease Management, PBM, Vision
  Benefits Offered: Behavioral Health, Dental, Disease Management, Long-Term Care, Prescription, Vision, Wellness, AD&D, Life, LTD, STD

Type of Coverage
Commercial, Individual, Medicare, Supplemental Medicare, Medicaid, Family, Military, Veterans, Group

Geographic Areas Served
Statewide

Accreditation Certification
NCQA

Key Personnel
CEO, GA/AL Health Plans . . . . Junior Harewood

11 VIVA Health
417 20th Street N
Suite 100
Birmingham, AL 35203
Toll-Free: 888-294-7780
Phone: 205-558-7474
www.vivahealth.com
Secondary Address: 2107b Eastern Boulevard, Montgomery, AL 36117, 800-633-1542
Year Founded: 1995
Number of Affiliated Hospitals: 70
Total Enrollment: 90,000
State Enrollment: 90,000

Healthplan and Services Defined
  PLAN TYPE: HMO
  Other Type: Medicare
  Plan Specialty: Medicare
  Benefits Offered: Dental, Prescription, Medicare

Type of Coverage
Medicare, Supplemental Medicare

Geographic Areas Served
Statewide

Key Personnel
Chief Executive Officer . . . . Patrick Tsang
Chief Operating Officer . . . . Cardwell Feagin

ALASKA

Health Insurance Coverage Status and Type of Coverage by Age

Category	All Persons Number	All Persons %	Under 19 years Number	Under 19 years %	Under 65 years Number	Under 65 years %
Total population	706 *(2)*	100.0 *(0.0)*	190 *(2)*	100.0 *(0.0)*	617 *(3)*	100.0 *(0.0)*
Covered by some type of health insurance	620 *(6)*	87.8 *(0.8)*	172 *(3)*	90.6 *(1.3)*	531 *(7)*	86.1 *(0.9)*
Covered by private health insurance	457 *(10)*	64.8 *(1.5)*	111 *(5)*	58.2 *(2.6)*	402 *(10)*	65.2 *(1.6)*
Employer-based	382 *(10)*	54.2 *(1.4)*	87 *(5)*	45.7 *(2.7)*	339 *(10)*	55.0 *(1.5)*
Direct purchase	52 *(4)*	7.4 *(0.6)*	9 *(2)*	4.7 *(1.1)*	39 *(4)*	6.4 *(0.6)*
TRICARE	69 *(7)*	9.8 *(1.0)*	26 *(4)*	13.4 *(2.0)*	59 *(6)*	9.6 *(1.1)*
Covered by public health insurance	248 *(10)*	35.2 *(1.3)*	74 *(5)*	38.7 *(2.7)*	164 *(9)*	26.5 *(1.5)*
Medicaid	154 *(9)*	21.8 *(1.2)*	71 *(5)*	37.1 *(2.6)*	141 *(9)*	22.8 *(1.4)*
Medicare	99 *(3)*	14.0 *(0.5)*	2 *(1)*	1.1 *(0.8)*	14 *(3)*	2.3 *(0.4)*
VA Care	29 *(3)*	4.2 *(0.4)*	2 *(1)*	0.9 *(0.5)*	19 *(2)*	3.1 *(0.4)*
Not covered at any time during the year	86 *(6)*	12.2 *(0.8)*	18 *(2)*	9.4 *(1.3)*	85 *(6)*	13.9 *(0.9)*

Note: Numbers in thousands; Figures cover civilian noninstitutionalized population in 2019; N/A indicates that data was not available; Z represents or rounds to zero; Margin of error appears in parenthesis and is calculated using replicate weights.
Source: U.S. Census Bureau, American Community Survey, Table HI-05. Health Insurance Coverage Status and Type of Coverage by State and Age for All People: 2019

Alaska

12 Aetna Health of Alaska
151 Farmington Avenue
Hartford, CT 06156
Toll-Free: 800-872-3862
www.aetna.com
Subsidiary of: CVS Health / Aetna Inc.
For Profit Organization: Yes

Healthplan and Services Defined
PLAN TYPE: PPO
Other Type: POS
Model Type: Network
Plan Specialty: Behavioral Health, EPO, Lab, PBM, Radiology
Benefits Offered: Behavioral Health, Dental, Disease Management, Long-Term Care, Physical Therapy, Podiatry, Prescription, Psychiatric, Vision, Wellness, Life, LTD, STD

Type of Coverage
Commercial, Supplemental Medicare, Student health

Type of Payment Plans Offered
POS, FFS

Geographic Areas Served
Statewide

Subscriber Information
Average Monthly Fee Per Subscriber
(Employee + Employer Contribution):
Employee Only (Self): Varies
Employee & 2 Family Members: Varies
Average Annual Deductible Per Subscriber:
Employee Only (Self): Varies
Employee & 2 Family Members: Varies
Average Subscriber Co-Payment:
Primary Care Physician: Varies
Prescription Drugs: Varies

Key Personnel
Chief Network Officer.................John J. Wagner

13 Moda Health Alaska
601 West 5th Avenue
Suite 305
Alaska, AK 99501
Toll-Free: 877-605-3229
medical@modahealth.com
www.modahealth.com
Mailing Address: P.O. Box 40384, Portland, OR 97240-0384
Subsidiary of: Moda Health Plan, Inc.
Year Founded: 1955
Total Enrollment: 800,000

Healthplan and Services Defined
PLAN TYPE: Multiple
Other Type: PPO, POS, Dental
Plan Specialty: Dental
Benefits Offered: Chiropractic, Dental, Disease Management, Home Care, Inpatient SNF, Physical Therapy, Podiatry, Prescription, Psychiatric, Vision, Wellness

Type of Coverage
Commercial, Individual, Medicare

Subscriber Information
Average Monthly Fee Per Subscriber
(Employee + Employer Contribution):
Employee Only (Self): Varies
Medicare: Varies
Average Annual Deductible Per Subscriber:
Employee Only (Self): Varies
Medicare: Varies
Average Subscriber Co-Payment:
Primary Care Physician: Varies
Non-Network Physician: Varies
Prescription Drugs: Varies
Hospital ER: Varies
Home Health Care: Varies
Home Health Care Max. Days/Visits Covered: Varies
Nursing Home: Varies
Nursing Home Max. Days/Visits Covered: Varies

Accreditation Certification
URAC

Key Personnel
Chief Executive Officer..................Robert Gootee
President................William Johnson, MD, MBA
Senior Vice President................Robin Richardson
Senior Vice President....................Scott Loftin

14 Premera Blue Cross Blue Shield of Alaska
3800 Centerpoint Drive
Suite 940
Anchorage, AK 99503
Toll-Free: 800-508-4722
www.premera.com/ak/visitor
Secondary Address: P.O. 91060, Seattle, WA 98111-9160
Subsidiary of: Premera
For Profit Organization: Yes
Year Founded: 1952
Number of Primary Care Physicians: 3,300

Healthplan and Services Defined
PLAN TYPE: PPO
Other Type: EPO
Model Type: Network
Plan Specialty: Dental, Vision
Benefits Offered: Behavioral Health, Dental, Disease Management, Home Care, Inpatient SNF, Long-Term Care, Prescription, Vision, Wellness, Life, LTD, STD

Type of Coverage
Commercial, Individual, Medicare, Supplemental Medicare

Geographic Areas Served
Alaska and Washington, excluding Clark County

Accreditation Certification
AAAHC, URAC, TJC

Key Personnel
SVP.....................................Jim Grazko
Media Contact.....................Courtney Wallace
425-381-8470
courtney.wallace@premera.com

15 UnitedHealthcare of Alaska
5995 Plaza Drive
Cypress, CA 90630
Toll-Free: 888-545-5205
Phone: 714-952-1121
www.uhc.com
Subsidiary of: UnitedHealth Group
For Profit Organization: Yes

Healthplan and Services Defined
  PLAN TYPE: HMO/PPO
  Model Type: Network
  Plan Specialty: Behavioral Health, Dental, Disease Management, PBM, Vision
  Benefits Offered: Behavioral Health, Dental, Disease Management, Long-Term Care, Prescription, Vision, Wellness, Life, LTD, STD

Type of Coverage
  Commercial, Individual, Medicare, Supplemental Medicare, Medicaid, Family, Group

Geographic Areas Served
  Statewide. Alaska is covered by the California Branch

ARIZONA

Health Insurance Coverage Status and Type of Coverage by Age

Category	All Persons Number	All Persons %	Under 19 years Number	Under 19 years %	Under 65 years Number	Under 65 years %
Total population	7,166 *(3)*	100.0 *(0.0)*	1,744 *(5)*	100.0 *(0.0)*	5,871 *(4)*	100.0 *(0.0)*
Covered by some type of health insurance	6,357 *(23)*	88.7 *(0.3)*	1,583 *(11)*	90.8 *(0.6)*	5,073 *(23)*	86.4 *(0.4)*
Covered by private health insurance	4,490 *(37)*	62.7 *(0.5)*	1,002 *(16)*	57.4 *(0.9)*	3,793 *(33)*	64.6 *(0.6)*
Employer-based	3,629 *(39)*	50.6 *(0.5)*	875 *(17)*	50.2 *(1.0)*	3,298 *(36)*	56.2 *(0.6)*
Direct purchase	898 *(22)*	12.5 *(0.3)*	115 *(8)*	6.6 *(0.5)*	499 *(19)*	8.5 *(0.3)*
TRICARE	242 *(11)*	3.4 *(0.2)*	40 *(4)*	2.3 *(0.3)*	138 *(10)*	2.4 *(0.2)*
Covered by public health insurance	2,750 *(30)*	38.4 *(0.4)*	652 *(18)*	37.4 *(1.0)*	1,499 *(30)*	25.5 *(0.5)*
Medicaid	1,492 *(31)*	20.8 *(0.4)*	637 *(18)*	36.5 *(1.0)*	1,336 *(30)*	22.8 *(0.5)*
Medicare	1,413 *(11)*	19.7 *(0.2)*	20 *(5)*	1.2 *(0.3)*	163 *(10)*	2.8 *(0.2)*
VA Care	212 *(7)*	3.0 *(0.1)*	3 *(1)*	0.1 *(0.1)*	92 *(6)*	1.6 *(0.1)*
Not covered at any time during the year	809 *(23)*	11.3 *(0.3)*	161 *(10)*	9.2 *(0.6)*	798 *(23)*	13.6 *(0.4)*

Note: Numbers in thousands; Figures cover civilian noninstitutionalized population in 2019; N/A indicates that data was not available; Z represents or rounds to zero; Margin of error appears in parenthesis and is calculated using replicate weights.
Source: U.S. Census Bureau, American Community Survey, Table HI-05. Health Insurance Coverage Status and Type of Coverage by State and Age for All People: 2019

Arizona

16 Aetna Health of Arizona
151 Farmington Avenue
Hartford, CT 06156
Toll-Free: 800-872-3862
www.aetna.com
Subsidiary of: CVS Health / Aetna Inc.
For Profit Organization: Yes
Year Founded: 1988

Healthplan and Services Defined
  PLAN TYPE: HMO/PPO
  Other Type: POS
  Model Type: Network
  Plan Specialty: Behavioral Health, Dental, Lab, PBM, Vision, Radiology
  Benefits Offered: Behavioral Health, Dental, Disease Management, Long-Term Care, Physical Therapy, Podiatry, Prescription, Psychiatric, Vision, Wellness, Life, LTD, STD

Type of Coverage
  Commercial, Supplemental Medicare, Catastrophic, Student health

Type of Payment Plans Offered
  POS, Capitated, Combination FFS & DFFS

Geographic Areas Served
  Statewide

Network Qualifications
  Minimum Years of Practice: 2
  Pre-Admission Certification: Yes

Peer Review Type
  Utilization Review: Yes

Publishes and Distributes Report Card: Yes

Accreditation Certification
  NCQA

Specialty Managed Care Partners
  Behavioral Health, Prescription, Dental, Vision

17 Aetna Medicaid Administrators LLC
4500 E Cotton Center Boulevard
Phoenix, AZ 85040
Phone: 602-659-1100
www.aetnabetterhealth.com
Subsidiary of: CVS Health / Aetna Inc.
For Profit Organization: Yes

Healthplan and Services Defined
  PLAN TYPE: HMO/PPO
  Model Type: Network
  Plan Specialty: Behavioral Health, Vision, Worker's Compensation, Programs for needy families
  Benefits Offered: Behavioral Health, Long-Term Care, Psychiatric, Vision, Worker's Compensation, LTD, STD

Type of Coverage
  Commercial, Medicaid

Geographic Areas Served
  Regional plans under the Aetna Better Health brand in California, Florida, Illinois, Kentucky, Louisiana, Maryland, Michigan, New Jersey, New York, Ohio, Pennsylvania, Texas, Virginia, and West Virginia

Key Personnel
  Chief Medical Officer .... Linda Kurian

18 AHCCCS/Medicaid
1 East Washington Street
Suite 1700
Phoenix, AZ 85004
Toll-Free: 800-348-4058
www.uhc.com
Subsidiary of: UnitedHealth Group
For Profit Organization: Yes

Healthplan and Services Defined
  PLAN TYPE: Other
  Other Type: Medicaid
  Model Type: Network
  Benefits Offered: Dental, Disease Management, Prescription, Vision, Wellness

Type of Coverage
  Medicaid

Geographic Areas Served
  Available in Apache, Cochise, Coconino, Graham, Greenlee, La Paz, Maricopa, Mohave, Navajo, Pima, Santa Cruz, Yavapai, Yuma

Key Personnel
  CEO, UnitedHealthcare .... Brian Thompson
  Chief Medical Officer............... Anne Docimo, MD
  Chief Operating Officer................... Krista Nelson
  Chief Financial Officer.................... Jeff Putnam

19 Allwell from Arizona Complete Health
P.O. Box 10420
Van Nuys, AZ 91410
Toll-Free: 800-977-7522
allwell.azcompletehealth.com
Subsidiary of: Centene Corporation
For Profit Organization: Yes

Healthplan and Services Defined
  PLAN TYPE: Medicare
  Model Type: Network
  Benefits Offered: Dental, Prescription

Type of Coverage
  Medicare, Supplemental Medicare, Medicare Advantage

Geographic Areas Served
  Pima, Cochise, Santa Cruz, Pinal, Yuma, Gila, Graham, Greenlee, and La Paz counties

20 Ambetter from Arizona Complete Health
Tempe, AZ 85281
Toll-Free: 866-918-4450
ambetter.azcompletehealth.com

Subsidiary of: Centene Corporation
For Profit Organization: Yes

Healthplan and Services Defined
 PLAN TYPE: Other
 Model Type: Network
 Plan Specialty: Lab
 Benefits Offered: Behavioral Health, Disease Management, Physical Therapy, Prescription, Wellness, Maternity and newborn care

Type of Coverage
 Health Insurance Marketplace

Geographic Areas Served
 Maricopa and Pima counties

---

21 Arizona Complete Health
Tempe, AZ 85281
Toll-Free: 888-788-4408
www.azcompletehealth.com
Subsidiary of: Centene Corporation
For Profit Organization: Yes
Year Founded: 2005

Healthplan and Services Defined
 PLAN TYPE: Other
 Model Type: Network
 Benefits Offered: Dental, Prescription

Type of Coverage
 Medicaid

Geographic Areas Served
 Cochise, Graham, Greenlee, La Paz, Pima, Pinal, Santa Cruz, Yuma, Maricopa, and Gila counties, plus San Carlos Apache Reservation and Tohono O'odham Nation

---

22 Arizona Foundation for Medical Care
19420 N 59th Ave
Suite B221
Glendale, AZ 85308-6888
Toll-Free: 800-624-4277
Phone: 602-252-4042
info@azfmc.com
www.azfmc.com
Non-Profit Organization: Yes
Year Founded: 1969
Number of Affiliated Hospitals: 77
Number of Primary Care Physicians: 4,516
Total Enrollment: 175,000

Healthplan and Services Defined
 PLAN TYPE: Multiple
 Other Type: HMO, PPO, POS, EPO
 Model Type: Group, Network
 Plan Specialty: Chiropractic, Disease Management, EPO, Worker's Compensation, PPO, POS, Medical Management, Case Management, Utilization Management, Wellness Services, 24/7 Nurse Line
 Benefits Offered: Disease Management, Wellness, Maternity Management
 Offers Demand Management Patient Information Service: Yes

 DMPI Services Offered: 24-Hour Nurse Care Line

Type of Coverage
 Commercial, Individual, Indemnity

Type of Payment Plans Offered
 POS

Geographic Areas Served
 Statewide

Network Qualifications
 Pre-Admission Certification: Yes

Peer Review Type
 Utilization Review: Yes
 Case Management: Yes

Accreditation Certification
 TJC, URAC, NCQA

Key Personnel
 Director of Operations . . . . Kerry Kovaleski
 Executive Vice President . . . . Tracey Mitchell

Specialty Managed Care Partners
 American Health Holding

---

23 Avesis: Arizona
10400 N 25th Avenue
Suite 200
Phoenix, AZ 85012
Toll-Free: 855-214-6777
www.avesis.com
Secondary Address: Executive Office, 10324 S Dilfield Road, Owings Mills, MD 21117, 800-643-1132
Subsidiary of: Guardian Life Insurance Company
Year Founded: 1978
Number of Primary Care Physicians: 25,000
Total Enrollment: 3,500,000

Healthplan and Services Defined
 PLAN TYPE: Multiple
 Model Type: Network
 Plan Specialty: Dental, Vision, Hearing, Medicare/Medicaid
 Benefits Offered: Dental, Vision

Type of Coverage
 Commercial, Medicare, Supplemental Medicare, Medicaid

Type of Payment Plans Offered
 POS, Capitated, Combination FFS & DFFS

Geographic Areas Served
 Statewide

Publishes and Distributes Report Card: Yes

Accreditation Certification
 AAAHC
 TJC Accreditation

Key Personnel
 Chief Executive Officer . . . . Sean Slovenski

24 Banner - University Care Advantage
2701 E Elvira Road
Tuscon, AZ 85756
Toll-Free: 877-874-3930
www.banneruca.com
Subsidiary of: Banner Health - University of Arizona Health Plans

Healthplan and Services Defined
PLAN TYPE: HMO
Benefits Offered: Chiropractic, Dental, Podiatry, Prescription, Vision, Wellness

Type of Coverage
Medicare

Geographic Areas Served
Cochise, Gila, Graham, Greenlee, La Paz, Maricopa, Pima, Pinal, Santa Cruz, and Yuma counties

25 Banner - University Family Care
2701 E Elvira Road
Tuscon, AZ 85756
Toll-Free: 833-516-1007
www.banneruca.com
Subsidiary of: Banner Health - University of Arizona Health Plans

Healthplan and Services Defined
PLAN TYPE: Medicare
Benefits Offered: Dental, Disease Management, Long-Term Care, Prescription, Wellness, Child wellness

Type of Coverage
Medicare

Geographic Areas Served
Cochise, Gila, Graham, Greenlee, La Paz, Maricopa, Pima, Pinal, Santa Cruz, and Yuma counties

26 Blue Cross & Blue Shield of Arizona
2444 West Las Palmaritas Drive
Phoenix, AZ 85021
Phone: 602-864-4100
www.azblue.com
Secondary Address: Flagstaff Customer Service Officer, 1500 E Cedar Avenue, Suite 56, Flagstaff, AZ 86004
Non-Profit Organization: Yes
Year Founded: 1939
Number of Affiliated Hospitals: 65
Number of Primary Care Physicians: 1,611
Total Enrollment: 1,500,000
State Enrollment: 1,500,000

Healthplan and Services Defined
PLAN TYPE: HMO/PPO
Model Type: Network
Benefits Offered: Behavioral Health, Chiropractic, Dental, Prescription, Wellness, STD

Type of Coverage
Commercial, Individual, Indemnity, Supplemental Medicare

Geographic Areas Served
Statewide

Accreditation Certification
URAC
TJC Accreditation, Medicare Approved, Utilization Review, Pre-Admission Certification, State Licensure, Quality Assurance Program

Key Personnel
President/CEO . . . . Pam D. Kehaly
Chairman of the Board . . . . Richard H. Kehaly
Chief Medical Officer . . . . Cara Christ, MD, MS
Chief Operating Officer . . . . Paige Rothermel
Chief Admin. Officer . . . . Deanna Salazar
Chief Marketing Officer . . . . Lori Turner
CFO/Chief Risk Officer . . . . Mark El-Tawil

27 Care1st Health Plan Arizona
1870 W Rio Salado Parkway
Phoenix, AZ 85281
Toll-Free: 866-560-4042
Phone: 602-778-1800
Fax: 602-778-1863
www.care1staz.com/az
Subsidiary of: WellCare Health Plans
For Profit Organization: Yes
Year Founded: 2003
Total Enrollment: 50,000

Healthplan and Services Defined
PLAN TYPE: HMO
Benefits Offered: Disease Management, Wellness

Type of Coverage
Medicare

Geographic Areas Served
Maricopa County and Pima County

Accreditation Certification
NCQA

Key Personnel
Plan President . . . . Scott Cummings
Director, Operations . . . . Brent Ratterree
VP, Finance . . . . Deena Sigel
Medical Director . . . . Ed Fess, MD

28 CareCentrix: Arizona
7740 N 16th Street
Suite 100
Phoenix, AZ 85020
Toll-Free: 800-808-1902
carecentrix.com
Year Founded: 1996
Number of Primary Care Physicians: 8,000

Healthplan and Services Defined
PLAN TYPE: HMO
Benefits Offered: Home Care, Physical Therapy, Durable Medical Equipment, Occupational & Respiratory Therapy, Orthotics, Prosthetics

Key Personnel
Dir., Network Management . . . . David L. Chartrand

29 Cigna HealthCare of Arizona
25500 N Norterra Drive
Building B
Phoenix, AZ 85085
Toll-Free: 800-997-1654
www.cigna.com
Secondary Address: 5310 E High Street, Suite 200, Phoenix, AZ 85054, 480-426-6700
Subsidiary of: Cigna Corporation
For Profit Organization: Yes

Healthplan and Services Defined
PLAN TYPE: HMO
Other Type: POS
Model Type: IPA, Network
Benefits Offered: Behavioral Health, Chiropractic, Complementary Medicine, Disease Management, Home Care, Inpatient SNF, Long-Term Care, Physical Therapy, Podiatry, Prescription, Psychiatric, Transplant, Vision, Wellness

Type of Coverage
Commercial, Individual, Medicare

Type of Payment Plans Offered
POS

Accreditation Certification
NCQA

Key Personnel
Market President. . . . . Kim Shepard

30 Cigna Medical Group
25500 N Norterra Drive
Phoenix, AZ 85085
Toll-Free: 800-356-0665
www.cigna.com/cmgaz
Subsidiary of: Cigna HealthCare of Arizona / Cigna Corporation
For Profit Organization: Yes
Year Founded: 1971

Healthplan and Services Defined
PLAN TYPE: HMO
Model Type: Staff
Plan Specialty: Primary care, pediatrics
Benefits Offered: Podiatry, Prescription, Vision, After-Hours Nurseline, General Surgery, Hearing, Ophthalmology, Outpatient Surgery

Key Personnel
President/General Manager . . . . Jeff Holt

31 Delta Dental of Arizona
5656 West Talavi Boulevard
Glendale, AZ 85306
Toll-Free: 800-352-6132
Phone: 602-938-3131
www.deltadentalaz.com
Mailing Address: P.O. Box 43000, Phoenix, AZ 85080-3000
Non-Profit Organization: Yes
Year Founded: 1972
State Enrollment: 892,000

Healthplan and Services Defined
PLAN TYPE: Dental
Other Type: Vision
Model Type: Network
Plan Specialty: Dental, Vision
Benefits Offered: Dental, Vision

Type of Coverage
Commercial, Individual, Indemnity

Type of Payment Plans Offered
FFS

Geographic Areas Served
Statewide

Accreditation Certification
NCQA

Key Personnel
President & CEO . . . . Allan Allford
VP, Financial Officer . . . . Mark Anderson
VP, Business Development . . . . Brad Clothier
VP of Operations. . . . . Craig Livesay
VP of Marketing & Comm. . . . . Scott Pederson
General Counsel . . . . Leslie Hess

32 Employers Dental Services
3430 E Sunrise
Suite 160
Tuscon, AZ 85718
Toll-Free: 800-722-9772
Phone: 520-696-4343
edscs@principal.com
www.employersdental.com
Subsidiary of: Principal Financial Group
Year Founded: 1974
Owned by an Integrated Delivery Network (IDN): Yes
Number of Primary Care Physicians: 1,340
Total Enrollment: 130,000
State Enrollment: 130,000

Healthplan and Services Defined
PLAN TYPE: Dental
Model Type: Group, Individual
Plan Specialty: Dental, Vision
Benefits Offered: Dental, Prescription, Vision, Prepaid

Type of Coverage
DHMO, Orthodontic

Geographic Areas Served
Arizona Statewide

Peer Review Type
Utilization Review: Yes
Case Management: Yes

Accreditation Certification
Utilization Review, Quality Assurance Program

33 Health Choice Arizona
410 N 44th Street
Suite 920
Phoenix, AZ 85008
Toll-Free: 800-322-8670
Phone: 480-968-6866
comments@healthchoiceaz.com
www.healthchoiceaz.com
Subsidiary of: Blue Cross Blue Shield of Arizona
For Profit Organization: Yes
Year Founded: 1990
Number of Affiliated Hospitals: 4
Number of Primary Care Physicians: 132
Total Enrollment: 115,000

Healthplan and Services Defined
PLAN TYPE: HMO
Model Type: IPA
Plan Specialty: Services to AHCCCS members
Benefits Offered: Behavioral Health, Dental, Disease Management, Prescription, Wellness, Care Coordination, Maternal Child Health

Type of Coverage
Medicaid, Managed Medicaid

Geographic Areas Served
Apache, Coconino, Gila, Maricopa, Mohave, Navajo, Pinal, and Yavapai counties

Network Qualifications
Pre-Admission Certification: Yes

Peer Review Type
Utilization Review: Yes
Second Surgical Opinion: Yes
Case Management: Yes

Accreditation Certification
URAC
Utilization Review

Key Personnel
CEO . . . . Shawn Nau
   928-214-9321
   shawn.nau@steward.org
Chief Operating Officer. . . . . Troy Smith
VP, Operations . . . . Diana Alvarez
   480-350-2237
   diana.alvarez@steward.org

34 Health Net of Arizona
1230 W Washington Street
Suite 401
Tempe, AZ 85281
Toll-Free: 877-878-7983
Phone: 520-376-1680
www.healthnet.com

Subsidiary of: Centene Corporation
For Profit Organization: Yes

Healthplan and Services Defined
PLAN TYPE: HMO
Model Type: Network
Plan Specialty: Behavioral Health

Type of Coverage
Commercial, Individual, Medicare, Supplemental Medicare

Geographic Areas Served
Statewide

35 Humana Health Insurance of Arizona
2231 E Camelback Road
Suite 400
Phoenix, AZ 85016
Toll-Free: 800-889-0301
Phone: 602-760-1700
www.humana.com
Subsidiary of: Humana Inc.
For Profit Organization: Yes
Year Founded: 1984

Healthplan and Services Defined
PLAN TYPE: HMO/PPO
Model Type: IPA
Benefits Offered: Dental, Disease Management, Prescription, Transplant, Vision, Wellness, Life, LTD, STD

Type of Coverage
Commercial, Individual, Medicare, Medicaid

Type of Payment Plans Offered
POS, Combination FFS & DFFS

Geographic Areas Served
Apache, Cochise, Coconino, Gila, Graham, Greenlee, La Paz, Maricipa, Mohave, Navajo, Pima, Pinal, Santa Cruz, Yavapai, Yuma counties

Peer Review Type
Utilization Review: Yes
Second Surgical Opinion: Yes
Case Management: Yes

Publishes and Distributes Report Card: Yes

Accreditation Certification
URAC, NCQA, CORE
TJC Accreditation

Key Personnel
Market VP . . . . Brian Sullivan

Specialty Managed Care Partners
Enters into Contracts with Regional Business Coalitions: Yes

36 Magellan Complete Care of Arizona
4800 North Scottdale Road
Suite 4400
Scottsdale, AZ 85251
Toll-Free: 800-424-5891
www.mccofaz.com
Subsidiary of: Magellan Health

For Profit Organization: Yes

Healthplan and Services Defined
  PLAN TYPE: Other
  Plan Specialty: Behavioral Health
  Benefits Offered: Behavioral Health, Psychiatric

Type of Coverage
  Medicaid, Specialty plan for individuals with

Geographic Areas Served
  Maricopa, Gila, and Pinal counties

Key Personnel
  Media Contact.......................... Lilly Ackley
    860-507-1923
    ackleyl@magellanhealth.com
  Investor Contact .... Joe Bogdan
    860-507-1910
    jbogdan@magellanhealth.com

---

37 Magellan Health
4800 N Scottsdale Road
Suite 4400
Scottsdale, AZ 85251
MagellanHealthComInquiries@magellanhealth.com
www.magellanhealth.com
For Profit Organization: Yes

Healthplan and Services Defined
  PLAN TYPE: Other
  Plan Specialty: ASO, Behavioral Health, Diagnostic imaging
    & specialty pharma services
  Benefits Offered: Behavioral Health, Long-Term Care,
    Prescription

Type of Coverage
  Medicare, Medicaid

Key Personnel
  Chief Executive Officer .... Barry M. Smith
  Chief Financial Officer .... Jonathan N. Rubin
  General Counsel .... Daniel N. Gregoire
  Human Resources................. Caskie Lewis-Clapper
  Chief Technology Officer .... Srini Koushik

---

38 Magellan Rx Management
4800 N Scottsdale Road
Suite 4400
Scottsdale, AZ 85251
www.magellanrx.com
Subsidiary of: Magellan Health
For Profit Organization: Yes

Healthplan and Services Defined
  PLAN TYPE: Other
  Other Type: PBM
  Plan Specialty: PBM

Key Personnel
  President & CEO..................... Mostafa Kamal
  VP, Account Management .... Barbie Hoglund

---

39 Mercy Care Plan/Mercy Care Advantage
4350 East Cotton Center Boulevard
Building D
Phoenix, AZ 85040
Toll-Free: 800-624-3879
Phone: 602-263-3000
www.mercycareaz.org
Subsidiary of: Southwest Catholic Health Network
Non-Profit Organization: Yes
Year Founded: 1985
Total Enrollment: 325,000
State Enrollment: 325,000

Healthplan and Services Defined
  PLAN TYPE: Multiple
  Other Type: HMO, Medicare
  Model Type: Group
  Benefits Offered: Disease Management, Long-Term Care,
    Prescription, Wellness

Type of Coverage
  Medicare, Medicaid

Geographic Areas Served
  Cochise, Gila, Graham, Greenlee, La Paz, Maricopa, Pima,
  Pinal, Santa Cruz, Yavapai, Yuma counties

Key Personnel
  President/CEO .... Lorry Bottrill
  Chief Operations Officer .... Brad Hargens
  Chief Medical Officer .... Gagandeep Singh, MD

---

40 NIA Magellan
4800 N Scottsdale Road
Suite 4400
Scottsdale, AZ 85251
Toll-Free: 877-NIA-9762
www.niahealthcare.com
Subsidiary of: Magellan Health
For Profit Organization: Yes
Year Founded: 1995

Healthplan and Services Defined
  PLAN TYPE: Other
  Plan Specialty: Radiology, Radiology benefits management

Key Personnel
  Chief Medical Officer............... Michael J. Pentecost
  Dir., Business Dev. .... Justin Beck

---

41 Outlook Benefit Solutions
1550 E McKellips Road
Suite 112
Mesa, AZ 85203
Toll-Free: 800-342-7188
Phone: 480-461-9001
Fax: 480-461-9021
customerservice@outlookvision.com
www.outlookvision.com
Year Founded: 1990
Federally Qualified: Yes

Healthplan and Services Defined
 PLAN TYPE: Vision
 Plan Specialty: Vision, Discount program
 Benefits Offered: Prescription, Vision, Hearing

Type of Coverage
 Commercial, Individual

Geographic Areas Served
 Available nationwide, except for AK, CT, MT, RI, VT and WA

---

42 Pivot Health
14300 N Northsight Boulevard
Suite 220
Scottsdale, AZ 85260
Toll-Free: 866-566-2707
pivothealth.com
Year Founded: 2015

Healthplan and Services Defined
 PLAN TYPE: Other
 Other Type: Supplemental

Type of Coverage
 Short-term; Supplemental; Zero Dedu

Geographic Areas Served
 Alabama, Arizona, Arkansas, the District of Columbia, Florida, Georgia, Illinois, Indiana, Iowa, Kentucky, Michigan, Mississippi, Nebraska, Ohio, Oklahoma, Pennsylvania, Tennessee, Texas, Virginia, West Virginia, and Wisconsin

Key Personnel
 Chief Executive Officer . . . . Jeff Smedsrud
 VP of Sales & Marketing . . . . Kyle Dietz

---

43 Preferred Therapy Providers
23460 North 19th Avenue
Suite 250
Phoenix, AZ 85027
Toll-Free: 800-664-5240
Phone: 623-869-9101
www.preferredtherapy.com
For Profit Organization: Yes
Year Founded: 1992
Physician Owned Organization: No
Federally Qualified: No
Number of Referral/Specialty Physicians: 3,000

Healthplan and Services Defined
 PLAN TYPE: HMO/PPO
 Model Type: Network
 Plan Specialty: Physical, Occupational, Speech Therapies
 Benefits Offered: Physical Therapy, Ocupational Therapy, Speech Therapy
 Offers Demand Management Patient Information Service: No

Type of Coverage
 Commercial

Geographic Areas Served
 35 states

Network Qualifications
 Pre-Admission Certification: No

Publishes and Distributes Report Card: No

Accreditation Certification
 NCQA, AAPPO

Key Personnel
 President . . . . Steven Allred
 Marketing/Comms. Manager . . . . Cathy Stell
 Contracting/Network Dev. . . . . Debbie Rutherford

Specialty Managed Care Partners
 Enters into Contracts with Regional Business Coalitions: No

---

44 SilverScript Insurance Company
Toll-Free: 833-537-3385
silverscript.com
Subsidiary of: Aetna Medicare
Year Founded: 2006

Healthplan and Services Defined
 PLAN TYPE: Medicare
 Plan Specialty: Medicare Part D
 Benefits Offered: Prescription

Type of Coverage
 Medicare

Geographic Areas Served
 SilverScript Choice: Nationwide and the District of Columbia; SilverScript Plus: Nationwide and the District of Columbia, except Alaska

Key Personnel
 President/CEO. . . . . Todd Meek

---

45 Total Dental Administrators
2800 N 44th Street
Suite 500
Phoenix, AZ 85008
Toll-Free: 888-422-1995
Fax: 602-266-1948
www.tdadental.com
Secondary Address: 6985 Union Park Center, Suite 675, Salt Lake City, UT 84047
Subsidiary of: Blue Cross Blue Shield of South Carolina

Healthplan and Services Defined
 PLAN TYPE: Dental
 Plan Specialty: PPO, Prepaid
 Benefits Offered: Dental, Vision

Type of Coverage
 Indemnity

Key Personnel
 President/CEO . . . . Jeremy Spencer

46 TriWest Healthcare Alliance

P.O. Box 42049
Phoenix, AZ 85080-2049
Toll-Free: 877-226-8749
Phone: 602-564-2000
triwest@triwest.com
www.triwest.com
Subsidiary of: Health Care Service Corporation
For Profit Organization: Yes
Year Founded: 1996

Healthplan and Services Defined
PLAN TYPE: Other
Model Type: Network
Plan Specialty: Behavioral Health
Benefits Offered: Behavioral Health, Inpatient SNF, Prescription, Outpatient, Limited Newborn Care

Type of Coverage
Individual, Administrator of Community Care Net

Geographic Areas Served
VA Region 3, VA Region 5A, VA Region 5B, VA Region 6

Key Personnel
President & CEO . . . . David McIntyre, Jr.
Chief Financial Officer. . . . . Elizabeth Dodd
CAO . . . . James Griffith
VP, Human Capital . . . . Jeanne Ong
Chief Planning Officer. . . . . Julie A. Townsend
SVP, Strategic Comm. . . . . Donna Hoffmeier
Chief Medical Officer. . . . . James L. Robbins, MD

47 United Concordia of Arizona

2198 E Camelback Road
Suite 260
Phoenix, AZ 85016
Phone: 602-667-2200
www.unitedconcordia.com
For Profit Organization: Yes
Year Founded: 1971
Number of Primary Care Physicians: 104,000
Total Enrollment: 8,800,000

Healthplan and Services Defined
PLAN TYPE: Dental
Model Type: Network
Plan Specialty: Dental
Benefits Offered: Dental

Type of Coverage
Commercial, Individual, Military personnel & families

Geographic Areas Served
Nationwide

Accreditation Certification
URAC

Key Personnel
President/CEO . . . . Edward Shellard, DMD
Chairman of the Board . . . . Tim Constantine
Chief Dental Officer. . . . . Quinn Dufurrena, DDS, JD
Chief Operating Officer. . . . . Daniel J. Wright

48 UnitedHealthcare Community Plan Arizona

UnitedHealthcare Customer Service
P.O. Box 30769
Salt Lake City, UT 85004
Toll-Free: 800-348-4058
Fax: 801-478-7582
www.uhccommunityplan.com/arizona
Mailing Address: P.O. Box 5290, Kingston, NY 12402-5290
Subsidiary of: UnitedHealth Group
For Profit Organization: Yes

Healthplan and Services Defined
PLAN TYPE: Multiple
Model Type: Network
Benefits Offered: Behavioral Health, Dental, Home Care, Podiatry, Prescription, Vision, Wellness, Hearing, Acupuncture, Chiropractic

Type of Coverage
Medicare, Medicaid, CHIP

Geographic Areas Served
Statewide

Key Personnel
CEO, Community Plan AZ . . . . Jean Kalbacher
jean_kalbacher@uhc.com

49 UnitedHealthcare of Arizona

1 East Washington Street
Suite 900
Phoenix, AZ 85004
Toll-Free: 888-545-5205
Phone: 602-255-8455
www.uhc.com
Subsidiary of: UnitedHealth Group
For Profit Organization: Yes
Year Founded: 1984

Healthplan and Services Defined
PLAN TYPE: HMO/PPO
Model Type: Network
Plan Specialty: Behavioral Health, Dental, Vision
Benefits Offered: Behavioral Health, Dental, Disease Management, Prescription, Vision, Wellness, AD&D, Life

Type of Coverage
Commercial, Individual, Medicare, Supplemental Medicare, Medicaid, Family, Group

Geographic Areas Served
Statewide

Key Personnel
CEO, Arizona & New Mexico. . . . . Heather Kane

ARKANSAS

Health Insurance Coverage Status and Type of Coverage by Age

Category	All Persons Number	All Persons %	Under 19 years Number	Under 19 years %	Under 65 years Number	Under 65 years %
Total population	2,963 *(2)*	100.0 *(0.0)*	741 *(4)*	100.0 *(0.0)*	2,455 *(4)*	100.0 *(0.0)*
Covered by some type of health insurance	2,692 *(13)*	90.9 *(0.4)*	698 *(6)*	94.1 *(0.7)*	2,187 *(13)*	89.1 *(0.5)*
Covered by private health insurance	1,757 *(22)*	59.3 *(0.7)*	348 *(11)*	47.0 *(1.5)*	1,481 *(21)*	60.3 *(0.8)*
Employer-based	1,386 *(20)*	46.8 *(0.7)*	298 *(11)*	40.2 *(1.5)*	1,261 *(19)*	51.4 *(0.8)*
Direct purchase	388 *(12)*	13.1 *(0.4)*	46 *(5)*	6.2 *(0.6)*	224 *(10)*	9.1 *(0.4)*
TRICARE	92 *(7)*	3.1 *(0.3)*	16 *(3)*	2.1 *(0.4)*	49 *(6)*	2.0 *(0.2)*
Covered by public health insurance	1,303 *(16)*	44.0 *(0.6)*	379 *(11)*	51.1 *(1.5)*	808 *(17)*	32.9 *(0.7)*
Medicaid	787 *(16)*	26.6 *(0.6)*	376 *(11)*	50.8 *(1.5)*	715 *(17)*	29.1 *(0.7)*
Medicare	614 *(6)*	20.7 *(0.2)*	4 *(1)*	0.5 *(0.2)*	120 *(6)*	4.9 *(0.2)*
VA Care	94 *(4)*	3.2 *(0.1)*	2 *(1)*	0.2 *(0.1)*	41 *(4)*	1.7 *(0.2)*
Not covered at any time during the year	271 *(12)*	9.1 *(0.4)*	43 *(5)*	5.9 *(0.7)*	268 *(12)*	10.9 *(0.5)*

Note: Numbers in thousands; Figures cover civilian noninstitutionalized population in 2019; N/A indicates that data was not available; Z represents or rounds to zero; Margin of error appears in parenthesis and is calculated using replicate weights.

Source: U.S. Census Bureau, American Community Survey, Table HI-05. Health Insurance Coverage Status and Type of Coverage by State and Age for All People: 2019

Arkansas

50 Ambetter from Arkansas Health & Wellness
P.O. Box 842737
Dallas, TX 75284-2737
Toll-Free: 877-617-0390
ambetter.arhealthwellness.com
Subsidiary of: Centene Corporation
For Profit Organization: Yes

Healthplan and Services Defined
PLAN TYPE: Other
Model Type: Network
Benefits Offered: Behavioral Health, Dental, Physical Therapy, Prescription, Vision, Maternity and newborn care

Type of Coverage
Individual, Medicare, Health Insurance Marketplace

Geographic Areas Served
Statewide

Key Personnel
President & CEO .... John P. Ryan

51 Arkansas Blue Cross Blue Shield
P.O. Box 2181
Little Rock, AR 72203-2181
Toll-Free: 800-238-8379
www.arkansasbluecross.com
Non-Profit Organization: Yes
Year Founded: 1948

Healthplan and Services Defined
PLAN TYPE: Multiple
Other Type: HMO, Medicare
Model Type: Network
Plan Specialty: Dental, Vision
Benefits Offered: Chiropractic, Dental, Home Care, Inpatient SNF, Physical Therapy, Podiatry, Prescription, Vision, Worker's Compensation, Life, Mental Health, Substance Abuse, Emergency, Short-Term, Federal Employees

Type of Coverage
Commercial, Individual, Medicare, Supplemental Medicare
Catastrophic Illness Benefit: Varies per case

Geographic Areas Served
Statewide

Subscriber Information
Average Subscriber Co-Payment:
Home Health Care: Varies
Nursing Home: Varies

Accreditation Certification
TJC, URAC, NCQA

Key Personnel
President/CEO .... Curtis Barnett
EVP/Chief Admin. Officer .... Kathy Ryan
EVP/COO/Treasurer .... Gray Dillard
SVP, Claims/Membership .... Marcus James
Chief Financial Officer .... Scott Winter
VP/Chief Medical Officer .... Mark Jansen, MD
SVP/Chief Legal Officer .... Tim Gauger
VP/Chief Actuary .... Victor Davis
VP/Information Technology .... David Martin

52 Arkansas Health & Wellness
1 Allied Drive
Suite 2520
Little Rock, AR 72202
Toll-Free: 800-294-3557
www.arhealthwellness.com
Subsidiary of: Centene Corporation
For Profit Organization: Yes
Year Founded: 1996

Healthplan and Services Defined
PLAN TYPE: Multiple
Model Type: Network
Plan Specialty: Integrated provider network & administrative services

Type of Coverage
Individual, Medicare

Geographic Areas Served
Statewide

Key Personnel
Chief Executive Officer .... John P. Ryan

53 Arkansas Total Care
P.O. Box 25010
Little Rock, AR 72221
Toll-Free: 866-282-6280
www.arkansastotalcare.com
Subsidiary of: Arkansas Health & Wellness / Centene Corporation
For Profit Organization: Yes

Healthplan and Services Defined
PLAN TYPE: Other
Model Type: Network
Plan Specialty: Behavioral Health
Benefits Offered: Behavioral Health, Home Care, Inpatient SNF, Physical Therapy, Prescription, Range of services for people with IDD and behavioral health needs

Type of Coverage
Individual

Geographic Areas Served
Statewide

Key Personnel
President & CEO .... John P. Ryan

54 Delta Dental of Arkansas
P.O. Box 6247
Sherwood, AR 72124
Toll-Free: 800-462-5410
Phone: 501-835-3400
Fax: 877-992-1854
www.deltadentalar.com
Mailing Address: P.O. Box 15965, Little Rock, AR 72231

Non-Profit Organization: Yes
Year Founded: 1982
Total Enrollment: 2,000,000

Healthplan and Services Defined
  PLAN TYPE: Dental
  Other Type: Vision
  Model Type: Network
  Plan Specialty: Dental, Vision
  Benefits Offered: Dental, Vision

Type of Coverage
  Commercial, Individual, Group

Type of Payment Plans Offered
  DFFS

Geographic Areas Served
  Statewide

Publishes and Distributes Report Card: Yes

Key Personnel
  President/CEO . . . . Kristin Merlo
  Vice President, Ops. . . . . Jimmy Anthony
  VP, Information Tech. . . . . Caleb Castleberry
  Vice President, Marketing . . . . Dave Hawsey
  Vice President, Legal . . . . Katie Mehdizadegan
  Chief Financial Officer . . . . Debi Lowtharp

55 Frazier Insurance Agency
808 Reservoir Road
Suite B
Little Rock, AR 72227
Phone: 501-225-1818
Fax: 501-223-8682
frazieragency.com

Healthplan and Services Defined
  PLAN TYPE: HMO/PPO
  Benefits Offered: Wellness, AD&D, Life

Type of Coverage
  Medicare

Geographic Areas Served
  Statewide

Key Personnel
  Partner/Agent. . . . . Toni Frazier
  Partner. . . . . William Richard Frazier

56 HealthSCOPE Benefits
27 Corporate Hill Drive
Little Rock, AR 72205
Toll-Free: 800-972-3025
www.healthscopebenefits.com
For Profit Organization: Yes
Year Founded: 1985
Total Enrollment: 650,000

Healthplan and Services Defined
  PLAN TYPE: Other
  Plan Specialty: Healthcare management services

Type of Coverage
  Catastrophic Illness Benefit: Maximum $1M

Type of Payment Plans Offered
  POS, DFFS, FFS, Combination FFS & DFFS

Geographic Areas Served
  Nationwide

Network Qualifications
  Minimum Years of Practice: 3
  Pre-Admission Certification: Yes

Peer Review Type
  Utilization Review: Yes
  Second Surgical Opinion: Yes
  Case Management: Yes

Accreditation Certification
  TJC, URAC
  Utilization Review, State Licensure

Key Personnel
  Chief Executive Officer . . . . Joe K. Edwards
  President . . . . Mary Catherine Person
  VP, Business Development . . . . Tom Bartlett
  Dir., Quality Assurance. . . . . Jennifer Spencer
  SVP, Solutions & Legal . . . . Brett Edwards
  SVP of Operations. . . . . Darren Ashby
  Chief Information Officer . . . . Tim Beasley

Specialty Managed Care Partners
  American Health Holdings, PHCS, Advance PCS, Caremark, CCN
  Enters into Contracts with Regional Business Coalitions: Yes
  Alaska Business Coalition

Employer References
  American Greetings, Alcoa, MedCath, Whirlpool

57 Humana Health Insurance of Arkansas
5206 Village Parkway
Suite 4
Rogers, AR 72758
Toll-Free: 800-434-4207
Phone: 479-418-7140
Fax: 479-273-2516
www.humana.com
Subsidiary of: Humana Inc.
For Profit Organization: Yes

Healthplan and Services Defined
  PLAN TYPE: HMO/PPO
  Model Type: Network
  Plan Specialty: Dental, Vision
  Benefits Offered: Dental, Prescription, Vision, Life, LTD, STD

Type of Coverage
  Commercial, Medicare

Geographic Areas Served
  Statewide

Accreditation Certification
  URAC, NCQA, CORE

58 Mercy Clinic Arkansas
214 Carter Street
Berryville, AR 72616
Phone: 870-423-3355
mercy.net
Subsidiary of: IBM Watson Health
Non-Profit Organization: Yes
Year Founded: 1986
Number of Affiliated Hospitals: 44
Number of Primary Care Physicians: 700
Number of Referral/Specialty Physicians: 2,000

Healthplan and Services Defined
PLAN TYPE: HMO
Benefits Offered: Behavioral Health, Disease Management, Home Care, Inpatient SNF, Physical Therapy, Podiatry, Vision, Wellness, Non-Surgical Weight Loss; Urgent Care; Dermatology; Rehabilitation; Breast Cancer; Orthopedics; Ostoclerosis; Pediatrics

Geographic Areas Served
Arkansas

Key Personnel
President, Arkansas......................Scott Cooper

59 UnitedHealthcare Community Plan Arkansas
UnitedHealthcare Customer Service
P.O. Box 30769
Salt Lake City, UT 84130-0769
Toll-Free: 888-545-5205
www.uhccommunityplan.com/ar
Subsidiary of: UnitedHealth Group
For Profit Organization: Yes

Healthplan and Services Defined
PLAN TYPE: Medicare
Other Type: Medicaid
Model Type: Network
Benefits Offered: Dental, Home Care, Podiatry, Prescription, Vision, Hearing

Type of Coverage
Medicare, Medicaid

Geographic Areas Served
Statewide

60 UnitedHealthcare of Arkansas
1401 West Capitol Avenue
Suite 375
Little Rock, AR 72201
Toll-Free: 888-545-5205
Phone: 501-664-7700
www.uhc.com
Subsidiary of: UnitedHealth Group
For Profit Organization: Yes

Healthplan and Services Defined
PLAN TYPE: HMO/PPO
Model Type: Network
Plan Specialty: Behavioral Health, Dental, Disease Management, PBM, Vision
Benefits Offered: Behavioral Health, Dental, Disease Management, Long-Term Care, Prescription, Vision, Wellness, Life, LTD, STD

Type of Coverage
Commercial, Individual, Medicare, Supplemental Medicare, Medicaid, Family, Group

Type of Payment Plans Offered
POS, FFS

Geographic Areas Served
Statewide

Network Qualifications
Pre-Admission Certification: Yes

Peer Review Type
Utilization Review: Yes

Publishes and Distributes Report Card: Yes

Accreditation Certification
URAC, NCQA
TJC Accreditation, Medicare Approved, Utilization Review, Pre-Admission Certification, State Licensure, Quality Assurance Program

Key Personnel
CFO, SE Region......................Eric H. Johnson
CEO, Mid-South......................Steve Wilson

Specialty Managed Care Partners
Enters into Contracts with Regional Business Coalitions: Yes

CALIFORNIA

Health Insurance Coverage Status and Type of Coverage by Age

Category	All Persons Number	All Persons %	Under 19 years Number	Under 19 years %	Under 65 years Number	Under 65 years %
Total population	38,998 *(6)*	100.0 *(0.0)*	9,405 *(10)*	100.0 *(0.0)*	33,259 *(7)*	100.0 *(0.0)*
Covered by some type of health insurance	35,996 *(42)*	92.3 *(0.1)*	9,071 *(16)*	96.4 *(0.2)*	30,313 *(42)*	91.1 *(0.1)*
Covered by private health insurance	24,913 *(86)*	63.9 *(0.2)*	5,434 *(41)*	57.8 *(0.4)*	22,057 *(84)*	66.3 *(0.3)*
Employer-based	20,687 *(87)*	53.0 *(0.2)*	4,715 *(43)*	50.1 *(0.5)*	18,916 *(89)*	56.9 *(0.3)*
Direct purchase	4,729 *(49)*	12.1 *(0.1)*	721 *(20)*	7.7 *(0.2)*	3,448 *(44)*	10.4 *(0.1)*
TRICARE	678 *(18)*	1.7 *(Z)*	170 *(10)*	1.8 *(0.1)*	449 *(17)*	1.4 *(0.1)*
Covered by public health insurance	14,749 *(73)*	37.8 *(0.2)*	4,017 *(42)*	42.7 *(0.4)*	9,330 *(73)*	28.1 *(0.2)*
Medicaid	9,926 *(77)*	25.5 *(0.2)*	3,970 *(43)*	42.2 *(0.5)*	8,764 *(74)*	26.4 *(0.2)*
Medicare	6,100 *(22)*	15.6 *(0.1)*	67 *(8)*	0.7 *(0.1)*	689 *(20)*	2.1 *(0.1)*
VA Care	585 *(13)*	1.5 *(Z)*	11 *(3)*	0.1 *(Z)*	284 *(10)*	0.9 *(Z)*
Not covered at any time during the year	3,002 *(42)*	7.7 *(0.1)*	334 *(14)*	3.6 *(0.2)*	2,946 *(42)*	8.9 *(0.1)*

Note: Numbers in thousands; Figures cover civilian noninstitutionalized population in 2019; N/A indicates that data was not available; Z represents or rounds to zero; Margin of error appears in parenthesis and is calculated using replicate weights.
Source: U.S. Census Bureau, American Community Survey, Table HI-05. Health Insurance Coverage Status and Type of Coverage by State and Age for All People: 2019

California

61 Aetna Better Health of California
10260 Meanley Drive
San Diego, CA 92131
Toll-Free: 855-772-9076
Fax: 844-453-1150
memberservices_ca@aetna.com
www.aetnabetterhealth.com/california
Subsidiary of: CVS Health / Aetna Inc.
For Profit Organization: Yes

Healthplan and Services Defined
PLAN TYPE: HMO/PPO
Other Type: POS
Model Type: Network
Plan Specialty: Behavioral Health, EPO, Lab, PBM, Radiology
Benefits Offered: Behavioral Health, Dental, Disease Management, Long-Term Care, Physical Therapy, Podiatry, Prescription, Psychiatric, Vision, Wellness, Life, LTD, STD

Type of Coverage
Commercial, Supplemental Medicare, Medicaid, Catastrophic, Student health, Medi-cal

Geographic Areas Served
Statewide

Key Personnel
CEO .... Verne Brizendine

62 Alameda Alliance for Health
1240 South Loop Road
Alameda, CA 94502
Phone: 510-747-4500
www.alamedaalliance.org
Non-Profit Organization: Yes
Year Founded: 1996
Federally Qualified: Yes
Number of Affiliated Hospitals: 15
Number of Primary Care Physicians: 4,000
Total Enrollment: 140,000
State Enrollment: 110,000

Healthplan and Services Defined
PLAN TYPE: HMO
Model Type: Network
Plan Specialty: Dental
Benefits Offered: Dental, Prescription, Vision, Medi-Cal, Alliance Group Care

Type of Coverage
Individual, Government Sponsored Programs

Type of Payment Plans Offered
POS

Geographic Areas Served
Alameda County

Peer Review Type
Second Surgical Opinion: Yes

Accreditation Certification
NCQA
State Licensure

Key Personnel
Chief Executive Officer .... Scott E. Coffin
Chief Operations Officer .... Matthew Woodruff
Chief Financial Officer .... Gil Riojas
Chief Medical Officer .... Steve O'Brien, MD
Chief Analytics Officer .... Tiffany Cheang

63 Alameda Alliance Group Care Plan
1240 South Loop Road
Alameda, CA 94502
Phone: 510-747-4567
www.alamedaalliance.org/visitors/health-plans/group-care
Subsidiary of: Alameda Alliance for Health
Non-Profit Organization: Yes
Federally Qualified: Yes
Number of Affiliated Hospitals: 15
Number of Primary Care Physicians: 4,000

Healthplan and Services Defined
PLAN TYPE: Other
Plan Specialty: Employer-sponsored plan serving IHSS workers
Benefits Offered: Behavioral Health, Chiropractic, Dental, Inpatient SNF, Prescription, Vision, Wellness, Acupuncture

Geographic Areas Served
Alameda County

64 Alameda Medi-Cal Plan
1240 South Loop Road
Alameda, CA 94502
Phone: 510-747-4567
www.alamedaalliance.org/visitors/health-plans/medi-cal
Subsidiary of: Alameda Alliance for Health
Non-Profit Organization: Yes
Federally Qualified: Yes
Number of Affiliated Hospitals: 15
Number of Primary Care Physicians: 4,000

Healthplan and Services Defined
PLAN TYPE: Other
Plan Specialty: Serving families and children, people with disabilities, and seniors through the state-sponsored Medi-Cal plan
Benefits Offered: Dental, Inpatient SNF, Vision, Wellness

Geographic Areas Served
Alameda County

Key Personnel
Chief Executive Officer .... Scott E. Coffin
Chief Operations Officer .... Matthew Woodruff
Chief Financial Officer .... Gil Riojas
Chief Medical Officer .... Steve O'Brien, MD
Chief Analytics Officer .... Tiffany Cheang

65 Alignment Health Plan
1100 W Town and Country Road
Suite 1600
Orange, CA 92868
Toll-Free: 866-634-2247
www.alignmenthealthplan.com

Healthplan and Services Defined
PLAN TYPE: Medicare

Type of Coverage
Medicare, Supplemental Medicare

Geographic Areas Served
Los Angeles, Northern Orange County, San Bernardino, Riverside, Stanislaus, San Joaquin and Santa Clara

Key Personnel
President/CEO .... John Kao

66 Allied Pacific IPA
1668 S. Garfield Avenue
2nd Floor
Alhambra, CA 91801
Toll-Free: 877-282-8272
Phone: 626-282-0288
www.alliedipa.com
Secondary Address: 568 W. Garvey Avenue, Monterey Park, CA 91754
Year Founded: 1992
Physician Owned Organization: Yes
Number of Primary Care Physicians: 800

Healthplan and Services Defined
PLAN TYPE: HMO
Other Type: IPA
Model Type: IPA
Benefits Offered: Disease Management, Wellness

Type of Coverage
Commercial, Individual

Key Personnel
Chair........................... Kenneth T. Sim, MD

67 Anthem Blue Cross of California
2000 Corporate Center Drive
Newbury Park, CA 91320
Toll-Free: 800-331-1476
www.anthem.com/ca
Subsidiary of: Anthem, Inc.
For Profit Organization: Yes

Healthplan and Services Defined
PLAN TYPE: HMO/PPO
Model Type: Network
Plan Specialty: Behavioral Health, Dental, Disease Management, Lab, PBM, Vision, Radiology
Benefits Offered: Behavioral Health, Dental, Disease Management, Inpatient SNF, Physical Therapy, Prescription, Psychiatric, Transplant, Vision, Wellness, Life

Type of Coverage
Commercial, Individual, Medicare, Supplemental Medicare, Medicaid, Minimum coverage

Geographic Areas Served
Santa Clara, San Joaquin, Stanislaus, Merced, and Tulare

Accreditation Certification
URAC

Key Personnel
President, CA Commercial. .... Beth Andersen
VP & GM, Large Group CA .... Kathy Martella

68 BEST Life and Health Insurance Co.
17701 Mitchell N
Irvine, CA 92614-6028
Toll-Free: 800-433-0088
Fax: 208-893-5040
cs@bestlife.com
www.bestlife.com
Mailing Address: P.O. Box 890, Meridian, ID 83680-0890
For Profit Organization: Yes
Year Founded: 1970
Number of Affiliated Hospitals: 5,005
Number of Primary Care Physicians: 772,292
Total Enrollment: 90,000

Healthplan and Services Defined
PLAN TYPE: PPO
Model Type: PPO/Indemnity
Benefits Offered: Dental, Disease Management, Vision, Wellness, Life, STD

Type of Coverage
Commercial

Geographic Areas Served
AK, AL, AR, AZ, CA, CO, DC, FL, GA, HI, ID, IL, IN, KS, KY, LA, MD, MI, MS, MO, MT, NC, ND, NE, NM, NV, OH, OK, OR, PA, SC, SD, TN, TX, UT, VA, WA, WY

Network Qualifications
Pre-Admission Certification: Yes

Peer Review Type
Case Management: Yes

Accreditation Certification
URAC, NCQA
Quality Assurance Program

69 Blue Shield of California
601 12th Street
Oakland, CA 94607
Toll-Free: 800-393-6130
Phone: 510-607-2000
www.blueshieldca.com
Non-Profit Organization: Yes
Year Founded: 1939
Total Enrollment: 4,380,000
State Enrollment: 4,380,000

Healthplan and Services Defined
PLAN TYPE: HMO/PPO

Plan Specialty: Dental, Vision
Benefits Offered: Behavioral Health, Chiropractic, Dental, Home Care, Inpatient SNF, Podiatry, Prescription, Vision, Life, Benefits vary depending on the plan

Type of Coverage
Commercial, Individual, Medicare, Supplemental Medicare, Medicaid

Geographic Areas Served
Statewide

Accreditation Certification
NCQA

Key Personnel
President/CEO . . . . Paul S. Markovich
SVP/CFO . . . . Sandra Clarke
SVP/General Counsel . . . . Hope Scott
SVP/Chief Actuary . . . . Amy Yao
SVP/Chief Info. Officer . . . . Lisa Davis

70 Blue Shield of California Promise Cal MediConnect Plans
601 Potrero Grande Drive
Montery Park, CA 91755
Toll-Free: 855-905-3825
Fax: 323-889-5416
care1st.com
Subsidiary of: Blue Shield of California

Healthplan and Services Defined
PLAN TYPE: Other
Plan Specialty: Combines Medicare and Medi-Cal benefits into a single plan.
Benefits Offered: Behavioral Health, Long-Term Care, Prescription

Type of Coverage
Medicare, Medicaid

Geographic Areas Served
Los Angeles and San Diego counties

Key Personnel
President/CEO . . . . Kristen Cerf

71 Blue Shield of California Promise Health Plan
601 Potrero Grande Drive
Monterey Park, CA 91755
Toll-Free: 855-905-3825
Fax: 323-889-5416
www.blueshieldca.com/promise
Subsidiary of: Blue Shield of California
For Profit Organization: Yes
Year Founded: 1994
Total Enrollment: 320,000

Healthplan and Services Defined
PLAN TYPE: HMO
Benefits Offered: Dental, Disease Management, Wellness, Cal MediConnect, Medi-Cal

Type of Coverage
Commercial, Medicare, Supplemental Medicare, Medicaid

Geographic Areas Served
Los Angeles, Orange, San Bernardino, Riverside and San Diego counties

Accreditation Certification
NCQA

Key Personnel
President/CEO . . . . Kristen Cerf

72 Blue Shield Promise Medi-Cal
601 Potrero Grande Drive
Monterey Park, CA 91755
Toll-Free: 800-605-2556
Fax: 323-889-6236
www.blueshieldca.com/promise/medi-cal
Subsidiary of: Blue Shield of California
Year Founded: 1994

Healthplan and Services Defined
PLAN TYPE: Other
Plan Specialty: Contracted to provide Medi-Cal health benefits to recipients.
Benefits Offered: Disease Management, Wellness

Type of Coverage
Medicare, Supplemental Medicare

Geographic Areas Served
Los Angeles, San Diego

Accreditation Certification
NCQA

73 Brand New Day
5455 Garden Grove Boulevard
Suite 500
Westminster, CA 92683
Toll-Free: 866-255-4795
Fax: 657-400-1208
bndhmo.com
Subsidiary of: Bright HealthCare
For Profit Organization: Yes
Year Founded: 1985

Healthplan and Services Defined
PLAN TYPE: HMO
Plan Specialty: Behavioral Health
Benefits Offered: Behavioral Health, Dental, Disease Management, Prescription, Psychiatric, Vision, Wellness

Type of Coverage
Individual, Medicare, Medicaid

Geographic Areas Served
Statewide

Key Personnel
Chief Operating Officer . . . . Jeff Davis

74 Bright Now! Dental
3358 South Bristol Street
Santa Ana, CA 92704
Toll-Free: 844-400-7645
Phone: 714-361-2141
www.brightnow.com
Secondary Address: 1601 W 17th Street, Suite G, Santa Ana, CA 92706, 714-567-9255
Subsidiary of: Smile Brands Inc.
Year Founded: 1998
Number of Primary Care Physicians: 300
Number of Referral/Specialty Physicians: 416

Healthplan and Services Defined
PLAN TYPE: Dental
Model Type: Staff, Network
Plan Specialty: Dental
Benefits Offered: Dental

Type of Payment Plans Offered
Capitated

Geographic Areas Served
AZ, CA, CO, FL, IN, MD, OH, OR, PA, TN, TX, UT, VA, WA

Subscriber Information
Average Monthly Fee Per Subscriber
(Employee + Employer Contribution):
Employee Only (Self): $40.00
Employee & 1 Family Member: $75.00
Employee & 2 Family Members: $110.00

Network Qualifications
Pre-Admission Certification: Yes

Key Personnel
President/CEO . . . . Steven C. Bilt
Chief Financial Officer . . . . John Slack
Chief Information Officer . . . . George Suda

Specialty Managed Care Partners
Enters into Contracts with Regional Business Coalitions: No

75 California Dental Network
23291 Mill Creek Drive
Suite 100
Laguna Hills, CA 92653
Toll-Free: 877-433-6825
Fax: 949-830-1655
www.caldental.net
Subsidiary of: DentaQuest Ventures
Total Enrollment: 85,000

Healthplan and Services Defined
PLAN TYPE: Dental
Plan Specialty: Dental
Benefits Offered: Dental

Type of Coverage
Individual

Geographic Areas Served
Statewide

Key Personnel
CEO . . . . Brian Watts

76 California Foundation for Medical Care
PO Box 2425
Riverside, CA 92516
Toll-Free: 800-334-7341
Fax: 951-686-1692
www.cfmcnet.org
For Profit Organization: Yes
Number of Affiliated Hospitals: 250
Number of Primary Care Physicians: 29,000
Number of Referral/Specialty Physicians: 5,000

Healthplan and Services Defined
PLAN TYPE: PPO
Plan Specialty: Behavioral Health, EPO, Lab, Worker's Compensation, UR, Chemical Dependency Centers, Surgical Centers
Benefits Offered: Worker's Compensation

Geographic Areas Served
Statewide

Key Personnel
President . . . . Carolyn Temple
661-616-4814
ctemple@kernfmc.com
Vice President . . . . Dolores L. Green
661-616-4814
dgreen@rcmadocs.org
Director . . . . John Nacol
707-544-2010

77 California Health & Wellness
1740 Creekside Oaks Drive
Suite 200
Sacramento, CA 95833
Toll-Free: 877-658-0305
www.cahealthwellness.com
Subsidiary of: Centene Corporation
For Profit Organization: Yes
Year Founded: 2013

Healthplan and Services Defined
PLAN TYPE: Other
Model Type: Network
Benefits Offered: Behavioral Health, Dental, Disease Management, Inpatient SNF, Vision

Type of Coverage
Medicaid, Medi-Cal

Key Personnel
CEO, Centene Corporation . . . . Michael Neidorff

78 CalOptima
505 City Parkway West
Orange, CA 92868
Toll-Free: 888-587-8088
Phone: 714-246-8500
www.caloptima.org

For Profit Organization: Yes
Year Founded: 1993
Owned by an Integrated Delivery Network (IDN): Yes
Number of Primary Care Physicians: 1,551
Total Enrollment: 758,970
State Enrollment: 758,970

Healthplan and Services Defined
PLAN TYPE: HMO
Model Type: Group
Plan Specialty: ASO, Behavioral Health, Chiropractic, Dental, Disease Management, EPO, Lab, MSO, PBM, Vision, Radiology, Worker's Compensation
Benefits Offered: Behavioral Health, Chiropractic, Dental, Disease Management, Home Care, Prescription, Vision, Wellness

Type of Coverage
Individual, Supplemental Medicare, Medicaid, Medi-Cal

Geographic Areas Served
Orange County

Key Personnel
Chief Executive Officer . . . . Michael Hunn
Chief HR Officer. . . . . Brigette Hoey
Chief Operating Officer . . . . Yungkyung Kim
Chief Financial Officer . . . . Nancy Huang
Chief Medical Officer . . . . Richard Pitts, DO, PhD

---

79 CareMore Health Plan
12900 Park Plaza Drive
Suite 150, MS-6150
Cerritos, CA 90703
Toll-Free: 888-291-1358
Phone: 562-622-2800
ProviderRelations@caremore.com
www.caremore.com
Subsidiary of: Anthem, Inc.

Healthplan and Services Defined
PLAN TYPE: Medicare
Plan Specialty: Seniors healthcare
Benefits Offered: Home Care

Type of Coverage
Medicare

Geographic Areas Served
Arizona, California, Colorado, Connecticut, DC, Iowa, Nevada, Tennessee, Texas, Virginia

Key Personnel
Interim President. . . . . Greg Garza
VP, Operations . . . . Alexis Megeath
Staff VP, Finance. . . . . David Hsieh
Chief Medical Officer . . . . Andrew Aronson, MD
Chief Information Officer . . . . Kathleen Linder

---

80 CenCal Health
4050 Calle Real
Santa Barbara, CA 93110
Toll-Free: 800-421-2560
Phone: 805-685-9525
info@cencalhealth.org
www.cencalhealth.org
Secondary Address: 1288 Morro Street, Suite 100, San Luis Obispo, CA 93401
Non-Profit Organization: Yes
Year Founded: 1983
Number of Primary Care Physicians: 275
Number of Referral/Specialty Physicians: 1,250
Total Enrollment: 175,000

Healthplan and Services Defined
PLAN TYPE: HMO
Benefits Offered: Complementary Medicine, Disease Management, Physical Therapy, Prescription, Vision, Wellness

Type of Coverage
Individual, Medicare, Medicaid, Medi-Cal, Healthy Families

Geographic Areas Served
Santa Barbara and San Luis Obispo counties

Key Personnel
Chief Executive Officer. . . . . Marina Owen
Chief Operating Officer . . . . Paul Jaconette
Chief Financial Officer. . . . . David Ambrose

---

81 Central California Alliance for Health
1600 Green Hills Road
Suite 101
Scotts Valley, CA 95066-4981
Toll-Free: 800-700-3874
Phone: 831-430-5500
www.ccah-alliance.org
Secondary Address: 950 East Blanco Road, Suite 101, Salinas, CA 93901-3400, 831-755-6000
Non-Profit Organization: Yes
Year Founded: 1996
Physician Owned Organization: No
Federally Qualified: No
Number of Primary Care Physicians: 9,500
Total Enrollment: 346,000
State Enrollment: 346,000

Healthplan and Services Defined
PLAN TYPE: HMO
Model Type: County Org Health System
Benefits Offered: Behavioral Health, Chiropractic, Long-Term Care, Prescription, Vision, Medi-Cal, Healthy Families, Healthy Kids, Alliance Care Access for Infants and Mothers, Alliance Care IHSS
Offers Demand Management Patient Information Service: No

Geographic Areas Served
Santa Cruz, Monterey and Merced counties

Network Qualifications
Pre-Admission Certification: No

Publishes and Distributes Report Card: No

Key Personnel
Chief Executive Officer . . . . Stephanie Sonnenshine
Chief Financial Officer . . . . Lisa Ba
Chief Medical Officer . . . . Maurice Herbelin, MD, MBA
Administrative Officer . . . . Scott Fortner
Chief Information Officer . . . . Cecil Newton
Chief Operating Officer . . . . Van Wong, CHIE
Communications Director . . . . Linda Gorman

Specialty Managed Care Partners
Enters into Contracts with Regional Business Coalitions: No

---

82 Central Health Medicare Plan
1540 Bridgegate Drive
Diamond Bar, CA 91765
Toll-Free: 866-314-2427
memberservices@centralhealthplan.com
www.centralhealthplan.com
Year Founded: 2004
Number of Primary Care Physicians: 6,000

Healthplan and Services Defined
PLAN TYPE: Medicare
Other Type: HMO
Benefits Offered: Chiropractic, Dental, Home Care, Inpatient SNF, Physical Therapy, Podiatry, Vision, Wellness, Diagnostics/Labs/Imaging, Rehabilitation, Medical Equipment

Type of Coverage
Medicare, Supplemental Medicare

Geographic Areas Served
Los Angeles, Riverside, San Bernadino, Orange, San Benito, San Joaquin, and Ventura counties

---

83 Chinese Community Health Plan
445 Grant Avenue
Suite 700
San Francisco, CA 94108
Toll-Free: 888-775-7888
Phone: 415-834-2118
Fax: 415-955-8818
memberservices@cchphealthplan.com
www.cchphealthplan.com
Secondary Address: 386 Gellert Boulevard, Daly City, CA 94105, 415-834-2118
For Profit Organization: Yes
Year Founded: 1986
Owned by an Integrated Delivery Network (IDN): Yes
Number of Primary Care Physicians: 3,000
Total Enrollment: 23,000
State Enrollment: 23,000

Healthplan and Services Defined
PLAN TYPE: HMO
Model Type: IPA
Benefits Offered: Dental, Prescription, Vision, Wellness, Acupuncture Services, Worldwide Emergency

Type of Coverage
Individual, Medicare

Geographic Areas Served
San Francisco, Northern San Mateo

Subscriber Information
Average Monthly Fee Per Subscriber
(Employee + Employer Contribution):
Employee Only (Self): $218.00
Employee & 1 Family Member: $419.00
Employee & 2 Family Members: $384.53
Average Subscriber Co-Payment:
Primary Care Physician: $10.00
Non-Network Physician: Not covered
Prescription Drugs: $6.00
Hospital ER: $25.00
Home Health Care Max. Days/Visits Covered: None except mental
Nursing Home Max. Days/Visits Covered: 10 days

Network Qualifications
Pre-Admission Certification: Yes

Peer Review Type
Utilization Review: Yes
Second Surgical Opinion: Yes
Case Management: Yes

Accreditation Certification
TJC Accreditation, Medicare Approved, Utilization Review, Pre-Admission Certification, State Licensure, Quality Assurance Program

Key Personnel
Sales Manager . . . . Yolanda Lee
415-955-8000
Yolanda.Lee@CCHPHealthPlan.com
CEO . . . . Deena Louie
CEO, Chinese Hospital . . . . Jian Zhang

Specialty Managed Care Partners
Enters into Contracts with Regional Business Coalitions: No

---

84 ChiroSource, Inc. / Chiropractic Health Plan of California
PO Box 190
Clayton, CA 94517
Toll-Free: 800-680-9997
Fax: 888-972-9732
info@chirosource.com
www.chpc.com
Secondary Address: Chiropractic Health Plan of California, 800-995-2442
For Profit Organization: Yes
Year Founded: 1997

Healthplan and Services Defined
PLAN TYPE: Multiple
Model Type: Network
Plan Specialty: Chiropractic, Physical Medicine, Accupuncture, Massage
Benefits Offered: Worker's Compensation, Health-Group & Individual, Medicare Advantage, IME Networks

Type of Coverage
PPO, EPO, POS, MPN, HCN, IME

Type of Payment Plans Offered
FFS

Geographic Areas Served
National

Network Qualifications
Pre-Admission Certification: Yes

Peer Review Type
Utilization Review: Yes

Publishes and Distributes Report Card: No

Key Personnel
Vice President .... Ron Cataldo

Specialty Managed Care Partners
Enters into Contracts with Regional Business Coalitions: Yes

---

85 Cigna HealthCare of California
One Front Street
7th Floor
San Francisco, CA 94111
Toll-Free: 800-997-1654
www.cigna.com
Subsidiary of: Cigna Corporation
For Profit Organization: Yes
Year Founded: 1978

Healthplan and Services Defined
PLAN TYPE: HMO
Other Type: POS
Plan Specialty: Behavioral Health, Dental, Substance Abuse Centers
Benefits Offered: Behavioral Health, Dental, Life

Type of Coverage
Commercial, Individual

Key Personnel
President/General Manager .... Peter Welch

---

86 Coastal TPA, Inc.
10 Ragsdale Drive
Suite 102
Moterey, CA 93940
Toll-Free: 800-564-7475
Phone: 831-754-3800
Fax: 831-754-3830
info@coastalmgmt.com
www.coastalmgmt.com
For Profit Organization: Yes
Year Founded: 1961

Healthplan and Services Defined
PLAN TYPE: PPO
Plan Specialty: Third party claims administration and proprietary regional PPO.
Benefits Offered: Dental, Disease Management, Prescription, Vision, PPO Network

Type of Coverage
Commercial

Catastrophic Illness Benefit: Unlimited

Type of Payment Plans Offered
FFS

Geographic Areas Served
Monterey, Santa Cruz, San Benito, San Luis Obispo and Santa Clara counties

Peer Review Type
Utilization Review: No
Second Surgical Opinion: Yes
Case Management: No

Accreditation Certification
NCQA

Average Claim Compensation
Physician's Fees Charged: 70%
Hospital's Fees Charged: 85%

---

87 Community Health Group
2420 Fenton Street
100
Chula Vista, CA 91914
Toll-Free: 800-224-7766
Phone: 619-422-0422
info@chgsd.com
www.chgsd.com
Non-Profit Organization: Yes
Year Founded: 1982
Number of Affiliated Hospitals: 28
Number of Primary Care Physicians: 488
Number of Referral/Specialty Physicians: 1,820
Total Enrollment: 146,000
State Enrollment: 146,000

Healthplan and Services Defined
PLAN TYPE: HMO
Model Type: Network
Plan Specialty: Behavioral Health, Disease Management, Lab, Vision, Radiology, UR
Benefits Offered: Behavioral Health, Disease Management, Home Care, Inpatient SNF, Physical Therapy, Podiatry, Prescription, Psychiatric, Transplant, Wellness
Offers Demand Management Patient Information Service: Yes

Type of Coverage
Medi-Cal, CommuniCare Advantage
Catastrophic Illness Benefit: None

Type of Payment Plans Offered
Capitated, FFS

Geographic Areas Served
San Diego county

Network Qualifications
Pre-Admission Certification: Yes

Peer Review Type
Utilization Review: Yes
Second Surgical Opinion: Yes
Case Management: Yes

Publishes and Distributes Report Card: Yes

Accreditation Certification
NCQA
Utilization Review, Pre-Admission Certification, State Licensure, Quality Assurance Program

Key Personnel
Chief Executive Officer . . . . Norma Diaz

Specialty Managed Care Partners
Enters into Contracts with Regional Business Coalitions: No

---

88 Concern
2490 Hospital Drive
Suite 310
Mountain View, CA 94040
Toll-Free: 800-344-4222
info@concernhealth.com
www.concernhealth.com
Non-Profit Organization: Yes

Healthplan and Services Defined
PLAN TYPE: Other
Other Type: EAP
Benefits Offered: Behavioral Health, Psychiatric, Wellness

Type of Coverage
Commercial, EAP

Geographic Areas Served
Silicon Valley

Key Personnel
Chief Executive Officer . . . . Cecile Currier

---

89 Contra Costa Health Services
1220 Morello Avenue
Suite 200
Martinez, CA 94553
Toll-Free: 800-232-4636
cchealth.org
Non-Profit Organization: Yes
Year Founded: 1973
Federally Qualified: Yes
Number of Affiliated Hospitals: 1
Total Enrollment: 140,000

Healthplan and Services Defined
PLAN TYPE: HMO
Model Type: Staff, Network
Benefits Offered: Behavioral Health, Disease Management, Wellness, 24-hour psychiatric emergency services

Geographic Areas Served
Contra Costa County

Peer Review Type
Utilization Review: Yes
Second Surgical Opinion: Yes
Case Management: Yes

Publishes and Distributes Report Card: Yes

Accreditation Certification
URAC Accreditation
TJC Accreditation, Medicare Approved, Utilization Review, State Licensure, Quality Assurance Program

Key Personnel
Director . . . . Anna Roth, RN, MS
925-957-5403
Health Officer . . . . Chris Farnitano
COO/CFO . . . . Patrick Godley
925-957-5405
Communications Officer . . . . Kim McCarl
925-957-2681

Specialty Managed Care Partners
Enters into Contracts with Regional Business Coalitions: Yes

---

90 Delta Dental of California
P.O. Box 997330
Sacramento, CA 95899-7330
Toll-Free: 800-765-6003
www.deltadentalins.com
Secondary Address: DeltaCare USA Customer Service, P.O. Box 1803, Alpharetta, GA 30023, 800-422-4234
Subsidiary of: Delta Dental
Non-Profit Organization: Yes
Year Founded: 1955

Healthplan and Services Defined
PLAN TYPE: Dental
Other Type: Dental PPO
Model Type: Network
Plan Specialty: Dental
Benefits Offered: Dental

Type of Coverage
Commercial, Individual

Type of Payment Plans Offered
DFFS, Capitated, FFS

Geographic Areas Served
Statewide

Network Qualifications
Pre-Admission Certification: No

Peer Review Type
Utilization Review: Yes
Second Surgical Opinion: Yes
Case Management: Yes

Publishes and Distributes Report Card: Yes

Key Personnel
President & CEO . . . . Anthony S. Barth
Chief Financial Officer . . . . Michael Castro
Chief Operating Officer . . . . Nilesh Patel
Chief Information Officer . . . . Kirsten Garen
Chief Legal Officer . . . . Michael Hankinson

Specialty Managed Care Partners
PMI Dental Health Plan
Enters into Contracts with Regional Business Coalitions: Yes

91 Dental Alternatives Insurance Services
Toll-Free: 800-445-8119
Fax: 714-429-1261
info@gotodais.com
www.gotodais.com
Subsidiary of: SafeGuard Health Plans, Inc.
For Profit Organization: Yes
Year Founded: 1977
Total Enrollment: 390,000

Healthplan and Services Defined
PLAN TYPE: Dental
Model Type: IPA
Plan Specialty: Dental
Benefits Offered: Dental
Offers Demand Management Patient Information Service: Yes

Network Qualifications
Pre-Admission Certification: Yes

Peer Review Type
Utilization Review: Yes
Second Surgical Opinion: Yes
Case Management: Yes

Publishes and Distributes Report Card: Yes

Accreditation Certification
NCQA

Specialty Managed Care Partners
Enters into Contracts with Regional Business Coalitions: Yes

92 Dental Benefit Providers: California
425 Market Street
Suite 12
San Francisco, CA 94105
Phone: 415-778-3800
www.dbp.com
Mailing Address: P.O. Box 30567, Salt Lake City, UT 84130-0567
Subsidiary of: UnitedHealth Group
For Profit Organization: Yes
Year Founded: 1984
Number of Primary Care Physicians: 125,000
Total Enrollment: 6,600,000

Healthplan and Services Defined
PLAN TYPE: Dental
Model Type: IPA
Plan Specialty: ASO, Dental, EPO, DHMO, PPO, CSO, Preventive, Claims Repricing and Network Access
Benefits Offered: Dental

Type of Coverage
Indemnity, Medicare, Medicaid

Type of Payment Plans Offered
POS, DFFS, Capitated, FFS

Geographic Areas Served
48 states including District of Columbia, Puerto Rico and Virgin Islands

Accreditation Certification
NCQA

93 Dental Health Services of California
3780 Kilroy Airport Way
Suite 750
Long Beach, CA 90806
Toll-Free: 800-637-6453
www.dentalhealthservices.com
For Profit Organization: Yes
Year Founded: 1974
Physician Owned Organization: Yes
Federally Qualified: Yes
Number of Primary Care Physicians: 1,000
Number of Referral/Specialty Physicians: 400
Total Enrollment: 90,000

Healthplan and Services Defined
PLAN TYPE: Dental
Model Type: Network
Plan Specialty: Dental
Benefits Offered: Dental

Type of Coverage
Commercial, Individual
Catastrophic Illness Benefit: None

Type of Payment Plans Offered
DFFS

Geographic Areas Served
California, Washington, and Oregon

Subscriber Information
Average Monthly Fee Per Subscriber
(Employee + Employer Contribution):
Employee Only (Self): Varies
Employee & 1 Family Member: Varies
Employee & 2 Family Members: Varies

Network Qualifications
Pre-Admission Certification: Yes

Peer Review Type
Second Surgical Opinion: Yes
Case Management: Yes

Publishes and Distributes Report Card: Yes

Accreditation Certification
Dhm
TJC Accreditation, Utilization Review, State Licensure, Quality Assurance Program

Key Personnel
Founder .... Godfrey Pernell

Specialty Managed Care Partners
United Association, 7up
Enters into Contracts with Regional Business Coalitions: No

94 Dentistat
455 Los Gatos Boulevard
Suite 206
Los Gatos, CA 95032
Toll-Free: 800-336-8250
info@dentistat.com
www.dentistat.com
For Profit Organization: Yes

Year Founded: 1968
Number of Primary Care Physicians: 80,000

Healthplan and Services Defined
PLAN TYPE: Dental
Model Type: Network
Plan Specialty: Dental, Network management services for the dental industry.
Benefits Offered: Dental

Type of Payment Plans Offered
DFFS, Capitated, FFS, Combination FFS & DFFS

Geographic Areas Served
Nationwide

Accreditation Certification
NCQA
Utilization Review, Quality Assurance Program

Key Personnel
President . . . . Bret Guenther

Specialty Managed Care Partners
Enters into Contracts with Regional Business Coalitions: Yes

95 eHealthInsurance Services, Inc.
2625 Augustine Drive
Santa Clara, CA 95054
Toll-Free: 877-456-7180
www.ehealthinsurance.com
Subsidiary of: eHealth, Inc.
Year Founded: 1997
Total Enrollment: 5,000,000

Healthplan and Services Defined
PLAN TYPE: Multiple
Plan Specialty: Dental, Vision
Benefits Offered: Behavioral Health, Chiropractic, Dental, Disease Management, Home Care, Inpatient SNF, Podiatry, Prescription, Vision, Wellness, Life, STD, Benefits vary according to plan

Type of Coverage
Commercial, Individual, Medicare, Supplemental Medicare

Geographic Areas Served
Nationwide, including the District of Columbia

Key Personnel
Chief Executive Officer . . . . Scott N. Flanders
Chief Operating Officer . . . . Dave Francis
Chief Financial Officer . . . . Derek Yung
Chief Technology Officer . . . . Bill Billings
Chief Marketing Officer . . . . Tim Hannan
SVP, Human Resources . . . . Christopher Hoffman
SVP, Sales & Operations . . . . Dave Nicklaus
SVP/General Counsel . . . . Scott Giesler

96 Fdn. for Medical Care of Kern & Santa Barbara Counties
5701 Truxtun Avenue
Suite 100
Bakersfield, CA 93309
Phone: 661-327-7581
Fax: 661-327-5129
sales@kernfmc.com
www.kernfmc.com
Number of Affiliated Hospitals: 400
Number of Primary Care Physicians: 30,000
Number of Referral/Specialty Physicians: 7,000

Healthplan and Services Defined
PLAN TYPE: PPO
Model Type: IPA, Group, Network
Benefits Offered: Dental, Disease Management, Prescription, Wellness
Offers Demand Management Patient Information Service: Yes

Type of Payment Plans Offered
POS, DFFS, FFS, Combination FFS & DFFS

Geographic Areas Served
Kern and Santa Barbara counties

Network Qualifications
Pre-Admission Certification: Yes

Peer Review Type
Utilization Review: Yes
Second Surgical Opinion: Yes
Case Management: Yes

Accreditation Certification
TJC Accreditation, Medicare Approved, Utilization Review, Pre-Admission Certification, State Licensure

Key Personnel
Chief Executive Officer . . . . Carolyn J. Temple
Chief Operating Officer . . . . Deborah Hankins
Manager, Finance . . . . Larissa Wright
Manager, Customer Service . . . . Annette Charlton
Provider Relations . . . . Kelly Swartz

Specialty Managed Care Partners
Enters into Contracts with Regional Business Coalitions: No

97 First Health
Toll-Free: 800-226-5116
www.firsthealth.com
Subsidiary of: Aetna, Inc.
For Profit Organization: Yes
Year Founded: 1984
Number of Affiliated Hospitals: 134
Number of Primary Care Physicians: 1,923
Number of Referral/Specialty Physicians: 5,744
Total Enrollment: 2,000,000
State Enrollment: 585,000

Healthplan and Services Defined
PLAN TYPE: PPO
Model Type: Network
Benefits Offered: Disease Management, Wellness

Type of Payment Plans Offered
DFFS

Geographic Areas Served
State of Oklahoma and contiguous border cities of Missouri, Arkansas, Kansas and Texas

Average Claim Compensation
Physician's Fees Charged: 72%
Hospital's Fees Charged: 62%

98 GEMCare Health Plan
4550 California Avenue
Suite 100
Bakersfield, CA 93309
Toll-Free: 800-414-5860
Phone: 661-716-7100
Fax: 661-716-9200
gemcare.com
Subsidiary of: Dignity Health Medical Network
Year Founded: 1992
Number of Primary Care Physicians: 120
Number of Referral/Specialty Physicians: 200

Healthplan and Services Defined
PLAN TYPE: Medicare
Model Type: IPA

Type of Coverage
Medicare, Supplemental Medicare

Geographic Areas Served
Kern County, including Bakersfield and the outlying communities of Arvin, Delano, Lake Isabella, Shafter, Taft, Tehachapi and Wasco

99 Golden West Dental & Vision
Camarillo, CA 93010
Toll-Free: 866-926-8078
www.goldenwestdental.com
Subsidiary of: Anthem, Inc.
For Profit Organization: Yes
Year Founded: 1974

Healthplan and Services Defined
PLAN TYPE: Multiple
Plan Specialty: Dental, Vision
Benefits Offered: Dental, Vision
Offers Demand Management Patient Information Service: Yes

Type of Payment Plans Offered
Capitated, Combination FFS & DFFS

Geographic Areas Served
Statewide

Peer Review Type
Second Surgical Opinion: Yes

Publishes and Distributes Report Card: Yes

Average Claim Compensation
Physician's Fees Charged: 80%

Specialty Managed Care Partners
Enters into Contracts with Regional Business Coalitions: Yes

100 Health Net Dental
Toll-Free: 800-977-7307
www.hndental.com
For Profit Organization: Yes

Healthplan and Services Defined
PLAN TYPE: Dental
Model Type: Network
Plan Specialty: Dental
Benefits Offered: Dental

Type of Coverage
Individual, Dental coverage for Healthy Familie

Geographic Areas Served
Los Angeles and Sacramento County

101 Health Net Federal Services (HNFS)
2025 Aerojet Road
Mail Code CA-169-01-27
Rancho Cordova, CA 95742
Toll-Free: 844-866-9378
www.hnfs.com
Subsidiary of: Centene Corporation
For Profit Organization: Yes
Total Enrollment: 8,500,000

Healthplan and Services Defined
PLAN TYPE: Multiple
Model Type: Network
Plan Specialty: Behavioral Health
Benefits Offered: Behavioral Health, Anger management; DUI program; alcohol & drug assessments

Type of Coverage
Commercial, Individual, Medicare, Supplemental Medicare

Geographic Areas Served
Alaska, Arizona, California, Colorado, Hawaii, Idaho, Iowa (except the Rock Island Arsenal area), Kansas, Minnesota, Missouri, (except the St. Louis area), Montana, Nebraska, Nevada, New Mexico, North Dakota, Oregon, South Dakota, Texas (areas of Western Texas only), Utah, Washington, and Wyoming

Key Personnel
Chief Operating Officer . . . . Susan J. Pietrykowski
Chief Financial Officer . . . . Joseph P. Semith
Vice President, Ops. Ezra M. Easley
Media Contact . . . . Molly Tuttle
molly.m.tuttle@healthnet.com

102 Health Net of California
21281 Burbank Boulevard
Woodland Hills, CA 91367
Toll-Free: 888-926-4988
ifp.healthnetcalifornia.com
Secondary Address: 21650 Oxnard Street, Woodland Hills, CA 91367
Subsidiary of: Centene Corporation
For Profit Organization: Yes
Year Founded: 1977

Healthplan and Services Defined
PLAN TYPE: HMO
Model Type: Network
Plan Specialty: Behavioral Health

Type of Coverage
Commercial, Individual, Medicare, Supplemental Medicare, Medi-Cal

Geographic Areas Served
Statewide

Key Personnel
President . . . . Brian Ternan

103 Health Net, Inc.
21281 Burbank Blvd
Woodland Hills, CA 91367
Toll-Free: 877-527-8409
www.healthnet.com
Secondary Address: 11931 Foundation Place D, Rancho Cordova, CA 95670
Subsidiary of: Centene Corporation
For Profit Organization: Yes
Year Founded: 1979
Total Enrollment: 6,100,000

Healthplan and Services Defined
PLAN TYPE: Multiple
Model Type: IPA, Group
Plan Specialty: Behavioral Health, PBM, Substance abuse and employee assistance programs.
Benefits Offered: Behavioral Health, Chiropractic, Dental, Disease Management, Prescription, Vision, Wellness, Benefits vary according to plan
Offers Demand Management Patient Information Service: Yes

Type of Coverage
Commercial, Individual, Medicare, Supplemental Medicare, Health Net Medi-Cal
Catastrophic Illness Benefit: Covered

Type of Payment Plans Offered
POS, DFFS, FFS

Geographic Areas Served
Statewide

Peer Review Type
Utilization Review: Yes
Second Surgical Opinion: Yes
Case Management: Yes

Publishes and Distributes Report Card: Yes

Accreditation Certification
NCQA
TJC Accreditation, Medicare Approved, Utilization Review, Pre-Admission Certification, State Licensure, Quality Assurance Program

Key Personnel
Chief Executive Officer . . . . Brian Ternan
Chief Medical Officer . . . . Alex Y. Chen
Chief Operating Officer . . . . Kerri Balbone
Chief Financial Officer. . . . . Jessica Sellner
Contact, Federal Services . . . . Molly Tuttle
molly.tuttle@healthnet.com

Specialty Managed Care Partners
Enters into Contracts with Regional Business Coalitions: Yes

104 Health Plan of San Joaquin
7751 South Manthey Road
French Camp, CA 95231-9802
Toll-Free: 888-936-7526
Phone: 209-942-6340
Fax: 209-942-6305
www.hpsj.com
Secondary Address: 1025 J. Street, Modesto, CA 95354
Non-Profit Organization: Yes
Year Founded: 1996
Number of Primary Care Physicians: 180
Number of Referral/Specialty Physicians: 1,400
Total Enrollment: 335,000
State Enrollment: 335,000

Healthplan and Services Defined
PLAN TYPE: HMO
Benefits Offered: Behavioral Health, Dental, Inpatient SNF, Podiatry, Prescription, Vision, Wellness
Offers Demand Management Patient Information Service: Yes
DMPI Services Offered: 24 Hour Nurse Advice Hotline

Type of Coverage
Commercial, Individual, Medicaid, Medi-Cal

Geographic Areas Served
San Joaquin and Stanislaus counties

Key Personnel
CEO. . . . . Michael Schrader
CFO . . . . Michelle Tetreault
Chief Medical Officer . . . . Lakshmi Dhanvanthari
Chief Operations Officer. . . . . Lizeth Granados
Chief Information Officer. . . . . Cheron Vail
Medical Director . . . . Dorcas C. Yao, MD
VP, External Affairs. . . . . David Hurst

105 Health Plan of San Mateo
801 Gateway Boulevard
Suite 100
South San Francisco, CA 94080
Toll-Free: 800-735-2929
Phone: 650-616-0050
Fax: 650-616-0060
info@hpsm.org
www.hpsm.org
Non-Profit Organization: Yes
Year Founded: 1987
Number of Affiliated Hospitals: 12
Number of Primary Care Physicians: 197
Total Enrollment: 130,000
State Enrollment: 130,000

Healthplan and Services Defined
PLAN TYPE: HMO
Model Type: IPA

Benefits Offered: Dental, Disease Management, Long-Term Care, Prescription, Vision, Wellness

Type of Coverage
Individual, Medicaid, Medi-Cal, Healthy Families, Healthy

Type of Payment Plans Offered
Capitated, FFS

Geographic Areas Served
San Mateo county

Key Personnel
CEO .... Maya Altman
CFO .... Trent Ehrgood
CIO .... Eben Yong
CCO .... Ian Johansson
Int. Chief Med. Officer .... Richard Moore
Chief HR Officer .... Vicki Simpson

106 Health Services Los Angeles County

313 N Figueroa Street
Los Angeles, CA 90012
Toll-Free: 844-804-0055
dhs.lacounty.gov/wps/portal/dhs
Subsidiary of: Los Angeles County Department of Health Services
Non-Profit Organization: Yes
Federally Qualified: Yes
Number of Affiliated Hospitals: 4
Total Enrollment: 600,000

Healthplan and Services Defined
PLAN TYPE: Other
Model Type: municipal health system
Plan Specialty: Juvenile Justice System, children in Foster Care
Benefits Offered: Disease Management, Inpatient SNF, Physical Therapy, Prescription, Wellness, AIDS Drug Assistance Program; Pediatrics

Type of Coverage
Catastrophic Illness Benefit: Unlimited

Geographic Areas Served
Los Angeles County

Subscriber Information
Average Monthly Fee Per Subscriber
    (Employee + Employer Contribution):
        Employee Only (Self): $143.05
        Employee & 1 Family Member: $286.15
        Employee & 2 Family Members: $332.01
Average Subscriber Co-Payment:
    Primary Care Physician: $5.00
    Prescription Drugs: $4.00
    Home Health Care Max. Days/Visits Covered: Unlimited
    Nursing Home Max. Days/Visits Covered: 60 days

Network Qualifications
Pre-Admission Certification: Yes

Peer Review Type
Utilization Review: Yes
Second Surgical Opinion: Yes
Case Management: Yes

Accreditation Certification
TJC Accreditation, Medicare Approved, Utilization Review, State Licensure, Quality Assurance Program

Key Personnel
Director .... Christina R. Ghaly, MD

107 Humana Health Insurance of California

1 Park Plaza
Suite 470
Irvine, CA 92614
Phone: 949-623-1447
www.humana.com
Secondary Address: 516 W Shaw Avenue, Suite 200, Fresno, CA 93704, 559-221-2522
Subsidiary of: Humana Inc.
For Profit Organization: Yes

Healthplan and Services Defined
PLAN TYPE: HMO/PPO
Model Type: Network
Plan Specialty: Dental, Vision
Benefits Offered: Dental, Prescription, Vision, Life, LTD, STD, Benefits vary according to plan

Type of Coverage
Commercial, Medicare

Geographic Areas Served
Statewide

Accreditation Certification
URAC, NCQA, CORE

Key Personnel
Market VP .... Brian Sullivan

108 Inter Valley Health Plan

300 S Park Avenue
P.O. Box 6002
Pomona, CA 91769-6002
Toll-Free: 800-251-8191
info@ivhp.com
www.ivhp.com
Non-Profit Organization: Yes
Year Founded: 1979
Owned by an Integrated Delivery Network (IDN): No
Federally Qualified: Yes
Number of Affiliated Hospitals: 16
Number of Primary Care Physicians: 1,638
Number of Referral/Specialty Physicians: 2,672
Total Enrollment: 18,900

Healthplan and Services Defined
PLAN TYPE: Medicare
Model Type: Network
Benefits Offered: Behavioral Health, Dental, Home Care, Inpatient SNF, Physical Therapy, Prescription, Psychiatric, Transplant, Wellness

Type of Coverage
Medicare
Catastrophic Illness Benefit: Unlimited

Type of Payment Plans Offered
Capitated

Geographic Areas Served
Southern California counties including Los Angeles, Riverside, San Bernardino, and Orange

Network Qualifications
Pre-Admission Certification: No

Peer Review Type
Utilization Review: Yes
Second Surgical Opinion: Yes
Case Management: Yes

Accreditation Certification
URAC, PBGH, CCHRI
TJC Accreditation, Medicare Approved, Utilization Review, State Licensure, Quality Assurance Program

Key Personnel
President/CEO .... Micheal A. Nelson
VP, Finance/CFO .... Bruce Brown
VP, Health Plan Operation .... Susan Tenorio
Chief Medical Officer .... Kenneth E. Smith, MD
Chief Information Officer .... Bill Chen

Average Claim Compensation
Physician's Fees Charged: 75%
Hospital's Fees Charged: 55%

Specialty Managed Care Partners
Vision Service Plan

---

109 Kaiser Permanente
1 Kaiser Plaza
Oakland, CA 94612
Toll-Free: 800-813-2000
healthy.kaiserpermanente.org
Non-Profit Organization: Yes
Year Founded: 1945
Number of Affiliated Hospitals: 39
Number of Primary Care Physicians: 23,271
Total Enrollment: 12,400,000

Healthplan and Services Defined
PLAN TYPE: HMO/PPO
Model Type: Group
Benefits Offered: Dental, Disease Management, Home Care, Inpatient SNF, Long-Term Care, Physical Therapy, Podiatry, Prescription, Psychiatric, Transplant, Vision, Wellness, Benefits vary according to plan
Offers Demand Management Patient Information Service: Yes

Type of Coverage
Commercial, Individual, Medicare, Supplemental Medicare, Medicaid
Catastrophic Illness Benefit: Covered

Type of Payment Plans Offered
POS

Geographic Areas Served
California, Colorado, Georgia, Hawaii, Maryland, Oregon, Virginia, Washington and the District of Columbia

Network Qualifications
Pre-Admission Certification: Yes

Peer Review Type
Utilization Review: Yes
Second Surgical Opinion: Yes
Case Management: Yes

Publishes and Distributes Report Card: Yes

Accreditation Certification
NCQA
TJC Accreditation, Medicare Approved, Utilization Review, Pre-Admission Certification, State Licensure, Quality Assurance Program

Key Personnel
Chair/CEO .... Greg A. Adams
EVP/CIO/CTO .... Diane Comer
EVP/CFO .... Kathy Lancaster
SVP, Government Relations .... Anthony A. Barrueta
SVP/Chief Comms. Officer .... Catherine Hernandez
SVP, Chief Legal Officer .... Vanessa M. Benavides
EVP/Chief Medical Officer .... Andrew Bindman, MD

Specialty Managed Care Partners
Enters into Contracts with Regional Business Coalitions: No

---

110 Kaiser Permanente Northern California
3600 Broadway
Oakland, CA 94611
Toll-Free: 800-464-4000
Phone: 510-752-1000
thrive.kaiserpermanente.org/care-near-northern-california
Subsidiary of: Kaiser Permanente
Non-Profit Organization: Yes
Year Founded: 1945
Number of Affiliated Hospitals: 237
Number of Primary Care Physicians: 8,000
Total Enrollment: 4,383,328
State Enrollment: 4,383,328

Healthplan and Services Defined
PLAN TYPE: HMO/PPO
Model Type: Group, Network
Benefits Offered: Disease Management, Home Care, Inpatient SNF, Long-Term Care, Physical Therapy, Podiatry, Prescription, Psychiatric, Transplant, Vision, Wellness, Benefits vary according to plan

Type of Coverage
Commercial, Individual, Medicare, Medicaid

Type of Payment Plans Offered
POS, Combination FFS & DFFS

Geographic Areas Served
Central Valley, Diablo, East Bay, Fresno, Greater Southern Alameda County, Marin-Sonoma, Napa-Solano, Greater Sacramento, Greater San Francisco, Peninsula and South Bay

Subscriber Information
Average Monthly Fee Per Subscriber
(Employee + Employer Contribution):
Employee Only (Self): Varies by plan

Network Qualifications
Pre-Admission Certification: Yes

Publishes and Distributes Report Card: Yes

Accreditation Certification
TJC Accreditation, Medicare Approved, Utilization Review, Pre-Admission Certification, State Licensure, Quality Assurance Program

Key Personnel
Regional President . . . . Carrie Owen Plietz
Media Contact . . . . Kerri Leedy
559-307-6491

Specialty Managed Care Partners
Enters into Contracts with Regional Business Coalitions: Yes

---

111 Kaiser Permanente Southern California
9455 Clairemont Mesa Boulevard
San Diego, CA 92123
thrive.kaiserpermanente.org/care-near-you/southern-californi
Subsidiary of: Kaiser Permanente
Non-Profit Organization: Yes
Year Founded: 1945
Number of Primary Care Physicians: 7,600
Total Enrollment: 4,608,507
State Enrollment: 4,608,507

Healthplan and Services Defined
PLAN TYPE: Multiple
Model Type: Network
Benefits Offered: Disease Management, Home Care, Inpatient SNF, Long-Term Care, Physical Therapy, Podiatry, Prescription, Psychiatric, Transplant, Vision, Wellness, Benefits vary according to plan

Type of Coverage
Commercial, Individual, Medicare, Medicaid

Geographic Areas Served
Antelope Valley, Baldwin Park, Downey, Kern County, Los Angeles, Orange County, Panorama City, Riverside County, San Bernadino County, San Diego, South Bay, Ventura County, West Los Angeles & Woodland Hills

Key Personnel
Regional President . . . . Julie Miller-Phipps
Media Contact. . . . . Terry Kanakri
626-660-6543

---

112 Kern Family Health Care
2900 Buck Owens Blvd.
Bakersfield, CA 93308
Toll-Free: 800-391-2000
Phone: 661-664-5000
louiei@khs-net.com
www.kernfamilyhealthcare.com
Secondary Address: 9700 Stockdale Highway, Bakersfield, CA 93311, 661-632-1590
Subsidiary of: Kern Health Systems
Non-Profit Organization: Yes
Number of Affiliated Hospitals: 10

Number of Primary Care Physicians: 213
Number of Referral/Specialty Physicians: 400
Total Enrollment: 97,000
State Enrollment: 90,074

Healthplan and Services Defined
PLAN TYPE: HMO
Model Type: Network
Benefits Offered: Behavioral Health, Chiropractic, Dental, Disease Management, Prescription, Vision, Wellness
Offers Demand Management Patient Information Service: Yes
DMPI Services Offered: 24 Hour Nurse Advice Hotline

Type of Coverage
Individual, Medicaid, Medi-Cal

Key Personnel
Chief Executive Officer . . . . Doug Hayward
Chief Financial Officer . . . . Robert Landis
Chief Operations Officer. . . . . Alan Avery
Chief Medical Officer. . . . . Dr. Martha E. Tasinga
Chief Information Officer . . . . Richard Pruitt
Manager, Marketing . . . . Louis Iturriria
661-664-5120
louiei@khs-net.com

---

113 L.A. Care Health Plan
1055 W 7th Street
10th Floor
Los Angeles, CA 90017
Toll-Free: 888-452-2273
www.lacare.org
Non-Profit Organization: Yes
Year Founded: 1997
Total Enrollment: 2,000,000

Healthplan and Services Defined
PLAN TYPE: HMO
Benefits Offered: Behavioral Health, Dental, Home Care, Inpatient SNF, Physical Therapy, Prescription, Transplant, Vision, Wellness, Asthma Care; Cancer Clinical Trials; Diabetic Care; Diagnostic/Labs/Imaging Services; Durable Medical Equipment; Hospice

Type of Coverage
Individual, Medicare, Medicaid

Geographic Areas Served
Los Angeles county

Key Personnel
Chief Executive Officer. . . . . John Baackes
Chief Operating Officer . . . . Acacia B. Reed
Chief Financial Officer. . . . . Marie Montgomery
Chief Medical Officer . . . . Richard Seidman
General Counsel . . . . Augustavia Haydel
Chief Compliance Officer . . . . Tom Mapp
Chief Information Officer . . . . Tom MacDougall

114 Lakeside Community Healthcare Network
191 S Buena Vista Street
Suite 200
Burbank, CA 91505
Phone: 818-557-2671
For Profit Organization: Yes
Year Founded: 1997
Number of Primary Care Physicians: 300
Number of Referral/Specialty Physicians: 1,500
Total Enrollment: 250,000
State Enrollment: 250,000

Healthplan and Services Defined
PLAN TYPE: HMO
Model Type: IPA

Geographic Areas Served
San Fernando, San Gabriel, and Santa Clarita Valleys. Parts of Ventura and San Bernadino counties

Key Personnel
Dir., Network Management . . . . Julie Feind

115 Landmark Healthplan of California
2629 Townsgate Rd.
Suite 235
Westlake Village, CA 91361
Toll-Free: 800-298-4875
Fax: 800-547-9784
www.lhp-ca.com
For Profit Organization: Yes
Year Founded: 1985
Number of Referral/Specialty Physicians: 4,500
Total Enrollment: 150,000

Healthplan and Services Defined
PLAN TYPE: HMO/PPO
Model Type: IPA, Network
Plan Specialty: Chiropractic, Acupuncture
Benefits Offered: Chiropractic, Acupuncture

Type of Coverage
Commercial

Type of Payment Plans Offered
Combination FFS & DFFS

Geographic Areas Served
Statewide

Network Qualifications
Pre-Admission Certification: Yes

Peer Review Type
Utilization Review: Yes
Case Management: Yes

Key Personnel
President/CEO . . . . George W. Vieth, Jr
VP/CFO . . . . Thomas P. Klammer
VP, Sales . . . . Greg Clure
   800-298-4875

116 Liberty Dental Plan of California
340 Commerce
Suite 100
Irvine, CA 92602
Toll-Free: 888-703-6999
www.libertydentalplan.com
Mailing Address: P.O. Box 26110, Santa Ana, CA 92799-6110
For Profit Organization: Yes
Year Founded: 2001
Total Enrollment: 3,000,000

Healthplan and Services Defined
PLAN TYPE: Dental
Other Type: Dental HMO
Plan Specialty: Dental
Benefits Offered: Dental

Type of Coverage
Commercial, Individual, Medicare, Medicaid, Medi-Cal

Geographic Areas Served
Statewide

Accreditation Certification
NCQA

Key Personnel
CA Dental Director . . . . Charag Sarkari

117 Managed Health Network, Inc.
2370 Kerner Boulevard
San Rafael, CA 94901
Toll-Free: 800-327-2133
productinfo@mhn.com
www.mhn.com
Subsidiary of: Health Net, Inc.
For Profit Organization: Yes
Number of Affiliated Hospitals: 1,500
Number of Primary Care Physicians: 63,000
Total Enrollment: 7,300,000

Healthplan and Services Defined
PLAN TYPE: Other
Plan Specialty: Behavioral Health, Substance abuse and employee assistance programs (EAPs).
Benefits Offered: Behavioral Health, Disease Management, Wellness, Work/life balance, employee productivity and organizational effectiveness.

Geographic Areas Served
Nationwide

Accreditation Certification
URAC

118 March Vision Care
6601 Center Drive W
Suite 200
Los Angeles, CA 90045
Toll-Free: 877-627-2456
marchinfo@marchvisioncare.com
www.marchvisioncare.com
For Profit Organization: Yes

California

Healthplan and Services Defined
PLAN TYPE: Vision
Plan Specialty: Vision
Benefits Offered: Vision

Type of Coverage
Commercial, Medicare, Medicaid

Geographic Areas Served
Nationwide

Key Personnel
Founder & CEO . . . . Glenville A March, Jr, MD

119 Medcore Medical Group
2609 E Hammer Lane
Stockton, CA 95210
Toll-Free: 877-963-2673
Phone: 209-320-2650
Fax: 209-320-2644
medcoreipa.com
Year Founded: 1985

Healthplan and Services Defined
PLAN TYPE: Other
Model Type: IPA

Geographic Areas Served
San Joaquin County

Key Personnel
Chief Operating Officer . . . . Maria Martinez

120 Medica HealthCare Plans, Inc
9100 S Dadeland Boulevard
Suite 1250
Miami, FL 33156
Toll-Free: 800-407-9069
Fax: 501-262-7070
MemberServices@uhcsouthflorida.com
www.medicaplans.com
Mailing Address: P.O. Box 30770, Salt Lake City, UT 81303-0770
Number of Affiliated Hospitals: 23
Number of Primary Care Physicians: 912
Total Enrollment: 12,000

Healthplan and Services Defined
PLAN TYPE: Medicare
Benefits Offered: Chiropractic, Dental, Disease Management, Inpatient SNF, Podiatry, Prescription, Psychiatric, Vision, Wellness

Type of Coverage
Medicare, Supplemental Medicare

Geographic Areas Served
Miami-Dade & Broward counties

121 Molina Healthcare
200 Oceangate
Suite 100
Long Beach, CA 90802
Toll-Free: 888-562-5442
Phone: 562-435-3666
www.molinahealthcare.com
For Profit Organization: Yes
Year Founded: 1980
Total Enrollment: 3,400,000

Healthplan and Services Defined
PLAN TYPE: Medicare
Other Type: Madicaid
Benefits Offered: Disease Management, Physical Therapy, Wellness

Type of Coverage
Medicare, Supplemental Medicare, Medicaid

Geographic Areas Served
California, Florida, Idaho, Illinois, Michigan, Mississippi, New Mexico, New York, Ohio, Puerto Rico, South Carolina, Texas, Utah, Washington and Wisconsin

Key Personnel
President/CEO. . . . . Joseph Zubretsky
Chief Financial Officer . . . . Mark Keim
Chief Legal Officer. . . . . Jeff Barlow, JD
EVP, Health Plans. . . . . Marc Russo
EVP, Health Plan Services . . . . James Woys

122 Molina Healthcare of California
200 Oceangate
Suite 100
Long Beach, CA 90802
Toll-Free: 800-526-8196
www.molinahealthcare.com
Subsidiary of: Molina Healthcare, Inc.
For Profit Organization: Yes
Year Founded: 1989

Healthplan and Services Defined
PLAN TYPE: Medicare
Model Type: Network
Plan Specialty: Dental, PBM, Vision, Integrated Medicare/Medicaid (Duals)
Benefits Offered: Dental, Prescription, Vision, Wellness, Life

Type of Coverage
Individual, Medicare, Supplemental Medicare, Medicaid

Geographic Areas Served
Statewide

Key Personnel
President/Chair. . . . . John Kotal

123 On Lok Lifeways
1333 Bush Street
San Francisco, CA 94109
Phone: 415-292-8888
Fax: 415-292-8745
info@onlok.org

www.onlok.org
Non-Profit Organization: Yes
Year Founded: 1971
Number of Affiliated Hospitals: 7
Number of Primary Care Physicians: 10
Number of Referral/Specialty Physicians: 100
Total Enrollment: 1,000
State Enrollment: 942

Healthplan and Services Defined
  PLAN TYPE: HMO
  Model Type: Staff
  Benefits Offered: Dental, Home Care, Long-Term Care, Physical Therapy, Podiatry, Prescription, Vision, Wellness

Type of Coverage
  Medicaid
  Catastrophic Illness Benefit: Covered

Geographic Areas Served
  San Francisco, Fremont, Newark, Union City and Santa Clara County

Accreditation Certification
  TJC Accreditation, Medicare Approved, Utilization Review, Pre-Admission Certification, State Licensure, Quality Assurance Program

Key Personnel
  CEO .... Grace Li
  CFO .... Gary Campanella
  COO .... David C. Nolan
  Chief Medical Officer .... Jay Luxenberg, MD
  Chief, Gov. Affairs .... Eileen Kunz, MPH
  Chief Development Officer .... John V. Blazek

---

124 OptumRx
Irvine, CA
Toll-Free: 800-356-3477
www.optum.com

Healthplan and Services Defined
  PLAN TYPE: Other
  Other Type: PBM
  Benefits Offered: Prescription

Key Personnel
  Chief Excutive Officer .... Heather Cianfrocco

---

125 Pacific Foundation for Medical Care
3510 Unocal Place
Suite 108
Santa Rosa, CA 95403
Toll-Free: 800-548-7677
Phone: 707-525-4281
Fax: 707-525-4311
pfmc.org
Non-Profit Organization: Yes
Year Founded: 1957
Number of Primary Care Physicians: 34,000

Healthplan and Services Defined
  PLAN TYPE: Multiple
  Model Type: Network
  Plan Specialty: EPO, PPO, LOCO

Geographic Areas Served
  counties: Alameda, Butte, Colusa, Contra Costa, El Dorado, Glenn, Imperial, Lake, Lassen, Marin, Mendocino, Modoc, Napa, Nevada, Placer, Plumas, Sacramento, San Diego, San Francisco, Shasta, Sierra, Siskiyou, Solano, Sonoma, Sutter, Tehama, Trinity,Yolo, Yuba

Network Qualifications
  Pre-Admission Certification: Yes

Peer Review Type
  Utilization Review: Yes
  Second Surgical Opinion: Yes
  Case Management: Yes

Publishes and Distributes Report Card: No

Key Personnel
  Chief Executive Officer .... John Nicol
    jnacol@rhs.org
  President .... Dan Lightfoot, MD
  Medical Director .... William Pitt, MD
  Contact .... Kathy Pass
    705-525-4281
    kpass@rhs.org

Specialty Managed Care Partners
  Enters into Contracts with Regional Business Coalitions: No

---

126 Pacific Health Alliance
1525 Rollins Road
Suite B
Burlingame, CA 94010
Toll-Free: 800-533-4742
Fax: 650-375-5820
pha@pacifichealthalliance.com
www.pacifichealthalliance.com
For Profit Organization: Yes
Year Founded: 1986
Number of Affiliated Hospitals: 400
Number of Primary Care Physicians: 50,000
Number of Referral/Specialty Physicians: 1,500
Total Enrollment: 338,000
State Enrollment: 197,000

Healthplan and Services Defined
  PLAN TYPE: PPO
  Model Type: Group
  Plan Specialty: Behavioral Health, Chiropractic, EPO, Lab, Worker's Compensation, UR
  Benefits Offered: Behavioral Health, Chiropractic, Dental, Home Care, Inpatient SNF, Long-Term Care, Physical Therapy, Podiatry, Psychiatric, Transplant, Vision, Worker's Compensation

Type of Coverage
  Commercial, Individual, Indemnity

Type of Payment Plans Offered
  DFFS, FFS

Geographic Areas Served
  Nationwide

Network Qualifications
Pre-Admission Certification: Yes

Peer Review Type
Utilization Review: Yes
Second Surgical Opinion: Yes
Case Management: Yes

Publishes and Distributes Report Card: No

Accreditation Certification
TJC Accreditation, Medicare Approved, Utilization Review, Pre-Admission Certification, State Licensure, Quality Assurance Program

Average Claim Compensation
Physician's Fees Charged: 70%
Hospital's Fees Charged: 75%

Specialty Managed Care Partners
Daughters of Charity, Saint Rose Hospital, San Monterry
Enters into Contracts with Regional Business Coalitions: No

---

127 Partnership HealthPlan of California
4665 Business Center Drive
Fairfield, CA 94534-1675
Toll-Free: 800-863-4155
Fax: 707-863-4117
www.partnershiphp.org
Secondary Address: 3688 Avtech Parkway, Redding, CA 96002, 855-798-8760
Non-Profit Organization: Yes
Year Founded: 1994
Total Enrollment: 560,000

Healthplan and Services Defined
PLAN TYPE: Other
Other Type: Medi-Cal
Benefits Offered: Behavioral Health, Chiropractic, Dental, Home Care, Inpatient SNF, Long-Term Care, Podiatry, Prescription, Vision, Durable Medical Equipment; Hospice; Prenatal Care; Substance Abuse; Transportation; Labs & Imaging; Pediatrics; and more

Type of Coverage
Individual, Medicare, Medicaid

Geographic Areas Served
counties: Del Norte, Humboldt, Lake, Lassen, Marin, Mendocino, Modoc, Napa, Shasta, Siskiyou, Solano, Sonoma, Trinity and Yolo

Accreditation Certification
NCQA

Key Personnel
Chief Executive Officer . . . . Liz Gibboney
Chief Operating Officer . . . . Sonja Bjork
Chief Financial Officer . . . . Patti McFarland
Administrative Officer. . . . . Sue Monez
Chief Information Officer. . . . . Kirt Kemp
Chief Medical Officer . . . . Robert Moore, MD

---

128 Premier Access Insurance/Access Dental
P.O. Box 659010
Sacramento, CA 95865-9010
Toll-Free: 888-634-6074
Phone: 916-920-2500
Fax: 916-563-9000
info@premierlife.com
www.premierlife.com
Subsidiary of: Guardian Life Insurance Co.
For Profit Organization: Yes
Year Founded: 1989
Number of Primary Care Physicians: 1,000
Total Enrollment: 125,000

Healthplan and Services Defined
PLAN TYPE: PPO
Other Type: Dental
Model Type: Network
Plan Specialty: Dental
Benefits Offered: Dental

Type of Payment Plans Offered
FFS

Geographic Areas Served
California, Nevada, Utah, Arizona

Accreditation Certification
TJC Accreditation, Medicare Approved, Utilization Review, Pre-Admission Certification, State Licensure, Quality Assurance Program

Key Personnel
President & CEO . . . . Deanna M. Mulligan

---

129 Primecare Dental Plan
10700 Civic Center Drive
Suite 100-A
Rancho Cucamonga, CA 91730
Toll-Free: 800-937-3400
unumdentalhmo.net
For Profit Organization: Yes
Year Founded: 1983
Physician Owned Organization: Yes
Total Enrollment: 17,000

Healthplan and Services Defined
PLAN TYPE: Dental
Model Type: Staff
Plan Specialty: Dental
Benefits Offered: Dental
Offers Demand Management Patient Information Service: Yes

Type of Coverage
Commercial, Individual

Type of Payment Plans Offered
DFFS, Capitated

Geographic Areas Served
Alameda, Butte, Colusa, Contra Costa, El Dorado, Fresno, Glenn, Kern, Kings, Los Angeles, Madera, Mariposa, Merced Monterey, Napa, Nevada, Orange, Placer, Riverside, Sacramento, San Benito, San Bernardino, San Diego, San Francisco, San Joaquin, San Luis Opispo, San Mateo, Santa

Barbara, Santa Clara, Santa Cruz, Shasta, Siskiyou, Solano, Sonoma, Stanislaus, Sutter, Tehama, Tuolumne, Tulare, Ventura, Yolo, and Yuba counties

Network Qualifications
Pre-Admission Certification: Yes

Peer Review Type
Utilization Review: Yes

Publishes and Distributes Report Card: No

Accreditation Certification
URAC, NCQA
Utilization Review

Key Personnel
President & CEO . . . . Rick McKenney

Specialty Managed Care Partners
Enters into Contracts with Regional Business Coalitions: No

130 PTPN
26635 W Agoura Road
Suite 250
Calabasas, CA 91302
Toll-Free: 800-766-7876
www.ptpn.com
Year Founded: 1985
Number of Primary Care Physicians: 3,500

Healthplan and Services Defined
PLAN TYPE: PPO
Other Type: Rehab Network
Model Type: Network
Plan Specialty: Outpatient Rehabilitation (Physical, Occupational and Speech Therapy)
Benefits Offered: Physical Therapy, Worker's Compensation, Occupational Therapy; Speech Therapy; Physical Therapy; Hand Therapy; Speech/Language Therapy; and Pediatric Therapy

Type of Payment Plans Offered
DFFS

Geographic Areas Served
Nationwide

Network Qualifications
Minimum Years of Practice: 3

Peer Review Type
Utilization Review: Yes

Accreditation Certification
NCQA

Key Personnel
President . . . . Michael Weinper
VP/COO . . . . Stevyn Voyles
Dir., Quality Assurance . . . . Michel Kaye

131 San Francisco Health Plan
50 Beale Street
12th Floor
San Francisco, CA 94119
Toll-Free: 800-288-5555
Phone: 415-547-7818
Fax: 415-547-7826
www.sfhp.org
Mailing Address: P.O. Box 194247
Year Founded: 1994
Number of Affiliated Hospitals: 6
Number of Primary Care Physicians: 2,300
Total Enrollment: 145,000
State Enrollment: 145,000

Healthplan and Services Defined
PLAN TYPE: HMO
Benefits Offered: Dental, Disease Management, Prescription, Vision, Wellness

Type of Coverage
Medicare, Medicaid, Medi-Cal, Healthy Families, Healthy

Geographic Areas Served
San Francisco

Key Personnel
Chief Executive Officer . . . . John F Grgurina, Jr
Chief Financial Officer . . . . Skip Bishop
Chief Medical Officer . . . . Jim Glauber, MD
Chief Information Officer . . . . Darin Moore
Compliance Officer . . . . Nina Maruyama
Human Res. Consultant . . . . Kate Gormley
Dir., System Development . . . . Cecil Newton
Dir., Business Services . . . . Van Wong

132 Santa Clara Family Health Foundations Inc
6201 San Ignacio Avenue
San Jose, CA 95119
Toll-Free: 800-260-2055
Phone: 408-376-2000
www.scfhp.com
Mailing Address: P.O. Box 18880, San Jose, CA 95158
Non-Profit Organization: Yes
Year Founded: 1997
Number of Affiliated Hospitals: 6
Number of Primary Care Physicians: 742
Number of Referral/Specialty Physicians: 3,490
Total Enrollment: 245,000
State Enrollment: 245,000

Healthplan and Services Defined
PLAN TYPE: HMO
Benefits Offered: Behavioral Health, Disease Management, Long-Term Care, Prescription, Wellness
Offers Demand Management Patient Information Service: Yes
DMPI Services Offered: 24 hour nurse advice line

Type of Coverage
Commercial, Medicaid, Medicare Advantage SNP, Medi-Cal, H

Geographic Areas Served
Santa Clara County

Subscriber Information
Average Monthly Fee Per Subscriber
   (Employee + Employer Contribution):
      Employee & 2 Family Members: $18 max per family

Key Personnel
Chief Executive Officer . . . . Christine M. Tomcala
Chief Information Officer . . . . Jonathan Tomayo
Chief Medical Officer . . . . Laurie Nakahira
Chief Financial Officer . . . . Neal Jarecki
Chief Compliance Officer. . . . . Robin L. Larmer
VP, Human Resources . . . . Sharon Valdez
Chief Operating Officer . . . . Christine K. Turner

Specialty Managed Care Partners
Medimpact

133 Sant, Community Physicians
7370 N Palm
Suite 101
Fresno, CA 93711
Toll-Free: 800-652-2900
Phone: 559-228-5400
Fax: 559-228-2958
www.santehealth.net
Year Founded: 1980
Number of Primary Care Physicians: 1,200
Total Enrollment: 120,000

Healthplan and Services Defined
PLAN TYPE: HMO/PPO
Model Type: IPA
Benefits Offered: Wellness

Type of Coverage
medi-cal

Type of Payment Plans Offered
FFS

Geographic Areas Served
Fresno, Madera and Kings counties

Network Qualifications
Pre-Admission Certification: Yes

Peer Review Type
Utilization Review: Yes
Case Management: Yes

Publishes and Distributes Report Card: Yes

Accreditation Certification
TJC Accreditation, Medicare Approved, Utilization Review, Pre-Admission Certification, State Licensure, Quality Assurance Program

Specialty Managed Care Partners
Enters into Contracts with Regional Business Coalitions: Yes

134 SCAN Health Plan
P.O. Box 22616
Long Beach, CA 90801-5616
Toll-Free: 800-559-3500
memberservices@scanhealthplan.com
www.scanhealthplan.com

Non-Profit Organization: Yes
Year Founded: 1977
Number of Affiliated Hospitals: 151
Number of Primary Care Physicians: 6,560
Number of Referral/Specialty Physicians: 17,186
Total Enrollment: 128,272
State Enrollment: 12,283

Healthplan and Services Defined
PLAN TYPE: HMO
Plan Specialty: Medicare
Benefits Offered: Dental, Prescription, Vision

Type of Coverage
Medicare

Geographic Areas Served
los angeles, san bernardino, sonoma, napa, san diego, ventura, orange, san francisco, riverside, santa clara, stanislaus county

Subscriber Information
Average Annual Deductible Per Subscriber:
   Medicare: $0
Average Subscriber Co-Payment:
   Primary Care Physician: $0-$5
   Hospital ER: $75
   Home Health Care: $0
   Nursing Home: $0
   Nursing Home Max. Days/Visits Covered: 100

Key Personnel
CEO & President . . . . Sachin H. Jain
Chief Financial Officer . . . . Vinod Mohan
General Counsel . . . . Janet Kornblatt
Chief Operations Officer. . . . . Nancy J. Monk
Chief Information Officer . . . . Josh Goode
Chief Pharmacy Officer . . . . Sharon K. Jhawar
SVP, National Sales. . . . . David Milligan
Chief Medical Executive. . . . . Romilla Batra

135 Sharp Health Plan
8520 Tech Way
Suite 200
San Diego, CA 92123
Toll-Free: 800-359-2002
Phone: 858-499-8300
customer.service@sharp.com
www.sharphealthplan.com
Subsidiary of: Sharp HealthCare
Non-Profit Organization: Yes
Year Founded: 1992
Number of Affiliated Hospitals: 13
Number of Primary Care Physicians: 1,700
Total Enrollment: 49,000
State Enrollment: 49,000

Healthplan and Services Defined
PLAN TYPE: HMO
Model Type: Network
Benefits Offered: Dental, Prescription, Vision, Wellness

Type of Coverage
Medicare

Geographic Areas Served
San Diego and Southern Riverside counties

Key Personnel
President/CEO . . . . Melissa Hayden-Cook
VP/CFO . . . . Rita Datko
VP/COO . . . . Leslie Pels-Beck
VP/Chief Medical Officer . . . . Cary Shames, MD
VP Business Development. . . . . Michael Bryd

136 Stanislaus Foundation for Medical Care
2339 St Pauls Way
Modesto, CA 95355
Toll-Free: 800-962-7362
Phone: 209-527-2430
Fax: 209-524-8773
fmc@stanislausmedicalsociety.com
stanfoundation.com
Mailing Address: P.O. Box 576007, Modesto, CA 95357-6007
Non-Profit Organization: Yes
Year Founded: 1957
Physician Owned Organization: Yes
Number of Affiliated Hospitals: 400
Number of Primary Care Physicians: 27,000
Number of Referral/Specialty Physicians: 5,000

Healthplan and Services Defined
PLAN TYPE: PPO
Model Type: Network
Benefits Offered: Dental, Prescription, Vision, Worker's Compensation
Offers Demand Management Patient Information Service: Yes

Geographic Areas Served
Stanislaus, Tuolumne counties

Network Qualifications
Pre-Admission Certification: Yes

Publishes and Distributes Report Card: No

Key Personnel
President of SFMC . . . . David Shiba, MD
Executive Director. . . . . Joanne Chipponeri

Specialty Managed Care Partners
Enters into Contracts with Regional Business Coalitions: No

137 Taylor Benefits Insurance Agency
4820 Harwood Road
Suite 130
San Jose, CA 95124
Toll-Free: 800-903-6066
Phone: 408-358-7502
Fax: 408-723-8201
taylorbenefitsinsurance.com
Year Founded: 1987

Healthplan and Services Defined
PLAN TYPE: Multiple
Benefits Offered: Behavioral Health, Dental, Inpatient SNF, Long-Term Care, Prescription, Vision, Wellness, Life, Short-and-long-term disability; Substance Abuse; Maternity & Newborn Care; Rehabiliation; Labs; Pediatrics

Geographic Areas Served
Plans available for employers statewide

Key Personnel
Principal . . . . Todd Taylor
   todd@taylorbenefits.net
Administrative Assistant . . . . Ronda Agpaoa
   ronda@taylorbenefits.net
Principal . . . . Jennifer Taylor
   jennifer@taylorbenefits.net

138 Trinity Health of California
Saint Agnes Medical Center
1303 E Herndon Avenue
Fresno, CA 93720
Phone: 559-450-3000
www.trinity-health.org
Secondary Address: 20555 Victor Parkway, Livonia, MI 48152-7018, 734-343-1000
Subsidiary of: Trinity Health
Non-Profit Organization: Yes
Year Founded: 2013
Number of Affiliated Hospitals: 92
Total Enrollment: 30,000,000

Healthplan and Services Defined
PLAN TYPE: Other
Benefits Offered: Disease Management, Home Care, Long-Term Care, Psychiatric, Hospice programs, PACE (Program of All Inclusive Care for the Elderly)

Geographic Areas Served
San Joaquin Valley

Key Personnel
President/CEO . . . . Michael A. Slubowski
Chief Operating Officer . . . . Benjamin R. Carter

139 United Concordia of California
516 W Shaw Avenue
Suite 200
Fresno, CA 93704
Phone: 559-228-0400
www.unitedconcordia.com
For Profit Organization: Yes
Year Founded: 1971
Number of Primary Care Physicians: 104,000
Total Enrollment: 8,800,000

Healthplan and Services Defined
PLAN TYPE: Dental
Model Type: Network
Plan Specialty: Dental
Benefits Offered: Dental

Type of Coverage
Commercial, Individual, Military personnel & families

Geographic Areas Served
Nationwide

Accreditation Certification
URAC

140 UnitedHealthcare Community Plan California

UnitedHealthcare Customer Service
P.O. Box 30769
Salt Lake City, UT 84130-0769
Toll-Free: 888-545-5205
www.uhccommunityplan.com/ca
Subsidiary of: UnitedHealth Group
For Profit Organization: Yes

Healthplan and Services Defined
PLAN TYPE: Medicare
Other Type: Medicaid
Model Type: Network
Benefits Offered: Home Care, Prescription, Vision, Wellness, NurseLine, Lab & X-Ray

Type of Coverage
Medicare, Medicaid

Geographic Areas Served
San Diego

Key Personnel
CEO, Community Plan CA . . . . Kevin Kandalaft
kevin_kandalaft@uhc.com

141 UnitedHealthcare of Northern California

2300 Clayton Road
Suite 1000
Concord, CA 94520
Toll-Free: 888-545-5205
Phone: 925-246-1300
www.uhc.com
Subsidiary of: UnitedHealth Group
For Profit Organization: Yes

Healthplan and Services Defined
PLAN TYPE: HMO/PPO
Model Type: Network
Plan Specialty: Behavioral Health, Dental, Disease Management, PBM, Vision
Benefits Offered: Behavioral Health, Dental, Disease Management, Long-Term Care, Prescription, Vision, Wellness, Life, LTD, STD

Type of Coverage
Commercial, Individual, Medicare, Supplemental Medicare, Medicaid, Family, Group
Catastrophic Illness Benefit: Covered

Type of Payment Plans Offered
DFFS, Capitated

Geographic Areas Served
Statewide

Subscriber Information
Average Monthly Fee Per Subscriber
(Employee + Employer Contribution):
Employee Only (Self): Varies
Employee & 1 Family Member: Varies
Employee & 2 Family Members: Varies
Medicare: Varies
Average Annual Deductible Per Subscriber:
Employee Only (Self): Varies
Employee & 1 Family Member: Varies
Employee & 2 Family Members: Varies
Medicare: Varies

Publishes and Distributes Report Card: Yes

Accreditation Certification
NCQA
TJC Accreditation, Utilization Review, State Licensure

Key Personnel
CEO, Northern California . . . . Steve Cain

Specialty Managed Care Partners
Enters into Contracts with Regional Business Coalitions: Yes

142 UnitedHealthcare of Southern California

4365 Executive Drive
Suite 500
San Diego, CA 92121
Toll-Free: 866-270-5785
www.uhc.com
Subsidiary of: UnitedHealth Group
For Profit Organization: Yes

Healthplan and Services Defined
PLAN TYPE: HMO/PPO
Model Type: Network
Plan Specialty: Behavioral Health, Dental, Disease Management, PBM, Vision
Benefits Offered: Behavioral Health, Dental, Disease Management, Long-Term Care, Prescription, Vision, Wellness, Life, LTD, STD

Type of Coverage
Commercial, Individual, Medicare, Supplemental Medicare, Medicaid, Family, Group
Catastrophic Illness Benefit: Covered

Type of Payment Plans Offered
DFFS, Capitated

Geographic Areas Served
Statewide

Subscriber Information
Average Monthly Fee Per Subscriber
(Employee + Employer Contribution):
Employee Only (Self): Varies
Employee & 1 Family Member: Varies
Employee & 2 Family Members: Varies
Medicare: Varies
Average Annual Deductible Per Subscriber:
Employee Only (Self): Varies
Employee & 1 Family Member: Varies
Employee & 2 Family Members: Varies
Medicare: Varies

Publishes and Distributes Report Card: Yes

Accreditation Certification
NCQA
TJC Accreditation, Utilization Review, State Licensure

Key Personnel
CEO, West Region . . . . Dan Rosenthal

Specialty Managed Care Partners
Enters into Contracts with Regional Business Coalitions: Yes

143 University HealthCare Alliance
7999 Gateway Boulevard
Suite 200
Newark, CA 95460
uha_communications@stanfordhealthcare.org
universityhealthcarealliance.org
Subsidiary of: Stanford Health Care / Stanford Medicine
For Profit Organization: Yes
Year Founded: 2011

Healthplan and Services Defined
PLAN TYPE: PPO
Model Type: Network

Geographic Areas Served
San Francisco Bay area

Key Personnel
President/CEO..................... Catherine Krna
Chief Financial Officer............... Mike Weatherford
Chief Operating Officer............. Michael O'Connell

144 Ventura County Health Care Plan
2220 E Gonzales Rd
Suite 210 B
Oxnard, CA 93036
Toll-Free: 800-600-8247
Phone: 805-981-5050
Fax: 805-981-5051
VCHCP.Memberservices@ventura.org
www.vchealthcareplan.org
Non-Profit Organization: Yes
Year Founded: 1993

Healthplan and Services Defined
PLAN TYPE: HMO
Benefits Offered: Behavioral Health, Disease Management, Prescription, Wellness

Geographic Areas Served
Ventura County

Accreditation Certification
NCQA

145 Vision Plan of America
3250 Wilshire Boulevard
Suite 1610
Los Angeles, CA 90010
Toll-Free: 800-400-4872
Fax: 213-384-0084
info@visionplanofamerica.com
www.visionplanofamerica.com
For Profit Organization: Yes
Year Founded: 1986

Healthplan and Services Defined
PLAN TYPE: Vision
Model Type: IPA
Plan Specialty: Dental, Vision
Benefits Offered: Dental, Vision

Type of Coverage
Commercial, Individual

Type of Payment Plans Offered
POS, Capitated

Geographic Areas Served
Nationwide

Peer Review Type
Case Management: Yes

Key Personnel
President & CEO................. Stuart Needleman, OD

146 VSP Vision Care
Rancho Cordova, CA 95670
Toll-Free: 800-877-7195
vsp.com
Subsidiary of: VSP Global
Year Founded: 1955
Total Enrollment: 88,000,000

Healthplan and Services Defined
PLAN TYPE: Vision
Plan Specialty: Vision
Benefits Offered: Vision

Geographic Areas Served
Nationwide, Canada, Australia, and the UK

Key Personnel
President & CEO, Global.............. Michael J. Guyette
President, VSP Vision........... Kate Renwick-Espinosa

147 Western Dental & Orthodontics
530 South Main Street
Orange, CA 92868
Toll-Free: 866-316-9409
corporate@westerndental.com
westerndental.com
For Profit Organization: Yes
Year Founded: 1903
Number of Primary Care Physicians: 2,000
Total Enrollment: 123,880

Healthplan and Services Defined
PLAN TYPE: Dental
Other Type: Dental HMO
Model Type: Staff
Plan Specialty: Dental
Benefits Offered: Dental

Type of Coverage
Commercial, Individual, Medicare, Supplemental Medicare, Medicaid

Geographic Areas Served
California, Nevada, Arizona

Key Personnel
Chief Executive Officer................. Daniel Crowley
President......................... Jeffrey Miller
Chief Financial Officer............ William Dembereckyj

VP, Operations .... Patricia Mahony

148 Western Health Advantage
2349 Gateway Oaks Drive
Suite 100
Sacramento, CA 95833
Toll-Free: 888-227-5942
Phone: 916-563-2250
Fax: 916-568-0126
memberservices@westernhealth.com
www.westernhealth.com
Non-Profit Organization: Yes
Year Founded: 1996
Total Enrollment: 92,000
State Enrollment: 92,000

Healthplan and Services Defined
   PLAN TYPE: HMO
   Model Type: Network
   Benefits Offered: Behavioral Health, Chiropractic, Disease Management, Prescription, Wellness, 24/7 Nurse hotline, 24/7 Travel Assistance

Type of Coverage
   Commercial, Individual

Geographic Areas Served
   Sacramento, Yolo, Solano, El Dorado, Placer, Colusa, Napa, Sonoma, Marin counties

Key Personnel
   President/CEO .... Garry Maisel
   Chief Financial Officer .... Rita Ruecker
   Chief Legal Officer .... Rebecca Downing
   Chief Information Officer .... Glenn Hamburg
   Chief Medical Officer................. Khuram Arif, MD
   Chief Marketing/Branding .... Rick Heron
   Chief Client Services .... Glenn Hamburg
   Chief Sales Officer..................... Bill Figenshu

COLORADO

Health Insurance Coverage Status and Type of Coverage by Age

Category	All Persons Number	All Persons %	Under 19 years Number	Under 19 years %	Under 65 years Number	Under 65 years %
Total population	5,664 *(3)*	100.0 *(0.0)*	1,331 *(4)*	100.0 *(0.0)*	4,835 *(4)*	100.0 *(0.0)*
Covered by some type of health insurance	5,211 *(17)*	92.0 *(0.3)*	1,258 *(9)*	94.5 *(0.6)*	4,386 *(17)*	90.7 *(0.3)*
Covered by private health insurance	4,016 *(28)*	70.9 *(0.5)*	870 *(14)*	65.4 *(1.0)*	3,554 *(26)*	73.5 *(0.5)*
Employer-based	3,249 *(31)*	57.4 *(0.5)*	739 *(16)*	55.5 *(1.1)*	3,018 *(29)*	62.4 *(0.6)*
Direct purchase	754 *(16)*	13.3 *(0.3)*	103 *(7)*	7.8 *(0.5)*	508 *(14)*	10.5 *(0.3)*
TRICARE	230 *(12)*	4.1 *(0.2)*	57 *(6)*	4.3 *(0.5)*	164 *(11)*	3.4 *(0.2)*
Covered by public health insurance	1,785 *(28)*	31.5 *(0.5)*	430 *(14)*	32.3 *(1.0)*	990 *(28)*	20.5 *(0.6)*
Medicaid	967 *(27)*	17.1 *(0.5)*	426 *(14)*	32.0 *(1.1)*	875 *(26)*	18.1 *(0.5)*
Medicare	886 *(6)*	15.6 *(0.1)*	6 *(2)*	0.4 *(0.1)*	92 *(6)*	1.9 *(0.1)*
VA Care	143 *(8)*	2.5 *(0.1)*	2 *(1)*	0.1 *(0.1)*	81 *(6)*	1.7 *(0.1)*
Not covered at any time during the year	453 *(17)*	8.0 *(0.3)*	73 *(8)*	5.5 *(0.6)*	449 *(16)*	9.3 *(0.3)*

Note: Numbers in thousands; Figures cover civilian noninstitutionalized population in 2019; N/A indicates that data was not available; Z represents or rounds to zero; Margin of error appears in parenthesis and is calculated using replicate weights.
Source: U.S. Census Bureau, American Community Survey, Table HI-05. Health Insurance Coverage Status and Type of Coverage by State and Age for All People: 2019

Colorado

149 Aetna Health of Colorado
151 Farmington Avenue
Hartford, CT 06156
Toll-Free: 800-872-3862
www.aetna.com
Subsidiary of: CVS Health / Aetna Inc.
For Profit Organization: Yes
Year Founded: 1987

Healthplan and Services Defined
PLAN TYPE: HMO/PPO
Other Type: POS
Model Type: Network
Plan Specialty: Behavioral Health, Vision
Benefits Offered: Behavioral Health, Dental, Disease Management, Home Care, Physical Therapy, Podiatry, Prescription, Vision, Worker's Compensation, Life

Type of Coverage
Commercial, Student health

Type of Payment Plans Offered
POS, Capitated, FFS, Combination FFS & DFFS

Geographic Areas Served
Statewide

Peer Review Type
Case Management: Yes

Publishes and Distributes Report Card: Yes

Accreditation Certification
TJC Accreditation, Medicare Approved, Utilization Review, Pre-Admission Certification, State Licensure, Quality Assurance Program

Key Personnel
Senior Network Manager .... David Jacobs

Specialty Managed Care Partners
Enters into Contracts with Regional Business Coalitions: Yes

150 AlphaDentalPlan.com
6200 South Syracuse Way
Suite 460
Greenwood Village, CO 80111
Toll-Free: 800-807-0706
Phone: 303-744-3007
www.alphadentalplan.com
Subsidiary of: Beta Health Association, Inc.
For Profit Organization: Yes
Year Founded: 1990
Physician Owned Organization: Yes

Healthplan and Services Defined
PLAN TYPE: Dental
Plan Specialty: Dental, Vision
Benefits Offered: Dental, Vision, Life, LTD, STD

Type of Coverage
Commercial, Individual, Indemnity

Accreditation Certification
State Dental Board

Key Personnel
President & CEO .... Rod Henningsen

151 American Dental Group
6755 Earl Drive
Suite 108
Colorado Springs, CO 80918
Toll-Free: 800-633-3010
Phone: 719-633-3000
adg@americandentalgroup.org
www.americandentalgroup.org
Mailing Address: P.O. Box 25517, Colorado Springs, CO 80936
For Profit Organization: Yes
Year Founded: 1992
Physician Owned Organization: Yes

Healthplan and Services Defined
PLAN TYPE: Dental
Other Type: Vision
Model Type: Group
Plan Specialty: Dental, Vision
Benefits Offered: Dental, Prescription, Vision

Type of Coverage
Commercial, Individual

Type of Payment Plans Offered
DFFS, FFS, Combination FFS & DFFS

Geographic Areas Served
Colorado, Maryland

Key Personnel
Chief Executive Officer .... Christopher Sisco
VP, Operations .... Tiffany Sisco
Marketing Director .... Leslie Massey

152 Anthem Blue Cross & Blue Shield of Colorado
700 Broadway
Denver, CO 80203
Toll-Free: 800-331-1476
www.anthem.com
Subsidiary of: Anthem, Inc.
For Profit Organization: Yes
Year Founded: 1978

Healthplan and Services Defined
PLAN TYPE: HMO/PPO
Model Type: Network
Plan Specialty: Behavioral Health, Dental, Disease Management, Lab, PBM, Vision, Radiology
Benefits Offered: Behavioral Health, Dental, Disease Management, Inpatient SNF, Physical Therapy, Prescription, Psychiatric, Transplant, Vision, Wellness, Life, Benefits vary according to plan

Type of Coverage
Commercial, Individual, Medicare, Supplemental Medicare

Geographic Areas Served
Statewide

Accreditation Certification
URAC, NCQA

Key Personnel
President . . . . Charles Ritz

153 Beta Health Association, Inc.
6200 South Syracuse Way
Suite 460
Greenwood Village, CO 80111
Toll-Free: 800-807-0706
Phone: 303-744-3007
www.betadental.com
For Profit Organization: Yes
Year Founded: 1990
Physician Owned Organization: Yes

Healthplan and Services Defined
PLAN TYPE: Dental
Plan Specialty: Dental, Vision
Benefits Offered: Dental, Vision, Life, LTD, STD

Type of Coverage
Commercial, Individual, Indemnity
Catastrophic Illness Benefit: Unlimited

Geographic Areas Served
48 states

Publishes and Distributes Report Card: Yes

Accreditation Certification
State Dental Board

Key Personnel
President & CEO. . . . . Rod Henningsen

Specialty Managed Care Partners
Enters into Contracts with Regional Business Coalitions: Yes

154 Boulder Valley Individual Practice Association
6676 Gunpark Drive
Suite B
Boulder, CO 80301
Phone: 303-530-3405
Fax: 303-530-2441
info@bvipa.com
www.bvipa.com
Non-Profit Organization: Yes
Year Founded: 1978
Physician Owned Organization: Yes
Number of Affiliated Hospitals: 4
Number of Primary Care Physicians: 561
Total Enrollment: 300,000

Healthplan and Services Defined
PLAN TYPE: PPO
Model Type: IPA
Offers Demand Management Patient Information Service: Yes

Type of Payment Plans Offered
POS

Geographic Areas Served
Boulder, Lafayette, Longmont & Louisville

Network Qualifications
Pre-Admission Certification: Yes

Peer Review Type
Utilization Review: Yes
Second Surgical Opinion: Yes
Case Management: Yes

Publishes and Distributes Report Card: No

Accreditation Certification
TJC Accreditation, Utilization Review, State Licensure

Key Personnel
President. . . . . Susan Roach, MD
Vice President . . . . Drigan Weider, MD
Treasurer . . . . Mary Louder, MD
Medical Director . . . . Adam Palazzari, MD

Specialty Managed Care Partners
Enters into Contracts with Regional Business Coalitions: No

155 Bright Health Colorado
10333 E Dry Creek Rd
Suite 150
Englewood, CO 80112
Toll-Free: 844-667-5502
Phone: 833-356-1182
brighthealthplan.com
Year Founded: 2015
Number of Primary Care Physicians: 5,000

Healthplan and Services Defined
PLAN TYPE: HMO
Benefits Offered: Prescription, Wellness

Geographic Areas Served
Statewide

Key Personnel
President/CEO. . . . . G. Mike Mikan
Chief Financial Officer . . . . Cathy Smith

156 Cigna HealthCare of Colorado
2000 South Colorado Boulevard
Suites 1100 & 1200
Denver, CO 80222
Toll-Free: 800-997-1654
www.cigna.com
Subsidiary of: Cigna Corporation
For Profit Organization: Yes
Number of Affiliated Hospitals: 80

Healthplan and Services Defined
PLAN TYPE: HMO
Other Type: POS
Plan Specialty: Behavioral Health, Dental, Vision
Benefits Offered: Behavioral Health, Dental, Disease Management, Prescription, Vision, Wellness, Life, LTD, STD
Offers Demand Management Patient Information Service: Yes

Type of Coverage
Commercial, Individual
Catastrophic Illness Benefit: Covered

Type of Payment Plans Offered
POS, Combination FFS & DFFS

Network Qualifications
Pre-Admission Certification: Yes

Peer Review Type
Utilization Review: Yes
Second Surgical Opinion: Yes
Case Management: Yes

Publishes and Distributes Report Card: Yes

Accreditation Certification
NCQA
TJC Accreditation, Medicare Approved, Utilization Review, Pre-Admission Certification, State Licensure, Quality Assurance Program

Key Personnel
Pres., Mountain States . . . . John Roble

Specialty Managed Care Partners
Enters into Contracts with Regional Business Coalitions: Yes

---

157 Colorado Access
11100 E Bethany Drive
Aurora, CO 80014
Toll-Free: 800-511-5010
customer.service@coaccess.com
www.coaccess.com
Non-Profit Organization: Yes
Year Founded: 1994

Healthplan and Services Defined
PLAN TYPE: HMO
Benefits Offered: Behavioral Health, Dental, Disease Management, Psychiatric, Wellness

Type of Coverage
Medicaid

Geographic Areas Served
Statewide

Key Personnel
President/CEO. . . . . Marshall Thomas, MD
SVP/CFO . . . . Philip J Reed
COO/SVP, Plan Operations . . . . April Abrahamson
VP of Legal Services . . . . Ann Edelman
Chief Medical Officer/SVP. . . . . Alexis Giese, MD
Chief Information Officer . . . . Paula Kautzmann

---

158 Delta Dental of Colorado
4582 S Ulster Street
Suite 800
Denver, CO 80237
Toll-Free: 800-233-0860
Phone: 303-741-9300
customer_service@ddpco.com
www.deltadentalco.com
Non-Profit Organization: Yes
Year Founded: 1958
Number of Primary Care Physicians: 3,200
State Enrollment: 1,000,000

Healthplan and Services Defined
PLAN TYPE: Dental
Model Type: Network
Plan Specialty: Dental
Benefits Offered: Dental

Type of Coverage
Commercial, Individual

Type of Payment Plans Offered
DFFS

Geographic Areas Served
Statewide

Publishes and Distributes Report Card: Yes

Key Personnel
President & CEO . . . . Helen Drexler
Chief Financial Officer . . . . Greg Vochis
Network/Clinical Mgmt. . . . . Cheryl Lerner, MD
General Counsel . . . . Dave Gerbus, JD
VP, Marketing/Member Exp. . . . . Kathy Jacoby

---

159 Denver Health Medical Plan
777 Bannock Street
MC6000
Denver, CO 80204
Toll-Free: 800-700-8140
Phone: 303-602-2100
www.denverhealthmedicalplan.com
Non-Profit Organization: Yes
Year Founded: 1997
Total Enrollment: 100,000

Healthplan and Services Defined
PLAN TYPE: HMO
Benefits Offered: Chiropractic, Home Care, Inpatient SNF, Physical Therapy, Podiatry, Psychiatric, Transplant, Vision, Wellness

Type of Coverage
Commercial, Medicare, Medicare Advantage, CHP+

Geographic Areas Served
Denver metro area

Key Personnel
Chief Executive Officer . . . . Robin D. Wittenstein
Marketing/PR Officer . . . . Rob Borland
Chief Nursing Officer . . . . Kathy Boyle
Chief Financial Officer . . . . Peg Burnett
Director of Public Health . . . . Bill Burman
Chief Operating Officer . . . . Kris Gaw

---

160 Friday Health Plans
700 Main Street
Suite 100
Alamosa, CO 81101
Toll-Free: 800-475-8466
www.fridayhealthplans.com
Subsidiary of: Friday Health Plans, Inc.
Non-Profit Organization: Yes
Year Founded: 1972
Total Enrollment: 5,000

Healthplan and Services Defined
   PLAN TYPE: HMO
   Benefits Offered: Dental, Disease Management, Home Care, Inpatient SNF, Podiatry, Prescription, Vision, Wellness, Life

Type of Coverage
   Commercial, Individual, Medicare

Geographic Areas Served
   Southern Colorado, San Luis Valley, Arkansas Valley, Durango, Pueblo, Colorado Springs, Denver

Key Personnel
   Co-Founder/CEO .... Salvatore Gentile
   Co-Founder/President .... David Pinkert
   Chief Operating Officer .... Jennifer Mueller
   Chief Marketing Officer .... Tracy Faigin
   303-888-4803
   tracy.faigin@fridayhealthplans.com

---

161 Humana Health Insurance of Colorado
5310 N Nevada Ave.
Colorado Springs, CO 80918
Toll-Free: 800-871-6270
Phone: 719-532-7700
Fax: 719-531-7089
www.humana.com
Secondary Address: 6300 S Syracuse Way, Suite 555, Centennial, CO 80111, 866-355-6152
Subsidiary of: Humana Inc.
For Profit Organization: Yes
Year Founded: 1987

Healthplan and Services Defined
   PLAN TYPE: HMO/PPO
   Plan Specialty: Dental, Vision
   Benefits Offered: Dental, Disease Management, Transplant, Vision

Type of Coverage
   Commercial, Individual, Group, Medicare

Geographic Areas Served
   Statewide

Accreditation Certification
   URAC, NCQA

Key Personnel
   Market VP .... Brian Sullivan

---

162 Kaiser Permanente Northern Colorado
2950 E Harmony Road
Suite 190
Fort Collins, CO 80528
Phone: 303-338-3800
thrive.kaiserpermanente.org/care-near-northern-colorado
Subsidiary of: Kaiser Permanente
Non-Profit Organization: Yes
Year Founded: 1969
Number of Affiliated Hospitals: 5
Number of Primary Care Physicians: 400
Total Enrollment: 636,904
State Enrollment: 636,904

Healthplan and Services Defined
   PLAN TYPE: HMO
   Model Type: Network
   Benefits Offered: Disease Management, Home Care, Inpatient SNF, Long-Term Care, Physical Therapy, Podiatry, Prescription, Psychiatric, Transplant, Vision, Wellness, Benefits vary according to plan

Type of Coverage
   Commercial, Individual, Medicare, Supplemental Medicare, Medicaid

Geographic Areas Served
   Denver, Boulder, Fort Collins, Loveland, Greeley and surrounding areas

Accreditation Certification
   NCQA

Key Personnel
   Regional President .... Mike Ramseier
   Pres./Exec. Med. Dir. .... Jeffrey Krawcek, MD, MBOE
   Media Contact .... Amy Whited
   303-344-7518

---

163 Kaiser Permanente Southern Colorado
1400 E. Boulder St.
Colorado Springs, CO 80909
Phone: 719-365-5000
thrive.kaiserpermanente.org/care-near-southern-colorado
Subsidiary of: Kaiser Permanente
Non-Profit Organization: Yes
Year Founded: 1969
Number of Affiliated Hospitals: 9
Number of Primary Care Physicians: 1,200
Total Enrollment: 636,904
State Enrollment: 636,904

Healthplan and Services Defined
   PLAN TYPE: HMO/PPO
   Model Type: Network
   Benefits Offered: Disease Management, Home Care, Inpatient SNF, Long-Term Care, Physical Therapy, Podiatry, Prescription, Psychiatric, Transplant, Vision, Wellness, Benefits vary according to plan

Type of Coverage
   Commercial, Individual, Medicare, Supplemental Medicare, Medicaid

Geographic Areas Served
   Colorado Springs, Pueblo

Accreditation Certification
   NCQA

Key Personnel
   Regional President .... Mike Ramseier
   Pres./Exec. Med. Dir. .... Jeffrey Krawcek, MD
   Media Contact .... Nick Riper
   303-344-7619

164 Pueblo Health Care
400 W 16th Street
Pueblo, CO 81003
Phone: 719-584-4000
www.pueblohealthcare.com
Number of Primary Care Physicians: 270

Healthplan and Services Defined
PLAN TYPE: PPO
Model Type: Network

Geographic Areas Served
Pueblo Market Area

Key Personnel
Executive Director....................... Ann Bellah
   719-584-4371
   ann_bellah@parkviewmc.com
Provider Relations .... Sandra Proud
   719-584-4642
   sandra_proud@parkviewmc.com

165 Rocky Mountain Health Plans
2775 Crossroads Boulevard
Grand Junction, CO 81506
Toll-Free: 800-346-4643
Phone: 970-243-7050
www.rmhp.org
Mailing Address: P.O. Box 10600, Grand Junction, CO 81502-5600
Subsidiary of: Rocky Mountain Health Maintenance Organization
Non-Profit Organization: Yes
Year Founded: 1974
Owned by an Integrated Delivery Network (IDN): Yes
Number of Affiliated Hospitals: 107
Number of Primary Care Physicians: 2,630
Number of Referral/Specialty Physicians: 6,866
Total Enrollment: 236,962
State Enrollment: 236,962

Healthplan and Services Defined
PLAN TYPE: HMO/PPO
Other Type: HSA
Model Type: Mixed
Benefits Offered: Disease Management, Home Care, Prescription, Wellness

Type of Coverage
Commercial, Individual, Medicare, Supplemental Medicare
Catastrophic Illness Benefit: Unlimited

Type of Payment Plans Offered
FFS

Geographic Areas Served
Statewide

Network Qualifications
Minimum Years of Practice: 3
Pre-Admission Certification: Yes

Peer Review Type
Utilization Review: Yes
Second Surgical Opinion: Yes

Case Management: Yes

Publishes and Distributes Report Card: Yes

Accreditation Certification
NCQA
Medicare Approved, Utilization Review, Pre-Admission Certification, State Licensure, Quality Assurance Program

Key Personnel
President/CEO .... Steven ErkenBrack
COO.............................. Laurel Walters
CFO.............................. Pat Duncan
VP, Human Resources................. Jan Rohr
VP, Legal & Govt Affairs............ Mike Huotari
Chief Marketing Officer............. Neil Waldron
Chief Medical Officer......... Kevin R Fitzgerald, MD

Specialty Managed Care Partners
Delta Dental, Landmark Chiropractic, Vision Service Plan, Life Strategies

166 United Concordia of Colorado
4401 Deer Path Road
Harrisburg, PA 17110
Phone: 717-260-6800
www.unitedconcordia.com
For Profit Organization: Yes
Year Founded: 1971
Number of Primary Care Physicians: 104,000
Total Enrollment: 8,800,000

Healthplan and Services Defined
PLAN TYPE: Dental
Model Type: Network
Plan Specialty: Dental
Benefits Offered: Dental

Type of Coverage
Commercial, Individual, Military personnel & families

Geographic Areas Served
Nationwide

Accreditation Certification
URAC

Key Personnel
Sales Executive .... Brice Heller

167 UnitedHealthcare Community Plan Colorado
UnitedHealthcare Customer Service
P.O. Box 30769
Salt Lake City, UT 84130-0769
Toll-Free: 888-545-5205
www.uhccommunityplan.com/co
Subsidiary of: UnitedHealth Group
For Profit Organization: Yes

Healthplan and Services Defined
PLAN TYPE: Medicare
Other Type: Medicaid
Model Type: Network
Benefits Offered: Dental, Podiatry, Prescription, Vision, Wellness, Hearing

Type of Coverage
Medicare, Medicaid

Geographic Areas Served
Adams, Arapahoe, Boulder, Broomfield, Denver, Douglas, El Paso, Fremont, Jefferson, Larimer, Pueblo, and Weld

168 UnitedHealthcare of Colorado
6465 S Greenwood Plaza Boulevard
Suite 300
Centennial, CO 80111
Toll-Free: 866-574-6088
Phone: 720-441-6311
www.uhc.com
Subsidiary of: UnitedHealth Group
For Profit Organization: Yes
Year Founded: 1986

Healthplan and Services Defined
PLAN TYPE: HMO/PPO
Model Type: Network
Plan Specialty: Behavioral Health, Dental, Disease Management, MSO, PBM, Vision
Benefits Offered: Behavioral Health, Chiropractic, Complementary
Medicine, Dental, Disease Management, Home Care, Inpatient SNF, Long-Term Care, Physical Therapy, Podiatry, Prescription, Psychiatric, Transplant, Vision, Wellness, AD&D, Life, Benefits vary according to plan

Type of Coverage
Commercial, Individual, Medicare, Medicaid, Family, Military, Veterans, Group

Type of Payment Plans Offered
DFFS, FFS, Combination FFS & DFFS

Geographic Areas Served
HMO: Front Range Colorado; PPO/POS: Statewide

Subscriber Information
Average Monthly Fee Per Subscriber
(Employee + Employer Contribution):
Employee Only (Self): Varies

Network Qualifications
Pre-Admission Certification: Yes

Peer Review Type
Case Management: Yes

Publishes and Distributes Report Card: Yes

Accreditation Certification
URAC, NCQA
State Licensure, Quality Assurance Program

Key Personnel
CEO, Colorado & Wyoming................ Marc Neely

Average Claim Compensation
Physician's Fees Charged: 70%
Hospital's Fees Charged: 55%

Specialty Managed Care Partners
United Behavioral Health
Enters into Contracts with Regional Business Coalitions: No

CONNECTICUT

Health Insurance Coverage Status and Type of Coverage by Age

Category	All Persons Number	%	Under 19 years Number	%	Under 65 years Number	%
Total population	3,515 *(1)*	100.0 *(0.0)*	773 *(4)*	100.0 *(0.0)*	2,905 *(2)*	100.0 *(0.0)*
Covered by some type of health insurance	3,307 *(11)*	94.1 *(0.3)*	746 *(5)*	96.5 *(0.5)*	2,702 *(11)*	93.0 *(0.4)*
Covered by private health insurance	2,440 *(20)*	69.4 *(0.6)*	498 *(10)*	64.4 *(1.2)*	2,077 *(20)*	71.5 *(0.7)*
Employer-based	2,081 *(23)*	59.2 *(0.6)*	457 *(10)*	59.1 *(1.3)*	1,864 *(22)*	64.2 *(0.7)*
Direct purchase	423 *(11)*	12.0 *(0.3)*	41 *(3)*	5.3 *(0.4)*	246 *(9)*	8.5 *(0.3)*
TRICARE	48 *(5)*	1.4 *(0.1)*	10 *(2)*	1.3 *(0.3)*	30 *(4)*	1.0 *(0.1)*
Covered by public health insurance	1,303 *(19)*	37.1 *(0.5)*	284 *(11)*	36.7 *(1.3)*	726 *(18)*	25.0 *(0.6)*
Medicaid	766 *(19)*	21.8 *(0.6)*	283 *(11)*	36.5 *(1.4)*	673 *(19)*	23.2 *(0.6)*
Medicare	648 *(5)*	18.4 *(0.2)*	2 *(1)*	0.2 *(0.1)*	71 *(5)*	2.5 *(0.2)*
VA Care	55 *(3)*	1.6 *(0.1)*	1 *(1)*	0.1 *(0.1)*	22 *(3)*	0.8 *(0.1)*
Not covered at any time during the year	207 *(11)*	5.9 *(0.3)*	27 *(4)*	3.5 *(0.5)*	203 *(11)*	7.0 *(0.4)*

Note: Numbers in thousands; Figures cover civilian noninstitutionalized population in 2019; N/A indicates that data was not available; Z represents or rounds to zero; Margin of error appears in parenthesis and is calculated using replicate weights.
Source: U.S. Census Bureau, American Community Survey, Table HI-05. Health Insurance Coverage Status and Type of Coverage by State and Age for All People: 2019

Connecticut

169 Aetna Health of Connecticut
151 Farmington Avenue
Hartford, CT 06156
Toll-Free: 800-872-3862
www.aetna.com
Subsidiary of: CVS Health / Aetna Inc.
For Profit Organization: Yes
Year Founded: 1853

Healthplan and Services Defined
PLAN TYPE: HMO/PPO
Other Type: POS
Model Type: Network
Plan Specialty: Behavioral Health, Dental, EPO, Lab, PBM, Vision, Radiology
Benefits Offered: Behavioral Health, Dental, Disease Management, Long-Term Care, Physical Therapy, Podiatry, Prescription, Psychiatric, Vision, Wellness, Life, LTD, STD

Type of Coverage
Commercial, Individual, Medicare, Medicaid, Student health

Geographic Areas Served
Statewide

170 Aetna Inc.
151 Farmington Avenue
Hartford, CT 06156
Toll-Free: 800-872-3862
www.aetna.com
Subsidiary of: CVS Health
For Profit Organization: Yes
Year Founded: 1853
Number of Affiliated Hospitals: 5,667
Number of Primary Care Physicians: 664,301
Total Enrollment: 46,500,000

Healthplan and Services Defined
PLAN TYPE: Multiple
Other Type: POS
Model Type: Network
Plan Specialty: Behavioral Health, Dental, Lab, PBM, Vision, Radiology
Benefits Offered: Behavioral Health, Dental, Disease Management, Long-Term Care, Physical Therapy, Podiatry, Prescription, Psychiatric, Vision, Wellness, Life, LTD, STD

Type of Coverage
Commercial, Medicare, Medicaid, Public sector, Retirees, Part-time

Type of Payment Plans Offered
FFS

Geographic Areas Served
Nationwide

Key Personnel
President/CEO, CVS Health . . . . Karen S. Lynch
EVP/CFO, CVS Health . . . . Shawn Guertin
EVP/COO, CVS Health . . . . Jonathan C. Roberts
EVP/CMO, CVS Health . . . . Sree Chaguturu, MD
President, HCB, Aetna . . . . Dan Finke

171 Aetna Student Health Agency Inc.
151 Farmington Avenue
Hartford, CT 06156
Toll-Free: 877-480-4161
www.aetnastudenthealth.com
Subsidiary of: CVS Health / Aetna Inc.
For Profit Organization: Yes

Healthplan and Services Defined
PLAN TYPE: HMO/PPO
Other Type: POS
Model Type: Network
Plan Specialty: Disease Management, Vision
Benefits Offered: Dental, Prescription, Vision, Wellness, Life

Type of Coverage
Individual

Geographic Areas Served
Nationwide

Key Personnel
Chief Medical Officer. . . . . Wendy Shanahan-Richards

172 Anthem Blue Cross & Blue Shield of Connecticut
108 Leigus Road
Wallingford, CT 06492
Toll-Free: 800-922-4670
www.anthem.com
Subsidiary of: Anthem, Inc.
For Profit Organization: Yes

Healthplan and Services Defined
PLAN TYPE: HMO/PPO
Model Type: Network
Plan Specialty: Behavioral Health, Dental, Disease Management, Lab, PBM, Vision, Radiology
Benefits Offered: Behavioral Health, Dental, Disease Management, Inpatient SNF, Physical Therapy, Prescription, Psychiatric, Transplant, Vision, Wellness, Life

Type of Coverage
Commercial, Individual, Medicare, Supplemental Medicare, Catastrophic

Geographic Areas Served
Statewide

Accreditation Certification
URAC, NCQA

Key Personnel
President . . . . Lou Gianquinto

173 CareCentrix
20 Church Street
12th Floor
Hartford, CT 06103
Toll-Free: 800-808-1902
carecentrix.com

Secondary Address: 100 First Stamford Place, 2nd Floor W, Stamford, CT 06902
Year Founded: 1996
Number of Primary Care Physicians: 8,000

Healthplan and Services Defined
PLAN TYPE: HMO
Benefits Offered: Home Care, Physical Therapy, Durable Medical Equipment; Occupational & Respiratory Therapy; Orthotics; Prosthetics

Geographic Areas Served
Arizona, Connecticut, Florida, Georgia, Kansas, and New York

Key Personnel
Chief Executive Officer . . . . John Driscoll
President/COO. . . . . Laizer Kornwasser
Chief Medical Officer. . . . . Dr. Michael Cantor
Chief Compliance Officer. . . . . Gisele Molloy
Chief Customer Officer . . . . Tom Gaffney
Chief Legal Officer. . . . . Alison Gilligan
Chief Financial Officer. . . . . Steve Horowitz

174 Cigna Corporation
900 Cottage Grove Road
Bloomfield, CT 06002
Toll-Free: 800-997-1654
www.cigna.com
For Profit Organization: Yes
Year Founded: 1982
Total Enrollment: 19,000,000

Healthplan and Services Defined
PLAN TYPE: Multiple
Benefits Offered: Behavioral Health, Dental, Disease Management, Prescription, Vision, Wellness, AD&D, Life, LTD, STD

Type of Coverage
Commercial, Individual, Medicare, Supplemental Medicare, Medicaid, Part-time and hourly workers; Union

Geographic Areas Served
Nationwide

Accreditation Certification
URAC, NCQA

Key Personnel
Chairman/CEO . . . . David M. Cordani
President, Gov. Business . . . . Chuck Berg
Chief Financial Officer . . . . Brian Evanko
EVP/Chief HR Officer . . . . Cindy Ryan
EVP/General Counsel . . . . Nicole Jones
President, US Commercial . . . . Mike Triplett

175 Cigna HealthCare of Connecticut
900 Cottage Grove Road
C8NAS
Hartford, CT 06152-7314
Toll-Free: 800-997-1654
www.cigna.com

Secondary Address: 612 Wheelers Farm Road, Milford, CT 06461, 203-874-1122
Subsidiary of: Cigna Corporation
For Profit Organization: Yes

Healthplan and Services Defined
PLAN TYPE: HMO
Other Type: POS
Plan Specialty: Behavioral Health, Dental, Vision
Benefits Offered: Behavioral Health, Dental, Disease Management, Prescription, Vision, AD&D, Life, LTD, STD

Type of Coverage
Commercial, Individual

Type of Payment Plans Offered
POS, DFFS, Capitated, FFS, Combination FFS & DFFS

Peer Review Type
Utilization Review: Yes
Second Surgical Opinion: Yes
Case Management: Yes

Publishes and Distributes Report Card: Yes

Accreditation Certification
URAC, NCQA
Utilization Review, Pre-Admission Certification, State Licensure, Quality Assurance Program

Key Personnel
President . . . . Wendy Sherry

Average Claim Compensation
Physician's Fees Charged: 1%
Hospital's Fees Charged: 1%

Specialty Managed Care Partners
Quest
Enters into Contracts with Regional Business Coalitions: Yes

176 Cigna-HealthSpring
900 Cottage Grove Road
Bloomfield, CT 06002
Toll-Free: 800-668-3813
cigna.com/medicare
Subsidiary of: Cigna Corporation
For Profit Organization: Yes

Healthplan and Services Defined
PLAN TYPE: Medicare
Other Type: Medicaid
Benefits Offered: Prescription

Type of Coverage
Medicare, Supplemental Medicare, Medicaid

Geographic Areas Served
Nationwide

Key Personnel
President & CEO . . . . David M. Cordani

177 ConnectiCare
4551 Main Street
Bridgeport, CT 06606
Toll-Free: 800-251-7722
info@connecticare.com
www.connecticare.com
Secondary Address: 835 Wolcott Street, Waterbury, CT 06705
For Profit Organization: Yes
Year Founded: 1981
Owned by an Integrated Delivery Network (IDN): Yes

Healthplan and Services Defined
PLAN TYPE: HMO/PPO
Other Type: POS
Model Type: IPA, HMO, POS
Plan Specialty: Disease Management, Vision, UR
Benefits Offered: Behavioral Health, Chiropractic, Complementary Medicine, Dental, Disease Management, Home Care, Inpatient SNF, Physical Therapy, Podiatry, Prescription, Psychiatric, Transplant, Vision, Wellness

Type of Coverage
Commercial, Individual, Medicare, Medicare Advantage
Catastrophic Illness Benefit: Unlimited

Type of Payment Plans Offered
Capitated, FFS

Geographic Areas Served
Statewide

Peer Review Type
Utilization Review: Yes
Second Surgical Opinion: Yes
Case Management: Yes

Publishes and Distributes Report Card: Yes

Accreditation Certification
TJC, NCQA
Utilization Review, Pre-Admission Certification, State Licensure, Quality Assurance Program

Key Personnel
President .... Eric Galvin
SVP/COO .... Robert A. Kosior
SVP, Sales & Marketing .... Brian Pagliaro

Average Claim Compensation
Physician's Fees Charged: 100%
Hospital's Fees Charged: 100%

Specialty Managed Care Partners
United Behavioral Health, Express Scripts
Enters into Contracts with Regional Business Coalitions: No

Employer References
Federal Government, Hartford Insurance Company, United Technologies, State of Connecticut

178 Harvard Pilgrim Health Care Connecticut
City Place II
185 Asylum Street, 2nd Floor
Hartford, CT 06103
Toll-Free: 888-888-4742
www.harvardpilgrim.org

Non-Profit Organization: Yes
Year Founded: 1973
Number of Affiliated Hospitals: 179
Number of Referral/Specialty Physicians: 53,000

Healthplan and Services Defined
PLAN TYPE: HMO
Benefits Offered: Prescription

Geographic Areas Served
Statewide

Peer Review Type
Utilization Review: Yes
Second Surgical Opinion: No
Case Management: Yes

Publishes and Distributes Report Card: No

Accreditation Certification
TJC Accreditation, Medicare Approved, Utilization Review, Pre-Admission Certification, State Licensure, Quality Assurance Program

Key Personnel
VP, Regional Market .... Jason Madrak

Specialty Managed Care Partners
Enters into Contracts with Regional Business Coalitions: No

179 Oxford Health Plans
48 Monroe Turnpike
Trumbull, CT 06611
Toll-Free: 800-444-6222
www.oxhp.com
Subsidiary of: UnitedHealth Group
For Profit Organization: Yes
Year Founded: 1984
Owned by an Integrated Delivery Network (IDN): Yes

Healthplan and Services Defined
PLAN TYPE: HMO/PPO
Model Type: IPA, Network, POS
Benefits Offered: Behavioral Health, Chiropractic, Complementary Medicine, Dental, Disease Management, Home Care, Inpatient SNF, Podiatry, Prescription, Psychiatric, Transplant, Vision, Wellness
Offers Demand Management Patient Information Service: Yes

Type of Coverage
Commercial, Individual, Indemnity, Medicare, Catastrophic
Catastrophic Illness Benefit: Varies per case

Type of Payment Plans Offered
FFS

Geographic Areas Served
Connecticut: Fairfield, New Haven, Litchfield, Hartford, Middlesex, New London, Tolland & Windham counties; New Jersey: Essex, Hudson, Middlesex, Monmouth, Morris, Ocean, Passaic & Somerset counties; New York: Bronx, Dutchess, Kings, Nassau, New York, Putnam, Queens, Richmond, Rockland, Suffolk, & Westchester counties

Peer Review Type
Utilization Review: Yes
Second Surgical Opinion: Yes

Case Management: Yes

Publishes and Distributes Report Card: Yes

Accreditation Certification
NCQA
TJC Accreditation, Medicare Approved, Utilization Review, Pre-Admission Certification, State Licensure, Quality Assurance Program

Key Personnel
EVP, Operations & CIO . . . . Steve H. Black
EVP, Medical Delivery . . . . Paul C. Conlin
EVP & General Counsel . . . . Daniel N. Gregoire
EVP & CMO . . . . Alan M. Muney, MD
EVP & CFO . . . . Kurt B. Thompson
Medical Director . . . . James Dillard, MD
EVP, Sales/Business Dev. . . . . Kevin R. Hill

Specialty Managed Care Partners
Enters into Contracts with Regional Business Coalitions: Yes

180 Trinity Health of New England
1000 Asylum Avenue
5th Floor
Hartford, CT 06105
Toll-Free: 860-714-1400
www.trinityhealthofne.org
Secondary Address: Mercy Medical Center, 271 Carew Street, Springfield, MA 01104
Subsidiary of: Trinity Health
Non-Profit Organization: Yes
Year Founded: 2013
Number of Affiliated Hospitals: 5
Number of Primary Care Physicians: 837
Number of Referral/Specialty Physicians: 1,500
Total Enrollment: 30,000,000
State Enrollment: 3,000,000

Healthplan and Services Defined
PLAN TYPE: Other
Benefits Offered: Disease Management, Home Care, Long-Term Care, Psychiatric, Hospice programs, PACE (Program of All Inclusive Care for the Elderly)

Key Personnel
President/CEO . . . . Reginald J. Eadie, MD, MBA
Chief Financial Officer . . . . Jennifer Schneider, CPA
Chief Clinical Executive . . . . Syed A. Hussain, MD

181 UnitedHealthcare Community Plan Connecticut
UnitedHealthcare Customer Service
P.O. Box 30769
Salt Lake City, UT 84130-0769
Toll-Free: 888-545-5205
www.uhccommunityplan.com/ct
Subsidiary of: UnitedHealth Group
For Profit Organization: Yes

Healthplan and Services Defined
PLAN TYPE: Medicare
Other Type: Medicaid
Model Type: Network
Benefits Offered: Prescription, Hospitals, Doctors

Type of Coverage
Medicare, Medicaid

Geographic Areas Served
Fairfield, Hartford, Litchfield, New Haven, New London, Tolland, and Windham

182 UnitedHealthcare of Connecticut
185 Asylum Street
Hartford, CT 06103
Toll-Free: 888-545-5205
Phone: 860-702-5000
www.uhc.com
Subsidiary of: UnitedHealth Group
For Profit Organization: Yes
Year Founded: 1991

Healthplan and Services Defined
PLAN TYPE: HMO/PPO
Model Type: Network
Plan Specialty: Behavioral Health, Dental, Disease Management, PBM, Vision
Benefits Offered: Behavioral Health, Dental, Disease Management, Long-Term Care, Prescription, Vision, Wellness, Life, LTD, STD

Type of Coverage
Individual, Medicare, Supplemental Medicare, Medicaid, Catastrophic, Family, Military, Veterans, Group

Geographic Areas Served
Statewide

Key Personnel
CEO, New England . . . . Tim Archer

DELAWARE

Health Insurance Coverage Status and Type of Coverage by Age

Category	All Persons Number	All Persons %	Under 19 years Number	Under 19 years %	Under 65 years Number	Under 65 years %
Total population	956 (2)	100.0 (0.0)	215 (2)	100.0 (0.0)	771 (2)	100.0 (0.0)
Covered by some type of health insurance	894 (6)	93.4 (0.6)	205 (3)	95.2 (1.4)	708 (7)	91.9 (0.8)
Covered by private health insurance	678 (13)	70.9 (1.4)	132 (6)	61.4 (2.8)	551 (12)	71.5 (1.6)
Employer-based	568 (13)	59.4 (1.3)	118 (6)	54.9 (2.8)	490 (13)	63.6 (1.6)
Direct purchase	130 (6)	13.6 (0.6)	14 (3)	6.4 (1.2)	64 (5)	8.3 (0.6)
TRICARE	42 (5)	4.4 (0.6)	8 (3)	3.5 (1.3)	25 (4)	3.2 (0.6)
Covered by public health insurance	378 (12)	39.5 (1.3)	86 (6)	39.7 (3.0)	196 (12)	25.4 (1.5)
Medicaid	198 (11)	20.8 (1.1)	85 (6)	39.5 (2.9)	177 (11)	23.0 (1.5)
Medicare	207 (3)	21.6 (0.3)	1 (1)	0.4 (0.3)	25 (3)	3.3 (0.3)
VA Care	24 (2)	2.5 (0.2)	0 (0)	0.0 (0.0)	9 (2)	1.2 (0.2)
Not covered at any time during the year	63 (6)	6.6 (0.6)	10 (3)	4.8 (1.4)	62 (6)	8.1 (0.8)

Note: Numbers in thousands; Figures cover civilian noninstitutionalized population in 2019; N/A indicates that data was not available; Z represents or rounds to zero; Margin of error appears in parenthesis and is calculated using replicate weights.
Source: U.S. Census Bureau, American Community Survey, Table HI-05. Health Insurance Coverage Status and Type of Coverage by State and Age for All People: 2019

Delaware

183 Delta Dental of Delaware
One Delta Drive
Mechanicsburg, PA 17055-6999
Toll-Free: 800-932-0783
www.deltadentalins.com
Mailing Address: P.O. Box 1803, Alpharetta, GA 30023
Non-Profit Organization: Yes

Healthplan and Services Defined
PLAN TYPE: Dental
Other Type: Dental PPO
Plan Specialty: Dental
Benefits Offered: Dental

Type of Coverage
Commercial, Individual

Geographic Areas Served
Statewide

Key Personnel
President/CEO . . . . Michael Castro
Chief Financial Officer . . . . Alicia Weber
Chief Legal Officer . . . . Michael Hankinson
Chief Information Officer . . . . Dominic Titcombe
Chief Operating Officer . . . . Roy Gilbert

184 Highmark BCBS Delaware
P.O. Box 226
Pittsburgh, DE 15230-0226
Toll-Free: 800-633-2563
www.highmarkbcbsde.com
Subsidiary of: Highmark Blue Cross Blue Shield
Non-Profit Organization: Yes
Year Founded: 1935

Healthplan and Services Defined
PLAN TYPE: HMO/PPO
Model Type: IPA, Network
Benefits Offered: Dental, Disease Management, Prescription, Vision, Wellness

Type of Coverage
Commercial, Individual, Medicare, Supplemental Medicare

Type of Payment Plans Offered
Combination FFS & DFFS

Geographic Areas Served
Statewide

Key Personnel
Customer Service . . . . Becca Bartlett
Manager, Underwriting . . . . Tim Rzepski
Market Facing Analytics . . . . Dave Stuart

185 Mid-Atlantic Behavioral Health
910 S Chapel Street
Suite 102
Newark, DE 19713
Phone: 302-224-1400
www.midatlanticbh.com

Secondary Address: 3521 Silverside Road, Suite 2F1, Wilmington, DE 19810

Healthplan and Services Defined
PLAN TYPE: Multiple
Plan Specialty: Behavioral Health
Benefits Offered: Behavioral Health, Psychiatric

Type of Payment Plans Offered
FFS

Geographic Areas Served
Maryland, Virginia, West Virginia, North Carolina, Pennsylvania, Delaware & Washington DC

Network Qualifications
Minimum Years of Practice: 2
Pre-Admission Certification: Yes

Peer Review Type
Utilization Review: No
Second Surgical Opinion: No
Case Management: No

Publishes and Distributes Report Card: No

Accreditation Certification
TJC Accreditation, Medicare Approved, Utilization Review, Pre-Admission Certification, State Licensure, Quality Assurance Program

Key Personnel
Practice Director . . . . Traci Bolander, Psy. D
Practice Development . . . . Curtis Bolander

Specialty Managed Care Partners
Enters into Contracts with Regional Business Coalitions: No

186 Trinity Health of Delaware
St. Francis Healthcare
701 North Clayton Street
Wilmington, DE 19805
Phone: 302-421-4100
www.trinity-health.org
Subsidiary of: Trinity Health
Non-Profit Organization: Yes
Year Founded: 1924
Total Enrollment: 30,000,000

Healthplan and Services Defined
PLAN TYPE: Other
Benefits Offered: Disease Management, Home Care, Long-Term Care, Psychiatric, Hospice programs, PACE (Program of All Inclusive Care for the Elderly)

Key Personnel
President/CEO . . . . Michael A. Slubowski
Chief Operating Officer . . . . Benjamin R. Carter

187 UnitedHealthcare Community Plan Delaware
UnitedHealthcare Customer Service
P.O. Box 30769
Salt Lake City, UT 84130-0769
Toll-Free: 888-545-5205
www.uhccommunityplan.com/de

Subsidiary of: UnitedHealth Group
For Profit Organization: Yes

Healthplan and Services Defined
  PLAN TYPE: Medicare
  Other Type: Medicaid
  Model Type: Network
  Benefits Offered: Dental, Home Care, Podiatry, Prescription, Vision, Wellness, Hearing, Chiropractic

Type of Coverage
  Medicare, Medicaid

Geographic Areas Served
  Statewide

DISTRICT OF COLUMBIA

Health Insurance Coverage Status and Type of Coverage by Age

Category	All Persons Number	All Persons %	Under 19 years Number	Under 19 years %	Under 65 years Number	Under 65 years %
Total population	697 *(1)*	100.0 *(0.0)*	138 *(2)*	100.0 *(0.0)*	611 *(1)*	100.0 *(0.0)*
Covered by some type of health insurance	672 *(4)*	96.5 *(0.6)*	136 *(2)*	98.0 *(0.9)*	588 *(5)*	96.1 *(0.7)*
Covered by private health insurance	506 *(10)*	72.6 *(1.4)*	84 *(5)*	60.4 *(3.6)*	451 *(9)*	73.8 *(1.5)*
Employer-based	427 *(10)*	61.4 *(1.4)*	64 *(5)*	45.9 *(3.2)*	385 *(10)*	62.9 *(1.5)*
Direct purchase	90 *(7)*	13.0 *(1.0)*	18 *(4)*	13.1 *(2.8)*	71 *(6)*	11.7 *(1.0)*
TRICARE	14 *(3)*	2.1 *(0.5)*	5 *(2)*	3.6 *(1.6)*	12 *(3)*	2.0 *(0.6)*
Covered by public health insurance	238 *(10)*	34.2 *(1.4)*	59 *(5)*	42.9 *(3.8)*	161 *(10)*	26.3 *(1.6)*
Medicaid	173 *(10)*	24.8 *(1.4)*	58 *(5)*	41.7 *(3.8)*	151 *(10)*	24.7 *(1.6)*
Medicare	92 *(3)*	13.2 *(0.4)*	2 *(1)*	1.1 *(0.7)*	15 *(3)*	2.5 *(0.4)*
VA Care	10 *(2)*	1.4 *(0.4)*	1 *(1)*	0.7 *(1.0)*	6 *(2)*	1.0 *(0.4)*
Not covered at any time during the year	25 *(4)*	3.5 *(0.6)*	3 *(1)*	2.0 *(0.9)*	24 *(4)*	3.9 *(0.7)*

Note: Numbers in thousands; Figures cover civilian noninstitutionalized population in 2019; N/A indicates that data was not available; Z represents or rounds to zero; Margin of error appears in parenthesis and is calculated using replicate weights.
Source: U.S. Census Bureau, American Community Survey, Table HI-05. Health Insurance Coverage Status and Type of Coverage by State and Age for All People: 2019

District of Columbia

188 Aetna Health of District of Columbia
151 Farmington Avenue
Hartford, CT 06156
Toll-Free: 888-238-6258
www.aetnadcgov.com
Subsidiary of: CVS Health / Aetna Inc.
For Profit Organization: Yes

Healthplan and Services Defined
PLAN TYPE: HMO/PPO
Other Type: POS
Model Type: Network
Plan Specialty: Behavioral Health, EPO, Lab, PBM, Radiology
Benefits Offered: Behavioral Health, Dental, Disease Management, Long-Term Care, Physical Therapy, Podiatry, Prescription, Psychiatric, Vision, Wellness, Life, LTD, STD

Type of Coverage
Commercial, Student health

Geographic Areas Served
Statewide

Key Personnel
VP, Head of Public Policy .... Bonnie Washington
Dir., Ops, Govt. Affairs .... Christopher Amidei

189 AmeriHealth Caritas District of Columbia
1250 Maryland Avenue
Suite 500
Washington, DC 20024
Toll-Free: 800-408-7511
Phone: 202-408-4720
www.amerihealthcaritasdc.com
For Profit Organization: Yes
Year Founded: 1987
Total Enrollment: 100,000
State Enrollment: 100,000

Healthplan and Services Defined
PLAN TYPE: Other
Plan Specialty: Behavioral Health, Dental
Benefits Offered: Prescription

Type of Coverage
Medicaid

Geographic Areas Served
District of Columbia

Publishes and Distributes Report Card: Yes

Accreditation Certification
NCQA

Key Personnel
Market President .... Karen M. Dale
Compliance Director .... Brian Geesaman
Local Operations Director .... James R. Christian
Dental Director........................ Nathan Fletcher
Director, Marketing................... Keith Maccannon
Chief Medical Officer .... Lavdena A. Orr, MD

Specialty Managed Care Partners
Enters into Contracts with Regional Business Coalitions: Yes

190 Delta Dental of the District of Columbia
One Delta Drive
Mechanicsburg, PA 17055-6999
Toll-Free: 800-932-0783
www.deltadentalins.com
Non-Profit Organization: Yes

Healthplan and Services Defined
PLAN TYPE: Dental
Other Type: Dental PPO
Plan Specialty: Dental
Benefits Offered: Dental

Type of Coverage
Commercial, Individual

Geographic Areas Served
District of Columbia

Key Personnel
President & CEO...................... Micheal Castro
Chief Financial Officer................... Alicia Weber
Chief Legal Officer .... Michael Hankinson
Chief Information Officer .... Dominic Titcombe
Chief Operating Officer .... Roy Gilbert

191 Quality Plan Administrators
7824 Eastern Avenue NW
Suite 100
Washington, DC 20012
Toll-Free: 800-900-4112
Phone: 202-722-2744
Fax: 202-291-5703
quality@qpatpa.com
qualityplanadmin.com
For Profit Organization: Yes
Year Founded: 1986
Number of Primary Care Physicians: 175
Total Enrollment: 90,000

Healthplan and Services Defined
PLAN TYPE: HMO/PPO
Plan Specialty: Dental, Vision
Benefits Offered: Dental, Vision

Type of Coverage
Commercial, Government, municipalities, correct

Key Personnel
President/CEO................... Milton Bernard, DDS

192 UnitedHealthcare Community Plan District of Columbia
UnitedHealthcare Customer Service
P.O. Box 30769
Salt Lake City, UT 84130-0769
Toll-Free: 888-545-5205
www.uhccommunityplan.com/dc
Subsidiary of: UnitedHealth Group

For Profit Organization: Yes

Healthplan and Services Defined
PLAN TYPE: Medicare
Other Type: Medicaid
Model Type: Network
Benefits Offered: Dental, Home Care, Podiatry, Prescription, Vision

Type of Coverage
Medicare, Medicaid

Geographic Areas Served
District of Columbia

Key Personnel
CEO, Community Plan MD/DC . . . . Kathlyn Wee
kathlyn.wee@uhc.com

Peer Review Type
Utilization Review: Yes
Second Surgical Opinion: Yes
Case Management: Yes

Publishes and Distributes Report Card: Yes

Accreditation Certification
TJC Accreditation, Medicare Approved, Utilization Review, Pre-Admission Certification, State Licensure, Quality Assurance Program

Key Personnel
CEO, Mid-Atlantic . . . . Joe Ochipinti

Specialty Managed Care Partners
Enters into Contracts with Regional Business Coalitions: Yes

---

193 UnitedHealthcare of the District of Columbia
800 King Farm Boulevard
Suite 600
Rockville, MD 20850
Toll-Free: 888-545-5205
Phone: 240-683-6984
www.uhc.com
Subsidiary of: UnitedHealth Group
Non-Profit Organization: Yes
Year Founded: 1976

Healthplan and Services Defined
PLAN TYPE: HMO/PPO
Model Type: Network
Benefits Offered: Dental, Disease Management, Prescription, Vision, Wellness, Life, LTD, STD

Type of Coverage
Group, Small Business

Geographic Areas Served
Statewide. The District of Columbia is covered by the Maryland branch

Subscriber Information
Average Monthly Fee Per Subscriber
(Employee + Employer Contribution):
Employee Only (Self): $104.00-135.00
Employee & 1 Family Member: $143.00-184.00
Employee & 2 Family Members: $331.00-440.00
Medicare: $112.00-156.00
Average Annual Deductible Per Subscriber:
Employee Only (Self): $100.00-250.00
Employee & 1 Family Member: $500.00-1500.00
Employee & 2 Family Members: $200.00-500.00
Medicare: $0
Average Subscriber Co-Payment:
Primary Care Physician: $5.00/10.00
Non-Network Physician: Deductible
Prescription Drugs: $5.00/10.00
Hospital ER: $25.00/50.00
Home Health Care: $5.00/10.00

Network Qualifications
Pre-Admission Certification: Yes

FLORIDA

Health Insurance Coverage Status and Type of Coverage by Age

Category	All Persons Number	%	Under 19 years Number	%	Under 65 years Number	%
Total population	21,157 *(5)*	100.0 *(0.0)*	4,480 *(9)*	100.0 *(0.0)*	16,729 *(6)*	100.0 *(0.0)*
Covered by some type of health insurance	18,372 *(45)*	86.8 *(0.2)*	4,137 *(18)*	92.4 *(0.4)*	13,995 *(44)*	83.7 *(0.3)*
Covered by private health insurance	13,216 *(71)*	62.5 *(0.3)*	2,457 *(29)*	54.9 *(0.7)*	11,016 *(63)*	65.9 *(0.4)*
Employer-based	9,682 *(69)*	45.8 *(0.3)*	1,962 *(29)*	43.8 *(0.7)*	8,599 *(64)*	51.4 *(0.4)*
Direct purchase	3,576 *(50)*	16.9 *(0.2)*	440 *(19)*	9.8 *(0.4)*	2,369 *(45)*	14.2 *(0.3)*
TRICARE	772 *(23)*	3.6 *(0.1)*	137 *(12)*	3.1 *(0.3)*	455 *(21)*	2.7 *(0.1)*
Covered by public health insurance	7,780 *(46)*	36.8 *(0.2)*	1,818 *(30)*	40.6 *(0.7)*	3,535 *(46)*	21.1 *(0.3)*
Medicaid	3,663 *(49)*	17.3 *(0.2)*	1,796 *(30)*	40.1 *(0.7)*	3,023 *(44)*	18.1 *(0.3)*
Medicare	4,782 *(17)*	22.6 *(0.1)*	30 *(5)*	0.7 *(0.1)*	543 *(15)*	3.2 *(0.1)*
VA Care	613 *(14)*	2.9 *(0.1)*	10 *(3)*	0.2 *(0.1)*	264 *(12)*	1.6 *(0.1)*
Not covered at any time during the year	2,784 *(45)*	13.2 *(0.2)*	343 *(16)*	7.6 *(0.4)*	2,734 *(45)*	16.3 *(0.3)*

Note: Numbers in thousands; Figures cover civilian noninstitutionalized population in 2019; N/A indicates that data was not available; Z represents or rounds to zero; Margin of error appears in parenthesis and is calculated using replicate weights.
Source: U.S. Census Bureau, American Community Survey, Table HI-05. Health Insurance Coverage Status and Type of Coverage by State and Age for All People: 2019

Florida

194 Aetna Better Health of Florida
8200 NW 41st Street
Suite 125
Doral, FL 33166
Toll-Free: 800-441-5501
Fax: 959-888-4124
www.aetnabetterhealth.com/florida
Mailing Address: P.O. Box 63578, Phoenix, AZ 85082-1925
Subsidiary of: CVS Health / Aetna Inc.
For Profit Organization: Yes

Healthplan and Services Defined
PLAN TYPE: HMO/PPO
Other Type: POS
Model Type: Network
Plan Specialty: Behavioral Health, Dental, EPO, Lab, PBM, Vision, Radiology
Benefits Offered: Behavioral Health, Dental, Disease Management, Long-Term Care, Physical Therapy, Podiatry, Prescription, Psychiatric, Wellness, Life, LTD, STD

Type of Coverage
Commercial, Medicare, Medicaid, Catastrophic, Student health

Geographic Areas Served
Statewide

Key Personnel
CEO.............................. Jennifer A. Sweet

195 Allwell from Sunshine Health
PO Box 459089
Fort Lauderdale, FL 33345-9089
Toll-Free: 877-935-8022
wellcare.sunshinehealth.com
Subsidiary of: Centene Corporation
For Profit Organization: Yes

Healthplan and Services Defined
PLAN TYPE: Medicare
Model Type: Network
Benefits Offered: Dental, Prescription

Type of Coverage
Medicare, Supplemental Medicare, Medicare Advantage

Geographic Areas Served
Duval, Miami-Dade, Hillsborough, Pasco, Pinellas, Orange, Osceola, Seminole, Broward, Palm Beach, Polk, Volusia, Baker, Duval, Hardee, Hernando, Lake, Manatee, Marion, and Martin counties

196 Ambetter from Sunshine Health
1301 International Parkway
4th Floor
Sunrise, FL 33323
Toll-Free: 877-687-1169
ambetter.sunshinehealth.com
Subsidiary of: Centene Corporation
For Profit Organization: Yes

Healthplan and Services Defined
PLAN TYPE: Other
Model Type: Network
Benefits Offered: Behavioral Health, Dental, Physical Therapy, Prescription, Vision

Type of Coverage
Health Insurance Marketplace

Geographic Areas Served
Alachua, Broward, Charlotte, Citrus, Clay, Duval, Flagler, Hernando, Highlands, Hillsborough, Lake, Marion, Manatee, Miami-Dade, Okeechobee, Orange, Osceola, Palm Beach, Pasco, Pinellas, Polk, Putnam, Sarasota, Seminole, St. Lucie, and Volusia counties

197 AvMed
9400 S Dadeland Boulevard
Miami, FL 33156
Toll-Free: 800-882-8633
Phone: 305-671-5437
www.avmed.org
Subsidiary of: SantaFe HealthCare, Inc.
Non-Profit Organization: Yes
Year Founded: 1969
Total Enrollment: 230,000
State Enrollment: 230,000

Healthplan and Services Defined
PLAN TYPE: Medicare
Plan Specialty: Dental, Nurse On Call Program
Benefits Offered: Behavioral Health, Dental, Prescription, Wellness

Type of Coverage
Medicare

Type of Payment Plans Offered
POS

Geographic Areas Served
Miami-Dade counties

Subscriber Information
Average Annual Deductible Per Subscriber:
    Employee Only (Self): $0
    Employee & 1 Family Member: $0
    Employee & 2 Family Members: $0
    Medicare: $0

Accreditation Certification
NCQA

Key Personnel
President/CEO .... Larry Schreiber
President/COO .... James M. Repp
SVP, Human Resources .... Christine Shipley
SVP/CIO............................. Eric Johnson
SVP/CFO........................... Randall L. Stuart
SVP, General Counsel................ Steven M. Ziegler

Specialty Managed Care Partners
Enters into Contracts with Regional Business Coalitions: No

198 AvMed Ft. Lauderdale
1340 W Sunrise Boulevard
Suite 370
Ft. Lauderdale, FL 33323
Toll-Free: 800-882-8633
Phone: 954-462-2520
www.avmed.org
Non-Profit Organization: Yes
Year Founded: 1973
Federally Qualified: Yes
Total Enrollment: 230,000
State Enrollment: 230,000

Healthplan and Services Defined
PLAN TYPE: Medicare
Model Type: IPA
Plan Specialty: Nurse On Call Program
Benefits Offered: Behavioral Health, Dental, Disease Management, Prescription, Wellness

Type of Coverage
Medicare

Geographic Areas Served
Broward County

Accreditation Certification
TJC, NCQA

199 AvMed Gainesville
4300 NW 89th Boulevard
Gainesville, FL 32606
Toll-Free: 800-882-8633
Phone: 352-372-8400
www.avmed.org
Non-Profit Organization: Yes
Year Founded: 1986
Total Enrollment: 230,000
State Enrollment: 230,000

Healthplan and Services Defined
PLAN TYPE: HMO
Model Type: IPA
Plan Specialty: Nurse On Call Program
Benefits Offered: Behavioral Health, Dental, Disease Management, Prescription, Wellness

Type of Coverage
Commercial, Individual
Catastrophic Illness Benefit: Unlimited

Type of Payment Plans Offered
POS, DFFS, Combination FFS & DFFS

Geographic Areas Served
Alachua, Bradford, Citrus, Columbia, Dixie, Gilchrist, Hamilton, Levy, Marion, Suwannee and Union counties

Accreditation Certification
NCQA

Average Claim Compensation
Physician's Fees Charged: 85%
Hospital's Fees Charged: 70%

Specialty Managed Care Partners
Enters into Contracts with Regional Business Coalitions: No

200 Capital Health Plan
2140 Centerville Place
Tallahassee, FL 32308
Toll-Free: 877-247-6512
Phone: 850-383-3311
memberservices@chp.org
www.capitalhealth.com
Mailing Address: P.O. Box 15349, Tallahassee, FL 32317-5349
Subsidiary of: Blue Cross Blue Shield of Florida
Non-Profit Organization: Yes
Year Founded: 1982
Owned by an Integrated Delivery Network (IDN): Yes
Number of Primary Care Physicians: 150
Number of Referral/Specialty Physicians: 400
Total Enrollment: 135,000
State Enrollment: 135,000

Healthplan and Services Defined
PLAN TYPE: HMO
Model Type: Staff, Mixed Model
Plan Specialty: Chiropractic, Lab, Vision, Radiology, UR
Benefits Offered: Behavioral Health, Chiropractic, Disease Management, Home Care, Inpatient SNF, Physical Therapy, Podiatry, Prescription, Psychiatric, Transplant, Vision, Wellness

Type of Coverage
Commercial, Medicare, Supplemental Medicare, Catastrophic
Catastrophic Illness Benefit: Unlimited

Geographic Areas Served
Calhoun, Franklin, Gadsden, Jefferson, Leon, Liberty and Wakulla counties

Peer Review Type
Second Surgical Opinion: Yes

Publishes and Distributes Report Card: Yes

Accreditation Certification
NCQA

Key Personnel
President & CEO . . . . John Hogan

Specialty Managed Care Partners
Enters into Contracts with Regional Business Coalitions: Yes

201 CareCentrix: Florida
9119 Corporate Lake Drive
Suite 300
Tampa, FL 33634
Toll-Free: 800-808-1902
carecentrix.com
Subsidiary of: CareCentrix,Inc.
Year Founded: 1996
Number of Primary Care Physicians: 8,000

Healthplan and Services Defined
PLAN TYPE: HMO

Benefits Offered: Home Care, Physical Therapy, Durable Medical Equipment; Occupational & Respiratory Therapy; Orthotics; Prosthetics

Key Personnel
Area VP, IT .... Fran Lanham

202 CarePlus Health Plans
11430 NW 20th Street
Suite 300
Miami, FL 33172
Toll-Free: 800-794-5907
cphp_memberservices@careplus-hp.com
www.careplushealthplans.com
Subsidiary of: Humana
Year Founded: 2003
Total Enrollment: 111,000
State Enrollment: 111,000

Healthplan and Services Defined
PLAN TYPE: Medicare
Benefits Offered: Prescription

Type of Coverage
Medicare

Geographic Areas Served
Miami-Dade, Broward, Palm Beach, Hillsborough, Pinellas, Pasco, Polk, Lake, Marion, Sumter, Orange, Osceola, Seminole, Brevard, Indian River, Martin, Okeechobee, St. Lucie and Duval counties

Accreditation Certification
AAAHC

Key Personnel
President/CEO .... Bruce Dale Broussard
Director/CFO..................... Brian Andrew Kane

203 Cigna HealthCare of Florida
1571 Sawgrass Corporate Parkway
Suite 140
Sunrise, FL 33323
Toll-Free: 800-997-1654
www.cigna.com
Subsidiary of: Cigna Corporation
For Profit Organization: Yes

Healthplan and Services Defined
PLAN TYPE: HMO
Other Type: POS
Model Type: Network
Plan Specialty: Behavioral Health, Dental
Benefits Offered: Behavioral Health, Dental, Disease Management, Prescription, Transplant, Vision, Wellness, Life, LTD, STD

Type of Coverage
Commercial, Individual

Type of Payment Plans Offered
POS, DFFS, FFS, Combination FFS & DFFS

Geographic Areas Served
Statewide

Network Qualifications
Minimum Years of Practice: 3

Peer Review Type
Second Surgical Opinion: Yes
Case Management: Yes

Publishes and Distributes Report Card: Yes

Accreditation Certification
NCQA
TJC Accreditation, Medicare Approved, Utilization Review, Pre-Admission Certification, State Licensure, Quality Assurance Program

Key Personnel
Market President .... Giselle Cushing

204 Clear Health Alliance
9250 W Flagler Street
Miami, FL 33174
Toll-Free: 844-406-2398
www.clearhealthalliance.com
Subsidiary of: Simply Healthcare Plans, Inc. / Anthem, Inc.
For Profit Organization: Yes
Year Founded: 2010

Healthplan and Services Defined
PLAN TYPE: Medicare
Model Type: Network
Plan Specialty: Disease Management, Specialty Medicaid plan for individuals with HIV/AIDS in Florida.
Benefits Offered: Behavioral Health, Dental, Disease Management, Prescription, Psychiatric, Nonemergency transportation services

Type of Coverage
Medicare, Medicaid

205 Dimension Health
5881 NW 151st Street
Suite 201
Hialeah, FL 33014
Toll-Free: 800-483-4992
Phone: 305-823-7664
info@dimensionhealth.com
www.dimensionhealth.com
Year Founded: 1985
Number of Affiliated Hospitals: 51

Healthplan and Services Defined
PLAN TYPE: PPO
Model Type: Network
Benefits Offered: Disease Management, Wellness, Worker's Compensation

Type of Coverage
Commercial

Type of Payment Plans Offered
POS, DFFS, Capitated, FFS, Combination FFS & DFFS

Network Qualifications
Pre-Admission Certification: Yes

Peer Review Type
Utilization Review: Yes
Second Surgical Opinion: Yes
Case Management: Yes

Publishes and Distributes Report Card: No

Key Personnel
President/CEO .... Creta Diehs
   305-823-7664
   cdiehs@dimensionhealth.com
Office Mngr./Asst. to CEO .... Rosemary Osorio
   305-823-7664
   rosorio@dimensionhealth.com
Provider Relations Coord................. Melissa Macias
   mmacias@dimensionhealth.com

Specialty Managed Care Partners
Enters into Contracts with Regional Business Coalitions: No

206 Florida Blue
P.O. Box 1798
Jacksonville, FL 32231-0014
Toll-Free: 800-352-2583
www.floridablue.com
Secondary Address: Medicare Mail, P.O. Box 45296, Jacksonville, FL 32232-5296
Subsidiary of: Blue Cross and Blue Shield of Florida, Inc.
Non-Profit Organization: Yes
Year Founded: 1985
Owned by an Integrated Delivery Network (IDN): Yes

Healthplan and Services Defined
PLAN TYPE: HMO
Plan Specialty: Dental
Benefits Offered: Behavioral Health, Chiropractic, Complementary Medicine, Dental, Disease Management, Home Care, Inpatient SNF, Physical Therapy, Podiatry, Prescription, Psychiatric, Transplant, Wellness, AD&D, Life, Critical illness
Offers Demand Management Patient Information Service: Yes
DMPI Services Offered: Nurse Line 24x7x365, Health Coaching, Support for Chronic Conditions, Health Risk Assessments, Web Tools & Resources

Type of Coverage
Commercial, Individual, Indemnity, Medicare

Type of Payment Plans Offered
FFS

Geographic Areas Served
Statewide

Subscriber Information
Average Subscriber Co-Payment:
   Primary Care Physician: Varies
   Non-Network Physician: Varies
   Prescription Drugs: Varies
   Hospital ER: Varies
   Home Health Care: Varies
   Nursing Home: Varies

Network Qualifications
Pre-Admission Certification: Yes

Peer Review Type
Utilization Review: Yes

Publishes and Distributes Report Card: No

Accreditation Certification
Utilization Review

Key Personnel
President/CEO .... Patrick Geraghty

Specialty Managed Care Partners
Prime Therapeutics, LLC-PBM and Mental Health Network (MHnet), Health Dialog, Accordant and Quest Diagnostics
Enters into Contracts with Regional Business Coalitions: Yes

Employer References
State of Florida, Gevity HR (formerly Staff Leasing), Publix, Lincare, Miami Dade County

207 Florida Health Care Plan, Inc.
2450 Mason Avenue
Daytona Beach, FL 32114
Toll-Free: 800-352-9824
www.fhcp.com
Subsidiary of: Blue Cross and Blue Shield of Florida, Inc.
Non-Profit Organization: Yes
Year Founded: 1974
Owned by an Integrated Delivery Network (IDN): Yes
Federally Qualified: Yes

Healthplan and Services Defined
PLAN TYPE: HMO
Benefits Offered: Behavioral Health, Chiropractic, Dental, Disease Management, Home Care, Inpatient SNF, Podiatry, Prescription, Psychiatric, Transplant, Vision, Wellness

Type of Coverage
Commercial, Individual, Medicare, Supplemental Medicare
Catastrophic Illness Benefit: Varies per case

Geographic Areas Served
Volusia, Flagler, Brevard and Seminole counties

Publishes and Distributes Report Card: Yes

Accreditation Certification
TJC, NCQA

Key Personnel
President/CEO..................... David C. Schandel
Chief Financial Officer .... Melanie Ruel
Chief Medical Officer .... Joseph Zuckerman, MD
Chief Information Officer .... Tim Moylan
Compliance Officer .... Robert Gilliland
Quality Management .... Joann Adams, RN, CPHQ

Specialty Managed Care Partners
Enters into Contracts with Regional Business Coalitions: Yes

208 Freedom Health
5403 N Church Avenue
Tampa, FL 33614
Toll-Free: 800-401-2740
Fax: 813-506-6150
www.freedomhealth.com
Mailing Address: P.O. Box 151137, Tampa, FL 33684

Physician Owned Organization: Yes

Healthplan and Services Defined
PLAN TYPE: Medicare
Benefits Offered: Prescription, Wellness

Type of Coverage
Supplemental Medicare, Medicaid

Geographic Areas Served
Brevard, Broward, Charlotte, Citrus, Collier, Hernando, Hillsborough, Indian River, Lake, Lee, Manatee, Marion, Martin, Miami-Dade, Orange, Osceola, Palm Beach, Pasco, Pinellas, Polk, Sarasota, Seminole, St. Lucie, Sumter and Volusia counties

Accreditation Certification
NCQA

Key Personnel
Chief Executive Officer . . . . Rupesh Shah

---

209 Health First Health Plans
6450 US Highway 1
Rockledge, FL 32955
Toll-Free: 800-716-7737
Phone: 321-434-4335
www.healthfirsthealthplans.org
Non-Profit Organization: Yes
Year Founded: 1995
Number of Affiliated Hospitals: 8
Number of Referral/Specialty Physicians: 4,000

Healthplan and Services Defined
PLAN TYPE: Medicare
Model Type: Network
Benefits Offered: Behavioral Health, Chiropractic, Disease Management, Home Care, Inpatient SNF, Long-Term Care, Physical Therapy, Podiatry, Prescription, Psychiatric, Transplant, Vision, Wellness

Type of Coverage
Commercial, Medicare
Catastrophic Illness Benefit: Covered

Type of Payment Plans Offered
FFS

Geographic Areas Served
Brevard and Indian River counties

Peer Review Type
Utilization Review: Yes
Second Surgical Opinion: Yes
Case Management: Yes

Accreditation Certification
NCQA

Key Personnel
President & CEO. Steven P. Johnson

Average Claim Compensation
Physician's Fees Charged: 110%

Specialty Managed Care Partners
SXC, Ameripharm

Employer References
Boeing/McDonnell Douglas Corp., ITT, Computer Science Raytheon, Intersil Corp.

---

210 Health First Medicare Plans
6450 US Highway 1
Rockledge, FL 32955
Toll-Free: 800-716-7737
Phone: 321-434-4335
www.health-first.org/health_plans/medicare
Subsidiary of: Health First Health Plans
Year Founded: 1997
Number of Affiliated Hospitals: 8
Number of Referral/Specialty Physicians: 4,000

Healthplan and Services Defined
PLAN TYPE: Medicare
Other Type: HMO-POS

Type of Coverage
Medicare

Geographic Areas Served
Brevard and Indian River counties

Key Personnel
President/CEO. . . . . Steven P. Johnson

---

211 Healthchoice
1414 Kuhl Avenue
Orlando, FL 32806
Toll-Free: 866-500-5048
www.healthchoiceorlando.org
Subsidiary of: Orlando Health
For Profit Organization: Yes
Year Founded: 1984
Number of Affiliated Hospitals: 9

Healthplan and Services Defined
PLAN TYPE: PPO
Plan Specialty: Behavioral Health, Worker's Compensation, UR, Pediatrics
Benefits Offered: Behavioral Health, Disease Management

Type of Coverage
Commercial
Catastrophic Illness Benefit: Varies per case

Type of Payment Plans Offered
FFS

Geographic Areas Served
Central Florida

Peer Review Type
Utilization Review: Yes
Second Surgical Opinion: Yes
Case Management: Yes

Publishes and Distributes Report Card: Yes

Accreditation Certification
AAAHC
TJC Accreditation, Medicare Approved, Utilization Review, Pre-Admission Certification, State Licensure, Quality Assurance Program

Specialty Managed Care Partners
Enters into Contracts with Regional Business Coalitions: Yes

212 HealthNetwork
301 Clematis Street
Suite 3000
West Palm Beach, FL 33401
Toll-Free: 800-200-9416
healthnetwork.com
For Profit Organization: Yes

Healthplan and Services Defined
PLAN TYPE: Multiple
Plan Specialty: Dental, Vision
Benefits Offered: Dental, Prescription, Vision, Wellness, Short-term

Type of Coverage
Commercial, Individual, Medicare

Key Personnel
Chief Executive Officer . . . . Jeremy Kayne
General Counsel/COO . . . . Erika Sullivan
Creative Director . . . . Janna Gilleland
Chief Technology Officer . . . . James Beams

213 HealthSun
9250 W. Flagler Street
Suite 600
Miami, FL 33174
Toll-Free: 877-207-4900
Phone: 305-234-9292
Fax: 305-234-9275
info@healthsun.com
www.healthsun.com
Subsidiary of: Anthem, Inc.
Year Founded: 2005
Number of Affiliated Hospitals: 19

Healthplan and Services Defined
PLAN TYPE: Medicare
Benefits Offered: Prescription, Transportation Services

Type of Coverage
Medicare

Geographic Areas Served
Miami-Dade and Broward counties

Key Personnel
President/CEO. . . . . Ron Schutzen

214 Humana Health Insurance of Florida
9965 San Jose Boulevard
Suite 12
Jacksonville, FL 32257
Toll-Free: 800-639-1133
Phone: 904-376-1234
Fax: 904-376-1270
www.humana.com
Secondary Address: 7218 West Colonial Drive, Orlando, FL 32818, 407-241-3000
Subsidiary of: Humana Inc.

For Profit Organization: Yes
Year Founded: 1962

Healthplan and Services Defined
PLAN TYPE: HMO/PPO
Model Type: IPA
Plan Specialty: Dental, Vision
Benefits Offered: Dental, Disease Management, Prescription, Vision, Wellness, Life, LTD, STD

Type of Coverage
Commercial, Individual

Type of Payment Plans Offered
POS

Geographic Areas Served
Statewide

Subscriber Information
Average Annual Deductible Per Subscriber:
Employee Only (Self): $0
Medicare: $0
Average Subscriber Co-Payment:
Primary Care Physician: $10.00
Prescription Drugs: $7.00
Hospital ER: $25.00

Network Qualifications
Pre-Admission Certification: Yes

Peer Review Type
Utilization Review: Yes
Second Surgical Opinion: Yes
Case Management: Yes

Publishes and Distributes Report Card: Yes

Accreditation Certification
URAC, NCQA, CORE
TJC Accreditation, Medicare Approved, Utilization Review, Pre-Admission Certification, State Licensure, Quality Assurance Program

Key Personnel
Market VP. . . . . Mack Perry

Specialty Managed Care Partners
Enters into Contracts with Regional Business Coalitions: Yes

215 Leon Medical Centers Health Plan
8600 NW 41st Street
Suite 201
Doral, FL 33166
Toll-Free: 866-393-5366
Phone: 305-229-7461
membersupport@lmchealthplans.com
www.lmchealthplans.com
Subsidiary of: HealthSpring, Inc.
For Profit Organization: Yes
Year Founded: 2005
Number of Affiliated Hospitals: 5
Number of Primary Care Physicians: 600
Total Enrollment: 42,000
State Enrollment: 42,000

Healthplan and Services Defined
PLAN TYPE: HMO
Benefits Offered: Chiropractic, Dental, Inpatient SNF, Podiatry, Prescription, Psychiatric, Vision, Wellness

Type of Coverage
Supplemental Medicare, Medicare Advantage

Geographic Areas Served
Miami-Dade County

Key Personnel
President/CEO . . . . Albert Maury
   albert.maury@lmchealthplans.com
Vice President, IT . . . . Jennifer Velasquez
   jennifer.velasquez@lmchealthplans.com
COO . . . . Guillermo Gurdian
   guillermo.gurdian@lmchealthplans.com
VP, Medical Director . . . . Luis Fernandez
   luis.fernandez@lmchealthplans.com
Director of Finance . . . . Mercy Kirkpatrick
   mercy.kirpatrick@lmchealthplans.com

216 Liberty Dental Plan of Florida
PO Box 15149
Tampa, FL 33684-5149
Toll-Free: 888-352-7924
Fax: 888-334-6034
www.libertydentalplan.com
For Profit Organization: Yes
Total Enrollment: 2,000,000

Healthplan and Services Defined
PLAN TYPE: Dental
Other Type: Dental HMO
Plan Specialty: Dental
Benefits Offered: Dental

Type of Coverage
Commercial, Medicare, Medicaid, Unions

Geographic Areas Served
Statewide

Accreditation Certification
NCQA

Key Personnel
Pres. Liberty Florida. . . . . Heather Stearns

217 Magellan Complete Care of Florida
4800 North Scottdale Road
Suite 4400
Scottsdale, AZ 85251
Toll-Free: 800-327-8613
FLMCCCustomerService@magellanhealth.com
www.magellancompletecareoffl.com
Subsidiary of: Magellan Health
For Profit Organization: Yes

Healthplan and Services Defined
PLAN TYPE: Other
Plan Specialty: Behavioral Health
Benefits Offered: Behavioral Health, Psychiatric

Type of Coverage
Medicaid, Specialty plan for individuals with

Geographic Areas Served
Region 4: Baker, Clay, Duval, Flagler, Nassau, St. Johns and Volusia. Region 5: Pasco and Pinellas. Region 7: Brevard, Orange, Osceola, and Seminole

Key Personnel
President, Complete Care. . . . . Chrissie Cooper
President, Behavioral . . . . Gus Giraldo

218 Molina Healthcare of Florida
8300 NW 33rd Street
Suite 400
Miami, FL 33122
Toll-Free: 866-422-2541
www.molinahealthcare.com
Subsidiary of: Molina Healthcare, Inc.
For Profit Organization: Yes

Healthplan and Services Defined
PLAN TYPE: Medicare
Model Type: Network
Plan Specialty: Dental, PBM, Vision, Integrated Medicare/Medicaid (Duals)
Benefits Offered: Dental, Prescription, Vision, Wellness, Life

Type of Coverage
Individual, Medicare, Supplemental Medicare, Medicaid

Geographic Areas Served
Statewide

Key Personnel
President/Chair . . . . Mike Jones
Chief Medical Officer. . . . . Mark Bloom, MD

219 Neighborhood Health Partnership
Miami, FL
www.uhc.com/nhpfl
Subsidiary of: UnitedHealthcare
For Profit Organization: Yes
Year Founded: 1993
Number of Primary Care Physicians: 1,282
Total Enrollment: 108,000
State Enrollment: 141,178

Healthplan and Services Defined
PLAN TYPE: HMO
Other Type: POS
Plan Specialty: Behavioral Health, Chiropractic
Benefits Offered: Disease Management, Home Care, Prescription, Transplant, Wellness, Durable Medical Equipment

Type of Coverage
Commercial, Medicare

Type of Payment Plans Offered
Capitated

Geographic Areas Served
Orange, Seminole, Osceola, Flagler, Lake, Volusia, Hillsborough, Pasco, Pinellas, Sarasota, Polk, Hernando, and Lee counties

Peer Review Type
Utilization Review: Yes

Publishes and Distributes Report Card: Yes

Accreditation Certification
NCQA

Key Personnel
CEO, Community Plan . . . . Michael Lawton

---

220 One Call Care Management
841 Prudential Drive
Suite 204
Jacksonville, FL 32207
Toll-Free: 866-697-2680
www.onecallcm.com
Secondary Address: 8501 Fallbrook Avenue, West Hills, CA 91304
For Profit Organization: Yes
Year Founded: 1993

Healthplan and Services Defined
PLAN TYPE: Other
Plan Specialty: Worker's Compensation
Benefits Offered: Dental, Home Care, Long-Term Care, Physical Therapy, Wellness, Worker's Compensation

Type of Payment Plans Offered
POS, DFFS, FFS, Combination FFS & DFFS

Geographic Areas Served
Nationwide

Network Qualifications
Pre-Admission Certification: Yes

Publishes and Distributes Report Card: No

Accreditation Certification
Utilization Review, Quality Assurance Program

Key Personnel
President & CEO . . . . Thomas Warsop
Chief Financial Officer. . . . . Fred Pensotti
Chief Operating Officer . . . . Chris Watson
Business Devel. Officer . . . . Robert Zeccardi
Chief Product Officer. . . . . Will Smith

Specialty Managed Care Partners
Enters into Contracts with Regional Business Coalitions: No

---

221 Optimum HealthCare, Inc
5403 North Church Avenue
Tampa, FL 33614
Toll-Free: 866-245-5360
Fax: 813-506-6150
www.youroptimumhealthcare.com
Mailing Address: P.O. Box 151137, Tampa, FL 33684

Healthplan and Services Defined
PLAN TYPE: HMO

Type of Coverage
Medicare, Medicaid

Geographic Areas Served
Brevard, Broward, Charlotte, Citrus, Collier, Hernando, Hillsborough, Indian River, Lake, Lee, Manatee, Marion, Martin, Orange, Osceola, Palm Beach, Pasco, Pinellas, Polk, Sarasota, Seminole, St. Lucie, Sumter and Volusia counties

Accreditation Certification
NCQA

---

222 Preferred Care Partners
9100 S Dadeland Boulevard
Suite 1250
Miami, FL 33156
Toll-Free: 866-231-7201
Fax: 501-262-7070
MemberServices@uhcsouthflorida.com
www.mypreferredcare.com
Mailing Address: P.O. Box 30770, Salt Lake City, UT 84130-0770
Number of Affiliated Hospitals: 18
Number of Primary Care Physicians: 917
Total Enrollment: 45,000

Healthplan and Services Defined
PLAN TYPE: Multiple
Benefits Offered: Dental, Prescription, Vision, Hearing, Transportation, Fitness Programs

Type of Coverage
Supplemental Medicare, Catastrophic

Geographic Areas Served
Miami-Dade, Broward, and Palm Beach counties

Accreditation Certification
URAC

Key Personnel
President . . . . Justo Pozo
CEO . . . . Joseph Caruncho

---

223 Simply Healthcare Plans, Inc.
9250 W Flagler Street
Suite 600
Miami, FL 33174
Toll-Free: 877-577-0115
Info@simplyhealthcareplans.com
simplyhealthcareplans.com
Subsidiary of: Amerigroup / Anthem, Inc.
For Profit Organization: Yes
Year Founded: 2010
Total Enrollment: 560,000

Healthplan and Services Defined
PLAN TYPE: Medicare
Model Type: Network
Plan Specialty: Behavioral Health, Dental, Disease Management, Lab, Vision, Managed health care for people enrolled in Medicaid and/or Medicare programs.

Benefits Offered: Behavioral Health, Dental, Disease Management, Long-Term Care, Podiatry, Prescription, Vision, Wellness

Type of Coverage
Medicare, Medicaid

Key Personnel
President . . . . Holly Prince
Chief Operating Officer . . . . Suzanna Roberts

---

224 Sunshine Health
P.O. Box 459089
Fort Lauderdale, FL 33345-9089
Toll-Free: 800-955-8770
Phone: 866-796-0530
www.sunshinehealth.com
Subsidiary of: Centene Corporation
For Profit Organization: Yes

Healthplan and Services Defined
PLAN TYPE: Other
Model Type: Network
Plan Specialty: Lab
Benefits Offered: Behavioral Health, Home Care, Inpatient SNF, Physical Therapy, Podiatry, Prescription, Vision

Type of Coverage
Medicaid

Geographic Areas Served
Statewide

Key Personnel
Plan President/CEO . . . . Nathan Landsbaum

---

225 Trinity Health of Florida
1700 McMullen Booth Rd
Suite A21
Clearwater, FL 33759
Toll-Free: 800-229-2273
www.trinity-health.org
Secondary Address: Holy Cross Hospital, 4725 N Federal Highway, Fort Lauderdale, FL 33308
Subsidiary of: Trinity Health
Non-Profit Organization: Yes
Year Founded: 2013
Total Enrollment: 30,000,000

Healthplan and Services Defined
PLAN TYPE: Other
Benefits Offered: Disease Management, Home Care, Long-Term Care, Psychiatric, Hospice programs, PACE (Program of All Inclusive Care for the Elderly)

Geographic Areas Served
South Florida

Key Personnel
President/CEO . . . . Tommy Inzina

---

226 United Concordia of Florida
8932 Chambore Dr
Jacksonville, FL 32256
Phone: 904-998-7244
www.unitedconcordia.com
For Profit Organization: Yes
Year Founded: 1971
Number of Primary Care Physicians: 104,000
Total Enrollment: 8,800,000

Healthplan and Services Defined
PLAN TYPE: Dental
Plan Specialty: Dental
Benefits Offered: Dental

Type of Coverage
Commercial, Individual, Military personnel & families

Geographic Areas Served
Nationwide

Accreditation Certification
URAC

Key Personnel
Senior Dental Network Svc . . . . Cynthia Byndas
Contact . . . . Beth Rutherford
717-260-7659
beth.rutherford@ucci.com

---

227 UnitedHealthcare Community Plan Florida
UnitedHealthcare Customer Service
P.O. Box 30769
Salt Lake City, UT 84130-0769
Toll-Free: 888-545-5205
www.uhccommunityplan.com/fl
Subsidiary of: UnitedHealth Group
For Profit Organization: Yes

Healthplan and Services Defined
PLAN TYPE: Multiple
Model Type: Network
Benefits Offered: Dental, Home Care, Podiatry, Prescription, Vision, Wellness, Hearing, Acupuncture, Chiropractic

Type of Coverage
Medicare, Medicaid, CHIP

Geographic Areas Served
Brevard, Charlotte, Clay, Duval, Flagler, Hernando, Hillsborough, Indian River, Lee, Manatee, Orange, Osceola, Pasco, Pinellas, Polk, Sarasota, Seminole, and St. Johns. Some plans statewide

Key Personnel
CEO, Community Plan FL . . . . Michael Lawton
michael_s_lawton@uhc.com

228 UnitedHealthcare of Florida
9009 Corporate Lake Drive
Suite 200
Tampa, FL 33634
Toll-Free: 866-515-7403
Phone: 727-480-9851
www.uhc.com
Subsidiary of: UnitedHealth Group
For Profit Organization: Yes
Owned by an Integrated Delivery Network (IDN): Yes

Healthplan and Services Defined
 PLAN TYPE: HMO/PPO
 Model Type: Network
 Plan Specialty: Behavioral Health, Dental, Disease Management, PBM, Vision
 Benefits Offered: Behavioral Health, Chiropractic, Dental, Disease Management, Home Care, Inpatient SNF, Physical Therapy, Podiatry, Prescription, Psychiatric, Transplant, Vision, Wellness, AD&D, Life, LTD, STD

Type of Coverage
 Commercial, Individual, Medicare, Supplemental Medicare, Medicaid, Catastrophic, Family, Military, Veterans, Group

Geographic Areas Served
 Statewide

Subscriber Information
 Average Monthly Fee Per Subscriber
  (Employee + Employer Contribution):
   Employee Only (Self): Varies

Peer Review Type
 Case Management: Yes

Accreditation Certification
 TJC, NCQA

Key Personnel
 CEO, Florida............................ Nick Zaffiris

Specialty Managed Care Partners
 Own Network
 Enters into Contracts with Regional Business Coalitions: Yes

229 UnitedHealthcare of South Florida
3100 SW 145th Avenue
Miramar, FL 33027
Toll-Free: 800-310-7622
www.uhc.com
Subsidiary of: UnitedHealth Group
For Profit Organization: Yes
Year Founded: 1970

Healthplan and Services Defined
 PLAN TYPE: HMO/PPO
 Model Type: Network
 Plan Specialty: ASO, Behavioral Health, Chiropractic, Dental, Disease Management, PBM, Vision
 Benefits Offered: Behavioral Health, Chiropractic, Complementary Medicine, Dental, Disease Management, Long-Term Care, Physical Therapy, Podiatry, Prescription, Psychiatric, Vision, Wellness, AD&D, Life, LTD, STD

Type of Coverage
 Commercial, Individual, Medicare, Supplemental Medicare, Medicaid, Catastrophic, Family, Military, Veterans, Group, Catastrophic Illness Benefit: Varies per case

Type of Payment Plans Offered
 POS, DFFS, Capitated, FFS, Combination FFS & DFFS

Geographic Areas Served
 Palm Beach, Broward & Dade counties

Subscriber Information
 Average Subscriber Co-Payment:
  Primary Care Physician: $5.00-15.00
  Non-Network Physician: Varies
  Prescription Drugs: $5.00-10.00
  Hospital ER: $100.00

Network Qualifications
 Pre-Admission Certification: Yes

Peer Review Type
 Utilization Review: Yes
 Second Surgical Opinion: Yes
 Case Management: Yes

Publishes and Distributes Report Card: Yes

Accreditation Certification
 AAAHC, URAC, NCQA
 TJC Accreditation, Medicare Approved, Utilization Review, Pre-Admission Certification, State Licensure, Quality Assurance Program

Key Personnel
 CEO, Florida............................ Nick Zaffiris

Specialty Managed Care Partners
 Enters into Contracts with Regional Business Coalitions: No

230 WellCare Health Plans, Inc.
P.O. Box 31370
Tampa, FL 33631
Toll-Free: 800-960-2530
www.wellcare.com
Secondary Address: 7700 Forsyth Boulevard, St. Louis, MO 63105
For Profit Organization: Yes
Year Founded: 1985
Total Enrollment: 6,300,000

Healthplan and Services Defined
 PLAN TYPE: Medicare
 Model Type: Network
 Plan Specialty: Dental, PBM, Vision, Integrated Medicare/Medicaid (Duals)
 Benefits Offered: Dental, Prescription, Vision, Wellness, Life

Type of Coverage
 Individual, Medicare, Supplemental Medicare, Medicaid

Geographic Areas Served
 Nationwide

Accreditation Certification
 URAC

Key Personnel
 Chief Executive Officer............. Kenneth A. Burdick

Chief Financial Officer.................... Drew Asher
General Counsel/Secretary................. Anat Hakim

GEORGIA

Health Insurance Coverage Status and Type of Coverage by Age

Category	All Persons Number	All Persons %	Under 19 years Number	Under 19 years %	Under 65 years Number	Under 65 years %
Total population	10,420 *(4)*	100.0 *(0.0)*	2,662 *(9)*	100.0 *(0.0)*	8,928 *(6)*	100.0 *(0.0)*
Covered by some type of health insurance	9,023 *(32)*	86.6 *(0.3)*	2,465 *(15)*	92.6 *(0.5)*	7,544 *(31)*	84.5 *(0.3)*
Covered by private health insurance	6,860 *(45)*	65.8 *(0.4)*	1,520 *(24)*	57.1 *(0.9)*	6,027 *(43)*	67.5 *(0.5)*
Employer-based	5,652 *(46)*	54.2 *(0.4)*	1,303 *(23)*	49.0 *(0.9)*	5,185 *(44)*	58.1 *(0.5)*
Direct purchase	1,227 *(24)*	11.8 *(0.2)*	166 *(11)*	6.2 *(0.4)*	822 *(21)*	9.2 *(0.2)*
TRICARE	420 *(17)*	4.0 *(0.2)*	108 *(9)*	4.1 *(0.3)*	296 *(16)*	3.3 *(0.2)*
Covered by public health insurance	3,272 *(30)*	31.4 *(0.3)*	1,042 *(22)*	39.2 *(0.8)*	1,839 *(29)*	20.6 *(0.3)*
Medicaid	1,791 *(30)*	17.2 *(0.3)*	1,021 *(23)*	38.3 *(0.9)*	1,558 *(29)*	17.4 *(0.3)*
Medicare	1,705 *(12)*	16.4 *(0.1)*	25 *(4)*	1.0 *(0.2)*	274 *(12)*	3.1 *(0.1)*
VA Care	261 *(11)*	2.5 *(0.1)*	7 *(3)*	0.2 *(0.1)*	150 *(9)*	1.7 *(0.1)*
Not covered at any time during the year	1,398 *(31)*	13.4 *(0.3)*	197 *(14)*	7.4 *(0.5)*	1,383 *(31)*	15.5 *(0.3)*

Note: Numbers in thousands; Figures cover civilian noninstitutionalized population in 2019; N/A indicates that data was not available; Z represents or rounds to zero; Margin of error appears in parenthesis and is calculated using replicate weights.
Source: U.S. Census Bureau, American Community Survey, Table HI-05. Health Insurance Coverage Status and Type of Coverage by State and Age for All People: 2019

Georgia

231 Aetna Health of Georgia
PO Box 14079
Lexington, KY 40512-4079
Toll-Free: 800-445-5299
www.aetna.com
Subsidiary of: CVS Health / Aetna Inc.
For Profit Organization: Yes

Healthplan and Services Defined
PLAN TYPE: HMO/PPO
Other Type: POS
Model Type: Network
Plan Specialty: Behavioral Health, Dental, EPO, Lab, PBM, Vision, Radiology
Benefits Offered: Behavioral Health, Dental, Disease Management, Long-Term Care, Physical Therapy, Podiatry, Prescription, Psychiatric, Vision, Wellness, Life, LTD, STD

Type of Coverage
Commercial, Medicare, Supplemental Medicare, Medicaid, Catastrophic, Student health

Geographic Areas Served
Statewide

Key Personnel
Market Pres., GA & Gulf............Cynthia Follmer
Medical Director......................David Epstein

232 Alliant Health Plans
P.O. Box 2667
Dalton, GA 30722
Toll-Free: 800-811-4793
Fax: 866-634-8917
customerservice@alliantplans.com
www.alliantplans.com
Non-Profit Organization: Yes
Year Founded: 1998
Physician Owned Organization: Yes
Number of Affiliated Hospitals: 9,999
Number of Primary Care Physicians: 500,000
Total Enrollment: 15,000
State Enrollment: 15,000

Healthplan and Services Defined
PLAN TYPE: HMO/PPO
Model Type: PSHCC

Type of Coverage
Commercial, Individual

Geographic Areas Served
Statewide

Key Personnel
Chief Executive Officer................Mark Mixer
Chief Operating Officer...............Amanda Reed
Chief Financial Officer............Joe Caldwell, RN

233 Allwell from Peach State Health Plan
1100 Circle 75 Parkway
Suite 1100
Atlanta, GA 30339
Toll-Free: 844-890-2326
allwell.pshpgeorgia.com
Subsidiary of: Centene Corporation
For Profit Organization: Yes

Healthplan and Services Defined
PLAN TYPE: Medicare
Model Type: Network
Benefits Offered: Dental, Prescription

Type of Coverage
Medicare, Supplemental Medicare, Medicare Advantage

234 Ambetter from Peach State Health Plan
1100 Circle 75 Parkway
Suite 1100
Atlanta, GA 30339
Toll-Free: 877-687-1180
Phone: 678-556-2300
ambetter.pshpgeorgia.com
Subsidiary of: Centene Corporation
For Profit Organization: Yes

Healthplan and Services Defined
PLAN TYPE: Other
Model Type: Network
Plan Specialty: Lab
Benefits Offered: Behavioral Health, Physical Therapy, Prescription, Wellness

Type of Coverage
Medicaid, Health Insurance Marketplace

235 Amerigroup Georgia
740 West Peachtree Street NW
Atlanta, GA 30308
Toll-Free: 800-600-4441
Phone: 678-587-4840
GAmembers@amerigroup.com
www.myamerigroup.com/ga
Subsidiary of: Anthem, Inc.
For Profit Organization: Yes
Year Founded: 2006
Total Enrollment: 300,000

Healthplan and Services Defined
PLAN TYPE: Medicare
Benefits Offered: Prescription

Type of Coverage
Medicaid, PeachCare for Kids

Accreditation Certification
NCQA

Key Personnel
President/CEO......................Melvin Lindsey

236 Anthem Blue Cross & Blue Shield of Georgia
3350 Peachtree Road
Atlanta, GA 30326
Toll-Free: 800-331-1476
Phone: 404-842-8000
www.anthem.com
Subsidiary of: Anthem, Inc.
For Profit Organization: Yes

Healthplan and Services Defined
  PLAN TYPE: HMO/PPO
  Model Type: Network
  Plan Specialty: ASO, Behavioral Health, Chiropractic, Dental, Disease Management, Lab, PBM, Vision, Radiology, Worker's Compensation, UR
  Benefits Offered: Behavioral Health, Chiropractic, Dental, Disease Management, Home Care, Inpatient SNF, Physical Therapy, Podiatry, Prescription, Psychiatric, Transplant, Vision, Wellness, Worker's Compensation, Life

Type of Coverage
  Commercial, Individual, Medicare, Supplemental Medicare, Medicaid, Catastrophic

Geographic Areas Served
  Statewide

Accreditation Certification
  URAC, NCQA

Key Personnel
  President . . . . Robert Bunch

237 Cigna HealthCare of Georgia
3500 Piedmont Road
Suite 200
Atlanta, GA 30305
Toll-Free: 800-997-1654
www.cigna.com
Subsidiary of: Cigna Corporation
For Profit Organization: Yes

Healthplan and Services Defined
  PLAN TYPE: HMO
  Other Type: POS
  Plan Specialty: Behavioral Health, Dental, Vision
  Benefits Offered: Behavioral Health, Dental, Disease Management, Prescription, Vision, AD&D, Life, LTD, STD

Type of Coverage
  Commercial, Individual

Type of Payment Plans Offered
  POS

Geographic Areas Served
  Statewide

Accreditation Certification
  URAC, NCQA

Key Personnel
  Market President . . . . Bonnie Evelyn

238 CompBenefits Corporation
100 Mansell Court East
Suite 400
Roswell, GA 30076
Toll-Free: 800-295-6279
Phone: 404-365-0074
Fax: 404-233-2366
www.compbenefits.com
Subsidiary of: Humana
Year Founded: 1978
Owned by an Integrated Delivery Network (IDN): Yes

Healthplan and Services Defined
  PLAN TYPE: HMO/PPO
  Model Type: Network, HMO, PPO, POS, TPA
  Plan Specialty: ASO, Dental, Vision
  Benefits Offered: Dental, Vision

Type of Coverage
  Commercial, Individual

Type of Payment Plans Offered
  DFFS, Capitated, FFS

Publishes and Distributes Report Card: Yes

Key Personnel
  President & CEO . . . . Bruce D. Broussard
  Chief Medical Officer . . . . William H. Shrank
  Human Resources. . . . . Tim Huval
  Chief Financial Officer . . . . Brian Kane
  General Counsel . . . . Christopher M. Todoroff

Specialty Managed Care Partners
  Enters into Contracts with Regional Business Coalitions: Yes

Employer References
  Royal Caribbean Cruise Line, Tupperware

239 Delta Dental Insurance Company
1130 Sanctuary Parkway
Suite 600
Alpharetta, GA 30009
Toll-Free: 800-521-2651
www.deltadentalins.com
Mailing Address: P.O. Box 1809, Alpharetta, GA 30023-1809
Non-Profit Organization: Yes

Healthplan and Services Defined
  PLAN TYPE: Dental
  Plan Specialty: Dental
  Benefits Offered: Dental

Type of Coverage
  Commercial, Individual

Type of Payment Plans Offered
  POS, DFFS, FFS

Geographic Areas Served
  Alabama, Florida, Georgia, Louisiana, Mississippi, Montana, Nevada, Texas and Utah

Key Personnel
  Dir., Technology . . . . Navin Prabhu

240 Humana Health Insurance of Georgia
1200 Ashwood Parkway
Suite 250
Atlanta, GA 30338
Toll-Free: 800-986-9527
Phone: 770-508-2388
Fax: 770-391-1423
www.humana.com
Secondary Address: 100 Mansell Court East, Suite 125, Roswell, GA 30076, 770-643-3564
Subsidiary of: Humana Inc.
For Profit Organization: Yes
Year Founded: 1961

Healthplan and Services Defined
  PLAN TYPE: HMO/PPO
  Model Type: Network
  Plan Specialty: Dental, Vision
  Benefits Offered: Behavioral Health, Chiropractic, Dental, Disease Management, Prescription, Psychiatric, Transplant, Vision, Wellness, Worker's Compensation, Life, LTD, STD

Type of Coverage
  Commercial, Individual, Medicare, Supplemental Medicare

Geographic Areas Served
  Statewide

Accreditation Certification
  URAC, NCQA, CORE

Key Personnel
  Market VP, GA/AL . . . . John Dammann

241 Kaiser Permanente Georgia
3495 Piedmont Road NE
Atlanta, GA 30305
Phone: 404-364-7000
thrive.kaiserpermanente.org/care-near-georgia
Subsidiary of: Kaiser Permanente
Non-Profit Organization: Yes
Year Founded: 1985
Number of Affiliated Hospitals: 26
Number of Primary Care Physicians: 500
Total Enrollment: 312,899
State Enrollment: 312,899

Healthplan and Services Defined
  PLAN TYPE: HMO
  Model Type: Network
  Benefits Offered: Disease Management, Prescription, Vision, Wellness, Benefits vary according to plan

Type of Coverage
  Commercial, Individual, Medicare, Supplemental Medicare, Medicaid

Geographic Areas Served
  Atlanta, Athens

Key Personnel
  Regional President . . . . Pamela Shipley
  Pres./Exec. Med. Dir. . . . . Nkem Chukwumerije, MD
  Media Contact . . . . Kevin McClelland
  404-949-5187

242 Northeast Georgia Health Partners
465 EE Butler Parkway
Gainesville, GA 30501
Phone: 770-219-6600
Fax: 770-219-6609
www.healthpartnersnetwork.com
Non-Profit Organization: Yes
Number of Affiliated Hospitals: 6
Number of Primary Care Physicians: 750
Number of Referral/Specialty Physicians: 75

Healthplan and Services Defined
  PLAN TYPE: PPO
  Benefits Offered: Behavioral Health, Home Care, Physical Therapy, Podiatry, Prescription, Psychiatric, Wellness, Labs; Occupational & Speech Therapy; Durable Medical Equipment; Hearing Center

Type of Coverage
  Commercial

Geographic Areas Served
  Banks, Barrow, Dawson, Forsyth, Gwinnett (City of Buford only), Habersham, Hall, Jackson, Lumpkin, Rabun, Stephens, Towns, Union and White counties

Accreditation Certification
  NCQA

Key Personnel
  VP, Managed Care . . . . Steven McNeilly
  Executive Director . . . . Wanda Katich
  Operations Manager . . . . Kathryn Riner
  Project Manager . . . . Jennifer Nicholson

243 Peach State Health Plan
1100 Circle 75 Parkway
Suite 1100
Atlanta, GA 30339
Toll-Free: 800-704-1484
Phone: 678-556-2300
www.pshpgeorgia.com
Subsidiary of: Centene Corporation
For Profit Organization: Yes

Healthplan and Services Defined
  PLAN TYPE: Other
  Model Type: Network
  Benefits Offered: Behavioral Health, Dental, Wellness

Type of Coverage
  Medicaid, PeachCare for Kids, Planning for He

Geographic Areas Served
  Statewide

Key Personnel
  President/CEO . . . . Patrick Healy
  Medical Director . . . . Steve Dziabis

244 Secure Health PPO Newtork
577 Mulberry Street
Suite 1000
Macon, GA 31201
Toll-Free: 800-648-7563
Phone: 478-314-2400
www.shpg.com
Mailing Address: P.O. Box 4088, Macon, GA 31028
For Profit Organization: Yes
Year Founded: 1992
Physician Owned Organization: Yes
Number of Affiliated Hospitals: 16
Number of Primary Care Physicians: 950
Total Enrollment: 68,000
State Enrollment: 68,000

Healthplan and Services Defined
PLAN TYPE: PPO
Other Type: TPA
Benefits Offered: Disease Management, Prescription, Wellness, EAP

Type of Coverage
Commercial

Geographic Areas Served
Statewide

Peer Review Type
Utilization Review: Yes
Case Management: Yes

Accreditation Certification
URAC

Key Personnel
President/CEO . . . . Albert Ertel

245 Trinity Health of Georgia
Saint Mary's Health Care System
1230 Baxter Street
Athens, GA 30606
Phone: 706-389-3000
www.trinity-health.org
Secondary Address: Saint Joseph's Health System, 424 Decatur Street SE, Atlanta, GA 30312, 678-843-8500
Subsidiary of: Trinity Health
Non-Profit Organization: Yes
Year Founded: 2013
Total Enrollment: 30,000,000

Healthplan and Services Defined
PLAN TYPE: Other
Benefits Offered: Disease Management, Home Care, Long-Term Care, Psychiatric, Hospice programs, PACE (Program of All Inclusive Care for the Elderly)

Geographic Areas Served
Atlanta and Southeast Georgia

Key Personnel
President/CEO . . . . Michael A. Slubowski
Chief Operating Officer . . . . Benjamin R. Carter

246 United Concordia of Georgia
9635 Ventana Way
Suite 100
Alpharetta, GA 30022
Phone: 678-893-8650
www.unitedconcordia.com
For Profit Organization: Yes
Year Founded: 1971
Number of Primary Care Physicians: 104,000
Total Enrollment: 8,800,000

Healthplan and Services Defined
PLAN TYPE: Dental
Plan Specialty: Dental
Benefits Offered: Dental

Type of Coverage
Commercial, Individual, Military personnel & families

Geographic Areas Served
Nationwide

Accreditation Certification
URAC

Key Personnel
Sales Manager . . . . Donyale Drawdy
Contact. . . . . Beth Rutherford
717-260-7659
beth.rutherford@ucci.com

247 UnitedHealthcare Community Plan Georgia
UnitedHealthcare Customer Service
P.O. Box 30769
Salt Lake City, UT 84130-0769
Toll-Free: 888-545-5205
www.uhccommunityplan.com/ga
Subsidiary of: UnitedHealth Group
For Profit Organization: Yes

Healthplan and Services Defined
PLAN TYPE: Medicare
Other Type: Medicaid
Model Type: Network
Benefits Offered: Dental, Home Care, Podiatry, Prescription, Vision, Wellness, Hearing, Acupuncture, Chiropractic

Type of Coverage
Medicare, Medicaid

Geographic Areas Served
Varies by plan

248 UnitedHealthcare of Georgia
3720 Davinci Court
Suite 300
Norcross, GA 30092
Toll-Free: 888-545-5205
Phone: 760-509-2413
www.uhc.com
Secondary Address: 2310 Parklake Drive NE, Atlanta, GA 30345
Subsidiary of: UnitedHealth Group
For Profit Organization: Yes

Year Founded: 1980

Healthplan and Services Defined
PLAN TYPE: HMO/PPO
Model Type: Network
Plan Specialty: Behavioral Health, Dental, Disease Management, PBM, Vision
Benefits Offered: Behavioral Health, Dental, Disease Management, Long-Term Care, Physical Therapy, Prescription, Vision, Wellness, Life, LTD, STD

Type of Coverage
Individual, Medicare, Supplemental Medicare, Medicaid, Catastrophic, Family, Military, Veterans, Group, Catastrophic Illness Benefit: Unlimited

Type of Payment Plans Offered
POS, FFS

Geographic Areas Served
Statewide

Network Qualifications
Pre-Admission Certification: Yes

Peer Review Type
Utilization Review: Yes
Case Management: Yes

Publishes and Distributes Report Card: Yes

Accreditation Certification
NCQA
TJC Accreditation, Medicare Approved, Utilization Review, Pre-Admission Certification, State Licensure, Quality Assurance Program

Key Personnel
CEO, GA/AL Health Plans .... Junior Harewood

Specialty Managed Care Partners
Enters into Contracts with Regional Business Coalitions: Yes

HAWAII

Health Insurance Coverage Status and Type of Coverage by Age

Category	All Persons Number	All Persons %	Under 19 years Number	Under 19 years %	Under 65 years Number	Under 65 years %
Total population	1,359 *(3)*	100.0 *(0.0)*	315 *(1)*	100.0 *(0.0)*	1,093 *(3)*	100.0 *(0.0)*
Covered by some type of health insurance	1,302 *(5)*	95.8 *(0.4)*	306 *(3)*	97.2 *(0.7)*	1,038 *(5)*	95.0 *(0.5)*
Covered by private health insurance	1,034 *(11)*	76.1 *(0.8)*	218 *(6)*	69.1 *(1.9)*	849 *(11)*	77.6 *(1.0)*
Employer-based	869 *(12)*	63.9 *(0.9)*	176 *(6)*	56.0 *(2.0)*	731 *(11)*	66.9 *(1.0)*
Direct purchase	176 *(9)*	12.9 *(0.7)*	25 *(3)*	7.8 *(1.0)*	108 *(8)*	9.9 *(0.7)*
TRICARE	106 *(7)*	7.8 *(0.5)*	37 *(4)*	11.7 *(1.2)*	84 *(6)*	7.6 *(0.6)*
Covered by public health insurance	493 *(9)*	36.3 *(0.7)*	105 *(5)*	33.5 *(1.7)*	240 *(9)*	21.9 *(0.8)*
Medicaid	245 *(9)*	18.0 *(0.7)*	104 *(5)*	33.0 *(1.7)*	213 *(9)*	19.5 *(0.8)*
Medicare	275 *(3)*	20.2 *(0.2)*	1 *(1)*	0.4 *(0.2)*	22 *(3)*	2.0 *(0.2)*
VA Care	34 *(3)*	2.5 *(0.2)*	1 *(1)*	0.2 *(0.2)*	16 *(2)*	1.5 *(0.2)*
Not covered at any time during the year	56 *(5)*	4.2 *(0.4)*	9 *(2)*	2.8 *(0.7)*	55 *(5)*	5.0 *(0.5)*

Note: Numbers in thousands; Figures cover civilian noninstitutionalized population in 2019; N/A indicates that data was not available; Z represents or rounds to zero; Margin of error appears in parenthesis and is calculated using replicate weights.
Source: U.S. Census Bureau, American Community Survey, Table HI-05. Health Insurance Coverage Status and Type of Coverage by State and Age for All People: 2019

Hawaii

249 AlohaCare
1357 Kapiolani Boulevard
Suite 1250
Honolulu, HI 96814
Toll-Free: 877-973-0712
Phone: 808-973-0712
www.alohacare.org
Secondary Address: 210 Imi Kala Street, Suite 206, Wailuku, HI 96793
Non-Profit Organization: Yes
Year Founded: 1994
Number of Affiliated Hospitals: 25
Number of Primary Care Physicians: 855
Number of Referral/Specialty Physicians: 1,833
Total Enrollment: 70,000

Healthplan and Services Defined
PLAN TYPE: HMO
Benefits Offered: Dental, Prescription, Vision, Wellness, Hearing; X-rays & Labs; Acupuncture; 24-hour Nurse Advice Line

Type of Coverage
Medicare, Supplemental Medicare

Geographic Areas Served
Oahu, Kauai, Molokai, Lanai, Maui, Hawaii

Peer Review Type
Case Management: Yes

Publishes and Distributes Report Card: Yes

Key Personnel
Interim CEO . . . . Francoise Culley-Trotman, .
CMO . . . . Gary Okamoto
CFO. . . . . Bruce Lane
CIO . . . . Todd Morgan

250 AlohaCare Advantage Plus
1357 Kapiolani Boulevard
Suite 1250
Honolulu, HI 96814
Toll-Free: 866-973-6395
Phone: 808-973-1657
www.alohacare.org
Non-Profit Organization: Yes
Year Founded: 1994

Healthplan and Services Defined
PLAN TYPE: Medicare
Other Type: HMO SNP
Benefits Offered: Dental, Prescription, Wellness

Type of Coverage
Medicare, Medicaid, Medicare Part A, B

Geographic Areas Served
Oahu, Kauai, Molokai, Lanai, Maui, Hawaii

Key Personnel
Chairman . . . . David Derauf
Vice Chair. . . . . Irene Carpenter
Treasure. . . . . BJ Ott
Secretary . . . . Emanuel Kintu
CEO. . . . . Francoise Culley-Trotman
Chief Financial Officer . . . . Bruce Lane
Chief Medical Officer . . . . Gary Okamoto

251 Hawaii Medical Assurance Association
737 Bishop Street
Suite 1200
Honolulu, HI 96813
Toll-Free: 800-621-6998
Phone: 808-591-0088
Fax: 808-591-0463
www.hmaa.com
Secondary Address: Customer Service Center , 888-941-4622
For Profit Organization: Yes
Year Founded: 1989

Healthplan and Services Defined
PLAN TYPE: PPO
Benefits Offered: Chiropractic, Dental, Prescription, Vision, Wellness, AD&D, Life, Acupuncture

Type of Coverage
Commercial

Geographic Areas Served
Hawaii

Accreditation Certification
URAC

Key Personnel
Chairman, COO, CFO . . . . John Henry Felix
Director. . . . . Gail Mukaihata Hannemann
Director . . . . Dennis Y.V. Kwan
Director . . . . Warren Price III
President & CEO . . . . William C. McCorriston

252 Hawaii Medical Service Association
HMSA Building
818 Keeaumoku Street
Honolulu, HI 96814
hmsa.com
State Enrollment: 700,000

Healthplan and Services Defined
PLAN TYPE: HMO/PPO
Benefits Offered: Dental, Physical Therapy, Prescription, Vision, Wellness

Type of Coverage
Commercial, Individual, Medicare, Medicaid

Geographic Areas Served
Hawaii

Key Personnel
President & CEO . . . . Mark M. Mugiishi
Chief Operating Officer . . . . David R. Herndon
Chief Health Officer . . . . David Underriner
Chief Information Officer . . . . Rick Hopfer
Chief Financial Officer . . . . Gina L. Marting
General Counsel . . . . Jennifer A. Walker

253　Humana Health Insurance of Hawaii

733 Bishop Street
Suite 2100
Honolulu, HI 96813
Phone: 808-540-2570
Fax: 808-548-7618
www.humana.com
Subsidiary of: Humana Inc.
For Profit Organization: Yes

Healthplan and Services Defined
PLAN TYPE: HMO/PPO
Model Type: Network
Plan Specialty: Dental, Vision
Benefits Offered: Dental, Vision, Life, LTD, STD

Type of Coverage
Commercial

Geographic Areas Served
Statewide

Accreditation Certification
URAC, NCQA, CORE

Key Personnel
Sales Director................Jose L. Cabrera, Jr., MBA

254　Kaiser Permanente Hawaii

1010 Pensacola Street
Honolulu, HI 96814
Phone: 808-432-2000
www.kpinhawaii.org
Subsidiary of: Kaiser Permanente
Non-Profit Organization: Yes
Year Founded: 1958
Number of Affiliated Hospitals: 20
Number of Primary Care Physicians: 600
Total Enrollment: 252,840
State Enrollment: 252,840

Healthplan and Services Defined
PLAN TYPE: HMO
Model Type: Group
Plan Specialty: Obstetrics/gynecology, orthopedics, cardiothoracic and vascular surgery, neurosurgery, oncology, gastroenterology
Benefits Offered: Behavioral Health, Chiropractic, Complementary Medicine, Disease Management, Prescription, Vision, Wellness, Worker's Compensation, Benefits vary according to plan
Offers Demand Management Patient Information Service: Yes

Type of Coverage
Commercial, Individual, Medicare, Medicaid
Catastrophic Illness Benefit: Unlimited

Type of Payment Plans Offered
POS, Capitated, FFS

Geographic Areas Served
Oahu, Maui, Hawaii Island, Kauai

Subscriber Information
Average Subscriber Co-Payment:
Home Health Care Max. Days/Visits Covered: Unlimited
Nursing Home: Skilled nursing fac.
Nursing Home Max. Days/Visits Covered: Skilled nursing fac.

Network Qualifications
Pre-Admission Certification: No

Peer Review Type
Utilization Review: Yes
Case Management: Yes

Publishes and Distributes Report Card: Yes

Accreditation Certification
NCQA, UNICEF/WHO Baby Friendly
TJC Accreditation, Medicare Approved, Utilization Review, State Licensure, Quality Assurance Program

Key Personnel
Market President......................Greg Christian
Pres./Medical Director..................John Yang, MD
Media Contact..........................Laura Lott
  808-432-5916

Specialty Managed Care Partners
Enters into Contracts with Regional Business Coalitions: Yes

255　UnitedHealthcare Community Plan Hawaii

UnitedHealthcare Customer Service
P.O. Box 30769
Salt Lake City, UT 84130-0769
Toll-Free: 888-545-5205
www.uhccommunityplan.com/hi
Subsidiary of: UnitedHealth Group
For Profit Organization: Yes

Healthplan and Services Defined
PLAN TYPE: Medicare
Other Type: Medicaid
Model Type: Network
Benefits Offered: Dental, Home Care, Podiatry, Prescription, Vision, Wellness, Acupuncture, Chiropractic

Type of Coverage
Medicare, Medicaid

Geographic Areas Served
Honolulu. Other plans statewide

Key Personnel
CEO, Community Plan HI..............Dave Heywood
  david_w_heywood@uhc.com

256　UnitedHealthcare of Hawaii

1132 Bishop Street
Suite 400
Honolulu, HI 96813
Toll-Free: 888-980-8728
www.uhc.com
Subsidiary of: UnitedHealth Group
For Profit Organization: Yes
Year Founded: 1986

Healthplan and Services Defined
PLAN TYPE: HMO/PPO
Model Type: Network

Plan Specialty: Behavioral Health, Dental, Disease Management, PBM, Vision

Benefits Offered: Behavioral Health, Dental, Disease Management, Long-Term Care, Prescription, Vision, Wellness, Life, LTD, STD

Type of Coverage

Medicare, Supplemental Medicare, Medicaid, Catastrophic, Family, Military, Veterans, Group,

Catastrophic Illness Benefit: Covered

Type of Payment Plans Offered

DFFS, Capitated

Geographic Areas Served

Statewide

Subscriber Information

Average Monthly Fee Per Subscriber
(Employee + Employer Contribution):
Employee Only (Self): $120.00
Employee & 1 Family Member: $240.00
Employee & 2 Family Members: $375.00

Average Annual Deductible Per Subscriber:
Employee & 2 Family Members: Varies

Average Subscriber Co-Payment:
Primary Care Physician: $5.00-10.00
Prescription Drugs: $5.00/10.00/25.00
Hospital ER: $50.00
Nursing Home Max. Days/Visits Covered: 120 per year

Publishes and Distributes Report Card: Yes

Accreditation Certification

NCQA

TJC Accreditation, Utilization Review, State Licensure

Key Personnel

CEO, WA/OR/MT/AK/HI .... Gary Daniels
VP, Quality .... Kie Kawano

Specialty Managed Care Partners

Enters into Contracts with Regional Business Coalitions: Yes

IDAHO

Health Insurance Coverage Status and Type of Coverage by Age

Category	All Persons Number	All Persons %	Under 19 years Number	Under 19 years %	Under 65 years Number	Under 65 years %
Total population	1,765 *(1)*	100.0 *(0.0)*	475 *(3)*	100.0 *(0.0)*	1,481 *(2)*	100.0 *(0.0)*
Covered by some type of health insurance	1,574 *(10)*	89.2 *(0.5)*	451 *(5)*	95.0 *(0.8)*	1,291 *(10)*	87.2 *(0.6)*
Covered by private health insurance	1,235 *(16)*	70.0 *(0.9)*	300 *(10)*	63.1 *(2.0)*	1,059 *(16)*	71.5 *(1.1)*
Employer-based	939 *(18)*	53.2 *(1.0)*	251 *(10)*	52.8 *(2.0)*	869 *(18)*	58.7 *(1.2)*
Direct purchase	307 *(13)*	17.4 *(0.7)*	46 *(6)*	9.6 *(1.2)*	191 *(12)*	12.9 *(0.8)*
TRICARE	64 *(6)*	3.6 *(0.4)*	12 *(3)*	2.5 *(0.6)*	37 *(6)*	2.5 *(0.4)*
Covered by public health insurance	573 *(14)*	32.5 *(0.8)*	172 *(8)*	36.3 *(1.8)*	296 *(13)*	20.0 *(0.9)*
Medicaid	283 *(12)*	16.0 *(0.7)*	172 *(9)*	36.2 *(1.8)*	256 *(12)*	17.3 *(0.8)*
Medicare	317 *(4)*	18.0 *(0.3)*	2 *(1)*	0.3 *(0.2)*	40 *(4)*	2.7 *(0.3)*
VA Care	57 *(4)*	3.2 *(0.2)*	Z *(Z)*	0.1 *(0.1)*	24 *(3)*	1.6 *(0.2)*
Not covered at any time during the year	191 *(10)*	10.8 *(0.5)*	24 *(4)*	5.0 *(0.8)*	190 *(10)*	12.8 *(0.6)*

Note: Numbers in thousands; Figures cover civilian noninstitutionalized population in 2019; N/A indicates that data was not available; Z represents or rounds to zero; Margin of error appears in parenthesis and is calculated using replicate weights.
Source: U.S. Census Bureau, American Community Survey, Table HI-05. Health Insurance Coverage Status and Type of Coverage by State and Age for All People: 2019

Idaho

257 Aetna Health of Idaho
151 Farmington Avenue
Hartford, CT 06156
Toll-Free: 800-872-3862
www.aetna.com
Subsidiary of: CVS Health / Aetna Inc.
For Profit Organization: Yes

Healthplan and Services Defined
PLAN TYPE: HMO/PPO
Other Type: POS
Model Type: Network
Plan Specialty: Behavioral Health, EPO, Lab, PBM, Radiology
Benefits Offered: Behavioral Health, Dental, Disease Management, Long-Term Care, Physical Therapy, Podiatry, Prescription, Psychiatric, Vision, Wellness, Life, LTD, STD

Type of Coverage
Commercial, Student health

Type of Payment Plans Offered
POS, FFS

Geographic Areas Served
Statewide

Key Personnel
Chief Network Officer................... John J. Wagner

258 Blue Cross of Idaho Health Service, Inc.
3000 East Pine Avenue
Meridian, ID 83642
Toll-Free: 800-274-4018
Phone: 208-345-4550
Fax: 208-331-7311
www.bcidaho.com
Mailing Address: P.O. Box 7408, Boise, ID 83707
Subsidiary of: Blue Cross and Blue Shield Association
Non-Profit Organization: Yes
Year Founded: 1945
Number of Affiliated Hospitals: 44
Number of Primary Care Physicians: 1,631
Total Enrollment: 563,000
State Enrollment: 563,000

Healthplan and Services Defined
PLAN TYPE: HMO/PPO
Model Type: IPA, Group, Network
Plan Specialty: ASO, Chiropractic, Dental, Disease Management
Benefits Offered: Chiropractic, Dental, Disease Management, Prescription, Vision, Wellness

Type of Coverage
Commercial, Individual, Indemnity, Medicare, Supplemental Medicare

Type of Payment Plans Offered
POS, DFFS, FFS

Geographic Areas Served
Statewide

Subscriber Information
Average Subscriber Co-Payment:
Prescription Drugs: Varies
Hospital ER: Varies
Home Health Care: Varies
Nursing Home: Varies

Network Qualifications
Pre-Admission Certification: Yes

Peer Review Type
Utilization Review: Yes
Case Management: Yes

Publishes and Distributes Report Card: Yes

Accreditation Certification
TJC Accreditation, Pre-Admission Certification, State Licensure

Key Personnel
President/CEO....................... Charlene Maher
Chief Financial Officer..................... Dave Ward
Chief Information Officer.............. Sameer Sonalkar
General Counsel.................... Brian Wonderlich
Media Contact....................... Bret Rumbeck
bret.rumbeck@bcidaho.com

Specialty Managed Care Partners
Wellpoint Pharmacy Management, Dental through Blue Cross of Idaho, Vision through VSP, Life Insurance, EAP through Business Psychology Associates
Enters into Contracts with Regional Business Coalitions: No

259 Delta Dental of Idaho
555 East Parkcenter Boulevard
Boise, ID 83706
Toll-Free: 800-356-7586
Phone: 208-489-3580
customerservice@deltadentalid.com
www.deltadentalid.com
Non-Profit Organization: Yes
Year Founded: 1971
Total Enrollment: 75,000,000

Healthplan and Services Defined
PLAN TYPE: Dental
Other Type: Dental PPO
Model Type: Network
Plan Specialty: Dental
Benefits Offered: Dental

Type of Coverage
Commercial, Individual, Medicare

Type of Payment Plans Offered
DFFS

Geographic Areas Served
Statewide

Network Qualifications
Pre-Admission Certification: Yes

Publishes and Distributes Report Card: Yes

Key Personnel
Chair................................. Kyle Siemen

Director of Sales . . . . Don Murray
   dmurray@deltadentalid.com
CEO/President . . . . Greg Donaca

260 Humana Health Insurance of Idaho
3597 E Monarch Sky Ln
Suite 240
Meridian, ID 83646
Phone: 208-319-3400
Fax: 208-888-7298
www.humana.com
Subsidiary of: Humana Inc.
For Profit Organization: Yes

Healthplan and Services Defined
   PLAN TYPE: HMO/PPO
   Model Type: Network
   Plan Specialty: Dental, Vision
   Benefits Offered: Dental, Vision, Life, LTD, STD

Type of Coverage
   Commercial

Geographic Areas Served
   Statewide

Accreditation Certification
   URAC, NCQA, CORE

Key Personnel
   Regional Market President . . . . Jesse Gamez

261 Molina Healthcare of Idaho
950 W Bannock St.
Suite 100
Boise, ID 83702
Phone: 844-239-4913
www.molinahealthcare.com
Subsidiary of: Molina Healthcare, Inc.
For Profit Organization: Yes

Healthplan and Services Defined
   PLAN TYPE: Medicare
   Model Type: Network
   Plan Specialty: Dental, PBM, Vision, Integrated
      Medicare/Medicaid (Duals)
   Benefits Offered: Dental, Prescription, Vision, Wellness, Life

Type of Coverage
   Individual, Medicare, Supplemental Medicare, Medicaid

Geographic Areas Served
   Statewide

Key Personnel
   President, ID/UT. . . . . Brandon Hendrickson

262 Primary Health Medical Group
10482 W Carlton Bay Drive
Garden City, ID 83714
Toll-Free: 800-481-9777
Phone: 208-955-6500
Fax: 208-955-6502
information@primaryhealth.com
www.primaryhealth.com
Year Founded: 1996
Physician Owned Organization: Yes

Healthplan and Services Defined
   PLAN TYPE: Multiple
   Model Type: IPA
   Plan Specialty: ASO
   Benefits Offered: Behavioral Health, Chiropractic, Dental,
      Disease Management, Home Care, Inpatient SNF, Physical
      Therapy, Podiatry, Prescription, Psychiatric, Transplant,
      Vision, Wellness, AD&D, Life

Type of Coverage
   Commercial, Individual, Indemnity

Type of Payment Plans Offered
   POS, DFFS

Geographic Areas Served
   Southwest Idaho

Accreditation Certification
   NCQA

Key Personnel
   Chief Operating Officer . . . . Steve Judy
   Director of Information . . . . Paul Castronova

263 Regence BlueShield of Idaho
P.O. Box 1106
Lewiston, ID 83501
Toll-Free: 888-675-6570
www.regence.com
Secondary Address: Regence Corporate, P.O. Box 1071,
   Portland, OR 97207
Subsidiary of: Regence
Non-Profit Organization: Yes
Year Founded: 1946
Total Enrollment: 2,400,000
State Enrollment: 151,299

Healthplan and Services Defined
   PLAN TYPE: Multiple
   Model Type: Network
   Benefits Offered: Dental, Prescription, Vision, Wellness, Life,
      Preventive Care

Type of Coverage
   Commercial, Individual, Supplemental Medicare

Geographic Areas Served
   statewide

Accreditation Certification
   URAC

Key Personnel
   President. . . . . Mark Ruszczyk
   Dir., Public Affairs. . . . . Tara Harrison

264 Trinity Health of Idaho
Saint Alphonsus Health System
1055 N Curtis Road
Boise, ID 83706
Phone: 208-367-2121
webmaster@saintalphonsus.org
www.trinity-health.org
Subsidiary of: Trinity Health
Non-Profit Organization: Yes
Year Founded: 2013
Number of Affiliated Hospitals: 4
Number of Primary Care Physicians: 1,400
Total Enrollment: 30,000,000
State Enrollment: 700,000

Healthplan and Services Defined
PLAN TYPE: Other
Benefits Offered: Disease Management, Home Care, Long-Term Care, Psychiatric, Hospice programs, PACE (Program of All Inclusive Care for the Elderly)

Geographic Areas Served
Boise and Nampa, Idaho and Ontario and Baker City, and Oregon

Key Personnel
Chief Executive Officer .... Richard J. Gilfillan
Chief Financial Officer .... Lannie Checketts
Chief Nursing Officer.................... Shelley Harris
Chief HR Officer...................... Heather Sprague
Chief Compliance Officer............... Jennifer Johnson
VP/General Counsel .... Stephanie Westermeier
Interim CMO.......................... Charles Davis

Subscriber Information
Average Monthly Fee Per Subscriber
(Employee + Employer Contribution):
Employee Only (Self): $120.00
Employee & 1 Family Member: $240.00
Employee & 2 Family Members: $375.00
Average Annual Deductible Per Subscriber:
Employee & 2 Family Members: Varies
Average Subscriber Co-Payment:
Primary Care Physician: $5.00-10.00
Prescription Drugs: $5.00/10.00/25.00
Hospital ER: $50.00
Nursing Home Max. Days/Visits Covered: 120 per year

Publishes and Distributes Report Card: Yes

Accreditation Certification
NCQA
TJC Accreditation, Utilization Review, State Licensure

Key Personnel
CEO, NV/UT/ID .... Donald Giancursio

Specialty Managed Care Partners
Enters into Contracts with Regional Business Coalitions: Yes

265 UnitedHealthcare of Idaho
322 E Front Street
Suite 400
Boise, ID 83702
Toll-Free: 888-545-5205
www.uhc.com
Subsidiary of: UnitedHealth Group
For Profit Organization: Yes
Year Founded: 1986

Healthplan and Services Defined
PLAN TYPE: HMO/PPO
Model Type: Network
Plan Specialty: Behavioral Health, Dental, Disease Management, PBM, Vision
Benefits Offered: Behavioral Health, Dental, Disease Management, Long-Term Care, Prescription, Vision, Wellness, Life, LTD, STD

Type of Coverage
Individual, Medicare, Supplemental Medicare, Medicaid, Catastrophic, Family, Military, Veterans, Group, Catastrophic Illness Benefit: Covered

Type of Payment Plans Offered
DFFS, Capitated

Geographic Areas Served
Statewide

ILLINOIS

Health Insurance Coverage Status and Type of Coverage by Age

Category	All Persons Number	All Persons %	Under 19 years Number	Under 19 years %	Under 65 years Number	Under 65 years %
Total population	12,488 *(3)*	100.0 *(0.0)*	2,982 *(6)*	100.0 *(0.0)*	10,507 *(5)*	100.0 *(0.0)*
Covered by some type of health insurance	11,565 *(25)*	92.6 *(0.2)*	2,861 *(10)*	96.0 *(0.3)*	9,600 *(24)*	91.4 *(0.2)*
Covered by private health insurance	8,760 *(45)*	70.1 *(0.4)*	1,898 *(23)*	63.6 *(0.7)*	7,578 *(43)*	72.1 *(0.4)*
Employer-based	7,466 *(42)*	59.8 *(0.3)*	1,746 *(23)*	58.5 *(0.7)*	6,821 *(41)*	64.9 *(0.4)*
Direct purchase	1,534 *(24)*	12.3 *(0.2)*	159 *(9)*	5.3 *(0.3)*	871 *(23)*	8.3 *(0.2)*
TRICARE	155 *(9)*	1.2 *(0.1)*	32 *(5)*	1.1 *(0.2)*	103 *(8)*	1.0 *(0.1)*
Covered by public health insurance	4,184 *(36)*	33.5 *(0.3)*	1,054 *(21)*	35.4 *(0.7)*	2,297 *(37)*	21.9 *(0.3)*
Medicaid	2,274 *(35)*	18.2 *(0.3)*	1,042 *(21)*	35.0 *(0.7)*	2,071 *(35)*	19.7 *(0.3)*
Medicare	2,147 *(12)*	17.2 *(0.1)*	15 *(4)*	0.5 *(0.1)*	262 *(10)*	2.5 *(0.1)*
VA Care	208 *(7)*	1.7 *(0.1)*	4 *(2)*	0.1 *(0.1)*	88 *(5)*	0.8 *(0.1)*
Not covered at any time during the year	923 *(25)*	7.4 *(0.2)*	120 *(9)*	4.0 *(0.3)*	907 *(24)*	8.6 *(0.2)*

Note: Numbers in thousands; Figures cover civilian noninstitutionalized population in 2019; N/A indicates that data was not available; Z represents or rounds to zero; Margin of error appears in parenthesis and is calculated using replicate weights.
Source: U.S. Census Bureau, American Community Survey, Table HI-05. Health Insurance Coverage Status and Type of Coverage by State and Age for All People: 2019

Illinois

266 Aetna Better Health of Illinois
3200 Highland Avenue
MC F661
Downers Grove, IL 60515
Toll-Free: 866-329-4701
Fax: 855-254-1791
ABHILContactusMem@aetna.com
www.aetnabetterhealth.com/illinois
Subsidiary of: CVS Health / Aetna Inc.
For Profit Organization: Yes

Healthplan and Services Defined
PLAN TYPE: HMO/PPO
Other Type: POS
Model Type: Network
Plan Specialty: Behavioral Health, Dental, EPO, Lab, PBM, Vision, Radiology
Benefits Offered: Behavioral Health, Dental, Disease Management, Long-Term Care, Physical Therapy, Podiatry, Prescription, Psychiatric, Vision, Wellness, Life, LTD, STD

Type of Coverage
Commercial, Medicaid, Student health

Geographic Areas Served
Statewide

Key Personnel
CEO .... Kimberly S. Foltz

267 Aetna Health of Illinois
151 Farmington Avenue
Hartford, CT 06156
Toll-Free: 800-872-3862
www.aetna.com
Subsidiary of: CVS Health / Aetna Inc.
For Profit Organization: Yes
Year Founded: 1984

Healthplan and Services Defined
PLAN TYPE: HMO/PPO
Other Type: POS
Model Type: Network
Plan Specialty: Behavioral Health, Dental, Worker's Compensation
Benefits Offered: Behavioral Health, Dental, Long-Term Care, Wellness, Worker's Compensation, Life, LTD, STD

Type of Coverage
Commercial, Individual, Medicare, Supplemental Medicare, Medicaid, Student health

Type of Payment Plans Offered
POS, DFFS, Capitated, FFS, Combination FFS & DFFS

Geographic Areas Served
Bond, Boone, Calhoun, Champaign, Christian, Clark, Clinton, Coles, Crawford, Cumberland, DeWitt, Douglas, Edgar, Effingham, Fayette, Ford, Greene, Iroquois, Jasper, Jersey, Kankakee, LaSalle, Lee, Logan, Macon, Macoupin, Madison, Marshall, McLean, Menard, Monroe, Montgomery, Morgan, Moultrie, Ogle, Peoria, Piatt, Sangaman, Saint Clair, Shelby, Stark, Stephenson, Tazewell, Vermilion, Washington, Whiteside, Will, Winnebago, Woodford counties

Network Qualifications
Pre-Admission Certification: Yes

Peer Review Type
Utilization Review: Yes
Second Surgical Opinion: Yes
Case Management: Yes

Accreditation Certification
NCQA
TJC Accreditation, Medicare Approved, Utilization Review, Pre-Admission Certification, State Licensure, Quality Assurance Program

Key Personnel
VP, Government Programs .... Michael Kavouras, Esq.

Employer References
Horace Mann, Verizon, Pepsi, Sarah Bush Lincoln Health, Walgreen's

268 Allwell from IlliniCare Health
P.O. Box 92050
Elk Grove Village, IL 60009-2050
Toll-Free: 855-766-1736
allwell.illinicare.com
Subsidiary of: Centene Corporation

Healthplan and Services Defined
PLAN TYPE: Medicare
Model Type: Network
Benefits Offered: Dental, Prescription

Type of Coverage
Medicare, Supplemental Medicare, Medicare Advantage

Geographic Areas Served
Cook, Kane, and Will counties

269 Ambetter from IlliniCare Health
999 Oakmont Laza Drive
Suite 400
Westmont, IL 60059
Toll-Free: 855-745-5507
ambetter.illinicare.com
Subsidiary of: Centene Corporation

Healthplan and Services Defined
PLAN TYPE: Other
Model Type: Network
Plan Specialty: Lab
Benefits Offered: Behavioral Health, Disease Management, Physical Therapy, Prescription, Wellness, Maternity and newborn care

Type of Coverage
Health Insurance Marketplace

Geographic Areas Served
Cook and DuPage counties

270 Blue Cross & Blue Shield of Illinois
300 East Randolph Street
Chicago, IL 60601-5099
Toll-Free: 800-654-7385
www.bcbsil.com
Subsidiary of: Health Care Service Corporation
Year Founded: 1936
Total Enrollment: 8,000,000
State Enrollment: 8,000,000

Healthplan and Services Defined
PLAN TYPE: HMO/PPO
Benefits Offered: Disease Management, Physical Therapy, Prescription, Wellness

Type of Coverage
Commercial, Individual, Supplemental Medicare, Medicaid, Healthy Kids, Healthy Families

Type of Payment Plans Offered
POS, FFS

Geographic Areas Served
Statewide

Key Personnel
President .... Stephen Harris
VP/CMO .... Derek J. Robinson, MD
Media Contact .... John Simley
312-653-0558
john_simley@bcbsil.com

Specialty Managed Care Partners
Prime Therapeutics

271 BlueCross BlueShield Association
225 North Michigan Avenue
Chicago, IL 60601
Toll-Free: 888-630-2583
www.bcbs.com
Secondary Address: 1310 G Street NW, Washington, DC 20005
Total Enrollment: 107,000,000

Healthplan and Services Defined
PLAN TYPE: Medicare
Benefits Offered: Chiropractic, Disease Management, Home Care, Inpatient SNF, Physical Therapy, Podiatry, Prescription, Psychiatric, Wellness

Type of Coverage
Individual, Medicare

Geographic Areas Served
Nationwide, including the District of Columbia and Puerto Rico

Subscriber Information
Average Monthly Fee Per Subscriber
(Employee + Employer Contribution):
Employee Only (Self): Varies
Medicare: Varies
Average Annual Deductible Per Subscriber:
Employee Only (Self): Varies
Medicare: Varies
Average Subscriber Co-Payment:
Primary Care Physician: Varies
Non-Network Physician: Varies
Prescription Drugs: Varies
Hospital ER: Varies
Home Health Care: Varies
Home Health Care Max. Days/Visits Covered: Varies
Nursing Home: Varies
Nursing Home Max. Days/Visits Covered: Varies

Key Personnel
President/CEO .... Kim A. Keck
EVP/CFO..................... Christina Y. Fisher
EVP, Business Operations .... Jennifer Vachon
SVP, Government Programs .... William A. Breskin
SVP/General Counsel..................... Scott Nehs

272 Celtic Insurance Company
233 S Wacker Dr.
Suite 700
Chicago, OH 60606
Toll-Free: 800-477-7870
Phone: 312-619-3000
Fax: 800-749-3340
celticinsurancecompany.com
Subsidiary of: Centene Corporation
Year Founded: 1978

Healthplan and Services Defined
PLAN TYPE: PPO

Type of Coverage
Individual

Geographic Areas Served
All states except NY

Key Personnel
VP, HR/CIO .... Barbara Basham

273 Cigna HealthCare of Illinois
525 W Monroe Street
Suite 1650
Chicago, IL 60661-3629
Toll-Free: 800-997-1654
www.cigna.com
Subsidiary of: Cigna Corporation
For Profit Organization: Yes
Year Founded: 1982

Healthplan and Services Defined
PLAN TYPE: HMO
Other Type: POS
Plan Specialty: Behavioral Health, Dental
Benefits Offered: Behavioral Health, Dental, Disease Management, Prescription, Vision, Wellness, AD&D, Life, LTD, STD

Type of Coverage
Commercial, Individual, Medicare, Supplemental Medicare, Medicaid, Part-time and hourly workers; Union

Geographic Areas Served
Statewide

274 CNA
CNA Center
151 N Franklin Street
Chicago, IL 60606
Toll-Free: 877-262-2727
Phone: 312-822-5000
www.cna.com
Year Founded: 1987
Owned by an Integrated Delivery Network (IDN): Yes

Healthplan and Services Defined
  PLAN TYPE: Other
  Model Type: Network
  Plan Specialty: Dental, Disease Management, Lab, MSO, Vision, Radiology, Worker's Compensation, UR
  Benefits Offered: Behavioral Health, Chiropractic, Dental, Disease Management, Home Care, Inpatient SNF, Long-Term Care, Physical Therapy, Podiatry, Prescription, Psychiatric, Transplant, Vision, Wellness, Worker's Compensation, AD&D, Life, LTD, STD

Type of Coverage
  Commercial, Individual, Indemnity, Medicaid, Catastrophic

Type of Payment Plans Offered
  POS

Geographic Areas Served
  Nation wide

Network Qualifications
  Pre-Admission Certification: Yes

Peer Review Type
  Utilization Review: Yes
  Case Management: Yes

Publishes and Distributes Report Card: Yes

Accreditation Certification
  URAC
  TJC Accreditation, Pre-Admission Certification

Key Personnel
  Chairman & CEO .... Dino E. Robusto
  CFO .... Al Miralles
  COO .... Michael Costonis
  Chief Underwriting Off .... Douglas M. Worman

Specialty Managed Care Partners
  Enters into Contracts with Regional Business Coalitions: Yes

275 Dearborn National
1020 31st Street
Downers Grove, IL 60515
Toll-Free: 800-348-4512
Secondary Address: 701 E 22nd Street, Lombard, IL 60148
Subsidiary of: Health Care Service Corporation
Year Founded: 1969
Total Enrollment: 3,000,000
State Enrollment: 3,000,000

Healthplan and Services Defined
  PLAN TYPE: Other
  Model Type: Group, Network
  Plan Specialty: Vision
  Benefits Offered: Vision, Life, LTD, STD

Type of Coverage
  Commercial, Individual

Key Personnel
  President/CEO .... Mike Witwer

276 Delta Dental of Illinois
111 Shuman Boulevard
Naperville, IL 60563
Toll-Free: 800-335-8215
Phone: 630-718-4700
askdelta@deltadentalil.com
www.deltadentalil.com
Non-Profit Organization: Yes
Year Founded: 1967
Total Enrollment: 2,000,000
State Enrollment: 1,000,000

Healthplan and Services Defined
  PLAN TYPE: Dental
  Other Type: Dental PPO
  Model Type: Network
  Plan Specialty: Dental
  Benefits Offered: Dental

Type of Coverage
  Commercial, Individual

Geographic Areas Served
  Statewide

Peer Review Type
  Utilization Review: Yes

Key Personnel
  President & CEO .... John Maples
  Dental Network Admin .... Lynne Williams
  Corp. Communications .... Lyndsay Bradshaw
  VP, Service Operations .... Terry Maddox
  Underwriting Manager .... Laurend Doumba
  IT Project Manager .... Eita Harshman
  Small Bus. Sales Manager .... Steve Soyke
  Director, Compliance .... Carolyn Shanahan
  Corporate Counsel .... Alexandra Kotelon

277 Dental Network of America
701 East 22nd Street
Suite 300
Lombard, IL 60148
Toll-Free: 800-972-7565
Phone: 630-691-1133
general_inquiry@dnoa.com
www.dnoa.com
Subsidiary of: Health Care Service Corporation
For Profit Organization: Yes
Year Founded: 1985
Federally Qualified: Yes

Number of Primary Care Physicians: 80,000
Total Enrollment: 6,200,000

Healthplan and Services Defined
PLAN TYPE: Dental
Other Type: TPA, Dental PPO
Plan Specialty: ASO, Dental, Dental, Fully Insured
Benefits Offered: Dental

Type of Coverage
Commercial, Individual, Indemnity, Group

Type of Payment Plans Offered
Capitated

Geographic Areas Served
Nationwide

Network Qualifications
Pre-Admission Certification: Yes

Peer Review Type
Utilization Review: Yes

Key Personnel
Dental Director . . . . Timothy Custer

278 HCSC Insurance Services Company
300 E. Randolph St.
Chicago, IL 60601
Phone: 800-654-7385
hcsc.com
Subsidiary of: Blue Cross Blue Shield Association
Non-Profit Organization: Yes
Year Founded: 1936
Number of Primary Care Physicians: 9,400
State Enrollment: 220,000

Healthplan and Services Defined
PLAN TYPE: HMO
Benefits Offered: Behavioral Health, Dental, Disease Management, Psychiatric, Wellness

Geographic Areas Served
Statewide

Key Personnel
President/CEO . . . . Maurice Smith
SVP/COO . . . . Mike Frank
SVP/CFO . . . . James Walsh
SVP/Chief Legal Officer . . . . Catherine Nelson
SVP/Chief Admin. Officer . . . . Jill Wolowitz

279 Health Alliance
3310 Fields South Drive
Champaign, IL 61822
Toll-Free: 877-686-1168
www.healthalliance.org
For Profit Organization: Yes
Year Founded: 1980
Physician Owned Organization: Yes
Federally Qualified: Yes

Healthplan and Services Defined
PLAN TYPE: HMO/PPO
Plan Specialty: Dental, Vision
Benefits Offered: Dental, Disease Management, Prescription, Vision, Wellness

Type of Coverage
Commercial, Individual, Medicare, Medicaid

Geographic Areas Served
Illinois and Central Iowa

Publishes and Distributes Report Card: Yes

Accreditation Certification
NCQA

280 Health Alliance Medicare
3310 Fields South Drive
Champaign, IL 61822
Toll-Free: 887-686-1168
memberservices@healthalliance.org
www.healthalliance.org
Year Founded: 1997
Number of Primary Care Physicians: 3,000
Total Enrollment: 255,494

Healthplan and Services Defined
PLAN TYPE: Medicare
Other Type: HMO/PPO
Benefits Offered: Prescription

Type of Coverage
Medicare, Supplemental Medicare

Accreditation Certification
NCQA

281 Health Care Service Corporation (HCSC)
300 E. Randolph St.
Chicago, IL 60601
Toll-Free: 800-654-7385
Phone: 312-653-6000
www.hcsc.com
For Profit Organization: Yes
Year Founded: 1936
Number of Affiliated Hospitals: 8,200
Number of Primary Care Physicians: 258,000
Total Enrollment: 16,000,000
State Enrollment: 16,000,000

Healthplan and Services Defined
PLAN TYPE: HMO/PPO
Model Type: Network
Plan Specialty: Chiropractic, Dental, Disease Management, Lab, Vision, Radiology, UR
Benefits Offered: Chiropractic, Dental, Disease Management, Home Care, Inpatient SNF, Physical Therapy, Podiatry, Prescription, Psychiatric, Transplant, Vision, Wellness, AD&D, Life, LTD, STD

Type of Coverage
Commercial, Individual, Indemnity, Supplemental Medicare, Catastrophic

Geographic Areas Served
Illinois, Montana, New Mexico, Oklahoma, Texas

Peer Review Type
Second Surgical Opinion: Yes

Accreditation Certification
NCQA

Key Personnel
President/CEO .... Maureen Smith
SVP/COO .... Mike Frank
SVP/Chief Legal Officer .... Catherine Nelson
SVP/CFO .... James Walsh
SVP/Chief Admin. Officer .... Jill Wolowitz

282 Humana Health Insurance of Illinois
2301 W 22nd Street
Suite 301
Oak Brook, IL 60523
Toll-Free: 800-569-2492
Phone: 630-794-5950
Fax: 630-794-0107
www.humana.com
Subsidiary of: Humana Inc.
For Profit Organization: Yes
Year Founded: 1972

Healthplan and Services Defined
PLAN TYPE: HMO/PPO
Model Type: Network
Plan Specialty: Behavioral Health, Chiropractic, Dental, Disease Management, Lab, PBM, Vision, Worker's Compensation, UR
Benefits Offered: Behavioral Health, Chiropractic, Complementary Medicine, Dental, Disease Management, Home Care, Inpatient SNF, Long-Term Care, Physical Therapy, Prescription, Psychiatric, Transplant, Vision, Wellness, Worker's Compensation, AD&D, Life, LTD, STD

Type of Coverage
Commercial, Individual, Indemnity, Medicare, Supplemental Medicare, Medicaid, Catastrophic

Type of Payment Plans Offered
POS, DFFS, Capitated, FFS

Geographic Areas Served
Statewide

Network Qualifications
Pre-Admission Certification: Yes

Peer Review Type
Utilization Review: Yes
Second Surgical Opinion: Yes
Case Management: Yes

Publishes and Distributes Report Card: Yes

Accreditation Certification
URAC, NCQA, CORE
TJC Accreditation, Medicare Approved, Utilization Review, Pre-Admission Certification, State Licensure, Quality Assurance Program

Key Personnel
Pres., North Central Reg. .... Chuck Dow

Specialty Managed Care Partners
Behavioral Health, Disease Management, PBM, Worker's Compensation
Enters into Contracts with Regional Business Coalitions: Yes
Midwest Business Group on Health, Mercer Coalition

283 Liberty Dental Plan of Illinois
P.O. Box 401086
Santa Ana, NV 89140
Toll-Free: 888-352-7924
www.libertydentalplan.com
For Profit Organization: Yes
Total Enrollment: 2,000,000

Healthplan and Services Defined
PLAN TYPE: Dental
Other Type: Dental HMO
Plan Specialty: Dental
Benefits Offered: Dental

Type of Coverage
Commercial, Medicare, Medicaid, Unions

Geographic Areas Served
Statewide

Accreditation Certification
NCQA

Key Personnel
SVP, Government Programs .... Dave Meadows

284 Meridian Health Plan of Illinois
300 South Riverside Plaza
Suite 500
Chicago, IL 60606
Toll-Free: 866-606-3700
memberservices.il@mhplan.com
www.mhplan.com
Total Enrollment: 750,000
State Enrollment: 240,000

Healthplan and Services Defined
PLAN TYPE: Medicare

Type of Coverage
Medicare, Medicaid

Geographic Areas Served
Statewide

Accreditation Certification
URAC, NCQA

Key Personnel
President .... Karen Brach

285 Molina Healthcare of Illinois
1520 Kensington Road
Suite 212
Oak Brook, IL 60523
Toll-Free: 855-687-7861
www.molinahealthcare.com
Secondary Address: 1 West Old State Capital Plaza, Suite 300, Springfield, IL 62701

Subsidiary of: Molina Healthcare, Inc.
For Profit Organization: Yes

Healthplan and Services Defined
    PLAN TYPE: Medicare
    Model Type: Network
    Plan Specialty: Dental, PBM, Vision, Integrated
        Medicare/Medicaid (Duals)
    Benefits Offered: Dental, Prescription, Vision, Wellness, Life

Type of Coverage
    Individual, Medicare, Supplemental Medicare, Medicaid

Geographic Areas Served
    Statewide

Key Personnel
    Plan President .... Matt Wolf
    Chief Medical Officer .... Varsha Chandramouli, MD

286 OSF Healthcare
800 NE Glen Oak Avenue
Peoria, IL 61603-3200
Toll-Free: 800-421-5700
www.osfhealthcare.org
Subsidiary of: Sisters of the Third Order of St Francis
Non-Profit Organization: Yes
Number of Affiliated Hospitals: 14
Number of Primary Care Physicians: 1,103
Number of Referral/Specialty Physicians: 692
Total Enrollment: 1,500,000

Healthplan and Services Defined
    PLAN TYPE: HMO
    Model Type: Network
    Plan Specialty: Integrated Healthcare Network of Facilities
    Benefits Offered: Behavioral Health, Disease Management,
        Wellness

Geographic Areas Served
    Illinois and Michigan

Key Personnel
    Chief Executive Officer .... Bob Sehring
    Media Relations .... Shelli Dankoff
        shelli.j.dankoff@osfhealthcare.org
    CFO .... Michael Allen

287 Preferred Network Access
1510 W 75th Street
Suite 250
Darien, IL 60561
Phone: 630-493-0905
www.pna-usa.net
For Profit Organization: Yes
Year Founded: 1995
Number of Affiliated Hospitals: 113
Number of Primary Care Physicians: 34,000
Number of Referral/Specialty Physicians: 250
Total Enrollment: 316,000
State Enrollment: 316,000

Healthplan and Services Defined
    PLAN TYPE: PPO
    Plan Specialty: Group, Health
    Benefits Offered: Home Care, Physical Therapy, Wellness,
        Worker's Compensation, Occupational Health

Type of Coverage
    Commercial

Geographic Areas Served
    Illinois, Indiana, Wisconsin

Key Personnel
    President .... Joseph M Zerega

288 Trinity Health of Illinois
Mercy Health System
2525 S Michigan Avenue
Chicago, IL 60616
Phone: 312-567-2000
www.trinity-health.org
Secondary Address: Layola University Medical Center, 2160 S
    First Avenue, Maywood, IL 60153, 888-584-7888
Subsidiary of: Trinity Health
Non-Profit Organization: Yes
Year Founded: 2013
Total Enrollment: 30,000,000

Healthplan and Services Defined
    PLAN TYPE: Other
    Benefits Offered: Disease Management, Home Care,
        Long-Term Care, Psychiatric, Hospice programs, PACE
        (Program of All Inclusive Care for the Elderly)

Geographic Areas Served
    Greater Chicago

Key Personnel
    President/CEO, Mercy .... Carol L. Garikes Schneider
    Chief Medical Officer .... Michael Davenport
    Chief HR Officer .... Diane Hargreaves
    Chief Operating Officer .... Joan Ormsby
    President/CEO, Trinity IL .... Shawn Vincent

289 Trustmark
400 Field Drive
Lake Forest, IL 60045
Phone: 847-615-1500
bgosman@trustmarkbenefits.com
www.trustmarkbenefits.com
Year Founded: 1913
Total Enrollment: 1,100,000

Healthplan and Services Defined
    PLAN TYPE: PPO
    Other Type: TPA
    Model Type: Network
    Plan Specialty: Benefits Administration
    Benefits Offered: Behavioral Health, Dental, Home Care,
        Prescription, Transplant, Vision, Wellness

Type of Coverage
    Commercial

Geographic Areas Served
    Nationwide

Accreditation Certification
  URAC
  Utilization Review, Pre-Admission Certification

Key Personnel
  President/CEO . . . . Nancy Eckrich
  Chief Clinical Leader. Meera Atkins
  Chief Operating Officer. . . . . Lloyd Sarrel
  Chief Financial Officer. . . . . Clare Smith
  Chief Information Officer . . . . Brooke Terry
  VP, Marketing. . . . . Steve Horvath
  VP, Human Resources . . . . Dave Kenney

---

290 Trustmark Companies
400 Field Drive
Lake Forest, IL 60045
Phone: 847-615-1500
Fax: 847-615-3910
customercare@trustmarksolutions.com
www.trustmarkcompanies.com
For Profit Organization: Yes
Year Founded: 1913
Federally Qualified: Yes
Total Enrollment: 475,000

Healthplan and Services Defined
  PLAN TYPE: PPO
  Other Type: Self-funded
  Model Type: Network
  Plan Specialty: Behavioral Health, Dental, Lab
  Benefits Offered: Behavioral Health, Dental, Disease
    Management, Prescription, Vision, Wellness, AD&D, Life,
    LTD, STD, Major Medical, Nurse Line, Health Advocacy
    Service

Type of Coverage
  Commercial, Indemnity

Type of Payment Plans Offered
  FFS

Geographic Areas Served
  Nationwide

Network Qualifications
  Pre-Admission Certification: Yes

Peer Review Type
  Utilization Review: Yes
  Second Surgical Opinion: Yes

Accreditation Certification
  TJC Accreditation, Utilization Review, State Licensure

Key Personnel
  President/CEO . . . . Kevin Slawin
  SVP/General Counsel . . . . Steve Auburn
  SVP/CFO/Treasurer. . . . . Phil Goss
  SVP, Human Resources. . . . . Kristin Zelkowitz
  SVP, CIO . . . . Brad Bodell

---

291 UniCare Illinois
233 S Wacker Drive
Chicago, IL 60606
Toll-Free: 800-379-0274
www.unicare.com
Subsidiary of: Anthem, Inc.
For Profit Organization: Yes
Year Founded: 1995

Healthplan and Services Defined
  PLAN TYPE: HMO/PPO
  Model Type: Network
  Benefits Offered: Behavioral Health, Chiropractic,
    Complementary
Medicine, Dental, Disease Management, Home Care,
Inpatient SNF, Long-Term Care, Physical Therapy,
Podiatry, Prescription, Psychiatric, Transplant,
Vision, Wellness, Worker's Compensation, AD&D,
Life, LTD, STD

Type of Coverage
  Commercial, Individual, Medicare, Supplemental Medicare

Type of Payment Plans Offered
  POS

Geographic Areas Served
  Statewide

Network Qualifications
  Pre-Admission Certification: Yes

Peer Review Type
  Utilization Review: Yes
  Second Surgical Opinion: Yes

Accreditation Certification
  URAC, NCQA
  TJC Accreditation, State Licensure

Specialty Managed Care Partners
  Enters into Contracts with Regional Business Coalitions: Yes

---

292 UnitedHealthcare of Illinois
60 W Superior Street
Chicago, IL 60654
Toll-Free: 888-545-5205
Phone: 872-241-1585
www.uhc.com
Subsidiary of: UnitedHealth Group
For Profit Organization: Yes

Healthplan and Services Defined
  PLAN TYPE: HMO/PPO
  Model Type: Network
  Plan Specialty: Behavioral Health, Dental, Disease
    Management, PBM, Vision
  Benefits Offered: Behavioral Health, Chiropractic, Dental,
    Disease Management, Home Care, Inpatient SNF,
    Long-Term Care, Podiatry, Prescription, Psychiatric,
    Transplant, Vision, Wellness, Life, LTD, STD

Type of Coverage
  Individual, Medicare, Supplemental Medicare, Medicaid,
  Catastrophic, Family, Military, Veterans, Group

Geographic Areas Served
Statewide

Key Personnel
CEO, Illinois . . . . Tom Kunst

INDIANA

Health Insurance Coverage Status and Type of Coverage by Age

Category	All Persons Number	%	Under 19 years Number	%	Under 65 years Number	%
Total population	6,632 *(1)*	100.0 *(0.0)*	1,664 *(5)*	100.0 *(0.0)*	5,584 *(3)*	100.0 *(0.0)*
Covered by some type of health insurance	6,053 *(19)*	91.3 *(0.3)*	1,545 *(10)*	92.9 *(0.6)*	5,010 *(19)*	89.7 *(0.3)*
Covered by private health insurance	4,610 *(31)*	69.5 *(0.5)*	1,060 *(16)*	63.7 *(1.0)*	3,985 *(27)*	71.4 *(0.5)*
Employer-based	3,900 *(33)*	58.8 *(0.5)*	973 *(16)*	58.5 *(1.0)*	3,596 *(30)*	64.4 *(0.5)*
Direct purchase	811 *(18)*	12.2 *(0.3)*	88 *(8)*	5.3 *(0.4)*	436 *(15)*	7.8 *(0.3)*
TRICARE	110 *(8)*	1.7 *(0.1)*	25 *(4)*	1.5 *(0.3)*	72 *(7)*	1.3 *(0.1)*
Covered by public health insurance	2,232 *(23)*	33.7 *(0.3)*	551 *(15)*	33.1 *(0.9)*	1,214 *(24)*	21.7 *(0.4)*
Medicaid	1,171 *(25)*	17.7 *(0.4)*	544 *(15)*	32.7 *(0.9)*	1,067 *(24)*	19.1 *(0.4)*
Medicare	1,197 *(8)*	18.0 *(0.1)*	11 *(2)*	0.6 *(0.1)*	180 *(7)*	3.2 *(0.1)*
VA Care	144 *(7)*	2.2 *(0.1)*	2 *(2)*	0.1 *(0.1)*	62 *(5)*	1.1 *(0.1)*
Not covered at any time during the year	578 *(19)*	8.7 *(0.3)*	119 *(9)*	7.1 *(0.6)*	574 *(19)*	10.3 *(0.3)*

Note: Numbers in thousands; Figures cover civilian noninstitutionalized population in 2019; N/A indicates that data was not available; Z represents or rounds to zero; Margin of error appears in parenthesis and is calculated using replicate weights.
Source: U.S. Census Bureau, American Community Survey, Table HI-05. Health Insurance Coverage Status and Type of Coverage by State and Age for All People: 2019

Indiana

293 Aetna Health of Indiana
151 Farmington Avenue
Hartford, CT 06156
Toll-Free: 800-872-3862
www.aetna.com
Subsidiary of: CVS Health / Aetna Inc.
For Profit Organization: Yes
Year Founded: 1995

Healthplan and Services Defined
   PLAN TYPE: HMO/PPO
   Other Type: POS
   Model Type: Network
   Plan Specialty: Dental, Vision
   Benefits Offered: Chiropractic, Complementary Medicine, Dental, Home Care, Inpatient SNF, Long-Term Care, Podiatry, Prescription, Psychiatric, Transplant, Vision, Wellness

Type of Coverage
   Commercial, Student health

Geographic Areas Served
   Statewide

294 Allwell from Managed Health Services
550 N Meridian Street
Suite 101
Indianapolis, IN 46204
Toll-Free: 855-766-1541
allwell.mhsindiana.com
Subsidiary of: Centene Corporation

Healthplan and Services Defined
   PLAN TYPE: Medicare
   Model Type: Network
   Benefits Offered: Dental, Prescription

Type of Coverage
   Medicare, Supplemental Medicare, Medicare Advantage

Geographic Areas Served
   Statewide

295 Ambetter from Managed Health Services
550 N Meridian Street
Suite 101
Indianapolis, IN 46204
Toll-Free: 877-687-1182
ambetter.mhsindiana.com
Subsidiary of: Centene Corporation

Healthplan and Services Defined
   PLAN TYPE: Other
   Model Type: Network
   Plan Specialty: Lab
   Benefits Offered: Behavioral Health, Disease Management, Physical Therapy, Prescription, Wellness, Maternity and newborn care

Type of Coverage
   Health Insurance Marketplace

Geographic Areas Served
   Statewide

296 American Health Network
10689 N Pennsylvania Street
Suite 200
Indianapolis, IN 46280
Toll-Free: 888-255-2246
Phone: 317-580-6309
www.ahni.com
Secondary Address: 2500 Corporate Exchange, Suite 100, Columbus, OH 43229, 614-794-4500
Subsidiary of: Optum
Year Founded: 1994
Number of Primary Care Physicians: 200

Healthplan and Services Defined
   PLAN TYPE: PPO
   Plan Specialty: Lab, Vision, Family Medicine, General Surgery, Pain Management, Pediatrics
   Benefits Offered: Physical Therapy, Podiatry

Type of Payment Plans Offered
   Capitated

Geographic Areas Served
   Indiana

Accreditation Certification
   TJC Accreditation, State Licensure

Key Personnel
   President . . . . Ben Park, MD

297 American Specialty Health
12800 N. Meridian St.
Carmel, IN 46032
Toll-Free: 800-848-3555
Fax: 619-237-3859
www.ashcompanies.com
For Profit Organization: Yes
Year Founded: 1987
Total Enrollment: 25,900,000

Healthplan and Services Defined
   PLAN TYPE: HMO
   Model Type: Network
   Plan Specialty: Chiropractic
   Benefits Offered: Chiropractic, Complementary Medicine, Wellness, Acupuncture

Type of Coverage
   Commercial, Supplemental Medicare

Type of Payment Plans Offered
   POS, Capitated

Geographic Areas Served
   Nationwide - ASH Network, California - ASH Plans

Network Qualifications
   Pre-Admission Certification: Yes

Peer Review Type
Utilization Review: Yes
Case Management: Yes

Accreditation Certification
URAC, NCQA, HITRUST

Key Personnel
Chairman/CEO/Co-Founder . . . . George T. DeVries III
President/COO . . . . Robert White
CFO/EVP . . . . Marcel Danko
Chief Legal Officer/EVP . . . . Erin Hiley

Specialty Managed Care Partners
Enters into Contracts with Regional Business Coalitions: Yes

298 Anthem Blue Cross & Blue Shield of Indiana
220 Virginia Avenue
Indianapolis, IN 46204
Toll-Free: 800-331-1476
Phone: 888-525-2571
www.anthem.com
Subsidiary of: Anthem, Inc.
For Profit Organization: Yes
Year Founded: 1990
Number of Affiliated Hospitals: 105
Number of Primary Care Physicians: 3,532
Number of Referral/Specialty Physicians: 8,475
Total Enrollment: 900,000

Healthplan and Services Defined
PLAN TYPE: HMO/PPO
Model Type: Network
Benefits Offered: Behavioral Health, Chiropractic, Complementary Medicine, Dental, Disease Management, Home Care, Inpatient SNF, Physical Therapy, Podiatry, Prescription, Psychiatric, Transplant, Vision, Wellness

Type of Coverage
Medicare, Supplemental Medicare

Type of Payment Plans Offered
DFFS, FFS, Combination FFS & DFFS

Geographic Areas Served
Statewide

Subscriber Information
Average Annual Deductible Per Subscriber:
  Employee Only (Self): Varies $250-$5000
  Employee & 2 Family Members: Varies $2500-$10000
Average Subscriber Co-Payment:
  Primary Care Physician: Varies $25/20%
  Non-Network Physician: 20%
  Prescription Drugs: Varies $15/$30/$0
  Hospital ER: 20%
  Home Health Care: 20%
  Home Health Care Max. Days/Visits Covered: 100 days
  Nursing Home Max. Days/Visits Covered: 60 days

Network Qualifications
Pre-Admission Certification: Yes

Peer Review Type
Utilization Review: Yes
Second Surgical Opinion: No

Case Management: Yes

Publishes and Distributes Report Card: Yes

Accreditation Certification
URAC, NCQA
TJC Accreditation, Medicare Approved, Utilization Review, Pre-Admission Certification, State Licensure, Quality Assurance Program

Key Personnel
President . . . . Beth Keyser

299 Anthem, Inc.
220 Virginia Avenue
Indianapolis, IN 46204
Toll-Free: 800-331-1476
www.antheminc.com
For Profit Organization: Yes
Year Founded: 2004
Total Enrollment: 79,000,000

Healthplan and Services Defined
PLAN TYPE: HMO/PPO
Model Type: Network
Plan Specialty: Behavioral Health, Dental, Vision
Benefits Offered: Behavioral Health, Dental, Vision, Life, LTD, STD

Type of Coverage
Commercial, Individual, Medicare, Supplemental Medicare, Medicaid, Federal employee program

Key Personnel
President/CEO . . . . Gail K. Boudreaux
EVP/CFO . . . . John E. Gallina
EVP/CAO . . . . Gloria McCarthy
EVP/Chief Legal Officer . . . . Blair Todt

300 Ascension At Home
St Vincent Home Health & Hospice
2015 Jackson Street
Anderson, IN 46016
Phone: 765-203-2616
Fax: 765-643-0153
ascensionathome.com
Subsidiary of: Ascension
Non-Profit Organization: Yes

Healthplan and Services Defined
PLAN TYPE: Other
Plan Specialty: Disease Management
Benefits Offered: Dental, Disease Management, Home Care, Wellness, Ambulance & Transportation; Nursing Service; Short-and-long-term care management planning; Hospice

Geographic Areas Served
Texas, Alabama, Indiana, Kansas, Michigan, Mississippi, Oklahoma, Wisconsin

Key Personnel
President . . . . David Grams
Chair/CEO . . . . James A. Deal

301 CareSource Indiana
P.O. Box 8738
Dayton, OH 45401-8738
Toll-Free: 877-806-9284
Phone: 937-224-3300
www.caresource.com
Non-Profit Organization: Yes
Total Enrollment: 1,000,000

Healthplan and Services Defined
PLAN TYPE: Medicare
Benefits Offered: Behavioral Health, Dental, Disease Management, Prescription, Vision, 24-hour Nurse Advice Line; Durable Medical Equipment

Type of Coverage
Individual, Medicare, Medicaid

Geographic Areas Served
Statewide

Key Personnel
President, Indiana Market . . . . Steve Smitherman

302 Cigna HealthCare of Indiana
11595 N Meridian Street
Suite 500
Carmel, IN 46032
Toll-Free: 800-997-1654
www.cigna.com
Subsidiary of: Cigna Corporation
For Profit Organization: Yes
Year Founded: 1982

Healthplan and Services Defined
PLAN TYPE: HMO
Other Type: POS
Plan Specialty: Behavioral Health, Dental
Benefits Offered: Behavioral Health, Dental, Disease Management, Prescription, Vision, Wellness, AD&D, Life, LTD, STD

Type of Coverage
Commercial, Individual, Medicare, Supplemental Medicare, Medicaid

Geographic Areas Served
Statewide

Key Personnel
Market Pres., Midwest . . . . Brian Marsella

303 Deaconess Health Plans
600 Mary St
Evansville, IN 47747
Phone: 812-450-5000
www.deaconess.com
Year Founded: 1892
Physician Owned Organization: Yes
Number of Affiliated Hospitals: 7

Healthplan and Services Defined
PLAN TYPE: PPO
Model Type: Network
Plan Specialty: Behavioral Health, Chiropractic, Lab, Radiology
Benefits Offered: Disease Management, Podiatry, Prescription, Wellness

Type of Coverage
Individual

Geographic Areas Served
Illinois, Indiana, Kentucky

Peer Review Type
Utilization Review: Yes
Second Surgical Opinion: No
Case Management: Yes

Accreditation Certification
TJC Accreditation, Medicare Approved, Utilization Review, Pre-Admission Certification, State Licensure, Quality Assurance Program

Key Personnel
President . . . . James R. Porter
Chief Executive Officer . . . . Shawn McCoy
Chief Financial Officer . . . . Cheryl Wathen
Chief Operating Officer . . . . Lynn Lingafelter

Average Claim Compensation
Physician's Fees Charged: 1%
Hospital's Fees Charged: 1%

304 Encore Health Network
8520 Allison Pointe Boulevard
Suite 200
Indianapolis, IN 46250-4299
Toll-Free: 888-574-8180
Phone: 317-621-4250
Fax: 317-621-2388
encoreconnect.com
Subsidiary of: The HealthCare Group, LLC
Year Founded: 1986

Healthplan and Services Defined
PLAN TYPE: PPO
Benefits Offered: Vision, Worker's Compensation

Type of Coverage
Commercial, Individual

Geographic Areas Served
Select Indiana markets

Key Personnel
President . . . . Bruce Smiley

305 Healthy Indiana Plan
Toll-Free: 877-438-4479
www.in.gov/fssa/hip
Year Founded: 2007

Healthplan and Services Defined
PLAN TYPE: HMO
Benefits Offered: Behavioral Health, Disease Management, Home Care, Inpatient SNF, Prescription, Wellness

Type of Coverage
Individual

Geographic Areas Served
Statewide

306 Humana Health Insurance of Indiana
7035 E 96th Street
Suite F
Indianapolis, IN 46250
Toll-Free: 866-355-6170
Phone: 317-558-5670
Fax: 502-508-8169
www.humana.com
Secondary Address: 7525 E Virginia Street, Suite 430, Evansville, IN 47715, 888-652-9151
Subsidiary of: Humana Inc.
For Profit Organization: Yes
Year Founded: 1986

Healthplan and Services Defined
PLAN TYPE: HMO/PPO
Model Type: IPA
Benefits Offered: Disease Management, Wellness

Type of Coverage
Commercial, Individual, Medicare, Medicaid

Geographic Areas Served
(Southern Indiana) Boone, Clark, Crawford, Delaware, Dubois, Floyd, Gibson, Hamilton, Hancock, Harrison, Hendricks, Howard, Jackson, Jefferson, Jennings, Johnson, Knox, Lake, LaPorte, Madison, Marrion, Morgan, Orange, Pike, Porter, Posey, Scott, Shelby, Spencer, Tipton, Vanderburgh, Warrick, Washington

Accreditation Certification
URAC, NCQA, CORE

Key Personnel
Regional President .... Kathie Mancini

307 Managed Health Services
550 N Meridian Street
Suite 101
Indianapolis, IN 46204
Toll-Free: 877-647-4848
www.mhsindiana.com
Subsidiary of: Centene Corporation

Healthplan and Services Defined
PLAN TYPE: Other
Model Type: Network
Benefits Offered: Dental, Disease Management, Vision

Type of Coverage
Medicaid, Hoosier Healthwise, Hoosier Care Co

Key Personnel
President/CEO...................... Kevin O'Toole
Chief Operating Officer .... Dana Moell
Chief Medical Officer............. A. Joel Feldman, MD
Chief Financial Officer .... Bill Wilson, CPA

308 MDwise
2955 N Meridian Street
Suite 201
Indianapolis, IN 46208
Toll-Free: 800-356-1204
www.mdwise.org
Subsidiary of: McLaren Health Care
Non-Profit Organization: Yes
Year Founded: 1994

Healthplan and Services Defined
PLAN TYPE: Multiple

Type of Coverage
Individual, Medicare, Medicaid

Geographic Areas Served
Indiana

Key Personnel
President/CEO...................... Jessica Cromer
VP/General Counsel .... Patricia Hebenstreit, JD
VP, Health Services .... Rebecca Trapp
VP, Health Plan Operation............. Torriaun Everett
Medical Director .... Jeffrey Wheeler

309 Mid America Health
1499 Windhorst Way
Suite 100
Greenwood, IN 46143
Toll-Free: 888-309-8239
Fax: 317-972-7969
mahweb.com
For Profit Organization: Yes
Year Founded: 1986

Healthplan and Services Defined
PLAN TYPE: Multiple
Plan Specialty: Behavioral Health, Dental, Vision
Benefits Offered: Physical Therapy, Psychiatric

Geographic Areas Served
Correctional facilities, county jails, military installations and long-term care facilities nationwide

Key Personnel
President........................... Patrick Murphy
  patrick@mahweb.com
VP of Operations .... Jose Lopez
  jlopez@mahweb.com
Marketing/Sales Director............. Elizabeth McClure
  emcclure@mahweb.com

310 Parkview Total Health
Toll-Free: 800-666-4449
Phone: 260-266-5510
www.parkviewtotalhealth.com
Non-Profit Organization: Yes
Year Founded: 1992

Healthplan and Services Defined
PLAN TYPE: PPO
Benefits Offered: Disease Management, Wellness

Indiana

Type of Coverage
Commercial

Geographic Areas Served
Indiana & Northwestern Ohio

Network Qualifications
Pre-Admission Certification: Yes

Peer Review Type
Utilization Review: Yes
Second Surgical Opinion: No
Case Management: Yes

Accreditation Certification
TJC Accreditation, Medicare Approved, Utilization Review, Pre-Admission Certification, State Licensure, Quality Assurance Program

Key Personnel
Wellness Coordinator . . . . Courntey Drummond
Wellness Coordinator . . . . Amanda Vanwagner
Dir. of Business Devel. . . . . Melissa McKown

Employer References
Parkview Hospitals, East Allen County Schools, Guardian Industries, Chore Timer Brook, Tomkins

311 Physicians Health Plan of Northern Indiana
1700 Magnavox Way
Suite 201
Fort Wayne, IN 46804
Toll-Free: 800-982-6257
Phone: 260-432-6690
Fax: 260-432-0493
custsvc@phpni.com
www.phpni.com
Non-Profit Organization: Yes
Year Founded: 1983
Physician Owned Organization: Yes
Federally Qualified: Yes

Healthplan and Services Defined
PLAN TYPE: HMO
Model Type: IPA, POS
Benefits Offered: Behavioral Health, Dental, Disease Management, Home Care, Physical Therapy, Podiatry, Prescription, Psychiatric, Transplant, Vision, Wellness, AD&D, Life, LTD, STD
Offers Demand Management Patient Information Service: Yes

Type of Coverage
Commercial, Individual
Catastrophic Illness Benefit: Unlimited

Type of Payment Plans Offered
POS, DFFS, FFS, Combination FFS & DFFS

Geographic Areas Served
40 Northern Indiana counties

Peer Review Type
Utilization Review: Yes
Case Management: Yes

Publishes and Distributes Report Card: Yes

Accreditation Certification
Utilization Review, Pre-Admission Certification, State Licensure, Quality Assurance Program

Key Personnel
Chair . . . . James C. Stevens
President/CEO . . . . Gary Shearer

Specialty Managed Care Partners
Enters into Contracts with Regional Business Coalitions: Yes

312 Renaissance Dental
P.O. Box 1596
Indianapolis, IN 46206-4596
Toll-Free: 800-963-4596
Fax: 800-963-4597
renaissancefamily.com
Total Enrollment: 13,100,000

Healthplan and Services Defined
PLAN TYPE: Dental
Plan Specialty: Dental
Benefits Offered: Dental

Type of Coverage
Supplemental Medicare

Geographic Areas Served
Arkansas, Georgia, Florida, Indiana, Kentucky, Michigan, New Mexico, New York, North Carolina, South Carolina, Ohio, Tennessee, Texas, and Nevada

Key Personnel
President & CEO . . . . Robert P. Mulligan
Chief Operating Officer . . . . Jeff Kolesar
VP, Market Development . . . . John Feeney

313 Sagamore Health Network
11595 N Meridian Street
Suite 600
Carmel, IN 46032
Toll-Free: 800-364-3469
Phone: 317-573-2886
www.sagamorehn.com
Subsidiary of: Cigna
Year Founded: 1985

Healthplan and Services Defined
PLAN TYPE: PPO
Model Type: IPA

Geographic Areas Served
Entire state of Indiana, Kentucky, Illinois, Michigan and Ohio

Accreditation Certification
URAC
TJC Accreditation, Medicare Approved, Utilization Review, Pre-Admission Certification, State Licensure, Quality Assurance Program

314 SIHO Insurance Services
417 Washington Street
Columbus, IN 47201
Toll-Free: 800-443-2980
Phone: 812-378-7070
memberservices@siho.org
www.siho.org
Mailing Address: P.O. Box 1787, Columbus, IN 47202-1787
Non-Profit Organization: Yes
Year Founded: 1987
Physician Owned Organization: Yes

Healthplan and Services Defined
PLAN TYPE: HMO
Model Type: IPA, Network, POS
Plan Specialty: ASO, Dental, Disease Management, Vision
Benefits Offered: Behavioral Health, Chiropractic, Dental, Disease Management, Home Care, Inpatient SNF, Long-Term Care, Physical Therapy, Prescription, Transplant, Vision, Wellness, AD&D, Life, STD

Type of Coverage
Individual, Indemnity, Medicaid
Catastrophic Illness Benefit: Unlimited

Type of Payment Plans Offered
POS, DFFS, FFS

Geographic Areas Served
Bloomington, Columbus, Evansville, Indianapolis and Seymour

Network Qualifications
Pre-Admission Certification: Yes

Peer Review Type
Utilization Review: Yes
Case Management: Yes

Publishes and Distributes Report Card: Yes

Accreditation Certification
TJC Accreditation, Utilization Review, Pre-Admission Certification, State Licensure

Key Personnel
Chief Executive Officer . . . . John Sadtler
VP of Medical Management . . . . Hoskins Mary

Specialty Managed Care Partners
Caremark Rx
Enters into Contracts with Regional Business Coalitions: Yes

Employer References
Columbus Regional Hospital, Enkei America, Seymour Memorial Hospital, Seymour Tubing

315 Trinity Health of Indiana
Saint Joseph Health System
5215 Holy Cross Parkway
Mishawaka, IN 46545
Phone: 574-335-5633
www.trinity-health.org
Subsidiary of: Trinity Health
Non-Profit Organization: Yes
Year Founded: 2013

Total Enrollment: 30,000,000

Healthplan and Services Defined
PLAN TYPE: Other
Benefits Offered: Disease Management, Home Care, Long-Term Care, Psychiatric, Hospice programs, PACE (Program of All Inclusive Care for the Elderly)

Geographic Areas Served
North Central Indiana

Key Personnel
Chief Executive Officer . . . . Chad W. Towner
Chief Financial Officer . . . . Kevin Higdon
General Counsel. . . . . Jason Schultz
Chief Nursing Officer . . . . Loretta Schmidt
Chief Medical Officer . . . . Genevieve Lankowicz

316 UnitedHealthcare Community Plan Indiana
UnitedHealthcare Customer Service
P.O. Box 30769
Salt Lake City, UT 84130-0769
Toll-Free: 888-545-5205
www.uhccommunityplan.com/in
Subsidiary of: UnitedHealth Group
For Profit Organization: Yes

Healthplan and Services Defined
PLAN TYPE: Medicare
Other Type: Medicaid
Model Type: Network
Benefits Offered: Prescription, Hospitals, Doctors

Type of Coverage
Medicare, Medicaid

Geographic Areas Served
Adams, Allen, Brown, DeKalb, Elkhart, Grant, Hancock, Hendricks, Henry, Huntington, Jay, Johnson, Kosciusko, La Porte, Lagrange, Lake, Marion, Monroe, Montgomery, Morgan, Noble, Porter, Posey, St. Joseph, Steuben, Vanderburgh, Warrick, Wells, and Whitley

Key Personnel
CEO, Health Plan IN. . . . . Charlotte MacBeth
charlotte_macbeth@uhc.com

317 UnitedHealthcare of Indiana
7440 Woodland Drive
Indianapolis, IN 46278
Toll-Free: 800-273-8115
www.uhc.com
Subsidiary of: UnitedHealth Group
For Profit Organization: Yes
Year Founded: 1986

Healthplan and Services Defined
PLAN TYPE: HMO/PPO
Model Type: Network
Plan Specialty: Behavioral Health, Dental, Disease Management, PBM, Vision
Benefits Offered: Behavioral Health, Chiropractic, Dental, Disease Management, Home Care, Inpatient SNF,

Long-Term Care, Podiatry, Prescription, Psychiatric, Transplant, Vision, Wellness, Life, LTD, STD

Type of Coverage
Commercial, Individual, Medicare, Supplemental Medicare, Medicaid, Catastrophic, Family, Military, Veterans, Group

Type of Payment Plans Offered
POS

Geographic Areas Served
Statewide

Subscriber Information
Average Monthly Fee Per Subscriber
 (Employee + Employer Contribution):
  Employee Only (Self): Varies per plan
  Employee & 2 Family Members: Variers per plan
Average Annual Deductible Per Subscriber:
  Employee Only (Self): Varies per plan
  Employee & 2 Family Members: Varies per plan
Average Subscriber Co-Payment:
  Primary Care Physician: Varies per plan

Accreditation Certification
TJC

Key Personnel
CEO, IN/KY......................... Kim Sonerholm

IOWA

Health Insurance Coverage Status and Type of Coverage by Age

Category	All Persons Number	%	Under 19 years Number	%	Under 65 years Number	%
Total population	3,112 *(1)*	100.0 *(0.0)*	765 *(4)*	100.0 *(0.0)*	2,580 *(2)*	100.0 *(0.0)*
Covered by some type of health insurance	2,956 *(10)*	95.0 *(0.3)*	743 *(5)*	97.1 *(0.5)*	2,426 *(10)*	94.0 *(0.4)*
Covered by private health insurance	2,277 *(21)*	73.2 *(0.7)*	506 *(10)*	66.1 *(1.4)*	1,935 *(20)*	75.0 *(0.8)*
Employer-based	1,869 *(23)*	60.1 *(0.7)*	465 *(11)*	60.8 *(1.5)*	1,745 *(22)*	67.6 *(0.9)*
Direct purchase	460 *(11)*	14.8 *(0.3)*	45 *(4)*	5.9 *(0.5)*	220 *(10)*	8.5 *(0.4)*
TRICARE	55 *(4)*	1.8 *(0.1)*	11 *(2)*	1.4 *(0.3)*	35 *(4)*	1.3 *(0.2)*
Covered by public health insurance	1,123 *(18)*	36.1 *(0.6)*	280 *(11)*	36.6 *(1.3)*	604 *(18)*	23.4 *(0.7)*
Medicaid	603 *(17)*	19.4 *(0.6)*	278 *(11)*	36.3 *(1.3)*	550 *(17)*	21.3 *(0.7)*
Medicare	587 *(5)*	18.9 *(0.2)*	3 *(1)*	0.4 *(0.2)*	69 *(5)*	2.7 *(0.2)*
VA Care	80 *(5)*	2.6 *(0.1)*	2 *(1)*	0.3 *(0.2)*	34 *(4)*	1.3 *(0.1)*
Not covered at any time during the year	156 *(10)*	5.0 *(0.3)*	22 *(4)*	2.9 *(0.5)*	154 *(10)*	6.0 *(0.4)*

Note: Numbers in thousands; Figures cover civilian noninstitutionalized population in 2019; N/A indicates that data was not available; Z represents or rounds to zero; Margin of error appears in parenthesis and is calculated using replicate weights.
Source: U.S. Census Bureau, American Community Survey, Table HI-05. Health Insurance Coverage Status and Type of Coverage by State and Age for All People: 2019

Iowa

318 Amerigroup Iowa
P.O. Box 61010
Virginia Beach, IA 23466-1010
Toll-Free: 800-600-4441
Phone: 866-805-4589
www.myamerigroup.com/ia
Subsidiary of: Anthem, Inc.
For Profit Organization: Yes
Year Founded: 2016

Healthplan and Services Defined
 PLAN TYPE: Medicare
 Plan Specialty: Behavioral Health, Disease Management, Lab, Vision, Managed health care for people in public programs. Mental health and substance abuse services.
 Benefits Offered: Behavioral Health, Disease Management, Physical Therapy, Podiatry, Prescription, Vision, Wellness

Type of Coverage
 Medicaid

Key Personnel
 Dir., Long Term Services .... Kelly Espeland
 Director, Operations .... Jill Cook
 Mgr., Provider Relations.................... Julie Stuhr

319 Delta Dental of Iowa
P.O. Box 9010
Johnston, IA 50131-9010
Toll-Free: 800-544-0718
IndividualProduct@deltadentalia.com
www.deltadentalia.com
Non-Profit Organization: Yes
Year Founded: 1970

Healthplan and Services Defined
 PLAN TYPE: Dental
 Other Type: Dental PPO
 Model Type: Network
 Plan Specialty: Dental
 Benefits Offered: Dental

Type of Coverage
 Commercial

Type of Payment Plans Offered
 DFFS

Geographic Areas Served
 Statewide

Publishes and Distributes Report Card: Yes

Key Personnel
 President & CEO........................ Jeff Russell
 VP, Operations .... Liz Myers
 VP & Dental Director .... Jeffrey Chaffin
 VP, Finance & Controller................ Sherry Perkins
 VP, Marketing .... April Schmaltz
 VP, Technology .... Todd Herren

320 Healthy and Well Kids in Iowa (Hawki)
Toll-Free: 800-257-8563
Fax: 515-457-7701
hawk-i@dhs.state.ia.us
dhs.iowa.gov/hawki

Healthplan and Services Defined
 PLAN TYPE: HMO
 Plan Specialty: Chiropractic, Dental, Vision
 Benefits Offered: Behavioral Health, Chiropractic, Dental, Home Care, Prescription, Vision, Wellness

Geographic Areas Served
 Statewide

321 Humana Health Insurance of Iowa
3100 100th Street
Urbandale, IA 50322
Toll-Free: 866-653-7275
Phone: 515-400-8464
Fax: 515-278-7002
www.humana.com
Subsidiary of: Humana Inc.
For Profit Organization: Yes
Year Founded: 1961
Federally Qualified: Yes

Healthplan and Services Defined
 PLAN TYPE: HMO/PPO
 Model Type: Staff
 Plan Specialty: Dental
 Benefits Offered: Behavioral Health, Chiropractic, Dental, Disease Management, Prescription, Psychiatric, Wellness, Worker's Compensation, Life, LTD, STD

Type of Coverage
 Commercial, Individual, Supplemental Medicare

Geographic Areas Served
 Statewide

Accreditation Certification
 URAC, NCQA, CORE

Key Personnel
 Pres., North Central Reg. .... Chuck Dow

322 Iowa Total Care
636 E Grand Avenue
Des Moines, IA 50309
Toll-Free: 833-404-1061
Phone: 515-376-6214
www.iowatotalcare.com
Secondary Address: Imaging Center 4, P.O. Box 2027, Cedar Rapids, IA 52406
Subsidiary of: Centene Corporation
For Profit Organization: Yes

Healthplan and Services Defined
 PLAN TYPE: Other
 Model Type: Network
 Benefits Offered: Behavioral Health, Prescription, Vision, Wellness

Type of Coverage
Medicaid

Key Personnel
President/CEO .... Mitch Wasden

323 Medical Associates
1500 Associates Drive
Dubuque, IA 52002
Toll-Free: 800-648-6868
Phone: 563-584-3000
www.mahealthcare.com
Non-Profit Organization: Yes
Year Founded: 1982
Physician Owned Organization: Yes
Number of Primary Care Physicians: 170
Number of Referral/Specialty Physicians: 1,000
Total Enrollment: 45,000

Healthplan and Services Defined
PLAN TYPE: HMO
Model Type: Group
Plan Specialty: EPO
Benefits Offered: Behavioral Health, Chiropractic, Complementary Medicine, Home Care, Inpatient SNF, Physical Therapy, Podiatry, Prescription, Psychiatric, Transplant, Vision, Wellness

Type of Coverage
Commercial, Indemnity, Medicare, Supplemental Medicare

Type of Payment Plans Offered
POS

Geographic Areas Served
Iowa-Wisconsin-Illinois tri-state area

Accreditation Certification
NCQA

Key Personnel
Chief Executive Officer .... John Tallent
Director of Finance .... Jill Mitchell
Chief Operating Officer .... Zach Keeling

324 Mercy Health Network
1755 59th Place
West Des Moines, IA 50266
Phone: 515-358-8027
Fax: 515-358-8931
mhninfo@mercydesmoines.org
mercyone.org
Year Founded: 1998
Number of Affiliated Hospitals: 25

Healthplan and Services Defined
PLAN TYPE: HMO
Plan Specialty: Lab, Radiology, Cardiac Care
Benefits Offered: Chiropractic, Dental, Disease Management, Home Care, Physical Therapy, Podiatry, Prescription, Vision, Wellness

Type of Coverage
Individual

Geographic Areas Served
Clinton, Des Moines, Dubuque, North Iowa, Siouxland, Waterloo/Cedar Falls

Key Personnel
CEO .... John M. Starcher, Jr.
President/COO, Core Ops. .... Brian Smith
Chief Legal Officer .... Michael Bezney
Chief Financial Officer .... Deborah Bloomfield

325 Sanford Health Plan
300 Cherapa Place
Suite 201
Sioux Falls, SD 57103
Toll-Free: 888-234-2042
memberservices@sanfordhealth.org
www.sanfordhealthplan.org
Non-Profit Organization: Yes
Year Founded: 1996
Number of Affiliated Hospitals: 349
Total Enrollment: 50,000

Healthplan and Services Defined
PLAN TYPE: HMO
Model Type: IPA
Plan Specialty: Commercial Group
Benefits Offered: Disease Management, Home Care, Long-Term Care, Prescription, Wellness

Type of Coverage
Commercial, Individual, Medicare, Supplemental Medicare, Sec 125, TPA, Individual, Lg Group

Geographic Areas Served
Northwest Iowa, Southwest Minnesota, South Dakota

Accreditation Certification
NCQA

326 Trinity Health of Iowa
Mercy Health Network
1755 59th Place
West Des Moines, IA 50266
Phone: 515-358-8027
Fax: 515-358-8931
MHNinfo@mercydesmoines.org
www.trinity-health.org/iowa
Non-Profit Organization: Yes
Year Founded: 2013
Number of Affiliated Hospitals: 40

Healthplan and Services Defined
PLAN TYPE: Other
Benefits Offered: Disease Management, Home Care, Long-Term Care, Physical Therapy, Psychiatric, Hospice programs, Senior Living

Geographic Areas Served
Iowa, Nebraska, and South Dakota

Key Personnel
CEO. .... Bob Ritz
VP, Quality & Safety .... Stephanie Baron

VP, Marketing/Comm. Janell Pittman
jpittman@mercydesmoines.org
VP/General Counsel . . . . Marcia Smith
VP, Network Affiliates . . . . Mike Trachta
mtrachta@mercydesmoines.org
SVP, Operations/CFO . . . . Mike Wegner

327 UnitedHealthcare Community Plan Iowa

UnitedHealthcare Customer Service
P.O. Box 30769
Salt Lake City, UT 84130-0769
Toll-Free: 888-545-5205
www.uhccommunityplan.com/iowa
Subsidiary of: UnitedHealth Group
For Profit Organization: Yes

Healthplan and Services Defined
PLAN TYPE: Multiple
Model Type: Network
Benefits Offered: Home Care, Podiatry, Prescription, Wellness, Hearing

Type of Coverage
Medicare, Medicaid, CHIP

Geographic Areas Served
Appanoose, Benton, Black Hawk, Boone, Bremer, Buchanan, Butler, Carroll, Cedar, Chickasaw, Clarke, Clayton, Clinton, Dallas, Davis, Delaware, Des Moines, Fayette, Floyd, Greene, Grundy, Guthrie, Hamilton, Hardin, Henry, Iowa, Jackson, Jasper, Jefferson, Johnson, Jones, Keokuk, Linn, Louisa, Lucas, Madison, Mahaska, Marion, Marshall, Mills, Monroe, Muscatine, Polk, Pottawattamie, Poweshiek, Scott, Story, Tama, Van Buren, Wapello, Warren, Washington, Wayne, & Webster

328 UnitedHealthcare of Iowa

1089 Jordan Creek Parkway
Suite 320
West Des Moines, IA 50266
Toll-Free: 888-545-5205
www.uhc.com
Subsidiary of: UnitedHealth Group
For Profit Organization: Yes
Year Founded: 1984

Healthplan and Services Defined
PLAN TYPE: HMO/PPO
Model Type: Network
Plan Specialty: Behavioral Health, Dental, Disease Management, PBM, Vision
Benefits Offered: Behavioral Health, Dental, Disease Management, Long-Term Care, Prescription, Vision, Wellness, Life, LTD, STD

Type of Coverage
Commercial, Individual, Indemnity, Medicare, Supplemental Medicare, Medicaid, Catastrophic, Family, Military, Veterans, Group

Type of Payment Plans Offered
POS, DFFS, FFS

Geographic Areas Served
Statewide

Network Qualifications
Pre-Admission Certification: Yes

Peer Review Type
Utilization Review: Yes
Second Surgical Opinion: Yes
Case Management: Yes

Publishes and Distributes Report Card: Yes

Accreditation Certification
TJC Accreditation, Medicare Approved, Utilization Review, Pre-Admission Certification, State Licensure, Quality Assurance Program

Key Personnel
CEO, Community Plan IA . . . . Alissa Weber
CEO, IA/KS/NE/Central IL . . . . Rob Broomfield

329 Wellmark Blue Cross Blue Shield

1331 Grand Avenue
Des Moines, IA 50309
Toll-Free: 800-524-9242
Phone: 515-376-4500
www.wellmark.com
Secondary Address: 600 3rd Avenue SE, Suite 200, Cedar Rapids, IA 52401, 319-294-5950
Year Founded: 1939

Healthplan and Services Defined
PLAN TYPE: HMO
Model Type: IPA
Plan Specialty: ASO, Chiropractic, Disease Management, Lab, Vision, Radiology, UR
Benefits Offered: Chiropractic, Disease Management, Home Care, Inpatient SNF, Physical Therapy, Podiatry, Prescription, Psychiatric, Transplant, Vision, Wellness
Offers Demand Management Patient Information Service: Yes

Type of Coverage
Commercial, Individual, Indemnity, Medicare, Supplemental Medicare, Medicaid

Type of Payment Plans Offered
POS, Capitated

Geographic Areas Served
Iowa and South Dakota

Network Qualifications
Pre-Admission Certification: Yes

Peer Review Type
Utilization Review: Yes

Publishes and Distributes Report Card: Yes

Accreditation Certification
URAC, NCQA
TJC Accreditation, Medicare Approved, Utilization Review, Pre-Admission Certification, State Licensure, Quality Assurance Program

Key Personnel
President/CEO . . . . Cory R. Harris
EVP/CFO/Treasurer . . . . David Brown

EVP/CIO .... Paul Eddy
SVP/Chief Legal Officer .... John T. Clendenin
SVP, Operations .... Jared Landin

KANSAS

Health Insurance Coverage Status and Type of Coverage by Age

Category	All Persons Number	All Persons %	Under 19 years Number	Under 19 years %	Under 65 years Number	Under 65 years %
Total population	2,852 *(3)*	100.0 *(0.0)*	740 *(4)*	100.0 *(0.0)*	2,392 *(4)*	100.0 *(0.0)*
Covered by some type of health insurance	2,589 *(11)*	90.8 *(0.4)*	697 *(6)*	94.2 *(0.7)*	2,132 *(11)*	89.1 *(0.5)*
Covered by private health insurance	2,121 *(17)*	74.4 *(0.6)*	508 *(9)*	68.7 *(1.1)*	1,822 *(15)*	76.2 *(0.6)*
Employer-based	1,701 *(18)*	59.6 *(0.6)*	448 *(9)*	60.6 *(1.2)*	1,588 *(18)*	66.4 *(0.7)*
Direct purchase	446 *(12)*	15.6 *(0.4)*	51 *(4)*	6.9 *(0.6)*	242 *(11)*	10.1 *(0.4)*
TRICARE	109 *(7)*	3.8 *(0.2)*	32 *(4)*	4.3 *(0.5)*	77 *(6)*	3.2 *(0.3)*
Covered by public health insurance	845 *(12)*	29.6 *(0.4)*	220 *(8)*	29.7 *(1.1)*	400 *(12)*	16.7 *(0.5)*
Medicaid	380 *(13)*	13.3 *(0.5)*	218 *(8)*	29.4 *(1.1)*	342 *(12)*	14.3 *(0.5)*
Medicare	508 *(5)*	17.8 *(0.2)*	3 *(1)*	0.4 *(0.1)*	63 *(4)*	2.7 *(0.2)*
VA Care	69 *(4)*	2.4 *(0.1)*	2 *(1)*	0.3 *(0.2)*	32 *(3)*	1.3 *(0.1)*
Not covered at any time during the year	262 *(11)*	9.2 *(0.4)*	43 *(5)*	5.8 *(0.7)*	260 *(11)*	10.9 *(0.5)*

Note: Numbers in thousands; Figures cover civilian noninstitutionalized population in 2019; N/A indicates that data was not available; Z represents or rounds to zero; Margin of error appears in parenthesis and is calculated using replicate weights.
Source: U.S. Census Bureau, American Community Survey, Table HI-05. Health Insurance Coverage Status and Type of Coverage by State and Age for All People: 2019

Kansas

330 Advance Insurance Company of Kansas
1133 SW Topeka Boulevard
Topeka, KS 66629
Toll-Free: 800-530-5989
Phone: 785-273-9804
Fax: 785-290-0727
claims@advanceinsurance.com
www.advanceinsurance.com
Subsidiary of: Blue Cross & Blue Shield of Kansas
For Profit Organization: Yes
Total Enrollment: 121,000

Healthplan and Services Defined
  PLAN TYPE: Multiple
  Benefits Offered: AD&D, Life, LTD, STD

Geographic Areas Served
  all counties in Kansas except Johnson and Wyandotte

Key Personnel
  President . . . . Treena Mason
  VP/COO. . . . . Mike Eichten

331 Aetna Health of Kansas
151 Farmington Avenue
Hartford, CT 06156
Toll-Free: 866-851-0754
www.aetnastateofkansas.com
Subsidiary of: CVS Health / Aetna Inc.
For Profit Organization: Yes

Healthplan and Services Defined
  PLAN TYPE: HMO/PPO
  Other Type: POS
  Model Type: Network
  Plan Specialty: Behavioral Health, Dental, EPO, Lab, PBM, Vision, Radiology
  Benefits Offered: Behavioral Health, Dental, Disease Management, Long-Term Care, Physical Therapy, Podiatry, Prescription, Psychiatric, Vision, Wellness, Life, LTD, STD

Type of Coverage
  Commercial, Student health

Type of Payment Plans Offered
  POS, FFS

Geographic Areas Served
  Statewide

Key Personnel
  Sales Director . . . . Syd Warner

332 Aetna Health of Kansas
9401 Indian Creek Parkway
Suite 1300
Overland Park, KS 66210
Toll-Free: 855-221-5656
www.www.aetnabetterhealth.com/kansas
Subsidiary of: CVS Health / Aetna Inc.
For Profit Organization: Yes

Healthplan and Services Defined
  PLAN TYPE: HMO/PPO
  Other Type: POS
  Model Type: Network
  Plan Specialty: Behavioral Health, Dental, EPO, Lab, PBM, Vision, Radiology
  Benefits Offered: Behavioral Health, Dental, Disease Management, Long-Term Care, Physical Therapy, Podiatry, Prescription, Psychiatric, Vision, Wellness, Life, LTD, STD

Type of Coverage
  Commercial, Medicare, Medicaid, Student health

Geographic Areas Served
  Statewide

Key Personnel
  Provider Network Manager . . . . Irene Hermreck

333 Allwell from Sunflower Health Plan
8325 Lenexa Drive
Suite 410
Lenexa, KS 66214
Toll-Free: 855-565-9519
allwell.sunflowerhealthplan.com
Subsidiary of: Centene Corporation
For Profit Organization: Yes

Healthplan and Services Defined
  PLAN TYPE: Medicare
  Model Type: Network
  Benefits Offered: Dental, Prescription

Type of Coverage
  Medicare, Supplemental Medicare, Medicare Advantage

Geographic Areas Served
  Johnson, Leavenworth, Miami, Wyandotte, Cherokee, Crawford, and Sedgwick counties

334 Ambetter from Sunflower Health Plan
8325 Lenexa Drive
Suite 200
Lenexa, KS 66214
Toll-Free: 844-518-9505
ambetter.sunflowerhealthplan.com
Subsidiary of: Centene Corporation
For Profit Organization: Yes

Healthplan and Services Defined
  PLAN TYPE: Other
  Model Type: Network
  Plan Specialty: Lab
  Benefits Offered: Behavioral Health, Disease Management, Physical Therapy, Prescription, Wellness, Maternity and newborn care

Type of Coverage
  Health Insurance Marketplace

Geographic Areas Served
  Johnson, Leavenworth, Miami, and Wyandotte counties

335 Ascension At Home
Via Christi Home Health
1035 N Emporia, Suite 230
Wichita, KS 76214
Phone: 316-268-8588
Fax: 316-264-1265
ascensionathome.com
Subsidiary of: Ascension
Non-Profit Organization: Yes

Healthplan and Services Defined
PLAN TYPE: Other
Plan Specialty: Disease Management
Benefits Offered: Dental, Disease Management, Home Care, Wellness, Ambulance & Transportation; Nursing Service; Short-and-long-term care management planning; Hospice

Geographic Areas Served
Texas, Alabama, Indiana, Kansas, Michigan, Mississippi, Oklahoma, Wisconsin

Key Personnel
President.............................David Grams
Chair/CEO ....James A. Deal

336 Blue Cross and Blue Shield of Kansas
1133 SW Topeka Boulevard
Topeka, KS 66629
Toll-Free: 800-432-3990
Phone: 785-291-4180
www.bcbsks.com
For Profit Organization: Yes
Year Founded: 1942
Total Enrollment: 916,695
State Enrollment: 916,695

Healthplan and Services Defined
PLAN TYPE: HMO
Model Type: Staff
Benefits Offered: Behavioral Health, Chiropractic, Disease Management, Inpatient SNF, Podiatry, Prescription, Psychiatric, Wellness

Type of Coverage
Commercial, Individual

Geographic Areas Served
All counties in Kansas except Johnson and Wyandotte

Subscriber Information
Average Annual Deductible Per Subscriber:
    Employee Only (Self): $1,000
    Employee & 2 Family Members: $2,000
Average Subscriber Co-Payment:
    Primary Care Physician: $15.00
    Prescription Drugs: $5.00
    Hospital ER: $50.00

Accreditation Certification
TJC, URAC

Key Personnel
President/CEO.........................Matt All
VP, Finance ....Jeff Bergman
VP, Operations.....................Holly Graves
VP, HR & Admin. Services..............Nicki Flanagan
SVP, Provider/Gov Affairs.......John K. Fong, MD, MBA
VP, IT Services/CIO ....Matt Langdon
VP, Legal Services.....................Clay Britton
VP, Sales/Operations..................Treena Mason

337 CareCentrix: Kansas
6130 Sprint Parkway
Suite 200
Overland Park, KS 66211
Toll-Free: 800-808-1902
carecentrix.com
Year Founded: 1996
Number of Primary Care Physicians: 8,000
Total Enrollment: 26,000,000

Healthplan and Services Defined
PLAN TYPE: HMO
Benefits Offered: Home Care, Physical Therapy, Durable Medical Equipment; Occupational & Respiratory Therapy; Orthotics; Prosthetics

338 Delta Dental of Kansas
1619 N Waterfront Parkway
P.O. Box 789769
Wichita, KS 67278-9769
Toll-Free: 800-733-5823
Phone: 316-264-1099
Fax: 316-462-3392
moreinfo@deltadentalks.com
www.deltadentalks.com
Secondary Address: 11300 Tomahawk Creek Parkway, Pinnacle Corporate Centre, Suite 350, Leawood, KS 66211, 913-381-4928
Non-Profit Organization: Yes
Year Founded: 1972

Healthplan and Services Defined
PLAN TYPE: Dental
Other Type: Dental PPO
Model Type: Network
Plan Specialty: Dental
Benefits Offered: Dental

Type of Coverage
Commercial, Individual

Type of Payment Plans Offered
DFFS

Geographic Areas Served
Statewide

Network Qualifications
Pre-Admission Certification: Yes

Publishes and Distributes Report Card: Yes

Key Personnel
President & CEO ....Dean Newton
Chief Sales Officer ....Natalie Daney
Chief Financial Officer ....Bryce Dougherty
Chief Operating Officer................Patrick Tuttle
In-House Counsel.....................Jennifer Bauer

Kansas

VP, Information . . . . Bob Ebenkamp
Controller . . . . Michael Ellis

339 Health Partners of Kansas
550 N Lorraine Street
Wichita, KS 67214
Phone: 316-652-1327
www.hpkansas.com
Subsidiary of: Wesley Medical Center
For Profit Organization: Yes
Year Founded: 1987
Number of Affiliated Hospitals: 149
Number of Primary Care Physicians: 1,000
Number of Referral/Specialty Physicians: 6,000
Total Enrollment: 95,000
State Enrollment: 95,000

Healthplan and Services Defined
PLAN TYPE: PPO
Model Type: IPA, Network
Benefits Offered: Worker's Compensation, Network Rental, Provider Servicing, Provider Credentialing

Type of Coverage
Catastrophic Illness Benefit: Maximum $1M

Type of Payment Plans Offered
POS, DFFS, Capitated, FFS, Combination FFS & DFFS

Geographic Areas Served
Statewide

Network Qualifications
Pre-Admission Certification: Yes

Peer Review Type
Utilization Review: Yes
Second Surgical Opinion: Yes
Case Management: Yes

Key Personnel
President . . . . Gaylee Dolloff
Vice President . . . . Teresa Montenegro

Specialty Managed Care Partners
Enters into Contracts with Regional Business Coalitions: No

340 Humana Health Insurance of Kansas
7311 W 132nd Street
Suite 200
Overland Park, KS 66213
Toll-Free: 800-842-6188
Phone: 913-217-3333
Fax: 913-217-3245
www.humana.com
Subsidiary of: Humana Inc.
For Profit Organization: Yes
Year Founded: 1985

Healthplan and Services Defined
PLAN TYPE: HMO/PPO
Model Type: IPA
Plan Specialty: Dental, Vision
Benefits Offered: Dental, Disease Management, Prescription, Vision, Wellness, Life, LTD, STD

Type of Coverage
Commercial, Individual

Geographic Areas Served
Kansas City metro area

Subscriber Information
Average Monthly Fee Per Subscriber
(Employee + Employer Contribution):
Employee Only (Self): $150.44
Employee & 1 Family Member: $354.06
Employee & 2 Family Members: $354.06
Medicare: $196.48
Average Subscriber Co-Payment:
Primary Care Physician: $5.00
Non-Network Physician: Not covered
Prescription Drugs: $5.00
Hospital ER: $25.00
Home Health Care: $0
Nursing Home: $0
Nursing Home Max. Days/Visits Covered: 60 days

Accreditation Certification
URAC, NCQA, CORE

Key Personnel
Sales Director . . . . David Brown

Average Claim Compensation
Physician's Fees Charged: 70%
Hospital's Fees Charged: 60%

Specialty Managed Care Partners
Enters into Contracts with Regional Business Coalitions: Yes

341 Mercy Clinic Kansas
220 N Pennsylvania Avenue
Columbus, KS 66725
Phone: 620-429-2545
mercy.net
Subsidiary of: IBM Watson Health
Non-Profit Organization: Yes
Number of Affiliated Hospitals: 44
Number of Primary Care Physicians: 700
Number of Referral/Specialty Physicians: 2,000

Healthplan and Services Defined
PLAN TYPE: HMO
Benefits Offered: Behavioral Health, Disease Management, Home Care, Physical Therapy, Podiatry, Vision, Wellness, Non-Surgical Weight Loss; Urgent Care; Dermatology; Rehabilitation; Breast Cancer; Orthopedics; Ostoclerosis; Pediatrics

Geographic Areas Served
Arkansas, Kansas, Missouri, and Oklahoma

Key Personnel
President, Joplin/Kansas . . . . Tracy Godfrey, MD

342 PCC Preferred Chiropractic Care

555 North McLean Boulevard
Suite 301
Wichita, KS 67203
Toll-Free: 800-611-3048
Phone: 316-263-7800
Fax: 316-263-7814
providerrelations@pccnetwork.com
www.pccnetwork.com
For Profit Organization: Yes
Year Founded: 1984
Physician Owned Organization: No
Federally Qualified: No
Number of Primary Care Physicians: 3,500
Total Enrollment: 5,000,000

Healthplan and Services Defined
PLAN TYPE: PPO
Model Type: Network
Plan Specialty: Chiropractic
Benefits Offered: Chiropractic, Disease Management, Wellness, Worker's Compensation
Offers Demand Management Patient Information Service: Yes
DMPI Services Offered: Chiropractic, Physical Therapy

Type of Coverage
Medicaid

Type of Payment Plans Offered
POS, DFFS, Capitated, FFS, Combination FFS & DFFS

Geographic Areas Served
Nationwide

Network Qualifications
Pre-Admission Certification: No

Peer Review Type
Utilization Review: Yes
Second Surgical Opinion: Yes
Case Management: No

Publishes and Distributes Report Card: No

Accreditation Certification
URAC, NCQA

Key Personnel
President and CEO . . . . Brad Dopps

Average Claim Compensation
Physician's Fees Charged: 80%

Specialty Managed Care Partners
Enters into Contracts with Regional Business Coalitions: Yes

Employer References
Preferred Health Systems, fiserv, Health Partners of Kansas

343 Preferred Mental Health Management

7309 E 21st N Street
Suite 110
Wichita, KS 67206
Toll-Free: 800-819-9571
Phone: 316-262-0444
www.pmhm.com
Subsidiary of: Family Health America
Year Founded: 1987
Number of Affiliated Hospitals: 1,900
Number of Primary Care Physicians: 10,500
Number of Referral/Specialty Physicians: 4,000
Total Enrollment: 400,000

Healthplan and Services Defined
PLAN TYPE: Multiple
Model Type: Network
Plan Specialty: Mental Health
Benefits Offered: Behavioral Health, Prescription, Psychiatric, Substance Abuse
Offers Demand Management Patient Information Service: Yes

Type of Coverage
Work

Geographic Areas Served
Nationwide including Puerto Rico

Network Qualifications
Minimum Years of Practice: 6
Pre-Admission Certification: Yes

Peer Review Type
Utilization Review: Yes

Publishes and Distributes Report Card: Yes

Accreditation Certification
URAC, NCQA
TJC Accreditation, Utilization Review, Pre-Admission Certification, State Licensure, Quality Assurance Program

Key Personnel
President/CEO . . . . Les Ruthven, PhD
316-262-0444

Specialty Managed Care Partners
Enters into Contracts with Regional Business Coalitions: No

344 Preferred Vision Care

P.O. Box 26025
Overland Park, KS 66225-6025
Phone: 913-451-1672
Fax: 913-451-1704
customerservice@preferredvisioncare.com
preferredvisioncare.com
For Profit Organization: Yes
Owned by an Integrated Delivery Network (IDN): Yes

Healthplan and Services Defined
PLAN TYPE: Vision
Other Type: PPO
Model Type: Network
Plan Specialty: Vision
Benefits Offered: Vision

Type of Coverage
Commercial
Catastrophic Illness Benefit: Unlimited

Type of Payment Plans Offered
POS, DFFS

Network Qualifications
Pre-Admission Certification: No

151

Peer Review Type
 Utilization Review: Yes
 Second Surgical Opinion: Yes
 Case Management: Yes

Publishes and Distributes Report Card: Yes

Accreditation Certification
 URAC
 Quality Assurance Program

Key Personnel
 CEO .... Paul J. Disser

Specialty Managed Care Partners
 Enters into Contracts with Regional Business Coalitions: Yes

345 ProviDRs Care Network
238 N Waco
Wichita, KS 67202
Toll-Free: 800-801-9772
Phone: 316-683-4111
Fax: 316-683-1271
customerservice@providrscare.net
www.providrscare.net
Subsidiary of: Medical Society Medical Review Foundation
For Profit Organization: Yes
Year Founded: 1985
Physician Owned Organization: Yes
Number of Affiliated Hospitals: 173
Number of Primary Care Physicians: 14,000
Total Enrollment: 152,000

Healthplan and Services Defined
 PLAN TYPE: PPO
 Model Type: Group
 Benefits Offered: Behavioral Health, Chiropractic, Home Care, Physical Therapy, Podiatry, Psychiatric, Transplant, Worker's Compensation

Type of Coverage
 Commercial, Individual

Type of Payment Plans Offered
 POS

Geographic Areas Served
 Kansas, Southwest Missouri; parts of Oklahoma and Nebraska; 1 county in Colorado

Subscriber Information
 Average Monthly Fee Per Subscriber
 (Employee + Employer Contribution):
  Employee Only (Self): $3.00
  Employee & 1 Family Member: $3.00
  Employee & 2 Family Members: $3.00
 Average Annual Deductible Per Subscriber:
  Employee Only (Self): Varies
  Employee & 1 Family Member: Varies
 Average Subscriber Co-Payment:
  Primary Care Physician: Varies
  Non-Network Physician: Varies
  Prescription Drugs: Varies
  Hospital ER: Varies

Network Qualifications
 Pre-Admission Certification: Yes

Peer Review Type
 Utilization Review: Yes
 Second Surgical Opinion: Yes
 Case Management: No

Publishes and Distributes Report Card: No

Accreditation Certification
 URAC
 TJC Accreditation, Medicare Approved, Utilization Review, Pre-Admission Certification, State Licensure, Quality Assurance Program

Key Personnel
 Chief Executive Officer .... Karen Cox
  316-683-0665
  karencox@providrscare.net
 Chief Operating Officer................... Justin Leitzen
  316-683-0604
  justinleitzen@providrscare.net
 Claims Manager .... Jeanne Hingst
  316-683-4111
  jeannehingst@providrscare.net
 Director of Claims/Info .... Nikki Sade
  316-683-0805
  nikkisade@providrscare.net

Specialty Managed Care Partners
 Enters into Contracts with Regional Business Coalitions: No

Employer References
 Western Resources, Kansas Health Insurance Association, Medicalodges, County of Reno Kansas, National Cooperative of Refineries Association

346 Sunflower Health Plan
8325 Lenexa Drive
Suite 200
Lenexa, KS 66214
Toll-Free: 877-644-4623
www.sunflowerhealthplan.com
Subsidiary of: Centene Corporation
For Profit Organization: Yes

Healthplan and Services Defined
 PLAN TYPE: Other
 Model Type: Network
 Benefits Offered: Behavioral Health, Prescription, Vision

Type of Coverage
 Medicaid

Key Personnel
 President/CEO...................... Michael Stephens
 Chief Operating Officer .... Jonalan Smith

347 UnitedHealthcare Community Plan Kansas
UnitedHealthcare Customer Service
P.O. Box 30769
Salt Lake City, UT 84130-0769
Toll-Free: 888-545-5205
www.uhccommunityplan.com/ks

Subsidiary of: UnitedHealth Group
For Profit Organization: Yes

Healthplan and Services Defined
PLAN TYPE: Medicare
Other Type: Medicaid
Model Type: Network
Benefits Offered: Dental, Prescription, Hearing, Acupuncture, Chiropractic

Type of Coverage
Medicare, Medicaid

Geographic Areas Served
Butler, Cowley, Douglas, Franklin, Harvey, Jackson, Jefferson, Johnson, Leavenworth, Miami, Osage, Sedgwick, Sumner, and Wyandotte. Other plans statewide

Key Personnel
CEO, Community Plan KS .... Kevin Sparks
kevin_sparks@uhc.com

---

348 UnitedHealthcare of Kansas
6860 W 115th Street
Overland Park, KS 66211
Toll-Free: 877-542-9238
www.uhc.com
Subsidiary of: UnitedHealth Group
For Profit Organization: Yes

Healthplan and Services Defined
PLAN TYPE: HMO/PPO
Model Type: Network
Plan Specialty: Behavioral Health, Dental, Disease Management, PBM, Vision
Benefits Offered: Behavioral Health, Dental, Disease Management, Long-Term Care, Prescription, Vision, Wellness, Life, LTD, STD

Type of Coverage
Individual, Medicare, Supplemental Medicare, Medicaid, Catastrophic, Family, Military, Veterans, Group

Geographic Areas Served
Statewide

Key Personnel
CEO, IA/KS/NE/Central IL............. Rob Broomfield

KENTUCKY

Health Insurance Coverage Status and Type of Coverage by Age

Category	All Persons Number	%	Under 19 years Number	%	Under 65 years Number	%
Total population	4,385 *(2)*	100.0 *(0.0)*	1,059 *(5)*	100.0 *(0.0)*	3,653 *(4)*	100.0 *(0.0)*
Covered by some type of health insurance	4,102 *(13)*	93.6 *(0.3)*	1,013 *(7)*	95.7 *(0.5)*	3,373 *(13)*	92.3 *(0.4)*
Covered by private health insurance	2,795 *(25)*	63.7 *(0.6)*	588 *(13)*	55.5 *(1.2)*	2,351 *(25)*	64.4 *(0.7)*
Employer-based	2,320 *(27)*	52.9 *(0.6)*	523 *(14)*	49.5 *(1.3)*	2,087 *(26)*	57.1 *(0.7)*
Direct purchase	513 *(14)*	11.7 *(0.3)*	56 *(5)*	5.3 *(0.5)*	268 *(11)*	7.3 *(0.3)*
TRICARE	121 *(8)*	2.8 *(0.2)*	22 *(3)*	2.1 *(0.3)*	79 *(6)*	2.2 *(0.2)*
Covered by public health insurance	1,893 *(24)*	43.2 *(0.5)*	470 *(13)*	44.4 *(1.2)*	1,177 *(24)*	32.2 *(0.7)*
Medicaid	1,135 *(25)*	25.9 *(0.6)*	466 *(13)*	44.0 *(1.2)*	1,034 *(24)*	28.3 *(0.7)*
Medicare	899 *(8)*	20.5 *(0.2)*	7 *(2)*	0.7 *(0.2)*	184 *(8)*	5.0 *(0.2)*
VA Care	118 *(5)*	2.7 *(0.1)*	2 *(1)*	0.2 *(0.1)*	51 *(4)*	1.4 *(0.1)*
Not covered at any time during the year	283 *(14)*	6.4 *(0.3)*	45 *(5)*	4.3 *(0.5)*	280 *(13)*	7.7 *(0.4)*

Note: Numbers in thousands; Figures cover civilian noninstitutionalized population in 2019; N/A indicates that data was not available; Z represents or rounds to zero; Margin of error appears in parenthesis and is calculated using replicate weights.
Source: U.S. Census Bureau, American Community Survey, Table HI-05. Health Insurance Coverage Status and Type of Coverage by State and Age for All People: 2019

Kentucky

349 Aetna Better Health of Kentucky
9900 Corporate Campus Drive
Suite 1000
Louisville, KY 40223
Toll-Free: 855-300-5528
Fax: 855-454-5578
www.aetnabetterhealth.com/kentucky
Mailing Address: P.O. Box 65195, Phoenix, AZ 85082-6125
Subsidiary of: CVS Health / Aetna Inc.
For Profit Organization: Yes

Healthplan and Services Defined
PLAN TYPE: HMO/PPO
Other Type: POS
Model Type: Network
Plan Specialty: Behavioral Health, EPO, Lab, PBM, Radiology
Benefits Offered: Behavioral Health, Dental, Disease Management, Long-Term Care, Physical Therapy, Podiatry, Prescription, Psychiatric, Vision, Wellness, Life, LTD, STD

Type of Coverage
Commercial, Medicaid, Student health

Type of Payment Plans Offered
POS, FFS

Geographic Areas Served
Statewide

Key Personnel
CEO . . . . Jonathan Copley
Network Relations Manager . . . . Michelle Marrs
Dir., Quality Management . . . . Jennifer Ruehl Nachreiner

350 Aetna Medicare
P.O. Box 14088
Lexington, KY 40512
Toll-Free: 855-335-1407
www.aetnamedicare.com
Subsidiary of: CVS Health / Aetna Inc.
For Profit Organization: Yes

Healthplan and Services Defined
PLAN TYPE: Medicare
Model Type: Network
Benefits Offered: Chiropractic, Dental, Disease Management, Home Care, Inpatient SNF, Physical Therapy, Prescription, Psychiatric, Vision, Wellness

Type of Coverage
Individual, Medicare, Supplemental Medicare

Geographic Areas Served
Available in multiple states

Subscriber Information
Average Monthly Fee Per Subscriber
 (Employee + Employer Contribution):
  Employee Only (Self): Varies
  Medicare: Varies
Average Annual Deductible Per Subscriber:
  Employee Only (Self): Varies
  Medicare: Varies
Average Subscriber Co-Payment:
  Primary Care Physician: Varies
  Non-Network Physician: Varies
  Prescription Drugs: Varies
  Hospital ER: Varies
  Home Health Care: Varies
  Home Health Care Max. Days/Visits Covered: Varies

Key Personnel
President. . . . . Christopher Ciano

351 Anthem Blue Cross & Blue Shield of Kentucky
1792 Alysheba Way
Suite 200
Lexington, KY 40509
Toll-Free: 800-331-1476
Phone: 859-226-5300
www.anthem.com
Secondary Address: 13550 Triton Park Boulevard, Louisville, KY 40223, 800-880-2583
Subsidiary of: Anthem, Inc.
For Profit Organization: Yes

Healthplan and Services Defined
PLAN TYPE: HMO/PPO
Model Type: Network
Plan Specialty: Behavioral Health, Dental, Disease Management, Lab, PBM, Vision, Radiology
Benefits Offered: Behavioral Health, Dental, Disease Management, Inpatient SNF, Physical Therapy, Prescription, Psychiatric, Transplant, Vision, Wellness, Life

Type of Coverage
Commercial, Individual, Medicare, Supplemental Medicare, Catastrophic

Geographic Areas Served
Statewide

Accreditation Certification
URAC, NCQA

Key Personnel
President, Medicaid KY. . . . . Kennan Wethington

352 CareSource Kentucky
10200 Forest Green Boulevard
Suite 400
Louisville, KY 40223
Phone: 502-213-4700
www.caresource.com
Non-Profit Organization: Yes
Total Enrollment: 1,900,000

Healthplan and Services Defined
PLAN TYPE: Medicare
Benefits Offered: Chiropractic, Dental, Podiatry, Prescription, Psychiatric, Vision

Type of Coverage
Medicare, Medicaid

Geographic Areas Served
Statewide

Key Personnel
Dir., Administration . . . . Samantha Harrison
Regulatory Contract Mgr. . . . . Brian K. Staples
Quality Improvement Mgr. . . . . Sanggil Tsai
Dir., Pharmacy Operations . . . . Joe Vennari
President, KY & WV . . . . Michael Taylor

353 CareSource West Virginia
230 N Main Street
Dayton, OH 45402
Phone: 937-224-3300
www.caresource.com
Non-Profit Organization: Yes
Total Enrollment: 1,900,000

Healthplan and Services Defined
PLAN TYPE: Medicare

Type of Coverage
Medicare, Medicaid

Geographic Areas Served
West Virginia counties: Barbour, Boone, Calhoun, Clay, Doddridge, Fayette, Gilmer, Harrison, Jackson, Logan, Marion, Monongalia, Pleasants, Preston, Raleigh, Ritchie, Roane, Taylor, Tyler, Wetzel, Wirt and Wood

Key Personnel
President, KY & WV . . . . Michael Taylor

354 Delta Dental of Kentucky
10100 Linn Station Road
Louisville, KY 40223
Toll-Free: 800-955-2030
Fax: 877-224-0052
kentucky.deltadental.com
Non-Profit Organization: Yes
Year Founded: 1966
Number of Primary Care Physicians: 4,000

Healthplan and Services Defined
PLAN TYPE: Dental
Other Type: Dental PPO
Model Type: IPA
Plan Specialty: Dental
Benefits Offered: Dental

Type of Coverage
Commercial, Individual

Type of Payment Plans Offered
DFFS

Geographic Areas Served
Statewide

Peer Review Type
Utilization Review: Yes
Second Surgical Opinion: Yes
Case Management: Yes

Publishes and Distributes Report Card: Yes

Key Personnel
President/CEO . . . . J. Jude Thompson
VP/Chief Finance Officer. . . . . Chris Green
VP/Adminstrative Officer . . . . Angie Zuvon Nenni
VP/Chief Revenue Officer . . . . Brian Hart
VP/Information Officer. Ron Story

Specialty Managed Care Partners
Enters into Contracts with Regional Business Coalitions: Yes

355 Humana Inc.
Humana Tower
500 West Main Street
Louisville, KY 40202
Toll-Free: 800-457-4708
www.humana.com
For Profit Organization: Yes
Year Founded: 1961
Total Enrollment: 10,000,000

Healthplan and Services Defined
PLAN TYPE: Multiple
Model Type: Network
Plan Specialty: Dental, Vision
Benefits Offered: Dental, Prescription, Vision, Life, LTD, STD

Type of Coverage
Commercial, Individual, Medicare, Supplemental Medicare, Medicaid

Geographic Areas Served
Statewide

Accreditation Certification
URAC, NCQA

Key Personnel
President & CEO . . . . Bruce D. Broussard
Chief Strategy Officer . . . . Vishal Agrawal, MD
CFO . . . . Susan M. Diamond
CAO. . . . . Tim Huval
Chief Medical Officer . . . . William H. Shrank, MD
Chief Legal Officer . . . . Joseph Ventura

356 Humana Medicare
Humana Correspondence Office
P.O. Box 14601
Lexington, KY 40512-4601
Toll-Free: 800-457-4708
www.humana.com/medicare
Subsidiary of: Humana Inc.
For Profit Organization: Yes

Healthplan and Services Defined
PLAN TYPE: Medicare
Benefits Offered: Chiropractic, Dental, Home Care, Inpatient SNF, Physical Therapy, Podiatry, Prescription, Psychiatric, Vision, Wellness

Type of Coverage
Individual, Medicare, Supplemental Medicare

Geographic Areas Served
Available in multiple states

Subscriber Information
Average Monthly Fee Per Subscriber
(Employee + Employer Contribution):
Employee Only (Self): Varies
Medicare: Varies
Average Annual Deductible Per Subscriber:
Employee Only (Self): Varies
Medicare: Varies
Average Subscriber Co-Payment:
Primary Care Physician: Varies
Non-Network Physician: Varies
Prescription Drugs: Varies
Hospital ER: Varies
Home Health Care: Varies
Home Health Care Max. Days/Visits Covered: Varies
Nursing Home: Varies
Nursing Home Max. Days/Visits Covered: Varies

Accreditation Certification
URAC, NCQA, CORE

Key Personnel
Segment President, Retail . . . . Alan Wheatley

357 Passport Health Plan
5100 Commerce Crossings Drive
Louisville, KY 40229
Toll-Free: 800-578-0603
Phone: 502-585-7900
www.passporthealthplan.com
Subsidiary of: AmeriHealth Mercy Health Plan
Non-Profit Organization: Yes
Year Founded: 1997
Total Enrollment: 300,000
State Enrollment: 300,000

Healthplan and Services Defined
PLAN TYPE: HMO

Type of Coverage
Medicaid

Geographic Areas Served
Jefferson, Oldham, Trimble, Carroll, Henry, Shelby, Spencer, Bullitt, Nelson, Washington, Marion, Larue, Hardin, Grayson, Meade, Breckinridge counties

Accreditation Certification
NCQA

Key Personnel
Chief Executive Officer. . . . . Scott A. Bowers
Chief Financial Officer. . . . . Scott Worthington
VP/Chief Medical Officer . . . . . . Stephen J. Houghland, MD
VP/Chief Marketing . . . . Jill Joseph Bell
VP, Human Resources . . . . Gary Bensing
Chief Operations Officer. . . . . Shawn Elman

358 Rural Carrier Benefit Plan
P.O. Box 14079
Lexington, KY 40512-4079
Toll-Free: 800-638-8432
www.rcbphealth.com
Subsidiary of: Aetna Inc.

Healthplan and Services Defined
PLAN TYPE: PPO
Benefits Offered: Disease Management, Prescription, Vision, Wellness, Cancer Treatment; Kidney Dialysis; 24-hour Nurse Line; Travel Assistance Program; Healthy Maternity; Quest Lab Program

Type of Coverage
Commercial, Individual

Type of Payment Plans Offered
Capitated, FFS

Subscriber Information
Average Monthly Fee Per Subscriber
(Employee + Employer Contribution):
Employee Only (Self): $73.11
Employee & 2 Family Members: $119.87
Average Annual Deductible Per Subscriber:
Employee & 2 Family Members: $350.00
Average Subscriber Co-Payment:
Primary Care Physician: 10%
Prescription Drugs: $20 - $30
Hospital ER: $0

359 UnitedHealthcare Community Plan Kentucky
UnitedHealthcare Customer Service
P.O. Box 30769
Salt Lake City, UT 84130-0769
Toll-Free: 888-545-5205
www.uhccommunityplan.com/ky
Subsidiary of: UnitedHealth Group
For Profit Organization: Yes

Healthplan and Services Defined
PLAN TYPE: Medicare
Other Type: Medicaid
Model Type: Network
Benefits Offered: Dental, Prescription, Wellness

Type of Coverage
Medicare, Medicaid

Geographic Areas Served
Boone, Bullitt, Campbell, Fayette, Franklin, Hardin, Jefferson, Jessamine, Kenton, Larue, Madison, Marion, Nelson, Oldham, Shelby, Spencer, and Woodford

Key Personnel
CEO, Community Plan KY . . . . Krista Hensel
krista_hensel@uhc.com

360 UnitedHealthcare of Kentucky

9100 Shelbyville Road
Suite 270
Louisville, KY 40222
Toll-Free: 888-545-5205
Phone: 502-318-1863
Fax: 502-318-1874
www.uhc.com
Subsidiary of: UnitedHealth Group
For Profit Organization: Yes
Year Founded: 1986

Healthplan and Services Defined
PLAN TYPE: HMO/PPO
Model Type: Network
Plan Specialty: Behavioral Health, Dental, Disease Management, PBM, Vision
Benefits Offered: Behavioral Health, Chiropractic, Dental, Disease Management, Long-Term Care, Prescription, Vision, Wellness, Life, LTD, STD

Type of Coverage
Individual, Medicare, Supplemental Medicare, Medicaid, Catastrophic, Family, Military, Veterans, Group, Catastrophic Illness Benefit: Maximum $1M

Type of Payment Plans Offered
POS

Geographic Areas Served
Central Kentucky: 99 counties

Subscriber Information
Average Monthly Fee Per Subscriber
(Employee + Employer Contribution):
Employee Only (Self): $139.00
Employee & 1 Family Member: $282.00
Employee & 2 Family Members: $445.00
Medicare: $0
Average Annual Deductible Per Subscriber:
Employee Only (Self): $0
Employee & 1 Family Member: $0
Employee & 2 Family Members: $0
Average Subscriber Co-Payment:
Primary Care Physician: $10.00
Non-Network Physician: Not covered
Prescription Drugs: $7.00
Hospital ER: $50.00
Home Health Care: 20%
Nursing Home: Not covered

Network Qualifications
Pre-Admission Certification: Yes

Peer Review Type
Utilization Review: Yes
Second Surgical Opinion: No
Case Management: Yes

Publishes and Distributes Report Card: Yes

Accreditation Certification
TJC Accreditation, Utilization Review, Pre-Admission Certification, State Licensure, Quality Assurance Program

Key Personnel
CEO, IN/KY . . . . Kim Sonerholm

Average Claim Compensation
Physician's Fees Charged: 1%
Hospital's Fees Charged: 1%

Specialty Managed Care Partners
Enters into Contracts with Regional Business Coalitions: Yes

LOUISIANA

Health Insurance Coverage Status and Type of Coverage by Age

Category	All Persons Number	%	Under 19 years Number	%	Under 65 years Number	%
Total population	4,540 *(3)*	100.0 *(0.0)*	1,149 *(5)*	100.0 *(0.0)*	3,817 *(4)*	100.0 *(0.0)*
Covered by some type of health insurance	4,135 *(14)*	91.1 *(0.3)*	1,099 *(9)*	95.6 *(0.6)*	3,418 *(14)*	89.5 *(0.4)*
Covered by private health insurance	2,625 *(30)*	57.8 *(0.7)*	555 *(14)*	48.3 *(1.2)*	2,247 *(28)*	58.9 *(0.7)*
Employer-based	2,160 *(29)*	47.6 *(0.6)*	486 *(13)*	42.3 *(1.1)*	1,941 *(28)*	50.9 *(0.7)*
Direct purchase	509 *(16)*	11.2 *(0.4)*	59 *(7)*	5.2 *(0.6)*	321 *(16)*	8.4 *(0.4)*
TRICARE	121 *(9)*	2.7 *(0.2)*	27 *(5)*	2.4 *(0.4)*	76 *(9)*	2.0 *(0.2)*
Covered by public health insurance	2,013 *(24)*	44.3 *(0.5)*	589 *(14)*	51.2 *(1.2)*	1,318 *(24)*	34.5 *(0.6)*
Medicaid	1,320 *(23)*	29.1 *(0.5)*	585 *(14)*	50.9 *(1.2)*	1,205 *(23)*	31.6 *(0.6)*
Medicare	848 *(10)*	18.7 *(0.2)*	4 *(1)*	0.4 *(0.1)*	154 *(8)*	4.0 *(0.2)*
VA Care	101 *(6)*	2.2 *(0.1)*	2 *(2)*	0.2 *(0.1)*	47 *(4)*	1.2 *(0.1)*
Not covered at any time during the year	404 *(14)*	8.9 *(0.3)*	50 *(7)*	4.4 *(0.6)*	399 *(14)*	10.5 *(0.4)*

Note: Numbers in thousands; Figures cover civilian noninstitutionalized population in 2019; N/A indicates that data was not available; Z represents or rounds to zero; Margin of error appears in parenthesis and is calculated using replicate weights.
Source: U.S. Census Bureau, American Community Survey, Table HI-05. Health Insurance Coverage Status and Type of Coverage by State and Age for All People: 2019

Louisiana

361 Aetna Better Health of Louisiana
2400 Veterans Memorial Boulevard
Suite 200
Kenner, LA 70062
Toll-Free: 855-242-0802
Fax: 866-776-2813
AetnaBetterHealth-LA-MemberServices@Aetna.com
www.aetnabetterhealth.com/louisiana
Subsidiary of: CVS Health / Aetna Inc.
For Profit Organization: Yes

Healthplan and Services Defined
  PLAN TYPE: HMO/PPO
  Other Type: POS
  Model Type: Network
  Plan Specialty: Behavioral Health, Dental, EPO, Lab, PBM, Vision, Radiology
  Benefits Offered: Behavioral Health, Dental, Disease Management, Long-Term Care, Physical Therapy, Podiatry, Prescription, Psychiatric, Vision, Wellness, Life, LTD, STD

Type of Coverage
  Commercial, Medicaid, Student health

Type of Payment Plans Offered
  POS, FFS

Geographic Areas Served
  Statewide with some exceptions

Key Personnel
  CEO .... Rick Born

362 Allwell from Louisiana Healthcare Connections
P.O. Box 84180
Baton Rouge, LA 70884
Toll-Free: 855-766-1572
allwell.louisianahealthconnect.com
Subsidiary of: Centene Corporation
For Profit Organization: Yes

Healthplan and Services Defined
  PLAN TYPE: Medicare
  Model Type: Network
  Benefits Offered: Dental, Prescription

Type of Coverage
  Medicare, Supplemental Medicare, Medicare Advantage

Geographic Areas Served
  Ascension, East Baton Rouge, Iberville, Livingston, Pointe Coupee, St. James, Tangipahoa, Washington, West Baton Rouge, St. Tammany, Acadia, Lafayette, St. Landry, and St. Martin parishes

363 Blue Cross and Blue Shield of Louisiana
5525 Reitz Avenue
Baton Rouge, LA 70809
Toll-Free: 800-495-2583
Phone: 225-295-2527
www.bcbsla.com
Secondary Address: 4508 Coliseum Boulevard, Suite A, Alexandria, LA 71303, 318-442-8107
For Profit Organization: Yes
Year Founded: 1934
Number of Affiliated Hospitals: 39
Number of Primary Care Physicians: 962
Number of Referral/Specialty Physicians: 2,219
Total Enrollment: 1,800,000
State Enrollment: 1,800,000

Healthplan and Services Defined
  PLAN TYPE: HMO/PPO
  Model Type: Network
  Benefits Offered: Behavioral Health, Disease Management, Prescription, Wellness

Type of Coverage
  Commercial, Individual, Medicare, Supplemental Medicare
  Catastrophic Illness Benefit: Maximum $2M

Type of Payment Plans Offered
  POS

Geographic Areas Served
  statewide

Subscriber Information
  Average Subscriber Co-Payment:
    Primary Care Physician: 10%/20%
    Home Health Care: Varies

Network Qualifications
  Pre-Admission Certification: Yes

Peer Review Type
  Utilization Review: Yes

Publishes and Distributes Report Card: No

Accreditation Certification
  URAC, NCQA
  TJC Accreditation, Medicare Approved, Utilization Review, Pre-Admission Certification, State Licensure, Quality Assurance Program

Key Personnel
  President/CEO .... I. Steven Udvarhelyi
  Chair.......................... Jerome (Jerry) Greig
  Vice Chair .... Judy P. Miller
  SVP/Chief HR Officer .... Sherri Enight
  Chief Information Officer .... Sue Kozik
  EVP/COO......................... Bryan Camerlinck

Specialty Managed Care Partners
  Enters into Contracts with Regional Business Coalitions: Yes

364 DINA Dental Plan
101 Parklane Blvd
Suite 301
Sugar Land, TX 77478
Toll-Free: 866-436-3093
Fax: 281-313-7155
info@dinadental.com
www.dinadental.com
Subsidiary of: FCL Dental
For Profit Organization: Yes
Year Founded: 1978

Healthplan and Services Defined
PLAN TYPE: Dental
Model Type: Group
Plan Specialty: Dental
Benefits Offered: Dental

Type of Coverage
Commercial, Individual

Geographic Areas Served
Louisiana

Peer Review Type
Second Surgical Opinion: Yes

Publishes and Distributes Report Card: No

Specialty Managed Care Partners
Enters into Contracts with Regional Business Coalitions: No

365 Humana Health Insurance of Louisiana
747 Veterans Memorial Blvd.
Metairie, LA 70005
Phone: 504-667-4366
Fax: 504-219-5142
www.humana.com
Secondary Address: 1655 E Bert Kouns Industrial Loop, Suite 200, Shreveport, LA 71105, 318-383-5969
Subsidiary of: Humana Inc.
For Profit Organization: Yes
Year Founded: 1985
Physician Owned Organization: Yes
Federally Qualified: Yes

Healthplan and Services Defined
PLAN TYPE: HMO/PPO
Model Type: Network
Plan Specialty: Dental, Vision
Benefits Offered: Behavioral Health, Chiropractic, Dental, Disease Management, Home Care, Inpatient SNF, Physical Therapy, Podiatry, Prescription, Psychiatric, Transplant, Vision, Wellness, Life, LTD, STD

Type of Coverage
Commercial, Individual, Indemnity, Medicare
Catastrophic Illness Benefit: Unlimited

Type of Payment Plans Offered
POS, Combination FFS & DFFS

Geographic Areas Served
Statewide, excluding Monroe

Subscriber Information
Average Monthly Fee Per Subscriber
(Employee + Employer Contribution):
Employee Only (Self): $189.31
Employee & 1 Family Member: $378.62
Employee & 2 Family Members: $530.07
Average Subscriber Co-Payment:
Primary Care Physician: $15.00
Prescription Drugs: $10/$25/$40
Home Health Care Max. Days/Visits Covered: 60 days

Network Qualifications
Pre-Admission Certification: Yes

Peer Review Type
Utilization Review: Yes
Second Surgical Opinion: Yes
Case Management: Yes

Publishes and Distributes Report Card: Yes

Accreditation Certification
URAC, NCQA, CORE
Medicare Approved, Utilization Review, Pre-Admission Certification, State Licensure, Quality Assurance Program

Key Personnel
Market Pres., Medicaid .... Tony Mollica

Specialty Managed Care Partners
CMS Healthcare, Medimpact
Enters into Contracts with Regional Business Coalitions: Yes
Chamber of Commerce

Employer References
State of Louisiana, Exxon-Mobil, Shell, Chevron, Sears

366 Louisiana Healthcare Connections
8585 Archives Avenue
Suite 310
Baton Rouge, LA 70809
Toll-Free: 866-595-8133
www.louisianahealthconnect.com
Subsidiary of: Centene Corporation
For Profit Organization: Yes

Healthplan and Services Defined
PLAN TYPE: Other
Model Type: Network
Benefits Offered: Behavioral Health, Dental, Disease Management, Prescription, Vision

Type of Coverage
Medicaid

Key Personnel
VP, Operations .... Joe Sullivan

367 Peoples Health
3838 N Causeway Boulevard
Suite 2200
Metairie, LA 70002
Toll-Free: 800-222-8600
Phone: 504-849-4685
www.peopleshealth.com

Mailing Address: PO Box 7890, Metairie, LA 70010
For Profit Organization: Yes
Year Founded: 1994
Total Enrollment: 80,000
State Enrollment: 80,000

Healthplan and Services Defined
PLAN TYPE: Medicare
Plan Specialty: Lab, Radiology
Benefits Offered: Dental, Disease Management, Home Care, Prescription, Wellness

Type of Coverage
Commercial, Medicare

Geographic Areas Served
Statewide

Accreditation Certification
NCQA

Key Personnel
Chief Executive Officer .... Warren Murrell
VP, Finance/Controller .... Emmet Geary
General Counsel......................... Alden Kellogg
Chief Information Officer................... Colin Hulin
SVP, Network Development .... Thomas Gennaro
VP, Health Services .... Jane E. Olds

368 Starmount
8485 Goodwood Boulevard
Baton Rouge, LA 70806
Toll-Free: 888-400-9304
starmountlife.com
Mailing Address: P.O. Box 98100, Baton Rouge, LA 70898-9100
Subsidiary of: Unum Group

Healthplan and Services Defined
PLAN TYPE: Dental
Benefits Offered: Dental, Prescription, Vision, Life, Hearing aids

Geographic Areas Served
Available in 41 states

Key Personnel
Chief Operating Officer.................... Rob Keene
CEO of Unum Group .... Rick McKenney

369 UnitedHealthcare Community Plan Louisiana
UnitedHealthcare Customer Service
P.O. Box 30769
Salt Lake City, UT 84130-0769
Toll-Free: 888-545-5205
www.uhccommunityplan.com/la
Subsidiary of: UnitedHealth Group
For Profit Organization: Yes

Healthplan and Services Defined
PLAN TYPE: Medicare
Other Type: Medicaid
Model Type: Network
Benefits Offered: Dental, Podiatry, Prescription, Wellness

Type of Coverage
Medicare, Medicaid

Geographic Areas Served
Acadia, Assumption, Bienville, Bossier, Caddo, Claiborne, De Soto, East Baton Rouge, East Feliciana, Evangeline, Iberia, Iberville, Jefferson, Lafayette, Lafourche, Orleans, Ouachita, Plaquemines, Pointe Coupee, Rapides, Red River, St. Bernard, St. Charles, St. James, St. John The Baptist, St. Landry, St. Mary, Terrebonne, Vermilion, Webster, West Baton Rouge, and West Feliciana. Other plans statewide

Key Personnel
CEO, Community Plan LA .... Karl Lirette
karl.lirette@uhc.com

370 UnitedHealthcare of Louisiana
3838 N Causeway Boulevard
Suite 2600
Metairie, LA 70002
Toll-Free: 800-826-1981
www.uhc.com
Subsidiary of: UnitedHealth Group
For Profit Organization: Yes
Year Founded: 1986

Healthplan and Services Defined
PLAN TYPE: HMO/PPO
Model Type: Network
Plan Specialty: Behavioral Health, Dental, Disease Management, PBM, Vision
Benefits Offered: Behavioral Health, Dental, Disease Management, Long-Term Care, Prescription, Vision, Wellness, Life, LTD, STD

Type of Coverage
Individual, Medicare, Supplemental Medicare, Medicaid, Catastrophic, Family, Military, Veterans, Group

Geographic Areas Served
Ascension, Assumption, East Baton Rouge, East Feliciana, Iberville, Jefferson, LaFourche, Livingston, Orleans, Plaquemines, Point Coupee, St. Bernard, St. Charles, St. Helena, St. James, St. Tammany, Tangipahoa, Terrabona, West Baton Rouge, West Feliciana

Subscriber Information
Average Monthly Fee Per Subscriber
(Employee + Employer Contribution):
Employee Only (Self): $129.45
Employee & 1 Family Member: $261.04
Employee & 2 Family Members: $422.40
Average Annual Deductible Per Subscriber:
Employee Only (Self): $5.00
Average Subscriber Co-Payment:
Primary Care Physician: $10.00
Prescription Drugs: $10.00
Hospital ER: $50.00

Network Qualifications
Pre-Admission Certification: Yes

Peer Review Type
   Utilization Review: Yes

Publishes and Distributes Report Card: No

Accreditation Certification
   TJC Accreditation, Medicare Approved, Utilization Review, Pre-Admission Certification, State Licensure, Quality Assurance Program

Key Personnel
   CEO, Louisiana .... Stephen L. Wilson, Jr.

Specialty Managed Care Partners
   Enters into Contracts with Regional Business Coalitions: No

---

371 Vantage Health Plan
130 DeSiard Street
Suite 300
Monroe, LA 71201
Toll-Free: 888-823-1910
Phone: 318-361-0900
www.vantagehealthplan.com
For Profit Organization: Yes
Year Founded: 1994
Number of Referral/Specialty Physicians: 7,000
Total Enrollment: 55,000
State Enrollment: 55,000

Healthplan and Services Defined
   PLAN TYPE: HMO
   Plan Specialty: Lab, Radiology
   Benefits Offered: Behavioral Health, Chiropractic, Disease Management, Home Care, Inpatient SNF, Physical Therapy, Prescription, Wellness, Durable Medical Equipment

Type of Coverage
   Medicare, Supplemental Medicare

Geographic Areas Served
   Statewide

Network Qualifications
   Pre-Admission Certification: Yes

Key Personnel
   Executive Vice President................... Mike Breard
   Chief Financial Officer .... Rhonda Haygood
   Chief Information Officer .... Landon Wright

Specialty Managed Care Partners
   Caremark Rx

---

372 Vantage Medicare Advantage
122 St. John Street
Monroe, LA 71201
Toll-Free: 888-823-1910
Phone: 318-361-0900
www.vantagehealthplan.com
Secondary Address: 130 DeSiard Street, Suite 300, Monroe, LA 71201, 318-361-0900
Year Founded: 1994
Total Enrollment: 14,000

Healthplan and Services Defined
   PLAN TYPE: Medicare
   Other Type: Medicare PPO
   Plan Specialty: Dental, Vision
   Benefits Offered: Home Care, Inpatient SNF, Prescription, Vision

Type of Coverage
   Medicare, Supplemental Medicare

Geographic Areas Served
   Bossier, Caddo, Caldwell, Jackson, Lincoln, Morehouse, Rapides, Ouachita, richland, and Union Parishes

Key Personnel
   Executive Vice President................... Mike Breard
   Chief Financial Officer .... Rhonda Haygood
   Chief Information Officer .... Landon Wright

MAINE

Health Insurance Coverage Status and Type of Coverage by Age

Category	All Persons Number	All Persons %	Under 19 years Number	Under 19 years %	Under 65 years Number	Under 65 years %
Total population	1,328 *(1)*	100.0 *(0.0)*	262 *(2)*	100.0 *(0.0)*	1,050 *(2)*	100.0 *(0.0)*
Covered by some type of health insurance	1,221 *(7)*	92.0 *(0.5)*	247 *(4)*	94.4 *(1.1)*	944 *(7)*	89.9 *(0.7)*
Covered by private health insurance	922 *(11)*	69.5 *(0.9)*	172 *(6)*	65.6 *(2.2)*	755 *(10)*	71.9 *(0.9)*
Employer-based	727 *(13)*	54.8 *(1.0)*	151 *(6)*	57.6 *(2.2)*	645 *(11)*	61.4 *(1.1)*
Direct purchase	199 *(9)*	15.0 *(0.6)*	19 *(3)*	7.2 *(1.2)*	110 *(7)*	10.5 *(0.7)*
TRICARE	48 *(5)*	3.6 *(0.4)*	8 *(2)*	2.9 *(0.9)*	25 *(4)*	2.4 *(0.4)*
Covered by public health insurance	513 *(10)*	38.6 *(0.8)*	92 *(6)*	35.3 *(2.1)*	244 *(10)*	23.3 *(1.0)*
Medicaid	260 *(10)*	19.5 *(0.8)*	91 *(6)*	34.9 *(2.1)*	212 *(10)*	20.2 *(0.9)*
Medicare	315 *(3)*	23.7 *(0.3)*	1 *(1)*	0.4 *(0.2)*	47 *(3)*	4.4 *(0.3)*
VA Care	44 *(3)*	3.3 *(0.2)*	1 *(1)*	0.3 *(0.2)*	18 *(2)*	1.7 *(0.2)*
Not covered at any time during the year	107 *(7)*	8.0 *(0.5)*	15 *(3)*	5.6 *(1.1)*	106 *(7)*	10.1 *(0.7)*

Note: Numbers in thousands; Figures cover civilian noninstitutionalized population in 2019; N/A indicates that data was not available; Z represents or rounds to zero; Margin of error appears in parenthesis and is calculated using replicate weights.
Source: U.S. Census Bureau, American Community Survey, Table HI-05. Health Insurance Coverage Status and Type of Coverage by State and Age for All People: 2019

Maine

373 Aetna Health of Maine
151 Farmington Avenue
Hartford, CT 06156
Toll-Free: 800-872-3862
www.aetna.com
Subsidiary of: CVS Health / Aetna Inc.
For Profit Organization: Yes

Healthplan and Services Defined
PLAN TYPE: HMO/PPO
Other Type: POS
Model Type: Network
Plan Specialty: Behavioral Health, Dental, EPO, Lab, PBM, Vision, Radiology
Benefits Offered: Behavioral Health, Dental, Disease Management, Long-Term Care, Physical Therapy, Podiatry, Prescription, Psychiatric, Vision, Wellness, Life, LTD, STD

Type of Coverage
Commercial, Medicare, Medicaid, Student health

Geographic Areas Served
Statewide

Key Personnel
President, North Atlantic . . . . Michael Cole

374 Anthem Blue Cross & Blue Shield of Maine
2 Gannett Drive
South Portland, ME 04106
Toll-Free: 800-331-1476
Phone: 207-536-9026
www.anthem.com
Subsidiary of: Anthem, Inc.
For Profit Organization: Yes

Healthplan and Services Defined
PLAN TYPE: HMO/PPO
Model Type: Network
Plan Specialty: Behavioral Health, Dental, Disease Management, Lab, PBM, Vision, Radiology
Benefits Offered: Behavioral Health, Dental, Disease Management, Inpatient SNF, Physical Therapy, Prescription, Psychiatric, Transplant, Vision, Wellness, Life

Type of Coverage
Commercial, Individual, Medicare, Supplemental Medicare, Catastrophic

Geographic Areas Served
Statewide

Accreditation Certification
URAC, NCQA

Key Personnel
President . . . . Denise McDonough
VP, Provider Engagement. . . . . Andrew Ellis

375 Community Health Options
150 Mill Street
Lewiston, ME 04240
Toll-Free: 855-624-6463
healthoptions.org
Secondary Address: Mail Stop 200, P.O. Box 1121, Lewiston, ME 04243
Non-Profit Organization: Yes

Healthplan and Services Defined
PLAN TYPE: HMO/PPO

Geographic Areas Served
Maine and New Hampshire

Key Personnel
President & CEO. . . . . Kevin Lewis
SVP, Operations Officer . . . . Robert Hillman
SVP, Clinical Officer . . . . Maggie Kelley
SVP, Information Officer . . . . Will Kilbreth

376 Harvard Pilgrim Health Care Maine
1 Market Street
3rd Floor
Portland, ME 04101
Toll-Free: 888-888-4742
www.harvardpilgrim.org
Non-Profit Organization: Yes
Year Founded: 1977
Number of Affiliated Hospitals: 179
Number of Referral/Specialty Physicians: 53,000
Total Enrollment: 3,000,000

Healthplan and Services Defined
PLAN TYPE: Multiple
Model Type: Network
Plan Specialty: ASO, Behavioral Health, Chiropractic, Dental, Disease Management, EPO, Lab, MSO, PBM, Vision, Radiology, Worker's Compensation, UR
Benefits Offered: Behavioral Health, Chiropractic, Disease Management, Home Care, Inpatient SNF, Long-Term Care, Physical Therapy, Podiatry, Prescription, Psychiatric, Transplant, Vision, Wellness

Type of Coverage
Commercial, Individual, Indemnity, Medicare, Supplemental Medicare, Medicaid

Geographic Areas Served
Statewide

Peer Review Type
Utilization Review: Yes
Second Surgical Opinion: Yes
Case Management: Yes

Publishes and Distributes Report Card: Yes

Accreditation Certification
NCQA
TJC Accreditation, Medicare Approved, Utilization Review, Pre-Admission Certification, State Licensure, Quality Assurance Program

Key Personnel
Vice President. . . . . Bill Whitmore

Client Manager.......................... Steve Conley

Average Claim Compensation
Physician's Fees Charged: 51%
Hospital's Fees Charged: 40%

Specialty Managed Care Partners
Enters into Contracts with Regional Business Coalitions: No

---

377 Martin's Point HealthCare
331 Veranda Street
Portland, ME 04103
Toll-Free: 800-322-0280
Phone: 207-828-2402
Fax: 207-828-2433
www.martinspoint.org
Non-Profit Organization: Yes
Year Founded: 1981
Total Enrollment: 70,000

Healthplan and Services Defined
PLAN TYPE: Multiple
Benefits Offered: Disease Management, Prescription, Wellness, No co-pay for: routine physical exams/hearing tests/eye exams/mammograms/prostrate & pap exams/bone mass/flu vaccines.

Type of Coverage
Commercial, Medicare, Military

Geographic Areas Served
Maine, New Hampshire, Vermont, Northeastern New York

Subscriber Information
Average Monthly Fee Per Subscriber
(Employee + Employer Contribution):
Employee Only (Self): Varies
Medicare: Varies
Average Annual Deductible Per Subscriber:
Employee Only (Self): Varies
Medicare: Varies
Average Subscriber Co-Payment:
Primary Care Physician: Varies
Prescription Drugs: Varies
Hospital ER: Varies

Key Personnel
President/CEO..................... David Howes, MD
Chief Financial Officer................. Amanda Jackson
Chief Medical Officer............. Jonathan Harvey, MD
COO/Delivery System .... Sandra Monfiletto
Chief Information Officer.............. Jeffrey L. Brown
Chief HR Officer....................... Teresa Nizza

---

378 Northeast Delta Dental Maine
1022 Portland Road
Suite 2
Saco, ME 04072-9674
Phone: 207-282-0404
Fax: 207-282-0505
nedelta@nedelta.com
www.nedelta.com
Mailing Address: P.O. Box 2002, Concord, NH 03302-2002

Non-Profit Organization: Yes
Year Founded: 1961
Total Enrollment: 936,000

Healthplan and Services Defined
PLAN TYPE: Dental
Other Type: Dental PPO
Plan Specialty: ASO, Dental
Benefits Offered: Dental

Type of Coverage
Commercial, Individual

Geographic Areas Served
Maine, New Hampshire and Vermont

Key Personnel
President/CEO........................ Thomas Raffio
Chair, Maine .... Don Oakes
VP, Sales .... Jodie Hittle
SVP, Operations .... William H. Lambrukos
General Counsel.................... Erica Bodwell, Esq.
SVP, Finance .... Francis Boucher

---

379 UnitedHealthcare Community Plan Maine
UnitedHealthcare Customer Service
P.O. Box 30769
Salt Lake City, UT 84130-0769
Toll-Free: 888-545-5205
www.uhccommunityplan.com/me
Subsidiary of: UnitedHealth Group
For Profit Organization: Yes

Healthplan and Services Defined
PLAN TYPE: Medicare
Other Type: Medicaid
Model Type: Network
Benefits Offered: Dental, Podiatry, Prescription

Type of Coverage
Medicare, Medicaid

Geographic Areas Served
Androscoggin, Cumberland, Franklin, Kennebec, Knox, Lincoln, Oxford, Sagadahoc, Waldo, and York

---

380 UnitedHealthcare of Maine
950 Winter Street
Waltham, MA 02451
Toll-Free: 888-545-5205
Phone: 866-414-1959
www.uhc.com
Subsidiary of: UnitedHealth Group
For Profit Organization: Yes
Year Founded: 1977

Healthplan and Services Defined
PLAN TYPE: HMO/PPO
Model Type: Network
Plan Specialty: Behavioral Health, Dental, Disease Management, Lab, PBM, Vision, Radiology
Benefits Offered: Behavioral Health, Chiropractic, Dental, Disease Management, Long-Term Care, Physical Therapy, Prescription, Vision, Wellness, AD&D, Life, LTD, STD

Type of Coverage
   Commercial, Individual, Indemnity, Medicare, Supplemental Medicare, Medicaid, Catastrophic, Family, Military, Veterans, Group

Geographic Areas Served
   Statewide. Maine is covered by the Massachusetts branch

Network Qualifications
   Pre-Admission Certification: Yes

Peer Review Type
   Utilization Review: Yes
   Second Surgical Opinion: Yes
   Case Management: Yes

Publishes and Distributes Report Card: Yes

Accreditation Certification
   TJC, NCQA

Key Personnel
   CEO, New England...................... Tim Archer

Specialty Managed Care Partners
   Enters into Contracts with Regional Business Coalitions: Yes

MARYLAND

Health Insurance Coverage Status and Type of Coverage by Age

Category	All Persons Number	All Persons %	Under 19 years Number	Under 19 years %	Under 65 years Number	Under 65 years %
Total population	5,946 *(2)*	100.0 *(0.0)*	1,411 *(4)*	100.0 *(0.0)*	5,009 *(4)*	100.0 *(0.0)*
Covered by some type of health insurance	5,589 *(15)*	94.0 *(0.3)*	1,363 *(8)*	96.6 *(0.5)*	4,661 *(15)*	93.1 *(0.3)*
Covered by private health insurance	4,398 *(32)*	74.0 *(0.5)*	927 *(15)*	65.7 *(1.1)*	3,738 *(29)*	74.6 *(0.6)*
Employer-based	3,753 *(33)*	63.1 *(0.6)*	812 *(16)*	57.6 *(1.1)*	3,284 *(30)*	65.6 *(0.6)*
Direct purchase	729 *(18)*	12.3 *(0.3)*	93 *(8)*	6.6 *(0.6)*	465 *(18)*	9.3 *(0.4)*
TRICARE	229 *(12)*	3.9 *(0.2)*	61 *(6)*	4.3 *(0.4)*	167 *(11)*	3.3 *(0.2)*
Covered by public health insurance	1,991 *(25)*	33.5 *(0.4)*	490 *(14)*	34.8 *(1.0)*	1,113 *(24)*	22.2 *(0.5)*
Medicaid	1,096 *(25)*	18.4 *(0.4)*	478 *(14)*	33.9 *(1.0)*	982 *(23)*	19.6 *(0.5)*
Medicare	1,018 *(12)*	17.1 *(0.2)*	18 *(4)*	1.3 *(0.3)*	141 *(10)*	2.8 *(0.2)*
VA Care	112 *(5)*	1.9 *(0.1)*	4 *(2)*	0.2 *(0.1)*	60 *(4)*	1.2 *(0.1)*
Not covered at any time during the year	357 *(15)*	6.0 *(0.3)*	48 *(6)*	3.4 *(0.5)*	348 *(15)*	6.9 *(0.3)*

Note: Numbers in thousands; Figures cover civilian noninstitutionalized population in 2019; N/A indicates that data was not available; Z represents or rounds to zero; Margin of error appears in parenthesis and is calculated using replicate weights.
Source: U.S. Census Bureau, American Community Survey, Table HI-05. Health Insurance Coverage Status and Type of Coverage by State and Age for All People: 2019

Maryland

381 Aetna Better Health of Maryland
509 Progress Drive
Suite 117
Linthicum, MD 21090-2256
Toll-Free: 866-827-2710
Fax: 844-348-0621
MarylandProviderRelationsDepartment@Aetna.com
www.aetnabetterhealth.com/maryland
Subsidiary of: CVS Health / Aetna Inc.
For Profit Organization: Yes

Healthplan and Services Defined
PLAN TYPE: HMO/PPO
Other Type: POS
Model Type: Network
Plan Specialty: Behavioral Health, EPO, Lab, PBM, Radiology
Benefits Offered: Behavioral Health, Dental, Disease Management, Long-Term Care, Physical Therapy, Podiatry, Prescription, Psychiatric, Vision, Wellness, Life, LTD, STD

Type of Coverage
Commercial, Medicaid, Student health

Type of Payment Plans Offered
DFFS, Capitated, FFS

Geographic Areas Served
Statewide

Key Personnel
CEO................................. Angelo D. Edge
Chief Medical Officer.......... Nina F. Miles Everett, MD

382 American Postal Workers Union (APWU) Health Plan
799 Cromwell Park Drive
Suite K-Z
Glen Burnie, MD 21061
Toll-Free: 800-222-2798
Fax: 410-424-1588
www.apwuhp.com
Year Founded: 1960
Number of Affiliated Hospitals: 6,000
Number of Primary Care Physicians: 600,000
Total Enrollment: 205,000
State Enrollment: 205,000

Healthplan and Services Defined
PLAN TYPE: PPO
Plan Specialty: Behavioral Health, Dental, Disease Management
Benefits Offered: Behavioral Health, Dental, Disease Management, Prescription, Wellness
Offers Demand Management Patient Information Service: Yes
DMPI Services Offered: 24 Hour Nurse Advisory Line

Type of Payment Plans Offered
FFS

Geographic Areas Served
Nationwide - APWU/The American Postal Workers Union Health Plan is health insurance for federal employees and retirees

Subscriber Information
Average Monthly Fee Per Subscriber
 (Employee + Employer Contribution):
  Employee Only (Self): $36.80-177.20 varies
  Employee & 2 Family Members: $82.80-398.66 varies
Average Annual Deductible Per Subscriber:
  Employee Only (Self): $250
Average Subscriber Co-Payment:
  Primary Care Physician: 15%
  Prescription Drugs: 25%
  Hospital ER: 15% - 30%
  Home Health Care Max. Days/Visits Covered: 10 - 30%

Key Personnel
President .... Mark Dimondstein
Director......................... Sarah Jane Rodriguez

383 Amerigroup Maryland
7550 Teague Road
Suite 500
Hanover, MD 21076
Toll-Free: 800-600-4441
Phone: 410-859-5800
Fax: 800-964-3627
www.myamerigroup.com/md
Subsidiary of: Anthem, Inc.
For Profit Organization: Yes
Year Founded: 1999

Healthplan and Services Defined
PLAN TYPE: Medicare
Plan Specialty: Behavioral Health, Dental, Disease Management, Vision, Taking Care of Baby and Me program
Benefits Offered: Behavioral Health, Dental, Disease Management, Prescription, Vision

Type of Coverage
Medicare, Medicaid

Accreditation Certification
NCQA

Key Personnel
VP, Finance .... Kevin Criswell

384 Avesis: Maryland
10324 S Dolfield Road
Owings Mills, MD 21117
Toll-Free: 800-643-1132
www.avesis.com
Subsidiary of: Guardian Life Insurance Company
Year Founded: 1978
Number of Primary Care Physicians: 25,000
Total Enrollment: 3,500,000

Healthplan and Services Defined
PLAN TYPE: PPO

Other Type: Vision, Dental
Model Type: Network
Plan Specialty: Dental, Vision, Hearing
Benefits Offered: Dental, Vision

Type of Coverage
Commercial

Type of Payment Plans Offered
POS, Capitated, Combination FFS & DFFS

Geographic Areas Served
Nationwide and Puerto Rico

Publishes and Distributes Report Card: Yes

Accreditation Certification
AAAHC
TJC Accreditation

Key Personnel
Accountant .... Mary Griffin

---

385 CareFirst BlueCross BlueShield
Canton Tower
1501 S Clinton Street
Baltimore, MD 21224
Toll-Free: 800-544-8703
Phone: 855-300-7751
individual.carefirst.com
Secondary Address: Union Center Plaza, 840 First Street NE, Washington, DC 20065, 202-479-8000
Non-Profit Organization: Yes
Year Founded: 1984
Number of Primary Care Physicians: 5,500
Total Enrollment: 3,300,000

Healthplan and Services Defined
PLAN TYPE: HMO/PPO
Model Type: Network
Benefits Offered: Dental, Prescription, Vision

Type of Coverage
Commercial, Individual, Medicare
Catastrophic Illness Benefit: Unlimited

Geographic Areas Served
Maryland, the District of Columbia and parts of Northern Virginia

Accreditation Certification
NCQA
TJC Accreditation, Medicare Approved, Utilization Review, Pre-Admission Certification, State Licensure, Quality Assurance Program

Key Personnel
President/CEO .... Brian D. Pieninck
EVP/CFO............................. Jenny Smith
VP/CMO .... Tich Changamire, MD
EVP/General Counsel .... Meryl Burgin
EVP/Chief HR Officer................. Angela Celestin
EVP, Goverment Affairs .... Wanda Oneferu-Bey

Specialty Managed Care Partners
Enters into Contracts with Regional Business Coalitions: Yes

---

386 Denta-Chek of Maryland
10400 Little Patuxet Parkway
Suite 260
Columbia, MD 21044
Toll-Free: 888-478-8833
Phone: 410-997-3300
Fax: 410-997-3796
info@dentachek.com
www.dentachek.com
Non-Profit Organization: Yes
Year Founded: 1981
Number of Primary Care Physicians: 300
Number of Referral/Specialty Physicians: 200
Total Enrollment: 10,000

Healthplan and Services Defined
PLAN TYPE: Dental
Model Type: IPA
Plan Specialty: Dental
Benefits Offered: Dental

Type of Coverage
Catastrophic Illness Benefit: None

Type of Payment Plans Offered
POS, Combination FFS & DFFS

Geographic Areas Served
Statewide

Subscriber Information
Average Monthly Fee Per Subscriber
(Employee + Employer Contribution):
Employee Only (Self): $16.00
Employee & 1 Family Member: $22.00
Employee & 2 Family Members: $28.00
Medicare: $0
Average Annual Deductible Per Subscriber:
Employee Only (Self): $0
Employee & 1 Family Member: $0
Employee & 2 Family Members: $0
Medicare: $0
Average Subscriber Co-Payment:
Non-Network Physician: $0
Prescription Drugs: $0
Hospital ER: $0
Home Health Care: $0
Nursing Home: $0

Network Qualifications
Pre-Admission Certification: Yes

Peer Review Type
Utilization Review: Yes
Second Surgical Opinion: Yes
Case Management: Yes

Publishes and Distributes Report Card: No

Accreditation Certification
State Licensure, Quality Assurance Program

Specialty Managed Care Partners
Enters into Contracts with Regional Business Coalitions: No

387 Jai Medical Systems
301 International Circle
Hunt Valley, MD 21030
Toll-Free: 888-524-1999
www.jaimedicalsystems.com
Subsidiary of: Managed Care Organization Inc.
For Profit Organization: Yes
Year Founded: 1997

Healthplan and Services Defined
  PLAN TYPE: HMO
  Plan Specialty: Dental, Lab, Radiology
  Benefits Offered: Behavioral Health, Dental, Disease Management, Home Care, Inpatient SNF, Prescription, Vision, Substance abuse treatment, HIV/AIDS treatment, Family planning services, Diabetes care

Type of Coverage
  Individual

Geographic Areas Served
  Statewide

Key Personnel
  CEO . . . . Jai Seunarine
  Chief Financial Officer . . . . Tim Barrett
  Medical Director . . . . Aye Lwin
  HR Manager. . . . . Landy Castillo
  Medical Assistant . . . . Nessa Williams
  Chief Information Officer . . . . Devon Bowers
  Data Analyst. . . . . Robert Frey

388 Kaiser Permanente Mid-Atlantic
2101 E. Jefferson Street
Rockville, MD 20852
Toll-Free: 800-777-7904
Phone: 301-816-2424
Fax: 301-816-7119
thrive.kaiserpermanente.org/care-near-mid-atlantic
Subsidiary of: Kaiser Permanente
Non-Profit Organization: Yes
Year Founded: 1945
Number of Affiliated Hospitals: 48
Number of Primary Care Physicians: 1,500
Total Enrollment: 750,552
State Enrollment: 750,552

Healthplan and Services Defined
  PLAN TYPE: Multiple
  Model Type: Network
  Benefits Offered: Disease Management, Prescription, Vision, Wellness, Benefits vary according to plan

Type of Coverage
  Commercial, Individual, Medicare, Supplemental Medicare, Medicaid

Geographic Areas Served
  Virginia, Maryland and the District of Columbia

Key Personnel
  Regional President . . . . Ruth E. Williams-Brinkley
  President/CEO . . . . Richard S. Isaacs, MD
  Media Contact . . . . Marisa Lavine
  202-289-9917

389 Priority Partners Health Plans
7231 Parkway Drive
Suite 100
Hanover, MD 21076
Toll-Free: 800-654-9728
www.ppmco.org
Subsidiary of: John Hopkins HealthCare LLC/Maryland Community Health System
Non-Profit Organization: Yes
Year Founded: 1996
Total Enrollment: 250,000
State Enrollment: 250,000

Healthplan and Services Defined
  PLAN TYPE: HMO
  Benefits Offered: Behavioral Health, Dental, Prescription, Vision

Type of Coverage
  Medicaid

Type of Payment Plans Offered
  Capitated, FFS

Geographic Areas Served
  Maryland

Peer Review Type
  Second Surgical Opinion: Yes

Publishes and Distributes Report Card: Yes

Accreditation Certification
  TJC, NCQA, JACHO, HMO

390 Spectera Eyecare Networks
10175 Little Patuxent Parkway
6th Floor
Columbia, MD 21044
Toll-Free: 800-638-3120
www.spectera.com
Mailing Address: P.O. Box 30978, Salt Lake City, UT 84130
Subsidiary of: UnitedHealth Group
For Profit Organization: Yes
Year Founded: 1964
Number of Primary Care Physicians: 24,000
Total Enrollment: 12,500,000

Healthplan and Services Defined
  PLAN TYPE: Multiple
  Model Type: Network
  Plan Specialty: Vision
  Benefits Offered: Disease Management, Vision

Type of Coverage
  Commercial, Individual

Type of Payment Plans Offered
  POS, DFFS, Capitated

Subscriber Information
  Average Monthly Fee Per Subscriber
  (Employee + Employer Contribution):

Employee Only (Self): Varies
Average Annual Deductible Per Subscriber:
Employee & 2 Family Members: Varies
Average Subscriber Co-Payment:
Primary Care Physician: Varies

Network Qualifications
Pre-Admission Certification: Yes

Publishes and Distributes Report Card: Yes

Specialty Managed Care Partners
United Heath Group
Enters into Contracts with Regional Business Coalitions: No

---

391 Superior Vision
881 Elkridge Landing Rd.
Suite 300
Linthicum, MD 21090
Toll-Free: 800-243-1401
Phone: 410-752-0121
Fax: 410-752-8969
www.superiorvision.com
Subsidiary of: Versant Health
For Profit Organization: Yes
Year Founded: 1993

Healthplan and Services Defined
PLAN TYPE: Vision
Model Type: Group
Plan Specialty: Vision
Benefits Offered: Vision

Type of Coverage
Commercial, Indemnity, Medicaid, Catastrophic

Geographic Areas Served
Nationwide

Accreditation Certification
AAPI, NCQA

---

392 Trinity Health of Maryland
Holy Cross Health
1500 Forest Glen Road
Silver Spring, MD 20910
Phone: 301-754-7000
www.trinity-health.org
Subsidiary of: Trinity Health
Non-Profit Organization: Yes
Year Founded: 2013
Number of Affiliated Hospitals: 2
Total Enrollment: 30,000,000

Healthplan and Services Defined
PLAN TYPE: Other
Benefits Offered: Disease Management, Home Care, Long-Term Care, Psychiatric, Hospice programs, PACE (Program of All Inclusive Care for the Elderly)

Geographic Areas Served
Montgomery, Prince Georges and Howard counties

Key Personnel
President/CEO .... Norvell V. Coots

Chief Medical Officer .... Blair M. Eig
Chief Strategy Officer .... Kristin Feliciano
Chief Financial Officer .... Anne Gillis
Chief Development Officer .... Wendy Friar
Chief Quality Officer .... Yancy Phillips
General Counsel .... Elizabeth Simpson

---

393 United Concordia of Maryland
11311 McCormick Road
Suite 170
Hunt Valley, MD 21031
Phone: 443-866-9500
www.unitedconcordia.com
For Profit Organization: Yes
Year Founded: 1971
Number of Primary Care Physicians: 104,000
Total Enrollment: 8,800,000

Healthplan and Services Defined
PLAN TYPE: Dental
Plan Specialty: Dental
Benefits Offered: Dental

Type of Coverage
Commercial, Individual, Military personnel & families

Geographic Areas Served
Nationwide

Accreditation Certification
URAC

Key Personnel
Professional Relations .... Tim Dodd
Contact .... Beth Rutherford
   717-260-7659
   beth.rutherford@ucci.com

---

394 UnitedHealthcare Community Plan Maryland
UnitedHealthcare Customer Service
P.O. Box 30769
Salt Lake City, UT 84130-0769
Toll-Free: 888-545-5205
www.uhccommunityplan.com/md
Subsidiary of: UnitedHealth Group
For Profit Organization: Yes

Healthplan and Services Defined
PLAN TYPE: Medicare
Other Type: Medicaid
Model Type: Network
Benefits Offered: Dental, Podiatry, Prescription, Vision

Type of Coverage
Medicare, Medicaid

Geographic Areas Served
Montgomery

Key Personnel
CEO, Community Plan MD/DC .... Kathlyn Wee
   kathlyn.wee@uhc.com

395 UnitedHealthcare of Maryland
6220 Old Dobbin Lane
Suite 100
Columbia, MD 21045
Toll-Free: 888-545-5205
Phone: 443-201-1186
www.uhc.com
Secondary Address: 800 King Farm Boulevard, Suite 600, Rockville, MD 20850
Subsidiary of: UnitedHealth Group
Non-Profit Organization: Yes
Year Founded: 1976

Healthplan and Services Defined
  PLAN TYPE: HMO/PPO
  Model Type: Network
  Plan Specialty: Behavioral Health, Dental, Disease Management, PBM, Vision
  Benefits Offered: Behavioral Health, Dental, Disease Management, Long-Term Care, Prescription, Vision, Wellness, Life, LTD, STD

Type of Coverage
  Individual, Medicare, Supplemental Medicare, Medicaid, Catastrophic, Family, Military, Veterans, Group

Geographic Areas Served
  Maryland, Virginia, and the District of Columbia

Subscriber Information
  Average Monthly Fee Per Subscriber
    (Employee + Employer Contribution):
      Employee Only (Self): $104.00-135.00
      Employee & 1 Family Member: $143.00-184.00
      Employee & 2 Family Members: $331.00-440.00
      Medicare: $112.00-156.00
  Average Annual Deductible Per Subscriber:
      Employee Only (Self): $100.00-250.00
      Employee & 1 Family Member: $500.00-1500.00
      Employee & 2 Family Members: $200.00-500.00
      Medicare: $0
  Average Subscriber Co-Payment:
      Primary Care Physician: $5.00/10.00
      Non-Network Physician: Deductible
      Prescription Drugs: $5.00/10.00
      Hospital ER: $25.00/50.00
      Home Health Care: $5.00/10.00

Network Qualifications
  Pre-Admission Certification: Yes

Peer Review Type
  Utilization Review: Yes
  Second Surgical Opinion: Yes
  Case Management: Yes

Publishes and Distributes Report Card: Yes

Accreditation Certification
  TJC Accreditation, Medicare Approved, Utilization Review, Pre-Admission Certification, State Licensure, Quality Assurance Program

Key Personnel
  CEO, Mid-Atlantic...................Joe Ochipinti

Specialty Managed Care Partners
  Enters into Contracts with Regional Business Coalitions: Yes

396 Versant Health
Po Box 1416
Latham, MD 12110
Toll-Free: 800-571-3366
Fax: 410-752-8969
www.versanthealth.com
For Profit Organization: Yes
Year Founded: 2017

Healthplan and Services Defined
  PLAN TYPE: Vision
  Model Type: Group
  Plan Specialty: Vision
  Benefits Offered: Vision

Type of Coverage
  Commercial, Indemnity, Medicaid, Catastrophic

Geographic Areas Served
  Nationwide

Key Personnel
  Chief Executive Officer...................James Reid
  Chief Operating Officer...............Maynard McAlpin
  Chief Financial Officer..................Kimberly Davis
  Chief Medical Officer...............Mark Ruchman, MD

MASSACHUSETTS

Health Insurance Coverage Status and Type of Coverage by Age

Category	All Persons Number	All Persons %	Under 19 years Number	Under 19 years %	Under 65 years Number	Under 65 years %
Total population	6,821 *(1)*	100.0 *(0.0)*	1,446 *(5)*	100.0 *(0.0)*	5,684 *(3)*	100.0 *(0.0)*
Covered by some type of health insurance	6,617 *(10)*	97.0 *(0.2)*	1,424 *(5)*	98.5 *(0.2)*	5,485 *(10)*	96.5 *(0.2)*
Covered by private health insurance	5,068 *(28)*	74.3 *(0.4)*	1,008 *(15)*	69.7 *(1.0)*	4,336 *(26)*	76.3 *(0.5)*
Employer-based	4,305 *(29)*	63.1 *(0.4)*	922 *(14)*	63.8 *(0.9)*	3,868 *(28)*	68.1 *(0.5)*
Direct purchase	961 *(20)*	14.1 *(0.3)*	103 *(7)*	7.1 *(0.5)*	578 *(17)*	10.2 *(0.3)*
TRICARE	79 *(6)*	1.2 *(0.1)*	12 *(3)*	0.9 *(0.2)*	43 *(5)*	0.8 *(0.1)*
Covered by public health insurance	2,461 *(30)*	36.1 *(0.4)*	500 *(15)*	34.6 *(1.0)*	1,387 *(30)*	24.4 *(0.5)*
Medicaid	1,499 *(30)*	22.0 *(0.4)*	498 *(15)*	34.4 *(1.0)*	1,309 *(29)*	23.0 *(0.5)*
Medicare	1,221 *(8)*	17.9 *(0.1)*	5 *(2)*	0.4 *(0.1)*	147 *(6)*	2.6 *(0.1)*
VA Care	98 *(5)*	1.4 *(0.1)*	2 *(1)*	0.1 *(0.1)*	36 *(3)*	0.6 *(0.1)*
Not covered at any time during the year	204 *(10)*	3.0 *(0.2)*	22 *(3)*	1.5 *(0.2)*	199 *(10)*	3.5 *(0.2)*

Note: Numbers in thousands; Figures cover civilian noninstitutionalized population in 2019; N/A indicates that data was not available; Z represents or rounds to zero; Margin of error appears in parenthesis and is calculated using replicate weights.
Source: U.S. Census Bureau, American Community Survey, Table HI-05. Health Insurance Coverage Status and Type of Coverage by State and Age for All People: 2019

Massachusetts

397 Aetna Health of Massachusetts
151 Farmington Avenue
Hartford, CT 06156
Toll-Free: 800-872-3862
www.aetna.com
Subsidiary of: CVS Health / Aetna Inc.
For Profit Organization: Yes
Year Founded: 1987

Healthplan and Services Defined
PLAN TYPE: HMO/PPO
Other Type: POS
Model Type: IPA, Network
Plan Specialty: Behavioral Health, EPO, Lab, PBM, Radiology
Benefits Offered: Behavioral Health, Dental, Disease Management, Long-Term Care, Physical Therapy, Podiatry, Prescription, Psychiatric, Vision, Life, LTD, STD

Type of Coverage
Commercial, Student health
Catastrophic Illness Benefit: Covered

Geographic Areas Served
Statewide

Peer Review Type
Second Surgical Opinion: Yes
Case Management: Yes

Publishes and Distributes Report Card: Yes

Accreditation Certification
NCQA

Key Personnel
President, North Atlantic . . . . Michael Cole

398 Allways Health Partners
399 Revolution Drive
Somerville, MA 02145
Toll-Free: 866-414-5533
allwayshealthpartners.org
Non-Profit Organization: Yes
Year Founded: 1986
Owned by an Integrated Delivery Network (IDN): Yes
Number of Affiliated Hospitals: 41
Number of Primary Care Physicians: 2,800
Number of Referral/Specialty Physicians: 10,400
Total Enrollment: 430,000
State Enrollment: 430,000

Healthplan and Services Defined
PLAN TYPE: HMO
Model Type: Network
Plan Specialty: ASO, Behavioral Health, Disease Management, Medicaid Focus
Benefits Offered: Behavioral Health, Complementary Medicine, Dental, Disease Management, Home Care, Prescription, Vision, Wellness

Type of Coverage
Commercial, Medicaid
Catastrophic Illness Benefit: Covered

Geographic Areas Served
Most of Massachusetts counties

Network Qualifications
Pre-Admission Certification: Yes

Peer Review Type
Utilization Review: Yes
Second Surgical Opinion: Yes
Case Management: Yes

Publishes and Distributes Report Card: Yes

Accreditation Certification
State of MA
TJC Accreditation, Medicare Approved, Utilization Review, Pre-Admission Certification, State Licensure, Quality Assurance Program

Key Personnel
Interim President/CEO . . . . Steven Tringale
Chief Operating Officer . . . . Mark McCormick
Chief Financial Officer . . . . Joseph C. Capezza
Chief, Stategy/Marketing . . . . Tim Walsh
Chief Medical Officer . . . . Anton B. Dodek, MD

Specialty Managed Care Partners
Beacon Health Strategies
Enters into Contracts with Regional Business Coalitions: No

399 Araz Group
7201 West 78th Street
Bloomington, MN 55439
Toll-Free: 800-444-3005
Phone: 952-896-1200
www.araz.com
For Profit Organization: Yes
Year Founded: 1982
Number of Primary Care Physicians: 71,000
Total Enrollment: 250,000
State Enrollment: 160,000

Healthplan and Services Defined
PLAN TYPE: PPO
Plan Specialty: UR
Benefits Offered: Behavioral Health, Disease Management, Prescription, Worker's Compensation, AD&D, LTD, STD

Type of Coverage
Commercial, Medicare

Geographic Areas Served
Minnesota, Western Wisconsin, Northern Iowa, North and South Dakota

Accreditation Certification
Pre-Admission Certification

Key Personnel
Founder & CEO . . . . Nazie Eftekhari
President . . . . Amir Eftekhari

Specialty Managed Care Partners
Intracorp

400 Avesis: Massachusetts
790 Turnpike St.
Suite 202
North Andover, MA 01845
Toll-Free: 855-214-6777
Phone: 978-681-6400
www.avesis.com
Subsidiary of: Guardian Life Insurance Co.
Year Founded: 1978
Number of Primary Care Physicians: 25,000
Total Enrollment: 3,500,000

Healthplan and Services Defined
PLAN TYPE: PPO
Other Type: Vision, Dental
Model Type: Network
Plan Specialty: Dental, Vision
Benefits Offered: Dental, Vision

Type of Coverage
Commercial

Type of Payment Plans Offered
POS, Capitated, Combination FFS & DFFS

Geographic Areas Served
Nationwide and Puerto Rico

Publishes and Distributes Report Card: Yes

Accreditation Certification
AAAHC
TJC Accreditation

Key Personnel
VP, Regional Sales .... Lawrence Ford

401 Blue Cross & Blue Shield of Massachusetts
101 Huntington Avenue
Suite 1300
Boston, MA 02199
Toll-Free: 800-262-2583
www.bcbsma.com
Mailing Address: P.O. Box 9134 N., Quincy, MA 02171-9134
Non-Profit Organization: Yes
Year Founded: 1937
Number of Affiliated Hospitals: 74
Number of Primary Care Physicians: 20,266
Total Enrollment: 2,900,000
State Enrollment: 2,900,000

Healthplan and Services Defined
PLAN TYPE: HMO
Model Type: Network
Plan Specialty: Dental, Group Medical
Benefits Offered: Behavioral Health, Chiropractic, Complementary Medicine, Dental, Disease Management, Home Care, Inpatient SNF, Long-Term Care, Physical Therapy, Podiatry, Prescription, Psychiatric, Transplant, Vision, Wellness, AD&D, Life, LTD, STD
Offers Demand Management Patient Information Service: Yes
DMPI Services Offered: 24-Hour Nurse Care Line

Type of Coverage
Medicare, Group Insurance

Type of Payment Plans Offered
FFS

Geographic Areas Served
Massachusetts & Southern New Hampshire

Subscriber Information
Average Monthly Fee Per Subscriber
(Employee + Employer Contribution):
Employee Only (Self): Varies by plan

Network Qualifications
Pre-Admission Certification: Yes

Peer Review Type
Utilization Review: Yes

Accreditation Certification
NCQA
TJC Accreditation, Medicare Approved, Utilization Review, Pre-Admission Certification, State Licensure

Key Personnel
President/CEO .... Andrew Dreyfus
Chief Operating Officer .... Richard Lynch
Chief Financial Officer .... Andreana Santangelo
Chief Legal Officer.................... Stephanie Lovell
SVP, Corp Communications.............. Jay McQuaide
Chief Physician Executive .... Bruce Nash, MD
EVP, Sales/Marketing.................. Patrick Gilligan

Specialty Managed Care Partners
Express Scripts

402 DentaQuest
465 Medford Street
Boston, MA 02129-1454
Toll-Free: 888-278-7310
www.dentaquest.com
Subsidiary of: DentaQuest Ventures
Year Founded: 1980
Number of Primary Care Physicians: 750
Total Enrollment: 27,000,000

Healthplan and Services Defined
PLAN TYPE: Dental
Plan Specialty: Dental
Benefits Offered: Dental

Type of Coverage
Individual, Medicare, Medicaid

Geographic Areas Served
Arizona, California, Colorado, Florida, Georgia, Idaho, Illinois, Indiana, Kentucky, Louisiana, Maryland, Massachusetts, Michicgan, Minnesota, Mississippi, Missouri, New Hampshire, New Jersey, New Mexico, New York, Ohio, Rhode Island, Pennsylvania, North Carolina, South Carolina, Tennessee, Texas, Utah, Virginia, Washington, Wisconsin

Key Personnel
President/CEO......................... Steve Pollock
EVP/COO............................. Kamila Chytil
EVP/CFO .... Akhil Sharma
Chief Legal Officer .... David Abelman
EVP, Chief Sales Officer................... Bob Lynn

403 Fallon Health
10 Chestnut Street
Worcester, MA 01608
Non-Profit Organization: Yes
Year Founded: 1977

Healthplan and Services Defined
PLAN TYPE: Multiple
Benefits Offered: Behavioral Health, Chiropractic, Dental, Disease Management, Home Care, Inpatient SNF, Physical Therapy, Podiatry, Prescription, Psychiatric, Vision, Wellness

Type of Coverage
Individual, Medicare, Medicaid

Geographic Areas Served
Statewide

Key Personnel
President & CEO . . . . Richard P. Burke

404 Harvard Pilgrim Health Care Massachusetts
93 Worcester Street
Wellesley, MA 02481
Toll-Free: 888-888-4742
Phone: 617-509-1000
www.harvardpilgrim.org
Secondary Address: Landmark Center, 401 Park Drive, Suite 401, East Boston, MA 02215-3325
Non-Profit Organization: Yes
Year Founded: 1977
Number of Affiliated Hospitals: 183
Number of Referral/Specialty Physicians: 53,000
Total Enrollment: 3,000,000

Healthplan and Services Defined
PLAN TYPE: Multiple
Model Type: Network
Plan Specialty: ASO, Behavioral Health, Chiropractic, Dental, Disease Management, EPO, Lab, MSO, PBM, Vision, Radiology, Worker's Compensation, UR
Benefits Offered: Behavioral Health, Chiropractic, Disease Management, Home Care, Inpatient SNF, Long-Term Care, Physical Therapy, Podiatry, Prescription, Psychiatric, Transplant, Vision, Wellness

Type of Coverage
Commercial, Individual, Indemnity, Medicare, Supplemental Medicare, Medicaid

Geographic Areas Served
Statewide

Peer Review Type
Utilization Review: Yes
Second Surgical Opinion: Yes
Case Management: Yes

Publishes and Distributes Report Card: Yes

Accreditation Certification
NCQA
TJC Accreditation, Medicare Approved, Utilization Review, Pre-Admission Certification, State Licensure, Quality Assurance Program

Key Personnel
President/CEO . . . . Michael Carson
Chief Financial Officer . . . . Charles Goheen
Chief Legal Officer . . . . Tisa Hughes
Chief Information Officer . . . . Deborah Norton
Chief Medical Officer . . . . Michael Sherman, MD

Average Claim Compensation
Physician's Fees Charged: 51%
Hospital's Fees Charged: 40%

Specialty Managed Care Partners
Enters into Contracts with Regional Business Coalitions: No

405 Health New England
One Monarch Place
Suite 1500
Springfield, MA 01144-1500
Toll-Free: 800-310-2835
Phone: 413-787-4004
healthnewengland.org
Non-Profit Organization: Yes
Year Founded: 1985
Number of Affiliated Hospitals: 23
Number of Primary Care Physicians: 4,300
Total Enrollment: 200,000
State Enrollment: 200,000

Healthplan and Services Defined
PLAN TYPE: HMO/PPO
Model Type: IPA
Plan Specialty: ASO, Disease Management
Benefits Offered: Behavioral Health, Chiropractic, Complementary Medicine, Dental, Disease Management, Home Care, Inpatient SNF, Physical Therapy, Podiatry, Prescription, Psychiatric, Transplant, Vision, Wellness

Type of Coverage
Commercial, Medicare, Medicaid, Catastrophic
Catastrophic Illness Benefit: Maximum $1M

Type of Payment Plans Offered
POS

Geographic Areas Served
Berkshire, Franklin, Hampden, Hampshire and Worcester counties in Massachusetts, and Hartford and Tolland counties in Connecticut

Peer Review Type
Utilization Review: Yes
Second Surgical Opinion: Yes
Case Management: Yes

Publishes and Distributes Report Card: Yes

Accreditation Certification
NCQA
TJC Accreditation, Medicare Approved, Utilization Review, Pre-Admission Certification, State Licensure, Quality Assurance Program

Key Personnel
Interim President/CEO . . . . Marion A. McGowan
VP, Sales & Marketing . . . . Ashley Allen
VP, Info Technology . . . . Ken Bernard

VP/CMO .... Laurie Gianturco, MD
VP/General Counsel .... Susan O'Connor, Esq.
VP/Interim CFO .... Richard Swift

Average Claim Compensation
Physician's Fees Charged: 59%
Hospital's Fees Charged: 49%

Specialty Managed Care Partners
Enters into Contracts with Regional Business Coalitions: No

406 Health Plans, Inc.
1500 West Park Drive
Suite 330
Westborough, MA 01581
Toll-Free: 800-532-7575
Phone: 508-752-2480
Fax: 508-754-9664
www.healthplansinc.com
Mailing Address: PO Box: 5199, Westborough, 01581
Subsidiary of: Harvard Pilgrim
Year Founded: 1981

Healthplan and Services Defined
PLAN TYPE: PPO
Other Type: TPA
Model Type: Network
Plan Specialty: ASO, Behavioral Health, Chiropractic, Dental, Disease Management, EPO, Lab, PBM, Vision, Radiology, UR
Benefits Offered: Home Care, Inpatient SNF, Long-Term Care, Physical Therapy, Podiatry, Prescription, Psychiatric, Transplant, Vision, Wellness, Worker's Compensation, AD&D, Life, LTD, STD

Geographic Areas Served
New England, South Carolina, Florida

Accreditation Certification
TJC Accreditation, Pre-Admission Certification

Key Personnel
President & CEO .... Deborah Hodges
Sen. VP of Sales .... Drew Rozmiarek
Chief Information Officer .... Chuck Moulter
VP, Operations .... Chris Parr
VP, Financial Operations .... Joan Recore

407 Medical Center Healthnet Plan
529 Main Street
Suite 500
Charlestown, MA 02129
Toll-Free: 800-792-4355
Phone: 617-748-6000
memberquestions@bmchp.org
www.bmchp.org
Non-Profit Organization: Yes
Year Founded: 1997
Number of Affiliated Hospitals: 60
Number of Primary Care Physicians: 3,000
Number of Referral/Specialty Physicians: 12,000
Total Enrollment: 300,000
State Enrollment: 300,000

Healthplan and Services Defined
PLAN TYPE: HMO
Benefits Offered: Disease Management, Prescription, Wellness

Type of Coverage
Individual

Geographic Areas Served
statewide

Key Personnel
President .... Heather Thiltgen
Chief Financial Officer .... Jim Collins
Chief Operating Officer .... Lynn Bowman
Chief Information Officer .... Kim Sinclair
Chief Medical Officer .... Jonathan Welch, MD
Chief Legal Officer .... Ellen Weinstein

408 Senior Whole Health Massachusetts
58 Charles Street
Cambridge, MA 02141
Toll-Free: 888-566-3526
Phone: 617-494-5353
Fax: 617-494-5599
www.seniorwholehealth.com
Subsidiary of: Magellan Health
For Profit Organization: Yes
Year Founded: 2004

Healthplan and Services Defined
PLAN TYPE: Medicare
Benefits Offered: Home Care, Long-Term Care, Psychiatric

Type of Coverage
Medicare, Medicaid, Specialty plan for seniors requirin

Geographic Areas Served
Statewide

409 Sun Life Financial
One Sun Life Executive Park
Wellesley Hills, MA 02481
Toll-Free: 800-786-5433
USWeb_General_Information@sunlife.com
www.sunlife.com
Secondary Address: SC 2350, Wellesley Hills, MA 02481
For Profit Organization: Yes
Year Founded: 1865

Healthplan and Services Defined
PLAN TYPE: Multiple
Plan Specialty: Dental, Vision
Benefits Offered: Dental, Vision, Wellness, AD&D, Life, LTD, STD

Type of Coverage
Commercial, Individual

Geographic Areas Served
Nationwide

Subscriber Information
Average Monthly Fee Per Subscriber
(Employee + Employer Contribution):

Employee Only (Self): Varies by plan

Accreditation Certification
NCQA

Key Personnel
President . . . . Dan Fishbein, MD
SVP/CFO. . . . . Neil Haynes
SVP/Chief Info. Officer . . . . Paula Bartgis
VP, Marketing. . . . . Ed Milano
VP, Human Resources. . . . . Tammi Wortham

410 Tufts Health Medicare Plan
705 Mt Auburn Street
Watertown, MA 02472
www.tuftshealthplan.com
Non-Profit Organization: Yes
Year Founded: 1979

Healthplan and Services Defined
PLAN TYPE: Medicare
Benefits Offered: Chiropractic, Dental, Disease Management, Home Care, Inpatient SNF, Physical Therapy, Podiatry, Prescription, Psychiatric, Vision, Wellness

Type of Coverage
Individual, Medicare, Medicaid

Geographic Areas Served
Massachusetts, Connecticut, New Hampshire, Rhode Island

Subscriber Information
Average Monthly Fee Per Subscriber
(Employee + Employer Contribution):
Employee Only (Self): Varies
Medicare: Varies
Average Annual Deductible Per Subscriber:
Employee Only (Self): Varies
Medicare: Varies
Average Subscriber Co-Payment:
Primary Care Physician: Varies
Non-Network Physician: Varies
Prescription Drugs: Varies
Hospital ER: Varies
Home Health Care: Varies
Home Health Care Max. Days/Visits Covered: Varies
Nursing Home: Varies
Nursing Home Max. Days/Visits Covered: Varies

Key Personnel
President/CEO . . . . Cain A. Hayes
Chief Medical Officer . . . . Michael Sherman, MD

411 Tufts Health Plan
705 Mt Auburn Street
Watertown, MA 02472
www.tuftshealthplan.com
Non-Profit Organization: Yes
Year Founded: 1979
Number of Affiliated Hospitals: 110
Number of Primary Care Physicians: 25,000
Number of Referral/Specialty Physicians: 12,500
Total Enrollment: 1,170,000

Healthplan and Services Defined
PLAN TYPE: Multiple
Other Type: POS
Model Type: IPA
Plan Specialty: ASO, Behavioral Health, Chiropractic, Disease Management, EPO, Lab, PBM, Vision, Radiology, UR, Pharmacy
Benefits Offered: Behavioral Health, Chiropractic, Complementary Medicine, Disease Management, Home Care, Inpatient SNF, Physical Therapy, Podiatry, Prescription, Psychiatric, Transplant, Vision, Wellness

Type of Coverage
Commercial, Individual, Medicare, Supplemental Medicare, Medicaid, HSA, HRA

Type of Payment Plans Offered
POS, DFFS, FFS, Combination FFS & DFFS

Geographic Areas Served
Massachusetts, New Hampshire and Rhode Island

Subscriber Information
Average Monthly Fee Per Subscriber
(Employee + Employer Contribution):
Employee Only (Self): $190.00-220.00
Employee & 2 Family Members: $800.00-950.00
Medicare: $150.00
Average Annual Deductible Per Subscriber:
Employee Only (Self): $1000.00
Employee & 1 Family Member: $500.00
Employee & 2 Family Members: $3000.00
Average Subscriber Co-Payment:
Primary Care Physician: $10.00
Non-Network Physician: 20%
Prescription Drugs: $10/20/35
Hospital ER: $50.00
Home Health Care: $0
Home Health Care Max. Days/Visits Covered: 120 days
Nursing Home: $0
Nursing Home Max. Days/Visits Covered: 120 days

Network Qualifications
Pre-Admission Certification: No

Peer Review Type
Utilization Review: Yes
Case Management: Yes

Publishes and Distributes Report Card: Yes

Accreditation Certification
TJC, AAPI, NCQA

Key Personnel
President/CEO . . . . Cain A. Hayes
Chief Medical Officer . . . . Michael Sherman

Average Claim Compensation
Physician's Fees Charged: 75%
Hospital's Fees Charged: 70%

Specialty Managed Care Partners
Advance PCS, Private Healthe Care Systems

Employer References
Commonwealth of Massachuestts, Fleet Boston, Roman Catholic Archdiocese of Boston, City of Boston, State Street Corporation

412 UniCare Massachusetts
Brickstone Square
Eight Floor
Andover, MA 01810
Toll-Free: 866-755-2680
Phone: 978-470-1795
www.unicare.com
Subsidiary of: Anthem, Inc.
Year Founded: 1985

Healthplan and Services Defined
  PLAN TYPE: HMO/PPO
  Model Type: Network
  Benefits Offered: Behavioral Health, Chiropractic, Complementary
Medicine, Dental, Disease Management, Home Care, Inpatient SNF, Long-Term Care, Physical Therapy, Podiatry, Prescription, Psychiatric, Transplant, Vision, Wellness, Worker's Compensation, AD&D, Life, LTD, STD

Type of Coverage
  Commercial, Individual, Indemnity, Medicare

Geographic Areas Served
  Massachusetts, Southern New Hampshire & Rhode Island

Subscriber Information
  Average Monthly Fee Per Subscriber
    (Employee + Employer Contribution):
      Employee Only (Self): Varies
      Employee & 1 Family Member: Varies
      Employee & 2 Family Members: Varies
      Medicare: Varies
  Average Annual Deductible Per Subscriber:
      Employee Only (Self): Varies
      Employee & 1 Family Member: Varies
      Employee & 2 Family Members: Varies
      Medicare: Varies
  Average Subscriber Co-Payment:
      Primary Care Physician: Varies
      Non-Network Physician: Varies
      Prescription Drugs: Varies
      Hospital ER: Varies
      Home Health Care: Varies
      Home Health Care Max. Days/Visits Covered: Varies
      Nursing Home: Varies
      Nursing Home Max. Days/Visits Covered: Varies

Network Qualifications
  Pre-Admission Certification: Yes

Peer Review Type
  Utilization Review: Yes
  Second Surgical Opinion: Yes
  Case Management: Yes

Publishes and Distributes Report Card: No

Accreditation Certification
  URAC
  TJC Accreditation, Medicare Approved, Utilization Review, Pre-Admission Certification, State Licensure, Quality Assurance Program

413 UnitedHealthcare Community Plan Massachusetts
UnitedHealthcare Customer Service
P.O. Box 30769
Salt Lake City, UT 84130-0769
Toll-Free: 888-545-5205
www.uhccommunityplan.com/ma
Subsidiary of: UnitedHealth Group
For Profit Organization: Yes

Healthplan and Services Defined
  PLAN TYPE: Medicare
  Other Type: Medicaid
  Model Type: Network
  Benefits Offered: Dental, Prescription, Vision, Wellness

Type of Coverage
  Medicare, Medicaid

Geographic Areas Served
  Bristol, Essex, Hampden, Middlesex, Norfolk, Plymouth, Suffolk, and Worcester

Key Personnel
  CEO, Community Plan MA . . . . John Madondo
    john_madondo@uhc.com

414 UnitedHealthcare of Massachusetts
950 Winter Street
Waltham, MA 02451
Toll-Free: 888-545-5205
Phone: 866-414-1959
www.uhc.com
Subsidiary of: UnitedHealth Group
For Profit Organization: Yes

Healthplan and Services Defined
  PLAN TYPE: HMO/PPO
  Model Type: Network
  Plan Specialty: Behavioral Health, Dental, Disease Management, PBM, Vision
  Benefits Offered: Behavioral Health, Dental, Disease Management, Long-Term Care, Prescription, Vision, Wellness, Life, LTD, STD
  Offers Demand Management Patient Information Service: Yes

Type of Coverage
  Individual, Medicare, Supplemental Medicare, Medicaid, Catastrophic, Family, Military, Veterans, Group, Catastrophic Illness Benefit: None

Type of Payment Plans Offered
  POS, FFS

Geographic Areas Served
  Massachusetts, Vermont, New Hampsire, Maine

Subscriber Information
  Average Monthly Fee Per Subscriber
    (Employee + Employer Contribution):
      Employee Only (Self): $150.00
      Employee & 2 Family Members: $300.00

Network Qualifications
  Pre-Admission Certification: Yes

Peer Review Type
  Utilization Review: Yes
  Second Surgical Opinion: Yes
  Case Management: Yes

Publishes and Distributes Report Card: Yes

Accreditation Certification
  AAPI, NCQA
  TJC Accreditation, Medicare Approved, Utilization Review,
    Pre-Admission Certification, State Licensure, Quality
    Assurance Program

Key Personnel
  CEO, New England....................... Tim Archer

Average Claim Compensation
  Physician's Fees Charged: 70%
  Hospital's Fees Charged: 80%

Specialty Managed Care Partners
  Enters into Contracts with Regional Business Coalitions: Yes

MICHIGAN

Health Insurance Coverage Status and Type of Coverage by Age

Category	All Persons Number	%	Under 19 years Number	%	Under 65 years Number	%
Total population	9,879 *(1)*	100.0 *(0.0)*	2,280 *(5)*	100.0 *(0.0)*	8,150 *(4)*	100.0 *(0.0)*
Covered by some type of health insurance	9,308 *(17)*	94.2 *(0.2)*	2,203 *(8)*	96.6 *(0.3)*	7,584 *(18)*	93.1 *(0.2)*
Covered by private health insurance	7,015 *(35)*	71.0 *(0.4)*	1,475 *(16)*	64.7 *(0.7)*	5,805 *(32)*	71.2 *(0.4)*
Employer-based	5,976 *(34)*	60.5 *(0.3)*	1,354 *(16)*	59.4 *(0.7)*	5,188 *(32)*	63.7 *(0.4)*
Direct purchase	1,293 *(21)*	13.1 *(0.2)*	136 *(8)*	5.9 *(0.3)*	725 *(18)*	8.9 *(0.2)*
TRICARE	132 *(7)*	1.3 *(0.1)*	22 *(3)*	1.0 *(0.1)*	75 *(6)*	0.9 *(0.1)*
Covered by public health insurance	3,829 *(29)*	38.8 *(0.3)*	855 *(17)*	37.5 *(0.7)*	2,143 *(29)*	26.3 *(0.4)*
Medicaid	2,154 *(31)*	21.8 *(0.3)*	850 *(17)*	37.3 *(0.7)*	1,940 *(29)*	23.8 *(0.4)*
Medicare	1,988 *(10)*	20.1 *(0.1)*	11 *(2)*	0.5 *(0.1)*	304 *(8)*	3.7 *(0.1)*
VA Care	200 *(7)*	2.0 *(0.1)*	3 *(1)*	0.1 *(0.1)*	81 *(5)*	1.0 *(0.1)*
Not covered at any time during the year	571 *(18)*	5.8 *(0.2)*	78 *(6)*	3.4 *(0.3)*	566 *(17)*	6.9 *(0.2)*

Note: Numbers in thousands; Figures cover civilian noninstitutionalized population in 2019; N/A indicates that data was not available; Z represents or rounds to zero; Margin of error appears in parenthesis and is calculated using replicate weights.
Source: U.S. Census Bureau, American Community Survey, Table HI-05. Health Insurance Coverage Status and Type of Coverage by State and Age for All People: 2019

Michigan

415 Aetna Better Health of Michigan
28588 Northwestern Highway
Suite 380B
Southfield, MI 48034
Toll-Free: 866-316-3784
www.aetnabetterhealth.com/michigan
Subsidiary of: CVS Health / Aetna Inc.
For Profit Organization: Yes

Healthplan and Services Defined
  PLAN TYPE: HMO/PPO
  Other Type: POS
  Model Type: Network
  Plan Specialty: Behavioral Health, EPO, Lab, PBM, Radiology
  Benefits Offered: Behavioral Health, Dental, Disease Management, Long-Term Care, Physical Therapy, Podiatry, Prescription, Psychiatric, Vision, Wellness, Life, LTD, STD

Type of Coverage
  Commercial, Medicaid, Catastrophic, Student health

Geographic Areas Served
  Statewide

Key Personnel
  CEO . . . . Beverly Allen

416 Ascension At Home
Crittenton Medical Plaza
2251 Squirrel Road, Suite 320
Auburn Hills, MI 48326
Toll-Free: 888-246-6322
Fax: 877-561-7891
ascensionathome.com
Subsidiary of: Ascension
Non-Profit Organization: Yes

Healthplan and Services Defined
  PLAN TYPE: Other
  Plan Specialty: Disease Management
  Benefits Offered: Dental, Disease Management, Home Care, Wellness, Ambulance & Transportation; Nursing Service; Short-and-long-term care management planning; Hospice

Geographic Areas Served
  Texas, Alabama, Indiana, Kansas, Michigan, Mississippi, Oklahoma, Wisconsin

Key Personnel
  President . . . . David Grams
  Chair/CEO . . . . James A. Deal

417 Blue Care Network of Michigan
20500 Civic Center Drive
Southfield, MI 48076
Toll-Free: 855-237-3501
www.bcbsm.com
Subsidiary of: Blue Cross Blue Shield of Michigan
Non-Profit Organization: Yes
Year Founded: 1998
Federally Qualified: Yes
Number of Primary Care Physicians: 6,000
Number of Referral/Specialty Physicians: 23,000
Total Enrollment: 900,000

Healthplan and Services Defined
  PLAN TYPE: HMO
  Model Type: IPA, Network
  Plan Specialty: Lab, Radiology
  Benefits Offered: Behavioral Health, Disease Management, Prescription, Psychiatric, Wellness

Type of Coverage
  Commercial, Individual, Medicare, Medicaid
  Catastrophic Illness Benefit: Covered

Geographic Areas Served
  Statewide

Peer Review Type
  Case Management: Yes

Publishes and Distributes Report Card: Yes

Accreditation Certification
  NCQA

Key Personnel
  President/CEO . . . . Daniel J. Loepp
  EVP, Financial Officer . . . . Paul L. Mozak
  SVP, Information Officer . . . . William M. Fandrich
  SVP/Chief Medical Officer . . . . James D. Grant, MD

Specialty Managed Care Partners
  Enters into Contracts with Regional Business Coalitions: Yes

Employer References
  General Motors, Ford Motor Company, State of Michigan, Federal Employee Program, Daimler Chrysler

418 Blue Care Network of Michigan
20500 Civic Center Drive
Southfield, MI 48076
Toll-Free: 855-237-3501
www.bcbsm.com
Non-Profit Organization: Yes
Year Founded: 1998
Federally Qualified: Yes
Number of Affiliated Hospitals: 152
Number of Primary Care Physicians: 6,100
Number of Referral/Specialty Physicians: 22,700
State Enrollment: 900,000

Healthplan and Services Defined
  PLAN TYPE: HMO
  Model Type: Network
  Plan Specialty: Dental, Lab, Vision, Radiology
  Benefits Offered: Behavioral Health, Dental, Disease Management, Physical Therapy, Prescription, Psychiatric, Vision, Wellness

Type of Coverage
  Commercial, Individual
  Catastrophic Illness Benefit: Varies per case

Type of Payment Plans Offered
  POS, Capitated, Combination FFS & DFFS

Geographic Areas Served
Muskegon, Newago, Oceana & Ottawa counties

Peer Review Type
Utilization Review: Yes
Second Surgical Opinion: Yes

Publishes and Distributes Report Card: Yes

Key Personnel
President/CEO . . . . Daniel J. Loepp
EVP/CFO. . . . . Paul L. Mozak
Chief Medical Officer. . . . . James D. Grant, MD
SVP/CIO . . . . William M. Fandrich
Chief Operating Officer . . . . Darrell E. Middleton

419 Blue Cross Blue Shield of Michigan
20500 Civic Center Drive
Southfield, MI 48076
Toll-Free: 855-237-3501
www.bcbsm.com
Year Founded: 1939
Number of Affiliated Hospitals: 152
Number of Primary Care Physicians: 32,000
Total Enrollment: 6,100,000
State Enrollment: 4,500,000

Healthplan and Services Defined
PLAN TYPE: Multiple
Model Type: Network
Benefits Offered: Chiropractic, Disease Management, Home Care, Inpatient SNF, Physical Therapy, Podiatry, Prescription, Psychiatric, Wellness

Type of Coverage
Commercial, Individual, Medicare, Supplemental Medicare, Medicaid

Geographic Areas Served
Blue Care Network available in 26 counties in southeastern Michigan. PPO plans available statewide

Subscriber Information
Average Monthly Fee Per Subscriber
  (Employee + Employer Contribution):
    Employee Only (Self): Varies
    Medicare: Varies
Average Annual Deductible Per Subscriber:
    Employee Only (Self): Varies
    Medicare: Varies
Average Subscriber Co-Payment:
    Primary Care Physician: Varies
    Non-Network Physician: Varies
    Prescription Drugs: Varies
    Hospital ER: Varies
    Home Health Care: Varies
    Home Health Care Max. Days/Visits Covered: Varies
    Nursing Home: Varies
    Nursing Home Max. Days/Visits Covered: Varies

Key Personnel
President/CEO . . . . Daniel J. Loepp
EVP/CFO. . . . . Paul L. Mozak
EVP/COO. . . . . Darrell E. Middleton
EVP/Health Plan Business . . . . Kenneth R. Dallafior

Chief Medical Officer. . . . . James D. Grant, MD
Corporate Compliance. . . . . Michele A. Samuels

420 ConnectCare
4000 Wellness Drive
Midland, MI 48670
Toll-Free: 888-646-2429
Phone: 989-839-1629
Fax: 989-389-1626
info@connectcare.com
www.connectcare.com
Subsidiary of: MidMichigan Health Network LLC
Non-Profit Organization: Yes
Year Founded: 1993
Physician Owned Organization: Yes
Owned by an Integrated Delivery Network (IDN): Yes
Federally Qualified: No
Number of Affiliated Hospitals: 5,000
Number of Referral/Specialty Physicians: 90,000
Total Enrollment: 17,000
State Enrollment: 36,000

Healthplan and Services Defined
PLAN TYPE: PPO
Model Type: Network
Benefits Offered: Behavioral Health, Dental, Home Care, Inpatient SNF, Long-Term Care, Physical Therapy, Podiatry, Prescription, Psychiatric, Wellness

Type of Coverage
Commercial, Indemnity

Type of Payment Plans Offered
POS, DFFS

Geographic Areas Served
Domiciled in central Michigan, with primary counties served including Clare, Gladwin, Gratiot, Isabella, Midland, Montcalm and Roscommon. Arrangement with national PPO's for coverage of downstate and those enrollees residing outside of Michigan

Subscriber Information
Average Annual Deductible Per Subscriber:
    Employee Only (Self): $275.00
    Employee & 2 Family Members: $550.00

Network Qualifications
Pre-Admission Certification: Yes

Peer Review Type
Utilization Review: Yes
Second Surgical Opinion: Yes
Case Management: Yes

Accreditation Certification
NCQA
Quality Assurance Program

421 Delta Dental of Michigan
4100 Okemos Road
Okemos, MI 48864
Toll-Free: 800-524-0149
www.deltadentalmi.com

Mailing Address: P.O. Box 9089, Farmington Hills, MI 48333-9089
Subsidiary of: Delta Dental Plans Association
Number of Primary Care Physicians: 5,000
Total Enrollment: 14,200,000

Healthplan and Services Defined
PLAN TYPE: Dental
Plan Specialty: Dental
Benefits Offered: Dental

Type of Coverage
Commercial, Individual

Geographic Areas Served
Michigan, Ohio, Indiana and Tennessee

Key Personnel
CEO .... Goran Jurkovic

---

422 Dencap Dental Plans
45 E Milwaukee Street
Detroit, MI 48202
Toll-Free: 888-988-3384
Phone: 313-972-1400
Fax: 313-972-4662
info@dencap.com
www.dencap.com
Year Founded: 1984
Number of Primary Care Physicians: 200
State Enrollment: 20,000

Healthplan and Services Defined
PLAN TYPE: Dental
Model Type: Network
Plan Specialty: Dental
Benefits Offered: Dental

Type of Coverage
Commercial, Individual

Type of Payment Plans Offered
DFFS, FFS

Geographic Areas Served
Southeastern Michigan

Subscriber Information
Average Monthly Fee Per Subscriber
(Employee + Employer Contribution):
Employee Only (Self): Varies

Peer Review Type
Case Management: Yes

Publishes and Distributes Report Card: Yes

Accreditation Certification
Utilization Review, Quality Assurance Program

Key Personnel
CEO .... Joe Lentine, Jr
Provider Relations Dir .... Frank Berge

Specialty Managed Care Partners
Midwest and Dentals, Great Expression

---

423 DenteMax
25925 Telegraph Road
Suite 400
Southfield, MI 48033
Toll-Free: 800-752-1547
Fax: 888-586-0296
customerservices@dentemax.com
www.dentemax.com
Subsidiary of: Dental Network of America
For Profit Organization: Yes
Year Founded: 1985
Number of Primary Care Physicians: 273,000
Total Enrollment: 4,500,000

Healthplan and Services Defined
PLAN TYPE: Dental
Other Type: Dental PPO
Plan Specialty: Dental
Benefits Offered: Dental

Type of Coverage
Commercial, Individual
Catastrophic Illness Benefit: None

Type of Payment Plans Offered
DFFS

Geographic Areas Served
Nationwide

Subscriber Information
Average Monthly Fee Per Subscriber
(Employee + Employer Contribution):
Employee Only (Self): Varies by plan

Network Qualifications
Pre-Admission Certification: No

Peer Review Type
Utilization Review: Yes

Accreditation Certification
Quality Assurance Program

Key Personnel
President/CEO .... Melissa Wagner
VP, Sales & Marketing .... Kim Sharbatz

---

424 Golden Dental Plans
29377 Hoover Road
Warren, MI 48093
Toll-Free: 800-451-5918
info@goldendentalplans.com
www.goldendentalplans.com
Year Founded: 1984
Number of Primary Care Physicians: 3,200
Total Enrollment: 130,000

Healthplan and Services Defined
PLAN TYPE: Dental
Other Type: Dental HMO
Model Type: Network
Plan Specialty: Dental
Benefits Offered: Dental

Type of Coverage
Individual

Type of Payment Plans Offered
DFFS

Geographic Areas Served
Southeast Michigan

Accreditation Certification
Utilization Review, Pre-Admission Certification

---

425 HAP-Health Alliance Plan: Flint
2050 S Linden Road
Flint, MI 48532
Toll-Free: 800-422-4641
www.hap.org
Secondary Address: 2850 W Grand Boulevard, Detroit, MI 48202, 313-872-8100
Non-Profit Organization: Yes
Year Founded: 1979
Federally Qualified: Yes
Number of Affiliated Hospitals: 29
Number of Primary Care Physicians: 900
Number of Referral/Specialty Physicians: 1,800
Total Enrollment: 650,000
State Enrollment: 650,000

Healthplan and Services Defined
PLAN TYPE: HMO/PPO
Model Type: Network
Plan Specialty: Lab, Radiology
Benefits Offered: Behavioral Health, Chiropractic, Complementary Medicine, Disease Management, Home Care, Inpatient SNF, Long-Term Care, Physical Therapy, Podiatry, Prescription, Psychiatric, Transplant, Vision, Wellness, Women's Health
Offers Demand Management Patient Information Service: Yes

Type of Coverage
Commercial, Individual, Medicare, Supplemental Medicare, Medicaid, Catastrophic, TPA
Catastrophic Illness Benefit: Unlimited

Type of Payment Plans Offered
POS, DFFS, Capitated, Combination FFS & DFFS

Geographic Areas Served
Commercial Product: Bay, Genesee, Huron, Lapeer, Livingston, Midland, Northern Oakland counties, Saginaw, Sanilac, Shiawassee, Tuscola. Full counties: Arenac, Sanilac and St Clair

Subscriber Information
Average Monthly Fee Per Subscriber
(Employee + Employer Contribution):
Employee Only (Self): Varies by plan

Network Qualifications
Pre-Admission Certification: Yes

Peer Review Type
Utilization Review: Yes
Second Surgical Opinion: Yes
Case Management: Yes

Publishes and Distributes Report Card: Yes

Accreditation Certification
NCQA
TJC Accreditation, Medicare Approved, Utilization Review, Pre-Admission Certification, State Licensure, Quality Assurance Program

Specialty Managed Care Partners
American Healthways
Enters into Contracts with Regional Business Coalitions: No

Employer References
General Motors, Delphi, Covenant Health Partners

---

426 HAP-Health Alliance Plan: Senior Medicare Plan
2850 W Grand Boulevard
Detroit, MI 48202
Toll-Free: 800-422-4641
Phone: 313-872-8100
msweb1@hap.org
www.hap.org
Non-Profit Organization: Yes
Number of Affiliated Hospitals: 29
Number of Primary Care Physicians: 900
Number of Referral/Specialty Physicians: 1,800
Total Enrollment: 14,000
State Enrollment: 14,000

Healthplan and Services Defined
PLAN TYPE: Medicare
Benefits Offered: Chiropractic, Disease Management, Home Care, Inpatient SNF, Physical Therapy, Podiatry, Prescription, Psychiatric, Vision, Wellness

Type of Coverage
Individual, Medicare, MIChild

Geographic Areas Served
Health Plus Senior Medicare Coverage Plans available only within Michigan

Subscriber Information
Average Monthly Fee Per Subscriber
(Employee + Employer Contribution):
Employee Only (Self): Varies
Medicare: Varies
Average Annual Deductible Per Subscriber:
Employee Only (Self): Varies
Medicare: Varies
Average Subscriber Co-Payment:
Primary Care Physician: Varies
Non-Network Physician: Varies
Prescription Drugs: Varies
Hospital ER: Varies
Home Health Care: Varies
Home Health Care Max. Days/Visits Covered: Varies
Nursing Home: Varies
Nursing Home Max. Days/Visits Covered: Varies

427 Health Alliance Medicare
2850 W Grand Boulevard
Detroit, MI 48202
Toll-Free: 800-422-4641
Phone: 313-872-8100
msweb1@hap.org
www.hap.org/medicare
Non-Profit Organization: Yes
Total Enrollment: 383,000

Healthplan and Services Defined
PLAN TYPE: Medicare
Other Type: HMO/PPO, POS
Benefits Offered: Chiropractic, Dental, Home Care, Inpatient SNF, Physical Therapy, Podiatry, Prescription, Psychiatric, Wellness, Worldwide Emergency, Fitness Benefits, Hearing Exams, Preventive Services, Eye Exams & Eyeglasses, Urgent Care, Hospice

Type of Coverage
Individual, Medicare, Group Medicare Plans

Geographic Areas Served
Statewide

Subscriber Information
Average Monthly Fee Per Subscriber
(Employee + Employer Contribution):
Employee Only (Self): Varies
Medicare: Varies
Average Annual Deductible Per Subscriber:
Employee Only (Self): Varies
Medicare: Varies
Average Subscriber Co-Payment:
Primary Care Physician: Varies
Non-Network Physician: Varies
Prescription Drugs: Varies
Hospital ER: Varies
Home Health Care: Varies
Home Health Care Max. Days/Visits Covered: Varies
Nursing Home: Varies
Nursing Home Max. Days/Visits Covered: Varies

Key Personnel
President/CEO . . . . Michael Genord

428 Health Alliance Plan
2850 W Grand Boulevard
Detroit, MI 48202
Toll-Free: 800-422-4641
Phone: 313-872-8100
www.hap.org
Non-Profit Organization: Yes
Year Founded: 1979
Number of Affiliated Hospitals: 157
Number of Primary Care Physicians: 18,000
Number of Referral/Specialty Physicians: 1,000
Total Enrollment: 650,000
State Enrollment: 650,000

Healthplan and Services Defined
PLAN TYPE: HMO/PPO
Other Type: EPO
Model Type: Staff
Benefits Offered: Dental, Disease Management, Prescription, Vision, Wellness, Alternative Medicine
Offers Demand Management Patient Information Service: Yes
DMPI Services Offered: Health Education Classes

Type of Coverage
Commercial, Individual, Medicare, Supplemental Medicare, Medicaid, Catastrophic

Type of Payment Plans Offered
POS, Capitated, FFS, Combination FFS & DFFS

Geographic Areas Served
Statewide

Network Qualifications
Pre-Admission Certification: Yes

Peer Review Type
Utilization Review: Yes
Second Surgical Opinion: No
Case Management: Yes

Publishes and Distributes Report Card: Yes

Accreditation Certification
NCQA
TJC Accreditation, Medicare Approved, Utilization Review, Pre-Admission Certification, State Licensure, Quality Assurance Program

Key Personnel
President/CEO . . . . Michael Genord, MD
Chief Financial Officer. Laurie Doran
VP, Human Resources . . . . Derick Adams, Esq.
SVP, Sales & Marketing . . . . Margaret Anderson
Chief Operating Officer. Mike Treash
Chief Medical Officer . . . . Charles Bloom, DO

Specialty Managed Care Partners
Enters into Contracts with Regional Business Coalitions: Yes

429 Humana Health Insurance of Michigan
18610 Fenkell Street
Suite A
Detroit, MI 48223
Toll-Free: 800-649-0059
Phone: 313-437-6532
Fax: 313-273-8375
www.humana.com
Secondary Address: 13685 Eureka Road, Southgate, MI 48195, 734-767-5006
Subsidiary of: Humana Inc.
For Profit Organization: Yes

Healthplan and Services Defined
PLAN TYPE: HMO/PPO
Plan Specialty: ASO
Benefits Offered: Disease Management, Prescription, Wellness

Type of Coverage
Commercial, Individual

Geographic Areas Served
Statewide

Accreditation Certification
URAC, NCQA, CORE

Key Personnel
Regional President . . . . Kathie Mancini

Specialty Managed Care Partners
Caremark Rx

Employer References
Tricare

430 McLaren Health Plan
G-3245 Beecher Road
Flint, MI 48532
Toll-Free: 888-327-0671
Fax: 833-540-8648
www.mclarenhealthplan.org
For Profit Organization: Yes
Year Founded: 2003
Number of Affiliated Hospitals: 14
Number of Primary Care Physicians: 490

Healthplan and Services Defined
PLAN TYPE: HMO
Benefits Offered: Home Care, Prescription, Hospice care

Type of Coverage
Commercial, Medicaid

Geographic Areas Served
Michigan and Indiana

Key Personnel
President/CEO . . . . Nancy Jenkins

431 Meridian Health Plan
1 Campus Martius
Suite 700
Detroit, MI 48226
Toll-Free: 888-437-0606
memberservices.mi@mhplan.com
www.mhplan.com
Subsidiary of: Wellcare Health Plans Inc.
Number of Primary Care Physicians: 45,000
Total Enrollment: 750,000

Healthplan and Services Defined
PLAN TYPE: HMO

Type of Coverage
Medicare, Medicaid

Geographic Areas Served
Michigan, Iowa, Illinois, Ohio, Indiana, Kentucky

Accreditation Certification
URAC, NCQA

432 Michigan Complete Health
1 Campus Martius
Suite 700
Detroit, MI 48226
Toll-Free: 844-239-7387
mmp.michigancompletehealth.com
Mailing Address: P.O. Box 3060, Farmington, MO 63640-3060
Subsidiary of: Centene Corporation
For Profit Organization: Yes

Healthplan and Services Defined
PLAN TYPE: Medicare
Model Type: Network
Benefits Offered: Dental, Home Care, Prescription, Vision, Hearing

Type of Coverage
Medicare, Medicaid, Medicare-Medicaid Plan

Geographic Areas Served
Macomb and Wayne counties

Key Personnel
President/CEO . . . . Amy Williams

433 Molina Healthcare of Michigan
880 West Long Lake Road
Troy, MI 48098
Toll-Free: 888-898-7969
www.molinahealthcare.com
Subsidiary of: Molina Healthcare, Inc.
For Profit Organization: Yes
Year Founded: 1980
Physician Owned Organization: Yes

Healthplan and Services Defined
PLAN TYPE: Medicare
Model Type: Network
Plan Specialty: Integrated Medicare/Medicaid (Duals)
Benefits Offered: Chiropractic, Dental, Home Care, Inpatient SNF, Long-Term Care, Podiatry, Vision

Type of Coverage
Commercial, Medicare, Supplemental Medicare, Medicaid

Accreditation Certification
URAC, NCQA

Key Personnel
President . . . . Christine Surdock
Chief Medical Officer . . . . David Donigian, MD

434 Paramount Care of Michigan
214 E. Elm St.
Suite 107
Monroe, MI 48162
Toll-Free: 800-462-3589
Phone: 419-887-2525
paramount.memberservices@promedica.org
www.paramounthealthcare.com
Mailing Address: PO Box 928, Toledo, OH 43697-0497
Subsidiary of: ProMedica Health System
For Profit Organization: Yes
Year Founded: 1988
Number of Affiliated Hospitals: 34
Number of Primary Care Physicians: 1,900
Total Enrollment: 187,000

Healthplan and Services Defined
PLAN TYPE: HMO/PPO

Benefits Offered: Disease Management, Prescription, Wellness

Type of Coverage
Commercial, Medicare

Geographic Areas Served
Southeast Michigan

Accreditation Certification
NCQA

Key Personnel
President .... Lori Johnston
Chief Financial Officer .... Jeff Martin
Chief Operating Officer .... Jered Wilson

Specialty Managed Care Partners
Express Scripts

---

435 Physicians Health Plan of Mid-Michigan
1400 East Michigan Avenue
Lansing, MI 48912
Toll-Free: 800-562-6197
Phone: 517-364-8400
Fax: 517-364-8460
www.phpmichigan.com
Mailing Address: P.O. Box 30377, Lansing, MI 48909-7877
Subsidiary of: Sparrow Health System
Non-Profit Organization: Yes
Year Founded: 1980
Owned by an Integrated Delivery Network (IDN): Yes
Number of Affiliated Hospitals: 31
Number of Primary Care Physicians: 3,100
Total Enrollment: 68,942
State Enrollment: 68,942

Healthplan and Services Defined
PLAN TYPE: HMO/PPO
Model Type: IPA
Plan Specialty: Behavioral Health, Chiropractic, Dental, Disease Management, Lab, PBM, Vision, Radiology, UR
Benefits Offered: Behavioral Health, Chiropractic, Dental, Disease Management, Home Care, Inpatient SNF, Physical Therapy, Podiatry, Prescription, Psychiatric, Transplant, Vision, Wellness, AD&D, Life, STD, FSA

Type of Coverage
Commercial, Medicaid, Catastrophic, PPO, TPA
Catastrophic Illness Benefit: Unlimited

Type of Payment Plans Offered
POS, DFFS

Geographic Areas Served
Clinton, Eaton, Gratiot, Ionia, Ingham, Isabella, Montcalm, Saginaw and Shiawassee counties

Subscriber Information
Average Subscriber Co-Payment:
Primary Care Physician: $10.00
Non-Network Physician: 20%
Prescription Drugs: $10.00/25.00/40.00
Hospital ER: $50.00
Home Health Care: $0
Nursing Home: $0

Nursing Home Max. Days/Visits Covered: 100

Network Qualifications
Pre-Admission Certification: Yes

Peer Review Type
Utilization Review: Yes
Second Surgical Opinion: Yes
Case Management: Yes

Publishes and Distributes Report Card: No

Accreditation Certification
URAC, NCQA
Medicare Approved, Utilization Review, Pre-Admission Certification, State Licensure, Quality Assurance Program

Key Personnel
President/CEO........................ Dennis J Reese

Specialty Managed Care Partners
United Behavioral Health
Enters into Contracts with Regional Business Coalitions: No

---

436 Priority Health
1257 East Beltline Ave. NE
Grand Rapids, MI 49525
Toll-Free: 800-942-0954
Phone: 616-942-0954
www.priorityhealth.com
Non-Profit Organization: Yes
Year Founded: 1985
Physician Owned Organization: Yes
Owned by an Integrated Delivery Network (IDN): Yes
Federally Qualified: No
Number of Affiliated Hospitals: 5,000
Number of Referral/Specialty Physicians: 617,000
Total Enrollment: 596,220

Healthplan and Services Defined
PLAN TYPE: Multiple
Model Type: IPA
Plan Specialty: ASO, Behavioral Health, Chiropractic, Dental, Disease Management, EPO, Lab, MSO, PBM, Vision, Radiology, UR
Benefits Offered: Behavioral Health, Chiropractic, Complementary Medicine, Dental, Disease Management, Home Care, Inpatient SNF, Long-Term Care, Physical Therapy, Podiatry, Prescription, Psychiatric, Transplant, Vision, Wellness, AD&D, Life, LTD, STD
Offers Demand Management Patient Information Service: No

Type of Coverage
Commercial, Individual, Indemnity, Medicare, Medicaid
Catastrophic Illness Benefit: Varies per case

Type of Payment Plans Offered
DFFS, Capitated, FFS, Combination FFS & DFFS

Geographic Areas Served
69 counties in Michigan

Subscriber Information
Average Monthly Fee Per Subscriber
(Employee + Employer Contribution):
Employee Only (Self): Varies
Employee & 1 Family Member: Varies

Employee & 2 Family Members: Varies
Medicare: Varies
Average Annual Deductible Per Subscriber:
Employee Only (Self): Varies
Employee & 1 Family Member: Varies
Employee & 2 Family Members: Varies
Medicare: Varies
Average Subscriber Co-Payment:
Primary Care Physician: Varies
Non-Network Physician: Varies
Prescription Drugs: Varies
Hospital ER: Varies
Home Health Care: Varies
Home Health Care Max. Days/Visits Covered: Varies
Nursing Home: Varies
Nursing Home Max. Days/Visits Covered: Varies

Network Qualifications
Pre-Admission Certification: No

Peer Review Type
Utilization Review: Yes
Case Management: Yes

Publishes and Distributes Report Card: No

Accreditation Certification
NCQA
Utilization Review, Pre-Admission Certification, State Licensure, Quality Assurance Program

Key Personnel
President . . . . Praveen Thadani
SVP, Information Services . . . . Christopher Crook
SVP, Government Markets . . . . Joyce Chan Russell
VP, Marketing . . . . Nathan Foco
SVP/Chief Medical Officer . . . . James Forshee, MD
SVP, Finance . . . . Nick Gates

Specialty Managed Care Partners
Enters into Contracts with Regional Business Coalitions: Yes
National Federation of Independent Business

437 PriorityHealth Medicare Plans
1257 E Beltline NE
Grand Rapids, MI 49525-4501
Toll-Free: 800-942-0954
Phone: 616-942-0954
www.priorityhealth.com/medicare
Subsidiary of: PriorityHealth

Healthplan and Services Defined
PLAN TYPE: Medicare
Benefits Offered: Chiropractic, Dental, Disease Management, Home Care, Inpatient SNF, Physical Therapy, Podiatry, Prescription, Psychiatric, Vision, Wellness

Type of Coverage
Individual, Medicare, Medicaid

Geographic Areas Served
Lower Michigan

Subscriber Information
Average Monthly Fee Per Subscriber
(Employee + Employer Contribution):
Employee Only (Self): Varies
Medicare: Varies
Average Annual Deductible Per Subscriber:
Employee Only (Self): Varies
Medicare: Varies
Average Subscriber Co-Payment:
Primary Care Physician: Varies
Non-Network Physician: Varies
Prescription Drugs: Varies
Hospital ER: Varies
Home Health Care: Varies
Home Health Care Max. Days/Visits Covered: Varies
Nursing Home: Varies
Nursing Home Max. Days/Visits Covered: Varies

Accreditation Certification
NCQA

Key Personnel
President/CEO . . . . Praveen Thadani

438 SVS Vision
118 Cass Avenue
Mount Clemens, MI 48043
Toll-Free: 800-787-4600
customerservice@svsvision.com
www.svsvision.com
For Profit Organization: Yes
Year Founded: 1974
Total Enrollment: 390,000

Healthplan and Services Defined
PLAN TYPE: Vision
Other Type: Vision Plan
Plan Specialty: Vision
Benefits Offered: Vision, Services limited to vision care

Type of Payment Plans Offered
DFFS

Geographic Areas Served
Michigan; Illinois; Ohio; Indiana; Kentucky; Missouri; Georgia; New York

Subscriber Information
Average Monthly Fee Per Subscriber
(Employee + Employer Contribution):
Employee Only (Self): Varies by plan

Network Qualifications
Pre-Admission Certification: Yes

Peer Review Type
Utilization Review: Yes
Second Surgical Opinion: Yes
Case Management: Yes

Key Personnel
President/CFO . . . . Kenneth Stann
CEO . . . . Robert G. Farrell, Jr., OD
EVP/COO . . . . Lisa Stann
EVP/CAO . . . . David Cassell

Michigan

439 Total Health Care
3011 W Grand Boulevard
Suite 1600
Detroit, MI 48202
Toll-Free: 800-826-2862
Phone: 313-871-2000
www.thcmi.com
Non-Profit Organization: Yes
Year Founded: 1973
Owned by an Integrated Delivery Network (IDN): Yes
Number of Affiliated Hospitals: 28
Number of Primary Care Physicians: 1,850
Number of Referral/Specialty Physicians: 4,500
Total Enrollment: 90,000
State Enrollment: 90,000

Healthplan and Services Defined
PLAN TYPE: HMO
Other Type: PPN, POS
Model Type: Staff
Plan Specialty: Lab, Radiology
Benefits Offered: Behavioral Health, Chiropractic, Complementary
Medicine, Disease Management, Home Care, Inpatient SNF, Long-Term Care, Physical Therapy, Podiatry, Prescription, Psychiatric, Transplant, Vision, Wellness, Worker's Compensation, Alternative Treatments, Durable Medical Equipment, Speech, OT
24-hour Nurse Advice Line
Offers Demand Management Patient Information Service: Yes
DMPI Services Offered: Educational Classes and Programs

Type of Coverage
Commercial, Individual, Medicare, Medicaid

Type of Payment Plans Offered
Combination FFS & DFFS

Geographic Areas Served
Michigan

Subscriber Information
Average Monthly Fee Per Subscriber
  (Employee + Employer Contribution):
    Employee Only (Self): $67.12
    Employee & 2 Family Members: $164.88
  Average Subscriber Co-Payment:
    Primary Care Physician: $10.00
    Hospital ER: $40.00

Accreditation Certification
TJC, NCQA

Key Personnel
Chief Executive Officer................Randy Narowitz
Office Manager........................Nancy Kowal

Specialty Managed Care Partners
RxAmerica

Employer References
Federal Government, State of Michigan, American Airlines, Detroit Board of Education, Wayne County Employees

440 Trinity Health
20555 Victor Parkway
Livonia, MI 48152-7018
Phone: 734-343-1000
www.trinity-health.org
Subsidiary of: Trinity Health
Non-Profit Organization: Yes
Year Founded: 2013
Number of Affiliated Hospitals: 92
Number of Primary Care Physicians: 3,600
Total Enrollment: 30,000,000

Healthplan and Services Defined
PLAN TYPE: Other
Benefits Offered: Disease Management, Home Care, Long-Term Care, Psychiatric, Hospice programs, PACE (Program of All Inclusive Care for the Elderly)

Geographic Areas Served
California, Connecticut, Delaware, Florida, Georgia, Idaho, Illinois, Indiana, Iowa, Nebraska, Maryland, Massachusetts, Michigan, New Jersey, New York, Ohio, and Pennsylvania

Key Personnel
Chief Executive Officer............Michael A. Slubowski
Chief Operating Officer..............Benjamin R. Carter
Human Resources.....................Edmund F. Hodge
EVP, Chief Legal Officer...................Linda Ross
Chief Clinical Officer....................Daniel J. Roth
Interim CFO......................Cynthia A. Clemence

441 Trinity Health of Michigan
Saint Joseph Mercy Health System
5301 McAuley Drive
Ypsilanti, MI 48197
Phone: 734-712-3456
www.trinity-health.org
Secondary Address: Mercy Health, 200 Jefferson Avenue SE, Grand Rapids, MI 49503, 616-685-5000
Subsidiary of: Trinity Health
Non-Profit Organization: Yes
Year Founded: 2013
Total Enrollment: 30,000,000

Healthplan and Services Defined
PLAN TYPE: Other
Benefits Offered: Disease Management, Home Care, Long-Term Care, Psychiatric, Hospice programs, PACE (Program of All Inclusive Care for the Elderly)

Geographic Areas Served
Statewide

Key Personnel
President/CEO.........................Rob Casalou
Chief Financial Officer..................Michael Gusho
Chief HR Officer..........................Ane McNeil
VP, Philanthropy........................Fran Petonic
Chief Marketing Officer.............Michele Szczypka
VP, Strategy...........................Steve Paulus

442 UniCare Michigan
3200 Greenfield Road
Dearborn, MI 48120
Toll-Free: 800-564-0938
Phone: 313-336-5550
www.unicare.com
Subsidiary of: Anthem, Inc.
For Profit Organization: Yes
Year Founded: 1995

Healthplan and Services Defined
PLAN TYPE: HMO
Model Type: Network
Benefits Offered: Behavioral Health, Chiropractic, Complementary Medicine, Dental, Disease Management, Home Care, Inpatient SNF, Long-Term Care, Physical Therapy, Podiatry, Prescription, Psychiatric, Transplant, Vision, Wellness, Life

Type of Coverage
Commercial, Individual, Supplemental Medicare, Medicaid

Geographic Areas Served
Statewide

Network Qualifications
Pre-Admission Certification: Yes

Peer Review Type
Utilization Review: Yes
Second Surgical Opinion: Yes
Case Management: Yes

Publishes and Distributes Report Card: Yes

Accreditation Certification
URAC, NCQA
TJC Accreditation, Utilization Review, Pre-Admission Certification, State Licensure, Quality Assurance Program

Specialty Managed Care Partners
WellPoint Pharmacy Management, WellPoint Dental Services, WellPoint Behavioral Health
Enters into Contracts with Regional Business Coalitions: Yes

443 United Concordia of Michigan
4401 Deer Path Road
Harrisburg, PA 17110
Phone: 717-260-6800
www.unitedconcordia.com
For Profit Organization: Yes
Year Founded: 1971
Number of Primary Care Physicians: 104,000
Total Enrollment: 8,800,000

Healthplan and Services Defined
PLAN TYPE: Dental
Plan Specialty: Dental
Benefits Offered: Dental

Type of Coverage
Commercial, Individual, Military personnel & families

Geographic Areas Served
Nationwide

Accreditation Certification
URAC

Key Personnel
Contact............................ Beth Rutherford
717-260-7659
beth.rutherford@ucci.com

444 UnitedHealthcare Community Plan Michigan
UnitedHealthcare Customer Service
P.O. Box 30769
Salt Lake City, UT 84130-0769
Toll-Free: 888-545-5205
www.uhccommunityplan.com/mi
Subsidiary of: UnitedHealth Group
For Profit Organization: Yes

Healthplan and Services Defined
PLAN TYPE: Medicare
Other Type: Medicaid
Model Type: Network
Benefits Offered: Dental, Prescription, Chiropractic

Type of Coverage
Medicare, Medicaid

Geographic Areas Served
Allegan, Barry, Bay, Berrien, Branch, Calhoun, Gratiot, Hillsdale, Kalamazoo, Kent, Mecosta, Montcalm, Newaygo, Ottawa, Saginaw, Sanilac, St. Joseph, Tuscola, Van Buren, and Washtenaw

Key Personnel
CEO, Community Plan MI .... Dennis Mouras
dmouras@uhc.com

445 UnitedHealthcare of Michigan
143 S Kalamazoo Mall
Kalamazoo, MI 49007
Toll-Free: 888-545-5205
Phone: 269-345-2561
www.uhc.com
Subsidiary of: UnitedHealth Group
Year Founded: 1977

Healthplan and Services Defined
PLAN TYPE: HMO/PPO
Model Type: Network
Plan Specialty: Behavioral Health, Dental, Disease Management, Lab, PBM, Vision, Radiology
Benefits Offered: Behavioral Health, Chiropractic, Dental, Disease Management, Physical Therapy, Prescription, Vision, Wellness, AD&D, Life, LTD, STD

Type of Coverage
Commercial, Individual, Indemnity, Medicare, Supplemental Medicare, Medicaid, Catastrophic, Family, Military, Veterans, Group

Geographic Areas Served
Statewide

Network Qualifications
Pre-Admission Certification: Yes

Peer Review Type
Utilization Review: Yes
Second Surgical Opinion: Yes
Case Management: Yes

Publishes and Distributes Report Card: Yes

Accreditation Certification
TJC, NCQA

Key Personnel
President/CEO, WI/MI .... Dustin Hinton

Specialty Managed Care Partners
Enters into Contracts with Regional Business Coalitions: Yes

---

446 Upper Peninsula Health Plan
853 W Washington Street
Marquette, MI 49855
Toll-Free: 800-835-2556
Phone: 906-225-7500
Fax: 906-225-7690
uphpwebmaster@uphp.com
www.uphp.com
Year Founded: 1998
Total Enrollment: 47,000
State Enrollment: 47,000

Healthplan and Services Defined
PLAN TYPE: HMO

Type of Coverage
Medicaid

Accreditation Certification
NCQA

Key Personnel
Chief Executive Officer............... Melissa Holmquist
Dir., Quality Management.............. Anne Levandoski
Corporate Communications .... Carly Harrington
   906-225-7158
   charrington@uphp.com

MINNESOTA

Health Insurance Coverage Status and Type of Coverage by Age

Category	All Persons Number	All Persons %	Under 19 years Number	Under 19 years %	Under 65 years Number	Under 65 years %
Total population	5,581 *(1)*	100.0 *(0.0)*	1,378 *(4)*	100.0 *(0.0)*	4,689 *(3)*	100.0 *(0.0)*
Covered by some type of health insurance	5,308 *(13)*	95.1 *(0.2)*	1,336 *(7)*	96.9 *(0.4)*	4,419 *(14)*	94.2 *(0.3)*
Covered by private health insurance	4,234 *(25)*	75.9 *(0.4)*	973 *(12)*	70.6 *(0.9)*	3,613 *(23)*	77.1 *(0.5)*
Employer-based	3,495 *(22)*	62.6 *(0.4)*	899 *(12)*	65.2 *(0.9)*	3,274 *(21)*	69.8 *(0.5)*
Direct purchase	851 *(12)*	15.2 *(0.2)*	78 *(5)*	5.6 *(0.4)*	396 *(11)*	8.4 *(0.2)*
TRICARE	80 *(5)*	1.4 *(0.1)*	16 *(3)*	1.2 *(0.2)*	47 *(5)*	1.0 *(0.1)*
Covered by public health insurance	1,835 *(20)*	32.9 *(0.4)*	433 *(13)*	31.4 *(0.9)*	972 *(19)*	20.7 *(0.4)*
Medicaid	963 *(20)*	17.3 *(0.4)*	430 *(13)*	31.2 *(0.9)*	885 *(20)*	18.9 *(0.4)*
Medicare	955 *(6)*	17.1 *(0.1)*	3 *(1)*	0.2 *(0.1)*	93 *(5)*	2.0 *(0.1)*
VA Care	130 *(5)*	2.3 *(0.1)*	1 *(Z)*	0.1 *(Z)*	40 *(3)*	0.9 *(0.1)*
Not covered at any time during the year	273 *(13)*	4.9 *(0.2)*	42 *(5)*	3.1 *(0.4)*	270 *(13)*	5.8 *(0.3)*

Note: Numbers in thousands; Figures cover civilian noninstitutionalized population in 2019; N/A indicates that data was not available; Z represents or rounds to zero; Margin of error appears in parenthesis and is calculated using replicate weights.
Source: U.S. Census Bureau, American Community Survey, Table HI-05. Health Insurance Coverage Status and Type of Coverage by State and Age for All People: 2019

Minnesota

447 Aetna Health of Minnesota
151 Farmington Avenue
Hartford, CT 06156
Toll-Free: 800-872-3862
www.aetna.com
Subsidiary of: CVS Health / Aetna Inc.
For Profit Organization: Yes

Healthplan and Services Defined
PLAN TYPE: PPO
Other Type: POS
Benefits Offered: Dental

Type of Coverage
Commercial, Student Health

Type of Payment Plans Offered
POS, DFFS, Combination FFS & DFFS

Geographic Areas Served
Statewide

Peer Review Type
Second Surgical Opinion: Yes
Case Management: Yes

Accreditation Certification
AAAHC, URAC
TJC Accreditation

448 Americas PPO
7201 W 78th Street
Suite 100
Bloomington, MN 55439
Phone: 952-806-1200
www.americasppo.com
Subsidiary of: Araz Group Inc
For Profit Organization: Yes
Year Founded: 1982
Physician Owned Organization: No
Number of Affiliated Hospitals: 260
Number of Primary Care Physicians: 18,000
Number of Referral/Specialty Physicians: 71,000
State Enrollment: 245,000

Healthplan and Services Defined
PLAN TYPE: PPO
Model Type: Staff, Group
Benefits Offered: Behavioral Health, Wellness, Worker's
  Compensation, Maternity
Offers Demand Management Patient Information Service: No

Type of Coverage
Commercial, Individual, Medicaid
Catastrophic Illness Benefit: Maximum $1M

Type of Payment Plans Offered
DFFS, Capitated

Geographic Areas Served
Minnesota, South Dakota, North Dakota, Western Wisconsin

Subscriber Information
Average Monthly Fee Per Subscriber
  (Employee + Employer Contribution):
    Employee Only (Self): Varies by plan
Average Annual Deductible Per Subscriber:
  Employee Only (Self): $500.00
  Employee & 1 Family Member: $500.00
  Employee & 2 Family Members: $750.00
Average Subscriber Co-Payment:
  Primary Care Physician: $15.00
  Non-Network Physician: $500.00-1000.00
  Prescription Drugs: $10.00/15.00
  Hospital ER: $150.00
  Nursing Home: Varies

Network Qualifications
Pre-Admission Certification: Yes

Peer Review Type
Utilization Review: Yes
Case Management: Yes

Publishes and Distributes Report Card: No

Accreditation Certification
URAC
TJC Accreditation, Utilization Review, Pre-Admission
  Certification, State Licensure, Quality Assurance Program

Key Personnel
President . . . . Amir Eftekhari
Founder and CEO. . . . . Nazie Eftekhari

Specialty Managed Care Partners
Enters into Contracts with Regional Business Coalitions: Yes

449 Avesis: Minnesota
904 Oak Pond Court
Sartell, MN 56377
Toll-Free: 800-522-0258
www.avesis.com
Subsidiary of: Guardian Life Insurance Co.
Year Founded: 1978
Number of Primary Care Physicians: 25,000
Total Enrollment: 3,500,000

Healthplan and Services Defined
PLAN TYPE: PPO
Other Type: Vision, Dental
Model Type: Network
Plan Specialty: Dental, Vision, Hearing
Benefits Offered: Dental, Vision

Type of Coverage
Commercial

Type of Payment Plans Offered
POS, Capitated, Combination FFS & DFFS

Geographic Areas Served
Statewide

Publishes and Distributes Report Card: Yes

Accreditation Certification
AAAHC
TJC Accreditation

Key Personnel
VP, Regional Sales . . . . Christine Pieper
612-481-1644
cpieper@avesis.com

---

450 Blue Cross & Blue Shield of Minnesota
3535 Blue Cross Road
Eagan, MN 55122-1154
Toll-Free: 800-382-2000
Phone: 651-662-8000
www.bluecrossmn.com
Mailing Address: P.O. Box 64560, St. Paul, MN 55164-0560
Subsidiary of: Blue Cross Blue Shield
Non-Profit Organization: Yes
Year Founded: 1933
Owned by an Integrated Delivery Network (IDN): Yes
Number of Affiliated Hospitals: 30
Number of Primary Care Physicians: 8,000
Total Enrollment: 2,700,000
State Enrollment: 2,700,000

Healthplan and Services Defined
PLAN TYPE: HMO
Model Type: Network
Plan Specialty: Medical
Benefits Offered: Disease Management, Prescription, Wellness, Life

Type of Coverage
Individual, Medicare, Supplemental Medicare

Geographic Areas Served
Statewide

Network Qualifications
Pre-Admission Certification: Yes

Peer Review Type
Utilization Review: Yes
Second Surgical Opinion: Yes

Publishes and Distributes Report Card: Yes

Accreditation Certification
URAC, NCQA

Key Personnel
President/CEO . . . . Dana Erickson
SVP/COO . . . . Carey Smith
SVP/CFO . . . . John Uribe
SVP/Chief Medical Officer . . . . Mark Steffen, MD, MPH
Chief Legal Officer . . . . Scott Lynch
SVP/Chief HR Officer . . . . Julie Loosbrock

Specialty Managed Care Partners
Enters into Contracts with Regional Business Coalitions: No

Employer References
General Mills/Pillsbury, Northwest Airlines, Target

---

451 Delta Dental of Minnesota
500 Washington Avenue S
Minneapolis, MN 55415
Toll-Free: 800-553-9536
www.deltadentalmn.org
Non-Profit Organization: Yes
Year Founded: 1969
Number of Primary Care Physicians: 5,133

Healthplan and Services Defined
PLAN TYPE: Dental
Other Type: Dental PPO
Model Type: Network
Plan Specialty: ASO, Dental
Benefits Offered: Dental

Type of Coverage
Commercial, Individual, Group
Catastrophic Illness Benefit: None

Geographic Areas Served
Minnesota and North Dakota

Key Personnel
President/CEO . . . . Rodney Young
SVP/CFO . . . . Tamera Robinson
SVP/COO/CIO . . . . Michael McGuire
VP/General Counsel . . . . Stephanie Albert
VP, Sales . . . . David Anderson
VP, Medical Services . . . . Eileen Crespo, MD
Chief Marketing Officer . . . . Tim Quinn
VP, Human Resources . . . . Judy Peterson
Media Contact . . . . Clarise Tushie-Lessard
612-224-3341
ctushie-lessard@deltadentalmn.org

---

452 HealthEZ
7201 West 78th Street
Bloomington, MN 55439
Toll-Free: 800-948-9450
Phone: 952-896-1208
service@healthez.com
www.healthez.com
For Profit Organization: Yes
Year Founded: 1982
Number of Primary Care Physicians: 71,000

Healthplan and Services Defined
PLAN TYPE: PPO
Other Type: Dental, Vision, Life
Benefits Offered: Dental, Disease Management, Prescription, Psychiatric, Vision, Wellness, Life, HSA, Case management, High-risk maternity management

Type of Coverage
Individual

Geographic Areas Served
Minnesota, North Dakota, and South Dakota

Key Personnel
President . . . . Amir Eftekhari
952-896-1204
amir.eftekhari@healthez.com
Founder/CEO . . . . Nazie Eftekhari
VP, Care Management . . . . Joann Damawand
Mgr., Claims/Operations . . . . Dawn Potter
Chief Medical Officer . . . . Jacquelyn Conley, MD
Chief Financial Officer . . . . Josh Kutzler

453 HealthPartners
8170 33rd Avenue S
Bloomington, MN 55425
Toll-Free: 800-883-2177
Phone: 952-883-6000
www.healthpartners.com
Non-Profit Organization: Yes
Year Founded: 1957
Owned by an Integrated Delivery Network (IDN): Yes

Healthplan and Services Defined
PLAN TYPE: HMO
Model Type: Staff, Network
Benefits Offered: Behavioral Health, Chiropractic, Dental, Disease Management, Home Care, Inpatient SNF, Physical Therapy, Prescription, Psychiatric, Transplant, Vision, Worker's Compensation

Type of Coverage
Commercial, Individual, Indemnity, Medicare, Supplemental Medicare, Medicaid
Catastrophic Illness Benefit: Unlimited

Type of Payment Plans Offered
POS, Combination FFS & DFFS

Geographic Areas Served
Minnesota and 8 counties in Northwestern Wisconsin

Peer Review Type
Utilization Review: Yes
Case Management: Yes

Accreditation Certification
URAC, NCQA

Key Personnel
President & CEO.........................Andrea Walsh
EVP, Chief Admin Officer..................Jim Eppel
SVP, General Counsel....................Nancy Evert
Chief Operating Officer...............Nance McClure
Co-Medical Officer...............Steven Connelly, MD
Co-Medical Officer...................Brian Rank, MD
SVP, Human Resources....................Calvin Allen

Specialty Managed Care Partners
Alere, Accordant, RMS
Enters into Contracts with Regional Business Coalitions: Yes

Employer References
University of MN, St Paul Public Schools, The College of St Catherine

454 Healthplex
PO Box 211672
Eagan, NY 55121
Toll-Free: 800-662-1220
info@healthplex.com
www.healthplex.com
For Profit Organization: Yes
Year Founded: 1977
Number of Primary Care Physicians: 2,855
Number of Referral/Specialty Physicians: 448
Total Enrollment: 3,500,000

Healthplan and Services Defined
PLAN TYPE: Dental
Other Type: Dental HMO/PPO
Model Type: IPA
Plan Specialty: Dental
Benefits Offered: Dental

Type of Coverage
Commercial, Individual, Indemnity

Type of Payment Plans Offered
POS, DFFS, Capitated, FFS, Combination FFS & DFFS

Geographic Areas Served
New Jersey & New York

Subscriber Information
Average Monthly Fee Per Subscriber
 (Employee + Employer Contribution):
  Employee Only (Self): $159.00
  Employee & 1 Family Member: $264.00
  Employee & 2 Family Members: $350.00
Average Annual Deductible Per Subscriber:
  Employee Only (Self): $0
  Employee & 1 Family Member: $0
  Employee & 2 Family Members: $0

Network Qualifications
Pre-Admission Certification: No

Peer Review Type
Utilization Review: Yes
Second Surgical Opinion: Yes
Case Management: Yes

Accreditation Certification
NCQA
Utilization Review, Quality Assurance Program

Key Personnel
President/CEO.....................Christopher Schmidt

Specialty Managed Care Partners
Enters into Contracts with Regional Business Coalitions: Yes

455 Hennepin Health
Minneapolis Grain Exchange Building
400 South Fourth Street, Suite 201
Minneapolis, MN 55415
Phone: 612-596-1036
hennepinhealth@hennepin.us
www.hennepinhealth.org
Non-Profit Organization: Yes
Year Founded: 2012
Total Enrollment: 24,176

Healthplan and Services Defined
PLAN TYPE: HMO
Model Type: Network
Benefits Offered: Behavioral Health, Chiropractic, Dental, Disease Management, Home Care, Podiatry, Prescription, Psychiatric, Vision, Substance Abuse Care; Hearing; Durable Medical Equipment; Family Planning

Type of Coverage
Medicaid

Type of Payment Plans Offered
 Combination FFS & DFFS

Geographic Areas Served
 Hennepin County

Subscriber Information
 Average Subscriber Co-Payment:
  Primary Care Physician: $0
  Non-Network Physician: $0
  Home Health Care: $0
  Nursing Home: $0

Peer Review Type
 Utilization Review: Yes
 Case Management: Yes

Key Personnel
 Chief Executive Officer .... Anne Kanyusik Yoakum
 Chief Financial Officer .... Abdirahman Abdi
 Medical Director .... Marc Manley
 Chief Compliance Officer .... Teresa Julkowski
 Director of Operations .... Mary Rowan

---

456 Humana Health Insurance of Minnesota
12600 Whitewater Drive
Suite 150
Minnetonka, MN 55343
Toll-Free: 877-367-6990
Phone: 952-253-3540
Fax: 952-938-2787
www.humana.com
Subsidiary of: Humana Inc.
For Profit Organization: Yes

Healthplan and Services Defined
 PLAN TYPE: HMO/PPO
 Model Type: Network
 Plan Specialty: Dental, Vision
 Benefits Offered: Dental, Vision, Life, LTD, STD

Type of Coverage
 Commercial, Individual

Geographic Areas Served
 Statewide

Accreditation Certification
 URAC, NCQA, CORE

Key Personnel
 Market VP .... Tracey Wilbourn
 Pres., North Central Reg. .... Chuck Dow

---

457 Medica
401 Carlson Parkway
Minnetonka, MN 55305
Toll-Free: 800-952-3455
Phone: 952-945-8000
www.medica.com
Subsidiary of: Medica Holding Company
Non-Profit Organization: Yes
Year Founded: 1975
Total Enrollment: 150,000

Healthplan and Services Defined
 PLAN TYPE: HMO
 Model Type: IPA
 Benefits Offered: Behavioral Health, Disease Management, Prescription

Type of Coverage
 Commercial, Individual, Medicare, Supplemental Medicare, Pet insurance

Type of Payment Plans Offered
 FFS

Geographic Areas Served
 Iowa, Kansas, Minnesota, Nebraska, North Dakota, and Wisconsin

Peer Review Type
 Utilization Review: Yes
 Second Surgical Opinion: Yes
 Case Management: Yes

Publishes and Distributes Report Card: Yes

Accreditation Certification
 NCQA
 TJC Accreditation, Medicare Approved, Utilization Review, Pre-Admission Certification, State Licensure, Quality Assurance Program

Key Personnel
 President & CEO .... John Naylor
 SVP, Financial Officer .... Mark Baird
 VP, Human Resources .... Lynn Altmann
 SVP, General Counsel .... Jim Jacobson
 Chief Operations Officer .... Robert Geyer
 VP, General Manager .... Geoff Bartsh
 SVP, Government Programs .... Tom Lindquist
 SVP, Marketing .... Kelly Lindberg
 SVP, Medical Officer .... John R. Mach, Jr., MD

Average Claim Compensation
 Physician's Fees Charged: 65%
 Hospital's Fees Charged: 60%

---

458 Optum Complex Medical Conditions
11000 Optum Circle
MN Office 102
Eden Prairie, MN 55344
Toll-Free: 877-801-3507
Fax: 877-897-5338
cmc_client_services@optum.com
www.myoptumhealthcomplexmedical.com
Mailing Address: P.O. Box 1459, Minneapolis, MN 55440-1459
Subsidiary of: UnitedHealth Group
For Profit Organization: Yes
Year Founded: 1986

Healthplan and Services Defined
 PLAN TYPE: Multiple
 Model Type: Network
 Plan Specialty: Complex medical conditions including transplantation, cancer, kidney disease, congenital heart disease and infertility.

Type of Payment Plans Offered
POS, Capitated, FFS

Geographic Areas Served
Nationwide

Peer Review Type
Utilization Review: Yes
Case Management: Yes

Publishes and Distributes Report Card: Yes

Accreditation Certification
URAC
Utilization Review, Quality Assurance Program

Key Personnel
President & COO .... John Prince

Specialty Managed Care Partners
Enters into Contracts with Regional Business Coalitions: Yes

---

459 Spirit Dental & Vision
55 5th Street E
Suite 500
St. Paul, MN 55101
Toll-Free: 844-833-8440
www.spiritdental.com
Subsidiary of: Direct Benefits Inc.
For Profit Organization: Yes

Healthplan and Services Defined
PLAN TYPE: Dental
Plan Specialty: Dental, Vision
Benefits Offered: Dental, Vision

Geographic Areas Served
statewide

Key Personnel
President .... Tom Mayer

---

460 UCare
500 Stinson Boulevard NE
Minneapolis, MN 55413
Toll-Free: 800-688-2534
Phone: 612-676-6500
home.ucare.org
Secondary Address: 4310 Menard Drive, Suite 600, Hermantown, MN 55811, 218-336-4260
Non-Profit Organization: Yes
Year Founded: 1984
Owned by an Integrated Delivery Network (IDN): Yes
Number of Primary Care Physicians: 43,000
Total Enrollment: 147,000

Healthplan and Services Defined
PLAN TYPE: Multiple
Model Type: Network
Benefits Offered: Behavioral Health, Chiropractic, Dental, Disease Management, Home Care, Inpatient SNF, Physical Therapy, Podiatry, Prescription, Psychiatric, Transplant, Vision, Wellness, Disability Plans available

Type of Coverage
Individual, Medicare, Supplemental Medicare, Medicaid

Catastrophic Illness Benefit: Unlimited

Type of Payment Plans Offered
POS

Geographic Areas Served
Statewide

Network Qualifications
Pre-Admission Certification: Yes

Peer Review Type
Utilization Review: Yes
Second Surgical Opinion: Yes
Case Management: Yes

Publishes and Distributes Report Card: Yes

Accreditation Certification
NCQA
Medicare Approved, Utilization Review, Pre-Admission Certification, State Licensure, Quality Assurance Program

Key Personnel
President/CEO......................... Mark Traynor
SVP/CAO .... Hilary Marden-Resnik
SVP/CFO .... Beth Monsrud
SVP, Public Affairs/Mkt .... Ghita Worcester
Chief Executive Officer............ Hilary Marden-Resnik
EVP/Chief Info. Officer .... Darin McDonald
EVP/Chief Financial Off.................. Beth Monsrud
EVP/Chief Legal Officer................. Daniel Santos
EVP/Chief Admin. Officer .... Pat Schmitt
EVP/Chief Marketing Off................ Ghita Worcester

Specialty Managed Care Partners
Enters into Contracts with Regional Business Coalitions: Yes

---

461 UnitedHealth Group
P.O. Box 1459
Minneapolis, MN 55440-1459
Toll-Free: 800-328-5979
www.unitedhealthgroup.com
For Profit Organization: Yes
Year Founded: 1974
Total Enrollment: 70,000,000

Healthplan and Services Defined
PLAN TYPE: Multiple
Model Type: Network
Plan Specialty: Behavioral Health, Dental, Disease Management, PBM, Vision
Benefits Offered: Behavioral Health, Dental, Disease Management, Long-Term Care, Prescription, Vision, Wellness, Life, LTD, STD

Type of Coverage
Individual, Medicare, Supplemental Medicare, Medicaid, Catastrophic, Family, Military, Veterans, Group

Geographic Areas Served
All 50 states, the District of Columbia, most U.S. territories & 130 countries

Key Personnel
Chief Executive Officer .... Andrew Witty
Chief Financial Officer..................... John Rex

Chief Operating Officer	Dirk McMahon
Chief Marketing Officer	Terry M. Clark
Chief Development Officer	Richard Mattera
Chief Medical Officer	Richard Migliori
Chief Strategy Officer	Dan Schumacher
Chief Communications Off.	Jennifer Smoter
CEO, UnitedHealthcare	Brian Thompson

462 UnitedHealthcare of Minnesota

12700 Whitewater Dr.
Minnetonka, MN 55343
Toll-Free: 888-545-5205
www.uhc.com
Subsidiary of: UnitedHealth Group
For Profit Organization: Yes
Year Founded: 1977

Healthplan and Services Defined
PLAN TYPE: HMO/PPO
Model Type: Network
Plan Specialty: Behavioral Health, Dental, Disease Management, Lab, PBM, Vision, Radiology
Benefits Offered: Behavioral Health, Chiropractic, Dental, Disease Management, Long-Term Care, Physical Therapy, Prescription, Vision, Wellness, AD&D, Life, LTD, STD

Type of Coverage
Commercial, Individual, Indemnity, Medicare, Supplemental Medicare, Medicaid, Catastrophic, Family, Military, Veterans, Group

Geographic Areas Served
Minnesota, North Dakota, South Dakota, Virgin Islands, and Puerto Rico

Network Qualifications
Pre-Admission Certification: Yes

Peer Review Type
Utilization Review: Yes
Second Surgical Opinion: Yes
Case Management: Yes

Publishes and Distributes Report Card: Yes

Accreditation Certification
TJC, NCQA

Key Personnel
CEO, MN/ND/SD .... Brett Edelson

Specialty Managed Care Partners
Enters into Contracts with Regional Business Coalitions: Yes

MISSISSIPPI

Health Insurance Coverage Status and Type of Coverage by Age

Category	All Persons Number	All Persons %	Under 19 years Number	Under 19 years %	Under 65 years Number	Under 65 years %
Total population	2,905 *(2)*	100.0 *(0.0)*	745 *(6)*	100.0 *(0.0)*	2,431 *(3)*	100.0 *(0.0)*
Covered by some type of health insurance	2,528 *(15)*	87.0 *(0.5)*	699 *(7)*	93.9 *(0.7)*	2,056 *(15)*	84.6 *(0.6)*
Covered by private health insurance	1,705 *(27)*	58.7 *(0.9)*	341 *(12)*	45.8 *(1.6)*	1,457 *(26)*	59.9 *(1.0)*
Employer-based	1,338 *(26)*	46.1 *(0.9)*	286 *(13)*	38.5 *(1.7)*	1,238 *(25)*	50.9 *(1.0)*
Direct purchase	357 *(12)*	12.3 *(0.4)*	41 *(5)*	5.5 *(0.6)*	209 *(10)*	8.6 *(0.4)*
TRICARE	115 *(9)*	4.0 *(0.3)*	26 *(4)*	3.5 *(0.6)*	71 *(8)*	2.9 *(0.3)*
Covered by public health insurance	1,145 *(20)*	39.4 *(0.7)*	380 *(12)*	51.0 *(1.6)*	681 *(19)*	28.0 *(0.8)*
Medicaid	697 *(20)*	24.0 *(0.7)*	378 *(12)*	50.8 *(1.6)*	610 *(19)*	25.1 *(0.8)*
Medicare	573 *(7)*	19.7 *(0.3)*	4 *(2)*	0.6 *(0.2)*	110 *(7)*	4.5 *(0.3)*
VA Care	69 *(5)*	2.4 *(0.2)*	1 *(1)*	0.1 *(0.1)*	29 *(3)*	1.2 *(0.1)*
Not covered at any time during the year	377 *(15)*	13.0 *(0.5)*	46 *(5)*	6.1 *(0.7)*	375 *(15)*	15.4 *(0.6)*

Note: Numbers in thousands; Figures cover civilian noninstitutionalized population in 2019; N/A indicates that data was not available; Z represents or rounds to zero; Margin of error appears in parenthesis and is calculated using replicate weights.
Source: U.S. Census Bureau, American Community Survey, Table HI-05. Health Insurance Coverage Status and Type of Coverage by State and Age for All People: 2019

Mississippi

463 Allegiance Life & Health Insurance Company
2806 S Garfield Street
P.O. Box 3507
Missoula, MT 59806-3507
Toll-Free: 800-737-3137
Phone: 406-523-3122
Fax: 406-523-3124
inquire@askallegiance.com
www.allegiancelifeandhealth.com
Subsidiary of: Cigna
For Profit Organization: Yes
Year Founded: 1981

Healthplan and Services Defined
PLAN TYPE: HMO
Benefits Offered: Dental, Vision, Wellness, Pharmacy

Type of Coverage
Commercial, Individual

Geographic Areas Served
Statewide

Key Personnel
President & Owner .... Dirk Visser

464 Allwell from Magnolia Health
111 E Capitol Street
Suite 500
Jackson, MS 39201
Toll-Free: 844-786-7711
allwell.magnoliahealthplan.com
Subsidiary of: Centene Corporation
For Profit Organization: Yes

Healthplan and Services Defined
PLAN TYPE: Medicare
Model Type: Network
Benefits Offered: Dental, Prescription

Type of Coverage
Medicare, Supplemental Medicare, Medicare Advantage

Geographic Areas Served
George, Harrison, Hinds, Jackson, Madison, Rankin, Stone, DeSoto, Lafayette, Panola, and Tate counties

465 Ambetter from Magnolia Health
111 E Capitol Street
Suite 500
Jackson, MS 39201
Toll-Free: 877-687-1187
ambetter.magnoliahealthplan.com
Subsidiary of: Centene Corporation
For Profit Organization: Yes

Healthplan and Services Defined
PLAN TYPE: Other
Model Type: Network
Benefits Offered: Behavioral Health, Disease Management, Physical Therapy, Prescription, Wellness, Maternity and newborn care

Type of Coverage
Health Insurance Marketplace

Geographic Areas Served
Statewide

466 Health Link PPO
808 Varsity Drive
Tupelo, MS 38801
Toll-Free: 888-855-2740
Phone: 662-377-3868
Fax: 662-377-7599
www.healthlinkppo.com
Subsidiary of: North Mississippi Medical Center
Non-Profit Organization: Yes
Year Founded: 1986
Number of Affiliated Hospitals: 30
Number of Primary Care Physicians: 1,500
Total Enrollment: 155,070

Healthplan and Services Defined
PLAN TYPE: PPO
Benefits Offered: Dental, Long-Term Care, Prescription, Transplant, Vision, Life, LTD, STD, Major Medical

Type of Coverage
Commercial, Individual

Geographic Areas Served
Mississippi and northwest Alabama

Accreditation Certification
NCQA
Medicare Approved, Utilization Review, Pre-Admission Certification, State Licensure, Quality Assurance Program

467 Humana Health Insurance of Mississippi
772 Lake Harbour Drive
Suite 3
Ridgeland, MS 39157
Toll-Free: 866-945-4376
Phone: 601-605-5130
Fax: 601-856-5222
www.humana.com
Secondary Address: 2650 Beach Boulevard, Suite 31A, Biloxi, MS 39531, 228-271-6800
Subsidiary of: Humana Inc.
For Profit Organization: Yes

Healthplan and Services Defined
PLAN TYPE: HMO/PPO
Plan Specialty: ASO
Benefits Offered: Disease Management, Prescription, Wellness

Type of Coverage
Commercial, Individual, Medicare

Geographic Areas Served
Statewide

Accreditation Certification
URAC, NCQA

Key Personnel
President, Gulf States . . . . Matt Berger

Specialty Managed Care Partners
Caremark Rx

Employer References
Tricare

---

468 Magnolia Health
111 E Capitol Street
Suite 500
Jackson, MS 39201
Toll-Free: 866-912-6285
www.magnoliahealthplan.com
Subsidiary of: Centene Corporation
For Profit Organization: Yes

Healthplan and Services Defined
PLAN TYPE: Multiple
Plan Specialty: Medicaid, Mississippi Children's Health Insurance Program (CHIP)
Benefits Offered: Behavioral Health, Disease Management, Prescription, Wellness, Maternity & Newborn Care; Transportation

Type of Coverage
Individual, Medicare, Medicaid

Geographic Areas Served
Statewide

Key Personnel
President/CEO . . . . Aaron Sisk

---

469 Molina Healthcare of Mississippi
188 E Capitol Street
Suite 700
Jackson, MS 39201
Toll-Free: 844-809-8438
www.molinahealthcare.com
Subsidiary of: Monlina Healthcare, Inc.
For Profit Organization: Yes
Year Founded: 1980

Healthplan and Services Defined
PLAN TYPE: Medicare
Plan Specialty: Dental, PBM, Vision, intergrated Medicare/Medicaid (Duals)
Benefits Offered: Dental, Prescription, Vision, Wellness, Life

Geographic Areas Served
Statewide

Key Personnel
President . . . . Bridget Galatas
Chief Medical Officer . . . . Thomas Joiner, MD

---

470 UnitedHealthcare Community Plan Mississippi
UnitedHealthcare Customer Service
P.O. Box 30769
Salt Lake City, UT 84130-0769
Toll-Free: 888-545-5205
www.uhccommunityplan.com/ms
Subsidiary of: UnitedHealth Group
For Profit Organization: Yes

Healthplan and Services Defined
PLAN TYPE: Multiple
Model Type: Network
Benefits Offered: Dental, Prescription, Vision

Type of Coverage
Medicare, Medicaid, CHIP

Geographic Areas Served
Benton, Copiah, Desoto, George, Hancock, Harrison, Hinds, Holmes, Jackson, Lafayette, Lawrence, Madison, Marion, Marshall, Panola, Quitman, Rankin, Scott, Simpson, Smith, Stone, Tate, and Yazoo. Other plans are statewide

Key Personnel
CEO, Community Plan MS . . . . J. Michael Parnell, PhD, RN

---

471 UnitedHealthcare of Mississippi
795 Woodlands Parkway
Suite 301
Ridgeland, MS 39157
Toll-Free: 888-545-5205
Phone: 866-574-6088
www.uhc.com
Subsidiary of: UnitedHealth Group
For Profit Organization: Yes
Year Founded: 1992

Healthplan and Services Defined
PLAN TYPE: HMO/PPO
Model Type: Network
Plan Specialty: Behavioral Health, Dental, Disease Management, PBM, Vision
Benefits Offered: Behavioral Health, Dental, Disease Management, Long-Term Care, Prescription, Vision, Wellness, Life, LTD, STD

Type of Coverage
Commercial, Individual, Indemnity, Medicare, Supplemental Medicare, Medicaid, Catastrophic, Family, Military, Veterans, Group

Type of Payment Plans Offered
FFS

Geographic Areas Served
Statewide

Network Qualifications
Pre-Admission Certification: Yes

Peer Review Type
Utilization Review: Yes
Second Surgical Opinion: Yes
Case Management: Yes

Publishes and Distributes Report Card: Yes

Accreditation Certification
NCQA
TJC Accreditation, Medicare Approved, Utilization Review, Pre-Admission Certification, State Licensure, Quality Assurance Program

Key Personnel
CEO, Mississippi . . . . Stephen L. Wilson, Jr.

Specialty Managed Care Partners
Enters into Contracts with Regional Business Coalitions: Yes

Health Insurance Coverage Status and Type of Coverage by Age

Category	All Persons Number	%	Under 19 years Number	%	Under 65 years Number	%
Total population	6,021 *(2)*	100.0 *(0.0)*	1,447 *(6)*	100.0 *(0.0)*	4,998 *(4)*	100.0 *(0.0)*
Covered by some type of health insurance	5,417 *(19)*	90.0 *(0.3)*	1,352 *(8)*	93.5 *(0.5)*	4,400 *(19)*	88.0 *(0.4)*
Covered by private health insurance	4,196 *(30)*	69.7 *(0.5)*	925 *(13)*	64.0 *(0.9)*	3,617 *(27)*	72.4 *(0.5)*
Employer-based	3,438 *(31)*	57.1 *(0.5)*	813 *(14)*	56.2 *(0.9)*	3,165 *(30)*	63.3 *(0.6)*
Direct purchase	803 *(17)*	13.3 *(0.3)*	105 *(8)*	7.3 *(0.5)*	463 *(16)*	9.3 *(0.3)*
TRICARE	163 *(9)*	2.7 *(0.1)*	31 *(4)*	2.1 *(0.3)*	103 *(9)*	2.1 *(0.2)*
Covered by public health insurance	1,941 *(20)*	32.2 *(0.3)*	472 *(14)*	32.7 *(1.0)*	946 *(20)*	18.9 *(0.4)*
Medicaid	874 *(19)*	14.5 *(0.3)*	466 *(14)*	32.2 *(1.0)*	780 *(19)*	15.6 *(0.4)*
Medicare	1,176 *(8)*	19.5 *(0.1)*	8 *(2)*	0.6 *(0.2)*	182 *(8)*	3.6 *(0.2)*
VA Care	163 *(7)*	2.7 *(0.1)*	2 *(1)*	0.1 *(0.1)*	72 *(5)*	1.4 *(0.1)*
Not covered at any time during the year	604 *(19)*	10.0 *(0.3)*	95 *(7)*	6.5 *(0.5)*	598 *(18)*	12.0 *(0.4)*

Note: Numbers in thousands; Figures cover civilian noninstitutionalized population in 2019; N/A indicates that data was not available; Z represents or rounds to zero; Margin of error appears in parenthesis and is calculated using replicate weights.
Source: U.S. Census Bureau, American Community Survey, Table HI-05. Health Insurance Coverage Status and Type of Coverage by State and Age for All People: 2019

Missouri

472 Allwell from Home State Health
11720 Borman Drive
St. Louis, MO 63146
Toll-Free: 855-766-1452
allwell.homestatehealth.com
Subsidiary of: Centene Corporation
For Profit Organization: Yes

Healthplan and Services Defined
PLAN TYPE: Medicare
Model Type: Network
Benefits Offered: Dental, Prescription

Type of Coverage
Medicare, Supplemental Medicare, Medicare Advantage

Geographic Areas Served
Barry, Cass, Christian, Clay, Crawford, Dallas, Franklin, Greene, Jackson, Jasper, Jefferson, Lawrence, Lincoln, McDonald, Newton, Platte, Polk, St. Charles, Warren, Washington, and Webster counties

473 Ambetter from Home State Health
11720 Borman Drive
St. Louis, MO 63146
Toll-Free: 855-650-3789
ambetter.homestatehealth.com
Subsidiary of: Centene Corporation
For Profit Organization: Yes

Healthplan and Services Defined
PLAN TYPE: Other
Model Type: Network
Plan Specialty: Lab
Benefits Offered: Behavioral Health, Disease Management, Physical Therapy, Prescription, Wellness, Maternity and newborn care

Type of Coverage
Health Insurance Marketplace

Geographic Areas Served
Andrew, Atchison, Barry, Barton, Bates, Benton, Buchanan, Caldwell, Carroll, Cass, Cedar, Christian, Clay, Clinton, Dade, Dallas, Daviess, DeKalb, Douglas, Frankling, Gentry, Greene, Grundy, Harrison, Henry, Hickory, Holt, Jackson, Jasper, Jefferson, Johnson, Laclede, Lafayette, Lawrence, Lincoln, Livingston, McDonald, Mercer, Newton, Nodaway, Ozark, Pettis, Platte, Polk, Ray, Saline, St. Charles, St. Clair, St. Louis, Stone, Taney, Vernon, Warren, Webster, Wright

474 American Health Care Alliance
9229 Ward Parkway
Suite 300
Kansas City, MO 64114
Toll-Free: 800-870-6252
customerservice@ahappo.com
www.americanhealthcareallianceonline.com
Mailing Address: P.O. Box 8530, Kansas City, MO 64114-0530

Year Founded: 1990
Number of Affiliated Hospitals: 5,745
Number of Primary Care Physicians: 190,736
Number of Referral/Specialty Physicians: 285,353
Total Enrollment: 942,000
State Enrollment: 860,000

Healthplan and Services Defined
PLAN TYPE: PPO
Model Type: Network of PPOs
Benefits Offered: Behavioral Health, Chiropractic, Complementary Medicine, Dental, Home Care, Physical Therapy, Podiatry, Prescription, Psychiatric, Vision, Wellness
Offers Demand Management Patient Information Service: Yes

Geographic Areas Served
Nationwide

Subscriber Information
Average Annual Deductible Per Subscriber:
   Employee Only (Self): Varies
   Employee & 1 Family Member: Varies
   Employee & 2 Family Members: Varies
   Medicare: Varies
Average Subscriber Co-Payment:
   Primary Care Physician: Varies
   Non-Network Physician: Varies
   Prescription Drugs: Varies
   Hospital ER: Varies
   Home Health Care: Varies
   Nursing Home: Varies

Publishes and Distributes Report Card: Yes

Accreditation Certification
AAAHC, URAC, AAPI, NCQA
TJC Accreditation, Medicare Approved, Utilization Review, Pre-Admission Certification, State Licensure

Key Personnel
Executive Vice President.................Phil Mehelic
Director Client Service..................Lisa Enslinger

475 Anthem Blue Cross & Blue Shield of Missouri
1831 Chestnut Street
St Louis, MO 63103
Toll-Free: 800-331-1476
Phone: 314-923-4444
www.anthem.com
Subsidiary of: Anthem, Inc.
For Profit Organization: Yes

Healthplan and Services Defined
PLAN TYPE: HMO/PPO
Model Type: Network
Plan Specialty: Behavioral Health, Dental, Disease Management, Lab, PBM, Vision, Radiology
Benefits Offered: Behavioral Health, Dental, Disease Management, Inpatient SNF, Physical Therapy, Prescription, Psychiatric, Transplant, Vision, Wellness, Life

Type of Coverage
Commercial, Individual, Medicare, Supplemental Medicare, Catastrophic

Geographic Areas Served
All of Missouri, excluding 30 counties in the Kansas City area

Accreditation Certification
URAC, NCQA

Key Personnel
President . . . . Stephanie Vojicic

476 Blue Cross Blue Shield of Kansas City
One Pershing Square
2301 Main Street
Kansas City, MO 64108
Toll-Free: 800-875-3596
Phone: 816-395-2222
www.bluekc.com
Non-Profit Organization: Yes
Year Founded: 1982

Healthplan and Services Defined
PLAN TYPE: PPO
Model Type: Network
Benefits Offered: Behavioral Health, Chiropractic, Dental, Physical Therapy, Podiatry, Prescription, Psychiatric

Type of Coverage
Commercial, Individual, Medicare, Supplemental Medicare, Travel Insurance
Catastrophic Illness Benefit: Maximum $2M

Type of Payment Plans Offered
POS, FFS

Geographic Areas Served
Serving 32 counties in greater Kansas City (including Johnson and Wyandotte) and northwestern Missouri

Network Qualifications
Pre-Admission Certification: Yes

Peer Review Type
Utilization Review: Yes

Publishes and Distributes Report Card: No

Accreditation Certification
URAC, NCQA

Key Personnel
President/CEO . . . . Erin Stucky
SVP/CFO. . . . . Henri Cournand
SVP, Compliance . . . . Scott McAdams
EVP, Market Innovation . . . . Jenny Hously
SVP/Chief of Staff. . . . . Kim White
SVP/CMO . . . . Greg Sweat, MD
SVP, COO. . . . . Ron Rowe

Specialty Managed Care Partners
Enters into Contracts with Regional Business Coalitions: Yes

477 Centene Corporation
Centene Plaza
7700 Forsyth Boulevard
St. Louis, MO 63105
Phone: 314-725-4477
www.centene.com
For Profit Organization: Yes
Year Founded: 1984
Total Enrollment: 15,000,000

Healthplan and Services Defined
PLAN TYPE: HMO/PPO
Model Type: Network
Plan Specialty: Behavioral Health, Dental, PBM, Vision
Benefits Offered: Behavioral Health, Dental, Vision, Wellness, Life, Correctional health services

Type of Coverage
Commercial, Individual, Medicare, Supplemental Medicare, Medicaid

Geographic Areas Served
Arizona, Arkansas, California, Florida, Georgia, Indiana, Illinois, Kansas, Louisiana, Massachusetts, Michigan, Mississippi, Missouri, Ohio, South Carolina, Texas, Washington, Wisconsin

Accreditation Certification
URAC, NCQA, CORE Phase III Certified

Key Personnel
Chief Executive Officer. . . . . Sarah M. London
President/COO . . . . Brent Layton
Chief Financial Officer. Drew Asher
Chief Admin. Officer. . . . . Shannon Bagley

478 Children's Mercy Pediatric Care Network
2420 Pershing Road
Suite G10
Kansas City, MO 64141
Toll-Free: 888-670-7261
www.cmics.org
Mailing Address: P.O. Box 411596, Kansas City, MO 64141
Non-Profit Organization: Yes
Year Founded: 1996
Owned by an Integrated Delivery Network (IDN): Yes
Number of Affiliated Hospitals: 31
Number of Primary Care Physicians: 200
Number of Referral/Specialty Physicians: 2,400
Total Enrollment: 49,976
State Enrollment: 49,976

Healthplan and Services Defined
PLAN TYPE: HMO
Model Type: Network, Medicaid
Benefits Offered: Behavioral Health, Dental, Disease Management, Home Care, Inpatient SNF, Physical Therapy, Podiatry, Prescription, Psychiatric, Vision, Wellness

Type of Coverage
Medicaid
Catastrophic Illness Benefit: None

Geographic Areas Served
Cass, Clay, Henry, Jackson, Johnson, Lafayette, Platte, Ray, St. Claire counties in Missouri

Subscriber Information
Average Monthly Fee Per Subscriber
(Employee + Employer Contribution):
Employee Only (Self): $0.00
Employee & 1 Family Member: $0.00
Employee & 2 Family Members: $0.00

Peer Review Type
Utilization Review: Yes
Second Surgical Opinion: Yes
Case Management: Yes

Publishes and Distributes Report Card: Yes

Key Personnel
Executive Director............................ Bob Finuf
Director, IT................................. Bob Clark
Director, Finance....................... Suzie Dunaway
Medical Director.................... Doug Blowey, MD
Dir., Medical Economics.................... Kent Pack
Dir., Intergrated Care................ Matthew Combes

Average Claim Compensation
Physician's Fees Charged: 50%
Hospital's Fees Charged: 60%

Specialty Managed Care Partners
Enters into Contracts with Regional Business Coalitions: Yes

Employer References
State of Missouri, Division of Medical Services, State of Kansas, SRS

479 Cox Healthplans
Medical Mile Plaza
3200 S National, Building B
Springfield, MO 65807
Toll-Free: 800-205-7665
Phone: 417-269-2900
Fax: 417-269-2949
www.coxhealthplans.com
Mailing Address: P.O. Box 5750, Springfield, MO 65801-5750
Subsidiary of: CoxHealth
For Profit Organization: Yes
Number of Primary Care Physicians: 1,000
Number of Referral/Specialty Physicians: 5,000
Total Enrollment: 5,000
State Enrollment: 1,964

Healthplan and Services Defined
PLAN TYPE: HMO/PPO
Benefits Offered: Disease Management, Prescription, Wellness

Type of Coverage
Commercial, Individual

Type of Payment Plans Offered
POS

Geographic Areas Served
Statewide

Key Personnel
President................................... Matt Aug
Chief Information Officer................. Susan Butts
Chief Financial Officer .... Lisa Odom

Specialty Managed Care Partners
Caremark Rx

480 Delta Dental of Missouri
12399 Gravois Road
St. Louis, MO 63127
Toll-Free: 800-392-1167
Phone: 314-656-3000
service@deltadentalmo.com
www.deltadentalmo.com
Mailing Address: P.O. Box 8690, St. Louis, MO 63126-0690
Non-Profit Organization: Yes
Year Founded: 1958
Owned by an Integrated Delivery Network (IDN): Yes
State Enrollment: 1,900,000

Healthplan and Services Defined
PLAN TYPE: Dental
Other Type: Dental PPO
Model Type: Group
Plan Specialty: Dental, Vision
Benefits Offered: Dental, Vision

Type of Coverage
Commercial

Geographic Areas Served
Missouri and South Carolina

Publishes and Distributes Report Card: No

Key Personnel
President/CEO .... E.B. Rob Goren
CFO/Corporate Counsel .... Barbara C. Bentrup
COO/Chief Dental Officer.......... Ronald E. Inge, DDS
Chief Actuary................... Jonathan R. Jennings
CIO .... Karl A. Mudra
Sales/Marketing Officer .... Jim Barone

Specialty Managed Care Partners
Enters into Contracts with Regional Business Coalitions: No

481 Dental Health Alliance
2323 Grand Boulevard
Kansas City, MO 64108
Toll-Free: 800-522-1313
ppoinforequests@sunlife.com
www.dha.com
Subsidiary of: Sunlife Financial
Year Founded: 1994
Number of Primary Care Physicians: 74,000
Total Enrollment: 1,700,000

Healthplan and Services Defined
PLAN TYPE: Dental
Other Type: Dental PPO Network
Model Type: Network, Dental PPO Network
Plan Specialty: Dental
Benefits Offered: Dental

Type of Coverage
Commercial

Type of Payment Plans Offered
POS, FFS, Combination FFS & DFFS

Geographic Areas Served
Nationwide

Network Qualifications
Pre-Admission Certification: No

Peer Review Type
Utilization Review: Yes

---

482 Dental Source: Dental Health Care Plans
101 Parklane Boulevard
Suite 301
Sugar Land, TX 77478
Toll-Free: 877-493-6282
Phone: 866-481-9473
Fax: 281-313-7155
www.densource.com
Subsidiary of: FCL Dental
For Profit Organization: Yes
Number of Primary Care Physicians: 149
State Enrollment: 1,500

Healthplan and Services Defined
PLAN TYPE: Dental
Other Type: Dental HMO
Model Type: Network
Plan Specialty: Dental
Benefits Offered: Dental

Type of Coverage
Commercial, Individual, Indemnity

Geographic Areas Served
Kansas and Missouri

---

483 Essence Healthcare
13900 Riverport Drive
Maryland Heights, MO 63043
Toll-Free: 866-509-5398
Phone: 314-209-2700
Fax: 888-480-2577
customerservice@essencehealthcare.com
www.essencehealthcare.com
Secondary Address: 3330 S National Avenue, Suite 100, Springfield, MO 65807
Year Founded: 2004
Total Enrollment: 60,000

Healthplan and Services Defined
PLAN TYPE: Medicare
Benefits Offered: Chiropractic, Dental, Disease Management, Home Care, Inpatient SNF, Physical Therapy, Podiatry, Prescription, Psychiatric, Vision, Wellness

Type of Coverage
Individual, Medicare

Geographic Areas Served
Missouri: Boone, Christian, Greene, Jefferson, Stone, Saint Louis, Saint Louis City, Saint Charles, Saint Francois, and Taney counties. Illinois: Madison, Monroe, and Saint Clair counties

Subscriber Information
Average Monthly Fee Per Subscriber
(Employee + Employer Contribution):
Employee Only (Self): Varies
Medicare: Varies
Average Annual Deductible Per Subscriber:
Employee Only (Self): Varies
Medicare: Varies
Average Subscriber Co-Payment:
Primary Care Physician: Varies
Non-Network Physician: Varies
Prescription Drugs: Varies
Hospital ER: Varies
Home Health Care: Varies
Home Health Care Max. Days/Visits Covered: Varies
Nursing Home: Varies
Nursing Home Max. Days/Visits Covered: Varies

Key Personnel
President & CEO . . . . Richard Jones
Chief Compliance Officer . . . . Erin Venable
Chief Operating Officer . . . . Martha Butler
Chief Medical Officer . . . . Deborah Zimmerman, MD
VP, Sales & Marketing . . . . Joel Andersen
Claims & Customer Service . . . . Dawn Walter

---

484 Government Employees Health Association (GEHA)
310 NE Mulberry Street
Lee's Summit, MO 64086
Toll-Free: 800-821-6136
www.geha.com
Non-Profit Organization: Yes
Year Founded: 1964

Healthplan and Services Defined
PLAN TYPE: Other
Plan Specialty: Dental, Vision, Federal employees
Benefits Offered: Dental, Disease Management, Prescription, Vision, Wellness, Life

Type of Coverage
Commercial, Medicare
Catastrophic Illness Maximum Benefit: $5,000

Type of Payment Plans Offered
FFS

Geographic Areas Served
Nationwide

Network Qualifications
Pre-Admission Certification: Yes

Accreditation Certification
URAC

Key Personnel
President & CEO . . . . Arthur A. Nizza

Average Claim Compensation
Hospital's Fees Charged: 85%

485 HealthLink HMO
St. Louis, MO 63103
Toll-Free: 800-624-2356
www.healthlink.com
For Profit Organization: Yes
Year Founded: 1985

Healthplan and Services Defined
PLAN TYPE: Multiple
Benefits Offered: Dental, Vision, Wellness, Worker's Compensation, Life, LTD, STD, Reinsurance

Type of Coverage
Catastrophic Illness Benefit: Varies per case

Geographic Areas Served
Arkansas, Illinois, Missouri, Ohio, Kentucky, and Indiana

Network Qualifications
Pre-Admission Certification: Yes

Peer Review Type
Utilization Review: Yes
Second Surgical Opinion: No
Case Management: Yes

Accreditation Certification
URAC
Utilization Review, Pre-Admission Certification, Quality Assurance Program

Specialty Managed Care Partners
WellPoint Pharmacy Management, Cigna Behavioral Health, Vision Service Plan
Enters into Contracts with Regional Business Coalitions: Yes
Gateway Purchases

Employer References
Local fifty benefits service trust, Jefferson City Public Schools, ConAgra

486 Home State Health Plan
11720 Borman Drive
St. Louis, MO 63146
Toll-Free: 855-694-4663
www.homestatehealth.com
Subsidiary of: Centene Corporation
For Profit Organization: Yes

Healthplan and Services Defined
PLAN TYPE: Other
Benefits Offered: Behavioral Health, Dental, Disease Management, Wellness, Children's health

Type of Coverage
Medicaid

Key Personnel
Plan President/CEO . . . . Jeff Johnston

487 Humana Health Insurance of Missouri
909 E Montclair
Suite 108
Springfield, MO 65807
Toll-Free: 800-951-0128
Phone: 417-227-5700
Fax: 417-882-2015
www.humana.com
Secondary Address: 10805 Sunset Office Drive, Suite 300, St. Louis, MO 63127, 314-238-2537
Subsidiary of: Humana Inc.
For Profit Organization: Yes

Healthplan and Services Defined
PLAN TYPE: HMO/PPO
Model Type: Network
Plan Specialty: Dental, Vision
Benefits Offered: Dental, Vision, Life, LTD, STD

Type of Coverage
Commercial, Individual

Geographic Areas Served
Statewide

Accreditation Certification
URAC, NCQA, CORE

Key Personnel
Pres., Kansas/Missouri . . . . Bob Hayworth

488 Liberty Dental Plan of Missouri
P.O. Box 26110
Santa Ana, CA 92799-6110
Toll-Free: 888-352-7924
Fax: 888-334-6034
www.libertydentalplan.com
For Profit Organization: Yes
Year Founded: 2001
Total Enrollment: 3,000,000

Healthplan and Services Defined
PLAN TYPE: Dental
Other Type: Dental HMO
Plan Specialty: Dental
Benefits Offered: Dental

Type of Coverage
Commercial, Individual, Medicare, Medicaid, Unions

Geographic Areas Served
Statewide

Accreditation Certification
NCQA

Key Personnel
Provider Network Manager . . . . Molly Majors
  888-703-6999
  mmajors@libertydentalplan.com
Provider Network Manager . . . . Daniel Flott
  888-703-6999
  dflott@libertydentalplan.com
Provider Network Manager . . . . Bryan McMillan
  888-703-6999
  bmcmillan@libertydentalplan.com

489 Med-Pay
1650 Battlefield
Suite 300
Springfield, MO 65804-3706
Toll-Free: 800-777-9087
Phone: 417-886-6886
Fax: 417-890-0741
www.med-pay.com
Year Founded: 1983
State Enrollment: 26,000

Healthplan and Services Defined
PLAN TYPE: Other
Other Type: TPA, HSA, HRA
Model Type: Network
Plan Specialty: ASO, Behavioral Health, Chiropractic, Dental, Disease Management, Lab, MSO, PBM, Vision, Radiology
Benefits Offered: Behavioral Health, Chiropractic, Dental, Disease Management, Home Care, Inpatient SNF, Long-Term Care, Physical Therapy, Prescription, Transplant, Vision
Offers Demand Management Patient Information Service: Yes

Type of Coverage
Commercial, Individual

Geographic Areas Served
Statewide

Accreditation Certification
State of MO
Utilization Review

Specialty Managed Care Partners
HCC, BCBS, Healthlink
Enters into Contracts with Regional Business Coalitions: Yes

490 Mercy Clinic Missouri
615 South New Ballas Road
Saint Louis, MO 63141
Phone: 314-251-6000
mercy.net
Subsidiary of: IBM Watson Health
Non-Profit Organization: Yes
Number of Affiliated Hospitals: 44
Number of Primary Care Physicians: 700
Number of Referral/Specialty Physicians: 2,000

Healthplan and Services Defined
PLAN TYPE: HMO
Benefits Offered: Behavioral Health, Disease Management, Home Care, Physical Therapy, Vision, Wellness, Non-Surgical Weight Loss, Urgent Care, Dermatology, Rehabilitation, Breast Cancer, Orthopedics, Otosclerosis, Pediatrics

Type of Coverage
Commercial, Individual

Geographic Areas Served
Arkansas, Kansas, Missouri, Oklahoma

Key Personnel
President/CEO......................... Steve Mackin
Chief Financial Officer................. Cheryl Matejka
COO/Chief Strategist .... Shannon Sock
SVP/General Counsel .... Philip Wheeler

491 UnitedHealthcare Community Plan Missouri
UnitedHealthcare Customer Service
P.O. Box 30769
Salt Lake City, UT 84130-0769
Toll-Free: 888-545-5205
www.uhccommunityplan.com/mo
Subsidiary of: UnitedHealth Group
For Profit Organization: Yes

Healthplan and Services Defined
PLAN TYPE: Medicare
Other Type: Medicaid
Model Type: Network
Benefits Offered: Dental, Home Care, Prescription, Vision, Wellness

Type of Coverage
Medicare, Medicaid

Geographic Areas Served
Varies by plan

Key Personnel
CEO, Community Plan MO................ Jamie Bruce
jamie_bruce@uhc.com

492 UnitedHealthcare of Missouri
13655 Riverport Drive
Maryland Heights, MO 63043
Toll-Free: 888-545-5205
Phone: 314-592-7000
www.uhc.com
Subsidiary of: UnitedHealth Group
For Profit Organization: Yes

Healthplan and Services Defined
PLAN TYPE: HMO/PPO
Model Type: Network
Plan Specialty: Behavioral Health, Dental, Disease Management, PBM, Vision
Benefits Offered: Behavioral Health, Dental, Disease Management, Long-Term Care, Prescription, Vision, Life, LTD, STD

Type of Coverage
Individual, Medicare, Supplemental Medicare, Medicaid, Catastrophic, Family, Military, Veterans, Group

Geographic Areas Served
Statewide

Key Personnel
CEO, MO/Central IL...................... Pat Quinn

MONTANA

Health Insurance Coverage Status and Type of Coverage by Age

Category	All Persons Number	All Persons %	Under 19 years Number	Under 19 years %	Under 65 years Number	Under 65 years %
Total population	1,054 *(1)*	100.0 *(0.0)*	242 *(2)*	100.0 *(0.0)*	850 *(2)*	100.0 *(0.0)*
Covered by some type of health insurance	967 *(6)*	91.7 *(0.5)*	227 *(3)*	93.8 *(0.9)*	764 *(6)*	89.8 *(0.7)*
Covered by private health insurance	698 *(10)*	66.3 *(0.9)*	139 *(5)*	57.4 *(2.0)*	578 *(9)*	68.0 *(1.1)*
Employer-based	512 *(12)*	48.6 *(1.1)*	115 *(5)*	47.7 *(2.1)*	468 *(11)*	55.0 *(1.3)*
Direct purchase	195 *(8)*	18.5 *(0.8)*	23 *(3)*	9.4 *(1.3)*	115 *(7)*	13.6 *(0.8)*
TRICARE	40 *(4)*	3.8 *(0.4)*	9 *(2)*	3.7 *(1.0)*	26 *(4)*	3.0 *(0.5)*
Covered by public health insurance	428 *(9)*	40.6 *(0.9)*	102 *(6)*	42.0 *(2.3)*	230 *(10)*	27.0 *(1.1)*
Medicaid	222 *(9)*	21.0 *(0.9)*	101 *(6)*	41.8 *(2.3)*	201 *(9)*	23.6 *(1.1)*
Medicare	224 *(3)*	21.3 *(0.3)*	1 *(1)*	0.3 *(0.2)*	26 *(2)*	3.0 *(0.3)*
VA Care	44 *(4)*	4.2 *(0.4)*	Z *(Z)*	0.1 *(0.1)*	19 *(3)*	2.2 *(0.3)*
Not covered at any time during the year	87 *(6)*	8.3 *(0.5)*	15 *(2)*	6.2 *(0.9)*	87 *(6)*	10.2 *(0.7)*

Note: Numbers in thousands; Figures cover civilian noninstitutionalized population in 2019; N/A indicates that data was not available; Z represents or rounds to zero; Margin of error appears in parenthesis and is calculated using replicate weights.
Source: U.S. Census Bureau, American Community Survey, Table HI-05. Health Insurance Coverage Status and Type of Coverage by State and Age for All People: 2019

Montana

493 Blue Cross & Blue Shield of Montana
3645 Alice Street
P.O. Box 4309
Helena, MT 59604-4309
Toll-Free: 800-447-7828
www.bcbsmt.com
Subsidiary of: Health Care Service Corporation
Non-Profit Organization: Yes
Year Founded: 1986
Owned by an Integrated Delivery Network (IDN): Yes
Federally Qualified: Yes
Number of Affiliated Hospitals: 58
Number of Primary Care Physicians: 1,900
Number of Referral/Specialty Physicians: 2,800
Total Enrollment: 300,000
State Enrollment: 300,000

Healthplan and Services Defined
  PLAN TYPE: HMO
  Model Type: Network
  Plan Specialty: ASO, Behavioral Health, Chiropractic, Dental, Disease Management, EPO, Lab, MSO, PBM, Vision, Radiology, Worker's Compensation, UR
  Benefits Offered: Behavioral Health, Chiropractic, Complementary
Medicine, Dental, Disease Management, Home Care, Inpatient SNF, Long-Term Care, Physical Therapy, Podiatry, Prescription, Psychiatric, Transplant, Vision, Wellness, Worker's Compensation, AD&D, Life, LTD, STD
  Offers Demand Management Patient Information Service: Yes

Type of Coverage
  Commercial, Individual, Indemnity, Medicare, Supplemental Medicare, Catastrophic
  Catastrophic Illness Benefit: Varies per case

Type of Payment Plans Offered
  POS, DFFS, Capitated

Geographic Areas Served
  Beaverhead, Big Horn, Blaine, Broadwater, Carbon, Carter, Cascade, Choteau, Custer, Deer Lodge, Flathead, Glacier, Hill, Jefferson, Lake, Lewis and Clark, Liberty, Lincoln, Madison, McCone, Meagher, Mineral, Missoula, Musselshell, Pondera, Ravalli, Sanders, Silver Bow, Stillwater, Sweet Grass, Teton, Wheatland, Yellowstone

Subscriber Information
  Average Subscriber Co-Payment:
    Primary Care Physician: $15
    Non-Network Physician: Deductible
    Hospital ER: $75.00
    Home Health Care: No deductible
    Home Health Care Max. Days/Visits Covered: 180 days
    Nursing Home: $300 per admit co-pay
    Nursing Home Max. Days/Visits Covered: 60 days

Network Qualifications
  Pre-Admission Certification: Yes

Peer Review Type
  Utilization Review: Yes
  Second Surgical Opinion: Yes
  Case Management: Yes

Publishes and Distributes Report Card: Yes

Accreditation Certification
  URAC

Key Personnel
  Presiden . . . . Collette Hanson
  VP, Sales & Account Mngmt . . . . Corey Palmer
  Media Contact . . . . John Doran
    406-437-6195
    John_Doran@bcbsmt.com
  Media Contact . . . . Jesse Zentz
    406-437-6182
    Jesse_Zentz@bcbsmt.com

Specialty Managed Care Partners
  Behavioral Health, Chiropractic, Dental, Disease Management, Home Care, Inpatient SNF, and more
  Enters into Contracts with Regional Business Coalitions: Yes

Employer References
  Montana University System, Evening Post Publishing Company, Costco Wholesale, State of Montana, Huntley Project Schools

494 HCSC Insurance Services Company Montana
3645 Alice St.
Helena, MT 59601
Phone: 406-437-5000
hcsc.com
Subsidiary of: Blue Cross Blue Shield Association
Non-Profit Organization: Yes
Year Founded: 1936

Healthplan and Services Defined
  PLAN TYPE: HMO
  Benefits Offered: Behavioral Health, Dental, Disease Management, Psychiatric, Wellness

Key Personnel
  President, MT Plan . . . . Collette Hanson

495 Mountain Health Co-Op
810 Hialeah Ct.
Helena, ID 59604
Toll-Free: 855-477-2900
information@mhc.coop
mhc.coop
Mailing Address: P.O. Box 5358, Helena, MT 59601
Non-Profit Organization: Yes
Year Founded: 2013

Healthplan and Services Defined
  PLAN TYPE: HMO
  Plan Specialty: Behavioral Health
  Benefits Offered: Chiropractic, Inpatient SNF, Physical Therapy, Prescription, Wellness, Labs & X-Ray; Occupational & Speech Therapy; Maternity

Geographic Areas Served
Idaho, Montana, Wyoming

Key Personnel
Chair .... Raymond Rogers
Media Contact .... Karen Early
    208-917-1605
    kearly@mhc.com

---

496 UnitedHealthcare of Montana
1111 3rd Avenue
Suite 1100
Seattle, WA 98101
Toll-Free: 888-545-5205
Phone: 206-926-0251
www.uhc.com
Subsidiary of: UnitedHealth Group
For Profit Organization: Yes
Year Founded: 1986

Healthplan and Services Defined
PLAN TYPE: HMO/PPO
Model Type: Network
Plan Specialty: Behavioral Health, Dental, Disease Management, MSO, PBM, Vision
Benefits Offered: Behavioral Health, Chiropractic, Complementary Medicine, Dental, Disease Management, Home Care, Inpatient SNF, Long-Term Care, Physical Therapy, Podiatry, Prescription, Psychiatric, Transplant, Vision, Wellness, AD&D, Life

Type of Coverage
Commercial, Individual, Medicare, Supplemental Medicare, Medicaid, Family, Military, Veterans, Group

Type of Payment Plans Offered
DFFS, FFS, Combination FFS & DFFS

Geographic Areas Served
Statewide. Montana is covered by the Washington branch

Subscriber Information
Average Monthly Fee Per Subscriber
    (Employee + Employer Contribution):
        Employee Only (Self): Varies
Average Subscriber Co-Payment:
    Primary Care Physician: $10
    Prescription Drugs: $10/15/30
    Hospital ER: $50

Network Qualifications
Pre-Admission Certification: Yes

Peer Review Type
Case Management: Yes

Publishes and Distributes Report Card: Yes

Accreditation Certification
URAC, NCQA
State Licensure, Quality Assurance Program

Key Personnel
CEO, WA/OR/MT/AK/HI .... Gary Daniels

Average Claim Compensation
Physician's Fees Charged: 70%
Hospital's Fees Charged: 55%

Specialty Managed Care Partners
United Behavioral Health
Enters into Contracts with Regional Business Coalitions: No

NEBRASKA

Health Insurance Coverage Status and Type of Coverage by Age

Category	All Persons Number	All Persons %	Under 19 years Number	Under 19 years %	Under 65 years Number	Under 65 years %
Total population	1,904 *(1)*	100.0 *(0.0)*	502 *(3)*	100.0 *(0.0)*	1,603 *(2)*	100.0 *(0.0)*
Covered by some type of health insurance	1,746 *(8)*	91.7 *(0.4)*	474 *(5)*	94.3 *(0.8)*	1,446 *(8)*	90.2 *(0.5)*
Covered by private health insurance	1,432 *(13)*	75.2 *(0.7)*	351 *(7)*	69.9 *(1.4)*	1,249 *(12)*	77.9 *(0.7)*
Employer-based	1,145 *(13)*	60.1 *(0.7)*	308 *(7)*	61.3 *(1.4)*	1,078 *(12)*	67.2 *(0.8)*
Direct purchase	317 *(10)*	16.7 *(0.5)*	46 *(5)*	9.1 *(0.9)*	194 *(9)*	12.1 *(0.6)*
TRICARE	63 *(5)*	3.3 *(0.2)*	13 *(2)*	2.6 *(0.4)*	41 *(4)*	2.6 *(0.3)*
Covered by public health insurance	539 *(11)*	28.3 *(0.6)*	138 *(7)*	27.4 *(1.5)*	248 *(11)*	15.5 *(0.7)*
Medicaid	244 *(11)*	12.8 *(0.6)*	136 *(7)*	27.1 *(1.5)*	215 *(11)*	13.4 *(0.7)*
Medicare	326 *(3)*	17.1 *(0.2)*	2 *(1)*	0.4 *(0.2)*	35 *(3)*	2.2 *(0.2)*
VA Care	51 *(3)*	2.7 *(0.2)*	1 *(Z)*	0.1 *(0.1)*	20 *(2)*	1.2 *(0.1)*
Not covered at any time during the year	158 *(8)*	8.3 *(0.4)*	28 *(4)*	5.7 *(0.8)*	157 *(8)*	9.8 *(0.5)*

Note: Numbers in thousands; Figures cover civilian noninstitutionalized population in 2019; N/A indicates that data was not available; Z represents or rounds to zero; Margin of error appears in parenthesis and is calculated using replicate weights.
Source: U.S. Census Bureau, American Community Survey, Table HI-05. Health Insurance Coverage Status and Type of Coverage by State and Age for All People: 2019

Nebraska

497 Ameritas
5900 O Street
Lincoln, NE 68501-1889
Toll-Free: 800-751-1112
Fax: 402-467-7335
www.ameritas.com
For Profit Organization: Yes
Year Founded: 1990

Healthplan and Services Defined
PLAN TYPE: Multiple
Model Type: Staff
Plan Specialty: ASO, Dental, Vision
Benefits Offered: Dental, Vision, Life, Disability

Type of Coverage
Commercial, Individual

Type of Payment Plans Offered
POS, DFFS, Capitated, Combination FFS & DFFS

Geographic Areas Served
Nationwide

Peer Review Type
Utilization Review: Yes
Second Surgical Opinion: Yes
Case Management: Yes

Publishes and Distributes Report Card: Yes

Accreditation Certification
Medicare Approved

Key Personnel
President & CEO . . . . William W. Lester

498 Blue Cross & Blue Shield of Nebraska
1919 Aksarben Drive
P.O. Box 3248
Omaha, NE 68180
Toll-Free: 800-422-2763
Phone: 402-982-7000
Fax: 402-392-4153
sales@nebraskablue.com
www.nebraskablue.com
Secondary Address: 1233 Lincoln Mall, Lincoln, NE 68508, 402-458-4800
Year Founded: 1939
Total Enrollment: 717,000
State Enrollment: 717,000

Healthplan and Services Defined
PLAN TYPE: PPO
Model Type: Network
Benefits Offered: Behavioral Health, Chiropractic, Dental, Disease Management, Home Care, Inpatient SNF, Long-Term Care, Physical Therapy, Podiatry, Prescription, Psychiatric, Vision

Type of Coverage
Commercial, Individual, Medicare, Supplemental Medicare

Geographic Areas Served
Statewide

Publishes and Distributes Report Card: No

Key Personnel
President/CEO . . . . Steven H. Grandfield
Chief Financial Officer . . . . Chad Werner
EVP, Operations . . . . Susan Courtney
Chief Information Officer . . . . Rama Kolli
Chief Medical Officer . . . . Josette Gordon-Simet, MD
VP, Marketing/Comms. Kim Arnold

499 Delta Dental of Nebraska
1807 N 169th Plaza
Omaha, NE 68118
Toll-Free: 800-736-0710
www.deltadentalne.org
Non-Profit Organization: Yes
Year Founded: 1969

Healthplan and Services Defined
PLAN TYPE: Dental
Other Type: Dental PPO
Model Type: Network
Plan Specialty: ASO, Dental
Benefits Offered: Dental

Type of Coverage
Commercial, Individual
Catastrophic Illness Benefit: None

Geographic Areas Served
Statewide

Key Personnel
President . . . . Rodney Young
Office Administrator. . . . . Sally Gutowski
Sales Manager . . . . Barbara Jensen
Media Contact. . . . . Clarise Tushie-Lessard
   612-224-3341
   ctushie-lessard@deltadentalmn.org

500 Medica with CHI Health
331 Village Point Plaza
Suite 304
Omaha, NE 68118
Toll-Free: 800-918-6892
www.medica.com
Subsidiary of: UniNet Health Care
Number of Affiliated Hospitals: 30
Number of Primary Care Physicians: 1,400

Healthplan and Services Defined
PLAN TYPE: HMO
Benefits Offered: Behavioral Health, Chiropractic, Dental, Disease Management, Prescription, Wellness

Geographic Areas Served
Buffalo, Burt, Butler, Cass, Colfax, Cuming, Dodge, Douglas, Fillmore, Hall, Johnson, Lancaster, Nance, Nemaha, Nuckolls, Otoe, Pawnee, Saline, Sarpy, Saunders, Seward, Thayer or Washington counties

Key Personnel
President & CEO . . . . John Naylor
VP, Human Resources . . . . Lynn Altmann
SVP, Financial Officer . . . . Mark Baird
VP, General Manager . . . . Geoff Bartsh
SVP, General Counsel . . . . Jim Jacobson
SVP, Government Programs. . . . . Tom Lindquist
Chief Medical Officer . . . . John R. Mach, MD

501 Medica: Nebraska

331 Village Point Plaza
Suite 304
Omaha, NE 68118
Toll-Free: 800-918-6892
medica.com
Year Founded: 1974
Number of Affiliated Hospitals: 170
Number of Primary Care Physicians: 7,200
Total Enrollment: 150,000

Healthplan and Services Defined
PLAN TYPE: HMO
Benefits Offered: Behavioral Health, Chiropractic, Dental, Disease Management, Prescription, Wellness, AD&D, Life

Type of Coverage
Medicare

Geographic Areas Served
Statewide

Key Personnel
President & CEO . . . . John Naylor
VP, Human Resources . . . . Lynn Altmann
SVP, Financial Officer . . . . Mark Baird
VP, General Manager . . . . Geoff Bartsh
SVP, General Counsel . . . . Jim Jacobson
SVP, Government Programs. . . . . Tom Lindquist
Chief Medical Officer . . . . John R. Mach, MD

502 Midlands Choice

8420 W Dodge Road
Suite 210
Omaha, NE 68114
Phone: 402-390-8233
www.midlandschoice.com
For Profit Organization: Yes
Year Founded: 1993
Physician Owned Organization: Yes
Number of Affiliated Hospitals: 320
Number of Primary Care Physicians: 20,000
Total Enrollment: 615,000

Healthplan and Services Defined
PLAN TYPE: PPO
Model Type: PPO Network

Geographic Areas Served
Iowa, Nebraska, South Dakota, Colorado, and portions of Wyoming, Kansas, Missouri, Illinois, Wisconsin and Minnesota

Accreditation Certification
URAC

Key Personnel
President/CEO . . . . Greta Vaught
VP/Privacy Officer. . . . . Daniel McCulley

Specialty Managed Care Partners
Enters into Contracts with Regional Business Coalitions: No

503 Mutual of Omaha

3300 Mutual of Omaha Plaza
Omaha, NE 68175
www.mutualofomaha.com
For Profit Organization: Yes
Year Founded: 1909
Number of Affiliated Hospitals: 43
Number of Primary Care Physicians: 673
Number of Referral/Specialty Physicians: 1,718
Total Enrollment: 54,418
State Enrollment: 28,978

Healthplan and Services Defined
PLAN TYPE: HMO/PPO
Other Type: POS
Model Type: IPA
Plan Specialty: ASO, Behavioral Health, Chiropractic, Disease Management, Lab, Vision, Radiology, UR
Benefits Offered: Behavioral Health, Chiropractic, Disease Management, Home Care, Inpatient SNF, Long-Term Care, Physical Therapy, Podiatry, Prescription, Psychiatric, Transplant, Vision, Wellness, AD&D, Life, LTD, STD, Critical Illness, EAP

Type of Coverage
Commercial, Individual, Indemnity, Medicare, Supplemental Medicare, Medicaid
Catastrophic Illness Benefit: Covered

Type of Payment Plans Offered
POS, Combination FFS & DFFS

Geographic Areas Served
Iowa: Harrison, Mills & Pottawattamie counties; Nebraska: Burt, Butler, Cass, Colfas, Cuming, Oakota, Dixon, Filmore, Johnson, Lancaster, Madison, Otoe, Salone, Saunders, Seuard, Stanton, Dodge, Douglas, Sampy, Washington counties

Subscriber Information
Average Monthly Fee Per Subscriber
 (Employee + Employer Contribution):
  Employee Only (Self): Varies by plan
Average Annual Deductible Per Subscriber:
  Employee Only (Self): $0.00
Average Subscriber Co-Payment:
  Primary Care Physician: $15.00
  Prescription Drugs: $15.00
  Hospital ER: $50.00
  Home Health Care: $25.00
  Home Health Care Max. Days/Visits Covered: Unlimited
  Nursing Home: $0.00
  Nursing Home Max. Days/Visits Covered: 100 days

Nebraska

Network Qualifications
Pre-Admission Certification: Yes

Peer Review Type
Utilization Review: Yes
Second Surgical Opinion: No
Case Management: Yes

Publishes and Distributes Report Card: Yes

Accreditation Certification
URAC, NCQA
TJC Accreditation, Utilization Review, Pre-Admission Certification, State Licensure, Quality Assurance Program

Key Personnel
Chairman/CEO .... James T. Blackledge
Chief Financial Officer .... Richard Hrabchak
Chief Information Officer .... Michael Lechtenberger
Chief Admin. Officer .... Liz Mazzotta

Average Claim Compensation
Physician's Fees Charged: 75%
Hospital's Fees Charged: 60%

Specialty Managed Care Partners
Enters into Contracts with Regional Business Coalitions: No

Employer References
Mutual of Omaha, Forest National Bank, Nebraska Furniture Mart, Saint Joseph Hospital

504 Mutual of Omaha Dental Insurance
3300 Mutual of Omaha Plaza
Omaha, NE 68175
www.mutualofomaha.com/dental
For Profit Organization: Yes
Year Founded: 1985

Healthplan and Services Defined
PLAN TYPE: Dental
Model Type: Network
Plan Specialty: Dental
Benefits Offered: Dental

Type of Coverage
Commercial, Individual

Peer Review Type
Utilization Review: Yes
Second Surgical Opinion: Yes
Case Management: Yes

Publishes and Distributes Report Card: Yes

Accreditation Certification
TJC Accreditation, Medicare Approved, Utilization Review, Pre-Admission Certification, State Licensure, Quality Assurance Program

Key Personnel
Chief Executive Officer .... James Blackledge
Chief Financial Officer .... Vibhu Sharma
General Counsel .... Nancy Crawford
Chief Information Officer .... Michael Lechtenberger
CAO .... Stacy Scholtz

Specialty Managed Care Partners
Enters into Contracts with Regional Business Coalitions: No

505 Nebraska Total Care
2525 N 117th Avenue
Suite 100
Omaha, NE 68164-9988
Toll-Free: 844-385-2192
www.nebraskatotalcare.com
Subsidiary of: Centene Corporation
For Profit Organization: Yes

Healthplan and Services Defined
PLAN TYPE: Other
Model Type: Network
Benefits Offered: Behavioral Health, Disease Management, Prescription, Vision, Wellness

Type of Coverage
Medicaid

Key Personnel
Plan President/CEO .... Health Phillips
Director, Contracting .... Tim Easton

506 UnitedHealthcare Community Plan Nebraska
UnitedHealthcare Customer Service
P.O. Box 30769
Salt Lake City, UT 84130-0769
Toll-Free: 888-545-5205
www.uhccommunityplan.com/ne
Subsidiary of: UnitedHealth Group
For Profit Organization: Yes

Healthplan and Services Defined
PLAN TYPE: Medicare
Other Type: Medicaid
Model Type: Network
Benefits Offered: Dental, Home Care, Podiatry, Prescription, Vision, Wellness, Acupuncture, Chiropractic, Hearing

Type of Coverage
Medicare, Medicaid

Geographic Areas Served
Adams, Buffalo, Burt, Cass, Dodge, Douglas, Gage, Hall, Lancaster, Madison, Otoe, Saline, Sarpy, Saunders, Seward, and Washington. Other plans statewide

Key Personnel
CEO, Community Plan NE .... Jeff Stafford
jeff_stafford@uhc.com

507 UnitedHealthcare of Nebraska
2717 North 118th Street
Suite 300
Omaha, NE 68164
Toll-Free: 888-545-5205
Phone: 402-445-5000
www.uhc.com
Subsidiary of: UnitedHealth Group
For Profit Organization: Yes
Year Founded: 1984

Healthplan and Services Defined
PLAN TYPE: HMO/PPO
Model Type: Network
Plan Specialty: ASO, Behavioral Health, Chiropractic, Dental, Disease Management, Lab, MSO, PBM, Vision, Radiology
Benefits Offered: Behavioral Health, Dental, Disease Management, Long-Term Care, Prescription, Vision, Wellness, Life, LTD, STD

Type of Coverage
Commercial, Individual, Medicare, Supplemental Medicare, Medicaid, Catastrophic, Family, Military, Veterans, Group

Type of Payment Plans Offered
POS, DFFS, FFS

Geographic Areas Served
Iowa: Cass, Fremont, Harrison, Mills, Mononas, Page, Pottawattsmie, Shelby, Woodbury counties; Nebraska: Buffalo, Burt, Butler, Dodge, Douglas, Gage, Hale, Jefferson, Johnson, Lancaster, Madison, Nemaha, Otoe, Pierce, Platte, Saline, Sarpy, Seward, & Washington counties

Subscriber Information
Average Subscriber Co-Payment:
    Primary Care Physician: $10.00
    Non-Network Physician: Deductible
    Prescription Drugs: $10.00
    Hospital ER: $50.00

Network Qualifications
Pre-Admission Certification: Yes

Peer Review Type
Utilization Review: Yes
Second Surgical Opinion: Yes
Case Management: Yes

Publishes and Distributes Report Card: Yes

Accreditation Certification
TJC Accreditation, Medicare Approved, Utilization Review, Pre-Admission Certification, State Licensure, Quality Assurance Program

Key Personnel
CEO, Midlands . . . . Kathy Mallatt
CEO, IA/KS/NE/Central IL . . . . Rob Broomfield

NEVADA

Health Insurance Coverage Status and Type of Coverage by Age

Category	All Persons Number	All Persons %	Under 19 years Number	Under 19 years %	Under 65 years Number	Under 65 years %
Total population	3,043 *(2)*	100.0 *(0.0)*	725 *(3)*	100.0 *(0.0)*	2,550 *(3)*	100.0 *(0.0)*
Covered by some type of health insurance	2,696 *(14)*	88.6 *(0.5)*	667 *(6)*	92.0 *(0.9)*	2,208 *(14)*	86.6 *(0.6)*
Covered by private health insurance	1,977 *(20)*	65.0 *(0.7)*	448 *(9)*	61.8 *(1.2)*	1,736 *(19)*	68.1 *(0.7)*
Employer-based	1,637 *(23)*	53.8 *(0.8)*	390 *(11)*	53.8 *(1.5)*	1,514 *(22)*	59.4 *(0.9)*
Direct purchase	340 *(13)*	11.2 *(0.4)*	51 *(6)*	7.0 *(0.8)*	222 *(11)*	8.7 *(0.4)*
TRICARE	110 *(8)*	3.6 *(0.3)*	20 *(4)*	2.7 *(0.5)*	67 *(7)*	2.6 *(0.3)*
Covered by public health insurance	1,028 *(18)*	33.8 *(0.6)*	239 *(9)*	33.0 *(1.3)*	557 *(18)*	21.8 *(0.7)*
Medicaid	543 *(19)*	17.8 *(0.6)*	238 *(9)*	32.8 *(1.3)*	483 *(17)*	18.9 *(0.7)*
Medicare	531 *(5)*	17.5 *(0.2)*	2 *(1)*	0.3 *(0.1)*	60 *(4)*	2.4 *(0.2)*
VA Care	95 *(5)*	3.1 *(0.2)*	Z *(Z)*	0.1 *(0.1)*	45 *(4)*	1.8 *(0.2)*
Not covered at any time during the year	348 *(14)*	11.4 *(0.5)*	58 *(6)*	8.0 *(0.9)*	341 *(14)*	13.4 *(0.6)*

Note: Numbers in thousands; Figures cover civilian noninstitutionalized population in 2019; N/A indicates that data was not available; Z represents or rounds to zero; Margin of error appears in parenthesis and is calculated using replicate weights.
Source: U.S. Census Bureau, American Community Survey, Table HI-05. Health Insurance Coverage Status and Type of Coverage by State and Age for All People: 2019

Nevada

508 Ambetter from SilverSummit Healthplan
6100 Neil Rd.
Reno, NV 89511
Toll-Free: 866-263-8134
ambetter.silversummithealthplan.com
Subsidiary of: Centene Corporation
For Profit Organization: Yes

Healthplan and Services Defined
 PLAN TYPE: Other
 Model Type: Network
 Plan Specialty: Lab
 Benefits Offered: Behavioral Health, Disease Management, Physical Therapy, Prescription, Wellness, Maternity and newborn care

Type of Coverage
 Health Insurance Marketplace

Geographic Areas Served
 Statewide

---

509 Anthem Blue Cross & Blue Shield of Nevada
9133 W Russell Road
Las Vegas, NV 89148
Toll-Free: 800-331-1476
Phone: 702-586-6100
www.anthem.com
Secondary Address: 5250 S Virginia Street, Reno, NV 89502, 775-448-4000
Subsidiary of: Anthem, Inc.
For Profit Organization: Yes

Healthplan and Services Defined
 PLAN TYPE: HMO/PPO
 Model Type: Network
 Plan Specialty: Behavioral Health, Dental, Disease Management, Lab, PBM, Vision, Radiology
 Benefits Offered: Behavioral Health, Dental, Disease Management, Inpatient SNF, Physical Therapy, Prescription, Psychiatric, Transplant, Vision, Wellness, Life

Type of Coverage
 Commercial, Individual, Medicare, Supplemental Medicare, Medicaid, Catastrophic

Geographic Areas Served
 Statewide

Accreditation Certification
 URAC, NCQA

Key Personnel
 President . . . . Mike Murphy

---

510 Behavioral Healthcare Options, Inc.
2716 N Tenaya Way
Las Vegas, NV 89128
Toll-Free: 800-873-2246
Phone: 702-364-1484
www.bhoptions.com
Subsidiary of: UnitedHealthcare
For Profit Organization: Yes
Year Founded: 1991

Healthplan and Services Defined
 PLAN TYPE: PPO
 Model Type: Group
 Plan Specialty: Behavioral Health, Mental health, addiction treatment, employee assistance, work-life services
 Benefits Offered: Behavioral Health, Psychiatric

Geographic Areas Served
 Nationwide

Accreditation Certification
 URAC

---

511 Health Plan of Nevada
2720 N Tenaya Way
Las Vegas, NV 89128
Toll-Free: 800-777-1840
Phone: 702-242-7300
www.healthplanofnevada.com
Subsidiary of: United HealthCare Services, Inc.
For Profit Organization: Yes
Year Founded: 1982
Total Enrollment: 418,000
State Enrollment: 25,576

Healthplan and Services Defined
 PLAN TYPE: HMO
 Other Type: POS, Medicare
 Model Type: Network
 Benefits Offered: Disease Management, Prescription, Wellness

Type of Coverage
 Commercial, Individual, Medicare, Supplemental Medicare, Medicaid

Geographic Areas Served
 Statewide

Accreditation Certification
 NCQA

Key Personnel
 President/CEO . . . . Jonathan W Bunker

Specialty Managed Care Partners
 Express Scripts

---

512 Hometown Health Plan
10315 Professional Circle
Reno, NV 89521
Toll-Free: 800-336-0123
Phone: 775-982-3232
Fax: 775-982-3741
customer_service@hometownhealth.com
www.hometownhealth.com
Subsidiary of: Renown Health
Non-Profit Organization: Yes
Year Founded: 1988
Owned by an Integrated Delivery Network (IDN): Yes

Number of Affiliated Hospitals: 19
Number of Primary Care Physicians: 256
Number of Referral/Specialty Physicians: 8,917
Total Enrollment: 32,000
State Enrollment: 10,000

Healthplan and Services Defined
　PLAN TYPE: Multiple
　Model Type: Network
　Plan Specialty: ASO, Behavioral Health, Chiropractic, Dental, Disease Management, EPO, Lab, PBM, Vision, Radiology, Worker's Compensation, UR
　Benefits Offered: Behavioral Health, Chiropractic, Complementary Medicine, Dental, Disease Management, Home Care, Inpatient SNF, Physical Therapy, Podiatry, Prescription, Psychiatric, Transplant, Vision, Wellness, Worker's Compensation, AD&D, Life, LTD, STD, Accupuncture
　Offers Demand Management Patient Information Service: Yes

Type of Coverage
　Commercial, Individual, Medicare, Supplemental Medicare

Geographic Areas Served
　Statewide

Subscriber Information
　Average Monthly Fee Per Subscriber
　　(Employee + Employer Contribution):
　　　Employee Only (Self): Varies
　　　Employee & 1 Family Member: Varies
　　　Employee & 2 Family Members: Varies
　　　Medicare: Varies
　Average Annual Deductible Per Subscriber:
　　　Employee Only (Self): Varies
　　　Employee & 1 Family Member: Varies
　　　Employee & 2 Family Members: Varies
　　　Medicare: Varies
　Average Subscriber Co-Payment:
　　　Primary Care Physician: Varies
　　　Non-Network Physician: Varies
　　　Prescription Drugs: Varies
　　　Hospital ER: Varies
　　　Home Health Care: Varies
　　　Home Health Care Max. Days/Visits Covered: Varies
　　　Nursing Home: Varies
　　　Nursing Home Max. Days/Visits Covered: Varies

Accreditation Certification
　TJC

Key Personnel
　President/CEO . . . . Ty Windfeldt

513　Humana Health Insurance of Nevada
770 E Warm Springs Road
Suite 340
Las Vegas, NV 89119
Phone: 702-837-4401
Fax: 702-562-0134
www.humana.com
Subsidiary of: Humana Inc.
For Profit Organization: Yes

Healthplan and Services Defined
　PLAN TYPE: HMO/PPO
　Model Type: Network
　Plan Specialty: Dental, Vision
　Benefits Offered: Dental, Vision, Life, LTD, STD

Type of Coverage
　Commercial, Individual

Geographic Areas Served
　Statewide

Accreditation Certification
　URAC, NCQA, CORE

514　Liberty Dental Plan of Nevada
6385 S. Rainbow Blvd.
Suite 200
Las Vegas, NV 89118
Toll-Free: 888-700-0643
www.libertydentalplan.com
For Profit Organization: Yes
Total Enrollment: 2,000,000

Healthplan and Services Defined
　PLAN TYPE: Dental
　Other Type: Dental HMO
　Plan Specialty: Dental
　Benefits Offered: Dental

Type of Coverage
　Commercial, Medicare, Medicaid, Unions

Geographic Areas Served
　Statewide

Accreditation Certification
　NCQA

Key Personnel
　NEV Dental Officer . . . . Amy Tongsiri

515　Nevada Preferred Healthcare Providers
1510 Meadow Wood Lane
Reno, NV 89502
Toll-Free: 800-776-6959
Phone: 775-356-1159
Fax: 775-356-5746
www.universalhealthnet.com
Subsidiary of: Universal Health Services, Inc.
Non-Profit Organization: Yes
Year Founded: 1991
Number of Affiliated Hospitals: 70
Number of Primary Care Physicians: 4,483
Total Enrollment: 150,000
State Enrollment: 150,000

Healthplan and Services Defined
　PLAN TYPE: PPO
　Other Type: EPO
　Model Type: Network
　Plan Specialty: EPO, Worker's Compensation
　Benefits Offered: Behavioral Health, Chiropractic, Home Care, Physical Therapy, Podiatry, Psychiatric, Transplant, Wellness, Worker's Compensation

Nevada Guide to U.S. HMOs & PPOs 2023

Type of Coverage
  Commercial, Individual

Type of Payment Plans Offered
  POS, DFFS, FFS, Combination FFS & DFFS

Geographic Areas Served
  Nevada, and limited areas in Utah

Network Qualifications
  Pre-Admission Certification: Yes

Peer Review Type
  Utilization Review: Yes
  Second Surgical Opinion: Yes
  Case Management: Yes

Publishes and Distributes Report Card: No

Specialty Managed Care Partners
  Enters into Contracts with Regional Business Coalitions: Yes

Employer References
  State of Nevada, CCN, PPO USA GEHA, Valley Health System, Pepperpill

516 Prominence Health Plan
1510 Meadow Wood Lane
Reno, NV 89502
Toll-Free: 800-433-3077
Phone: 775-770-9300
Secondary Address: 6900 I-40 West Amarillo, Amarillo, TX 79106
Subsidiary of: Universal Health Services, Inc.
For Profit Organization: Yes
Year Founded: 1993
Number of Affiliated Hospitals: 34
Number of Primary Care Physicians: 4,000
Number of Referral/Specialty Physicians: 1,500

Healthplan and Services Defined
  PLAN TYPE: HMO/PPO
  Other Type: POS
  Model Type: Group, Network
  Plan Specialty: ASO, Behavioral Health, Chiropractic, Dental, Disease Management, EPO, MSO, PBM, Vision, Radiology, Worker's Compensation
  Benefits Offered: Behavioral Health, Chiropractic, Complementary Medicine, Dental, Disease Management, Home Care, Inpatient SNF, Long-Term Care, Physical Therapy, Podiatry, Prescription, Psychiatric, Transplant, Vision, Wellness, Worker's Compensation, Routine PE, pre and post-natal care, well baby/well child care, mammography, GYN, prostate screenings

Type of Payment Plans Offered
  POS, DFFS, FFS, Combination FFS & DFFS

Geographic Areas Served
  Nevada and border communities in California and Arizona

Subscriber Information
  Average Monthly Fee Per Subscriber
    (Employee + Employer Contribution):
      Employee Only (Self): Varies by plan
  Average Subscriber Co-Payment:
    Nursing Home: Varies

Network Qualifications
  Pre-Admission Certification: Yes

Peer Review Type
  Utilization Review: Yes
  Second Surgical Opinion: Yes
  Case Management: Yes

Accreditation Certification
  NCQA
  TJC Accreditation, Medicare Approved, Pre-Admission Certification

Key Personnel
  President/CEO .... David Livingston
  Director of Operations .... Marjorie Henriksen

517 SilverSummit Healthplan
6100 Neil Rd.
Reno, NV 89511
Toll-Free: 844-366-2880
www.silversummithealthplan.com
Subsidiary of: Centene Corporation
For Profit Organization: Yes

Healthplan and Services Defined
  PLAN TYPE: Other
  Model Type: Network
  Benefits Offered: Dental, Prescription, Vision, Wellness

Type of Coverage
  Medicaid

Key Personnel
  President & CEO .... Garrett Leaf

518 UnitedHealthcare Community Plan Nevada
UnitedHealthcare Customer Service
P.O. Box 30769
Salt Lake City, UT 84130-0769
Toll-Free: 888-545-5205
www.uhccommunityplan.com/nv
Subsidiary of: UnitedHealth Group
For Profit Organization: Yes

Healthplan and Services Defined
  PLAN TYPE: Other
  Other Type: Medicaid
  Model Type: Network
  Benefits Offered: Dental

Type of Coverage
  Medicaid

Geographic Areas Served
  Clark and Washoe

Key Personnel
  Pres., Community Plan NV .... Kelly Simonson
    kelly.simonson@uhc.com

519 UnitedHealthcare of Nevada

2720 N Tenaya Way
Las Vegas, NV 89128
Toll-Free: 888-545-5205
www.uhc.com
Subsidiary of: UnitedHealth Group
For Profit Organization: Yes
Year Founded: 1984

Healthplan and Services Defined
 PLAN TYPE: HMO/PPO
 Other Type: POS
 Model Type: Network
 Plan Specialty: Behavioral Health, Dental, Disease Management, PBM, Vision
 Benefits Offered: Behavioral Health, Dental, Disease Management, Long-Term Care, Prescription, Vision, Wellness, Life, LTD, STD

Type of Coverage
 Individual, Medicare, Supplemental Medicare, Medicaid, Catastrophic, Family, Military, Veterans, Group

Type of Payment Plans Offered
 POS, DFFS, Capitated, FFS

Geographic Areas Served
 Statewide

Subscriber Information
 Average Monthly Fee Per Subscriber
  (Employee + Employer Contribution):
   Employee Only (Self): $39.00
 Average Annual Deductible Per Subscriber:
   Employee Only (Self): $0
   Employee & 1 Family Member: $0
   Employee & 2 Family Members: $0
   Medicare: $0
 Average Subscriber Co-Payment:
   Primary Care Physician: $0.00
   Prescription Drugs: $10.00
   Hospital ER: $50.00
   Home Health Care: Varies
   Home Health Care Max. Days/Visits Covered: Unlimited
   Nursing Home: Varies
   Nursing Home Max. Days/Visits Covered: 100 days

Peer Review Type
 Case Management: Yes

Publishes and Distributes Report Card: Yes

Key Personnel
 CEO, NV/UT/ID .... Donald Giancursio

NEW HAMPSHIRE

Health Insurance Coverage Status and Type of Coverage by Age

Category	All Persons Number	All Persons %	Under 19 years Number	Under 19 years %	Under 65 years Number	Under 65 years %
Total population	1,343 *(1)*	100.0 *(0.0)*	277 *(2)*	100.0 *(0.0)*	1,098 *(2)*	100.0 *(0.0)*
Covered by some type of health insurance	1,259 *(8)*	93.7 *(0.6)*	267 *(3)*	96.3 *(0.9)*	1,014 *(8)*	92.4 *(0.7)*
Covered by private health insurance	1,015 *(13)*	75.6 *(1.0)*	196 *(5)*	70.9 *(2.0)*	852 *(11)*	77.6 *(1.0)*
Employer-based	839 *(13)*	62.4 *(1.0)*	179 *(6)*	64.5 *(2.0)*	755 *(13)*	68.8 *(1.2)*
Direct purchase	190 *(8)*	14.1 *(0.6)*	15 *(2)*	5.5 *(0.8)*	100 *(6)*	9.1 *(0.6)*
TRICARE	31 *(4)*	2.3 *(0.3)*	5 *(2)*	1.7 *(0.6)*	16 *(3)*	1.5 *(0.3)*
Covered by public health insurance	431 *(11)*	32.1 *(0.8)*	79 *(6)*	28.4 *(2.1)*	194 *(11)*	17.7 *(1.0)*
Medicaid	177 *(10)*	13.2 *(0.8)*	78 *(6)*	28.1 *(2.1)*	160 *(10)*	14.6 *(0.9)*
Medicare	271 *(3)*	20.2 *(0.3)*	1 *(1)*	0.4 *(0.2)*	35 *(3)*	3.2 *(0.3)*
VA Care	35 *(3)*	2.6 *(0.2)*	Z *(Z)*	Z *(Z)*	13 *(2)*	1.2 *(0.2)*
Not covered at any time during the year	84 *(8)*	6.3 *(0.6)*	10 *(2)*	3.7 *(0.9)*	84 *(7)*	7.6 *(0.7)*

Note: Numbers in thousands; Figures cover civilian noninstitutionalized population in 2019; N/A indicates that data was not available; Z represents or rounds to zero; Margin of error appears in parenthesis and is calculated using replicate weights.
Source: U.S. Census Bureau, American Community Survey, Table HI-05. Health Insurance Coverage Status and Type of Coverage by State and Age for All People: 2019

New Hampshire

520 Able Insurance Agency
130 Broadway
Concord, NH 03301
Phone: 603-225-6677
able2insure.com

Healthplan and Services Defined
PLAN TYPE: HMO
Benefits Offered: Wellness, Worker's Compensation, Life

Geographic Areas Served
Greater Concord Area

Key Personnel
Principal .... PJ Cistulli
  pjcj@able2insure.com
Producer .... Angela Chicoine
  angela@able2insure.com
Agent .... Kathy Coleman
  kathy@able2insure.com
Marketing Coordinator .... Samantha Sharff
  samanthaleec@gmail.com

521 Ambetter from NH Health Families
2 Executive Park Drive
Bedford, NH 03110
Toll-Free: 844-265-1278
ambetter.nhhealthyfamilies.com
Subsidiary of: Centene Corporation
For Profit Organization: Yes

Healthplan and Services Defined
PLAN TYPE: Other
Model Type: Network
Plan Specialty: Lab
Benefits Offered: Behavioral Health, Disease Management, Physical Therapy, Prescription, Wellness, Maternity and newborn care

Type of Coverage
Health Insurance Marketplace

522 Anthem Blue Cross & Blue Shield of New Hampshire
1155 Elm Street
Suite 200
Manchester, NH 03101-1505
Toll-Free: 800-331-1476
www.anthem.com
Subsidiary of: Anthem, Inc.
For Profit Organization: Yes

Healthplan and Services Defined
PLAN TYPE: HMO/PPO
Model Type: Network
Plan Specialty: Behavioral Health, Dental, Disease Management, Lab, PBM, Vision, Radiology
Benefits Offered: Behavioral Health, Dental, Disease Management, Inpatient SNF, Physical Therapy, Prescription, Psychiatric, Transplant, Vision, Wellness, Life

Type of Coverage
Commercial, Individual, Medicare, Supplemental Medicare, Catastrophic

Geographic Areas Served
Statewide

Accreditation Certification
URAC, NCQA

Key Personnel
President .... Lisa Guertin

523 Harvard Pilgrim Health Care New Hampshire
650 Elm Street
Suite 700
Manchester, NH 03101-2596
Toll-Free: 888-888-4742
www.harvardpilgrim.org
Non-Profit Organization: Yes
Year Founded: 1977
Number of Affiliated Hospitals: 179
Number of Referral/Specialty Physicians: 53,000
Total Enrollment: 3,000,000

Healthplan and Services Defined
PLAN TYPE: HMO/PPO
Benefits Offered: Wellness

Type of Coverage
Individual, Medicare

Geographic Areas Served
Statewide

Accreditation Certification
NCQA

Key Personnel
VP, Operations NH Market .... William Brewster, MD

524 Humana Health Insurance of New Hampshire
1 New Hampshire Avenue
Suite 125
Portsmouth, NH 03801
Toll-Free: 800-967-2370
www.humana.com
Subsidiary of: Humana Inc.
For Profit Organization: Yes

Healthplan and Services Defined
PLAN TYPE: HMO/PPO
Model Type: Network
Plan Specialty: Dental, Vision
Benefits Offered: Dental, Vision, Life, LTD, STD

Type of Coverage
Commercial

Geographic Areas Served
Statewide

Accreditation Certification
URAC, NCQA, CORE

525 NH Healthy Families
2 Executive Park Drive
Bedford, NH 03110
Toll-Free: 866-769-3085
www.nhhealthyfamilies.com
Subsidiary of: Centene Corporation
For Profit Organization: Yes

Healthplan and Services Defined
PLAN TYPE: Other
Model Type: Network
Benefits Offered: Behavioral Health, Disease Management, Prescription, Vision

Type of Coverage
Medicaid

Key Personnel
President/CEO.......................... Clyde White

526 Northeast Delta Dental
One Delta Drive
P.O. Box 2002
Concord, NH 03302-2002
Toll-Free: 800-537-1715
Phone: 603-223-1000
Fax: 603-223-1199
nedelta@nedelta.com
www.nedelta.com
Non-Profit Organization: Yes
Year Founded: 1961
Total Enrollment: 936,000

Healthplan and Services Defined
PLAN TYPE: Dental
Other Type: Dental PPO
Model Type: Network
Plan Specialty: ASO, Dental
Benefits Offered: Dental

Type of Coverage
Commercial, Individual
Catastrophic Illness Benefit: None

Geographic Areas Served
Maine, New Hampshire and Vermont

Key Personnel
President/CEO....................... Thomas Raffio
Chair.............................. David B. Staples
SVP, Finance..................... Francis R. Boucher
SVP, Operations .... William H. Lambrukos

527 UnitedHealthcare of New Hampshire
950 Winter Street
Waltham, MA 02451
Toll-Free: 888-545-5205
Phone: 866-414-1959
www.uhc.com
Subsidiary of: UnitedHealth Group
For Profit Organization: Yes
Year Founded: 1986

Healthplan and Services Defined
PLAN TYPE: HMO/PPO
Model Type: Network
Plan Specialty: Behavioral Health, Dental, Disease Management, MSO, PBM, Vision
Benefits Offered: Behavioral Health, Chiropractic, Complementary Medicine, Dental, Disease Management, Home Care, Inpatient SNF, Long-Term Care, Physical Therapy, Podiatry, Prescription, Psychiatric, Transplant, Vision, Wellness, AD&D, Life, LTD, STD

Type of Coverage
Commercial, Individual, Medicare, Supplemental Medicare, Medicaid, Catastrophic, Family, Military, Veterans, Group

Type of Payment Plans Offered
DFFS, FFS, Combination FFS & DFFS

Geographic Areas Served
Statewide. New Hampshire is covered by the Massachusetts branch

Subscriber Information
Average Monthly Fee Per Subscriber
(Employee + Employer Contribution):
Employee Only (Self): Varies
Average Subscriber Co-Payment:
Primary Care Physician: $10
Prescription Drugs: $10/15/30
Hospital ER: $50

Network Qualifications
Pre-Admission Certification: Yes

Peer Review Type
Case Management: Yes

Publishes and Distributes Report Card: Yes

Accreditation Certification
URAC, NCQA
State Licensure, Quality Assurance Program

Key Personnel
CEO, New England....................... Tim Archer

Average Claim Compensation
Physician's Fees Charged: 70%
Hospital's Fees Charged: 55%

Specialty Managed Care Partners
United Behavioral Health
Enters into Contracts with Regional Business Coalitions: No

528 Well Sense Health Plan
1155 Elm Street
Suite 600
Manchester, NH 03101
Toll-Free: 877-492-6965
NHmembers@wellsense.org
www.wellsense.org
Subsidiary of: Boston Medical Center Health Plan, Inc.
Non-Profit Organization: Yes
Number of Affiliated Hospitals: 46
Number of Primary Care Physicians: 1,751
Number of Referral/Specialty Physicians: 3,112

Healthplan and Services Defined
PLAN TYPE: Other
Other Type: Medicaid
Benefits Offered: Behavioral Health, Prescription, Vision, Wellness

Type of Coverage
Medicaid

Geographic Areas Served
New Hampshire

Key Personnel
Chief Medical Officer	Jonathan Welch, MD
Director, Operations	Carol Iacopino
Executive Director	Lisabritt Solsky

NEW JERSEY

Health Insurance Coverage Status and Type of Coverage by Age

Category	All Persons Number	All Persons %	Under 19 years Number	Under 19 years %	Under 65 years Number	Under 65 years %
Total population	8,776 *(2)*	100.0 *(0.0)*	2,042 *(5)*	100.0 *(0.0)*	7,340 *(3)*	100.0 *(0.0)*
Covered by some type of health insurance	8,084 *(19)*	92.1 *(0.2)*	1,953 *(9)*	95.7 *(0.4)*	6,662 *(19)*	90.8 *(0.3)*
Covered by private health insurance	6,290 *(34)*	71.7 *(0.4)*	1,367 *(15)*	66.9 *(0.7)*	5,427 *(32)*	73.9 *(0.4)*
Employer-based	5,437 *(37)*	62.0 *(0.4)*	1,236 *(16)*	60.6 *(0.7)*	4,875 *(34)*	66.4 *(0.5)*
Direct purchase	1,034 *(24)*	11.8 *(0.3)*	140 *(10)*	6.9 *(0.5)*	640 *(22)*	8.7 *(0.3)*
TRICARE	87 *(7)*	1.0 *(0.1)*	20 *(3)*	1.0 *(0.2)*	54 *(6)*	0.7 *(0.1)*
Covered by public health insurance	2,778 *(27)*	31.7 *(0.3)*	644 *(16)*	31.5 *(0.8)*	1,421 *(27)*	19.4 *(0.4)*
Medicaid	1,452 *(26)*	16.5 *(0.3)*	633 *(16)*	31.0 *(0.8)*	1,280 *(26)*	17.4 *(0.4)*
Medicare	1,540 *(8)*	17.6 *(0.1)*	16 *(3)*	0.8 *(0.1)*	184 *(7)*	2.5 *(0.1)*
VA Care	96 *(5)*	1.1 *(0.1)*	2 *(1)*	0.1 *(0.1)*	37 *(4)*	0.5 *(Z)*
Not covered at any time during the year	692 *(19)*	7.9 *(0.2)*	88 *(8)*	4.3 *(0.4)*	677 *(19)*	9.2 *(0.3)*

Note: Numbers in thousands; Figures cover civilian noninstitutionalized population in 2019; N/A indicates that data was not available; Z represents or rounds to zero; Margin of error appears in parenthesis and is calculated using replicate weights.
Source: U.S. Census Bureau, American Community Survey, Table HI-05. Health Insurance Coverage Status and Type of Coverage by State and Age for All People: 2019

New Jersey

529 Aetna Better Health of New Jersey
3 Independence Way
Suite 400
Princeton, NJ 08540-6626
Toll-Free: 855-232-3596
www.aetnabetterhealth.com/newjersey
Subsidiary of: CVS Health / Aetna Inc.
For Profit Organization: Yes

Healthplan and Services Defined
PLAN TYPE: HMO/PPO
Other Type: POS
Model Type: Network
Plan Specialty: Behavioral Health, EPO, Lab, PBM, Radiology
Benefits Offered: Behavioral Health, Dental, Disease Management, Long-Term Care, Physical Therapy, Podiatry, Prescription, Psychiatric, Vision, Wellness, Life, LTD, STD

Type of Coverage
Commercial, Medicare, Supplemental Medicare, Medicaid, Student Health

Geographic Areas Served
Statewide

Key Personnel
CEO .... Joseph W. Manger

530 Amerigroup District of Columbia
609 H Street NE
Suite 200
Washington, NJ 20002
Toll-Free: 800-600-4441
mpsweb@amerigroup.com
www.myamerigroup.com/nj
Subsidiary of: Anthem, Inc.
For Profit Organization: Yes

Healthplan and Services Defined
PLAN TYPE: Medicare
Plan Specialty: Dental, Lab, Vision
Benefits Offered: Dental, Disease Management, Long-Term Care, Physical Therapy, Prescription, Vision

Type of Coverage
Medicaid

Geographic Areas Served
Statewide

Key Personnel
Plan President .... Linda Elam

531 Amerigroup New Jersey
101 Woods Avenue
Iselin, NJ 08830
Toll-Free: 800-600-4441
mpsweb@amerigroupcorp.com
www.myamerigroup.com/nj
Subsidiary of: Anthem, Inc.
For Profit Organization: Yes
Year Founded: 1996

Healthplan and Services Defined
PLAN TYPE: Medicare
Plan Specialty: Dental, Lab, Vision
Benefits Offered: Dental, Disease Management, Long-Term Care, Physical Therapy, Prescription, Vision

Type of Coverage
Medicaid

Geographic Areas Served
Statewide

Key Personnel
Mgr., Ancillary Contracts .... Yvonne McNab-Capraun

532 AmeriHealth New Jersey
259 Prospect Plains Road
Building M
Cranbury, NJ 08512-3706
Toll-Free: 888-968-7241
www.amerihealthnj.com
Total Enrollment: 265,000

Healthplan and Services Defined
PLAN TYPE: HMO/PPO
Benefits Offered: Dental, Disease Management, Prescription, Vision, Wellness

Type of Coverage
Commercial, Individual

Geographic Areas Served
New Jersey

Key Personnel
Market President....................... Mike Munoz
Networking Operations................ Ken Kobylowski
Vice President of Sales .... Ryan J. Petrizzi
Senior Medical Director .... Frank L. Urbano

533 Atlanticare Health Plans
2500 English Creek Avenue
Egg Harbor Township, NJ 08234
Toll-Free: 888-569-1000
Phone: 609-407-2300
webmaster@atlanticare.org
www.atlanticare.org
Subsidiary of: Geisinger Health System
Non-Profit Organization: Yes
Year Founded: 1993
Number of Affiliated Hospitals: 36
Number of Primary Care Physicians: 600
Number of Referral/Specialty Physicians: 4,000
Total Enrollment: 150,000
State Enrollment: 150,000

Healthplan and Services Defined
PLAN TYPE: HMO/PPO
Model Type: IPA
Plan Specialty: ASO, Behavioral Health, Worker's Compensation, UR

Benefits Offered: Behavioral Health

Type of Payment Plans Offered
Combination FFS & DFFS

Geographic Areas Served
Southeastern New Jersey

Subscriber Information
Average Subscriber Co-Payment:
Primary Care Physician: $10.00
Non-Network Physician: $20.00
Prescription Drugs: $15.00
Hospital ER: $50.00
Home Health Care: $60
Nursing Home: $120

Network Qualifications
Pre-Admission Certification: Yes

Peer Review Type
Utilization Review: Yes
Second Surgical Opinion: Yes
Case Management: Yes

Accreditation Certification
TJC, URAC, NCQA

Key Personnel
Chief Finance Officer . . . . Walt Greiner

Specialty Managed Care Partners
Horizon BC/BS of NJ

---

534 CHN PPO
300 American Metro Boulevard
Suite 170
Hamilton, NJ 08619
Toll-Free: 800-225-4246
Phone: 800-293-9795
www.chn.com
Subsidiary of: Consolidated Services Group
For Profit Organization: Yes
Year Founded: 1986
Number of Affiliated Hospitals: 165
Number of Primary Care Physicians: 116,000
Number of Referral/Specialty Physicians: 57,550
Total Enrollment: 975,000

Healthplan and Services Defined
PLAN TYPE: PPO
Model Type: Network
Plan Specialty: Behavioral Health, Chiropractic, EPO, Lab, Vision, Radiology, Worker's Compensation, UR
Benefits Offered: Behavioral Health, Chiropractic, Disease Management, Home Care, Inpatient SNF, Long-Term Care, Physical Therapy, Podiatry, Psychiatric, Transplant, Vision, Wellness, Worker's Compensation

Type of Coverage
Catastrophic Illness Benefit: Varies per case

Type of Payment Plans Offered
POS, DFFS, FFS

Geographic Areas Served
Connecticut, New Jersey & New York

Subscriber Information
Average Monthly Fee Per Subscriber
(Employee + Employer Contribution):
Employee Only (Self): Varies
Employee & 1 Family Member: Varies
Employee & 2 Family Members: Varies
Medicare: Varies
Average Annual Deductible Per Subscriber:
Employee Only (Self): Varies
Employee & 1 Family Member: Varies
Employee & 2 Family Members: Varies
Medicare: Varies
Average Subscriber Co-Payment:
Primary Care Physician: Varies
Non-Network Physician: Varies
Prescription Drugs: Varies
Hospital ER: Varies
Home Health Care: Varies
Home Health Care Max. Days/Visits Covered: Varies
Nursing Home: Varies
Nursing Home Max. Days/Visits Covered: Varies

Network Qualifications
Pre-Admission Certification: Yes

Peer Review Type
Utilization Review: Yes
Second Surgical Opinion: Yes
Case Management: Yes

Accreditation Certification
URAC, AAPI
TJC Accreditation, Medicare Approved, Utilization Review, Pre-Admission Certification, State Licensure, Quality Assurance Program

Key Personnel
President/CEO . . . . Craig Goldstein
SVP, Financial Operations . . . . Lee Ann Iannelli

Average Claim Compensation
Physician's Fees Charged: 33%
Hospital's Fees Charged: 40%

Specialty Managed Care Partners
Enters into Contracts with Regional Business Coalitions: Yes

---

535 Cigna HealthCare of New Jersey
44 Whippany Road
Morristown, NJ 07960
Toll-Free: 800-997-1654
www.cigna.com
Subsidiary of: Cigna Corporation
For Profit Organization: Yes
Year Founded: 1982

Healthplan and Services Defined
PLAN TYPE: HMO
Other Type: POS
Plan Specialty: Behavioral Health, Dental
Benefits Offered: Behavioral Health, Dental, Disease Management, Prescription, Vision, Wellness, AD&D, Life, LTD, STD

New Jersey

Type of Coverage
  Commercial, Individual, Medicare, Supplemental Medicare, Medicaid

Geographic Areas Served
  Statewide

Key Personnel
  President . . . . Dave Kobus

536 Delta Dental of New Jersey
1639 Route 10
Parsippany, NJ 07054
Toll-Free: 800-452-9310
www.deltadentalnj.com
Mailing Address: P.O. Box 16354, Little Rock, AR 72231
Non-Profit Organization: Yes
Year Founded: 1969
Total Enrollment: 1,700,000

Healthplan and Services Defined
  PLAN TYPE: Dental
  Other Type: Dental HMO/PPO/POS
  Model Type: Staff
  Plan Specialty: Dental
  Benefits Offered: Dental

Type of Coverage
  Commercial

Type of Payment Plans Offered
  POS, DFFS, Capitated, FFS, Combination FFS & DFFS

Geographic Areas Served
  New Jersey and Connecticut

Key Personnel
  President/CEO . . . . Dennis G. Wilson
  SVP, CFO . . . . Michael Rodrigues
  Chief Marketing Officer . . . . Randy Stodard
  Chief Information Officer . . . . Justin Lahullier, MD
  SVP, General Counsel . . . . Paul Di Maio
  SVP, Operations . . . . Lori Acker

537 Horizon Blue Cross Blue Shield of New Jersey
P.O. Box 820
Newark, NJ 07101
Toll-Free: 800-355-2583
www.horizonblue.com
Non-Profit Organization: Yes
Year Founded: 1932
Total Enrollment: 3,500,000
State Enrollment: 3,500,000

Healthplan and Services Defined
  PLAN TYPE: HMO/PPO
  Other Type: POS
  Model Type: Staff, Network
  Benefits Offered: Behavioral Health, Dental, Prescription, Psychiatric, Vision, Worker's Compensation
  Offers Demand Management Patient Information Service: Yes

Type of Coverage
  Commercial, Individual, Indemnity, Medicare
  Catastrophic Illness Benefit: None

Geographic Areas Served
  Statewide

Peer Review Type
  Utilization Review: Yes
  Second Surgical Opinion: Yes
  Case Management: Yes

Accreditation Certification
  AAAHC, URAC, NCQA
  TJC Accreditation, Medicare Approved, Utilization Review, Pre-Admission Certification, State Licensure, Quality Assurance Program

Key Personnel
  President/CEO . . . . Gary D. St. Hilaire
  SVP, Operations . . . . Mark L. Barnard
  EVP/CFO . . . . Douglas R. Simpson
  SVP/Chief HR Officer . . . . Steven J. Krupinski
  SVP/General Counsel . . . . Jennifer Velez

Specialty Managed Care Partners
  Enters into Contracts with Regional Business Coalitions: Yes

538 Horizon NJ Health
1700 American Blvd.
Pennington, NJ 08534
Toll-Free: 800-682-9090
www.horizonnjhealth.com
Subsidiary of: Horizon Blue Cross Blue Shield of NJ
Year Founded: 1993
Total Enrollment: 854,000
State Enrollment: 854,000

Healthplan and Services Defined
  PLAN TYPE: PPO
  Model Type: Network
  Benefits Offered: Dental, Disease Management, Prescription, Vision, Wellness

Type of Coverage
  Individual, Medicaid

Geographic Areas Served
  Statewide

Accreditation Certification
  URAC

Key Personnel
  President . . . . Karen Clark
  Controller/Subsidiary CFO . . . . James Dalessio
  Marketing/Communications . . . . Len Kudgis
  VP, Clinical Affairs/CMO . . . . Philip M Bonaparte, MD
  Media Contact . . . . Carol Chernack
    609-718-9290
    carol_chernack@horizonnjhealth.com

539 Humana Health Insurance of New Jersey
1075 RXR Plaza
Uniondale, NJ 11556
Phone: 516-247-2021
www.humana.com
Secondary Address: 3000 Atrium Way, Suite 200, Mt. Laurel, NJ 08054, 866-355-5861
Subsidiary of: Humana Inc.
For Profit Organization: Yes

Healthplan and Services Defined
PLAN TYPE: HMO/PPO
Model Type: Network
Plan Specialty: Dental, Vision
Benefits Offered: Dental, Vision, Life, LTD, STD

Type of Coverage
Commercial

Geographic Areas Served
Statewide

Accreditation Certification
URAC, NCQA, CORE

540 Liberty Dental Plan of New Jersey
P.O. Box 26110
Santa Ana, CA 92799-6110
Toll-Free: 888-352-7924
www.libertydentalplan.com
For Profit Organization: Yes
Year Founded: 2001
Total Enrollment: 3,000,000

Healthplan and Services Defined
PLAN TYPE: Dental
Other Type: Dental HMO
Plan Specialty: Dental
Benefits Offered: Dental

Type of Coverage
Commercial, Individual, Medicare, Medicaid, Unions

Geographic Areas Served
Statewide

Accreditation Certification
NCQA

Key Personnel
NJ Dental Director . . . . Peter Fuentes
   pfuentes@libertydentalplan.com

541 QualCare
30 Knightsbridge Road
Piscataway, NJ 08854
Toll-Free: 800-992-6613
Phone: 732-562-0833
info@qualcareinc.com
www.qualcareinc.com
Subsidiary of: QualCare Alliance Networks, Inc.
For Profit Organization: Yes
Year Founded: 1993
Federally Qualified: Yes
Number of Affiliated Hospitals: 100
Number of Primary Care Physicians: 9,000
Number of Referral/Specialty Physicians: 14,000
Total Enrollment: 900,000
State Enrollment: 900,000

Healthplan and Services Defined
PLAN TYPE: Multiple
Other Type: POS, TPA
Model Type: Network
Plan Specialty: ASO, Behavioral Health, Chiropractic, Dental, Disease Management, EPO, Lab, MSO, PBM, Vision, Radiology, Worker's Compensation, UR
Benefits Offered: Behavioral Health, Chiropractic, Complementary
Medicine, Dental, Disease Management, Home Care, Inpatient SNF, Long-Term Care, Physical Therapy, Podiatry, Prescription, Psychiatric, Transplant, Vision, Wellness, Worker's Compensation, AD&D, Life, LTD, STD
   Offers Demand Management Patient Information Service: Yes

Type of Coverage
Commercial

Type of Payment Plans Offered
FFS

Geographic Areas Served
New Jersey, Pennsylvania, New York

Peer Review Type
Utilization Review: Yes
Second Surgical Opinion: Yes
Case Management: Yes

Publishes and Distributes Report Card: Yes

Accreditation Certification
AAAHC, TJC, AAPI, NCQA
Medicare Approved, Utilization Review, State Licensure, Quality Assurance Program

Key Personnel
VP/CFO . . . . Janet Buggle
VP, Network/Delivery . . . . Jennifer Lagasca
Medical Director . . . . Michael McNeil, MD

Specialty Managed Care Partners
Multiplan

542 Trinity Health of New Jersey
St Francis Medical Center
601 Hamilton Avenue
Trenton, NJ 08629
Phone: 609-599-5000
www.trinity-health.org
Subsidiary of: Trinity Health
Non-Profit Organization: Yes
Year Founded: 2013
Total Enrollment: 30,000,000

Healthplan and Services Defined
PLAN TYPE: Other

Benefits Offered: Disease Management, Home Care, Long-Term Care, Psychiatric, Hospice programs, PACE (Program of All Inclusive Care for the Elderly)

Geographic Areas Served
Central New Jersey

Key Personnel
President . . . . Daniel P. Moen
Chief Finance Officer . . . . Mark Kelly
SVP, CMO . . . . C. James Romano

543 UnitedHealthcare Community Plan New Jersey
UnitedHealthcare Customer Service
P.O. Box 30769
Salt Lake City, UT 84130-0769
Toll-Free: 888-545-5205
www.uhccommunityplan.com/nj
Subsidiary of: UnitedHealth Group
For Profit Organization: Yes

Healthplan and Services Defined
PLAN TYPE: Medicare
Other Type: Medicaid
Model Type: Network
Benefits Offered: Home Care, Prescription, Wellness

Type of Coverage
Medicare, Medicaid

Geographic Areas Served
Atlantic, Bergen, Burlington, Camden, Cumberland, Essex, Gloucester, Hudson, Hunterdon, Mercer, Middlesex, Monmouth, Morris, Ocean, Passaic, Salem, Somerset, Sussex, and Union

Key Personnel
CEO, Community Plan NJ . . . . Charles Wayland
charles_wayland@uhc.com

544 UnitedHealthcare of New Jersey
111 S Wood Ave
Suite 2
Iselin, NJ 08830
Toll-Free: 888-545-5205
Phone: 732-623-1000
www.uhc.com
Subsidiary of: UnitedHealth Group
For Profit Organization: Yes

Healthplan and Services Defined
PLAN TYPE: HMO/PPO
Model Type: Network
Plan Specialty: Behavioral Health, Dental, Disease Management, PBM, Vision
Benefits Offered: Behavioral Health, Dental, Disease Management, Long-Term Care, Prescription, Vision, Wellness, Life, LTD, STD

Type of Coverage
Individual, Medicare, Supplemental Medicare, Medicaid, Catastrophic, Family, Military, Veterans, Group

Geographic Areas Served
Statewide

Key Personnel
CEO, Healthplan NJ/PA/DE . . . . Paul Marden

545 Zelis Healthcare
2 Crossroads Drive
Bedminster, NJ 07921
Phone: 888-311-3505
www.zelis.com
Subsidiary of: Zelis Healthcare
For Profit Organization: Yes
Year Founded: 2016
Owned by an Integrated Delivery Network (IDN): Yes

Healthplan and Services Defined
PLAN TYPE: PPO
Plan Specialty: Dental, Worker's Compensation
Benefits Offered: Dental, Worker's Compensation

Type of Coverage
Individual

NEW MEXICO

Health Insurance Coverage Status and Type of Coverage by Age

Category	All Persons Number	All Persons %	Under 19 years Number	Under 19 years %	Under 65 years Number	Under 65 years %
Total population	2,059 *(2)*	100.0 *(0.0)*	502 *(3)*	100.0 *(0.0)*	1,686 *(3)*	100.0 *(0.0)*
Covered by some type of health insurance	1,854 *(11)*	90.0 *(0.6)*	473 *(5)*	94.3 *(0.9)*	1,484 *(11)*	88.0 *(0.7)*
Covered by private health insurance	1,106 *(17)*	53.7 *(0.8)*	217 *(8)*	43.2 *(1.6)*	906 *(16)*	53.7 *(1.0)*
Employer-based	900 *(18)*	43.7 *(0.9)*	185 *(9)*	37.0 *(1.7)*	778 *(18)*	46.1 *(1.1)*
Direct purchase	215 *(10)*	10.5 *(0.5)*	26 *(4)*	5.2 *(0.8)*	129 *(8)*	7.6 *(0.5)*
TRICARE	84 *(5)*	4.1 *(0.3)*	16 *(2)*	3.1 *(0.5)*	49 *(4)*	2.9 *(0.3)*
Covered by public health insurance	1,031 *(17)*	50.1 *(0.8)*	286 *(9)*	57.0 *(1.7)*	671 *(17)*	39.8 *(1.0)*
Medicaid	688 *(17)*	33.4 *(0.8)*	284 *(9)*	56.6 *(1.8)*	623 *(16)*	37.0 *(0.9)*
Medicare	422 *(5)*	20.5 *(0.3)*	4 *(1)*	0.7 *(0.3)*	62 *(5)*	3.7 *(0.3)*
VA Care	65 *(4)*	3.2 *(0.2)*	1 *(1)*	0.2 *(0.2)*	29 *(3)*	1.7 *(0.2)*
Not covered at any time during the year	205 *(12)*	10.0 *(0.6)*	29 *(4)*	5.7 *(0.9)*	202 *(11)*	12.0 *(0.7)*

Note: Numbers in thousands; Figures cover civilian noninstitutionalized population in 2019; N/A indicates that data was not available; Z represents or rounds to zero; Margin of error appears in parenthesis and is calculated using replicate weights.
Source: U.S. Census Bureau, American Community Survey, Table HI-05. Health Insurance Coverage Status and Type of Coverage by State and Age for All People: 2019

New Mexico

546 Allwell from Western Sky Community Care
5300 Homestead Road NE
Albuquerque, NM 87110
Toll-Free: 833-543-0246
allwell.westernskycommunitycare.com
Subsidiary of: Centene Corporation
For Profit Organization: Yes

Healthplan and Services Defined
PLAN TYPE: Medicare
Model Type: Network
Benefits Offered: Dental, Prescription

Type of Coverage
Medicare, Supplemental Medicare, Medicare Advantage

Geographic Areas Served
Bernalillo, Cibola, Sandoval, and Valencia counties

547 Blue Cross & Blue Shield of New Mexico
4373 Alexander Blvd. NE
Albuquerque, NM 87107
Toll-Free: 800-835-8699
Phone: 505-291-3500
www.bcbsnm.com
Secondary Address: 5701 Balloon Fiesta Parkway NE, Albuquerque, NM 87107
Subsidiary of: Health Care Service Corporation
Non-Profit Organization: Yes
Year Founded: 1940
Owned by an Integrated Delivery Network (IDN): Yes
Number of Affiliated Hospitals: 54
Number of Primary Care Physicians: 3,322
Number of Referral/Specialty Physicians: 6,742
Total Enrollment: 550,000
State Enrollment: 550,000

Healthplan and Services Defined
PLAN TYPE: HMO/PPO
Other Type: EPO, CDHP
Model Type: Network
Plan Specialty: ASO, Behavioral Health
Benefits Offered: Dental, Disease Management, Prescription, Vision, Wellness, Medical, Case Management
Offers Demand Management Patient Information Service: Yes
DMPI Services Offered: Fully Insured

Type of Coverage
Commercial, Individual, Indemnity, Supplemental Medicare, Medicaid

Geographic Areas Served
Statewide

Network Qualifications
Pre-Admission Certification: Yes

Peer Review Type
Utilization Review: Yes
Second Surgical Opinion: Yes

Publishes and Distributes Report Card: Yes

Accreditation Certification
NCQA

Key Personnel
President . . . . Janice Torrez
Media Contact . . . . Becky Kenny
  505-816-2012
  becky_kenny@bcbsnm.com

Specialty Managed Care Partners
Pharmacy Manager, Prime Theraputics

548 Delta Dental of New Mexico
100 Sun Avenue NE
Suite 400
Albuquerque, NM 87109
Toll-Free: 877-395-9420
Phone: 505-855-7111
Fax: 505-883-7444
www.deltadentalnm.com
Non-Profit Organization: Yes
Year Founded: 1971
Number of Primary Care Physicians: 979
State Enrollment: 468,219

Healthplan and Services Defined
PLAN TYPE: Dental
Other Type: Dental PPO
Model Type: Group
Plan Specialty: ASO, Dental, Vision
Benefits Offered: Dental, Vision
Offers Demand Management Patient Information Service: Yes

Type of Coverage
Commercial

Geographic Areas Served
Statewide

Network Qualifications
Pre-Admission Certification: Yes

Publishes and Distributes Report Card: Yes

Key Personnel
President/CEO . . . . Lou Volk, III
Director, Operations . . . . Cynthia Lucero-Ali
Director, Public Affairs. . . . . John Martinez
Dir., Product Management. . . . . Nathalie Casado
Sr. Admin., Corp. Service . . . . Maria Lopez
VP, Sales/Marketing . . . . JoLou Trujillo-Ottino

Specialty Managed Care Partners
Enters into Contracts with Regional Business Coalitions: Yes

549 HCSC Insurance Services Company New Mexico
5701 Balloon Fiesta Pkywy NE
Albuquerque, NM 87113
Toll-Free: 800-835-8699
hcsc.com
Subsidiary of: Blue Cross Blue Shield Association
Non-Profit Organization: Yes

Year Founded: 1936
Number of Primary Care Physicians: 16,700
State Enrollment: 550,000

Healthplan and Services Defined
PLAN TYPE: HMO
Benefits Offered: Behavioral Health, Dental, Disease Management, Psychiatric, Wellness

Type of Coverage
Individual

Geographic Areas Served
Statewide

Key Personnel
President, NM Plan . . . . Janice Torrez

550 Humana Health Insurance of New Mexico
4904 Alameda Boulevard NE
Suite A
Albuquerque, NM 87113
Toll-Free: 800-681-0680
Phone: 505-468-0500
Fax: 505-468-0554
www.humana.com
Subsidiary of: Humana Inc.
For Profit Organization: Yes

Healthplan and Services Defined
PLAN TYPE: HMO/PPO

Type of Coverage
Commercial, Individual

Geographic Areas Served
Statewide

Accreditation Certification
URAC, NCQA, CORE

551 Molina Healthcare of New Mexico
400 Tijeras Avenue NW
Suite 200
Albuquerque, NM 87102
Toll-Free: 866-440-0127
www.molinahealthcare.com
Subsidiary of: Molina Healthcare, Inc.
For Profit Organization: Yes

Healthplan and Services Defined
PLAN TYPE: Medicare
Model Type: Network
Plan Specialty: Dental, PBM, Vision, Integrated Medicare/Medicaid (Duals)
Benefits Offered: Dental, Prescription, Vision, Wellness, Life

Type of Coverage
Individual, Medicare, Supplemental Medicare, Medicaid

Geographic Areas Served
Statewide

Key Personnel
Chief Medical Officer . . . . Irene Ortiz, MD

552 Presbyterian Health Plan
9521 San Mateo Boulevard NE
Albuquerque, NM 87113
Toll-Free: 800-356-2219
Phone: 505-923-5700
info@phs.org
www.phs.org
Non-Profit Organization: Yes
Year Founded: 1908
Number of Affiliated Hospitals: 28
Number of Primary Care Physicians: 18,843
Number of Referral/Specialty Physicians: 4,850
Total Enrollment: 400,000
State Enrollment: 400,000

Healthplan and Services Defined
PLAN TYPE: HMO
Other Type: POS
Model Type: Contracted Network
Benefits Offered: Disease Management, Inpatient SNF, Prescription

Type of Coverage
Commercial, Medicare, Medicaid

Type of Payment Plans Offered
POS, DFFS, Capitated, FFS

Geographic Areas Served
Statewide

Subscriber Information
Average Monthly Fee Per Subscriber
(Employee + Employer Contribution):
Employee Only (Self): Varies by plan
Average Subscriber Co-Payment:
Primary Care Physician: $10.00
Prescription Drugs: $0
Hospital ER: $50.00

Accreditation Certification
NCQA

Key Personnel
Chair/President/CEO. Dale Maxwell
Vice Chair . . . . Teresa Kline

Employer References
State of New Mexico, Albuquerque Public Schools, Intel Corporation

553 Presbyterian Medicare Advantage Plans
The Cooper Center
9521 San Mateo Boulevard NE
Albuquerque, NM 87113
Toll-Free: 800-979-5343
Phone: 505-923-6060
info@phs.org
www.phs.org
Mailing Address: P.O. Box 27489, Albuquerque, NM 87125

Healthplan and Services Defined
PLAN TYPE: Medicare
Benefits Offered: Chiropractic, Dental, Disease Management, Home Care, Inpatient SNF, Physical Therapy, Podiatry,

Prescription, Psychiatric, Vision, Wellness, Hearing; Rehabilitation; Durable Medical Equipment; Transportation

Type of Coverage
Individual, Medicare

Geographic Areas Served
Bernalillo, Cibola, Rio Arriba, Sandoval, Santa Fe, Socorro, Torrance and Valencia

Key Personnel
Chair . . . . Katharine Winograd
Vice Chair . . . . Brian Burnett

554 United Concordia of New Mexico
4401 Deer Path Road
Harrisburg, PA 17110
Phone: 717-260-6800
www.unitedconcordia.com
For Profit Organization: Yes
Year Founded: 1971
Number of Primary Care Physicians: 104,000
Total Enrollment: 8,800,000

Healthplan and Services Defined
PLAN TYPE: Dental
Plan Specialty: Dental
Benefits Offered: Dental

Type of Coverage
Commercial, Individual, Military personnel & families

Geographic Areas Served
Nationwide

Accreditation Certification
URAC

Key Personnel
Contact. . . . . Beth Rutherford
717-260-7659
beth.rutherford@ucci.com

555 UnitedHealthcare Community Plan New Mexico
UnitedHealthcare Customer Service
P.O. Box 30769
Salt Lake City, UT 84130-0769
Toll-Free: 888-545-5205
www.uhccommunityplan.com/nm
Subsidiary of: UnitedHealth Group
For Profit Organization: Yes

Healthplan and Services Defined
PLAN TYPE: Medicare
Other Type: Medicaid
Model Type: Network
Benefits Offered: Dental, Home Care, Podiatry, Prescription, Vision, Wellness

Type of Coverage
Medicare, Medicaid

Geographic Areas Served
Dona Ana, Grant, Hidalgo, Luna, and Sierra

Key Personnel
CEO, Community Plan NM . . . . Drew Peterson

556 UnitedHealthcare of New Mexico
8220 San Pedro Drive NE
Suite 300
Albuquerque, NM 87113
Toll-Free: 888-545-5205
Phone: 877-236-0826
www.uhc.com
Subsidiary of: UnitedHealth Group
For Profit Organization: Yes

Healthplan and Services Defined
PLAN TYPE: HMO/PPO
Model Type: Network
Plan Specialty: Behavioral Health, Dental, Disease Management, PBM, Vision
Benefits Offered: Behavioral Health, Dental, Disease Management, Long-Term Care, Prescription, Vision, Wellness, Life, LTD, STD

Type of Coverage
Individual, Medicare, Supplemental Medicare, Medicaid, Catastrophic, Family, Military, Veterans, Group

Geographic Areas Served
Statewide

Key Personnel
VP, Health Services. Tracy Townsend

557 Western Sky Community Care
5300 Homestead Road NE
Albuquerque, NM 87110
Toll-Free: 844-543-8996
www.westernskycommunitycare.com
Subsidiary of: Centene Corporation
For Profit Organization: Yes

Healthplan and Services Defined
PLAN TYPE: Other
Model Type: Network
Benefits Offered: Behavioral Health, Dental, Prescription, Vision, Wellness

Type of Coverage
Medicaid

NEW YORK

Health Insurance Coverage Status and Type of Coverage by Age

Category	All Persons Number	All Persons %	Under 19 years Number	Under 19 years %	Under 65 years Number	Under 65 years %
Total population	19,213 (3)	100.0 (0.0)	4,264 (7)	100.0 (0.0)	16,012 (4)	100.0 (0.0)
Covered by some type of health insurance	18,206 (20)	94.8 (0.1)	4,164 (10)	97.6 (0.2)	15,031 (20)	93.9 (0.1)
Covered by private health insurance	12,970 (58)	67.5 (0.3)	2,628 (28)	61.6 (0.6)	11,120 (56)	69.4 (0.3)
Employer-based	10,926 (56)	56.9 (0.3)	2,230 (27)	52.3 (0.6)	9,646 (52)	60.2 (0.3)
Direct purchase	2,504 (35)	13.0 (0.2)	436 (17)	10.2 (0.4)	1,736 (33)	10.8 (0.2)
TRICARE	170 (8)	0.9 (Z)	38 (4)	0.9 (0.1)	107 (7)	0.7 (Z)
Covered by public health insurance	7,611 (56)	39.6 (0.3)	1,763 (30)	41.3 (0.7)	4,574 (56)	28.6 (0.3)
Medicaid	4,930 (54)	25.7 (0.3)	1,753 (30)	41.1 (0.7)	4,300 (54)	26.9 (0.3)
Medicare	3,471 (16)	18.1 (0.1)	20 (3)	0.5 (0.1)	436 (13)	2.7 (0.1)
VA Care	249 (7)	1.3 (Z)	4 (1)	0.1 (Z)	99 (5)	0.6 (Z)
Not covered at any time during the year	1,007 (20)	5.2 (0.1)	101 (8)	2.4 (0.2)	981 (20)	6.1 (0.1)

Note: Numbers in thousands; Figures cover civilian noninstitutionalized population in 2019; N/A indicates that data was not available; Z represents or rounds to zero; Margin of error appears in parenthesis and is calculated using replicate weights.
Source: U.S. Census Bureau, American Community Survey, Table HI-05. Health Insurance Coverage Status and Type of Coverage by State and Age for All People: 2019

New York

558 Aetna Better Health of New York
55 West 125th Street
Suite 1300
New York, NY 10027
Toll-Free: 855-456-9126
www.aetnabetterhealth.com/ny
Subsidiary of: CVS Health / Aetna Inc.
For Profit Organization: Yes

Healthplan and Services Defined
PLAN TYPE: HMO/PPO
Other Type: POS
Model Type: Network
Plan Specialty: Behavioral Health, EPO, Lab, PBM, Radiology
Benefits Offered: Behavioral Health, Dental, Disease Management, Long-Term Care, Physical Therapy, Podiatry, Prescription, Psychiatric, Vision, Wellness, Life, LTD, STD

Type of Coverage
Commercial, Medicare, Supplemental Medicare, Medicaid, Student health

Geographic Areas Served
Statewide

Key Personnel
CEO .... Kevin P. Nelson

559 Aetna Health of New York
151 Farmington Avenue
Hartford, CT 06156
Toll-Free: 800-872-3862
www.aetna.com
Subsidiary of: CVS Health / Aetna Inc.
For Profit Organization: Yes
Year Founded: 1986
Number of Affiliated Hospitals: 61
Number of Primary Care Physicians: 2,691
Total Enrollment: 154,162
State Enrollment: 154,162

Healthplan and Services Defined
PLAN TYPE: HMO/PPO
Model Type: Network
Plan Specialty: Behavioral Health, Dental, EPO, Lab, PBM, Vision, Radiology
Benefits Offered: Behavioral Health, Dental, Disease Management, Long-Term Care, Physical Therapy, Podiatry, Prescription, Psychiatric, Vision, Wellness, Life, LTD, STD

Type of Coverage
Commercial, Supplemental Medicare, Medicaid, Student health
Catastrophic Illness Benefit: Varies per case

Type of Payment Plans Offered
POS, Capitated

Geographic Areas Served
Statewide

Network Qualifications
Pre-Admission Certification: Yes

Peer Review Type
Utilization Review: Yes
Second Surgical Opinion: No
Case Management: Yes

Publishes and Distributes Report Card: Yes

Accreditation Certification
NCQA
TJC Accreditation, Medicare Approved, Utilization Review, Pre-Admission Certification, State Licensure, Quality Assurance Program

Key Personnel
President, North Atlantic .... Michael Cole

Specialty Managed Care Partners
Enters into Contracts with Regional Business Coalitions: Yes

560 Affinity Health Plan
1776 Eastchester Road
Bronx, NY 10461
Toll-Free: 866-247-5678
Fax: 718-794-7804
mainoffice@affinityplan.org
www.affinityplan.org
Non-Profit Organization: Yes
Year Founded: 1986
Number of Affiliated Hospitals: 60
Number of Primary Care Physicians: 1,400
Number of Referral/Specialty Physicians: 5,000
Total Enrollment: 265,000
State Enrollment: 265,000

Healthplan and Services Defined
PLAN TYPE: HMO
Model Type: Staff
Benefits Offered: Behavioral Health, Prescription

Type of Coverage
Individual, Medicaid

Geographic Areas Served
NY Metropolitan Area

Accreditation Certification
TJC Accreditation, Medicare Approved, Utilization Review, State Licensure

Key Personnel
President/CEO .... Michael G. Murphy
Chief Compliance Officer .... Lisa Mingione
Chief Medical Officer .... Scott Breidbart, MD
Chief Marketing Officer .... Denise J. Pesich
Director, Medicaid .... Adrian Roberts
Chief Financial Officer .... Steve Giasi

561 BlueCross BlueShield of Western New York

257 W Genesee Street
Suite 100
Buffalo, NY 14202-2657
Toll-Free: 800-544-2583
Phone: 716-884-2800
www.bcbswny.com
Mailing Address: P.O. Box 80, Buffalo, NY 14240-0080
Non-Profit Organization: Yes
Year Founded: 1936
Total Enrollment: 555,405
State Enrollment: 197,194

Healthplan and Services Defined
 PLAN TYPE: HMO/PPO
 Other Type: POS, EPO
 Plan Specialty: Dental, Lab, Vision
 Benefits Offered: Dental, Disease Management, Prescription, Vision, Wellness

Type of Coverage
 Commercial, Medicare, Supplemental Medicare, Medicaid

Geographic Areas Served
 Statewide

Key Personnel
 President/CEO .... David W. Anderson
 EVP/CFO .... Stephen T. Swift
 VP, Operations .... Kerri Garrison
 VP, Commercial Sales.................... Paul Valley

Specialty Managed Care Partners
 Wellpoint Pharmacy Management

562 BlueShield of Northeastern New York

40 Century Hill Drive
Latham, NY 12110
Toll-Free: 800-888-1238
Phone: 518-220-4600
customerservice@bsneny.com
www.bsneny.com
Mailing Address: P.O. Box 15013, Albany, NY 12212
Non-Profit Organization: Yes
Year Founded: 1946
Total Enrollment: 193,498
State Enrollment: 72,563

Healthplan and Services Defined
 PLAN TYPE: HMO/PPO
 Other Type: POS, EPO
 Plan Specialty: Dental
 Benefits Offered: Dental, Disease Management, Prescription, Wellness

Type of Coverage
 Commercial, Medicare, Supplemental Medicare, Medicaid

Type of Payment Plans Offered
 POS, FFS

Geographic Areas Served
 Albany, Clinton, Columbia, Essex, Fulton, Green, Montgomery, Schoharie, Schenectedy, Warren and Washington counties

Accreditation Certification
 NCQA

Key Personnel
 President/CEO .... David W. Anderson
 Chief Financial Officer .... Stephen T. Swift
 SVP/General Counsel .... Kenneth J. Sodaro, Esq.
 VP, Commerical Officer .... Paul Valley
 VP, Operations .... Kerri Garrison

Specialty Managed Care Partners
 Wellpoint Pharmacy Management

563 CareCentrix: New York

1 Huntington Quadrangle
Suite 3N02
Melville, NY 11747
Toll-Free: 800-808-1902
carecentrix.com
Year Founded: 1996
Number of Primary Care Physicians: 8,000

Healthplan and Services Defined
 PLAN TYPE: HMO
 Benefits Offered: Home Care, Physical Therapy, LTD, STD, Durable Medical Equipment; Occupational & Respiratory Theraoy; Orthotics; Prosthetics

Geographic Areas Served
 Statewide

Key Personnel
 SVP, Business Development .... Judy Platkin

564 CDPHP Medicare Plan

500 Patroon Creek Boulevard
Albany, NY 12206-1057
Toll-Free: 888-248-6522
Phone: 518-641-3950
www.cdphp.com
Year Founded: 1984
Total Enrollment: 400,000

Healthplan and Services Defined
 PLAN TYPE: Medicare
 Benefits Offered: Chiropractic, Dental, Disease Management, Home Care, Inpatient SNF, Physical Therapy, Podiatry, Prescription, Psychiatric, Vision, Wellness

Type of Coverage
 Individual, Medicare

Geographic Areas Served
 Statewide

Subscriber Information
 Average Monthly Fee Per Subscriber
  (Employee + Employer Contribution):
   Employee Only (Self): Varies
   Medicare: Varies
 Average Annual Deductible Per Subscriber:
   Employee Only (Self): Varies
   Medicare: Varies
 Average Subscriber Co-Payment:
   Primary Care Physician: Varies

Non-Network Physician: Varies
Prescription Drugs: Varies
Hospital ER: Varies
Home Health Care: Varies
Home Health Care Max. Days/Visits Covered: Varies
Nursing Home: Varies
Nursing Home Max. Days/Visits Covered: Varies

565 CDPHP: Capital District Physicians' Health Plan
500 Patroon Creek Boulevard
Albany, NY 12206-1057
Toll-Free: 800-777-2273
Phone: 518-641-3700
www.cdphp.com
Non-Profit Organization: Yes
Year Founded: 1984
Number of Primary Care Physicians: 5,000
Total Enrollment: 350,000
State Enrollment: 350,000

Healthplan and Services Defined
PLAN TYPE: HMO/PPO
Other Type: POS, ASO
Model Type: IPA
Benefits Offered: Dental, Disease Management, Prescription, Wellness

Type of Coverage
Commercial, Individual, Medicare, Medicaid

Geographic Areas Served
Albany, Broome, Chenango, Columbia, Delaware, Dutchess, Essex, Fulton, Greene, Hamilton, Herkimer, Madison, Montgomery, Oneida, Orange, Ostego, Rensselaer, Saratoga, Schenectady, Schoharie, Tioga, Ulster, Warren, and Washington counties

Subscriber Information
Average Monthly Fee Per Subscriber
  (Employee + Employer Contribution):
    Employee Only (Self): $64.41
    Employee & 2 Family Members: $175.47
Average Subscriber Co-Payment:
  Primary Care Physician: $10
  Prescription Drugs: $5-20

Accreditation Certification
NCQA

Key Personnel
President/CEO.................... John D. Bennett, MD
Chief Operating Officer............... Barbara A. Downs
SVP, General Counsel .... Frederick B. Galt
SVP, Strategy Officer .... Robert R. Hinckley
SVP, Financial Officer................ Bethany R. Smith
Chief Medical Officer........... Anthony Marinello, MD
SVP, Marketing .... Brian J. Morrissey

566 Davis Vision
Capital Region Health Park, Suite 301
711 Troy-Schenectady Road
Latham, NY 12110
Toll-Free: 800-773-2847
providerhelp@versanthealth.com
www.davisvision.com
Secondary Address: Davis Vision Corporate Headquarters, 175 E Houston Street, San Antonio, TX 78205, 800-328-4728
Subsidiary of: Versant Health
For Profit Organization: Yes
Year Founded: 1964
Number of Primary Care Physicians: 30,000
Total Enrollment: 55,000,000

Healthplan and Services Defined
PLAN TYPE: Vision
Model Type: Network
Plan Specialty: Vision
Benefits Offered: Vision
Offers Demand Management Patient Information Service: Yes

Type of Payment Plans Offered
DFFS, Capitated, FFS

Geographic Areas Served
National & Puerto Rico, Guam, Saipan, Dominican Republic

Subscriber Information
Average Monthly Fee Per Subscriber
  (Employee + Employer Contribution):
    Employee Only (Self): Varies by plan
    Medicare: Varies

Network Qualifications
Pre-Admission Certification: No

Peer Review Type
Utilization Review: Yes
Second Surgical Opinion: Yes
Case Management: Yes

Publishes and Distributes Report Card: Yes

Accreditation Certification
NCQA, COLTS Certification
TJC Accreditation

Key Personnel
Chief Executive Officer.................... James Reid
Chief Financial Officer..................... Kim Davis
Chief Operating Officer .... Maynard McAlpin
Chief Medical Officer.............. Mark Ruchman, MD

Average Claim Compensation
Physician's Fees Charged: 75%

Specialty Managed Care Partners
Enters into Contracts with Regional Business Coalitions: Yes

567 Delta Dental of New York
One Delta Drive
Mechanicsburg, PA 17055-6999
Toll-Free: 800-932-0783
www.deltadentalins.com
Mailing Address: P.O. Box 1803, Alpharetta, GA 30023

Non-Profit Organization: Yes

Healthplan and Services Defined
  PLAN TYPE: Dental
  Other Type: Dental PPO
  Plan Specialty: Dental
  Benefits Offered: Dental

Type of Coverage
  Commercial, Individual

Geographic Areas Served
  Statewide

Key Personnel
  President & CEO .... Mike Castro
  Chief Financial Officer................... Alicia Weber
  Chief Legal Officer .... Michael Hankinson
  Chief Information Officer .... Dominic Titcombe
  Chief Operating Officer .... Roy Gilbert

568 Dentcare Delivery Systems
333 Earle Ovington Boulevard
Uniondale, NY 11553-3608
Toll-Free: 800-468-0608
Phone: 516-542-2200
Fax: 516-794-3186
www.dentcaredeliverysystems.org
Subsidiary of: Healthplex
Non-Profit Organization: Yes
Year Founded: 1978

Healthplan and Services Defined
  PLAN TYPE: Dental
  Model Type: IPA
  Plan Specialty: Dental
  Benefits Offered: Dental

Type of Coverage
  Commercial, Individual
  Catastrophic Illness Benefit: None

Type of Payment Plans Offered
  FFS

Geographic Areas Served
  Statewide

Accreditation Certification
  NCQA
  Utilization Review, Quality Assurance Program

Key Personnel
  Treasurer .... Deborah Wissing

569 Elderplan
6323 Seventh Avenue
Brooklyn, NY 11220
Toll-Free: 866-360-1934
Fax: 718-759-3643
memberservices@elderplan.org
www.elderplan.org
Subsidiary of: MJHS
Non-Profit Organization: Yes
Year Founded: 1985

Number of Affiliated Hospitals: 35
Number of Primary Care Physicians: 1,200
Number of Referral/Specialty Physicians: 3,800
Total Enrollment: 16,000
State Enrollment: 15,000

Healthplan and Services Defined
  PLAN TYPE: Medicare
  Other Type: Medicare Advantage
  Model Type: Network
  Plan Specialty: ASO, Behavioral Health, Chiropractic,
    Dental, Disease Management, EPO, Lab, Vision, Radiology
  Benefits Offered: Behavioral Health, Chiropractic,
    Complementary
Medicine, Dental, Disease Management, Home Care,
Inpatient SNF, Long-Term Care, Physical Therapy,
Podiatry, Prescription, Psychiatric, Transplant,
Vision, Hearing; Durable Medical Equipment; Speech
Therapy; Transportation

Type of Coverage
  Medicare

Type of Payment Plans Offered
  FFS

Geographic Areas Served
  Brooklyn, Bronx, Manhattan, Queens, Staten Island; Nassau,
  Suffolk, Westchester, Rockland, Putnam & Monroe counties

Subscriber Information
  Average Monthly Fee Per Subscriber
    (Employee + Employer Contribution):
      Medicare: No premium
  Average Annual Deductible Per Subscriber:
      Medicare: $0.00
  Average Subscriber Co-Payment:
      Primary Care Physician: $0.00 co-pay
      Prescription Drugs: $5.00/9.00
      Hospital ER: $50.00
      Home Health Care: $0.00
      Home Health Care Max. Days/Visits Covered: 365 days
      Nursing Home Max. Days/Visits Covered: 200 days

Network Qualifications
  Pre-Admission Certification: Yes

Peer Review Type
  Utilization Review: Yes
  Second Surgical Opinion: Yes
  Case Management: Yes

Publishes and Distributes Report Card: No

Accreditation Certification
  TJC Accreditation, Medicare Approved, Utilization Review,
    State Licensure, Quality Assurance Program

Specialty Managed Care Partners
  HomeFirst, Maxore
  Enters into Contracts with Regional Business Coalitions: Yes

570 EmblemHealth
55 Water Street
New York, NY 10041-8190
www.emblemhealth.com

Non-Profit Organization: Yes
Year Founded: 1985

Healthplan and Services Defined
  PLAN TYPE: Other
  Model Type: IPA
  Plan Specialty: ASO, Chiropractic, Dental, Disease Management, EPO, Vision, Radiology
  Benefits Offered: Behavioral Health, Chiropractic, Complementary Medicine, Dental, Disease Management, Home Care, Inpatient SNF, Physical Therapy, Podiatry, Prescription, Psychiatric, Transplant, Vision, Wellness

Type of Payment Plans Offered
  Capitated

Geographic Areas Served
  City employees and retirees under 65: Queens, Nassau, Suffolk

Accreditation Certification
  URAC, NCQA
  TJC Accreditation, Medicare Approved, Utilization Review, Pre-Admission Certification, State Licensure, Quality Assurance Program

Key Personnel
  President & CEO .... Karen M. Ignagni
  Administrative Officer .... Michael Palmateer
  Chief Legal Officer .... Jeffrey D. Chansler
  Human Resources .... Donna Hughes
  Chief Compliance Officer .... Debra M. Lightner

---

571 EmblemHealth Enhanced Care Plus (HARP)
55 Water Street
New York, NY 10041-8190
www.emblemhealth.com
Subsidiary of: EmblemHealth
Non-Profit Organization: Yes

Healthplan and Services Defined
  PLAN TYPE: Other
  Benefits Offered: Behavioral Health, Dental, Home Care, Inpatient SNF, Prescription, Psychiatric, Vision, Wellness, Maternity care; Therapy for TB; Hospice; Labs & X-Ray; Substance Abuse services; Durable Medical Equipment; HIV testing

Geographic Areas Served
  Bronx, Queens, Brooklyn, Manhattan, Staten Island, Nassau, Suffolk and Westchester

Key Personnel
  President & CEO .... Karen M. Ignagni
  Administrative Officer .... Michael Palmateer
  Chief Legal Officer .... Jeffrey D. Chansler
  Human Resources .... Donna Hughes
  Chief Compliance Officer .... Debra M. Lightner

---

572 Empire BlueCross BlueShield
15 MetroTech Center
Brooklyn, NY 11201
Toll-Free: 800-331-1476
www.empireblue.com
Subsidiary of: Anthem, Inc.

Healthplan and Services Defined
  PLAN TYPE: HMO/PPO
  Model Type: Network
  Plan Specialty: Behavioral Health, Dental, Disease Management, Lab, PBM, Vision, Radiology
  Benefits Offered: Behavioral Health, Dental, Disease Management, Inpatient SNF, Physical Therapy, Prescription, Psychiatric, Transplant, Vision, Wellness, Life

Type of Coverage
  Commercial, Individual, Medicare, Supplemental Medicare, Medicaid, Catastrophic

Geographic Areas Served
  Serving the 28 eastern and southeastern counties of New York State

Accreditation Certification
  URAC

Key Personnel
  President/CEO .... Alan Murray

---

573 Excellus BlueCross BlueShield
165 Court Street
Rochester, NY 14647
Toll-Free: 877-883-9577
www.excellusbcbs.com
Secondary Address: Utica Business Park, 12 Rhoads Drive, Utica, NY 13502
Non-Profit Organization: Yes
Year Founded: 1985
Total Enrollment: 1,500,000

Healthplan and Services Defined
  PLAN TYPE: HMO
  Model Type: IPA
  Benefits Offered: Disease Management, Prescription, Wellness

Type of Coverage
  Individual, Medicare

Type of Payment Plans Offered
  POS, Combination FFS & DFFS

Geographic Areas Served
  Central New York, the Rochester area and Utica-Watertown

Publishes and Distributes Report Card: Yes

Accreditation Certification
  NCQA
  TJC Accreditation, Medicare Approved, Utilization Review, State Licensure, Quality Assurance Program

Key Personnel
  President/CEO .... James R. Reed

---

574 Fidelis Care
25-01 Jackson Avenue
Long Island City, NY 11101
Toll-Free: 888-343-3547
www.fideliscare.org
Subsidiary of: Centene Corporation

For Profit Organization: Yes
Year Founded: 1993
Number of Primary Care Physicians: 42,000
Total Enrollment: 625,000
State Enrollment: 625,000

Healthplan and Services Defined
  PLAN TYPE: Multiple
  Model Type: Network
  Benefits Offered: Behavioral Health, Chiropractic, Dental, Disease Management, Home Care, Inpatient SNF, Physical Therapy, Podiatry, Prescription, Psychiatric, Vision, Wellness

Type of Coverage
  Individual, Medicare, Medicaid, Health Insurance Marketplace

Geographic Areas Served
  53 counties in New York State

Subscriber Information
  Average Monthly Fee Per Subscriber
    (Employee + Employer Contribution):
      Employee Only (Self): Varies
      Medicare: Varies
  Average Annual Deductible Per Subscriber:
      Employee Only (Self): Varies
      Medicare: Varies
  Average Subscriber Co-Payment:
      Primary Care Physician: Varies
      Non-Network Physician: Varies
      Prescription Drugs: Varies
      Hospital ER: Varies
      Home Health Care: Varies
      Home Health Care Max. Days/Visits Covered: Varies
      Nursing Home: Varies
      Nursing Home Max. Days/Visits Covered: Varies

Key Personnel
  Chief Executive Officer................Thomas Halloran
  President/COO.........................David Thomas
  Chief Medical Officer............Vincent Marchello, MD
  VP, Communications...................Darla Skiermont

575 GHI Medicare Plan
55 Water Street
New York, NY 10041-8190
www.emblemhealth.com
Subsidiary of: EmblemHealth
Year Founded: 1931
Total Enrollment: 53,000

Healthplan and Services Defined
  PLAN TYPE: Medicare
  Benefits Offered: Chiropractic, Dental, Disease Management, Home Care, Inpatient SNF, Physical Therapy, Podiatry, Prescription, Psychiatric, Vision, Wellness

Type of Coverage
  Individual, Medicare

Geographic Areas Served
  Statwide

Subscriber Information
  Average Monthly Fee Per Subscriber
    (Employee + Employer Contribution):
      Employee Only (Self): Varies
      Medicare: Varies
  Average Annual Deductible Per Subscriber:
      Employee Only (Self): Varies
      Medicare: Varies
  Average Subscriber Co-Payment:
      Primary Care Physician: Varies
      Non-Network Physician: Varies
      Prescription Drugs: Varies
      Hospital ER: Varies
      Home Health Care: Varies
      Home Health Care Max. Days/Visits Covered: Varies
      Nursing Home: Varies
      Nursing Home Max. Days/Visits Covered: Varies

Key Personnel
  President/CEO......................Karen M. Ignagni
  EVP/Chief Admin Officer............Michael . Palmateer
  Chief Legal Officer.................Jeffrey D. Chansler
  Chief H.R. Officer....................Donna Hughes
  Chief Compliance Officer............Debra M. Lightner

576 Guardian Life Insurance Company of America
10 Hudson Yards
New York, NY 10001
Toll-Free: 888-482-7342
www.guardianlife.com
Subsidiary of: Guardian
For Profit Organization: Yes
Year Founded: 1860
Owned by an Integrated Delivery Network (IDN): Yes
Number of Affiliated Hospitals: 2,966
Number of Primary Care Physicians: 121,815
Number of Referral/Specialty Physicians: 193,137
Total Enrollment: 205,677

Healthplan and Services Defined
  PLAN TYPE: HMO/PPO
  Model Type: Network
  Plan Specialty: Chiropractic, Dental, Disease Management, Lab, PBM, Vision, Radiology, UR
  Benefits Offered: Behavioral Health, Chiropractic, Complementary Medicine, Dental, Disease Management, Home Care, Physical Therapy, Podiatry, Prescription, Psychiatric, Vision, Wellness, AD&D, Life, LTD, STD

Type of Coverage
  Commercial, Individual, Indemnity

Type of Payment Plans Offered
  Combination FFS & DFFS

Geographic Areas Served
  Nationwide

Subscriber Information
  Average Monthly Fee Per Subscriber
    (Employee + Employer Contribution):
      Employee Only (Self): Varies by plan

Peer Review Type
Utilization Review: Yes
Second Surgical Opinion: Yes
Case Management: Yes

Publishes and Distributes Report Card: Yes

Accreditation Certification
URAC, NCQA

Key Personnel
President/CEO .... Andrew J. McMahon
EVP/CIO .... Dean A. Del Vecchio
EVP/General Counsel .... Kermitt Brooks
EVP/CFO .... Kevin Molloy
EVP/Human Resources .... Stacey Hoin
Chief Investment Officer .... Jean LaTorre

Specialty Managed Care Partners
Health Net
Enters into Contracts with Regional Business Coalitions: Yes

---

577 Healthfirst
100 Church Street
New York, NY 10007
Toll-Free: 888-260-1010
healthfirst.org
Non-Profit Organization: Yes
Number of Affiliated Hospitals: 6

Healthplan and Services Defined
PLAN TYPE: Multiple
Benefits Offered: Dental, Inpatient SNF, Physical Therapy, Vision, Wellness

Type of Coverage
Medicare, Medicaid, Child Health Plus; Managed Long Ter

Geographic Areas Served
New York City, Long Island, Westchester County, Orange County, Sullivan County

Key Personnel
President & CEO .... Pat Wang
Chief Operating Officer .... Steve Black
Cheif Financial Officer .... John J. Bermel
Chief Clinical Officer .... Jay Schechtman, MD
Chief Legal Officer .... Linda Tiano
Human Resources........................ Sean Kane
Chief Information Officer .... G.T. Sweeney

---

578 Humana Health Insurance of New York
125 Wolf Road
Suite 501
Albany, NY 12205
Toll-Free: 800-967-2370
Fax: 518-435-0412
www.humana.com
Secondary Address: 290 Elwood Davis Road, Suite 225, Liverpool, NY 13088
Subsidiary of: Humana Inc.
For Profit Organization: Yes

Healthplan and Services Defined
PLAN TYPE: HMO/PPO
Model Type: Network
Plan Specialty: Dental, Vision
Benefits Offered: Dental, Vision, Life, LTD, STD

Type of Coverage
Commercial

Geographic Areas Served
Statewide

Accreditation Certification
URAC, NCQA, CORE

Key Personnel
Senior Market Manager .... Andre Dowdie

---

579 Independent Health
511 Farber Lakes Drive
Buffalo, NY 14221
Toll-Free: 800-501-3439
Phone: 716-631-3001
www.independenthealth.com
Non-Profit Organization: Yes
Year Founded: 1980
Number of Affiliated Hospitals: 35
Number of Primary Care Physicians: 1,125
Number of Referral/Specialty Physicians: 1,626
Total Enrollment: 365,000
State Enrollment: 365,000

Healthplan and Services Defined
PLAN TYPE: HMO/PPO
Model Type: IPA
Plan Specialty: EPO
Benefits Offered: Behavioral Health, Chiropractic, Dental, Disease Management, Home Care, Inpatient SNF, Physical Therapy, Podiatry, Prescription, Psychiatric, Transplant, Vision, Wellness

Type of Coverage
Commercial, Individual, Indemnity, Medicare, Medicaid, Choice
Catastrophic Illness Benefit: Varies per case

Type of Payment Plans Offered
POS, Combination FFS & DFFS

Geographic Areas Served
Allegany, Cattaraugus, Chautauqua, Erie, Genesee, Niagara, Orleans & Wyoming counties of western New York

Subscriber Information
Average Monthly Fee Per Subscriber (Employee + Employer Contribution):
Employee Only (Self): Varies by plan

Network Qualifications
Pre-Admission Certification: Yes

Peer Review Type
Utilization Review: Yes
Second Surgical Opinion: Yes
Case Management: Yes

Publishes and Distributes Report Card: No

Accreditation Certification
TJC, NCQA

Utilization Review, Pre-Admission Certification, State Licensure, Quality Assurance Program

Key Personnel
President/CEO . . . . Michael W. Cropp, MD
EVP/COO . . . . John Rodgers
EVP/CFO . . . . James A. Dunlop, Jr.
EVP, General Counsel . . . . John Mineo
Chief Medical Officer . . . . Anthony J. Billittier, MD
EVP, Human Resources. . . . . Patricia Clabeaux

Specialty Managed Care Partners
Enters into Contracts with Regional Business Coalitions: No

580 Independent Health Medicare Plan
511 Farber Lakes Drive
Buffalo, NY 14221
Toll-Free: 800-501-3439
Phone: 716-631-3001
www.independenthealth.com
Non-Profit Organization: Yes
Year Founded: 1980

Healthplan and Services Defined
PLAN TYPE: Medicare
Benefits Offered: Chiropractic, Dental, Disease Management, Home Care, Inpatient SNF, Physical Therapy, Podiatry, Prescription, Psychiatric, Vision, Wellness

Type of Coverage
Individual, Medicare

Geographic Areas Served
Statewide

Subscriber Information
Average Monthly Fee Per Subscriber
  (Employee + Employer Contribution):
    Employee Only (Self): Varies
    Medicare: Varies
Average Annual Deductible Per Subscriber:
    Employee Only (Self): Varies
    Medicare: Varies
Average Subscriber Co-Payment:
    Primary Care Physician: Varies
    Non-Network Physician: Varies
    Prescription Drugs: Varies
    Hospital ER: Varies
    Home Health Care: Varies
    Home Health Care Max. Days/Visits Covered: Varies
    Nursing Home: Varies
    Nursing Home Max. Days/Visits Covered: Varies

Key Personnel
President/CEO . . . . Michael W Cropp, MD
EVP/COO . . . . John Rodgers
EVP/CFO . . . . James A. Dunlop, Jr.
EVP, General Counsel . . . . John Mineo
EVP, Chief Med. Officer . . . . Anthony J. Billittier, MD
EVP, Chief HR Officer . . . . Patricia Clabeaux

581 Liberty Dental Plan of New York
50 Charles Lindberg Blvd.
Suite 504
New York, NY 11553
Toll-Free: 833-276-0853
www.libertydentalplan.com
For Profit Organization: Yes
Total Enrollment: 540,000
State Enrollment: 540,000

Healthplan and Services Defined
PLAN TYPE: Dental
Other Type: Dental HMO
Plan Specialty: Dental
Benefits Offered: Dental

Type of Coverage
Commercial, Medicare, Medicaid, Unions

Geographic Areas Served
Statewide

Accreditation Certification
NCQA

Key Personnel
President & CEO. . . . . Amir Neshat
EVP, Compliance Officer. . . . . John Carvelli
Chief Financial Officer . . . . Maja Kapic
General Counsel . . . . Steve Sohn
President, NE Region . . . . Anne Weeks
National Dental Officer . . . . Peter Fuentes
NY Dental Director . . . . Susan Weiss

582 MagnaCare
One Penn Plaza
53rd Floor
New York, NY 10119
Toll-Free: 800-235-7267
Phone: 516-282-8000
www.magnacare.com
Secondary Address: 1600 Stewart Avenue, Suite 700, Westbury, NY 11590
For Profit Organization: Yes
Year Founded: 1990
Number of Affiliated Hospitals: 260
Number of Primary Care Physicians: 70,000
Number of Referral/Specialty Physicians: 58,000
Total Enrollment: 1,326,000
State Enrollment: 928,200

Healthplan and Services Defined
PLAN TYPE: PPO
Model Type: Network
Plan Specialty: ASO, Behavioral Health, Chiropractic, Dental, Lab, Radiology, Worker's Compensation, UR
Benefits Offered: Behavioral Health, Chiropractic, Dental, Home Care, Inpatient SNF, Physical Therapy, Podiatry, Prescription, Psychiatric, Worker's Compensation, Correctional health services

Type of Coverage
Commercial, Individual, Leased Network Arrangement

Type of Payment Plans Offered
DFFS

Geographic Areas Served
New Jersey and New York

Subscriber Information
Average Monthly Fee Per Subscriber
(Employee + Employer Contribution):
Employee Only (Self): Varies
Average Subscriber Co-Payment:
Home Health Care: Varies
Home Health Care Max. Days/Visits Covered: Varies
Nursing Home: Varies
Nursing Home Max. Days/Visits Covered: Varies

Network Qualifications
Pre-Admission Certification: Yes

Peer Review Type
Utilization Review: Yes
Second Surgical Opinion: No
Case Management: Yes

Accreditation Certification
TJC Accreditation, Utilization Review, Pre-Admission Certification, State Licensure, Quality Assurance Program

Key Personnel
President & CFO . . . . Jim Cusumano
Chief Operating Officer . . . . Brian Murray
Chairman . . . . Joseph Berardo, Jr
Chief Compliance Officer . . . . Joseph Brennan
Chief Medical Officer . . . . Bartley Bryt, MD
SVP, Human Resources . . . . Julie Bank

Average Claim Compensation
Physician's Fees Charged: 50%
Hospital's Fees Charged: 60%

Specialty Managed Care Partners
American Psych Systems, Intra State Choice Management Chiropractic

Employer References
Local 947, District Council of Painters #9

583 Meritain Health

300 Corporate Parkway
Amherst, NY 14226
Toll-Free: 888-324-5789
service@meritain.com
www.meritain.com
Subsidiary of: Aetna Inc.
For Profit Organization: Yes
Year Founded: 1983

Healthplan and Services Defined
PLAN TYPE: Multiple
Model Type: Network
Plan Specialty: Dental, Disease Management, Vision, Radiology, UR
Benefits Offered: Dental, Prescription, Vision
Offers Demand Management Patient Information Service: Yes

Type of Coverage
Commercial

Geographic Areas Served
Nationwide

Accreditation Certification
URAC
TJC Accreditation, Medicare Approved, Utilization Review, Pre-Admission Certification, State Licensure, Quality Assurance Program

Key Personnel
President/CEO, CVS Health . . . . Karen S. Lynch
ED, Local Market Dev. . . . . Michael Ciarrocchi
Head, National Accounts . . . . Stacey Meade, CEBS

Average Claim Compensation
Physician's Fees Charged: 78%
Hospital's Fees Charged: 90%

584 MetroPlus Health Plan

160 Water Street
3rd Floor
New York, NY 10038
Toll-Free: 800-303-9626
Fax: 212-908-8601
www.metroplus.org
Subsidiary of: New York City Health Hospitals Corporation
Non-Profit Organization: Yes
Year Founded: 1985
Owned by an Integrated Delivery Network (IDN): Yes
Number of Affiliated Hospitals: 11
Number of Primary Care Physicians: 12,000
Total Enrollment: 500,000
State Enrollment: 500,000

Healthplan and Services Defined
PLAN TYPE: Medicare
Model Type: Network
Benefits Offered: Dental, Disease Management, Prescription, Vision, Wellness, Nurse management line, TeleHealth

Type of Coverage
Medicare, Medicaid, Child Health Plus, Family Health Pl

Geographic Areas Served
Brooklyn, Bronx, Manhattan and Queens

Accreditation Certification
TJC Accreditation

Key Personnel
President/CEO . . . . Talya Schwartz, MD
Chief Medical Officer . . . . Sanjiv S. Shah, MD
Chief Financial Officer . . . . John Cuda
Chief of Staff . . . . Meryl Weinberg
Chief HR Officer . . . . Ryan Harris
Chief Information Officer . . . . Ganesh Ramratan

Specialty Managed Care Partners
Enters into Contracts with Regional Business Coalitions: Yes

585 Molina Healthcare of New York

5232 Witz Drive
North Syracuse, NY 13212
Toll-Free: 800-223-7242
molinahealthcare.com

Subsidiary of: Molina Healthcare, Inc.
For Profit Organization: Yes
Year Founded: 1980

Healthplan and Services Defined
PLAN TYPE: Medicare
Plan Specialty: Dental, PBM, Vision, Integrated Medicare/Medicaid (Duals)
Benefits Offered: Dental, Prescription, Vision, Wellness, Life

Geographic Areas Served
Statewide

Key Personnel
President .... Jack Stephenson
Chief Medical Officer............. Mumtaz Ibrahim, MD

---

586 MVP Health Care
625 State Street
P.O. Box 2207
Schenectady, NY 12301-2207
Toll-Free: 800-777-4793
Phone: 518-370-4793
Fax: 518-370-0830
mvphealthcare.com
Non-Profit Organization: Yes
Total Enrollment: 700,000

Healthplan and Services Defined
PLAN TYPE: Multiple
Benefits Offered: Chiropractic, Dental, Disease Management, Home Care, Inpatient SNF, Physical Therapy, Podiatry, Prescription, Psychiatric, Vision, Wellness

Type of Coverage
Commercial, Individual, Medicare

Geographic Areas Served
New York, Vermont

Accreditation Certification
NCQA

Key Personnel
CEO/Director .... Denise Gonick, Esq.
President/COO .... Christopher Del Vecchio
EVP/CFO......................... Karla A. Austen
EVP, General Counsel .... Monice Barbero
VP, Human Resources .... Lynn Manning
Chief Information Officer .... Michael Della Villa
VP/Chief Actuary .... Kathleen Fish
VP, Marketing/Comm.................... Ted Herman
VP, Pharmacy....................... Jim Hopsicker
VP, Client Engagement................. Augusta Martin
VP, Sales .... Kelly Smith

---

587 Nova Healthcare Administrators
6400 Main Street
Suite 210
Williamsville, NY 14221
Toll-Free: 800-999-5703
AskNova@novahealthcare.com
www.novahealthcare.com
Subsidiary of: Independent Health Association, Inc.

For Profit Organization: Yes
Year Founded: 1982
Total Enrollment: 210,000

Healthplan and Services Defined
PLAN TYPE: Multiple
Plan Specialty: ASO, Dental
Benefits Offered: Dental, Disease Management, Prescription, Wellness

Type of Coverage
Commercial, Indemnity

Geographic Areas Served
Nationwide

Network Qualifications
Pre-Admission Certification: Yes

Peer Review Type
Utilization Review: Yes
Second Surgical Opinion: Yes
Case Management: Yes

Key Personnel
President .... James Walleshauser

Specialty Managed Care Partners
Express Scripts

---

588 Oscar Health
295 Lafayette Street
New York, NY 10012
Toll-Free: 855-672-2788
guides@hioscar.com
www.hioscar.com
Subsidiary of: Mulberry Health, Inc.
For Profit Organization: Yes
Year Founded: 2012

Healthplan and Services Defined
PLAN TYPE: PPO
Benefits Offered: Inpatient SNF, Physical Therapy, Prescription, Psychiatric, Wellness, Labs & Imaging; Occupational & Speech Therapy

Type of Coverage
Medicare

Geographic Areas Served
New York, California, and Texas

Key Personnel
Co-Founder .... Joshua Kushner
Co-Founder .... Mario Schlosser

---

589 Senior Whole Health New York
450 Fashion Ave.
New York, NY 10123
Toll-Free: 877-353-0188
Phone: 212-946-6600
www.seniorwholehealth.com
Subsidiary of: Magellan Health
For Profit Organization: Yes
Year Founded: 2004

Healthplan and Services Defined
PLAN TYPE: Medicare
Benefits Offered: Home Care, Long-Term Care, Psychiatric

Type of Coverage
Medicare, Medicaid, Specialty plan for seniors requirin

Geographic Areas Served
Statewide

590 Trinity Health of New York
Saint Joseph's Health
301 Prospect Avenue
Syracuse, NY 13203
Phone: 315-448-5111
www.trinity-health.org
Secondary Address: St. Peter's Health Partners, 315 S Manning Boulevard, Albany, NY 12208, 518-525-1111
Subsidiary of: Trinity Health
Non-Profit Organization: Yes
Year Founded: 2013
Total Enrollment: 30,000,000

Healthplan and Services Defined
PLAN TYPE: Other
Benefits Offered: Disease Management, Home Care, Long-Term Care, Psychiatric, Hospice programs, PACE (Program of All Inclusive Care for the Elderly)

Geographic Areas Served
Western New York and Albany

Key Personnel
President/CEO .... Leslie Paul Luke
VP, Integrity/Compliance .... Jennifer Reschke Bolster
COO .... Janet L. Ready
Chief Nursing Officer .... AnneMarie W. Czyz, RN
Chief Information Officer .... Charles J. Fennell
VP, Development .... Vincent J. Kuss
Chief Strategy Officer .... Mark E. Murphy
Chief Financial Officer .... Meredith Price
General Counsel .... Regina McGraw, RN, JD
Chief Medical Officer .... Joseph W. Spinale

591 United Concordia of New York
4401 Deer Path Road
Harrisburg, PA 17110
Toll-Free: 800-232-0366
www.unitedconcordia.com
Secondary Address: 159 Express Street, Plainview, NY 11803, 516-827-6720
For Profit Organization: Yes
Year Founded: 1971
Number of Primary Care Physicians: 104,000
Total Enrollment: 8,800,000

Healthplan and Services Defined
PLAN TYPE: Dental
Plan Specialty: Dental
Benefits Offered: Dental

Type of Coverage
Commercial, Individual, Military personnel & families

Geographic Areas Served
Nationwide

Accreditation Certification
URAC

Key Personnel
Contact .... Beth Rutherford
717-260-7659
beth.rutherford@ucci.com

592 UnitedHealthcare Community Plan New York
UnitedHealthcare Customer Service
P.O. Box 30769
Salt Lake City, UT 84130-0769
Toll-Free: 888-545-5205
www.uhccommunityplan.com/new-york
Subsidiary of: UnitedHealth Group
For Profit Organization: Yes

Healthplan and Services Defined
PLAN TYPE: Multiple
Model Type: Network
Benefits Offered: Dental, Home Care, Podiatry, Prescription, Vision, Wellness, Hearing

Type of Coverage
Medicare, Medicaid, CHIP

Geographic Areas Served
Varies by plan

Key Personnel
CEO, Community Plan NY .... Dan Benardette
dan_b_benardette@uhc.com

593 UnitedHealthcare of New York
1 Pennsylvania Plaza
Suite 8
New York, NY 10119
Toll-Free: 866-633-2446
www.uhc.com
Secondary Address: 13 Cornell Road, 2nd Floor, New York, NY 12110
Subsidiary of: UnitedHealth Group
For Profit Organization: Yes
Year Founded: 1987
Federally Qualified: Yes

Healthplan and Services Defined
PLAN TYPE: HMO/PPO
Model Type: Network
Plan Specialty: Behavioral Health, Dental, Disease Management, PBM, Vision
Benefits Offered: Behavioral Health, Dental, Disease Management, Long-Term Care, Prescription, Vision, Wellness, Life, LTD, STD

Type of Coverage
Individual, Medicare, Supplemental Medicare, Medicaid, Catastrophic, Family, Military, Veterans, Group

Type of Payment Plans Offered
DFFS, Capitated

Geographic Areas Served
Statewide

Network Qualifications
Pre-Admission Certification: Yes

Peer Review Type
Utilization Review: Yes
Second Surgical Opinion: Yes
Case Management: Yes

Publishes and Distributes Report Card: Yes

Accreditation Certification
TJC Accreditation, Medicare Approved, Utilization Review, Pre-Admission Certification, State Licensure, Quality Assurance Program

Key Personnel
CEO, Health Plan NY/NJ . . . . Michael McGuire
CEO, Community Plan NY . . . . Dan Bernadette

Specialty Managed Care Partners
Enters into Contracts with Regional Business Coalitions: Yes

---

594 Univera Healthcare

205 Park Club Lane
Buffalo, NY 14221
Toll-Free: 800-499-1275
Phone: 716-847-1480
www.univerahealthcare.com
Mailing Address: P.O. Box 211256, Eagan, MN 55121
Subsidiary of: The Lifetime Healthcare Companies
Non-Profit Organization: Yes
Number of Affiliated Hospitals: 35
Number of Primary Care Physicians: 5,700
Total Enrollment: 1,500,000
State Enrollment: 1,500,000

Healthplan and Services Defined
PLAN TYPE: HMO
Model Type: Network
Plan Specialty: ASO, Behavioral Health, Chiropractic, Dental, Disease Management, EPO, Lab, MSO, PBM, Vision, Radiology, Worker's Compensation, UR
Benefits Offered: Behavioral Health, Chiropractic, Complementary Medicine, Dental, Disease Management, Home Care, Inpatient SNF, Long-Term Care, Physical Therapy, Podiatry, Prescription, Psychiatric, Transplant, Vision, Wellness, Worker's Compensation, Life

Type of Coverage
Commercial, Individual, Medicare

Geographic Areas Served
Allegany, Cattaraugus, Chautauqua, Erie, Genesee, Niagara, Orleans and Wyoming counties

Subscriber Information
Average Monthly Fee Per Subscriber
(Employee + Employer Contribution):
Employee Only (Self): Varies by plan
Average Subscriber Co-Payment:
Primary Care Physician: Varies
Prescription Drugs: Varies

Publishes and Distributes Report Card: Yes

Accreditation Certification
NCQA

Key Personnel
President . . . . Arthur G. Wingerter
Chief Executive Officer. . . . . Christopher C. Booth
Chief Medical Officer . . . . Richard P. Vienne
VP, Sales . . . . Pamela J. Pawenski
VP, Communications . . . . Peter B Kates
716-857-4495
peter.kates@univerahealthcare.com

NORTH CAROLINA

Health Insurance Coverage Status and Type of Coverage by Age

Category	All Persons Number	All Persons %	Under 19 years Number	Under 19 years %	Under 65 years Number	Under 65 years %
Total population	10,281 *(4)*	100.0 *(0.0)*	2,455 *(8)*	100.0 *(0.0)*	8,569 *(6)*	100.0 *(0.0)*
Covered by some type of health insurance	9,124 *(26)*	88.7 *(0.3)*	2,313 *(12)*	94.2 *(0.4)*	7,424 *(25)*	86.6 *(0.3)*
Covered by private health insurance	6,852 *(40)*	66.6 *(0.4)*	1,378 *(20)*	56.1 *(0.8)*	5,833 *(37)*	68.1 *(0.4)*
Employer-based	5,373 *(46)*	52.3 *(0.4)*	1,152 *(21)*	46.9 *(0.8)*	4,856 *(43)*	56.7 *(0.5)*
Direct purchase	1,506 *(26)*	14.6 *(0.3)*	167 *(10)*	6.8 *(0.4)*	913 *(24)*	10.7 *(0.3)*
TRICARE	427 *(17)*	4.2 *(0.2)*	107 *(8)*	4.4 *(0.3)*	306 *(16)*	3.6 *(0.2)*
Covered by public health insurance	3,587 *(31)*	34.9 *(0.3)*	1,017 *(19)*	41.4 *(0.8)*	1,924 *(31)*	22.5 *(0.4)*
Medicaid	1,849 *(28)*	18.0 *(0.3)*	1,009 *(19)*	41.1 *(0.8)*	1,646 *(28)*	19.2 *(0.3)*
Medicare	1,943 *(11)*	18.9 *(0.1)*	10 *(2)*	0.4 *(0.1)*	283 *(8)*	3.3 *(0.1)*
VA Care	290 *(8)*	2.8 *(0.1)*	4 *(2)*	0.2 *(0.1)*	146 *(7)*	1.7 *(0.1)*
Not covered at any time during the year	1,157 *(26)*	11.3 *(0.3)*	142 *(9)*	5.8 *(0.4)*	1,145 *(26)*	13.4 *(0.3)*

Note: Numbers in thousands; Figures cover civilian noninstitutionalized population in 2019; N/A indicates that data was not available; Z represents or rounds to zero; Margin of error appears in parenthesis and is calculated using replicate weights.
Source: U.S. Census Bureau, American Community Survey, Table HI-05. Health Insurance Coverage Status and Type of Coverage by State and Age for All People: 2019

North Carolina

595 Aetna Health of North Carolina
151 Farmington Avenue
Hartford, CT 06156
Toll-Free: 800-872-3862
www.aetna.com
Subsidiary of: CVS Health / Aetna Inc.
For Profit Organization: Yes

Healthplan and Services Defined
PLAN TYPE: HMO/PPO
Other Type: POS
Model Type: Network
Plan Specialty: Behavioral Health, EPO, Lab, PBM, Radiology
Benefits Offered: Behavioral Health, Dental, Disease Management, Long-Term Care, Physical Therapy, Podiatry, Prescription, Psychiatric, Vision, Wellness, Life, LTD, STD

Type of Coverage
Commercial, Student health

Geographic Areas Served
Statewide

Key Personnel
Market Pres., Mid-South.................Jim Bostian

596 Ambetter of North Carolina
Centene Plaza
7700 Forsyth Boulevard
St. Louis, MO 63105
Toll-Free: 833-863-1310
www.ambetterofnorthcarolina.com
For Profit Organization: Yes

Healthplan and Services Defined
PLAN TYPE: Other
Model Type: Network
Plan Specialty: Lab
Benefits Offered: Behavioral Health, Disease Management, Physical Therapy, Prescription, Wellness

Type of Coverage
Health Insurance Marketplace

Geographic Areas Served
Durham and Wake counties

597 Blue Cross Blue Shield of North Carolina
4615 Univerisity Drive
Durham, NC 27707
Toll-Free: 800-665-8037
Phone: 919-698-8460
www.bluecrossnc.com
Mailing Address: P.O. Box 2291, DurhamNC 27702-2291
Non-Profit Organization: Yes
Year Founded: 1933
Total Enrollment: 3,810,000

Healthplan and Services Defined
PLAN TYPE: HMO/PPO
Model Type: Network
Plan Specialty: ASO, Behavioral Health, Chiropractic, Dental, Disease Management, Lab, PBM, Vision, Radiology, UR
Benefits Offered: Behavioral Health, Chiropractic, Complementary Medicine, Dental, Disease Management, Home Care, Inpatient SNF, Long-Term Care, Physical Therapy, Podiatry, Prescription, Psychiatric, Transplant, Vision, Wellness, AD&D, Life, LTD, STD

Type of Coverage
Commercial, Individual, Supplemental Medicare

Type of Payment Plans Offered
POS, DFFS, FFS, Combination FFS & DFFS

Geographic Areas Served
Statewide

Peer Review Type
Utilization Review: Yes
Second Surgical Opinion: Yes
Case Management: Yes

Accreditation Certification
NCQA
State Licensure

Key Personnel
President/CEO........................Tunde Sotunde
SVP/COO/Member Experience............Karla Mizelle
SVP/CFO..............................Mitch Perry

Average Claim Compensation
Physician's Fees Charged: 43%
Hospital's Fees Charged: 35%

598 Cigna HealthCare of North Carolina
11016 Rushmore Drive
Suite 300
Charlotte, NC 28277
Toll-Free: 800-997-1654
www.cigna.com
Subsidiary of: Cigna Corporation
For Profit Organization: Yes

Healthplan and Services Defined
PLAN TYPE: HMO
Other Type: POS
Plan Specialty: Behavioral Health, Dental
Benefits Offered: Behavioral Health, Dental, Disease Management, Prescription, Vision, Wellness, AD&D, Life, LTD, STD

Type of Coverage
Commercial, Individual, Medicare, Supplemental Medicare, Medicaid, Part-time and hourly workers; Union

Geographic Areas Served
Statewide

Key Personnel
Market Pres., Carolinas...................Charles Pitts

599 Crescent Health Solutions
1200 Ridgefield Boulevard
Suite 215
Asheville, NC 28806
Toll-Free: 800-707-7726
Phone: 828-670-9145
Fax: 828-670-9155
www.crescenths.com
Year Founded: 1999
Physician Owned Organization: Yes
Number of Affiliated Hospitals: 4,000
Number of Primary Care Physicians: 1,900
Number of Referral/Specialty Physicians: 2,400
Total Enrollment: 40,000
State Enrollment: 40,000

Healthplan and Services Defined
PLAN TYPE: PPO
Benefits Offered: Disease Management, Prescription, Wellness, Case Management, UR, TPA Services

Type of Coverage
Commercial, Individual

Geographic Areas Served
North Carolina, South Carolina, Georgia, and Oklahoma

Peer Review Type
Utilization Review: Yes
Case Management: Yes

600 Delta Dental of North Carolina
4242 Six Forks Road
Suite 970
Raleigh, NC 27609
Toll-Free: 800-662-8856
www.deltadentalnc.org
Secondary Address: Claims Mailing Address, P.O. Box 9085, Farmington Hills, MI 48333-9085
Non-Profit Organization: Yes

Healthplan and Services Defined
PLAN TYPE: Dental
Other Type: Dental PPO
Plan Specialty: Dental
Benefits Offered: Dental

Type of Coverage
Commercial, Individual

Type of Payment Plans Offered
POS, DFFS, FFS

Geographic Areas Served
Statewide

Key Personnel
President/CEO . . . . Curtis Ladig
Director of Operations . . . . Tia Jones
Director of Marketing . . . . Katie Williams
VP, Sales . . . . Debbie Jones

601 Envolve Vision
1151 Falls Road, Suite 2000
P.O. Box 7548
Rocky Mount, NC 27804
Toll-Free: 800-334-3937
Fax: 877-940-9243
visionbenefits.envolvehealth.com
For Profit Organization: Yes
Number of Primary Care Physicians: 20,000

Healthplan and Services Defined
PLAN TYPE: Vision
Model Type: Network
Plan Specialty: Vision
Benefits Offered: Vision

Type of Coverage
Commercial, Medicare, Supplemental Medicare, Medicaid

Type of Payment Plans Offered
POS, DFFS, Capitated, FFS, Combination FFS & DFFS

Geographic Areas Served
Nationwide

Peer Review Type
Utilization Review: Yes
Case Management: Yes

Accreditation Certification
AAAHC, NCQA, State Licensure

Key Personnel
President/CEO . . . . David Lavely
SVP, Information Systems . . . . Juan Marrero
SVP, Regulatory Affairs . . . . Larry Keeley
SVP, Finance . . . . George Verrastro
Chief Operating Officer . . . . Michael Grover

Employer References
Wilmer-Hutchins Independent School District

602 FirstCarolinaCare
42 Memorial Drive
Pinehurst, NC 28374
Phone: 910-715-8100
www.firstcarolinacare.com
Subsidiary of: FirstHealth of the Carolinas
Non-Profit Organization: Yes
Total Enrollment: 13,000
State Enrollment: 13,000

Healthplan and Services Defined
PLAN TYPE: HMO
Offers Demand Management Patient Information Service: Yes
DMPI Services Offered: Nurse Helpline

Type of Coverage
Individual

Geographic Areas Served
Statewide

Key Personnel
President . . . . Craig Humphrey

603 Humana Health Insurance of North Carolina
6135 Park South Drive
Suite 510
Charlotte, NC 28210
Toll-Free: 800-211-2389
Phone: 704-643-1009
www.humana.com
Secondary Address: 1863 Hendersonville Road, Suite 122, Asheville, NC 28803, 828-772-3090
Subsidiary of: Humana Inc.
For Profit Organization: Yes

Healthplan and Services Defined
PLAN TYPE: HMO/PPO
Plan Specialty: ASO
Benefits Offered: Disease Management, Prescription, Wellness

Type of Coverage
Commercial, Individual

Geographic Areas Served
Statewide

Accreditation Certification
URAC, NCQA, CORE

Key Personnel
Market VP .... Kathleen Schwarzwalder

Specialty Managed Care Partners
Caremark Rx

Employer References
Tricare

604 MedCost
165 Kimel Park Drive
Winston Salem, NC 27103
Toll-Free: 800-217-5097
www.medcost.com
Secondary Address: 1915 Rexford Road, Suite 430, Charlotte, NC 28211, 704-525-1473
Subsidiary of: Carolinas HealthCare System
For Profit Organization: Yes
Year Founded: 1983
Number of Affiliated Hospitals: 191
Number of Primary Care Physicians: 12,349
Number of Referral/Specialty Physicians: 21,295
Total Enrollment: 670,000
State Enrollment: 670,000

Healthplan and Services Defined
PLAN TYPE: PPO
Model Type: Network
Plan Specialty: UR, PPO Network, Maternity Management, Case Management, Nurse Coaching
Benefits Offered: Behavioral Health, Dental, Home Care, Inpatient SNF, Long-Term Care, Physical Therapy, Podiatry, Psychiatric, Transplant, Vision, Wellness, Medical, Hospice, Durable Medical Equipment

Type of Coverage
Commercial

Type of Payment Plans Offered
FFS

Geographic Areas Served
North Carolina, South Carolina, and Virginia

Subscriber Information
Average Subscriber Co-Payment:
Primary Care Physician: Varies
Non-Network Physician: Varies
Prescription Drugs: Varies
Hospital ER: Varies
Home Health Care: Varies
Home Health Care Max. Days/Visits Covered: Varies
Nursing Home: Varies
Nursing Home Max. Days/Visits Covered: Varies

Peer Review Type
Utilization Review: Yes
Second Surgical Opinion: Yes
Case Management: Yes

Publishes and Distributes Report Card: Yes

Accreditation Certification
URAC

Key Personnel
Senior Vice President .... Kathryn Showalter
Chief Financial Officer .... Greg Bray

605 United Concordia of North Carolina
10700 Sikes Place
Suite 331
Charlotte, NC 28277
Phone: 704-845-8224
www.unitedconcordia.com
For Profit Organization: Yes
Year Founded: 1971
Number of Primary Care Physicians: 104,000
Total Enrollment: 8,800,000

Healthplan and Services Defined
PLAN TYPE: Dental
Plan Specialty: Dental
Benefits Offered: Dental

Type of Coverage
Commercial, Individual, Military personnel & families

Geographic Areas Served
Nationwide

Accreditation Certification
URAC

Key Personnel
Contact............................ Beth Rutherford
717-260-7659
beth.rutherford@ucci.com

606 UnitedHealthcare Community Plan North Carolina

UnitedHealthcare Customer Service
P.O. Box 30769
Salt Lake City, UT 84130-0769
Toll-Free: 888-545-5205
www.uhccommunityplan.com/nc
Subsidiary of: UnitedHealth Group
For Profit Organization: Yes

Healthplan and Services Defined
  PLAN TYPE: Medicare
  Other Type: Medicaid
  Model Type: Network
  Benefits Offered: Dental, Home Care, Podiatry, Prescription, Vision, Wellness, Hearing

Type of Coverage
  Medicare, Medicaid

Geographic Areas Served
  Alamance, Buncombe, Caswell, Catawba, Chatham, Cumberland, Davidson, Davie, Durham, Forsyth, Guilford, Henderson, Mecklenburg, Orange, Person, Randolph, Rockingham, Rowan, Stokes, Wake, Wilkes, and Yadkin. Other plans statewide

Key Personnel
  CEO, Community Plan NC.............. Anita Bachmann
    anita.bachmann@uhc.com

607 UnitedHealthcare of North Carolina

8601 Six Forks Rd.
Raleigh, NC 27615
Toll-Free: 833-579-2430
www.uhc.com
Secondary Address: 6101 Carnegie Boulevard, Charlotte, NC 28209
Subsidiary of: UnitedHealth Group
For Profit Organization: Yes
Year Founded: 1985

Healthplan and Services Defined
  PLAN TYPE: HMO/PPO
  Model Type: Network
  Plan Specialty: Behavioral Health, Dental, Disease Management, PBM, Vision
  Benefits Offered: Behavioral Health, Dental, Disease Management, Long-Term Care, Prescription, Vision, Wellness, Life, LTD, STD

Type of Coverage
  Individual, Medicare, Supplemental Medicare, Medicaid, Catastrophic, Family, Military, Veterans, Group, Catastrophic Illness Benefit: Maximum $2M

Type of Payment Plans Offered
  POS, DFFS, FFS, Combination FFS & DFFS

Geographic Areas Served
  Statewide

Subscriber Information
  Average Subscriber Co-Payment:
    Primary Care Physician: $10.00
    Non-Network Physician: 20%
    Prescription Drugs: $10.00
    Hospital ER: $35.00
    Home Health Care: $0
    Home Health Care Max. Days/Visits Covered: 30 days
    Nursing Home: 20%
    Nursing Home Max. Days/Visits Covered: 30 days

Network Qualifications
  Pre-Admission Certification: Yes

Peer Review Type
  Utilization Review: Yes
  Second Surgical Opinion: No
  Case Management: Yes

Publishes and Distributes Report Card: Yes

Accreditation Certification
  TJC Accreditation, Utilization Review, Pre-Admission Certification, State Licensure, Quality Assurance Program

Key Personnel
  CEO, NC Medicare................... Anita Bachmann

NORTH DAKOTA

Health Insurance Coverage Status and Type of Coverage by Age

Category	All Persons Number	All Persons %	Under 19 years Number	Under 19 years %	Under 65 years Number	Under 65 years %
Total population	744 (2)	100.0 (0.0)	187 (3)	100.0 (0.0)	630 (2)	100.0 (0.0)
Covered by some type of health insurance	693 (5)	93.1 (0.7)	173 (4)	92.2 (1.5)	580 (5)	91.9 (0.8)
Covered by private health insurance	588 (9)	79.1 (1.2)	143 (5)	76.2 (2.2)	511 (8)	81.1 (1.3)
Employer-based	457 (9)	61.5 (1.3)	124 (5)	66.4 (2.3)	431 (9)	68.3 (1.4)
Direct purchase	142 (7)	19.0 (1.0)	17 (2)	9.1 (1.3)	86 (6)	13.6 (1.0)
TRICARE	29 (4)	3.9 (0.5)	7 (2)	3.8 (1.1)	22 (4)	3.5 (0.6)
Covered by public health insurance	202 (8)	27.2 (1.0)	38 (4)	20.5 (2.4)	92 (8)	14.6 (1.2)
Medicaid	90 (7)	12.1 (1.0)	38 (4)	20.3 (2.4)	78 (7)	12.4 (1.2)
Medicare	122 (2)	16.4 (0.3)	Z (Z)	0.2 (0.1)	13 (2)	2.0 (0.3)
VA Care	24 (3)	3.3 (0.3)	Z (Z)	Z (Z)	10 (2)	1.6 (0.3)
Not covered at any time during the year	51 (5)	6.9 (0.7)	15 (3)	7.8 (1.5)	51 (5)	8.1 (0.8)

Note: Numbers in thousands; Figures cover civilian noninstitutionalized population in 2019; N/A indicates that data was not available; Z represents or rounds to zero; Margin of error appears in parenthesis and is calculated using replicate weights.
Source: U.S. Census Bureau, American Community Survey, Table HI-05. Health Insurance Coverage Status and Type of Coverage by State and Age for All People: 2019

North Dakota

608 Aetna Health of North Dakota
151 Farmington Avenue
Hartford, CT 06156
Toll-Free: 800-872-3862
www.aetna.com
Subsidiary of: CVS Health / Aetna Inc.
For Profit Organization: Yes

Healthplan and Services Defined
PLAN TYPE: PPO
Other Type: POS
Model Type: Network
Plan Specialty: Behavioral Health, EPO, Lab, PBM, Radiology
Benefits Offered: Behavioral Health, Disease Management, Long-Term Care, Physical Therapy, Podiatry, Prescription, Psychiatric, Wellness, Life, LTD, STD

Type of Coverage
Commercial, Student health

Type of Payment Plans Offered
POS, FFS

Geographic Areas Served
Statewide

Key Personnel
Operations Manager .... Rita Pfeifer

609 Medica: North Dakota
1711 Gold Drive South
Suite 210
Fargo, ND 58103
Phone: 701-293-4700
www.medica.com
Non-Profit Organization: Yes
Year Founded: 1974
Number of Affiliated Hospitals: 158
Number of Primary Care Physicians: 24,000
Total Enrollment: 150,000

Healthplan and Services Defined
PLAN TYPE: HMO
Model Type: IPA
Benefits Offered: Behavioral Health, Chiropractic, Dental, Disease Management, Prescription, Wellness, AD&D, Life, LTD, STD
Offers Demand Management Patient Information Service: Yes

Type of Coverage
Medicare
Catastrophic Illness Benefit: Covered

Type of Payment Plans Offered
Capitated, FFS, Combination FFS & DFFS

Geographic Areas Served
Aitkin, Anoka, Becker, Beltrami, Benton, Big Stone, Blue Earth, Brown, Carlton, Carver, Cass, Chisago, Clay, Clearwater, Cottonwood, Crow Wing, Dakota, Dodge, Douglas, Fillmore, Goodhue, Grant, Hennepin, Hubbard, Isanti, Itaska, Kanabec, Kandiyohi, Koochiching, Jackson, Lac Qui Parle, Lake, Le Sueur, Lincoln, Lyon, Mahnomen, McLeod, Meeker, Mille Lacs, Morrison, Murray, Nicollet, Norman, Olnsted, Otter Tail, Pine, Polk, Pope, Ramsey, Renville, Rice, Rock, Scott

Subscriber Information
Average Monthly Fee Per Subscriber
(Employee + Employer Contribution):
Employee Only (Self): Varies by plan
Average Subscriber Co-Payment:
Primary Care Physician: $15.00
Non-Network Physician: Deductible + 20%
Prescription Drugs: $11.00
Hospital ER: $60.00
Home Health Care: 20%
Nursing Home: 20%

Network Qualifications
Pre-Admission Certification: Yes

Peer Review Type
Utilization Review: Yes
Second Surgical Opinion: Yes
Case Management: Yes

Publishes and Distributes Report Card: Yes

Accreditation Certification
NCQA
TJC Accreditation, Medicare Approved, Utilization Review, Pre-Admission Certification, State Licensure, Quality Assurance Program

Average Claim Compensation
Physician's Fees Charged: 65%
Hospital's Fees Charged: 60%

Specialty Managed Care Partners
Express Scrips, Vision Service Plan, National Healthcare Resources, Cigna Behavioral Resources
Enters into Contracts with Regional Business Coalitions: Yes

Employer References
Construction Industry Laborers Welfare Fund-Jefferson City, District 9 Machinists (Missouri/Welfare Plan), Government Employees Hospital Association/GEHA, Missouri Highway & Transportation Department/Highway Patrol

610 Noridian Healthcare Services Inc.
900 42nd Street South
Fargo, ND 58103-6055
Toll-Free: 800-575-9643
noridiansolutions@noridian.com
noridiansolutions.com
For Profit Organization: Yes

Healthplan and Services Defined
PLAN TYPE: PPO
Plan Specialty: Dental, Vision
Benefits Offered: Dental, Long-Term Care, Vision, AD&D, Life, LTD, STD

Type of Coverage
Commercial, Individual, Indemnity

Geographic Areas Served
North Dakota and Northwest Minnesota

611 UnitedHealthcare of North Dakota
9700 Health Care Lane
Minnetonka, MN 55343
Toll-Free: 888-545-5205
www.uhc.com
Subsidiary of: UnitedHealth Group
For Profit Organization: Yes
Year Founded: 1977

Healthplan and Services Defined
   PLAN TYPE: HMO/PPO
   Model Type: Network
   Plan Specialty: Behavioral Health, Dental, Disease Management, Lab, PBM, Vision, Radiology
   Benefits Offered: Behavioral Health, Dental, Disease Management, Home Care, Long-Term Care, Physical Therapy, Prescription, Psychiatric, Vision, Wellness, AD&D, Life, LTD, STD
   Offers Demand Management Patient Information Service: Yes

Type of Coverage
   Commercial, Individual, Indemnity, Medicare, Supplemental Medicare, Medicaid, Catastrophic, Family, Military, Veterans, Group, Retirees
   Catastrophic Illness Benefit: Varies per case

Geographic Areas Served
   Statewide. North Dakota is covered by the Minnesota branch

Publishes and Distributes Report Card: Yes

Accreditation Certification
   TJC Accreditation, Medicare Approved

Key Personnel
   CEO, MN/ND/SD . . . . Brett Edelson

Specialty Managed Care Partners
   Enters into Contracts with Regional Business Coalitions: Yes

OHIO

Health Insurance Coverage Status and Type of Coverage by Age

Category	All Persons Number	%	Under 19 years Number	%	Under 65 years Number	%
Total population	11,515 *(2)*	100.0 *(0.0)*	2,736 *(7)*	100.0 *(0.0)*	9,541 *(4)*	100.0 *(0.0)*
Covered by some type of health insurance	10,757 *(22)*	93.4 *(0.2)*	2,605 *(10)*	95.2 *(0.3)*	8,793 *(22)*	92.2 *(0.2)*
Covered by private health insurance	7,939 *(41)*	68.9 *(0.4)*	1,739 *(20)*	63.5 *(0.7)*	6,758 *(37)*	70.8 *(0.4)*
Employer-based	6,809 *(46)*	59.1 *(0.4)*	1,606 *(21)*	58.7 *(0.8)*	6,149 *(41)*	64.4 *(0.4)*
Direct purchase	1,346 *(20)*	11.7 *(0.2)*	136 *(8)*	5.0 *(0.3)*	699 *(17)*	7.3 *(0.2)*
TRICARE	196 *(10)*	1.7 *(0.1)*	40 *(5)*	1.5 *(0.2)*	124 *(10)*	1.3 *(0.1)*
Covered by public health insurance	4,283 *(34)*	37.2 *(0.3)*	992 *(19)*	36.3 *(0.7)*	2,376 *(34)*	24.9 *(0.4)*
Medicaid	2,311 *(33)*	20.1 *(0.3)*	985 *(19)*	36.0 *(0.7)*	2,119 *(32)*	22.2 *(0.3)*
Medicare	2,203 *(12)*	19.1 *(0.1)*	12 *(2)*	0.4 *(0.1)*	298 *(10)*	3.1 *(0.1)*
VA Care	257 *(9)*	2.2 *(0.1)*	3 *(1)*	0.1 *(0.1)*	113 *(7)*	1.2 *(0.1)*
Not covered at any time during the year	758 *(22)*	6.6 *(0.2)*	131 *(9)*	4.8 *(0.3)*	748 *(22)*	7.8 *(0.2)*

Note: Numbers in thousands; Figures cover civilian noninstitutionalized population in 2019; N/A indicates that data was not available; Z represents or rounds to zero; Margin of error appears in parenthesis and is calculated using replicate weights.
Source: U.S. Census Bureau, American Community Survey, Table HI-05. Health Insurance Coverage Status and Type of Coverage by State and Age for All People: 2019

Ohio

612 Aetna Better Health of Ohio
7400 W Campus Road
New Albany, OH 43054
Toll-Free: 855-364-0974
www.aetnabetterhealth.com/ohio
Subsidiary of: CVS Health / Aetna Inc.
For Profit Organization: Yes

Healthplan and Services Defined
  PLAN TYPE: HMO/PPO
  Other Type: POS
  Model Type: Network
  Plan Specialty: Behavioral Health, Dental, EPO, Lab, PBM, Vision, Radiology
  Benefits Offered: Behavioral Health, Dental, Disease Management, Long-Term Care, Physical Therapy, Podiatry, Prescription, Psychiatric, Vision, Wellness, Life, LTD, STD

Type of Coverage
  Commercial, Medicare, Medicaid, Student health

Type of Payment Plans Offered
  POS

Geographic Areas Served
  Statewide

Subscriber Information
  Average Subscriber Co-Payment:
    Prescription Drugs: $5.00
    Home Health Care Max. Days/Visits Covered: Unlimited

Network Qualifications
  Pre-Admission Certification: No

Peer Review Type
  Utilization Review: Yes
  Second Surgical Opinion: Yes
  Case Management: Yes

Publishes and Distributes Report Card: Yes

Accreditation Certification
  NCQA
  TJC Accreditation, Utilization Review, Pre-Admission Certification, State Licensure, Quality Assurance Program

Specialty Managed Care Partners
  Enters into Contracts with Regional Business Coalitions: Yes

613 Allwell from Buckeye Health Plan
4349 Easton Way
Suite 300
Columbus, OH 43219
Toll-Free: 855-766-1851
allwell.buckeyehealthplan.com
Subsidiary of: Centene Corporation
For Profit Organization: Yes

Healthplan and Services Defined
  PLAN TYPE: Other
  Model Type: Network
  Benefits Offered: Dental, Prescription

Type of Coverage
  Medicare, Supplemental Medicare, Medicare Advantage

Geographic Areas Served
  Statewide

614 Ambetter from Buckeye Health Plan
4349 Easton Way
Suite 300
Columbus, OH 43219
Toll-Free: 877-687-1189
ambetter.buckeyehealthplan.com
Subsidiary of: Centene Corporation
For Profit Organization: Yes

Healthplan and Services Defined
  PLAN TYPE: Other
  Model Type: Network
  Plan Specialty: Lab
  Benefits Offered: Behavioral Health, Disease Management, Physical Therapy, Prescription, Wellness, Maternity and newborn care

Type of Coverage
  Health Insurance Marketplace

Geographic Areas Served
  Allen, Butler, Carroll, Champaign, Clark, Columbiana, Cuyahoga, Darke, Geauga, Greene, Hamilton, Harrison, Lake, Logan, Lorain, Lucas, Mahoning, Medina, Montgomery, Portage, Preble, Shelby, Stark, Summit, Trumbull, Van Wert, and Warren counties

615 American Health Network Ohio
2500 Corporate Exchange
Suite 100
Columbus, OH 43229
Toll-Free: 833-319-9364
Phone: 614-794-4500
www.ahni.com

Healthplan and Services Defined
  PLAN TYPE: PPO
  Plan Specialty: Lab, Vision, Family Medicine, General Surgery, Pain Management, Pediatrics
  Benefits Offered: Physical Therapy, Podiatry

Geographic Areas Served
  Ohio

616 Anthem Blue Cross & Blue Shield of Ohio
4361 Irwin Simpson Road
Mason, OH 45040
Toll-Free: 800-331-1476
www.anthem.com
Secondary Address: 6740 N High Street, Worthington, OH 43085
Subsidiary of: Anthem, Inc.
For Profit Organization: Yes
Year Founded: 1944
Owned by an Integrated Delivery Network (IDN): Yes
Number of Affiliated Hospitals: 568

Number of Primary Care Physicians: 25,000
Number of Referral/Specialty Physicians: 61,728

Healthplan and Services Defined
PLAN TYPE: HMO/PPO
Plan Specialty: ASO, Behavioral Health, Chiropractic, Dental, Disease Management, Lab, PBM, Vision, Radiology, Worker's Compensation, UR
Benefits Offered: Behavioral Health, Chiropractic, Dental, Disease Management, Home Care, Inpatient SNF, Physical Therapy, Podiatry, Prescription, Psychiatric, Transplant, Vision, Wellness, Worker's Compensation
Offers Demand Management Patient Information Service: Yes
DMPI Services Offered: Iris Program, Care Wise (24/7 Nurse Line), Dental, Vision

Type of Coverage
Commercial, Individual, Indemnity, Medicare, Catastrophic

Type of Payment Plans Offered
POS, DFFS, Capitated, FFS

Geographic Areas Served
Statewide

Subscriber Information
Average Monthly Fee Per Subscriber
(Employee + Employer Contribution):
    Employee Only (Self): Proprietary
    Employee & 1 Family Member: Proprietary
    Employee & 2 Family Members: Proprierary
    Medicare: Proprietary
Average Annual Deductible Per Subscriber:
    Employee Only (Self): Proprietary
    Employee & 1 Family Member: Proprietary
    Employee & 2 Family Members: Proprietary
    Medicare: Proprietary

Network Qualifications
Pre-Admission Certification: Yes

Peer Review Type
Utilization Review: Yes
Second Surgical Opinion: Yes
Case Management: Yes

Accreditation Certification
URAC, NCQA
TJC Accreditation, Medicare Approved, Utilization Review, Pre-Admission Certification, State Licensure, Quality Assurance Program

Key Personnel
President . . . . Steve Martenet

Specialty Managed Care Partners
Anthem Dental, Anthem Prescription Management LLC, Anthem Vision, Anthem Life

---

617 Aultcare Corporation
2600 Sixth Street SW
Canton, OH 44710
Toll-Free: 800-344-8858
Phone: 330-363-6360
www.aultcare.com
Non-Profit Organization: Yes

Year Founded: 1985
Number of Affiliated Hospitals: 30
Number of Primary Care Physicians: 3,500
Number of Referral/Specialty Physicians: 6,800
Total Enrollment: 500,000
State Enrollment: 5,151

Healthplan and Services Defined
PLAN TYPE: HMO/PPO
Model Type: Network
Benefits Offered: Chiropractic, Dental, Disease Management, Inpatient SNF, Podiatry, Vision, Wellness, Worker's Compensation, STD, Flexible Spending Accounts

Type of Coverage
Commercial, Individual

Geographic Areas Served
Carroll, Holmes, Stark, Summit, Tuscarawas and Wayne counties

Network Qualifications
Pre-Admission Certification: Yes

Peer Review Type
Utilization Review: Yes
Second Surgical Opinion: Yes
Case Management: Yes

Accreditation Certification
NCQA

Key Personnel
CEO/President . . . . Rick Haines

Employer References
Maytag, Timken Company

---

618 Buckeye Health Plan
4349 Easton Way
Suite 300
Columbus, OH 43219
Toll-Free: 866-246-4358
www.buckeyehealthplan.com
Subsidiary of: Centene Corporation
For Profit Organization: Yes

Healthplan and Services Defined
PLAN TYPE: Other
Model Type: Network
Benefits Offered: Behavioral Health, Dental, Disease Management, Vision, Wellness

Type of Coverage
Medicaid

Geographic Areas Served
Statewide

Key Personnel
President/CEO . . . . Steven Province
Chief Medical Officer . . . . Brad Lucas, MD
SVP, Leg. & Gov. Affairs . . . . Eric Poklar
SVP, Operations . . . . Jay Scherler
VP, Network Development . . . . Natalie Lukaszewicz

619 Buckeye Health Plan - MyCare Ohio
4349 Easton Way
Suite 120
Columbus, OH 43219
Toll-Free: 866-549-8289
mmp.buckeyehealthplan.com
Subsidiary of: Centene Corporation
For Profit Organization: Yes

Healthplan and Services Defined
PLAN TYPE: Other
Model Type: Network
Benefits Offered: Prescription

Type of Coverage
Medicare, Medicaid, Medicare-Medicaid Plan

Geographic Areas Served
Clark, Cuyahoga, Fulton, Geauga, Greene, Lake, Lorain, Lucas, Medina, Montgomery, Ottawa, and Wood counties

620 CareSource Ohio
230 N Main Street
Dayton, OH 45402
Toll-Free: 844-607-2830
Phone: 937-224-3300
www.caresource.com
Secondary Address: 5900 Landerbrook Drive, Suite 300, Mayfield Heights, OH 44124, 216-839-1001
Non-Profit Organization: Yes
Total Enrollment: 1,900,000

Healthplan and Services Defined
PLAN TYPE: Medicare
Other Type: Medicaid

Type of Coverage
Medicare, Medicaid

Geographic Areas Served
Statewide

Key Personnel
President & CEO . . . . Erhardt Preitauer
COO . . . . Jai Pillai
CFO . . . . David Goltz
CIO . . . . Devon Valencia
CAO . . . . Dan McCabe
President, Ohio Market . . . . Steve Ringel

621 Delta Dental of Ohio
8044 Montgomery Rd.
Cincinnati, OH 45236
Toll-Free: 800-524-0149
www.deltadentaloh.com
Mailing Address: P.O. Box 9085, Farmington Hills, MI 48333-9085
Non-Profit Organization: Yes
Year Founded: 1960

Healthplan and Services Defined
PLAN TYPE: Dental
Other Type: Dental PPO
Plan Specialty: Dental
Benefits Offered: Dental

Type of Coverage
Commercial

Type of Payment Plans Offered
POS

Geographic Areas Served
Statewide

Peer Review Type
Second Surgical Opinion: Yes
Case Management: No

Publishes and Distributes Report Card: Yes

Accreditation Certification
Utilization Review

Key Personnel
VP, Finance . . . . Jennifer Needham, CPA
Exec. Dir., Sales/Account . . . . Bryan Leddy
Senior Account Manager . . . . Cathy Dorocak
Account Executive . . . . Daniel Parker

Specialty Managed Care Partners
Enters into Contracts with Regional Business Coalitions: Yes

622 EyeMed Vision Care
4000 Luxottica Place
Mason, OH 45040
https://eyemed.com
Subsidiary of: Luxxotica
For Profit Organization: Yes
Year Founded: 1988
Total Enrollment: 43,000,000

Healthplan and Services Defined
PLAN TYPE: Vision
Plan Specialty: Vision
Benefits Offered: Vision

Type of Coverage
Commercial

Key Personnel
President . . . . Lukas Ruecker

623 Humana Health Insurance of Ohio
3252 Geier Drive
Cincinnati, OH 45209
Phone: 513-830-1821
Fax: 513-442-7668
www.humana.com
Secondary Address: 4071 Lee Road, Suite 135, Cleveland, OH 44128, 216-706-8610
Subsidiary of: Humana Inc.
For Profit Organization: Yes
Year Founded: 1979
Owned by an Integrated Delivery Network (IDN): Yes

Healthplan and Services Defined
PLAN TYPE: HMO/PPO
Model Type: Group

Plan Specialty: ASO, Dental, Vision, Radiology, Worker's Compensation
Benefits Offered: Behavioral Health, Chiropractic, Disease Management, Inpatient SNF, Physical Therapy, Podiatry, Prescription, Psychiatric, Transplant, Vision, Wellness
Offers Demand Management Patient Information Service: Yes

Type of Coverage
Commercial, Individual, Medicare, Medicaid

Type of Payment Plans Offered
POS, DFFS, Capitated, FFS, Combination FFS & DFFS

Geographic Areas Served
Statewide

Subscriber Information
Average Subscriber Co-Payment:
Home Health Care: $0
Nursing Home: $0

Peer Review Type
Utilization Review: Yes
Case Management: Yes

Publishes and Distributes Report Card: No

Accreditation Certification
URAC, NCQA, CORE
Utilization Review, Pre-Admission Certification, State Licensure, Quality Assurance Program

Key Personnel
Regional President . . . . Kathie Mancini

Specialty Managed Care Partners
Enters into Contracts with Regional Business Coalitions: No

---

624 Medical Mutual
2060 E 9th Street
Cleveland, OH 44115-1355
Toll-Free: 800-382-5729
www.medmutual.com
Year Founded: 1934

Healthplan and Services Defined
PLAN TYPE: HMO
Model Type: Staff
Benefits Offered: Prescription

Type of Coverage
Commercial, Individual, Medicare

Type of Payment Plans Offered
DFFS, Capitated, FFS, Combination FFS & DFFS

Geographic Areas Served
Statewide

Publishes and Distributes Report Card: Yes

Accreditation Certification
NCQA

Key Personnel
Chairman, President & CEO . . . . Rick Chiricosta
EVP, Chief Health Officer . . . . Kathy Golovan
EVP, Financial Officer . . . . Ray Mueller
Chief Information Officer . . . . John Kish
Chief Medical Officer . . . . Tere Koenig
Chief Marketing Officer . . . . Steffany Larkins

Specialty Managed Care Partners
Enters into Contracts with Regional Business Coalitions: Yes

---

625 Medical Mutual Services
PO Box 5700
Cleveland, OH 44101
Toll-Free: 800-367-3762
www.mutualhealthservices.com
Number of Primary Care Physicians: 24,000
Total Enrollment: 144,000

Healthplan and Services Defined
PLAN TYPE: PPO
Benefits Offered: Chiropractic, Physical Therapy, Podiatry, Psychiatric

Type of Coverage
Commercial, Self Funded, Insurance Companies

Geographic Areas Served
South Carolina, Georgia, Ohio

Accreditation Certification
TJC, NCQA

---

626 MediGold
6150 East Broad Street
Suite EE320
Columbus, OH 43213-1574
Toll-Free: 800-964-4525
Fax: 833-256-2871
www.medigold.com
Subsidiary of: Mount Carmel Health Plan
Non-Profit Organization: Yes
Year Founded: 1997
Federally Qualified: Yes
Number of Affiliated Hospitals: 23
Number of Primary Care Physicians: 1,050
Number of Referral/Specialty Physicians: 1,850
Total Enrollment: 55,000
State Enrollment: 55,000

Healthplan and Services Defined
PLAN TYPE: Medicare
Model Type: Network, Medicare
Benefits Offered: Behavioral Health, Chiropractic, Dental, Disease Management, Home Care, Inpatient SNF, Physical Therapy, Podiatry, Prescription, Psychiatric, Vision, Wellness, Medical, OP Services, Drug Coverage

Type of Coverage
Individual, Medicare
Catastrophic Illness Benefit: Unlimited

Type of Payment Plans Offered
Combination FFS & DFFS

Geographic Areas Served
33 counties in Ohio

Subscriber Information
Average Monthly Fee Per Subscriber
(Employee + Employer Contribution):

Employee Only (Self): Varies
Medicare: Varies
Average Annual Deductible Per Subscriber:
Employee Only (Self): Varies
Medicare: Varies
Average Subscriber Co-Payment:
Primary Care Physician: Varies
Non-Network Physician: Varies
Prescription Drugs: Varies
Hospital ER: Varies
Home Health Care: Varies
Home Health Care Max. Days/Visits Covered: Varies
Nursing Home: Varies
Nursing Home Max. Days/Visits Covered: Varies

Network Qualifications
Pre-Admission Certification: Yes

Peer Review Type
Utilization Review: Yes
Case Management: Yes

Publishes and Distributes Report Card: Yes

Accreditation Certification
TJC Accreditation, Medicare Approved, Utilization Review, Pre-Admission Certification, State Licensure, Quality Assurance Program

Key Personnel
President/CEO .... Mike Demand, PhD
Chief Admin Officer .... Chuck Alvarado
VP, Network Management .... Matt Barrett
VP, Finance .... Juan Fraiz
VP, Health Services .... Karen Phillippi
VP, Compliance/Governance .... Larry Pliskin, JD
CMO/Medical Director .... Greg Wise, MD

Specialty Managed Care Partners
PBM-CAREMARK

Employer References
Timken, Mount Carmel Trinity

---

627 Molina Healthcare of Ohio
3000 Corporate Exchange Drive
Columbus, OH 43231
Toll-Free: 800-642-4168
www.molinahealthcare.com
Subsidiary of: Molina Healthcare, Inc.
For Profit Organization: Yes
Year Founded: 1980
Physician Owned Organization: Yes

Healthplan and Services Defined
PLAN TYPE: Medicare
Model Type: Network
Plan Specialty: Integrated Medicare/Medicaid (Duals)
Benefits Offered: Chiropractic, Dental, Home Care, Inpatient SNF, Long-Term Care, Podiatry, Vision

Type of Coverage
Commercial, Medicare, Supplemental Medicare, Medicaid

Accreditation Certification
URAC, NCQA

Key Personnel
President .... Ami Cole
Chief Medical Officer.............. Kimberly Chen, MD

---

628 Ohio Health Choice
P.O. Box 2090
Akron, OH 44309-2090
Toll-Free: 800-554-0027
contactus@ohiohealthchoice.com
www.ohiohealthchoice.com
Mailing Address: P.O. Box 3619, Akron, OH 44309-3619
For Profit Organization: Yes
Year Founded: 1982
Number of Affiliated Hospitals: 189
Number of Primary Care Physicians: 38,000
Number of Referral/Specialty Physicians: 3,600
Total Enrollment: 370,000
State Enrollment: 370,000

Healthplan and Services Defined
PLAN TYPE: PPO
Model Type: Network
Plan Specialty: Chiropractic, Disease Management, EPO, UR
Benefits Offered: Behavioral Health, Chiropractic, Disease Management, Home Care, Inpatient SNF, Long-Term Care, Physical Therapy, Podiatry, Psychiatric, Transplant, Wellness, Audiology, durable medical equipment, sleep disorder services, speech therapy

Type of Coverage
Commercial, Individual, Indemnity, Medicare

Type of Payment Plans Offered
POS, FFS

Geographic Areas Served
Throughout Ohio as well as the contiguous counties of Boone, Boyd, Campbell, Grant and Kenton in Kentucky; Dearborn in Indiana; Mercer and Erie in Pennsylvania; and Wood, Hancock and Ohio in West Virginia

Peer Review Type
Utilization Review: Yes
Second Surgical Opinion: Yes
Case Management: Yes

---

629 Ohio State University Health Plan Inc.
700 Ackerman Road
Suite 1007
Columbus, OH 43202
Toll-Free: 800-678-6269
Phone: 614-292-4700
OSUHealthPlanCS@osumc.edu
www.osuhealthplan.com
Non-Profit Organization: Yes
Year Founded: 1991
Number of Affiliated Hospitals: 95
Number of Primary Care Physicians: 3,250
Number of Referral/Specialty Physicians: 7,950
Total Enrollment: 52,000
State Enrollment: 52,000

Healthplan and Services Defined
  PLAN TYPE: Multiple
  Model Type: IPA
  Plan Specialty: ASO, Behavioral Health, Disease Management, EPO
  Benefits Offered: Behavioral Health, Chiropractic, Complementary Medicine, Dental, Disease Management, Home Care, Inpatient SNF, Physical Therapy, Podiatry, Prescription, Psychiatric, Transplant, Vision, Wellness
  Offers Demand Management Patient Information Service: Yes
  DMPI Services Offered: Faculty and Staff Assistance Program, University Health Connection

Type of Payment Plans Offered
  DFFS, Capitated, Combination FFS & DFFS

Geographic Areas Served
  Ohio State University employees and their dependents

Subscriber Information
  Average Annual Deductible Per Subscriber:
    Employee Only (Self): $0
    Employee & 1 Family Member: $0
    Employee & 2 Family Members: $0
    Medicare: $0
  Average Subscriber Co-Payment:
    Primary Care Physician: $15.00
    Non-Network Physician: 30%
    Prescription Drugs: 20% (generic)
    Hospital ER: $75.00
    Home Health Care: 20%
    Home Health Care Max. Days/Visits Covered: Unlimited
    Nursing Home: $0
    Nursing Home Max. Days/Visits Covered: 60 days

Network Qualifications
  Pre-Admission Certification: Yes

Peer Review Type
  Utilization Review: Yes
  Second Surgical Opinion: No
  Case Management: Yes

Publishes and Distributes Report Card: No

Accreditation Certification
  NCQA
  TJC Accreditation, Medicare Approved, Utilization Review, Pre-Admission Certification, State Licensure, Quality Assurance Program

Key Personnel
  CEO/CFO/CAO .... Kelly Hamilton
  Medical Director .... Rob Cooper, MD

Specialty Managed Care Partners
  Enters into Contracts with Regional Business Coalitions: No

Employer References
  Ohio State University

---

630 Paramount Elite Medicare Plan
PO Box 928
Toledo, OH 43697-0497
Toll-Free: 800-462-3589
Phone: 419-887-2525
Fax: 419-887-2047
paramount.memberservices@promedica.org
www.paramounthealthcare.com
Subsidiary of: ProMedica Health System
Year Founded: 1988
Number of Affiliated Hospitals: 34
Number of Primary Care Physicians: 1,900
Total Enrollment: 187,000

Healthplan and Services Defined
  PLAN TYPE: Medicare
  Other Type: HMO
  Benefits Offered: Chiropractic, Dental, Disease Management, Home Care, Inpatient SNF, Physical Therapy, Podiatry, Prescription, Psychiatric, Vision

Type of Coverage
  Individual, Medicare

Geographic Areas Served
  Ohio: Lucas and Wood counties; Michigan: Monroe County

Subscriber Information
  Average Monthly Fee Per Subscriber (Employee + Employer Contribution):
    Employee Only (Self): Varies
    Medicare: Varies
  Average Annual Deductible Per Subscriber:
    Employee Only (Self): Varies
    Medicare: Varies
  Average Subscriber Co-Payment:
    Primary Care Physician: Varies
    Non-Network Physician: Varies
    Prescription Drugs: Varies
    Hospital ER: Varies
    Home Health Care: Varies
    Home Health Care Max. Days/Visits Covered: Varies
    Nursing Home: Varies
    Nursing Home Max. Days/Visits Covered: Varies

Key Personnel
  President .... Lori Johnston
  Chief Financial Officer .... Jeff Martin
  Chief Operating Officer .... Jered Wilson

---

631 Paramount Health Care
PO Box 928
Toledo, OH 43697-0497
Toll-Free: 800-462-3589
Phone: 419-887-2525
paramount.memberservices@promedica.org
www.paramounthealthcare.com
Subsidiary of: ProMedica Health System
For Profit Organization: Yes
Year Founded: 1988
Number of Affiliated Hospitals: 34
Number of Primary Care Physicians: 1,900

Number of Referral/Specialty Physicians: 900
Total Enrollment: 187,000

Healthplan and Services Defined
  PLAN TYPE: HMO/PPO
  Model Type: Network
  Benefits Offered: Dental, Prescription, Vision, Worker's Compensation

Type of Coverage
  Commercial, Individual, Medicare, Medicaid

Geographic Areas Served
  Northwest Ohio and Southeast Michigan

Subscriber Information
  Average Monthly Fee Per Subscriber
    (Employee + Employer Contribution):
      Employee Only (Self): Varies by plan
  Average Annual Deductible Per Subscriber:
      Employee Only (Self): Varies
      Employee & 1 Family Member: Varies
      Employee & 2 Family Members: Varies
  Average Subscriber Co-Payment:
      Primary Care Physician: Varies
      Prescription Drugs: Varies
      Hospital ER: $25.00
      Home Health Care: $0
      Home Health Care Max. Days/Visits Covered: Unlimited
      Nursing Home: $0
      Nursing Home Max. Days/Visits Covered: 100 days

Network Qualifications
  Pre-Admission Certification: Yes

Peer Review Type
  Second Surgical Opinion: Yes

Publishes and Distributes Report Card: Yes

Accreditation Certification
  URAC, NCQA

Key Personnel
  President .... Lori Johnston
  Chief Financial Officer .... Jeff Martin
  Chief Operating Officer .... Jered Wilson

---

632 Prime Time Health Medicare Plan
2600 Sixth Street SW
Canton, OH 44710
Toll-Free: 800-577-5084
Phone: 330-363-7407
www.primetimehealthplan.com
Mailing Address: P.O. Box 6905, Canton, OH 44706
Subsidiary of: Aultcare
Year Founded: 1997
Total Enrollment: 20,000
State Enrollment: 20,000

Healthplan and Services Defined
  PLAN TYPE: Medicare
  Benefits Offered: Chiropractic, Dental, Disease Management, Home Care, Inpatient SNF, Physical Therapy, Podiatry, Prescription, Psychiatric, Vision, Wellness

Type of Coverage
  Individual, Medicare, Medicaid

Geographic Areas Served
  Portage, Medina, Summit, Stark, Carroll, Columbiana, Holmes, Harrison, Trumbull, Mahoning, Tuscarawas and Wayne counties

Subscriber Information
  Average Monthly Fee Per Subscriber
    (Employee + Employer Contribution):
      Employee Only (Self): Varies
      Medicare: Varies
  Average Annual Deductible Per Subscriber:
      Employee Only (Self): Varies
      Medicare: Varies
  Average Subscriber Co-Payment:
      Primary Care Physician: Varies
      Non-Network Physician: Varies
      Prescription Drugs: Varies
      Hospital ER: Varies
      Home Health Care: Varies
      Home Health Care Max. Days/Visits Covered: Varies
      Nursing Home: Varies
      Nursing Home Max. Days/Visits Covered: Varies

Key Personnel
  President/CEO .... Rick Haines

---

633 S&S HealthCare Strategies
1385 Kemper Meadow Drive
Cincinnati, OH 45240
Toll-Free: 800-717-2872
Phone: 513-772-8866
Fax: 513-772-9174
servicedesk@ss-healthcare.com
www.ss-healthcare.com
Subsidiary of: International Managed Care Strategies
Year Founded: 1994

Healthplan and Services Defined
  PLAN TYPE: Other
  Plan Specialty: Third Party Administrator
  Benefits Offered: Dental, Prescription, Vision

Type of Payment Plans Offered
  POS, DFFS, FFS

Peer Review Type
  Second Surgical Opinion: No
  Case Management: No

Publishes and Distributes Report Card: Yes

Specialty Managed Care Partners
  Enters into Contracts with Regional Business Coalitions: Yes

---

634 SummaCare Medicare Advantage Plan
1200 East Market Street
Akron, OH 44305-4018
Toll-Free: 800-996-8411
www.summacare.com
Subsidiary of: Summa Health System
For Profit Organization: Yes

Year Founded: 1993
Physician Owned Organization: Yes
Number of Affiliated Hospitals: 60
Number of Primary Care Physicians: 10,000
Total Enrollment: 26,000
State Enrollment: 73,724

Healthplan and Services Defined
  PLAN TYPE: Medicare
  Model Type: IPA, PPO, POS
  Benefits Offered: Behavioral Health, Chiropractic, Complementary Medicine, Dental, Disease Management, Home Care, Inpatient SNF, Physical Therapy, Podiatry, Prescription, Psychiatric, Transplant, Vision, Wellness, AD&D, Life
  Offers Demand Management Patient Information Service: Yes
  DMPI Services Offered: Nurses Line

Type of Coverage
  Medicare
  Catastrophic Illness Benefit: Covered

Type of Payment Plans Offered
  POS, DFFS, FFS

Geographic Areas Served
  Northeast Ohio: Cuyahoga, Geauga, Medina, Portage, Stark, Summit, Wayne, Tuscarawas, Ashtabula, Caroll, Mahoning, Trumbull & Lorain counties

Subscriber Information
  Average Monthly Fee Per Subscriber
    (Employee + Employer Contribution):
      Employee Only (Self): Proprietary
  Average Annual Deductible Per Subscriber:
      Employee Only (Self): $0
      Employee & 1 Family Member: $0
      Employee & 2 Family Members: $0
      Medicare: $45.00
  Average Subscriber Co-Payment:
      Primary Care Physician: $5.00/10.00
      Prescription Drugs: $5.00/10.00
      Hospital ER: $50.00
      Home Health Care: $0 if in-network
      Home Health Care Max. Days/Visits Covered: 30 days
      Nursing Home: $0 if in-network
      Nursing Home Max. Days/Visits Covered: 100 days

Network Qualifications
  Pre-Admission Certification: Yes

Peer Review Type
  Utilization Review: Yes
  Second Surgical Opinion: Yes
  Case Management: Yes

Accreditation Certification
  NCQA
  TJC Accreditation, Medicare Approved, Utilization Review, Pre-Admission Certification, State Licensure, Quality Assurance Program

Key Personnel
  President .... Bill Epling
  Chief Medical Officer .... Charles A. Zonfa, MD
  Chief Operations Officer .... Stephen Adamson
  Chief Financial Officer .... Alan Fehlner
  VP, Marketing .... Michelle Bisson
  VP, Commercial Sales .... Kevin Cavalier

Specialty Managed Care Partners
  Enters into Contracts with Regional Business Coalitions: Yes
  Akron Regional Development Board, Canton Regional Chamber of Commerce, Home Builders Association

Employer References
  Goodyear, Summa Health System, Cuyahoga County, University of Akron, Akron Public Schools

---

635 Superior Dental Care
6683 Centerville Business Parkway
Centerville, OH 45459
Toll-Free: 800-762-3159
Phone: 937-438-0283
www.superiordental.com
Year Founded: 1986
Physician Owned Organization: Yes

Healthplan and Services Defined
  PLAN TYPE: Dental
  Model Type: Network, POS
  Plan Specialty: Dental
  Benefits Offered: Dental, Vision

Type of Payment Plans Offered
  FFS

Geographic Areas Served
  Nationwide

Publishes and Distributes Report Card: Yes

Key Personnel
  Chairman .... Richard W. Portune
  President .... L. Don Shumaker

---

636 The Dental Care Plus Group
100 Crowne Point Place
Cincinnati, OH 45241
Toll-Free: 800-367-9466
Phone: 513-554-1100
Fax: 513-554-3187
www.dentalcareplus.com
For Profit Organization: Yes
Year Founded: 1986
Physician Owned Organization: Yes
Number of Primary Care Physicians: 246,000
Total Enrollment: 300,000

Healthplan and Services Defined
  PLAN TYPE: Multiple
  Model Type: IPA
  Plan Specialty: Dental, Vision
  Benefits Offered: Dental, Vision

Type of Payment Plans Offered
  POS

Geographic Areas Served
  Ohio, Kentucky and Indiana

Peer Review Type
Utilization Review: Yes

Key Personnel
President/CEO/CFO . . . . Robert C. Hodgkins, Jr.
Marketing/Communications . . . . Julie Lange

637 Trinity Health of Ohio
Mount Carmel Health System
6001 E Broad Street
Columbus, OH 43213
Phone: 614-234-6000
www.trinity-health.org
Subsidiary of: Trinity Health
Non-Profit Organization: Yes
Year Founded: 2013
Number of Primary Care Physicians: 257
Number of Referral/Specialty Physicians: 1,250
Total Enrollment: 30,000,000

Healthplan and Services Defined
PLAN TYPE: Other
Benefits Offered: Disease Management, Home Care, Long-Term Care, Psychiatric, Hospice programs, PACE (Program of All Inclusive Care for the Elderly)

Geographic Areas Served
Greater Central Ohio

Key Personnel
President . . . . Daniel Wendorff
Medical Director . . . . Loren Ledheiser
Chief Operating Officer . . . . Michael Ceballos

638 UnitedHealthcare Community Plan Ohio
UnitedHealthcare Customer Service
P.O. Box 30769
Salt Lake City, UT 84130-0769
Toll-Free: 888-545-5205
www.uhccommunityplan.com/oh
Subsidiary of: UnitedHealth Group
For Profit Organization: Yes

Healthplan and Services Defined
PLAN TYPE: Medicare
Other Type: Medicaid
Model Type: Network
Benefits Offered: Dental, Home Care, Podiatry, Prescription, Vision, Wellness, Hearing, Acupuncture, Chiropractic

Type of Coverage
Medicare, Medicaid

Geographic Areas Served
Varies by plan

Key Personnel
CEO, Community Plan OH . . . . Scott Waulters

639 UnitedHealthcare of Ohio
3608 Euclid Avenue
Cleveland, OH 44114
Toll-Free: 888-835-9637
www.uhc.com
Secondary Address: 4342 Harrison Avenue, Cincinnati, OH 45211
Subsidiary of: UnitedHealth Group
For Profit Organization: Yes
Year Founded: 1980

Healthplan and Services Defined
PLAN TYPE: HMO/PPO
Model Type: Network
Plan Specialty: Behavioral Health, Dental, Disease Management, PBM, Vision
Benefits Offered: Behavioral Health, Dental, Disease Management, Long-Term Care, Prescription, Vision, Wellness, Life, LTD, STD

Type of Coverage
Individual, Medicare, Supplemental Medicare, Medicaid, Catastrophic, Family, Military, Veterans, Group

Geographic Areas Served
Statewide

Subscriber Information
Average Subscriber Co-Payment:
Primary Care Physician: $15.00
Prescription Drugs: $15.00

Accreditation Certification
NCQA

Key Personnel
CEO, Ohio . . . . Kurt Lewis

OKLAHOMA

Health Insurance Coverage Status and Type of Coverage by Age

Category	All Persons Number	%	Under 19 years Number	%	Under 65 years Number	%
Total population	3,872 *(2)*	100.0 *(0.0)*	1,005 *(3)*	100.0 *(0.0)*	3,256 *(3)*	100.0 *(0.0)*
Covered by some type of health insurance	3,319 *(14)*	85.7 *(0.3)*	919 *(7)*	91.4 *(0.6)*	2,707 *(14)*	83.2 *(0.4)*
Covered by private health insurance	2,474 *(18)*	63.9 *(0.5)*	529 *(10)*	52.6 *(0.9)*	2,095 *(17)*	64.3 *(0.5)*
Employer-based	1,966 *(21)*	50.8 *(0.5)*	449 *(9)*	44.7 *(0.9)*	1,784 *(20)*	54.8 *(0.6)*
Direct purchase	512 *(12)*	13.2 *(0.3)*	63 *(5)*	6.2 *(0.5)*	302 *(10)*	9.3 *(0.3)*
TRICARE	161 *(9)*	4.2 *(0.2)*	41 *(5)*	4.1 *(0.5)*	109 *(9)*	3.4 *(0.3)*
Covered by public health insurance	1,337 *(13)*	34.5 *(0.3)*	435 *(10)*	43.3 *(1.0)*	743 *(14)*	22.8 *(0.4)*
Medicaid	670 *(13)*	17.3 *(0.3)*	418 *(10)*	41.6 *(1.0)*	607 *(13)*	18.7 *(0.4)*
Medicare	724 *(6)*	18.7 *(0.2)*	21 *(4)*	2.1 *(0.4)*	131 *(6)*	4.0 *(0.2)*
VA Care	131 *(4)*	3.4 *(0.1)*	2 *(1)*	0.2 *(0.1)*	62 *(4)*	1.9 *(0.1)*
Not covered at any time during the year	553 *(14)*	14.3 *(0.3)*	86 *(6)*	8.6 *(0.6)*	549 *(14)*	16.8 *(0.4)*

Note: Numbers in thousands; Figures cover civilian noninstitutionalized population in 2019; N/A indicates that data was not available; Z represents or rounds to zero; Margin of error appears in parenthesis and is calculated using replicate weights.
Source: U.S. Census Bureau, American Community Survey, Table HI-05. Health Insurance Coverage Status and Type of Coverage by State and Age for All People: 2019

Oklahoma

640 Aetna Health of Oklahoma
151 Farmington Avenue
Hartford, CT 06156
Toll-Free: 800-872-3862
www.aetna.com
Subsidiary of: CVS Health / Aetna Inc.
For Profit Organization: Yes

Healthplan and Services Defined
PLAN TYPE: HMO/PPO
Other Type: POS
Model Type: Network
Plan Specialty: Behavioral Health, EPO, Lab, PBM, Radiology
Benefits Offered: Behavioral Health, Dental, Disease Management, Long-Term Care, Physical Therapy, Podiatry, Prescription, Psychiatric, Vision, Wellness, Life, LTD, STD

Type of Coverage
Commercial, Student health

Geographic Areas Served
Statewide

Key Personnel
Market Pres., So. Central . . . . LaMonte Thomas

641 Ascension At Home
Jane Phillips Regional Home Care
219 N Virginia
Bartlesville, OK 74003
Phone: 918-907-3010
Fax: 844-721-8184
ascensionathome.com
Subsidiary of: Ascension
Non-Profit Organization: Yes

Healthplan and Services Defined
PLAN TYPE: Other
Plan Specialty: Disease Management
Benefits Offered: Dental, Disease Management, Home Care, Wellness, Ambulance & Transportation; Nursing Service; Short-and-long-term care management planning; Hospice

Geographic Areas Served
Texas, Alabama, Indiana, Kansas, Michigan, Mississippi, Oklahoma, Wisconsin

Key Personnel
President. . . . . David Grams
Chair/CEO . . . . James A. Deal

642 Blue Cross & Blue Shield of Oklahoma
1400 S Boston
Tulsa, OK 74119
Toll-Free: 800-942-5837
Phone: 918-551-3500
www.bcbsok.com
Secondary Address: 7777E 42nd Place, Tulsa, OK 74145
Subsidiary of: Health Care Service Corporation
Non-Profit Organization: Yes

Year Founded: 1940
Number of Affiliated Hospitals: 88
Number of Primary Care Physicians: 1,551
Number of Referral/Specialty Physicians: 6,000
Total Enrollment: 700,000
State Enrollment: 700,000

Healthplan and Services Defined
PLAN TYPE: HMO/PPO
Model Type: IPA
Plan Specialty: ASO, Behavioral Health, Chiropractic, Dental, Disease Management, Lab, MSO, PBM, Vision, Radiology, UR
Benefits Offered: Behavioral Health, Chiropractic, Dental, Disease Management, Home Care, Inpatient SNF, Long-Term Care, Physical Therapy, Podiatry, Prescription, Psychiatric, Transplant, Vision, Worker's Compensation, Life, LTD, STD

Type of Coverage
Commercial, Individual, Indemnity, Medicare, Supplemental Medicare, Student health, Short-term

Type of Payment Plans Offered
POS, FFS

Geographic Areas Served
Statewide

Subscriber Information
Average Annual Deductible Per Subscriber:
  Employee Only (Self): $500.00
Average Subscriber Co-Payment:
  Primary Care Physician: $10.00
  Prescription Drugs: 10/20/30%

Network Qualifications
Pre-Admission Certification: Yes

Peer Review Type
Utilization Review: Yes
Second Surgical Opinion: Yes
Case Management: Yes

Accreditation Certification
URAC

Key Personnel
President. . . . . Joseph R. Cunningham, MD
Communications/Pub Rel. . . . . Lauren Cusick
  918-551-2002
  lauren_cusick@bcbsok.com

Specialty Managed Care Partners
Enters into Contracts with Regional Business Coalitions: Yes

Employer References
Federal Employee Program, The Williams Companies, OneOK, Helmerich & Payne, Bank of Oklahoma

643 CommunityCare
Williams Center Tower II
2 West 2nd Street, Suite 100
Tulsa, OK 74103
Toll-Free: 800-278-7563
Phone: 918-594-5200
www.ccok.com

For Profit Organization: Yes
Total Enrollment: 500,000

Healthplan and Services Defined
PLAN TYPE: Multiple
Benefits Offered: Disease Management, Prescription, Vision, Wellness

Type of Coverage
Commercial, Medicare, Supplemental Medicare

Type of Payment Plans Offered
POS

Geographic Areas Served
Oklahoma

Key Personnel
President/CEO .... Bob Bush
SVP/CFO .... Jeff Butcher
SVP/Chief Medical Officer .... Lee Mills
VP, Operations .... Sherri White

644 Delta Dental of Oklahoma
16 NW 63rd Street
Oklahoma City, OK 73116
Toll-Free: 800-522-0188
Phone: 405-607-2100
customerservice@deltadentalok.org
www.deltadentalok.org
Secondary Address: Customer Service Department, P.O. Box 54709, Oklahoma City, OK 73154-1709
Non-Profit Organization: Yes
Year Founded: 1973
Number of Primary Care Physicians: 1,700
Total Enrollment: 1,000,000

Healthplan and Services Defined
PLAN TYPE: Dental
Other Type: Dental PPO
Model Type: Network
Plan Specialty: ASO, Dental
Benefits Offered: Dental

Type of Coverage
Commercial, Individual, Group
Catastrophic Illness Benefit: None

Geographic Areas Served
Statewide

Subscriber Information
Average Subscriber Co-Payment:
Prescription Drugs: $0
Home Health Care: $0
Nursing Home: $0

Key Personnel
President & CEO .... John Gladden
Chief Financial Officer .... Ashley Albright
Chief Operating Officer .... Tania Foss
Chief Information Officer .... David Jones
Vice President of Sales .... Lan Miller

645 HCSC Insurance Services Company Oklahoma
1400 S. Boston Ave.
Tulsa, OK 74119
Phone: 918-560-3500
hcsc.com
Subsidiary of: Blue Cross Blue Shield Association
Non-Profit Organization: Yes
Year Founded: 1936
Number of Primary Care Physicians: 21,700
Total Enrollment: 830,000
State Enrollment: 830,000

Healthplan and Services Defined
PLAN TYPE: HMO
Benefits Offered: Behavioral Health, Dental, Disease Management, Psychiatric, Wellness

Geographic Areas Served
Statewide

Key Personnel
President, OK Plan. .... Stephania Grober

646 Humana Health Insurance of Oklahoma
6808 S Memorial Drive
Suite 202
Tulsa, OK 74133
Toll-Free: 800-681-0637
Phone: 918-237-4707
Fax: 918-499-2297
www.humana.com
Subsidiary of: Humana Inc.
For Profit Organization: Yes

Healthplan and Services Defined
PLAN TYPE: HMO/PPO
Model Type: Network
Plan Specialty: Dental, Vision
Benefits Offered: Dental, Vision, Life, LTD, STD

Type of Coverage
Commercial, Individual

Geographic Areas Served
Statewide

Accreditation Certification
URAC, NCQA, CORE

Key Personnel
Senior Manager..................... Jeremy Driggers

647 Mercy Clinic Oklahoma
4300 W Memorial Road
Oklahoma City, OK 73120
Phone: 405-755-1515
mercy.net
Subsidiary of: IBM Watson Health
Non-Profit Organization: Yes
Number of Affiliated Hospitals: 44
Number of Primary Care Physicians: 700
Number of Referral/Specialty Physicians: 2,000

Oklahoma

Healthplan and Services Defined
  PLAN TYPE: HMO
  Benefits Offered: Behavioral Health, Disease Management, Home Care, Inpatient SNF, Physical Therapy, Podiatry, Vision, Wellness, Non-Surgical Weight Loss; Urgent Care; Dermatology; Rehabilitation; Breast Cancer; Orthopedics; Ostoclerosis; Pediatrics

Geographic Areas Served
  Arkansas, Kansas, Missouri, and Oklahoma

Key Personnel
  Regional Strategy Officer . . . . Jim Gebhart

Type of Coverage
  Commercial, Individual, Medicare, Supplemental Medicare, Medicaid, Catastrophic, Family, Military, Veterans, Group

Geographic Areas Served
  Statewide. Oklahoma is covered by the Texas branch

Network Qualifications
  Pre-Admission Certification: Yes

Publishes and Distributes Report Card: Yes

Accreditation Certification
  AAPI, NCQA

Key Personnel
  CEO, TX/OK . . . . David Milich

Specialty Managed Care Partners
  Enters into Contracts with Regional Business Coalitions: Yes

648 UnitedHealthcare Community Plan Oklahoma

UnitedHealthcare Customer Service
P.O. Box 30769
Salt Lake City, UT 84130-0769
Toll-Free: 888-545-5205
www.uhccommunityplan.com/ok
Subsidiary of: UnitedHealth Group
For Profit Organization: Yes

Healthplan and Services Defined
  PLAN TYPE: Medicare
  Other Type: Medicaid
  Model Type: Network
  Benefits Offered: Dental, Home Care, Podiatry, Prescription, Vision, Wellness, Hearing, Acupuncture, Chiropractic

Type of Coverage
  Medicare, Medicaid

Geographic Areas Served
  Adair, Canadian, Cherokee, Cleveland, Craig, Creek, Delaware, Grady, Kingfisher, Lincoln, Logan, McClain, Muskogee, Oklahoma, Osage, Pottawatomie, Seminole, Sequoyah, Tulsa, and Wagoner

Key Personnel
  CEO, Community Plan OK . . . . Keith Derks
    keith_derks@uhc.com

649 UnitedHealthcare of Oklahoma

1250 S Capital of Texas Highway
Suite 1
Austin, TX 78746
Toll-Free: 888-545-5205
Phone: 512-347-2600
www.uhc.com
Subsidiary of: UnitedHealth Group
For Profit Organization: Yes
Year Founded: 1986

Healthplan and Services Defined
  PLAN TYPE: HMO/PPO
  Model Type: Network
  Plan Specialty: Behavioral Health, Dental, Disease Management, PBM, Vision
  Benefits Offered: Behavioral Health, Dental, Disease Management, Long-Term Care, Prescription, Vision, Wellness, AD&D, Life, LTD, STD

OREGON

Health Insurance Coverage Status and Type of Coverage by Age

Category	All Persons Number	%	Under 19 years Number	%	Under 65 years Number	%
Total population	4,175 *(2)*	100.0 *(0.0)*	914 *(4)*	100.0 *(0.0)*	3,418 *(4)*	100.0 *(0.0)*
Covered by some type of health insurance	3,876 *(14)*	92.8 *(0.3)*	877 *(6)*	95.9 *(0.6)*	3,123 *(14)*	91.4 *(0.4)*
Covered by private health insurance	2,840 *(26)*	68.0 *(0.6)*	574 *(13)*	62.8 *(1.4)*	2,396 *(25)*	70.1 *(0.7)*
Employer-based	2,298 *(28)*	55.0 *(0.7)*	518 *(14)*	56.6 *(1.5)*	2,100 *(28)*	61.4 *(0.8)*
Direct purchase	598 *(14)*	14.3 *(0.3)*	59 *(6)*	6.5 *(0.6)*	321 *(12)*	9.4 *(0.4)*
TRICARE	86 *(7)*	2.1 *(0.2)*	13 *(3)*	1.4 *(0.3)*	47 *(5)*	1.4 *(0.2)*
Covered by public health insurance	1,606 *(23)*	38.5 *(0.5)*	344 *(12)*	37.6 *(1.3)*	874 *(22)*	25.6 *(0.6)*
Medicaid	874 *(23)*	20.9 *(0.5)*	340 *(12)*	37.2 *(1.3)*	787 *(22)*	23.0 *(0.6)*
Medicare	822 *(7)*	19.7 *(0.2)*	5 *(1)*	0.5 *(0.1)*	92 *(5)*	2.7 *(0.2)*
VA Care	121 *(5)*	2.9 *(0.1)*	2 *(1)*	0.2 *(0.1)*	53 *(4)*	1.5 *(0.1)*
Not covered at any time during the year	299 *(13)*	7.2 *(0.3)*	38 *(5)*	4.1 *(0.6)*	295 *(13)*	8.6 *(0.4)*

Note: Numbers in thousands; Figures cover civilian noninstitutionalized population in 2019; N/A indicates that data was not available; Z represents or rounds to zero; Margin of error appears in parenthesis and is calculated using replicate weights.
Source: U.S. Census Bureau, American Community Survey, Table HI-05. Health Insurance Coverage Status and Type of Coverage by State and Age for All People: 2019

Oregon

650 Aetna Health of Oregon
151 Farmington Avenue
Hartford, CT 06156
Toll-Free: 800-872-3862
www.aetna.com
Subsidiary of: CVS Health / Aetna Inc.
For Profit Organization: Yes

Healthplan and Services Defined
PLAN TYPE: PPO
Other Type: POS
Model Type: Network
Plan Specialty: Behavioral Health, EPO, Lab, PBM, Radiology
Benefits Offered: Behavioral Health, Disease Management, Long-Term Care, Physical Therapy, Podiatry, Prescription, Psychiatric, Wellness, Life, LTD, STD

Type of Coverage
Commercial, Student health

Type of Payment Plans Offered
POS, FFS

Geographic Areas Served
Statewide

Key Personnel
Chief Network Officer................... John J. Wagner

651 AllCare Health
1701 NE 7th Street
Grants Pass, OR 97526
Phone: 541-471-4106
Fax: 541-471-1524
www.allcarehealth.com
Secondary Address: 100 East Main Street, Suite B, Medford, OR 97501, 541-734-5520
Year Founded: 1995
Number of Primary Care Physicians: 1,500
Total Enrollment: 54,000
State Enrollment: 54,000

Healthplan and Services Defined
PLAN TYPE: Medicare
Plan Specialty: Medicaid
Benefits Offered: Chiropractic, Dental, Disease Management, Home Care, Inpatient SNF, Physical Therapy, Podiatry, Prescription, Psychiatric, Vision, Wellness

Type of Coverage
Individual, Medicare, Medicaid

Geographic Areas Served
Southern Oregon (Josephine, Jackson, Curry counties and Glendale and Azalea in Douglas County)

Subscriber Information
Average Monthly Fee Per Subscriber
(Employee + Employer Contribution):
Employee Only (Self): Varies
Medicare: Varies
Average Annual Deductible Per Subscriber:
Employee Only (Self): Varies
Medicare: Varies
Average Subscriber Co-Payment:
Primary Care Physician: Varies
Non-Network Physician: Varies
Prescription Drugs: Varies
Hospital ER: Varies
Home Health Care: Varies
Home Health Care Max. Days/Visits Covered: Varies
Nursing Home: Varies
Nursing Home Max. Days/Visits Covered: Varies

Key Personnel
Chair .... Thomas Eagan
Vice Chair........................ Katherine Johnston
Secretary/Treasurer..................... Jessica Durant

652 Atrio Health Plans
2965 Ryan Drive SE
Salem, OR 97301
Toll-Free: 877-672-8620
Fax: 541-672-8670
www.atriohp.com

Healthplan and Services Defined
PLAN TYPE: Medicare
Other Type: HMO, PPO
Benefits Offered: Chiropractic, Dental, Disease Management, Home Care, Inpatient SNF, Physical Therapy, Podiatry, Prescription, Psychiatric, Vision, Wellness

Type of Coverage
Individual, Medicare

Geographic Areas Served
Douglas, Klamath, Josephine, Jackson, Marion, Polk, and Deschutes counties

Subscriber Information
Average Monthly Fee Per Subscriber
(Employee + Employer Contribution):
Employee Only (Self): Varies
Medicare: Varies
Average Annual Deductible Per Subscriber:
Employee Only (Self): Varies
Medicare: Varies
Average Subscriber Co-Payment:
Primary Care Physician: Varies
Non-Network Physician: Varies
Prescription Drugs: Varies
Hospital ER: Varies
Home Health Care: Varies
Home Health Care Max. Days/Visits Covered: Varies
Nursing Home: Varies
Nursing Home Max. Days/Visits Covered: Varies

Accreditation Certification
URAC

Key Personnel
President & CEO..................... Wendy Edwards
Chief of Information .... Julianne Matzell
Chief Operations Officer................. Dana Franke
General Counsel .... Charles Wilson

Chief Finance Officer . . . . Michelle Murphy
Chief Medical Officer. . . . . Steven Paulissen, MD

653 CareOregon Health Plan
315 SW Fifth Avenue
Portland, OR 97204
Toll-Free: 800-224-4840
Phone: 503-416-4100
customerservice@careoregon.org
www.careoregon.org
Non-Profit Organization: Yes
Year Founded: 1993
Number of Affiliated Hospitals: 33
Number of Primary Care Physicians: 950
Number of Referral/Specialty Physicians: 3,000
Total Enrollment: 250,000
State Enrollment: 250,000

Healthplan and Services Defined
PLAN TYPE: Medicare
Plan Specialty: Dental
Benefits Offered: Dental, Prescription, Vision, Wellness, Maternity and Family Planning

Type of Coverage
Medicare

Geographic Areas Served
20 counties in Oregon. careOregon Advantage is available for residents of Clackamas, Clatsop, Columbia, Jackson, Josephine, Marion, Multnomah, Polk and Washington counties

Key Personnel
President/CEO . . . . Eric C. Hunter
Chief Financial Officer . . . . Teresa Learn
Chief Operating Officer . . . . Amy Dowd
Chief Medical Officer . . . . Amit Shah, MD

654 Dental Health Services of Oregon
Toll-Free: 866-756-4259
www.dentalhealthservices.com
For Profit Organization: Yes
Year Founded: 1974

Healthplan and Services Defined
PLAN TYPE: Dental
Plan Specialty: Dental
Benefits Offered: Dental

Geographic Areas Served
California, Oregon, and Washington State

Accreditation Certification
URAC, NCQA

Key Personnel
Founder . . . . Godfrey Pernell

655 First Choice Health
10260 SW Greenburg Road
Suite 400
Portland, OR 97223
Phone: 877-287-2922
Fax: 503-652-8087
www.fchn.com
For Profit Organization: Yes
Year Founded: 1996
Number of Affiliated Hospitals: 94
Number of Primary Care Physicians: 980
Number of Referral/Specialty Physicians: 1,793

Healthplan and Services Defined
PLAN TYPE: PPO
Benefits Offered: Wellness

Type of Coverage
Commercial, Individual, Private & Public Plans, Geo-specifi

Geographic Areas Served
Washington, Oregon, Alaska, Idaho, Montana, Wyoming, and select areas of North Dakota and South Dakota

Key Personnel
Chief Executive Officer . . . . Jaja Okigwe
Chief Medical Officer . . . . John Robinson, MD

656 Health Net Health Plan of Oregon
13221 SW 68th Parkway
Tigard, OR 97223
Toll-Free: 888-802-7001
www.healthnet.com
Subsidiary of: Centene Corporation
For Profit Organization: Yes

Healthplan and Services Defined
PLAN TYPE: HMO
Model Type: Network
Plan Specialty: Behavioral Health

Type of Coverage
Commercial, Individual, Medicare, Supplemental Medicare

Geographic Areas Served
Statewide

Key Personnel
Chief Medical Officer . . . . Jeanne Savage, MD

657 Kaiser Permanente Northwest
500 NE Multnomah Street
Suite 100
Portland, OR 97232
Phone: 503-813-3860
thrive.kaiserpermanente.org
Subsidiary of: Kaiser Permanente
Non-Profit Organization: Yes
Year Founded: 1977
Number of Affiliated Hospitals: 47
Number of Primary Care Physicians: 1,200
Total Enrollment: 620,848
State Enrollment: 620,848

Healthplan and Services Defined
  PLAN TYPE: HMO
  Model Type: Network
  Plan Specialty: Dental, Lab, Radiology
  Benefits Offered: Behavioral Health, Dental, Disease Management, Prescription, Vision, Wellness, Worker's Compensation, Benefits vary according to plan

Type of Coverage
  Individual, Medicare, Supplemental Medicare, Medicaid

Geographic Areas Served
  Oregon & SW Washington

Accreditation Certification
  NCQA

Key Personnel
  Regional President .... Jeff Collins
  President/CEO.......................... Leong Koh, MD
  Dental Director .... John J. Snyder, DMD

---

658 LifeMap
P.O. Box 1271, MS E8L
Portland, OR 97207-1271
Toll-Free: 800-794-5390
Fax: 855-854-4570
lifemapco.com
Subsidiary of: Cambia Health Solutions
Year Founded: 1984

Healthplan and Services Defined
  PLAN TYPE: Other
  Plan Specialty: Short-term Medical
  Benefits Offered: Dental, Vision, AD&D, Life, LTD, STD

Type of Coverage
  Commercial, Individual

Geographic Areas Served
  Alaska, Idaho, Montana, Oregon, Utah, Washington, and Wyoming

Key Personnel
  President & CEO.......................... Chris Blanton
  Director of Finance .... Randy Lowell
  VP, Sales & Marketing.................... Peter Mueller
  Operations & Technology .... Scott Wilkinson
  VP, Rick Management .... Jim Clark

---

659 Managed HealthCare Northwest
422 East Burnside Street, Suite 215
P.O. Box 4629
Portland, OR 97208-4629
Phone: 503-413-5800
Fax: 503-413-5801
www.mhninc.com
Subsidiary of: Legacy Health & Adventist Medical Center
For Profit Organization: Yes
Year Founded: 1988
Number of Affiliated Hospitals: 21
Number of Primary Care Physicians: 1,228
Number of Referral/Specialty Physicians: 4,757
Total Enrollment: 125,000

Healthplan and Services Defined
  PLAN TYPE: PPO
  Model Type: Network
  Plan Specialty: Worker's Compensation, MCO, Precertification, Utilization Review
  Benefits Offered: Disease Management, Wellness, Worker's Compensation, MCO, Precertification, Utilization Review, Case Management

Type of Coverage
  Commercial, Individual

Geographic Areas Served
  Oregon: Clackamas, Clatsop, Columbia, Coos, Hood River, Lane, Marion, Multnomah, Polk, Wasco, Washington & Yamhill; Washington: Clark, Cowlitz, Klickitat & Skamania counties

Peer Review Type
  Utilization Review: Yes
  Second Surgical Opinion: Yes
  Case Management: Yes

Publishes and Distributes Report Card: No

Key Personnel
  Interim President/CEO..................... David Pyle
  Provider Relations...................... Nita Patterson

Specialty Managed Care Partners
  Enters into Contracts with Regional Business Coalitions: Yes

---

660 Moda Health Oregon
601 SW Second Avenue
Portland, OR 97204
Phone: 855-718-1767
individualplans@modahealth.com
modahealth.com
Mailing Address: P.O. Box 40384, Portland, OR 97240-0384
Year Founded: 1955

Healthplan and Services Defined
  PLAN TYPE: Multiple
  Plan Specialty: Dental, Disease Management, Health Coaches
  Benefits Offered: Behavioral Health, Complementary Medicine, Dental, Disease Management, Physical Therapy, Prescription, Wellness

Type of Coverage
  Individual

Geographic Areas Served
  Statewide, Alaska, and Washington

Key Personnel
  Chief Executive Officer .... Robert Gootee
  President .... William Johnson, MD, MBA
  Executive Vice President .... Steve Wynne

---

661 PacificSource Health Plans
555 International Way
Springfield, OR 97477
Toll-Free: 888-977-9299
www.pacificsource.com
Non-Profit Organization: Yes

Year Founded: 1933
Number of Referral/Specialty Physicians: 46,300
Total Enrollment: 275,000

Healthplan and Services Defined
PLAN TYPE: Multiple
Plan Specialty: Dental, PBM, Vision
Benefits Offered: Dental, Disease Management, Prescription, Vision, Wellness

Type of Coverage
Commercial, Individual, Medicare

Type of Payment Plans Offered
POS, Combination FFS & DFFS

Geographic Areas Served
Oregon, Montana & Idaho

Key Personnel
President/CEO . . . . Ken Provencher
EVP, Operating Officer . . . . Erick Doolen
EVP, Financial Officer . . . . Peter Davidson
EVP, Medical Officer . . . . Edward McEachern, MD
EVP/Strategy & Marketing . . . . Sharon Thomson

662 PacificSource Health Plans
555 International Way
Springfield, OR 97477
Toll-Free: 888-977-9299
www.pacificsource.com
Non-Profit Organization: Yes
Year Founded: 1933
Number of Referral/Specialty Physicians: 46,300
Total Enrollment: 275,000

Healthplan and Services Defined
PLAN TYPE: HMO/PPO
Benefits Offered: Dental, Disease Management, Prescription, Vision, Wellness

Type of Coverage
Commercial, Individual

Type of Payment Plans Offered
POS, Combination FFS & DFFS

Geographic Areas Served
Oregon, Idaho & Montana

663 Providence Health Plan
P.O. Box 4327
Portland, OR 97208-4327
Toll-Free: 800-878-4445
Phone: 503-574-7500
healthplans.providence.org
Non-Profit Organization: Yes
Year Founded: 1985

Healthplan and Services Defined
PLAN TYPE: Multiple
Model Type: IPA, Group, PHO
Plan Specialty: Disease Management, EPO, Vision, UR
Benefits Offered: Behavioral Health, Chiropractic, Complementary Medicine, Disease Management, Home Care, Inpatient SNF, Physical Therapy, Podiatry, Prescription, Psychiatric, Transplant, Vision, Wellness

Type of Coverage
Commercial, Individual, Medicare, Medicaid

Type of Payment Plans Offered
POS, FFS

Geographic Areas Served
Oregon: Clackamas, Clark, Columbia, Crook, Deschutes, Hood River, Jefferson, Lane, Marion, Multnomah, Washington, Wheeler; Washington: Clark

Peer Review Type
Utilization Review: Yes
Second Surgical Opinion: Yes
Case Management: Yes

Publishes and Distributes Report Card: Yes

Accreditation Certification
NCQA
Medicare Approved, Utilization Review, Pre-Admission Certification, State Licensure, Quality Assurance Program

Key Personnel
Chief Executive Officer . . . . Michael Cotton
Chief Financial Officer . . . . Michael White
Chief Medical Officer . . . . Robert Gluckman
Adminstrative Officer. . . . . Alison Schrupp
Chief Compliance Officer. . . . . Carrie Smith
Chief Marketing Officer . . . . Brad Garrigues

Average Claim Compensation
Physician's Fees Charged: 55%
Hospital's Fees Charged: 48%

Specialty Managed Care Partners
PBH Behavioral Health, ARGUS (PBM), Complementary Health Care, Well Partner
Enters into Contracts with Regional Business Coalitions: No

Employer References
Providence Health System, PeaceHealth, Portland Public School District, Oregon PERS, Tektonix

664 Regence BlueCross BlueShield of Oregon
100 SW Market Street
Portland, OR 97201
Toll-Free: 888-675-6570
www.regence.com
Subsidiary of: Regence
Non-Profit Organization: Yes
Total Enrollment: 2,400,000
State Enrollment: 730,000

Healthplan and Services Defined
PLAN TYPE: Multiple
Model Type: Network
Benefits Offered: Dental, Prescription, Vision, Wellness, Life, Preventive Care

Type of Coverage
Commercial, Individual, Supplemental Medicare

Geographic Areas Served
statewide

Oregon

Key Personnel
President . . . . Angela Dowling

665 Regence BlueCross BlueShield of Utah
2890 E Cottonwood Pkwy
Cottonwood Heights, UT 84121
Toll-Free: 888-367-2119
www.regence.com
Subsidiary of: Regence
Non-Profit Organization: Yes
Total Enrollment: 2,400,000
State Enrollment: 330,000

Healthplan and Services Defined
PLAN TYPE: Multiple
Model Type: Network
Benefits Offered: Dental, Prescription, Vision, Wellness, Life, Preventive Care

Type of Coverage
Commercial, Individual, Supplemental Medicare

Geographic Areas Served
Oregon and Utah

Key Personnel
President. . . . . Jim Swayze

666 Samaritan Health Plan Operations
2300 NW Walnut Boulevard
Corvallis, OR 97330
Toll-Free: 800-832-4580
Phone: 541-768-4550
www.samhealthplans.org
Subsidiary of: Samaritan Health Services
Year Founded: 1993

Healthplan and Services Defined
PLAN TYPE: Multiple
Benefits Offered: Chiropractic, Dental, Disease Management, Home Care, Inpatient SNF, Physical Therapy, Podiatry, Prescription, Psychiatric, Vision, Wellness

Type of Coverage
Commercial, Individual, Medicare

Geographic Areas Served
Statewide

Key Personnel
Chief Executive Officer . . . . Bruce Butler
Chair, Board of Directors. . . . . Doug Boysen
Chief Medical Officer . . . . Kevin Ewanchyna, MD
Chief Financial Officer . . . . Daniel B. Smith

667 Trillium Community Health Plan
555 International Way
Building B
Springfield, OR 97477
Toll-Free: 877-600-5472
Phone: 541-485-2155
Fax: 866-703-0958
www.trilliumohp.com

Secondary Address: 13221 Sw 68th Pkwy, Suite 200, Eugene, OR 97440-3940
Subsidiary of: Centene Corporation
For Profit Organization: Yes

Healthplan and Services Defined
PLAN TYPE: Other
Benefits Offered: Chiropractic, Dental, Disease Management, Home Care, Inpatient SNF, Physical Therapy, Podiatry, Prescription, Psychiatric, Vision, Wellness, Durable Medical Equipment; Hearing Aids

Type of Coverage
Medicaid

Geographic Areas Served
Serving Eugene, Springfield and the following counties: Benton, Clackamas, Clatsop, Deschutes, Douglas, Hood River, Jackson, Josephine, Klamath, Lane, Lincoln, Linn, Malheur, Marion, Polk, Umatilla, Wasco, Washington and Yamhill

Accreditation Certification
NCQA

Key Personnel
Interim Plan Pres./CEO . . . . Justin Lyman
Chief Operating Officer . . . . Suellen Narducci
Chief Medical Officer . . . . Jeanne Savage, MD
VP, Network Development. . . . . Amy Hill

668 United Concordia of Oregon
4401 Deer Path Road
Harrisburg, PA 17110
Phone: 717-260-6800
www.unitedconcordia.com
For Profit Organization: Yes
Year Founded: 1971
Number of Primary Care Physicians: 104,000
Total Enrollment: 8,800,000

Healthplan and Services Defined
PLAN TYPE: Dental
Plan Specialty: Dental
Benefits Offered: Dental

Type of Coverage
Commercial, Individual, Military personnel & families

Geographic Areas Served
Nationwide

Accreditation Certification
URAC

Key Personnel
Contact. . . . . Beth Rutherford
717-260-7659
beth.rutherford@ucci.com

669 UnitedHealthcare of Oregon
5 Centerpointe Drive
Suite 600
Lake Oswego, OR 97035
Toll-Free: 888-545-5205
Phone: 503-603-7355
www.uhc.com
Subsidiary of: UnitedHealth Group
For Profit Organization: Yes

Healthplan and Services Defined
 PLAN TYPE: HMO/PPO
 Model Type: Network
 Plan Specialty: Behavioral Health, Dental, Disease Management, PBM, Vision
 Benefits Offered: Behavioral Health, Dental, Disease Management, Long-Term Care, Prescription, Vision, Wellness, Life, LTD, STD

Type of Coverage
 Individual, Medicare, Supplemental Medicare, Medicaid, Catastrophic, Family, Military, Veterans, Group

Geographic Areas Served
 Statewide

Key Personnel
 CEO, WA/OR/MT/AK/HI .... Gary Daniels

670 Wellcare By Trillium Advantage
P.O. Box 11756
Eugene, OR 97440
Toll-Free: 844-867-1156
www.trilliumadvantage.com
Subsidiary of: Centene Corporation
For Profit Organization: Yes

Healthplan and Services Defined
 PLAN TYPE: Medicare
 Model Type: Network
 Plan Specialty: Lab
 Benefits Offered: Behavioral Health, Dental, Home Care, Inpatient SNF, Physical Therapy, Podiatry, Vision, Wellness, Hearing, Chiropractic

Type of Coverage
 Medicare

Geographic Areas Served
 Lane county

Accreditation Certification
 NCQA

671 Willamette Dental Group
6950 NE Campus Way
Hillsboro, OR 97124
Toll-Free: 855-433-6825
Fax: 503-952-2200
info@willamettedental.com
www.willamettedental.com
For Profit Organization: Yes
Year Founded: 1970

Healthplan and Services Defined
 PLAN TYPE: Dental
 Model Type: Staff
 Plan Specialty: Dental
 Benefits Offered: Dental

Type of Coverage
 Individual

Type of Payment Plans Offered
 POS, FFS

Geographic Areas Served
 Oregon, Washington and Idaho

Peer Review Type
 Case Management: Yes

Publishes and Distributes Report Card: No

Key Personnel
 President & CEO .... Dr. Eugene Skourtes, DMD

Specialty Managed Care Partners
 Enters into Contracts with Regional Business Coalitions: No

PENNSYLVANIA

Health Insurance Coverage Status and Type of Coverage by Age

Category	All Persons Number	%	Under 19 years Number	%	Under 65 years Number	%
Total population	12,593 *(2)*	100.0 *(0.0)*	2,804 *(6)*	100.0 *(0.0)*	10,284 *(4)*	100.0 *(0.0)*
Covered by some type of health insurance	11,867 *(21)*	94.2 *(0.2)*	2,676 *(12)*	95.4 *(0.3)*	9,569 *(22)*	93.0 *(0.2)*
Covered by private health insurance	9,052 *(35)*	71.9 *(0.3)*	1,779 *(19)*	63.5 *(0.7)*	7,526 *(36)*	73.2 *(0.3)*
Employer-based	7,448 *(39)*	59.1 *(0.3)*	1,615 *(19)*	57.6 *(0.7)*	6,691 *(40)*	65.1 *(0.4)*
Direct purchase	1,868 *(23)*	14.8 *(0.2)*	172 *(8)*	6.1 *(0.3)*	950 *(20)*	9.2 *(0.2)*
TRICARE	191 *(11)*	1.5 *(0.1)*	33 *(5)*	1.2 *(0.2)*	112 *(10)*	1.1 *(0.1)*
Covered by public health insurance	4,732 *(31)*	37.6 *(0.2)*	1,069 *(18)*	38.1 *(0.6)*	2,502 *(30)*	24.3 *(0.3)*
Medicaid	2,536 *(30)*	20.1 *(0.2)*	1,061 *(18)*	37.9 *(0.6)*	2,260 *(29)*	22.0 *(0.3)*
Medicare	2,567 *(11)*	20.4 *(0.1)*	15 *(2)*	0.5 *(0.1)*	338 *(9)*	3.3 *(0.1)*
VA Care	255 *(6)*	2.0 *(0.1)*	2 *(1)*	0.1 *(Z)*	99 *(6)*	1.0 *(0.1)*
Not covered at any time during the year	726 *(22)*	5.8 *(0.2)*	128 *(9)*	4.6 *(0.3)*	716 *(21)*	7.0 *(0.2)*

Note: Numbers in thousands; Figures cover civilian noninstitutionalized population in 2019; N/A indicates that data was not available; Z represents or rounds to zero; Margin of error appears in parenthesis and is calculated using replicate weights.
Source: U.S. Census Bureau, American Community Survey, Table HI-05. Health Insurance Coverage Status and Type of Coverage by State and Age for All People: 2019

Pennsylvania

672 Aetna Better Health of Pennsylvania
1422 Union Meeting Road
Blue Bell, PA 19422
Toll-Free: 866-638-1232
www.aetnabetterhealth.com/pennsylvania
Subsidiary of: CVS Health / Aetna Inc.
For Profit Organization: Yes

Healthplan and Services Defined
PLAN TYPE: HMO/PPO
Other Type: POS
Model Type: Network
Plan Specialty: Behavioral Health, EPO, Lab, PBM, Radiology
Benefits Offered: Behavioral Health, Dental, Disease Management, Long-Term Care, Physical Therapy, Podiatry, Prescription, Psychiatric, Vision, Wellness, Life, LTD, STD

Type of Coverage
Commercial, Medicaid, Student health

Geographic Areas Served
Statewide

Key Personnel
CEO . . . . Jason Rottman

673 Allwell from PA Health & Wellness
300 Corporate Center Drive
Camp Hill, PA 17011
Toll-Free: 855-766-1456
allwell.pahealthwellness.com
Subsidiary of: Centene Corporation
For Profit Organization: Yes

Healthplan and Services Defined
PLAN TYPE: Medicare
Model Type: Network
Benefits Offered: Dental, Prescription

Type of Coverage
Medicare, Supplemental Medicare, Medicare Advantage

674 Ambetter from PA Health & Wellness
5 Penn Center Boulevard
Suite 300
Pittsburgh, PA 15205
Toll-Free: 833-510-4727
ambetter.pahealthwellness.com
Subsidiary of: Centene Corporation
For Profit Organization: Yes

Healthplan and Services Defined
PLAN TYPE: Other
Model Type: Network
Plan Specialty: Lab
Benefits Offered: Behavioral Health, Disease Management, Physical Therapy, Prescription, Wellness, Maternity and newborn care

Type of Coverage
Health Insurance Marketplace

Geographic Areas Served
Bucks, Montgomery, and Philadelphia

675 American HealthCare Group
733 Washington Road
Suite 102
Pittsburgh, PA 15228
Phone: 412-563-8800
Fax: 412-563-8319
american-healthcare.net
For Profit Organization: Yes
Year Founded: 1996

Healthplan and Services Defined
PLAN TYPE: Other
Model Type: Network
Plan Specialty: ASO, Chiropractic, Dental, MSO, Worker's Compensation
Benefits Offered: Behavioral Health, Chiropractic, Complementary Medicine, Dental, Disease Management, Home Care, Inpatient SNF, Long-Term Care, Physical Therapy, Podiatry, Prescription, Psychiatric, Transplant, Vision, Wellness, Worker's Compensation, School wellness programs, on-site immunizations, support services for public housing

Type of Coverage
Medicare

Type of Payment Plans Offered
FFS

Geographic Areas Served
Pennsylvania, Eastern Ohio, Northwestern Virginia

Peer Review Type
Utilization Review: Yes
Second Surgical Opinion: Yes
Case Management: Yes

Accreditation Certification
State Licensure

Key Personnel
President & CEO. . . . . Robert E. Hagan, Jr.
 412-563-7804
 bhagan@american-healthcare.net
Accounts Recievable . . . . Lynn Hagan
 412-563-7805
 lhagan@american-healthcare.net
Dir., Health Benefits. . . . . Erin Hart
 412-563-7807
 ehart@american-healthcare.net
Dir., Wellness Services . . . . Liz Hagan Kanche
 412-563-7854
 lhkanche@american-healthcare.net
Marketing Manager . . . . Sarah Kelly
 skelly@american-healthcare.net

676 AmeriHealth Pennsylvania
1901 Market Street
Philadelphia, PA 19103-1480
Toll-Free: 866-681-7373
www.amerihealth.com
Year Founded: 1995
Total Enrollment: 265,000

Healthplan and Services Defined
PLAN TYPE: HMO/PPO
Benefits Offered: Dental, Disease Management, Prescription, Vision, Wellness

Type of Coverage
Commercial, Individual

Geographic Areas Served
Pennsylvania

677 Capital BlueCross
2500 Elmerton Avenue
Harrisburg, PA 17177
www.capbluecross.com
Non-Profit Organization: Yes
Year Founded: 1938

Healthplan and Services Defined
PLAN TYPE: HMO/PPO
Plan Specialty: Dental, Vision
Benefits Offered: Dental, Home Care, Inpatient SNF, Physical Therapy, Prescription, Psychiatric, Transplant, Vision, Wellness

Type of Coverage
Commercial

Type of Payment Plans Offered
FFS

Geographic Areas Served
21 counties in central Pennsylvania and the Lehigh Valley

Peer Review Type
Second Surgical Opinion: Yes
Case Management: Yes

Accreditation Certification
TJC Accreditation, Medicare Approved, Utilization Review, Pre-Admission Certification, State Licensure, Quality Assurance Program

Key Personnel
President/CEO . . . . Todd A. Shamash
SVP/CFO . . . . T. Ralph Woodward
SVP/CMO . . . . Jennifer Chambers, MD, MBA
EVP/COO . . . . Glenn Heisey
SVP, Human Resources . . . . Jodi Woleslagle

678 Delta Dental of Pennsylvania
One Delta Drive
Mechanicsburg, PA 17055-6999
Toll-Free: 800-932-0783
www.deltadentalins.com
Mailing Address: P.O. Box 1803, Alpharetta, GA 30023
Non-Profit Organization: Yes

Healthplan and Services Defined
PLAN TYPE: Dental
Other Type: Dental PPO
Plan Specialty: Dental
Benefits Offered: Dental

Type of Coverage
Commercial, Individual

Geographic Areas Served
Statewide

Key Personnel
President & CEO . . . . Michael Castro
Chief Financial Officer . . . . Alicia Weber
Chief Legal Officer . . . . Michael Hankinson
Chief Information Officer . . . . Dominic Titcombe
Chief Operating Officer . . . . Roy Gilbert

679 Devon Health Services
6970 O'Bannon Dr.
Las Vegas, NV 89117
Toll-Free: 866-434-3173
sales@devonhealthinc.com
www.devonhealthinc.com
Subsidiary of: GFAR Health Services
For Profit Organization: Yes
Year Founded: 1991
Physician Owned Organization: Yes

Healthplan and Services Defined
PLAN TYPE: PPO
Model Type: Network
Plan Specialty: Chiropractic, Dental, Lab, Vision, Radiology, Worker's Compensation, Group Health & Pharmacy Plans; Acupuncture
Benefits Offered: Chiropractic, Dental, Inpatient SNF, Physical Therapy, Vision, Worker's Compensation, Group Health & Pharmacy Plans

Type of Coverage
Commercial

Type of Payment Plans Offered
DFFS, FFS, Combination FFS & DFFS

Geographic Areas Served
Pennsylvania, New Jersey, and Delaware

Publishes and Distributes Report Card: No

Key Personnel
President . . . . Dean Vaden

Average Claim Compensation
Physician's Fees Charged: 55%
Hospital's Fees Charged: 58%

Specialty Managed Care Partners
Medimpact
Enters into Contracts with Regional Business Coalitions: Yes

Employer References
Mid-Jersey trucking Industry & Local 701 Welfare Fund, Pennsylvania Public School Health Care Trust, International Brotherhood of Teamsters

680 Gateway Health
Four Gateway Center
444 Liberty Ave, Suite 2100
Pittsburgh, PA 15222-1222
Toll-Free: 800-392-1147
Phone: 412-255-4640
www.gatewayhealthplan.com
Mailing Address: P.O.Box: 22278, Pittsburgh, PA 15222
For Profit Organization: Yes
Year Founded: 1992
Number of Affiliated Hospitals: 170
State Enrollment: 320,000

Healthplan and Services Defined
PLAN TYPE: HMO
Other Type: Medicaid
Model Type: Network
Plan Specialty: Dental, Disease Management, Vision, UR, Prospective Care Managment; Dual Eligibility; Chronic Special Needs
Benefits Offered: Chiropractic, Dental, Disease Management, Home Care, Inpatient SNF, Physical Therapy, Podiatry, Prescription, Transplant, Vision, Wellness

Type of Coverage
Medicare, Medicaid

Type of Payment Plans Offered
DFFS, Capitated, FFS

Geographic Areas Served
Allegheny, Armstrong, Beaver, Berks, Blair, Butler, Cambria, Clarion, Cumberland, Dauphin, Erie, Fayette, Greene, Indiana, Jefferson, Lawrence, Lehigh, Mercer, Montour, Northumberland, Schulkill, Somerset, Washington and Westmoreland counties

Peer Review Type
Utilization Review: Yes
Second Surgical Opinion: Yes
Case Management: Yes

Accreditation Certification
NCQA
Utilization Review, State Licensure, Quality Assurance Program

Key Personnel
President & CEO . . . . Cain A. Hayes Darnley
Chief Financial Officer. . . . . Ja'ron Bridges
SVP, Health Services . . . . Glenn Pomerantz, MD
Chief Operations Officer. . . . . Ellen Duffield

Specialty Managed Care Partners
Clarity Vision, Dental Benefit Providers, National Imaging Association, Merck-Medco

681 Geisinger Health Plan
100 North Academy Avenue
Danville, PA 17822
Toll-Free: 800-275-6401
www.geisinger.org/health-plan
Non-Profit Organization: Yes
Year Founded: 1985
Number of Affiliated Hospitals: 110
Number of Primary Care Physicians: 3,500
Number of Referral/Specialty Physicians: 27,000
Total Enrollment: 540,000

Healthplan and Services Defined
PLAN TYPE: HMO/PPO
Model Type: Network
Benefits Offered: Chiropractic, Dental, Disease Management, Home Care, Inpatient SNF, Physical Therapy, Podiatry, Prescription, Psychiatric, Vision, Wellness

Type of Coverage
Commercial, Individual, Medicare, Supplemental Medicare, CHIP

Geographic Areas Served
42 counties in Pennsylvania

Accreditation Certification
NCQA

Key Personnel
President/CEO . . . . Jaewon Ryu, MD

682 Health Partners Plans
901 Market Street
Suite 500
Philadelphia, PA 19107
Phone: 215-849-9606
contact@hpplans.com
www.healthpartnersplans.com
Non-Profit Organization: Yes
Year Founded: 1984
Physician Owned Organization: Yes
Number of Affiliated Hospitals: 43
Number of Primary Care Physicians: 6,400
Total Enrollment: 263,200

Healthplan and Services Defined
PLAN TYPE: Medicare
Other Type: Medicaid
Benefits Offered: Chiropractic, Dental, Disease Management, Home Care, Inpatient SNF, Physical Therapy, Podiatry, Prescription, Psychiatric, Vision, Wellness

Type of Coverage
Medicare, Medicaid, CHIP

Geographic Areas Served
Bucks, Chester, Delaware, Lancaster, Lehigh, Montgomery, Northampton, and Philadelphia counties

Key Personnel
President/CEO . . . . Denise Napier
SVP/CFO. . . . . Kevin Clancy
Chief Legal Officer . . . . Johnna Baker
COO . . . . Joe Brand

683 HealthAmerica Pennsylvania
3721 TecPort Drive
P.O. Box 67103
Harrisburg, PA 17106-7103
Toll-Free: 800-654-5988
www.coventryhealthcare.com/HealthAmerica

Secondary Address: 11 Stanwix Street, Suite 2300, Pittsburgh, PA 15222, 800-735-4404
Subsidiary of: Coventry Health Care / Aetna Inc.
For Profit Organization: Yes
Year Founded: 1974
Owned by an Integrated Delivery Network (IDN): Yes

Healthplan and Services Defined
PLAN TYPE: HMO/PPO
Model Type: Network
Plan Specialty: ASO, Behavioral Health, Chiropractic, Dental, Disease Management, Lab, Vision, Radiology
Benefits Offered: Behavioral Health, Chiropractic, Complementary Medicine, Dental, Disease Management, Home Care, Inpatient SNF, Physical Therapy, Podiatry, Prescription, Psychiatric, Transplant, Vision, Wellness

Type of Coverage
Commercial, Individual, Medicare, Medicaid

Type of Payment Plans Offered
POS, Capitated, FFS

Geographic Areas Served
Statewide

Peer Review Type
Utilization Review: Yes
Case Management: Yes

Accreditation Certification
TJC, NCQA
Medicare Approved, Utilization Review, Pre-Admission Certification, State Licensure, Quality Assurance Program

Specialty Managed Care Partners
ValueOptions, CareMark, Dominion Dental (WPA) Delta Dental (EPA), Quest Diagnostics (EPA) LabCorp (WPA), National Vision Administrators (NVA)

Employer References
Federal Government, Penn State University, US Airways, City of Pittsburgh, General Motors

---

684 Highmark Blue Cross Blue Shield
120 5th Ave
Pittsburgh, PA 15222
Toll-Free: 800-816-5527
www.highmarkbcbs.com
Mailing Address: P.O. Box 226, Pittsburgh, PA 15222
Non-Profit Organization: Yes
Year Founded: 1996
Owned by an Integrated Delivery Network (IDN): Yes

Healthplan and Services Defined
PLAN TYPE: HMO/PPO
Model Type: IPA
Benefits Offered: Dental, Disease Management, Prescription, Vision, Wellness
Offers Demand Management Patient Information Service: Yes

Type of Coverage
Commercial, Individual
Catastrophic Illness Benefit: Unlimited

Type of Payment Plans Offered
POS, DFFS, Capitated, FFS, Combination FFS & DFFS

Geographic Areas Served
Western and Northeastern Pennsylvania

Peer Review Type
Utilization Review: Yes
Second Surgical Opinion: No
Case Management: Yes

Publishes and Distributes Report Card: No

Accreditation Certification
URAC, NCQA
Medicare Approved, Pre-Admission Certification, State Licensure

Key Personnel
President/CEO/Chairman . . . . David L. Holmberg
Chief Legal Officer. . . . . Carolyn Duronio
Chief Marketing Officer. . . . . Cindy Donohoe

Average Claim Compensation
Physician's Fees Charged: 50%
Hospital's Fees Charged: 61%

Specialty Managed Care Partners
Enters into Contracts with Regional Business Coalitions: No

---

685 Highmark Blue Shield
Fifth Avenue Place
120 Fifth Avenue
Pittsburgh, PA 15222-3099
Toll-Free: 800-241-5704
Phone: 412-544-7000
www.highmarkblueshield.com
Non-Profit Organization: Yes
Year Founded: 1932
Total Enrollment: 5,300,000

Healthplan and Services Defined
PLAN TYPE: PPO
Model Type: Network
Benefits Offered: Disease Management, Prescription, Wellness

Type of Payment Plans Offered
POS, DFFS, Combination FFS & DFFS

Geographic Areas Served
Central Pennsylvania

Peer Review Type
Second Surgical Opinion: Yes

Publishes and Distributes Report Card: Yes

Accreditation Certification
URAC, NCQA

Key Personnel
President/CEO . . . . David L. Holmberg

Specialty Managed Care Partners
Enters into Contracts with Regional Business Coalitions: Yes

686 Humana Health Insurance of Pennsylvania
5000 Ritter Road
Suite 101
Mechanicsburg, PA 17055
Toll-Free: 866-355-5861
Phone: 717-766-6040
Fax: 717-795-1951
www.humana.com
Secondary Address: 325 Sentry Parkway, Suite 200, Blue Bell, PA 19422
Subsidiary of: Humana Inc.
For Profit Organization: Yes

Healthplan and Services Defined
PLAN TYPE: HMO/PPO
Model Type: Network
Plan Specialty: Dental, Vision
Benefits Offered: Dental, Vision, Life, LTD, STD

Type of Coverage
Commercial

Geographic Areas Served
Statewide

Accreditation Certification
URAC, NCQA, CORE

687 Independence Blue Cross
1919 Market Street
2nd Floor
Philadelphia, PA 19103
Toll-Free: 800-275-2583
www.ibx.com
Non-Profit Organization: Yes
Year Founded: 1986
Total Enrollment: 8,000,000
State Enrollment: 3,000,000

Healthplan and Services Defined
PLAN TYPE: HMO/PPO
Benefits Offered: Behavioral Health, Dental, Prescription, Vision, Worker's Compensation, AD&D, Life, LTD, STD

Type of Coverage
Individual, Indemnity, Medicaid

Type of Payment Plans Offered
DFFS, FFS, Combination FFS & DFFS

Geographic Areas Served
Southeastern Pennsylvania

Network Qualifications
Pre-Admission Certification: Yes

Peer Review Type
Utilization Review: Yes
Second Surgical Opinion: No
Case Management: Yes

Publishes and Distributes Report Card: Yes

Accreditation Certification
NCQA
TJC Accreditation, Medicare Approved, Utilization Review, Pre-Admission Certification, State Licensure, Quality Assurance Program

Key Personnel
President/CEO.................... Gregory E. Deavens
SVP, Operations .... Anthony J. Maleno
EVP/CFO/Treasurer .... Juan Lopez
General Counsel/Secretary............. Thomas A. Hutton
SVP/Chief Info. Officer............. Michael R. Vennera
Chief Medical Officer.................... Rodrigo Cerd

Specialty Managed Care Partners
Magellan Behavioral Health, United Concorida, Medco Health Solutions
Enters into Contracts with Regional Business Coalitions: Yes

688 InterGroup Services
5835 Ellsworth Ave., 2nd Floor
Pittsburgh, PA 15232
Phone: 412-363-0600
Fax: 412-363-0900
www.igs-ppo.com
Secondary Address: 1 S Bacton Hill Road, 2nd Floor, Malvern, PA 19355, 800-537-9389
For Profit Organization: Yes
Year Founded: 1985

Healthplan and Services Defined
PLAN TYPE: PPO
Model Type: Network
Plan Specialty: ASO, Behavioral Health, Chiropractic, EPO, Lab, MSO, PBM, Vision, Radiology, Worker's Compensation
Benefits Offered: Behavioral Health, Disease Management, Prescription, Wellness, Worker's Compensation

Type of Coverage
Commercial

Geographic Areas Served
Pennsylvania, New Jersey, Delaware and West Virginia

Network Qualifications
Pre-Admission Certification: Yes

Specialty Managed Care Partners
Chiropractic Network

689 PA Health & Wellness
5 Penn Center Boulevard
Suite 300
Pittsburgh, PA 15276
Toll-Free: 844-626-6813
www.pahealthwellness.com
Subsidiary of: Centene Corporation
For Profit Organization: Yes
Year Founded: 2016

Healthplan and Services Defined
PLAN TYPE: Other
Model Type: Network
Benefits Offered: Behavioral Health, Dental, Disease Management, Prescription, Vision

Type of Coverage
Medicaid, Community HealthChoices

Key Personnel
President/CEO . . . . Justin Davis

690 Penn Highlands Healthcare
204 Hospital Avenue
DuBois, PA 15801
Phone: 814-371-2200
www.phhealthcare.org
Non-Profit Organization: Yes
Year Founded: 2011
Number of Affiliated Hospitals: 5
Number of Primary Care Physicians: 361

Healthplan and Services Defined
PLAN TYPE: PPO
Model Type: IPA
Plan Specialty: ASO, Behavioral Health, Disease Management, EPO, Lab, MSO, Radiology, Worker's Compensation, UR
Benefits Offered: Behavioral Health, Chiropractic, Disease Management, Home Care, Inpatient SNF, Long-Term Care, Physical Therapy, Podiatry, Psychiatric, Transplant, Wellness, Worker's Compensation
Offers Demand Management Patient Information Service: Yes

Type of Coverage
Commercial

Type of Payment Plans Offered
POS, DFFS, Combination FFS & DFFS

Geographic Areas Served
Cameron, Centre, Clarion, Clearfield, Elk, Forest, Jefferson and McKean counties

Network Qualifications
Pre-Admission Certification: Yes

Peer Review Type
Utilization Review: Yes
Second Surgical Opinion: No
Case Management: Yes

Publishes and Distributes Report Card: Yes

Accreditation Certification
AAAHC, URAC
TJC Accreditation, Medicare Approved, Pre-Admission Certification, State Licensure

Key Personnel
Chief Executive Officer . . . . Steven M. Fontaine

Average Claim Compensation
Physician's Fees Charged: 1%
Hospital's Fees Charged: 1%

Specialty Managed Care Partners
Enters into Contracts with Regional Business Coalitions: No

691 Preferred Health Care
Urban Place
480 New Holland Ave, Suite 7203
Lancaster, PA 17602
Phone: 717-560-9290
Fax: 717-560-2312
info@phcunity.com
www.phcunity.com
Non-Profit Organization: Yes
Year Founded: 1984
Number of Affiliated Hospitals: 19
Number of Primary Care Physicians: 1,900

Healthplan and Services Defined
PLAN TYPE: PPO
Model Type: Network
Offers Demand Management Patient Information Service: Yes

Type of Payment Plans Offered
FFS

Geographic Areas Served
Statewide

Peer Review Type
Utilization Review: Yes
Case Management: Yes

Accreditation Certification
TJC Accreditation, Medicare Approved, Utilization Review, Pre-Admission Certification, State Licensure, Quality Assurance Program

Key Personnel
President/CEO. . . . . Eric E. Buck
VP, Operations. . . . . Sherry Wolgemuth
Dir., Info. Technology . . . . Doug Smith

692 Preferred Healthcare System
P.O. Box 1015
Duncansville, PA 16635
Toll-Free: 800-238-9900
Phone: 814-317-5063
Fax: 814-317-5139
www.phsppo.com
For Profit Organization: Yes
Year Founded: 1985
Physician Owned Organization: Yes
Number of Affiliated Hospitals: 14

Healthplan and Services Defined
PLAN TYPE: PPO
Model Type: Network
Plan Specialty: ASO, Behavioral Health, Chiropractic, Dental, Disease Management, EPO, PBM, Vision, Worker's Compensation, Health
Benefits Offered: Behavioral Health, Chiropractic, Complementary Medicine, Dental, Disease Management, Home Care, Inpatient SNF, Long-Term Care, Physical Therapy, Podiatry, Prescription, Psychiatric, Transplant, Vision, Wellness, AD&D, Life, STD, Durable Medical Equipment

Type of Coverage
Commercial, Individual, Indemnity
Catastrophic Illness Benefit: Maximum $1M

Type of Payment Plans Offered
Combination FFS & DFFS

Geographic Areas Served
South Central Pennsylvania

Peer Review Type
Utilization Review: Yes
Second Surgical Opinion: Yes

Publishes and Distributes Report Card: No

Accreditation Certification
TJC Accreditation, Utilization Review, Pre-Admission Certification, State Licensure, Quality Assurance Program

Key Personnel
President .... Maureen Frucella
Chief Executive Officer .... Brian Brumbaugh

Average Claim Compensation
Physician's Fees Charged: 70%
Hospital's Fees Charged: 70%

Specialty Managed Care Partners
Enters into Contracts with Regional Business Coalitions: Yes

693 South Central Preferred Health Network
3421 Concord Road
York, PA 17402
Toll-Free: 800-842-1768
Phone: 717-851-6800
www.scp-ppo.com
Non-Profit Organization: Yes
Year Founded: 1992
Number of Affiliated Hospitals: 16
Number of Primary Care Physicians: 6,150
Number of Referral/Specialty Physicians: 1,275
Total Enrollment: 33,000
State Enrollment: 33,000

Healthplan and Services Defined
PLAN TYPE: PPO
Model Type: PHO
Plan Specialty: Behavioral Health, Chiropractic, Radiology
Benefits Offered: Behavioral Health, Chiropractic, Home Care, Inpatient SNF, Long-Term Care, Physical Therapy, Podiatry, Psychiatric, Transplant

Type of Coverage
Catastrophic Illness Benefit: None

Type of Payment Plans Offered
Capitated

Geographic Areas Served
Cumberland, Dauphin, Lebanon, Perry and Northern York counties

Subscriber Information
Average Monthly Fee Per Subscriber
(Employee + Employer Contribution):
Employee Only (Self): $6.75 per employee

Network Qualifications
Pre-Admission Certification: No

Peer Review Type
Utilization Review: Yes

Average Claim Compensation
Physician's Fees Charged: 64%
Hospital's Fees Charged: 70%

694 Trinity Health of Pennsylvania
One West Elm Street
Suite 100 54th Street
Conshohocken, PA 19428
Phone: 610-567-6000
www.trinity-health.org
Secondary Address: St Mary Medical Center, 1201 Langhorne-Newtown Road, Langhorne, PA 19047, 215-710-2000
Subsidiary of: Trinity Health
Non-Profit Organization: Yes
Year Founded: 2013
Number of Primary Care Physicians: 183
Total Enrollment: 30,000,000

Healthplan and Services Defined
PLAN TYPE: Other
Benefits Offered: Disease Management, Home Care, Long-Term Care, Psychiatric, Hospice programs, PACE (Program of All Inclusive Care for the Elderly)

Geographic Areas Served
Statewide

Key Personnel
President/CEO .... Susan Croushore

695 United Concordia Dental
4401 Deer Path Road
Harrisburg, PA 17110
Phone: 717-260-6800
www.unitedconcordia.com
Subsidiary of: Highmark, Inc.
For Profit Organization: Yes
Year Founded: 1971
Number of Primary Care Physicians: 104,000
Total Enrollment: 8,800,000

Healthplan and Services Defined
PLAN TYPE: Dental
Plan Specialty: Dental
Benefits Offered: Dental

Type of Coverage
Commercial, Individual

Geographic Areas Served
Nationwide

Accreditation Certification
URAC

Key Personnel
President & COO .... Timothy J. Constantine

Contact. . . . . Beth Rutherford
717-260-7659
beth.rutherford@ucci.com

696 United Concordia of Pennsylvania
4401 Deer Path Road
Harrisburg, PA 17110
Phone: 717-260-6800
www.unitedconcordia.com
For Profit Organization: Yes
Year Founded: 1971
Number of Primary Care Physicians: 104,000
Total Enrollment: 8,800,000

Healthplan and Services Defined
PLAN TYPE: Dental
Plan Specialty: Dental
Benefits Offered: Dental

Type of Coverage
Commercial, Individual, Military personnel & families

Geographic Areas Served
Nationwide

Accreditation Certification
URAC

Key Personnel
Contact. . . . . Beth Rutherford
717-260-7659
beth.rutherford@ucci.com

697 UnitedHealthcare Community Plan Pennsylvania
UnitedHealthcare Customer Service
P.O. Box 30769
Salt Lake City, UT 84130-0769
Toll-Free: 888-545-5205
www.uhccommunityplan.com/pa
Subsidiary of: UnitedHealth Group
For Profit Organization: Yes

Healthplan and Services Defined
PLAN TYPE: Multiple
Model Type: Network
Benefits Offered: Dental, Home Care, Podiatry, Prescription, Vision, Wellness, Hearing

Type of Coverage
Medicare, Medicaid, CHIP

Geographic Areas Served
Varies by plan

Key Personnel
CEO, Community Plan PA . . . . Blair Boroch
bboroch@uhc.com

698 UnitedHealthcare of Pennsylvania
2 Allegheny Center
Suite 600
Pittsburgh, PA 15212
Toll-Free: 888-545-5205
www.uhc.com
Secondary Address: 100 E Penn Square, Philadelphia, PA 19107, 215-832-4500
Subsidiary of: UnitedHealth Group
For Profit Organization: Yes

Healthplan and Services Defined
PLAN TYPE: HMO/PPO
Model Type: Network
Plan Specialty: Behavioral Health, Dental, Disease Management, PBM, Vision
Benefits Offered: Behavioral Health, Dental, Disease Management, Long-Term Care, Prescription, Vision, Wellness, Life, LTD, STD

Type of Coverage
Individual, Medicare, Supplemental Medicare, Medicaid, Catastrophic, Family, Military, Veterans, Group

Type of Payment Plans Offered
DFFS

Geographic Areas Served
Statewide

Publishes and Distributes Report Card: Yes

Accreditation Certification
AAPI, NCQA

Key Personnel
CEO, Healthplan NJ/PA/DE . . . . Paul Marden

699 UPMC Health Plan
600 Grant Street
Pittsburgh, PA 15219
Toll-Free: 844-220-4785
www.upmchealthplan.com
Subsidiary of: University of Pittsburgh Medical Center
For Profit Organization: Yes
Year Founded: 1996
Physician Owned Organization: Yes
Number of Affiliated Hospitals: 125
Number of Primary Care Physicians: 23,300
Total Enrollment: 150,000
State Enrollment: 150,000

Healthplan and Services Defined
PLAN TYPE: Multiple
Benefits Offered: Behavioral Health, Chiropractic, Complementary Medicine, Dental, Disease Management, Home Care, Inpatient SNF, Physical Therapy, Podiatry, Prescription, Psychiatric, Transplant, Vision, Wellness

Type of Coverage
Commercial, Individual, Medicare, Medicaid

Type of Payment Plans Offered
POS

Geographic Areas Served
26 counties in western Pennsylvania

Subscriber Information
Average Monthly Fee Per Subscriber
(Employee + Employer Contribution):
Employee Only (Self): Varies
Employee & 1 Family Member: Varies
Employee & 2 Family Members: Varies
Medicare: Varies
Average Annual Deductible Per Subscriber:
Employee Only (Self): Varies
Employee & 1 Family Member: Varies
Employee & 2 Family Members: Varies
Medicare: Varies
Average Subscriber Co-Payment:
Primary Care Physician: Varies
Non-Network Physician: Varies
Prescription Drugs: Varies
Hospital ER: Varies
Home Health Care: Varies
Home Health Care Max. Days/Visits Covered: Varies
Nursing Home: Varies
Nursing Home Max. Days/Visits Covered: Varies

Accreditation Certification
NCQA

Key Personnel
President/CEO . . . . Diane Holder

---

700 UPMC Susquehanna
700 High Street
Williamsport, PA 17701
Phone: 570-321-1000
www.susquehannahealth.org
For Profit Organization: Yes
Year Founded: 1994
Physician Owned Organization: Yes
Number of Affiliated Hospitals: 6
Number of Primary Care Physicians: 600

Healthplan and Services Defined
PLAN TYPE: PPO
Model Type: Network
Plan Specialty: Disease Management, Lab, Cancer, Orthopedics, Heart & Vascular, Maternity Care
Benefits Offered: Disease Management, Home Care, Long-Term Care, Prescription, Psychiatric, Wellness

Type of Coverage
Catastrophic Illness Benefit: Maximum $2M

Geographic Areas Served
Central & Northeastern Pennsylvania

Subscriber Information
Average Monthly Fee Per Subscriber
(Employee + Employer Contribution):
Employee Only (Self): $140
Employee & 1 Family Member: $275
Employee & 2 Family Members: $410
Average Annual Deductible Per Subscriber:
Employee Only (Self): $500
Average Subscriber Co-Payment:
Primary Care Physician: $30.00
Non-Network Physician: $52.00
Hospital ER: $75.00
Home Health Care: 15%
Home Health Care Max. Days/Visits Covered: 100 days
Nursing Home Max. Days/Visits Covered: 30/confinement

Network Qualifications
Pre-Admission Certification: Yes

Peer Review Type
Utilization Review: Yes
Second Surgical Opinion: Yes

Publishes and Distributes Report Card: No

Accreditation Certification
Medicare Approved, Utilization Review, Pre-Admission Certification, State Licensure, Quality Assurance Program

Key Personnel
President/CEO . . . . Steven P. Johnson, Jr

Specialty Managed Care Partners
Enters into Contracts with Regional Business Coalitions: Yes

---

701 Vale-U-Health
800 Plaza Drive
Suite 230
Belle Vernon, PA 15012
Phone: 724-379-4011
Fax: 724-379-4354
cmw@vuhealth.com
www.valeuhealth.com
Non-Profit Organization: Yes
Year Founded: 1995
Number of Affiliated Hospitals: 1
Number of Primary Care Physicians: 156
Total Enrollment: 2,375

Healthplan and Services Defined
PLAN TYPE: PPO
Model Type: PHO
Plan Specialty: Radiology
Benefits Offered: Disease Management, Podiatry, Psychiatric, Wellness, 40 specialties including allergy & immunology, cardiology, dermatology & geriatrics.

Type of Coverage
Commercial, Individual
Catastrophic Illness Benefit: Covered

Geographic Areas Served
Monongahela Valley

Subscriber Information
Average Annual Deductible Per Subscriber:
Employee Only (Self): $200.00
Employee & 1 Family Member: $400.00
Employee & 2 Family Members: $400.00

Peer Review Type
Case Management: Yes

Accreditation Certification
TJC, CARF, COA and AOA

Key Personnel
Chief Executive Officer . . . . Susan Flynn
  smf@vuhealth.com
Director of Operations . . . . Lois J. Weaver
  ljw@vuhealth.com
Care & Quality Management . . . . Trina L. Curcio
  tlc@vuhealth.com
Claims Adjudicator . . . . Hillary Rodenz
  hrodenz@vuhealth.com

702 Valley Preferred
1605 N Cedar Crest Boulevard
Suite 411
Allentown, PA 18104-2351
Toll-Free: 800-955-6620
Phone: 610-969-0485
Fax: 610-969-0439
info@valleypreferred.com
www.valleypreferred.com
Non-Profit Organization: Yes
Year Founded: 1994
Physician Owned Organization: Yes
Federally Qualified: Yes
Number of Affiliated Hospitals: 18
Number of Primary Care Physicians: 778
Number of Referral/Specialty Physicians: 2,977
Total Enrollment: 174,309
State Enrollment: 174,309

Healthplan and Services Defined
  PLAN TYPE: Multiple
  Model Type: PHO

Geographic Areas Served
  Lehigh, Northampton, Berks, Bucks, Montgomery, Dauphin, Schuylkill, Columbia, Luzerne, Carbon and Lackawanna counties

Accreditation Certification
  TJC, NCQA

Key Personnel
Chair . . . . Gregory G. Kile
Executive Director . . . . Mark Wendling, MD
Associate Executive Dir. . . . . Laura J. Mertz, CBC
Medical Director . . . . Joseph A. Habig II, MD
Associate Medical Dir. . . . . Nicole Sully, DO

Specialty Managed Care Partners
  Enters into Contracts with Regional Business Coalitions: No
  NPRHCC

703 Value Behavioral Health of Pennsylvania
PO Box 1840
Cranberry Township, PA 16066
Toll-Free: 877-615-8503
pawebmaster@beaconhealthoptions.com
www.vbh-pa.com
Subsidiary of: A Beacon Health Options Company
For Profit Organization: Yes
Year Founded: 1999
Physician Owned Organization: Yes
Number of Referral/Specialty Physicians: 6,000
Total Enrollment: 22,000,000

Healthplan and Services Defined
  PLAN TYPE: PPO
  Model Type: Network
  Plan Specialty: ASO, Behavioral Health, UR
  Benefits Offered: Behavioral Health, Psychiatric, EAP

Type of Coverage
  Commercial, Indemnity, Medicaid

Type of Payment Plans Offered
  POS, DFFS, Combination FFS & DFFS

Geographic Areas Served
  Armstrong, Beaver, Butler, Crawford, Fayette, Greene, Indiana, Lawrence, Mercer, Venango, Washington and Westmoreland counties

Peer Review Type
  Case Management: Yes

Publishes and Distributes Report Card: Yes

Accreditation Certification
  TJC, URAC, NCQA, CARF, COA and AOA

Key Personnel
Chief Executive Officer . . . . Roxanne Kennedy
Medical Director . . . . Mike Usman

PUERTO RICO

Health Insurance Coverage Status and Type of Coverage by Age

Category	All Persons Number	%	Under 18 years Number	%	Under 65 years Number	%
Total population	N/A	-	N/A	-	N/A	-
Covered by some type of health insurance	N/A	N/A	N/A	N/A	N/A	N/A
Covered by private health insurance	N/A	N/A	N/A	N/A	N/A	N/A
Employer-based	N/A	N/A	N/A	N/A	N/A	N/A
Direct purchase	N/A	N/A	N/A	N/A	N/A	N/A
TRICARE	N/A	N/A	N/A	N/A	N/A	N/A
Covered by public health insurance	N/A	N/A	N/A	N/A	N/A	N/A
Medicaid	N/A	N/A	N/A	N/A	N/A	N/A
Medicare	N/A	N/A	N/A	N/A	N/A	N/A
VA Care	N/A	N/A	N/A	N/A	N/A	N/A
Not covered at any time during the year	N/A	N/A	N/A	N/A	N/A	N/A

Note: Figures cover civilian noninstitutionalized population in 2019; N/A indicates that data was not available.
Source: U.S. Census Bureau, American Community Survey, Table HI-05. Health Insurance Coverage Status and Type of Coverage by State and Age for All People: 2019

Puerto Rico

704 First Medical Health Plan
Lote #510 00966, Frontage Road
Guaynabo, PR 00966
Toll-Free: 888-318-0274
Phone: 787-474-3999
www.firstmedicalpr.com
For Profit Organization: Yes
Year Founded: 1977
Number of Affiliated Hospitals: 12
Total Enrollment: 180,000
State Enrollment: 180,000

Healthplan and Services Defined
  PLAN TYPE: Multiple
  Plan Specialty: Dental
  Benefits Offered: Dental, Disease Management, Wellness

Key Personnel
  President . . . . Francisco J. Artau Feliciano

705 Humana Health Insurance of Puerto Rico
383 F.D. Roosevelt Avenue
San Juan, PR 00918
Toll-Free: 800-314-3121
Fax: 888-899-6762
www.humana.pr
Secondary Address: Caribbean Cinemas Building Office #10, Barceloneta, PR 00617
Subsidiary of: Humana Inc.
For Profit Organization: Yes

Healthplan and Services Defined
  PLAN TYPE: HMO/PPO
  Model Type: Network
  Plan Specialty: Dental, Vision
  Benefits Offered: Dental, Vision, Life, LTD, STD

Type of Coverage
  Commercial

Accreditation Certification
  URAC, NCQA, CORE

Key Personnel
  President, Puerto Rico . . . . Luis A. Torres Olivera
  Finance Director, PR . . . . Jose Mercado

706 InnovaCare Health
173 Bridge Plaza N
Fort Lee, NJ 07024
Phone: 201-969-2300
info@innovacarehealth.com
innovacarehealth.com

Healthplan and Services Defined
  PLAN TYPE: Medicare

Type of Coverage
  Medicare

Geographic Areas Served
  Puerto Rico & Florida

Key Personnel
  President & CEO . . . . Richard Shinto, MD
  Chief Financial Officer . . . . Douglas Malton
  General Counsel . . . . Leslie Prizant
  Administrative Officer . . . . Penelope Kokkinides
  Chief Accounting Officer . . . . Michael J. Sortino
  Chief Actuary Officer . . . . Jonathan A. Meyers
  Chief Medical Officer . . . . Waldemar Rios, M.D,

707 Medical Card System (MCS)
MCS Plaza, 1st Fl, Suite 105, 255
Ave. Ponce de Leon
San Juan, PR 00916-1919
Toll-Free: 888-758-1616
Phone: 787-281-2800
www.mcs.com.pr
For Profit Organization: Yes
Year Founded: 1983
Number of Affiliated Hospitals: 57
Number of Primary Care Physicians: 11
Total Enrollment: 300,000

Healthplan and Services Defined
  PLAN TYPE: Multiple
  Model Type: Group, Network
  Plan Specialty: ASO, Behavioral Health, Chiropractic, Dental, Disease Management, EPO, Lab, MSO, PBM, Vision, Radiology
  Benefits Offered: Behavioral Health, Chiropractic, Complementary Medicine, Dental, Disease Management, Home Care, Inpatient SNF, Physical Therapy, Podiatry, Prescription, Psychiatric, Transplant, Vision, Wellness, Life, LTD

Type of Coverage
  Commercial, Individual, Indemnity, Medicare, Supplemental Medicare, Medicaid, Catastrophic

Type of Payment Plans Offered
  POS, Capitated

Geographic Areas Served
  Statewide

Subscriber Information
  Average Monthly Fee Per Subscriber
    (Employee + Employer Contribution):
      Employee Only (Self): Varies
      Employee & 1 Family Member: Varies
      Employee & 2 Family Members: Varies
      Medicare: Varies
  Average Annual Deductible Per Subscriber:
      Employee Only (Self): Varies
      Employee & 1 Family Member: Varies
      Employee & 2 Family Members: Varies
      Medicare: Varies
  Average Subscriber Co-Payment:
      Primary Care Physician: Varies
      Non-Network Physician: Varies
      Prescription Drugs: Varies
      Hospital ER: Varies
      Home Health Care: Varies
      Home Health Care Max. Days/Visits Covered: Varies

Nursing Home: Varies
Nursing Home Max. Days/Visits Covered: Varies

Network Qualifications
Pre-Admission Certification: Yes

Peer Review Type
Utilization Review: Yes
Second Surgical Opinion: Yes
Case Management: Yes

Accreditation Certification
Medicare Approved, Pre-Admission Certification, State Licensure

Key Personnel
Chief Compliance Officer . . . . Maite Morales Martinez
EVP, Clinical Operations . . . . Ixel Rivera
SVP, Human Resources . . . . Gretchen Muniz
Chief Medical Officer . . . . Ines Hernandez, MD

Employer References
Sensormatic, El Nuevo Dia, Pan Pepin, Nypro Puerto Rico, Cardinal Health

708 MMM Holdings
350 Carlos E Chardon Avenue
Suite 500
San Juan, PR 00918
Phone: 787-622-3000
www.mmm-pr.com
Subsidiary of: Anthem, Inc.
For Profit Organization: Yes
Year Founded: 2001
Total Enrollment: 126,000

Healthplan and Services Defined
PLAN TYPE: Multiple

Type of Coverage
Individual, Medicare, Medicaid

Geographic Areas Served
Puerto Rico

Accreditation Certification
NCQA

Key Personnel
President . . . . Orlando Gonzalez
Chief Executive Officer . . . . Richard Shinto
Chief Operating Officer . . . . Manuel Sanchez Sierra
Chief Financial Officer . . . . Carlos Vivaldi
Medical Director . . . . Benjamin Guardiola

709 Molina Healthcare of Puerto Rico
654 Av. Luis Munoz Rivera
Suite 907
San Juan, PR 00918
Toll-Free: 877-335-3305
www.molinahealthcare.com
Subsidiary of: Molina Healthcare, Inc.
For Profit Organization: Yes

Healthplan and Services Defined
PLAN TYPE: Medicare
Model Type: Network
Plan Specialty: Dental, PBM, Vision, Integrated Medicare/Medicaid (Duals)
Benefits Offered: Dental, Prescription, Vision, Wellness, Life

Type of Coverage
Individual, Medicare, Supplemental Medicare, Medicaid

Geographic Areas Served
Statewide

Key Personnel
President . . . . Zivany Garcia-Velazquez

710 Triple-S Salud
1441 Avenida Franklin D. Roosevelt
San Juan, PR 00920
Toll-Free: 800-981-3241
Phone: 787-774-6060
Fax: 787-706-2833
salud.grupotriples.com
Subsidiary of: Blue Cross Blue Shield of Puerto Rico
Year Founded: 1959

Healthplan and Services Defined
PLAN TYPE: Multiple
Benefits Offered: Chiropractic, Dental, Disease Management, Home Care, Inpatient SNF, Physical Therapy, Podiatry, Prescription, Psychiatric, Vision, Wellness

Type of Coverage
Individual, Medicare, Supplemental Medicare

Geographic Areas Served
Puerto Rico

Accreditation Certification
TJC, URAC, NCQA

711 UnitedHealthcare of Puerto Rico
9700 Health Care Lane
Minnetonka, MN 55343
Toll-Free: 888-545-5205
www.uhc.com
Subsidiary of: UnitedHealth Group
Year Founded: 1977

Healthplan and Services Defined
PLAN TYPE: HMO/PPO
Model Type: Network
Plan Specialty: Behavioral Health, Dental, Disease Management, Lab, PBM, Vision, Radiology
Benefits Offered: Behavioral Health, Chiropractic, Dental, Disease Management, Long-Term Care, Physical Therapy, Prescription, Vision, Wellness, AD&D, Life, LTD, STD

Type of Coverage
Commercial, Individual, Indemnity, Medicare, Supplemental Medicare, Medicaid, Catastrophic, Family, Military, Veterans, Group

Geographic Areas Served
Statewide. Puerto Rico is covered by the Minnesota branch

Network Qualifications
Pre-Admission Certification: Yes

Peer Review Type
  Utilization Review: Yes
  Second Surgical Opinion: Yes
  Case Management: Yes

Publishes and Distributes Report Card: Yes

Accreditation Certification
  TJC, NCQA

Specialty Managed Care Partners
  Enters into Contracts with Regional Business Coalitions: Yes

RHODE ISLAND

Health Insurance Coverage Status and Type of Coverage by Age

Category	All Persons Number	All Persons %	Under 19 years Number	Under 19 years %	Under 65 years Number	Under 65 years %
Total population	1,044 *(1)*	100.0 *(0.0)*	220 *(2)*	100.0 *(0.0)*	863 *(1)*	100.0 *(0.0)*
Covered by some type of health insurance	1,001 *(6)*	95.9 *(0.6)*	216 *(3)*	98.1 *(0.7)*	821 *(6)*	95.2 *(0.7)*
Covered by private health insurance	765 *(13)*	73.3 *(1.3)*	161 *(6)*	73.0 *(2.9)*	661 *(12)*	76.5 *(1.4)*
Employer-based	633 *(14)*	60.7 *(1.4)*	141 *(7)*	64.2 *(2.9)*	577 *(14)*	66.8 *(1.6)*
Direct purchase	161 *(9)*	15.4 *(0.9)*	22 *(3)*	10.0 *(1.6)*	101 *(8)*	11.7 *(0.9)*
TRICARE	21 *(3)*	2.0 *(0.3)*	4 *(1)*	1.7 *(0.5)*	11 *(2)*	1.3 *(0.3)*
Covered by public health insurance	378 *(12)*	36.2 *(1.1)*	73 *(5)*	33.2 *(2.5)*	205 *(11)*	23.8 *(1.3)*
Medicaid	212 *(11)*	20.4 *(1.1)*	72 *(5)*	32.8 *(2.5)*	186 *(11)*	21.6 *(1.2)*
Medicare	205 *(5)*	19.7 *(0.4)*	2 *(1)*	0.9 *(0.5)*	33 *(4)*	3.9 *(0.5)*
VA Care	22 *(2)*	2.1 *(0.2)*	Z *(1)*	0.2 *(0.3)*	6 *(2)*	0.7 *(0.2)*
Not covered at any time during the year	43 *(6)*	4.1 *(0.6)*	4 *(2)*	1.9 *(0.7)*	42 *(6)*	4.8 *(0.7)*

Note: Numbers in thousands; Figures cover civilian noninstitutionalized population in 2019; N/A indicates that data was not available; Z represents or rounds to zero; Margin of error appears in parenthesis and is calculated using replicate weights.
Source: U.S. Census Bureau, American Community Survey, Table HI-05. Health Insurance Coverage Status and Type of Coverage by State and Age for All People: 2019

Rhode Island

712 Aetna Health of Rhode Island
151 Farmington Avenue
Hartford, CT 06156
Toll-Free: 800-872-3862
www.aetna.com
Subsidiary of: CVS Health / Aetna Inc.
For Profit Organization: Yes

Healthplan and Services Defined
  PLAN TYPE: PPO
  Other Type: POS
  Model Type: Network
  Plan Specialty: Behavioral Health, EPO, Lab, PBM, Radiology
  Benefits Offered: Behavioral Health, Disease Management, Long-Term Care, Physical Therapy, Podiatry, Prescription, Psychiatric, Wellness, Life, LTD, STD

Type of Coverage
  Commercial, Student health

Type of Payment Plans Offered
  POS, FFS

Geographic Areas Served
  Statewide

Key Personnel
  President, North Atlantic . . . . Michael Cole

713 Blue Cross & Blue Shield of Rhode Island
500 Exchange Street
Providence, RI 02903
Toll-Free: 877-353-1258
Phone: 401-574-2911
www.bcbsri.com
Subsidiary of: Health and Wellness Institute
Non-Profit Organization: Yes
Year Founded: 1939
Number of Primary Care Physicians: 100,000
Total Enrollment: 600,000

Healthplan and Services Defined
  PLAN TYPE: HMO
  Model Type: Staff
  Plan Specialty: Dental, Vision
  Benefits Offered: Dental, Disease Management, Home Care, Inpatient SNF, Prescription, Vision, Wellness

Type of Coverage
  Commercial, Individual, Medicare

Type of Payment Plans Offered
  DFFS

Geographic Areas Served
  Statewide

Subscriber Information
  Average Monthly Fee Per Subscriber
    (Employee + Employer Contribution):
      Employee Only (Self): Varies
      Employee & 1 Family Member: Varies
      Employee & 2 Family Members: Varies
      Medicare: Varies
  Average Annual Deductible Per Subscriber:
      Employee Only (Self): Varies
      Employee & 1 Family Member: Varies
      Employee & 2 Family Members: Varies

Peer Review Type
  Case Management: Yes

Publishes and Distributes Report Card: Yes

Accreditation Certification
  URAC, NCQA

Key Personnel
  President/CEO . . . . Martha Wofford
  EVP/CFO. . . . . Mark Stewart
  EVP/Chief Legal Officer. . . . . Michele Lederberg
  EVP/Chief Medical Officer. . . . . Matt Collins, MD

714 CVS Caremark
One CVS Drive
Woonsocket, RI 02895
Toll-Free: 800-746-7287
www.caremark.com
Mailing Address: P.O. Box 6590, Lee's Summit, MO 64064-6590
Subsidiary of: CVS Health
For Profit Organization: Yes
Year Founded: 1963
Owned by an Integrated Delivery Network (IDN): Yes
Number of Affiliated Hospitals: 650
Number of Primary Care Physicians: 60,000
Total Enrollment: 70,000,000

Healthplan and Services Defined
  PLAN TYPE: Other
  Other Type: PBM
  Model Type: Staff
  Plan Specialty: Disease Management, PBM
  Benefits Offered: Disease Management, Prescription

Type of Payment Plans Offered
  POS, DFFS, FFS

Geographic Areas Served
  Nationwide

Peer Review Type
  Second Surgical Opinion: Yes
  Case Management: Yes

Publishes and Distributes Report Card: Yes

Accreditation Certification
  TJC, URAC

Key Personnel
  President. . . . . Alan M. Lotvin, MD

Specialty Managed Care Partners
  Enters into Contracts with Regional Business Coalitions: Yes

715 Neighborhood Health Plan of Rhode Island
910 Douglas Pike
Smithfield, RI 02917
Phone: 401-459-6075
www.nhpri.org
Non-Profit Organization: Yes
Year Founded: 1994
Number of Primary Care Physicians: 900
Number of Referral/Specialty Physicians: 2,700
Total Enrollment: 190,000
State Enrollment: 190,000

Healthplan and Services Defined
PLAN TYPE: HMO
Model Type: Network
Benefits Offered: Behavioral Health, Disease Management, Inpatient SNF, Prescription, Wellness

Type of Coverage
Commercial, Individual, Medicare, Medicaid

Peer Review Type
Case Management: Yes

Publishes and Distributes Report Card: Yes

Accreditation Certification
NCQA

Key Personnel
President/CEO.........................Peter M. Marino
Chief Financial Officer..................Michelle Sears
Chief Medical Officer..............Marylou Buyse, MD

716 Tufts Health Plan: Rhode Island
75 Fountain Street
Providence, RI 02902
www.tuftshealthplan.com
Secondary Address: 705 Mt Auburn Street, Watertown, MA 02742, 617-972-9400
Non-Profit Organization: Yes
Year Founded: 1979
Number of Affiliated Hospitals: 90
Number of Primary Care Physicians: 25,000
Number of Referral/Specialty Physicians: 12,500
Total Enrollment: 1,018,589

Healthplan and Services Defined
PLAN TYPE: Multiple
Model Type: IPA
Plan Specialty: ASO, Behavioral Health, Chiropractic, Disease Management, EPO, Lab, PBM, Vision, Radiology, UR, Pharmacy
Benefits Offered: Behavioral Health, Chiropractic, Complementary Medicine, Disease Management, Home Care, Inpatient SNF, Physical Therapy, Podiatry, Prescription, Psychiatric, Transplant, Vision, Wellness

Type of Coverage
Commercial, Individual, Medicare, Supplemental Medicare, Medicaid

Type of Payment Plans Offered
POS, DFFS, FFS, Combination FFS & DFFS

Geographic Areas Served
Massachusetts, New Hampshire and Rhode Island

Subscriber Information
Average Monthly Fee Per Subscriber
(Employee + Employer Contribution):
Employee Only (Self): $190.00-220.00
Employee & 2 Family Members: $800.00-950.00
Medicare: $150.00
Average Annual Deductible Per Subscriber:
Employee Only (Self): $1000.00
Employee & 1 Family Member: $500.00
Employee & 2 Family Members: $3000.00
Average Subscriber Co-Payment:
Primary Care Physician: $10.00
Non-Network Physician: 20%
Prescription Drugs: $10/20/35
Hospital ER: $50.00
Home Health Care: $0
Home Health Care Max. Days/Visits Covered: 120 days
Nursing Home: $0
Nursing Home Max. Days/Visits Covered: 120 days

Network Qualifications
Pre-Admission Certification: No

Peer Review Type
Utilization Review: Yes
Case Management: Yes

Publishes and Distributes Report Card: Yes

Accreditation Certification
TJC, AAPI, NCQA

Key Personnel
President/CEO.........................Cain A. Hayes
Chief Medical Officer............Michael Sherman, MD

Average Claim Compensation
Physician's Fees Charged: 75%
Hospital's Fees Charged: 70%

Specialty Managed Care Partners
Advance PCS, Private Healthe Care Systems

Employer References
Commonwealth of Massachuestts, Fleet Boston, Roman Catholic Archdiocese of Boston, City of Boston, State Street Corporation

717 UnitedHealthcare Community Plan Rhode Island
UnitedHealthcare Customer Service
P.O. Box 30769
Salt Lake City, UT 84130-0769
Toll-Free: 888-545-5205
www.uhccommunityplan.com/ri
Subsidiary of: UnitedHealth Group
For Profit Organization: Yes

Healthplan and Services Defined
PLAN TYPE: Multiple
Model Type: Network
Benefits Offered: Dental, Home Care, Podiatry, Prescription, Vision, Wellness, Hearing

Type of Coverage
  Medicare, Medicaid, CHIP

Geographic Areas Served
  Statewide

Key Personnel
  CEO, Community Plan RI . . . . Patrice Cooper
    pcooper@uhc.com

---

718 UnitedHealthcare of Rhode Island
475 Kilvert Street
Warwick, RI 02886
Toll-Free: 888-545-5205
Phone: 401-737-6900
www.uhc.com
Subsidiary of: UnitedHealth Group
For Profit Organization: Yes
Year Founded: 1983
Owned by an Integrated Delivery Network (IDN): Yes

Healthplan and Services Defined
PLAN TYPE: HMO/PPO
Model Type: Network
Plan Specialty: Behavioral Health, Chiropractic, Dental, Disease Management, Lab, PBM, Vision, Radiology
Benefits Offered: Behavioral Health, Dental, Disease Management, Long-Term Care, Prescription, Vision, Wellness, Life, LTD, STD

Type of Coverage
  Commercial, Individual, Medicare, Supplemental Medicare, Medicaid, Catastrophic, Family, Military, Veterans, Group

Type of Payment Plans Offered
  Combination FFS & DFFS

Geographic Areas Served
  Statewide

Publishes and Distributes Report Card: Yes

Accreditation Certification
  AAPI, NCQA

Key Personnel
  CEO, New England. . . . . Tim Archer

Specialty Managed Care Partners
  G Tec, State of RI

SOUTH CAROLINA

Health Insurance Coverage Status and Type of Coverage by Age

Category	All Persons Number	All Persons %	Under 19 years Number	Under 19 years %	Under 65 years Number	Under 65 years %
Total population	5,049 *(3)*	100.0 *(0.0)*	1,182 *(5)*	100.0 *(0.0)*	4,131 *(4)*	100.0 *(0.0)*
Covered by some type of health insurance	4,501 *(17)*	89.2 *(0.3)*	1,113 *(8)*	94.2 *(0.6)*	3,588 *(17)*	86.8 *(0.4)*
Covered by private health insurance	3,345 *(28)*	66.3 *(0.6)*	662 *(14)*	56.0 *(1.2)*	2,787 *(28)*	67.4 *(0.7)*
Employer-based	2,649 *(32)*	52.5 *(0.6)*	565 *(15)*	47.8 *(1.2)*	2,356 *(31)*	57.0 *(0.7)*
Direct purchase	705 *(19)*	14.0 *(0.4)*	83 *(7)*	7.0 *(0.6)*	416 *(17)*	10.1 *(0.4)*
TRICARE	252 *(12)*	5.0 *(0.2)*	46 *(5)*	3.9 *(0.4)*	152 *(11)*	3.7 *(0.3)*
Covered by public health insurance	1,875 *(23)*	37.1 *(0.4)*	503 *(14)*	42.5 *(1.2)*	981 *(22)*	23.8 *(0.5)*
Medicaid	948 *(22)*	18.8 *(0.4)*	499 *(14)*	42.2 *(1.2)*	833 *(22)*	20.2 *(0.5)*
Medicare	1,043 *(8)*	20.7 *(0.2)*	6 *(2)*	0.5 *(0.1)*	151 *(7)*	3.7 *(0.2)*
VA Care	165 *(7)*	3.3 *(0.1)*	2 *(1)*	0.2 *(0.1)*	75 *(6)*	1.8 *(0.1)*
Not covered at any time during the year	548 *(17)*	10.8 *(0.3)*	69 *(7)*	5.8 *(0.6)*	543 *(17)*	13.2 *(0.4)*

Note: Numbers in thousands; Figures cover civilian noninstitutionalized population in 2019; N/A indicates that data was not available; Z represents or rounds to zero; Margin of error appears in parenthesis and is calculated using replicate weights.

Source: U.S. Census Bureau, American Community Survey, Table HI-05. Health Insurance Coverage Status and Type of Coverage by State and Age for All People: 2019

South Carolina

719 Absolute Total Care - Healthy Connections Medicaid
100 Center Point Circle
Suite 100
Columbia, SC 29201
Toll-Free: 866-433-6041
www.absolutetotalcare.com
Subsidiary of: Centene Corporation
For Profit Organization: Yes

Healthplan and Services Defined
PLAN TYPE: Other
Model Type: Network
Benefits Offered: Behavioral Health, Disease Management, Prescription, Vision

Type of Coverage
Medicaid

Key Personnel
President/CEO .... John McClellan

720 Absolute Total Care - Healthy Connections Prime
100 Center Point Circle
Columbia, SC 29210
Toll-Free: 855-735-4398
mmp.absolutetotalcare.com
Subsidiary of: Centene Corporation
For Profit Organization: Yes

Healthplan and Services Defined
PLAN TYPE: Medicare
Model Type: Network
Benefits Offered: Prescription

Type of Coverage
Medicare, Medicaid, Medicare-Medicaid Plan

Geographic Areas Served
Upstate Region: Abbeville, Allendale, Anderson, Bamberg, Barnwell, Chester, Edgefield, Fairfield, Greenville, Greenwood, Kershaw, Laurens, Lexington, McCormick, Newberry, Pickens, Richland, Saluda, Spartanburg, and Union. Coastal Region: Beaufort, Berkeley, Calhoun, Charleston, Chesterfield, Clarendon, Colleton, Dillon, Florence, Georgetown, Hampton, Jasper, Lee, Marion, Marlboro, Orangeburg, and Williamsburg

721 Access One Consumer Health, Inc.
84 Villa Road
Greenville, SC 29615
Toll-Free: 800-896-1962
www.accessonedmpo.com
For Profit Organization: Yes

Healthplan and Services Defined
PLAN TYPE: Other
Other Type: Discount Plans
Benefits Offered: Dental, Prescription, Vision, Hearing, Chiropractic

Type of Coverage
Commercial, Individual

Key Personnel
President/CEO .... Mark Spinner

722 Aetna Health of South Carolina
151 Farmington Avenue
Hartford, CT 06156
Toll-Free: 800-872-3862
www.aetna.com
Subsidiary of: CVS Health / Aetna Inc.
For Profit Organization: Yes

Healthplan and Services Defined
PLAN TYPE: PPO
Other Type: POS
Model Type: Network
Plan Specialty: Behavioral Health, EPO, Lab, PBM, Radiology
Benefits Offered: Behavioral Health, Dental, Disease Management, Long-Term Care, Physical Therapy, Podiatry, Prescription, Psychiatric, Vision, Wellness, Life, LTD, STD

Type of Coverage
Commercial, Supplemental Medicare, Student health

Geographic Areas Served
29 counties

723 Allwell from Absolute Total Care
100 Center Point Circle
Columbia, SC 29210
Toll-Free: 855-766-1497
allwell.absolutetotalcare.com
Subsidiary of: Centene Corporation
For Profit Organization: Yes

Healthplan and Services Defined
PLAN TYPE: Medicare
Model Type: Network
Benefits Offered: Dental, Prescription

Type of Coverage
Medicare, Supplemental Medicare, Medicare Advantage

Geographic Areas Served
Abbeville, Allendale, Anderson, Bamberg, Barnwell, Beaufort, Berkeley, Calhoun, Charleston, Chester, Chesterfield, Clarendon, Colleton, Dillon, Edgefield, Fairfield, Florence, Georgetown, Greenville, Greenwood, Hampton, Jasper, Kershaw, Laurens, Lee, Marion, Marlboro, McCormick, Newberry, Orangeburg, Pickens, Richland, Saluda, Spartanburg, Union, and Williamsburg counties

724 Ambetter from Absolute Total Care
1441 Main Street
Suite 900
Columbia, SC 29201
Toll-Free: 833-270-5443
ambetter.absolutetotalcare.com
Subsidiary of: Centene Corporation
For Profit Organization: Yes

Healthplan and Services Defined
PLAN TYPE: Other
Model Type: Network
Plan Specialty: Lab
Benefits Offered: Behavioral Health, Disease Management, Physical Therapy, Prescription, Wellness, Maternity and newborn care

Type of Coverage
Health Insurance Marketplace

Geographic Areas Served
Charleston

725 Blue Cross & Blue Shield of South Carolina
I-20 East At Alpine Rd.
Columbia, SC 29219
Toll-Free: 800-288-2227
Phone: 803-788-0222
www.southcarolinablues.com
For Profit Organization: Yes
Year Founded: 1946
Number of Affiliated Hospitals: 64
Number of Primary Care Physicians: 3,434
Number of Referral/Specialty Physicians: 5,473
Total Enrollment: 950,000
State Enrollment: 950,000

Healthplan and Services Defined
PLAN TYPE: HMO/PPO
Model Type: Network
Plan Specialty: ASO, Behavioral Health, Chiropractic, Dental, Disease Management, EPO, Lab, PBM, Vision, Radiology, UR
Benefits Offered: Behavioral Health, Chiropractic, Complementary Medicine, Dental, Disease Management, Physical Therapy, Podiatry, Prescription, Psychiatric, Transplant, Vision, Wellness
Offers Demand Management Patient Information Service: Yes

Type of Coverage
Commercial, Individual, Medicare

Type of Payment Plans Offered
POS, DFFS, Capitated, FFS, Combination FFS & DFFS

Geographic Areas Served
Statewide

Network Qualifications
Pre-Admission Certification: Yes

Peer Review Type
Utilization Review: Yes
Second Surgical Opinion: Yes

Publishes and Distributes Report Card: Yes

Accreditation Certification
URAC, NCQA
TJC Accreditation, Utilization Review, Pre-Admission Certification, State Licensure, Quality Assurance Program

Key Personnel
President . . . . Davis S. Pankau

Specialty Managed Care Partners
Enters into Contracts with Regional Business Coalitions: Yes

726 BlueChoice Health Plan of South Carolina
P.O. Box 6170
Columbia, SC 29260-6170
Toll-Free: 800-868-2528
www.bluechoicesc.com
For Profit Organization: Yes
Year Founded: 1984
Owned by an Integrated Delivery Network (IDN): Yes
Federally Qualified: Yes
Number of Affiliated Hospitals: 68
Number of Primary Care Physicians: 7,700
Number of Referral/Specialty Physicians: 4,199
Total Enrollment: 205,000
State Enrollment: 205,000

Healthplan and Services Defined
PLAN TYPE: Multiple
Model Type: IPA
Plan Specialty: ASO, Disease Management, EPO, PBM, Vision, UR
Benefits Offered: Behavioral Health, Chiropractic, Complementary Medicine, Dental, Disease Management, Home Care, Inpatient SNF, Physical Therapy, Podiatry, Prescription, Psychiatric, Transplant, Vision, Wellness, AD&D, Life, LTD, STD, EAP
Offers Demand Management Patient Information Service: Yes

Type of Coverage
Commercial, Individual, Medicare, Medicaid, Medicare Advantage
Catastrophic Illness Benefit: Maximum $2M

Type of Payment Plans Offered
POS, DFFS, Combination FFS & DFFS

Geographic Areas Served
Statewide

Subscriber Information
Average Annual Deductible Per Subscriber:
   Employee Only (Self): $0
   Employee & 1 Family Member: $0
   Employee & 2 Family Members: $0
Average Subscriber Co-Payment:
   Primary Care Physician: $15.00
   Non-Network Physician: $25.00
   Prescription Drugs: $3 tier
   Hospital ER: 10%
   Home Health Care: 10%
   Home Health Care Max. Days/Visits Covered: Unlimited
   Nursing Home Max. Days/Visits Covered: 120 days

Network Qualifications
Pre-Admission Certification: Yes

Peer Review Type
Utilization Review: Yes
Second Surgical Opinion: Yes
Case Management: Yes

Publishes and Distributes Report Card: Yes

Accreditation Certification
NCQA
Quality Assurance Program

Key Personnel
President .... Scott Graves

Average Claim Compensation
Physician's Fees Charged: 65%
Hospital's Fees Charged: 65%

Specialty Managed Care Partners
Companion Benefit Alternatives (CBA)

Employer References
Alltel Corporation, Bank of America, Kimberley Clark, BellSouth, United Parcel Service

---

727 Cigna HealthCare of South Carolina
11016 Rushmore Drive
Suite 300
Charlotte, NC 28277
Toll-Free: 800-997-1654
www.cigna.com
Subsidiary of: Cigna Corporation
For Profit Organization: Yes
Year Founded: 1982

Healthplan and Services Defined
PLAN TYPE: HMO
Other Type: POS
Plan Specialty: Behavioral Health, Dental
Benefits Offered: Behavioral Health, Dental, Disease Management, Prescription, Vision, Wellness, AD&D, Life, LTD, STD

Type of Coverage
Commercial, Individual, Medicare, Supplemental Medicare, Medicaid, Part-time and hourly workers; Union

Geographic Areas Served
Statewide

Key Personnel
Market Pres., Carolinas .... Charles Pitts

---

728 Delta Dental of South Carolina
12399 Gravois Road
St. Louis, MO 63127-1702
Toll-Free: 800-529-3268
Phone: 803-731-2495
service@deltadentalmo.com
www.DELTADENTALSC.COM
Mailing Address: P.O. Box 8690, St. Louis, MO 63126-0690
Non-Profit Organization: Yes
Year Founded: 1969

Total Enrollment: 1,900,000

Healthplan and Services Defined
PLAN TYPE: Dental
Other Type: Dental PPO
Model Type: Network
Plan Specialty: ASO, Dental
Benefits Offered: Dental

Type of Coverage
Commercial, Individual
Catastrophic Illness Benefit: None

Geographic Areas Served
South Carolina and Missouri

Key Personnel
President/CEO .... E.B. Rob Goren
CFO/Corporate Counsel .... Barbara C. Bentrup
COO/Chief Dental Officer.............. Ronald E. Inge
Chief Actuary.................... Jonathan R. Jennings
Chief Information Officer .... Karl A. Mudra
Sales/Marketing Officer .... Jim Barone

---

729 Humana Health Insurance of South Carolina
240 Harbison Boulevard
Suite H
Columbia, SC 29212
Toll-Free: 877-486-2622
Phone: 803-865-7663
Fax: 803-865-1760
www.humana.com
Secondary Address: 1025 Woodruff Road, Suite J108, Greenville, SC 29607, 864-968-2307
Subsidiary of: Humana Inc.
For Profit Organization: Yes

Healthplan and Services Defined
PLAN TYPE: HMO/PPO
Model Type: Network
Plan Specialty: Dental, Vision
Benefits Offered: Dental, Vision, Life, LTD, STD

Type of Coverage
Commercial

Geographic Areas Served
Statewide

Accreditation Certification
URAC, NCQA, CORE

Key Personnel
Market Director........................ Brent Minter

---

730 InStil Health
P.O. Box 100294
Mail Code AG-795
Columbia, SC 29202-3294
Toll-Free: 800-444-5445
www.myinstil.com
Subsidiary of: Celerian Group
For Profit Organization: Yes
Total Enrollment: 30,000

Healthplan and Services Defined
  PLAN TYPE: Medicare
  Plan Specialty: ASO
  Benefits Offered: Behavioral Health, Disease Management, Home Care, Physical Therapy, Psychiatric, Wellness

Type of Coverage
  Medicare, Supplemental Medicare

Accreditation Certification
  URAC

Key Personnel
  Network Manager . . . . Sandy Collins
  Provider Relations . . . . Carlotta Rose
    carlotta.rose@myinstil.com
  Service Consultant . . . . Julie Drew
  Assistant VP . . . . Jennifer N. Mashura
    jennifer.mashura@myinstil.com

---

731 Molina Healthcare of South Carolina
4105 Faber Place Drive
Suite 470
North Charleston, SC 29405
Toll-Free: 855-882-3901
www.molinahealthcare.com
Subsidiary of: Molina Healthcare, Inc.
For Profit Organization: Yes

Healthplan and Services Defined
  PLAN TYPE: Medicare
  Model Type: Network
  Plan Specialty: Dental, PBM, Vision, Integrated Medicare/Medicaid (Duals)
  Benefits Offered: Dental, Prescription, Vision, Wellness, Life

Type of Coverage
  Individual, Medicare, Supplemental Medicare, Medicaid

Geographic Areas Served
  Statewide

Key Personnel
  President . . . . Dora Wilson
  Chief Medical Officer . . . . Rick Shrouds, MD

---

732 Select Health of South Carolina
P.O. Box 40849
Charleston, SC 29423
Toll-Free: 800-741-6605
Phone: 843-569-1759
www.selecthealthofsc.com
Subsidiary of: AmeriHealth Mercy
For Profit Organization: Yes
Total Enrollment: 330,000
State Enrollment: 330,000

Healthplan and Services Defined
  PLAN TYPE: HMO
  Model Type: Medicaid
  Plan Specialty: Medicaid
  Benefits Offered: Chiropractic, Disease Management, Home Care, Inpatient SNF, Physical Therapy, Prescription, Psychiatric, Transplant, Vision, Wellness, Transportation; Hearing; Durable Medical Equipment; Family Planning; Labs & X-rays; Speech Therapy

Type of Coverage
  Medicaid

Geographic Areas Served
  Statewide

Peer Review Type
  Case Management: Yes

Publishes and Distributes Report Card: Yes

Accreditation Certification
  TJC, URAC, NCQA

Key Personnel
  Market President . . . . Courtnay Thompson
  Market CMO . . . . Kirt Caton, MD
  Dir., Provider Network. . . . . Peggy Vickery

---

733 UnitedHealthcare Community Plan South Carolina
UnitedHealthcare Customer Service
P.O. Box 30769
Salt Lake City, UT 84130-0769
Toll-Free: 888-545-5205
www.uhccommunityplan.com/sc
Subsidiary of: UnitedHealth Group
For Profit Organization: Yes

Healthplan and Services Defined
  PLAN TYPE: Medicare
  Other Type: Medicaid
  Model Type: Network
  Benefits Offered: Prescription, Hospitals, Doctors

Type of Coverage
  Medicare, Medicaid

Geographic Areas Served
  Statewide

---

734 UnitedHealthcare of South Carolina
107 Westpark Boulevard
Suite 110
Columbia, SC 29210
Toll-Free: 888-545-5205
Phone: 803-274-2819
www.uhc.com
Subsidiary of: UnitedHealth Group
For Profit Organization: Yes

Healthplan and Services Defined
  PLAN TYPE: HMO/PPO
  Model Type: Network
  Plan Specialty: Behavioral Health, Dental, Disease Management, PBM, Vision
  Benefits Offered: Behavioral Health, Dental, Disease Management, Long-Term Care, Prescription, Vision, Wellness, Life, LTD, STD

Type of Coverage
  Individual, Medicare, Supplemental Medicare, Medicaid, Catastrophic, Family, Military, Veterans, Group

Geographic Areas Served
Statewide

Accreditation Certification
AAPI, NCQA

Key Personnel
CEO, NC/SC Medicare . . . . Thomas O'Connor

SOUTH DAKOTA

Health Insurance Coverage Status and Type of Coverage by Age

Category	All Persons Number	All Persons %	Under 19 years Number	Under 19 years %	Under 65 years Number	Under 65 years %
Total population	867 *(1)*	100.0 *(0.0)*	226 *(2)*	100.0 *(0.0)*	720 *(1)*	100.0 *(0.0)*
Covered by some type of health insurance	779 *(6)*	89.8 *(0.7)*	209 *(4)*	92.2 *(1.4)*	632 *(6)*	87.8 *(0.8)*
Covered by private health insurance	622 *(8)*	71.8 *(0.9)*	150 *(5)*	66.5 *(2.0)*	535 *(7)*	74.3 *(1.0)*
Employer-based	471 *(10)*	54.4 *(1.1)*	126 *(5)*	55.5 *(2.3)*	445 *(10)*	61.8 *(1.3)*
Direct purchase	153 *(7)*	17.7 *(0.8)*	24 *(3)*	10.5 *(1.4)*	92 *(6)*	12.8 *(0.9)*
TRICARE	31 *(3)*	3.6 *(0.4)*	7 *(2)*	2.9 *(0.7)*	21 *(3)*	2.9 *(0.4)*
Covered by public health insurance	267 *(8)*	30.7 *(0.9)*	67 *(5)*	29.4 *(2.1)*	124 *(8)*	17.2 *(1.1)*
Medicaid	114 *(8)*	13.1 *(0.9)*	66 *(5)*	29.0 *(2.1)*	102 *(8)*	14.2 *(1.0)*
Medicare	163 *(3)*	18.8 *(0.4)*	1 *(Z)*	0.4 *(0.2)*	21 *(3)*	2.9 *(0.4)*
VA Care	32 *(3)*	3.7 *(0.3)*	Z *(Z)*	Z *(Z)*	13 *(2)*	1.8 *(0.3)*
Not covered at any time during the year	88 *(6)*	10.2 *(0.7)*	18 *(3)*	7.8 *(1.4)*	88 *(6)*	12.2 *(0.8)*

Note: Numbers in thousands; Figures cover civilian noninstitutionalized population in 2019; N/A indicates that data was not available; Z represents or rounds to zero; Margin of error appears in parenthesis and is calculated using replicate weights.
Source: U.S. Census Bureau, American Community Survey, Table HI-05. Health Insurance Coverage Status and Type of Coverage by State and Age for All People: 2019

South Dakota

735 Avera Health Plans
5300 S Broadland Lane
Sioux Falls, SD 57108
Toll-Free: 855-692-8372
Phone: 605-322-4545
sales@averahealthplans.com
www.averahealthplans.com
Total Enrollment: 63,000
State Enrollment: 63,000

Healthplan and Services Defined
PLAN TYPE: HMO
Benefits Offered: Disease Management, Prescription, Wellness, Health Education, EAP

Type of Coverage
Commercial, Individual

Type of Payment Plans Offered
POS

Geographic Areas Served
Statewide

Accreditation Certification
URAC

736 DakotaCare
2600 W 49th Street
Sioux Falls, SD 57105
Toll-Free: 800-325-5598
www.dakotacare.com
Subsidiary of: Avera Health
For Profit Organization: Yes
Year Founded: 1986
Physician Owned Organization: Yes
Number of Affiliated Hospitals: 74
Number of Primary Care Physicians: 825
Number of Referral/Specialty Physicians: 950
Total Enrollment: 118,600
State Enrollment: 24,310

Healthplan and Services Defined
PLAN TYPE: HMO
Model Type: IPA
Plan Specialty: ASO, Behavioral Health, Chiropractic, Dental, Disease Management, Lab, PBM, Vision, Radiology, UR
Benefits Offered: Behavioral Health, Chiropractic, Complementary Medicine, Dental, Disease Management, Home Care, Inpatient SNF, Physical Therapy, Podiatry, Prescription, Psychiatric, Transplant, Vision, Wellness, AD&D, Life, LTD, STD
Offers Demand Management Patient Information Service: No

Type of Payment Plans Offered
POS, FFS

Geographic Areas Served
HMO: all counties in South Dakota; TPA: Nationwide

Subscriber Information
Average Monthly Fee Per Subscriber
   (Employee + Employer Contribution):
      Employee Only (Self): Varies by plan
Average Annual Deductible Per Subscriber:
   Employee & 1 Family Member: $1500
Average Subscriber Co-Payment:
   Primary Care Physician: $25.00
   Non-Network Physician: $25.00
   Hospital ER: $150.00

Network Qualifications
Pre-Admission Certification: Yes

Peer Review Type
Utilization Review: Yes
Case Management: Yes

Publishes and Distributes Report Card: No

Accreditation Certification
URAC
Utilization Review, Pre-Admission Certification, State Licensure, Quality Assurance Program

Specialty Managed Care Partners
Prescription benefits - CVS Caremark, Chiropractic - CASD, Transplant - Optum, Dental Benefits - Companion Life, Life Insurance Benefits - Companion Life, Sun Life Standard, STD/LTD - Companion Life
Enters into Contracts with Regional Business Coalitions: No

737 Delta Dental of South Dakota
720 North Euclid Avenue
Pierre, SD 57501
Toll-Free: 877-841-1478
Phone: 605-224-7345
Fax: 605-494-2566
benefit@deltadentalsd.com
www.deltadentalsd.com
Mailing Address: PO Box 1157, Pierre, SD 57501
Non-Profit Organization: Yes
Year Founded: 1963
Total Enrollment: 60,000,000
State Enrollment: 340,000

Healthplan and Services Defined
PLAN TYPE: Dental
Other Type: Dental PPO
Model Type: Network
Plan Specialty: ASO, Dental
Benefits Offered: Dental

Type of Coverage
Commercial, Individual
Catastrophic Illness Benefit: None

Geographic Areas Served
Statewide

Key Personnel
President & CEO . . . . Scott Jones
VP, Operations . . . . Mick Heckenlaible
VP, Finance . . . . Kirby Scott
VP, Underwriting . . . . Jeff Miller

VP, Information Tech . . . . Gene Tetzlaff

738 First Choice of the Midwest
100 S Spring Avenue
Suite 220
Sioux Falls, SD 57104-3660
Toll-Free: 888-246-9949
Phone: 605-332-5955
Fax: 605-332-5953
info@1choicem.com
www.1choicem.com
Mailing Address: P.O. Box 5078, Sioux Falls, SD 57117-5078
For Profit Organization: Yes
Year Founded: 1997
Owned by an Integrated Delivery Network (IDN): Yes
Number of Referral/Specialty Physicians: 6,924
Total Enrollment: 87,000
State Enrollment: 25,000

Healthplan and Services Defined
  PLAN TYPE: PPO
  Model Type: Network, Open Staff
  Plan Specialty: ASO, Behavioral Health, Chiropractic, Disease Management, EPO, Lab, Radiology, Worker's Compensation
  Benefits Offered: Behavioral Health, Chiropractic, Complementary Medicine, Home Care, Inpatient SNF, Long-Term Care, Physical Therapy, Podiatry, Prescription, Psychiatric, Transplant, Vision, Wellness, Worker's Compensation, Durable Medical Equipment

Type of Payment Plans Offered
  DFFS

Geographic Areas Served
  Colorado, Idaho, Iowa, Minnesota, Montana, Nebraska, North Dakota, South Dakota, Utah, and Wyoming

Network Qualifications
  Pre-Admission Certification: No

Accreditation Certification
  TJC, NCQA

Average Claim Compensation
  Physician's Fees Charged: 85%
  Hospital's Fees Charged: 90%

Specialty Managed Care Partners
  Enters into Contracts with Regional Business Coalitions: Yes

739 UnitedHealthcare of South Dakota
9700 Health Care Lane
Minnetonka, MN 55343
Toll-Free: 888-545-5205
www.uhc.com
Subsidiary of: UnitedHealth Group
For Profit Organization: Yes
Year Founded: 1977

Healthplan and Services Defined
  PLAN TYPE: HMO/PPO
  Model Type: Network
  Plan Specialty: Behavioral Health, Dental, Disease Management, Lab, PBM, Vision, Radiology
  Benefits Offered: Behavioral Health, Chiropractic, Dental, Disease Management, Long-Term Care, Physical Therapy, Prescription, Vision, Wellness, AD&D, Life, LTD, STD

Type of Coverage
  Commercial, Individual, Indemnity, Medicare, Supplemental Medicare, Medicaid, Catastrophic, Family, Military, Veterans, Group

Geographic Areas Served
  Statewide. South Dakota is covered by the Minnesota branch

Network Qualifications
  Pre-Admission Certification: Yes

Peer Review Type
  Utilization Review: Yes
  Second Surgical Opinion: Yes
  Case Management: Yes

Publishes and Distributes Report Card: Yes

Accreditation Certification
  TJC, NCQA

Key Personnel
  CEO, MN/ND/SD . . . . Brett Edelson

Specialty Managed Care Partners
  Enters into Contracts with Regional Business Coalitions: Yes

740 Wellmark Blue Cross & Blue Shield of South Dakota
1601 W Madison Street
Sioux Falls, SD 57104
Toll-Free: 800-524-9242
Phone: 605-373-7200
www.wellmark.com
Secondary Address: 1331 Grand Avenue, Des Moines, IA 50309, 515-376-4500
For Profit Organization: Yes
Owned by an Integrated Delivery Network (IDN): Yes
Number of Affiliated Hospitals: 6,000
Number of Primary Care Physicians: 600,000
Total Enrollment: 1,800,000
State Enrollment: 300,000

Healthplan and Services Defined
  PLAN TYPE: Multiple
  Model Type: Network
  Plan Specialty: ASO, Behavioral Health, Chiropractic, Dental, Disease Management, EPO, Lab, PBM, Vision, Radiology, UR
  Benefits Offered: Behavioral Health, Chiropractic, Complementary Medicine, Dental, Disease Management, Home Care, Inpatient SNF, Physical Therapy, Podiatry, Prescription, Psychiatric, Transplant, Vision, Wellness, AD&D, Life, LTD, STD

Type of Coverage
  Commercial, Individual, Indemnity, Medicare, Supplemental Medicare, Medicaid, Catastrophic
  Catastrophic Illness Benefit: Maximum $1M

Geographic Areas Served
South Dakota and Iowa

Publishes and Distributes Report Card: Yes

Accreditation Certification
AAAHC, TJC, URAC, NCQA

Key Personnel
Chairman/CEO.........................John D. Forsyth
Chairman/President/CEO ....Jose E. Almeida
CFO/Chief Admin. Officer..............Peter S. Hellman

Specialty Managed Care Partners
American Health Ways

TENNESSEE

Health Insurance Coverage Status and Type of Coverage by Age

Category	All Persons Number	All Persons %	Under 19 years Number	Under 19 years %	Under 65 years Number	Under 65 years %
Total population	6,719 *(3)*	100.0 *(0.0)*	1,600 *(7)*	100.0 *(0.0)*	5,608 *(5)*	100.0 *(0.0)*
Covered by some type of health insurance	6,038 *(20)*	89.9 *(0.3)*	1,520 *(9)*	95.0 *(0.5)*	4,932 *(19)*	87.9 *(0.4)*
Covered by private health insurance	4,439 *(34)*	66.1 *(0.5)*	939 *(18)*	58.7 *(1.1)*	3,810 *(33)*	67.9 *(0.6)*
Employer-based	3,564 *(35)*	53.0 *(0.5)*	817 *(17)*	51.0 *(1.1)*	3,274 *(34)*	58.4 *(0.6)*
Direct purchase	905 *(20)*	13.5 *(0.3)*	104 *(8)*	6.5 *(0.5)*	538 *(17)*	9.6 *(0.3)*
TRICARE	252 *(12)*	3.7 *(0.2)*	53 *(6)*	3.3 *(0.4)*	160 *(11)*	2.9 *(0.2)*
Covered by public health insurance	2,431 *(27)*	36.2 *(0.4)*	652 *(19)*	40.7 *(1.2)*	1,351 *(26)*	24.1 *(0.5)*
Medicaid	1,318 *(28)*	19.6 *(0.4)*	647 *(19)*	40.5 *(1.1)*	1,175 *(27)*	21.0 *(0.5)*
Medicare	1,269 *(10)*	18.9 *(0.2)*	7 *(2)*	0.4 *(0.1)*	191 *(8)*	3.4 *(0.2)*
VA Care	187 *(8)*	2.8 *(0.1)*	1 *(1)*	0.1 *(0.1)*	90 *(6)*	1.6 *(0.1)*
Not covered at any time during the year	682 *(20)*	10.1 *(0.3)*	80 *(7)*	5.0 *(0.5)*	676 *(20)*	12.1 *(0.4)*

Note: Numbers in thousands; Figures cover civilian noninstitutionalized population in 2019; N/A indicates that data was not available; Z represents or rounds to zero; Margin of error appears in parenthesis and is calculated using replicate weights.
Source: U.S. Census Bureau, American Community Survey, Table HI-05. Health Insurance Coverage Status and Type of Coverage by State and Age for All People: 2019

Tennessee

741 Aetna Health of Tennessee
151 Farmington Avenue
Hartford, CT 06156
Toll-Free: 800-872-3862
www.aetna.com
Subsidiary of: CVS Health / Aetna Inc.
For Profit Organization: Yes

Healthplan and Services Defined
  PLAN TYPE: HMO/PPO
  Other Type: POS
  Model Type: Network
  Plan Specialty: Behavioral Health, EPO, Lab, PBM, Radiology
  Benefits Offered: Behavioral Health, Dental, Disease Management, Long-Term Care, Physical Therapy, Podiatry, Prescription, Psychiatric, Vision, Wellness, Life, LTD, STD

Type of Coverage
  Commercial, Student health

Geographic Areas Served
  Statewide

742 Ambetter of Tennessee
P.O. Box 5010
Farmington, MO 63640-5010
Toll-Free: 833-709-4735
www.ambetteroftennessee.com
Subsidiary of: Centene Corporation
For Profit Organization: Yes

Healthplan and Services Defined
  PLAN TYPE: Other
  Model Type: Network
  Plan Specialty: Lab
  Benefits Offered: Behavioral Health, Disease Management, Physical Therapy, Prescription, Wellness, Maternity and newborn care

Type of Coverage
  Health Insurance Marketplace

Geographic Areas Served
  Bledsoe, Bradley, Fayette, Franklin, Grundy, Hamilton, Haywood, Lauderdale, Marion, McMinn, Meigs, Polk, Rhea, Sequatchie, Shelby, and Tipton counties

743 Amerigroup Tennessee
22 Century Boulevard
Suite 220
Nashville, TN 37214
Toll-Free: 800-600-4441
Phone: 615-231-6065
www.myamerigroup.com/tn
Subsidiary of: Anthem, Inc.
For Profit Organization: Yes
Year Founded: 2007

Healthplan and Services Defined
  PLAN TYPE: Medicare
  Plan Specialty: Behavioral Health, Dental, Vision, Taking Care of Baby and Me Program
  Benefits Offered: Behavioral Health, Dental, Prescription, Vision

Geographic Areas Served
  Statewide

Accreditation Certification
  NCQA

Key Personnel
  Director, Contracting.................Stephanie Dowell

744 Baptist Health Services Group
350 N Humphreys Boulevard
4th Floor
Memphis, TN 38120
Toll-Free: 800-522-2474
Phone: 901-227-2474
bhsginfo@bmhcc.org
www.bhsgonline.org
Subsidiary of: Baptist Memorial Health Care Corporation
Non-Profit Organization: Yes
Year Founded: 1984
Number of Affiliated Hospitals: 50
Number of Primary Care Physicians: 4,000
Number of Referral/Specialty Physicians: 2,073
Total Enrollment: 423,244

Healthplan and Services Defined
  PLAN TYPE: Other
  Model Type: Network, Provider Spons. Network
  Plan Specialty: Disease Management, Lab, Worker's Compensation
  Benefits Offered: Disease Management, Home Care, Long-Term Care, Physical Therapy, Podiatry, Transplant, Wellness, Orthopedics; Diabeties; Dialysis; Durable Medical Equipment; Occupational Therapy; Prosthetics
  Offers Demand Management Patient Information Service: No

Geographic Areas Served
  E Arkansas, SW Kentucky, N Mississipi, SE Missouri, and W Tennessee

Subscriber Information
  Average Monthly Fee Per Subscriber
    (Employee + Employer Contribution):
      Employee Only (Self): n/a
  Average Annual Deductible Per Subscriber:
    Employee Only (Self): n/a
  Average Subscriber Co-Payment:
    Primary Care Physician: n/a

Publishes and Distributes Report Card: No

Average Claim Compensation
  Physician's Fees Charged: 1%
  Hospital's Fees Charged: 1%

Specialty Managed Care Partners
  Enters into Contracts with Regional Business Coalitions: Yes

745 Blue Cross & Blue Shield of Tennessee
1 Cameron Hill Circle
Chattanooga, TN 37402
Toll-Free: 800-565-9140
Phone: 423-535-5600
www.bcbst.com
Secondary Address: 85 North Danny Thomas Boulevard, Memphis, TN 38103-2398, 901-544-2111
Non-Profit Organization: Yes
Year Founded: 1945
Number of Affiliated Hospitals: 130
Number of Primary Care Physicians: 2,490
Number of Referral/Specialty Physicians: 15,000
Total Enrollment: 3,500,000
State Enrollment: 3,500,000

Healthplan and Services Defined
PLAN TYPE: Multiple
Plan Specialty: Dental, Disease Management, Vision
Benefits Offered: Dental, Disease Management, Prescription, Vision, Wellness

Type of Coverage
Medicare, Medicaid

Geographic Areas Served
Statewide

Key Personnel
President/CEO .... JD Hickey
EVP/CFO .... John Giblin
EVP/COO .... Scott Pierce
SVP, Operations/CMO .... Robin Young
Chief Gov. Relations Off. .... Dakasha Winton
SVP, Chief HR Officer .... Roy Vaughn
SVP, General Counsel .... Anne Hance
SVP/Chief Comms. Officer .... Dalya Qualls White

Specialty Managed Care Partners
Magellen Health Services

Employer References
State, local and government employees

746 Cigna HealthCare of Tennessee
1000 Corporate Centre Drive
Suite 500
Franklin, TN 37067
Toll-Free: 800-997-1654
www.cigna.com
Subsidiary of: Cigna Corporation
For Profit Organization: Yes

Healthplan and Services Defined
PLAN TYPE: HMO
Other Type: POS
Plan Specialty: Behavioral Health, Dental, Vision
Benefits Offered: Behavioral Health, Dental, Disease Management, Prescription, Vision, AD&D, Life, LTD, STD

Type of Coverage
Commercial, Individual

Type of Payment Plans Offered
POS

Geographic Areas Served
Statewide

Key Personnel
Pres., MidSouth Market .... Greg Allen

747 Delta Dental of Tennessee
240 Venture Circle
Nashville, TN 37228
Toll-Free: 800-223-3104
Fax: 615-244-8108
information@deltadentaltn.com
tennessee.deltadental.com
Non-Profit Organization: Yes
Year Founded: 1965
State Enrollment: 1,400,000

Healthplan and Services Defined
PLAN TYPE: Dental
Other Type: Dental PPO
Model Type: Network
Plan Specialty: ASO, Dental
Benefits Offered: Dental

Type of Coverage
Commercial, Individual
Catastrophic Illness Benefit: None

Geographic Areas Served
Statewide

Key Personnel
President/CEO .... Philip A. Wenk
Senior VP, Operations .... Kaye Martin
Chief Financial Officer .... Jeff Ballard
VP, Sales/Account Manager .... Jay Reavis

748 FCL Dental
101 Parklane Boulevard
Suite 301
Sugar Land, TX 77478
Phone: 866-912-7131
Fax: 281-313-7155
info@dentalsolutionsplus.com
dentalsolutionsplus.com
Subsidiary of: FCL Dental
For Profit Organization: Yes
Year Founded: 1986

Healthplan and Services Defined
PLAN TYPE: Dental
Other Type: Dental HMO
Plan Specialty: Dental, Vision
Benefits Offered: Dental, Vision

Subscriber Information
Average Annual Deductible Per Subscriber:
    Employee Only (Self): $0
    Employee & 1 Family Member: $0
    Employee & 2 Family Members: $0
    Medicare: $0
Average Subscriber Co-Payment:
    Primary Care Physician: $9.00

749 Health Choice LLC
1661 International Place
Suite 150
Memphis, TN 38120
Phone: 901-821-6700
Fax: 901-821-4900
contactus@myhealthchoice.com
www.myhealthchoice.com
Year Founded: 1985
Number of Affiliated Hospitals: 24
Number of Primary Care Physicians: 1,400
Total Enrollment: 518,000
State Enrollment: 518,000

Healthplan and Services Defined
PLAN TYPE: PPO
Model Type: PHO
Plan Specialty: ASO, Behavioral Health, Chiropractic, Disease Management, EPO, Lab, MSO, PBM, Radiology, Worker's Compensation, UR

Type of Payment Plans Offered
DFFS, FFS, Combination FFS & DFFS

Geographic Areas Served
Tennessee: Shelby, Tipton, Fayette; Arkansas: Crittenden, Cross; Mississippi: Tunica, Desoto; Missouri: Pemiscott

Network Qualifications
Pre-Admission Certification: Yes

Peer Review Type
Utilization Review: Yes
Second Surgical Opinion: Yes
Case Management: Yes

Accreditation Certification
AAAHC
TJC Accreditation, Medicare Approved, Utilization Review, Pre-Admission Certification, State Licensure, Quality Assurance Program

Key Personnel
President/CEO . . . . George Wortham, MD

Specialty Managed Care Partners
Lakeside Behavioral Health, Med Impact PEM
Memphis Business Group On Health

Employer References
City of Memphis Employees, Shelby County Government, Memphis Light Gas and Water, Methodist HealthCare Associates, St. Jude Children's Hospital

750 Humana Health Insurance of Tennessee
6515 Poplar Avenue
Suite 108
Memphis, TN 38119
Toll-Free: 866-254-1218
Fax: 901-685-0194
www.humana.com
Secondary Address: 320 Seven Springs Way, Suite 200, Brentwood, TN 37027, 877-365-1197
Subsidiary of: Humana Inc.
For Profit Organization: Yes

Healthplan and Services Defined
PLAN TYPE: HMO/PPO
Plan Specialty: ASO
Benefits Offered: Disease Management, Prescription, Wellness

Type of Coverage
Commercial, Individual

Geographic Areas Served
Statewide

Accreditation Certification
URAC, NCQA, CORE

Key Personnel
President, Medicare . . . . Doug Haaland

Specialty Managed Care Partners
Caremark Rx

Employer References
Tricare

751 UnitedHealthcare Community Plan Tennessee
UnitedHealthcare Customer Service
P.O. Box 30769
Salt Lake City, UT 84130-0769
Toll-Free: 888-545-5205
www.uhccommunityplan.com/tn
Subsidiary of: UnitedHealth Group
For Profit Organization: Yes

Healthplan and Services Defined
PLAN TYPE: Medicare
Other Type: Medicaid
Model Type: Network
Benefits Offered: Dental, Home Care, Podiatry, Prescription, Vision, Wellness, Acupuncture, Chiropractic

Type of Coverage
Medicare, Medicaid

Geographic Areas Served
Statewide

Key Personnel
CEO, Community Plan TN. . . . . Ute Strand
ute_w_strand@uhc.com

752 UnitedHealthcare of Tennessee
10 Cadillac Drive
Suite 200
Brentwood, TN 37027
Toll-Free: 800-695-1273
www.uhc.com
Subsidiary of: UnitedHealth Group
For Profit Organization: Yes
Year Founded: 1992

Healthplan and Services Defined
PLAN TYPE: HMO/PPO
Model Type: Network

Plan Specialty: ASO, Behavioral Health, Chiropractic, Dental, Disease Management, EPO, Lab, MSO, PBM, Vision, Radiology, UR

Benefits Offered: Behavioral Health, Dental, Disease Management, Long-Term Care, Prescription, Vision, Wellness, AD&D, Life, LTD, STD

Type of Coverage

Commercial, Individual, Indemnity, Medicare, Supplemental Medicare, Medicaid, Catastrophic, Family, Military, Veterans, Group,

Catastrophic Illness Benefit: Covered

Geographic Areas Served
Statewide

Network Qualifications
Pre-Admission Certification: Yes

Accreditation Certification
AAPI, NCQA

Key Personnel
CEO, Mid-South........................ Steve Wilson

Specialty Managed Care Partners
United Health Group, Spectra, United Behavioral Health
Enters into Contracts with Regional Business Coalitions: Yes

TEXAS

Health Insurance Coverage Status and Type of Coverage by Age

Category	All Persons Number	All Persons %	Under 19 years Number	Under 19 years %	Under 65 years Number	Under 65 years %
Total population	28,514 *(6)*	100.0 *(0.0)*	7,808 *(11)*	100.0 *(0.0)*	24,861 *(9)*	100.0 *(0.0)*
Covered by some type of health insurance	23,280 *(67)*	81.6 *(0.2)*	6,813 *(27)*	87.3 *(0.3)*	19,692 *(69)*	79.2 *(0.3)*
Covered by private health insurance	17,619 *(82)*	61.8 *(0.3)*	4,130 *(39)*	52.9 *(0.5)*	15,738 *(78)*	63.3 *(0.3)*
Employer-based	14,657 *(80)*	51.4 *(0.3)*	3,577 *(38)*	45.8 *(0.5)*	13,613 *(74)*	54.8 *(0.3)*
Direct purchase	3,040 *(46)*	10.7 *(0.2)*	476 *(16)*	6.1 *(0.2)*	2,129 *(41)*	8.6 *(0.2)*
TRICARE	821 *(26)*	2.9 *(0.1)*	193 *(14)*	2.5 *(0.2)*	562 *(23)*	2.3 *(0.1)*
Covered by public health insurance	8,076 *(53)*	28.3 *(0.2)*	2,881 *(41)*	36.9 *(0.5)*	4,631 *(53)*	18.6 *(0.2)*
Medicaid	4,533 *(52)*	15.9 *(0.2)*	2,843 *(41)*	36.4 *(0.5)*	4,018 *(49)*	16.2 *(0.2)*
Medicare	4,002 *(22)*	14.0 *(0.1)*	46 *(6)*	0.6 *(0.1)*	562 *(18)*	2.3 *(0.1)*
VA Care	618 *(15)*	2.2 *(0.1)*	12 *(3)*	0.2 *(Z)*	341 *(13)*	1.4 *(0.1)*
Not covered at any time during the year	5,234 *(67)*	18.4 *(0.2)*	995 *(25)*	12.7 *(0.3)*	5,169 *(67)*	20.8 *(0.3)*

Note: Numbers in thousands; Figures cover civilian noninstitutionalized population in 2019; N/A indicates that data was not available; Z represents or rounds to zero; Margin of error appears in parenthesis and is calculated using replicate weights.
Source: U.S. Census Bureau, American Community Survey, Table HI-05. Health Insurance Coverage Status and Type of Coverage by State and Age for All People: 2019

Texas

753 Aetna Better Health of Texas
P.O. Box 569150
Dallas, TX 75356-9150
Toll-Free: 800-556-1555
Fax: 866-510-3710
www.aetnabetterhealth.com/texas
Subsidiary of: CVS Health / Aetna Inc.
For Profit Organization: Yes

Healthplan and Services Defined
PLAN TYPE: HMO/PPO
Other Type: POS
Model Type: Network
Plan Specialty: Behavioral Health, EPO, Lab, PBM, Radiology
Benefits Offered: Behavioral Health, Dental, Disease Management, Long-Term Care, Physical Therapy, Podiatry, Prescription, Psychiatric, Vision, Wellness, Life, LTD, STD

Type of Coverage
Commercial, Medicaid, Student health

Geographic Areas Served
Statewide

Key Personnel
CEO .... Stephanie Rogers
Chief Medical Officer .... Heidi Schwarzwald, MD
Chief Financial Officer .... Jeffrey Roscoe

754 Alliance Regional Health Network
1501 S Coulter Street
Amarillo, TX 79106
Phone: 806-354-1000
Fax: 806-354-1122
www.nwtexashealthcare.com
Subsidiary of: Northwest Texas Healthcare System
For Profit Organization: Yes
Year Founded: 1986
Number of Affiliated Hospitals: 25
Number of Primary Care Physicians: 550
Total Enrollment: 80,000
State Enrollment: 80,000

Healthplan and Services Defined
PLAN TYPE: PPO
Model Type: Network
Plan Specialty: Behavioral Health, Radiology, Blood Management Program; Diabetes; Sleep Disorders; Surgery
Benefits Offered: Behavioral Health, Disease Management, Prescription, Wellness, Worker's Compensation, Occupational therapy

Geographic Areas Served
Northwest Texas

Network Qualifications
Pre-Admission Certification: Yes

Accreditation Certification
Medicare Approved, Utilization Review, State Licensure, Quality Assurance Program

Key Personnel
Chief Executive Officer .... Ryan Chandler
Chief Operating Officer .... Sandy Ethridge
Chief Medical Officer .... Brian Weis, MD
Chief Nursing Officer .... Patti Thompson

Employer References
City of Amarillo, Affilate Foods, Potter County, TPMHMR/State Center, Boys Ranch

755 Allwell from Superior HealthPlan
7990 IH 10 West
Suite 300
San Antonio, TX 78230
Toll-Free: 844-796-6811
allwell.superiorhealthplan.com
Subsidiary of: Centene Corporation
For Profit Organization: Yes

Healthplan and Services Defined
PLAN TYPE: Medicare
Model Type: Network
Benefits Offered: Dental, Prescription

Type of Coverage
Medicare, Supplemental Medicare, Medicare Advantage

756 Ambetter from Superior HealthPlan
5900 E. Ben White Blvd.
Austin, TX 78741
Toll-Free: 877-687-1196
ambetter.superiorhealthplan.com
Subsidiary of: Centene Corporation
For Profit Organization: Yes

Healthplan and Services Defined
PLAN TYPE: Other
Model Type: Network
Plan Specialty: Lab
Benefits Offered: Behavioral Health, Disease Management, Physical Therapy, Prescription, Wellness, Maternity and newborn care

Type of Coverage
Health Insurance Marketplace

Geographic Areas Served
Bandera, Bastrop, Bell, Bexar, Blanco, Brazoria, Brazos, Brooks, Burleson, Burnet, Caldwell, Cameron, Collin, Comal, Concho, Dallas, Denton, El Paso, Fayette, Fort Bend, Gillespie, Grimes, Harris, Hays, Hidalgo, Hunt, Kendall, Kerr, Lee, Llano, Madison, Mason, McCulloch, Mclennan, Medina, Menard, Montgomery, Parker, Rockwell, Starr, Tarrant, Travis, Willacy, and Williamson counties

757 American National Insurance Company
One Moody Plaza
1 Moody Avenue
Galveston, TX 77550
www.americannational.com
Total Enrollment: 5,000,000

Healthplan and Services Defined
PLAN TYPE: PPO
Benefits Offered: AD&D, Life

Type of Coverage
Supplemental Medicare, Supplemental health, credit disabil

Geographic Areas Served
Nationwide and Puerto Rico

Key Personnel
President & CEO . . . . Robert L. Moody

758 American PPO
391 East Las Colinas Boulevard
Suite 130
Irving, TX 75039
Phone: 972-533-0081
Fax: 972-871-2005
www.americanppo.com
For Profit Organization: Yes
Year Founded: 2000
Number of Affiliated Hospitals: 305
Number of Primary Care Physicians: 10,000
Number of Referral/Specialty Physicians: 13,000

Healthplan and Services Defined
PLAN TYPE: PPO
Model Type: Network
Benefits Offered: Behavioral Health, Chiropractic, Dental, Disease Management, Home Care, Inpatient SNF, Long-Term Care, Physical Therapy, Prescription, Vision
Offers Demand Management Patient Information Service: Yes

Type of Coverage
Commercial

Type of Payment Plans Offered
Combination FFS & DFFS

Geographic Areas Served
Arkansas, Louisiana, Mississippi, Missouri, Oklahoma, Tennessee and Texas

Specialty Managed Care Partners
Enters into Contracts with Regional Business Coalitions: Yes

759 Amerigroup Texas
2505 N Highway 360 Service Road E
Suite 300
Grand Prairie, TX 75050
Toll-Free: 800-600-4441
mpsweb@amerigroupcorp.com
www.myamerigroup.com/tx
Subsidiary of: Anthem, Inc.
For Profit Organization: Yes
Year Founded: 1996

Healthplan and Services Defined
PLAN TYPE: Medicare
Plan Specialty: STAR/STAR Kids programs; CHIP
Benefits Offered: Prescription

Type of Coverage
Medicaid

Accreditation Certification
URAC, NCQA

Key Personnel
Chief Financial Officer. . . . . Debbie Hefley

760 Ascension At Home
9430 Research Boulevard
Bldg. 2, Suite 310
Austin, TX 78759
Phone: 512-863-3842
Fax: 888-965-4954
ascensionathome.com
Secondary Address: Providence Home Care, 301 Owen Lane, Waco, TX 76710, 254-523-6970
Subsidiary of: Ascension

Healthplan and Services Defined
PLAN TYPE: Other
Plan Specialty: Disease Management
Benefits Offered: Dental, Disease Management, Home Care, Vision, Wellness, Ambulance & Transportation; Nursing Service; Short-and-long-term care management planning; Hospice

Geographic Areas Served
Texas, Alabama, Indiana, Kansas, Michigan, Mississippi, Oklahoma, Wisconsin

Key Personnel
Chief Executive Officer . . . . Darcy Burthay

761 Avesis: Texas
Toll-Free: 855-214-6777
www.avesis.com
Subsidiary of: Guardian Life Insurance Co.
Year Founded: 1978
Number of Primary Care Physicians: 25,000
Total Enrollment: 3,500,000

Healthplan and Services Defined
PLAN TYPE: PPO
Other Type: Vision, Dental
Model Type: Network
Plan Specialty: Dental, Vision, Hearing
Benefits Offered: Dental, Vision

Type of Coverage
Commercial

Type of Payment Plans Offered
POS, Capitated, Combination FFS & DFFS

Geographic Areas Served
Nationwide and Puerto Rico

Publishes and Distributes Report Card: Yes

Accreditation Certification
AAAHC, NCQA
TJC Accreditation

Key Personnel
Regional VP, Center/Mid W . . . . Melissa Jones

762　Blue Cross & Blue Shield of Texas
1001 E Lookout Drive
Richardson, TX 75082
Phone: 972-766-6900
media@bcbstx.com
www.bcbstx.com
Secondary Address: 9442 Capital of Texas Highway N, Suite 500, Arboretum Plaza II, Austin, TX 78759, 800-336-5696
Subsidiary of: Health Care Service Corporation
Year Founded: 1984
Number of Affiliated Hospitals: 500
Number of Primary Care Physicians: 80,000
Total Enrollment: 6,000,000
State Enrollment: 6,000,000

Healthplan and Services Defined
　PLAN TYPE: HMO/PPO
　Model Type: Network
　Plan Specialty: Behavioral Health, Disease Management, Lab
　Benefits Offered: Behavioral Health, Disease Management, Physical Therapy, Prescription, Psychiatric, Wellness

Type of Coverage
　Commercial, Individual, Medicare, Supplemental Medicare, Medicaid
　Catastrophic Illness Benefit: Unlimited

Type of Payment Plans Offered
　POS, DFFS, Capitated, FFS, Combination FFS & DFFS

Geographic Areas Served
　Statewide

Subscriber Information
　Average Monthly Fee Per Subscriber
　　(Employee + Employer Contribution):
　　　Employee Only (Self): Varies by plan
　Average Subscriber Co-Payment:
　　　Home Health Care Max. Days/Visits Covered: 60 days
　　　Nursing Home Max. Days/Visits Covered: 60 days

Network Qualifications
　Pre-Admission Certification: Yes

Peer Review Type
　Utilization Review: Yes
　Second Surgical Opinion: Yes
　Case Management: Yes

Publishes and Distributes Report Card: Yes

Accreditation Certification
　NCQA
　TJC Accreditation, Medicare Approved, Utilization Review, Pre-Admission Certification, State Licensure, Quality Assurance Program

Key Personnel
　President . . . . James G. Springfield, MD
　Chief Medical Officer. Mark Chassay
　DSVP, Sales & Marketing . . . . Darrell Beckett
　VP, Government Relations . . . . Pati McCandles
　DSVP, Health Care Deliv. . . . . Shara McClure

Average Claim Compensation
　Physician's Fees Charged: 1%
　Hospital's Fees Charged: 1%

Specialty Managed Care Partners
　Magellen Behavioral Health
　Enters into Contracts with Regional Business Coalitions: Yes

Employer References
　American Airlines, Halliburton, Texas Instruments, Texas A&M System, JBS

763　Blue Shield Promise AdvantageOptimum Plan
601 Potrero Grande Drive
Monterey Park, CA 91755
Toll-Free: 855-203-3874
www.blueshieldca.com/promise/medicare
Subsidiary of: Blue Shield of California

Healthplan and Services Defined
　PLAN TYPE: Medicare
　Benefits Offered: Behavioral Health, Long-Term Care, Prescription

Type of Coverage
　Medicare

764　Care N' Care
1701 River Run
Suite 402
Fort Worth, TX 76107
Toll-Free: 800-994-1076
cnchealthplan.com
Year Founded: 2008

Healthplan and Services Defined
　PLAN TYPE: Medicare
　Other Type: HMO & PPO
　Benefits Offered: Dental, Home Care, Physical Therapy, Podiatry, Prescription, Durable Medical Equipment; Labs & X-rays; Occupational & Speech Therapy; Outpatient Surgery; Therapeutic Radiology

Geographic Areas Served
　Tarrant, Johnson, Dallas, Collin, Denton, Rockwall and parts of Parker County

Key Personnel
　Chief Executive Officer . . . . Wendy Karsten
　Chief Medical Officer. . . . . David Sand, MD
　SVP, Sales & Operations . . . . Scott Hancock
　Compliance Director . . . . Nakia Smith

765　Careington Solutions
7400 Gaylord Parkway
Frisco, TX 75034
Toll-Free: 800-290-0523
www1.careington.com
Year Founded: 1979

Healthplan and Services Defined
　PLAN TYPE: Other
　Other Type: DHMO
　Plan Specialty: Dental
　Benefits Offered: Dental

Type of Coverage
Commercial, Individual

Geographic Areas Served
Statewide

Key Personnel
Chief Executive Officer................. Barbara Fasola
Chief Financial Officer .... Melissa Baumann
Sales & Marketing..................... Stewart Sweda
General Counsel................ Amanda Rinker Horton
SVP, Sales & Marketing .... Chuck Misasi
SVP, Client Relations................... Wendy Sideris
Chief Information Officer .... Rashmi Jain

766 Christus Health Plan
919 Hidden Ridge Drive
Irving, TX 75038
Toll-Free: 844-282-3025
Fax: 210-766-8851
CHRISTUS.HP.MemberService.Inquiry@christushealth.org
www.christushealthplan.org

Healthplan and Services Defined
PLAN TYPE: Multiple
Benefits Offered: Dental, Disease Management, Inpatient SNF, Vision, Wellness

Type of Coverage
Individual, Medicare

Geographic Areas Served
Texas and New Mexico

Key Personnel
Chief Executive Officer .... Nancy Horstmann

767 Cigna HealthCare of Texas
2800 N Loop W
Houston, TX 77092
Toll-Free: 800-997-1654
www.cigna.com
Subsidiary of: Cigna Corporation
For Profit Organization: Yes
Year Founded: 1995

Healthplan and Services Defined
PLAN TYPE: HMO
Other Type: POS
Plan Specialty: Behavioral Health, Dental, Vision
Benefits Offered: Behavioral Health, Dental, Disease Management, Prescription, Vision, AD&D, Life, LTD, STD

Type of Coverage
Commercial, Individual

Type of Payment Plans Offered
POS, DFFS, Capitated, FFS, Combination FFS & DFFS

Geographic Areas Served
Statewide

Peer Review Type
Utilization Review: Yes
Second Surgical Opinion: Yes

Case Management: Yes

Publishes and Distributes Report Card: Yes

Accreditation Certification
URAC, NCQA
Utilization Review, Pre-Admission Certification, State Licensure, Quality Assurance Program

Key Personnel
Market Pres., North TX/OK .... Keith Barnes
Market Pres., South TX/LA .... Jim Hickey

Average Claim Compensation
Physician's Fees Charged: 1%
Hospital's Fees Charged: 1%

Specialty Managed Care Partners
Quest
Enters into Contracts with Regional Business Coalitions: Yes

768 Community First Health Plans
12238 Silicon Drive
Suite 100
San Antonio, TX 78249
Toll-Free: 800-434-2347
Phone: 210-227-2347
www.cfhp.com
Subsidiary of: University Health System
Non-Profit Organization: Yes
Year Founded: 1995
Total Enrollment: 110,000
State Enrollment: 110,000

Healthplan and Services Defined
PLAN TYPE: HMO/PPO
Benefits Offered: Disease Management, Wellness

Type of Coverage
Commercial, Medicaid, CHIP

Geographic Areas Served
Bexar and surrounding seven counties

Key Personnel
President/CEO .... Theresa Scepanski
Chief Financial Officer .... Daverick Isaac
Chief Medical Officer .... Priti Mody-Bailey, MD

769 Concentra
5080 Spectrum Drive
Suite 1200W
Addison, TX 75001
Toll-Free: 866-944-6046
www.concentra.com
For Profit Organization: Yes

Healthplan and Services Defined
PLAN TYPE: Other
Plan Specialty: Worker's Compensation, Workers' compensation and occupational health (wellness, ergonomics, drug screening and occupational therapy)
Benefits Offered: Wellness, Worker's Compensation

Type of Coverage
Commercial

Key Personnel
President & CEO .... Keith Newton
Chief Financial Officer .... Su Zan Nelson
SVP, Human Resources .... Dani Kendall
Chief Information Officer .... Jim Talalai
Chief Medical Officer .... John Anderson, MD
EVP, Marketing & Sales .... John deLorimier

770 Consumers Direct Insurance Services (CDIS)
14785 Preston Road
Suite 550
Dallas, TX 75254
Toll-Free: 855-788-2583
info@cdisinsure.com
texasmedicarehealth.com
Subsidiary of: Blue Cross Blue Shield of Texas
Year Founded: 1997

Healthplan and Services Defined
  PLAN TYPE: Multiple
  Benefits Offered: Dental, Wellness

Type of Coverage
  Individual, Medicare, Supplemental Medicare, Medicaid, Short-term Insurance

Geographic Areas Served
  Illinois, New Mexico, Oklahoma, Texas

Key Personnel
President .... Scott Loochtan
Executive Vice President .... Jenn Hemann

771 FirstCare Health Plans
1206 W Campus Drive
Austin, TX 76502
Toll-Free: 800-431-7737
Phone: 512-257-6000
www.firstcare.com
Secondary Address: 7005 Salem Park Drive, Suite 100 (1st Floor), Lubbock, TX 79424, 806-784-4300
Subsidiary of: Covenant Health
For Profit Organization: Yes
Year Founded: 1985
Number of Affiliated Hospitals: 210
Number of Primary Care Physicians: 18,900

Healthplan and Services Defined
  PLAN TYPE: Multiple

Type of Coverage
  Commercial, Individual, Medicaid, CHIP

Geographic Areas Served
  143 counties in Texas

Key Personnel
President/CEO .... Jeff Ingrum

772 Galaxy Health Network
2261 Brookhollow Plaza Drive
Suite 106
Arlington, TX 76006
Toll-Free: 800-975-3322
Phone: 817-633-5822
Fax: 817-633-5729
www.galaxyhealth.net
Mailing Address: P.O. Box 201425, Arlington, TX 76006
For Profit Organization: Yes
Year Founded: 1993
Number of Affiliated Hospitals: 2,700
Number of Primary Care Physicians: 400,000
Number of Referral/Specialty Physicians: 47,000
Total Enrollment: 3,500,000
State Enrollment: 3,200,000

Healthplan and Services Defined
  PLAN TYPE: PPO
  Model Type: Network
  Benefits Offered: Disease Management, Prescription, Wellness
  Offers Demand Management Patient Information Service: Yes

Type of Coverage
  Catastrophic Illness Benefit: Varies per case

Type of Payment Plans Offered
  POS, DFFS, FFS, Combination FFS & DFFS

Geographic Areas Served
  Nationwide

Subscriber Information
  Average Monthly Fee Per Subscriber
    (Employee + Employer Contribution):
      Employee Only (Self): Varies by plan
  Average Annual Deductible Per Subscriber:
    Employee Only (Self): $500.00
    Employee & 1 Family Member: $1000.00
    Employee & 2 Family Members: $1000.00
  Average Subscriber Co-Payment:
    Primary Care Physician: $10.00

Network Qualifications
  Pre-Admission Certification: Yes

Peer Review Type
  Utilization Review: Yes
  Second Surgical Opinion: Yes
  Case Management: Yes

Publishes and Distributes Report Card: Yes

Accreditation Certification
  URAC
  Utilization Review, Pre-Admission Certification, State Licensure, Quality Assurance Program

Specialty Managed Care Partners
  Enters into Contracts with Regional Business Coalitions: Yes

773 HCSC Insurance Services Company Texas
1001 E. Lookout Dr.
Richardson, TX 75082
Phone: 912-766-6900
hcsc.com
Subsidiary of: Blue Cross Blue Shield Association
Non-Profit Organization: Yes
Year Founded: 1936
Number of Primary Care Physicians: 137,600
Total Enrollment: 5,700,000
State Enrollment: 5,700,000

Healthplan and Services Defined
PLAN TYPE: HMO
Benefits Offered: Behavioral Health, Dental, Disease Management, Psychiatric, Wellness

Geographic Areas Served
Statewide

Key Personnel
President, TX Plan .... James Springfield

774 HealthSmart
222 West Las Colinas Boulevard
Suite 500N
Irving, TX 75039
Toll-Free: 800-687-0500
Phone: 214-574-3546
www.healthsmart.com
For Profit Organization: Yes
Year Founded: 1983
Total Enrollment: 1,000,000

Healthplan and Services Defined
PLAN TYPE: PPO
Model Type: Network
Plan Specialty: MSO, PBM
Benefits Offered: Disease Management, Wellness, Business intelligence; web-based reporting; employer clinics

Type of Coverage
Catastrophic Illness Benefit: Varies per case

Type of Payment Plans Offered
POS, DFFS, FFS, Combination FFS & DFFS

Subscriber Information
Average Monthly Fee Per Subscriber
 (Employee + Employer Contribution):
  Employee Only (Self): Varies
  Employee & 1 Family Member: Varies
  Employee & 2 Family Members: Varies
  Medicare: Varies
Average Annual Deductible Per Subscriber:
  Employee Only (Self): Varies
  Employee & 1 Family Member: Varies
  Employee & 2 Family Members: Varies
  Medicare: Varies
Average Subscriber Co-Payment:
  Primary Care Physician: Varies
  Non-Network Physician: Varies
  Hospital ER: Varies
  Home Health Care: Varies
  Home Health Care Max. Days/Visits Covered: Varies
  Nursing Home: Varies
  Nursing Home Max. Days/Visits Covered: Varies

Network Qualifications
Minimum Years of Practice: 1
Pre-Admission Certification: Yes

Peer Review Type
Utilization Review: Yes
Second Surgical Opinion: Yes
Case Management: Yes

Publishes and Distributes Report Card: Yes

Accreditation Certification
URAC
Medicare Approved, Utilization Review, Pre-Admission Certification, State Licensure, Quality Assurance Program

Key Personnel
Chief Executive Officer .... Phil Christianson
VP, Client Services................... Marc Zech
Chief Clinical Officer .... Pamela Coffey
EVP, Corporate Compliance............. Sarah Bittner
Chief Financial Officer .... Matt Kelso

Specialty Managed Care Partners
Enters into Contracts with Regional Business Coalitions: Yes

Employer References
Garland ISD, Richardson ISD, Nokia, Tenet Health System, Gulf Stream Aerospace

775 Horizon Health Corporation
1965 Lakepointe Drive
Suite 100
Lewisville, TX 75057
Toll-Free: 800-931-4646
bhs@horizonhealth.com
https://horizonhealth.com
Subsidiary of: Universal Health Solutions, Inc.
For Profit Organization: Yes
Year Founded: 1981
Number of Affiliated Hospitals: 2,000
Number of Primary Care Physicians: 17,000
Number of Referral/Specialty Physicians: 18,531
Total Enrollment: 120,000

Healthplan and Services Defined
PLAN TYPE: PPO
Model Type: Staff
Plan Specialty: Behavioral Health, UR
Benefits Offered: Behavioral Health, Psychiatric, Rehabilitation Services

Type of Coverage
Commercial, Indemnity

Type of Payment Plans Offered
POS, DFFS, Capitated, FFS, Combination FFS & DFFS

Geographic Areas Served
All 50 United States, Canada, Puerto Rico, Mexico, England, and the Virgin Islands

Subscriber Information
Average Monthly Fee Per Subscriber
(Employee + Employer Contribution):
Employee & 2 Family Members: Varies by plan

Network Qualifications
Pre-Admission Certification: Yes

Peer Review Type
Utilization Review: Yes
Case Management: Yes

Publishes and Distributes Report Card: Yes

Accreditation Certification
URAC, NCQA

Key Personnel
EVP/COO .... Cory Thomas
Chief Financial Officer .... Sue Adams
SVP, Clinical Practice .... Rebecca Dvorak, RN

Specialty Managed Care Partners
Enters into Contracts with Regional Business Coalitions: Yes
Employer Health Coalition

Employer References
American Greetings, Saint Gobain Corporation, Broodwing, Jeld-Wen, The Pep Boys

---

776 Humana Health Insurance of Texas
8119 Datapoint Drive
San Antonio, TX 78229
Toll-Free: 800-611-1456
Phone: 210-615-5100
Fax: 210-617-1251
www.humana.com
Secondary Address: 1221 S MoPac Expressway, Suite 300, Austin, TX 78746, 800-967-2971
Subsidiary of: Humana Inc.
For Profit Organization: Yes
Year Founded: 1983

Healthplan and Services Defined
PLAN TYPE: HMO/PPO
Model Type: Network
Benefits Offered: Disease Management, Prescription, Wellness
Offers Demand Management Patient Information Service: Yes

Type of Coverage
Commercial, Individual
Catastrophic Illness Benefit: Covered

Geographic Areas Served
Statewide

Peer Review Type
Utilization Review: Yes
Second Surgical Opinion: Yes
Case Management: Yes

Publishes and Distributes Report Card: Yes

Accreditation Certification
URAC, NCQA, CORE

TJC Accreditation, Medicare Approved, Utilization Review, Pre-Admission Certification, State Licensure, Quality Assurance Program

Key Personnel
Market VP .... Gloria A. Rodriguez

Average Claim Compensation
Physician's Fees Charged: 80%
Hospital's Fees Charged: 80%

Specialty Managed Care Partners
Enters into Contracts with Regional Business Coalitions: Yes

---

777 KelseyCare Advantage
11511 Shadow Creek Parkway
Pearland, TX 77584
Toll-Free: 866-302-9336
Phone: 713-442-5646
www.kelseycareadvantage.com

Healthplan and Services Defined
PLAN TYPE: Multiple
Other Type: HMO/POS
Benefits Offered: Behavioral Health, Chiropractic, Dental, Disease Management, Home Care, Podiatry, Prescription, Vision, Wellness, Hearing; Outpatient Rehabilitation; Prosthetic

Type of Coverage
Medicare, Medicare Advantage

Type of Payment Plans Offered
POS

Geographic Areas Served
Harris, Brazoria, Fort Bend, Montgomery, Galveston, Liberty, San Jacinto, Waller, Walker, Austin, Wharton, Chambers, and Grimes counties

Key Personnel
President .... Marnie Matheny
VP, Operations .... Theresa Devivar
Medical Director .... Dr. Donald Aga

---

778 Liberty Dental Plan of Texas
P.O. Box 26110
Santa Ana, CA 92799-6110
Toll-Free: 888-352-7924
www.libertydentalplan.com
For Profit Organization: Yes
Year Founded: 2008
Total Enrollment: 200,000
State Enrollment: 200,000

Healthplan and Services Defined
PLAN TYPE: Dental
Other Type: Dental HMO
Plan Specialty: Dental
Benefits Offered: Dental

Type of Coverage
Commercial, Individual, Medicare, Medicaid, Unions

Geographic Areas Served
Statewide

Accreditation Certification
NCQA

Key Personnel
Texas Dental Director . . . . Oscar Frank Wood
drwood@libertydentalplan.com
Network Manager, Texas . . . . Deborah Kinder
dkinder@libertydentalplan.com
Network Manager, Texas . . . . Michele Rodriguez
micheler@libertydentalplan.com

779 MHNet Behavioral Health
MHN Professional Relations
P.O. Box 10086
San Rafael, CA 94912-9874
Toll-Free: 844-966-0298
MHN.ProviderServices@Healthnet.com
www.mhn.com/members/behavioral-health.html
For Profit Organization: Yes
Year Founded: 1985
Number of Affiliated Hospitals: 134
Number of Referral/Specialty Physicians: 2,000
Total Enrollment: 2,000,000

Healthplan and Services Defined
PLAN TYPE: Multiple
Model Type: IPA
Plan Specialty: Behavioral Health, Employee Assistance Programs and Managed Behavioral Health Care
Benefits Offered: Behavioral Health, Psychiatric
Offers Demand Management Patient Information Service: Yes
DMPI Services Offered: Psychiatric Illness

Type of Payment Plans Offered
POS, DFFS, Capitated, FFS, Combination FFS & DFFS

Geographic Areas Served
Nationwide

Network Qualifications
Minimum Years of Practice: 1
Pre-Admission Certification: Yes

Peer Review Type
Utilization Review: Yes
Second Surgical Opinion: Yes
Case Management: Yes

Publishes and Distributes Report Card: Yes

Accreditation Certification
URAC, NCQA

Key Personnel
President, Aetna Inc. Karen S. Lynch
Business Development . . . . Jon Groff
Outpatient Case Manager . . . . Karen Almstedt

Average Claim Compensation
Physician's Fees Charged: 30%
Hospital's Fees Charged: 30%

Specialty Managed Care Partners
Enters into Contracts with Regional Business Coalitions: Yes

780 Molina Healthcare of Texas
1660 Westridge Cir N
Irving, TX 75038
Toll-Free: 877-665-4622
www.molinahealthcare.com
Subsidiary of: Molina Healthcare, Inc.
For Profit Organization: Yes
Year Founded: 1980
Physician Owned Organization: Yes

Healthplan and Services Defined
PLAN TYPE: Medicare
Model Type: Network
Plan Specialty: Integrated Medicare/Medicaid (Duals)
Benefits Offered: Chiropractic, Dental, Home Care, Inpatient SNF, Long-Term Care, Podiatry, Vision

Type of Coverage
Commercial, Medicare, Supplemental Medicare, Medicaid

Accreditation Certification
URAC, NCQA

Key Personnel
President/CEO . . . . Chris Coffey
Chief Medical Officer . . . . Cheryl Shafer, MD

781 Ora Quest Dental Plans
101 Parklane Boulevard
Suite 301
Sugar Land, TX 77478
Toll-Free: 800-660-6064
Phone: 281-313-7170
Fax: 281-313-7155
info@oraquest.com
www.oraquest.com
Subsidiary of: FCL Dental
For Profit Organization: Yes

Healthplan and Services Defined
PLAN TYPE: Dental
Other Type: Dental HMO
Model Type: Network
Plan Specialty: Dental
Benefits Offered: Dental

Type of Coverage
Commercial, Individual, Medicare, Medicaid

Subscriber Information
Average Annual Deductible Per Subscriber:
Employee Only (Self): $0

782 Parkland Community Health Plan
P.O. Box 569005
Dallas, TX 75356-9005
Toll-Free: 888-672-2277
www.parklandhmo.com
Non-Profit Organization: Yes
Year Founded: 1999
Number of Affiliated Hospitals: 25
Number of Primary Care Physicians: 3,000

Healthplan and Services Defined
PLAN TYPE: HMO
Model Type: Network
Benefits Offered: Behavioral Health, Chiropractic, Disease Management, Home Care, Inpatient SNF, Physical Therapy, Podiatry, Prescription, Psychiatric, Transplant, Vision, Wellness

Type of Coverage
Medicaid, Medicaid STAR, CHIP

Type of Payment Plans Offered
POS, FFS

Geographic Areas Served
Dallas, Collin, Ellis, Hunt, Kaufman, Navarro and Rockwall counties

Network Qualifications
Pre-Admission Certification: Yes

Peer Review Type
Utilization Review: Yes
Second Surgical Opinion: Yes
Case Management: Yes

Accreditation Certification
Utilization Review, Pre-Admission Certification, State Licensure, Quality Assurance Program

Key Personnel
President & CEO . . . . Frederick P. Cerise, MD
EVP, Financial Officer . . . . Richard Humphrey
Chief Operating Officer . . . . David Lopez
Chief Medical Officer . . . . Roberto De La Cruz, MD

Specialty Managed Care Partners
Comprehensive Behavioral Care, Block Vision

---

783 Scott & White Health Plan
1206 West Campus Drive
Temple, TX 76508
www.swhp.org
Non-Profit Organization: Yes
Year Founded: 1982
Owned by an Integrated Delivery Network (IDN): Yes
Number of Affiliated Hospitals: 18
Number of Primary Care Physicians: 1,000
Total Enrollment: 200,000
State Enrollment: 200,000

Healthplan and Services Defined
PLAN TYPE: Multiple
Other Type: POS, CDHP
Model Type: Group
Benefits Offered: Behavioral Health, Dental, Disease Management, Home Care, Inpatient SNF, Long-Term Care, Physical Therapy, Podiatry, Prescription, Psychiatric, Transplant, Vision, Life
Offers Demand Management Patient Information Service: Yes
DMPI Services Offered: Secondary prevention of Coronary Artery Disease, Pediatric Asthma, Diabetes Mellitius, Congestive Heart Failure, Hypertension

Type of Coverage
Commercial, Individual, Medicare, Medicare cost

Catastrophic Illness Benefit: Covered

Type of Payment Plans Offered
DFFS, Capitated

Geographic Areas Served
77 counties in the Central, East, North, and West Texas regions

Subscriber Information
Average Monthly Fee Per Subscriber
  (Employee + Employer Contribution):
    Employee Only (Self): Varies by plan
Average Annual Deductible Per Subscriber:
  Employee Only (Self): $0.00
  Employee & 1 Family Member: $0.00
  Employee & 2 Family Members: $0.00
Average Subscriber Co-Payment:
  Primary Care Physician: $10.00
  Prescription Drugs: $5.00/20.00/50.00
  Hospital ER: $75.00
  Home Health Care: $10.00
  Nursing Home: $0

Network Qualifications
Pre-Admission Certification: No

Peer Review Type
Utilization Review: Yes
Second Surgical Opinion: No
Case Management: Yes

Publishes and Distributes Report Card: Yes

Accreditation Certification
NCQA
TJC Accreditation, Medicare Approved, Utilization Review, State Licensure, Quality Assurance Program

Key Personnel
President/CEO . . . . Jeff Ingrum

Average Claim Compensation
Physician's Fees Charged: 57%
Hospital's Fees Charged: 43%

Employer References
Texas A&M, ERS, Wiliamson County

---

784 Script Care, Ltd.
6380 Folsom Drive
Beaumont, TX 77706
Toll-Free: 800-880-9988
customerservice@scriptcare.com
www.scriptcare.com
Year Founded: 1989
Number of Primary Care Physicians: 60,000

Healthplan and Services Defined
PLAN TYPE: PPO
Other Type: PBM
Plan Specialty: PBM
Benefits Offered: Prescription

Type of Coverage
Individual

Type of Payment Plans Offered
Capitated, FFS

Geographic Areas Served
Nationwide

Subscriber Information
Average Subscriber Co-Payment:
    Prescription Drugs: Variable

Peer Review Type
Case Management: Yes

Key Personnel
CEO . . . . Jim Brown
VP Sales/Marketing . . . . Tab Bryan

785 Seton Healthcare Family
P.O. Box 14545
Austin, TX 78761
Toll-Free: 866-272-2507
Phone: 512-421-5667
Fax: 512-421-4431
SetonHealthPlan@seton.org
www.seton.net/health-plan/
Subsidiary of: Ascension
Non-Profit Organization: Yes
Year Founded: 1902
Number of Affiliated Hospitals: 100
Total Enrollment: 15,000

Healthplan and Services Defined
PLAN TYPE: HMO
Benefits Offered: Behavioral Health, Disease Management, Long-Term Care, Physical Therapy, Podiatry, Prescription, Wellness, Cancer; Cardiac; Orthopedic; Plastic & Reconstructive Surgery; Pediatric;Dermatology; Trauma & Emergency

Type of Coverage
Commercial

Geographic Areas Served
Central Texas

Key Personnel
President/CEO . . . . Joseph Impicciche, JD

786 Sterling Insurance
P.O. Box 26580
Austin, TX 78755-0580
Toll-Free: 800-688-0010
Fax: 888-670-0146
www.cigna.com/sterlinginsurance/
Subsidiary of: CIGNA/Sterling Life Insurance
Total Enrollment: 44,000
State Enrollment: 44,000

Healthplan and Services Defined
PLAN TYPE: Medicare
Benefits Offered: Prescription, Life

Type of Coverage
Individual, Medicare, Supplemental Medicare

Geographic Areas Served
39 States

787 Superior HealthPlan
5900 E. Ben White Blvd.
Austin, TX 78741
Toll-Free: 877-687-1196
www.superiorhealthplan.com
Subsidiary of: Centene Corporation
For Profit Organization: Yes
Year Founded: 1999

Healthplan and Services Defined
PLAN TYPE: Multiple
Model Type: Network
Benefits Offered: Varies by plan

Type of Coverage
Medicare, Medicaid, Medicare-Medicaid Plan, CHIP

Geographic Areas Served
Varies by plan

Key Personnel
Chief Executive Officer. . . . . Mark Sanders
Sr. Dir., Finance . . . . Alaine Heselmeyer
Clinical Manager . . . . Dalia Dimerson
Mgr., Contract & Network . . . . Megan Cass

788 Texas HealthSpring
2800 North Loop West
Houston, TX 77092
Phone: 832-553-3300
www.cigna.com/medicare/cigna-healthspring
Subsidiary of: Cigna Corporation
For Profit Organization: Yes
Year Founded: 2000

Healthplan and Services Defined
PLAN TYPE: Medicare

Type of Coverage
Medicare, Medicaid

Geographic Areas Served
Houston, Golden Triangle & Valley, North Texas & Lubbock

789 UniCare Texas
3820 American Drive
Plano, TX 75075
Toll-Free: 888-747-4535
www.unicare.com
Secondary Address: 106 East Sixth Street, Suite 333, Austin, TX 78701
Subsidiary of: Anthem, Inc.
For Profit Organization: Yes
Year Founded: 1995

Healthplan and Services Defined
PLAN TYPE: HMO/PPO
Model Type: Network
Plan Specialty: Dental, EPO, Lab, Radiology

Benefits Offered: Dental, Inpatient SNF, Long-Term Care, Prescription, Transplant, Wellness, AD&D, Life, LTD, STD, EAP

Type of Coverage
Individual, Indemnity, Medicare, Supplemental Medicare

Geographic Areas Served
Statewide

Network Qualifications
Pre-Admission Certification: Yes

Peer Review Type
Utilization Review: Yes
Second Surgical Opinion: Yes
Case Management: Yes

Publishes and Distributes Report Card: No

Accreditation Certification
URAC, NCQA
TJC Accreditation, Utilization Review, Pre-Admission Certification, State Licensure, Quality Assurance Program

Specialty Managed Care Partners
Wellpoint Pharmacy Management, Wellpoint Dental Services, Wellpoint Behavioral Health
Enters into Contracts with Regional Business Coalitions: No

---

790 United Concordia of Texas
5546 Merkens Drive
San Antonio, TX 78240
Phone: 210-677-0500
www.unitedconcordia.com
For Profit Organization: Yes
Year Founded: 1971
Number of Primary Care Physicians: 104,000
Total Enrollment: 8,800,000

Healthplan and Services Defined
PLAN TYPE: Dental
Plan Specialty: Dental
Benefits Offered: Dental

Type of Coverage
Commercial, Individual, Military personnel & families

Geographic Areas Served
Nationwide

Accreditation Certification
URAC

Key Personnel
Sales Director...................... Christi Harvey
Contact............................. Beth Rutherford
717-260-7659
beth.rutherford@ucci.com

---

791 UnitedHealthcare Community Plan Texas
UnitedHealthcare Customer Service
P.O. Box 30769
Salt Lake City, UT 84130-0769
Toll-Free: 888-545-5205
www.uhccommunityplan.com/tx
Subsidiary of: UnitedHealth Group
For Profit Organization: Yes

Healthplan and Services Defined
PLAN TYPE: Multiple
Model Type: Network
Benefits Offered: Dental, Home Care, Podiatry, Prescription, Vision, Wellness, Hearing, Acupuncture, Chiropractic

Type of Coverage
Medicare, Medicaid, CHIP

Geographic Areas Served
Varies by plan

Key Personnel
CEO, Community Plan TX................. Don Langer
don_langer@uhc.com

---

792 UnitedHealthcare of Texas
1250 S Capital of Texas Highway
Suite 1
Austin, TX 78746
Toll-Free: 888-545-5205
Phone: 512-347-2600
www.uhc.com
Secondary Address: 1311 W President George Bush Highway, Richardson, TX 75080
Subsidiary of: UnitedHealth Group
For Profit Organization: Yes
Year Founded: 1986

Healthplan and Services Defined
PLAN TYPE: HMO/PPO
Model Type: Network
Plan Specialty: Behavioral Health, Dental, Disease Management, PBM, Vision
Benefits Offered: Behavioral Health, Dental, Disease Management, Long-Term Care, Prescription, Vision, Wellness, AD&D, Life, LTD, STD

Type of Coverage
Commercial, Individual, Medicare, Supplemental Medicare, Medicaid, Catastrophic, Family, Military, Veterans, Group

Geographic Areas Served
Texas and Oklahoma

Network Qualifications
Pre-Admission Certification: Yes

Publishes and Distributes Report Card: Yes

Accreditation Certification
AAPI, NCQA

Key Personnel
CEO, TX/OK .... David Milich

Specialty Managed Care Partners
Enters into Contracts with Regional Business Coalitions: Yes

---

793 USA Managed Care Organization
4609 Bee Caves Road
Suite 200
Austin, TX 78746
Toll-Free: 800-872-0020
info@usamco.com

www.usamco.com
Secondary Address: 7301 North 16th Street, Suite 201, Phoenix, AZ 85020
For Profit Organization: Yes
Year Founded: 1984
Number of Affiliated Hospitals: 5,000
Number of Primary Care Physicians: 430,000
Total Enrollment: 5,427,579
State Enrollment: 1,118,582

Healthplan and Services Defined
   PLAN TYPE: PPO
   Model Type: Group
   Plan Specialty: Behavioral Health, Chiropractic, Dental, Disease Management, EPO, Lab, PBM, Vision, Radiology, Worker's Compensation, UR
   Benefits Offered: Behavioral Health, Chiropractic, Dental, Disease Management, Physical Therapy, Prescription, Vision, Wellness, Worker's Compensation

Type of Coverage
   Commercial, Medicare

Type of Payment Plans Offered
   POS, DFFS, FFS, Combination FFS & DFFS

Network Qualifications
   Pre-Admission Certification: Yes

Peer Review Type
   Utilization Review: Yes
   Second Surgical Opinion: Yes
   Case Management: Yes

Publishes and Distributes Report Card: No

Accreditation Certification
   TJC Accreditation, Pre-Admission Certification, State Licensure, Quality Assurance Program

Key Personnel
   President and CEO . . . . Michael Bogle

Average Claim Compensation
   Physician's Fees Charged: 34%
   Hospital's Fees Charged: 32%

---

794 UTMB HealthCare Systems
301 University Boulevard
Galveston, TX 77555-0144
Phone: 409-772-1011
www.utmb.edu
Subsidiary of: The University of Texas Medical Branch
Non-Profit Organization: Yes
Year Founded: 1998
Total Enrollment: 1,000

Healthplan and Services Defined
   PLAN TYPE: HMO
   Benefits Offered: Disease Management

Type of Coverage
   Commercial, Medicare, CHIP

Geographic Areas Served
   Statewide

Key Personnel
   President . . . . Ben G. Raimer, MD

---

795 Valley Baptist Health Plan
2101 Pease Street
Harlingen, TX 78550
Toll-Free: 855-720-7448
www.valleybaptist.net
Subsidiary of: Valley Baptist Insurance Company
Non-Profit Organization: Yes
Total Enrollment: 22,000
State Enrollment: 12,004

Healthplan and Services Defined
   PLAN TYPE: HMO
   Plan Specialty: Lab, Surgical and Medical Weight Loss Program
   Benefits Offered: Behavioral Health, Chiropractic, Dental, Disease Management, Home Care, Inpatient SNF, Physical Therapy, Podiatry, Prescription, Psychiatric, Transplant, Vision, Wellness, Durable Medical Equipment; Orthopedics; Rehabilitation

Type of Coverage
   Commercial

Type of Payment Plans Offered
   POS

Geographic Areas Served
   Statewide

Subscriber Information
   Average Monthly Fee Per Subscriber
      (Employee + Employer Contribution):
         Employee Only (Self): Varies
         Employee & 1 Family Member: Varies
         Employee & 2 Family Members: Varies
         Medicare: Varies
   Average Annual Deductible Per Subscriber:
      Employee Only (Self): Varies
      Employee & 1 Family Member: Varies
      Employee & 2 Family Members: Varies
      Medicare: Varies
   Average Subscriber Co-Payment:
      Primary Care Physician: Varies
      Non-Network Physician: Varies
      Prescription Drugs: Varies
      Hospital ER: Varies
      Home Health Care: Varies
      Home Health Care Max. Days/Visits Covered: Varies
      Nursing Home: Varies
      Nursing Home Max. Days/Visits Covered: Varies

Key Personnel
   Chief Executive Officer . . . . Manny Vela
   Chief Financial Officer . . . . Marco Rodriguez
   Chief Nursing Officer . . . . Stephen Hill
   Chief Operating Officer . . . . Archie Drake

Specialty Managed Care Partners
   Express Scripts

796 WellCare TexanPlus

Wellcare Health Plans
P.O. Box 31370
Tampa, FL 78760-9909
Toll-Free: 877-285-1987
www.wellcare.com/texas
Subsidiary of: WellCare Health Plans
For Profit Organization: Yes
Total Enrollment: 42,000

Healthplan and Services Defined
   PLAN TYPE: Multiple
   Benefits Offered: Chiropractic, Dental, Disease Management, Home Care, Inpatient SNF, Physical Therapy, Podiatry, Prescription, Psychiatric, Vision, Wellness

Type of Coverage
   Individual, Medicare

Geographic Areas Served
   Statewide

Subscriber Information
   Average Monthly Fee Per Subscriber
      (Employee + Employer Contribution):
         Employee Only (Self): Varies
         Medicare: Varies
   Average Annual Deductible Per Subscriber:
         Employee Only (Self): Varies
         Medicare: Varies
   Average Subscriber Co-Payment:
         Primary Care Physician: Varies
         Non-Network Physician: Varies
         Prescription Drugs: Varies
         Hospital ER: Varies
         Home Health Care: Varies
         Home Health Care Max. Days/Visits Covered: Varies
         Nursing Home: Varies
         Nursing Home Max. Days/Visits Covered: Varies

UTAH

Health Insurance Coverage Status and Type of Coverage by Age

Category	All Persons Number	All Persons %	Under 19 years Number	Under 19 years %	Under 65 years Number	Under 65 years %
Total population	3,178 *(2)*	100.0 *(0.0)*	983 *(3)*	100.0 *(0.0)*	2,817 *(3)*	100.0 *(0.0)*
Covered by some type of health insurance	2,872 *(16)*	90.3 *(0.5)*	901 *(6)*	91.7 *(0.7)*	2,513 *(16)*	89.2 *(0.6)*
Covered by private health insurance	2,496 *(20)*	78.5 *(0.6)*	769 *(11)*	78.3 *(1.1)*	2,278 *(19)*	80.9 *(0.7)*
Employer-based	2,053 *(23)*	64.6 *(0.7)*	650 *(13)*	66.2 *(1.3)*	1,939 *(22)*	68.8 *(0.8)*
Direct purchase	472 *(18)*	14.8 *(0.6)*	117 *(9)*	11.9 *(0.9)*	353 *(16)*	12.5 *(0.6)*
TRICARE	80 *(6)*	2.5 *(0.2)*	19 *(3)*	1.9 *(0.3)*	54 *(5)*	1.9 *(0.2)*
Covered by public health insurance	657 *(14)*	20.7 *(0.4)*	161 *(10)*	16.4 *(1.0)*	312 *(14)*	11.1 *(0.5)*
Medicaid	307 *(14)*	9.7 *(0.5)*	160 *(10)*	16.3 *(1.0)*	275 *(14)*	9.8 *(0.5)*
Medicare	385 *(5)*	12.1 *(0.2)*	2 *(1)*	0.2 *(0.1)*	41 *(4)*	1.4 *(0.1)*
VA Care	46 *(4)*	1.5 *(0.1)*	1 *(1)*	0.1 *(0.1)*	21 *(2)*	0.8 *(0.1)*
Not covered at any time during the year	307 *(16)*	9.7 *(0.5)*	82 *(7)*	8.3 *(0.7)*	303 *(16)*	10.8 *(0.6)*

Note: Numbers in thousands; Figures cover civilian noninstitutionalized population in 2019; N/A indicates that data was not available; Z represents or rounds to zero; Margin of error appears in parenthesis and is calculated using replicate weights.
Source: U.S. Census Bureau, American Community Survey, Table HI-05. Health Insurance Coverage Status and Type of Coverage by State and Age for All People: 2019

Utah

797 Altius Health Plans
10150 S Centennial Parkway
Suite 450
Sandy, UT 84070
Toll-Free: 800-365-1334
www.coventryhealthcare.com/Altius
Subsidiary of: Coventry Health Care / Aetna Inc.
For Profit Organization: Yes
Year Founded: 1998
Number of Affiliated Hospitals: 46
Number of Primary Care Physicians: 3,800
Number of Referral/Specialty Physicians: 1,850
Total Enrollment: 148,000
State Enrollment: 84,000

Healthplan and Services Defined
PLAN TYPE: Multiple
Model Type: Group, POS
Plan Specialty: Behavioral Health, Chiropractic, Disease Management, Lab, PBM, Vision, Radiology, UR
Benefits Offered: Behavioral Health, Chiropractic, Dental, Disease Management, Home Care, Inpatient SNF, Physical Therapy, Podiatry, Prescription, Psychiatric, Transplant, Vision, Wellness
Offers Demand Management Patient Information Service: Yes

Type of Coverage
Commercial, Medicaid, Catastrophic
Catastrophic Illness Benefit: Unlimited

Type of Payment Plans Offered
POS, DFFS

Geographic Areas Served
Utah, Idaho, Wyoming, and Nevada

Subscriber Information
Average Monthly Fee Per Subscriber
(Employee + Employer Contribution):
Employee Only (Self): Varies
Employee & 1 Family Member: Varies
Employee & 2 Family Members: Varies
Medicare: Varies
Average Annual Deductible Per Subscriber:
Employee Only (Self): Varies
Employee & 1 Family Member: Varies
Employee & 2 Family Members: Varies
Medicare: Varies
Average Subscriber Co-Payment:
Primary Care Physician: $15.00
Non-Network Physician: 70%
Prescription Drugs: Varies
Hospital ER: Varies
Home Health Care: Varies
Home Health Care Max. Days/Visits Covered: 60 visits
Nursing Home: Varies
Nursing Home Max. Days/Visits Covered: 60 visits

Network Qualifications
Pre-Admission Certification: Yes

Peer Review Type
Utilization Review: Yes
Second Surgical Opinion: Yes
Case Management: Yes

Publishes and Distributes Report Card: Yes

Accreditation Certification
URAC
TJC Accreditation, Medicare Approved, Utilization Review, Pre-Admission Certification, State Licensure, Quality Assurance Program

Key Personnel
VP, Network Development . . . . Kevin Lawlor

Specialty Managed Care Partners
Horizon Behavioral Health, ESI

Employer References
Federal Government, State of Utah, Davis County School District, Wells Fargo, DMBA

798 BridgeSpan Health
2890 E Cottonwood Parkway
Salt Like City, UT 84121
Toll-Free: 855-857-9944
www.bridgespanhealth.com
Subsidiary of: Cambia Health Solutions
Non-Profit Organization: Yes
Year Founded: 2012

Healthplan and Services Defined
PLAN TYPE: HMO
Benefits Offered: Behavioral Health, Physical Therapy, Prescription, Wellness, Abulance Care; Hospice; Labs & Imaging; Maternity; Substance Abuse; Rehabilitation; Pediatrics

Geographic Areas Served
Idaho, Oregon, Utah, and Washington

Key Personnel
President . . . . Chris Blanton

799 Emi Health
5101 S Commerce Street
Murray, UT 84107
Toll-Free: 800-662-5850
Subsidiary of: Educators Mutual
Non-Profit Organization: Yes
Year Founded: 1935
Physician Owned Organization: Yes
Federally Qualified: Yes
Number of Affiliated Hospitals: 25
Number of Primary Care Physicians: 3,500
Total Enrollment: 6,000
State Enrollment: 65,000

Healthplan and Services Defined
PLAN TYPE: HMO/PPO
Model Type: Network
Plan Specialty: Behavioral Health, Chiropractic, Disease Management, Radiology, UR

Benefits Offered: Behavioral Health, Chiropractic, Complementary Medicine, Dental, Disease Management, Home Care, Inpatient SNF, Physical Therapy, Podiatry, Prescription, Psychiatric, Transplant, Vision, Wellness, AD&D, Life, LTD, STD
Offers Demand Management Patient Information Service: Yes
DMPI Services Offered: Wellness Web

Type of Coverage
Commercial, Individual

Type of Payment Plans Offered
POS

Geographic Areas Served
counties: Box Elder; Cache; Davis; Salt Lake; Weber

Subscriber Information
Average Monthly Fee Per Subscriber (Employee + Employer Contribution):
Employee Only (Self): Varies by plan
Average Annual Deductible Per Subscriber:
Employee Only (Self): $0
Employee & 1 Family Member: $0
Employee & 2 Family Members: $0
Medicare: $0
Average Subscriber Co-Payment:
Primary Care Physician: $5.00
Prescription Drugs: 30%
Hospital ER: $25.00
Home Health Care: $0
Nursing Home: $0

Network Qualifications
Pre-Admission Certification: Yes

Peer Review Type
Utilization Review: Yes
Second Surgical Opinion: No
Case Management: Yes

Publishes and Distributes Report Card: Yes

Accreditation Certification
TJC Accreditation, Utilization Review, Pre-Admission Certification, State Licensure, Quality Assurance Program

Key Personnel
President/CEO . . . . Steven C. Morrison

Specialty Managed Care Partners
Enters into Contracts with Regional Business Coalitions: No

---

800 Humana Health Insurance of Utah
9815 South Monroe Street
Suite 300
Sandy, UT 84070
Toll-Free: 800-884-8328
Phone: 801-256-6200
Fax: 801-256-0782
www.humana.com
Subsidiary of: Humana Inc.
For Profit Organization: Yes

Healthplan and Services Defined
PLAN TYPE: HMO/PPO
Model Type: Network
Plan Specialty: Dental, Vision
Benefits Offered: Dental, Vision, Life, LTD, STD

Type of Coverage
Commercial, Individual

Geographic Areas Served
Statewide

Accreditation Certification
URAC, NCQA, CORE

Key Personnel
Market Manager . . . . Nathan Brown
Regional Market President . . . . Jesse Gamez

---

801 Intermountain Healthcare
36 S State Street
Salt Lake City, UT 84111
Phone: 801-442-2000
www.intermountainhealthcare.org
Non-Profit Organization: Yes
Year Founded: 1975
Number of Affiliated Hospitals: 22
Number of Primary Care Physicians: 1,600
Total Enrollment: 750,000

Healthplan and Services Defined
PLAN TYPE: HMO
Benefits Offered: Chiropractic, Complementary Medicine, Dental, Home Care, Inpatient SNF, Long-Term Care, Podiatry, Prescription, Psychiatric, Transplant, Vision, Wellness, Worker's Compensation

Type of Coverage
Commercial, Individual, Medicare, Medicaid

Geographic Areas Served
Utah and SE Idaho

Accreditation Certification
NCQA

Key Personnel
President/CEO. . . . . A. Marc Harrison, MD
Chief Operating Officer. . . . . Robert W. Allen
Chief Physician Executive . . . . Mark Briesacher
Chief Development Officer. . . . . David L. Flood
Chief Financial Officer. . . . . Bert Zimmerli

---

802 Molina Healthcare of Utah
7050 Union Park Center
Suite 200
Midvale, UT 84047
Toll-Free: 888-483-0760
www.molinahealthcare.com
Subsidiary of: Molina Healthcare, Inc.
For Profit Organization: Yes
Year Founded: 1980
Physician Owned Organization: Yes

Healthplan and Services Defined
PLAN TYPE: Medicare
Model Type: Network
Plan Specialty: Integrated Medicare/Medicaid (Duals)

Benefits Offered: Chiropractic, Dental, Home Care, Inpatient SNF, Long-Term Care, Podiatry, Vision

Type of Coverage
Commercial, Medicare, Supplemental Medicare, Medicaid

Accreditation Certification
URAC, NCQA

Key Personnel
President, ID/UT................. Brandon Hendrickson
Chief Medical Officer........... Chandrakala Gowda, MD

803 Opticare of Utah
1901 W Parkway Boulevard
Salt Lake City, UT 84119
Phone: 801-869-2020
sales@opticarevisionservices.com
www.opticareofutah.com
For Profit Organization: Yes
Year Founded: 1985
Number of Referral/Specialty Physicians: 40
Total Enrollment: 150,000
State Enrollment: 150,000

Healthplan and Services Defined
PLAN TYPE: Vision
Other Type: Optical
Model Type: Network
Plan Specialty: Vision
Benefits Offered: Vision

Type of Payment Plans Offered
POS, Capitated, FFS

Geographic Areas Served
Statewide

Subscriber Information
Average Subscriber Co-Payment:
Primary Care Physician: Varies

Network Qualifications
Pre-Admission Certification: Yes

Peer Review Type
Utilization Review: Yes
Second Surgical Opinion: Yes
Case Management: Yes

Key Personnel
CEO/ABO......................... Aaron Schubach
800-363-0950
aaron@standardoptical.net

Specialty Managed Care Partners
Enters into Contracts with Regional Business Coalitions: Yes

Employer References
State of Utah Employees

804 Premier Access Insurance/Access Dental
P.O. Box 659010
Sacramento, CA 95865-9010
Toll-Free: 888-634-6074
Phone: 916-920-2500
Fax: 916-646-9000
info@premierlife.com
www.premierppo.com
Subsidiary of: Guardian Life Insurance Co.
For Profit Organization: Yes
Year Founded: 1989
Number of Primary Care Physicians: 1,000

Healthplan and Services Defined
PLAN TYPE: PPO
Other Type: Dental
Plan Specialty: Dental
Benefits Offered: Dental

805 Public Employees Health Program
560 East 200 South
Salt Lake City, UT 84102-2099
Toll-Free: 800-765-7347
Phone: 801-366-7555
www.pehp.org
Secondary Address: 20 North Main Street, Suite 206, St. George, UT 84770, 801-366-7775
Subsidiary of: Utah Retirement Systems
Non-Profit Organization: Yes
Year Founded: 1977
Number of Affiliated Hospitals: 49
Number of Primary Care Physicians: 12,000
Number of Referral/Specialty Physicians: 2,900
Total Enrollment: 177,854
State Enrollment: 177,854

Healthplan and Services Defined
PLAN TYPE: PPO
Model Type: Network
Plan Specialty: Dental, Disease Management, Lab, PBM, Radiology, UR
Benefits Offered: Dental, Disease Management, Home Care, Prescription, Transplant, Wellness, AD&D, Life, LTD

Type of Coverage
Supplemental Medicare, Children's Health Insurance Program
Catastrophic Illness Benefit: None

Type of Payment Plans Offered
FFS

Subscriber Information
Average Monthly Fee Per Subscriber
(Employee + Employer Contribution):
Employee Only (Self): Varies by plan
Employee & 1 Family Member: $583.00
Average Annual Deductible Per Subscriber:
Employee Only (Self): $0
Employee & 1 Family Member: $0
Employee & 2 Family Members: $0
Medicare: $0
Average Subscriber Co-Payment:

Primary Care Physician: $15.00
Non-Network Physician: 15.00 + 30%
Prescription Drugs: 20%
Hospital ER: $80.00
Home Health Care Max. Days/Visits Covered: Unlimited

Network Qualifications
Pre-Admission Certification: No

Peer Review Type
Utilization Review: Yes
Second Surgical Opinion: Yes
Case Management: Yes

Publishes and Distributes Report Card: Yes

Accreditation Certification
TJC Accreditation, Medicare Approved, State Licensure

Key Personnel
Managing Director . . . . R. Chet Loftis
Provider Relations . . . . Cortney Larson

Average Claim Compensation
Physician's Fees Charged: 70%
Hospital's Fees Charged: 80%

Specialty Managed Care Partners
Managed Mental Healthcare, Chiropratic Health Plan, IHC Auesst
Enters into Contracts with Regional Business Coalitions: Yes

Employer References
State of Utah, Jordon School District, Salt Lake County, Salt Lake City, Utah School Boards Association

806 SelectHealth
5381 S Green Street
Murray, UT 84123
Toll-Free: 800-538-5038
Non-Profit Organization: Yes

Healthplan and Services Defined
PLAN TYPE: HMO

Type of Coverage
Commercial, Individual

Geographic Areas Served
Utah and Idaho

Accreditation Certification
NCQA

807 Total Dental Administrators
6985 Union Park Center
Suite 675
Salt Lake City, UT 84047
Toll-Free: 888-422-1995
Fax: 801-268-9873
www.tdadental.com
Secondary Address: 2800 N 44th Street, Suite 500, Phoenix, AZ 85008
Subsidiary of: Blue Cross Blue Shielf of South Carolina

Healthplan and Services Defined
PLAN TYPE: Dental
Plan Specialty: PPO, Prepaid
Benefits Offered: Dental

Type of Coverage
Indemnity

Key Personnel
President/CEO . . . . Jeremy Spencer

808 United Healthcare Dental
P.O. 30567
Salt Lake City, UT 84130-0567
www.uhcdental.com
Subsidiary of: UnitedHealth Group
For Profit Organization: Yes
Year Founded: 1984

Healthplan and Services Defined
PLAN TYPE: Dental
Model Type: IPA
Plan Specialty: ASO, Dental, EPO, DHMO, PPO, CSO, Preventive, Claims Repricing and Network Access
Benefits Offered: Dental

Type of Coverage
Indemnity, Medicare, Medicaid

Type of Payment Plans Offered
POS, DFFS, Capitated, FFS

Geographic Areas Served
48 states including District of Columbia, Puerto Rico and Virgin Islands

Accreditation Certification
NCQA

Key Personnel
CEO. . . . . Colleen Van Ham

809 UnitedHealthcare of Utah
2525 Lake Park Boulevard
Salt Lake City, UT 84120
Toll-Free: 888-545-5205
www.uhc.com
Subsidiary of: UnitedHealth Group
For Profit Organization: Yes

Healthplan and Services Defined
PLAN TYPE: HMO/PPO
Model Type: Network
Plan Specialty: Behavioral Health, Dental, Disease Management, PBM, Vision
Benefits Offered: Behavioral Health, Dental, Disease Management, Long-Term Care, Prescription, Vision, Wellness, Life, LTD, STD

Type of Coverage
Individual, Medicare, Supplemental Medicare, Medicaid, Catastrophic, Family, Military, Veterans, Group

Geographic Areas Served
Statewide

Key Personnel
CEO, NV/UT/ID . . . . Donald Giancursio

810 University Health Plans
6053 Fashion Square Drive
Suite 110
Murray, UT 84107
Toll-Free: 888-271-5870
Fax: 801-281-6121
uuhp@hsc.utah.edu
uhealthplan.utah.edu
Non-Profit Organization: Yes
Number of Affiliated Hospitals: 28
Number of Primary Care Physicians: 1,750
Total Enrollment: 86,000
State Enrollment: 50,000

Healthplan and Services Defined
  PLAN TYPE: HMO/PPO
    Benefits Offered: Disease Management, Wellness

Type of Coverage
  Commercial, Medicare, Medicaid

Geographic Areas Served
  Statewide

VERMONT

Health Insurance Coverage Status and Type of Coverage by Age

Category	All Persons Number	All Persons %	Under 19 years Number	Under 19 years %	Under 65 years Number	Under 65 years %
Total population	618 (Z)	100.0 (0.0)	125 (2)	100.0 (0.0)	496 (1)	100.0 (0.0)
Covered by some type of health insurance	590 (3)	95.5 (0.5)	122 (2)	97.9 (0.7)	469 (3)	94.4 (0.6)
Covered by private health insurance	425 (8)	68.8 (1.3)	75 (4)	60.2 (2.8)	348 (7)	70.1 (1.5)
Employer-based	338 (8)	54.7 (1.2)	67 (3)	53.6 (2.7)	301 (7)	60.6 (1.5)
Direct purchase	97 (5)	15.8 (0.8)	8 (1)	6.1 (1.1)	51 (4)	10.3 (0.8)
TRICARE	14 (3)	2.3 (0.4)	3 (1)	2.1 (0.9)	8 (2)	1.6 (0.5)
Covered by public health insurance	259 (7)	42.0 (1.1)	54 (4)	43.5 (2.9)	140 (7)	28.3 (1.4)
Medicaid	142 (7)	22.9 (1.1)	54 (4)	43.1 (2.9)	128 (7)	25.8 (1.4)
Medicare	139 (2)	22.5 (0.4)	1 (1)	0.7 (0.5)	20 (2)	4.1 (0.4)
VA Care	15 (1)	2.5 (0.2)	Z (Z)	0.1 (0.1)	6 (1)	1.1 (0.2)
Not covered at any time during the year	28 (3)	4.5 (0.5)	3 (1)	2.1 (0.7)	28 (3)	5.6 (0.6)

Note: Numbers in thousands; Figures cover civilian noninstitutionalized population in 2019; N/A indicates that data was not available; Z represents or rounds to zero; Margin of error appears in parenthesis and is calculated using replicate weights.
Source: U.S. Census Bureau, American Community Survey, Table HI-05. Health Insurance Coverage Status and Type of Coverage by State and Age for All People: 2019

Vermont

811 Blue Cross & Blue Shield of Vermont
445 Industrial Lane
Berlin, VT 05602-0186
Toll-Free: 800-247-2583
customerservice@bcbsvt.com
www.bluecrossvt.org
Mailing Address: P.O. Box 186, Montpelier, VT 05601-0186
Subsidiary of: Blue Cross Blue Shield Association
Non-Profit Organization: Yes
Year Founded: 1944
Total Enrollment: 180,000
State Enrollment: 54,023

Healthplan and Services Defined
 PLAN TYPE: PPO
 Model Type: Network
 Plan Specialty: Behavioral Health, Chiropractic, Disease Management, PBM, Vision, UR
 Benefits Offered: Behavioral Health, Chiropractic, Physical Therapy, Prescription, Psychiatric, Vision, AD&D, Life, LTD, STD, Alternative Healthcare discounts, Vermont Medigap Blue

Type of Coverage
 Commercial, Individual, Indemnity, Medicare, Supplemental Medicare, Catastrophic
 Catastrophic Illness Benefit: Maximum $1M

Type of Payment Plans Offered
 Capitated

Geographic Areas Served
 Statewide

Subscriber Information
 Average Monthly Fee Per Subscriber
  (Employee + Employer Contribution):
   Employee Only (Self): Varies by plan
 Average Annual Deductible Per Subscriber:
   Employee Only (Self): $400.00
   Employee & 1 Family Member: $400.00
   Employee & 2 Family Members: $200.00
 Average Subscriber Co-Payment:
   Primary Care Physician: $10.00
   Prescription Drugs: $10.00/20.00/35.00
   Hospital ER: $50.00
   Home Health Care: $40.00

Network Qualifications
 Pre-Admission Certification: Yes

Peer Review Type
 Utilization Review: Yes
 Second Surgical Opinion: No
 Case Management: Yes

Publishes and Distributes Report Card: No

Accreditation Certification
 Utilization Review, State Licensure, Quality Assurance Program

Key Personnel
 President/CEO . . . . Don George
 VP/COO . . . . Dawn Schneiderman
 VP, Consumer Services . . . . Catherine Hamilton, PhD
 VP, Chief Medical Officer . . . . Joshua Plavin, MD, MPH
 General Counsel . . . . Rebecca Heintz
 VP/Treasurer/CFO . . . . Ruth Greene

Average Claim Compensation
 Physician's Fees Charged: 85%
 Hospital's Fees Charged: 92%

Specialty Managed Care Partners
 Magellan, Restat
 Enters into Contracts with Regional Business Coalitions: Yes

812 Northeast Delta Dental Vermont
12 Bacon Street
Suite B
Burlington, VT 05401-6140
Phone: 802-658-7839
Fax: 802-865-4430
nedelta@nedelta.com
www.nedelta.com
Non-Profit Organization: Yes
Year Founded: 1961
Number of Primary Care Physicians: 1,802
Total Enrollment: 930,000

Healthplan and Services Defined
 PLAN TYPE: Dental
 Other Type: Dental PPO
 Plan Specialty: ASO, Dental
 Benefits Offered: Dental, Vision

Type of Coverage
 Commercial, Individual

Geographic Areas Served
 Vermont, Maine, New Hampshire

Key Personnel
 President/CEO . . . . Thomas Raffio
 Chair . . . . David A. Solomon, DDS
 Vice Chair . . . . Theron Main, DDS
 Treasurer . . . . Katherine A. O'Connell, CPA
 Secretary . . . . Richard W. Park
 Legal Counsel . . . . William Mason, Esq.
 Senior Vice President . . . . William H. Lambrukos

813 UnitedHealthcare of Vermont
950 Winter Street
Waltham, MA 02451
Toll-Free: 888-545-5205
Phone: 866-414-1959
www.uhc.com
Subsidiary of: UnitedHealth Group
For Profit Organization: Yes
Year Founded: 1986

Healthplan and Services Defined
 PLAN TYPE: HMO/PPO
 Model Type: Network
 Plan Specialty: Behavioral Health, Dental, Disease Management, MSO, PBM, Vision

Benefits Offered: Behavioral Health, Chiropractic, Complementary Medicine, Dental, Disease Management, Home Care, Inpatient SNF, Long-Term Care, Physical Therapy, Podiatry, Prescription, Psychiatric, Transplant, Vision, Wellness, AD&D, Life, LTD, STD

Type of Coverage
Commercial, Individual, Medicare, Supplemental Medicare, Medicaid, Catastrophic, Family, Military, Veterans, Group

Type of Payment Plans Offered
DFFS, FFS, Combination FFS & DFFS

Geographic Areas Served
Statewide. Vermont is covered by the Massachusetts branch

Subscriber Information
Average Monthly Fee Per Subscriber
 (Employee + Employer Contribution):
  Employee Only (Self): Varies
Average Subscriber Co-Payment:
 Primary Care Physician: $10
 Prescription Drugs: $10/15/30
 Hospital ER: $50

Network Qualifications
Pre-Admission Certification: Yes

Peer Review Type
Case Management: Yes

Publishes and Distributes Report Card: Yes

Accreditation Certification
URAC, NCQA
State Licensure, Quality Assurance Program

Key Personnel
CEO, New England...................... Tim Archer

Average Claim Compensation
Physician's Fees Charged: 70%
Hospital's Fees Charged: 55%

Specialty Managed Care Partners
United Behavioral Health
Enters into Contracts with Regional Business Coalitions: No

VIRGINIA

Health Insurance Coverage Status and Type of Coverage by Age

Category	All Persons Number	All Persons %	Under 19 years Number	Under 19 years %	Under 65 years Number	Under 65 years %
Total population	8,304 (6)	100.0 (0.0)	1,975 (6)	100.0 (0.0)	6,972 (8)	100.0 (0.0)
Covered by some type of health insurance	7,645 (23)	92.1 (0.3)	1,879 (9)	95.1 (0.4)	6,326 (23)	90.7 (0.3)
Covered by private health insurance	6,196 (38)	74.6 (0.4)	1,367 (19)	69.2 (0.9)	5,304 (36)	76.1 (0.5)
Employer-based	4,991 (40)	60.1 (0.5)	1,136 (18)	57.5 (0.9)	4,489 (35)	64.4 (0.5)
Direct purchase	1,094 (18)	13.2 (0.2)	134 (8)	6.8 (0.4)	650 (19)	9.3 (0.3)
TRICARE	644 (20)	7.7 (0.2)	169 (9)	8.6 (0.5)	481 (19)	6.9 (0.3)
Covered by public health insurance	2,551 (28)	30.7 (0.3)	573 (18)	29.0 (0.9)	1,276 (27)	18.3 (0.4)
Medicaid	1,133 (25)	13.6 (0.3)	551 (16)	27.9 (0.8)	1,014 (25)	14.5 (0.4)
Medicare	1,466 (7)	17.7 (0.1)	17 (4)	0.9 (0.2)	194 (7)	2.8 (0.1)
VA Care	250 (10)	3.0 (0.1)	15 (2)	0.7 (0.1)	160 (8)	2.3 (0.1)
Not covered at any time during the year	658 (22)	7.9 (0.3)	97 (7)	4.9 (0.4)	646 (22)	9.3 (0.3)

Note: Numbers in thousands; Figures cover civilian noninstitutionalized population in 2019; N/A indicates that data was not available; Z represents or rounds to zero; Margin of error appears in parenthesis and is calculated using replicate weights.
Source: U.S. Census Bureau, American Community Survey, Table HI-05. Health Insurance Coverage Status and Type of Coverage by State and Age for All People: 2019

Virginia

814 Aetna Better Health of Virginia
9881 Mayland Drive
Richmond, VA 23233
Toll-Free: 800-279-1878
Fax: 866-207-8901
www.aetnabetterhealth.com/virginia
Mailing Address: P.O. Box 63518, Phoenix, AZ 85082-3518
Subsidiary of: CVS Health / Aetna Inc.
For Profit Organization: Yes
Year Founded: 1984

Healthplan and Services Defined
  PLAN TYPE: HMO/PPO
  Other Type: POS
  Model Type: Network
  Plan Specialty: Behavioral Health, Dental, EPO, Lab, PBM, Vision, Radiology
  Benefits Offered: Behavioral Health, Dental, Disease Management, Long-Term Care, Physical Therapy, Podiatry, Prescription, Psychiatric, Vision, Wellness, Life, LTD, STD

Type of Coverage
  Commercial, Medicaid, Catastrophic, Student health

Type of Payment Plans Offered
  POS, DFFS

Geographic Areas Served
  Alexandria City, Arlington, Fairfax, Fairfax City, Falls Church City, Loudoun, Stafford, Spotsylvania, Fredericksburg City, Prince William County, Manassas City, Manassas Park City, Winchester City, Frederick County, Clarke County, Shenandoah County, Warren County and Page County

Subscriber Information
  Average Annual Deductible Per Subscriber:
    Employee Only (Self): Varies
    Employee & 1 Family Member: Varies
    Employee & 2 Family Members: Varies
    Medicare: Varies

Network Qualifications
  Pre-Admission Certification: Yes

Peer Review Type
  Utilization Review: No
  Second Surgical Opinion: Yes
  Case Management: Yes

Publishes and Distributes Report Card: Yes

Accreditation Certification
  NCQA
  TJC Accreditation, Utilization Review, Pre-Admission Certification, State Licensure, Quality Assurance Program

Key Personnel
  CEO .... Jerold Mammano
  Chief Operating Officer .... Paula Starnes, MHA

Specialty Managed Care Partners
  Enters into Contracts with Regional Business Coalitions: Yes

815 Amerigroup
P.O. Box 62947
Virginia Beach, VA 23466-2947
Toll-Free: 800-600-4441
mpsweb@amerigroup.com
www.amerigroup.com
Subsidiary of: Anthem, Inc.
For Profit Organization: Yes
Year Founded: 1994
Total Enrollment: 7,900,000

Healthplan and Services Defined
  PLAN TYPE: Medicare
  Model Type: Network
  Plan Specialty: Behavioral Health
  Benefits Offered: Behavioral Health, Long-Term Care, Psychiatric, Wellness

Type of Coverage
  Medicare, Medicaid

Geographic Areas Served
  Primarily serves New Jersey, Maryland, Washington DC, Georgia, Tennessee, Iowa, Texas, and Washington. Medicaid plans are also available in Arizona, New Jersey, New Mexico, Tennessee, Texas, and Washington

Key Personnel
  President, Medicaid .... Elena McFann
  Executive Vice President .... Felicia F. Norwood

816 Anthem Blue Cross & Blue Shield of Virginia
2015 Staples Mill Road
Richmond, VA 23230
Toll-Free: 800-331-1476
www.anthem.com
Subsidiary of: Anthem, Inc.
For Profit Organization: Yes
Year Founded: 1980
Total Enrollment: 2,800,000
State Enrollment: 2,800,000

Healthplan and Services Defined
  PLAN TYPE: HMO/PPO
  Model Type: Network
  Plan Specialty: ASO, Behavioral Health, Chiropractic, Dental, Disease Management, Lab, PBM, Vision, Radiology, Worker's Compensation, UR
  Benefits Offered: Behavioral Health, Chiropractic, Dental, Disease Management, Home Care, Inpatient SNF, Physical Therapy, Podiatry, Prescription, Psychiatric, Transplant, Vision, Wellness, Worker's Compensation, Life

Type of Coverage
  Commercial, Individual, Medicare, Catastrophic
  Catastrophic Illness Benefit: Unlimited

Type of Payment Plans Offered
  Capitated

Geographic Areas Served
  All of Virginia except for the City of Fairfax, the Town of Vienna and the area east of State Route 123

Subscriber Information
Average Subscriber Co-Payment:
Primary Care Physician: $5.00/10.00
Prescription Drugs: $5.00/10.00
Hospital ER: $25.00
Home Health Care Max. Days/Visits Covered: 100 days

Peer Review Type
Case Management: Yes

Publishes and Distributes Report Card: Yes

Accreditation Certification
URAC, NCQA
TJC Accreditation, Medicare Approved, Utilization Review, Pre-Admission Certification, State Licensure, Quality Assurance Program

Key Personnel
President .... Jeff Ricketts
Corperate Communications .... Scott Golden
804-354-5252
scott.golden@anthem.com

Specialty Managed Care Partners
Enters into Contracts with Regional Business Coalitions: Yes

Employer References
Commonwealth of Virginia, GE

---

817 CareFirst Blue Cross & Blue Shield of Virginia
10780 Parkridge Boulevard
Suite 300
Reston, VA 20191
Toll-Free: 800-544-8703
www.carefirst.com
Non-Profit Organization: Yes
Year Founded: 1985
Number of Affiliated Hospitals: 165
Number of Primary Care Physicians: 4,500
Number of Referral/Specialty Physicians: 15,068
Total Enrollment: 3,300,000

Healthplan and Services Defined
PLAN TYPE: HMO/PPO
Model Type: IPA
Plan Specialty: ASO, Behavioral Health, Dental, Vision
Benefits Offered: Behavioral Health, Chiropractic, Dental, Disease Management, Home Care, Physical Therapy, Podiatry, Prescription, Psychiatric, Transplant, Vision, Wellness

Type of Coverage
Commercial, Individual

Type of Payment Plans Offered
POS

Geographic Areas Served
Arlington County and portions of Fairfax and Prince William counties east of State Route 123

Accreditation Certification
NCQA

Key Personnel
President/CEO .... Brian D. Pienick

---

818 Delta Dental of Virginia
4818 Starkey Road
Roanoke, VA 24018
Toll-Free: 800-237-6060
Phone: 540-989-8000
www.deltadentalva.com
Secondary Address: 4860 Cox Road, Suite 130, Glen Allen, VA 23060
Non-Profit Organization: Yes
Year Founded: 1964
Total Enrollment: 68,000,000
State Enrollment: 2,000,000

Healthplan and Services Defined
PLAN TYPE: Dental
Other Type: Dental PPO/POS
Plan Specialty: Dental
Benefits Offered: Dental, Vision

Type of Coverage
Commercial, Individual

Type of Payment Plans Offered
FFS

Geographic Areas Served
Statewide

Accreditation Certification
TJC

Key Personnel
President & CEO .... Frank Lucia
Chairman .... Lyn Brooks

---

819 Dominion Dental Services
251 18th Street South
Suite 900
Arlington, VA 22202
Toll-Free: 888-518-5338
www.dominionnational.com
Mailing Address: P.O. Box 1126, Claims/Utilization, Elk Grove Village, IL 60009
For Profit Organization: Yes
Year Founded: 1996
Physician Owned Organization: Yes
Total Enrollment: 24,000,000
State Enrollment: 490,000

Healthplan and Services Defined
PLAN TYPE: Dental
Plan Specialty: Dental
Benefits Offered: Dental, Vision

Type of Coverage
Commercial, Individual

Type of Payment Plans Offered
DFFS, Capitated, Combination FFS & DFFS

Virginia — Guide to U.S. HMOs & PPOs 2023

Geographic Areas Served
Maryland; Delaware; Pennsylvania; District of Columbia; Virginia

Network Qualifications
Pre-Admission Certification: Yes

Peer Review Type
Utilization Review: Yes
Case Management: Yes

Publishes and Distributes Report Card: No

Accreditation Certification
NCQA

Key Personnel
President and COO .... Mike Davis
VP of Business Management .... Jay Rausch
VP of Operations .... Dave Orlando
VP of Accounting .... Dee Dee Brooks
Dental Director .... Wayne Silverman, DDS
Director of Marketing .... Jeff Schwab
Member Services .... Pete Harris

Specialty Managed Care Partners
Enters into Contracts with Regional Business Coalitions: Yes

820 EPIC Pharmacy Network
8703 Studley Road
Suite B
Mechanicsville, VA 23116-2016
Toll-Free: 800-876-3742
Phone: 804-559-4597
Fax: 804-559-2038
www.epicrx.com
Subsidiary of: EPIC Pharmacies, Inc.
For Profit Organization: Yes
Year Founded: 1992
Number of Primary Care Physicians: 1,400

Healthplan and Services Defined
PLAN TYPE: Multiple
Plan Specialty: PBM
Benefits Offered: Prescription

Geographic Areas Served
Mid-Atlantic states

Key Personnel
Chief Executive Officer .... Jay Romero
VP, Network Development .... Luke Gordon

821 Evolent Health
800 N Gelebe Road
Suite 500
Arlington, VA 22203
Phone: 571-389-6000
Fax: 571-389-6001
info@evolenthealth.com
www.evolenthealth.com
For Profit Organization: Yes
Year Founded: 2011

Healthplan and Services Defined
PLAN TYPE: Multiple
Benefits Offered: Disease Management, Prescription

Type of Coverage
Commercial, Medicare, Medicaid

Geographic Areas Served
Virginia, California, and Illinois

Key Personnel
Co-Founder/CEO .... Frank Williams
Co-Founder/President .... Seth Blackley
Co-Founder/COO .... Tom Peterson
CIO .... Anita Cattrell, PhD
CFO .... John Johnson
CMO .... Andrew Snyder, MD
VP/CCO .... Jordan Flynn
Chief Customer Officer .... Katie DiPerna Cook
Medical Info Officer .... Jesse James, MD
Chief Technology Officer .... Chad Pomeroy
Chief Accounting Officer .... Lydia Stone
EVP, Strategy .... John Tam, MD
General Counsel .... Jonathan Weinberg

822 Humana Health Insurance of Virginia
4191 Innslake Drive
Suite 100
Glen Allen, VA 23060
Toll-Free: 800-350-7213
Phone: 804-253-0060
Fax: 804-217-6514
www.humana.com
Secondary Address: 3800 Electric Road, Suite 406, Roanoke, VA 24018, 540-772-5762
Subsidiary of: Humana Inc.
For Profit Organization: Yes

Healthplan and Services Defined
PLAN TYPE: HMO/PPO
Model Type: Network
Plan Specialty: Dental, Vision
Benefits Offered: Dental, Vision, Life, LTD, STD

Type of Coverage
Commercial, Individual

Geographic Areas Served
Statewide

Accreditation Certification
URAC, NCQA, CORE

Key Personnel
Market Director .... Mnason Plumb

823 Magellan Complete Care of Virginia
4800 North Scottdale Road
Suite 4400
Scottsdale, AZ 85251
Toll-Free: 800-643-2273
www.magellanofvirginia.com
Subsidiary of: Magellan Health
For Profit Organization: Yes

Healthplan and Services Defined
  PLAN TYPE: Other
  Plan Specialty: Behavioral Health
  Benefits Offered: Behavioral Health, Psychiatric

Type of Coverage
  Medicaid, Specialty plan for individuals with

Geographic Areas Served
  Statewide

Key Personnel
  VP/General Manager . . . . Cornel Hubbard, JD, CCEP
  Dir., Clinical Care Srvcs . . . . Tricia Van Rossum

---

824 MedCost Virginia
812 Moorefield Park Drive
Suite 204
Richmond, VA 23236
Phone: 804-320-3837
Fax: 804-320-5984
jhoover@vhn.com
medcost.com
For Profit Organization: Yes
Year Founded: 1988
Physician Owned Organization: No
Federally Qualified: No
Number of Affiliated Hospitals: 300
Number of Primary Care Physicians: 92,000
Total Enrollment: 88,366
State Enrollment: 88,366

Healthplan and Services Defined
  PLAN TYPE: PPO
  Model Type: Network
  Plan Specialty: Worker's Compensation, Medical PPO
  Benefits Offered: Prescription
  Offers Demand Management Patient Information Service: No

Type of Coverage
  Commercial

Geographic Areas Served
  Virginia, North and South Carolina

Network Qualifications
  Pre-Admission Certification: Yes

Publishes and Distributes Report Card: No

Accreditation Certification
  Medicare; State License
  TJC Accreditation, Medicare Approved, Utilization Review, State Licensure

Average Claim Compensation
  Physician's Fees Charged: 79%
  Hospital's Fees Charged: 67%

Specialty Managed Care Partners
  Enters into Contracts with Regional Business Coalitions: Yes

---

825 Optima Health Plan
4417 Corporation Lane
Virginia Beach, VA 23462-3162
Toll-Free: 877-552-7401
Phone: 757-687-6030
Fax: 757-687-6031
healthplans@optimahealth.com
www.optimahealth.com
Secondary Address: 1604 Santa Rosa Road, Suite 100, Richmond, VA 23229, 804-510-7453
Subsidiary of: Sentara Health Plans
Non-Profit Organization: Yes
Year Founded: 1984
Federally Qualified: Yes
Number of Affiliated Hospitals: 12
Number of Primary Care Physicians: 15,000
Number of Referral/Specialty Physicians: 3,870
Total Enrollment: 551,000
State Enrollment: 551,000

Healthplan and Services Defined
  PLAN TYPE: HMO/PPO
  Other Type: POS
  Model Type: Network
  Plan Specialty: ASO, Behavioral Health, Chiropractic, Dental, PBM, Vision
  Benefits Offered: Behavioral Health, Chiropractic, Complementary Medicine, Dental, Disease Management, Home Care, Inpatient SNF, Long-Term Care, Physical Therapy, Podiatry, Prescription, Psychiatric, Transplant, Vision, Wellness
  Offers Demand Management Patient Information Service: Yes
  DMPI Services Offered: After hours nurse triage

Type of Coverage
  Commercial, Individual, Medicare, Medicaid
  Catastrophic Illness Benefit: Covered

Type of Payment Plans Offered
  FFS

Geographic Areas Served
  Selected counties in Virginia

Subscriber Information
  Average Monthly Fee Per Subscriber
    (Employee + Employer Contribution):
      Employee Only (Self): Varies by plan
      Medicare: Varies
  Average Annual Deductible Per Subscriber:
      Employee Only (Self): $0
      Employee & 1 Family Member: $0
      Employee & 2 Family Members: $0
      Medicare: Varies
  Average Subscriber Co-Payment:
      Primary Care Physician: $15.00
      Non-Network Physician: 70 %
      Prescription Drugs: 50/20%
      Hospital ER: 80%
      Home Health Care: 80%

Network Qualifications
  Pre-Admission Certification: Yes

Peer Review Type
    Utilization Review: Yes
    Second Surgical Opinion: No
    Case Management: Yes

Accreditation Certification
    URAC, NCQA

Key Personnel
    President . . . . Dennis A. Matheis
    SVP/COO . . . . Khaled Ghaly
    SVP/CFO . . . . Andy Hilbert
    Chief Medical Officer . . . . Thomas Lundquist, MD
    SVP, Sales & Marketing . . . . John E. DeGruttola
    SVP/CMO . . . . Thomas Lundquist, MD, FAAP

Specialty Managed Care Partners
    Cole Vision, American Specialty Health, Doral Dental, Sentara Mental Health
    Enters into Contracts with Regional Business Coalitions: Yes

Employer References
    City of Virginia Beach, City of Norfolk, Bank of America, Nexcom, CHKD

826 Piedmont Community Health Plan
2316 Atherholt Road
Lynchburg, VA 24501
Toll-Free: 800-400-7247
Phone: 434-947-4463
Fax: 434-947-3670
customer.service@pchp.net
www.pchp.net
Subsidiary of: Centra Health System
For Profit Organization: Yes
Year Founded: 1995
Physician Owned Organization: Yes
Total Enrollment: 30,000
State Enrollment: 30,000

Healthplan and Services Defined
    PLAN TYPE: Multiple
    Other Type: POS
    Benefits Offered: Disease Management, Prescription, Wellness

Type of Payment Plans Offered
    POS

Geographic Areas Served
    Cities of Lynchburg and Bedford and the counties of Albemarle, Amherst, Appomattox, Bedford, Buckingham, Campbell, Cumberland, Lunenburg, Nottoway and Price Edward

Key Personnel
    Marketing Executive . . . . Lori Carter
        434-947-4463

Specialty Managed Care Partners
    Caremark Rx

827 United Concordia of Virginia
4860 Cox Road
Suite 200
Glen Allen, VA 23060
Phone: 804-217-8336
www.unitedconcordia.com
For Profit Organization: Yes
Year Founded: 1971
Number of Primary Care Physicians: 104,000
Total Enrollment: 8,800,000

Healthplan and Services Defined
    PLAN TYPE: Dental
    Plan Specialty: Dental
    Benefits Offered: Dental

Type of Coverage
    Commercial, Individual, Military personnel & families

Geographic Areas Served
    Nationwide

Accreditation Certification
    URAC

Key Personnel
    Contact . . . . Beth Rutherford
        717-260-7659
        beth.rutherford@ucci.com

828 UnitedHealthcare Community Plan Virginia
UnitedHealthcare Customer Service
P.O. Box 30769
Salt Lake City, UT 84130-0769
Toll-Free: 888-545-5205
www.uhccommunityplan.com/va
Subsidiary of: UnitedHealth Group
For Profit Organization: Yes

Healthplan and Services Defined
    PLAN TYPE: Medicare
    Other Type: Medicaid
    Model Type: Network
    Benefits Offered: Dental, Home Care, Podiatry, Prescription, Vision, Wellness, Hearing, Acupuncture, Chiropractic

Type of Coverage
    Medicare, Medicaid

Geographic Areas Served
    Varies by plan

Key Personnel
    CEO, Community Plan VA . . . . Tameeka Smith
        tameeka_smith@uhc.com

829 UnitedHealthcare of Virginia
9020 Stony Point Parkway
Suite 400
Richmond, VA 23235
Toll-Free: 888-545-5205
Phone: 804-267-5200
www.uhc.com
Subsidiary of: UnitedHealth Group

For Profit Organization: Yes

Healthplan and Services Defined
  PLAN TYPE: HMO/PPO
  Model Type: Network
  Plan Specialty: Behavioral Health, Dental, Disease Management, PBM, Vision
  Benefits Offered: Behavioral Health, Dental, Disease Management, Long-Term Care, Prescription, Vision, Wellness, Life, LTD, STD

Type of Coverage
  Individual, Medicare, Supplemental Medicare, Medicaid, Catastrophic, Family, Military, Veterans, Group

Geographic Areas Served
  Statewide, and West Virgnia

Accreditation Certification
  TJC

Key Personnel
  CEO, Mid-Atlantic . . . . Joe Ochipinti

WASHINGTON

Health Insurance Coverage Status and Type of Coverage by Age

Category	All Persons Number	All Persons %	Under 19 years Number	Under 19 years %	Under 65 years Number	Under 65 years %
Total population	7,497 *(4)*	100.0 *(0.0)*	1,757 *(5)*	100.0 *(0.0)*	6,310 *(5)*	100.0 *(0.0)*
Covered by some type of health insurance	7,001 *(19)*	93.4 *(0.3)*	1,703 *(8)*	96.9 *(0.3)*	5,823 *(20)*	92.3 *(0.3)*
Covered by private health insurance	5,327 *(33)*	71.1 *(0.5)*	1,098 *(19)*	62.5 *(1.1)*	4,572 *(34)*	72.5 *(0.5)*
Employer-based	4,387 *(37)*	58.5 *(0.5)*	965 *(19)*	54.9 *(1.1)*	4,020 *(36)*	63.7 *(0.6)*
Direct purchase	946 *(16)*	12.6 *(0.2)*	99 *(6)*	5.7 *(0.4)*	524 *(17)*	8.3 *(0.3)*
TRICARE	315 *(15)*	4.2 *(0.2)*	76 *(7)*	4.3 *(0.4)*	216 *(13)*	3.4 *(0.2)*
Covered by public health insurance	2,641 *(29)*	35.2 *(0.4)*	685 *(19)*	39.0 *(1.1)*	1,505 *(30)*	23.9 *(0.5)*
Medicaid	1,484 *(30)*	19.8 *(0.4)*	679 *(19)*	38.6 *(1.1)*	1,347 *(30)*	21.4 *(0.5)*
Medicare	1,285 *(8)*	17.1 *(0.1)*	8 *(2)*	0.4 *(0.1)*	151 *(7)*	2.4 *(0.1)*
VA Care	191 *(7)*	2.5 *(0.1)*	3 *(1)*	0.2 *(0.1)*	96 *(6)*	1.5 *(0.1)*
Not covered at any time during the year	496 *(19)*	6.6 *(0.3)*	54 *(6)*	3.1 *(0.3)*	487 *(19)*	7.7 *(0.3)*

Note: Numbers in thousands; Figures cover civilian noninstitutionalized population in 2019; N/A indicates that data was not available; Z represents or rounds to zero; Margin of error appears in parenthesis and is calculated using replicate weights.
Source: U.S. Census Bureau, American Community Survey, Table HI-05. Health Insurance Coverage Status and Type of Coverage by State and Age for All People: 2019

Washington

830 Aetna Health of Washington
151 Farmington Avenue
Hartford, CT 06156
Toll-Free: 800-872-3862
www.aetna.com
Subsidiary of: CVS Health / Aetna Inc.
For Profit Organization: Yes

Healthplan and Services Defined
  PLAN TYPE: PPO
  Other Type: POS
  Model Type: Network
  Plan Specialty: Behavioral Health, EPO, Lab, PBM, Radiology
  Benefits Offered: Chiropractic, Dental, Disease Management, Home Care, Long-Term Care, Physical Therapy, Podiatry, Prescription, Vision

Type of Coverage
  Commercial, Student Health

Type of Payment Plans Offered
  Capitated

Geographic Areas Served
  Statewide

Publishes and Distributes Report Card: Yes

Accreditation Certification
  AAAHC

Key Personnel
  Chief Network Officer . . . . John J. Wagner

831 Ambetter from Coordinated Care
1145 Broadway
Suite 300
Tacoma, WA 98402
Toll-Free: 877-687-1197
ambetter.coordinatedcarehealth.com
Subsidiary of: Centene Corporation
For Profit Organization: Yes

Healthplan and Services Defined
  PLAN TYPE: Other
  Model Type: Network
  Plan Specialty: Lab
  Benefits Offered: Behavioral Health, Disease Management, Physical Therapy, Prescription, Wellness, Maternity and newborn care

Type of Coverage
  Health Insurance Marketplace

832 Amerigroup Washington
705 5th Avenue S
Suite 300
Seattle, WA 98104
Toll-Free: 800-600-4441
Phone: 206-695-7081
www.myamerigroup.com/wa
Subsidiary of: Anthem, Inc.
For Profit Organization: Yes
Year Founded: 2012

Healthplan and Services Defined
  PLAN TYPE: Medicare
  Plan Specialty: Behavioral Health, Disease Management, Managed health care for people in public programs.
  Benefits Offered: Behavioral Health, Disease Management, Prescription

Type of Coverage
  Medicaid

Geographic Areas Served
  Statewide

Key Personnel
  Plan President . . . . Anthony Woods
  Dir., Medicaid Operations . . . . Donnell Coxq

833 Asuris Northwest Health
528 E Spokane Falls Boulevard
Suite 301
Spokane, WA 99202
Toll-Free: 888-367-2109
www.asuris.com
Mailing Address: P.O. Box: 91130, Seattle, WA 98111-9230
Subsidiary of: Cambia Health Solutions
Non-Profit Organization: Yes
Year Founded: 1998
Total Enrollment: 71,000

Healthplan and Services Defined
  PLAN TYPE: Multiple
  Model Type: Network, TPA
  Plan Specialty: ASO, Behavioral Health, Chiropractic, Disease Management, Lab, Vision, Radiology
  Benefits Offered: Chiropractic, Dental, Disease Management, Home Care, Inpatient SNF, Physical Therapy, Podiatry, Prescription, Psychiatric, Vision, Wellness, AD&D, Life, LTD, STD

Type of Coverage
  Individual, Medicare, Supplemental Medicare, Medicaid

Geographic Areas Served
  Eastern Washington

Peer Review Type
  Utilization Review: Yes
  Second Surgical Opinion: Yes

Accreditation Certification
  URAC
  TJC Accreditation, Medicare Approved, State Licensure

Key Personnel
  President . . . . Brady Cass

Average Claim Compensation
  Physician's Fees Charged: 80%
  Hospital's Fees Charged: 80%

834 Community Health Plan of Washington
1111 3rd Avenue
Suite 400
Seattle, WA 98101
Toll-Free: 800-440-1561
Phone: 206-652-7213
Fax: 206-652-7040
customercare@chpw.org
www.chpw.org
Non-Profit Organization: Yes
Year Founded: 1992
Number of Affiliated Hospitals: 100
Number of Primary Care Physicians: 2,500
Number of Referral/Specialty Physicians: 14,000
Total Enrollment: 300,000
State Enrollment: 300,000

Healthplan and Services Defined
PLAN TYPE: Multiple
Benefits Offered: Behavioral Health, Dental, Disease Management, Prescription, Vision, Wellness

Type of Coverage
Commercial, Individual, Medicare, Medicaid

Geographic Areas Served
24 counties in Washington State

Subscriber Information
Average Monthly Fee Per Subscriber
(Employee + Employer Contribution):
Employee Only (Self): Varies
Employee & 1 Family Member: Varies
Employee & 2 Family Members: Varies
Medicare: Varies
Average Annual Deductible Per Subscriber:
Employee Only (Self): Varies
Employee & 1 Family Member: Varies
Employee & 2 Family Members: Varies
Medicare: Varies
Average Subscriber Co-Payment:
Primary Care Physician: Varies
Non-Network Physician: Varies
Prescription Drugs: Varies
Hospital ER: Varies
Home Health Care: Varies
Home Health Care Max. Days/Visits Covered: Varies
Nursing Home: Varies
Nursing Home Max. Days/Visits Covered: Varies

Key Personnel
Chief Executive Officer . . . . Leanne Berge, Esq.
Chief Operating Officer . . . . Alan Lederman
Chief Financial Officer . . . . Stacy Kessel
Chief Medical Officer . . . . Paul Sherman, MD
Chief of Health Services . . . . Patty Jones
External Relations . . . . Abie Castillo
Media Contact . . . . Jackie Micucci
206-652-7213

Specialty Managed Care Partners
Express Scripts

835 Coordinated Care
1145 Broadway
Suite 300
Tacoma, WA 98402
Toll-Free: 877-644-4613
coordinatedcaremember@centene.com
www.coordinatedcarehealth.com
Subsidiary of: Centene Corporation
For Profit Organization: Yes

Healthplan and Services Defined
PLAN TYPE: Multiple
Model Type: Network
Benefits Offered: Behavioral Health, Dental, Disease Management, Prescription, Vision

Type of Coverage
Medicaid, Foster Care

836 Delta Dental of Washington
P.O. Box 75688
Seattle, WA 98175
Toll-Free: 800-554-1907
www.deltadentalwa.com
Non-Profit Organization: Yes
Year Founded: 1954

Healthplan and Services Defined
PLAN TYPE: Dental
Other Type: Dental PPO
Model Type: Network
Plan Specialty: ASO, Dental
Benefits Offered: Dental

Type of Coverage
Commercial, Individual
Catastrophic Illness Benefit: None

Geographic Areas Served
Statewide

Key Personnel
President & CEO . . . . Mark Mitchke
COO & CFO . . . . Brad Berg
Human Resources . . . . Karen Aliabadi
VP, Underwriting . . . . Eric Lo
VP, Sales . . . . Linda Lay

837 Dental Health Services of Washington
100 West Harrison Street
Suite S-440, South Tower
Seattle, WA 98119
Toll-Free: 800-637-6453
Phone: 206-633-2300
Fax: 206-624-8755
membercare@dentalhealthservices.com
www.dentalhealthservicesportal.com
For Profit Organization: Yes
Year Founded: 1974
Physician Owned Organization: Yes
Federally Qualified: Yes
Number of Primary Care Physicians: 1,000

Number of Referral/Specialty Physicians: 400
Total Enrollment: 90,000

Healthplan and Services Defined
PLAN TYPE: Dental
Model Type: Network
Plan Specialty: Dental
Benefits Offered: Dental

Type of Coverage
Commercial, Individual
Catastrophic Illness Benefit: None

Geographic Areas Served
Washington

Subscriber Information
Average Monthly Fee Per Subscriber
(Employee + Employer Contribution):
Employee Only (Self): Varies
Employee & 1 Family Member: Varies
Employee & 2 Family Members: Varies

Network Qualifications
Pre-Admission Certification: Yes

Key Personnel
Founder . . . . Godfrey Pernell

---

838 First Choice Health
600 Univeristy Street
Suite 1400
Seattle, WA 98101-3129
Toll-Free: 800-467-5281
Fax: 206-667-8062
www.fchn.com
For Profit Organization: Yes
Year Founded: 1985
Number of Affiliated Hospitals: 369
Number of Primary Care Physicians: 107,000

Healthplan and Services Defined
PLAN TYPE: PPO
Benefits Offered: Behavioral Health, Wellness

Type of Coverage
Commercial, Individual, Private & Public Plans, Geo-specifi

Geographic Areas Served
Washington, Oregon, Alaska, Idaho, Montana, Wyoming, North Dakota and South Dakota

Key Personnel
Marketing/Sales Officer . . . . Curtis Taylor
President/CEO . . . . Jaja Okigwe

---

839 Humana Health Insurance of Washington
1498 SE Tech Center Place
Suite 300
Vancouver, WA 98683
Toll-Free: 800-781-4203
Phone: 360-253-7523
Fax: 360-253-7524
www.humana.com
Subsidiary of: Humana Inc.

For Profit Organization: Yes

Healthplan and Services Defined
PLAN TYPE: HMO/PPO
Model Type: Network
Plan Specialty: Dental, Vision
Benefits Offered: Dental, Disease Management, Prescription, Vision, Wellness, Life, LTD, STD

Type of Coverage
Commercial, Medicare

Geographic Areas Served
Statewide

Accreditation Certification
URAC, NCQA, CORE

Key Personnel
Regional Market President . . . . Jesse Gamez

---

840 Kaiser Permanente Washington
1300 Sw 27th St.
Renton, WA 98057
Toll-Free: 888-901-4636
healthy.kaiserpermanente.org/washington/
Subsidiary of: Kaiser Permanente
Non-Profit Organization: Yes

Healthplan and Services Defined
PLAN TYPE: HMO

---

841 LifeWise
7001 220th Street SW
Building 1
Mountlake Terrace, WA 98043
Toll-Free: 800-592-6804
www.lifewisewa.com
Secondary Address: 3900 East Sprague Ave., Spokane, WA 99220
For Profit Organization: Yes
Year Founded: 1986
Number of Primary Care Physicians: 9,000
Total Enrollment: 2,200,000

Healthplan and Services Defined
PLAN TYPE: PPO
Benefits Offered: Chiropractic, Acupuncture, Naturopathy

Geographic Areas Served
Washington and Alaska

Accreditation Certification
NCQA

Key Personnel
President & CEO . . . . Jim Havens

---

842 Molina Healthcare of Washington
21540 30th Drive SE
Suite 400
Bothell, WA 98021
Toll-Free: 800-869-7175
www.molinahealthcare.com

Secondary Address: 19120 SE 34th St., 2nd Floor, Vancouver, WA 98683
Subsidiary of: Molina Healthcare, Inc.
For Profit Organization: Yes

Healthplan and Services Defined
PLAN TYPE: Medicare
Model Type: Network
Plan Specialty: Dental, PBM, Vision, Integrated Medicare/Medicaid (Duals)
Benefits Offered: Dental, Prescription, Vision, Wellness, Life

Type of Coverage
Individual, Medicare, Supplemental Medicare, Medicaid

Geographic Areas Served
Statewide

Key Personnel
President .... Jay Fathi, MD
Chief Medical Officer .... Frances Gough, MD

843 United Concordia of Washington
4401 Deer Path Road
Harrisburg, PA 17110
Phone: 717-260-6800
www.unitedconcordia.com
For Profit Organization: Yes
Year Founded: 1971
Number of Primary Care Physicians: 104,000
Total Enrollment: 8,800,000

Healthplan and Services Defined
PLAN TYPE: Dental
Plan Specialty: Dental
Benefits Offered: Dental

Type of Coverage
Commercial, Individual, Military personnel & families

Geographic Areas Served
Nationwide

Accreditation Certification
URAC

Key Personnel
Contact. .... Beth Rutherford
717-260-7659
beth.rutherford@ucci.com

844 UnitedHealthcare Community Plan Washington
UnitedHealthcare Customer Service
P.O. Box 30769
Salt Lake City, UT 84130-0769
Toll-Free: 888-545-5205
www.uhccommunityplan.com/washington
Subsidiary of: UnitedHealth Group
For Profit Organization: Yes

Healthplan and Services Defined
PLAN TYPE: Medicare
Other Type: Medicaid
Model Type: Network
Benefits Offered: Dental, Home Care, Podiatry, Prescription, Vision, Wellness, Hearing, Acupuncture, Chiropractic

Type of Coverage
Medicare, Medicaid

Geographic Areas Served
Varies by plan

Key Personnel
CEO, Community Plan WA Genevieve D. Caruncho-Simpson
genevieve.cs@uhc.com

845 UnitedHealthcare of Washington
1111 3rd Avenue
Suite 1100
Seattle, WA 98101
Toll-Free: 888-545-5205
Phone: 206-926-0251
www.uhc.com
Subsidiary of: UnitedHealth Group
For Profit Organization: Yes

Healthplan and Services Defined
PLAN TYPE: HMO/PPO
Model Type: Network
Plan Specialty: Behavioral Health, Dental, Disease Management, PBM, Vision
Benefits Offered: Behavioral Health, Dental, Disease Management, Long-Term Care, Prescription, Vision, Wellness, Life, LTD, STD

Type of Coverage
Individual, Medicare, Supplemental Medicare, Medicaid, Catastrophic, Family, Military, Veterans, Group

Geographic Areas Served
Washington and Montana

Accreditation Certification
URAC

Key Personnel
CEO, WA/OR/MT/AK/HI .... Gary Daniels

WEST VIRGINIA

Health Insurance Coverage Status and Type of Coverage by Age

Category	All Persons Number	All Persons %	Under 19 years Number	Under 19 years %	Under 65 years Number	Under 65 years %
Total population	1,762 *(1)*	100.0 *(0.0)*	381 *(3)*	100.0 *(0.0)*	1,404 *(2)*	100.0 *(0.0)*
Covered by some type of health insurance	1,644 *(8)*	93.3 *(0.4)*	367 *(3)*	96.5 *(0.6)*	1,288 *(8)*	91.7 *(0.5)*
Covered by private health insurance	1,103 *(18)*	62.6 *(1.0)*	207 *(8)*	54.4 *(2.1)*	877 *(16)*	62.5 *(1.2)*
Employer-based	952 *(17)*	54.0 *(1.0)*	192 *(8)*	50.5 *(2.1)*	806 *(16)*	57.4 *(1.2)*
Direct purchase	180 *(8)*	10.2 *(0.5)*	14 *(3)*	3.6 *(0.7)*	81 *(6)*	5.7 *(0.4)*
TRICARE	44 *(5)*	2.5 *(0.3)*	8 *(2)*	2.0 *(0.6)*	25 *(4)*	1.8 *(0.3)*
Covered by public health insurance	838 *(14)*	47.5 *(0.8)*	181 *(8)*	47.4 *(2.0)*	486 *(14)*	34.6 *(1.0)*
Medicaid	468 *(14)*	26.6 *(0.8)*	179 *(8)*	46.9 *(2.0)*	421 *(14)*	30.0 *(1.0)*
Medicare	428 *(6)*	24.3 *(0.3)*	3 *(1)*	0.8 *(0.4)*	77 *(5)*	5.5 *(0.4)*
VA Care	67 *(4)*	3.8 *(0.3)*	1 *(1)*	0.3 *(0.2)*	31 *(4)*	2.2 *(0.3)*
Not covered at any time during the year	118 *(8)*	6.7 *(0.4)*	13 *(2)*	3.5 *(0.6)*	116 *(8)*	8.3 *(0.5)*

Note: Numbers in thousands; Figures cover civilian noninstitutionalized population in 2019; N/A indicates that data was not available; Z represents or rounds to zero; Margin of error appears in parenthesis and is calculated using replicate weights.
Source: U.S. Census Bureau, American Community Survey, Table HI-05. Health Insurance Coverage Status and Type of Coverage by State and Age for All People: 2019

West Virginia

846 Aetna Better Health of West Virginia
500 Virginia Street East
Suite 400
Charleston, WV 25301
Toll-Free: 888-348-2922
Fax: 844-255-7027
abh-wv-memberservices@aetna.com
www.aetnabetterhealth.com/westvirginia
Mailing Address: P.O. Box 67450, Phoenix, AZ 85082-7450
Subsidiary of: CVS Health / Aetna Inc.
For Profit Organization: Yes

Healthplan and Services Defined
PLAN TYPE: HMO/PPO
Other Type: POS
Model Type: Network
Plan Specialty: Behavioral Health, EPO, Lab, PBM, Radiology
Benefits Offered: Behavioral Health, Dental, Disease Management, Long-Term Care, Physical Therapy, Podiatry, Prescription, Psychiatric, Vision, Wellness, Life, LTD, STD

Type of Coverage
Commercial, Medicaid, Student health

Geographic Areas Served
Statewide

Key Personnel
CEO . . . . Todd White

847 Delta Dental of West Virginia
One Delta Drive
Mechanicsburg, PA 17055-6999
Toll-Free: 800-932-0783
www.deltadentalins.com
Mailing Address: P.O. Box 1803, Alpharetta, GA 30023
Non-Profit Organization: Yes

Healthplan and Services Defined
PLAN TYPE: Dental
Other Type: Dental PPO
Plan Specialty: Dental
Benefits Offered: Dental

Type of Coverage
Commercial, Individual

Geographic Areas Served
Statewide

Key Personnel
President/CEO . . . . Mike Castro
Chief Financial Officer . . . . Alicia Weber
Chief Legal Officer . . . . Mike Hankinson
Chief Operating Officer . . . . Roy Gilbert
Chief Information Officer . . . . Dominic Titcombe

848 Highmark BCBS West Virginia
300 Wharton Circle
Suite 150
Triadelphia, WV 26059
Toll-Free: 800-876-7639
Phone: 412-544-0100
www.highmarkbcbswv.com
Secondary Address: Fifth Avenue Place, 120 Fifth Avenue, Pittsburgh, PA 15222-3099, 412-544-7000
Subsidiary of: Highmark, Inc.
For Profit Organization: Yes
Year Founded: 1932
Number of Affiliated Hospitals: 65
Number of Primary Care Physicians: 1,400
Number of Referral/Specialty Physicians: 3,200
Total Enrollment: 5,300,000
State Enrollment: 500,000

Healthplan and Services Defined
PLAN TYPE: PPO
Model Type: Network, PPO, POS, TPA
Plan Specialty: ASO, Behavioral Health, Chiropractic, EPO, Lab, Radiology, UR, Case Management
Benefits Offered: Behavioral Health, Chiropractic, Home Care, Inpatient SNF, Long-Term Care, Physical Therapy, Podiatry, Prescription, Psychiatric, Transplant

Type of Coverage
Commercial, Individual, Supplemental Medicare

Type of Payment Plans Offered
POS, DFFS

Geographic Areas Served
West Virginia and Washington County, Ohio

Network Qualifications
Pre-Admission Certification: Yes

Peer Review Type
Utilization Review: Yes
Second Surgical Opinion: Yes
Case Management: Yes

Publishes and Distributes Report Card: No

Accreditation Certification
URAC

Key Personnel
President . . . . Deborah L. Rice-Johnson
Chief Medical Officer . . . . Charles Deshazer
Chief Executive Officer . . . . David L. Holmberg

Specialty Managed Care Partners
WV University, Charleston Area Medical Center (CAMC)
Enters into Contracts with Regional Business Coalitions: No

849 Mountain Health Trust/Physician Assured Access System

231 Capitol Street
Suite 310
Charleston, WV 25301
Toll-Free: 800-449-8466
Fax: 304-345-1581
www.mountainhealthtrust.com
Year Founded: 1996

Healthplan and Services Defined
PLAN TYPE: HMO
Benefits Offered: Dental, Disease Management, Home Care, Inpatient SNF, Prescription, Vision, Wellness, Hearing; Durable Medical Equipment; Midwife Services

Type of Coverage
Medicaid

Geographic Areas Served
Statewide

850 The Health Plan

1110 Main Street
Wheeling, OH 26003
Toll-Free: 800-624-6961
www.healthplan.org
Non-Profit Organization: Yes
Year Founded: 1979
Federally Qualified: Yes
Number of Affiliated Hospitals: 63
Number of Primary Care Physicians: 4,000
Number of Referral/Specialty Physicians: 1,000
Total Enrollment: 380,000
State Enrollment: 380,000

Healthplan and Services Defined
PLAN TYPE: HMO/PPO
Other Type: POS
Model Type: IPA
Plan Specialty: ASO, Disease Management, Worker's Compensation, UR, TPA
Benefits Offered: Behavioral Health, Chiropractic, Disease Management, Home Care, Inpatient SNF, Physical Therapy, Podiatry, Prescription, Psychiatric, Transplant, Vision, Worker's Compensation, AD&D, Life, LTD, STD
Offers Demand Management Patient Information Service: No

Type of Coverage
Individual, Medicare, Medicaid
Catastrophic Illness Benefit: Unlimited

Type of Payment Plans Offered
POS, DFFS

Geographic Areas Served
Ohio & Central West Virginia

Subscriber Information
Average Monthly Fee Per Subscriber
  (Employee + Employer Contribution):
    Employee Only (Self): Varies
    Medicare: Varies
Average Annual Deductible Per Subscriber:
    Employee Only (Self): Varies
    Medicare: Varies
Average Subscriber Co-Payment:
    Primary Care Physician: Varies
    Non-Network Physician: Varies
    Prescription Drugs: Varies
    Hospital ER: Varies
    Home Health Care: Varies
    Home Health Care Max. Days/Visits Covered: Varies
    Nursing Home: Varies
    Nursing Home Max. Days/Visits Covered: Varies

Network Qualifications
Pre-Admission Certification: Yes

Peer Review Type
Utilization Review: Yes
Second Surgical Opinion: Yes
Case Management: Yes

Publishes and Distributes Report Card: Yes

Accreditation Certification
NCQA
TJC Accreditation, Medicare Approved, Utilization Review, Pre-Admission Certification, State Licensure, Quality Assurance Program

Key Personnel
President/COO . . . . Jeffrey M. Knight
Chief Financial Officer . . . . Ryan Ralston
VP, Network Services . . . . Jason Landers
Chief Information Officer . . . . Ken (Buck) Bryan

851 UniCare West Virginia

200 Association Drive
Suite 200
Charleston, WV 25311
Toll-Free: 888-611-9958
www.unicare.com
Subsidiary of: Anthem, Inc.
For Profit Organization: Yes
Year Founded: 1985
Number of Affiliated Hospitals: 102
Number of Primary Care Physicians: 3,500
Number of Referral/Specialty Physicians: 8,000
Total Enrollment: 80,000

Healthplan and Services Defined
PLAN TYPE: HMO/PPO
Model Type: Network
Plan Specialty: Dental, Vision
Benefits Offered: Chiropractic, Dental, Physical Therapy, Prescription, Vision, Life

Type of Coverage
Medicare, Supplemental Medicare, Medicaid

Geographic Areas Served
Statewide

Subscriber Information
Average Monthly Fee Per Subscriber
  (Employee + Employer Contribution):
    Employee Only (Self): Varies

Employee & 1 Family Member: Varies
Employee & 2 Family Members: Varies
Medicare: Varies
Average Annual Deductible Per Subscriber:
Employee Only (Self): Varies
Employee & 1 Family Member: Varies
Employee & 2 Family Members: Varies
Medicare: Varies
Average Subscriber Co-Payment:
Primary Care Physician: Varies
Non-Network Physician: Varies
Prescription Drugs: Varies
Hospital ER: Varies
Home Health Care: Varies
Home Health Care Max. Days/Visits Covered: Varies
Nursing Home: Varies
Nursing Home Max. Days/Visits Covered: Varies

Network Qualifications
Pre-Admission Certification: Yes

Peer Review Type
Utilization Review: Yes
Second Surgical Opinion: Yes
Case Management: Yes

Publishes and Distributes Report Card: No

Accreditation Certification
URAC
TJC Accreditation, Medicare Approved, Utilization Review, Pre-Admission Certification, State Licensure, Quality Assurance Program

Key Personnel
President................................Tadd Haynes

852 UnitedHealthcare Community Plan West Virginia
UnitedHealthcare Customer Service
P.O. Box 30769
Salt Lake City, UT 84130-0769
Toll-Free: 888-545-5205
www.uhccommunityplan.com/wv
Subsidiary of: UnitedHealth Group
For Profit Organization: Yes

Healthplan and Services Defined
PLAN TYPE: Medicare
Other Type: Medicaid
Model Type: Network
Benefits Offered: Prescription, Hospitals, Doctors

Type of Coverage
Medicare, Medicaid

Geographic Areas Served
Barbour, Berkeley, Boone, Braxton, Brooke, Cabell, Calhoun, Clay, Doddridge, Fayette, Gilmer, Grant, Greenbrier, Hancock, Hardy, Jackson, Jefferson, Kanawha, Lewis, Lincoln, Logan, Marion, Marshall, Mason, McDowell, Mercer, Mingo, Monongalia, Nicholas, Ohio, Pendleton, Preston, Putnam, Randolph, Ritchie, Roane, Summers, Taylor, Tucker, Upshur, Wayne, Webster, Wetzel, Wirt, Wood, and Wyoming

853 UnitedHealthcare of West Virginia
9020 Stony Point Parkway
Suite 400
Richmond, VA 23235
Toll-Free: 888-545-5205
Phone: 804-267-5200
www.uhc.com
Subsidiary of: UnitedHealth Group
For Profit Organization: Yes
Year Founded: 1977

Healthplan and Services Defined
PLAN TYPE: HMO/PPO
Model Type: Network
Plan Specialty: Behavioral Health, Dental, Disease Management, Lab, PBM, Vision, Radiology
Benefits Offered: Behavioral Health, Chiropractic, Dental, Disease Management, Long-Term Care, Physical Therapy, Prescription, Vision, Wellness, AD&D, Life, LTD, STD

Type of Coverage
Commercial, Individual, Indemnity, Medicare, Supplemental Medicare, Medicaid, Catastrophic, Family, Military, Veterans, Group

Geographic Areas Served
Statewide. West Virginia is covered by the Virgnia branch

Network Qualifications
Pre-Admission Certification: Yes

Peer Review Type
Utilization Review: Yes
Second Surgical Opinion: Yes
Case Management: Yes

Publishes and Distributes Report Card: Yes

Accreditation Certification
TJC, NCQA

Key Personnel
CEO, Mid-Atlantic......................Joe Ochipinti

Specialty Managed Care Partners
Enters into Contracts with Regional Business Coalitions: Yes

WISCONSIN

Health Insurance Coverage Status and Type of Coverage by Age

Category	All Persons Number	All Persons %	Under 19 years Number	Under 19 years %	Under 65 years Number	Under 65 years %
Total population	5,751 *(1)*	100.0 *(0.0)*	1,345 *(4)*	100.0 *(0.0)*	4,758 *(3)*	100.0 *(0.0)*
Covered by some type of health insurance	5,423 *(12)*	94.3 *(0.2)*	1,294 *(5)*	96.2 *(0.3)*	4,432 *(12)*	93.2 *(0.3)*
Covered by private health insurance	4,275 *(25)*	74.3 *(0.4)*	939 *(11)*	69.8 *(0.8)*	3,665 *(23)*	77.0 *(0.5)*
Employer-based	3,552 *(26)*	61.8 *(0.4)*	878 *(12)*	65.3 *(0.8)*	3,307 *(24)*	69.5 *(0.5)*
Direct purchase	833 *(15)*	14.5 *(0.3)*	71 *(4)*	5.3 *(0.3)*	418 *(12)*	8.8 *(0.3)*
TRICARE	82 *(5)*	1.4 *(0.1)*	13 *(2)*	1.0 *(0.1)*	49 *(4)*	1.0 *(0.1)*
Covered by public health insurance	1,907 *(19)*	33.2 *(0.3)*	418 *(11)*	31.1 *(0.8)*	939 *(19)*	19.7 *(0.4)*
Medicaid	949 *(18)*	16.5 *(0.3)*	413 *(11)*	30.7 *(0.8)*	839 *(18)*	17.6 *(0.4)*
Medicare	1,095 *(6)*	19.0 *(0.1)*	8 *(2)*	0.6 *(0.1)*	127 *(5)*	2.7 *(0.1)*
VA Care	137 *(4)*	2.4 *(0.1)*	1 *(1)*	0.1 *(Z)*	54 *(4)*	1.1 *(0.1)*
Not covered at any time during the year	329 *(12)*	5.7 *(0.2)*	51 *(4)*	3.8 *(0.3)*	326 *(12)*	6.8 *(0.3)*

Note: Numbers in thousands; Figures cover civilian noninstitutionalized population in 2019; N/A indicates that data was not available; Z represents or rounds to zero; Margin of error appears in parenthesis and is calculated using replicate weights.
Source: U.S. Census Bureau, American Community Survey, Table HI-05. Health Insurance Coverage Status and Type of Coverage by State and Age for All People: 2019

Wisconsin

854 Aetna Health of Wisconsin
151 Farmington Avenue
Hartford, CT 06156
Toll-Free: 800-872-3862
www.aetna.com
Subsidiary of: CVS Health / Aetna Inc.
For Profit Organization: Yes

Healthplan and Services Defined
PLAN TYPE: PPO
Other Type: POS
Plan Specialty: Behavioral Health, EPO, Lab, PBM, Radiology
Benefits Offered: Behavioral Health, Dental, Disease Management, Long-Term Care, Physical Therapy, Podiatry, Prescription, Psychiatric, Wellness, Life, LTD, STD

Type of Coverage
Commercial, Student health

Type of Payment Plans Offered
POS, FFS

Geographic Areas Served
Statewide

Key Personnel
President, North Central . . . . Jim Boyman

855 Allwell from Managed Health Services Wisconsin
801 S 60th Street
Suite 200
West Allis, WI 53214
Toll-Free: 877-935-8024
allwell.mhswi.com
Subsidiary of: Centene Corporation
For Profit Organization: Yes

Healthplan and Services Defined
PLAN TYPE: Medicare
Model Type: Network
Benefits Offered: Dental, Prescription, Vision

Type of Coverage
Medicare, Supplemental Medicare, Medicare Advantage

Geographic Areas Served
Adams, Brown, Calumet, Clark, Columbia, Dodge, Fond du Lac, Green Lake, Jefferson, Kenosha, Kewaunee, Langlade, Lincoln, Manitowoc, Marathon, Marinette, Marquette, Menominee, Milwaukee, Oconto, Outagamie, Ozaukee, Portage, Racine, Shawano, Sheboygan, Taylor, Walworth, Washington, Waukesha, Waupaca, Waushara, Winnebago, and Wood counties

Subscriber Information
Average Subscriber Co-Payment:
Home Health Care: $0

856 American Family Insurance
6000 American Parkway
Madison, WI 53783
Toll-Free: 800-692-6326
www.amfam.com

Healthplan and Services Defined
PLAN TYPE: Multiple
Benefits Offered: Life

Type of Coverage
Commercial, Individual, Supplemental Medicare, Short-term

Geographic Areas Served
Arizona, Colorado, Georgia, Idaho, Illinois, Indiana, Iowa, Kansas, Minnesota, Missouri, Nebraska, Nevada, North Dakota, Ohio, Oregon, South Dakota, Utah, Washington, Wisconsin

Key Personnel
Chairman, President & CEO . . . . Jack Salzwedel

857 Anthem Blue Cross & Blue Shield of Wisconsin
6775 W Washington Street
Milwaukee, WI 53214
Toll-Free: 800-331-1476
Phone: 414-459-5057
www.anthem.com
Secondary Address: 480 Pilgrim Way, Green Bay, WI 54304
Subsidiary of: Anthem, Inc.
For Profit Organization: Yes

Healthplan and Services Defined
PLAN TYPE: HMO/PPO
Model Type: Network
Plan Specialty: ASO, Behavioral Health, Chiropractic, Dental, Disease Management, Lab, PBM, Vision, Radiology, Worker's Compensation, UR
Benefits Offered: Behavioral Health, Chiropractic, Dental, Disease Management, Home Care, Inpatient SNF, Physical Therapy, Podiatry, Prescription, Psychiatric, Transplant, Vision, Wellness, Worker's Compensation, Life

Type of Coverage
Commercial, Individual, Medicare, Supplemental Medicare, Medicaid, Catastrophic

Geographic Areas Served
Statewide

Accreditation Certification
URAC, NCQA

Key Personnel
President . . . . Paul Nobile
President, Medicaid WI . . . . Ted Osthelder

858 Ascension At Home
816 West Winneconne Avenue
Neenah, WI 54956
Phone: 920-727-2000
Fax: 844-887-0047
ascensionathome.com

Subsidiary of: Ascension
Non-Profit Organization: Yes

Healthplan and Services Defined
  PLAN TYPE: Other
  Plan Specialty: Disease Management
  Benefits Offered: Dental, Disease Management, Home Care, Wellness, Ambulance & Transportation; Nursing Service; Short-and-long-term care management planning; Hospice

Geographic Areas Served
  Texas, Alabama, Indiana, Kansas, Michigan, Mississippi, Oklahoma, Wisconsin

Key Personnel
  President . . . . David Grams
  Chair/CEO . . . . James A. Deal

---

859 Care Plus Dental Plans
3333 N Mayfair Rd
Wauwatosa, WI 53222
Toll-Free: 800-318-7007
Phone: 414-771-1711
www.careplusdentalplans.com
Subsidiary of: Dental Associates Ltd
Non-Profit Organization: Yes
Year Founded: 1983
Physician Owned Organization: Yes
Total Enrollment: 200,000

Healthplan and Services Defined
  PLAN TYPE: Dental
  Model Type: Staff
  Plan Specialty: Dental
  Benefits Offered: Dental, Prescription

Type of Coverage
  Commercial, Individual

Type of Payment Plans Offered
  Capitated

Geographic Areas Served
  Appleton, Fond Du Lac, Green Bay, Greenville, Kenosha, Milwaukee & Waukesha

Peer Review Type
  Utilization Review: Yes

Accreditation Certification
  AAAHC

Key Personnel
  Labor Account Executive . . . . Fred Manos
  Business Development . . . . James Schmitz
  Sr. Client Service Mgn . . . . Branda Boyd

---

860 ChiroCare of Wisconsin
3300 Fernbrook Lane
Suite 150
Plymouth, WI 55447
Toll-Free: 800-397-1541
Phone: 414-476-4733
www.chirocare.com
Subsidiary of: Fulcrum Health, Inc.
Non-Profit Organization: Yes
Year Founded: 1986
Number of Primary Care Physicians: 2,400
Total Enrollment: 150,000

Healthplan and Services Defined
  PLAN TYPE: PPO
  Model Type: IPA, Network
  Plan Specialty: Chiropractic, Complimentary Medicine Networks
  Benefits Offered: Chiropractic

Type of Coverage
  Commercial, Indemnity, Medicare, Supplemental Medicare, Medicaid

Type of Payment Plans Offered
  POS, DFFS, Capitated, FFS, Combination FFS & DFFS

Geographic Areas Served
  Minnesota, Wisconsin, North Dakota, South Dakota, Iowa, Illinois, and Nebraska

Network Qualifications
  Pre-Admission Certification: Yes

Peer Review Type
  Utilization Review: Yes
  Second Surgical Opinion: Yes
  Case Management: Yes

Accreditation Certification
  URAC, NCQA
  Quality Assurance Program

Key Personnel
  CEO . . . . Patricia Dennis

---

861 Dean Health Plan
1277 Deming Way
Madison, WI 53717
Toll-Free: 866-794-3326
www.deancare.com
Mailing Address: P.O. Box 56099, Madison, WI 53705
For Profit Organization: Yes
Year Founded: 1983
Physician Owned Organization: Yes
Federally Qualified: Yes
Number of Affiliated Hospitals: 28
Number of Primary Care Physicians: 4,700
Total Enrollment: 247,881

Healthplan and Services Defined
  PLAN TYPE: Multiple
  Model Type: Network
  Benefits Offered: Behavioral Health, Chiropractic, Dental, Disease Management, Home Care, Inpatient SNF, Physical Therapy, Podiatry, Prescription, Psychiatric, Transplant, Vision, Wellness
  Offers Demand Management Patient Information Service: Yes
  DMPI Services Offered: On Call Nurse Line

Type of Coverage
  Commercial, Individual, Indemnity, Medicare, Supplemental Medicare, Medicaid

Wisconsin

Type of Payment Plans Offered
Capitated

Geographic Areas Served
20 counties in Southern Wisconsin

Subscriber Information
Average Monthly Fee Per Subscriber
 (Employee + Employer Contribution):
  Employee Only (Self): Varies
  Employee & 1 Family Member: Varies
  Employee & 2 Family Members: Varies
  Medicare: Varies
Average Annual Deductible Per Subscriber:
  Employee Only (Self): Varies
  Employee & 1 Family Member: Varies
  Employee & 2 Family Members: Varies
  Medicare: Varies
Average Subscriber Co-Payment:
  Primary Care Physician: Varies
  Non-Network Physician: Varies
  Prescription Drugs: Varies
  Hospital ER: Varies
  Home Health Care: Varies
  Home Health Care Max. Days/Visits Covered: Varies
  Nursing Home: Varies
  Nursing Home Max. Days/Visits Covered: Varies

Network Qualifications
Pre-Admission Certification: Yes

Peer Review Type
Utilization Review: Yes

Publishes and Distributes Report Card: Yes

Accreditation Certification
NCQA

Key Personnel
President . . . . Les McPherson
Executive Director . . . . David Docherty
Director of Compliance . . . . Stephanie Cook
VP of Operations . . . . Kathy Killian
Chief Medical Offier . . . . Kevin Eichhorn, MD
Chief Financial Officer. . . . . Randy Ruplinger
General Counsel. . . . . Dean Sutton

Specialty Managed Care Partners
Enters into Contracts with Regional Business Coalitions: No

Employer References
State of Wisconsin Employees

862 Delta Dental of Wisconsin
P.O. Box 828
Stevens Point, WI 54481-0828
Toll-Free: 800-236-3712
www.deltadentalwi.com
Non-Profit Organization: Yes
Year Founded: 1962

Healthplan and Services Defined
 PLAN TYPE: Dental
 Other Type: Dental PPO
 Model Type: Network
 Plan Specialty: Dental, Vision
 Benefits Offered: Dental, Vision

Type of Coverage
Commercial, Individual

Type of Payment Plans Offered
POS, FFS

Geographic Areas Served
Statewide

Peer Review Type
Case Management: Yes

Publishes and Distributes Report Card: No

Accreditation Certification
TJC

Key Personnel
President & CEO . . . . Doug Ballweg
Director of Sales . . . . Kim Christophersen
Chief Actuary. . . . . Scott Meyer
Director, IT . . . . Michael Upright

Specialty Managed Care Partners
Enters into Contracts with Regional Business Coalitions: No

863 Dental Protection Plan
7130 W Greenfield Avenue
West Allis, WI 53214-4708
Phone: 414-259-9522
www.bayviewdentalcare.com
Subsidiary of: Bayview Dental Care
Year Founded: 1987

Healthplan and Services Defined
 PLAN TYPE: Dental
 Other Type: Dental HMO
 Plan Specialty: Dental
 Benefits Offered: Dental

Type of Coverage
Individual

Geographic Areas Served
Nationwide

Subscriber Information
Average Monthly Fee Per Subscriber
 (Employee + Employer Contribution):
  Employee Only (Self): $35/year

Peer Review Type
Case Management: Yes

Publishes and Distributes Report Card: Yes

864 EyeQuest
465 Medford Street
Boston, MA 02129-1454
Toll-Free: 888-278-7310
www.dentaquest.com/vision
Mailing Address: P.O. Box 2906, Milwaukee, WI 53201-2906
Subsidiary of: DentaQuest Ventures
Year Founded: 2008
Total Enrollment: 1,500,000

Healthplan and Services Defined
PLAN TYPE: Vision
Plan Specialty: Vision
Benefits Offered: Vision

Type of Coverage
Individual, Medicare, Medicaid

Geographic Areas Served
National

Key Personnel
President/CEO .... Steve Pollock
EVP/COO .... Kamila Chytil
EVP/CFO .... Akhil Sharma
Chief Legal Officer .... David Abelman
EVP, Chief Sales Officer .... Bob Lynn

---

865 Group Health Cooperative of Eau Claire
2503 N Hillcrest Parkway
Altoona, WI 54702
Toll-Free: 888-203-7770
Phone: 715-552-4300
Fax: 715-836-7683
www.group-health.com
Non-Profit Organization: Yes
Year Founded: 1976
Number of Primary Care Physicians: 7,700
Total Enrollment: 70,000

Healthplan and Services Defined
PLAN TYPE: HMO
Model Type: Network
Benefits Offered: Dental, Disease Management, Prescription, Wellness, Comprehensive Health
Offers Demand Management Patient Information Service: Yes
DMPI Services Offered: FirstCare Nurseline

Type of Coverage
Commercial, Medicaid, SSI
Catastrophic Illness Benefit: Varies per case

Geographic Areas Served
Barron, Buffalo, Chippewa, Clark, Dunn, Eau Claire, Jackson, Pepin, Rusk, Sawyer, Taylor, Trempealeau, Washburn, Ashland, Bayfield, Douglas, Burnett, Polk, St. Croix, Pierce, LaCrosse, Monroe, Juneau, Veronn, Crawford, Richland, Sauk, Columbia, Grant, Iowa, Lafayette, Green counties

Peer Review Type
Utilization Review: Yes
Second Surgical Opinion: Yes
Case Management: Yes

Publishes and Distributes Report Card: Yes

Accreditation Certification
AAAHC
TJC Accreditation, Medicare Approved, Utilization Review, State Licensure, Quality Assurance Program

Key Personnel
General Manager & CEO .... Peter Farrow
Chief Medical Officer .... Michele Bauer, MD
Chief Operating Officer .... Luke Johnson
Chief Financial Officer .... Bob Tanner

Specialty Managed Care Partners
CMS, OMNE
Enters into Contracts with Regional Business Coalitions: Yes

---

866 Group Health Cooperative of South Central Wisconsin
1265 John Q Hammons Drive
Madison, WI 53717-1962
Toll-Free: 800-605-4327
Phone: 608-828-4853
member_services@ghcscw.com
www.ghcscw.com
Secondary Address: 700 Regent Street, Suite 302, Madison, WI 53715
Non-Profit Organization: Yes
Year Founded: 1976
Owned by an Integrated Delivery Network (IDN): Yes
Federally Qualified: Yes
Total Enrollment: 80,000

Healthplan and Services Defined
PLAN TYPE: HMO
Model Type: Staff
Plan Specialty: Dental, Lab, Vision, Radiology
Benefits Offered: Chiropractic, Disease Management, Physical Therapy, Prescription, Vision, Wellness, Acupuncture
Offers Demand Management Patient Information Service: Yes

Type of Coverage
Commercial, Medicare, Medicaid

Type of Payment Plans Offered
DFFS, Capitated

Geographic Areas Served
Dane County

Publishes and Distributes Report Card: Yes

Accreditation Certification
AAAHC, NCQA
Medicare Approved, Utilization Review, Pre-Admission Certification, State Licensure, Quality Assurance Program

Key Personnel
Chair .... Ann Hoyt
Vice Chair .... Henry Sanders
Treasurer .... Bill Oemichen
Secretary .... Donna Twining
President/CEO .... Mark Huth, MD
CMO .... Chris Kastman, MD
CFO .... Bruce Quade
CIO .... Annette Fox

Specialty Managed Care Partners
UW Hospitals
Enters into Contracts with Regional Business Coalitions: Yes

867 Health Tradition
45 Nob Hill Road
Madison, WI 53713
Toll-Free: 877-832-1823
Phone: 608-395-6594
customerservice@healthtradition.com
www.healthtradition.com
For Profit Organization: Yes
Year Founded: 1986
Number of Affiliated Hospitals: 17
Number of Primary Care Physicians: 800
Number of Referral/Specialty Physicians: 100
Total Enrollment: 40,000
State Enrollment: 40,000

Healthplan and Services Defined
PLAN TYPE: HMO
Model Type: Group
Benefits Offered: Disease Management, Prescription, Wellness
Offers Demand Management Patient Information Service: Yes
DMPI Services Offered: 24 hour nurse line

Type of Coverage
Medicare, Medicaid
Catastrophic Illness Benefit: Maximum $2M

Type of Payment Plans Offered
POS, Combination FFS & DFFS

Geographic Areas Served
Iowa: Allamakee; Minnesota: Houston; Buffalo, Crawford, Fillmore, Jackson, La Crosse, Monroe, Trempealeau, Vernon, Winneshiek, Winona counties

Subscriber Information
Average Monthly Fee Per Subscriber
(Employee + Employer Contribution):
Employee Only (Self): Varies by plan
Average Annual Deductible Per Subscriber:
Employee Only (Self): $50.00
Employee & 1 Family Member: $100.00
Employee & 2 Family Members: $150.00
Average Subscriber Co-Payment:
Primary Care Physician: $0
Prescription Drugs: $11.00
Hospital ER: $25.00-50.00
Home Health Care: $0
Home Health Care Max. Days/Visits Covered: 345 days
Nursing Home: $0
Nursing Home Max. Days/Visits Covered: 60 days

Network Qualifications
Pre-Admission Certification: Yes

Peer Review Type
Utilization Review: Yes
Second Surgical Opinion: Yes
Case Management: Yes

Publishes and Distributes Report Card: No

Accreditation Certification
TJC Accreditation, Medicare Approved, Utilization Review, Pre-Admission Certification, State Licensure, Quality Assurance Program

Key Personnel
Director/Sales & Market . . . . Michael Eckstein

Average Claim Compensation
Physician's Fees Charged: 85%
Hospital's Fees Charged: 85%

Specialty Managed Care Partners
Franciscon Scam Health Care
Enters into Contracts with Regional Business Coalitions: No

868 Humana Health Insurance of Wisconsin
N19W24133 Riverwood Drive
Suite 300
Waukesha, WI 53188
Toll-Free: 800-289-0260
Phone: 262-408-4300
Fax: 920-632-9508
www.humana.com
Subsidiary of: Humana Inc.
For Profit Organization: Yes
Year Founded: 1985
Physician Owned Organization: Yes

Healthplan and Services Defined
PLAN TYPE: HMO/PPO
Model Type: IPA, Network
Plan Specialty: UR
Benefits Offered: Behavioral Health, Chiropractic, Dental, Disease Management, Home Care, Inpatient SNF, Physical Therapy, Podiatry, Prescription, Psychiatric, Transplant, Vision, Wellness, Worker's Compensation, AD&D, Life, LTD
Offers Demand Management Patient Information Service: Yes

Type of Coverage
Commercial, Individual

Type of Payment Plans Offered
POS, DFFS, Capitated, FFS, Combination FFS & DFFS

Geographic Areas Served
Dodge, Jefferson, Kenosha, Milwaukee, Ozaukee, Racine, Sheboygan, Walworth, Washington, Fond du Luc, Green, Montowoe, Rock & Waukesha counties

Peer Review Type
Utilization Review: Yes
Second Surgical Opinion: Yes
Case Management: Yes

Accreditation Certification
AAAHC, URAC, NCQA, CORE

Key Personnel
Market Pres., Great Lakes. . . . . Ryan Zikeli

Specialty Managed Care Partners
Aurora Behavioral, Chirotech, Accordant, Health Service

869 Managed Health Services Wisconsin
801 S 60th Street
Suite 200
Wauwatosa, WI 53214
Toll-Free: 888-713-6180
Phone: 414-246-5582
www.mhswi.com
Subsidiary of: Centene Corporation
For Profit Organization: Yes
Year Founded: 1984
Number of Affiliated Hospitals: 57
Number of Primary Care Physicians: 5,500
Number of Referral/Specialty Physicians: 1,255
Total Enrollment: 130,000
State Enrollment: 164,700

Healthplan and Services Defined
PLAN TYPE: Other
Model Type: IPA, Network
Benefits Offered: Disease Management, Prescription, Wellness
Offers Demand Management Patient Information Service: Yes

Type of Coverage
Medicaid
Catastrophic Illness Benefit: Varies per case

Type of Payment Plans Offered
POS, FFS

Geographic Areas Served
22 counties in Wisconsin, Northern Indiana, and Illinois, Racine, Kenosha; Indiana: Indianapolis; Illinois: Chicago

Subscriber Information
Average Monthly Fee Per Subscriber
(Employee + Employer Contribution):
Employee Only (Self): Varies
Employee & 1 Family Member: Varies
Employee & 2 Family Members: Varies
Medicare: Varies
Average Annual Deductible Per Subscriber:
Employee Only (Self): Varies
Employee & 1 Family Member: Varies
Employee & 2 Family Members: Varies
Medicare: Varies
Average Subscriber Co-Payment:
Primary Care Physician: $10.00/15.00
Non-Network Physician: 100%
Prescription Drugs: $5.00/10.00
Hospital ER: $25.00
Home Health Care: $0

Network Qualifications
Pre-Admission Certification: Yes

Peer Review Type
Utilization Review: Yes

Publishes and Distributes Report Card: Yes

Accreditation Certification
NCQA
TJC Accreditation, Medicare Approved, Utilization Review, Pre-Admission Certification, State Licensure, Quality Assurance Program

Key Personnel
Chairman .... John Finerty, Jr.
President/CEO .... Sherry Husa

Specialty Managed Care Partners
Enters into Contracts with Regional Business Coalitions: Yes

870 MercyHealth System
1000 Mineral Point Avenue
Janesville, WI 53547
Toll-Free: 888-396-3729
Phone: 815-971-5000
mcare@mhemail.org
mercyhealthsystem.org
Non-Profit Organization: Yes
Year Founded: 1889
Number of Affiliated Hospitals: 6
Number of Primary Care Physicians: 850

Healthplan and Services Defined
PLAN TYPE: HMO
Benefits Offered: Disease Management, Orthopedic surgery; neurosurgery; cancer care; plastic/reconstructive surgery; trauma centers

Geographic Areas Served
Southern Wisconsin and Northern Illinois counties

Key Personnel
President & CEO .... Javon R. Bea

871 Molina Healthcare of Wisconsin
11200 W Parkland Avenue
Milwaukee, WI 53224
Toll-Free: 888-999-2404
www.molinahealthcare.com
Subsidiary of: Molina Healthcare, Inc.
For Profit Organization: Yes

Healthplan and Services Defined
PLAN TYPE: Medicare
Model Type: Network
Plan Specialty: Dental, PBM, Vision, Integrated Medicare/Medicaid (Duals)
Benefits Offered: Dental, Prescription, Vision, Wellness, Life

Type of Coverage
Individual, Medicare, Supplemental Medicare, Medicaid

Geographic Areas Served
Statewide

Key Personnel
President .... Scott Johnson
Chief Medical Officer .... Raymond Zastrow, MD

872 Network Health Plan of Wisconsin
1570 Midway Place
Menasha, WI 54952
Toll-Free: 800-826-0940
Phone: 920-720-1300
www.networkhealth.com

Secondary Address: 16960 W. Greenfield Ave., Suite 5, Brookfield, WI 53005
Subsidiary of: Ascension Wisconsin
For Profit Organization: Yes
Year Founded: 1982
Total Enrollment: 118,000
State Enrollment: 67,812

Healthplan and Services Defined
PLAN TYPE: HMO
Model Type: Group, Network
Plan Specialty: Behavioral Health, Chiropractic, Disease Management, Lab
Benefits Offered: Chiropractic, Disease Management, Prescription, Wellness, Maternity care

Type of Coverage
Commercial, Medicare, Medicaid

Type of Payment Plans Offered
POS, Combination FFS & DFFS

Geographic Areas Served
Brown, Calumet, Dodge, Door, Fond du Lac, Green Lake, Kewaunee, Kenosha, Manitowoc, Marquette, Milwaukee, Outagamie, Ozaukee, Portage, Racine, Shawano, Sheboygan, Washington, Waukesha, Waupaca, Waushara, Winnebago counties

Subscriber Information
Average Monthly Fee Per Subscriber
    (Employee + Employer Contribution):
        Employee Only (Self): Varies
        Employee & 1 Family Member: Varies
        Employee & 2 Family Members: Varies
        Medicare: Varies
Average Annual Deductible Per Subscriber:
    Employee Only (Self): Varies
    Employee & 1 Family Member: Varies
    Employee & 2 Family Members: Varies
    Medicare: Varies
Average Subscriber Co-Payment:
    Primary Care Physician: $10.00
    Prescription Drugs: $5.00-7.00
    Home Health Care: $0

Network Qualifications
Pre-Admission Certification: Yes

Peer Review Type
Utilization Review: Yes
Second Surgical Opinion: No
Case Management: Yes

Publishes and Distributes Report Card: Yes

Accreditation Certification
NCQA
TJC Accreditation, Medicare Approved, Utilization Review, Pre-Admission Certification, State Licensure, Quality Assurance Program

Key Personnel
President/CEO . . . . Coreen Dicus-Johnson
CFO . . . . Brian Ollech
CAO . . . . Penny Ransom
General Counsel . . . . Kathryn Finerty
CMO . . . . Gregory Buran, MD
Chief Actuary . . . . Kevin Borchert

Specialty Managed Care Partners
Enters into Contracts with Regional Business Coalitions: Yes

---

873 Prevea Health Network
P.O. Box 19070
Green Bay, WI 54307
Toll-Free: 888-277-3832
Phone: 920-496-4700
www.prevea.com
For Profit Organization: Yes
Year Founded: 1996
Number of Affiliated Hospitals: 14
Number of Primary Care Physicians: 1,602
Total Enrollment: 119,712
State Enrollment: 15,706

Healthplan and Services Defined
PLAN TYPE: PPO
Model Type: Group
Plan Specialty: UR
Benefits Offered: Behavioral Health, Chiropractic, Disease Management, Home Care, Prescription, Transplant, Wellness, Allergy; Asthma; Cancer Rehab; Cardiac; Dermatology; Lab & Pathology; Pediatric; Reconstructive Plastic Surgery

Type of Coverage
Commercial, Supplemental Medicare

Geographic Areas Served
Northeast Wisconsin and Western Wisconsin's Chippewa Valley region

Subscriber Information
Average Annual Deductible Per Subscriber:
    Employee Only (Self): $0
    Employee & 1 Family Member: $0
    Employee & 2 Family Members: $0
    Medicare: $0
Average Subscriber Co-Payment:
    Primary Care Physician: $0

Accreditation Certification
TJC
Pre-Admission Certification

Key Personnel
President/CEO . . . . Ashok Rai, MD
VP/CMO . . . . Gregory Grose, MD
SVP/CFO . . . . Lorrie Jacobetti
SVP/COO . . . . Brian Charlier
SVP/HR/Risk Management . . . . Samantha Tonn
SVP/General Counsel . . . . Larry Gille
VP, Chief Quality Officer . . . . Paul Pritchard, MD
VP, Strategy/Development . . . . Kaitlin Brice
Chief Information Officer . . . . Shane Miller

Specialty Managed Care Partners
Express Scripts

874 Quartz Health Plan

840 Carolina Street
Sauk City, WI 53583
Toll-Free: 800-362-3310
Phone: 608-644-3430
quartzbenefits.com
Subsidiary of: Quartz Health Solutions, Inc
For Profit Organization: Yes
Year Founded: 1994
Number of Affiliated Hospitals: 44
Number of Primary Care Physicians: 908
Number of Referral/Specialty Physicians: 3,227
Total Enrollment: 340,000

Healthplan and Services Defined
PLAN TYPE: Multiple
Model Type: Network
Benefits Offered: Behavioral Health, Chiropractic, Dental, Disease Management, Home Care, Inpatient SNF, Physical Therapy, Podiatry, Prescription, Psychiatric, Transplant, Vision, Wellness

Type of Coverage
Commercial, Individual, Medicare, Medicaid

Type of Payment Plans Offered
POS, DFFS, FFS, Combination FFS & DFFS

Geographic Areas Served
20 counties in Southwestern and South Central Wisconsin; Parts of Illinois, Iowa, and Minnesota

Network Qualifications
Pre-Admission Certification: Yes

Peer Review Type
Utilization Review: Yes
Second Surgical Opinion: Yes
Case Management: Yes

Publishes and Distributes Report Card: Yes

Accreditation Certification
NCQA
Medicare Approved, Utilization Review, Pre-Admission Certification, State Licensure, Quality Assurance Program

Key Personnel
President/CEO .... Terry Bolz
Chief Operating Officer .... Debbie Schiffman
Chief Medical Officer .... Gary Lenth
VP/CFO/Treasurer .... Jim Hiveley
Chief Information Officer................ Marybeth Bay
SVP/Chief Actuary .... Kyle Brua

Specialty Managed Care Partners
Behavioral Health Consultation System, UW Hospital and Clinics, APS Healthcare
Enters into Contracts with Regional Business Coalitions: No

Employer References
University of Wisconsin Medical Foundation, Middleton Cross Plains School District, Rockwell Automation, Brakebush Brothers, Epic Systemss Corporation

875 Security Health Plan of Wisconsin

1515 Saint Joseph Avenue
P.O. Box 8000
Marshfield, WI 54449-8000
Toll-Free: 800-472-2363
Phone: 715-221-9555
Fax: 715-221-9500
www.securityhealth.org
Non-Profit Organization: Yes
Year Founded: 1986
Physician Owned Organization: Yes
Total Enrollment: 205,000
State Enrollment: 205,000

Healthplan and Services Defined
PLAN TYPE: Multiple
Model Type: Network
Plan Specialty: Behavioral Health, Chiropractic, Disease Management, EPO, Lab, PBM, Vision, Radiology, Worker's Compensation, UR
Benefits Offered: Behavioral Health, Chiropractic, Complementary Medicine, Dental, Disease Management, Home Care, Inpatient SNF, Long-Term Care, Podiatry, Prescription, Psychiatric, Transplant, Vision, Wellness, Worker's Compensation, AD&D, Durable Medical Equipment
Offers Demand Management Patient Information Service: Yes
DMPI Services Offered: Nurse Line, Health Information Line

Type of Coverage
Commercial, Individual, Indemnity, Medicare, Supplemental Medicare, Medicaid, TPA
Catastrophic Illness Benefit: Covered

Type of Payment Plans Offered
Capitated, FFS

Geographic Areas Served
Northern, Western and Central Wisconsin

Subscriber Information
Average Monthly Fee Per Subscriber
  (Employee + Employer Contribution):
    Employee Only (Self): Varies by plan
Average Annual Deductible Per Subscriber:
    Employee Only (Self): $200.00
    Employee & 2 Family Members: $100.00
    Medicare: $0
Average Subscriber Co-Payment:
    Primary Care Physician: $20.00
    Non-Network Physician: $20.00
    Prescription Drugs: $3.00
    Hospital ER: $50.00
    Home Health Care: $0
    Home Health Care Max. Days/Visits Covered: 40 days
    Nursing Home: $0
    Nursing Home Max. Days/Visits Covered: 30 days

Network Qualifications
Pre-Admission Certification: No

Peer Review Type
Utilization Review: Yes

Publishes and Distributes Report Card: Yes

Accreditation Certification
NCQA
Medicare Approved, Pre-Admission Certification

Key Personnel
Medical Director .... Robert Steiner, MD
Chief Medical Officer .... Eric Quivers, MD
Dir., Population Health .... Melissa DeGoede
Asst. Director of Claims .... Stephanie Bauer
Applications Development .... Roshan Lenora
Communications Manager .... Rebecca Normington
  715-221-9726
  normington.rebecca@securityhealth.org

Specialty Managed Care Partners
Enters into Contracts with Regional Business Coalitions: Yes

---

876 Trilogy Health Insurance
18000 West Sarah Lane
Suite 310
Brookfield, WI 53045
Toll-Free: 866-429-3241
Phone: 262-432-9140
www.trilogycares.com
For Profit Organization: Yes
Number of Affiliated Hospitals: 86
Number of Primary Care Physicians: 3,700
Total Enrollment: 5,000

Healthplan and Services Defined
  PLAN TYPE: PPO
  Other Type: HSA
  Benefits Offered: Disease Management, Prescription, Wellness, Worker's Compensation
  Offers Demand Management Patient Information Service: Yes
  DMPI Services Offered: 24-Hour Nurse Line

Type of Coverage
Commercial

Geographic Areas Served
54 counties in Wisconsin

Accreditation Certification
URAC

---

877 UnitedHealthcare Community Plan Wisconsin
UnitedHealthcare Customer Service
P.O. Box 30769
Salt Lake City, UT 84130-0769
Toll-Free: 888-545-5205
www.uhccommunityplan.com/wi
Subsidiary of: UnitedHealth Group
For Profit Organization: Yes

Healthplan and Services Defined
  PLAN TYPE: Medicare
  Other Type: Medicaid
  Model Type: Network
  Benefits Offered: Dental, Home Care, Podiatry, Prescription, Vision, Wellness, Hearing, Acupuncture, Chiropractic

Type of Coverage
Medicare, Medicaid

Key Personnel
CEO, Community Plan WI .... Kevin Moore
  kevin.moore@uhc.com

---

878 UnitedHealthcare of Wisconsin
10701 W Research Drive
Wauwatosa, WI 53226
Toll-Free: 888-545-5205
Phone: 414-443-4000
www.uhc.com
Subsidiary of: UnitedHealth Group
For Profit Organization: Yes

Healthplan and Services Defined
  PLAN TYPE: HMO/PPO
  Model Type: Network
  Plan Specialty: Behavioral Health, Dental, Disease Management, PBM, Vision
  Benefits Offered: Behavioral Health, Dental, Disease Management, Long-Term Care, Prescription, Vision, Wellness, Life, LTD, STD

Type of Coverage
Commercial, Individual, Medicare, Supplemental Medicare, Medicaid, Catastrophic, Family, Military, Veterans, Group

Geographic Areas Served
Statewide

Key Personnel
President/CEO, WI/MI .... Dustin Hinton

---

879 Wisconsin Physician's Service
1717 West Broadway
P.O. Box 8190
Madison, WI 53708-8190
Toll-Free: 888-915-4001
Fax: 608-223-3639
www.wpshealth.com
Non-Profit Organization: Yes
Year Founded: 1946
Owned by an Integrated Delivery Network (IDN): Yes
Number of Affiliated Hospitals: 129
Number of Primary Care Physicians: 14,500
Total Enrollment: 200,000
State Enrollment: 200,000

Healthplan and Services Defined
  PLAN TYPE: Multiple
  Model Type: Network
  Plan Specialty: ASO, Behavioral Health, Chiropractic, Dental, Disease Management, EPO, Lab, PBM, Vision, Radiology, Worker's Compensation, UR, Rational Med
  Benefits Offered: Behavioral Health, Chiropractic, Dental, Disease Management, Home Care, Inpatient SNF, Physical Therapy, Podiatry, Prescription, Psychiatric, Transplant, Vision, Wellness, AD&D, Life, LTD, STD
  Offers Demand Management Patient Information Service: Yes

Type of Coverage
  Commercial, Individual, Indemnity, Medicare, Supplemental
    Medicare, Catastrophic
  Catastrophic Illness Benefit: Varies per case

Type of Payment Plans Offered
  POS, DFFS

Geographic Areas Served
  Wisconsin and parts of Illinois

Subscriber Information
  Average Annual Deductible Per Subscriber:
    Employee Only (Self): $0
    Employee & 1 Family Member: $0
    Employee & 2 Family Members: $0
    Medicare: $0

Peer Review Type
  Case Management: Yes

Publishes and Distributes Report Card: Yes

Accreditation Certification
  AAAHC, URAC
  Medicare Approved, Utilization Review, State Licensure,
    Quality Assurance Program

Key Personnel
  President and CEO .... Mike Hamerlik
  Chief Financial Officer .... Vicki Bernards
  Chief Legal Officer..................... Frank Gumina
  Chief Admin. Officer .... Craig Campbell
  Administrative Officer .... Craig Campbell
  VP, Government Relations .... Rob Palmer

Specialty Managed Care Partners
  Delta Dental
  Enters into Contracts with Regional Business Coalitions: Yes

Employer References
  US Department of Defense

WYOMING

Health Insurance Coverage Status and Type of Coverage by Age

Category	All Persons Number	All Persons %	Under 19 years Number	Under 19 years %	Under 65 years Number	Under 65 years %
Total population	569 *(1)*	100.0 *(0.0)*	143 *(3)*	100.0 *(0.0)*	473 *(2)*	100.0 *(0.0)*
Covered by some type of health insurance	499 *(7)*	87.7 *(1.3)*	128 *(4)*	89.4 *(1.8)*	403 *(8)*	85.2 *(1.5)*
Covered by private health insurance	407 *(9)*	71.6 *(1.6)*	98 *(5)*	68.1 *(3.1)*	347 *(9)*	73.5 *(1.8)*
Employer-based	318 *(8)*	55.8 *(1.5)*	85 *(5)*	59.6 *(2.9)*	296 *(8)*	62.6 *(1.7)*
Direct purchase	91 *(7)*	16.0 *(1.2)*	11 *(2)*	7.5 *(1.7)*	51 *(6)*	10.8 *(1.2)*
TRICARE	22 *(3)*	3.9 *(0.6)*	5 *(1)*	3.5 *(1.0)*	13 *(3)*	2.8 *(0.6)*
Covered by public health insurance	166 *(5)*	29.2 *(0.9)*	34 *(4)*	24.0 *(2.7)*	71 *(5)*	15.1 *(1.1)*
Medicaid	66 *(5)*	11.7 *(0.9)*	34 *(4)*	23.7 *(2.6)*	58 *(5)*	12.3 *(1.1)*
Medicare	106 *(2)*	18.6 *(0.4)*	1 *(Z)*	0.4 *(0.2)*	11 *(2)*	2.4 *(0.4)*
VA Care	19 *(3)*	3.4 *(0.5)*	Z *(Z)*	0.3 *(0.2)*	8 *(2)*	1.7 *(0.4)*
Not covered at any time during the year	70 *(7)*	12.3 *(1.3)*	15 *(3)*	10.6 *(1.8)*	70 *(7)*	14.8 *(1.5)*

Note: Numbers in thousands; Figures cover civilian noninstitutionalized population in 2019; N/A indicates that data was not available; Z represents or rounds to zero; Margin of error appears in parenthesis and is calculated using replicate weights.
Source: U.S. Census Bureau, American Community Survey, Table HI-05. Health Insurance Coverage Status and Type of Coverage by State and Age for All People: 2019

Wyoming

880 Aetna Health of Wyoming
151 Farmington Avenue
Hartford, CT 06156
Toll-Free: 800-872-3862
www.aetna.com
Subsidiary of: CVS Health / Aetna Inc.
For Profit Organization: Yes

Healthplan and Services Defined
PLAN TYPE: PPO
Other Type: POS
Model Type: Network
Plan Specialty: Behavioral Health, EPO, Lab, PBM, Radiology
Benefits Offered: Behavioral Health, Dental, Disease Management, Long-Term Care, Physical Therapy, Podiatry, Prescription, Psychiatric, Wellness, Life, LTD, STD

Type of Coverage
Commercial, Student health

Type of Payment Plans Offered
POS, FFS

Geographic Areas Served
Statewide

Key Personnel
Senior Dir., Network Mgt. . . . . Kevin Lawlor

881 Blue Cross & Blue Shield of Wyoming
4000 House Avenue
Cheyenne, WY 82001
Toll-Free: 800-442-2376
www.bcbswy.com
Non-Profit Organization: Yes
Year Founded: 1976
Total Enrollment: 100,000
State Enrollment: 100,000

Healthplan and Services Defined
PLAN TYPE: HMO
Benefits Offered: Disease Management, Physical Therapy, Wellness

Type of Coverage
Commercial, Individual, Medicare, Medicaid

Type of Payment Plans Offered
FFS

Geographic Areas Served
Statewide

Key Personnel
President/CEO. . . . . Diane Gore
VP, Finance/CFO . . . . Jeremy Martinez
VP, Sales. . . . . Lee Shannon
SVP/CIO. . . . . Michael Wells

Specialty Managed Care Partners
Prime Therapeutics

Employer References
Tricare

882 Delta Dental of Wyoming
6705 Faith Drive
Cheyenne, WY 82009
Toll-Free: 800-735-3379
Phone: 307-632-3313
Fax: 307-632-7309
customerservice@deltadentalwy.org
www.deltadentalwy.org
Non-Profit Organization: Yes

Healthplan and Services Defined
PLAN TYPE: Dental
Other Type: Dental PPO
Model Type: Network
Plan Specialty: ASO, Dental
Benefits Offered: Dental

Type of Coverage
Commercial, Individual
Catastrophic Illness Benefit: None

Geographic Areas Served
Statewide

Accreditation Certification
URAC, NCQA

Key Personnel
President & CEO . . . . Kerry P. Hall
VP, Admin./Gov. Relations . . . . Patricia J. Guzman
Director of Accounting . . . . Jennifer R. Hanrahan

883 UnitedHealthcare of Wyoming
6465 S Greenwood Plaza Boulevard
Suite 300
Centennial, CO 80111
Toll-Free: 866-574-6088
Phone: 720-441-6311
www.uhc.com
Subsidiary of: UnitedHealth Group
For Profit Organization: Yes

Healthplan and Services Defined
PLAN TYPE: HMO/PPO
Model Type: Network
Plan Specialty: Behavioral Health, Dental, Disease Management, MSO, PBM, Vision
Benefits Offered: Behavioral Health, Chiropractic, Complementary
Medicine, Dental, Disease Management, Home Care, Inpatient SNF, Long-Term Care, Physical Therapy, Podiatry, Prescription, Psychiatric, Transplant, Vision, Wellness, AD&D, Life, Benefits vary according to plan

Type of Coverage
Commercial, Individual, Medicare, Medicaid, Family, Military, Veterans, Group

Type of Payment Plans Offered
DFFS, FFS, Combination FFS & DFFS

Geographic Areas Served
Statewide. Wyoming is covered by the Colorado branch

Subscriber Information
  Average Monthly Fee Per Subscriber
    (Employee + Employer Contribution):
      Employee Only (Self): Varies

Network Qualifications
  Pre-Admission Certification: Yes

Peer Review Type
  Case Management: Yes

Publishes and Distributes Report Card: Yes

Accreditation Certification
  URAC, NCQA
  State Licensure, Quality Assurance Program

Key Personnel
  CEO, Colorado & Wyoming................ Marc Neely

Average Claim Compensation
  Physician's Fees Charged: 70%
  Hospital's Fees Charged: 55%

Specialty Managed Care Partners
  United Behavioral Health
  Enters into Contracts with Regional Business Coalitions: No

Appendix A: Glossary of Terms

A

Access
A person's ability to obtain healthcare services.

Acute Care
Medical treatment rendered to people whose illnesses or medical problems are short-term or don't require long-term continuing care. Acute care facilities are hospitals that mainly treat people with short-term health problems.

Aggregate Indemnity
The maximum amount of payment provided by an insurer for each covered service for a group of insured people.

Aid to Families with Dependent Children (AFDC)
A state-based federal assistance program that provided cash payments to needy children (and their caretakers), who met certain income requirements. AFDC has now been replaced by a new block grant program (Temporary Assistance for Needy Families), but the requirements, or criteria, can still be used for determining eligibility for Medicaid.

Alliance
Large businesses, small businesses, and individuals who form a group for insurance coverage.

All-payer System
A proposed healthcare system in which, no matter who is paying, prices for health services and payment methods are the same. Federal or state government, a private insurance company, a self-insured employer plan, an individual, or any other payer would pay the same rates. Also called Multiple Payer system.

Ambulatory Care
All health services that are provided on an out-patient basis, that don't require overnight care. Also called out-patient care.

Ancillary Services
Supplemental services, including laboratory, radiology and physical therapy, that are provided along with medical or hospital care.

B

Beneficiary
A person who is eligible for or receiving benefits under an insurance policy or plan.

Benefits
The services that members are entitled to receive based on their health plan.

Blue Cross/Blue Shield
Non-profit, tax-exempt insurance service plans that cover hospital care, physician care and related services. Blue Cross and Blue Shield are separate organizations that have different benefits, premiums and policies. These organizations are in all states, and The Blue Cross and Blue Shield Association of America is their national organization.

Board Certified
Status granted to a medical specialist who completes required training and passes and examination in his/her specialized area. Individuals who have met all requirements, but have not completed the exam are referred to as "board eligible."

Board Eligible
Reference to medical specialists who have completed all required training but have not completed the exam in his/her specialized area.

C

Cafeteria Plan
This benefit plan gives employees a set amount of funds that they can choose to spend on a different benefit options, such as health insurance or retirement savings

Capitation
A fixed prepayment, per patient covered, to a healthcare provider to deliver medical services to a particular group of patients. The payment is the same no matter how many services or what type of services each patient actually gets. Under capitation, the provider is financially responsible.

Care Guidelines
A set of medical treatments for a particular condition or group of patients that has been reviewed and endorsed by a national organization, such as the Agency for Healthcare Policy Research.

Carrier
A private organization, usually an insurance company, that finances healthcare.

Carve-out
Medical services that are separated out and contracted for independently from any other benefits.

Case management
Intended to improve health outcomes or control costs, services and education are tailored to a patient's needs, which are designed to improve health outcomes and/or control costs

Catastrophic Health Insurance
Health insurance that provides coverage for treating severe or lengthy illnesses or disability.

CHAMPUS
(Civilian Health and Medical Program of the Uniformed Services) A health plan that serves the dependents of active duty military personnel and retired military personnel and their dependents.

Chronic Care
Treatment given to people whose health problems are long-term and continuing. Nu nursing homes, mental hospitals and rehabilitation facilities are chronic care facilities.

Appendix A: Glossary of Terms

Chronic Disease
A medical problem that will not improve, that lasts a lifetime, or recurs.

Claims
Bills for services. Doctors, hospitals, labs and other providers send billed claims to health insurance plans, and what the plans pay are called paid claims.

COBRA
(Consolidated Omnibus Budget Reconciliation Act of 1985) Designed to provide health coverage to workers between jobs, this legal act lets workers who leave a company buy health insurance from that company at the employer's group rate rather than an individual rate.

Co-insurance
A cost-sharing requirement under some health insurance policies in which the insured person pays some of the costs of covered services.

Cooperatives/Co-ops
HMOs that are managed by the members of the health plan or insurance purchasing arrangements in which businesses or other groups join together to gain the buying power of large employers or groups.

Co-pay
Flat fees or payments (often $5-10) that a patient pays for each doctor visit or prescription.

Cost Containment
The method of preventing healthcare costs from increasing beyond a set level by controlling or reducing inefficiency and waste in the healthcare system.

Cost Sharing
An insurance policy requires the insured person to pay a portion of the costs of covered services. Deductibles, co-insurance and co-payments are cost sharing.

Cost Shifting
When one group of patients does not pay for services, such as uninsured or Medicare patients, healthcare providers pass on the costs for these health services to other groups of patients.

Coverage
A person's healthcare costs are paid by their insurance or by the government..

Covered services
Treatments or other services for which a health plan pays at least part of the charge.

D

Deductible
The amount of money, or value of certain services (such as one physician visit), a patient or family must pay before costs (or percentages of costs) are covered by the health plan or insurance company, usually per year.

Diagnostic related groups (DRGs)
A system for classifying hospital stays according to the diagnosis of the medical problem being treated, for the purposes of payment.

Direct access
The ability to see a doctor or receive a medical service without a referral from your primary care physician.

Disease management
Programs for people who have chronic illnesses, such as asthma or diabetes, that try to encourage them to have a healthy lifestyle, to take medications as prescribed, and that coordinate care.

Disposable Personal Income
The amount of a person's income that is left over after money has been spent on basic necessities such as rent, food, and clothing.

E

Early and Periodic Screening, Diagnosis, and Treatment Program (EPSDT)
As part of the Medicaid program, the law requires that all states have a program for eligible children under age 21 to receive a medical assessment, medical treatments and other measures to correct any problems and treat chronic conditions.

Elective
A healthcare procedure that is not an emergency and that the patient and doctor plan in advance.

Emergency
A medical condition that starts suddenly and requires immediate care.

Employee Retirement Income Security Act (ERISA)
A Federal act, passed in 1974, that established new standards for employer-funded health benefit and pension programs. Companies that have self-funded health benefit plans operating under ERISA are not subject to state insurance regulations and healthcare legislation.

Employer Contribution
The contribution is the money a company pays for its employees' healthcare. Exclusions
Health conditions that are explicitly not covered in an insurance package and that your insurance will not pay for.

Exclusive Provider Organizations (EPO)/Exclusive Provider Arrangement (EPA)
An indemnity or service plan that provides benefits only if those hospitals or doctors with which it contracts provide the medical services, with some exceptions for emergency and out-of-area services.

F

Federal Employee Health Benefit Program (FEP)
Health insurance program for Federal workers and their dependents, established in 1959 under the Federal Employees Health Benefits Act. Federal employees may choose to participate in one of two or more plans.

Fee-for-Service
Physicians or other providers bill separately for each patient encounter or service they provide. This method of billing means the insurance company pays all or some set percentage of the fees that hospitals and doctors set and charge. This is still the main system of paying for healthcare services in the United States.

First Dollar Coverage
A system in which the insurer pays for all employee out-of-pocket healthcare costs. Under first dollar coverage, the beneficiary has no deductible and no co-payments.

Flex plan
An account that lets workers set aside pretax dollars to pay for medical benefits, childcare, and other services.

Formulary
A list of medications that a managed care company encourages or requires physicians to prescribe as necessary in order to reduce costs.

G

Gag clause
A contractual agreement between a managed care organization and a provider that restricts what the provider can say about the managed care company

Gatekeeper
The person in a managed care organization, often a primary care provider, who controls a patient's access to healthcare services and whose approval is required for referrals to other services or other specialists.

General Practice
Physicians without specialty training who provide a wide range of primary healthcare services to patients.

Global Budgeting
A way of containing hospital costs in which participating hospitals share a budget, agreeing together to set the maximum amount of money that will be paid for healthcare.

Group Insurance
Health insurance offered through business, union trusts or other groups and associations. The most common system of health insurance in the United States, in which the cost of insurance is based on the age, sex, health status and occupation of the people in the group.

Group model HMO
An HMO that contracts with an independent group practice to provide medical services

Guaranteed Issue
The requirement that an insurance plan accept everyone who applies for coverage and guarantee the renewal of that coverage as long as the covered person pays the policy premium.

H

Healthcare Benefits
The specific services and procedures covered by a health plan or insurer.

Healthcare Financing Administration (HCFA)
The federal government agency within the Department of Health and Human Services that directs the Medicare and Medicaid programs. HCFA also does research to support these programs and oversees more than a quarter of all healthcare costs in the United States.

Health Insurance
Financial protection against the healthcare costs caused by treating disease or accidental injury.

Health Insurance Portability and Accountability Act (HIPAA)
Also known as Kennedy-Kassebaum law, this guarantees that people who lose their group health insurance will have access to individual insurance, regardless of pre-existing medical problems. The law also allows employees to secure health insurance from their new employer when they switch jobs even if they have a pre-existing medical condition.

Health Insurance Purchasing Cooperatives (HIPCs)
Public or private organizations that get health insurance coverage for certain populations of people, combining everyone in a specific geographic region and basing insurance rates on the people in that area.

Health Maintenance Organization (HMO)
A health plan provides comprehensive medical services to its members for a fixed, prepaid premium. Members must use participating providers and are enrolled for a fixed period of time. HMOs can do business either on a for-profit or not-for-profit basis.

Health Plan Employer Data and Information Set (HEDIS)
Performance measures designed by the National Committee for Quality Assurance to give participating managed health plans and employers to information about the value of their healthcare and trends in their health plan performance compared with other health plans.

Home healthcare
Skilled nurses and trained aides who provide nursing services and related care to someone at home.

Hospice Care
Care given to terminally ill patients. Hospital Alliances
Groups of hospitals that join together to cut their costs by purchasing services and equipment in volume.

I

Indemnity Insurance
A system of health insurance in which the insurer pays for the costs of covered services after care has been given, and which usually defines the maximum amounts which will be paid for covered services. This is the most common type of insurance in the United States.

Independent Practice Association (IPA)
A group of private physicians who join together in an association to contract with a managed care organization.

Indigent Care
Care provided, at no cost, to people who do not have health insurance or are not covered by Medicare, Medicaid, or other public programs.

In-patient
A person who has been admitted to a hospital or other health facility, for a period of at least 24 hours.

Integrated Delivery System (IDS)
An organization that usually includes a hospital, a large medical group, and an insurer such as an HMO or PPO.

Integrated Provider (IP)
A group of providers that offer comprehensive and coordinated care, and usually provides a range of medical care facilities and service plans including hospitals, group practices, a health plan and other related healthcare services.

J

Joint Commission on the Accreditation of Healthcare Organizations (JCAHO)
A national private, non-profit organization that accredits healthcare organizations and agencies and sets guidelines for operation for these facilities.

L

Limitations
A "cap" or limit on the amount of services that may be provided. It may be the maximum cost or number of days that a service or treatment is covered.

Limited Service Hospital
A hospital, often located in a rural area, that provides a limited set of medical and surgical services.

Long-term Care
Healthcare, personal care and social services provided to people who have a chronic illness or disability and do not have full functional capacity. This care can take place in an institution or at home, on a long-term basis.

M

Malpractice Insurance
Coverage for medical professionals which pays the costs of legal fees and/or any damages assessed by the court in a lawsuit brought against a professional who has been charged with negligence.

Managed care
This term describes many types of health insurance, including HMOs and PPOs. They control the use of health services by their members so that they can contain healthcare costs and/or improve the quality of care.

Mandate
Law requiring that a health plan or insurance carrier must offer a particular procedure or type of coverage.

Means Test
An assessment of a person's or family's income or assets so that it can be determined if they are eligible to receive public support, such as Medicaid.

Medicaid
An insurance program for people with low incomes who are unable to afford healthcare. Although funded by the federal government, Medicaid is administered by each state. Following very broad federal guidelines, states determine specific benefits and amounts of payment for providers.

Medical IRAs
Personal accounts which, like individual retirement plans, allow a person to accumulate funds for future use. The money in these accounts must be used to pay for medical services. The employee decides how much money he or she will spend on healthcare.

Medically Indigent
A person who does not have insurance and is not covered by Medicaid, Medicare or other public programs.

Medicare
A federal program of medical care benefits created in 1965 designed for those over age 65 or permanently disabled. Medicare consists of two separate programs: A and B. Medicare Part A, which is automatic at age 65, covers hospital costs and is financed largely by employer payroll taxes. Medicare Part B covers outpatient care and is financed through taxes and individual payments toward a premium.

Medicare Supplements or Medigap
A privately-purchased health insurance policy available to Medicare beneficiaries to cover costs of care that Medicare does not pay. Some policies cover additional costs, such as preventive care, prescription drugs, or at-home care.

Member
The person enrolled in a health plan.

N

National Committee on Quality Assurance (NCQA)
An independent national organization that reviews and accredits managed care plans and measures the quality of care offered by managed care plans.

Network
A group of affiliated contracted healthcare providers (physicians, hospitals, testing centers, rehabilitation centers etc.), such as an HMO, PPO, or Point of Service plan.

Non-contributory Plan
A group insurance plan that requires no payment from employees for their healthcare coverage.

Non-participating Provider
A healthcare provider who is not part of a health plan. Usually patients must pay their own healthcare costs to see a non-participating provider.

Nurse practitioner
A nurse specialist who provides primary and/or specialty care to patients. In some states nurse practitioners do not have to be supervised by a doctor.

O

Open Enrollment Period
A specified period of time during which people are allowed to change health plans.

Open Panel
A right included in an HMO, which allows the covered person to get non-emergency covered services from a specialist without getting a referral from the primary care physician or gatekeeper.

Out of Pocket costs or expenditures
The amount of money that a person must pay for his or her healthcare, including: deductibles, co-pays, payments for services that are not covered, and/or health insurance premiums that are not paid by his or her employer.

Outcomes
Measures of the effectiveness of particular kinds of medical treatment. This refers to what is quantified to determine if a specific treatment or type of service works.

Out of Pocket Maximum
The maximum amount that a person must pay under a plan or insurance contract.

Outpatient Care
Healthcare services that do not require a patient to receive overnight care in a hospital.

P

Participating Physician or Provider
Healthcare providers who have contracted with a managed care plan to provide eligible healthcare services to members of that plan.

Payer
The organization responsible for the costs of healthcare services. A payer may be private insurance, the government, or an employer's self-funded plan.

Peer Review Organization (PRO or PSRO)
An agency that monitors the quality and appropriateness of medical care delivered to Medicare and Medicaid patients. Healthcare professionals in these agencies review other professionals with similar training and experience. [See Quality Improvement Organizations]

Percent of Poverty
A term that describes the income level a person or family must have to be eligible for Medicaid.

Physician Assistant
A health professional who provides primary and/or specialty care to patients under the supervision of a physician.

Physician Hospital Organizations (PHOs)
An organization that contracts with payers on behalf of one or more hospitals and affiliated physicians. Physicians still own their practices.

Play or Pay
This system would provide coverage for all people by requiring employers either to provide health insurance for their employees and dependents (play) or pay a contribution to a publicly-provided system that covers uninsured or unemployed people without private insurance (pay).

Point of Service (POS)
A type of insurance where each time healthcare services are needed, the patient can choose from different types of provider systems (indemnity plan, PPO or HMO). Usually, members are required to pay more to see PPO or non-participating providers than to see HMO providers.

Portability
A person's ability to keep his or her health coverage during times of change in health status or personal situation (such as change in employment or unemployment, marriage or divorce) or while moving between health plans.

Postnatal Care
Healthcare services received by a woman immediately following the delivery of her child

Pre-authorization
The process where, before a patient can be admitted to the hospital or receive other types of specialty services, the managed care company must approve of the proposed service in order to cover it.

Pre-existing Condition
A medical condition or diagnosis that began before coverage began under a current plan or insurance contract. The insurance company may provide coverage but will specifically exclude treatment for such a condition from that person's coverage for a certain period of time, often six months to a year.

Preferred Provider Organization (PPO)
A type of insurance in which the managed care company pays a higher percentage of the costs when a preferred (in-plan) provider is used. The participating providers have agreed to provide their services at negotiated discount fees.

Premium
The amount paid periodically to buy health insurance coverage. Employers and employees usually share the cost of premiums.

Premium Cap
The maximum amount of money an insurance company can charge for coverage.

Premium Tax
A state tax on insurance premiums.

Prepaid Group Practice
A type of HMO where participating providers receive a fixed payment in advance for providing particular healthcare services.

Preventive Care
Healthcare services that prevent disease or its consequences. It includes primary prevention to keep people from getting sick (such as immunizations), secondary prevention to detect early disease (such as Pap smears) and tertiary prevention to keep ill people or those at high risk of disease from getting sicker (such as helping someone with lung disease to quit smoking).

Primary Care
Basic or general routine office medical care, usually from an internist, obstetrician-gynecologist, family practitioner, or pediatrician.

Primary care provider (PCP)
The health professional who provides basic healthcare services. The PCP may control patients' access to the rest of the healthcare system through referrals.

Private Insurance
Health insurance that is provided by insurance companies such as commercial insurers and Blue Cross plans, self-funded plans sponsored by employers, HMOs or other managed care arrangements.

Provider
An individual or institution who provides medical care, including a physician, hospital, skilled nursing facility, or intensive care facility.

Provider-Sponsored Organization (PSO)
Healthcare providers (physicians and/or hospitals) who form an affiliation to act as insurer for an enrolled population.

Q

Quality Assessment
Measurement of the quality of care.

Quality Assurance and Quality Improvement
A systematic process to improve quality of healthcare by monitoring quality, finding out what is not working, and fixing the problems of healthcare delivery.

Quality Improvement Organization (QIO)
An organization contracting with HCFA to review the medical necessity and quality of care provided to Medicare beneficiaries.

Quality of care
How well health services result in desired health outcomes.

R

Rate Setting
These programs were developed by several states in the 1970's to establish in advance the amount that hospitals would be paid no matter how high or low their costs actually were in any particular year. (Also known as hospital rate setting or prospective reimbursement programs)

Referral system
The process through which a primary care provider authorizes a patient to see a specialist to receive additional care.

Reimbursement
The amount paid to providers for services they provide to patients.

Risk
The responsibility for profiting or losing money based on the cost of healthcare services provided. Traditionally, health insurance companies have carried the risk. Under capitation, healthcare providers bear risk.

S

Self-insured
A type of insurance arrangement where employers, usually large employers, pay for medical claims out of their own funds rather than contracting with an insurance company for coverage. This puts the employer at risk for its employees' medical expenses rather than an insurance company.

Single Payer System
A healthcare reform proposal in which healthcare costs are paid by taxes rather than by the employer and employee. All people would have coverage paid by the government.

Socialized Medicine
A healthcare system in which providers are paid by the government, and healthcare facilities are run by the government.

Staff Model HMO
A type of managed care where physicians are employees of the health plan, usually in the health plan's own health center or facility.

Standard Benefit Package
A defined set of benefits provided to all people covered under a health plan.

T

Third Party Administrator (TPA)
An organization that processes health plan claims but does not carry any insurance risk.

Third Party Payer
An organization other than the patient or healthcare provider involved in the financing of personal health services.

U

Uncompensated Care
Healthcare provided to people who cannot pay for it and who are not covered by any insurance. This includes both charity care which is not billed and the cost of services that were billed but never paid.

Underinsured

People who have some type of health insurance but not enough insurance to cover their the cost of necessary healthcare. This includes people who have very high deductibles of $1000 to $5000 per year, or insurance policies that have specific exclusions for costly services.

Underwriting

This process is the basis of insurance. It analyzes the health status and history, claims experience (cost), age and general health risks of the individual or group who is applying for insurance coverage.

Uninsured

People who do not have health insurance of any type. Over 80 percent of the uninsured are working adults and their family members.

Universal Coverage

This refers to the proposal that all people could get health insurance, regardless of the way that the system is financed.

Utilization Review

A program designed to help reduce unnecessary medical expenses by studying the appropriateness of when certain services are used and by how many patients they are used.

Utilization

How many times people use particular healthcare services during particular periods of time.

V

Vertical Integration

A healthcare system that includes the entire range of healthcare services from out-patient to hospital and long-term care.

W

Waiting Period

The amount of time a person must wait from the date he or she is accepted into a health plan (or from when he or she applies) until the insurance becomes effective and he or she can receive benefits.

Withhold

A percentage of providers' fees that managed care companies hold back from providers which is only given to them if the amount of care they provide (or that the entire plan provides) is under a budgeted amount for each quarter or the whole year.

Worker's Compensation Coverage

States require employers to provide coverage to compensate employees for work-related injuries or disabilities.

Source: Public Broadcasting Service, http://www.pbs.org/healthcarecrisis/glossary.htm. Reprinted with permission of www.issuestv.com and www.pbs.com.

Appendix B: Industry Websites

Alliance of Community Health Plans (ACHP)
http://www.achp.org
Offers information on health care so that it is safe, effective, patient-centered, timely, efficient and equitable. Members use this web site to collaborate, share strategies and work toward solutions to some of health care's biggest challenges.

America's Health Insurance Plans (AHIP)
http://www.ahip.org
AHIP is a national trade association representing nearly 1,300 member companies providing health insurance coverage to more than 200 million Americans.

American Academy of Medical Administrators (AAMA)
http://www.aameda.org
Supports individuals involved in medical administration at the executive—or middle-management levels. Promotes educational courses for the training of persons in medical administration. Conducts research. Offers placement service.

American Accreditation Healthcare Commission/URAC
http://www.urac.org
URAC (Utilization Review Accreditation Commission) is a 501(c)(3) non-profit charitable organization founded in 1990 to establish standards for the managed care industry. URAC's broad-based membership includes representation from all the constituencies affected by managed care - employers, consumers, regulators, health care providers, and the workers' compensation and managed care industries.

American Association of Healthcare Administrative Management (AAHAM)
http://www.aaham.org
A professional organization in healthcare administrative management that offers information, education and advocacy in the areas of reimbursement, admitting and registration, data management, medical records, patient relations and more. Founded in 1968, AAHAM represents a broad-based constituency of healthcare professionals through a comprehensive program of legislative and regulatory monitoring and its participation in industry groups such as ANSI, DISA and NUBC.

American Association of Integrated Healthcare Delivery Systems (AAIHDS)
http://www.aaihds.org
AAIHDS was founded in 1993 as a non-profit organization dedicated to the educational advancement of provider-based managed care professionals involved in integrated healthcare delivery.

American Association of Payers, Administrators and Networks (AAPAN)
http://www.aapan.org
The American Association of Payers, Administrators and Networks (AAPAN) is the only national association providing a unified, integrated voice for payers, administrators, networks and care management organizations operating in the commercial/government health and workers' compensation markets.

American College of Health Care Administrators (ACHCA)
http://achca.org
Founded in 1962, ACHCA provides superior educational programming, professional certification, and career development opportunities for its members. It identifies, recognizes, and supports long term care leaders, advocating for their mission and promoting excellence in their profession.

American College of Healthcare Executives (ACHE)
http://www.ache.org
International professional society of more than 30,000 healthcare executives, including credentialing and educational programs and sponsors the Congress on Healthcare Management. ACHE's publishing division, Health Administration Press, is one of the largest publishers of books.

American Association for Physician Leadership (AAPL)
https://www.physicianleaders.org
Supports physicians whose primary professional responsibility is the management of healthcare organizations. Provides for continuing education and certification of the physician executive. Offers specialized career planning, counseling, recruitment and placement services, and research and information data on physician managers.

American Health Care Association (AHCA)
http://www.ahcancal.org
A non-profit federation of affiliated state health organizations, representing more than 10,000 non-profit and for-profit assisted living, nursing facility, developmentally-disabled, and subacute care providers that care for more than 1.5 million elderly and disabled individuals nationally.

American Health Planning Association (AHPA)
http://www.ahpanet.org
A non-profit public interest organization that brings together individuals and organizations interested in the availability, affordability and equitable distribution of health services. AHPA supports community participation in health policy formulation and in the organization and operation of local health services.

American Health Quality Association (AHQA)
http://www.ahqa.org
The American Health Quality Association represents Quality Improvement Organizations (QIOs) and professionals working to improve the quality of health care in communities across America. QIOs share information about best practices with physicians, hospitals, nursing homes, home health agencies, and others. Working together with health care providers, QIOs identify opportunities and provide assistance for improvement.

American Medical Association (AMA)
http://www.ama-assn.org
Founded more than 150 years ago, the AMA's work includes the development and promotion of standards in medical practice, research, and education. This site offers medical information for physicians, medical students, other health professionals, and patients.

Society for Post-Acute and Long-Term Care Medicine (AMDA)
https://paltc.org
A professional association of medical directors, attending physicians, and others practicing in the long term care continuum, that provides education, advocacy, information, and professional development to promote the delivery of quality long term care medicine.

American Medical Group Association (AMGA)
http://www.amga.org
Association that supports various medical groups and organized systems of care at the national level.

Association of Family Medicine Residency Directors (AFMRD)
http://www.afmrd.org
Provides representation for residency directors at a national level and provides a political voice for them to appropriate arenas. Promotes cooperation and communication between residency programs and different branches of the family medicine specialty. Dedicated to improving of education of family physicians. Provides a network for mutual assistance among FP, residency directors.

Association of Family Medicine Administrators (AFMA)
https://afmaonline.org
Promotes professionalism in family medicine administration. Serves as a network for sharing of information and fellowship among members. Provides technical assistance to members and functions as a liaison to related professional organizations.

Association of Healthcare Internal Auditors (AHIA)
http://www.ahia.org
Promotes cost containment and increased productivity in health care institutions through internal auditing. Serves as a forum for the exchange of experience, ideas, and information among members; provides continuing professional education courses and informs members of developments in health care internal auditing. Offers employment clearinghouse services.

Case Management Society of America (CMSA)
http://www.cmsa.org
CMSA is an international, non-profit organization founded in 1990 dedicated to the support and development of the profession of case management through educational forums, networking opportunities and legislative involvement.

Centers for Medicare and Medicaid Services (CMS)
https://www.cms.gov
Formerly known as the Health Care Financing Administration (HCFA), this is the federal agency that administers Medicare, Medicaid and the State Children's Health Insurance Program (SCHIP). CMS provides health insurance for over 74 million Americans through these programs.

College of Healthcare Information Management Executives (CHIME)
https://chimecentral.org
Serves the professional development needs of healthcare CIOs, and advocating the more effective use of information management within healthcare.

Electronic Healthcare Network Accreditation Commission (EHNAC)
http://www.ehnac.org
A federally-recognized standards development organization and non-profit accrediting body designed to improve transactional quality, operational efficiency and data security in healthcare.

Healthcare Financial Management Association (HFMA)
http://www.hfma.org
HFMA is a membership organization for healthcare financial management executives and leaders. The association brings perspective and clarity to the industry's complex issues for the purpose of preparing members to succeed. Programs, publications and partnerships enhance the capabilities that strengthen not only individuals careers, but also the organizations from which members come.

Healthcare Information and Management Systems Society (HIMSS)
http://www.himss.org
The healthcare industry's membership organization exclusively focused on providing global leadership for the optimal use of healthcare information technology (IT) and management systems. HIMSS represents more than 20,000 individual members and over 300 corporate members leads healthcare public policy and industry practices through its advocacy, educational and professional development initiatives designed to promote information and management systems' contributions to ensuring quality patient care.

Healthfinder.gov
https://health.gov/myhealthfinder
A comprehensive guide to resources for health information from the federal government and related agencies.

The Joint Commission (JC)
http://www.jointcommission.org
An independent, not-for-profit organization, JC accredits and certifies more than 15,000 health care organizations and programs in the United States which is recognized nationwide as a symbol of quality that reflects an organization's commitment to meeting certain performance standards.

NAMCP Medical Directors Institute
https://namcp.org
NAMCP, a non-profit membership association, was established in 1991 to provide tools, education, and resources to medical directors, practicing physicians, and other healthcare professionals. The membership consists of medical directors and physicians from purchaser, plan, and provider healthcare delivery systems. NAMCP is accredited by the Accreditation Council for Continuing Medical Education (ACCME) to provide AMA PRA Category I credits to physicians.

National Association for Healthcare Quality (NAHQ)
http://www.nahq.org
Provides vital research, education, networking, certification and professional practice resources, designed to empower healthcare quality professionals from every specialty. This leading resource for healthcare quality professionals is an essential connection for leadership, excellence and innovation in healthcare quality.

National Association for Health Care Recruitment (NAHCR)
http://www.nahcr.com

Supports individuals employed directly by hospitals and other health care organizations which are involved in the practice of professional health care recruitment. Promotes sound principles of professional healthcare recruitment. Provides financial assistance to aid members in planning and implementing regional educational programs. Offers technical assistance and consultation services. Compiles statistics.

National Association Medical Staff Services (NAMSS)
http://www.namss.org

Supports individuals involved in the management and administration of health care provider services. Seeks to enhance the knowledge and experience of medical staff services professionals and promote the certification of those involved in the profession.

National Association of Dental Plans (NADP)
http://www.nadp.org

Promotes and advances the dental benefits industry to improve consumer access to affordable, quality dental care.

National Association of Insurance Commissioners (NAIC)
http://www.naic.org

The mission of the NAIC is to assist state insurance regulators, individually and collectively, in serving the public interest and achieving the following fundamental insurance regulatory goals in a responsive, efficient and cost effective manner, consistent with the wishes of its members: protect the public interest; promote competitive markets; facilitate the fair and equitable treatment of insurance consumers; promote the reliability, solvency and financial solidity of insurance institutions; and support and improve state regulation of insurance.

National Association of Medicaid Directors (NAMD)
https://medicaiddirectors.org

NAMD represents, elevates, and supports state and territorial Medicaid leaders to deliver high value services to the millions of people served by Medicaid and CHIP so they can achieve their best health and thrive in their communities.

National Committee for Quality Assurance (NCQA)
http://www.ncqa.org

The National Committee for Quality Assurance (NCQA) is a private, not-for-profit organization dedicated to assessing and reporting on the quality of managed care plans. Their efforts are organized around two activities, accreditation and performance measurement, which are complementary strategies for producing information to guide choice.

The National Institute for Health Care Management (NIHCM) Foundation
http://www.nihcm.org

A nonprofit, nonpartisan group that conducts research on health care issues. The Foundation disseminates research findings and analysis and holds forums and briefings for policy makers, the health care industry, consumers, the government, and the media to increase understanding of issues affecting the health care system.

National Quality Forum (NQF)
http://www.qualityforum.org

A not-for-profit membership organization created to develop and implement a national strategy for health care quality measurement and reporting, Prompted by the impact of health care quality on patient outcomes, workforce productivity, and health care costs. NQF has broad participation from all parts of the health care system, including national, state, regional, and local groups representing consumers, public and private purchasers, employers, health care professionals, provider organizations, health plans, accrediting bodies, labor unions, supporting industries, and organizations.

National Society of Certified Healthcare Business Consultants (NSCHBC)
https://www.nschbc.org

The NSCHBC is a national organization dedicated to serving the needs of consultants who provide ethical, confidential and professional advice to the healthcare industry. Membership by successful completion of certification examination only.

Professional Association of Health Care Office Management (PAHCOM)
https://my.pahcom.com

Supports office managers of small group and solo medical practices. Operates certification program for healthcare office managers.

U.S. Food and Drug Administration (USFDA)
https://www.fda.gov

A department of the U.S. Department of Health and Human Services, the Food and Drug Administration provides information regarding health, medicine and nutrition. Their MedWatch Safety Information and Adverse Event Reporting Program serves both healthcare professionals and the public. MedWatch provides clinical information about safety issues involving medical products, including prescription and over-the-counter drugs, biologics, dietary supplements, and medical devices *(http://www.fda.gov/medwatch)*.
Updated 12/2/2021

Plan Index

Dental

American Dental Group Colorado Springs, CO, 151

Beta Health Association, Inc. Greenwood Village, CO, 153
Bright Now! Dental Santa Ana, CA, 74

California Dental Network Laguna Hills, CA, 75
Care Plus Dental Plans Wauwatosa, WI, 859

Delta Dental Insurance Company Alpharetta, GA, 239
Delta Dental of Arizona Glendale, AZ, 31
Delta Dental of Arkansas Sherwood, AR, 54
Delta Dental of California Sacramento, CA, 90
Delta Dental of Colorado Denver, CO, 158
Delta Dental of Delaware Mechanicsburg, PA, 183
Delta Dental of Idaho Boise, ID, 259
Delta Dental of Illinois Naperville, IL, 276
Delta Dental of Iowa Johnston, IA, 319
Delta Dental of Kansas Wichita, KS, 338
Delta Dental of Kentucky Louisville, KY, 354
Delta Dental of Michigan Okemos, MI, 421
Delta Dental of Minnesota Minneapolis, MN, 451
Delta Dental of Missouri St. Louis, MO, 480
Delta Dental of Nebraska Omaha, NE, 499
Delta Dental of New Jersey Parsippany, NJ, 536
Delta Dental of New Mexico Albuquerque, NM, 548
Delta Dental of New York Mechanicsburg, PA, 567
Delta Dental of North Carolina Raleigh, NC, 600
Delta Dental of Ohio Cincinnati, OH, 621
Delta Dental of Oklahoma Oklahoma City, OK, 644
Delta Dental of Pennsylvania Mechanicsburg, PA, 678
Delta Dental of South Carolina St. Louis, MO, 728
Delta Dental of South Dakota Pierre, SD, 737
Delta Dental of Tennessee Nashville, TN, 747
Delta Dental of the District of Columbia Mechanicsburg, PA, 190
Delta Dental of Virginia Roanoke, VA, 818
Delta Dental of Washington Seattle, WA, 836
Delta Dental of West Virginia Mechanicsburg, PA, 847
Delta Dental of Wisconsin Stevens Point, WI, 862
Delta Dental of Wyoming Cheyenne, WY, 882
Dencap Dental Plans Detroit, MI, 422
Denta-Chek of Maryland Columbia, MD, 386
Dental Alternatives Insurance Services , TX, 91
Dental Benefit Providers: California San Francisco, CA, 92
Dental Health Alliance Kansas City, MO, 481
Dental Health Services of California Long Beach, CA, 93
Dental Health Services of Oregon , OR, 654
Dental Health Services of Washington Seattle, WA, 837
Dental Network of America Lombard, IL, 277
Dental Protection Plan West Allis, WI, 863
Dental Source: Dental Health Care Plans Sugar Land, TX, 482
DentaQuest Boston, MA, 402

Dentcare Delivery Systems Uniondale, NY, 568
DenteMax Southfield, MI, 423
Dentistat Los Gatos, CA, 94
DINA Dental Plan Sugar Land, TX, 364
Dominion Dental Services Arlington, VA, 819

Employers Dental Services Tuscon, AZ, 32

FCL Dental Sugar Land, TX, 748

Golden Dental Plans Warren, MI, 424

Health Net Dental , , 100
Healthplex Eagan, NY, 454

Liberty Dental Plan of California Irvine, CA, 116
Liberty Dental Plan of Florida Tampa, FL, 216
Liberty Dental Plan of Illinois Santa Ana, NV, 283
Liberty Dental Plan of Missouri Santa Ana, CA, 488
Liberty Dental Plan of Nevada Las Vegas, NV, 514
Liberty Dental Plan of New Jersey Santa Ana, CA, 540
Liberty Dental Plan of New York New York, NY, 581
Liberty Dental Plan of Texas Santa Ana, CA, 778

Mutual of Omaha Dental Insurance Omaha, NE, 504

Northeast Delta Dental Concord, NH, 526
Northeast Delta Dental Maine Saco, ME, 378
Northeast Delta Dental Vermont Burlington, VT, 812

Ora Quest Dental Plans Sugar Land, TX, 781

Primecare Dental Plan Rancho Cucamonga, CA, 129

Renaissance Dental Indianapolis, IN, 312

Spirit Dental & Vision St. Paul, MN, 459
Starmount Baton Rouge, LA, 368
Superior Dental Care Centerville, OH, 635

Total Dental Administrators Phoenix, AZ, 45
Total Dental Administrators Salt Lake City, UT, 807

United Concordia Dental Harrisburg, PA, 695
United Concordia of Arizona Phoenix, AZ, 47
United Concordia of California Fresno, CA, 139
United Concordia of Colorado Harrisburg, PA, 166
United Concordia of Florida Jacksonville, FL, 226
United Concordia of Georgia Alpharetta, GA, 246
United Concordia of Maryland Hunt Valley, MD, 393
United Concordia of Michigan Harrisburg, PA, 443
United Concordia of New Mexico Harrisburg, PA, 554
United Concordia of New York Harrisburg, PA, 591
United Concordia of North Carolina Charlotte, NC, 605
United Concordia of Oregon Harrisburg, PA, 668
United Concordia of Pennsylvania Harrisburg, PA, 696

United Concordia of Texas San Antonio, TX, 790
United Concordia of Virginia Glen Allen, VA, 827
United Concordia of Washington Harrisburg, PA, 843
United Healthcare Dental Salt Lake City, UT, 808

Western Dental & Orthodontics Orange, CA, 147
Willamette Dental Group Hillsboro, OR, 671

HMO

Aetna Better Health of California San Diego, CA, 61
Aetna Better Health of Florida Doral, FL, 194
Aetna Better Health of Illinois Downers Grove, IL, 266
Aetna Better Health of Kentucky Louisville, KY, 349
Aetna Better Health of Louisiana Kenner, LA, 361
Aetna Better Health of Maryland Linthicum, MD, 381
Aetna Better Health of Michigan Southfield, MI, 415
Aetna Better Health of New Jersey Princeton, NJ, 529
Aetna Better Health of New York New York, NY, 558
Aetna Better Health of Ohio New Albany, OH, 612
Aetna Better Health of Pennsylvania Blue Bell, PA, 672
Aetna Better Health of Texas Dallas, TX, 753
Aetna Better Health of Virginia Richmond, VA, 814
Aetna Better Health of West Virginia Charleston, WV, 846
Aetna Health of Arizona Hartford, CT, 16
Aetna Health of Colorado Hartford, CT, 149
Aetna Health of Connecticut Hartford, CT, 169
Aetna Health of District of Columbia Hartford, CT, 188
Aetna Health of Georgia Lexington, KY, 231
Aetna Health of Idaho Hartford, CT, 257
Aetna Health of Illinois Hartford, CT, 267
Aetna Health of Indiana Hartford, CT, 293
Aetna Health of Kansas Hartford, CT, 331
Aetna Health of Kansas Overland Park, KS, 332
Aetna Health of Maine Hartford, CT, 373
Aetna Health of Massachusetts Hartford, CT, 397
Aetna Health of New York Hartford, CT, 559
Aetna Health of North Carolina Hartford, CT, 595
Aetna Health of Oklahoma Hartford, CT, 640
Aetna Health of Tennessee Hartford, CT, 741
Aetna Medicaid Administrators LLC Phoenix, AZ, 17
Aetna Student Health Agency Inc. Hartford, CT, 171
Affinity Health Plan Bronx, NY, 560
Alameda Alliance for Health Alameda, CA, 62
Allegiance Life & Health Insurance Company Missoula, MT, 463
Alliant Health Plans Dalton, GA, 232
Allied Pacific IPA Alhambra, CA, 66
Allways Health Partners Somerville, MA, 398
AlohaCare Honolulu, HI, 249
American Specialty Health Carmel, IN, 297
AmeriHealth New Jersey Cranbury, NJ, 532
AmeriHealth Pennsylvania Philadelphia, PA, 676
Anthem Blue Cross & Blue Shield of Colorado Denver, CO, 152
Anthem Blue Cross & Blue Shield of Connecticut Wallingford, CT, 172
Anthem Blue Cross & Blue Shield of Georgia Atlanta, GA, 236

Anthem Blue Cross & Blue Shield of Indiana Indianapolis, IN, 298
Anthem Blue Cross & Blue Shield of Kentucky Lexington, KY, 351
Anthem Blue Cross & Blue Shield of Maine South Portland, ME, 374
Anthem Blue Cross & Blue Shield of Missouri St Louis, MO, 475
Anthem Blue Cross & Blue Shield of Nevada Las Vegas, NV, 509
Anthem Blue Cross & Blue Shield of New Hampshire Manchester, NH, 522
Anthem Blue Cross & Blue Shield of Ohio Mason, OH, 616
Anthem Blue Cross & Blue Shield of Virginia Richmond, VA, 816
Anthem Blue Cross & Blue Shield of Wisconsin Milwaukee, WI, 857
Anthem Blue Cross of California Newbury Park, CA, 67
Anthem, Inc. Indianapolis, IN, 299
Atlanticare Health Plans Egg Harbor Township, NJ, 533
Aultcare Corporation Canton, OH, 617
Avera Health Plans Sioux Falls, SD, 735
AvMed Gainesville Gainesville, FL, 199

Banner - University Care Advantage Tuscon, AZ, 24
Blue Care Network of Michigan Southfield, MI, 417, 418
Blue Cross & Blue Shield of Arizona Phoenix, AZ, 26
Blue Cross & Blue Shield of Illinois Chicago, IL, 270
Blue Cross & Blue Shield of Massachusetts Boston, MA, 401
Blue Cross & Blue Shield of Minnesota Eagan, MN, 450
Blue Cross & Blue Shield of Montana Helena, MT, 493
Blue Cross & Blue Shield of New Mexico Albuquerque, NM, 547
Blue Cross & Blue Shield of Oklahoma Tulsa, OK, 642
Blue Cross & Blue Shield of Rhode Island Providence, RI, 713
Blue Cross & Blue Shield of South Carolina Columbia, SC, 725
Blue Cross & Blue Shield of Texas Richardson, TX, 762
Blue Cross & Blue Shield of Wyoming Cheyenne, WY, 881
Blue Cross and Blue Shield of Alabama Birmingham, AL, 4
Blue Cross and Blue Shield of Kansas Topeka, KS, 336
Blue Cross and Blue Shield of Louisiana Baton Rouge, LA, 363
Blue Cross Blue Shield of North Carolina Durham, NC, 597
Blue Cross of Idaho Health Service, Inc. Meridian, ID, 258
Blue Shield of California Oakland, CA, 69
Blue Shield of California Promise Health Plan Monterey Park, CA, 71
BlueCross BlueShield of Western New York Buffalo, NY, 561
BlueShield of Northeastern New York Latham, NY, 562
Brand New Day Westminster, CA, 73
BridgeSpan Health Salt Like City, UT, 798
Bright Health Alabama Minneapolis, MN, 5
Bright Health Colorado Englewood, CO, 155

CalOptima Orange, CA, 78
Capital BlueCross Harrisburg, PA, 677
Capital Health Plan Tallahassee, FL, 200
Care1st Health Plan Arizona Phoenix, AZ, 27
CareCentrix Hartford, CT, 173
CareCentrix: Arizona Phoenix, AZ, 28
CareCentrix: Florida Tampa, FL, 201
CareCentrix: Kansas Overland Park, KS, 337
CareCentrix: New York Melville, NY, 563
CareFirst Blue Cross & Blue Shield of Virginia Reston, VA, 817
CareFirst BlueCross BlueShield Baltimore, MD, 385
CDPHP: Capital District Physicians' Health Plan Albany, NY, 565

CenCal Health Santa Barbara, CA, 80
Centene Corporation St. Louis, MO, 477
Central California Alliance for Health Scotts Valley, CA, 81
Children's Mercy Pediatric Care Network Kansas City, MO, 478
Chinese Community Health Plan San Francisco, CA, 83
Cigna HealthCare of Arizona Phoenix, AZ, 29
Cigna HealthCare of California San Francisco, CA, 85
Cigna HealthCare of Colorado Denver, CO, 156
Cigna HealthCare of Connecticut Hartford, CT, 175
Cigna HealthCare of Florida Sunrise, FL, 203
Cigna HealthCare of Georgia Atlanta, GA, 237
Cigna HealthCare of Illinois Chicago, IL, 273
Cigna HealthCare of Indiana Carmel, IN, 302
Cigna HealthCare of New Jersey Morristown, NJ, 535
Cigna HealthCare of North Carolina Charlotte, NC, 598
Cigna HealthCare of South Carolina Charlotte, NC, 727
Cigna HealthCare of Tennessee Franklin, TN, 746
Cigna HealthCare of Texas Houston, TX, 767
Cigna Medical Group Phoenix, AZ, 30
Colorado Access Aurora, CO, 157
Community First Health Plans San Antonio, TX, 768
Community Health Group Chula Vista, CA, 87
Community Health Options Lewiston, ME, 375
CompBenefits Corporation Roswell, GA, 238
ConnectiCare Bridgeport, CT, 177
Contra Costa Health Services Martinez, CA, 89
Cox Healthplans Springfield, MO, 479

DakotaCare Sioux Falls, SD, 736
Denver Health Medical Plan Denver, CO, 159

Emi Health Murray, UT, 799
Empire BlueCross BlueShield Brooklyn, NY, 572
Excellus BlueCross BlueShield Rochester, NY, 573

FirstCarolinaCare Pinehurst, NC, 602
Florida Blue Jacksonville, FL, 206
Florida Health Care Plan, Inc. Daytona Beach, FL, 207
Frazier Insurance Agency Little Rock, AR, 55
Friday Health Plans Alamosa, CO, 160

Gateway Health Pittsburgh, PA, 680
Geisinger Health Plan Danville, PA, 681
Group Health Cooperative of Eau Claire Altoona, WI, 865
Group Health Cooperative of South Central Wisconsin Madison, WI, 866
Guardian Life Insurance Company of America New York, NY, 576

HAP-Health Alliance Plan: Flint Flint, MI, 425
Harvard Pilgrim Health Care Connecticut Hartford, CT, 178
Harvard Pilgrim Health Care New Hampshire Manchester, NH, 523
Hawaii Medical Service Association Honolulu, HI, 252
HCSC Insurance Services Company Chicago, IL, 278
HCSC Insurance Services Company Montana Helena, MT, 494
HCSC Insurance Services Company New Mexico Albuquerque, NM, 549
HCSC Insurance Services Company Oklahoma Tulsa, OK, 645
HCSC Insurance Services Company Texas Richardson, TX, 773

Health Alliance Champaign, IL, 279
Health Alliance Plan Detroit, MI, 428
Health Care Service Corporation (HCSC) Chicago, IL, 281
Health Choice Arizona Phoenix, AZ, 33
Health Net Health Plan of Oregon Tigard, OR, 656
Health Net of Arizona Tempe, AZ, 34
Health Net of California Woodland Hills, CA, 102
Health New England Springfield, MA, 405
Health Plan of Nevada Las Vegas, NV, 511
Health Plan of San Joaquin French Camp, CA, 104
Health Plan of San Mateo South San Francisco, CA, 105
Health Tradition Madison, WI, 867
HealthAmerica Pennsylvania Harrisburg, PA, 683
HealthPartners Bloomington, MN, 453
Healthy and Well Kids in Iowa (Hawki) , IA, 320
Healthy Indiana Plan , IN, 305
Hennepin Health Minneapolis, MN, 455
Highmark BCBS Delaware Pittsburgh, DE, 184
Highmark Blue Cross Blue Shield Pittsburgh, PA, 684
Horizon Blue Cross Blue Shield of New Jersey Newark, NJ, 537
Humana Health Insurance of Alabama Madison, AL, 7
Humana Health Insurance of Arizona Phoenix, AZ, 35
Humana Health Insurance of Arkansas Rogers, AR, 57
Humana Health Insurance of California Irvine, CA, 107
Humana Health Insurance of Colorado Colorado Springs, CO, 161
Humana Health Insurance of Florida Jacksonville, FL, 214
Humana Health Insurance of Georgia Atlanta, GA, 240
Humana Health Insurance of Hawaii Honolulu, HI, 253
Humana Health Insurance of Idaho Meridian, ID, 260
Humana Health Insurance of Illinois Oak Brook, IL, 282
Humana Health Insurance of Indiana Indianapolis, IN, 306
Humana Health Insurance of Iowa Urbandale, IA, 321
Humana Health Insurance of Kansas Overland Park, KS, 340
Humana Health Insurance of Louisiana Metairie, LA, 365
Humana Health Insurance of Michigan Detroit, MI, 429
Humana Health Insurance of Minnesota Minnetonka, MN, 456
Humana Health Insurance of Mississippi Ridgeland, MS, 467
Humana Health Insurance of Missouri Springfield, MO, 487
Humana Health Insurance of Nevada Las Vegas, NV, 513
Humana Health Insurance of New Hampshire Portsmouth, NH, 524
Humana Health Insurance of New Jersey Uniondale, NJ, 539
Humana Health Insurance of New Mexico Albuquerque, NM, 550
Humana Health Insurance of New York Albany, NY, 578
Humana Health Insurance of North Carolina Charlotte, NC, 603
Humana Health Insurance of Ohio Cincinnati, OH, 623
Humana Health Insurance of Oklahoma Tulsa, OK, 646
Humana Health Insurance of Pennsylvania Mechanicsburg, PA, 686
Humana Health Insurance of Puerto Rico San Juan, PR, 705
Humana Health Insurance of South Carolina Columbia, SC, 729
Humana Health Insurance of Tennessee Memphis, TN, 750
Humana Health Insurance of Texas San Antonio, TX, 776
Humana Health Insurance of Utah Sandy, UT, 800
Humana Health Insurance of Virginia Glen Allen, VA, 822
Humana Health Insurance of Washington Vancouver, WA, 839

Humana Health Insurance of Wisconsin Waukesha, WI, 868

Independence Blue Cross Philadelphia, PA, 687
Independent Health Buffalo, NY, 579
Intermountain Healthcare Salt Lake City, UT, 801

Jai Medical Systems Hunt Valley, MD, 387

Kaiser Permanente Oakland, CA, 109
Kaiser Permanente Georgia Atlanta, GA, 241
Kaiser Permanente Hawaii Honolulu, HI, 254
Kaiser Permanente Northern California Oakland, CA, 110
Kaiser Permanente Northern Colorado Fort Collins, CO, 162
Kaiser Permanente Northwest Portland, OR, 657
Kaiser Permanente Southern Colorado Colorado Springs, CO, 163
Kaiser Permanente Washington Renton, WA, 840
Kern Family Health Care Bakersfield, CA, 112

L.A. Care Health Plan Los Angeles, CA, 113
Lakeside Community Healthcare Network Burbank, CA, 114
Landmark Healthplan of California Westlake Village, CA, 115
Leon Medical Centers Health Plan Doral, FL, 215

McLaren Health Plan Flint, MI, 430
Medica Minnetonka, MN, 457
Medica with CHI Health Omaha, NE, 500
Medica: Nebraska Omaha, NE, 501
Medica: North Dakota Fargo, ND, 609
Medical Associates Dubuque, IA, 323
Medical Center Healthnet Plan Charlestown, MA, 407
Medical Mutual Cleveland, OH, 624
Mercy Clinic Arkansas Berryville, AR, 58
Mercy Clinic Kansas Columbus, KS, 341
Mercy Clinic Missouri Saint Louis, MO, 490
Mercy Clinic Oklahoma Oklahoma City, OK, 647
Mercy Health Network West Des Moines, IA, 324
MercyHealth System Janesville, WI, 870
Meridian Health Plan Detroit, MI, 431
Mountain Health Co-Op Helena, ID, 495
Mountain Health Trust/Physician Assured Access System Charleston, WV, 849
Mutual of Omaha Omaha, NE, 503

Neighborhood Health Partnership Miami, FL, 219
Neighborhood Health Plan of Rhode Island Smithfield, RI, 715
Network Health Plan of Wisconsin Menasha, WI, 872

On Lok Lifeways San Francisco, CA, 123
Optima Health Plan Virginia Beach, VA, 825
Optimum HealthCare, Inc Tampa, FL, 221
OSF Healthcare Peoria, IL, 286
Oxford Health Plans Trumbull, CT, 179

PacificSource Health Plans Springfield, OR, 662
Paramount Care of Michigan Monroe, MI, 434
Paramount Health Care Toledo, OH, 631
Parkland Community Health Plan Dallas, TX, 782
Passport Health Plan Louisville, KY, 357

Physicians Health Plan of Mid-Michigan Lansing, MI, 435
Physicians Health Plan of Northern Indiana Fort Wayne, IN, 311
Preferred Therapy Providers Phoenix, AZ, 43
Presbyterian Health Plan Albuquerque, NM, 552
Priority Partners Health Plans Hanover, MD, 389
Prominence Health Plan Reno, NV, 516

Quality Plan Administrators Washington, DC, 191

Rocky Mountain Health Plans Grand Junction, CO, 165

San Francisco Health Plan San Francisco, CA, 131
Sanford Health Plan Sioux Falls, SD, 325
Santa Clara Family Health Foundations Inc San Jose, CA, 132
Sant, Community Physicians Fresno, CA, 133
SCAN Health Plan Long Beach, CA, 134
Select Health of South Carolina Charleston, SC, 732
SelectHealth Murray, UT, 806
Seton Healthcare Family Austin, TX, 785
Sharp Health Plan San Diego, CA, 135
SIHO Insurance Services Columbus, IN, 314

The Health Plan Wheeling, OH, 850
Total Health Care Detroit, MI, 439

UniCare Illinois Chicago, IL, 291
UniCare Massachusetts Andover, MA, 412
UniCare Michigan Dearborn, MI, 442
UniCare Texas Plano, TX, 789
UniCare West Virginia Charleston, WV, 851
UnitedHealthcare of Alabama Birmingham, AL, 10
UnitedHealthcare of Alaska Cypress, CA, 15
UnitedHealthcare of Arizona Phoenix, AZ, 49
UnitedHealthcare of Arkansas Little Rock, AR, 60
UnitedHealthcare of Colorado Centennial, CO, 168
UnitedHealthcare of Connecticut Hartford, CT, 182
UnitedHealthcare of Florida Tampa, FL, 228
UnitedHealthcare of Georgia Norcross, GA, 248
UnitedHealthcare of Hawaii Honolulu, HI, 256
UnitedHealthcare of Idaho Boise, ID, 265
UnitedHealthcare of Illinois Chicago, IL, 292
UnitedHealthcare of Indiana Indianapolis, IN, 317
UnitedHealthcare of Iowa West Des Moines, IA, 328
UnitedHealthcare of Kansas Overland Park, KS, 348
UnitedHealthcare of Kentucky Louisville, KY, 360
UnitedHealthcare of Louisiana Metairie, LA, 370
UnitedHealthcare of Maine Waltham, MA, 380
UnitedHealthcare of Maryland Columbia, MD, 395
UnitedHealthcare of Massachusetts Waltham, MA, 414
UnitedHealthcare of Michigan Kalamazoo, MI, 445
UnitedHealthcare of Minnesota Minnetonka, MN, 462
UnitedHealthcare of Mississippi Ridgeland, MS, 471
UnitedHealthcare of Missouri Maryland Heights, MO, 492
UnitedHealthcare of Montana Seattle, WA, 496
UnitedHealthcare of Nebraska Omaha, NE, 507
UnitedHealthcare of Nevada Las Vegas, NV, 519

UnitedHealthcare of New Hampshire Waltham, MA, 527
UnitedHealthcare of New Jersey Iselin, NJ, 544
UnitedHealthcare of New Mexico Albuquerque, NM, 556
UnitedHealthcare of New York New York, NY, 593
UnitedHealthcare of North Carolina Raleigh, NC, 607
UnitedHealthcare of North Dakota Minnetonka, MN, 611
UnitedHealthcare of Northern California Concord, CA, 141
UnitedHealthcare of Ohio Cleveland, OH, 639
UnitedHealthcare of Oklahoma Austin, TX, 649
UnitedHealthcare of Oregon Lake Oswego, OR, 669
UnitedHealthcare of Pennsylvania Pittsburgh, PA, 698
UnitedHealthcare of Puerto Rico Minnetonka, MN, 711
UnitedHealthcare of Rhode Island Warwick, RI, 718
UnitedHealthcare of South Carolina Columbia, SC, 734
UnitedHealthcare of South Dakota Minnetonka, MN, 739
UnitedHealthcare of South Florida Miramar, FL, 229
UnitedHealthcare of Southern California San Diego, CA, 142
UnitedHealthcare of Tennessee Brentwood, TN, 752
UnitedHealthcare of Texas Austin, TX, 792
UnitedHealthcare of the District of Columbia Rockville, MD, 193
UnitedHealthcare of Utah Salt Lake City, UT, 809
UnitedHealthcare of Vermont Waltham, MA, 813
UnitedHealthcare of Virginia Richmond, VA, 829
UnitedHealthcare of Washington Seattle, WA, 845
UnitedHealthcare of West Virginia Richmond, VA, 853
UnitedHealthcare of Wisconsin Wauwatosa, WI, 878
UnitedHealthcare of Wyoming Centennial, CO, 883
Univera Healthcare Buffalo, NY, 594
University Health Plans Murray, UT, 810
Upper Peninsula Health Plan Marquette, MI, 446
UTMB HealthCare Systems Galveston, TX, 794

Valley Baptist Health Plan Harlingen, TX, 795
Vantage Health Plan Monroe, LA, 371
Ventura County Health Care Plan Oxnard, CA, 144
VIVA Health Birmingham, AL, 11

Wellmark Blue Cross Blue Shield Des Moines, IA, 329
Western Health Advantage Sacramento, CA, 148

Medicare

Aetna Medicare Lexington, KY, 350
Alignment Health Plan Orange, CA, 65
AllCare Health Grants Pass, OR, 651
Allwell from Absolute Total Care Columbia, SC, 723
Allwell from Arizona Complete Health Van Nuys, AZ, 19
Allwell from Home State Health St. Louis, MO, 472
Allwell from IlliniCare Health Elk Grove Village, IL, 268
Allwell from Louisiana Healthcare Connections Baton Rouge, LA, 362
Allwell from Magnolia Health Jackson, MS, 464
Allwell from Managed Health Services Indianapolis, IN, 294
Allwell from Managed Health Services Wisconsin West Allis, WI, 855
Allwell from PA Health & Wellness Camp Hill, PA, 673
Allwell from Peach State Health Plan Atlanta, GA, 233
Allwell from Sunflower Health Plan Lenexa, KS, 333

Allwell from Sunshine Health Fort Lauderdale, FL, 195
Allwell from Superior HealthPlan San Antonio, TX, 755
Allwell from Western Sky Community Care Albuquerque, NM, 546
AlohaCare Advantage Plus Honolulu, HI, 250
Amerigroup Virginia Beach, VA, 815
Amerigroup District of Columbia Washington, NJ, 530
Amerigroup Georgia Atlanta, GA, 235
Amerigroup Iowa Virginia Beach, IA, 318
Amerigroup Maryland Hanover, MD, 383
Amerigroup New Jersey Iselin, NJ, 531
Amerigroup Tennessee Nashville, TN, 743
Amerigroup Texas Grand Prairie, TX, 759
Amerigroup Washington Seattle, WA, 832
Atrio Health Plans Salem, OR, 652
AvMed Miami, FL, 197
AvMed Ft. Lauderdale Ft. Lauderdale, FL, 198

Banner - University Family Care Tuscon, AZ, 25
Blue Shield Promise AdvantageOptimum Plan Monterey Park, CA, 763
BlueCross BlueShield Association Chicago, IL, 271

Care N' Care Fort Worth, TX, 764
CareMore Health Plan Cerritos, CA, 79
CareOregon Health Plan Portland, OR, 653
CarePlus Health Plans Miami, FL, 202
CareSource Indiana Dayton, OH, 301
CareSource Kentucky Louisville, KY, 352
CareSource Ohio Dayton, OH, 620
CareSource West Virginia Dayton, OH, 353
CDPHP Medicare Plan Albany, NY, 564
Central Health Medicare Plan Diamond Bar, CA, 82
Cigna-HealthSpring Bloomfield, CT, 176
Clear Health Alliance Miami, FL, 204

Elderplan Brooklyn, NY, 569
Essence Healthcare Maryland Heights, MO, 483

Freedom Health Tampa, FL, 208

GEMCare Health Plan Bakersfield, CA, 98
GHI Medicare Plan New York, NY, 575

HAP-Health Alliance Plan: Senior Medicare Plan Detroit, MI, 426
Health Alliance Medicare Champaign, IL, 280
Health Alliance Medicare Detroit, MI, 427
Health First Health Plans Rockledge, FL, 209
Health First Medicare Plans Rockledge, FL, 210
Health Partners Plans Philadelphia, PA, 682
HealthSun Miami, FL, 213
Humana Medicare Lexington, KY, 356

Independent Health Medicare Plan Buffalo, NY, 580
InnovaCare Health Fort Lee, NJ, 706
InStil Health Columbia, SC, 730
Inter Valley Health Plan Pomona, CA, 108

Medica HealthCare Plans, Inc Miami, FL, 120

MediGold Columbus, OH, 626
Meridian Health Plan of Illinois Chicago, IL, 284
MetroPlus Health Plan New York, NY, 584
Michigan Complete Health Detroit, MI, 432
Molina Healthcare Long Beach, CA, 121
Molina Healthcare of California Long Beach, CA, 122
Molina Healthcare of Florida Miami, FL, 218
Molina Healthcare of Idaho Boise, ID, 261
Molina Healthcare of Illinois Oak Brook, IL, 285
Molina Healthcare of Michigan Troy, MI, 433
Molina Healthcare of Mississippi Jackson, MS, 469
Molina Healthcare of New Mexico Albuquerque, NM, 551
Molina Healthcare of New York North Syracuse, NY, 585
Molina Healthcare of Ohio Columbus, OH, 627
Molina Healthcare of Puerto Rico San Juan, PR, 709
Molina Healthcare of South Carolina North Charleston, SC, 731
Molina Healthcare of Texas Irving, TX, 780
Molina Healthcare of Utah Midvale, UT, 802
Molina Healthcare of Washington Bothell, WA, 842
Molina Healthcare of Wisconsin Milwaukee, WI, 871

Paramount Elite Medicare Plan Toledo, OH, 630
Peoples Health Metairie, LA, 367
Presbyterian Medicare Advantage Plans Albuquerque, NM, 553
Prime Time Health Medicare Plan Canton, OH, 632
PriorityHealth Medicare Plans Grand Rapids, MI, 437

Senior Whole Health Massachusetts Cambridge, MA, 408
Senior Whole Health New York New York, NY, 589
SilverScript Insurance Company , , 44
Simply Healthcare Plans, Inc. Miami, FL, 223
Sterling Insurance Austin, TX, 786
SummaCare Medicare Advantage Plan Akron, OH, 634

Texas HealthSpring Houston, TX, 788
Tufts Health Medicare Plan Watertown, MA, 410

UnitedHealthcare Community Plan Arkansas Salt Lake City, UT, 59
UnitedHealthcare Community Plan California Salt Lake City, UT, 140
UnitedHealthcare Community Plan Colorado Salt Lake City, UT, 167
UnitedHealthcare Community Plan Connecticut Salt Lake City, UT, 181
UnitedHealthcare Community Plan Delaware Salt Lake City, UT, 187
UnitedHealthcare Community Plan District of Columbia Salt Lake City, UT, 192
UnitedHealthcare Community Plan Georgia Salt Lake City, UT, 247
UnitedHealthcare Community Plan Hawaii Salt Lake City, UT, 255
UnitedHealthcare Community Plan Indiana Salt Lake City, UT, 316
UnitedHealthcare Community Plan Kansas Salt Lake City, UT, 347
UnitedHealthcare Community Plan Kentucky Salt Lake City, UT, 359
UnitedHealthcare Community Plan Louisiana Salt Lake City, UT, 369
UnitedHealthcare Community Plan Maine Salt Lake City, UT, 379
UnitedHealthcare Community Plan Maryland Salt Lake City, UT, 394
UnitedHealthcare Community Plan Massachusetts Salt Lake City, UT, 413
UnitedHealthcare Community Plan Michigan Salt Lake City, UT, 444
UnitedHealthcare Community Plan Missouri Salt Lake City, UT, 491
UnitedHealthcare Community Plan Nebraska Salt Lake City, UT, 506

UnitedHealthcare Community Plan New Jersey Salt Lake City, UT, 543
UnitedHealthcare Community Plan New Mexico Salt Lake City, UT, 555
UnitedHealthcare Community Plan North Carolina Salt Lake City, UT, 606
UnitedHealthcare Community Plan Ohio Salt Lake City, UT, 638
UnitedHealthcare Community Plan Oklahoma Salt Lake City, UT, 648
UnitedHealthcare Community Plan South Carolina Salt Lake City, UT, 733
UnitedHealthcare Community Plan Tennessee Salt Lake City, UT, 751
UnitedHealthcare Community Plan Virginia Salt Lake City, UT, 828
UnitedHealthcare Community Plan Washington Salt Lake City, UT, 844
UnitedHealthcare Community Plan West Virginia Salt Lake City, UT, 852
UnitedHealthcare Community Plan Wisconsin Salt Lake City, UT, 877

Vantage Medicare Advantage Monroe, LA, 372

Wellcare By Trillium Advantage Eugene, OR, 670
WellCare Health Plans, Inc. Tampa, FL, 230

Multiple

Aetna Inc. Hartford, CT, 170
Altius Health Plans Sandy, UT, 797
American Family Insurance Madison, WI, 856
Ameritas Lincoln, NE, 497
Arizona Foundation for Medical Care Glendale, AZ, 22
Arkansas Blue Cross Blue Shield Little Rock, AR, 51
Arkansas Health & Wellness Little Rock, AR, 52
Asuris Northwest Health Spokane, WA, 833
Avesis: Arizona Phoenix, AZ, 23

Blue Cross & Blue Shield of Tennessee Chattanooga, TN, 745
Blue Cross Blue Shield of Michigan Southfield, MI, 419
BlueChoice Health Plan of South Carolina Columbia, SC, 726

ChiroSource, Inc. / Chiropractic Health Plan of California Clayton, CA, 84
Christus Health Plan Irving, TX, 766
Cigna Corporation Bloomfield, CT, 174
Community Health Plan of Washington Seattle, WA, 834
CommunityCare Tulsa, OK, 643
Consumers Direct Insurance Services (CDIS) Dallas, TX, 770
Coordinated Care Tacoma, WA, 835

Dean Health Plan Madison, WI, 861

eHealthInsurance Services, Inc. Santa Clara, CA, 95
EPIC Pharmacy Network Mechanicsville, VA, 820
Evolent Health Arlington, VA, 821

Fallon Health Worcester, MA, 403
Fidelis Care Long Island City, NY, 574
First Medical Health Plan Guaynabo, PR, 704
FirstCare Health Plans Austin, TX, 771

Golden West Dental & Vision Camarillo, CA, 99

Harvard Pilgrim Health Care Maine Portland, ME, 376
Harvard Pilgrim Health Care Massachusetts Wellesley, MA, 404
Health Net Federal Services (HNFS) Rancho Cordova, CA, 101
Health Net, Inc. Woodland Hills, CA, 103

Healthfirst New York, NY, 577
HealthLink HMO St. Louis, MO, 485
HealthNetwork West Palm Beach, FL, 212
Hometown Health Plan Reno, NV, 512
Humana Inc. Louisville, KY, 355

Kaiser Permanente Mid-Atlantic Rockville, MD, 388
Kaiser Permanente Southern California San Diego, CA, 111
KelseyCare Advantage Pearland, TX, 777

Magnolia Health Jackson, MS, 468
Martin's Point HealthCare Portland, ME, 377
MDwise Indianapolis, IN, 308
Medical Card System (MCS) San Juan, PR, 707
Mercy Care Plan/Mercy Care Advantage Phoenix, AZ, 39
Meritain Health Amherst, NY, 583
MHNet Behavioral Health San Rafael, CA, 779
Mid America Health Greenwood, IN, 309
Mid-Atlantic Behavioral Health Newark, DE, 185
MMM Holdings San Juan, PR, 708
Moda Health Alaska Alaska, AK, 13
Moda Health Oregon Portland, OR, 660
MVP Health Care Schenectady, NY, 586

Nova Healthcare Administrators Williamsville, NY, 587

Ohio State University Health Plan Inc. Columbus, OH, 629
Optum Complex Medical Conditions Eden Prairie, MN, 458

Pacific Foundation for Medical Care Santa Rosa, CA, 125
PacificSource Health Plans Springfield, OR, 661
Piedmont Community Health Plan Lynchburg, VA, 826
Preferred Care Partners Miami, FL, 222
Preferred Mental Health Management Wichita, KS, 343
Primary Health Medical Group Garden City, ID, 262
Priority Health Grand Rapids, MI, 436
Providence Health Plan Portland, OR, 663

QualCare Piscataway, NJ, 541
Quartz Health Plan Sauk City, WI, 874

Regence BlueCross BlueShield of Oregon Portland, OR, 664
Regence BlueCross BlueShield of Utah Cottonwood Heights, UT, 665
Regence BlueShield of Idaho Lewiston, ID, 263

Samaritan Health Plan Operations Corvallis, OR, 666
Scott & White Health Plan Temple, TX, 783
Security Health Plan of Wisconsin Marshfield, WI, 875
Spectera Eyecare Networks Columbia, MD, 390
Sun Life Financial Wellesley Hills, MA, 409
Superior HealthPlan Austin, TX, 787

Taylor Benefits Insurance Agency San Jose, CA, 137
The Dental Care Plus Group Cincinnati, OH, 636
Triple-S Salud San Juan, PR, 710
Tufts Health Plan Watertown, MA, 411
Tufts Health Plan: Rhode Island Providence, RI, 716

UCare Minneapolis, MN, 460
UnitedHealth Group Minneapolis, MN, 461
UnitedHealthcare Community Plan Arizona Salt Lake City, UT, 48
UnitedHealthcare Community Plan Florida Salt Lake City, UT, 227
UnitedHealthcare Community Plan Iowa Salt Lake City, UT, 327
UnitedHealthcare Community Plan Mississippi Salt Lake City, UT, 470
UnitedHealthcare Community Plan New York Salt Lake City, UT, 592
UnitedHealthcare Community Plan Pennsylvania Salt Lake City, UT, 697
UnitedHealthcare Community Plan Rhode Island Salt Lake City, UT, 717
UnitedHealthcare Community Plan Texas Salt Lake City, UT, 791
UPMC Health Plan Pittsburgh, PA, 699

Valley Preferred Allentown, PA, 702

WellCare TexanPlus Tampa, FL, 796
Wellmark Blue Cross & Blue Shield of South Dakota Sioux Falls, SD, 740
Wisconsin Physician's Service Madison, WI, 879

PPO

Aetna Better Health of Florida Doral, FL, 194
Aetna Better Health of Illinois Downers Grove, IL, 266
Aetna Better Health of Kentucky Louisville, KY, 349
Aetna Better Health of Louisiana Kenner, LA, 361
Aetna Better Health of Maryland Linthicum, MD, 381
Aetna Better Health of Michigan Southfield, MI, 415
Aetna Better Health of New Jersey Princeton, NJ, 529
Aetna Better Health of New York New York, NY, 558
Aetna Better Health of Ohio New Albany, OH, 612
Aetna Better Health of Pennsylvania Blue Bell, PA, 672
Aetna Better Health of Texas Dallas, TX, 753
Aetna Better Health of Virginia Richmond, VA, 814
Aetna Better Health of West Virginia Charleston, WV, 846
Aetna Health of Alabama Hartford, CT, 1
Aetna Health of Alaska Hartford, CT, 12
Aetna Health of Arizona Hartford, CT, 16
Aetna Health of Colorado Hartford, CT, 149
Aetna Health of Connecticut Hartford, CT, 169
Aetna Health of District of Columbia Hartford, CT, 188
Aetna Health of Georgia Lexington, KY, 231
Aetna Health of Idaho Hartford, CT, 257
Aetna Health of Illinois Hartford, CT, 267
Aetna Health of Indiana Hartford, CT, 293
Aetna Health of Kansas Hartford, CT, 331
Aetna Health of Kansas Overland Park, KS, 332
Aetna Health of Maine Hartford, CT, 373
Aetna Health of Massachusetts Hartford, CT, 397
Aetna Health of Minnesota Hartford, CT, 447
Aetna Health of New York Hartford, CT, 559
Aetna Health of North Carolina Hartford, CT, 595
Aetna Health of North Dakota Hartford, CT, 608
Aetna Health of Oklahoma Hartford, CT, 640
Aetna Health of Oregon Hartford, CT, 650
Aetna Health of Rhode Island Hartford, CT, 712
Aetna Health of South Carolina Hartford, CT, 722
Aetna Health of Tennessee Hartford, CT, 741

Aetna Health of Washington Hartford, CT, 830
Aetna Health of Wisconsin Hartford, CT, 854
Aetna Health of Wyoming Hartford, CT, 880
Aetna Medicaid Administrators LLC Phoenix, AZ, 17
Aetna Student Health Agency Inc. Hartford, CT, 171
Alliance Regional Health Network Amarillo, TX, 754
Alliant Health Plans Dalton, GA, 232
American Health Care Alliance Kansas City, MO, 474
American Health Network Indianapolis, IN, 296
American Health Network Ohio Columbus, OH, 615
American National Insurance Company Galveston, TX, 757
American Postal Workers Union (APWU) Health Plan Glen Burnie, MD, 382
American PPO Irving, TX, 758
Americas PPO Bloomington, MN, 448
AmeriHealth New Jersey Cranbury, NJ, 532
AmeriHealth Pennsylvania Philadelphia, PA, 676
Anthem Blue Cross & Blue Shield of Colorado Denver, CO, 152
Anthem Blue Cross & Blue Shield of Connecticut Wallingford, CT, 172
Anthem Blue Cross & Blue Shield of Georgia Atlanta, GA, 236
Anthem Blue Cross & Blue Shield of Indiana Indianapolis, IN, 298
Anthem Blue Cross & Blue Shield of Kentucky Lexington, KY, 351
Anthem Blue Cross & Blue Shield of Maine South Portland, ME, 374
Anthem Blue Cross & Blue Shield of Missouri St Louis, MO, 475
Anthem Blue Cross & Blue Shield of Nevada Las Vegas, NV, 509
Anthem Blue Cross & Blue Shield of New Hampshire Manchester, NH, 522
Anthem Blue Cross & Blue Shield of Ohio Mason, OH, 616
Anthem Blue Cross & Blue Shield of Virginia Richmond, VA, 816
Anthem Blue Cross & Blue Shield of Wisconsin Milwaukee, WI, 857
Anthem Blue Cross of California Newbury Park, CA, 67
Anthem, Inc. Indianapolis, IN, 299
Araz Group Bloomington, MN, 399
Atlanticare Health Plans Egg Harbor Township, NJ, 533
Aultcare Corporation Canton, OH, 617
Avesis: Maryland Owings Mills, MD, 384
Avesis: Massachusetts North Andover, MA, 400
Avesis: Minnesota Sartell, MN, 449
Avesis: Texas , TX, 761

Behavioral Health Systems Birmingham, AL, 3
Behavioral Healthcare Options, Inc. Las Vegas, NV, 510
BEST Life and Health Insurance Co. Irvine, CA, 68
Blue Cross & Blue Shield of Arizona Phoenix, AZ, 26
Blue Cross & Blue Shield of Illinois Chicago, IL, 270
Blue Cross & Blue Shield of Nebraska Omaha, NE, 498
Blue Cross & Blue Shield of New Mexico Albuquerque, NM, 547
Blue Cross & Blue Shield of Oklahoma Tulsa, OK, 642
Blue Cross & Blue Shield of South Carolina Columbia, SC, 725
Blue Cross & Blue Shield of Texas Richardson, TX, 762
Blue Cross & Blue Shield of Vermont Berlin, VT, 811
Blue Cross and Blue Shield of Alabama Birmingham, AL, 4
Blue Cross and Blue Shield of Louisiana Baton Rouge, LA, 363
Blue Cross Blue Shield of Kansas City Kansas City, MO, 476
Blue Cross Blue Shield of North Carolina Durham, NC, 597
Blue Cross of Idaho Health Service, Inc. Meridian, ID, 258
Blue Shield of California Oakland, CA, 69

BlueCross BlueShield of Western New York Buffalo, NY, 561
BlueShield of Northeastern New York Latham, NY, 562
Boulder Valley Individual Practice Association Boulder, CO, 154

California Foundation for Medical Care Riverside, CA, 76
Capital BlueCross Harrisburg, PA, 677
CareFirst Blue Cross & Blue Shield of Virginia Reston, VA, 817
CareFirst BlueCross BlueShield Baltimore, MD, 385
CDPHP: Capital District Physicians' Health Plan Albany, NY, 565
Celtic Insurance Company Chicago, OH, 272
Centene Corporation St. Louis, MO, 477
ChiroCare of Wisconsin Plymouth, WI, 860
CHN PPO Hamilton, NJ, 534
Coastal TPA, Inc. Moterey, CA, 86
Community First Health Plans San Antonio, TX, 768
Community Health Options Lewiston, ME, 375
CompBenefits Corporation Roswell, GA, 238
ConnectCare Midland, MI, 420
ConnectiCare Bridgeport, CT, 177
Cox Healthplans Springfield, MO, 479
Crescent Health Solutions Asheville, NC, 599

Deaconess Health Plans Evansville, IN, 303
Devon Health Services Las Vegas, NV, 679
Dimension Health Hialeah, FL, 205

Emi Health Murray, UT, 799
Empire BlueCross BlueShield Brooklyn, NY, 572
Encore Health Network Indianapolis, IN, 304

Fdn. for Medical Care of Kern & Santa Barbara Counties Bakersfield, CA, 96
First Choice Health Portland, OR, 655
First Choice Health Seattle, WA, 838
First Choice of the Midwest Sioux Falls, SD, 738
First Health , MD, 97
Frazier Insurance Agency Little Rock, AR, 55

Galaxy Health Network Arlington, TX, 772
Geisinger Health Plan Danville, PA, 681
Guardian Life Insurance Company of America New York, NY, 576

HAP-Health Alliance Plan: Flint Flint, MI, 425
Harvard Pilgrim Health Care New Hampshire Manchester, NH, 523
Hawaii Medical Assurance Association Honolulu, HI, 251
Hawaii Medical Service Association Honolulu, HI, 252
Health Alliance Champaign, IL, 279
Health Alliance Plan Detroit, MI, 428
Health Care Service Corporation (HCSC) Chicago, IL, 281
Health Choice LLC Memphis, TN, 749
Health Choice of Alabama Birmingham, AL, 6
Health Link PPO Tupelo, MS, 466
Health New England Springfield, MA, 405
Health Partners of Kansas Wichita, KS, 339
Health Plans, Inc. Westborough, MA, 406
HealthAmerica Pennsylvania Harrisburg, PA, 683
Healthchoice Orlando, FL, 211
HealthEZ Bloomington, MN, 452

HealthSmart Irving, TX, 774
Highmark BCBS Delaware Pittsburgh, DE, 184
Highmark BCBS West Virginia Triadelphia, WV, 848
Highmark Blue Cross Blue Shield Pittsburgh, PA, 684
Highmark Blue Shield Pittsburgh, PA, 685
Horizon Blue Cross Blue Shield of New Jersey Newark, NJ, 537
Horizon Health Corporation Lewisville, TX, 775
Horizon NJ Health Pennington, NJ, 538
Humana Health Insurance of Alabama Madison, AL, 7
Humana Health Insurance of Arizona Phoenix, AZ, 35
Humana Health Insurance of Arkansas Rogers, AR, 57
Humana Health Insurance of California Irvine, CA, 107
Humana Health Insurance of Colorado Colorado Springs, CO, 161
Humana Health Insurance of Florida Jacksonville, FL, 214
Humana Health Insurance of Georgia Atlanta, GA, 240
Humana Health Insurance of Hawaii Honolulu, HI, 253
Humana Health Insurance of Idaho Meridian, ID, 260
Humana Health Insurance of Illinois Oak Brook, IL, 282
Humana Health Insurance of Indiana Indianapolis, IN, 306
Humana Health Insurance of Iowa Urbandale, IA, 321
Humana Health Insurance of Kansas Overland Park, KS, 340
Humana Health Insurance of Louisiana Metairie, LA, 365
Humana Health Insurance of Michigan Detroit, MI, 429
Humana Health Insurance of Minnesota Minnetonka, MN, 456
Humana Health Insurance of Mississippi Ridgeland, MS, 467
Humana Health Insurance of Missouri Springfield, MO, 487
Humana Health Insurance of Nevada Las Vegas, NV, 513
Humana Health Insurance of New Hampshire Portsmouth, NH, 524
Humana Health Insurance of New Jersey Uniondale, NJ, 539
Humana Health Insurance of New Mexico Albuquerque, NM, 550
Humana Health Insurance of New York Albany, NY, 578
Humana Health Insurance of North Carolina Charlotte, NC, 603
Humana Health Insurance of Ohio Cincinnati, OH, 623
Humana Health Insurance of Oklahoma Tulsa, OK, 646
Humana Health Insurance of Pennsylvania Mechanicsburg, PA, 686
Humana Health Insurance of Puerto Rico San Juan, PR, 705
Humana Health Insurance of South Carolina Columbia, SC, 729
Humana Health Insurance of Tennessee Memphis, TN, 750
Humana Health Insurance of Texas San Antonio, TX, 776
Humana Health Insurance of Utah Sandy, UT, 800
Humana Health Insurance of Virginia Glen Allen, VA, 822
Humana Health Insurance of Washington Vancouver, WA, 839
Humana Health Insurance of Wisconsin Waukesha, WI, 868

Independence Blue Cross Philadelphia, PA, 687
Independent Health Buffalo, NY, 579
InterGroup Services Pittsburgh, PA, 688

Kaiser Permanente Oakland, CA, 109
Kaiser Permanente Northern California Oakland, CA, 110
Kaiser Permanente Southern Colorado Colorado Springs, CO, 163

Landmark Healthplan of California Westlake Village, CA, 115
LifeWise Mountlake Terrace, WA, 841

MagnaCare New York, NY, 582

Managed HealthCare Northwest Portland, OR, 659
MedCost Winston Salem, NC, 604
MedCost Virginia Richmond, VA, 824
Medical Mutual Services Cleveland, OH, 625
Midlands Choice Omaha, NE, 502
Mutual of Omaha Omaha, NE, 503

Nevada Preferred Healthcare Providers Reno, NV, 515
Noridian Healthcare Services Inc. Fargo, ND, 610
North Alabama Managed Care Inc Huntsville, AL, 8
Northeast Georgia Health Partners Gainesville, GA, 242

Ohio Health Choice Akron, OH, 628
Optima Health Plan Virginia Beach, VA, 825
Oscar Health New York, NY, 588
Oxford Health Plans Trumbull, CT, 179

Pacific Health Alliance Burlingame, CA, 126
PacificSource Health Plans Springfield, OR, 662
Paramount Care of Michigan Monroe, MI, 434
Paramount Health Care Toledo, OH, 631
Parkview Total Health , IN, 310
PCC Preferred Chiropractic Care Wichita, KS, 342
Penn Highlands Healthcare DuBois, PA, 690
Physicians Health Plan of Mid-Michigan Lansing, MI, 435
Preferred Health Care Lancaster, PA, 691
Preferred Healthcare System Duncansville, PA, 692
Preferred Network Access Darien, IL, 287
Preferred Therapy Providers Phoenix, AZ, 43
Premera Blue Cross Blue Shield of Alaska Anchorage, AK, 14
Premier Access Insurance/Access Dental Sacramento, CA, 128, 804
Prevea Health Network Green Bay, WI, 873
Prominence Health Plan Reno, NV, 516
ProviDRs Care Network Wichita, KS, 345
PTPN Calabasas, CA, 130
Public Employees Health Program Salt Lake City, UT, 805
Pueblo Health Care Pueblo, CO, 164

Quality Plan Administrators Washington, DC, 191

Rocky Mountain Health Plans Grand Junction, CO, 165
Rural Carrier Benefit Plan Lexington, KY, 358

Sagamore Health Network Carmel, IN, 313
Sant, Community Physicians Fresno, CA, 133
Script Care, Ltd. Beaumont, TX, 784
Secure Health PPO Newtork Macon, GA, 244
South Central Preferred Health Network York, PA, 693
Stanislaus Foundation for Medical Care Modesto, CA, 136

The Health Plan Wheeling, OH, 850
Trilogy Health Insurance Brookfield, WI, 876
Trustmark Lake Forest, IL, 289
Trustmark Companies Lake Forest, IL, 290

UniCare Illinois Chicago, IL, 291
UniCare Massachusetts Andover, MA, 412

UniCare Texas Plano, TX, 789
UniCare West Virginia Charleston, WV, 851
UnitedHealthcare of Alabama Birmingham, AL, 10
UnitedHealthcare of Alaska Cypress, CA, 15
UnitedHealthcare of Arizona Phoenix, AZ, 49
UnitedHealthcare of Arkansas Little Rock, AR, 60
UnitedHealthcare of Colorado Centennial, CO, 168
UnitedHealthcare of Connecticut Hartford, CT, 182
UnitedHealthcare of Florida Tampa, FL, 228
UnitedHealthcare of Georgia Norcross, GA, 248
UnitedHealthcare of Hawaii Honolulu, HI, 256
UnitedHealthcare of Idaho Boise, ID, 265
UnitedHealthcare of Illinois Chicago, IL, 292
UnitedHealthcare of Indiana Indianapolis, IN, 317
UnitedHealthcare of Iowa West Des Moines, IA, 328
UnitedHealthcare of Kansas Overland Park, KS, 348
UnitedHealthcare of Kentucky Louisville, KY, 360
UnitedHealthcare of Louisiana Metairie, LA, 370
UnitedHealthcare of Maine Waltham, MA, 380
UnitedHealthcare of Maryland Columbia, MD, 395
UnitedHealthcare of Massachusetts Waltham, MA, 414
UnitedHealthcare of Michigan Kalamazoo, MI, 445
UnitedHealthcare of Minnesota Minnetonka, MN, 462
UnitedHealthcare of Mississippi Ridgeland, MS, 471
UnitedHealthcare of Missouri Maryland Heights, MO, 492
UnitedHealthcare of Montana Seattle, WA, 496
UnitedHealthcare of Nebraska Omaha, NE, 507
UnitedHealthcare of Nevada Las Vegas, NV, 519
UnitedHealthcare of New Hampshire Waltham, MA, 527
UnitedHealthcare of New Jersey Iselin, NJ, 544
UnitedHealthcare of New Mexico Albuquerque, NM, 556
UnitedHealthcare of New York New York, NY, 593
UnitedHealthcare of North Carolina Raleigh, NC, 607
UnitedHealthcare of North Dakota Minnetonka, MN, 611
UnitedHealthcare of Northern California Concord, CA, 141
UnitedHealthcare of Ohio Cleveland, OH, 639
UnitedHealthcare of Oklahoma Austin, TX, 649
UnitedHealthcare of Oregon Lake Oswego, OR, 669
UnitedHealthcare of Pennsylvania Pittsburgh, PA, 698
UnitedHealthcare of Puerto Rico Minnetonka, MN, 711

UnitedHealthcare of Rhode Island Warwick, RI, 718
UnitedHealthcare of South Carolina Columbia, SC, 734
UnitedHealthcare of South Dakota Minnetonka, MN, 739
UnitedHealthcare of South Florida Miramar, FL, 229
UnitedHealthcare of Southern California San Diego, CA, 142
UnitedHealthcare of Tennessee Brentwood, TN, 752
UnitedHealthcare of Texas Austin, TX, 792
UnitedHealthcare of the District of Columbia Rockville, MD, 193
UnitedHealthcare of Utah Salt Lake City, UT, 809
UnitedHealthcare of Vermont Waltham, MA, 813
UnitedHealthcare of Virginia Richmond, VA, 829
UnitedHealthcare of Washington Seattle, WA, 845
UnitedHealthcare of West Virginia Richmond, VA, 853
UnitedHealthcare of Wisconsin Wauwatosa, WI, 878
UnitedHealthcare of Wyoming Centennial, CO, 883
University Health Plans Murray, UT, 810
University HealthCare Alliance Newark, CA, 143
UPMC Susquehanna Williamsport, PA, 700
USA Managed Care Organization Austin, TX, 793

Vale-U-Health Belle Vernon, PA, 701
Value Behavioral Health of Pennsylvania Cranberry Township, PA, 703

Zelis Healthcare Bedminster, NJ, 545

Vision

Envolve Vision Rocky Mount, NC, 601
EyeMed Vision Care Mason, OH, 622
EyeQuest Boston, MA, 864

March Vision Care Los Angeles, CA, 118

Opticare of Utah Salt Lake City, UT, 803
Outlook Benefit Solutions Mesa, AZ, 41

Preferred Vision Care Overland Park, KS, 344

Superior Vision Linthicum, MD, 391
SVS Vision Mount Clemens, MI, 438

Versant Health Latham, MD, 396
Vision Plan of America Los Angeles, CA, 145
VSP Vision Care Rancho Cordova, CA, 146

Personnel Index

A

Abelman, David DentaQuest, 402
Abelman, David EyeQuest, 864
Abrahamson, April Colorado Access, 157
Acker, Lori Delta Dental of New Jersey, 536
Ackley, Lilly Magellan Complete Care of Arizona, 36
Adams, Derick, Esq. Health Alliance Plan, 428
Adams, Greg A. Kaiser Permanente, 109
Adams, Joann, RN, CPHQ Florida Health Care Plan, Inc., 207
Adams, Sue Horizon Health Corporation, 775
Adamson, Stephen SummaCare Medicare Advantage Plan, 634
Aga, Dr. Donald KelseyCare Advantage, 777
Agpaoa, Ronda Taylor Benefits Insurance Agency, 137
Agrawal, Vishal, MD Humana Inc., 355
Albert, Stephanie Delta Dental of Minnesota, 451
Albright, Ashley Delta Dental of Oklahoma, 644
Aliabadi, Karen Delta Dental of Washington, 836
All, Matt Blue Cross and Blue Shield of Kansas, 336
Allen, Ashley Health New England, 405
Allen, Beverly Aetna Better Health of Michigan, 415
Allen, Calvin HealthPartners, 453
Allen, Greg Cigna HealthCare of Tennessee, 746
Allen, Michael OSF Healthcare, 286
Allen, Robert W. Intermountain Healthcare, 801
Allford, Allan Delta Dental of Arizona, 31
Allred, Steven Preferred Therapy Providers, 43
Almeida, Jose E. Wellmark Blue Cross & Blue Shield of South Dakota, 740
Almstedt, Karen MHNet Behavioral Health, 779
Altman, Maya Health Plan of San Mateo, 105
Altmann, Lynn Medica, 457
Altmann, Lynn Medica with CHI Health, 500
Altmann, Lynn Medica: Nebraska, 501
Alvarado, Chuck MediGold, 626
Alvarez, Diana Health Choice Arizona, 33
Ambrose, David CenCal Health, 80
Amidei, Christopher Aetna Health of District of Columbia, 188
Andersen, Beth Anthem Blue Cross of California, 67
Andersen, Joel Essence Healthcare, 483
Anderson, David Delta Dental of Minnesota, 451
Anderson, David W. BlueCross BlueShield of Western New York, 561
Anderson, David W. BlueShield of Northeastern New York, 562
Anderson, John, M.D. Concentra, 769
Anderson, Margaret Health Alliance Plan, 428
Anderson, Mark Delta Dental of Arizona, 31
Anthony, Jimmy Delta Dental of Arkansas, 54
Archer, Tim UnitedHealthcare of Connecticut, 182
Archer, Tim UnitedHealthcare of Maine, 380
Archer, Tim UnitedHealthcare of Massachusetts, 414
Archer, Tim UnitedHealthcare of New Hampshire, 527
Archer, Tim UnitedHealthcare of Rhode Island, 718
Archer, Tim UnitedHealthcare of Vermont, 813

Arif, Khuram, MD Western Health Advantage, 148
Arnold, Kim Blue Cross & Blue Shield of Nebraska, 498
Aronson, Andrew, MD CareMore Health Plan, 79
Artau Feliciano, Francisco J. First Medical Health Plan, 704
Ashby, Darren HealthSCOPE Benefits, 56
Asher, Drew WellCare Health Plans, Inc., 230
Asher, Drew Centene Corporation, 477
Atkins, Meera Trustmark, 289
Auburn, Steve Trustmark Companies, 290
Aug, Matt Cox Healthplans, 479
Austen, Karla A. MVP Health Care, 586
Avery, Alan Kern Family Health Care, 112

B

Ba, Lisa Central California Alliance for Health, 81
Baackes, John L.A. Care Health Plan, 113
Bachmann, Anita UnitedHealthcare Community Plan North Carolina, 606
Bachmann, Anita UnitedHealthcare of North Carolina, 607
Bagley, Shannon Centene Corporation, 477
Baird, Mark Medica, 457
Baird, Mark Medica with CHI Health, 500
Baird, Mark Medica: Nebraska, 501
Baker, Johnna Health Partners Plans, 682
Balbone, Kerri Health Net, Inc., 103
Ballard, Jeff Delta Dental of Tennessee, 747
Ballweg, Doug Delta Dental of Wisconsin, 862
Bank, Julie MagnaCare, 582
Barbero, Monice MVP Health Care, 586
Barlow, Jeff, JD Molina Healthcare, 121
Barnard, Mark L. Horizon Blue Cross Blue Shield of New Jersey, 537
Barnes, Keith Cigna HealthCare of Texas, 767
Barnett, Curtis Arkansas Blue Cross Blue Shield, 51
Baron, Stephanie Trinity Health of Iowa, 326
Barone, Jim Delta Dental of Missouri, 480
Barone, Jim Delta Dental of South Carolina, 728
Barrett, Matt MediGold, 626
Barrett, Tim Jai Medical Systems, 387
Barrueta, Anthony A. Kaiser Permanente, 109
Bartgis, Paula Sun Life Financial, 409
Barth, Anthony S. Delta Dental of California, 90
Bartlett, Becca Highmark BCBS Delaware, 184
Bartlett, Tom HealthSCOPE Benefits, 56
Bartsh, Geoff Medica, 457
Bartsh, Geoff Medica with CHI Health, 500
Bartsh, Geoff Medica: Nebraska, 501
Basham, Barbara Celtic Insurance Company, 272
Batra, Romilla SCAN Health Plan, 134
Bauer, Jennifer Delta Dental of Kansas, 338
Bauer, Michele, MD Group Health Cooperative of Eau Claire, 865
Bauer, Stephanie Security Health Plan of Wisconsin, 875
Baumann, Melissa Careington Solutions, 765

Personnel Index

Bay, Marybeth Quartz Health Plan, 874
Bea, Javon R. MercyHealth System, 870
Beams, James HealthNetwork, 212
Beasley, Tim HealthSCOPE Benefits, 56
Beck, Justin NIA Magellan, 40
Beckett, Darrell Blue Cross & Blue Shield of Texas, 762
Bellah, Ann Pueblo Health Care, 164
Benardette, Dan UnitedHealthcare Community Plan New York, 592
Benavides, Vanessa M. Kaiser Permanente, 109
Bennett, John D., MD CDPHP: Capital District Physicians' Health Plan, 565
Bensing, Gary Passport Health Plan, 357
Bentrup, Barbara C. Delta Dental of Missouri, 480
Bentrup, Barbara C. Delta Dental of South Carolina, 728
Berardo, Joseph, Jr MagnaCare, 582
Berg, Brad Delta Dental of Washington, 836
Berg, Chuck Cigna Corporation, 174
Berge, Frank Dencap Dental Plans, 422
Berge, Leanne, Esq. Community Health Plan of Washington, 834
Berger, Matt Humana Health Insurance of Mississippi, 467
Bergman, Jeff Blue Cross and Blue Shield of Kansas, 336
Bermel, John J. Healthfirst, 577
Bernadette, Dan UnitedHealthcare of New York, 593
Bernard, Ken Health New England, 405
Bernard, Milton, DDS Quality Plan Administrators, 191
Bernards, Vicki Wisconsin Physician's Service, 879
Bezney, Michael Mercy Health Network, 324
Billings, Bill eHealthInsurance Services, Inc., 95
Billittier, Anthony J., MD Independent Health, 579
Billittier, Anthony J., M.D. Independent Health Medicare Plan, 580
Bilt, Steven C. Bright Now! Dental, 74
Bindman, Andrew, MD Kaiser Permanente, 109
Bishop, Skip San Francisco Health Plan, 131
Bisson, Michelle SummaCare Medicare Advantage Plan, 634
Bittner, Sarah HealthSmart, 774
Bjork, Sonja Partnership HealthPlan of California, 127
Black, Steve Healthfirst, 577
Black, Steve H. Oxford Health Plans, 179
Blackledge, James Mutual of Omaha Dental Insurance, 504
Blackledge, James T. Mutual of Omaha, 503
Blackley, Seth Evolent Health, 821
Blanton, Chris LifeMap, 658
Blanton, Chris BridgeSpan Health, 798
Blazek, John V. On Lok Lifeways, 123
Bloom, Charles, DO Health Alliance Plan, 428
Bloom, Mark, MD Molina Healthcare of Florida, 218
Bloomfield, Deborah Mercy Health Network, 324
Blowey, Doug, MD Children's Mercy Pediatric Care Network, 478
Bodell, Brad Trustmark Companies, 290
Bodwell, Erica, Esq. Northeast Delta Dental Maine, 378
Bogdan, Joe Magellan Complete Care of Arizona, 36
Bogle, Michael USA Managed Care Organization, 793
Bolander, Curtis Mid-Atlantic Behavioral Health, 185
Bolander, Traci, Psy. D Mid-Atlantic Behavioral Health, 185
Bolz, Terry Quartz Health Plan, 874

Bonaparte, Philip M, MD Horizon NJ Health, 538
Booth, Christopher C. Univera Healthcare, 594
Borchert, Kevin Network Health Plan of Wisconsin, 872
Borland, Rob Denver Health Medical Plan, 159
Born, Rick Aetna Better Health of Louisiana, 361
Boroch, Blair UnitedHealthcare Community Plan Pennsylvania, 697
Bostian, Jim Aetna Health of North Carolina, 595
Bottrill, Lorry Mercy Care Plan/Mercy Care Advantage, 39
Boucher, Francis Northeast Delta Dental Maine, 378
Boucher, Francis R. Northeast Delta Dental, 526
Boudreaux, Gail K. Anthem, Inc., 299
Bowers, Devon Jai Medical Systems, 387
Bowers, Scott A. Passport Health Plan, 357
Bowman, Lynn Medical Center Healthnet Plan, 407
Boyd, Branda Care Plus Dental Plans, 859
Boyle, Kathy Denver Health Medical Plan, 159
Boyman, Jim Aetna Health of Wisconsin, 854
Boysen, Doug Samaritan Health Plan Operations, 666
Brach, Karen Meridian Health Plan of Illinois, 284
Bradshaw, Lyndsay Delta Dental of Illinois, 276
Brand, Joe Health Partners Plans, 682
Bray, Greg MedCost, 604
Breard, Mike Vantage Health Plan, 371
Breard, Mike Vantage Medicare Advantage, 372
Breidbart, Scott, MD Affinity Health Plan, 560
Brennan, Joseph MagnaCare, 582
Breskin, William A. BlueCross BlueShield Association, 271
Brewster, William, MD Harvard Pilgrim Health Care New Hampshire, 523
Brice, Kaitlin Prevea Health Network, 873
Bridges, Ja'ron Gateway Health, 680
Briesacher, Mark Intermountain Healthcare, 801
Britton, Clay Blue Cross and Blue Shield of Kansas, 336
Brizendine, Verne Aetna Better Health of California, 61
Brooks, Dee Dee Dominion Dental Services, 819
Brooks, Kermitt Guardian Life Insurance Company of America, 576
Brooks, Lyn Delta Dental of Virginia, 818
Broomfield, Rob UnitedHealthcare of Iowa, 328
Broomfield, Rob UnitedHealthcare of Kansas, 348
Broomfield, Rob UnitedHealthcare of Nebraska, 507
Broussard, Bruce D. CompBenefits Corporation, 238
Broussard, Bruce D. Humana Inc., 355
Broussard, Bruce Dale CarePlus Health Plans, 202
Brown, Bruce Inter Valley Health Plan, 108
Brown, David Wellmark Blue Cross Blue Shield, 329
Brown, David Humana Health Insurance of Kansas, 340
Brown, Jeffrey L. Martin's Point HealthCare, 377
Brown, Jim Script Care, Ltd., 784
Brown, Nathan Humana Health Insurance of Utah, 800
Brua, Kyle Quartz Health Plan, 874
Bruce, Jamie UnitedHealthcare Community Plan Missouri, 491
Brumbaugh, Brian Preferred Healthcare System, 692
Brumbeloe, Debbie North Alabama Managed Care Inc, 8
Bryan, Ken (Buck) The Health Plan, 850
Bryan, Tab Script Care, Ltd., 784

Bryd, Michael Sharp Health Plan, 135
Bryt, Bartley, MD MagnaCare, 582
Buck, Eric E. Preferred Health Care, 691
Buggle, Janet QualCare, 541
Bunch, Robert Anthem Blue Cross & Blue Shield of Georgia, 236
Bunker, Jonathan W Health Plan of Nevada, 511
Buran, Gregory, MD Network Health Plan of Wisconsin, 872
Burdick, Kenneth A. WellCare Health Plans, Inc., 230
Burgin, Meryl CareFirst BlueCross BlueShield, 385
Burke, Richard P. Fallon Health, 403
Burman, Bill Denver Health Medical Plan, 159
Burnett, Brian Presbyterian Medicare Advantage Plans, 553
Burnett, Peg Denver Health Medical Plan, 159
Burthay, Darcy Ascension At Home, 760
Bush, Bob CommunityCare, 643
Butcher, Jeff CommunityCare, 643
Butler, Bruce Samaritan Health Plan Operations, 666
Butler, Martha Essence Healthcare, 483
Butts, Susan Cox Healthplans, 479
Buyse, Marylou, MD Neighborhood Health Plan of Rhode Island, 715
Byndas, Cynthia United Concordia of Florida, 226

C

Cabrera, Jr., Jose L., MBA Humana Health Insurance of Hawaii, 253
Cain, Steve UnitedHealthcare of Northern California, 141
Caldwell, Joe, RN Alliant Health Plans, 232
Camerlinck, Bryan Blue Cross and Blue Shield of Louisiana, 363
Campanella, Gary On Lok Lifeways, 123
Campbell, Craig Wisconsin Physician's Service, 879
Cannon, Tina Behavioral Health Systems, 3
Cantor, Dr. Michael CareCentrix, 173
Capezza, Joseph C. Allways Health Partners, 398
Carpenter, Irene AlohaCare Advantage Plus, 250
Carson, Michael Harvard Pilgrim Health Care Massachusetts, 404
Carter, Benjamin R. Trinity Health of Alabama, 9
Carter, Benjamin R. Trinity Health of California, 138
Carter, Benjamin R. Trinity Health of Delaware, 186
Carter, Benjamin R. Trinity Health of Georgia, 245
Carter, Benjamin R. Trinity Health, 440
Carter, Lori Piedmont Community Health Plan, 826
Caruncho, Joseph Preferred Care Partners, 222
Caruncho-Simpson, Genevieve D. UnitedHealthcare Community Plan Washington, 844
Carvelli, John Liberty Dental Plan of New York, 581
Casado, Nathalie Delta Dental of New Mexico, 548
Casalou, Rob Trinity Health of Michigan, 441
Cass, Brady Asuris Northwest Health, 833
Cass, Megan Superior HealthPlan, 787
Cassell, David SVS Vision, 438
Castillo, Abie Community Health Plan of Washington, 834
Castillo, Landy Jai Medical Systems, 387
Castleberry, Caleb Delta Dental of Arkansas, 54
Castro, Michael Delta Dental of California, 90
Castro, Michael Delta Dental of Delaware, 183

Castro, Michael Delta Dental of Pennsylvania, 678
Castro, Micheal Delta Dental of the District of Columbia, 190
Castro, Mike Delta Dental of New York, 567
Castro, Mike Delta Dental of West Virginia, 847
Castronova, Paul Primary Health Medical Group, 262
Cataldo, Ron ChiroSource, Inc. / Chiropractic Health Plan of California, 84
Caton, Kirt, MD Select Health of South Carolina, 732
Cattrell, Anita, PhD Evolent Health, 821
Cavalier, Kevin SummaCare Medicare Advantage Plan, 634
Ceballos, Michael Trinity Health of Ohio, 637
Celestin, Angela CareFirst BlueCross BlueShield, 385
Cerd, Rodrigo Independence Blue Cross, 687
Cerf, Kristen Blue Shield of California Promise Cal MediConnect Plans, 70
Cerf, Kristen Blue Shield of California Promise Health Plan, 71
Cerise, Frederick P., M.D. Parkland Community Health Plan, 782
Chaffin, Jeffrey Delta Dental of Iowa, 319
Chaguturu, Sree, MD Aetna Inc., 170
Chambers, Jennifer, MD, MBA Capital BlueCross, 677
Chan Russell, Joyce Priority Health, 436
Chandler, Ryan Alliance Regional Health Network, 754
Chandramouli, Varsha, MD Molina Healthcare of Illinois, 285
Changamire, Tich, MD CareFirst BlueCross BlueShield, 385
Chansler, Jeffrey D. EmblemHealth, 570
Chansler, Jeffrey D. EmblemHealth Enhanced Care Plus (HARP), 571
Chansler, Jeffrey D. GHI Medicare Plan, 575
Charlier, Brian Prevea Health Network, 873
Charlton, Annette Fdn. for Medical Care of Kern & Santa Barbara Counties, 96
Chartrand, David L. CareCentrix: Arizona, 28
Chassay, Mark Blue Cross & Blue Shield of Texas, 762
Cheang, Tiffany Alameda Alliance for Health, 62
Cheang, Tiffany Alameda Medi-Cal Plan, 64
Checketts, Lannie Trinity Health of Idaho, 264
Chen, Alex Y. Health Net, Inc., 103
Chen, Bill Inter Valley Health Plan, 108
Chen, Kimberly, MD Molina Healthcare of Ohio, 627
Chernack, Carol Horizon NJ Health, 538
Chicoine, Angela Able Insurance Agency, 520
Chipponeri, Joanne Stanislaus Foundation for Medical Care, 136
Chiricosta, Rick Medical Mutual, 624
Christ, Cara, MD, MS Blue Cross & Blue Shield of Arizona, 26
Christian, Greg Kaiser Permanente Hawaii, 254
Christian, James R. AmeriHealth Caritas District of Columbia, 189
Christianson, Phil HealthSmart, 774
Christophersen, Kim Delta Dental of Wisconsin, 862
Chukwumerije, Nkem, MD Kaiser Permanente Georgia, 241
Chytil, Kamila DentaQuest, 402
Chytil, Kamila EyeQuest, 864
Cianfrocco, Heather OptumRx, 124
Ciano, Christopher Aetna Medicare, 350
Ciarrocchi, Michael Meritain Health, 583
Cistulli, PJ Able Insurance Agency, 520
Clabeaux, Patricia Independent Health, 579
Clabeaux, Patricia Independent Health Medicare Plan, 580
Clancy, Kevin Health Partners Plans, 682

Clark, Bob Children's Mercy Pediatric Care Network, 478
Clark, Jim LifeMap, 658
Clark, Karen Horizon NJ Health, 538
Clark, Sherree North Alabama Managed Care Inc, 8
Clark, Terry M. UnitedHealth Group, 461
Clarke, Sandra Blue Shield of California, 69
Clemence, Cynthia A. Trinity Health, 440
Clendenin, John T. Wellmark Blue Cross Blue Shield, 329
Clothier, Brad Delta Dental of Arizona, 31
Clure, Greg Landmark Healthplan of California, 115
Coffey, Chris Molina Healthcare of Texas, 780
Coffey, Pamela HealthSmart, 774
Coffin, Scott E. Alameda Alliance for Health, 62
Coffin, Scott E. Alameda Medi-Cal Plan, 64
Cole, Ami Molina Healthcare of Ohio, 627
Cole, Michael Aetna Health of Maine, 373
Cole, Michael Aetna Health of Massachusetts, 397
Cole, Michael Aetna Health of New York, 559
Cole, Michael Aetna Health of Rhode Island, 712
Coleman, Kathy Able Insurance Agency, 520
Collins, Jeff Kaiser Permanente Northwest, 657
Collins, Jim Medical Center Healthnet Plan, 407
Collins, Matt, M.D. Blue Cross & Blue Shield of Rhode Island, 713
Collins, Sandy InStil Health, 730
Combes, Matthew Children's Mercy Pediatric Care Network, 478
Comer, Diane Kaiser Permanente, 109
Conley, Jacquelyn, MD HealthEZ, 452
Conley, Steve Harvard Pilgrim Health Care Maine, 376
Conlin, Paul C. Oxford Health Plans, 179
Connelly, Steven, MD HealthPartners, 453
Constantine, Tim United Concordia of Arizona, 47
Constantine, Timothy J. United Concordia Dental, 695
Cook, Jill Amerigroup Iowa, 318
Cook, Stephanie Dean Health Plan, 861
Cooner, Danny Behavioral Health Systems, 3
Cooper, Chrissie Magellan Complete Care of Florida, 217
Cooper, Patrice UnitedHealthcare Community Plan Rhode Island, 717
Cooper, Rob, MD Ohio State University Health Plan Inc., 629
Cooper, Scott Mercy Clinic Arkansas, 58
Coots, Norvell V. Trinity Health of Maryland, 392
Copley, Jonathan Aetna Better Health of Kentucky, 349
Cordani, David M. Cigna Corporation, 174
Cordani, David M. Cigna-HealthSpring, 176
Costonis, Michael CNA, 274
Cotton, Michael Providence Health Plan, 663
Cournand, Henri Blue Cross Blue Shield of Kansas City, 476
Courtney, Susan Blue Cross & Blue Shield of Nebraska, 498
Cox, Karen ProviDRs Care Network, 345
Coxq, Donnell Amerigroup Washington, 832
Crawford, Nancy Mutual of Omaha Dental Insurance, 504
Crespo, Eileen, MD Delta Dental of Minnesota, 451
Criswell, Kevin Amerigroup Maryland, 383
Cromer, Jessica MDwise, 308
Crook, Christopher Priority Health, 436

Cropp, Michael W, M.D. Independent Health Medicare Plan, 580
Cropp, Michael W., MD Independent Health, 579
Croushore, Susan Trinity Health of Pennsylvania, 694
Crowley, Daniel Western Dental & Orthodontics, 147
Cuda, John MetroPlus Health Plan, 584
Culley-Trotman, Francoise, . AlohaCare, 249
Culley-Trotman, Francoise AlohaCare Advantage Plus, 250
Cummings, Scott Care1st Health Plan Arizona, 27
Cunningham, Joseph R., MD Blue Cross & Blue Shield of Oklahoma, 642
Curcio, Trina L. Vale-U-Health, 701
Currier, Cecile Concern, 88
Cushing, Giselle Cigna HealthCare of Florida, 203
Cusick, Lauren Blue Cross & Blue Shield of Oklahoma, 642
Custer, Timothy Dental Network of America, 277
Cusumano, Jim MagnaCare, 582
Czyz, AnneMarie W., RN Trinity Health of New York, 590

D

Dale, Karen M. AmeriHealth Caritas District of Columbia, 189
Dalessio, James Horizon NJ Health, 538
Dallafior, Kenneth R. Blue Cross Blue Shield of Michigan, 419
Damawand, Joann HealthEZ, 452
Dammann, John Humana Health Insurance of Alabama, 7
Dammann, John Humana Health Insurance of Georgia, 240
Daney, Natalie Delta Dental of Kansas, 338
Daniels, Gary UnitedHealthcare of Hawaii, 256
Daniels, Gary UnitedHealthcare of Montana, 496
Daniels, Gary UnitedHealthcare of Oregon, 669
Daniels, Gary UnitedHealthcare of Washington, 845
Danko, Marcel American Specialty Health, 297
Dankoff, Shelli OSF Healthcare, 286
Darnley, Cain A. Hayes Gateway Health, 680
Datko, Rita Sharp Health Plan, 135
Davenport, Michael Trinity Health of Illinois, 288
Davidson, Peter PacificSource Health Plans, 661
Davis, Charles Trinity Health of Idaho, 264
Davis, Jeff Brand New Day, 73
Davis, Justin PA Health & Wellness, 689
Davis, Kim Davis Vision, 566
Davis, Kimberly Versant Health, 396
Davis, Lisa Blue Shield of California, 69
Davis, Mike Dominion Dental Services, 819
Davis, Victor Arkansas Blue Cross Blue Shield, 51
De La Cruz, Roberto, M.D. Parkland Community Health Plan, 782
Deal, James A. Ascension At Home, 2, 300, 335, 416, 641, 858
Deavens, Gregory E. Independence Blue Cross, 687
DeGoede, Melissa Security Health Plan of Wisconsin, 875
DeGruttola, John E. Optima Health Plan, 825
Del Vecchio, Christopher MVP Health Care, 586
Del Vecchio, Dean A. Guardian Life Insurance Company of America, 576
Della Villa, Michael MVP Health Care, 586
deLorimier, John Concentra, 769
Demand, Mike, PhD MediGold, 626
Dembereckyj, William Western Dental & Orthodontics, 147

Dennis, Patricia ChiroCare of Wisconsin, 860
Derauf, David AlohaCare Advantage Plus, 250
Derks, Keith UnitedHealthcare Community Plan Oklahoma, 648
Deshazer, Charles Highmark BCBS West Virginia, 848
Devivar, Theresa KelseyCare Advantage, 777
DeVries III, George T. American Specialty Health, 297
Dhanvanthari, Lakshmi Health Plan of San Joaquin, 104
Di Maio, Paul Delta Dental of New Jersey, 536
Diamond, Susan M. Humana Inc., 355
Diaz, Norma Community Health Group, 87
Dicus-Johnson, Coreen Network Health Plan of Wisconsin, 872
Diehs, Creta Dimension Health, 205
Dietz, Kyle Pivot Health, 42
Dillard, Gray Arkansas Blue Cross Blue Shield, 51
Dillard, James, MD Oxford Health Plans, 179
Dimerson, Dalia Superior HealthPlan, 787
Dimondstein, Mark American Postal Workers Union (APWU) Health Plan, 382
DiPerna Cook, Katie Evolent Health, 821
Disser, Paul J. Preferred Vision Care, 344
Docherty, David Dean Health Plan, 861
Docimo, Anne, MD AHCCCS/Medicaid, 18
Dodd, Elizabeth TriWest Healthcare Alliance, 46
Dodd, Tim United Concordia of Maryland, 393
Dodek, Anton B., MD Allways Health Partners, 398
Dolloff, Gaylee Health Partners of Kansas, 339
Donaca, Greg Delta Dental of Idaho, 259
Donigian, David, MD Molina Healthcare of Michigan, 433
Donohoe, Cindy Highmark Blue Cross Blue Shield, 684
Doolen, Erick PacificSource Health Plans, 661
Dopps, Brad PCC Preferred Chiropractic Care, 342
Doran, John Blue Cross & Blue Shield of Montana, 493
Doran, Laurie Health Alliance Plan, 428
Dorocak, Cathy Delta Dental of Ohio, 621
Dougherty, Bryce Delta Dental of Kansas, 338
Doumba, Laurend Delta Dental of Illinois, 276
Dow, Chuck Humana Health Insurance of Illinois, 282
Dow, Chuck Humana Health Insurance of Iowa, 321
Dow, Chuck Humana Health Insurance of Minnesota, 456
Dowd, Amy CareOregon Health Plan, 653
Dowdie, Andre Humana Health Insurance of New York, 578
Dowell, Stephanie Amerigroup Tennessee, 743
Dowling, Angela Regence BlueCross BlueShield of Oregon, 664
Downing, Rebecca Western Health Advantage, 148
Downs, Barbara A. CDPHP: Capital District Physicians' Health Plan, 565
Drake, Archie Valley Baptist Health Plan, 795
Drawdy, Donyale United Concordia of Georgia, 246
Drew, Julie InStil Health, 730
Drexler, Helen Delta Dental of Colorado, 158
Dreyfus, Andrew Blue Cross & Blue Shield of Massachusetts, 401
Driggers, Jeremy Humana Health Insurance of Oklahoma, 646
Driscoll, John CareCentrix, 173
Drummond, Courntey Parkview Total Health, 310
Duffield, Ellen Gateway Health, 680
Dufurrena, Quinn, DDS, JD United Concordia of Arizona, 47

Dunaway, Suzie Children's Mercy Pediatric Care Network, 478
Duncan, Pat Rocky Mountain Health Plans, 165
Dunlop, Jr., James A. Independent Health, 579
Dunlop, Jr., James A. Independent Health Medicare Plan, 580
Durant, Jessica AllCare Health, 651
Duronio, Carolyn Highmark Blue Cross Blue Shield, 684
Dvorak, Rebecca, RN Horizon Health Corporation, 775
Dziabis, Steve Peach State Health Plan, 243

E

Eadie, Reginald J., MD, MBA Trinity Health of New England, 180
Eagan, Thomas AllCare Health, 651
Early, Karen Mountain Health Co-Op, 495
Easley, Ezra M. Health Net Federal Services (HNFS), 101
Easton, Tim Nebraska Total Care, 505
Ebenkamp, Bob Delta Dental of Kansas, 338
Eckrich, Nancy Trustmark, 289
Eckstein, Michael Health Tradition, 867
Eddy, Paul Wellmark Blue Cross Blue Shield, 329
Edelman, Ann Colorado Access, 157
Edelson, Brett UnitedHealthcare of Minnesota, 462
Edelson, Brett UnitedHealthcare of North Dakota, 611
Edelson, Brett UnitedHealthcare of South Dakota, 739
Edge, Angelo D. Aetna Better Health of Maryland, 381
Edwards, Brett HealthSCOPE Benefits, 56
Edwards, Joe K. HealthSCOPE Benefits, 56
Edwards, Wendy Atrio Health Plans, 652
Eftekhari, Amir Araz Group, 399
Eftekhari, Amir Americas PPO, 448
Eftekhari, Amir HealthEZ, 452
Eftekhari, Nazie Araz Group, 399
Eftekhari, Nazie Americas PPO, 448
Eftekhari, Nazie HealthEZ, 452
Ehrgood, Trent Health Plan of San Mateo, 105
Eichhorn, Kevin, M.D. Dean Health Plan, 861
Eichten, Mike Advance Insurance Company of Kansas, 330
Eig, Blair M. Trinity Health of Maryland, 392
El-Tawil, Mark Blue Cross & Blue Shield of Arizona, 26
Elam, Linda Amerigroup District of Columbia, 530
Ellis, Andrew Anthem Blue Cross & Blue Shield of Maine, 374
Ellis, Michael Delta Dental of Kansas, 338
Elman, Shawn Passport Health Plan, 357
Enight, Sherri Blue Cross and Blue Shield of Louisiana, 363
Enslinger, Lisa American Health Care Alliance, 474
Epling, Bill SummaCare Medicare Advantage Plan, 634
Eppel, Jim HealthPartners, 453
Epstein, David Aetna Health of Georgia, 231
Erickson, Dana Blue Cross & Blue Shield of Minnesota, 450
ErkenBrack, Steven Rocky Mountain Health Plans, 165
Ertel, Albert Secure Health PPO Newtork, 244
Espeland, Kelly Amerigroup Iowa, 318
Ethridge, Sandy Alliance Regional Health Network, 754
Evanko, Brian Cigna Corporation, 174
Evelyn, Bonnie Cigna HealthCare of Georgia, 237

Personnel Index

F

Everett, Torriaun MDwise, 308
Evert, Nancy HealthPartners, 453
Ewanchyna, Kevin, MD Samaritan Health Plan Operations, 666

Faigin, Tracy Friday Health Plans, 160
Fandrich, William M. Blue Care Network of Michigan, 417, 418
Farnitano, Chris Contra Costa Health Services, 89
Farrell, Jr., Robert G., O.D. SVS Vision, 438
Farrow, Peter Group Health Cooperative of Eau Claire, 865
Fasola, Barbara Careington Solutions, 765
Fathi, Jay, MD Molina Healthcare of Washington, 842
Feagin, Cardwell VIVA Health, 11
Feeney, John Renaissance Dental, 312
Fehlner, Alan SummaCare Medicare Advantage Plan, 634
Feind, Julie Lakeside Community Healthcare Network, 114
Feldman, A. Joel, MD Managed Health Services, 307
Feliciano, Kristin Trinity Health of Maryland, 392
Felix, John Henry Hawaii Medical Assurance Association, 251
Fennell, Charles J. Trinity Health of New York, 590
Fernandez, Luis Leon Medical Centers Health Plan, 215
Fess, Ed, MD Care1st Health Plan Arizona, 27
Figenshu, Bill Western Health Advantage, 148
Finerty, Kathryn Network Health Plan of Wisconsin, 872
Finerty, Jr., John Managed Health Services Wisconsin, 869
Finke, Dan Aetna Inc., 170
Finuf, Bob Children's Mercy Pediatric Care Network, 478
Fish, Kathleen MVP Health Care, 586
Fishbein, Dan, MD Sun Life Financial, 409
Fisher, Christina Y. BlueCross BlueShield Association, 271
Fitzgerald, Kevin R, MD Rocky Mountain Health Plans, 165
Flanagan, Nicki Blue Cross and Blue Shield of Kansas, 336
Flanagan, Shannon Behavioral Health Systems, 3
Flanders, Scott N. eHealthInsurance Services, Inc., 95
Fletcher, Nathan AmeriHealth Caritas District of Columbia, 189
Flood, David L. Intermountain Healthcare, 801
Flott, Daniel Liberty Dental Plan of Missouri, 488
Flynn, Jordan Evolent Health, 821
Flynn, Susan Vale-U-Health, 701
Foco, Nathan Priority Health, 436
Follmer, Cynthia Aetna Health of Alabama, 1
Follmer, Cynthia Aetna Health of Georgia, 231
Foltz, Kimberly S. Aetna Better Health of Illinois, 266
Fong, John K., MD, MBA Blue Cross and Blue Shield of Kansas, 336
Fontaine, Steven M. Penn Highlands Healthcare, 690
Ford, Lawrence Avesis: Massachusetts, 400
Forshee, James, MD Priority Health, 436
Forsyth, John D. Wellmark Blue Cross & Blue Shield of South Dakota, 740
Fortner, Scott Central California Alliance for Health, 81
Foss, Tania Delta Dental of Oklahoma, 644
Fox, Annette Group Health Cooperative of South Central Wisconsin, 866
Fraiz, Juan MediGold, 626
Francis, Dave eHealthInsurance Services, Inc., 95
Frank, Mike HCSC Insurance Services Company, 278
Frank, Mike Health Care Service Corporation (HCSC), 281
Franke, Dana Atrio Health Plans, 652
Frazier, Toni Frazier Insurance Agency, 55
Frazier, William Richard Frazier Insurance Agency, 55
Frey, Robert Jai Medical Systems, 387
Friar, Wendy Trinity Health of Maryland, 392
Frucella, Maureen Preferred Healthcare System, 692
Fuentes, Peter Liberty Dental Plan of New Jersey, 540
Fuentes, Peter Liberty Dental Plan of New York, 581

G

Gaffney, Tom CareCentrix, 173
Galatas, Bridget Molina Healthcare of Mississippi, 469
Gallina, John E. Anthem, Inc., 299
Galt, Frederick B. CDPHP: Capital District Physicians' Health Plan, 565
Galvin, Eric ConnectiCare, 177
Gamez, Jesse Humana Health Insurance of Idaho, 260
Gamez, Jesse Humana Health Insurance of Utah, 800
Gamez, Jesse Humana Health Insurance of Washington, 839
Garcia-Velazquez, Zivany Molina Healthcare of Puerto Rico, 709
Garen, Kirsten Delta Dental of California, 90
Garikes Schneider, Carol L. Trinity Health of Illinois, 288
Garrigues, Brad Providence Health Plan, 663
Garrison, Kerri BlueCross BlueShield of Western New York, 561
Garrison, Kerri BlueShield of Northeastern New York, 562
Garza, Greg CareMore Health Plan, 79
Gates, Nick Priority Health, 436
Gauger, Tim Arkansas Blue Cross Blue Shield, 51
Gaw, Kris Denver Health Medical Plan, 159
Geary, Emmet Peoples Health, 367
Gebhart, Jim Mercy Clinic Oklahoma, 647
Geesaman, Brian AmeriHealth Caritas District of Columbia, 189
Gennaro, Thomas Peoples Health, 367
Genord, Michael Health Alliance Medicare, 427
Genord, Michael, MD Health Alliance Plan, 428
Gentile, Salvatore Friday Health Plans, 160
George, Don Blue Cross & Blue Shield of Vermont, 811
Geraghty, Patrick Florida Blue, 206
Gerbus, Dave, JD Delta Dental of Colorado, 158
Geyer, Robert Medica, 457
Ghaly, Christina R., MD Health Services Los Angeles County, 106
Ghaly, Khaled Optima Health Plan, 825
Giancursio, Donald UnitedHealthcare of Idaho, 265
Giancursio, Donald UnitedHealthcare of Nevada, 519
Giancursio, Donald UnitedHealthcare of Utah, 809
Gianquinto, Lou Anthem Blue Cross & Blue Shield of Connecticut, 172
Gianturco, Laurie, MD Health New England, 405
Giasi, Steve Affinity Health Plan, 560
Gibboney, Liz Partnership HealthPlan of California, 127
Giblin, John Blue Cross & Blue Shield of Tennessee, 745
Giese, Alexis, MD Colorado Access, 157
Giesler, Scott eHealthInsurance Services, Inc., 95
Gilbert, Roy Delta Dental of Delaware, 183
Gilbert, Roy Delta Dental of the District of Columbia, 190

Gilbert, Roy Delta Dental of New York, 567
Gilbert, Roy Delta Dental of Pennsylvania, 678
Gilbert, Roy Delta Dental of West Virginia, 847
Gilfillan, Richard J. Trinity Health of Idaho, 264
Gille, Larry Prevea Health Network, 873
Gilleland, Janna HealthNetwork, 212
Gilligan, Alison CareCentrix, 173
Gilligan, Patrick Blue Cross & Blue Shield of Massachusetts, 401
Gilliland, Robert Florida Health Care Plan, Inc., 207
Gillis, Anne Trinity Health of Maryland, 392
Giraldo, Gus Magellan Complete Care of Florida, 217
Gladden, John Delta Dental of Oklahoma, 644
Glauber, Jim, M.D. San Francisco Health Plan, 131
Gluckman, Robert Providence Health Plan, 663
Godfrey, Tracy, MD Mercy Clinic Kansas, 341
Godley, Patrick Contra Costa Health Services, 89
Goheen, Charles Harvard Pilgrim Health Care Massachusetts, 404
Golden, Scott Anthem Blue Cross & Blue Shield of Virginia, 816
Goldstein, Craig CHN PPO, 534
Golovan, Kathy Medical Mutual, 624
Goltz, David CareSource Ohio, 620
Gonick, Denise, Esq. MVP Health Care, 586
Gonzalez, Orlando MMM Holdings, 708
Goode, Josh SCAN Health Plan, 134
Gootee, Robert Moda Health Alaska, 13
Gootee, Robert Moda Health Oregon, 660
Gordon, Luke EPIC Pharmacy Network, 820
Gordon-Simet, Josette, MD Blue Cross & Blue Shield of Nebraska, 498
Gore, Diane Blue Cross & Blue Shield of Wyoming, 881
Goren, E.B. Rob Delta Dental of Missouri, 480
Goren, E.B. Rob Delta Dental of South Carolina, 728
Gorman, Linda Central California Alliance for Health, 81
Gormley, Kate San Francisco Health Plan, 131
Goss, Phil Trustmark Companies, 290
Gough, Frances, MD Molina Healthcare of Washington, 842
Gowda, Chandrakala, MD Molina Healthcare of Utah, 802
Grams, David Ascension At Home, 2, 300, 335, 416, 641, 858
Granados, Lizeth Health Plan of San Joaquin, 104
Grandfield, Steven H. Blue Cross & Blue Shield of Nebraska, 498
Grant, James D., MD Blue Care Network of Michigan, 417, 418
Grant, James D., MD Blue Cross Blue Shield of Michigan, 419
Graves, Holly Blue Cross and Blue Shield of Kansas, 336
Graves, Scott BlueChoice Health Plan of South Carolina, 726
Grazko, Jim Premera Blue Cross Blue Shield of Alaska, 14
Green, Chris Delta Dental of Kentucky, 354
Green, Dolores L. California Foundation for Medical Care, 76
Greene, Ruth Blue Cross & Blue Shield of Vermont, 811
Gregoire, Daniel N. Magellan Health, 37
Gregoire, Daniel N. Oxford Health Plans, 179
Greig, Jerome (Jerry) Blue Cross and Blue Shield of Louisiana, 363
Greiner, Walt Atlanticare Health Plans, 533
Grgurina, John F, Jr San Francisco Health Plan, 131
Griffin, Mary Avesis: Maryland, 384
Griffith, James TriWest Healthcare Alliance, 46

Grober, Stephania HCSC Insurance Services Company Oklahoma, 645
Groff, Jon MHNet Behavioral Health, 779
Grose, Gregory, MD Prevea Health Network, 873
Grover, Michael Envolve Vision, 601
Guardiola, Benjamin MMM Holdings, 708
Guenther, Bret Dentistat, 94
Guertin, Lisa Anthem Blue Cross & Blue Shield of New Hampshire, 522
Guertin, Shawn Aetna Inc., 170
Gumina, Frank Wisconsin Physician's Service, 879
Gurdian, Guillermo Leon Medical Centers Health Plan, 215
Gusho, Michael Trinity Health of Michigan, 441
Gutowski, Sally Delta Dental of Nebraska, 499
Guyette, Michael J. VSP Vision Care, 146
Guzman, Patricia J. Delta Dental of Wyoming, 882

H

Haaland, Doug Humana Health Insurance of Tennessee, 750
Habig II, Joseph A., MD Valley Preferred, 702
Hagan, Lynn American HealthCare Group, 675
Hagan, Robert E., Jr. American HealthCare Group, 675
Hagan Kanche, Liz American HealthCare Group, 675
Haines, Rick Aultcare Corporation, 617
Haines, Rick Prime Time Health Medicare Plan, 632
Hakim, Anat WellCare Health Plans, Inc., 230
Hall, Kerry P. Delta Dental of Wyoming, 882
Halloran, Thomas Fidelis Care, 574
Hamburg, Glenn Western Health Advantage, 148
Hamerlik, Mike Wisconsin Physician's Service, 879
Hamilton, Catherine, PhD Blue Cross & Blue Shield of Vermont, 811
Hamilton, Kelly Ohio State University Health Plan Inc., 629
Hance, Anne Blue Cross & Blue Shield of Tennessee, 745
Hancock, Scott Care N' Care, 764
Hankins, Deborah Fdn. for Medical Care of Kern & Santa Barbara Counties, 96
Hankinson, Michael Delta Dental of California, 90
Hankinson, Michael Delta Dental of Delaware, 183
Hankinson, Michael Delta Dental of the District of Columbia, 190
Hankinson, Michael Delta Dental of New York, 567
Hankinson, Michael Delta Dental of Pennsylvania, 678
Hankinson, Mike Delta Dental of West Virginia, 847
Hannan, Tim eHealthInsurance Services, Inc., 95
Hanrahan, Jennifer R. Delta Dental of Wyoming, 882
Hanson, Collette Blue Cross & Blue Shield of Montana, 493
Hanson, Collette HCSC Insurance Services Company Montana, 494
Harewood, Junior UnitedHealthcare of Alabama, 10
Harewood, Junior UnitedHealthcare of Georgia, 248
Hargens, Brad Mercy Care Plan/Mercy Care Advantage, 39
Hargreaves, Diane Trinity Health of Illinois, 288
Harrington, Carly Upper Peninsula Health Plan, 446
Harris, Cory R. Wellmark Blue Cross Blue Shield, 329
Harris, Pete Dominion Dental Services, 819
Harris, Ryan MetroPlus Health Plan, 584
Harris, Shelley Trinity Health of Idaho, 264
Harris, Stephen Blue Cross & Blue Shield of Illinois, 270
Harrison, A. Marc, MD Intermountain Healthcare, 801

Harrison, Samantha CareSource Kentucky, 352
Harrison, Tara Regence BlueShield of Idaho, 263
Harshman, Eita Delta Dental of Illinois, 276
Hart, Brian Delta Dental of Kentucky, 354
Hart, Erin American HealthCare Group, 675
Harvey, Christi United Concordia of Texas, 790
Harvey, Jonathan, MD Martin's Point HealthCare, 377
Havens, Jim LifeWise, 841
Hawsey, Dave Delta Dental of Arkansas, 54
Haydel, Augustavia L.A. Care Health Plan, 113
Hayden-Cook, Melissa Sharp Health Plan, 135
Hayes, Cain A. Tufts Health Medicare Plan, 410
Hayes, Cain A. Tufts Health Plan, 411
Hayes, Cain A. Tufts Health Plan: Rhode Island, 716
Haygood, Rhonda Vantage Health Plan, 371
Haygood, Rhonda Vantage Medicare Advantage, 372
Haynes, Neil Sun Life Financial, 409
Haynes, Tadd UniCare West Virginia, 851
Hayward, Doug Kern Family Health Care, 112
Hayworth, Bob Humana Health Insurance of Missouri, 487
Healy, Patrick Peach State Health Plan, 243
Hebenstreit, Patricia, JD MDwise, 308
Heckenlaible, Mick Delta Dental of South Dakota, 737
Hefley, Debbie Amerigroup Texas, 759
Heintz, Rebecca Blue Cross & Blue Shield of Vermont, 811
Heisey, Glenn Capital BlueCross, 677
Heller, Brice United Concordia of Colorado, 166
Hellman, Peter S. Wellmark Blue Cross & Blue Shield of South Dakota, 740
Hemann, Jenn Consumers Direct Insurance Services (CDIS), 770
Hendrickson, Brandon Molina Healthcare of Idaho, 261
Hendrickson, Brandon Molina Healthcare of Utah, 802
Henningsen, Rod AlphaDentalPlan.com, 150
Henningsen, Rod Beta Health Association, Inc., 153
Henriksen, Marjorie Prominence Health Plan, 516
Hensel, Krista UnitedHealthcare Community Plan Kentucky, 359
Herbelin, Maurice, MD, MBA Central California Alliance for Health, 81
Herman, Ted MVP Health Care, 586
Hermreck, Irene Aetna Health of Kansas, 332
Hernandez, Catherine Kaiser Permanente, 109
Hernandez, Ines, MD Medical Card System (MCS), 707
Herndon, David R. Hawaii Medical Service Association, 252
Heron, Rick Western Health Advantage, 148
Herren, Todd Delta Dental of Iowa, 319
Heselmeyer, Alaine Superior HealthPlan, 787
Hess, Leslie Delta Dental of Arizona, 31
Heywood, Dave UnitedHealthcare Community Plan Hawaii, 255
Hickey, JD Blue Cross & Blue Shield of Tennessee, 745
Hickey, Jim Cigna HealthCare of Texas, 767
Higdon, Kevin Trinity Health of Indiana, 315
Hilbert, Andy Optima Health Plan, 825
Hiley, Erin American Specialty Health, 297
Hill, Amy Trillium Community Health Plan, 667
Hill, Jeff Behavioral Health Systems, 3
Hill, Kevin R. Oxford Health Plans, 179

Hill, Stephen Valley Baptist Health Plan, 795
Hillman, Robert Community Health Options, 375
Hinckley, Robert R. CDPHP: Capital District Physicians' Health Plan, 565
Hingst, Jeanne ProviDRs Care Network, 345
Hinton, Dustin UnitedHealthcare of Michigan, 445
Hinton, Dustin UnitedHealthcare of Wisconsin, 878
Hittle, Jodie Northeast Delta Dental Maine, 378
Hiveley, Jim Quartz Health Plan, 874
Hodge, Edmund F. Trinity Health, 440
Hodges, Deborah Health Plans, Inc., 406
Hodgkins, Robert C., Jr. The Dental Care Plus Group, 636
Hoey, Brigette CalOptima, 78
Hoffman, Christopher eHealthInsurance Services, Inc., 95
Hoffmeier, Donna TriWest Healthcare Alliance, 46
Hogan, John Capital Health Plan, 200
Hoglund, Barbie Magellan Rx Management, 38
Hoin, Stacey Guardian Life Insurance Company of America, 576
Holder, Diane UPMC Health Plan, 699
Holmberg, David L. Highmark Blue Cross Blue Shield, 684
Holmberg, David L. Highmark Blue Shield, 685
Holmberg, David L. Highmark BCBS West Virginia, 848
Holmquist, Melissa Upper Peninsula Health Plan, 446
Holt, Jeff Cigna Medical Group, 30
Hopfer, Rick Hawaii Medical Service Association, 252
Hopsicker, Jim MVP Health Care, 586
Horowitz, Steve CareCentrix, 173
Horstmann, Nancy Christus Health Plan, 766
Horvath, Steve Trustmark, 289
Houghland, Stephen J., MD Passport Health Plan, 357
Hously, Jenny Blue Cross Blue Shield of Kansas City, 476
Houston, Daniel J. Employers Dental Services, 32
Howes, David, MD Martin's Point HealthCare, 377
Hoyt, Ann Group Health Cooperative of South Central Wisconsin, 866
Hrabchak, Richard Mutual of Omaha, 503
Hsieh, David CareMore Health Plan, 79
Huang, Nancy CalOptima, 78
Hubbard, Cornel, JD, CCEP Magellan Complete Care of Virginia, 823
Hughes, Donna EmblemHealth, 570
Hughes, Donna EmblemHealth Enhanced Care Plus (HARP), 571
Hughes, Donna GHI Medicare Plan, 575
Hughes, Tisa Harvard Pilgrim Health Care Massachusetts, 404
Hulin, Colin Peoples Health, 367
Humphrey, Craig FirstCarolinaCare, 602
Humphrey, Richard Parkland Community Health Plan, 782
Hunn, Michael CalOptima, 78
Hunter, Eric C. CareOregon Health Plan, 653
Huotari, Mike Rocky Mountain Health Plans, 165
Hurst, David Health Plan of San Joaquin, 104
Husa, Sherry Managed Health Services Wisconsin, 869
Hussain, Syed A., MD Trinity Health of New England, 180
Huth, Mark, MD Group Health Cooperative of South Central Wisconsin, 866
Hutton, Thomas A. Independence Blue Cross, 687
Huval, Tim CompBenefits Corporation, 238
Huval, Tim Humana Inc., 355

I

Iacopino, Carol Well Sense Health Plan, 528
Iannelli, Lee Ann CHN PPO, 534
Ibrahim, Mumtaz, MD Molina Healthcare of New York, 585
Ignagni, Karen M. EmblemHealth, 570
Ignagni, Karen M. EmblemHealth Enhanced Care Plus (HARP), 571
Ignagni, Karen M. GHI Medicare Plan, 575
Impicciche, Joseph, JD Seton Healthcare Family, 785
Inge, Ronald E., DDS Delta Dental of Missouri, 480
Inge, Ronald E. Delta Dental of South Carolina, 728
Ingrum, Jeff FirstCare Health Plans, 771
Ingrum, Jeff Scott & White Health Plan, 783
Inzina, Tommy Trinity Health of Florida, 225
Isaac, Daverick Community First Health Plans, 768
Isaacs, Richard S., MD Kaiser Permanente Mid-Atlantic, 388
Iturriria, Louis Kern Family Health Care, 112

J

Jackson, Amanda Martin's Point HealthCare, 377
Jacobetti, Lorrie Prevea Health Network, 873
Jacobs, David Aetna Health of Colorado, 149
Jacobson, Jim Medica, 457
Jacobson, Jim Medica with CHI Health, 500
Jacobson, Jim Medica: Nebraska, 501
Jacoby, Kathy Delta Dental of Colorado, 158
Jaconette, Paul CenCal Health, 80
Jain, Rashmi Careington Solutions, 765
Jain, Sachin H. SCAN Health Plan, 134
James, Jesse, MD Evolent Health, 821
James, Marcus Arkansas Blue Cross Blue Shield, 51
Jansen, Mark, MD Arkansas Blue Cross Blue Shield, 51
Jarecki, Neal Santa Clara Family Health Foundations Inc, 132
Jenkins, Nancy McLaren Health Plan, 430
Jennings, Jonathan R. Delta Dental of Missouri, 480
Jennings, Jonathan R. Delta Dental of South Carolina, 728
Jensen, Barbara Delta Dental of Nebraska, 499
Jhawar, Sharon K. SCAN Health Plan, 134
Johansson, Ian Health Plan of San Mateo, 105
Johnson, Eric AvMed, 197
Johnson, Eric H. UnitedHealthcare of Arkansas, 60
Johnson, Jennifer Trinity Health of Idaho, 264
Johnson, John Evolent Health, 821
Johnson, Luke Group Health Cooperative of Eau Claire, 865
Johnson, Scott Molina Healthcare of Wisconsin, 871
Johnson, Steven P. Health First Health Plans, 209
Johnson, Steven P. Health First Medicare Plans, 210
Johnson, Steven P., Jr UPMC Susquehanna, 700
Johnson, William, MD, MBA Moda Health Alaska, 13
Johnson, William, MD, MBA Moda Health Oregon, 660
Johnston, Jeff Home State Health Plan, 486
Johnston, Katherine AllCare Health, 651
Johnston, Lori Paramount Care of Michigan, 434
Johnston, Lori Paramount Elite Medicare Plan, 630
Johnston, Lori Paramount Health Care, 631

Joiner, Thomas, MD Molina Healthcare of Mississippi, 469
Jones, David Delta Dental of Oklahoma, 644
Jones, Debbie Delta Dental of North Carolina, 600
Jones, Melissa Avesis: Texas, 761
Jones, Mike Molina Healthcare of Florida, 218
Jones, Nicole Cigna Corporation, 174
Jones, Patty Community Health Plan of Washington, 834
Jones, Richard Essence Healthcare, 483
Jones, Scott Delta Dental of South Dakota, 737
Jones, Tia Delta Dental of North Carolina, 600
Joseph Bell, Jill Passport Health Plan, 357
Judy, Steve Primary Health Medical Group, 262
Julkowski, Teresa Hennepin Health, 455
Jurkovic, Goran Delta Dental of Michigan, 421

K

Kalbacher, Jean UnitedHealthcare Community Plan Arizona, 48
Kamal, Mostafa Magellan Rx Management, 38
Kanakri, Terry Kaiser Permanente Southern California, 111
Kandalaft, Kevin UnitedHealthcare Community Plan California, 140
Kane, Brian CompBenefits Corporation, 238
Kane, Brian Andrew CarePlus Health Plans, 202
Kane, Heather UnitedHealthcare of Arizona, 49
Kane, Sean Healthfirst, 577
Kanyusik Yoakum, Anne Hennepin Health, 455
Kao, John Alignment Health Plan, 65
Kapic, Maja Liberty Dental Plan of New York, 581
Karsten, Wendy Care N' Care, 764
Kastman, Chris, MD Group Health Cooperative of South Central Wisconsin, 866
Kates, Peter B Univera Healthcare, 594
Katich, Wanda Northeast Georgia Health Partners, 242
Kautzmann, Paula Colorado Access, 157
Kavouras, Michael, Esq. Aetna Health of Illinois, 267
Kawano, Kie UnitedHealthcare of Hawaii, 256
Kaye, Michel PTPN, 130
Kayne, Jeremy HealthNetwork, 212
Keck, Kim A. BlueCross BlueShield Association, 271
Keeley, Larry Envolve Vision, 601
Keeling, Zach Medical Associates, 323
Keene, Rob Starmount, 368
Kehaly, Pam D. Blue Cross & Blue Shield of Arizona, 26
Kehaly, Richard H. Blue Cross & Blue Shield of Arizona, 26
Keim, Mark Molina Healthcare, 121
Kelley, Maggie Community Health Options, 375
Kellogg, Alden Peoples Health, 367
Kelly, Mark Trinity Health of New Jersey, 542
Kelly, Sarah American HealthCare Group, 675
Kelso, Matt HealthSmart, 774
Kemp, Kirt Partnership HealthPlan of California, 127
Kendall, Dani Concentra, 769
Kennedy, Roxanne Value Behavioral Health of Pennsylvania, 703
Kenney, Dave Trustmark, 289
Kenny, Becky Blue Cross & Blue Shield of New Mexico, 547
Kessel, Stacy Community Health Plan of Washington, 834

417

Keyser, Beth Anthem Blue Cross & Blue Shield of Indiana, 298
Kilbreth, Will Community Health Options, 375
Kile, Gregory G. Valley Preferred, 702
Killian, Kathy Dean Health Plan, 861
Kim, Yungkyung CalOptima, 78
Kinder, Deborah Liberty Dental Plan of Texas, 778
Kintu, Emanuel AlohaCare Advantage Plus, 250
Kirkpatrick, Mercy Leon Medical Centers Health Plan, 215
Kish, John Medical Mutual, 624
Klammer, Thomas P. Landmark Healthplan of California, 115
Kline, Teresa Presbyterian Health Plan, 552
Knight, Jeffrey M. The Health Plan, 850
Kobus, Dave Cigna HealthCare of New Jersey, 535
Kobylowski, Ken AmeriHealth New Jersey, 532
Koenig, Tere Medical Mutual, 624
Koh, Leong, MD Kaiser Permanente Northwest, 657
Kokkinides, Penelope InnovaCare Health, 706
Kolesar, Jeff Renaissance Dental, 312
Kolli, Rama Blue Cross & Blue Shield of Nebraska, 498
Kornblatt, Janet SCAN Health Plan, 134
Kornwasser, Laizer CareCentrix, 173
Kosior, Robert A. ConnectiCare, 177
Kotal, John Molina Healthcare of California, 122
Kotelon, Alexandra Delta Dental of Illinois, 276
Koushik, Srini Magellan Health, 37
Kovaleski, Kerry Arizona Foundation for Medical Care, 22
Kowal, Nancy Total Health Care, 439
Kozik, Sue Blue Cross and Blue Shield of Louisiana, 363
Krawcek, Jeffrey, MD, MBOE Kaiser Permanente Northern Colorado, 162
Krawcek, Jeffrey, MD Kaiser Permanente Southern Colorado, 163
Krna, Catherine University HealthCare Alliance, 143
Krupinski, Steven J. Horizon Blue Cross Blue Shield of New Jersey, 537
Kudgis, Len Horizon NJ Health, 538
Kunst, Tom UnitedHealthcare of Illinois, 292
Kunz, Eileen, MPH On Lok Lifeways, 123
Kurian, Linda Aetna Medicaid Administrators LLC, 17
Kushner, Joshua Oscar Health, 588
Kuss, Vincent J. Trinity Health of New York, 590
Kutzler, Josh HealthEZ, 452
Kwan, Dennis Y.V. Hawaii Medical Assurance Association, 251

L

Ladig, Curtis Delta Dental of North Carolina, 600
Lagasca, Jennifer QualCare, 541
Lahullier, Justin, MD Delta Dental of New Jersey, 536
Lambrukos, William H. Northeast Delta Dental Maine, 378
Lambrukos, William H. Northeast Delta Dental, 526
Lambrukos, William H. Northeast Delta Dental Vermont, 812
Lancaster, Kathy Kaiser Permanente, 109
Landers, Jason The Health Plan, 850
Landin, Jared Wellmark Blue Cross Blue Shield, 329
Landis, Robert Kern Family Health Care, 112
Landsbaum, Nathan Sunshine Health, 224
Lane, Bruce AlohaCare, 249

Lane, Bruce AlohaCare Advantage Plus, 250
Langdon, Matt Blue Cross and Blue Shield of Kansas, 336
Lange, Julie The Dental Care Plus Group, 636
Langer, Don UnitedHealthcare Community Plan Texas, 791
Lanham, Fran CareCentrix: Florida, 201
Lankowicz, Genevieve Trinity Health of Indiana, 315
Larkins, Steffany Medical Mutual, 624
Larmer, Robin L. Santa Clara Family Health Foundations Inc, 132
Larson, Cortney Public Employees Health Program, 805
LaTorre, Jean Guardian Life Insurance Company of America, 576
Lavely, David Envolve Vision, 601
Lavine, Marisa Kaiser Permanente Mid-Atlantic, 388
Lawlor, Kevin Altius Health Plans, 797
Lawlor, Kevin Aetna Health of Wyoming, 880
Lawton, Michael Neighborhood Health Partnership, 219
Lawton, Michael UnitedHealthcare Community Plan Florida, 227
Lay, Linda Delta Dental of Washington, 836
Layton, Brent Centene Corporation, 477
Leaf, Garrett SilverSummit Healthplan, 517
Learn, Teresa CareOregon Health Plan, 653
Lechtenberger, Michael Mutual of Omaha, 503
Lechtenberger, Michael Mutual of Omaha Dental Insurance, 504
Leddy, Bryan Delta Dental of Ohio, 621
Lederberg, Michele Blue Cross & Blue Shield of Rhode Island, 713
Lederman, Alan Community Health Plan of Washington, 834
Ledheiser, Loren Trinity Health of Ohio, 637
Lee, Yolanda Chinese Community Health Plan, 83
Leedy, Kerri Kaiser Permanente Northern California, 110
Leitzen, Justin ProviDRs Care Network, 345
Lenora, Roshan Security Health Plan of Wisconsin, 875
Lenth, Gary Quartz Health Plan, 874
Lentine, Joe, Jr Dencap Dental Plans, 422
Lerner, Cheryl, MD Delta Dental of Colorado, 158
Lester, William W. Ameritas, 497
Levandoski, Anne Upper Peninsula Health Plan, 446
Lewis, Kevin Community Health Options, 375
Lewis, Kurt UnitedHealthcare of Ohio, 639
Lewis-Clapper, Caskie Magellan Health, 37
Li, Grace On Lok Lifeways, 123
Lightfoot, Dan, MD Pacific Foundation for Medical Care, 125
Lightner, Debra M. EmblemHealth, 570
Lightner, Debra M. EmblemHealth Enhanced Care Plus (HARP), 571
Lightner, Debra M. GHI Medicare Plan, 575
Lindberg, Kelly Medica, 457
Linder, Kathleen CareMore Health Plan, 79
Lindquist, Tom Medica, 457
Lindquist, Tom Medica with CHI Health, 500
Lindquist, Tom Medica: Nebraska, 501
Lindsey, Melvin Amerigroup Georgia, 235
Lingafelter, Lynn Deaconess Health Plans, 303
Lirette, Karl UnitedHealthcare Community Plan Louisiana, 369
Livesay, Craig Delta Dental of Arizona, 31
Livingston, David Prominence Health Plan, 516
Lo, Eric Delta Dental of Washington, 836

Loepp, Daniel J. Blue Care Network of Michigan, 417, 418
Loepp, Daniel J. Blue Cross Blue Shield of Michigan, 419
Loftin, Scott Moda Health Alaska, 13
Loftis, R. Chet Public Employees Health Program, 805
London, Sarah M. Centene Corporation, 477
Loochtan, Scott Consumers Direct Insurance Services (CDIS), 770
Loosbrock, Julie Blue Cross & Blue Shield of Minnesota, 450
Lopez, David Parkland Community Health Plan, 782
Lopez, Jose Mid America Health, 309
Lopez, Juan Independence Blue Cross, 687
Lopez, Maria Delta Dental of New Mexico, 548
Lott, Laura Kaiser Permanente Hawaii, 254
Lotvin, Alan M., M.D. CVS Caremark, 714
Louder, Mary, MD Boulder Valley Individual Practice Association, 154
Louie, Deena Chinese Community Health Plan, 83
Lovell, Stephanie Blue Cross & Blue Shield of Massachusetts, 401
Lowell, Randy LifeMap, 658
Lowtharp, Debi Delta Dental of Arkansas, 54
Lucas, Brad, MD Buckeye Health Plan, 618
Lucero-Ali, Cynthia Delta Dental of New Mexico, 548
Lucia, Frank Delta Dental of Virginia, 818
Lukaszewicz, Natalie Buckeye Health Plan, 618
Lundquist, Thomas, M.D. Optima Health Plan, 825
Luxenberg, Jay, M.D. On Lok Lifeways, 123
Lwin, Aye Jai Medical Systems, 387
Lyman, Justin Trillium Community Health Plan, 667
Lynch, Karen S. Aetna Inc., 170
Lynch, Karen S. Meritain Health, 583
Lynch, Karen S. MHNet Behavioral Health, 779
Lynch, Richard Blue Cross & Blue Shield of Massachusetts, 401
Lynch, Scott Blue Cross & Blue Shield of Minnesota, 450
Lynn, Bob DentaQuest, 402
Lynn, Bob EyeQuest, 864

M

MacBeth, Charlotte UnitedHealthcare Community Plan Indiana, 316
Maccannon, Keith AmeriHealth Caritas District of Columbia, 189
MacDougall, Tom L.A. Care Health Plan, 113
Mach, John R., MD Medica with CHI Health, 500
Mach, John R., MD Medica: Nebraska, 501
Mach, Jr., John R., MD Medica, 457
Macias, Melissa Dimension Health, 205
Mackin, Steve Mercy Clinic Missouri, 490
Maddox, Terry Delta Dental of Illinois, 276
Madondo, John UnitedHealthcare Community Plan Massachusetts, 413
Madrak, Jason Harvard Pilgrim Health Care Connecticut, 178
Maher, Charlene Blue Cross of Idaho Health Service, Inc., 258
Mahony, Patricia Western Dental & Orthodontics, 147
Main, Theron, DDS Northeast Delta Dental Vermont, 812
Maisel, Garry Western Health Advantage, 148
Majors, Molly Liberty Dental Plan of Missouri, 488
Maleno, Anthony J. Independence Blue Cross, 687
Mallatt, Kathy UnitedHealthcare of Nebraska, 507
Malton, Douglas InnovaCare Health, 706

Mammano, Jerold Aetna Better Health of Virginia, 814
Mancini, Kathie Humana Health Insurance of Indiana, 306
Mancini, Kathie Humana Health Insurance of Michigan, 429
Mancini, Kathie Humana Health Insurance of Ohio, 623
Manger, Joseph W. Aetna Better Health of New Jersey, 529
Manley, Marc Hennepin Health, 455
Manning, Lynn MVP Health Care, 586
Manos, Fred Care Plus Dental Plans, 859
Maples, John Delta Dental of Illinois, 276
Mapp, Tom L.A. Care Health Plan, 113
March, Glenville A, Jr, MD March Vision Care, 118
Marchello, Vincent, MD Fidelis Care, 574
Marden, Paul UnitedHealthcare of New Jersey, 544
Marden, Paul UnitedHealthcare of Pennsylvania, 698
Marden-Resnik, Hilary UCare, 460
Marinello, Anthony, MD CDPHP: Capital District Physicians' Health Plan, 565
Marino, Peter M. Neighborhood Health Plan of Rhode Island, 715
Markovich, Paul S. Blue Shield of California, 69
Marrero, Juan Envolve Vision, 601
Marrs, Michelle Aetna Better Health of Kentucky, 349
Marsella, Brian Cigna HealthCare of Illinois, 273
Marsella, Brian Cigna HealthCare of Indiana, 302
Martella, Kathy Anthem Blue Cross of California, 67
Martenet, Steve Anthem Blue Cross & Blue Shield of Ohio, 616
Martin, Augusta MVP Health Care, 586
Martin, David Arkansas Blue Cross Blue Shield, 51
Martin, Jeff Paramount Care of Michigan, 434
Martin, Jeff Paramount Elite Medicare Plan, 630
Martin, Jeff Paramount Health Care, 631
Martin, Kaye Delta Dental of Tennessee, 747
Martinez, Jeremy Blue Cross & Blue Shield of Wyoming, 881
Martinez, John Delta Dental of New Mexico, 548
Martinez, Maria Medcore Medical Group, 119
Marting, Gina L. Hawaii Medical Service Association, 252
Maruyama, Nina San Francisco Health Plan, 131
Mary, Hoskins SIHO Insurance Services, 314
Mashura, Jennifer N. InStil Health, 730
Mason, Treena Advance Insurance Company of Kansas, 330
Mason, Treena Blue Cross and Blue Shield of Kansas, 336
Mason, William, Esq. Northeast Delta Dental Vermont, 812
Massey, Leslie American Dental Group, 151
Matejka, Cheryl Mercy Clinic Missouri, 490
Matheis, Dennis A. Optima Health Plan, 825
Matheny, Marnie KelseyCare Advantage, 777
Mattera, Richard UnitedHealth Group, 461
Matzell, Julianne Atrio Health Plans, 652
Maury, Albert Leon Medical Centers Health Plan, 215
Maxwell, Dale Presbyterian Health Plan, 552
Mayer, Tom Spirit Dental & Vision, 459
Mazzotta, Liz Mutual of Omaha, 503
McAdams, Scott Blue Cross Blue Shield of Kansas City, 476
McAlpin, Maynard Versant Health, 396
McAlpin, Maynard Davis Vision, 566
McCabe, Dan CareSource Ohio, 620

419

McCandles, Pati Blue Cross & Blue Shield of Texas, 762
McCarl, Kim Contra Costa Health Services, 89
McCarthy, Gloria Anthem, Inc., 299
McClellan, John Absolute Total Care - Healthy Connections Medicaid, 719
McClelland, Kevin Kaiser Permanente Georgia, 241
McClure, Elizabeth Mid America Health, 309
McClure, Nance HealthPartners, 453
McClure, Shara Blue Cross & Blue Shield of Texas, 762
McCormick, Mark Allways Health Partners, 398
McCorriston, William C. Hawaii Medical Assurance Association, 251
McCoy, Shawn Deaconess Health Plans, 303
McCulley, Daniel Midlands Choice, 502
McDonald, Darin UCare, 460
McDonough, Denise Anthem Blue Cross & Blue Shield of Maine, 374
McEachern, Edward, MD PacificSource Health Plans, 661
McFann, Elena Amerigroup, 815
McFarland, Patti Partnership HealthPlan of California, 127
McGowan, Marion A. Health New England, 405
McGraw, Regina, RN, JD Trinity Health of New York, 590
McGuire, Michael Delta Dental of Minnesota, 451
McGuire, Michael UnitedHealthcare of New York, 593
McIntyre, Jr., David TriWest Healthcare Alliance, 46
McKenney, Rick Primecare Dental Plan, 129
McKenney, Rick Starmount, 368
McKown, Melissa Parkview Total Health, 310
McMahon, Andrew J. Guardian Life Insurance Company of America, 576
McMahon, Dirk UnitedHealth Group, 461
McMillan, Bryan Liberty Dental Plan of Missouri, 488
McNab-Capraun, Yvonne Amerigroup New Jersey, 531
McNeil, Ane Trinity Health of Michigan, 441
McNeil, Michael, MD QualCare, 541
McNeilly, Steven Northeast Georgia Health Partners, 242
McPherson, Les Dean Health Plan, 861
McQuaide, Jay Blue Cross & Blue Shield of Massachusetts, 401
Meade, Stacey, CEBS Meritain Health, 583
Meadows, Dave Liberty Dental Plan of Illinois, 283
Meek, Todd SilverScript Insurance Company, 44
Megeath, Alexis CareMore Health Plan, 79
Mehdizadegan, Katie Delta Dental of Arkansas, 54
Mehelic, Phil American Health Care Alliance, 474
Mercado, Jose Humana Health Insurance of Puerto Rico, 705
Merlo, Kristin Delta Dental of Arkansas, 54
Mertz, Laura J., CBC Valley Preferred, 702
Meyer, Scott Delta Dental of Wisconsin, 862
Meyers, Jonathan A. InnovaCare Health, 706
Micucci, Jackie Community Health Plan of Washington, 834
Middleton, Darrell E. Blue Care Network of Michigan, 418
Middleton, Darrell E. Blue Cross Blue Shield of Michigan, 419
Migliori, Richard UnitedHealth Group, 461
Mikan, G. Mike Bright Health Alabama, 5
Mikan, G. Mike Bright Health Colorado, 155
Milano, Ed Sun Life Financial, 409
Miles Everett, Nina F., MD Aetna Better Health of Maryland, 381
Milich, David UnitedHealthcare of Oklahoma, 649

Milich, David UnitedHealthcare of Texas, 792
Miller, Jeff Delta Dental of South Dakota, 737
Miller, Jeffrey Western Dental & Orthodontics, 147
Miller, Judy P. Blue Cross and Blue Shield of Louisiana, 363
Miller, Lan Delta Dental of Oklahoma, 644
Miller, Shane Prevea Health Network, 873
Miller-Phipps, Julie Kaiser Permanente Southern California, 111
Milligan, David SCAN Health Plan, 134
Mills, Lee CommunityCare, 643
Mineo, John Independent Health, 579
Mineo, John Independent Health Medicare Plan, 580
Mingione, Lisa Affinity Health Plan, 560
Minter, Brent Humana Health Insurance of South Carolina, 729
Miralles, Al CNA, 274
Misasi, Chuck Careington Solutions, 765
Mitchell, Jill Medical Associates, 323
Mitchell, Tracey Arizona Foundation for Medical Care, 22
Mitchke, Mark Delta Dental of Washington, 836
Mixer, Mark Alliant Health Plans, 232
Mizelle, Karla Blue Cross Blue Shield of North Carolina, 597
Mody-Bailey, Priti, MD Community First Health Plans, 768
Moell, Dana Managed Health Services, 307
Moen, Daniel P. Trinity Health of New Jersey, 542
Mohan, Vinod SCAN Health Plan, 134
Mollica, Tony Humana Health Insurance of Louisiana, 365
Molloy, Gisele CareCentrix, 173
Molloy, Kevin Guardian Life Insurance Company of America, 576
Monez, Sue Partnership HealthPlan of California, 127
Monfiletto, Sandra Martin's Point HealthCare, 377
Monk, Nancy J. SCAN Health Plan, 134
Monsrud, Beth UCare, 460
Montenegro, Teresa Health Partners of Kansas, 339
Montgomery, Marie L.A. Care Health Plan, 113
Moody, Robert L. American National Insurance Company, 757
Moore, Darin San Francisco Health Plan, 131
Moore, Kevin UnitedHealthcare Community Plan Wisconsin, 877
Moore, Richard Health Plan of San Mateo, 105
Moore, Robert, MD Partnership HealthPlan of California, 127
Morales Martinez, Maite Medical Card System (MCS), 707
Morgan, Todd AlohaCare, 249
Morrison, Steven C. Emi Health, 799
Morrissey, Brian J. CDPHP: Capital District Physicians' Health Plan, 565
Moulter, Chuck Health Plans, Inc., 406
Mouras, Dennis UnitedHealthcare Community Plan Michigan, 444
Moylan, Tim Florida Health Care Plan, Inc., 207
Mozak, Paul L. Blue Care Network of Michigan, 417, 418
Mozak, Paul L. Blue Cross Blue Shield of Michigan, 419
Mudra, Karl A. Delta Dental of Missouri, 480
Mudra, Karl A. Delta Dental of South Carolina, 728
Mueller, Jennifer Friday Health Plans, 160
Mueller, Peter LifeMap, 658
Mueller, Ray Medical Mutual, 624
Mugiishi, Mark M. Hawaii Medical Service Association, 252
Mukaihata Hannemann, Gail Hawaii Medical Assurance Association, 251

Mulligan, Deanna M. Premier Access Insurance/Access Dental, 128
Mulligan, Robert P. Renaissance Dental, 312
Muney, Alan M., MD Oxford Health Plans, 179
Muniz, Gretchen Medical Card System (MCS), 707
Munoz, Mike AmeriHealth New Jersey, 532
Murphy, Mark E. Trinity Health of New York, 590
Murphy, Michael G. Affinity Health Plan, 560
Murphy, Michelle Atrio Health Plans, 652
Murphy, Mike Anthem Blue Cross & Blue Shield of Nevada, 509
Murphy, Patrick Mid America Health, 309
Murray, Alan Empire BlueCross BlueShield, 572
Murray, Brian MagnaCare, 582
Murray, Don Delta Dental of Idaho, 259
Murrell, Warren Peoples Health, 367
Myers, Liz Delta Dental of Iowa, 319

N

Nacol, John California Foundation for Medical Care, 76
Nakahira, Laurie Santa Clara Family Health Foundations Inc, 132
Napier, Denise Health Partners Plans, 682
Narducci, Suellen Trillium Community Health Plan, 667
Narowitz, Randy Total Health Care, 439
Nash, Bruce, M.D. Blue Cross & Blue Shield of Massachusetts, 401
Nau, Shawn Health Choice Arizona, 33
Naylor, John Medica, 457
Naylor, John Medica with CHI Health, 500
Naylor, John Medica: Nebraska, 501
Needham, Jennifer, CPA Delta Dental of Ohio, 621
Needleman, Stuart, OD Vision Plan of America, 145
Neely, Marc UnitedHealthcare of Colorado, 168
Neely, Marc UnitedHealthcare of Wyoming, 883
Nehs, Scott BlueCross BlueShield Association, 271
Neidorff, Michael California Health & Wellness, 77
Nelson, Catherine HCSC Insurance Services Company, 278
Nelson, Catherine Health Care Service Corporation (HCSC), 281
Nelson, Kevin P. Aetna Better Health of New York, 558
Nelson, Krista AHCCCS/Medicaid, 18
Nelson, Micheal A. Inter Valley Health Plan, 108
Nelson, Su Zan Concentra, 769
Neshat, Amir Liberty Dental Plan of New York, 581
Newton, Cecil Central California Alliance for Health, 81
Newton, Cecil San Francisco Health Plan, 131
Newton, Dean Delta Dental of Kansas, 338
Newton, Keith Concentra, 769
Nicholson, Jennifer Northeast Georgia Health Partners, 242
Nicklaus, Dave eHealthInsurance Services, Inc., 95
Nicol, John Pacific Foundation for Medical Care, 125
Nizza, Arthur A. Government Employees Health Association (GEHA), 484
Nizza, Teresa Martin's Point HealthCare, 377
Nobile, Paul Anthem Blue Cross & Blue Shield of Wisconsin, 857
Nolan, David C. On Lok Lifeways, 123
Normington, Rebecca Security Health Plan of Wisconsin, 875
Norton, Deborah Harvard Pilgrim Health Care Massachusetts, 404
Norwood, Felicia F. Amerigroup, 815

O

O'Brien, Steve, MD Alameda Alliance for Health, 62
O'Brien, Steve, MD Alameda Medi-Cal Plan, 64
O'Connell, Katherine A., CPA Northeast Delta Dental Vermont, 812
O'Connell, Michael University HealthCare Alliance, 143
O'Connor, Susan, Esq. Health New England, 405
O'Connor, Thomas UnitedHealthcare of South Carolina, 734
O'Toole, Kevin Managed Health Services, 307
Oakes, Don Northeast Delta Dental Maine, 378
Ochipinti, Joe UnitedHealthcare of the District of Columbia, 193
Ochipinti, Joe UnitedHealthcare of Maryland, 395
Ochipinti, Joe UnitedHealthcare of Virginia, 829
Ochipinti, Joe UnitedHealthcare of West Virginia, 853
Odom, Lisa Cox Healthplans, 479
Oemichen, Bill Group Health Cooperative of South Central Wisconsin, 866
Okamoto, Gary AlohaCare, 249
Okamoto, Gary AlohaCare Advantage Plus, 250
Okigwe, Jaja First Choice Health, 655, 838
Olds, Jane E. Peoples Health, 367
Ollech, Brian Network Health Plan of Wisconsin, 872
Oneferu-Bey, Wanda CareFirst BlueCross BlueShield, 385
Ong, Jeanne TriWest Healthcare Alliance, 46
Orlando, Dave Dominion Dental Services, 819
Ormsby, Joan Trinity Health of Illinois, 288
Orr, Lavdena A., MD AmeriHealth Caritas District of Columbia, 189
Ortiz, Irene, MD Molina Healthcare of New Mexico, 551
Osorio, Rosemary Dimension Health, 205
Osthelder, Ted Anthem Blue Cross & Blue Shield of Wisconsin, 857
Ott, BJ AlohaCare Advantage Plus, 250
Owen, Marina CenCal Health, 80
Owen Plietz, Carrie Kaiser Permanente Northern California, 110

P

Pack, Kent Children's Mercy Pediatric Care Network, 478
Pagliaro, Brian ConnectiCare, 177
Palazzari, Adam, MD Boulder Valley Individual Practice Association, 154
Palmateer, Michael EmblemHealth, 570
Palmateer, Michael EmblemHealth Enhanced Care Plus (HARP), 571
Palmateer, Michael . GHI Medicare Plan, 575
Palmer, Corey Blue Cross & Blue Shield of Montana, 493
Palmer, Rob Wisconsin Physician's Service, 879
Pankau, Davis S. Blue Cross & Blue Shield of South Carolina, 725
Park, Ben, MD American Health Network, 296
Park, Richard W. Northeast Delta Dental Vermont, 812
Parker, Daniel Delta Dental of Ohio, 621
Parnell, J. Michael, PhD, RN UnitedHealthcare Community Plan Mississippi, 470
Parr, Chris Health Plans, Inc., 406
Pass, Kathy Pacific Foundation for Medical Care, 125
Patel, Nilesh Delta Dental of California, 90
Patterson, Nita Managed HealthCare Northwest, 659
Patterson, William, MD Behavioral Health Systems, 3
Paul Luke, Leslie Trinity Health of New York, 590
Paulissen, Steven, M.D. Atrio Health Plans, 652

Paulus, Steve Trinity Health of Michigan, 441
Pawenski, Pamela J. Univera Healthcare, 594
Pederson, Scott Delta Dental of Arizona, 31
Pels-Beck, Leslie Sharp Health Plan, 135
Pensotti, Fred One Call Care Management, 220
Pentecost, Michael J. NIA Magellan, 40
Perkins, Sherry Delta Dental of Iowa, 319
Pernell, Godfrey Dental Health Services of California, 93
Pernell, Godfrey Dental Health Services of Oregon, 654
Pernell, Godfrey Dental Health Services of Washington, 837
Perry, Mack Humana Health Insurance of Florida, 214
Perry, Mitch Blue Cross Blue Shield of North Carolina, 597
Person, Mary Catherine HealthSCOPE Benefits, 56
Pesich, Denise J. Affinity Health Plan, 560
Peterson, Drew UnitedHealthcare Community Plan New Mexico, 555
Peterson, Judy Delta Dental of Minnesota, 451
Peterson, Tom Evolent Health, 821
Petonic, Fran Trinity Health of Michigan, 441
Petrizzi, Ryan J. AmeriHealth New Jersey, 532
Pfeifer, Rita Aetna Health of North Dakota, 608
Phillippi, Karen MediGold, 626
Phillips, Health Nebraska Total Care, 505
Phillips, Yancy Trinity Health of Maryland, 392
Pienick, Brian D. CareFirst Blue Cross & Blue Shield of Virginia, 817
Pieninck, Brian D. CareFirst BlueCross BlueShield, 385
Pieper, Christine Avesis: Minnesota, 449
Pierce, Scott Blue Cross & Blue Shield of Tennessee, 745
Pietrykowski, Susan J. Health Net Federal Services (HNFS), 101
Pillai, Jai CareSource Ohio, 620
Pinkert, David Friday Health Plans, 160
Pitt, William, MD Pacific Foundation for Medical Care, 125
Pittman, Janell Trinity Health of Iowa, 326
Pitts, Charles Cigna HealthCare of North Carolina, 598
Pitts, Charles Cigna HealthCare of South Carolina, 727
Pitts, Richard, DO, PhD CalOptima, 78
Platkin, Judy CareCentrix: New York, 563
Plavin, Joshua, MD, MPH Blue Cross & Blue Shield of Vermont, 811
Pliskin, Larry, JD MediGold, 626
Plumb, Mnason Humana Health Insurance of Virginia, 822
Poklar, Eric Buckeye Health Plan, 618
Pollock, Steve DentaQuest, 402
Pollock, Steve EyeQuest, 864
Pomerantz, Glenn, MD Gateway Health, 680
Pomeroy, Chad Evolent Health, 821
Porter, James R. Deaconess Health Plans, 303
Portune, Richard W. Superior Dental Care, 635
Potter, Dawn HealthEZ, 452
Pozo, Justo Preferred Care Partners, 222
Prabhu, Navin Delta Dental Insurance Company, 239
Preitauer, Erhardt CareSource Ohio, 620
Price, Meredith Trinity Health of New York, 590
Price III, Warren Hawaii Medical Assurance Association, 251
Prince, Holly Simply Healthcare Plans, Inc., 223
Prince, John Optum Complex Medical Conditions, 458

Pritchard, Paul, MD Prevea Health Network, 873
Prizant, Leslie InnovaCare Health, 706
Proud, Sandra Pueblo Health Care, 164
Provencher, Ken PacificSource Health Plans, 661
Province, Steven Buckeye Health Plan, 618
Pruitt, Richard Kern Family Health Care, 112
Putnam, Jeff AHCCCS/Medicaid, 18
Pyle, David Managed HealthCare Northwest, 659

Q

Quade, Bruce Group Health Cooperative of South Central Wisconsin, 866
Qualls White, Dalya Blue Cross & Blue Shield of Tennessee, 745
Quinn, Pat UnitedHealthcare of Missouri, 492
Quinn, Tim Delta Dental of Minnesota, 451
Quivers, Eric, MD Security Health Plan of Wisconsin, 875

R

Raffio, Thomas Northeast Delta Dental Maine, 378
Raffio, Thomas Northeast Delta Dental, 526
Raffio, Thomas Northeast Delta Dental Vermont, 812
Rai, Ashok, MD Prevea Health Network, 873
Raimer, Ben G., MD UTMB HealthCare Systems, 794
Ralston, Ryan The Health Plan, 850
Ramratan, Ganesh MetroPlus Health Plan, 584
Ramseier, Mike Kaiser Permanente Northern Colorado, 162
Ramseier, Mike Kaiser Permanente Southern Colorado, 163
Rank, Brian, MD HealthPartners, 453
Ransom, Penny Network Health Plan of Wisconsin, 872
Ratterree, Brent Care1st Health Plan Arizona, 27
Rausch, Jay Dominion Dental Services, 819
Ready, Janet L. Trinity Health of New York, 590
Reavis, Jay Delta Dental of Tennessee, 747
Recore, Joan Health Plans, Inc., 406
Reed, Acacia B. L.A. Care Health Plan, 113
Reed, Amanda Alliant Health Plans, 232
Reed, James R. Excellus BlueCross BlueShield, 573
Reed, Philip J Colorado Access, 157
Reese, Dennis J Physicians Health Plan of Mid-Michigan, 435
Reid, James Versant Health, 396
Reid, James Davis Vision, 566
Renwick-Espinosa, Kate VSP Vision Care, 146
Repp, James M. AvMed, 197
Reschke Bolster, Jennifer Trinity Health of New York, 590
Rex, John UnitedHealth Group, 461
Rice-Johnson, Deborah L. Highmark BCBS West Virginia, 848
Richardson, Robin Moda Health Alaska, 13
Ricketts, Jeff Anthem Blue Cross & Blue Shield of Virginia, 816
Riner, Kathryn Northeast Georgia Health Partners, 242
Ringel, Steve CareSource Ohio, 620
Rinker Horton, Amanda Careington Solutions, 765
Riojas, Gil Alameda Alliance for Health, 62
Riojas, Gil Alameda Medi-Cal Plan, 64
Rios, Waldemar, M.D. InnovaCare Health, 706
Riper, Nick Kaiser Permanente Southern Colorado, 163

Ritz, Bob Trinity Health of Iowa, 326
Ritz, Charles Anthem Blue Cross & Blue Shield of Colorado, 152
Rivera, Ixel Medical Card System (MCS), 707
Roach, Susan, MD Boulder Valley Individual Practice Association, 154
Robbins, James L., MD TriWest Healthcare Alliance, 46
Roberts, Adrian Affinity Health Plan, 560
Roberts, Jonathan C. Aetna Inc., 170
Roberts, Suzanna Simply Healthcare Plans, Inc., 223
Robinson, Derek J., MD Blue Cross & Blue Shield of Illinois, 270
Robinson, John, MD First Choice Health, 655
Robinson, Tamera Delta Dental of Minnesota, 451
Roble, John Cigna HealthCare of Colorado, 156
Robusto, Dino E. CNA, 274
Rodenz, Hillary Vale-U-Health, 701
Rodgers, John Independent Health, 579
Rodgers, John Independent Health Medicare Plan, 580
Rodrigues, Michael Delta Dental of New Jersey, 536
Rodriguez, Gloria A. Humana Health Insurance of Texas, 776
Rodriguez, Marco Valley Baptist Health Plan, 795
Rodriguez, Michele Liberty Dental Plan of Texas, 778
Rodriguez, Sarah Jane American Postal Workers Union (APWU) Health Plan, 382
Rogers, Raymond Mountain Health Co-Op, 495
Rogers, Stephanie Aetna Better Health of Texas, 753
Rohr, Jan Rocky Mountain Health Plans, 165
Romano, C. James Trinity Health of New Jersey, 542
Romero, Jay EPIC Pharmacy Network, 820
Roscoe, Jeffrey Aetna Better Health of Texas, 753
Rose, Carlotta InStil Health, 730
Rosenthal, Dan UnitedHealthcare of Southern California, 142
Ross, Linda Trinity Health, 440
Roth, Anna, RN, MS Contra Costa Health Services, 89
Roth, Daniel J. Trinity Health, 440
Rothermel, Paige Blue Cross & Blue Shield of Arizona, 26
Rottman, Jason Aetna Better Health of Pennsylvania, 672
Rowan, Mary Hennepin Health, 455
Rowe, Ron Blue Cross Blue Shield of Kansas City, 476
Rozmiarek, Drew Health Plans, Inc., 406
Rubin, Jonathan N. Magellan Health, 37
Ruchman, Mark, MD Versant Health, 396
Ruchman, Mark, MD Davis Vision, 566
Ruecker, Lukas EyeMed Vision Care, 622
Ruecker, Rita Western Health Advantage, 148
Ruehl Nachreiner, Jennifer Aetna Better Health of Kentucky, 349
Ruel, Melanie Florida Health Care Plan, Inc., 207
Rumbeck, Bret Blue Cross of Idaho Health Service, Inc., 258
Ruplinger, Randy Dean Health Plan, 861
Russell, Jeff Delta Dental of Iowa, 319
Russo, Marc Molina Healthcare, 121
Ruszczyk, Mark Regence BlueShield of Idaho, 263
Rutherford, Beth United Concordia of Florida, 226
Rutherford, Beth United Concordia of Georgia, 246
Rutherford, Beth United Concordia of Maryland, 393
Rutherford, Beth United Concordia of Michigan, 443
Rutherford, Beth United Concordia of New Mexico, 554
Rutherford, Beth United Concordia of New York, 591
Rutherford, Beth United Concordia of North Carolina, 605
Rutherford, Beth United Concordia of Oregon, 668
Rutherford, Beth United Concordia Dental, 695
Rutherford, Beth United Concordia of Pennsylvania, 696
Rutherford, Beth United Concordia of Texas, 790
Rutherford, Beth United Concordia of Virginia, 827
Rutherford, Beth United Concordia of Washington, 843
Rutherford, Debbie Preferred Therapy Providers, 43
Ruthven, Les, PhD Preferred Mental Health Management, 343
Ryan, Cindy Cigna Corporation, 174
Ryan, John P. Ambetter from Arkansas Health & Wellness, 50
Ryan, John P. Arkansas Health & Wellness, 52
Ryan, John P. Arkansas Total Care, 53
Ryan, Kathy Arkansas Blue Cross Blue Shield, 51
Ryu, Jaewon, MD Geisinger Health Plan, 681
Rzepski, Tim Highmark BCBS Delaware, 184

S

Sade, Nikki ProviDRs Care Network, 345
Sadtler, John SIHO Insurance Services, 314
Salazar, Deanna Blue Cross & Blue Shield of Arizona, 26
Salzwedel, Jack American Family Insurance, 856
Samuels, Michele A. Blue Cross Blue Shield of Michigan, 419
Sanchez Sierra, Manuel MMM Holdings, 708
Sand, David, MD Care N' Care, 764
Sanders, Henry Group Health Cooperative of South Central Wisconsin, 866
Sanders, Mark Superior HealthPlan, 787
Santangelo, Andreana Blue Cross & Blue Shield of Massachusetts, 401
Santos, Daniel UCare, 460
Sarkari, Charag Liberty Dental Plan of California, 116
Sarrel, Lloyd Trustmark, 289
Savage, Jeanne, MD Health Net Health Plan of Oregon, 656
Savage, Jeanne, MD Trillium Community Health Plan, 667
Scepanski, Theresa Community First Health Plans, 768
Schandel, David C. Florida Health Care Plan, Inc., 207
Schechtman, Jay, MD Healthfirst, 577
Scherler, Jay Buckeye Health Plan, 618
Schiffman, Debbie Quartz Health Plan, 874
Schlosser, Mario Oscar Health, 588
Schmaltz, April Delta Dental of Iowa, 319
Schmidt, Christopher Healthplex, 454
Schmidt, Loretta Trinity Health of Indiana, 315
Schmitt, Pat UCare, 460
Schmitz, James Care Plus Dental Plans, 859
Schneider, Jennifer, CPA Trinity Health of New England, 180
Schneiderman, Dawn Blue Cross & Blue Shield of Vermont, 811
Scholtz, Stacy Mutual of Omaha Dental Insurance, 504
Schrader, Michael Health Plan of San Joaquin, 104
Schreiber, Larry AvMed, 197
Schrupp, Alison Providence Health Plan, 663
Schubach, Aaron Opticare of Utah, 803
Schultz, Jason Trinity Health of Indiana, 315

423

Schumacher, Dan UnitedHealth Group, 461
Schutzen, Ron HealthSun, 213
Schwab, Jeff Dominion Dental Services, 819
Schwartz, Talya, MD MetroPlus Health Plan, 584
Schwarzwald, Heidi, MD Aetna Better Health of Texas, 753
Schwarzwalder, Kathleen Humana Health Insurance of North Carolina, 603
Scott, Hope Blue Shield of California, 69
Scott, Kirby Delta Dental of South Dakota, 737
Sears, Michelle Neighborhood Health Plan of Rhode Island, 715
Sehring, Bob OSF Healthcare, 286
Seidman, Richard L.A. Care Health Plan, 113
Sellner, Jessica Health Net, Inc., 103
Semith, Joseph P. Health Net Federal Services (HNFS), 101
Seunarine, Jai Jai Medical Systems, 387
Shafer, Cheryl, MD Molina Healthcare of Texas, 780
Shah, Amit, MD CareOregon Health Plan, 653
Shah, Rupesh Freedom Health, 208
Shah, Sanjiv S., MD MetroPlus Health Plan, 584
Shamash, Todd A. Capital BlueCross, 677
Shames, Cary, M.D. Sharp Health Plan, 135
Shanahan, Carolyn Delta Dental of Illinois, 276
Shanahan-Richards, Wendy Aetna Student Health Agency Inc., 171
Shannon, Lee Blue Cross & Blue Shield of Wyoming, 881
Sharbatz, Kim DenteMax, 423
Sharff, Samantha Able Insurance Agency, 520
Sharma, Akhil DentaQuest, 402
Sharma, Akhil EyeQuest, 864
Sharma, Vibhu Mutual of Omaha Dental Insurance, 504
Shearer, Gary Physicians Health Plan of Northern Indiana, 311
Shellard, Edward, DMD United Concordia of Arizona, 47
Shepard, Kim Cigna HealthCare of Arizona, 29
Sherman, Michael, MD Harvard Pilgrim Health Care Massachusetts, 404
Sherman, Michael, MD Tufts Health Medicare Plan, 410
Sherman, Michael Tufts Health Plan, 411
Sherman, Michael, MD Tufts Health Plan: Rhode Island, 716
Sherman, Paul, MD Community Health Plan of Washington, 834
Sherry, Wendy Cigna HealthCare of Connecticut, 175
Shiba, David, MD Stanislaus Foundation for Medical Care, 136
Shinto, Richard, M.D. InnovaCare Health, 706
Shinto, Richard MMM Holdings, 708
Shipley, Christine AvMed, 197
Shipley, Pamela Kaiser Permanente Georgia, 241
Showalter, Kathryn MedCost, 604
Shrank, William H. CompBenefits Corporation, 238
Shrank, William H., MD Humana Inc., 355
Shrouds, Rick, MD Molina Healthcare of South Carolina, 731
Shumaker, L. Don Superior Dental Care, 635
Sideris, Wendy Careington Solutions, 765
Siemen, Kyle Delta Dental of Idaho, 259
Sigel, Deena Care1st Health Plan Arizona, 27
Silverman, Wayne, DDS Dominion Dental Services, 819
Sim, Kenneth T., MD Allied Pacific IPA, 66
Simley, John Blue Cross & Blue Shield of Illinois, 270
Simonson, Kelly UnitedHealthcare Community Plan Nevada, 518

Simpson, Douglas R. Horizon Blue Cross Blue Shield of New Jersey, 537
Simpson, Elizabeth Trinity Health of Maryland, 392
Simpson, Vicki Health Plan of San Mateo, 105
Sinclair, Kim Medical Center Healthnet Plan, 407
Singh, Gagandeep, MD Mercy Care Plan/Mercy Care Advantage, 39
Sisco, Christopher American Dental Group, 151
Sisco, Tiffany American Dental Group, 151
Sisk, Aaron Magnolia Health, 468
Skiermont, Darla Fidelis Care, 574
Skourtes, Dr. Eugene, DMD Willamette Dental Group, 671
Slack, John Bright Now! Dental, 74
Slawin, Kevin Trustmark Companies, 290
Slovenski, Sean Avesis: Arizona, 23
Slubowski, Michael A. Trinity Health of Alabama, 9
Slubowski, Michael A. Trinity Health of California, 138
Slubowski, Michael A. Trinity Health of Delaware, 186
Slubowski, Michael A. Trinity Health of Georgia, 245
Slubowski, Michael A. Trinity Health, 440
Smedsrud, Jeff Pivot Health, 42
Smiley, Bruce Encore Health Network, 304
Smith, Barry M. Magellan Health, 37
Smith, Bethany R. CDPHP: Capital District Physicians' Health Plan, 565
Smith, Brian Mercy Health Network, 324
Smith, Carey Blue Cross & Blue Shield of Minnesota, 450
Smith, Carrie Providence Health Plan, 663
Smith, Cathy Bright Health Alabama, 5
Smith, Cathy Bright Health Colorado, 155
Smith, Clare Trustmark, 289
Smith, Daniel B. Samaritan Health Plan Operations, 666
Smith, Doug Preferred Health Care, 691
Smith, Jenny CareFirst BlueCross BlueShield, 385
Smith, Jonalan Sunflower Health Plan, 346
Smith, Kelly MVP Health Care, 586
Smith, Kenneth E., M.D. Inter Valley Health Plan, 108
Smith, Marcia Trinity Health of Iowa, 326
Smith, Maureen Health Care Service Corporation (HCSC), 281
Smith, Maurice HCSC Insurance Services Company, 278
Smith, Nakia Care N' Care, 764
Smith, Tameeka UnitedHealthcare Community Plan Virginia, 828
Smith, Troy Health Choice Arizona, 33
Smith, Will One Call Care Management, 220
Smitherman, Steve CareSource Indiana, 301
Smoter, Jennifer UnitedHealth Group, 461
Snyder, Andrew, MD Evolent Health, 821
Snyder, John J., DMD Kaiser Permanente Northwest, 657
Sock, Shannon Mercy Clinic Missouri, 490
Sodaro, Kenneth J., Esq. BlueShield of Northeastern New York, 562
Sohn, Steve Liberty Dental Plan of New York, 581
Solomon, David A., DDS Northeast Delta Dental Vermont, 812
Solsky, Lisabritt Well Sense Health Plan, 528
Sonalkar, Sameer Blue Cross of Idaho Health Service, Inc., 258
Sonerholm, Kim UnitedHealthcare of Indiana, 317
Sonerholm, Kim UnitedHealthcare of Kentucky, 360
Sonnenshine, Stephanie Central California Alliance for Health, 81

Sortino, Michael J. InnovaCare Health, 706
Sotunde, Tunde Blue Cross Blue Shield of North Carolina, 597
Soyke, Steve Delta Dental of Illinois, 276
Sparks, Kevin UnitedHealthcare Community Plan Kansas, 347
Spencer, Jennifer HealthSCOPE Benefits, 56
Spencer, Jeremy Total Dental Administrators, 45, 807
Spinale, Joseph W. Trinity Health of New York, 590
Spinner, Mark Access One Consumer Health, Inc., 721
Sprague, Heather Trinity Health of Idaho, 264
Springfield, James HCSC Insurance Services Company Texas, 773
Springfield, James G., MD Blue Cross & Blue Shield of Texas, 762
St. Hilaire, Gary D. Horizon Blue Cross Blue Shield of New Jersey, 537
Stafford, Jeff UnitedHealthcare Community Plan Nebraska, 506
Stann, Kenneth SVS Vision, 438
Stann, Lisa SVS Vision, 438
Staples, Brian K. CareSource Kentucky, 352
Staples, David B. Northeast Delta Dental, 526
Starcher, John M., Jr. Mercy Health Network, 324
Starnes, Paula, MHA Aetna Better Health of Virginia, 814
Stearns, Heather Liberty Dental Plan of Florida, 216
Steffen, Mark, MD, MPH Blue Cross & Blue Shield of Minnesota, 450
Steiner, Robert, MD Security Health Plan of Wisconsin, 875
Stell, Cathy Preferred Therapy Providers, 43
Stephens, Deborah L. Behavioral Health Systems, 3
Stephens, Michael Sunflower Health Plan, 346
Stephenson, Jack Molina Healthcare of New York, 585
Stevens, James C. Physicians Health Plan of Northern Indiana, 311
Stewart, Mark Blue Cross & Blue Shield of Rhode Island, 713
Stodard, Randy Delta Dental of New Jersey, 536
Stone, Lydia Evolent Health, 821
Story, Ron Delta Dental of Kentucky, 354
Strand, Ute UnitedHealthcare Community Plan Tennessee, 751
Strange, Kyle Behavioral Health Systems, 3
Stuart, Dave Highmark BCBS Delaware, 184
Stuart, Randall L. AvMed, 197
Stucky, Erin Blue Cross Blue Shield of Kansas City, 476
Stuhr, Julie Amerigroup Iowa, 318
Suda, George Bright Now! Dental, 74
Sullivan, Brian Humana Health Insurance of Arizona, 35
Sullivan, Brian Humana Health Insurance of California, 107
Sullivan, Brian Humana Health Insurance of Colorado, 161
Sullivan, Erika HealthNetwork, 212
Sullivan, Joe Louisiana Healthcare Connections, 366
Sully, Nicole, DO Valley Preferred, 702
Surdock, Christine Molina Healthcare of Michigan, 433
Sutton, Dean Dean Health Plan, 861
Swartz, Kelly Fdn. for Medical Care of Kern & Santa Barbara Counties, 96
Swayze, Jim Regence BlueCross BlueShield of Utah, 665
Sweat, Greg, MD Blue Cross Blue Shield of Kansas City, 476
Sweda, Stewart Careington Solutions, 765
Sweeney, G.T. Healthfirst, 577
Sweet, Jennifer A. Aetna Better Health of Florida, 194
Swift, Richard Health New England, 405
Swift, Stephen T. BlueCross BlueShield of Western New York, 561
Swift, Stephen T. BlueShield of Northeastern New York, 562
Szczypka, Michele Trinity Health of Michigan, 441

T

Talalai, Jim Concentra, 769
Tallent, John Medical Associates, 323
Tam, John, MD Evolent Health, 821
Tanner, Bob Group Health Cooperative of Eau Claire, 865
Tasinga, Dr. Martha E. Kern Family Health Care, 112
Taylor, Curtis First Choice Health, 838
Taylor, Jennifer Taylor Benefits Insurance Agency, 137
Taylor, Michael CareSource Kentucky, 352
Taylor, Michael CareSource West Virginia, 353
Taylor, Todd Taylor Benefits Insurance Agency, 137
Temple, Carolyn California Foundation for Medical Care, 76
Temple, Carolyn J. Fdn. for Medical Care of Kern & Santa Barbara Counties, 96
Tenorio, Susan Inter Valley Health Plan, 108
Ternan, Brian Health Net of California, 102
Ternan, Brian Health Net, Inc., 103
Terry, Brooke Trustmark, 289
Tetreault, Michelle Health Plan of San Joaquin, 104
Tetzlaff, Gene Delta Dental of South Dakota, 737
Thadani, Praveen Priority Health, 436
Thadani, Praveen PriorityHealth Medicare Plans, 437
Thiltgen, Heather Medical Center Healthnet Plan, 407
Thomas, Cory Horizon Health Corporation, 775
Thomas, David Fidelis Care, 574
Thomas, LaMonte Aetna Health of Oklahoma, 640
Thomas, Marshall, MD Colorado Access, 157
Thompson, Brian AHCCCS/Medicaid, 18
Thompson, Brian UnitedHealth Group, 461
Thompson, Courtnay Select Health of South Carolina, 732
Thompson, J. Jude Delta Dental of Kentucky, 354
Thompson, Kurt B. Oxford Health Plans, 179
Thompson, Patti Alliance Regional Health Network, 754
Thomson, Sharon PacificSource Health Plans, 661
Tiano, Linda Healthfirst, 577
Titcombe, Dominic Delta Dental of Delaware, 183
Titcombe, Dominic Delta Dental of the District of Columbia, 190
Titcombe, Dominic Delta Dental of New York, 567
Titcombe, Dominic Delta Dental of Pennsylvania, 678
Titcombe, Dominic Delta Dental of West Virginia, 847
Todoroff, Christopher M. CompBenefits Corporation, 238
Todt, Blair Anthem, Inc., 299
Tomayo, Jonathan Santa Clara Family Health Foundations Inc, 132
Tomcala, Christine M. Santa Clara Family Health Foundations Inc, 132
Tongsiri, Amy Liberty Dental Plan of Nevada, 514
Tonn, Samantha Prevea Health Network, 873
Torres Olivera, Luis A. Humana Health Insurance of Puerto Rico, 705
Torrez, Janice Blue Cross & Blue Shield of New Mexico, 547
Torrez, Janice HCSC Insurance Services Company New Mexico, 549
Towner, Chad W. Trinity Health of Indiana, 315
Townsend, Julie A. TriWest Healthcare Alliance, 46
Townsend, Tracy UnitedHealthcare of New Mexico, 556

Trachta, Mike Trinity Health of Iowa, 326
Trapp, Rebecca MDwise, 308
Traynor, Mark UCare, 460
Treash, Mike Health Alliance Plan, 428
Tringale, Steven Allways Health Partners, 398
Triplett, Mike Cigna Corporation, 174
Trujillo-Ottino, JoLou Delta Dental of New Mexico, 548
Tsai, Sanggil CareSource Kentucky, 352
Tsang, Patrick VIVA Health, 11
Turner, Christine K. Santa Clara Family Health Foundations Inc, 132
Turner, Lori Blue Cross & Blue Shield of Arizona, 26
Tushie-Lessard, Clarise Delta Dental of Minnesota, 451
Tushie-Lessard, Clarise Delta Dental of Nebraska, 499
Tuttle, Molly Health Net Federal Services (HNFS), 101
Tuttle, Molly Health Net, Inc., 103
Tuttle, Patrick Delta Dental of Kansas, 338
Twining, Donna Group Health Cooperative of South Central Wisconsin, 866

U

Udvarhelyi, I. Steven Blue Cross and Blue Shield of Louisiana, 363
Underriner, David Hawaii Medical Service Association, 252
Upright, Michael Delta Dental of Wisconsin, 862
Urbano, Frank L. AmeriHealth New Jersey, 532
Uribe, John Blue Cross & Blue Shield of Minnesota, 450
Usman, Mike Value Behavioral Health of Pennsylvania, 703

V

Vachon, Jennifer BlueCross BlueShield Association, 271
Vaden, Dean Devon Health Services, 679
Vail, Cheron Health Plan of San Joaquin, 104
Valdez, Sharon Santa Clara Family Health Foundations Inc, 132
Valencia, Devon CareSource Ohio, 620
Valley, Paul BlueCross BlueShield of Western New York, 561
Valley, Paul BlueShield of Northeastern New York, 562
Van Ham, Colleen United Healthcare Dental, 808
Van Rossum, Tricia Magellan Complete Care of Virginia, 823
Vanwagner, Amanda Parkview Total Health, 310
Vaughn, Roy Blue Cross & Blue Shield of Tennessee, 745
Vaught, Greta Midlands Choice, 502
Vela, Manny Valley Baptist Health Plan, 795
Velasquez, Jennifer Leon Medical Centers Health Plan, 215
Velez, Jennifer Horizon Blue Cross Blue Shield of New Jersey, 537
Venable, Erin Essence Healthcare, 483
Vennari, Joe CareSource Kentucky, 352
Vennera, Michael R. Independence Blue Cross, 687
Ventura, Joseph Humana Inc., 355
Verrastro, George Envolve Vision, 601
Vickery, Peggy Select Health of South Carolina, 732
Vienne, Richard P. Univera Healthcare, 594
Vieth, George W., Jr Landmark Healthplan of California, 115
Vincent, Shawn Trinity Health of Illinois, 288
Vines, Tim Blue Cross and Blue Shield of Alabama, 4
Visser, Dirk Allegiance Life & Health Insurance Company, 463
Vivaldi, Carlos MMM Holdings, 708

Vochis, Greg Delta Dental of Colorado, 158
Vojicic, Stephanie Anthem Blue Cross & Blue Shield of Missouri, 475
Volk, Lou, III Delta Dental of New Mexico, 548
Voyles, Stevyn PTPN, 130

W

Wagner, John J. Aetna Health of Alaska, 12
Wagner, John J. Aetna Health of Idaho, 257
Wagner, John J. Aetna Health of Oregon, 650
Wagner, John J. Aetna Health of Washington, 830
Wagner, Melissa DenteMax, 423
Waldron, Neil Rocky Mountain Health Plans, 165
Walker, Jennifer A. Hawaii Medical Service Association, 252
Wallace, Courtney Premera Blue Cross Blue Shield of Alaska, 14
Walleshauser, James Nova Healthcare Administrators, 587
Walsh, Andrea HealthPartners, 453
Walsh, James HCSC Insurance Services Company, 278
Walsh, James Health Care Service Corporation (HCSC), 281
Walsh, Tim Allways Health Partners, 398
Walter, Dawn Essence Healthcare, 483
Walters, Laurel Rocky Mountain Health Plans, 165
Wang, Pat Healthfirst, 577
Ward, Dave Blue Cross of Idaho Health Service, Inc., 258
Warner, Syd Aetna Health of Kansas, 331
Warsop, Thomas One Call Care Management, 220
Wasden, Mitch Iowa Total Care, 322
Washington, Bonnie Aetna Health of District of Columbia, 188
Wathen, Cheryl Deaconess Health Plans, 303
Watson, Chris One Call Care Management, 220
Watts, Brian California Dental Network, 75
Waulters, Scott UnitedHealthcare Community Plan Ohio, 638
Wayland, Charles UnitedHealthcare Community Plan New Jersey, 543
Weatherford, Mike University HealthCare Alliance, 143
Weaver, Lois J. Vale-U-Health, 701
Weber, Alicia Delta Dental of Delaware, 183
Weber, Alicia Delta Dental of the District of Columbia, 190
Weber, Alicia Delta Dental of New York, 567
Weber, Alicia Delta Dental of Pennsylvania, 678
Weber, Alicia Delta Dental of West Virginia, 847
Weber, Alissa UnitedHealthcare of Iowa, 328
Wee, Kathlyn UnitedHealthcare Community Plan District of Columbia, 192
Wee, Kathlyn UnitedHealthcare Community Plan Maryland, 394
Weeks, Anne Liberty Dental Plan of New York, 581
Wegner, Mike Trinity Health of Iowa, 326
Weider, Drigan, MD Boulder Valley Individual Practice Association, 154
Weinberg, Jonathan Evolent Health, 821
Weinberg, Meryl MetroPlus Health Plan, 584
Weinper, Michael PTPN, 130
Weinstein, Ellen Medical Center Healthnet Plan, 407
Weis, Brian, MD Alliance Regional Health Network, 754
Weiss, Susan Liberty Dental Plan of New York, 581
Welch, Jonathan, MD Medical Center Healthnet Plan, 407
Welch, Jonathan, MD Well Sense Health Plan, 528
Welch, Peter Cigna HealthCare of California, 85

Wells, Michael Blue Cross & Blue Shield of Wyoming, 881
Wendling, Mark, MD Valley Preferred, 702
Wendorff, Daniel Trinity Health of Ohio, 637
Wenk, Philip A. Delta Dental of Tennessee, 747
Werner, Chad Blue Cross & Blue Shield of Nebraska, 498
Westermeier, Stephanie Trinity Health of Idaho, 264
Wethington, Kennan Anthem Blue Cross & Blue Shield of Kentucky, 351
Wheatley, Alan Humana Medicare, 356
Wheeler, Jeffrey MDwise, 308
Wheeler, Philip Mercy Clinic Missouri, 490
White, Clyde NH Healthy Families, 525
White, Kim Blue Cross Blue Shield of Kansas City, 476
White, Michael Providence Health Plan, 663
White, Robert American Specialty Health, 297
White, Sherri CommunityCare, 643
White, Todd Aetna Better Health of West Virginia, 846
Whited, Amy Kaiser Permanente Northern Colorado, 162
Whitmore, Bill Harvard Pilgrim Health Care Maine, 376
Wilbourn, Tracey Humana Health Insurance of Minnesota, 456
Wilkinson, Scott LifeMap, 658
Williams, Amy Michigan Complete Health, 432
Williams, Frank Evolent Health, 821
Williams, Katie Delta Dental of North Carolina, 600
Williams, Lynne Delta Dental of Illinois, 276
Williams, Nessa Jai Medical Systems, 387
Williams-Brinkley, Ruth E. Kaiser Permanente Mid-Atlantic, 388
Wilson, Bill, CPA Managed Health Services, 307
Wilson, Charles Atrio Health Plans, 652
Wilson, Dennis G. Delta Dental of New Jersey, 536
Wilson, Dora Molina Healthcare of South Carolina, 731
Wilson, Jered Paramount Care of Michigan, 434
Wilson, Jered Paramount Elite Medicare Plan, 630
Wilson, Jered Paramount Health Care, 631
Wilson, Steve UnitedHealthcare of Arkansas, 60
Wilson, Steve UnitedHealthcare of Tennessee, 752
Wilson, Jr., Stephen L. UnitedHealthcare of Louisiana, 370
Wilson, Jr., Stephen L. UnitedHealthcare of Mississippi, 471
Windfeldt, Ty Hometown Health Plan, 512
Wingerter, Arthur G. Univera Healthcare, 594
Winograd, Katharine Presbyterian Medicare Advantage Plans, 553
Winter, Scott Arkansas Blue Cross Blue Shield, 51
Winton, Dakasha Blue Cross & Blue Shield of Tennessee, 745
Wise, Greg, MD MediGold, 626
Wissing, Deborah Dentcare Delivery Systems, 568
Wittenstein, Robin D. Denver Health Medical Plan, 159
Witty, Andrew UnitedHealth Group, 461
Witwer, Mike Dearborn National, 275
Wofford, Martha Blue Cross & Blue Shield of Rhode Island, 713
Woleslagle, Jodi Capital BlueCross, 677
Wolf, Matt Molina Healthcare of Illinois, 285
Wolgemuth, Sherry Preferred Health Care, 691

Wolowitz, Jill HCSC Insurance Services Company, 278
Wolowitz, Jill Health Care Service Corporation (HCSC), 281
Wonderlich, Brian Blue Cross of Idaho Health Service, Inc., 258
Wong, Van, CHIE Central California Alliance for Health, 81
Wong, Van San Francisco Health Plan, 131
Wood, Oscar Frank Liberty Dental Plan of Texas, 778
Woodruff, Matthew Alameda Alliance for Health, 62
Woodruff, Matthew Alameda Medi-Cal Plan, 64
Woods, Anthony Amerigroup Washington, 832
Woodward, T. Ralph Capital BlueCross, 677
Worcester, Ghita UCare, 460
Worman, Douglas M. CNA, 274
Wortham, George, MD Health Choice LLC, 749
Wortham, Tammi Sun Life Financial, 409
Worthington, Scott Passport Health Plan, 357
Woys, James Molina Healthcare, 121
Wright, Daniel J. United Concordia of Arizona, 47
Wright, Landon Vantage Health Plan, 371
Wright, Landon Vantage Medicare Advantage, 372
Wright, Larissa Fdn. for Medical Care of Kern & Santa Barbara Counties, 96
Wynne, Steve Moda Health Oregon, 660

Y

Yang, John, MD Kaiser Permanente Hawaii, 254
Yao, Amy Blue Shield of California, 69
Yao, Dorcas C., MD Health Plan of San Joaquin, 104
Yong, Eben Health Plan of San Mateo, 105
Young, Robin Blue Cross & Blue Shield of Tennessee, 745
Young, Rodney Delta Dental of Minnesota, 451
Young, Rodney Delta Dental of Nebraska, 499
Yung, Derek eHealthInsurance Services, Inc., 95

Z

Zaffiris, Nick UnitedHealthcare of Florida, 228
Zaffiris, Nick UnitedHealthcare of South Florida, 229
Zastrow, Raymond, MD Molina Healthcare of Wisconsin, 871
Zeccardi, Robert One Call Care Management, 220
Zech, Marc HealthSmart, 774
Zelkowitz, Kristin Trustmark Companies, 290
Zentz, Jesse Blue Cross & Blue Shield of Montana, 493
Zerega, Joseph M Preferred Network Access, 287
Zhang, Jian Chinese Community Health Plan, 83
Ziegler, Steven M. AvMed, 197
Zikeli, Ryan Humana Health Insurance of Wisconsin, 868
Zimmerli, Bert Intermountain Healthcare, 801
Zimmerman, Deborah, MD Essence Healthcare, 483
Zonfa, Charles A., MD SummaCare Medicare Advantage Plan, 634
Zubretsky, Joseph Molina Healthcare, 121
Zuckerman, Joseph, MD Florida Health Care Plan, Inc., 207
Zuvon Nenni, Angie Delta Dental of Kentucky, 354

Membership Enrollment Index

107,000,000	BlueCross BlueShield Association, 271	8,800,000	United Concordia of Oregon, 668
88,000,000	VSP Vision Care, 146	8,800,000	United Concordia of Pennsylvania, 696
79,000,000	Anthem, Inc., 299	8,800,000	United Concordia of Texas, 790
75,000,000	Delta Dental of Idaho, 259	8,800,000	United Concordia of Virginia, 827
70,000,000	CVS Caremark, 714	8,800,000	United Concordia of Washington, 843
70,000,000	UnitedHealth Group, 461	8,500,000	Health Net Federal Services (HNFS), 101
68,000,000	Delta Dental of Virginia, 818	8,000,000	Blue Cross & Blue Shield of Illinois, 270
60,000,000	Delta Dental of South Dakota, 737	8,000,000	Independence Blue Cross, 687
55,000,000	Davis Vision, 566	7,900,000	Amerigroup, 815
46,500,000	Aetna Inc., 170	7,300,000	Managed Health Network, Inc., 117
43,000,000	EyeMed Vision Care, 622	6,600,000	Dental Benefit Providers: California, 92
30,000,000	Trinity Health, 440	6,300,000	WellCare Health Plans, Inc., 230
30,000,000	Trinity Health of Alabama, 9	6,200,000	Dental Network of America, 277
30,000,000	Trinity Health of California, 138	6,100,000	Blue Cross Blue Shield of Michigan, 419
30,000,000	Trinity Health of Delaware, 186	6,100,000	Health Net, Inc., 103
30,000,000	Trinity Health of Florida, 225	6,000,000	Blue Cross & Blue Shield of Texas, 762
30,000,000	Trinity Health of Georgia, 245	5,700,000	HCSC Insurance Services Company Texas, 773
30,000,000	Trinity Health of Idaho, 264	5,427,579	USA Managed Care Organization, 793
30,000,000	Trinity Health of Illinois, 288	5,300,000	Highmark BCBS West Virginia, 848
30,000,000	Trinity Health of Indiana, 315	5,300,000	Highmark Blue Shield, 685
30,000,000	Trinity Health of Maryland, 392	5,000,000	American National Insurance Company, 757
30,000,000	Trinity Health of Michigan, 441	5,000,000	PCC Preferred Chiropractic Care, 342
30,000,000	Trinity Health of New England, 180	5,000,000	eHealthInsurance Services, Inc., 95
30,000,000	Trinity Health of New Jersey, 542	4,608,507	Kaiser Permanente Southern California, 111
30,000,000	Trinity Health of New York, 590	4,500,000	DenteMax, 423
30,000,000	Trinity Health of Ohio, 637	4,383,328	Kaiser Permanente Northern California, 110
30,000,000	Trinity Health of Pennsylvania, 694	4,380,000	Blue Shield of California, 69
27,000,000	DentaQuest, 402	3,810,000	Blue Cross Blue Shield of North Carolina, 597
26,000,000	CareCentrix: Kansas, 337	3,500,000	Avesis: Arizona, 23
25,900,000	American Specialty Health, 297	3,500,000	Avesis: Maryland, 384
24,000,000	Dominion Dental Services, 819	3,500,000	Avesis: Massachusetts, 400
22,000,000	Value Behavioral Health of Pennsylvania, 703	3,500,000	Avesis: Minnesota, 449
19,000,000	Cigna Corporation, 174	3,500,000	Avesis: Texas, 761
16,000,000	Health Care Service Corporation (HCSC), 281	3,500,000	Blue Cross & Blue Shield of Tennessee, 745
15,000,000	Centene Corporation, 477	3,500,000	Galaxy Health Network, 772
14,200,000	Delta Dental of Michigan, 421	3,500,000	Healthplex, 454
13,100,000	Renaissance Dental, 312	3,500,000	Horizon Blue Cross Blue Shield of New Jersey, 537
12,500,000	Spectera Eyecare Networks, 390	3,400,000	Molina Healthcare, 121
12,400,000	Kaiser Permanente, 109	3,300,000	CareFirst Blue Cross & Blue Shield of Virginia, 817
10,000,000	Humana Inc., 355	3,300,000	CareFirst BlueCross BlueShield, 385
8,800,000	United Concordia Dental, 695	3,000,000	Dearborn National, 275
8,800,000	United Concordia of Arizona, 47	3,000,000	Harvard Pilgrim Health Care Maine, 376
8,800,000	United Concordia of California, 139	3,000,000	Harvard Pilgrim Health Care Massachusetts, 404
8,800,000	United Concordia of Colorado, 166	3,000,000	Harvard Pilgrim Health Care New Hampshire, 523
8,800,000	United Concordia of Florida, 226	3,000,000	Liberty Dental Plan of California, 116
8,800,000	United Concordia of Georgia, 246	3,000,000	Liberty Dental Plan of Missouri, 488
8,800,000	United Concordia of Maryland, 393	3,000,000	Liberty Dental Plan of New Jersey, 540
8,800,000	United Concordia of Michigan, 443	2,900,000	Blue Cross & Blue Shield of Massachusetts, 401
8,800,000	United Concordia of New Mexico, 554	2,800,000	Anthem Blue Cross & Blue Shield of Virginia, 816
8,800,000	United Concordia of New York, 591	2,700,000	Blue Cross & Blue Shield of Minnesota, 450
8,800,000	United Concordia of North Carolina, 605	2,400,000	Regence BlueCross BlueShield of Oregon, 664

2,400,000	Regence BlueCross BlueShield of Utah, 665	650,000	Health Alliance Plan, 428
2,400,000	Regence BlueShield of Idaho, 263	650,000	HealthSCOPE Benefits, 56
2,200,000	LifeWise, 841	636,904	Kaiser Permanente Northern Colorado, 162
2,000,000	Delta Dental of Arkansas, 54	636,904	Kaiser Permanente Southern Colorado, 163
2,000,000	Delta Dental of Illinois, 276	625,000	Fidelis Care, 574
2,000,000	First Health, 97	620,848	Kaiser Permanente Northwest, 657
2,000,000	L.A. Care Health Plan, 113	615,000	Midlands Choice, 502
2,000,000	Liberty Dental Plan of Florida, 216	600,000	Blue Cross & Blue Shield of Rhode Island, 713
2,000,000	Liberty Dental Plan of Illinois, 283	600,000	Health Services Los Angeles County, 106
2,000,000	Liberty Dental Plan of Nevada, 514	596,220	Priority Health, 436
2,000,000	MHNet Behavioral Health, 779	563,000	Blue Cross of Idaho Health Service, Inc., 258
1,900,000	CareSource Kentucky, 352	560,000	Partnership HealthPlan of California, 127
1,900,000	CareSource Ohio, 620	560,000	Simply Healthcare Plans, Inc., 223
1,900,000	CareSource West Virginia, 353	555,405	BlueCross BlueShield of Western New York, 561
1,900,000	Delta Dental of South Carolina, 728	551,000	Optima Health Plan, 825
1,800,000	Blue Cross and Blue Shield of Louisiana, 363	550,000	Blue Cross & Blue Shield of New Mexico, 547
1,800,000	Wellmark Blue Cross & Blue Shield of South Dakota, 740	540,000	Geisinger Health Plan, 681
1,700,000	Delta Dental of New Jersey, 536	540,000	Liberty Dental Plan of New York, 581
1,700,000	Dental Health Alliance, 481	518,000	Health Choice LLC, 749
1,500,000	Blue Cross & Blue Shield of Arizona, 26	502,000	Behavioral Health Systems, 3
1,500,000	Excellus BlueCross BlueShield, 573	500,000	Aultcare Corporation, 617
1,500,000	EyeQuest, 864	500,000	CommunityCare, 643
1,500,000	OSF Healthcare, 286	500,000	MetroPlus Health Plan, 584
1,500,000	Univera Healthcare, 594	475,000	Trustmark Companies, 290
1,326,000	MagnaCare, 582	430,000	Allways Health Partners, 398
1,170,000	Tufts Health Plan, 411	423,244	Baptist Health Services Group, 744
1,100,000	Trustmark, 289	418,000	Health Plan of Nevada, 511
1,018,589	Tufts Health Plan: Rhode Island, 716	400,000	CDPHP Medicare Plan, 564
1,000,000	CareSource Indiana, 301	400,000	Preferred Mental Health Management, 343
1,000,000	Delta Dental of Oklahoma, 644	400,000	Presbyterian Health Plan, 552
1,000,000	HealthSmart, 774	390,000	Dental Alternatives Insurance Services, 91
975,000	CHN PPO, 534	390,000	SVS Vision, 438
950,000	Blue Cross & Blue Shield of South Carolina, 725	383,000	Health Alliance Medicare, 427
942,000	American Health Care Alliance, 474	380,000	The Health Plan, 850
936,000	Northeast Delta Dental, 526	370,000	Ohio Health Choice, 628
936,000	Northeast Delta Dental Maine, 378	365,000	Independent Health, 579
930,000	Northeast Delta Dental Vermont, 812	350,000	CDPHP: Capital District Physicians' Health Plan, 565
916,695	Blue Cross and Blue Shield of Kansas, 336	346,000	Central California Alliance for Health, 81
900,000	Anthem Blue Cross & Blue Shield of Indiana, 298	340,000	Quartz Health Plan, 874
900,000	Blue Care Network of Michigan, 417	338,000	Pacific Health Alliance, 126
900,000	QualCare, 541	335,000	Health Plan of San Joaquin, 104
854,000	Horizon NJ Health, 538	330,000	Select Health of South Carolina, 732
830,000	HCSC Insurance Services Company Oklahoma, 645	325,000	Mercy Care Plan/Mercy Care Advantage, 39
800,000	Moda Health Alaska, 13	320,000	Blue Shield of California Promise Health Plan, 71
758,970	CalOptima, 78	316,000	Preferred Network Access, 287
750,552	Kaiser Permanente Mid-Atlantic, 388	312,899	Kaiser Permanente Georgia, 241
750,000	Intermountain Healthcare, 801	300,000	Amerigroup Georgia, 235
750,000	Meridian Health Plan, 431	300,000	Blue Cross & Blue Shield of Montana, 493
750,000	Meridian Health Plan of Illinois, 284	300,000	Boulder Valley Individual Practice Association, 154
717,000	Blue Cross & Blue Shield of Nebraska, 498	300,000	Community Health Plan of Washington, 834
700,000	Blue Cross & Blue Shield of Oklahoma, 642	300,000	Medical Card System (MCS), 707
700,000	MVP Health Care, 586	300,000	Medical Center Healthnet Plan, 407
670,000	MedCost, 604	300,000	Passport Health Plan, 357
650,000	HAP-Health Alliance Plan: Flint, 425	300,000	The Dental Care Plus Group, 636

275,000	PacificSource Health Plans, 661, 662	144,000	Medical Mutual Services, 625
265,000	Affinity Health Plan, 560	140,000	Alameda Alliance for Health, 62
265,000	AmeriHealth New Jersey, 532	140,000	Contra Costa Health Services, 89
265,000	AmeriHealth Pennsylvania, 676	135,000	Capital Health Plan, 200
263,200	Health Partners Plans, 682	130,000	Employers Dental Services, 32
255,494	Health Alliance Medicare, 280	130,000	Golden Dental Plans, 424
252,840	Kaiser Permanente Hawaii, 254	130,000	Health Plan of San Mateo, 105
250,000	Araz Group, 399	130,000	Managed Health Services Wisconsin, 869
250,000	CareOregon Health Plan, 653	128,272	SCAN Health Plan, 134
250,000	Lakeside Community Healthcare Network, 114	126,000	MMM Holdings, 708
250,000	Priority Partners Health Plans, 389	125,000	Managed HealthCare Northwest, 659
247,881	Dean Health Plan, 861	125,000	Premier Access Insurance/Access Dental, 128
245,000	Santa Clara Family Health Foundations Inc, 132	123,880	Western Dental & Orthodontics, 147
236,962	Rocky Mountain Health Plans, 165	121,000	Advance Insurance Company of Kansas, 330
230,000	AvMed, 197	120,000	Horizon Health Corporation, 775
230,000	AvMed Ft. Lauderdale, 198	120,000	Sant, Community Physicians, 133
230,000	AvMed Gainesville, 199	119,712	Prevea Health Network, 873
210,000	Nova Healthcare Administrators, 587	118,600	DakotaCare, 736
205,677	Guardian Life Insurance Company of America, 576	118,000	Network Health Plan of Wisconsin, 872
205,000	American Postal Workers Union (APWU) Health Plan, 382	115,000	Health Choice Arizona, 33
205,000	BlueChoice Health Plan of South Carolina, 726	111,000	CarePlus Health Plans, 202
205,000	Security Health Plan of Wisconsin, 875	110,000	Community First Health Plans, 768
200,000	Care Plus Dental Plans, 859	108,000	Neighborhood Health Partnership, 219
200,000	Health New England, 405	100,000	AmeriHealth Caritas District of Columbia, 189
200,000	Liberty Dental Plan of Texas, 778	100,000	Blue Cross & Blue Shield of Wyoming, 881
200,000	Scott & White Health Plan, 783	100,000	Denver Health Medical Plan, 159
200,000	Wisconsin Physician's Service, 879	97,000	Kern Family Health Care, 112
193,498	BlueShield of Northeastern New York, 562	95,000	Health Partners of Kansas, 339
190,000	Neighborhood Health Plan of Rhode Island, 715	92,000	Western Health Advantage, 148
187,000	Paramount Care of Michigan, 434	90,000	BEST Life and Health Insurance Co., 68
187,000	Paramount Elite Medicare Plan, 630	90,000	Dental Health Services of California, 93
187,000	Paramount Health Care, 631	90,000	Dental Health Services of Washington, 837
180,000	Blue Cross & Blue Shield of Vermont, 811	90,000	Quality Plan Administrators, 191
180,000	First Medical Health Plan, 704	90,000	Total Health Care, 439
177,854	Public Employees Health Program, 805	90,000	VIVA Health, 11
175,000	Arizona Foundation for Medical Care, 22	88,366	MedCost Virginia, 824
175,000	CenCal Health, 80	87,000	First Choice of the Midwest, 738
174,309	Valley Preferred, 702	86,000	University Health Plans, 810
155,070	Health Link PPO, 466	85,000	California Dental Network, 75
154,162	Aetna Health of New York, 559	80,000	Alliance Regional Health Network, 754
152,000	ProviDRs Care Network, 345	80,000	Group Health Cooperative of South Central Wisconsin, 866
150,000	Atlanticare Health Plans, 533	80,000	Peoples Health, 367
150,000	ChiroCare of Wisconsin, 860	80,000	UniCare West Virginia, 851
150,000	Landmark Healthplan of California, 115	71,000	Asuris Northwest Health, 833
150,000	Medica, 457	70,000	AlohaCare, 249
150,000	Medica: Nebraska, 501	70,000	Group Health Cooperative of Eau Claire, 865
150,000	Medica: North Dakota, 609	70,000	Martin's Point HealthCare, 377
150,000	Nevada Preferred Healthcare Providers, 515	68,942	Physicians Health Plan of Mid-Michigan, 435
150,000	Opticare of Utah, 803	68,000	Secure Health PPO Newtork, 244
150,000	UPMC Health Plan, 699	66,000	North Alabama Managed Care Inc, 8
148,000	Altius Health Plans, 797	63,000	Avera Health Plans, 735
147,000	UCare, 460	60,000	Essence Healthcare, 483
146,000	Community Health Group, 87	55,000	MediGold, 626
145,000	San Francisco Health Plan, 131	55,000	Vantage Health Plan, 371

Membership Enrollment Index

54,418	Mutual of Omaha, 503	**24,176**	Hennepin Health, 455
54,000	AllCare Health, 651	**23,000**	Chinese Community Health Plan, 83
53,000	GHI Medicare Plan, 575	**22,000**	Valley Baptist Health Plan, 795
52,000	Ohio State University Health Plan Inc., 629	**20,000**	Prime Time Health Medicare Plan, 632
50,000	Care1st Health Plan Arizona, 27	**18,900**	Inter Valley Health Plan, 108
50,000	Sanford Health Plan, 325	**17,000**	ConnectCare, 420
49,976	Children's Mercy Pediatric Care Network, 478	**17,000**	Primecare Dental Plan, 129
49,000	Sharp Health Plan, 135	**16,000**	Elderplan, 569
47,000	Upper Peninsula Health Plan, 446	**15,000**	Alliant Health Plans, 232
45,000	Health Choice of Alabama, 6	**15,000**	Seton Healthcare Family, 785
45,000	Medical Associates, 323	**14,000**	HAP-Health Alliance Plan: Senior Medicare Plan, 426
45,000	Preferred Care Partners, 222	**14,000**	Vantage Medicare Advantage, 372
44,000	Sterling Insurance, 786	**13,000**	FirstCarolinaCare, 602
42,000	Leon Medical Centers Health Plan, 215	**12,000**	Medica HealthCare Plans, Inc, 120
42,000	WellCare TexanPlus, 796	**10,000**	Denta-Chek of Maryland, 386
40,000	Crescent Health Solutions, 599	**6,000**	Emi Health, 799
40,000	Health Tradition, 867	**5,000**	Cox Healthplans, 479
33,000	South Central Preferred Health Network, 693	**5,000**	Friday Health Plans, 160
32,000	Hometown Health Plan, 512	**5,000**	Trilogy Health Insurance, 876
30,000	InStil Health, 730	**2,375**	Vale-U-Health, 701
30,000	Piedmont Community Health Plan, 826	**1,000**	On Lok Lifeways, 123
26,000	SummaCare Medicare Advantage Plan, 634	**1,000**	UTMB HealthCare Systems, 794

Primary Care Physician Index

772,292	BEST Life and Health Insurance Co., 68	32,000	Blue Cross Blue Shield of Michigan, 419
664,301	Aetna Inc., 170	30,000	Davis Vision, 566
600,000	American Postal Workers Union (APWU) Health Plan, 382	30,000	Fdn. for Medical Care of Kern & Santa Barbara Counties, 96
600,000	Wellmark Blue Cross & Blue Shield of South Dakota, 740	29,000	California Foundation for Medical Care, 76
500,000	Alliant Health Plans, 232	27,000	Stanislaus Foundation for Medical Care, 136
430,000	USA Managed Care Organization, 793	25,000	Anthem Blue Cross & Blue Shield of Ohio, 616
400,000	Galaxy Health Network, 772	25,000	Avesis: Arizona, 23
273,000	DenteMax, 423	25,000	Avesis: Maryland, 384
258,000	Health Care Service Corporation (HCSC), 281	25,000	Avesis: Massachusetts, 400
246,000	The Dental Care Plus Group, 636	25,000	Avesis: Minnesota, 449
190,736	American Health Care Alliance, 474	25,000	Avesis: Texas, 761
137,600	HCSC Insurance Services Company Texas, 773	25,000	Tufts Health Plan, 411
125,000	Dental Benefit Providers: California, 92	25,000	Tufts Health Plan: Rhode Island, 716
121,815	Guardian Life Insurance Company of America, 576	24,000	Medica: North Dakota, 609
116,000	CHN PPO, 534	24,000	Medical Mutual Services, 625
107,000	First Choice Health, 838	24,000	Spectera Eyecare Networks, 390
104,000	United Concordia Dental, 695	23,300	UPMC Health Plan, 699
104,000	United Concordia of Arizona, 47	23,271	Kaiser Permanente, 109
104,000	United Concordia of California, 139	21,700	HCSC Insurance Services Company Oklahoma, 645
104,000	United Concordia of Colorado, 166	20,266	Blue Cross & Blue Shield of Massachusetts, 401
104,000	United Concordia of Florida, 226	20,000	Envolve Vision, 601
104,000	United Concordia of Georgia, 246	20,000	Midlands Choice, 502
104,000	United Concordia of Maryland, 393	18,900	FirstCare Health Plans, 771
104,000	United Concordia of Michigan, 443	18,843	Presbyterian Health Plan, 552
104,000	United Concordia of New Mexico, 554	18,000	Americas PPO, 448
104,000	United Concordia of New York, 591	18,000	Health Alliance Plan, 428
104,000	United Concordia of North Carolina, 605	17,000	Horizon Health Corporation, 775
104,000	United Concordia of Oregon, 668	16,700	HCSC Insurance Services Company New Mexico, 549
104,000	United Concordia of Pennsylvania, 696	15,000	Optima Health Plan, 825
104,000	United Concordia of Texas, 790	14,500	Wisconsin Physician's Service, 879
104,000	United Concordia of Virginia, 827	14,000	ProviDRs Care Network, 345
104,000	United Concordia of Washington, 843	13,000	North Alabama Managed Care Inc, 8
100,000	Blue Cross & Blue Shield of Rhode Island, 713	12,349	MedCost, 604
92,000	MedCost Virginia, 824	12,000	MetroPlus Health Plan, 584
80,000	Blue Cross & Blue Shield of Texas, 762	12,000	Public Employees Health Program, 805
80,000	Dental Network of America, 277	10,500	Preferred Mental Health Management, 343
80,000	Dentistat, 94	10,000	American PPO, 758
74,000	Dental Health Alliance, 481	10,000	SummaCare Medicare Advantage Plan, 634
71,000	Araz Group, 399	9,500	Central California Alliance for Health, 81
71,000	HealthEZ, 452	9,400	HCSC Insurance Services Company, 278
70,000	MagnaCare, 582	9,000	LifeWise, 841
63,000	Managed Health Network, Inc., 117	9,000	QualCare, 541
60,000	CVS Caremark, 714	8,000	Blue Cross & Blue Shield of Minnesota, 450
60,000	Script Care, Ltd., 784	8,000	CareCentrix, 173
50,000	Pacific Health Alliance, 126	8,000	CareCentrix: Arizona, 28
45,000	Meridian Health Plan, 431	8,000	CareCentrix: Florida, 201
43,000	UCare, 460	8,000	CareCentrix: Kansas, 337
42,000	Fidelis Care, 574	8,000	CareCentrix: New York, 563
38,000	Ohio Health Choice, 628	8,000	Kaiser Permanente Northern California, 110
34,000	Pacific Foundation for Medical Care, 125	7,700	BlueChoice Health Plan of South Carolina, 726
34,000	Preferred Network Access, 287	7,700	Group Health Cooperative of Eau Claire, 865

Primary Care Physician Index

7,600	Kaiser Permanente Southern California, 111		2,490	Blue Cross & Blue Shield of Tennessee, 745
7,500	Trinity Health of Alabama, 9		2,400	ChiroCare of Wisconsin, 860
7,200	Medica: Nebraska, 501		2,300	San Francisco Health Plan, 131
6,560	SCAN Health Plan, 134		2,000	Western Dental & Orthodontics, 147
6,400	Health Partners Plans, 682		1,923	First Health, 97
6,200	Health Choice of Alabama, 6		1,900	Blue Cross & Blue Shield of Montana, 493
6,150	South Central Preferred Health Network, 693		1,900	Crescent Health Solutions, 599
6,100	Blue Care Network of Michigan, 418, 417		1,900	Paramount Care of Michigan, 434
6,000	Central Health Medicare Plan, 82		1,900	Paramount Elite Medicare Plan, 630
5,700	Univera Healthcare, 594		1,900	Paramount Health Care, 631
5,500	CareFirst BlueCross BlueShield, 385		1,900	Preferred Health Care, 691
5,500	Managed Health Services Wisconsin, 869		1,850	Total Health Care, 439
5,133	Delta Dental of Minnesota, 451		1,802	Northeast Delta Dental Vermont, 812
5,000	Bright Health Colorado, 155		1,751	Well Sense Health Plan, 528
5,000	CDPHP: Capital District Physicians' Health Plan, 565		1,750	University Health Plans, 810
5,000	Delta Dental of Michigan, 421		1,700	Delta Dental of Oklahoma, 644
4,700	Dean Health Plan, 861		1,700	Sharp Health Plan, 135
4,516	Arizona Foundation for Medical Care, 22		1,638	Inter Valley Health Plan, 108
4,500	CareFirst Blue Cross & Blue Shield of Virginia, 817		1,631	Blue Cross of Idaho Health Service, Inc., 258
4,483	Nevada Preferred Healthcare Providers, 515		1,611	Blue Cross & Blue Shield of Arizona, 26
4,300	Health New England, 405		1,602	Prevea Health Network, 873
4,000	Alameda Alliance Group Care Plan, 63		1,600	Intermountain Healthcare, 801
4,000	Alameda Alliance for Health, 62		1,551	Blue Cross & Blue Shield of Oklahoma, 642
4,000	Alameda Medi-Cal Plan, 64		1,551	CalOptima, 78
4,000	Baptist Health Services Group, 744		1,500	AllCare Health, 651
4,000	Delta Dental of Kentucky, 354		1,500	Bright Health Alabama, 5
4,000	Prominence Health Plan, 516		1,500	Health Link PPO, 466
4,000	The Health Plan, 850		1,500	Kaiser Permanente Mid-Atlantic, 388
3,800	Altius Health Plans, 797		1,400	Affinity Health Plan, 560
3,700	Trilogy Health Insurance, 876		1,400	EPIC Pharmacy Network, 820
3,600	Trinity Health, 440		1,400	Health Choice LLC, 749
3,532	Anthem Blue Cross & Blue Shield of Indiana, 298		1,400	Highmark BCBS West Virginia, 848
3,500	Aultcare Corporation, 617		1,400	Medica with CHI Health, 500
3,500	Emi Health, 799		1,400	Trinity Health of Idaho, 264
3,500	Geisinger Health Plan, 681		1,340	Employers Dental Services, 32
3,500	PCC Preferred Chiropractic Care, 342		1,282	Neighborhood Health Partnership, 219
3,500	PTPN, 130		1,228	Managed HealthCare Northwest, 659
3,500	UniCare West Virginia, 851		1,200	Elderplan, 569
3,434	Blue Cross & Blue Shield of South Carolina, 725		1,200	Kaiser Permanente Northwest, 657
3,322	Blue Cross & Blue Shield of New Mexico, 547		1,200	Kaiser Permanente Southern Colorado, 163
3,300	Premera Blue Cross Blue Shield of Alaska, 14		1,200	Sant, Community Physicians, 133
3,250	Ohio State University Health Plan Inc., 629		1,125	Independent Health, 579
3,200	Delta Dental of Colorado, 158		1,103	OSF Healthcare, 286
3,200	Golden Dental Plans, 424		1,050	MediGold, 626
3,100	Physicians Health Plan of Mid-Michigan, 435		1,000	Cox Healthplans, 479
3,000	Chinese Community Health Plan, 83		1,000	Dental Health Services of California, 93
3,000	Health Alliance Medicare, 280		1,000	Dental Health Services of Washington, 837
3,000	Medical Center Healthnet Plan, 407		1,000	Health Partners of Kansas, 339
3,000	Parkland Community Health Plan, 782		1,000	Premier Access Insurance/Access Dental, 128, 804
2,855	Healthplex, 454		1,000	Scott & White Health Plan, 783
2,800	Allways Health Partners, 398		980	First Choice Health, 655
2,691	Aetna Health of New York, 559		979	Delta Dental of New Mexico, 548
2,630	Rocky Mountain Health Plans, 165		962	Blue Cross and Blue Shield of Louisiana, 363
2,500	Community Health Plan of Washington, 834		950	CareOregon Health Plan, 653

950	Secure Health PPO Newtork, 244		500	Kaiser Permanente Georgia, 241
917	Preferred Care Partners, 222		490	McLaren Health Plan, 430
912	Medica HealthCare Plans, Inc, 120		488	Community Health Group, 87
908	Quartz Health Plan, 874		400	Kaiser Permanente Northern Colorado, 162
900	HAP-Health Alliance Plan: Flint, 425		361	Penn Highlands Healthcare, 690
900	HAP-Health Alliance Plan: Senior Medicare Plan, 426		300	Bright Now! Dental, 74
900	Neighborhood Health Plan of Rhode Island, 715		300	Denta-Chek of Maryland, 386
855	AlohaCare, 249		300	Lakeside Community Healthcare Network, 114
850	MercyHealth System, 870		275	CenCal Health, 80
837	Trinity Health of New England, 180		270	Pueblo Health Care, 164
825	DakotaCare, 736		257	Trinity Health of Ohio, 637
800	Allied Pacific IPA, 66		256	Hometown Health Plan, 512
800	Health Tradition, 867		213	Kern Family Health Care, 112
778	Valley Preferred, 702		200	American Health Network, 296
750	DentaQuest, 402		200	Children's Mercy Pediatric Care Network, 478
750	Northeast Georgia Health Partners, 242		200	Dencap Dental Plans, 422
742	Santa Clara Family Health Foundations Inc, 132		197	Health Plan of San Mateo, 105
700	Mercy Clinic Arkansas, 58		183	Trinity Health of Pennsylvania, 694
700	Mercy Clinic Kansas, 341		180	Health Plan of San Joaquin, 104
700	Mercy Clinic Missouri, 490		175	Quality Plan Administrators, 191
700	Mercy Clinic Oklahoma, 647		170	Medical Associates, 323
673	Mutual of Omaha, 503		156	Vale-U-Health, 701
600	Atlanticare Health Plans, 533		150	Capital Health Plan, 200
600	Kaiser Permanente Hawaii, 254		149	Dental Source: Dental Health Care Plans, 482
600	Leon Medical Centers Health Plan, 215		132	Health Choice Arizona, 33
600	UPMC Susquehanna, 700		120	GEMCare Health Plan, 98
561	Boulder Valley Individual Practice Association, 154		11	Medical Card System (MCS), 707
550	Alliance Regional Health Network, 754		10	On Lok Lifeways, 123

Referral/Specialty Physician Index

617,000	Priority Health, 436		4,199	BlueChoice Health Plan of South Carolina, 726
285,353	American Health Care Alliance, 474		4,000	Atlanticare Health Plans, 533
193,137	Guardian Life Insurance Company of America, 576		4,000	Health First Health Plans, 209
90,000	ConnectCare, 420		4,000	Health First Medicare Plans, 210
71,000	Americas PPO, 448		4,000	Preferred Mental Health Management, 343
61,728	Anthem Blue Cross & Blue Shield of Ohio, 616		3,870	Optima Health Plan, 825
58,000	MagnaCare, 582		3,800	Elderplan, 569
57,550	CHN PPO, 534		3,600	Ohio Health Choice, 628
53,000	Harvard Pilgrim Health Care Connecticut, 178		3,490	Santa Clara Family Health Foundations Inc, 132
53,000	Harvard Pilgrim Health Care Maine, 376		3,227	Quartz Health Plan, 874
53,000	Harvard Pilgrim Health Care Massachusetts, 404		3,200	Highmark BCBS West Virginia, 848
53,000	Harvard Pilgrim Health Care New Hampshire, 523		3,112	Well Sense Health Plan, 528
47,000	Galaxy Health Network, 772		3,000	CareOregon Health Plan, 653
46,300	PacificSource Health Plans, 661, 662		3,000	Preferred Therapy Providers, 43
27,000	Geisinger Health Plan, 681		2,977	Valley Preferred, 702
23,000	Blue Care Network of Michigan, 417, 418		2,900	Public Employees Health Program, 805
21,295	MedCost, 604		2,800	Blue Cross & Blue Shield of Montana, 493
18,531	Horizon Health Corporation, 775		2,700	Neighborhood Health Plan of Rhode Island, 715
17,186	SCAN Health Plan, 134		2,672	Inter Valley Health Plan, 108
15,068	CareFirst Blue Cross & Blue Shield of Virginia, 817		2,400	Children's Mercy Pediatric Care Network, 478
15,000	Blue Cross & Blue Shield of Tennessee, 745		2,400	Crescent Health Solutions, 599
14,000	Community Health Plan of Washington, 834		2,219	Blue Cross and Blue Shield of Louisiana, 363
14,000	QualCare, 541		2,073	Baptist Health Services Group, 744
13,000	American PPO, 758		2,000	MHNet Behavioral Health, 779
12,500	Tufts Health Plan, 411		2,000	Mercy Clinic Arkansas, 58
12,500	Tufts Health Plan: Rhode Island, 716		2,000	Mercy Clinic Kansas, 341
12,000	Medical Center Healthnet Plan, 407		2,000	Mercy Clinic Missouri, 490
10,400	Allways Health Partners, 398		2,000	Mercy Clinic Oklahoma, 647
8,917	Hometown Health Plan, 512		1,850	Altius Health Plans, 797
8,475	Anthem Blue Cross & Blue Shield of Indiana, 298		1,850	MediGold, 626
8,000	UniCare West Virginia, 851		1,833	AlohaCare, 249
7,950	Ohio State University Health Plan Inc., 629		1,820	Community Health Group, 87
7,000	Fdn. for Medical Care of Kern & Santa Barbara Counties, 96		1,800	HAP-Health Alliance Plan: Flint, 425
7,000	Vantage Health Plan, 371		1,800	HAP-Health Alliance Plan: Senior Medicare Plan, 426
6,924	First Choice of the Midwest, 738		1,793	First Choice Health, 655
6,866	Rocky Mountain Health Plans, 165		1,718	Mutual of Omaha, 503
6,800	Aultcare Corporation, 617		1,626	Independent Health, 579
6,742	Blue Cross & Blue Shield of New Mexico, 547		1,500	Lakeside Community Healthcare Network, 114
6,000	Blue Cross & Blue Shield of Oklahoma, 642		1,500	Pacific Health Alliance, 126
6,000	Health Partners of Kansas, 339		1,500	Prominence Health Plan, 516
6,000	Value Behavioral Health of Pennsylvania, 703		1,500	Trinity Health of New England, 180
5,744	First Health, 97		1,400	Health Plan of San Joaquin, 104
5,473	Blue Cross & Blue Shield of South Carolina, 725		1,275	South Central Preferred Health Network, 693
5,000	Affinity Health Plan, 560		1,255	Managed Health Services Wisconsin, 869
5,000	California Foundation for Medical Care, 76		1,250	CenCal Health, 80
5,000	Cox Healthplans, 479		1,250	Trinity Health of Ohio, 637
5,000	Stanislaus Foundation for Medical Care, 136		1,000	Health Alliance Plan, 428
4,850	Presbyterian Health Plan, 552		1,000	Medical Associates, 323
4,757	Managed HealthCare Northwest, 659		1,000	The Health Plan, 850
4,500	Landmark Healthplan of California, 115		950	DakotaCare, 736
4,500	Total Health Care, 439		900	Paramount Health Care, 631

692	OSF Healthcare, 286	250	Preferred Network Access, 287
448	Healthplex, 454	200	Denta-Chek of Maryland, 386
416	Bright Now! Dental, 74	200	GEMCare Health Plan, 98
400	Capital Health Plan, 200	100	Health Tradition, 867
400	Dental Health Services of California, 93	100	On Lok Lifeways, 123
400	Dental Health Services of Washington, 837	75	Northeast Georgia Health Partners, 242
400	Kern Family Health Care, 112	40	Opticare of Utah, 803

Titles from Grey House

Visit www.GreyHouse.com for Product Information, Table of Contents, and Sample Pages.

Opinions Throughout History
Opinions Throughout History: Church & State
Opinions Throughout History: The Death Penalty
Opinions Throughout History: Diseases & Epidemics
Opinions Throughout History: Drug Use & Abuse
Opinions Throughout History: The Environment
Opinions Throughout History: Free Speech & Censorship
Opinions Throughout History: Gender: Roles & Rights
Opinions Throughout History: Globalization
Opinions Throughout History: Guns in America
Opinions Throughout History: Immigration
Opinions Throughout History: Law Enforcement in America
Opinions Throughout History: National Security vs. Civil & Privacy Rights
Opinions Throughout History: Presidential Authority
Opinions Throughout History: Robotics & Artificial Intelligence
Opinions Throughout History: Social Media Issues
Opinions Throughout History: Voters' Rights
Opinions Throughout History: War & the Military
Opinions Throughout History: Workers Rights & Wages

This is Who We Were
This is Who We Were: Colonial America (1492-1775)
This is Who We Were: 1880-1899
This is Who We Were: In the 1900s
This is Who We Were: In the 1910s
This is Who We Were: In the 1920s
This is Who We Were: A Companion to the 1940 Census
This is Who We Were: In the 1940s (1940-1949)
This is Who We Were: In the 1950s
This is Who We Were: In the 1960s
This is Who We Were: In the 1970s
This is Who We Were: In the 1980s
This is Who We Were: In the 1990s
This is Who We Were: In the 2000s
This is Who We Were: In the 2010s

Working Americans
Working Americans—Vol. 1: The Working Class
Working Americans—Vol. 2: The Middle Class
Working Americans—Vol. 3: The Upper Class
Working Americans—Vol. 4: Children
Working Americans—Vol. 5: At War
Working Americans—Vol. 6: Working Women
Working Americans—Vol. 7: Social Movements
Working Americans—Vol. 8: Immigrants
Working Americans—Vol. 9: Revolutionary War to the Civil War
Working Americans—Vol. 10: Sports & Recreation
Working Americans—Vol. 11: Inventors & Entrepreneurs
Working Americans—Vol. 12: Our History through Music
Working Americans—Vol. 13: Education & Educators
Working Americans—Vol. 14: African Americans
Working Americans—Vol. 15: Politics & Politicians
Working Americans—Vol. 16: Farming & Ranching
Working Americans—Vol. 17: Teens in America
Working Americans—Vol. 18: Health Care Workers

Grey House Health & Wellness Guides
The Autism Spectrum Handbook & Resource Guide
Autoimmune Disorders Handbook & Resource Guide
Cardiovascular Disease Handbook & Resource Guide
Dementia Handbook & Resource Guide
Diabetes Handbook & Resource Guide
Nutrition, Obesity & Eating Disorders Handbook & Resource Guide

Consumer Health
Complete Mental Health Resource Guide
Complete Resource Guide for Pediatric Disorders
Complete Resource Guide for People with Chronic Illness
Complete Resource Guide for People with Disabilities
Older Americans Information Resource
Parenting: Styles & Strategies

Education
Complete Learning Disabilities Resource Guide
Educators Resource Guide
The Comparative Guide to Elem. & Secondary Schools
Special Education: A Reference Book for Policy & Curriculum Development

General Reference
American Environmental Leaders
Constitutional Amendments
Encyclopedia of African-American Writing
Encyclopedia of Invasions & Conquests
Encyclopedia of Prisoners of War & Internment
Encyclopedia of the Continental Congresses
Encyclopedia of the United States Cabinet
Encyclopedia of War Journalism
The Environmental Debate
Financial Literacy Starter Kit
From Suffrage to the Senate
The Gun Debate: Gun Rights & Gun Control in the U.S.
Historical Warrior Peoples & Modern Fighting Groups
Human Rights and the United States
Political Corruption in America
Privacy Rights in the Digital Age
The Religious Right and American Politics
Speakers of the House of Representatives, 1789-2021
US Land & Natural Resources Policy
The Value of a Dollar 1600-1865 Colonial to Civil War
The Value of a Dollar 1860-2019

Business Information
Business Information Resources
The Complete Broadcasting Industry Guide: Television, Radio, Cable & Streaming
Directory of Mail Order Catalogs
Environmental Resource Handbook
Food & Beverage Market Place
The Grey House Guide to Homeland Security Resources
The Grey House Performing Arts Industry Guide
Guide to Healthcare Group Purchasing Organizations
Guide to U.S. HMOs and PPOs
Guide to Venture Capital & Private Equity Firms
Hudson's Washington News Media Contacts Guide
New York State Directory
Sports Market Place

Grey House Publishing | Salem Press | H.W. Wilson | 4919 Route, 22 PO Box 56, Amenia NY 12501-0056

Grey House Imprints

Visit www.GreyHouse.com for Product Information, Table of Contents, and Sample Pages.

Statistics & Demographics
America's Top-Rated Cities
America's Top-Rated Smaller Cities
The Comparative Guide to American Suburbs
Profiles of America
Profiles of California
Profiles of Florida
Profiles of Illinois
Profiles of Indiana
Profiles of Massachusetts
Profiles of Michigan
Profiles of New Jersey
Profiles of New York
Profiles of North Carolina & South Carolina
Profiles of Ohio
Profiles of Pennsylvania
Profiles of Texas
Profiles of Virginia
Profiles of Wisconsin

Canadian Resources
Associations Canada
Canadian Almanac & Directory
Canadian Environmental Resource Guide
Canadian Parliamentary Guide
Canadian Venture Capital & Private Equity Firms
Canadian Who's Who
Cannabis Canada
Careers & Employment Canada
Financial Post: Directory of Directors
Financial Services Canada
FP Bonds: Corporate
FP Bonds: Government
FP Equities: Preferreds & Derivatives
FP Survey: Industrials
FP Survey: Mines & Energy
FP Survey: Predecessor & Defunct
Health Guide Canada
Libraries Canada

Weiss Financial Ratings
Financial Literacy Basics
Financial Literacy: How to Become an Investor
Financial Literacy: Planning for the Future
Weiss Ratings Consumer Guides
Weiss Ratings Guide to Banks
Weiss Ratings Guide to Credit Unions
Weiss Ratings Guide to Health Insurers
Weiss Ratings Guide to Life & Annuity Insurers
Weiss Ratings Guide to Property & Casualty Insurers
Weiss Ratings Investment Research Guide to Bond & Money Market Mutual Funds
Weiss Ratings Investment Research Guide to Exchange-Traded Funds
Weiss Ratings Investment Research Guide to Stock Mutual Funds
Weiss Ratings Investment Research Guide to Stocks

Books in Print Series
American Book Publishing Record® Annual
American Book Publishing Record® Monthly
Books In Print®
Books In Print® Supplement
Books Out Loud™
Bowker's Complete Video Directory™
Children's Books In Print®
El-Hi Textbooks & Serials In Print®
Forthcoming Books®
Law Books & Serials In Print™
Medical & Health Care Books In Print™
Publishers, Distributors & Wholesalers of the US™
Subject Guide to Books In Print®
Subject Guide to Children's Books In Print®

Grey House Publishing | Salem Press | H.W. Wilson | 4919 Route, 22 PO Box 56, Amenia NY 12501-0056

Titles from Salem Press

Visit www.SalemPress.com for Product Information, Table of Contents, and Sample Pages.

LITERATURE
Critical Insights: Authors
Louisa May Alcott
Sherman Alexie
Isabel Allende
Maya Angelou
Isaac Asimov
Margaret Atwood
Jane Austen
James Baldwin
Saul Bellow
Roberto Bolano
Ray Bradbury
The Brontë Sisters
Gwendolyn Brooks
Albert Camus
Raymond Carver
Willa Cather
Geoffrey Chaucer
John Cheever
Joseph Conrad
Charles Dickens
Emily Dickinson
Frederick Douglass
T. S. Eliot
George Eliot
Harlan Ellison
Louise Erdrich
William Faulkner
F. Scott Fitzgerald
Gustave Flaubert
Horton Foote
Benjamin Franklin
Robert Frost
Neil Gaiman
Gabriel Garcia Marquez
Thomas Hardy
Nathaniel Hawthorne
Robert A. Heinlein
Lillian Hellman
Ernest Hemingway
Langston Hughes
Zora Neale Hurston
Henry James
Thomas Jefferson
James Joyce
Jamaica Kincaid
Stephen King
Martin Luther King, Jr.
Barbara Kingsolver
Abraham Lincoln
Mario Vargas Llosa
Jack London
James McBride
Cormac McCarthy
Herman Melville
Arthur Miller
Toni Morrison
Alice Munro
Tim O'Brien
Flannery O'Connor
Eugene O'Neill
George Orwell
Sylvia Plath
Edgar Allan Poe

Philip Roth
Salman Rushdie
J.D. Salinger
Mary Shelley
John Steinbeck
Amy Tan
Leo Tolstoy
Mark Twain
John Updike
Kurt Vonnegut
Alice Walker
David Foster Wallace
Edith Wharton
Walt Whitman
Oscar Wilde
Tennessee Williams
Virginia Woolf
Richard Wright
Malcolm X

Critical Insights: Works
Absalom, Absalom!
Adventures of Huckleberry Finn
Adventures of Tom Sawyer
Aeneid
All Quiet on the Western Front
Animal Farm
Anna Karenina
The Awakening
The Bell Jar
Beloved
Billy Budd, Sailor
The Book Thief
Brave New World
The Canterbury Tales
Catch-22
The Catcher in the Rye
The Color Purple
The Crucible
Death of a Salesman
The Diary of a Young Girl
Dracula
Fahrenheit 451
The Grapes of Wrath
Great Expectations
The Great Gatsby
Hamlet
The Handmaid's Tale
Harry Potter Series
Heart of Darkness
The Hobbit
The House on Mango Street
How the Garcia Girls Lost Their Accents
The Hunger Games Trilogy
I Know Why the Caged Bird Sings
In Cold Blood
The Inferno
Invisible Man
Jane Eyre
The Joy Luck Club
Julius Caesar
King Lear
The Kite Runner
Life of Pi
Little Women

Lolita
Lord of the Flies
The Lord of the Rings
Macbeth
The Metamorphosis
Midnight's Children
A Midsummer Night's Dream
Moby-Dick
Mrs. Dalloway
Nineteen Eighty-Four
The Odyssey
Of Mice and Men
The Old Man and the Sea
On the Road
One Flew Over the Cuckoo's Nest
One Hundred Years of Solitude
Othello
The Outsiders
Paradise Lost
The Pearl
The Poetry of Baudelaire
The Poetry of Edgar Allan Poe
A Portrait of the Artist as a Young Man
Pride and Prejudice
The Red Badge of Courage
Romeo and Juliet
The Scarlet Letter
Short Fiction of Flannery O'Connor
Slaughterhouse-Five
The Sound and the Fury
A Streetcar Named Desire
The Sun Also Rises
A Tale of Two Cities
The Tales of Edgar Allan Poe
Their Eyes Were Watching God
Things Fall Apart
To Kill a Mockingbird
War and Peace
The Woman Warrior

Critical Insights: Themes
The American Comic Book
American Creative Non-Fiction
The American Dream
American Multicultural Identity
American Road Literature
American Short Story
American Sports Fiction
The American Thriller
American Writers in Exile
Censored & Banned Literature
Civil Rights Literature, Past & Present
Coming of Age
Conspiracies
Contemporary Canadian Fiction
Contemporary Immigrant Short Fiction
Contemporary Latin American Fiction
Contemporary Speculative Fiction
Crime and Detective Fiction
Crisis of Faith
Cultural Encounters
Dystopia
Family
The Fantastic
Feminism

Grey House Publishing | Salem Press | H.W. Wilson | 4919 Route, 22 PO Box 56, Amenia NY 12501-0056

Titles from Salem Press

Visit www.SalemPress.com for Product Information, Table of Contents, and Sample Pages.

Flash Fiction
Gender, Sex and Sexuality
Good & Evil
The Graphic Novel
Greed
Harlem Renaissance
The Hero's Quest
Historical Fiction
Holocaust Literature
The Immigrant Experience
Inequality
LGBTQ Literature
Literature in Times of Crisis
Literature of Protest
Love
Magical Realism
Midwestern Literature
Modern Japanese Literature
Nature & the Environment
Paranoia, Fear & Alienation
Patriotism
Political Fiction
Postcolonial Literature
Pulp Fiction of the '20s and '30s
Rebellion
Russia's Golden Age
Satire
The Slave Narrative
Social Justice and American Literature
Southern Gothic Literature
Southwestern Literature
Survival
Technology & Humanity
Truth & Lies
Violence in Literature
Virginia Woolf & 20th Century Women Writers
War

Critical Insights: Film
Bonnie & Clyde
Casablanca
Alfred Hitchcock
Stanley Kubrick

Critical Approaches to Literature
Critical Approaches to Literature: Feminist
Critical Approaches to Literature: Moral
Critical Approaches to Literature: Multicultural
Critical Approaches to Literature: Psychological

Critical Surveys of Literature
Critical Survey of American Literature
Critical Survey of Drama
Critical Survey of Graphic Novels: Heroes & Superheroes
Critical Survey of Graphic Novels: History, Theme, and Technique
Critical Survey of Graphic Novels: Independents & Underground Classics
Critical Survey of Graphic Novels: Manga
Critical Survey of Long Fiction
Critical Survey of Mystery and Detective Fiction
Critical Survey of Mythology & Folklore: Gods & Goddesses
Critical Survey of Mythology & Folklore: Heroes and Heroines
Critical Survey of Mythology & Folklore: Love, Sexuality, and Desire
Critical Survey of Mythology & Folklore: World Mythology
Critical Survey of Poetry
Critical Survey of Poetry: Contemporary Poets
Critical Survey of Science Fiction & Fantasy Literature
Critical Survey of Shakespeare's Plays
Critical Survey of Shakespeare's Sonnets
Critical Survey of Short Fiction
Critical Survey of World Literature
Critical Survey of Young Adult Literature

Cyclopedia of Literary Characters & Places
Cyclopedia of Literary Characters
Cyclopedia of Literary Places

Introduction to Literary Context
American Poetry of the 20th Century
American Post-Modernist Novels
American Short Fiction
English Literature
Plays
World Literature

Magill's Literary Annual
Magill's Literary Annual, 2022
Magill's Literary Annual, 2021
Magill's Literary Annual, 2020
Magill's Literary Annual (Backlist Issues 2019-1977)

Masterplots
Masterplots, Fourth Edition
Masterplots, 2010-2018 Supplement

Notable Writers
Notable African American Writers
Notable American Women Writers
Notable Mystery & Detective Fiction Writers
Notable Writers of the American West & the Native American Experience
Novels into Film: Adaptations & Interpretation
Recommended Reading: 600 Classics Reviewed

Grey House Publishing | Salem Press | H.W. Wilson | 4919 Route, 22 PO Box 56, Amenia NY 12501-0056

Titles from Salem Press

Visit www.SalemPress.com for Product Information, Table of Contents, and Sample Pages.

HISTORY

The Decades
The 1910s in America
The Twenties in America
The Thirties in America
The Forties in America
The Fifties in America
The Sixties in America
The Seventies in America
The Eighties in America
The Nineties in America
The 2000s in America
The 2010s in America

Defining Documents in American History
Defining Documents: The 1900s
Defining Documents: The 1910s
Defining Documents: The 1920s
Defining Documents: The 1930s
Defining Documents: The 1950s
Defining Documents: The 1960s
Defining Documents: The 1970s
Defining Documents: The 1980s
Defining Documents: American Citizenship
Defining Documents: The American Economy
Defining Documents: The American Revolution
Defining Documents: The American West
Defining Documents: Business Ethics
Defining Documents: Capital Punishment
Defining Documents: Civil Rights
Defining Documents: Civil War
Defining Documents: The Constitution
Defining Documents: The Cold War
Defining Documents: Dissent & Protest
Defining Documents: Domestic Terrorism
Defining Documents: Drug Policy
Defining Documents: The Emergence of Modern America
Defining Documents: Environment & Conservation
Defining Documents: Espionage & Intrigue
Defining Documents: Exploration and Colonial America
Defining Documents: The First Amendment
Defining Documents: The Free Press
Defining Documents: The Great Depression
Defining Documents: The Great Migration
Defining Documents: The Gun Debate
Defining Documents: Immigration & Immigrant Communities
Defining Documents: The Legacy of 9/11
Defining Documents: LGBTQ+
Defining Documents: Manifest Destiny and the New Nation
Defining Documents: Native Americans
Defining Documents: Political Campaigns, Candidates & Discourse
Defining Documents: Postwar 1940s
Defining Documents: Prison Reform
Defining Documents: Secrets, Leaks & Scandals
Defining Documents: Slavery
Defining Documents: Supreme Court Decisions
Defining Documents: Reconstruction Era
Defining Documents: The Vietnam War
Defining Documents: U.S. Involvement in the Middle East
Defining Documents: World War I
Defining Documents: World War II

Defining Documents in World History
Defining Documents: The 17th Century
Defining Documents: The 18th Century
Defining Documents: The 19th Century
Defining Documents: The 20th Century (1900-1950)
Defining Documents: The Ancient World
Defining Documents: Asia
Defining Documents: Genocide & the Holocaust
Defining Documents: Nationalism & Populism
Defining Documents: Pandemics, Plagues & Public Health
Defining Documents: Renaissance & Early Modern Era
Defining Documents: The Middle Ages
Defining Documents: The Middle East
Defining Documents: Women's Rights

Great Events from History
Great Events from History: The Ancient World
Great Events from History: The Middle Ages
Great Events from History: The Renaissance & Early Modern Era
Great Events from History: The 17th Century
Great Events from History: The 18th Century
Great Events from History: The 19th Century
Great Events from History: The 20th Century, 1901-1940
Great Events from History: The 20th Century, 1941-1970
Great Events from History: The 20th Century, 1971-2000
Great Events from History: Modern Scandals
Great Events from History: African American History
Great Events from History: The 21st Century, 2000-2016
Great Events from History: LGBTQ Events
Great Events from History: Human Rights
Great Events from History: Women's History

Great Lives from History
Computer Technology Innovators
Fashion Innovators
Great Athletes
Great Athletes of the Twenty-First Century
Great Lives from History: African Americans
Great Lives from History: American Heroes
Great Lives from History: American Women
Great Lives from History: Asian and Pacific Islander Americans
Great Lives from History: Inventors & Inventions
Great Lives from History: Jewish Americans
Great Lives from History: Latinos
Great Lives from History: Scientists and Science
Great Lives from History: The 17th Century
Great Lives from History: The 18th Century
Great Lives from History: The 19th Century
Great Lives from History: The 20th Century
Great Lives from History: The 21st Century, 2000-2017
Great Lives from History: The Ancient World
Great Lives from History: The Incredibly Wealthy
Great Lives from History: The Middle Ages
Great Lives from History: The Renaissance & Early Modern Era
Human Rights Innovators
Internet Innovators
Music Innovators
Musicians and Composers of the 20th Century
World Political Innovators

Grey House Publishing | Salem Press | H.W. Wilson | 4919 Route, 22 PO Box 56, Amenia NY 12501-0056

Titles from Salem Press

Visit www.SalemPress.com for Product Information, Table of Contents, and Sample Pages.

History & Government
American First Ladies
American Presidents
The 50 States
The Ancient World: Extraordinary People in Extraordinary Societies
The Bill of Rights
The Criminal Justice System
The U.S. Supreme Court

SOCIAL SCIENCES
Civil Rights Movements: Past & Present
Countries, Peoples and Cultures
Countries: Their Wars & Conflicts: A World Survey
Education Today: Issues, Policies & Practices
Encyclopedia of American Immigration
Ethics: Questions & Morality of Human Actions
Issues in U.S. Immigration
Principles of Sociology: Group Relationships & Behavior
Principles of Sociology: Personal Relationships & Behavior
Principles of Sociology: Societal Issues & Behavior
Racial & Ethnic Relations in America
World Geography

HEALTH
Addictions, Substance Abuse & Alcoholism
Adolescent Health & Wellness
Aging
Cancer
Community & Family Health Issues
Integrative, Alternative & Complementary Medicine
Genetics and Inherited Conditions
Infectious Diseases and Conditions
Magill's Medical Guide
Nutrition
Parenting: Styles & Strategies
Psychology & Behavioral Health
Women's Health

Principles of Health
Principles of Health: Allergies & Immune Disorders
Principles of Health: Anxiety & Stress
Principles of Health: Depression
Principles of Health: Diabetes
Principles of Health: Nursing
Principles of Health: Obesity
Principles of Health: Pain Management
Principles of Health: Prescription Drug Abuse

SCIENCE
Ancient Creatures
Applied Science
Applied Science: Engineering & Mathematics
Applied Science: Science & Medicine
Applied Science: Technology
Biomes and Ecosystems
Earth Science: Earth Materials and Resources
Earth Science: Earth's Surface and History
Earth Science: Earth's Weather, Water and Atmosphere
Earth Science: Physics and Chemistry of the Earth
Encyclopedia of Climate Change
Encyclopedia of Energy
Encyclopedia of Environmental Issues
Encyclopedia of Global Resources
Encyclopedia of Mathematics and Society
Forensic Science
Notable Natural Disasters
The Solar System
USA in Space

Principles of Science
Principles of Anatomy
Principles of Astronomy
Principles of Behavioral Science
Principles of Biology
Principles of Biotechnology
Principles of Botany
Principles of Chemistry
Principles of Climatology
Principles of Computer-aided Design
Principles of Information Technology
Principles of Computer Science
Principles of Ecology
Principles of Energy
Principles of Fire Science
Principles of Geology
Principles of Marine Science
Principles of Mathematics
Principles of Microbiology
Principles of Modern Agriculture
Principles of Pharmacology
Principles of Physical Science
Principles of Physics
Principles of Programming & Coding
Principles of Robotics & Artificial Intelligence
Principles of Scientific Research
Principles of Sports Medicine & Kinesiology
Principles of Sustainability
Principles of Zoology

Grey House Publishing | Salem Press | H.W. Wilson | 4919 Route, 22 PO Box 56, Amenia NY 12501-0056

Titles from Salem Press

Visit www.SalemPress.com for Product Information, Table of Contents, and Sample Pages.

CAREERS

Careers: Paths to Entrepreneurship
Careers in Artificial Intelligence
Careers in the Arts: Fine, Performing & Visual
Careers in the Automotive Industry
Careers in Biology
Careers in Building Construction
Careers in Business
Careers in Chemistry
Careers in Communications & Media
Careers in Education & Training
Careers in Engineering
Careers in Environment & Conservation
Careers in Financial Services
Careers in Forensic Science
Careers in Gaming
Careers in Green Energy
Careers in Healthcare
Careers in Hospitality & Tourism
Careers in Human Services
Careers in Information Technology
Careers in Law, Criminal Justice & Emergency Services
Careers in the Music Industry
Careers in Manufacturing & Production
Careers in Nursing
Careers in Physics
Careers in Protective Services
Careers in Psychology & Behavioral Health
Careers in Public Administration
Careers in Sales, Insurance & Real Estate
Careers in Science & Engineering
Careers in Social Media
Careers in Sports & Fitness
Careers in Sports Medicine & Training
Careers in Technical Services & Equipment Repair
Careers in Transportation
Careers in Writing & Editing
Careers Outdoors
Careers Overseas
Careers Working with Infants & Children
Careers Working with Animals

BUSINESS

Principles of Business: Accounting
Principles of Business: Economics
Principles of Business: Entrepreneurship
Principles of Business: Finance
Principles of Business: Globalization
Principles of Business: Leadership
Principles of Business: Management
Principles of Business: Marketing

Grey House Publishing | Salem Press | H.W. Wilson | 4919 Route, 22 PO Box 56, Amenia NY 12501-0056

Titles from H.W. Wilson

Visit www.HWWilsonInPrint.com for Product Information, Table of Contents, and Sample Pages.

Core Collections
Children's Core Collection
Fiction Core Collection
Graphic Novels Core Collection
Middle & Junior High School Core
Public Library Core Collection: Nonfiction
Senior High Core Collection
Young Adult Fiction Core Collection

The Reference Shelf
Affordable Housing
Aging in America
Alternative Facts, Post-Truth and the Information War
The American Dream
Artificial Intelligence
The Business of Food
Campaign Trends & Election Law
College Sports
Democracy Evolving
The Digital Age
Embracing New Paradigms in Education
Food Insecurity & Hunger in the United States
Future of U.S. Economic Relations: Mexico, Cuba, & Venezuela
Global Climate Change
Guns in America
Hate Crimes
Immigration
Income Inequality
Internet Abuses & Privacy Rights
Internet Law
LGBTQ in the 21st Century
Marijuana Reform
Mental Health Awareness
National Debate Topic 2014/2015: The Ocean
National Debate Topic 2015/2016: Surveillance
National Debate Topic 2016/2017: US/China Relations
National Debate Topic 2017/2018: Education Reform
National Debate Topic 2018/2019: Immigration
National Debate Topic 2019/2021: Arms Sales
National Debate Topic 2020/2021: Criminal Justice Reform
National Debate Topic 2021/2022: Water Resources
National Debate Topic 2022/2023
New Frontiers in Space
Policing in 2020
Pollution
Prescription Drug Abuse
Propaganda and Misinformation
Racial Tension in a Postracial Age
Reality Television
Representative American Speeches, Annual Editions
Rethinking Work
Revisiting Gender
The South China Sea Conflict
Sports in America
The Supreme Court
The Transformation of American Cities
The Two Koreas
UFOs
Vaccinations
Voters' Rights
Whistleblowers

Current Biography
Current Biography Cumulative Index 1946-2021
Current Biography Monthly Magazine
Current Biography Yearbook

Readers' Guide to Periodical Literature
Abridged Readers' Guide to Periodical Literature
Readers' Guide to Periodical Literature

Indexes
Index to Legal Periodicals & Books
Short Story Index
Book Review Digest

Sears List
Sears List of Subject Headings
Sears: Lista de Encabezamientos de Materia

History
American Game Changers: Invention, Innovation & Transformation
American Reformers
Speeches of the American Presidents

Facts About Series
Facts About the 20th Century
Facts About American Immigration
Facts About China
Facts About the Presidents
Facts About the World's Languages

Nobel Prize Winners
Nobel Prize Winners: 1901-1986
Nobel Prize Winners: 1987-1991
Nobel Prize Winners: 1992-1996
Nobel Prize Winners: 1997-2001
Nobel Prize Winners: 2002-2018

Famous First Facts
Famous First Facts
Famous First Facts About American Politics
Famous First Facts About Sports
Famous First Facts About the Environment
Famous First Facts: International Edition

American Book of Days
The American Book of Days
The International Book of Days

Grey House Publishing | Salem Press | H.W. Wilson | 4919 Route, 22 PO Box 56, Amenia NY 12501-0056